Contemporary
Literary Criticism

Guide to Gale Literary Criticism Series

For criticism on	Consult these Gale series
Authors now living or who died after December 31, 1999	**CONTEMPORARY LITERARY CRITICISM (CLC)**
Authors who died between 1900 and 1999	**TWENTIETH-CENTURY LITERARY CRITICISM (TCLC)**
Authors who died between 1800 and 1899	**NINETEENTH-CENTURY LITERATURE CRITICISM (NCLC)**
Authors who died between 1400 and 1799	**LITERATURE CRITICISM FROM 1400 TO 1800 (LC)** **SHAKESPEAREAN CRITICISM (SC)**
Authors who died before 1400	**CLASSICAL AND MEDIEVAL LITERATURE CRITICISM (CMLC)**
Authors of books for children and young adults	**CHILDREN'S LITERATURE REVIEW (CLR)**
Dramatists	**DRAMA CRITICISM (DC)**
Poets	**POETRY CRITICISM (PC)**
Short story writers	**SHORT STORY CRITICISM (SSC)**
Asian American writers of the last two hundred years	**ASIAN AMERICAN LITERATURE (AAL)**
Black writers of the past two hundred years	**BLACK LITERATURE CRITICISM (BLC)** **BLACK LITERATURE CRITICISM SUPPLEMENT (BLCS)**
Hispanic writers of the late nineteenth and twentieth centuries	**HISPANIC LITERATURE CRITICISM (HLC)** **HISPANIC LITERATURE CRITICISM SUPPLEMENT (HLCS)**
Native North American writers and orators of the eighteenth, nineteenth, and twentieth centuries	**NATIVE NORTH AMERICAN LITERATURE (NNAL)**
Major authors from the Renaissance to the present	**WORLD LITERATURE CRITICISM, 1500 TO THE PRESENT (WLC)** **WORLD LITERATURE CRITICISM SUPPLEMENT (WLCS)**

ISSN 0091-3421

Volume 167

Contemporary Literary Criticism

Criticism of the Works
of Today's Novelists, Poets, Playwrights,
Short Story Writers, Scriptwriters, and
Other Creative Writers

Janet Witalec
PROJECT EDITOR

Contemporary Literary Criticism, Vol. 167

Project Editor
Janet Witalec

Editorial
Tom Burns, Jenny Cromie, Kathy D. Darrow, Jeffrey W. Hunter, Justin Karr, Ellen McGeagh, Lemma Shomali

Research
Nicodemus Ford, Sarah Genik, Tamara C. Nott, Tracie A. Richardson

Permissions
Margaret A. Chamberlain

Imaging and Multimedia
Lezlie Light, Kelly A. Quin, Luke Rademacher

Composition and Electronic Capture
Gary Leach

Manufacturing
Stacy L. Melson

© 2003 by Gale. Gale is an imprint of The Gale Group, Inc., a division of Thomson Learning, Inc.

Gale and Design™ and Thomson Learning™ are trademarks used herein under license.

For more information, contact
The Gale Group, Inc.
27500 Drake Rd.
Farmington Hills, MI 48331-3535
Or you can visit our internet site at
http://www.gale.com

ALL RIGHTS RESERVED
No part of this work covered by the copyright herein may be reproduced or used in any form or by any means—graphic, electronic, or mechanical, including photocopying, recording, taping, Web distribution, or information storage retrieval systems—without the written permission of the publisher.

This publication is a creative work fully protected by all applicable copyright laws, as well as by misappropriation, trade secret, unfair competition, and other applicable laws. The authors and editors of this work have added value to the underlying factual material herein through one or more of the following: unique and original selection, coordination, expression, arrangement, and classification of the information.

For permission to use material from the product, submit your request via the Web at http://www.gale-edit.com/permissions, or you may download our Permissions Request form and submit your request by fax or mail to:

Permisssions Department
The Gale Group, Inc.
27500 Drake Rd.
Farmington Hills, MI 48331-3535
Permissions Hotline:
248-699-8006 or 800-877-4253, ext. 8006
Fax 248-699-8074 or 800-762-4058

Since this page cannot legibly accommodate all copyright notices, the acknowledgments constitute an extension of the copyright notice.

While every effort has been made to secure permission to reprint material and to ensure the reliability of the information presented in this publication, the Gale Group neither guarantees the accuracy of the data contained herein nor assumes any responsibility for errors, omissions or discrepancies. Gale accepts no payment for listing; and inclusion in the publication of any organization, agency, institution, publication, service, or individual does not imply endorsement of the editors or publisher. Errors brought to the attention of the publisher and verified to the satisfaction of the publisher will be corrected in future editions.

LIBRARY OF CONGRESS CATALOG CARD NUMBER 76-46132
ISBN 0-7876-5963-0
ISSN 0091-3421

Printed in the United States of America
10 9 8 7 6 5 4 3 2 1

Contents

Preface vii

Acknowledgments xi

Literary Criticism Series Advisory Board xiii

Contemporary Southern Literature
Introduction 1
Representative Works 1
Criticism 2
Further Reading 131

Nicholas Delbanco 1942- 133
English-born American novelist, short story writer, essayist, travel writer, critic, and nonfiction writer

Gao Xingjian 1940- 182
Chinese-born French playwright, critic, novelist, translator, and essayist

Alice Walker 1944- 232
American novelist, essayist, poet, short story writer, editor, memoirist, and children's writer; entry devoted to Walker's novel The Color Purple *(1982)*

Literary Criticism Series Cumulative Author Index 345

Literary Criticism Series Cumulative Topic Index 435

CLC Cumulative Nationality Index 445

CLC-167 Title Index 459

Preface

Named "one of the twenty-five most distinguished reference titles published during the past twenty-five years" by *Reference Quarterly,* the *Contemporary Literary Criticism (CLC)* series provides readers with critical commentary and general information on more than 2,000 authors now living or who died after December 31, 1999. Volumes published from 1973 through 1999 include authors who died after December 31, 1959. Previous to the publication of the first volume of *CLC* in 1973, there was no ongoing digest monitoring scholarly and popular sources of critical opinion and explication of modern literature. *CLC,* therefore, has fulfilled an essential need, particularly since the complexity and variety of contemporary literature makes the function of criticism especially important to today's reader.

Scope of the Series

CLC provides significant passages from published criticism of works by creative writers. Since many of the authors covered in *CLC* inspire continual critical commentary, writers are often represented in more than one volume. There is, of course, no duplication of reprinted criticism.

Authors are selected for inclusion for a variety of reasons, among them the publication or dramatic production of a critically acclaimed new work, the reception of a major literary award, revival of interest in past writings, or the adaptation of a literary work to film or television.

Attention is also given to several other groups of writers—authors of considerable public interest—about whose work criticism is often difficult to locate. These include mystery and science fiction writers, literary and social critics, foreign authors, and authors who represent particular ethnic groups.

Each *CLC* volume contains individual essays and reviews taken from hundreds of book review periodicals, general magazines, scholarly journals, monographs, and books. Entries include critical evaluations spanning from the beginning of an author's career to the most current commentary. Interviews, feature articles, and other published writings that offer insight into the author's works are also presented. Students, teachers, librarians, and researchers will find that the general critical and biographical material in *CLC* provides them with vital information required to write a term paper, analyze a poem, or lead a book discussion group. In addition, complete biographical citations note the original source and all of the information necessary for a term paper footnote or bibliography.

Organization of the Book

A *CLC* entry consists of the following elements:

- The **Author Heading** cites the name under which the author most commonly wrote, followed by birth and death dates. Also located here are any name variations under which an author wrote, including transliterated forms for authors whose native languages use nonroman alphabets. If the author wrote consistently under a pseudonym, the pseudonym will be listed in the author heading and the author's actual name given in parenthesis on the first line of the biographical and critical information. Uncertain birth or death dates are indicated by question marks. Single-work entries are preceded by a heading that consists of the most common form of the title in English translation (if applicable) and the original date of composition.

- A **Portrait of the Author** is included when available.

- The **Introduction** contains background information that introduces the reader to the author, work, or topic that is the subject of the entry.

- The list of **Principal Works** is ordered chronologically by date of first publication and lists the most important works by the author. The genre and publication date of each work is given. In the case of foreign authors whose works have been translated into English, the English-language version of the title follows in brackets. Unless otherwise indicated, dramas are dated by first performance, not first publication.

- Reprinted **Criticism** is arranged chronologically in each entry to provide a useful perspective on changes in critical evaluation over time. The critic's name and the date of composition or publication of the critical work are given at the beginning of each piece of criticism. Unsigned criticism is preceded by the title of the source in which it appeared. All titles by the author featured in the text are printed in boldface type. Footnotes are reprinted at the end of each essay or excerpt. In the case of excerpted criticism, only those footnotes that pertain to the excerpted texts are included.

- A complete **Bibliographical Citation** of the original essay or book precedes each piece of criticism.

- Critical essays are prefaced by brief **Annotations** explicating each piece.

- Whenever possible, a recent **Author Interview** accompanies each entry.

- An annotated bibliography of **Further Reading** appears at the end of each entry and suggests resources for additional study. In some cases, significant essays for which the editors could not obtain reprint rights are included here. Boxed material following the further reading list provides references to other biographical and critical sources on the author in series published by Gale.

Indexes

A **Cumulative Author Index** lists all of the authors that appear in a wide variety of reference sources published by the Gale Group, including *CLC*. A complete list of these sources is found facing the first page of the Author Index. The index also includes birth and death dates and cross references between pseudonyms and actual names.

A **Cumulative Nationality Index** lists all authors featured in *CLC* by nationality, followed by the number of the *CLC* volume in which their entry appears.

A **Cumulative Topic Index** lists the literary themes and topics treated in the series as well as in *Literature Criticism from 1400 to 1800, Nineteenth-Century Literature Criticism, Twentieth-Century Literary Criticism,* and the *Contemporary Literary Criticism* Yearbook, which was discontinued in 1998.

An alphabetical **Title Index** accompanies each volume of *CLC*. Listings of titles by authors covered in the given volume are followed by the author's name and the corresponding page numbers where the titles are discussed. English translations of foreign titles and variations of titles are cross-referenced to the title under which a work was originally published. Titles of novels, dramas, nonfiction books, and poetry, short story, or essay collections are printed in italics, while individual poems, short stories, and essays are printed in roman type within quotation marks.

In response to numerous suggestions from librarians, Gale also produces an annual cumulative title index that alphabetically lists all titles reviewed in *CLC* and is available to all customers. Additional copies of this index are available upon request. Librarians and patrons will welcome this separate index; it saves shelf space, is easy to use, and is recyclable upon receipt of the next edition.

Citing *Contemporary Literary Criticism*

When writing papers, students who quote directly from any volume in the Literary Criticism Series may use the following general format to footnote reprinted criticism. The first example pertains to material drawn from periodicals, the second to material reprinted from books.

Alfred Cismaru, "Making the Best of It," *The New Republic* 207, no. 24 (December 7, 1992): 30, 32; excerpted and reprinted in *Contemporary Literary Criticism,* vol. 85, ed. Christopher Giroux (Detroit: The Gale Group, 1995), 73-4.

Yvor Winters, *The Post-Symbolist Methods* (Allen Swallow, 1967), 211-51; excerpted and reprinted in *Contemporary Literary Criticism,* vol. 85, ed. Christopher Giroux (Detroit: The Gale Group, 1995), 223-26.

Suggestions are Welcome

Readers who wish to suggest new features, topics, or authors to appear in future volumes, or who have other suggestions or comments are cordially invited to call, write, or fax the Project Editor:

Project Editor, Literary Criticism Series
The Gale Group
27500 Drake Road
Farmington Hills, MI 48331-3535
1-800-347-4253 (GALE)
Fax: 248-699-8054

Acknowledgments

The editors wish to thank the copyright holders of the criticism included in this volume and the permissions managers of many book and magazine publishing companies for assisting us in securing reproduction rights. We are also grateful to the staffs of the Detroit Public Library, the Library of Congress, the University of Detroit Mercy Library, Wayne State University Purdy/Kresge Library Complex, and the University of Michigan Libraries for making their resources available to us. Following is a list of the copyright holders who have granted us permission to reproduce material in this volume of *CLC*. Every effort has been made to trace copyright, but if omissions have been made, please let us know.

COPYRIGHTED MATERIAL IN *CLC*, VOLUME 167, WAS REPRODUCED FROM THE FOLLOWING PERIODICALS:

African American Review, v. 26, Spring 1992 for "Towards a Map of Mis(sed) Reading: The Presence of Absence in *The Color Purple*," by James C. Hall, v. 29, Spring 1995 for "Race and Domesticity in *The Color Purple*," by Linda Selzer. Reproduced by permission of the authors.—*ANQ,* v. 13, Winter 2000. Reproduced by permission.—*ARIEL,* v. 21, April 1990 for "'What She Got to Sing About?': Comedy and The Color Purple," by Priscilla L. Walton. Reproduced by permission of the publisher and the author.—*Boston Globe,* March 7, 2001; August 19, 2001. Reproduced by permission.—*Chicago Tribune Books,* July 23, 1989; February 4, 1990; October 1, 1995. Reproduced by permission.—*Christian Science Monitor,* v. LXXXI, September 1, 1989. Reproduced by permission.—*Chronicle of Higher Education,* v. 47, December 8, 2000. Reproduced by permission.—*Comparative Literature Studies,* v. 29, Fall 1992. Reproduced by permission.—*Contemporary Literature,* v. 25, Winter 1984; v. 32, Spring 1991. Reproduced by permission. —*Critique,* v. 28, Summer 1987; v. 29, Fall 1987. Reproduced by permission. —*Georgia Review,* v. LIV, Fall 2000. Reproduced by permission. —*Irish Times,* October 27, 2001. Reproduced by permission. —*Journal of Narrative Technique,* v. 16, Fall 1986; v. 19, Fall 1989. Reproduced by permission.—*Los Angeles Times Book Review,* August 7, 1983; December 17, 2000. Reproduced by permission.—*Los Angeles Times,* October 3, 1995; October 13, 2000; October 16, 2000; November 1, 2000; February 27, 2001. Reproduced by permission.—*MELUS,* v. 25, Fall-Winter 2000. Reproduced by permission. —*Michigan Quarterly Review,* v. XXXVI, Summer 1997 for "Half in Love with Easeful Death," by Steven G. Kellman. Reproduced by permission of the author. —*Midwest Quarterly,* v. 38, Spring 1997; Reproduced by permission. —*Mississippi Quarterly,* v. 50, Fall 1997. Reproduced by permission. —*Modern Drama,* v. 41, Fall 1998. Reproduced by permission. —*Modern Fiction Studies,* v. 34, Spring 1988. Reproduced by permission. —*Narrative,* v. 9, May 2001. Reproduced by permission.—*New Leader,* v. LXXXIV, January-February 2001. Reproduced by permission.—*New Republic,* v. 189, October 31, 1983. Reproduced by permission.—*New York Review of Books,* v. XLIV, October 9, 1997. Reproduced by permission. —*PMLA,* v. 106, October 1991. Reproduced by permission. —*Quadrant,* v. XLIV, April 2000 for "The Voice of One in the Wilderness,"; v. XLIV, September 2000 for "Journey without End," by Oliver Burckhardt. Reproduced by permission of the publisher and the author.—*Review of Contemporary Fiction,* v. XVIII, Spring 1998; v. XXI, Summer 2001. Reproduced by permission.—*Sewanee Review,* v. XCI, April 1983. Reproduced by permission. —*Southern Humanities Review,* v. XVIII, Summer 1984. Reproduced by permission.—*Southern Literary Journal,* v. 22, Spring 1990; v. 32, Fall 1999. Reproduced by permission.—*The Southern Quarterly,* v. 30, Winter-Spring 1992. Reproduced by permission.—*The Southern Review,* v. 33, Winter 1997 for "Toward a New Southern Poetry: Southern Poetry in Contemporary American Literary History," by Ernest Suarez. Reproduced by permission of the author. —*Spectator,* v. CCXLIX, October 9, 1982. Reproduced by permission. —*Studies in American Fiction,* v. 16, Spring 1988. Reproduced by permission. —*Studies in Short Fiction,* v. 30, Winter 1993. Reproduced by permission. —*Texas Studies in Literature and Language,* v. 36, Winter 1994 for "Humor, Subjectivity, Resistance: The Case of Laughter in *The Color Purple*," by Carole Anne Taylor. Reproduced by permission of the publisher and the author. —*Times Literary Supplement,* October 22, 1982; October 20, 2000; March 9, 2001; November 30, 2001. Reproduced by permission.—*Virginia Quarterly Review,* v. 77, Summer 2001. Reproduced by permission.—*Washington Post Book World,* January 14, 2001. Reproduced by permission.—*Washington Post,* February 8, 1990. Reproduced by permission.—*World Literature Today,* v. LXXIV, Autumn 2000; v. LXXV, Winter 2001. Reproduced by permission.

COPYRIGHTED MATERIAL IN *CLC*, VOLUME 167, WAS REPRODUCED FROM THE FOLLOWING BOOKS:

Bennett, Barbara. From *Introduction to Comic Visions, Female Voices: Contemporary Women Novelists and Southern Humor.* Louisiana State University Press, 1998. Copyright © 1998 by Louisiana State University Press. All rights reserved.

Reproduced by permission.—Buchanan, Harriette C. From "Lee Smith: The Storyteller's Voice," in *Southern Women Writers: The New Generation.* The University of Alabama Press, 1990. Copyright © 1990 by The University of Alabama Press. All rights reserved. Reproduced by permission.—Cawelti, John G. From "Cormac McCarthy: Restless Seekers," in *Southern Writers at Century's End.* Edited by Jeffrey J. Folks and James A. Perkins. The University Press of Kentucky, 1997. Copyright © 1997 by The University Press of Kentucky. All rights reserved. Reproduced by permission.—Chew, Martha. From "Rita Mae Brown: Feminist Theorist and Southern Novelist," in *Women Writers of the Contemporary South.* Edited by Peggy Whitman Prenshaw. University Press of Mississippi, 1984. Copyright © 1984 by *The Southern Quarterly.* All rights reserved. Reproduced by permission.—Gabbin, Joanne Veal. From "The Southern Imagination of Sonia Sanchez," in *Southern Women Writers: The New Generation.* The University of Alabama Press, 1990. Copyright © 1990 by The University of Alabama Press. All rights reserved. Reproduced by permission.—Gretlund, Jan Nordby. From "Josephine Humphreys's New Southerner," in *Frames of Southern Mind: Reflections on the Stoic, Bi-Racial & Existential South.* Odense University Press, 1998. Copyright © 1998 by Jan Nordby Gretlund and Odense University Press. All rights reserved. Reproduced by permission.—Lowe, John. From Introduction to *The Future of Southern Letters.* Edited by Jefferson Humphries and John Lowe. Oxford University Press, 1996. Copyright © 1996 by Oxford University Press. All rights reserved. Reproduced by permission.—Prenshaw, Peggy Whitman. From "The Construction of Confluence: The Female South and Eudora Welty's Art," in *The Late Novels of Eudora Welty.* Edited by Jan Nordby Gretlund and Karl-Heinz Westarp. University of South Carolina Press, 1998. Copyright © 1998 by University of South Carolina Press. All rights reserved. Reproduced by permission.—Spivey, Ted R. From "The City and the Quest for Cultural Values," in *Revival: Southern Writers in the Modern City.* University Presses of Florida, 1986. Copyright © 1986 by University Presses of Florida. All rights reserved. Reproduced by permission.—Yaeger, Patricia. From "Beyond the Hummingbird: Southern Women Writers and the Southern Gargantua," in *Haunted Bodies: Gender and Southern Texts.* Edited by Anne Goodwyn Jones and Susan V. Donaldson. University Press of Virginia, 1998. Copyright © 1998 by the Rector and Visitors of the University of Virginia. All rights reserved. Reproduced by permission.

PHOTOGRAPHS AND ILLUSTRATIONS APPEARING IN *CLC*, VOLUME 167, WERE RECEIVED FROM THE FOLLOWING SOURCES:

Delbanco, Nicholas, photograph. Reproduced by permission.—Gao Xingjian, photograph. Reuters/Archive Photos, Inc. Reproduced by permission.—Walker, Alice, photograph. © Roger Ressmeyer/Corbis. Reproduced with permission.

Literary Criticism Series Advisory Board

The members of the Gale Group Literary Criticism Series Advisory Board—reference librarians and subject specialists from public, academic, and school library systems—represent a cross-section of our customer base and offer a variety of informed perspectives on both the presentation and content of our literature criticism products. Advisory board members assess and define such quality issues as the relevance, currency, and usefulness of the author coverage, critical content, and literary topics included in our series; evaluate the layout, presentation, and general quality of our printed volumes; provide feedback on the criteria used for selecting authors and topics covered in our series; provide suggestions for potential enhancements to our series; identify any gaps in our coverage of authors or literary topics, recommending authors or topics for inclusion; analyze the appropriateness of our content and presentation for various user audiences, such as high school students, undergraduates, graduate students, librarians, and educators; and offer feedback on any proposed changes/enhancements to our series. We wish to thank the following advisors for their advice throughout the year.

Dr. Toby Burrows
Principal Librarian
The Scholars' Centre
University of Western Australia Library

David M. Durant
Reference Librarian, Joyner Library
East Carolina University

Steven R. Harris
English Literature Librarian
University of Tennessee

Mary Jane Marden
Literature and General Reference Librarian
St. Petersburg Jr. College

Mark Schumacher
Jackson Library
University of North Carolina at Greensboro

Gwen Scott-Miller
Fiction Department Manager
Seattle Public Library

Contemporary Southern Literature

INTRODUCTION

Discussion of Southern literature in the United States usually begins with the works of Edgar Allan Poe and climaxes with the Southern Renascence authors who wrote in the 1950s and 1960s—such as William Faulkner, Eudora Welty, Robert Penn Warren, and James Dickey, among others. The Renascence authors helped to define and solidify the image of Southern literature that still, in many respects, holds true today. Some of the hallmarks of this genre, as scholars have pointed out, are a concern with regionalism—with the geography, landscape, and local customs of the South; a respect for family, tradition, and history; and a particular fondness and talent for storytelling, whether through formal narrative or back-porch gossip. Interaction between Blacks and whites in the South also remains a key theme for many Southern writers, prompting continual reexamination of the relationship between the past and the present in their works. Because of their unique historic circumstance as natives of a slave-owning society defeated in the Civil War, "Southerners are always being asked to account for themselves," as Welty has noted. The very question of what it means to be a Southern writer is a recurring theme in Southern literature, with authors exploring the possible advantages and limitations of regionalism, as well as analyzing the qualities that constitute a Southern writer in exile.

Contemporary Southern writers continue to incorporate many of these same themes into their works, but they have also branched out in new directions. As many writers have migrated to urban centers, they have written of traditional Southern values challenged in various ways, as Ted R. Spivey has commented, and they have written about Southerners' assimilation into the new environment. Julius Rowan Raper has theorized about a postmodern Southern sensibility among writers who are nourished by the sense of place that connects them to the South, yet are less and less defined by it. Whether or not they physically live in the South, such writers are the inheritors of many of its historical burdens. But the contemporary, especially material, consumer culture, has also gained a foothold in the South. Bobbie Ann Mason's characters, for example, immerse themselves in pop culture gleaned in television programs, searching for meaning and relevance to their own lives. Cormac McCarthy's novels offer a critique of a failed white Southern culture, as the characters in his novels often retreat to exotic locales in search of more meaningful values. Still other writers, like Sonia Sanchez, fully embrace urban culture, while also being influenced by a rural Southern upbringing. Narrative and storytelling—either written, oral, passed from generation to generation, or from woman to woman—also remains an important facet of contemporary Southern literature. Scholars have frequently written about this aspect of the writings of Lee Smith, Fannie Flagg, and Josephine Humphreys, among other writers, as a particularly characteristic Southern trait. Whether overtly feminist, like the writing of Rita Mae Brown, or writing that deals with the daily interactions of ordinary women, women's narratives have become a strong force in Southern literature. Critics like Angelina Godwin Dvorak, Barbara Bennett, and Peggy Whitman Prenshaw have written about the recurring examinations of women in the South by Southern writers—for example, about the role of food and cooking in their lives; about their use of humor as a survival tactic and as social criticism; and about the sense of strength that Southern women derive from and impart to each other.

REPRESENTATIVE WORKS

Rita Mae Brown
Rubyfruit Jungle (novel) 1973
Southern Discomfort (novel) 1982

James Dickey
The Whole Motion: Collected Poems 1945-1992 (poetry) 1992

Clyde Edgerton
Walking across Egypt (novel) 1987

Fannie Flagg
Fried Green Tomatoes at the Whistle Stop Cafe (novel) 1987

Ernest Gaines
The Autobiography of Miss Jane Pittman (novel) 1971
A Lesson before Dying (novel) 1993

Shirley Ann Grau
The Black Prince and Other Stories (short stories) 1955
Evidence of Love (novel) 1977
Nine Women (short stories) 1985

Allan Gurganus
Oldest Living Confederate Widow Tells All (novel) 1989

Josephine Humphreys
Dreams of Sleep (novel) 1984
Rich in Love (novel) 1987
The Fireman's Fair (novel) 1991

Bobbie Ann Mason
Shiloh and Other Stories (short stories) 1982
In Country (novel) 1985

Peter Matthiessen
Killing Mister Watson (novel) 1990

Cormac McCarthy
Suttree (novel) 1979
All the Pretty Horses (novel) 1982
Blood Meridian; or, The Evening Reddens in the West (novel) 2001

Larry McMurtry
The Last Picture Show (novel) 1969

Toni Morrison
Beloved (novel) 1987

Walker Percy
Lancelot (novel) 1977

Sonia Sanchez
Homecoming (poetry) 1967
Sister Son/ji (drama) 1969

Lee Smith
Black Mountain Breakdown (novel) 1981
Oral History (novel) 1983

William Styron
The Confessions of Nat Turner (novel) 1967

Peter Taylor
Summons to Memphis (novel) 1986

Anne Tyler
Dinner at the Homesick Restaurant (novel) 1982

Alice Walker
The Color Purple (novel) 1982

Eudora Welty
One Writer's Beginnings (lectures) 1984
The Optimist's Daughter (novella) 1984

CRITICISM

Eudora Welty (essay date 1954)

SOURCE: Welty, Eudora. "Place and Time: The Southern Writer's Inheritance.'" *Mississippi Quarterly* 50, no. 4 (fall 1997): 545-51.

[*In the following essay, first published in 1954, Welty discusses some general characteristics of Southern literature and praises the work of such modern novelists as William Faulkner, Katherine Anne Porter, and Peter Taylor.*]

As this was being written, the new book by William Faulkner is about to come out in America—a long novel entitled *A Fable*. One never knows ahead what a new work by Mr. Faulkner will be like—that is one of the joys of living contemporaneously with a genius. Now in the prime of his life, in the mid-fifties, he may well be giving us his major work; the talk is that he himself has an inkling that this is so. We shall have it here before long, and meanwhile the American critics are all giving cry. They ought to know by now, though, that Faulkner's work is a whole, that cannot be satisfactorily analysed and accounted for, until it can be predicted—Lord save the day. That prose is indestructibly itself and alive, something passionate and uncompromising, that will never sit still and wait on what anybody thinks; it will never be a possum in the tree. It sheds its light from higher up than any of the boys can shoot it down.

In the present surge of writers coming out of the South, Faulkner is the Man—pride and joy and show piece. Still, Mr. Edmund Wilson has put himself on record as wondering why on earth Mr. Faulkner doesn't quit all this local stuff and come out of the South to write in civilization. He asks how writing like that can possibly come out of some little town in Mississippi. The marvellous thing is that such writing comes. Let Mr. Wilson try calling for some in another direction, and see how long it takes. Such writing does not happen often, anywhere.

In America, Southerners are always being asked to account for themselves in general; it's a national habit. If they hold themselves too proud, or let themselves go too quickly, to give a reasonable answer, it does not really matter—at least it does not matter to the Southerners. Now that the "Southern Renaissance" is a frequent term, and they are being asked to account for that, some try and others just go on writing. In one little Mississippi town on the river, seventeen authors are in the national print and a Pulitzer Prize winner edits the paper. It is also true that nobody is *buying* books in that town, or generally in the South. It seems that when it comes to books they are reading the old ones and writing the new ones. Southerners are, indeed, apart from and in addition to the giant Faulkner, writing a substantial part of the seriously considered novels, stories and poems of the day in America, and the most interesting criticism. One might just think that they are good at writing, and let it go at that.

There has always been a generous flow of writing to come out of the South. One can begin with Poe and come up through George Washington Cable, Joel Chandler Harris, James Branch Cabell, Julia Peterkin, Willa Cather, Ellen Glasgow, Stark Young, William Alexander Percy, and so on—there are many more. Before the famous *Southern Review* of the thirties there were two previous *Southern Reviews,* the first published more than a hundred years earlier in Charleston. There was the *Southern Literary Messenger,* to which Poe contributed, and there was, and still is, the *South Atlantic Quarterly,* which has been going on in Durham, N. C., for the last fifty years, with many creditable pieces in it, as Dr. W. B. Hamilton's recently published collection from it has made plain. There has been a high standard of journalism in the South, not everywhere, but continuously somewhere; one thinks of it as a tradition out of which came historians and critics like Herbert Agar, who edited the Louisville *Courier* before coming to England; of Virginius Dabney in Richmond, and of Hodding Carter in Greenville, Miss., the aforementioned Pulitzer prize winner.

It is nothing new or startling that Southerners do write—probably they *must* write. It is the way they are: born readers and reciters, great document holders, diary keepers, letter exchangers and savers, history tracers—and, outstaying the rest, great talkers. Emphasis in talk is on the narrative form and the verbatim conversation, for which time is needed. Children who grow up listening through rewarding stretches of unhurried time, reading in big lonely rooms, dwelling in the confidence of slow-changing places, are naturally more prone than other children to be entertained from the first by life and to feel free, encouraged, and then in no time compelled, to pass their pleasure on. They cannot help being impressed by a world around them where history has happened in the yard or come into the house, where all round the countryside big things happened and monuments stand to the memory of fiery deeds still to be heard from the lips of grandparents, the columns in the field or the familiar cedar avenue leading uphill to nothing, where such-and-such a house once stood. At least one version of an inextinguishable history of everybody and his grandfather is a community possession, not for a moment to be forgotten—just added to, with due care, mostly. The individual is much too cherished as such for his importance ever to grow *diminished* in a story. The rarity in a man is what is appreciated and encouraged.

All through their lives Southerners are thus brought up, without any occasion to give it wonder, to be intimate with, and observant of, the telling detail in a life that is changing ever so slowly—like a garden in a season—and is reluctant to be changing at all. Without the conscious surmise of how they may have come to find it out, they do habitually find out how to be curious and aware, and perhaps compassionate and certainly prejudiced, about the stories that can be watched in the happening, all the way—lifelong and generation-long stories. They are stories watched and participated in, if not by one member of the family, then without a break by another, allowing the continuous recital to be passed along in its full course—memory and event and the comprehension of it and being part of it scarcely marked off from one another in the present glow of hearing it again, telling it, feeling it, knowing it. Someday somebody is liable to write it, although nobody is quite so likely to read it. The main thing Southern writers learn is that the story, whatever it is, is not incredible. Of course, that is what they wind up being charged with—stark incredibility. Faulkner is all true—he is poetically the most accurate man alive, he has looked straight into the heart of the matter and got it down for good.

One thing Yoknapatawpha County has demonstrated is that deeper down than people, farther back than history, there is the Place. All Southerners must have felt that they were born somewhere in its story, and can see themselves in line. The South was beautiful as a place, things have happened to it, and it is beautiful still—sometimes to the eye, often to the memory; and beyond any doubt it has a tearing beauty for the vision of the Southern writer, in whose work Place is seen with Time walking on it—dramatically, portentously, mournfully, in ravishment, in remembrance, as the case may be—though without the humour this writing is full of, where would it be? It is a rural land, not industrialized yet—so that William Faulkner can still go out and get his deer—but threatened with industry now; and some towns are much bigger and are filling with strangers, though many, perhaps most, are still small, poor, self-contained, individual, only beginning to change round the edges. The South is in no way homogeneous and even in one state there will be five or six different regions, with different sets of notions, different turns of speech. And yet most of the South's body of memories and lore and states of mind are basically Anglo-Saxon or Celtic—with a small dash of Huguenot French here and there—all of it, most likely, having passed through Virginia at some time or other. In the eighteenth or nineteenth century everybody who was coming to the South came, and mostly they stayed. The Civil War and industry have brought its only visitors. And the writing, in a way, communicates out of this larger and older body of understanding, the inheritance that is more felt than seen, more evident and reliable in thought and dream than in present life, in all the racket of the highways with the trucks and the transports bearing down. Quiet places are still left, if you know where to find them; and inwardly, family life, customs, the way of looking at life, have hardly changed at all, and never will, it is safe to say, at the heart—pride and poverty and maybe a general pernicketiness prevailing. The essential landscape remains one to induce the kind of meditation from which real writing springs.

Place must have something to do with this fury of writing with which the South is charged. If one thing stands out in these writers, all quite different from another, it is that each feels passionately about Place. And not merely in the historical and prideful meaning of the word, but in the sensory meaning, the breathing world of sight and smell and sound, in its earth and water and sky its time and its seasons. In being so moved, the Southerners—one could almost indisputably say—are unique in America today. One would have to look to those other writers of remote parts, to the Irish and the Welsh—to find the same thing.

Literature does belong in essential ways to place, and always invokes place to speak in its fullest voice. To Southerners that assumption is so accepted, lies so deep in the bones, as never to have needed stating among themselves. It belongs to the privacies of writing. The movement of the twenties that was called, to begin with, the Fugitive, might never have quickened and burned so bright except out of defiance—that defiance that habitually springs up in Southerners in the face of what the North wants out of them. The ravishment of their countryside, industrialization, standardization, exploitation, and the general vulgarization of life, have ever, reasonably or not, been seen as one Northern thing to the individualist mind of the South. This new defiance was the kind of emotion that called up a self-conscious power; and the group of poets and essayists clustered round Vanderbilt University in Nashville, Tenn., in those days put all that into an eloquent statement, into the symbol of poetry, into a systematized ethical idea eventually to be christened Agrarianism. What they did was simply to see the South as an entity—historical, geographic, economic, aesthetic—and to take their stand to treat it as such, do or die. Strangely enough, they *did*. Perhaps there was something romantic and heroic about agrarianism, which history has trampled on; but their cause was not lost, for their ideas about writing, perhaps the heart of it all, persevered and triumphed. Their little group flourished and reached out, for the reason that they were, first of all, a group of creative minds, charged to bursting point with the poetic impulse. This was too much to defeat.

Their original organ was the little magazine called *The Fugitive,* green in the mind today for its poetry and criticism. The contributors have almost without exception been published ever since, all over the world; they were the original Southern galaxy of Robert Penn Warren, Allen Tate, John Crowe Ransom, Herbert Agar, Donald Davidson. The writers who came after them, whose early work was nearly all recognized by, and only by, the Agrarian group in its next established quarterly, *The Southern Review,* were not so consciously taking a stand; perhaps now it was not necessary. They wrote out of the same world, and the same instincts, inescapably so, but in their own way, echoing only by the coincidences of strong place feeling these earlier writers. It is likely that the new crop, paying all respect and honour to what had been done before them, would have written their stories and poems just the same, without the Agrarians: they simply would never have got published. *The Southern Review,* edited in Baton Rouge, La., by Robert Penn Warren and Cleanth Brooks and Albert Erskine—with Katherine Anne Porter, John Crowe Ransom, Allen Tate and others acting in close editorial connexion, while some of their finest work was appearing there—was of inestimable help to these new writers in giving them publication in austerely good company, under the blessing of discriminating editing, without ever seeking to alter or absorb them. This was to the good of everybody: the idea was, after all, to keep alight the individual vitality of the region. Eudora Welty is an example of the writers who owe publication of their earliest stories to acceptance by *The Southern Review*. Peter Taylor is another, published there and in a sister quarterly, the *Sewanee*. Of course there were up-and-coming Southern writers *not* appearing in *The Southern Review* or *Sewanee*—Carson McCullers, for instance, came out in Boston in a novel. But there were always enough writers to go round. For years *The Southern Review* did in fact bring out most of the best work of the time, by Warren, Tate, Ransom, Katherine Anne Porter, Caroline Gordon, &c., in an array seldom matched in the files of American magazines. Though *The Southern Review* is gone, *Kenyon* came, and it and the *Sewanee* have carried on the early ideas, though more critical than creative work is filling its pages these days.

Appearing this year in England are books by a number of these writers. *Brother to Dragons,* the brilliant long poem that is Robert Penn Warren's latest work, is an example of that act of Mr. Warren's imagination of drawing up together in one astonishing handful a hundred threads, of passions, deeds, convictions, curiosities and facts, symbols and searchings, holy and unholy, and shaking out before our eyes a resultant poem that is a wonder of dazzling pertinence and beauty. Always vigorous and magnetic, alive with thought and feeling, deeply probing, poetic, scholarly, proud and gay, bitter and affectionate, his work—poems, novels, stories, criticism—continues through the years to circle round the South, old and new, and illuminate it in new aspects and ways.

The Days Before, Katherine Anne Porter's newest book, is a notable collection of essays. It is to be hoped though that her famous stories, too, will soon be available in new editions on this side. Born in Texas, a descendant, it is said, of Daniel Boone—who, as pictured in a current United States advertisement of something, did his writing with a knife on the bark of a tree ("D. Boon kilt a bar here")—Miss Porter has perhaps the greatest purity and elegance of style of all living American writers. In thirty years of writing her output has not been large, and at home she has been asked to account for that, but has serenely continued to put forth perfect things in judicious amounts, just as it suits her. Reproaching her for little output is as illogical as trying to take down the performance of the moon because it is not out every night. Miss Porter's prose has lucidity and radiance, but one would not say it was lunar, for it is neither unearthly nor dreamlike nor particularly feminine. It has the rather more masculine power of mental and moral strength. She deals with states of mind, moral journeyings, with good and evil. She is not especially identified with place, or rather with one place, with her South: Miss Porter is a cosmopolitan in the good and the literal sense both. Within a range of three books of stories she has written of Mexico, Colorado, Germany, Texas, New Orleans, and the remembered South as handed down (with great strength of mind and no vapours) from her grandmother. In retrospect her writing seems to have the most sparingly allotted sensory images of any Southern prose one can think of, but those it has (the "Flowering Judas," the "Pale Horse, Pale Rider") are all the more extraordinarily powerful and compelling; in their role of symbols they control whole stories with the force of magic. It is to be hoped that all three books of stories will shortly be put within the easy reach of English readers; that they are not now is surprising.

Peter Taylor is another writer who one wishes were better known here. He is, in addition to being a good writer, and a young one, the authentic voice of a part of the South too seldom heard from out of the thick of the rumours and alarms of Caldwell and Cain—that of the "nice people." *A Woman of Means, The Long Fourth and Other Stories,* and the recent collection called *The Widows of Thornton* will all be known here, it is to be hoped, before long. Eudora Welty has a new book out this September in England, called *The Ponder Heart.* It is a long story, of comic design, set in a small town in Mississippi. One of Elizabeth Spencer's two novels *This Crooked Way,* is published in England, but the unpublished one is just as good: *Fire in the Morning.* Young and richly talented, a teacher in the University of Mississippi she is at present travelling in England and on the Continent on a Guggenheim Fellowship. Other strongly recommended new novels out of the South in recent months are *A Good Man,* by Jefferson Young, a sensitive study of race relations in a quiet, authentic, and tender voice; and *The Chain in the Heart,* by Hubert Creekmore, an historical novel of race, dealing with three generations of Negroes in the deep South and notable for its sincerity.

Note

1. The first American printing of "Place and Time: The Southern Writer's Inheritance," has been authorized by Eudora Welty and the *Times Literary Supplement,* where it first appeared on September 17, 1954. (A briefer version entitled "From Where I Live" was published in the *Della Review* in 1969.) The editor is thankful to Suzanne Marrs for helping to arrange publication rights, and to Hank Holmes of the Mississippi Department of Archives and History for supplying a copy of Welty's original typescript.

Ted R. Spivey (essay date 1986)

SOURCE: Spivey, Ted R. "The City and the Quest for Cultural Values." In *Revival: Southern Writers in the Modern City,* pp. 12-37. Gainsville: University Presses of Florida, 1986.

[*In the following essay, Spivey presents an overview of the role of the city in Southern life and the Southern literary imagination, noting that the South has traditionally—and mistakenly—been regarded as an agricultural society.*]

Like literary artists throughout Western civilization, many southern writers in the early twentieth century went to large cities to practice their art in order to escape increasing narcissistic and solipsistic tendencies in the provinces. To a greater extent than most other Western cultures the provinces of the South were caught up in an encompassing narcissism, a result of the persistent tendency of southern cultural leaders to look back to the largely imagined glory of the antebellum past. As Arnold Toynbee, Pitirim Sorokin, and other scholar-philosophers have noted, all of Western society after 1800 surrendered to an ever-increasing narcissism. Western culture, Sorokin tells us, became a "sensate" way of life based not so much on fundamental values of culture as on surface images, primarily on the images of imagined collective and individual greatness.[1] One outcome of the growing cultural narcissism was a collision of rival narcissistic cultures that resulted in World War I, the one event that more than any other brought to fruition the modernist movement in the arts.

As early as the mid-nineteenth century serious artists throughout the world had become aware of the decline of values brought about by narcissism and by the attitude that often accompanied such narcissism, puritanism. Narcissism in its extreme form, as analyzed by Christopher Lasch in *Culture of Narcissism* (1979), becomes solipsism. Eventually an ever-increasing narcissism threatens that group cooperation necessary for the life of societies, and a reaction sets in that takes the form of an enforced moralism, often called puritanism. After 1830 provincial societies even in advanced countries like France, England, and Germany were dogged by the growing tyranny of a stifling moralism, or Victorianism, as it came to be called in England. Minor artistic talents often clung to the provincial setting, becoming regional artists; but for most major talents after 1850 the cities beckoned as refuges from a moralism that threatened all new artistic endeavor. Cities offered the artist a freedom to experiment not found in the provinces. As Gertrude Stein once put it, what mattered was not so much what Paris gave the artist as what it did not take away. In great cities like Paris, London, Berlin, and New York, artists found the freedom to search for a revival of serious artistic values. When such herculean figures as Stravinsky, Picasso, Rodin, Joyce, Yeats, and Gropius brought forth art forms that were truly modern, they found that they had in fact challenged values in many areas other than the arts. Above all, they found that the integrity of the human being had been challenged by rapid scientific and technological advances. In 1900 Henry Adams maintained that the chief symbol of civilization was the dynamo and not, as in the past, the more human symbol of the Virgin Mary. Adams, like other modern philosophers and artists, saw the need for the revival of those humanistic and cultural values related to the full development of individuals so that humans would not feel dwarfed by their technological creations.

Robert Langbaum, in *Mysteries of Identity* (1977), maintains that the primary task of the great modern writer is "reconstituting" the twentieth-century self. For Langbaum the loss of human identity is the great modern problem: "Both Yeats and Lawrence, in their attempts to reconstitute the twentieth-century self, take into account the two opposite manifestations of lost identity—solipsism and collectivism."[2] Solipsism, as Lasch suggests, results from a pervasive narcissism that finally isolates individuals from each other, whereas collectivism, or totalitarianism, as Yeats called it, arises largely from the demands of a large number of people for a morality given and enforced by a dictatorship. Hannah Arendt and others have shown how totalitarianism flourishes in societies where the majority of people have little or no personal identity. The gradual loss of identity springs from both solipsism and the absence of a sense of the individual self and its relationship to others. The self, in fact, cannot believe in its own value without taking into account human relationship, as Langbaum suggests by quoting the psychologist Erik A. Erikson: "Societies create the only conditions under which human growth is possible."[3] The great artist then is called, along with other cultural leaders, to combat what Lasch calls the dominant syndrome of this century—the narcissistic-solipsistic syndrome—because, as Langbaum puts it, "No values or persons seem to the solipsist real or important enough to be worth the sacrifice or even postponement of one's own gratification."[4]

Langbaum's importance lies primarily in his analysis of new cultural forms on which creative societies may be built. Thus he counters the pessimism of Lasch, who sees narcissism as a personal and social cancer whose growth is seemingly impossible to check. Actually, of course, artists and other cultural leaders throughout the nineteenth and twentieth centuries have continually fought narcissism-solipsism and the dissolution of human values it brings about. The results of their efforts can in fact still be observed. I take these efforts to be part of the cultural renewal that Sorokin speaks of when he refutes Oswald Spengler's gloomy followers, saying that the "alleged death agony" of civilization has been but "the birth pangs of a new form of culture, the travail attending the release of new creative form."[5]

Possibly the greatest achievement of Western civilization since 1750 has been the ability of its various societies to discover new values as well as to revive old ones. For this reason, even more than for its science and technology, the West is imitated by all of the major societies of the world. Chinese musicians, for example, risk imprisonment to play Western music, and Japanese readers form groups to study William Faulkner or Thomas Hardy. Certain nations of the West have declined into totalitarianism, but evidence of meaningful Western cultural renewal since 1800 is revealed by the fact that major nations like Britain, France, and America—and many smaller ones also—have avoided totalitarianism and social disintegration (which always go together) by maintaining the spirit of freedom and creativity, by keeping an "open society," as Karl Popper has called such nations. One of the chief reasons for this growth is that the great cities have remained open to artistic experimentation and new ideas and have resisted the rigid puritanism of the provinces. Modern artists and philosophers put aside Victorianism without sinking into moral anarchy; they explored and revived human values and formed a new chapter in the development of cultural values even as much of Western culture was disintegrating. The best modern artists were witnesses to the enormous inhumanity and acts of violence of a century that is now regarded as a major transitional period in human history—transitional, let us hope (and as Sorokin maintains) to a new age of cultural formation.

All I have written thus far about modern artists and their encounter with the great city can be said of the nine significant southern writers I have chosen to examine. But these southerners, all of whom were deeply influenced by modern cities as well as by the great universities connected with them, also turned to the South to examine the culture of their region. In fact, they saw more clearly than many other artists, particularly other American artists, that the great cities exacted an enormous price in loss of cultural values and that the vision of creative freedom they offered was sometimes dimmed by those megalopolitan aspects of great cities about which Spengler writes. Modern literary artists as diverse as Baudelaire and Matthew Arnold, of course, have dealt with the numbing effect of cities like Paris and London, but they seldom have shown any awareness of values other than those of the great city itself. Major southern writers, on the other hand, even when they were most at war with the South, maintained a belief in certain cultural values that they absorbed from their native region. The two chief values they cling to, I suggest, are community-centeredness and hierarchy. Even when, like Wolfe or Ellison, the southern writer does not return to his native heath, he still maintains those values—and his adopted city is in part judged by them. Indeed, in the case of a writer like Wolfe, as Paschal Reeves has pointed out, the experience of extreme individualism in New York brings forth a vision of not only a southern but also an American community awareness. Wolfe was first drawn to Harvard and then to New York because he hoped to find a hierarchal leadership that would enable him to become a literary artist, but when he encountered the extreme individualism of megalopolitan New York he reacted by returning to his deeply held southern values and by bringing forth in his later works visions of communal existence. Wolfe and other southerners found in New York the remnants of an old cultural center that for a time provided hierarchal leadership, but they also found the megalopolitan individualistic spirit of urban sprawl.

Although largely disowned by southern writers of the Agrarian tradition, Thomas Wolfe is in fact typical of most of the better-known southern writers of this century. His sense of hierarchy not only drew him to the cultural values found in great cities like New York, London, and Berlin; it also led him to accept the influence of professors in two universities, North Carolina and Harvard. In fact, the university and its surrounding city have had in this century probably as much influence on southern writers as the great city itself. Universities like Vanderbilt and North Carolina played important roles in freeing many southerners from the grip of southern narcissism and puritanism. Like Wolfe, the Agrarians encountered a small center of culture in a southern university; and many went from Vanderbilt to other American universities as well as some of the great cities of the world. Some, like Wolfe, chose to live in the North, others returned to the South. Most of the Agrarians, like other southern writers, struggled to retain the old southern emphasis on certain cultural values like community-centeredness and to acquire at the same time the values of other regions and countries. Although some, like Warren and Styron, ceased to be southern in their outlook, most of the major writers remained stubbornly southern, often to the point of returning to live in the South and struggling with the problems they found there. They became, in a sense, revivers of culture in the South by reviving certain cultural values within themselves and then, as teachers and writers, helping others to revive these values, particularly in the realm of higher education.

The hierarchal attitude of southerners in regard to higher education meant that their attitude toward culture was largely shaped by the humanistic tradition of letters as handed down by professors who upheld a literary continuum from Shakespeare to Tennyson and Arnold. Southern writers went beyond their professors by accepting as their chief literary hierarchs such moderns as James Joyce and T. S. Eliot; several in their roles as professors and critics helped to bring these and other esteemed modern writers into the canon of Anglo-American letters. In fact, what they had learned about English literature prepared them for the emergence of Joyce and Eliot as literary leaders. After all, these southerners, particularly in the realm of culture and literary criticism, harked back to a tradition that began with Goethe, Wordsworth, and Coleridge, all of whom saw the need to restore cultural values in order to restore true community.

Wordsworth declared in his best poetry that visions of harmony leading to emotions of joy and love were necessary for a true restoration of community; his friend Coleridge, in his influential essays, proclaimed the need for the development of the imagination to allow humans to glimpse the essence underlying matter—essence, according to Coleridge, that was based on harmony and organic form and that gave meaning to all life. Culture was also a matter of personal development for the romantics. According to Arnold, in his famous essay "Sweetness and Light" in *Culture and Anarchy,* "Culture places human perfection in an *internal* condition, in the growth and predominance of our humanity proper, as distinguished from our animality. . . . Faith in machinery [is] our besetting danger."[6] Obsessions with material objects, Arnold says, can keep us from our true cultural activity, the quest for "the peace and satisfaction which are reached as we draw near to complete spiritual perfection, and not merely to moral perfection."[7] Yeats, whose ideas influenced Joyce and Eliot, emphasizes in his criticism the "return to imagination" and to "organic rhythms, which are the embodiment of the imagination."[8] For Yeats, as Richard Ellmann points out, unity of being was the most significant cultural value. In all of these injunctions of the romantic and neoromantic critics there was always an emphasis on moving forward toward a deeper personal life that denied the claims of both narcissism and materialism. This refined personal life was based on spiritual growth, an idea that attacked the puritan belief in the supremacy of morality as the great human good.

Southern writers in their hierarchal conservatism also held to Shakespeare and the Bible, as well as to certain tenets basic to the Judeo-Christian tradition, the chief of which is the primacy of love in the hierarchy of values. Love of God and neighbor have traditionally been for Christians and Jews the chief commandments, and love is considered to be the fulfillment of God's law. I do not mean to suggest that only southerners were aware of the need for love. One of the great themes of both nineteenth- and twentieth-century literature is love in all its various forms. In a wide-ranging study of literature since 1800, *The Romantic Heroic Ideal* (1982), James D. Wilson writes about love and voluntary cooperation: "In America, then, it was possible to see solipsism as antithetical to that kind of voluntary cooperation among citizens demanded by emergent democracies."[9] Wilson goes on to claim that "love can be for the hero a potentially redemptive force, but not if it is narcissistic."[10] Narcissism and puritanism continue into this century, and their presence encourages many writers to demand a principle that will bind people together. Jung wrote, late in his life, "The free society needs a bond of an affective nature, a principle of a kind like *caritas,* the Christian love of your neighbor." He follows this injunction with an even more pointed statement: "Where love stops, power begins, and violence and terror."[11]

Northern writers have been just as aware of the need for *caritas* as southern writers, although southern writers think of love in terms of a particular community, their own, and in terms of a hierarchal tradition of letters, with Shakespeare and the Bible representing the fountainhead of that tradition. Northern writers in this century, like southern writers, have sought the freedom of the great city in order to escape provincial puritanism, but they have often tended to become exiles in megalopolis before moving on to join artistic enclaves. The great southern writers, even when living in the North, have linked themselves to the southern community. Northern writers let go of much of the past, but southern writers at their best have continued to work out of their cultural heritage. A sense of the past as well as an awareness of the need for community drew the best southern writers to Joyce and Eliot. In these two writers they found men who could carry on the Anglo-American literary tradition and at the same time accept new concepts of mythology that grew out of James Frazer's *The Golden Bough.* It was Eliot's mythical method that enabled southern writers to discover their cultural roots.

The struggles of southern writers with the complexities of myth led them to understand the hidden and often misunderstood depths of their own culture. These struggles led them past pseudo-myths like that of the story of the great white mansion, which concentrated on the plantation splendors of the South. They were often able to discern the usefulness as well as the limitations of social myths like those connected with the Old South and the New South. But above all, the mythical method led them to look more deeply at the values of their own culture, to see how many of these values were dying, and to bring forth visions of cultural rebirth that were related to that revival of values necessary for individual and community existence. Through myth they hoped to find again the hidden unity—or context, in the anthropological sense—that lends coherence to a revived culture. With myth they could fight the forces of narcissism, puritanism (in the sense of fanatical moralism), and an ever-growing collectivism. But before I seek to define myth as it was developed in the work of Joyce and Eliot and then passed on to the southern writers, it is necessary to look briefly at that hierarchal, community-oriented culture which these writers inherited and which their work, in one sense, was dedicated to reviving.

* * *

The South has suffered from stereotyping more than most cultures of the Western world. The most pervasive stereotypes depict either a rural paradise or a rural hell. Actually, because of its close connections with Europe the South has been traditionally one of the most cosmopolitan regions in the nation.

Close examination of a society that is considered to have originated in a plantation economy reveals that the region's tobacco and rice plantations served in part as a sieve through which culture passed from Europe to the people of the early South. These plantations, however, were not part of either paradise or hell but rather part of an urban-rural continuum that included both New World and Old World cities and communal towns. They were part of what we would call today agribusiness. Owners of the first great plantations that became the models for the later upcountry plantations spent much of their lives in urban communities and traveled as extensively as their incomes permitted. Carl Bridenbaugh, discussing the differences between the Chesapeake gentry and the Carolina gentry, points to money as the central factor in the early development of what we now call the Deep South: "Unlike the illusory wealth of the Chesapeake gentry, that of the Carolinians was real; for its time, it was the big money. Upon favored possessors it conferred a precious endowment of abundant leisure and the coveted privilege of living in the city, at the same time that it sucked dry the rural low country." Yet, as Bridenbaugh shows, this early foundation of the Deep South was not based on a "grasping materialism" but instead was "circumscribed by a still powerful aristocratic tradition with a clear-cut standard of taste." What regulated behavior was "status, accepted as a yardstick."[12] Thus the social hierarchy of Britain extended into the South from earliest times.

The most important element of southern culture has always been the urban center. The European settlements in the American South were urban-based, beginning with the city of St. Augustine in 1565 and continuing in 1607 with Jamestown and later Williamsburg, Charleston (1670), New Orleans (1718), and Savannah (1733). The most important characteristic of the southern urban center, as Bridenbaugh suggests, was that it maintained a lifeline to certain European metropolises. This fact has continued to be important and accounts for a sometimes unexpected cosmopolitanism as well as a European-style decadence in the personalities of people who have lived at the center of southern culture. Brownell and Goldfield explain the position of the southern city in the British trade system: "Southern cities in the colonial period were basically creatures of British mercantilism. Their markets were defined by trade laws emanating from London and their very existence was in part the result of British colonial designs. In a 'typical' colonial economy, southern cities functioned as market centers for agricultural products destined for final processing in the mother metropolis." From its beginnings in colonial days the South, as Brownell and Goldfield indicate, was an urban-rural continuum: "The close interdependence with agriculture became a characteristic feature of southern urban growth."[13]

The majority of people who created the northern and western cultures of America thought of themselves as leaving behind the evils of Europe, carrying with them a few old ideas and techniques; but in the South there were always strong ties with the Old World that were never denied—that were, on the contrary, cherished. One of the many evidences of this is that little "isolationism" has ever existed in the South. In World Wars I and II southerners of all classes led the nation in volunteering to fight in Europe.

The second most important fact about the South and the one least understood is its kinship with the French and Spanish cultures in the New World. In his study *Myths and Realities: Societies of the Colonial South*, Bridenbaugh deals only with the Chesapeake and Carolina societies, ignoring the fact that the colonial South also included Florida and Texas of the Spanish colonial empire and Louisiana of the French colonial empire. The South is the least white—Anglo-Saxon—Protestant culture of the three major cultures of the United States. Like the French and the Spanish, southerners—many of whom in fact were French and Spanish—became deeply involved with large African and native American populations. Northerners and westerners, with a few notable exceptions, kept Indians and blacks at a great distance. The English throughout the world have always feared "going native," and this psychic fear was deep both in the Puritan forefathers who stayed at home and in those who went west.

The English element in the South, to be sure, has always been strong; and the southerner shares many attitudes with his northern countrymen. But existing side by side with "Englishness" in the southerner is that Latin element absorbed from the beginning by contacts with the Spanish in Florida and the West Indies and with the French in South Carolina and Louisiana. The "Englishness" of Southerners led them to hide from others and sometimes even from themselves their blood connections with Indians and blacks. These hidden connections are so vital and underestimated that I will return to deal with them at length later; it is impossible, for example, to understand much of William Faulkner's work without taking them into account.

The branding of the South as Protestant—and for many non-southern intellectuals it is indeed a brand—is a mistake, as much so as supposing that the South is basically white and Anglo-Saxon. The North and the West, until recently, were Protestant cultures, but the South began as a Catholic culture, both Roman Catholic and Anglo-Catholic, and, in a general religious sense, remained so, despite the rural Protestant elements. The Spanish and the French—even the Huguenots—brought with them a religious vision that was deeply bound to medieval Catholicism. And the settlers at Jamestown, Charleston, and Savannah brought with them an Anglicanism that had the imprimatur of the liturgical Catholicism of a conservative queen, Elizabeth I. Even Methodism began in America as a society within the Church of England; Francis Asbury, first bishop of the Methodist church, sought to preserve the hierarchal tradition in Anglicanism by keeping the title of bishop. Even the Baptists, and various Pentecostal sects both black and white, preserved in their religious life a lavish and sometimes outlandish communalism that is not found in the individualistic Protestantism of the North and West.

Two terms sum up the southern culture better than any others: community-centeredness and hierarchy. The southern emphasis of the community over the individual has its roots not only in the religiosity of the culture but also in the strong influences of the tribal life of Africans and Indians on the South. In fact, Bridenbaugh has said that in the colonial life of the Chesapeake and Carolina societies the "Negro supplied to each society its common determining human element."[14] As for hierarchy, the fact that the South was in many ways an extension of European society made southerners respect all the trappings of the hierarchal, aristocratic way of life that dominated Europe until the twentieth century. One who persists in thinking of the South as an Anglo-Saxon culture should study how the Irish and the Highland Scots—both groups that were originally Catholic, communal, and persecuted by the English and the Protestant Scots—found a way of life in the South that held a profound attraction for them. They and the Spanish, the French, the Africans, the Indians, the English Catholics, and the Anglicans finally combined to make a way of life far more complex than that society called to mind by clichés having to do with white mansions and backwoods Protestantism.

Many reasons can be found for the misunderstanding that non-southern Americans have about the South. In fact, southerners often feel they are better understood by Europeans than they are by other Americans—partly because most other Americans broke many of their ties with Europe, whereas those people who lived at the center of southern culture carefully cultivated their European roots. There is an even more important reason for these misunderstandings, one which has to do with several of the major social myths of America. The three great cultures of the United States have each been represented by certain myths. The North early became associated with mechanical inventiveness and self-improvement; it has since become the site of the largest financial-industrial complex in the world. The mythology of the West has dealt with shaping and harnessing natural forces and with containing and eliminating destructive human beings who exploited nature for personal gain—that is, with bringing "law and order" to untamed man and nature. The southern social myth centers around the plantation, which represented the union of the advantages of urban and rural life in order to bring European patterns of hierarchy and community to the New World. But the myth of the plantation has too often taken the form of what I call the story of the great white mansion, which deals with a house located in an idyllic natural setting replete with happy slaves and resplendent lords and ladies. An opposing myth of the South as one large concentration camp was bound to arise in reaction to these magnolia-blossom stories.

The chief social myths of a society by no means sum up all of the life, good and bad, of that society, but they do contain most of its major tasks, or missions, as a society, and therein lies much of their value. A culture that has no mission loses a sense of cohesiveness and dies unless new tasks are found. The failures associated with the southern mission were possibly greater and certainly more obvious than those of the North and West. For example, the failures of plantation life yielded stories of effete "ladies and gentlemen," on one hand, and of slave-driving fanatics on the other.

Pseudo-myth always gathers in clusters around true myth and eventually, according to Gresham's Law, drives it from the intellectual and the cultural marketplace. The Horatio Alger stories of the North, the dime novels of western banditry, and the moonlight-and-magnolia sagas—all pseudo-myths of America—have had great effect on huge audiences. Harmless at best, they become dangerous when taken literally. The southern pseudo-myths, which have a far more ridiculous quality about them than those of the other two regions, have often been taken literally by many Americans who passionately admire or hate southern culture.

The historical background of the southern pseudo-myths shows why they have led to such profound misunderstanding, even animosity, about the South. The aim of the Chesapeake settlers to create something like the English country estates (which were always closely connected with the life of London) and the phenomenon of the plantations of the Deep South (which were also urban-oriented) was never understood by early northern Protestants. This misunderstanding goes back to hostility during and before Reformation and Counter-Reformation wars between northern and southern Europe.

Since the days of Greek and Roman culture, agricultural and urban life-styles have always been more intimately connected in southern Europe than in northern Europe, which was not as strongly influenced by Roman culture. This difference continued into American colonial days, when anything Spanish was considered the devil's handiwork. Later many northerners and westerners looked at the South the way most English colonials looked at Spanish America, seeing only a society of decadent aristocrats tyrannizing a debased slave population—the sort of vision of Latin America we find in Herman Melville's story "Benito Cerino."

Henry Adams, one of America's most perceptive students of culture, found the South like another world. In *The Education of Henry Adams* (1907), he describes his visit to Mount Vernon. His usually acute mind could not square the greatness of George Washington with the place he was seeing, the meaning of which lay beyond his historical imagination and understanding. His mental confusion was representative of how deeply the North and South misunderstood each other in the nineteenth century. A culture is measured in part by those people in it who rise to eminence. This fact Adams could not accept; for him Washington could not be a part of the South. Yet no one who sprang from southern culture represented its eighteenth-century leadership better than George and Martha Washington. Not that they were typical; they simply epitomized a period of southern culture when Virginia led the South, in the way that Louis XIV personified French culture in the late seventeenth century. Stories about Washington, some real and some apocryphal, became an important part of southern as well as American mythology. Washington and his wife had the fine sense of hierarchy typical of the colonial South and also a sense of community not readily understood today, because since their day it has been assumed that the hierarchal patrician is aloof from the demands of community. It was neither Washington's intellect nor his money nor his ability to command soldiers that held together a community of soldiers and later a young nation, but simply his character, as Thomas Jefferson pointed out—the kind of character that made most Americans feel reverence and awe in his presence. Like all people, Washington had more weaknesses than history can properly record, but, like the early Spanish conquerers, the strength of his personality enabled him to do the work the times demanded. Like the Spanish conquerers, Washington was torn between the good life on an estate and the ambition that drove him into worldly affairs. In a 1976 biography of Washington, Noemie Emery describes the father of the nation: "There was no choice ever for the shy and driven half brother for whom fame and service, duty and ambition were inextricably interwoven and set into his bones and blood. His intermittent efforts at 'retirement' . . . were recuperations, repair between exertions, the background for his efforts and the repair for his belief."[15]

The South, as I have already suggested, has been fortunate to possess a literature that is one of the most acclaimed in the twentieth century. What has generally not been understood is that much of this literature is closely connected with the development of the modern urban centers in the South. In fact, the role of the urban center in both southern literature and southern culture has been ignored. The chief reason the southern urban centers have not received the kind of study they deserve is that the only urban center considered to be a true city by many people in the late twentieth century is the megalopolis, what John Kenneth Galbraith has more recently termed the "polyglot metropolis." Only very recently have we seen cities like Atlanta, Memphis, Houston, Dallas, and Miami turning into smaller versions of New York. Faulkner and O'Connor depicted Memphis and Atlanta as cities whose growth was shapeless, thereby signifying at least some of the chaos of megalopolis.

However, cities such as Savannah, Charleston, Richmond, San Antonio, Memphis, and New Orleans are now exploring the possibilities of participating in cultural renewal instead of allowing their inner cities to become museums surrounded by a polyglot metropolitan sprawl; we see more and more in the seventies and eighties a search for the role that inner cities can play in the cultural development of a region. Galbraith has contributed to the study of cities as types in his *Age of Uncertainty,* noting that in addition to the polyglot metropolis there are also the governmental city, the merchant city, the industrial city, and the bedroom city. What is still needed, however, is a contemporary concept of the American cultural city. Studies of the Italian Renaissance, for instance, have for many years dealt with certain European cities as cultural centers, but Americans have never believed in themselves as creators of urban cultural centers. When sophisticated Americans like Franklin, Jefferson, Henry James, or T. S. Eliot have sought urban culture, they have often turned to Europe. The continuing influence of European culture is responsible for causing southerners to seek ways in which the city can be made a center of cultural development.

American individualism and the myth of the frontier have made Americans in many cases forget the meaning of the city as a cultural center. Frederick Jackson Turner and other mythographers of American history would have us believe that the frontier is the dominant fact of American life. The experiences and stories of Americans living on the frontier have of course been an important part of American life; their importance should never be underestimated. But the frontier is not the dominant fact of cultural life in this country. Indeed, the frontier itself loses all meaning (except as the expression of individualism) unless it is seen as a part of the expansion of America to the Pacific coast.

The reason that the frontier has always held such sway over critics of America is that it was the place where two great dramas could be acted out. In fact, the entire New World was thought by many to be made for these dramas. The first is the exploitation of resources, both environmental and human. *Exploitation* sounds harsh to those who prefer the word *development*. But the idea behind this drama, call it what one will, is simply to strike it rich, either quickly (by finding gold or seizing someone else's) or, in a more extended manner, by setting up great estates and factories and marshaling huge labor gangs to create wealth. The other drama that is always present, sometimes as a reaction against the first, is the search for complete freedom from the demands or even the help of others, for the achievement of self-sufficiency as envisioned by Thoreau in *Walden* or by Emerson in "Self-Reliance." Huck Finn's story is a great mythic statement of this drama of the quest for a freedom beyond the demands of society, just as Daniel Boone's is a real-life version of it.

The American quest to develop natural resources and to find room for personal growth is not inherently evil. But when separated from culture, the concepts of development and freedom become absolutes that lead to the opposite of what is desired: absolute freedom, as Socrates once pointed out, leads finally to absolute tyranny. In other words, the myths on which the frontier was based had some creative results as long as they had a cultural basis. The concepts of freedom and development have been explored endlessly in this century, but the exploration of the meaning of culture still awaits our serious attention.

Culture represents the unification of humanity's values at a given time in a given geographical area. Sorokin says that "any great culture, instead of being a mere dumping place of a multitude of diverse cultural phenomena . . . represents a unity."[16] There have been thousands of individual cultures and there will probably be thousands more; like stars in the galaxies, cultures are always burning out and coming into being. The nature of humanity is such that it needs a certain amount of unity and order in its life to maintain a basis for creative activities, but unity and order alone are not enough; there must also be a certain amount of diversity to stimulate creativity so that boredom can be overcome.

The breakup of cultures all over the world has led to two responses that do not work over any length of time. One is to set up a rigid authoritarianism and enforce unity at any price. The other method is to allow complete diversity or "freedom." Extreme individualism, as polities have often shown in their decline, often leads to a demand for order at any price, which brings us back to centralized authority. Only through the development of those human and cultural values that make a true civilization possible can the extremes of totalitarianism on one hand and anarchy on the other be avoided. Culture accommodates freedom and individualism as well as order and responsibility and thus allows for a meaningful civilized existence. All known cultures have flaws that are evinced in the human failings of individual members. But the difference between a people with culture and a people without it is the difference between a certain amount of order, individual happiness, and a widespread distinctiveness on the one hand and political-state tyranny on the other.

Possibly the greatest single theme since 1850 of all the arts, and literature in particular, has been the growing collapse of cultural values in the West. But in the West, as opposed to other cultural areas of the world, there has been in the arts and other areas a strong creative effort to recover the values that undergird civilization. The best of our artists have recorded this effort to give new life to values. Nietzsche in the late nineteenth century saw that Western humanity's greatest need was what he called the transvaluation of all values. Creative writers in particular have sought in their best work to present visions of the possibility of this transvaluation. Historians also have sought to give us insight into basic values that still exist in our disintegrating culture.

As I have suggested, the best southern writers have long emphasized the central values of hierarchy and community even as cultural unity itself has steadily declined. With the decline of this unity there has been a tendency to forget these values and to see the South only in terms of certain pseudo-myths. The pseudo-myth that sees the South in terms of a great white mansion has led some to think of the region as once having been a "sacred community." There are other pseudo-myths, supported by James Baldwin and other writers, that portray the South as nothing but a concentration camp. All cultures are prone to certain delusions and evil practices. If such cultures survive it is because at least some of their members have worked to revive the culture's basic values.

Modern southerners have often doubted that their culture ever contained many important values worth reviving. For instance, one southern journalist, W. J. Cash, writes, with insufficient understanding of his region's culture, that the South has always been "simple in its culture, always inclined to lag, never having had within itself any very fecund principle of intellectual development."[17] Yet southern culture in this century has produced several of the most complex and advanced writers found anywhere in the twentieth century, not to mention colonial America's most influential intellectual, Thomas Jefferson. Obviously Cash never looked at southern culture as a whole; neither did he consider the role of mythology in southern history. Tindall may well be right when he asks, "Can it be that the historians have been looking in the wrong places, that they have failed to seek the key to the enigma where the poets have so readily found it—in the mythology that has had so much to do with shaping character, unifying society, developing a sense of community, of common ideals and shared goals, making the region conscious of its distinctiveness?"[18]

Yet myths, particularly social myths, often mislead southern writers. The social myths of the Old South and New South, now nearly worn out, have misled many into thinking there have been only two historical periods in southern life—one before the Civil War, based on slavery (when in fact only a relative handful of southerners owned more than five slaves and the majority never owned slaves at all), and the other after the Civil War, when the South tried to catch up with the North in industry and education. Actually there have been at least four periods of southern culture before 1945: from 1660 to 1763, when religious and commercial expansion were at a peak; from 1763 to 1819, when southern leaders like Jefferson helped unify the nation under federalism; from 1820 to 1865, when the so-called Cotton Kingdom and southern nationalism were dominant; and from 1877 to 1945, when the South, though still partly nationalistic, moved toward an acceptance of certain aspects of the dominant commercial-industrial life of the North.

I have already suggested that it is time to recognize that the South since 1945 has been in a new period which I call the restored South—restored, that is, to the dominant currents of American life. This restoration of the South to the American mainstream came in a period when those who lived in the major regions of the country, including various ethnic and racial groups—blacks and Hispanics in particular—were searching for a better understanding of their own ways of life. Southern creative writers and historians have been in the vanguard of this movement. In searching for values inherent in their own regional culture they have sometimes achieved visions of the meaning of culture in general and of the South in particular. Writers like Faulkner, Wolfe, Ellison, and Percy have even suggested the possibility of a new, unified national culture.

One reason why millions of readers everywhere in the world have found southern authors so appealing is that they have been prompted by an essential conservatism of spirit; the best modern southern writers have sought to recover memory and history. But they also have made the inner quest for renewal. In their search into history and memory, as well as into their psyches, they have discovered the real meaning of both death and rebirth; namely, that death has meaning only to those who can fully accept it and still desire life. These writers have seen life in the South as having once been communal because it was based on cultural values that united the region's urban centers with farms and plantations in an agribusiness complex. With the decline of southern culture they have perceived and written about the possibility of cultural rebirth taking place in this century.

With the rise to dominance of the megalopolis in the South as well as in the other civilized cultures of the world, many have forgotten the cultural beginnings of the city. Megalopolitan values are often read into the past by good historians and novelists who see nothing but the struggle of isolated individuals trying to grab the world's goods for themselves. But although the spirit of megalopolis had come by 1960 to dominate the cities and even the small towns of the world, surviving fragments of the old culture still existed, and attempts to revive the basic function of the city as a cultural center, rather than seeing it only in terms of the modern megalopolitan sprawl, continued to be made.

One of the best statements about the values underlying southern culture is Robert Manson Myers's *The Children of Pride,* a book of nearly two thousand pages devoted mainly to the letters of the Jones family of Midway, Georgia, in the nineteenth century. This work reveals the nature of the urban-rural continuum of southern culture in general and the role in particular that the city and agribusiness played in the development of the region. Above all, the letters testify to the continuation of culture in a family that began as a communal multi-ethnic group and became one of the great families of the South, with its members eventually playing leading roles both on farms and in cities. This family sums up the meaning of culture at its best in nineteenth-century America. Of the family itself Myers writes:

> Throughout the antebellum South the Midway people were justly known for their remarkable way of life. No planting community could boast deeper religious convictions, higher intellectual cultivation, gentler social refinement, or greater material wealth. The church was the very cornerstone of their being. . . . Education was second only to religion. . . . In a society thus fixed on the things of the mind and the spirit the people were virtuous and accomplished. If few were extravagantly rich, all were comfortably disposed; equality of rank and fortune generally prevailed, and social life was leisurely, gracious, and polite.[19]

Indications of the life of true culture in all aspects of the South continue to multiply with the growth of scholarly investigation, but what is now needed are large views of all three of the nation's major cultures that will show the unity underlying the diverse activities of different peoples in a region, as well as the elements of disharmony and chaos—the power of anticulture. The Emery biography of George Washington has some of this scope. The author begins her work by establishing the city as the central focus of life in Virginia, and London as the city that most influenced Virginia's culture; she quotes Hugh Jones, writing in 1724 in *The Present State of Virginia*: "The habits, life, customs, computations &c. of the Virginians are much the same as about London, which they esteem their home." Emery reveals the obsessive and brooding qualities of Washington, his coldness toward those on the lower rungs of the social ladder as well as toward his own mother: "The youthful acolyte at the shrine of aristocracy would never find much enchantment in the ignorance or antics of the poor." She also shows us Washington's ravenous land hunger, which drove him to acquire a "500-acre tract on Bullskin Creek in Frederick County, bought with his first saved cache of his surveying money, when he was slightly more than sixteen years of age."[20] Yet Emery also depicts Washington as a representative man in a culture directly linked to the very centers of European life, in which the hierarch held sway not only because of breeding but also because of an innate ability to unite disparate groups. Thus the biographer who plunges into the heart of Washington's life or that of a lesser person will find the thread of culture that makes possible the individual's creative acts and restrains those inevitable forces of entropy that exist at all times in people and societies.

In the later decades of this century one of the significant challenges of cultural history has been to perceive what was creative and destructive in past cultures, so that a cultural hierarch like Washington is neither idealized as a figure wrought in marble nor reviled as an absurd, even malevolent figure to be studied only because he must be debunked. The same may be said of the different stages of the development of the three American cultures and of American culture generally.

The cultural historian must also recognize that another challenge facing the modern age, particularly since 1960, has been to see that life is in many ways the opposite of what it was a hundred years ago. Then the forces of culture still held in check a growing personal and social chaos. Now, as the century closes, chaotic forces have been unleashed; but much good still remains within society and individuals. Fragments of culture exist, as do visions of cultural rebirth. For that rebirth to take place there must be a renewal of the city as cultural center; this renewal will lead in turn to the renewal of the urban-rural continuum. The question now is: can we prepare ourselves for new life and can we bear the pain of this renewal? The answer, I think, can be seen in the renewal process that is even now going on in certain southern cities.

Even as some cities have disintegrated from within since 1960, we have seen others renewing themselves. Charleston has been a prime example of cultural renewal. Chosen by Gian Carlo Menotti as the site for the greatest contemporary American art festival—an American Spoleto—Charleston is a living refutation of many pseudomyths about the South. It is and has always been a place of struggle and development where people from many parts of the world have found a home and where religious and civic freedoms have always been cherished. Charleston in the 1980s is a living reminder that individual as well as communal cultural revival is possible.

A study of the culture of early Charleston reveals that instead of being simply an urban area surrounded by plantations, it was actually a kind of city-state, in effect an urban-agricultural continuum governed culturally by a city center. The spirit of frontier individualism, together with the New South spirit of individual enterprise, tended to obscure this early urban and communal development of southern culture. Historian Blaine Brownell says of two cities that came into their own in the New South period, "In Memphis and Birmingham the spirit of the twentieth-century metropolis was traced back to the adventurous frontiersman rather than to the patriarchal planter."[21] Actually, both frontiersmen and planters played roles in developing upland cities like Memphis and Birmingham, but the basic southern culture that underlay these cities first grew in the Tidewater cities. By the end of the seventies both Memphis and Birmingham, in the new period of the restored South, were seeking a kind of urban renewal that would place greater emphasis than ever before on both communal and artistic forms of individual expression. With the growth of black political and economic power in Birmingham, Memphis, and other southern cities there came an even greater emphasis on urban community. Indeed, the southern black community is the most community-centered of all the different groups in the South. Increasing black and Hispanic influences inevitably mean more emphasis on communal activities. The revival, beginning in the sixties, of many southern cities—Savannah, Tampa, San Antonio, New Orleans, and Charleston, for example—was the work of representatives of four traditional southern communities: the gentry, the yeomanry, the Hispanics, and the black community. The urban renewal of San Antonio, for instance, was based in large part on the traditional Hispanic concern for communal life. Urban revival was also greatly aided by northerners newly arrived in the South as well as by Europeans and Latin Americans who were drawn to the South after 1945. Southern urban cultural development in the restored South forms an important chapter in American life of the late twentieth century.

Unless we view both urban revival and the growth of the arts in America as part of a larger cultural development, I believe we will not understand the emergence after 1960 of a long-range attempt to renew the nation's entire culture. If this development is not understood, then we are left only with an awareness of the decline of cultural forms everywhere. The powerful effect of cultural decline was seen in the sixties, when it drove counterculture advocates to try to create a new culture overnight. It has caused others to advocate a totally regulated society in which human emotions are eliminated. Amaury de Riencourt, attacking B. F. Skinner's utopian vision, tells us that "nothing specifically human remains in the Skinnerian world" and cites one of Skinner's most damning quotes: "To man *qua* man I say good riddance."[22]

Are there concrete signs that any kind of rebirth is really taking place amidst what seems to be overwhelming cultural decay? If we look at changes in language, the most basic of all cultural forms, in the South we definitely see new growth. Emory University linguist Lee Pederson states that although one southern speech pattern is passing away, another that is distinctly southern is coming into being: "Atlanta's speech is changing, but it is not changing to Northern speech, but to another version of Southern speech, quite different from Northern urban."[23] A large view of cultural history, as Sorokin tells us, indicates that cultural death and revival go on side by side. When one way of life dies, no instant vacuum is created into which flows some totally new way of life. For instance, when the urban culture of the Roman Empire died in the West between A.D. 400 and 700, the new rural societies did not totally cease to be Roman; neither were they swamped by the incoming barbarians. (In fact, the barbarians were looking for a new way of life when they invaded the dying Roman Empire.) A way of life that eventually became Western civilization had been emerging for several centuries from the wreckage of Greco-Roman culture. The concept of rebirth must be included in our understanding of culture, which should be seen, as R.

W. Collingwood maintains, not as something static but rather as a continual becoming. Collingwood thus refutes Oswald Spengler's concept of culture as a social entity without issue: "There is no static entity called culture, there is only a perpetual development.... And this conception of 'turning into', the conception of becoming, is the fundamental idea of all history."[24]

If a new culture is indeed emerging in the revived cities of America, one may well ask what it is that the various groups taking part in urban revival want most. The answer, I think, can be found in the searchings of American writers and other artists in the cultural centers of Europe and America during the early twentieth century. What they sought was a realization of their inner selves and the chance to express themselves as artists in an atmosphere removed from the puritanism and narcissism of the provinces. Their first concern had to be with cultural values connected with their own particular art form, but as they saw the culture of cities like New York and Paris slowly dissolving before the rising megalopolis, they also became concerned in their work with other cultural values—those related to the family, politics, religion, and the male-female relationship, among others. The spirit of megalopolis as defined by Spengler is that of individualistic effort without order, leading to what we now call urban sprawl. Its spirit is everywhere in the civilized world, but increasingly since 1960 provincial cities in America have fought this spirit, seeking to revive the freedom and creativity found in urban America and Europe earlier in the century. Cities like San Francisco, New Orleans, San Antonio, and Baltimore sought after World War II to capture the spirit of the earlier great cities. Spengler noted that the world's supercities devalue the provinces, but the great event in American urban culture in this century has been a movement toward restoring cities to what they always are at their best, cultural centers. Even the greatest of America's cities like New York, Philadelphia, and Chicago had by 1960 joined the attempt to rediscover their cultural roots, long concealed by the disorganization of urban sprawl.

Arnold Toynbee has defined the true city as a place where "the inhabitants of the built-up area are citizens in the non-material sense of having, and being conscious of having, a corporate social life." For Toynbee the true city provides both an order and a sense of freedom that make creativity possible. Out of this creativity comes cultural development, or, to put it the other way, creativity becomes possible because of the living culture of the city. We recognize the cultural quality of a city, Toynbee tells us, by the nature of its soul. Thus he says, of a city that became a megalopolis without first having created its own culture: "Los Angeles may swell physically to the size of a sub-continent, but the tropical luxuriance of its physical growth may never succeed in making a city of it. In order to become a city, it would have to evolve at least the rudiments of a soul. This is the essence of cityhood."[25]

Although we cannot easily define the word *soul,* we can see the effects of the quality of soul in certain cities—Paris, New Orleans, San Francisco. It is a quality existing even in the midst of the urban decay present in every city; it may be called joie de vivre, a sense of communal joy. This joy is possible because of the freedom and creativity related to culture. Artists are gifted at discovering this quality. Literary artists, in particular, plunge into the mythic basis of individual and social creativity that makes possible both culture and the quality of life associated with the intangible quality of soul. Robert Langbaum has written of W. B. Yeats: "All through his career Yeats was concerned with the question of how you get over from the flesh-and-blood creature to the mythical person who puts forth those magical powers from which all value and culture derive."[26] This mythic realm described by Langbaum is similar to what Jung meant by the archetypal realm or what Mircea Eliade means by the realm of the sacred. Culture has been defined as a system of values that helps to refine and develop the manners, taste, mind, and emotions of individuals and to promote creative interaction between groups. If this is so, then the modern writer's search for self-realization is in fact a quest to develop his inner qualities and to bring into being revived cultural values. He seeks, in short, to embody in his work an inner human quality that we associate with the word *soul.*

For Joseph Campbell the essence of myth is for the seeker who ventures into the immaterial realm of myth "to die to the world and to come to birth from within."[27] This inner development consists of an activation of symbols contained within the unconscious mind, symbols that are "inspirational, informative, initiatory, rendering a sense of illumination."[28] One of the great examples of this illuminative quality of a mythic symbol is Joyce's description in *Portrait of the Artist as a Young Man* of Stephen Dedalus's illumination when he sees a young girl walking on the beach. The girl becomes an anima archetype in the same manner that Beatrice became a symbol of love for Dante; she allows Stephen a glimpse into the realm of mythic experience. Deeply influenced by Dante, Joyce records the same sense of life renewal that Dante gives us in *La Vita Nuova,* a revival of life flowing from the illuminated awareness of love flowing from the anima achetype.

Jung, who was also a great influence on Joyce, has described the mythic life as the life of the archetype. A myth, in fact, is a collection of archetypes. For Campbell and Jung the chief archetype is the mandala, a mythic image that represents an essential unity contained within the continuum that makes up the life process. Mircea Eliade has written that the basis of myth is a continuum called life-death-rebirth. This continuum, as he demonstrates in *The Sacred and the Profane,* underlies the birth of culture. The mandala indeed points toward that unity which exists beneath the process of human history. Campbell in *The Mythic Image* demonstrates how the essence that Eliade calls the sacred is symbolized by the mandala in the building of cities that are the cultural centers of communities. For a primitive tribe the cultural center may be no more than a sacred stone or pool, but in a civilization the cultural center consists of buildings often constructed in the design of the mandala. Preserving the meaning associated with the mandala, the cultural center embraces the surrounding countryside, becoming then an urban-rural continuum. The revival in the late twentieth century of the city center as a cultural unit that seeks to embrace the surrounding suburbs is in fact an attempt to fight the megalopolitan concept of total urban sprawl and to proclaim the necessity of an urban-rural continuum to preserve cultural values.

Cultural revival in contemporary American cities does not by itself constitute the rebirth of culture but is, rather, one piece of evidence of the long search necessary for both mythic and cultural renewal. To the definitions of myth by Campbell, Eliade, and Jung, I add that of Alan Watts: myth in effect is a game of hide and seek.[29] Since the early romantic period the West has been searching for those symbols necessary to recover a unified context for new culture as well as such basic values as *caritas,* needed for social cohesiveness and a recognition of the proper balance between men and women, children and parents, leaders and followers.

This search for new cultural contexts is worldwide, as Alexander Solzhenitsyn made clear in a speech at Harvard University in 1978. A literary descendant of Tolstoi and Dostoevski, Solzhenitsyn is himself a member of that branch of existentialists that includes, along with the great Russian novelists, Kierkegaard, Jaspers, Berdyaev, Marcel, Buber, and the southern novelist-philosopher Walker Percy. Unlike such atheist existentialists as Sartre and Camus, who are far better known to the general public, the religious existentialists take into account the destructiveness inevitable in dying cultures, but they place a major emphasis on the continuing quest for those visions necessary for cultural renewal. In his Harvard address, Solzhenitsyn asserted that modern humanity is in a period of history similar to the transitional period between the Middle Ages and the Renaissance. The Russian novelist ended his speech by saying that we have nowhere to go but up, which is a simple statement of the fact that one complex of cultures is dead, though its values still remain, and another is struggling to be born through the revival of dying values.

Marion Montgomery, a southern novelist and critic, has rightly compared certain attitudes of Solzhenitsyn to those of the South. Montgomery even maintains that the Russian novelist bears witness to a "strikingly similar life, grown out of a common ground," to "that of the southern Agrarians."[30] Southern writers, he tells us, have a worldwide appeal, not only because they are linked with leading modern figures like Joyce and Eliot as well as with the Coleridge-Arnold tradition of English-culture criticism, but also because they are so remarkably similar to some European existential writers and philosophers. Their similarity to certain Russians in particular, like Solzhenitsyn, is due primarily to the fact that they accepted their own dying culture with all its imperfections and sought to find new visions and symbols on which cultural renewal could be based.

What is needed to fully explain the work of writers like Solzhenitsyn and the leading southerners is an active critical movement that examines how the quest for self-realization is related to the quest for cultural values. Part of this burgeoning movement are writers like Langbaum, who studies the quest for values and identity; Geoffrey Hartman, who takes into account the realm of the sacred in literature; and James D. Wilson, who examines in his work the relationship of love and solipsism to cultural values. Studies of the search for self-realization in literature have so far dealt primarily with the individualistic aspects of this quest. But now we see emerging—for example, in Langbaum's *Mysteries of Identity*—an attempt to show that much expressive art based on the quest motif, as opposed to mimetic art, is an effort not only to discover the depths of the human psyche but also to bring forth new cultural values. As contemporary authorities on myth like Joseph Campbell and Mircea Eliade have already shown, the mythic quests of individuals are necessary to bring to light those creative human powers needed to establish a living culture. More than most writers in the modern world the southerners were aware of this connection between the individual quest and communal needs; for them the community was always a central concern. The philosophical groundwork for much of what was most mythic and expressive in southern literature after 1920 was laid by a group called the Vanderbilt Agrarians, and it is necessary to look first at their work in relationship to the city before proceeding to better-known writers.

Notes

1. Pitirim A. Sorokin, *The Crisis of Our Age* (New York: E. P. Dutton, 1941), 13-29.
2. Robert Langbaum, *The Mysteries of Identity* (Chicago: University of Chicago Press, 1982), 144.
3. Ibid., 11.
4. Ibid., 5.
5. Sorokin, *Crisis,* 25, 26.

6. Quoted in Daniel G. Hoffman and Samuel Hynes, eds., *English Literary Criticism: Romantic and Victorian* (New York: Appleton-Century-Crofts, 1963), 245, 246.

7. Quoted ibid., 252.

8. Quoted ibid., 321.

9. James D. Wilson, *The Romantic Heroic Ideal* (Baton Rouge: Louisiana State University Press, 1982), 167.

10. Ibid., 194.

11. C. G. Jung, *The Undiscovered Self,* trans. R. F. C. Hall (New York: New American Library of World Literature, 1959), 117, 118.

12. Carl Bridenbaugh, *Myths and Realities: Societies of the Colonial South* (Baton Rouge: Louisiana State University Press, 1952), 116, 117.

13. Blaine A. Brownell and David R. Goldfield, *The City in Southern History* (Port Washington, N.Y.: Kennikat Press, 1977), 16.

14. Bridenbaugh, *Myths and Realities,* 6.

15. Noemie Emery, *Washington: A Biography* (New York: G. P. Putnam's Sons, 1976), 51.

16. Sorokin, *Crisis,* 17.

17. W. J. Cash, *The Mind of the South* (Garden City, N.Y.: Doubleday, 1954), 150.

18. George B. Tindall, *The Ethnic Southerners* (Baton Rouge: Louisiana State University Press, 1976), 42.

19. Robert Manson Myers, ed., *The Children of Pride* (New Haven: Yale University Press, 1972), 10.

20. Emery, *Washington,* 13, 15, 52.

21. Blaine A. Brownell, *The Urban Ethos in the South* (Baton Rouge: Louisiana State University Press, 1975), 212, 213.

22. Amaury de Riencourt, *Sex and Power in History* (New York: David McKay, 1974), 402.

23. Quoted in Larry Shealy, "The Southern Accent . . . We Ain't All Gomer Pyles," *Atlanta Journal and Constitution,* January 6, 1980, 1F, 10F.

24. R. W. Collingwood, "Oswald Spengler and the Theory of Historical Cycles," *Antiquity* 1 (1927): 323, 324.

25. Arnold J. Toynbee, "Cities in History," in *Cities of Destiny,* ed. Arnold J. Toynbee (New York: McGraw-Hill, 1967), 13.

26. Langbaum, *Mysteries,* 220.

27. Joseph Campbell, *The Masks of God: Creative Mythology* (New York: Viking Press, 1968), 678.

28. Ibid., 672.

29. Alan W. Watts, *The Two Hands of God* (New York: George Braziller, 1963), 1-46.

30. Marion Montgomery, "Solzhenitsyn as Southerner," in *Why the South Will Survive* (Athens: University of Georgia Press, 1981), 196.

Julius Rowan Raper (essay date spring 1990)

SOURCE: Raper, Julius Rowan. "Inventing Modern Southern Fiction: A Postmodern View." *Southern Literary Journal* 22, no. 2 (spring 1990): 3-18.

[*In the following essay, Raper explores the special role of a sense of place in traditional Southern fiction and suggests that postmodern Southern writers have deliberately reacted against their locale as a limitation in their works.*]

The possibility I want to explore,[1] that in modern Southern literature the sense of place takes on a role better played by a sense of self, arises from my irritation with a popular anthology of modern Southern short stories. The anthology, *Stories of the Modern South,* is a useful collection, as a supplement to novels or to a major anthology. It helps especially, we will see, with current writers like Doris Betts, Elizabeth Spencer, David Madden. But when I come to the selection for John Barth, I pause. And I become irritated. Not rageful, for reasons we will understand when we talk about rage. But not merely peeved either. Irritated. For the John Barth I want to teach is the postmodern Barth of tales like "Menelaiad" or the three novellas that make up *Chimera,* which may be the finest postmodern book yet written by an American. I want to teach John Barth both as a Southern writer and as the major American postmodernist. But the Barth story in the anthology is "Water-Message"—an episode from the eastern-shore Maryland boyhood of Barth's autobiographical character, Ambrose Mensch. Out of a perversity of memory I find myself referring to it as "1928 Story," which is, in fact, the title of the James Agee selection preceding it in the anthology. This slip, I think, is significant.

For Barth's "Water-Message" is very much a 1928 story. It is the sort of *memory* of childhood that the major Southern novelists were writing in 1928.1928 was a year when Thomas Wolfe was assigning his memories to Eugene Gant, a year when William Faulkner was wrestling with the boyhood of Quentin Compson, a year in which Ellen Glasgow was between the girlhoods of Dorinda Oakley and Jenny Blair Archbald.

When I remember these great models, I take the title of the anthology literally. These *are* stories of the *modern* South, and by 1928 Modern Southern Fiction had established itself as the type of writing that it has, in large part, remained. Given the anthology's title, then, the fireworks and magic of the major fiction of John Barth would probably be out of place. Moreover, when we consider the popular success of contemporary *realistic* Southern writers like Anne Tyler and Bobbie Ann Mason, we have to concede that the odds of Barth's postmodernism cutting significant roads into the domain of Modern Southern Fiction seem slim indeed. And thereby, I think, hangs a historical tale.

If we look back to the beginnings of Modern Southern Fiction between 1890 and 1930 or so, we find that although Ellen Glasgow had considerable help—from Mark Twain, George Washington Cable, Mary Noailles Murfree, Kate Chopin, and many others—she, as much as anyone, set the form that Modern Southern Fiction has followed during the past sixty years. For that reason, the pattern of her literary development bears on any discussion of the invention of Modern Southern Fiction. The phases of her development also point the way to alternatives latent within the tradition.

Glasgow began publishing in the late 1890s when the old models of local-color writing—Thomas Nelson Page, Joel Chandler Harris, Mary Noailles Murfree—were losing their appeal. Although she learned from the local colorists, she began as a literary revolutionary. Her first two novels were bursting at the seams with allusions to the scientific thinkers—Charles Darwin, Ernst Haeckel, Herbert Spencer, Thomas Huxley—who inspired the American literary naturalists of the 1890s. Her early novels are, in fact, first cousins of the naturalist fictions of Stephen Crane, Hamlin Garland, Frank Norris, and Theodore Dreiser. With her third novel, *The Voice of the People,* her first set totally in Virginia, she began to soften her programmatic naturalism and to settle into the mainstream of realistic American fiction that runs from Howells and James to Cather, Anderson, Lewis, Fitzgerald, and others. There she remained, with some excursions outside, for two-and-one-half decades. With *Barren Ground* (1925), however, she took up a major modernist theme, sexual repression, along with modernist techniques for exploring the unconscious mind. But by 1925, the great Southern modernists, Wolfe and Faulkner, were moving toward their first major novels, and Glasgow's days as the leading Southern realist were numbered.

By 1925, however, Glasgow's development included the four *major* movements that would influence Wolfe and Faulkner and, through them, what we call Modern Southern Fiction. These four movements or tendencies—local color, naturalism, realism, and modernism—all have left their mark on Southern fiction of the twentieth century, down to 1990. More important for our discussion here, all four share a characteristic that appeals profoundly to Southern readers and writers, a trait that makes it difficult for postmodernists to make deep inroads in Southern fiction. From the great web of interrelated elements that Louis Rubin has described as the Southernness of Southern literature, I wish to draw out a single thread and examine it.

Although Glasgow, and Modern Southern Fiction, began in revolt against the local-color writing of Page and others, aspects of local color remained part of her style and of Southern writing in general. For local color emphasized the *setting* of a story, the special character of a place, its customs, landscape, speech, dress. From local color comes a fidelity to minute details and accurate description that, in the twentieth century, critics and teachers of creative writing often take to be the hallmark of good writing (even though readers trained in New Criticism struggle in vain to locate such local texture in Homer or Aeschylus, who for reasons other than particularity stick around). Southern regionalists, especially John Crowe Ransom and his colleagues, would later eliminate what was merely quaint from the local-color approach and give a more philosophical and historical dimension to writing with a geographic focus. But fidelity to details and description remained a mark of their best work.

Such loyalty to setting also played a major part in the movement Glasgow turned to in rebelling against local color. For in novels associated with literary *naturalism,* the setting and the socioeconomic conditions have a vital part to play. They line up with heredity as the forces that work against the protagonist. For example, in Glasgow's first book *The Descendant* (1897), Michael Akershems' Virginia neighbors hound him out of the state in much the same way that the community in Faulkner's *Light in August* (1932) pursues Joe Christmas to his death. Naturalism is realism with a program; a major plank in this program holds that the setting must be created as a force capable of controlling, even crushing, the hero. In naturalist writing, as in local color, but for philosophical reasons, the sense of place, malicious as it often seems, remains a central force.

In Modern Southern Fiction the sense of place can become doubly destructive. For no matter how viciously Gothic the setting appears—witness Walter Hines Page's South as the abode of ghosts and mummies, or Faulkner's Mississippi as a barracks of ghosts—every Southerner knows in his or her heart, the way Tate's speaker does in "Ode to the Confederate Dead," that loyalty to the place and its people is required. This mixture of messages—that the place is destructive but demands loyalty—creates the impossible double bind, the stone paralysis, traditionally called the Hamlet problem, that becomes for modern Southerners the "Quentin problem." As Faulkner tells us, Quentin's spirit can never leave Jefferson, no matter to what New England college his body travels. Quentin drowns in his past, the fine dead sound of all his fathers' voices, as surely as he drowns in the Charles River. Loyalty to place is a double-edged sword, all blade, without a hilt to hold, as sure to wound the wielder as anyone. Yet fidelity to description of place remains a mainstay of Modern Southern Fiction—long after setting has begun to play a very different part in postmodern writing.

When Glasgow moved away from naturalism to the gentler mode associated with literary realism, she relinquished the deterministic program of naturalism—but she did not abandon its emphasis on details and description. If Christopher Blake in *The Deliverance* (1904) and Dorinda Oakley in *Barren Ground* (1925) manage to triumph over conditions in the post-war South, they nevertheless do so in settings that Glasgow establishes with loving and often lyrical attention to particulars. For modern realism implies verisimilitude; and verisimilitude since Balzac, in order to seem true, has depended on close attention to detailed descriptions of both characters and settings.

Glasgow's great modernist successors, Wolfe and Faulkner, Wright and Warren, Welty and present writers, are seldom accused of being skimpy with details. We know well the legendary, often maniacal, efforts of Wolfe to get the whole of his life down on paper, the more measured attempt of Faulkner to recapture his postage stamp of Mississippi, the crushing portrait Wright creates of Chicago as it destroys Bigger Thomas, Welty's success in capturing the flavors of a Southern reunion.

Much Modern Southern Fiction, at its very best—whether realist, naturalist, or modernist—succeeds in doing what Warren in "Blackberry Winter" suggests people generally cease doing at an early age. It turns Time into place and lovingly suspends them both:

> when you are nine years old, what you remember seems forever; for you remember everything and everything is important and stands big and full and fills up Time and is so solid that you can walk around and around it like a tree and look at it. You are aware that time passes, that there is movement in time, but that is not what Time is. Time is not a movement, a flowing, a wind then, but is, rather, a kind of climate in which things are, and when a thing happens it begins to live and keeps on living and stands solid in Time like the tree that you can walk around. And if there is a movement, the movement is not time itself, any more than a breeze is climate, and all the breeze does is to shake a little the leaves on the tree which is alive and solid. When you are nine, you know that there are things that you don't know, but you know that when you know something you know it.
>
> (1060)

"Blackberry Winter" is the story of an *ideal* Southern childhood that changes, at the moment a boy matures, into a *realistic* Southern manhood. The fixed order that young Seth holds to when he is nine—an order in which his father wears "strong cowhide boots" (1073), sits on "his mare over the heads of the other men" (1065), and all is right with Seth's world—is an order doomed by real time.

In the course of the story, all the absolutes young Seth counts on fragment into merely relative truths. Although change sets Seth free from the tree of solid, unmoving Time, he cannot experience that change as freedom. Instead, loss of his absolutes, illusory as they were, leaves Seth feeling like a "little son-of-a-bitch" who all the years since has followed the rage-filled tramp, the man who first threatened his order (1074). Seth has had to accept the changes that time brings, and because he has done so, he feels as though he has both been betrayed by and betrayed the static order over which his father presided—as though he too spat at the toe of his father's right boot (1073).

Warren's story brilliantly demonstrates the special role the sense of place plays in the Southern imagination, but we need to digress for a moment to provide a background. Seth's damaged self-esteem, his father's elevated posture, the tramp's dark rage are all essential elements of the Southern psyche, according to what Fred Hobson implies in his reading of the Southern past, *Tell About the South: The Southern Rage to Explain* (1983). So too, I suggest, are the separate reactions of Seth and his father to the process of fragmentation that change brings.

Hobson's book, an inclusive, helpful synthesis of Southern culture, argues persuasively that since the 1820s and 1830s when the "region was forced on the defensive . . . because of its peculiar institution, Negro slavery," the American South "has been on the defensive" (9), that when its view of the world is challenged it "becomes helpless and explodes in anger" (Weaver 389, qtd. in Hobson 10). Consequently, as Hobson demonstrates, when Southerners write about their region, they tend to fall either into a school of loyalists who insist upon the superiority of the South, or into a school of guilt and shame. Either way, they rage.

The split Hobson describes exists in "Blackberry Winter" in the contrast between young Seth's view of his father and mature Seth's estimate of himself. Young Seth know that "if the glob [of the tramp's spit] had hit [his] father's boot something would have happened" (Warren, 1073). The tramp too knows what that reaction would be, for his own black shoes first twitch, then take "a real step backward" (1073). In short, Seth's father has, once more in Southern fiction, turned back a challenge by threatening to respond to the tramp's rage, growing from the need to survive, with a superior rage, rage arising from loyalty to the established order of things. But though the tramp retreats, Seth's father's victory is powerless to protect the boy from all the changes around him. So Seth ends with guilt and shame for not preserving his father's exalted social posture.

Warren's story comes from the core of the Southern psyche. Our literature is filled with similar tales. To mention familiar names like Thomas Sutpen, Dorinda Oakley, Eugene Gant, Quentin Compson, Eva Birdsong, Rosa Coldfield, Gail Hightower, Percy Grimm, Bigger Thomas, Lancelot Lamar is to evoke memories of threatening change, wounded pride, outrage, and shame that overwhelm an individual's defenses against outbursts of destructive emotions.

Perception of the inevitable relationships between change, pride, shame, and rage has grown in recent years as our understanding of narcissistic rage has increased, largely through the work of Heinz Kohut and Kohut's school of Self Psychology. Kohut's work helps us comprehend the way that a history of guilt about slavery followed by repeated defenses against abolitionists, military invasion, reconstruction, and integration may have damaged what Kohut calls the core, or nuclear, self of generation of Southern parents. They, in turn, have turned to their offspring with their needs and defenses. Rageful fathers and needy mothers, whether in the South or Timbuktu, inadvertently rob children of the ideal models and supportive mirroring we now know children need if they are to develop their own strong, inward centers of security and initiative. Want of a solid core self, Kohut points out, leaves an individual oscillating between the extremes of low self-esteem and grandiosity that Hobson describes as his opposed schools of self-loathing and Southern loyalty. Grandiose loyalty may defend, for a moment or a lifetime, against self-loathing and emptiness. But grandiosity creates a false image of one's self and, because it is hollow, always remains in danger of fragmenting in the face of change, or any narcissistic blow, the way young Thomas Sutpen dissolves when told to go around to the back door of Pettibone's mansion. Like Sutpen, Kohut's narcissists try to ward off the devastating fear of fragmentation with modes of extreme behavior, including grandiose, rageful violence, like that which fuels Sutpen's career after the Pettibone incident.

Viewing *all* Southern fathers as rageful and all Southern mothers as hypochondriac and seductive, or vice versa, would, of course, be an injustice. Viewing a number of key literary fathers and mothers that way, however, appears to me to be a fair and useful generalization, one supported by knowledge of our literature and by what Hobson has shown us about the polemical history of the South.

In the South, we defend against rage and seduction, and against the sense of fragmentation and hollowness that are likely to result from flawed parenting, I suggest, with the extraordinary sense of place that is a mainstay still of Modern Southern Fiction—but, less and less, of modern Southern life. As Eudora Welty says in her famous essay on "Place in Fiction": "place has a good deal to do with making . . . characters real, that is, themselves, and keeping them so. . . . It is our describable outside that . . . may *save* us, or destroy us, in the world; it may be our *shield* against chaos, our mask against exposure" (540-41, emphasis mine). As Glasgow's Dorinda Oakley demonstrates, what we in the South lack from parents and community we find mirrored back to us from the landscape, even from barren ground. By default, we may employ the landscape, as Dorinda does, to mirror our desire, or our rage. Or we may use a strong sense of place, much the way Welty does, as a ballast against the chaos of rage.

Either way, we tend to fuse what the Greeks called *edos,* our dwelling-place or foundation, with *ethos,* our custom or habit, and then confuse both place and custom with *ethnos,* the Southern people. In short, we find our character in our place. In Welty's words, "Place . . . has the most delicate control over character . . . : by confining character, it defines it" (541). Welty is speaking of character in novels, of the way "the novel and its place have become one" (540). But she has put her finger on an aspect of Modern Southern Fiction that both feeds upon, and feeds, modern Southern life. In the South, the *people* (*ethnos*) and the place (*edos*) tend to become one.

Perhaps because Welty's sense of place is serene, her writing may seem, to those who grew up on the fictional fundamentalism of Wolfe and Faulkner or even Glasgow, supremely Episcopal. an anthropologist friend with an interest in Southern churches calls Episcopalianism "religion in its mildest form." If he is right, then Welty may well represent the Episcopal branch of Modern Southern Fiction—Modern Southern Fiction in its least rageful and violent form. I don't think it mere coincidence that Welty is also the writer who speaks with such sensitivity to the way place defines and shields character. Certainly, if her gentleness is desirable (and in life it may well be), then the counterbalance of place must be equally desirable.

But our familiar place of red clay and mules, of piney hills, hamlets, and grandparents soft as the underside of leaves, is vanishing, even in our fiction. The time may come when introducing pine hills and red clay, good old boys and hard-boiled virgins, into Southern stories would seem as great an exercise in nostalgia as moonlight and magnolias, plumed cavaliers and crinolined ladies, were when Glasgow began her campaign for "blood and irony." Where then will be our "shield against chaos," our defense against characters (or people) flying "to pieces" (Welty 541)?

That is what postmodern fiction asks us to consider: that in the postmodern world the dependence of character on stability of place is inevitably doomed by the speed with which modern environments are changed. At the same time, postmodernism tells us that, in the age of ideology, the fictional imagination has a special role to play in keeping us *free* from the verisimilitude, the seeming truth, that "controllers of reality," the advertisers and ideologues of the age, have a distinct interest in foisting upon us. Thus, in its view of verisimilitude, postmodern fiction moves in a direction contrary to Modern Southern Fiction.

About verisimilitude, Welty wrote in 1956:

> The world of appearance in the novel has got to *seem* actuality. . . . Place being brought to life in the round before the reader's eye is the readiest and gentlest and most honest and natural way this can be brought about. . . . The moment the place in which the novel happens is accepted as true, through it will begin to glow . . . the feeling and thought that inhabited the novel in the author's head and animated the whole of his work.
>
> (540, Welty's emphasis)

One year after Welty's important essay, however, a leading novelist with his finger on the pulse of a different world was proclaiming that the novel in which character is fixed by name, heredity, and private property was already an obsolete notion inherited from the time of Balzac (Robbe-Grillet 28). The same French novelist, six years later, pointed out that the contemporary author no longer asks his reader "to receive ready-made a world completed, full, closed upon itself, but on the contrary to participate in a creation, to invent in his turn the work—and the world—and thus to learn to invent his own life" (Robbe-Grillet 156).

Neither Welty, in stressing verisimilitude, nor Alain Robbe-Grillet, in calling for the continuous undercutting of verisimilitude, wrote out of frivolous, or even solely literary, motives. Welty wrote out of the Southern situation, out of the South's need to defend the self from chaos and fragmentation by providing a strong sense of place. Robbe-Grillet wrote in the heart of the Cold War, out of the desire to use literary imagination to liberate readers from narrow definitions of reality and behavior that the dominant ideologues clearly seek to impose on masses of people. For Welty, fiction grounds the self and makes it feel secure in its place. For Robbe-Grillet, it is the free play of imagination in fiction that best illustrates how we can invent our own world rather than accept what has been invented for us by Lenin or Hitler, Stalin or Madison Avenue. There is an almost scientific earnestness about Welty's wish to establish a sense of reality. In contrast, Robbe-Grillet associates verisimilitude with the dogmas of socialist realism (35-37), but he is earnest about the free play of fiction.

Modernism, as Welty shows, is the literature of memory (cf. Dasenbrock 518). The postmodern, for reasons Robbe-Grillet underscores, is a literature of imagination. The need today, he argues, is to reinvent the world, one free of the narrow mind sets of Nazis, Marxists, and advertising agencies. But a new reality can only be spun from a new self—and it is difficult to invent a new self, the way John Barth, John Fowles, Lawrence Durrell, Robert Coover, Philip Roth, and other postmodern novelists do, if one is preoccupied bolstering the old self with the comforts of a fixed place. Freeing the imagination, through parody, through the free invention of fantasy, through framing one reality with another more real, and through frame breaking (cf. Goffman 345-77) the way Barth does in *Chimera*, presumes either a secure sense of self—or a desperation about one's ability to hold on to the old self. Whereas Barth's own mix of despair and security moves him toward parody, frame breaking, and fantasy, Welty's special blend of desperation and security keeps her chiefly in the camp of memory.

I say "chiefly" because, in addition to her defense of the place called home, she speaks eloquently of the tyranny of the familiar when she writes:

> For the artist to be unwilling to move, mentally or spiritually or physically, out of the familiar is a sign that spiritual timidity or poverty or decay has come upon him; for what is familiar will then have turned into all that is tyrannical. . . . In fact, when we think in terms of the spirit, which are the terms of writing, is there a conception more stupefying than that of security?
>
> (546)

With Welty's position here the boldest of our postmodern authors would concur, and would applaud the clear defense of experimentation that follows: "No art ever came out of not risking your neck. And risk—experiment—is a considerable part of the joy of doing . . ." (546).

I also qualify Welty's commitment to the literature of memory because, even when most convinced by the verisimilitude of Welty's South, we cannot forget that her imaginative gifts can slip us, before we realize it, out of the frame of our familiar reality into the parallel world of the Olympians that stands behind works like *The Golden Apples* and "Death of a Traveling Salesman," or spin us into the circles through which Virgil and Dante still pass, with added humor, in "The Wide Net." Welty's use of the modernist mythic method, sometimes called symbolic mimesis, implies an ambivalence about, perhaps even impatience with, the reality we see in the light of common day. Her mythic parallels suggest what Barth's mythic stories do, that we live not solely in our place and time but also in the invisible place of the archetypes seen in dreams, in fantasies, and in enduring works of art.

But Barth's tales, like many postmodern works, turn the modernist mythic method on its head. They do not hesitate to deal directly, rather than obliquely, with the myths that underlie our culture. In *Chimera,* an author with Barth's own resumé says:

> Since myths themselves are among other things poetic distillations of our ordinary psychic experience and therefore point always to daily reality, to write realistic fictions which point always to mythic archetypes is in my opinion to take the wrong end of the mythopoeic stick, however meritorious such fictions may be in other respects. Better to address the archetypes directly.
>
> (199)

Later in the same trilogy of tales, an angry, militant feminist derides "the male-supremist character of the great body of our classic myths," proclaims mythology "the propaganda of the winners," and announces that she and her sisters-in-arms are going to rewrite "the grand myth . . . of heroic maleness" that all the smaller myths of the patriarchy support (277-78).

What Barth proposes here is frame breaking on a grand, yet playful, scale. Forget Robbe-Grillet's Cold War; Barth is out to strike a decisive blow in the eternal war between the sexes, a struggle in which, during the four thousand years since the overthrow of the matriarchy in the eastern Mediterranean, men have held the upper hand. But to do so, Barth must address directly the mythology, whether Greek, Judaic, Roman, Christian, or Cartesian, that has framed Western reality for four millennia. His program, as audacious as it is worthwhile, requires that he relinquish the sense of place that has been a mainstay of Modern Southern Fiction growing out of the local color, realist, and naturalist movements. *Chimera* may treat the major gender issues of the 1970s, but Barth has set it in the ancient Middle East.

Even though Barth appears alone, among Southern writers, in electing to dispense with the furnishings we expect in our novels, he is not alone in the larger literary world. Since Robbe-Grillet, many novelists, for reasons already discussed, have turned the reader's desire to be engrossed, even swamped, by the setting to good use as they work to liberate the imagination from the passivity and fatality associated with realism, naturalism, and derivative movements. In contemporary fictions, settings may appear to be engrossing realities. But they can just as easily be sets for a stage-managing narrator to strike, the way Lawrence Durrell undercut the reality of *Justine* (1957) altogether when he published *Balthazar* (1958), the second novel in the famous *Alexandria Quartet* (1957-1960).

If writers of the postmodern South respond to the inspiration of Barth and other fabulators, it may be, in part, because the sense of self in the post-Birmingham South is finally sufficiently solid—free enough of both guilt and shame—for our writers to dispense with grandiose loyalties grounded in the piety of place. Having rewritten their fathers as Atticus Finch (or maybe Gregory Peck) and Dr. King rather than the seductive Rhetts, morose Mr. Compsons, and raging W. O. Gants, and having reinvented their mothers in the image of Eudora Welty, I guess, rather than flirty Scarlett, narcissistic Mrs. Compson, or intrusive Amanda Wingfield,[2] the younger generation of Southern writers may not need to bolster the self with an all-encompassing sense of place. If these writers decide to step from the literature of memory into what Durrell calls the kingdom of the imagination, they will discover, in past Southern writing, substantial underground formations on which to set the foundations of this new fiction.

For even though the dominant tendency in Modern Southern Fiction since Glasgow has been attachment to real places, Southern writing has a distinguished heritage of framed stories and an important, often ignored, current of fantasy or magical writing. Admittedly, the Southwest humorists and later local colorists like Thomas Nelson Page, Joel Chandler Harris, and Charles Chesnutt took more interest in the *social* significance of framing a lower-class fiction with a superior reality than they did in the epistemological and ontological effects of frame breaking. They did not break frames to free the imagination but framed stories to feel superior to vernacular storytellers. Nevertheless, their tales provide textbook examples, as Barth must know, of the ways a story can be framed—from the beginning, the middle, the end, and all combinations of the three. If we include Mark Twain in the group, our humorists also appreciated the relative powers of various frames.

Equally promising for contemporary Southern writers pulled in the postmodern direction is the role fantasy has played in our fiction. Put aside Poe and James Branch Cabell, the greatest of our fantasists, and Mark Twain of *The Mysterious Stranger.* For the moment, recollect the ways Glasgow, Wolfe, and Faulkner used fantastical materials. Between 1913 and 1922, Glasgow's writing reached its lowest ebb; this is the decade when she was making the difficult transition from the surface realism of her early novels to the modernist psychological element in *Barren Ground* and later books. During this period, she used a series of experimental ghost stories, included in *The Shadowy Third and Other Stories* (1923), to break the frame of her nineteenth-century realism and open her psyche to the wider range of emotions and behaviors explored in the major works after 1924.

Similarly, Wolfe, at the end of *Look Homeward, Angel*, a novel that overwhelms readers and biographers with its loyalty to real life, was inspired to carry Eugene Gant out of the clockwork world of realism into the fantastical realm where the boy encounters the avatars of his past life. Here Eugene also confronts the ghost of his dead brother Ben, and receives instruction from beyond the grave that clarifies the quest lying ahead. If we write this ending off as rhetorical coda to a realistic novel, we overlook the historical facts that, in the Europe that Wolfe haunted during the middle 1920s, surrealism and expressionism were flourishing literary movements. Even Magic Realism, one of the widely accepted tendencies of our postmodern literature, had established itself as an active trend in German visual arts. These may be the techniques Wolfe draws upon to show that Eugene's dark double, his shadow, Ben, is now as deep a force in the younger brother's psyche as his mother, his father, and the avatars of his past selves are—that skeptical Ben too is one of the building blocks bearing the alphabet that spells out Eugene's great forgotten language. By reducing this ending to rhetoric, we would also overlook the way Wolfe anticipates the final chapter's descent into the dark magic of the unconscious with the important lyrical passages (about love, alcohol, death, rebirth) that increase in frequency through the final chapters. Like D. H. Lawrence, Wolfe employed heightened lyrical intensity—along with surreal, expressionist, and magical passages—to carry his readers into the collective unconscious, a domain postmodernists use every device available to reach.

When we look from Wolfe to Faulkner for foreshadowings of postmodern technique, three powerful instances come to mind. In *Light in August* (1932), it is difficult, within the frame of realistic fiction, to account for the demonic Player that directs Percy Grimm's pursuit of Joe Christmas as though Percy were a pawn in a chess game. An expanded postmodern reality, however, welcomes the magical synchronicity said to occur when archetypal roles emerge from the unconscious. In *Absalom, Absalom!* (1936), the reader has, first, to work in good *modernist* fashion to *construct* the story of the Sutpen family from the ragtag bits and pieces provided by the various narrators. Having constructed the story, however, the reader discovers his work is not done, that Faulkner has framed the Sutpen saga so that the story *deconstructs* itself. When we recognize that Quentin and Shreve have literally invented Eulalia and the possibly black blood of Charles Bon because fear of miscegenation seems to explain the self-destructive behavior of the major characters, an important option follows. If the reader accepts Bon's black blood as fact rather than the fiction of Quentin and Shreve—that is, if the reader's catharsis here is emotional and intellectual rather than aesthetic, if the reader is emotionally persuaded rather than aesthetically satisfied—the reader has been swamped by the fine dead values of all Quentin's fathers much the way Shreve has. But the deconstructive frame, by repeatedly reminding us that much of the novel was invented by the characters, not the author, gives the reader ground on which to stand above the rising flood of Quentin's fathers' voices. Finally, in "The Old People" (1940), the realist streak in modernism has to blink away the *multiple* avatars of the single deer who incarnates the spirit of the wilderness: I mean, the mature buck that young Ike McCaslin feels "come to the edge of the cane" before Walter Ewell shoots it (183); the "little spike buck" Ewell actually kills; and the "tremendous, unhurried" buck Sam Fathers salutes with "Oleh, Chief, . . . Grandfather" (184). The impact of the story, however, requires that we take the three-deer-in-one as the trinity of an Indian hunting cult into which Isaac is initiated by Sam Fathers and McCaslin Edmonds (187). Faulkner's Player and the immortal deer are devices more in tune with contemporary Magic Realism, with Gabriel García Márquez for example, than with realist writing. Faulkner's deconstructive frame for the Sutpen saga creates interpretative possibilities equal to those generated by frames in the most complex novels of Barth, Durrell, John Fowles, and Philip Roth.

Thus Faulkner, even more than Glasgow, Wolfe, or Welty, provides a foundation on which Southern novelists of Barth's generation and the next can build a postmodern fiction. Although Barth has embraced the *metafictional* and *frame-breaking* tendencies of contemporary fiction more completely than other major Southern novelists with whom I am familiar, a number of our leading writers appear pulled in the direction of Magic Realism.

For example: in Reynolds Price's *A Generous Man*, the epic hunt for a twenty-foot two-hundred-eighty-pound python was unbelievable and a liability when the novel appeared in 1966. In 1990, however, such devices seem audacious and loaded with significance—more so even than the boldness Price demonstrated when he moved into the inner world of Kate Vaiden. Walker Percy's magically ambiguous portrait of a madman in *Lancelot* (1977) is as dramatic and fantastical as Poe's famous monologues by lunatics. Or again: Doris Betts's popular story, "The Ugliest Pilgrim," threatens to break through into one of the deepest, darkest, therefore most magical corners of the Southern psyche when Flick, the black soldier, as well as Monty, the white soldier, calls in the night at Violet's hotel door (Forkner 49). And Elizabeth Spencer's tale, "The Finder," likewise strains the limits of Modern Southern Fiction by brilliantly presenting the consequence of suppressing the magic that the unconscious appears to contain. In "The Finder," in order to conform to the familiar and familial reality, Gavin Anderson abandons his extraordinary gift, the ability to locate missing objects, and, by so doing, denies the deep, wild part of himself (Forkner 429-30).

Finally, David Madden's story, "The Singer," demonstrates the value of Magic Realism relative to realism when a public audience demands that a film lecturer suspend his earnest *picture of conditions* in the mining regions of Kentucky so that the audience can concentrate on an extraordinary *story*. This story is a filmed account of a young girl, called the Singer, who is discovering the combined powers of the Orphic and Jesus archetypes in herself when she is mowed down by a motorcycle (Forkner 295-96).

Madden's story reminds us that modernism, the literature of memory, often sacrifices story to paint a picture of a character or, worse, of conditions. In contrast, the kingdom of imagination that the postmodern seeks to reclaim is, first and last, the realm of stories, stories that have a wholeness: a beginning, middle, and end; past, present, and future; memory, experience, *and* imagination. Whole stories we come to value more as our traditional mythologies lose their power and give way to modern mythologies devoid of human personality; I mean, the large explanatory systems we have inherited from Newton, Darwin, and Einstein—as well as from Marx and Freud, if we press them to their ground in history and instinct. We need myths, I think, that have a human face even when they wear the masks of Perseus, Bellerophon, Scheherazade, and Medusa, for Barth in *Chimera*, or the mask of the gnostics, for Durrell in the new *Avignon Quintet*, or the mask of the muse Erato, for Fowles in *Mantissa*. Despite the skepticism that postmodern writing commonly evokes, the movement has a good deal to offer, for it brings back the motions of the human spirit that come to consciousness in fantasies. It also restores the storytelling powers that shape deep fantasies into whole stories rather than character sketches.

But, even though the postmodern movement promises a return to story-telling and free imagination, are these sufficient reasons for writers to abandon the program of realistic Modern Southern Fiction? In the South, we have had a good literary thing going for more than eighty years—even New York knows we have. Why change a good thing? To this sensible and practical question, the contemporary Southern writer could reply that we have seen a New South and a new Southern Literature, a modern South and a Modern Literature, and that now the skylines of Atlanta, even Durham, show us we are becoming the Postmodern South. Consequently, a Postmodern Southern Literature appears as inevitable as the movements that came before.

A better response, however, to champions of Modern Southern Fiction would be to quote Welty once more, when she says that "No art ever came out of not risking you neck." Welty's assertion captures the spirit that has driven the novel since it began: an *old* novel, especially the same old novel, is a plain contradiction in terms. There will be a Postmodern Southern Fiction because it is there to write, and a novelist worth his salt cannot help but risk her neck. The *nature* of this new literature remains a mystery, for it must be as outrageous and unpredictable as the novel itself. It will be playful rather than scientifically earnest—deliberately less engrossing, but more liberating. And it will probably seem closer akin to philosophy, mythology, and post-Freudian psychology than is the sociological and historical literature of memory.

Notes

1. This essay was presented June 28, 1989, as part of the NEH Summer Institute, "The Southern Novel and the Southern Community," The University of North Carolina at Chapel Hill, June 12-July 20, 1989.

   In an earlier session of the Institute, novelist Max Steele and Professor Louis D. Rubin, Jr., engaged in a brief discussion in which each gave the other credit for initiating the Second Southern Literary Renaissance, of which Chapel Hill seems to be the center.

   Two recurring themes in the essay provide evidence of the way the two men worked together. The two themes go back to conversations overheard in Rubin's house in 1967 or '68, when the University of North Carolina's senior creative-writing honors seminar taught by Steele and Rubin met in Rubin's house. These were occasions I attended as a new assistant professor able to slip in, more or less, as a student. In this way I overheard the conversations of Rubin and Steele as well as other participants, who, from time to time, included Elizabeth Spencer, Daphne Athas, and, on occasion, Betty Smith.

   Part of the essay's argument about framed stories grows out of a conversation Rubin and Steele were having one evening when I walked in, about *Don Quixote* and the effects of framing one story with another. Other parts reflect Steele's remark one night about a story a student had written, I think, about a family graveyard. Steele said, "Even nostalgia's not what it used to be." This may have been the first "postmodern" comment I heard in Chapel Hill; it is still one of the best.

2. For their brothers, to Quentin, Eugene, and Jack Burden, they may have added James Cheney, Andrew Goodman, Michael Schwerner.

Works Cited

Barth, John. *Chimera*. New York: Random House, 1972.

Dasenbrock, Reed Way. "Lawrence Durrell and the Modes of Modernism." *Twentieth Century Literature* 33 (Fall-Winter 1987): 515-27.

Faulkner, William. *Go Down, Moses*. New York: Modern Library, 1942.

Forkner, Ben, and Patrick Samway, eds. *Stories of the Modern South*. New York: Penguin, 1986.

Goffman, Erving. *Frame Analysis: An Essay on the Organization of Experience*. Boston: Northeastern UP, 1986.

Hobson, Fred. *Tell About the South: The Southern Rage to Explain*. Baton Rouge: Louisiana State UP, 1983.

Robbe-Grillet, Alain. *For A New Novel: Essays on Fiction*. Trans Richard Howard. New York: Grove, 1965.

Warren, Robert Penn. "Blackberry Winter." *The Literature of the South*. Eds. Thomas Daniel Young et al. Glenview, IL: Scott, Foresman, 1968.

Weaver, Richard M. *The Southern Tradition at Bay: A History of Postbellum Thought*. Eds. George Core and M. E. Bradford. New Rochelle, NY: Arlington House, 1968.

Welty, Eudora. "Place in Fiction." *A Modern Southern Reader*. Eds. Ben Forkner and Patrick Samway. Atlanta: Peachtree, 1986.

John Lowe (essay date 1996)

SOURCE: Lowe, John. Introduction to *The Future of Southern Letters,* edited by Jefferson Humphries and John Lowe, pp. 3-19. New York: Oxford University Press, 1996.

[*In the following essay, Lowe discusses new directions in contemporary Southern fiction, including a reexamination of history, a more central treatment of popular culture, and a greater presence of women authors.*]

> *It is never, as one knows, the* subject, *but only the* treatment *that distinguishes the artist and poet.*
> Friedrich Schiller, "On Matthison's Poems" (1794)

> *We talk real funny down here*
> *We drink too much and we laugh too loud*
> *We're too dumb to make it in no northern town . . .*
> *We got no-necked oilmen from Texas*
> *And good ol' boys from Tennessee*
> *And college men from L.S.U.*
> *Went in dumb. Come out dumb too*
> *Hustlin' 'round Atlanta in their alligator shoes*
> *Gettin' drunk every weekend at the barbecues—*
> *We're Rednecks, we're rednecks*
> *And we don't know our ass from a hole in the ground.*
> Randy Newman, "Rednecks" (1974)

When Randy Newman's "Rednecks" came out two decades ago it seemed to speak for a moment when the South had one foot in its moonlit, magnolia-scented, but racist past, and the other in the age of pickup trucks, Sunbelt cities, and country rock. Today, even that moment seems dated. Although the racial agonies the song also speaks of still exist in all areas of the country, the southern "good old boy" has had to make room for professional women, educated African-Americans, and new immigrants like the Vietnamese, Cambodians, and Haitians. The rural past has been eclipsed by an ever-expanding urban present, centered on high-finance, high-tech wheeling-dealing, which takes place in high-rise postmodern skyscrapers, hub airports, and gigantic shopping malls. At the same time, the South still seems haunted by the gothic ghosts of its past, and religion's sway is as strong as ever, despite the development of a new southern hedonism. Maybe that accounts for the heavy irony in Newman's voice, as he initially seems to accept the stereotype; later he appears to be fighting it tooth and nail, waging a double-front deconstruction, first on the mythology of the South (much of it self-generated) and next on the secondary mythology, much of it negative, that continues to widely circulate in other regions of the country and abroad as well. And yet Newman, like most of our writers, finds much to celebrate too, even as he criticizes, and he seems to think that this cauldron of symbols and markers, bubbling over with a new brew of southern identity, offers much vitality, humor, and hope.

Newman's song attracted attention when it came out, sometimes not so much for what he was saying as for how he said, sang, and accompanied it. Perhaps Schiller's general principle about style fits many readers, including Newman's; it isn't the *South* they care about so much, but the stylistics of those who make it their subject. But I would hazard a guess that most of the writers in this volume, at any rate, and most *southern* readers, if not the majority of general readers, would quarrel with that. Content, when it has a stranglehold on the heart, *does* matter. What Newman is really addressing is the age-old southern rage against hypocritical attacks on southern culture, a rage surprisingly shared on occasion by southern women, African-Americans, and Jews, who have all on occasion risen to defend their region.

A Southern Grammatology

The most prominent voices in this debate have always been those of the South's artists. Subject and style are somewhat dictated by the times and the culture, but artists make conscious choices. Such a gift is accompanied by responsibility, so as dedicated South-watchers and aficionados of the literature that reflects it, we should continually ask this question: who writes down—or makes up—the image of the South for us today? Is it simply mirrored back to us from the ever-slicker news reports of our local TV station? If, as some suggest, the best images are found in the narratives of our native writers, are these authors faithful to the reality of life as we know it, or are they catering to the stereotypes they think a national audience (including southerners themselves) requires? Finally, who will be writing southern literature tomorrow, and about what, and why?

This volume seeks to answer these and other questions by letting many of our younger and more interesting writers speak for themselves, and for a region and a people whose contours and ticks they feel a need to chart. They may have other, more prominent concerns, too, but this charting and mapping of the culture inevitably follows, as a matter of course, because of who these writers have been, are, and will be: southerners. We also take some looks backward, at our joint past, which, despite the modernist and postmodernist zeitgeists, all too often dictates the future.

Books like these of course have to ponder definitions. Superficially, there has always been a debate about what states qualify as southern. In the nineteenth century, Maryland certainly would have been included; today, probably not. Most would be content to say the South consists of the former Confederacy plus Kentucky and Oklahoma, but we're still asking ourselves, is Texas part of the South? If not, are we willing to deny the profoundly southern qualities of the thoughtful and intricate writing in the novels of Beverly Lowry, the plays of Horton Foote, or the epics and bittersweet comedies of Larry McMurtry?

Then there's the question of permanence. Is being southern a category fixed for life? What do you do with the southern writer who leaves the South, both physically *and* in her fiction? One might ask, for instance, whether Richard Ford is really a southern writer. Most of his works unfold in distant places and concern easterners or Rocky Mountain folk. Nonetheless, does he—do they—speak under this patina with a southern nuance? Are the places they inhabit really metaphors for southern climes? Then there's the case of James Wilcox, a gifted comic writer who's been compared to Chekhov. His first four novels were set in Louisiana, but he's been using New York for most of his locales since then, probably because he's been living in Gotham for some time now. Yusef Komunyakaa now writes poetry in Indiana, not Louisiana. Cormac McCarthy recently won the National Book Award for his wonderful *All the Pretty Horses,* but much of it is set in Mexico. Gail Godwin has been confusing label-pasters for years with her shifting subjects and locales. Southern or not?

This is an old debate, after all; we've driven out some of our best writers, including Edgar Allan Poe, George Washington Cable, Charles Chesnutt, Carson McCullers, Robert Penn Warren, Allen Tate, and many others, and most of them began to write some non-southern narratives. Others, however, seemed relatively unaffected. Warren, to cite the most salient example, spent much of his life in Connecticut, but would anyone challenge the profoundly southern essence of his writing? But even those who chose to stay put can and do venture outside "southern" waters. What then? Do we include these texts in surveys, anthologies, and studies of southern literature? It seems likely we'll see many more examples of this syndrome in the future, as Americans in general and writers, perhaps, in particular, become more mobile and less fastened to their cultural bases. No doubt, however, as always, we'll see just as many writers *returning* to their "roots." Tony Kushner, a Louisianan, won the Pulitzer Prize for *Angels in America,* but there is little that is southern about the play. But does that necessarily mean that Kushner's future works won't be about the South? Other recent dramas have proved the vitality southern subjects have for the region's playwrights, such as Beth Henley, Marsha Norman, Tom Dent, Robert Harling, and Alfred Uhry, yet many of them have slipped easily in and out of southern themes.

Similarly, we have to ask ourselves what we mean when we say "literature." Does it include popular but definitely schlock productions—sex-grits-and-skyscrapers paperbacks with titles like *Atlanta* or *B'ham Ala*? Typically, a blurb for the former reads, "The inside story of the thundering emergence of a city of glass and steel—the men who built it, the women who bathed in its glamour, and loved in its shadows, and the shocking power-play that threatened to engulf their glittering dreams."

More problematic are the compelling narratives by talented storytellers that all the same seem calculated for a mass audience, especially in their obliging redecking of old stereotypes in new guises. I am thinking here of the work of Harry Crews, Pete Dexter, or, distressingly, much of Pat Conroy's wildly popular *Prince of Tides.* Catering to an audience-determined formula? Looking for the movie contract? Or are these necessarily compromising factors? What about novelist Lee Smith's recent foray into Nashville's music scene, surely one of the most interesting aspects of contemporary southern culture? A sellout, or an expansion of her natural canvas? And how does it compare with Harry Crews's similar mining of another musical realm in *The Gospel Singer,* a novel that garnered the praise of a master craftsman of the old school, Andrew Lytle?

One thing seems certain: most of today's southern narratives, highbrow or low, aspire to mirror a culture in the throes of dynamic and dramatic change, a condition that has often led to some of the greatest achievements in southern literature, such as *Cane, The Sound and the Fury, All the King's Men,* and *Meridian.*

As the outpouring of books like *Atlanta* reveals, however, not all of our musings on change have been of this gravity. In addition to the page-turners, what are we to do with the vastly popular books of southern good-old-boy humorists like the late Lewis Grizzard and Roy Blount Jr.? Their witticisms grew out of the fertile soil of change too; do such writers have any affinity with, or (gasp!) an actual influence on, "serious" comic writers like Clyde Edgerton, Barry Hannah, Larry Brown, Lewis Nordan, or Allan Gurganus? And for that matter, the new southern woman has a comic persona too, in the delightful fictions of Alice Childress, Ellen Gilchrist, Fannie Flagg, Rita Mae Brown, and Kaye Gibbons. Do we draw a strict line of separation between them and more commercially thinking women writers? And the debate still rages about John Kennedy Toole's *Confederacy of Dunces*; can such a popular, wildly funny book really be any good?

Once again, this is hardly a new conundrum. Southern readers and critics have always wondered what to do with "popular writers," especially when their works indubitably satisfy basic human yearnings for warmth, humor, and tenderness, without necessarily providing great art. The frontier humorists had to wait outside the academy for some time, and so did their heir, Mark Twain.

Popular *women* writers must face the charge of being melodramatic, sentimental, or both. This charge has its most obvious example in Margaret Mitchell, but one sees it again today in the chilly critical reception of a work such as Olive Ann Burns's runaway best-seller, *Cold Sassy Tree*. The current holder of the "popular" southern historical novel crown, however, is surely Anne Rivers Siddons, whose *Peachtree Road* not only limns her own native culture but also sets out a basic pattern (some would say formula) followed in her other romances, such as *The Outer Banks*, about North Carolina. Yet on reading V. S. Naipaul's interview with her in *A Turn in the South*, one is struck by her honesty, her concern for justice, and her constant examination of the implications of being southern, female, and an artist.

Burns and Siddons clearly loom far above the many hack writers who combine ample portions of sex and glitter with southern stereotypes. But again, how do we draw the line? Quo vadis, southern writer?

Resetting the Table

As my remarks already suggest, the future of southern letters won't lie entirely in the hands of white male southerners. The *greatest* change in southern letters has come in with the new canon. Without question, many of the very best and/or most popular contemporary writers from the region are female, African-American, or both.

Ernest Gaines and Alice Walker are surely candidates, along with Reynolds Price, for recognition as the greatest currently active southern writers.

But as always, the *living* canon—our current supply of active writers—shifts regularly, in unexpected ways. Most obviously, we never know when commanding or merely intriguing voices will be stilled, either by premature death, illness, or writer's block. We lost Henry Dumas, John Kennedy Toole, John O. Killens, and Raymond Andrews all too soon. Many regret that Ralph Ellison, Harper Lee, and others never followed up their brilliant first novels with others.

Some of the greatest writers in the tradition have continued to write well into old age; surviving and productive figures here include Elizabeth Spencer, Reynolds Price, Albert Murray, Shirley Ann Grau, Wendell Berry, David Madden, Maya Angelou, and Mary Lee Settle, and one devoutly hopes that our literary future will include new works by them. Often, writers we think we know well astonish us with something entirely new, unexpected, and utterly true, as in Peter Taylor's magnificent *Summons to Memphis,* or Douglas's *Can't Quit You Baby.* So even when our writers die after a long, productive career, as was the case recently with Taylor, Robert Penn Warren, Etheridge Knight, Walker Percy, and Frank Yerby, we wonder if they took a final manuscript with them. On the other hand, other great living writers, such as Eudora Welty and Margaret Walker Alexander, have seemingly halted their production.

The current state of southern letters, despite the losses mentioned above, is strong. The announcement of the 1993 Pulitzer Prizes in fiction and drama to two Louisiana natives follows the honors awarded to Allan Gurganus's *Oldest Living Confederate Widow Tells All* and Pete Dexter's *Paris Trout*. Ernest Gaines just received the prestigious MacArthur Award and, for *A Lesson before Dying,* the National Book Critics' Circle Award. Such acclaim and attention can only encourage and challenge developing and struggling writers of the South to press on.

Writers of the contemporary South differ dramatically from their predecessors; how could they not? In their lifetime the region has changed more than it had in all its previous history. But somehow southern writers, moving with the flow, see some kind of constant, enduring presence in southern settings. Place, despite dramatic changes, still casts the same old spell in many ways. New Orleans, in the works of poet Brenda Marie Osbey, novelist John Kennedy Toole, or short story writer Ellen Gilchrist, seems eternal and unique. The rippling fields and forests emerge with a contemporary menace but an ageless essence in the works of Cormac McCarthy, while Louise Shivers finds a sensual, smoky setting for her tale of contemporary passion in the North Carolina tobacco country. Charleston has never seemed so hip, so vibrant, but yet so traditional and tropical too, as in the fiction of Josephine Humphreys or Pat Conroy. Other writers from other places have added to this tradition recently. Peter Matthiessen's brooding, brutal, and beautiful depiction of the Florida frontier in *Killing Mr. Watson* reminds us that transplanted "Yankees" have frequently added to our store of verbal landscapes. Who can forget Marjorie Kinnan Rawlings's equally compelling vision of her beloved Florida?

Resetting the table has meant playing with some recipes as well. An often-overlooked component of Faulkner's continuing influence on southern letters has been evident in the experimental nature of much of southern fiction of the last few decades. One of the most impressive achievements here has been Jack Butler's *Jujitsu for Christ,* to my mind one of the true classics in the tradition. Another writer willing to take on almost any aesthetic dare is Barry Hannah, whose real achievement sometimes gets obscured by his occasional, inevitable failures. The women's movement and its focus on gender has undoubtedly encouraged writers to experiment in exploring issues that matter to their opposite sex, often in that sex's voice. Clyde Edgerton's *Raney,* Reynolds Price's *Kate Vaiden,* Ellen Douglas's *Rock Cried Out,* and Alice Walker's *Third Life of Grange Copeland* all fit this welcome pattern and seem to promise more to come. Writers have shown a willingness to cross ethnic and racial boundaries: Robert Olen Butler's *Good Scent from a Strange Mountain* concerns Vietnamese-Americans; Shirley Ann Grau has returned to the literary scene with her striking new novel *Roadwalkers,* about African-Americans caught in the Great Depression.

Similarly, recent attention in society at large to abused children and children's rights has coincided with a new interest in child narrators and characters in southern fiction; imaginative rethinking of southern classics such as *Huckleberry Finn* have lately emerged in works such as Padgett Powell's *Edisto,* Kaye Gibbons's *Ellen Foster,* and Dori Sanders's *Clover.*

As this collection's several essays on southern poetry demonstrate, innovation and experimentation continue to vitalize southern poetry. I would add that the lyrical tradition of poetry lives on, especially in Louisiana, where one finds Pinkie Gordon Lane, Mona Lisa Saloy, Tom Dent, Brenda Marie Osbey, and many others. Louisiana now also boasts Dave Smith, whose muscular, dark, and brooding work brings a contemporary resonance to an equally venerable tradition of masculine poetry, epitomized by Donald Davidson, Allen Tate, James Dickey, Jerry W. Ward Jr., Fred Chappell, Alvin Aubert, and, of course, Robert Penn Warren.

The elegant patterns of malaise charted by the late Walker Percy have found a more pedestrian expression in the recent and creative neorealism of writers such as Bobbie Ann Mason, Valerie Sayers, Larry Brown, Richard Ford, and Josephine Humphreys. And yet one of our contributors, Jack Butler, claims that the most uninteresting literature of all is that which seeks to expose the "essential meaningless and vapidity of life," a sentiment others surely share. Clearly, although certain threads appear to run in common through southern texts, attitudes and approaches toward them differ widely.

At least one sign of the newly catholic nature of southern studies may be found in the emerging courses, anthologies, and critical studies that reflect the new canon of southern literature and cultural studies. *The History of Southern Literature* (1985), edited by an older generation of scholars, offered the first proof of the paradigm shift. A more dramatic example, in the broader field of southern cultural studies, emerged in the best-selling and widely honored *Encyclopedia of Southern Culture* (1989), edited by Charles Reagan Wilson and William Ferris, which attempted to honor every aspect of the region's life and thought, from hushpuppies, kudzu, possums, and air-conditioning to architectural styles, dialect, recreation, and women's lives. Although the hundred-page section on "Black Life" is impressive, references to African-American culture appear throughout the many entries. Even more space is devoted to "Ethnic Life" and "Folklife." One is surprised and disappointed to find that only three of the forty writers identified as "major" in the folklife section are African-Americans. But the study as a whole constitutes a watershed in rethinking what southern "culture" is, incorporating much previously scorned material and peoples, and placing folk culture's value much higher in our collective consciousness. The *Encyclopedia* in many ways reflects a sea change in the academy, where the South's peoples and cultures are studied in inter-disciplinary, multicultural ways undreamed of only a few decades ago. Within literature, previously dismissed genres such as diaries, journals, cookbooks, autobiographies, work songs, spirituals, and the like now are studied alongside long-revered poems, novels, plays, essays, and sermons. The *Encyclopedia*'s writers and other "New New South" scholars practice a revisionist history, one that looks with a jaundiced eye on the old accounts of southern history while eagerly seeking out documents, photographs, maps, and any literary artifacts that point to a broader portrait of our past than we have previously suspected. This scholarship, with its attendent panels, symposia, festivals, and the like, which often involve the region's writers, has gradually fed into the creation of a new southern literature and will surely continue to have its effect in the decades to come.

REACCENTUATING THE PAST

The future of southern letters will always be partly dependent on our changing perceptions of its past. Twenty-five years ago, most southern literature courses focused on white male writers; even Eudora Welty and Flannery O'Connor were considered "minor" writers and not worthy of study, and the only black writer who made the list from time to time was Booker T. Washington, for obvious reasons. One often heard the argument that this was simply the result of an aesthetic evaluation; the "best" writers just turned out to be male. But of course literary hierarchies, which in turn led to literary histories, paralleled the old patterns of history. The record of the past was assumed to be a linear progression of "great events," which inevitably starred "great men."

Sweeping change in historiography, partly brought about by European historians such as Febvre, Bloch, and, most important, Braudel, has made history less a stitching together of great events than a mining of what Braudel calls "the structure of everyday life." Coincidentally or not, seismic forces operating in literary studies have had much the same effect. In 1996, southern literature courses often devote at least a third of their syllabi to African-American writers, and many works by women, black and white, have been brought into the classroom as well. The list of previously unknown—rather than merely neglected—writers grows apace. The remarkable *Civil War Diary of Sarah Morgan* has not only presented us with a memorable voice from the past but has also radically reshaped our sense of important moments in southern history, notably the Battle of Baton Rouge, the Battle of Port Hudson, and the Siege of Vicksburg. Morgan's reportage contrasts dramatically with Mary Chesnut's and complements the important work currently being done on the role women played in mourning practices, southern art, and the cult of the Lost Cause, a subject that has been brought to our attention in the important *The Confederate Image: Prints of the Lost Cause*, which in turn extends the groundbreaking (and somewhat opposed) work of Charles Reagan Wilson's *Baptized in Blood: The Religion of the Lost Cause, 1865-1920*, and Gaines Foster's *Ghosts of the Confederacy: Defeat, the Lost Cause, and the Emergence of the New South*.

These works of course represent only a fragment of important new studies coming out of southern history, women's studies, multicultural studies, American art history, and many other dynamic disciplines. One might argue that southern writers are unlikely to read such academic texts, but they certainly know when the public's tastes are being steered back toward regional literature, history, and culture, whether directly or indirectly, through a kind of "trickle-down" effect brought about by local newspapers, book reviews, or even magazine articles in *Southern Living, Southern Accents,* and the like.

One of the things that needs to be said here is that despite the changes listed above, the South in many ways continues to be a very conservative region, and it would be foolish to pretend that conservative elements in southern literature—and, indeed, literary criticism—have disappeared. Several of the essays in this book reflect that reality—particularly Fred Hobson's and Jefferson Humphries's.

Certainly many writers native to the region and from outside it have been turning to historical fiction lately. Many African-American writers have done so; southerners Margaret Walker Alexander and Alex Haley paved the way with *Jubilee* and *Roots,* respectively, following the lead of Frank Yerby, whose *Foxes of Harrow* ought to have been seen in that light too, and would have, if more people had realized that its author was black. All three of these novels went back in time to examine slavery from a black perspective, a venerable tradition that of course began with yet another southern genre, the slave narrative. In our time this tradition, recast in the historical novel, has found one of its greatest expressions in Ohio's Toni Morrison, in her Pulitzer Prize—winning *Beloved*. Another non-southerner, Sherley Anne Williams, preceded Morrison in searching out another vision of southern slavery in *Dessa Rose*. Nor is slavery the only time frame subject to inspection. Georgia's Alice Walker chose the 1930s (*The Color Purple*) and the 1960s of the civil rights movement (*Meridian*) for examination under her literary microscope. Similarly, Ernest Gaines has set most of his work in the past, most obviously in *The Autobiography of Miss Jane Pittman,* which examines both of the heroic epochs (emancipation and the civil rights movement) through the life of its title character. His magnificent new novel, *A Lesson before Dying,* goes back to a 1948 execution to help us ponder why so many young, black American men continue to be warehoused and put to death in today's up-to-date prisons. Gloria Naylor, who is no southerner but was conceived, she reminds us, in Mississippi, went to the legendary Georgia/South Carolina coast for her hit novel *Mama Day*, a book that shuttles easily between the legendary past and a disillusioning present.

Rita Mae Brown's Civil War novel *High Hearts* is a key example of how a writer associated with one school—in this case, comic "feminist" fiction—can easily switch gears in order to mine and rethink a classic southern genre. Something rather similar may be found in various pieces by the good-old-boy *enfant terrible* of southern letters, Barry Hannah, particularly in his justly famous short stories involving Jeb Stuart.

In his recent study *The Southern Writer in the Postmodern World,* Fred Hobson has made an interesting observation about Bobbie Ann Mason, who has frequently been criticized for writing a kind of "Kmart" realism, even when ostensibly pondering historical issues, such as Vietnam, in books like In Country. Hobson gives Mason credit for engaging such matters; argues that she shouldn't be expected to write historical fiction the way Warren or Faulkner would; and, most revealingly, notes the difficulty of coupling what he calls a "minimalist" style with historical subject matter. Hobson suggests, "Perhaps mythology—and a way to order one's life—can come from M*A*S*H as well as The Golden Bough" (Hobson 19-20).

Hobson seems on the verge of proclaiming folklore the successor of mythology. One of the great things about the rediscovery of Zora Neale Hurston and her work has been a renewed respect for southern folk culture (heretofore labeled "low culture"), and not just that of African-Americans. High-minded critics such as Mencken and others always blasted the South for its lack of "high culture"; recent literary criticism—certainly of African-American southern literature, but also of women's writing in the South (like that focused on Augusta Jane Evans in the nineteenth century, for instance, or the work of Ellen Douglas or Elizabeth Spencer in our own time)—has revealed a rich vein of folk culture that runs prominently through classic and little-known works of southern literature. One finds it in unexpected places, as in the description of the way southern belles fastened the buttons of Confederate soldier's uniforms onto their dresses in Thomas Nelson Page's Reconstruction novel, Red Rock, or the lovingly detailed quotidean rituals Welty provides in Delta Wedding, or the African-American folklore one finds in Raymond Andrews's or John Killens's fictional small towns. Will critical appreciation of these neglected aspects of southern writing encourage more of it?

New Southern Dialogics

All these issues and many more are taken up by the authors we have assembled here. In our lead essay, James Applewhite reveals the prominence and significance of the unsatisfactory father motif in southern letters; surely one extension of his theory would be that many of today's southern artists find the old approaches and stereotypes of their literary tradition moldy at best and are constantly seeking to replace outworn symbols with newer ones, while simultaneously trying to restore that sense of fidelity to the South's body and mind that originally animated the old symbols when they were generated.

In his apt metaphor describing the differentiation between writers and critics, Jack Butler suggests that the critics map the coastline, while the writers *are* the coastline. But this image also suggests that the real way we define the body of the South and its culture is through its boundaries and what they touch, a theory quite similar, in fact, to Fredrik Barth's formulation of what constitutes an ethnic group: not content but boundary, a constantly shifting line. And as Jefferson Humphries asserts in his essay here, any regional or national identity stems from at least two conflicting needs—the desire to create a narrative from within that codifies identity but also by the narrative constructed *without* that the first narrative inevitably responds to.)

Butler proclaims the need to be not just southern but "southern modern," to bring a novelty into the equation of rendering the New New South. But he, like Applewhite and many others in this volume, conjures up that old genie William Faulkner in the same breath, blending the present and the past to cast a new formula for southern writing, albeit set in his own vital language: "We think of a place; we think of the darkness and splendor of families; we think of a way of talking; we think of the Bible; and we think of black and white locked into a mutual if inharmonious fate."

And yet, as our writers constantly demonstrate, most of the changes—even the seismic eruption of postmodern southern humor have antecedents. Stephen Smith's jaunty ride through the trickster show of our literary humor demonstrates that that other rude, irreverent South, just back of the big house, lives on and on and on, even if it has to pitch its sideshow tent in Kmart's parking lot. His open eye for popular culture's role in this ongoing carnival makes for some joyful reading and some careful rethinking.

The ubiquitous presence of humor in southern discourse finds ample display in two other pieces in our collection. Fred Chappell's hilarious sendup of books such as this one displays, if nothing else, the boisterous survival of southern academic humor. He also wickedly skewers the expectations we and publishers have of southern writers. The fact that "Wil Hickson" speaks to us from 2001 (a "South Odyssey"?) confirms not only that there will be a future for southern letters but also that the quest for it will remain ever elusive, endless, and, one hopes, joyful. Ole Wil's short history of the Appal Lit Insurrection furnishes a kind of microcosm of the broader history of the set it seeks to separate from—"Grit Lit," southern literature itself.

Similarly, Jim Wayne Miller resurrects the legendary and irreverent Sut Lovingood to poke fun at our academic landmark, *The History of Southern Literature,* which is eloquently defended elsewhere in this volume by Fred Hobson. Nobody ever said that southern writers and scholars tend to agree!

The hip-flip mask of Chappell finds its counterpart in the dramatic jeremiad of Rodger Cunningham, who makes a startling application of postcolonialist theorists such as Edward Said to help us posit a different kind of future for Appalachia. In reaching out to the methodologies of other fields, Cunningham encourages us to remap what we think is familiar terrain.

Poet Kate Daniels employs a luminous prose to demonstrate how the post-modern writer's identity stems from a personal task: commemorating one's family. For in her brief memoir of a Richmond childhood, she locates the origins of narratives in the structures of everyday life, as they pass, as Zora Neale Hurston might say, from "mouth almighty" as it whiles away a summer's night on dimly lit front porches. Daniels shows us how these voices helped her both write and read poetry years later, in the North (where, like many, she finds out what it *really* means to be southern) and, later, in Louisiana.

Fred Hobson and Jefferson Humphries offer varying views of our subject from very different academic perches. Hobson, once a Pulitzer Prize-winning journalist and for many years an editor, teacher, and historian/scholar of southern literature, provides us with a shrewd and true-to-the-bone assessment of what the patterns mean in the long history of the southern literary canon. Among its many other virtues, Hobson's essay demonstrates decisively that academic critics have an extremely important role to play in identifying, supporting, and, yes, criticizing future southern writers. Understanding the errors of past scholars (especially their racism and sexism) plays a key role here, but Hobson takes pains to temper some recent and, he would say, unwarranted attacks on the elder generation's critical legacy. Hobson's even-handed and courageous approach skillfully untangles some knotted clusters of aesthetics and ideology, and coincidentally equips us with some valuable clues about how best to examine similar knots in our critical and literary discourse about contemporary and future writers. His piece is also a tribute to magnificent scholars such as Louis Rubin and Lewis Simpson, who in transforming their approaches to southern letters—most memorably in their seminal *History of Southern Literature* (1985)—helped steer us toward the multicultural, inter-disciplinary position the field now seems to favor. Hobson's essay offers a reminder, too, that no consideration of the South's literary future will be successful in effacing its past.

Jefferson Humphries appears to contradict much of what some other essayists here have written in his emphasis on the South as story, as idea, but in fact he usefully complements many of their pronouncements, particularly those of Fred Hobson. Humphries uses an adroit blend of contemporary theory and literary history (much of it drawn from the nineteenth century) to create a surprising congruence between Old South intellectual activity and recently fashionable theories of narrative. His employment of "narrative exigency" ties together many apparently disparate observations in this collection, and like Hobson and Olney, Humphries mines the past in order to understand the future.

No section of this volume speaks more eloquently of the continuing hold of place than the interview with Brenda Marie Osbey. Her comments on New Orleans offer proof of at least one area of traditional southern resonance that continues to pulse with generating, creative power. And yet Osbey speaks perceptively about the "quilt" of the South, noting the other distinct "patches" that have also retained a certain unique quality. She sees religion, a preoccupation with death and loss, remembrance, and a love for the land as common threads that hold the quilt together.

Osbey's meditations and wry comments find a contrast in Robert Olen Butler's conversation with Michael Sartisky. Butler provides fascinating insights on how it feels for a southern writer to achieve virtually overnight fame, as he did when he won the Pulitzer Prize. He also offers up quite a detailed autobiography, one that explains why writing about "the collision of cultures"—especially those of Vietnam and America—comes naturally to him, as it does for many southern writers. Readers pondering the question of who actually belongs in this latter group, or what makes an outsider a "southern writer," will find a compelling case study in Butler, who grew up in St. Louis, lived in New York for years, and then went to Vietnam. Ultimately, when his interviewer asks him to name the "place" that he identifies with most closely, he names Louisiana, his home for the last eight years.

Butler's musings on the influences and patterns in his life suggest the importance of autobiography in southern letters. James Olney brings his impressive expertise in this field to bear on the peculiarities of the southern "life narrative." His essay also typifies some of the most encouraging comparative work now being done, particularly in his pairing of works by a black man and a white woman—Mississippi's native son and daughter Richard Wright and Eudora Welty.

Olney's remarks may seem to address only the past, yet they are especially apropos now, when the personal memoir has been coming more to the fore of southern letters. Surely the civil rights-era witnessing of James Farmer, Anne Moody, Howell Raines, and many others has played a large role in establishing a contemporary version of the venerable tradition of the classic slave narratives, Washington's *Up from Slavery,* or Mary Chesnut or Sarah Morgan's Civil War diaries. Writers such as Reynolds Price, Maya Angelou, Albert Murray, and the many others collected in anthologies such as *A World Unsuspected* continue to write in this genre. Fiction itself has adapted this mode in make-believe memoirs, such as Gaines's memorable *Autobiography* of *Miss Jane Pittman,* or Allan Gurganus's best-seller, *Oldest Living Confederate Widow Tells All.* We can hardly speculate about the future of these traditions without meditating at length on their origins.

Dave Smith's musings over the problem of defining a "southern poet" rehearses many of the issues raised here by his fellow versifiers, James Applewhite, Fred Chappell, Kate Daniels, and Brenda Marie Osbey. But Smith also profitably zeroes in on a kind of "attitude of obligation, of piety, of something like a sacred respect" that one indeed notices both in the poems of this group and in their pronouncements about those poems.

Problems and Prospects in Southern Letters

This discussion would be incomplete without word of some exciting developments in southern letters that complement the suggestions of the writers in this volume. Jefferson Humphries's ongoing task of employing contemporary, frequently European criticism toward a rereading of southern letters is by no means unique. The dynamic Society for the Study of Southern Literature's bulging and informative newsletters offer eloquent testimony to the exciting new approaches to the field now being mounted by feminists, African-Americanists, Marxists, Hispanic-Americanists, deconstructionists, postcolonialists, and all other types of critics.

But much work remains to be done. Several essayists in this collection chide critics for neglecting Appalachian literature and culture. Someone should concurrently urge southernists to pay more attention to the South's French and Spanish legacies, especially the Cajun and Creole cultures in Louisiana. And then what about the new literature now being written by recent immigrants to the South from other countries such as Cuba, Vietnam, Haiti, and, more recently, China and India? Miami's scintillating Little Havana has already produced some original new writers, such as Virgil Suarez, and the Hispanic-American Renaissance in Texas, typified by the writing of Rolando Hinojosa, has been thriving for some time. More is sure to come as other groups coalesce and find their "southern" voice. One preliminary effect has been the Pulitzer Prize-winning novel *A Good Scent from a Strange Mountain,* by Louisiana's Robert Olen Butler, a group of stories centering on Vietnamese Americans on the Gulf Coast. Surely this community will be speaking in its own voice shortly, and we will need critics who know how to properly hear it and integrate it with the broader dialogic of the region.

These "emerging southerners," after all, are undergoing a more severe form of the "future shock" all southerners are experiencing, and all southern writers, regardless of their other affiliations, must come to grips with the literary traditions of the past that continue to inform and influence the future. As I have suggested, this has meant rethinking and reinventing all the subgenres of southern writing, including the historical novel, a subgenre explored by Rita Mae Brown, Ernest Gaines, Alice Walker, and others. This too is nothing new; as Mikhail Bakhtin usefully tells us,

> Every age re-accentuates in its own way the works of its most immediate past. The historical life of classic works is in fact the uninterrupted process of their social and ideological re-accentuation. Thanks to the intentional potential embedded in them, such works have proved capable of uncovering in each era and against ever new dialogizing backgrounds ever newer aspects of meaning; their semantic content literally continues to grow, to further create out of itself. Likewise their influence on subsequent creative works inevitably includes re-accentuation. New images in literature are very often created through a re-accentuation of old images, by translating them from one accentual register to another (from the comic plane to the tragic, for instance, or the other way around).
>
> (Bakhtin 421)

Richard Wright, in detailing the development of an authentic and southern African-American voice, affirmed the validity of Bakhtin's observation in a particular sense—that of liberation:

> We stole words from the grudging lips of the Lords of the Land, who did not want us to know too many of them or their meaning. And we charged this meager horde of stolen sounds with all the emotions and longings we had; we proceeded to build our language in inflections of voice, through tonal variety, by hurried speech, in honeyed drawls, by rolling our eyes, by flourishing our hands, by assigning to common, simple words new meanings, meanings which enable us to speak of revolt in the actual presence of the Lords of the Land without their being aware! Our secret language extended our understanding of what slavery meant and gave us the freedom to speak to our brothers in captivity; we polished our new words, caressed them, gave them new shape and color, a new order and tempo, until, though they were the words of the Lords of the Land, they became *our* words, *our* language.
>
> (Wright 40)

In another passage, Wright suggested that this process demanded of African-American southerners the qualities always exacted of "mighty artists." I do not wish to subtract one iota from the specificity this observation must continue to have in relation to the struggles of African-Americans; but the broader ramifications of dealing with a view imposed from outside a culture has been a problem for *all* southerners for some time now. Secondly, Wright's reference to "mighty artists" powerfully indicates the connection he sees between aesthetics and ideology. Many southern critics—most notably the Fugitives, but including many critics writing today—have denied this link. It is time, though, for this artificial barrier to come down.

This book attempts to demonstrate our own time's attempt to reaccentuate our traditions, while simultaneously building our own language and literature to fit today's needs and realities. Thankfully, the walls separating southerners from one another have been tumbling down; those that remain may be breached, paradoxically, by embracing each other's "secret language," by learning to listen on *all* the broadcasting frequencies. Our writers have preceded us in this endeavor; one of the things this collection proves is that southern writers read each other avidly and appreciatively. No "Melville never meeting Whitman" here. Praise gets heaped on quite a number of writers we weren't able to corral for this gathering, such as Lewis Nordan, Reynolds Price, Anne Tyler, Clyde Edgerton, James Alan McPherson, Louis Rubin, Cormac McCarthy, Robert Morgan, Ernest Gaines, Cleanth Brooks, David Bottoms, Charles Wright, William Styron, Gayl Jones, Willie Morris, Alice Walker, Barry Hannah, Bobbie Ann Mason, Lewis Simpson, and, especially often, Lee Smith, whose work places her in several camps.

What do writers look for in their peers? No doubt sheer pleasure and wonder lead the list, but they also find warnings of things to come, things hidden, things festering, that may be just beneath the surface of their own work as well. Writers prophesy to each other as well as to their general readers.

* * *

During his first presidential campaign, Jimmy Carter sounded a refrain that he had utilized frequently during his dynamic stint as governor of Georgia: namely, that the passage of the Civil Rights Act in the 1960s was the greatest thing that had ever happened to the South. Equally dramatic change followed as the nation experienced its first military defeat in Vietnam, bringing it in line with the South, which until then had labored under the heavy penumbra of a civil war that in many ways should have been forgotten. "The defeated South," already flexing its Sunbelt power, was now part of a "defeated" nation. As James Applewhite remarks in this volume, "Much tragedy is encoded, for the South and for the nation, in that allegiance beyond logic, beyond reason."

And now in the 1990s, with another southern president in the White House, with African-American mayors in place in most large southern cities, and a woman newly elected in her own right to the Senate from Texas (which already, like Kentucky before it, had elected a woman governor), the South, relocating its mythical allegiances, indeed sets many standards for the nation to follow. A space-age Atlanta—presided over by Ted and Jane, the postmodern Rhett and Scarlett—prepares to host the Olympics. Florida's boom into the power-state category was only slightly slowed by Hurricane Andrew. Southern-hatched crazes have swept the nation, including Cabbage Patch dolls, the mania for Arkansas-born Wal-Mart, and the appetite for Cajun and Tex-Mex food, Vidalia onions, and pickled okra. Nashville has become the nation's music and recording center, for southern music—gospel, jazz, blues, rock and roll, bluegrass, zydeco, country—has surely become not only America's only unique cultural product but the music of the sphere itself.

And yet the proud new cities also harbor the homeless; newly affluent citizens may well be drug addicts, alcoholics, philanderers, and worse. Environmental and governmental scandals proliferate, and oil busts, plant closings, urban blight, and substandard schools continue to breed tragedies worth writing about. The news from the New New South isn't all good. But whatever the story, the South's special trappings give it a unique appeal and an opportunity to mount messages of national concern through compelling regional metaphor and narrative.

For despite the oft-bemoaned homogenization of the nation, the South continues to have a special identity quite apart from the rest of the nation, even when that identity sometimes seems just as different from the South's own past. To choose only one of many subjects, today, as much as ever, change, loss, and an effort to limn the contours of a vanishing world appear to be vital impulses for many southern writers. The difference lies in the subjects "lost": not just the old plantation but also the plantation quarters (Ernest Gaines); not just the isolation of the mountains but also their crafts and customs (Lee Smith); not just Old New Orleans but also its decency and honor (Nancy Lemann). And charting a world of loss, of course, goes all the way back to George Washington Cable, William Faulkner, Jean Toomer, and Katherine Anne Porter, to name but a few of our elegists. No doubt we (or more likely, our grandchildren) will someday hear about the vanished world of Houston's fabled Galleria, or Miami's Fontainebleu, or Charlotte's Coliseum.

To take this subject of loss to a broader dimension: if Fred Hobson is right that a certain power has been lost in southern letters, is that because the old agonies of the South—particularly those connected with race—have somewhat abated? Or is it merely that what used to be seen as local tragedy has passed into the realm of the nation? To put a more positive interpretation on it, perhaps southerners have at long last accepted what Richard Wright asserted long ago, in an utterance that has even more relevance to southerners in particular than to

Americans as a whole: "The differences between black folk and white folk are not blood or color, and the ties that bind us are deeper than those that separate us. The common road of hope which we all have traveled has brought us into a stronger kinship than any words, laws, or legal claims" (Wright 146). As other barriers that divide us to continue to fall, and as long as our writers continue to travel this road of hope and to see the South as both a legacy and a challenge, there will always be a future for southern letters.

Works Cited

Bakhtin, Mikhail. *The Dialogic Imagination.* Ed. Michael Holquist. Trans. Caryl Emerson and Michael Holquist. Austin: U of Texas P, 1981.

Hobson, Fred C. *The Southern Writer in the Postmodern World.* Athens: U of Georgia P, 1991.

Wright, Richard. *Twelve Million Black Voices.* 1941; rpt. New York: Thunder's Mouth P, 1988.

Ernest Suarez (essay date winter 1997)

SOURCE: Suarez, Ernest. "Toward a New Southern Poetry: Southern Poetry in Contemporary American Literary History." *Southern Review* 33, no. 1 (winter 1997): 181-96.

[*In the following essay, Suarez examines the poetry of James Dickey and Robert Penn Warren as representative of the modern South, pointing out that their poetry is both regional and highly individual.*]

Robert Penn Warren's and James Dickey's verse published since the mid-1950s provides a basis for reevaluating the history not only of southern poetry but of contemporary American poetry. During the '50s, Warren and Dickey developed approaches that neither historical field has been able fully to accommodate; their work indicates how two categories that should overlap have instead formed distinct, and fragmentary, narratives. Considering the tensions between romantic and naturalistic tendencies in Warren's later poetry and Dickey's verse can suggest how these two men altered assumptions about the Southern Renascence, creating a foundation for a new southern poetry; but also how in doing so their work eventually conflicted with the critical assumptions shaping histories of contemporary poetry, with the result that their large body of influential and significant work has remained unaddressed in recent assessments. Current evaluations of southern and contemporary poetry remain incomplete because they fail to recognize the centrality of these two figures to recent poetry.

An overview will help set the stage for discussing their relationships to southern poetry and to post-World War II American poetry. Warren's career spanned the modern and postmodern eras. He graduated from Vanderbilt in 1925 and began publishing verse in the '20s. By 1946, when Dickey entered Vanderbilt after his military service, Warren had won the Pulitzer Prize in fiction for *All the King's Men,* had published a "selected poems," and had coauthored with Cleanth Brooks the most influential textbooks—*Understanding Poetry* and *Understanding Fiction*—of his generation. But after the publication of his first selected poems in 1943, Warren experienced a decade during which, by his admission, he could not finish a short poem. In 1954 he once again began completing lyrics, eventually resulting in *Promises,* which won the 1957 Pulitzer Prize. Over the next twenty-three years Warren published six books of poetry, three volumes of selected poems, and three long poems (*Audubon: A Vision, Chief Joseph of the Nez Perce,* and his radically revised *Brother to Dragons.*) He also won another Pulitzer for poetry, the National Book Award, the Bollingen Prize, and earned many other honors.

Dickey spent over a decade experimenting before he discovered the voice and approach that led to his first book, *Into the Stone* (1960). At this point Dickey had a tremendous creative outburst, producing six books of poetry over the next decade, a collected poems in 1968, and five more volumes of verse in the '70s and '80s. In 1993 he released *The Whole Motion: Poems, 1945-1992.* Among the honors bestowed upon him are the National Book Award, the Bollingen Prize, a Guggenheim Fellowship, and the Levinson Prize. Like Warren, he was elected to both the National Institute of Arts and Letters and the fifty-member American Academy of Arts and Sciences.

So it is certainly fair to say that neither Warren nor Dickey has been neglected. The quality and quantity of their poetry after the mid-'50s are no secret to many scholars, but—peculiarly—their role in defining southern poetry and their significance for contemporary poetry have yet to be adequately recognized, a situation due in large part to the ways these fields have been defined and represented by critics, teachers, and editors. Separate sets of critics, with disparate backgrounds, have developed the two areas of study, but in each instance—though with very different emphases—the poetry valued is tied to the topical and the social in a manner that affirms commentators' ideological expectations. The play between romantic and naturalistic elements in Warren's and Dickey's poetry resulted in work more various and complex than can be accommodated by current conceptions of what typifies southern or contemporary poetry.

Histories of recent poetry tend to be movement-centered, employing paradigms involving literary, political, and cultural protest. Books published before the mid-1980s by Cary Nelson, Robert von Hallberg, James

Breslin, Charles Altieri, Charles Molesworth, Laslo Gefin, and others formed the "first wave" of histories, which revolve around Beat, Confessional, Deep Image, Black Mountain, and New York poets, and express values associated with the New Left of the '60s and '70s. Since the mid-'80s, a second wave of studies has stressed feminist and L-A-N-G-U-A-G-E poets. But whereas the earlier analyses presented historical explications of poetic rebellions, the second wave has often adopted the discourse of postmodern theory. Like much deconstructive, Lacanian, feminist, New Historicist, and neo-Marxian criticism, the current crop of studies often posits a dominant "metanarrative" (a history of literature that promotes traditional Western values) that canonical texts reaffirm and that "marginalized" literature subverts. Consequently, '80s and '90s politics of diversity and marginalization underlie newer books by Peter Baker, Walter Kalaidjian, Peter Quartermain, Joseph M. Conte, Norman Finkelstein, George Hartley, Deborah Pope, Diana Wood, Jan Montefiore, and Liz Yorke.

For several reasons, Dickey's poetry and Warren's later verse have not fit under the umbrella of these studies. Warren is usually considered part of the generation against which contemporary poets have rebelled; he is identified with the Fugitives and the New Criticism. Dickey is regarded as excessively macho and sensationalistic. Neither is associated with any recent movements, and, most significant for my purposes, both focus on the contradictory dimensions of human experience by emphasizing the tension between romantic subjectivity and naturalistic fact, making their visions not easily adaptable to the didactic, politically oriented interpretations of verse that today's critics tend to favor.

Their relationship to southern literary history is even more complex. Critics' failure to recognize and credit the importance of Warren's later poetry and Dickey's verse to the region's poetry seems puzzling because their stress on the paradoxical coincides with the thematic and aesthetic assumptions that have dominated the study of southern literature for forty years. Beginning in the late '50s, scholars—Louis Rubin, Louise Cowan, John L. Stewart, Walter Sullivan, Hugh Holman, Lewis P. Simpson, Thomas Daniel Young, Floyd Watkins, and others—shaped a history that documented the Southern Renascence, roughly the period from 1920 to 1950. These critics appraised this literary awakening as the summit of southern writing, a perception that remains unchallenged. John Crowe Ransom, Allen Tate, Donald Davidson, Warren, and others put together the little magazine *The Fugitive* and wrote books of verse for which they received many accolades. As poets, critics, and teachers, these figures influenced both later southern poets, such as Randall Jarrell, and poets from other parts of the country, among them Robert Lowell, Theodore Roethke, and James Wright.

Warren's and Dickey's relationship to the Southern Renascence helps explain the failure to account for their importance to the region's literature. Despite Warren's Pulitzers in poetry in 1957 and 1979, critics continue to associate him—as poet, novelist, and critic—with the old order. This emphasis has overshadowed the formative influence of his later verse on contemporary poets, southern or otherwise. Dickey is not considered a latter-day Fugitive or Agrarian, but critics occasionally refer to him as the last in a line of southern poets affiliated with Vanderbilt—as a kind of afterword to the Renascence. Critics' inclination to see this three-decade "golden age" as the cynosure of the region's literary history makes them either neglect Warren's and Dickey's work of the last four decades or see it as a "Requiem for the Renaissance" (to adopt Walter Sullivan's phrase) instead of recognizing its role in fostering a vibrant new poetry practiced by a talented younger generation including Rodney Jones, Dave Smith, Betty Adcock, Yusef Komunyakaa, David Bottoms, T. R. Hummer, Ellen Bryant Voigt, and others.

Allen Tate's well-known essay "A Southern Mode of Imagination" helps clarify the transition from the Renascence to southern poetry of the last half-century. As I've stated, studies of southern high modernism have pursued the intricacies of paradox rather than the didactic ends of recent criticism. The consensus among critics of southern literature—and a premise advanced in Tate's essay—is that in contrast to the tendentious, often racist and topical "Confederate" poetry and prose of Sidney Lanier, William Gilmore Simms, Thomas Nelson Page, T. S. Stribling, and others who viewed the South as oppressed and contemned by the rest of the country, the best work of the Renascence became more actively self-conscious. Tate details the movement from the "rhetorical mode" to the "dialectical" to account for the great leap in quality of southern writing during the first half of the twentieth century. In a nutshell, Tate argues that southern literature improved because it stopped defending itself against "northern aggression" and became introspective, resulting in the exploration of cultural tensions through the writer's inner conflicts. Though the claim holds true for southern fiction, particularly Faulkner's novels, Tate jumped the gun in regard to the region's poetry. The Fugitive poets, and others he mentions, are more properly seen as transitional figures. Even Ransom's and Tate's best verse—consider "Antique Harvesters" or "Ode to the Confederate Dead"—though perhaps not propagandistic, nevertheless expresses a powerful nostalgia for a previous order. Critics of southern literature often share this nostalgia, which contributes to their failure to remark the limitations of Renascence poetry. In *The Southern Agrarians* (1988), Paul Conkin asserts that the Agrarians "remind us of what people lost in the transition from a proprietary economy to a collective economy. . . . Only the most insensitive and shallow person can listen, really listen, to the Agrarians without a poignant sense of loss." As recently as 1994, Louis Rubin—the dean of southern critics—ended an essay on the Fugitive poets by quoting Yeats: "All the Olympians; a thing never known again." Contrary to such assertions, southern poetry had to wait until the '50s, when Warren emerged from his decade-long drought and Dickey began to discover the themes and techniques that would mark his maturity, to find the type of poet that Tate identified.

Warren's and Dickey's ambivalent relationship to the social upheavals of the '50s illustrates this point. Raised in provincial, conservative surroundings in the segregated South, they continued to be affected by their upbringings even as they developed increasingly liberal convictions about social issues. As the attack on segregation intensified in the '50s, Warren and Dickey both wrote on race relations, declaring their support for the Civil Rights Movement and assuming more progressive positions than did the Fugitives and Agrarians. But both men viewed the budding New Left counterculture—typified by the Beats' romantic idealism—with suspicion, for they retained a belief in the contradictory nature of experience and held a profound distrust of utopian impulses. In essence, they became what Thomas Hill Schaub calls "chastened liberals," writers who explored their paradoxical views of the human condition by investigating a "universal" issue, in this case the relation between romanticism and naturalism.

Much Southern Renascence and contemporary poetry also displays romantic and naturalistic elements, but the dynamic interaction between these philosophies shapes Warren's and Dickey's poetic visions. Though the ideological assumptions of poets identified with the Renascence and with later movements are very different, each group's verse remains firmly anchored to the topical and social. Much recent poetry—by Robert Bly, Allen Ginsberg, Adrienne Rich, Gary Snyder, Carolyn Forché, and many others—contains a romantic component, yet contemporary social and political issues saturate their verse, as for example when Bly accesses the subconscious through the deep image—a romantic mode—in order to combat what he considers oppressive political (the Vietnam war) and repressive cultural (the loss of masculine instincts) phenomena.

Specific issues also shaped Ransom's and Tate's poetry, but less directly. Both poets often assumed what *seems* like a universal focus—for instance, the imagination's power to heal the dualism caused by scientific naturalism—but like the other Fugitives and Agrarians, Ransom and Tate linked such ideas to the decline of southern culture. Where Warren and Dickey use a wide array of dramatic situations to explore their paradoxes, reaching varied conclusions in different poems, Ransom's and Tate's works are guided and limited by traditional southern values, much as the poetry of Bly, Ginsberg, and others is shaped and constrained by New Left positions. Though much of Warren's verse, and some of Dickey's, remains rooted in regional and cultural specifics, their tendency to view experience as a dynamic between romantic subjectivity and naturalistic fact results in an ever-evolving interrogation and transformation of cultural myths. Though their poetry is not "ideologically neutral"—perhaps an impossibility—it is a poetry of ideas, and of varied conclusions, not verse that closes down on its subject and gives the impression of exhausting it, a point illustrated by Warren's "Rattlesnake Country" and Dickey's "Under Buzzards."

I select "Rattlesnake Country" because Warren dedicated it to Dickey, and "Under Buzzards" because Dickey dedicated it to Warren . . . but I could use practically any of their poems published after the mid-'50s to show how the interaction of romantic and naturalistic elements provides a more universal appeal—a maneuver that conflicts with the ideological parameters characterizing histories of southern and, particularly, contemporary poetry.

"Rattlesnake Country" is divided into five sections, the first four of which describe the narrator's experience at a ranch resort in the desert mountains of the Southwest. Warren stresses the division between humans and nature in the first part, then blurs it in subsequent sections. The poem's opening suggests a process that takes place in many of Warren's later poems: people—through their perceptions, imaginations, and actions—make a conscious or subconscious attempt to subordinate the world around them, to make it conform to their desires. But for Warren (unlike, say, the early Emerson), the success of this attempt is always conditional, tentative, doubtful.

> Arid that country and high, anger of sun on the
>   mountains, but
> One little patch of cool lawn:
>
>   Trucks
> Had brought in rich loam. Stonework
> Held it in place like a shelf, at one side backed
> By the length of the house porch, at one end
> By rock-fall. Above that, the mesquite, wolf-waiting.
>   Its turn
> Will, again, come.

In contradistinction to much contemporary poetry, Warren focuses on the fundamental, exploring humans' interaction with time and nature. The relatively uncomplicated attempt to order nature—the physical act of building a comfortable refuge in an inhospitable locale—is portrayed as transient, as doomed, because nature will inevitably reassert itself: "the mesquite, wolf-waiting. Its turn / Will, again, come."

The remainder of the first section picks up on this theme as Warren juxtaposes people's projections and conceptions of time with nature's forces:

> Meanwhile, wicker chairs, all day,
> Follow the shimmering shade of the lone cottonwood,
>   the way that
> Time, sadly seeking to know its own nature, follows
> The shadow on a sun-dial. All day,
> The sprinkler ejects its misty rainbow.
>
> All day,
> The sky shivers white with heat, the lake,
> For its fifteen miles of distance, stretches
> Tight under the white sky. It is stretched
> Tight as a mystic drumhead. It glitters like neurosis.
> You think it may scream, but nothing
> Happens. Except that, bit by bit, the mountains
> Get heavier all afternoon.

Warren's use of "all day," which is repeated and then isolated for emphasis, suggests how for the persona time proceeds slowly as he experiences contradictory sensations of lassitude and of anticipation. Isolated on the "One little patch of cool lawn," he thinks of his surroundings as patiently menacing. The "anger of sun" is on the mountains; the lake, "stretched / Tight as a mystic drumhead," "glitters like neurosis." He states, "You think it may scream, but nothing / Happens"; indeed, nothing happens because—as becomes particularly evident in the use of the word *neurosis*—the things he attributes to nature are his own projections. But this does not mean nature is benign, a point Warren highlights through the transition from "all day" to

> One day,
> When some secret, high drift of air comes eastward
>   over the lake,
> Ash, gray, sifts minutely down on
> Our lunch-time ice cream. Which is vanilla, and white.
>
> There is a forest fire on Mount Ti-Po-Ki, which
> Is at the western end of the lake.

Nature's omnipresent forces will assert themselves, but not necessarily according to people's projections or intent. The ash from the forest fire arrives on "some secret, high drift of air" as the people are, unassumingly, about to indulge in a cool treat to abate the heat. Warren pointedly identifies the ice cream as "vanilla, and white," suggesting innocence and naiveté.

Unlike much recent American poetry—think of Sylvia Plath's use of Nazis in "Daddy"—Warren's work does not use extrinsic elements to dramatize the narrator's anguish or a social ill. Instead, he typically employs the persona to explore a larger philosophical issue, in this case the relationship between human subjectivity and natural forces. Eschewing the fragmented politics of marginalization advanced by many poets and critics, Warren presents a world in which people, regardless of race, gender, or class, share a common humanity and the dilemmas that come with it.

In section two, Warren elaborates the boundary between humans and nature. The narrator awakens to look at the forest fire, but is lured to the lake instead:

> At night, in the dark room, not able to sleep, you
> May think of the red eyes of fire that
> Are winking from blackness. You may,
> As I once did, rise up and go from the house. But,
> When I got out, the moon had emerged from cloud,
>   and I
> Entered the lake. Swam miles out,
> Toward moonset. Motionless,
> Awash, metaphysically undone in that silvered and
> Unbreathing medium, and beyond
> Prayer or desire, saw
> The moon, slow, swag down, like an old woman's
>   belly.
>
> Going back to the house, I gave the now-dark lawn a
>   wide berth.
>
> At night the rattlers come out from the rock-fall.
> They lie on the damp grass for coolness.

Unlike the first section, in which the narrator's projections upon nature seem to be illusions, with nature operating at its own pace, section two shows people (Warren uses "you" to expand the focus) and the natural world interacting and sharing the same desires. Warren's description of the fire at night—"the red eyes of the fire that / Are winking from blackness"—points to this difference. In part two the forces that earlier made the narrator apprehensive begin to entice him. The fire winks at him, and the moon tempts him to enter the lake, in which he experiences a transcendental moment that takes him "beyond / Prayer or desire." But the section ends with the narrator avoiding snakes, which have assumed a threatening position. Nature's actions have attracted the narrator while people's actions have attracted nature; the snakes seek the comfort of the cool grassy lawn, a human artifice. The situation contains potential dangers.

In section three the cowboys' roundup cry—"*I-yee!*"—excites the narrator, but this relatively formal ritual cannot compete with violence's visceral seductions:

> The wranglers cry out.
>
> And nearer.
>
> But,
>
> Before I go for my quick coffee-scald and to the corral,
> I hear, much nearer, not far from my open window, a
>   croupy
> Gargle of laughter.
>
> It is Laughing Boy.

By the end of section four the narrator, inspired by the grotesque and primitivistic yard-hand Laughing Boy, is dousing rattlesnakes with gasoline:

> Whenever
> Laughing Boy really gets a rattler, he makes that sound like
> Croupy laughter. His face twists.
>
> Once I get one myself. I see, actually, the stub-buttoned tail
> Whip through pale flame down into earth-darkness.
>
> "The son-of-a-bitch," I am yelling, "did you see me, I got him!"
>
> I have gotten that stub-tailed son-of-a-bitch.
>
> I look up at the sky. Already, that early, the sky shivers
>   with whiteness.

Warren makes clear that the persona shares in the violence he attributes to nature in the opening section, a point suggested by the personification of the snake, which he twice calls a "son-of-a-bitch." In section two the distinction between humans and nature had dimmed, but it still existed; here Warren shows that people are part of nature. Like Dickey's depiction of the hillbillies who commit the rape in *Deliverance,* Warren's portrayal of Laughing Boy's and the narrator's ecstasy emphasizes humans' primitive, destructive impulses, as does the description of the blazing serpent plunging "down into earth-darkness."

The final section assesses the dynamic between people's romantic projections and the world as fact, and the poem foregrounds memory's ability to recall and arrange experience:

> I can't remember the names of the others who came there,
> The casual weekend-ers. But remember
>
> What I remember, but do not
> Know what it all means, unless the meaning inheres in
> The compulsion to try to convert what now is *was*
> Back into what was *is.*
>
>   I remember
> The need to enter the night-lake and swim out toward
> The distant moonset. Remember
> The blue-tattered flick of white flame at the rock-hole
> In the instant before I lifted up
> My eyes to the high sky that shivered in its hot whiteness.
>
> And sometimes—usually at dawn—I remember the cry on
>   the mountain.
>
> All I can do is to offer my testimony.

In offering his "testimony" the persona succumbs to—in Wallace Stevens's words—the "maker's rage to order," because for Warren, poetry's relationship to memory represents a romantic attempt to impart meaning to an otherwise chaotic naturalistic universe. The narrator wishes to "convert what now is *was* / Back into what was *is.*" He desires to give phenomena shape and form; but the attempt may be inherently futile because it requires the manipulations of memory. Indeed, in Warren's world, people often crave something beyond mere fact; they cannot rid themselves of the romantic desire to transcend nature.

The dilemmas found in Warren's later verse indicate a movement beyond the paradoxical emphasis that informs studies of the Southern Renascence. Largely because they focus on a culture that contained an almost inseparable fusion of enticements and atrocities, these studies value the contradictory, but they are often tinged with a regret—present not only in the criticism but in the literature—for the loss of a doomed and flawed past that was based on such appealing characteristics as an organic sense of community and esteem for family. Unlike Tate's "Ode to the Confederate Dead," which expresses terror at the impossibility of faith in a naturalistic world and which contrasts modern man's self-consciousness with the resolve of Rebel soldiers in battle, Warren's later work unfailingly confronts the naturalistic with the human desire to transform it, even when the poet is exploring traditional southern values. (For instance, in "Old-Time Childhood in Kentucky"—a poem about generational bonds—the discord between romantic "honor" and primitive blood-lust serves to check nostalgia.)

"Under Buzzards" shows how romantic and naturalistic tensions in Dickey's poetry differ from those in Warren, but with the similar result of distinguishing his verse from that privileged in histories of contemporary and southern poetry. Like the elder poet, Dickey embarks on a romantic quest. But for Warren there is never certainty, despite the abiding possibility of metaphysical enlightenment; Dickey's world contains less doubt, for the locates romantic impulses *within* a naturalistic world. For Dickey, any ultimate enlightenment is an illusion, but one that must be imaginatively engaged . . . whether the results are destructive, as in "The Fiend"; life-enhancing, as in "The Eagle's Mile"; or a mixture, as in "Madness." This volcanic composite often results in emotionally intense poems with conflicting ideological signals, a characteristic that has drawn socially oriented critics' wrath and that bears little relationship to the work of Ransom, Tate, Davidson, or Jarrell.

"Under Buzzards" is the second half of the two-poem sequence "Diabetes." The poems contain inaccuracies concerning the disease and its treatment (for instance, injecting insulin directly into one's veins is lethal), but Dickey's dramatic depiction of the persona's battle with diabetes typifies his poetry's philosophical foundations. As its typographical layout indicates, "Diabetes" revolves around conceptions of balance. In the first poem, "Sugar," the narrator discovers he is diabetic, speaks to a doctor, and achieves equilibrium—"A livable death at last"—by accepting his condition. In "Under Buzzards," the balance takes a different form, as Dickey describes the persona—a projection of the poet—and Warren climbing "Hogback Ridge":

> Heavy summer. Heavy. Companion, if we climb our
> mortal bodies
>   High with great effort, we shall find ourselves
>   Flying with the life
>   Of the birds of death. We have come up
>   Under buzzards   they face us
>
> Slowly   slowly circling   and as we watch them
> they turn us
>   Around, and you and I spin
>   Slowly, slowly rounding
>   Out the hill. We are level
>   Exactly on this moment; exactly on the same
>   bird- plane with those deaths. They are the salvation
> of our sense
>   Of glorious movement. Brother, it is right for us to
> face
>   Them every which way, and come to ourselves and
> come
>   From every direction
>   There is. Whirl and stand fast!
>   Whence cometh death, O Lord?
>   On the downwind, riding fire,
>
> Of Hogback Ridge.

Instead of the topical and social, Dickey portrays individuals' romantic attempts to access the elemental. In "Under Buzzards," as in much of his work, death—or its threat—energizes life: the characters find themselves "Flying with the life / Of the birds of death," and those birds are "the salvation of our sense / Of glorious movement." The position of the persona and his companion in relation to the buzzards—"We are level / Exactly on this moment; exactly on the same bird— / plane with those deaths"—reflects Dickey's desire to balance between a mundane "death-in-life" and discovering "life-in-death." In "Sugar" the emphasis is on stability—"Moderation, moderation, / My friend, and exercise"—but in "Under Buzzards" the characters seek a climactic confrontation with death, as Dickey uses biblical language ("Whence cometh death, O Lord?") and the characters swirl upon the mountaintop while beckoning death in the form of the birds, who are "riding fire," the updraft from a conflagration below.

But as the poem continues, the persona's resolve to transcend naturalism by imaginatively facing down death diminishes:

>   But listen: what is dead here?
>   They are not falling but waiting   but waiting
>   Riding, and they may know
>   The rotten, nervous sweetness of my blood.
>
>   Somewhere riding the updraft
>   Of a far forest fire, they sensed the city sugar
>   The doctors found in time.
>   My eyes are green as lettuce with my diet,
>   My weight is down,
>
> One pocket nailed with needles and injections, the
> other dragging
>   With sugar cubes to balance me in life
>   And hold my blood
>
> Level, level. Tell me, black riders, does this do any
> good?
>   Tell me what I need to know about my time
>   In the world. O out of the fiery
>
> Furnace of pine-woods, in the sap-smoke and crown-
> fire of needles,
>   Say when I'll die. When will the sugar rise boil-
> ing
>   Against me, and my brain be sweetened
>   to death?
>
>   *In heavy summer, like this day.*
> All right! Physicians, witness! I will shoot my veins
>   Full of insulin. Let the needle burn
>   In. From your terrible heads
>   The flight-blood drains   and you are falling
> back
>   Back to the body-raising
>
> Fire.

By juxtaposing the observation that the birds are "waiting" with the thought that "they may know / The rotten, nervous sweetness of my blood," Dickey conveys the narrator's anxiety. The next several stanzas express the desire to deal sensibly with the diabetes, but with recognition of moderation's price. A feeling that he is "nailed" and "dragging" supplants the earlier sensations of flight and "glorious movement." When he imagines the birds replying that he will die "*In heavy summer, like this day,*" he quickly medicates himself, causing the birds to retreat. But he soon rejects the cost of "blood balance," engaging in a romantic attempt to fuse with nature:

> Heavy summer. Heavy. My blood is clear
> For a time. Is it too clear? Heat waves are rising
> Without birds. But something is gone from me,
>   Friend. This is too sensible. Really it is better
> To know when to die   better for my blood
> To stream with the death-wish of birds.
>   You know, I had just as soon crush
> This doomed syringe

>   Between two mountain rocks, and bury this needle in
>   needles
>   Of trees. Companion, open that beer
>   How the body works   how hard it works
>   For its medical books is not
>   Everything: everything is how
>   Much glory is in it: heavy summer is right.
>
>   For a long drink of beer. Red sugar of my
>   eyeballs
>   Fells them turn blindly
>   In the fire   rising   turning   turning
>   Back to Hogback Ridge, and it is all
>   Delicious, brother: my body is turning   is flashing
>   unbalanced
>   sweetness everywhere, and I am calling my
>   birds.

As in Robinson Jeffers's "Vulture"—a poem and a poet much admired by Dickey—the narrator in "Under Buzzards" desires to "stream with the death-wish of birds." He rejects self-consciousness—"Is it too clear?"—for a "flashing" moment of "unbalanced" ecstasy, voicing the desire to obliterate consciousness by becoming part of the animal and elemental. The poem ends with the narrator imagining the red, sugary fire of his eyeball, representative of his impending death, and summoning the birds, which are "rising turning turning" much as the persona's "body is turning" over the blaze below—creating an image that can be likened to a funeral pyre, transforming and returning the narrator to an elemental condition.

Though the region's next generation of poets have not necessarily accented the dynamic between naturalism and romanticism, they have embraced Warren's and Dickey's conception of poetry; in large part, and ironically, this conception has inspired them because it is not traditionally southern: Warren's and Dickey's work is not dominated by local issues, and though a good deal of their verse is set in the South, a good deal is not. Many aspects of their poetry—the belief in humans' destructive potential, the mystical emphasis, the expressionistic use of sex and violence, the rhetorical cadences—are common to southern literature. But unlike the poets of the Renascence, they were able to see beyond the South (as the variety of dramatic situations they employ demonstrates), providing those talented poets who followed with an example of verse with an emotional and intellectual range.

Warren's and Dickey's profoundest influence on younger southern poets may be in their disposition against ideology. In 1956, Warren said that authentic poetry resulted from "a tentative spirit, and a kind of—well, I don't know exactly what's the word, except a lack of dogmatism in dealing with your own responses and your own ideas as they come along, a certain kind of freedom and lack of dogmatism under some notion of a shaping process." In "The Self as Agent," Dickey claimed that "the better the poet is, the more personalities he will have, and the more surely he will find the right forms to give each of them its being, its time and place, and its voice. A true poet can write with utter convincingness about 'his career' as a sex murderer, and then in the next poem with equal conviction about tenderness and children and self-sacrifice. . . . The poem is a window opening not on truth but on possibility." Similarly, Dave Smith, who has commented at length on Warren's and Dickey's influence on his work, claims that "I'm not interested and not capable of thinking in the sort of editorial way that [much contemporary] verse wants to mount. If you come at poetry from the point of view of loving the sound of language, but also loving the enactment of human experience, then you're not looking to make a point. You do not seek lyric purity nor a verse podium. You're looking to somehow just engender. Just be in the experience. I do not want to use the anecdote to somehow make a statement." Betty Adcock explains in her essay "Permanent Enchantments" that she read "Adrienne Rich and other poets of the '70s who were in effect seceding from the male tradition. . . . I determined not to accept the idea of a separate women's poetry whose only legitimate subjects were anger and victimhood. . . . [H]ad I been part of the then-forming circle of separatist feminists, I'd not have gained from James Dickey's early books the permission, flawed or not, those poems gave me to write about the South I knew; not an idealized country as set up by some of the Fugitives, but a flesh-and-blood place, strange and funny and horrifying and beautifully mysterious."

As Adcock's statement implies, younger southern poets sought verse different from that of both the Renascence and the then-regnant movements. Warren's and Dickey's work met their desire for a poetry that maintained a connection to the South but that spoke to the complexities of individual experience. Years earlier, Tate had claimed that "the great writer, the spokesman of a culture, carries within himself the fundamental dialectic of that culture: the deeper conflicts of which his contemporaries are only dimly aware." He was quite right, but the deeper conflict of southern culture was, for Ransom, Tate, Davidson, the early Warren, and others, still fueled by a nostalgia that in the final analysis is—like the work of many recent poets—too tightly bound to political ideology (consider *I'll Take My Stand*). Paradoxically, Warren and Dickey expanded southern poetry's focus by narrowing the conflict; each highlights individual subjectivity in a manner that addresses and engages universal issues. Understanding the way in which romantic and naturalistic tensions inform Warren's later verse and Dickey's poetry is central to recognizing this shift, and to comprehending how their careers have formed the basis for a distinctly new contemporary southern poetry.

Anthony Bukoski (essay date summer 1987)

SOURCE: Bukoski, Anthony. "The Burden of Home: Shirley Ann Grau's Fiction." *Critique* 28, no. 4 (summer 1987): 181-93.

[*In the following essay, Bukoski discusses Shirley Ann Grau's fiction in terms of her "home-consciousness"—her use of interior spaces, houses, and dispossession to develop theme and characterization.*]

In Shirley Ann Grau's fiction, houses provide a loci for the psychological and emotional lives of families.[1] Her fictional houses alienate, however, when they become representative of the failure of the family to provide direction to its members. This, I believe, partly answers the critics who see in Grau's work the "absence of . . . unifying symbol, or theme, or resolving incident."[2] When social and emotional life turns inharmonious inside a house, the sense we get of the place changes. In "Fever Flower" from *The Black Prince and Other Stories* (1955), the house becomes "very quiet and empty" (177)—an emotionally and psychologically safe place—when the child Maureen's parents are out and she is left with the maid. With her parents' return, however, the house changes. In a flash-forward, Grau shows us the result of their handiwork, the child as "a middle-aged, strikingly handsome woman" (178), three times divorced, who now lives in an expensive apartment for one on the west coast. Raised by a mother who was "not quite human. She [the mother] did not need anyone" (172), Maureen is marked for life by the charged emotional atmosphere of her childhood home. A similar scene occurs in "Ending" from *Nine Women* (1985), Grau's newest short story collection. When Barbara Eagleton's husband leaves for good, she can actually feel the empty house settling itself for the night. "She felt a sigh of relief run along beams and floors" (122). Grau's fictive landscapes often generate from such houses and their families.

Shirley Ann Grau wrote to me in April of 1984 that she does not think "at all abstractly about [her] fiction" (Letter). In a recent *Louisiana Literature* interview, she also says, "I never think in classifications. I just don't. That's not the way my mind works" (Parrill 7). Because in Grau's fiction the houses that shelter inhabitants are so regularly a party to, and a symbol of, the inhabitants' psychical, emotional, and physical distress, one must conclude that her patterns of imagery and symbolism, or at least her house symbols, derive from the subconscious. In five novels and many of her stories, characters fight the constricting regimen of domestic life and the houses which project it.

In *The Condor Passes* (1971), for example, young Anthony Caillet, shortly before his death, feels trapped in his mother's house. Its walls moving toward him, he fears he will be caught inside forever. When the boy's grandfather dies, Grau speaks of the old man's trapped spirit as escaping as the animal inside him might find "endless doors opening on echoing corridors, wind-swept walks, ultimate distances" (40). House walls also press in on Lucy Roundtree Evans in *Evidence of Love* (1977). To avoid complete dependence on her first husband, she runs imaginary errands and spends hours driving around when he is home. As she swings open the garage door, she feels pleased and relieved to be out. Late in life, her second husband, Stephen Henley, feels similarly claustrophobic. Finally having become as much prisoner as sheltered, he dies trying to open a door to the darkness outside his Florida retirement home. Only when his wife returns does his soul "stream . . . toward freedom" through the door she has opened (141). After his death, she herself feels as though she is "smothering" in the empty air of the place. Finally, in "Letting Go" from *Nine Women*, Mary Margaret MacIntyre flees the constricting regimen of her parents' lives and home, while in "Ending," Barbara Eagleton escapes her mother's questioning by fleeing outside only to feel "almost panicky" in the foggy night air (107).[3]

Shirley Ann Grau once described a house as "like a myopic vision" (*Evidence* 205). Because of its size and shape and the dimensions of those surrounding it, that house demanded from passersby a sort of near-sighted view of itself. Seen interiorly, one could think of the inhabitants as "near-sighted" in the sense that they were totally absorbed in their affairs. For characters not so enthralled by the home place, houses become symbols of isolation and alienation where domestic problems are exacerbated to the degree that characters as "inhabitors" have no alternative but to "disinhabit" their houses. Such walls project for the exile his or her loss of the emotional, even spiritual life, of the family.

I want to deal with this central motif or situation in four novels, *The Hard Blue Sky* (1958), *The House on Coliseum Street* (1961), *The Condor Passes* (1971) and *Evidence of Love* (1977), each containing a dispossessed character and a disinhabited house. Though some critics consider *The Keepers of the House* her best novel—it was awarded a Pulitzer Prize in 1964—I have chosen the other four because near the end of each, a character is separated from his or her house in ways more dramatic and convincing than in *The Keepers of the House,* where Margaret Carmichael's leaving one-third of the way through lacks the intensity of Annie Landry's leaving at the end of *The Hard Blue Sky,* Joan Mitchell's at the end of *The House on Coliseum Street,* Stanley's at the end of *The Condor Passes,* or Edward Milton Henley's and his son Stephen's leaving at the end of *Evidence of Love*.[4] All are logical outgrowths of the disharmony plaguing the lives of the people inside. Forced outside, these characters (and Margaret Carmichael from her great-grandmother's house) fail to establish a sense of identity, that narcissistic sense which often attends between a house and its inhabitants. They see and hear someone else inside the house's walls, not themselves or their reflection; yet, to remain psychologically whole, they must leave. Nothing can be gained by staying. In Grau's fiction, characters do not come home to a house as often as they flee in an attempt at psychological self-preservation.

The Hard Blue Sky, Grau's first novel, is set on an island off the Louisiana coast. Returning from the convent in New Orleans where she has gone after her mother's death, Annie Landry roams the island, increasingly disaffected with life there. Following her first sexual encounter, her alienation grows, especially with her father's house, whose walls seem to center and enclose all that bothers her. Trapped by the island's social and geographic boundaries and by the familial boundaries of Al Landry's house, "sometimes, when it was bright moonlight, she would wake up . . . and she would stagger up and pull open the door and send it slamming back into the wall before she could catch her breath again" (112). Other times in dry weather, she avoids the house entirely and finds private hiding places among the trees and grasses. Her first lover, Perique Lombas, does the same, though Annie's feeling of being trapped is more extreme and even increases when her widowed father marries a woman from Port Ronquille.

Annie spends the night of the wedding party roaming around outside. When she can no longer stand up, she sneaks in, thus avoiding the party in the front of the house. She liked the house empty, Grau writes, especially of the new stepmother Adele. "The whole house . . . she's got such a musky smell. You can tell it even on the front porch; you could tell it anywhere. If it wasn't raining I could stay out" (352).

The feeling of being hemmed in bothers others, too. At night, the grocer Julius Arcenaux can feel his wife's body filling the whole room, so that sometimes he ends up sleeping on the linoleum floor. Henry Livudais seeks room to breathe in the swamps and bayous where he elopes with a girl from Terre Haute, a neighboring island, in the process setting off inter-island warfare. The stepmother Adele herself has escaped Port Ronquille where her family frowned on her going with a fisherman. Finally, Inky D'Alfonso of the Pixie, a sailboat put in at Isle aux Chiens, suffers the heat and boredom of shipboard and island life as he awaits the sailboat owner's return.

Annie, however, is the character most circumscribed by her environment. Her father's house fails to provide her the emotional closeness she desires nor does she find it with Perique, who virtually turns his back on her. Her room "making small tight circles," she thinks, "Now . . . either I put my stuff in a suitcase or I don't. It's that simple. Now. Only when I look back on it tomorrow, I'll see that it wasn't. . . ." (360). Eventually, the house becomes increasingly remote to her. On one of her last stops, "she was a little surprised when she saw the house in front of her—the gray house where she'd been born and where, except for one year, she'd always lived. She walked all around, staring as if she'd never seen it before" (368). In the afternoon, she leaves with Inky.

Annie's abandoning the house is indicative of some larger abandonment of island custom, or perhaps of the culture as a whole. She takes not only an outsider as her lover but aids an islander from Terre Haute, whom she discovers hiding with a broken leg in a slough, thus symbolically renouncing Isle aux Chiens. Her father's house ceases to be the focus of her universe. No longer identifying with it—the house failing her in some way and she it—she heads for New Orleans, or Iberville where Inky knows someone who "always can use a man at the bar" (379). Sailing off, she foresakes her father's house but retains the memory of Perique, for "if things were ever really rough, she could tell the children about the man who nearly was their father" (381).

As Annie Landry prepares to leave her father's house on the island, Mamere Terrebone, perhaps the island's oldest resident, prepares for winter by laying in supplies and fixing her house. In contrast to Annie Landry, who flees out of self-preservation, Mamere Terrebone preserves herself another way: by building inward, fixed and rooted to one place. She relishes her house as the last defense against death, whom she has been fighting for the last ten years and who, she fears, might manage "to slip through a crack somewhere with the winter cold" (391). She buys food from the grocery and puts up the shutters. Finally, she locks the windows and places a heavy bar across the door. Like Mamere Terrebone, some of Grau's other characters are equally house-centered. In "One Summer" from *The Black Prince,* in *The Keepers of the House* (where Abigail Mason Tolliver defends the Howland estate from intruders), and in "Window's Walk" and "Home" from *Nine Women,* the house represents a vital light to its inhabitants.

More often, however, the human spirit, weary of light in Grau's fiction, inclines toward darkness, loneliness, or worse, extinction. Annie Landry is so inclined in *The Hard Blue Sky.* By isolating herself from others and their houses, she, in turn, is isolated. So is Joan Mitchell in *The House on Coliseum Street.* Her problems, like Annie's, are psycho-sexual. Both characters are incapable of connecting with others on any physical, emotional, or psychological plane. Alwyn Berland has written that not only in Annie Landry's "initiations into sex . . . [but] in a number of other ways [she] prepare[s] us for the central character of . . . *The House on Coliseum Street*" (81-82).

Through *that* house's doors go Aurelie Caillet and her daughters, each born while Aurelie was married to a different man. Joan Mitchell, oldest daughter and the novel's protagonist, appears most harmed by a home environment where Aurelie routinely takes new husbands and where Joan's half-sister, the household's reigning beauty, competes for the younger men of New Orleans. Neither socially active like her mother, nor beautiful or athletic like Doris, Joan lives mentally and emotionally detached. She works in the campus library and takes university classes, which she often skips. When she is overcome with fear of her emotional and physical needs, fear of that ancient demiurge that provides "the oleander bushes . . . glossy thriving poisonous leaves" and makes "the grass and vines [grow] so frantically you could see them move—the way you could see the heavy white moonflowers open on summer nights" (7), she rides streetcars. During these hour-long rides, she finds the stability that is lacking at home.

Her father's and Aurelie's latest husband's conditions have paralleled Joan's own. One became estranged from the house years ago, a few months after Joan's birth, and the other gradually withdraws to the third floor of the house, happy to be left alone. Then there is the tramp who one day appears from the slums along the levee. He makes his way to the neighborhood only to fall down on the uneven sidewalks, where he remains "directly in front of the Caillet house. His outflung hand . . . a few inches away from the wrought-iron pillar that supported the iron gate." The street, says Grau, "close[s] up on itself" at sight of him, "the windows that looked out on the front porches (the windows that were nearly always kept open for a cross breeze) . . . closing"—except Joan's (24-25).

To her, the house on Coliseum Street built by her great-great-grandfather provides little emotional succor. At first, emotional, then physical walls exclude her. Metaphors of displacement and alienation may sometimes be found in a character's unmet expectations of a house's decor, for houses become "home" as a result of personal associations; houses enclose life's more personal moments as they exclude the less-valued, the disordered, the impersonal. In time a house projects the owner, who sees him or herself reflected in its decor. In this way—whether in the real house or in the house as it is imagined in fiction—one enters a kind of narcissistic relationship with his or her surroundings. Some characters, however, must seek their identity beyond what should be the repose and safety of home.

Even as a child away at summer camp, Joan Mitchell does not miss her mother's house. Later, at her aunt's on the Gulf where she goes to have an abortion, she again realizes how little Aurelie's house in New Orleans means to her. She remembers hating her mother's "bronze lamp with the fringed shade" so much that as a child "she had carefully worked away at it until the tiny glass beads were all pulled off" (44). Home again, she goes upstairs in the house on Coliseum Street but regrets having returned and remembers, even as a child, how she wanted to go away. She is trapped, she thinks, just as she was four months earlier. Even her room's decor, the cracked dull finish of the mahogany furniture, seems alien, a reflection of her dissatisfaction with self and others. Missing is the sense of repose in a familiar, psychologically inviting place. In an effort to express herself in her surroundings, she thinks of doing over the room to suit her tastes. To do so would be to create, or to attempt to create, a new, more habitable emotional and psychological environment, one truer to her self and her experience. As is, the room does not reflect her anymore than her family does. "The good things are all down[stairs] or in Aurelie's room" (45), she thinks. In time—having made no attempt to change her domestic situation, not even her room's decor—she finds herself isolation from humans and from the walls they build around themselves and from their excluded families.

Aside from her car, she finds safety sitting at a hard steel desk on the next-to-highest floor of the library. With only the dust and carbolic odor of bindings surrounding her, she rests one-third of each day six floors above the earth. Joan chooses a place nobody else will work because it lacks air conditioning. Heretofore, the library staff tossed coins to see who would work where Joan Mitchell, the library's newest staff member, now goes willingly. Sometimes she ascends to the next level, a place without windows and whose faint yellow bulbs cast hardly any light. On the seventh floor repose uncatalogued items. High above the earth, she retreats to these windowless, cement rooms. Unlike the rooms in Aurelie's house, which Joan is dissatisfied with, the rooms on the uppermost library floor hold no associations for her and thus are suited to her psychological and emotional state. Ambivalent in her feelings toward her mother's house, she finds these rooms inviting, as they remind her of nothing in the past. Their concrete brick walls are unpainted; the rooms remain empty.

Throughout the novel, Joan senses the importance of rooms and heights. Her dislike of, or dissatisfaction with, rooms in the house on Coliseum Street is a manifestation of something deeper: perhaps fear of Aurelie's and Doris's attraction to men and her own sexuality. Heights provide distance from the fecundity of plant and human life below. On one of her nights spying on Michael, her former lover, "it seemed to her . . . that the whole dark was full of couples, the building, the bushes, the shrubs, the trees, even the leaves overhead. Soft wet sounds" (185). High up in the library, she peers through a single window on the west side and at home sees the tramp from twenty feet up. Though Shirley Ann Grau may not think abstractly about her fiction, she is undoubtedly aware here of the spatial worth of a house. In *The House on Coliseum Street,* she uses heights and the opposition between inside and outside places richly and evocatively. The dark center space of Joan's aunt's house, for example, becomes a kind of objective correlative of the psyche when Grau writes: "[going] down the long halls and the stairway" of her aunt's on the morning of the abortion, she, Joan, was "surprised to see how dark the center of the house was. She had never noticed it before" (138).[5]

Not long after her abortion and subsequent harassment of Michael, and having forgotten her key one night, she finds herself locked out of the house on Coliseum Street. She stands looking at the balcony across the second floor and at the glow from deep inside the narrow house. She stands where the tramp stood, or fell, on the broken sidewalks the summer before and thinks how, once the family knows she has caused Michael to lose his university teaching job, she will have to leave. Moving a chair "to the spot the sun would strike first . . . she curled up, huddled inside her . . . sweater, and waited" (242). For her, the tangible and intangible elements that make up the ethos *home* are missing. She is displaced. What she offers in emotional terms has been rejected by Aurelie, Doris, and Michael, so that finally, whether in the car, the library, or her house, Joan not only disinhabits places but becomes a disembodied spirit herself. "She wanted to move without anyone knowing she was moving. She wanted to slip like a ghost through walls" (182).

In an interview, Shirley Ann Grau once said that she "intended to emphasize the redemption theme" in the last chapter of *The House on Coliseum Street* (Schlueter 44). Joan's being huddled in the fetal position at the sun's rising suggests the possibility of rebirth and redemption. But redemption and acceptance into the house must come, if at all, only after Joan's exile. "I'll have to go away now," she thinks. "Once they know what I've done, I couldn't stay in the house. But I can go. It's only a question of where. My father knew I would have to leave some day. And he fixed it so I can go . . . she bowed slightly to the crisp busy figure on the other side of the grave" (241).

A "house full of bitches" (171), her half-sister Doris calls it. The house on Coliseum Street—a house which Paul Schlueter says is "totally lacking in roots and family security"—has in the past provided Joan little respite from the unsettling world. Now she finds herself completely shut out. "A lock is a psychological threshold," the philosopher Bachelard has written (81). Though not intentionally set, the locked door here serves as a metaphor of dispossession. Increasingly withdrawn from the universe inside, Joan now finds herself closed out physically as well. To be excluded is to be turned loose into a world now less familiar because of lacking the referent home. Such befalls Anthony Mitchell, whom Aurelie found too quiet and dull. Another husband, Herbert Norton, gradually disappeared from their breakfast table, then from their lives. Others before Joan were also deemed unfit to join house and family. This is a not uncommon occurrence: the character who turns away, or is turned away, from the emotional and psychological life of the family as it is represented in the house loses part of himself, loses *himself* perhaps. So estranged is Joan Mitchell from the family and the house on Coliseum Street that in the end, the world outside its walls could hardly be more foreign. Though her leaving may prove redemptive, whether it results in a return to the house on Coliseum Street is another matter.

Stanley, the black factotum in *The Condor Passes,* also preserves himself by leaving a house. Here, again, Grau relies on the motif of displacement and flight; only in *The Condor Passes,* enclosed places and spaces are presented in a somewhat different manner. It is a tribute to Ms. Grau's art that her houses and houseless wanderers never seem redundant. She accomplishes this by modifying her unifying symbol (as in *The Condor Passes*), by introducing it at a different time in the narrative (as in *The Keepers of the House*), or by varying the depth and intensity with which she examines this symbol. Sometimes, to borrow the visual imagery she often uses, she views a house "myopically"; at other times, she draws back, viewing a house and its inhabitants in broader terms. Unlike Grau's other fictions, the inhabitants of the Old Man's, Thomas Henry Oliver's, house in *The Condor Passes* are incapable of fleeing either the real, physical structure, or the genealogical "house" when things go wrong. Because Stanley is black and no family member, he survives. Trying to remain invisible, he hears or sees nothing, he says, just performs his duties.

Those remaining in the house lack the courage, strength, and perseverance to continue the Old Man's work. Where Robert Caillet, Anna, and Margaret (virtually anyone in the Old Man's family) have been corrupted, Stanley has remained intact, freer of sin and guilt; thus Grau changes her motif slightly. Stanley walks out into the rain only moments after the Old Man's death and as the drunken Robert and the daughters Margaret and Anna rush to the house—actually to the huge conservatory where the Old Man sits. "He [Stanley] took the limousine key from his pocket and dropped it on the counter. . . . He opened the door; the east wind pulled it from his fingers and slammed it inward. He did not bother closing it." After several decades of service, he leaves the family cold: their houses, cars, planes. He walks away from the house.

> Behind him he could still hear the shouting, voices strung out on the wind. . . . He didn't listen. Like the Old Man, he was finished here. . . . Rain poured into his eyes, blurring his vision. . . . It would be strange not coming back, not coming this way again, a little bit like being dead.
>
> (420-21)

Not so much an emotional or psychological part of the house as the others, he calls himself the "secret thief" of the things learned in their employment. Neither he nor his wife want any part of the real suffering of the house, however, any part of "their ghosts or their hauntings" (384). Just as have Joan Mitchell in *The House on Coliseum Street*, Margaret Carmichael in *The Keepers of the House*, or any number of Grau's characters, Stanley survives by leaving. Sometimes such figures are morally wrong to do so. The father in "The Man Outside" from *The Wind Shifting West* (1973) abandons his family, for instance. But those in *The Condor Passes* cannot escape. They are inextricably bound to the ethos of the house, to the air and spirit of Oliver history. To leave becomes impossible. Paying for their and the Old Man's indiscretions, their final punishment—like the characters in Sartre's *No Exit*—is each other and themselves. Anna and Robert live with the memory of their son Anthony's suicide-by-drowning in the Gulf, for example. Stanley says that he, Stanley, sees a grassy slope, then the beach and the water when he looks out from the porch at Porta Bella, but not so Anna and Robert. She stays on the other side of the house away from the porch and the lawn as though there's "something here she doesn't want to see." On the other hand, Robert goes to the beach when he is drunk. Stanley once sees him "shouting at the empty water" (383). The Old Man himself sits in the humid air of his tropical greenhouse, staring at the shiny leaves.

These characters' various houses represent them in different ways. The Old Man's house in New Orleans, Stanley says, is in "perfect shape, not a speck of rust, not a crack, not a dent, not a heel mark on the polished floor . . . like the house was built of stacks of dollar bills" (6-7). Reflected in its walls is an insistence upon order and detail; nothing there can be changed. Anna has her house before she even leaves the convent school. She sees it once, and the next day her father buys it. She spends the next several years remodeling and designing it. "*Open the door*," she thinks, "*key heavy and cool in my hand. Lovely door, oval leaded glass, cut facets to catch the light. I like the door most of all about the house.*" She has little doubt that "*people could see* [her] *reflection in these things*" were she to die (171). And Margaret's various dwellings represent her personality.

But characters flee these houses, too—Robert flees his wife Anna's; Anthony, who drowns himself, his mother's. Only Stanley survives by not falling under the Old Man's power. Stanley holds his self in reserve. Through it all, he maintains a sense of his own worth, never losing perspective on the family. Because he has managed to stay apart from them, in the end the house holds no power. He has escaped the Old Man's claims in a way others cannot.

In *Evidence of Love* finally, characters abandon not only a physical, architectural dwelling, but sometimes the house as it is rendered metaphorically as the human body. The motif of the character removed from his or her house appears on the first page when Edward Milton Henley's father moves to his club to avoid his wife's noisy irritability during her pregnancy. "A man maintained his own home, his own cave, in his own city," Grau writes. "Though he might never set foot inside during the long summer months, he knew his house waited for its master" (18). Though seeing to his son's financial security, the senior Henley neglects the boy's emotional and psychological well-being. Consequently, Edward Milton Henley grows up lacking a sense of rootedness to place, or to anything permanent for that matter. His life becomes a series of physical entanglements, some with men.

Whereas Edward Milton Henley follows his Dionysian energies, seeking in them some evidence of love, his son's life takes an opposite course. A Unitarian minister, the younger Henley pursues his interests in the classics, sometimes to the exclusion of all else. Having lived with his wife in the same house in Pennsylvania for over thirty-four years, he still cannot recall its color. Though he notices beauty in the world, he has little interest in anything else, even the house which has protected him from the elements these many years. When he retires to Florida, however, he begins to appreciate how a house can protect him psychologically from the encroaching dark, as Mamere Terrebone in *The Hard Blue Sky* is aware of her house. Not wanting to see his reflection outside the house at night, Stephen Henley draws the curtains to feel more secure. Eventually his surroundings control him. He complains of the Florida heat, the light, the tropical insects, all of them external enemies. "Our house was surrounded and protected by a magic white circle," he says, "a voodoo circle of malathion crystals carefully renewed each week" (107). Behind drawn curtains, with the air conditioning and electric lights on, he feels "insulated and completely apart" (109). Trapped by the house, by his many years, and by the changes he has suffered moving south, he fails in the same way his house does. Where the house is ventilated by louvers in the doors, windows, and roof—he calls his house a mechanical house and "a wind-up toy" (109)—so has his life been precisely ordered. Early on, he says, "I began carefully writing down a complete plan for my life. A timetable [which] I have managed to keep quite closely to. . . ." (93). One night as the mechanical house fails during a power blackout, so does his body. In his agony, and desperately seeking in logic some solution to his problems, some evidence of love, he even forgets his wife's name. Returning from a meeting, Lucy Roundtree Evans finds him dead inside the house. Until she opens the door, thus freeing his spirit, she can feel it trapped within "hissing and singing" (141). She herself stands fifty feet away from the house to await the police.

Lucy serves Stephen's father, the wheelchair-bound Edward Milton Henley, in a similar way. Earlier Edward Henley's fourth wife, who heretofore rarely left their house, one day simply walks out, leaving the front door open. Now it is his turn to leave. "Locked inside" a crumbling body, he likens his ribs to the collapsing roof timbers of a deserted house—the house-body metaphor. In a final act of mercy, his daughter-in-law gives him extra Seconal tablets to hasten his death. As she waits for his soul to free itself from the house of the body, she reads a magazine, ironically called *House and Garden*.

For those who find in houses evocative symbols, "house-holders," a few other human symbols are so significant. Bachelard observes that, "Without it [a house] man would be a dispersed being. It maintains him through the storms of the heavens and through those of life. It is body and soul . . . the human being's first world. Life begins well, it begins enclosed, protected, all warm in the bosom of the house" (Bachelard 7). An integrating force, a house holds the promise of physical and psychological well-being; it promises safety and respite from trouble.

Exploring the history or decor of Shirley Ann Grau's fictional houses is less productive than exploring her use of the spatial value of a house and her examination of that missing narcissistic sense that a house reflects none other than oneself. For Grau, the house is center and substance of each fictional world. Relying upon spatial values, she succeeds in gathering characters and readers about an ancient symbol of sheltering places and spaces. Her houses can represent the final hope of those struggling against the outer dark like Mamere Terrebone in *The Hard Blue Sky* and Abigail Mason Tolliver in *The Keepers of the House*. More often they represent an often-destructive shelter from which to escape. Annie Landry in *The Hard Blue Sky*, Joan Mitchell in *The House on Coliseum Street*, the young Margaret Carmichael in *The Keeper of the House*, the child-suicide Anthony and Stanley in *The Condor Passes*, Edward Henley and his son Stephen with his Florida retirement home: all foresake the walls of a house because they are not mirrored in them. Finding not gratification but threat therein and torn by the life they find, they look elsewhere.

From *The Black Prince*, her first book, to *Nine Women*, her most recent, Shirley Ann Grau has found resonance and meaning in the image and symbol of houses and in the motif of the character displaced from them. Her comprehensive house-consciousness—her using interior places and spaces, heights, and the disordered impersonal world just beyond the threshold—all suggest a writer deeply aware of the symbolic nature of houses in her own and her characters' lives. Her fictional houses have provided her work with a unifying symbol and incident, an organizing pattern which critics of her work have failed to notice. Her readers share the human core both of those who must build inward in order to survive and of those who must leave such inwardly leaning or inclining walls to go outward.

Notes

1. Some of the ideas in this paper appear in my review of Grau's *Nine Women* in *Louisiana Literature*, Vol. 3, no.2.

2. More than twenty years ago, Alwyn Berland found Grau's three published books "less achieved than promising" and complained that Grau's work generally ended "with a kind of meaningless inconsequence: the sum of the parts *should* have been more substantial than the whole" (78-79). Berland, perhaps already sensing Grau's house consciousness, used metaphors of architecture to explain what she saw as Grau's aesthetic shortcomings. "[I]t is an architectural defect which Miss Grau's talent suffers from." Missing in Grau's "construction," which is often "done in beautifully polished stone . . . is the keystone . . . the firm center, the center of a vision, and hence the conviction of why her characters behaves as they do" (81-84), Berland wrote.

Louise Y. Gosset also found Grau's fiction to be "largely without a dominant theme" (193). And Ann Pearson has asked, "What, if any, overall purpose does this talented writer have in her fiction" (47). Pearson continues: Grau's "only definable vision of the world lies in her perception of the ever present closeness of nature, that 'hard blue sky' which rules the lives of her characters. Thus, nature is her vision, the focal point of her best fiction" (47-48). In his comments on Grau in *Contemporary Novelists*, Chester Eisinger also sees her lacking "the complex vision that enables her both to see around and to penetrate deeply into her subject" (515). Remarkably, not one of these critics has paid attention to the house-as-focal point of Grau's fiction, especially as houses and their inhabitants' reactions to them comprise a major part of Grau's fictive universe.

3. Grau's houses signify differently depending upon the context of the fiction. In "One Summer" from *The Black Prince* a young man, attempting to accept the difficult loss of his grandfather, wanders

the neighborhood at night instead of participating in the grandfather's wake. In a kind of epiphany, "Mac" Addams recalls seeing the old man two days earlier. "He'd just been sitting there, waiting. . . . And I understood then. . . . Why old people wanted to be left alone. . . . *One Day I'll be that afraid.*" By avoiding human company—because "loneliness is more bearable than company . . . it's a kind of preparation for that coming final loneliness"—Mac for the first time confronts his own mortality. "All the hot noisy outside had come down to this: our green-painted clapboard house. . . . But somehow I couldn't go inside" (252-54).

In another story, "The Way of a Man," William kills his father and has to sleep out in the fog: "[M]ost nights he would not have minded that," Grau writes. "But tonight . . . the fog would be cold and the night was going to be long" (208). In "The Man Outside" from *The Wind Shifting West* (a story originally entitled "Stranger at the Window"), a wanderer returns to find the doors of his own house barred to him. An outsider also figures in "Homecoming" when the protagonist refuses to allow a dead soldier's memory to become part of her house and in so doing makes him a sort of spiritual exile shut out from both house *and* memory.

4. Margaret Carmichael's leaving is not meant to be climatic, thus its position earlier in the novel. Because she is only partly black, she is forced out by the black family in her great-grandmother's house. Finding shelter in "a hollow tree trunk, up the slope about a mile," Margaret stays away from the house as much as she can, while keeping alive some notion of home:

> She always waited until the steady dripping of the night ice ended, then she stopped feeding her fire and watched it go out. She never once stomped the coals—somewhere in the back of her memory was a warning never to kill a fire on your hearth. Way back, from a story long ago—she did not think about it, did not question or wonder, she merely obeyed. The same way she never put a hat on a bed, nor entered and left a house by anything but the same individual door.
>
> (91)

Finally leaving for good, she lives with a white man and, years later, secretly marries him, at which point she tells the great-grandmother: "I buried my blood with you. . . . I'm using only the other half now" (103). Eventually, Will Howland's granddaughter defends the house against the night riders who have found out about his indiscretion. "The Howland they wanted was dead. His Negro wife was dead. Their children disappeared. And so they were wrecking the only thing that was left of him, of them. First the barn and then the house. . . ." (285). Abigail Mason Tolliver embraces the house, however. Her history as well as her grandfather's lives inside. When Will Howland was alive, Grau writes, "[S]ometimes he felt the age of the house, felt the people who had lived in it peer over his shoulder, wondering and watching what he was doing. . . . It seemed to him too . . . that he could hear their breathing, all of them, dozens of them, breathing together, deep and steady, the way they had when they were alive" (133-34). The Howland house is a place of collective human endeavor, a locus of the collective psyche of the family.

5. Whether in fact or fiction, attics and cellars often signify differently; so, likewise, do thresholds, center spaces of houses, and backdoors convey meaning, and gates, doors, locks, latches and still smaller interior places and spaces like drawers and chests. Grau betrays her awareness of the psychologically resonant places of a house when she mentions the "dark center" of Joan's aunt's and has Margaret Carmichael in *The Keepers of the House* cherish her makeshift hearth, the "heart" of the house in the tree trunk.

Grau appears even more interested in heights, especially as they appear in *The House on Coliseum Street* and *Nine Women*. Bachelard calls the attic a place of "detachment, privacy, and rumination" (17). Joan Mitchell feels detached in her second floor room and upstairs in the library. So, too, do the girl, "the young black female of illegitimate birth" (17) in "The Beginning" and Myra Rowland in "Widow's Walk," both from *Nine Women*. In the latter, Myra Rowland succumbs to a kind of ecstasy as, high atop the house, she "watched the constellations swing up and out of the ocean and traced the twin bands of the Milky Way." The only human sounds are "filtered by distance," Grau writes. Up on the widow's walk—and, presumably, closer to her dead husband—Myra Rowland would "fall asleep . . . waking only to the first light and bird cries, her hair drenched and dripping with dew and night fog, her lips smiling with quiet joy" (79).

Works Cited

Bachelard, Gaston. *The Poetics of Space*. Boston: Beacon, 1969.

Berland, Alwyn. "The Fiction of Shirley Ann Grau." *Critique* 6 (1963).

Gossett, Louise Y. *Violence in Recent Southern Fiction*. Durham: Duke Univ. Press, 1965.

Grau, Shirley Ann. *The Black Prince and Other Stories.* New York: Knopf, 1955.

———. *The Condor Passes.* New York: Knopf, 1971.

———. *Evidence of Love.* New York: Knopf, 1977.

———. *The Hard Blue Sky.* New York: Knopf, 1958.

———. *The House on Coliseum Street.* New York: Knopf, 1961.

———. *The Keepers of the House.* New York: Knopf, 1964.

———. "Letter to the Author." 5 April 1984.

———. *Nine Women.* New York: Knopf, 1985.

———. *The Wind Shifting West.* New York: Knopf, 1973.

Parrill, William. "The Art of the Novel: An Interview with Shirley Ann Grau." *Louisiana Literature,* Spring 1985.

Pearson, Ann. "Shirley Ann Grau: Nature is the Vision." *Critique* 17 (1975).

Schlueter, Paul. *Shirley Ann Grau.* Boston: Twayne Publishers, 1981.

Vinson, James, ed. *Contemporary Novelists,* 3rd ed. New York: St. Martin's, 1982.

Joanne Veal Gabbin (essay date 1990)

SOURCE: Gabbin, Joanne Veal. "The Southern Imagination of Sonia Sanchez." In *Southern Women Writers: The New Generation,* pp. 180-203. Tuscaloosa: The University of Alabama Press, 1990.

[*In the following essay, Gabbin focuses on the literary career of Sonia Sanchez, stressing her blending of political and personal, urban and rural elements in her works.*]

> Death is a five o'clock door forever changing time. And wars end. Sometimes too late. I am here. Still in Mississippi. Near the graves of my past. We are at peace . . . I have my sweet/astringent memories because we dared to pick up the day and shake its tail until it became evening. A time for us. Blackness, Black people. Anybody can grab the day and make it stop. Can you my friends? Or maybe it's better if I ask:
>
> Will you?[1]

The woman who utters this challenge at the end of Sonia Sanchez's play *Sister Son/ji* has the gift of second sight: she is a visionary, a prophet, a revealer of truths. She has touched love, births, deaths, danger, tumult, upheaval, and change and has distilled from these experiences "sweet/astringent memories." Willing to pick up the day and "shake its tail until it became evening," she helped to bring into being an order that transformed time and defied death itself.

In many ways, *Sister Son/ji* becomes a metaphor for the poet herself and the visionary quality and sense of the past that pervade much of her poetry. Like *Sister Son/ji,* Sonia Sanchez has been a singer during turbulent times, a translator of the needs and dreams of black people. Sanchez has written to challenge black people—all people—to change the world, "to make people understand . . . that we are here to perpetuate humanity, to figure out what it means to be a human being,"[2] "to show what is wrong with the way that we are living and what is wrong with this country . . . to correct misinterpretation and bring love, understanding, and information to those who need it."[3] If this all sounds idealistic, it is. For Sanchez matured as a writer in an era in which ideas took on an elasticity heretofore unheard of. It was a time when a visionary president challenged the nation to land a man on the moon before the end of the decade; when a black power movement, led by such political thinkers as Malcolm X, Stokely Carmichael, H. Rap Brown, Angela Davis, Huey P. Newton, and Elijah Muhammad, ushered in a change in race relations in America; when 250,000 people, culminating several difficult years of boycotts, sit-ins, voter registration drives, marches, and riots, marched on Washington to make America accountable to black and poor people. It was a time when Americans protested an undeclared war in Vietnam, and the country mourned and immortalized its fallen heroes: John F. Kennedy, Robert Kennedy, and Martin Luther King, Jr. This era shaped the mettle of the poet, and like the Mississippi woman, Sanchez has become an armed prophet whose voice is at once a prod and a sword.

In her eight volumes of poetry, which appeared between 1969 and 1987, Sanchez's voice is sometimes abrasive but never as profane as the conditions she knows must be eradicated; her tone ranges from gentle to derisive, yet the message is one of redeeming realism. Also undergirding her poetic expression is a deep concern for heritage; for the sovereignty of time with all its ramifications of birth, change, rebirth, and death; for the impress of the past and memories; and for nurture, nature, and God. Moreover, these themes reveal Sanchez's strong Southern imagination, one that was born in the impressionable times of her youth in Alabama, where the tensions of struggle were fed with mama's milk.

Homecoming (1969), Sanchez's first book of poems, is her pledge of allegiance to blackness, to black love, to black heroes, and to her own realization as a woman, an artist, and a revolutionary. The language and the typography are experimental; they are aberrations of standard middle-class Americanese and traditional

Western literary forms. As such, they reflect her view of American society, which perceives blacks as aberrations and exploits them through commercialism, drugs, brutality, and institutionalized racism. In this book and the poetry that follows, the vernacular and the forms are clear indications of her fierce determination to redefine her art and rail against Western aesthetics. *Homecoming* also introduces us to a poet who is saturated with the sound and sense of black speech and black music, learned at the knees of Birmingham women discovering themselves full voiced and full spirited. The rhythm and color of black speech—the rapping, reeling, explosive syllables—are her domain, for she is steeped in the tradition of linguistic virtuosity that Stephen Henderson talks about in *Understanding the New Black Poetry*. Black music, especially the jazz sounds of John Coltrane, Ornette Coleman, and Pharoah Sanders, pulse, riff, and slide through her poetry.

In her second volume, *We a BadddDDD People* (1970), Sanchez is wielding a survival sword that rips away the enemy's disguise and shears through the facade of black ignorance and reactionism. Arranged in three groups, "Survival Poems," "Love/Songs/Chants," and "TCB/EN Poems," the poems extend the attack begun in *Homecoming* and tell black people how to survive in a country of death traps (drugs, suicide, sexual exploitation, psychological slaughter via the mass media) and televised assassination. Her message, however, is not one of unrelieved gloom, for it is rooted in optimism and faith: "know and love yourself." Like Sterling A. Brown's "Strong Men" and Margaret Walker's "For My People," "We A BadddDDD People," the title poem of the volume, is a praise song that celebrates black love, talent, courage, and continuity. The poems appear rooted in a courage learned early from aunts who spit in the face of Southern racism and sisters who refused to be abused by white men or black men. In this volume, Sanchez reveals her unmistakable signature, the singing/chanting voice. Inflections, idiom, intonations—skillfully represented by slashes, capitalization (or the lack of it), and radical and rhythmic spelling—emphasize her link with the community and her role as ritual singer.

In *It's a New Day* (1971), a collection of poems "for young brothas and sistuhs," Sanchez nurtures young minds, minds that must know their beauty and worth if the nation is to be truly free. Her belief in the seed-forced of the young led her to write the children's story *The Adventures of Small Head, Square Head and Fat Head* (1973).

In 1973, her fourth volume, *Love Poems*, appeared. Haki Madhubuti calls this "a book of laughter and hurt, smiles and missed moments."[4] The poems are collages of the images, sounds, aromas, and textures of woman-love. With the clarity and precision of Japanese ink sketches, Sanchez skillfully uses the haiku to evoke emotion:

>   did ya ever cry
>   Black man, did ya ever cry
>   til you knocked all over?[5]

Using the haiku, the ballad, and other traditional forms that advance her preference for tightness, brevity, and gemlike intensity, she fingers the raw edges of a woman's hurt and betrayal:

>   When he came home
>   from her
>   he poured me on
>   the bed and slid
>   into me like glass.
>   And there was
>   the sound of splinters.[6]

The poet also celebrates the magic that love has to transform and transcend:

>   i gather up
>   each sound
>   you left behind
>   and stretch them
>   on our bed.
>   each nite
>   i breathe you
>   and become high . . .[7]

A Blues Book for Blue Black Magical Women (1974) is a dramatic departure from the poetry of earlier volumes. The scope here is large and sweeping. The language is no longer the raw vernacular of *Homecoming*, though, as in *We A BadddDDD People*, it is possessed by the rhythms of the chants and rituals. At its most prosaic, it is laden with the doctrine of the Nation of Islam and ideologically correct images. At its best, it is intimate, luminous, and apocalyptic. Tucked inside *A Blues Book* is a striking spiritual odyssey that reveals the poet's growing awareness of the psychological and spiritual features of her face.

In 1978, Sanchez culled some of her best poetry from earlier volumes in *I've Been a Woman: New and Selected Poems*. To these she adds a collection of haiku and tankas that is dominated by the theme of love: the sensual love of a man, the love of old people and young, the love for a father and spiritual mothers. She brings to this theme a style that is replete with irony, wit, and understatement. And in most of her poetry, her feelings are intensified and her symbols, those of nurturing, birth, growth, freedom, civilization, are deeply feminine. Here, as Margaret Walker Alexander states, is poetry of "consistently high artistry that reflects her womanliness—her passion, power, perfume, and prescience."[8]

In *homegirls & handgrenades* (1984), Sanchez shows the further deepening of the poet's consciousness, for it is a sterling example of her going inside herself, inside the past, to pull out of her residual memory deeply personal experience. From the past, she draws images that explode the autobiographical into universal truths. The predominant genre in this volume is the sketch, much like those that stud Jean Toomer's *Cane*. Bubba, "the black panther of Harlem," lost in a sea of drugs and unfulfilled dreams; Norma, black genius that lay unmined; or the old "bamboo-creased" woman in "Just Don't Never Give Up on Love" all live again and vividly show Sanchez distilling "sweet/astringent memories" from her own experience.

Distinguishing much of her poetry is a prophetic voice that brings the weight of her experience to articulating the significant truths about liberation and love, self-actualization and being, spiritual growth and continuity, heroes, and the cycles of life. Her vision is original because it is both new (a fresh rearrangement of knowledge) and faithful to the "origins" of its inspiration. Therefore, it is not surprising that in her most recent volume of poetry, *Under a Soprano Sky* (1987), the mature voice of the poet is giving expression to the sources of her spiritual strength, establishing and reestablishing connections that recognize the familyhood of man/womankind, and singing, as another Lady did, of society's strange fruit sacrificed on the altars of political megalomania, economic greed, and social misunderstanding.

Throughout her poetry, which will be the focus of this study, Sanchez demonstrates the complexity of her Southern imagination. Though she spent a relatively short period of her life in the South, her way of looking at the world is generously soaked in the values she learned during her childhood in Birmingham, Alabama. The importance of the family and love relationships, her fascination with the past and her ancestry, her search for identity amid the chaos and deracination of the North, her communion with nature, her exploration of the folk culture, her response to an evangelical religious experience, and her embracing of a militancy nurtured in fear and rage are Southern attitudes that inform her poetry. Especially in *A Blues Book, I've Been a Woman*, and *Under a Soprano Sky*, Sanchez's fascination with the concept of time, her faith in the lessons of the past, and her deep notion of continuity firmly root her in the tradition of southern imagination.

In *The Immoderate Past: The Southern Writer and History*, Hugh Holman explores the relationship between the concept of time and the Southern writer:

> The imagination of the Southerner for over one hundred and seventy-five years has been historical. The imagination of the Puritans was essentially typological, catching fire as it saw men and events as types of Christian principles. The imagination of the New England romantics was fundamentally symbolic, translating material objects into ideal forms and ideas. The Southerner has always had his imaginative faculties excited by events in time and has found the most profound truths of the present and the future in the interpretation of the past.[9]

In part two of *A Blues Book*, the poet invites her readers to:

> Come into Black geography
> you, seated like Manzu's cardinal,
> come up through tongues
> multiplying memories
> and to avoid descent
> among wounds
> cruising like ships,
> climb into these sockets
> golden with brine.[10]

Describing history as the spiritual landscape of events and images, she invites the reader to travel back in time, through what George Kent calls her "spiritual autobiography," her "own psychological and spiritual evolution in the past."[11] Sanchez has the past define the features of her identity and uncover her origins. Calling on the earth mother as the inspiration and guide on the journey, she implores her to reveal the truths locked in time:

> Come ride my birth, earth mother
> tell me how i have become, became
> this woman with razor blades between
> her teeth.
>
>   sing me my history O earth mother
> about tongues multiplying memories
> about breaths contained in straw.[12]

The poet realizes that the essential clues to who she is are there in the dusty corners of history, in the myths and tales preserved by "tongues multiplying memories," in the seemingly inconsequential bits that can be gleaned from those who live in the spirit and in the flesh. Because she is in tune with her oral tradition, she shares with other Southern black writers, such as Ralph Ellison, Richard Wright, Margaret Walker, Ernest Gaines, Maya Angelou, and Alice Walker, what Ellison calls some of the advantages of the South:

> I believe that a black Southern writer who does know his traditions has some of the advantages which William Faulkner or other white Southern writers have had: the advantage of contact with a long accumulation of history in a given place; an experience which has been projected in other forms of artistic expression, which has traditional values and variants, and which has been refined by being defined by generations of people who have told what it seemed to be: "This is the life of black men here. . . ."

> This is one of the advantages of the South. In the stories you get the texture of an experience and the projection of values, and the distillation of a kind of wisdom.[13]

For Sanchez, who she is and who she is to become have much to do with the texture of experience, the values, and the wisdom alive in the folk community of Birmingham, Alabama.

Sonia Sanchez was born in Birmingham on September 9, 1934. Her parents, Wilson L. Driver and Lena Jones Driver, faced with naming a second girl (the first daughter was named Patricia), gladly turned over the task to relatives, who returned quickly enough with the name Wilsonia Benita. The communal name turned out to be a portent of the role relatives would play in her upbringing, for when she was one year old, her mother died in childbirth, and she thus began a series of moves from one relative's home to another during the next nine years.

After her mother's death, Wilsonia and her sister were cared for by her father's mother. Elizabeth "Mama" Driver, whom Sanchez describes as a "heavy-set, dark complected woman," was the head deaconess in the African Methodist Episcopal Church. In an interview, Sanchez remembers her grandmother: "My grandmother spoiled my sister and me outrageously. She loved us to death . . . she loved us so much that she used to walk us to Tuggle Elementary School. This old, old woman used to walk very slowly up that hill. . . ."[14] Mama Driver brought the girls into the circle of the rituals of the A. M. E. Church. They experienced the sonorous roar of the minister, who strode across the pulpit of the wood frame church; the buzz of the congregation when a sister got "happy" and threw her pocketbook "clean across the aisle"; and the wonderment of the spirituals when all those choir members, dressed in white, sounded like the angels at the gates of the city.

Sanchez remembers the many occasions her grandmother had allowed them to sit quietly at her knees while she talked with the women who visited their modest house in a Birmingham housing development. In "Dear Mama" in her most recent book, *Under a Soprano Sky,* she recalls vividly the Saturday afternoons when she "crawled behind the couch" and listened to the old deaconesses as they told of their lives "spent on so many things":

> And history began once again. I received it and let it circulate in my blood. I learned on those Saturday afternoons about women rooted in themselves, raising themselves in dark America, discharging their pain without ever stopping. I learned about women fighting men back when they hit them: "Don't never let no mens hit you mo than once girl." I learned about "womens waking up they mens" in the nite with pans of hot grease and the compromises reached after the smell of hot grease had penetrated their sleepy brains. I learned about loose women walking their abandoned walk down front in church, crossing their legs instead of their hands to God. And I crept into my eyes. Alone with my daydreams of being woman. Adult. Powerful. Loving. Like them. Allowing nobody to rule me if I didn't want to be.
>
> And when they left. When those old bodies had gathered up their sovereign smells. After they had kissed and packed up beans snapped and cakes cooked and laughter bagged. After they had called out their last goodbyes, I crawled out of my place. Surveyed the room. Then walked over to the couch where some had sat for hours and bent my head and smelled their evening smells. I screamed out loud, "oooweeee! Ain't that stinky!" and I laughed laughter from a thousand corridors. And you turned Mama, closed the door, chased me round the room until I crawled into a corner where your large body could not reach me. But your laughter pierced the little alcove where I sat laughing at the night. And your humming sprinkled my small space. Your humming about you Jesus and how one day he was gonna take you home. . . .[15]

Mama Driver also gave the children a sense of continuity as she acquainted them with the long line of aunts, uncles, and cousins who made up their extended family. She acquainted them with a community that held dear the notion of family ties and took for granted the willingness of family members to take another member in: "My life flows from you Mama. My style comes from a long line of Louises who picked me up in the nite to keep me from wetting the bed. A long line of Sarahs who fed me and my sister and fourteen other children from watery soups and beans and a lot of imagination. A long line of Lizzies who made me understand love. Sharing. Holding a child up to the stars. Holding your tribe in a grip of love. A long line of Black people holding each other up against silence."[16]

When Mama Driver died, the small frail child of five experienced the manufactured adult mystery of death and the insensitivity of relatives who shut children out of this fact of nature. As a way of managing the loss and the pain, she withdrew behind a veil of stuttering that remained with her for the next twelve years. When she and her sister lived with her father and his second wife, the stuttering protected her from the brunt of her stepmother's cruelty. In part two of *A Blues Book,* she raises the specter of this woman:

> And YOU U U U U U U—step/mother.
> woman of my father's youth
> who stands at a mirror
> elaborate with smells
> all shiny like my new copper penny.
> telling me through a parade of smiles
> you are to be my new mother. and your painted lips
> outlined against time become time
> and i look on time and hear you
> who threw me in angry afternoon closets
> till i slipped beneath the cracks

> like light. and time stopped.
> and i turned into myself
> a young girl breathing in crusts
> and listened to those calling me.
>
> to/ no matter what they do
> be/ they won't find me
> chanted/ no matter what they say
> i won't come out.[17]

The collective images of the woman—her stepmother's resentment, her rages, her neglect, and her authoritarianism that weighed heavily on the two girls—had the effect of distorting time itself ("and your painted lips / outlined against time"). The mature sensibility records the prominence of the cruel punishment that loomed prodigiously in the child's mind ("and time stopped / and i turned into myself") and indelibly marks her personality. She, the youngest, had hidden behind her "black braids and stutters"; she, the strange one, the quiet one, would not come out. When her father learned of his second wife's treatment of the children, he sent them to live with relatives, and they remained with relatives or friends until their father married again and took them to New York, reenacting the solemn ceremony that many thousands of black people performed as they migrated to Northern cities.

Reflecting on her childhood, Sanchez said that, despite the unhappy experiences, she had "a good Southern girlhood."[18] Her grandmother had initiated her into the rituals of black life; aunts and uncles and cousins had given connections, continuity to her sense of self, and Birmingham, Alabama, had rooted her in a history of black struggle, with its lessons of fear, segregation, rebellion, and an awareness of her place. Years later, in her first published poem, she urges from her subconscious the memory of a cousin who, when made to move from her seat on the bus, spits in the white driver's face.

From 1944 until she graduated from Hunter College, Wilsonia Driver lived in Harlem at 152d and St. Nicholas Place, where there was "no space." In the small apartment she shared with her sister, her father, and his third wife, she felt hemmed in. Her tiny bedroom, whose window faced a redbrick wall, further mocked her sense of loss, now far from the greener, open space of the South. She also felt hemmed in by the kind, yet restrictive, care of her new stepmother and by the unwritten expectation placed on a young girl growing up in an environment that did not offer its girl-women protection but demanded that they protect themselves or run the risk of scorn and censure:

> coming out from alabama
> to the island city of perpetual adolescence
> where i drink my young breasts
> and stay thirsty
> always hungry for more than the
> georgewashingtonhighschoolhuntercollegedays
> of america.
> remember parties
> where we'd grindddDDDD
> and grindddDDDD
> but not too close
> cuz if you gave it up
> everybody would know. and tell.[19]

In those early Harlem days, the young girl was hungry for more than the restrictions of the island city, so she daydreamed and began to write. In an *Essence* magazine article, Sanchez recalls that she started writing because it was a way to express herself without the annoying stuttering. She remembers writing a poem about George Washington's crossing of the Delaware. The poem, which was left out while she rushed to rewash dishes, was found by her sister, who began reading the poem to their parents in a singsong rhyme. "I reached for the poem, but she pulled it away and finished reading it to everybody in the kitchen. They all laughed. I don't really remember it as cruel laughter, but I was a very sensitive little girl. So I was very much upset and after that I began hiding my poems. I doubt if anyone knew I was still writing."[20]

This incident recalls a similar experience related by Richard Wright in his book *Black Boy*. After he read one of his stories to a woman in his neighborhood, he realizes that she cannot possibly understand his desire to write: "God only knows what she thought. My environment contained nothing more alien that writing or the desire to express one's self in writing."[21] According to Ladell Payne in *Black Novelists and the Southern Literary Tradition*, Richard Wright's life of imagination sustained him in his estrangement but also served to isolate him further from his family and community.[22] Similarly for Sanchez, from the very beginning, writing was a solitary endeavor that simultaneously isolated her from others and gave her the distance that she needed to see herself, her family, and community reconstituted in a new light.

As the young woman matured, her estrangement extended into most areas of her life. At Hunter College, she wanted more than the benign indifference that left her sense of self unnourished. She was not only alienated from those at school, but she was also separated from those on her block. They left the serious-eyed, quiet, college girl alone.[23] However, in "Bubba" in *homegirls & handgrenades,* the poet remembers one who saw more in her than she was prepared to acknowledge: "One summer day, I remember Bubba and I banging the ball against the filling station. Handball champs we were. The king and queen of handball we were. And we talked as we played. He asked me if I ever talked to trees or rivers or things like that. And I who walked with voices for years denied the different tongues populating my mouth. I stood still denying the commonplace things of my private childhood. And his eyes pinned me against the filling station wall and my eyes became small and lost their color."[24]

And the alienation reached her in her home. She had not really known her father. Though she lived with him from the time she was ten until she left college, on many levels, they remained strangers. "A Poem for My Father" in *We A BadddDDD People* and "Poem at Thirty" in *Homecoming* tell poignantly of this relationship.

But more significantly, the young poet felt alienated from herself and her roots. In *A Blues Book,* she recalls those times when she "moved in liquid dreams":

> and i dressed myself
> in foreign words
>   became a proper painted
>   european Black faced american
>   going to theatre parties and bars
>
> and cocktail parties and bars
> and downtown village apartments
> and bars and ate good cheese
> and caviar with wine that
> made my stomach stretch for artificial warmth.
>
> danced with white friends who
> included me because that was
> the nice thing to do in the late
> fifties and early sixties
>
> and i lost myself
> down roads
> i had never walked.
>
> and my name was
> without honor
> and i became a
> stranger at my birthright.[25]

Perhaps it was this sense that she had lost her birthright that turned her thoughts to her past. And the South became the place where the mysteries of her past could be discovered. There too was the knowledge of her mother.

It was not until she graduated from college that she learned anything about her mother. When her father showed her a photograph of Lena Jones Driver, a beautiful Latin-looking woman with fair skin and dark eyes, she became aware of the void that existed in her life. On a pilgrimage to the South in 1980, she found a wizened old man who held the knowledge that had long since been lost in county records. He told her that her mother was the daughter of a black plantation worker and her white boss by the name of Jones. The revelation convinced the poet of her intimacy with historical events and finds its way into her upcoming novel, *After Saturday Night Comes Sunday,* in which a woman who is going crazy because of a man must spiritually find her mother's mother. Only then, when she had traversed the void, can she become the kind of woman she is capable of becoming. In *After Saturday Night Comes Sunday,* as in part two of *A Blues Book,* the reader experiences an almost cinematographic sensation, as Sanchez reverses the projector, making the frames from the past flick in rapid retrogression. In much the manner of Alejo Carpentier as he envisions a "journey back to the source" (*Guerra Del Tiempo*), the poet manipulates time and harnesses the power and magic of the rivers to give birth to herself:

> tell me. tellLLLLLL me. earth mother
> for i want to rediscover me. the secret of me
> the river of me. the morning ease of me.
> i want my body to carry my words like aqueducts.
> i want to make the world my diary
> and speak rivers.[26]

The ritual invocation of the earth mother has its analogue in the rituals of the Orisha, the Yoruba gods. As if drawing on the Jungian collective unconscious, the poet reveals a close relationship between the riverain goddesses who reside at the bottom of the river, and Earth, whom they recognize as the pure force, the *ashe,* the power to make things happen.[27] In *Flash of the Spirit,* Robert Farris Thompson gives a description of one of the riverain goddesses, who has an uncanny resemblance to the spirituality revealed in *A Blues Book*:

> Divination literature tells us that Oshun was once married to Ifa but fell into a more passionate involvement with the fiery thunder god, who carried her into his vast brass palace, where she ruled with him; she bore him twins and accumulated, as mothers of twins in Yorubaland are want to do, money and splendid things galore.... When she died, she took these things to the bottom of the river. There she reigns in glory, within the sacred depths, fully aware that so much treasure means that she must counter inevitable waves of jealousy with witchcraft, by constant giving, constant acts of intricate generosity. Even so, she is sometimes seen crowned, in images of warlock capacity and power, brandishing a lethal sword, ready to burn and destroy immoral persons who incur her wrath, qualities vividly contrasting with her sweetness, love, and calm.[28]

Oshun, in fact, can well be a metaphor for Sanchez's power. For in her poems, one senses a power that is feminine, and consciously so. It comes from her understanding of her connections with the universe, her connections with her ancestors, and her strong matrilineal ties with a universe that has given to its kind not only the responsibility but, indeed, the power to bear the children and nurture seed. Her power comes from a faith in continuity; seeds grow into flowers and produce their own seeds. Sanchez clearly presents the life cycle and cherishes it.

Sanchez calls the phenomenon that makes sense out of these mystical connections and recurrent archetypal images "residual memory." It is her capacity to draw on this memory that deepens the implications of her poetry. And on another level, it provides a source of implications that even the poet cannot fathom. Some would call this simply—inspiration.

In speaking about how she writes, Sanchez explains a process in which one sees the art of the poet and the role of the prophet merging. In an interview that appeared in *Essence* magazine (July 1979), she says that sometimes lines of poetry come and she jots them down and that sometimes a feeling comes and she will write down lines that respond to that feeling. Often for Sanchez, the inspiration comes after rereading a favorite book or the work of a poet she admires. During her best time for reflection—early in the morning, from twelve midnight until four, she reads and reworks lines, "fussing at those things that obviously don't work."[29] However, sometimes the poet gives way to the prophet, whose voice "derives its authority, not from some inner reservoir, but from an outside . . . source."[30] Sanchez says: "Sometimes I actually see something that moves me or makes me angry or whatever, and then line by line just pours out from God knows where. Whenever people compliment me after a reading or tell me they enjoyed one of my books, I'll say, 'Thank you so much.' But inside I'll say to myself, 'It's not just me.' Everything that you or I could write has been written before; there's that energy there in the universe for us to pull from. Many of us just become attuned to that energy."[31]

It was this energy that helped Sanchez begin her career as a writer. While attending New York University, she began to write seriously. At NYU, she took a course from poet Louise Bogan, a prolific writer and teacher who disliked intensely "bad writing and bad writers."[32] Sanchez found Bogan fascinating and sincerely interested in her growth as a writer, and she did not sense in her the patronization and indifference that she had encountered at Hunter.

Encouraged by this experience, she organized a writers' workshop that met every Wednesday night in the village; there she met Amiri Baraka (LeRoi Jones) and Larry Neal, the poet-critics who became the architects of the black arts movement, and began to read with them in jazz night spots. She also joined the New York CORE and the Reform Democrats Club. At this time, she was married to Albert Sanchez, a first-generation Puerto Rican American. He did not understand her intense commitment to causes or her need to write. After four years of marriage and the birth of her first child, Sanchez found herself moving away from the narrowly defined bounds of that relationship:

> and visions came from the wall.
> bodies without heads, laughter without mouths.
> then faces crawling on the walls
> like giant spiders,
> came toward me
> and my legs buckled and
>   i cried out.[33]

And when the break was complete, she

> woke up alone
> to the middle sixties
> full of the rising wind of history . . .[34]

In 1967, Sanchez started teaching at San Francisco State College. Her two-year tenure there was marked by student unrest, demonstrations, and the fledgling stretching of the black power movement. She found herself in the midst of the struggle to make black studies a part of the college's offerings. She, along with psychologist Nathan Hare, played a significant role in the establishment of the first black studies program in the country. She also began to document the ironies and nuances of the overall struggle for black awareness in poems that would appear in her first volume, *Homecoming*.

Also during this time, Sanchez met poet Etheridge Knight through Gwendolyn Brooks and Dudley Randall. While he was in prison, they began to correspond, and in 1969, they married. Twin sons, Mungu and Morani, were born to them. After little more than a year, the marriage ended in an uneasy alliance. "Poem for Etheridge," "last poem i'm gonna write bout us," and other poems in *We A BadddDDD People* and *Love Poems* reveal the often poignant, sometimes tragic nature of their relationship. However, what is significant in these poems is the ability of the poet to transcend the bounds of her own experience and speak with an authority that comes from going many times to her own personal wailing wall. For example, in "Poem No. 8," Sanchez brilliantly captures the sense of interminable waiting that only a woman knows intimately:

> i've been a woman
>   with my legs stretched by the wind
>   rushing the day
>   thinking i heard your voice
>   while it was only the night
>   moving over
>   making room for the dawn.[35]

From 1967 to 1975, Sanchez was intensely involved in continuing her career as a poet and a teacher. During that time, she completed nine books and published her poems and plays in several periodicals, including *Black Scholar, Black Theatre, Black World, Journal of Black Poetry, Liberator, Massachusetts Review, Minnesota Review, New York Quarterly,* and the *Tulane Drama Review*. She also taught at the University of Pittsburgh, Rutgers University, Manhattan Community College, and Amherst College. While at Amherst, from 1972 to 1975, she taught one of the first courses on black women writers offered in an American college. For a brief period from 1972 to 1975, she was a member of the Nation of Islam, directing its cultural and educational program and writing for *Muhammad Speaks*. She resigned from the Nation of Islam in 1975 and one year later came to Philadelphia to teach at the University of Pennsylvania. After a year, Sanchez began teaching at Temple University, where she has taught Afro-American studies, English, Pan-African studies, and creative writing since then.

In 1978, Sanchez published *I've Been a Woman: New and Selected Poems*. In this volume, she concludes with a group of new poems that fall under the rubric "Generations." These poems attest to the significance she places on the vestiges of the past that have been gathered to bring meaning, value, direction, and inspiration to an individual's present.

In "A Poem of Praise," which is dedicated to Gerald Penny, a student who died on September 23, 1973, and to the Brothers of Amherst College, Sanchez reconciles the loss of a young warrior by giving promise to the cycles of his life. The truth of the poem is that the man has been on earth and has experienced a life that is no less beautiful, dramatic, or meaningful because it has been short. One sees the poet developing a view of the universe that holds man as a traveler, who comes from another space, walks from the morning through day, to evening, tasting "in himself the world":[36]

> In your days made up of dreams
> in your eyes made of dawn
> you walked toward old age,
> child of the rainbow
> child of beauty
> through the broad fields
> and your eyes gained power
> and your limbs grew long like yellow corn
> an abundance of life
> an abundance of joy
> with beauty before you, you walked
> toward old age.[37]

This traveler brings to mind another one who came "trailing clouds of glory." William Wordsworth's youth must travel from the East, farther from the splendid vision of celestial light that was his when he was born. However, consistent with the teaching of Islam (during the writing of this poem, the poet was a follower of the teachings of Elijah Muhammad), Sanchez envisions a universe in which the young man walks toward the light, wisdom, and rebirth:

> For i am man
> and i must
> run with the evening tide
> must hold up my hands
> for my life is opening
> before me.

> I am going to walk far to the East
> i hope to find a good morning
> somewhere.[38]

This youth need not content himself with the memory of radiance that once was, for life moves in cycles and progresses toward endings that have, at their center, beginnings.

Sanchez's poetic kinship with Native American tribal poets is striking here. There is the same understanding of "the cyclic continuities" that make up the circle of life.[39] There is the same respect for the generative power of language, a language that is medicinal, rooted in nature, dignified, and spare. Kenneth Lincoln, in his book *Native American Renaissance*, writes:

> Oral tribal poetry remains for the most part organic, for tribal poets see themselves as essentially keepers of the sacred word bundle. . . . They regard rhythm, vision, craft, nature, and words as gifts that precede and continue beyond any human life. The people are born into and die out of a language that gives them being. Song-poets in this respect discover, or better rediscover, nature's poems. They never pretend to have invented a "poetic" world apart from nature, but instead believe they are permitted to husband songs as one tends growing things; they give thanks that the songs have chosen them as singers.[40]

In a real way, Sanchez's attitude about her purpose as a poet is rooted in a way of thinking about the world that is similar to that of the poet-singers of more than five hundred Native American cultures who send out the voice. Her early Southern experience watered her sensibility—the greening of her mind—and nourished her purpose as a poet: to create positive values for her community. She writes in "The Poet as a Creator of Social Values" that the poet is a manipulator of symbols and language—images that have been planted by experience in the collective subconscious of a people. She believes that "the poet has the power to create new or intensified meaning and experience" and, depending on the visibility of the poet and the efficacy of the poetry itself, "create, preserve or destroy social values."[41]

However, even more than these conditions, the poet's power depends on the clarity of her vision, her ability to interpret human nature, and her willingness to speak in tongues that will confirm her vision. For Sanchez, poetry is "subconscious conversation." She says, "When I say something on stage, I make them remember similar experiences that they have not even brought up, but I bring them up and say look remember and people say, 'Yes, I remember.'" And given this process, "poetry is as much the work of those who understand it as those who make it."[42] Thus, when Sanchez eulogizes the Amherst student whose life ended prematurely, she is sending a voice among the people who hear and speak:

> There is nothing which does not
>   come to an end
> And to live seventeen years is good
>   in the sight of God.[43]

The cycle-of-life theme that provides the frame for "A Song of Praise" gets a deeper, subtler exploration in "Kwa mama zetu waliotuzaa." Significantly, the poem begins with the line, "death is a five o'clock door forever changing time," which first appeared in *Sister Son/ji*, a play written in 1970. By repeating the line, the poet emphasizes the consistency, the predictability, and the weight she attributes to this theme. According to critic Joyce Ann Joyce:

> This line along with the title of the poem echoes the "In the beginning / there was no end" of *Blues Book*. Just as Sister Son/ji reaches out to the audience and asks if they will "grab the day and make it stop," "Kwa mama zetu waliotuzaa" illustrates how the physical, temporal, historical reality becomes an embodiment of the spiritual. For if we grab the day and make it stop, we will see that death is a concrete reality (a five o'clock door) that rules the process of life. For the death of the natural world brings forth the birth of the spiritual (forever changing time) as Sister Son/ji learns.[44]

The lines that follow dramatically show the cyclic nature of life and ironically reveal the human attempt to still a process that is as unrelenting as waves against a shore:

>   and it was morning without sun or shadow;
> a morning already afternoon. sky. cloudy with incense.
>   and it was morning male in speech;
> feminine in memory.
> but i am speaking of everyday occurrences:
> of days unrolling bandages for civilized wounds;
> of guady women chanting rituals under a waterfall of
>   stars;
> of men freezing their sperms in diamond-studded
>   wombs;
> of children abandoned to a curfew of marble.[45]

The poem, whose title translates "for our mother who gave us birth," is at once a praise poem for the mothers (biological and spiritual) of black women and a eulogy for Shirley Graham DuBois, biographer, teacher and lecturer, whose career spanned over forty years and took her to Africa, Asia, and Europe. In the opening passages, the poet remembers her father's third wife, Geraldine Driver, a kind, caring Southern woman who was saddled with notions of her place and feared breaking loose to ride out her potential. Here, however, in memorializing her (she died of cancer in Detroit), Sanchez uses the symbolism of nature to represent continuity, growth, fruitfulness, and joy, and in effect, she undercuts the pain and unfulfillment that were hers in life:

>   mother. i call out to you
>   traveling up the congo. i am preparing a place for
>   you:
>   nite made of female rain
>   i am ready to sing her song
>   prepare a place for her
>   she comes to you out of turquoise pain.
>
>   restring her eyes for me
>   restring her body for me
>   restring her peace for me
>
> no longer full of pain, may she walk
> bright with orange smiles, may she walk
> as it was long ago, may she walk
>
> abundant with lightning steps, may she walk
> abundant with green trails, may she walk
> abundant with rainbows, may she walk
> as it was long ago, may she walk . . .[46]

For Shirley Graham DuBois, who was "a bearer of roots," who taught the poet the truth of the African past, who "painted the day with palaces," Sanchez, in broad sweeps of pantheism, calls up the bells, Olokun (the goddess of the sea), the spirits of day and night. For through their persistence, their repetitiveness, their predictability, they reassure the poet of her mentor's continuity and her triumphal passage to the land of the ancestors.

At several turns in the poem, the privileged perception cuts through the eulogy:

> as morning is the same as nite death and life are one.
>   . . . . .
>
> at the center of death is birth
>   . . . . .
>
> death is coming. the whole world hears
> the buffalo walk of death passing thru the
> archway of new life.[47]

From the very first metaphor, the poem is unified by the epigrams concerning death. Death is one with life and continuity; at its center is a beginning.

The dimensions of Sanchez's Southern imagination become imposing in *homegirls & handgrenades*. Her fascination with time and the past, her communion with nature, her reverence for the folk, her search for identity and self-actualization through meaningful relationships, and her intense spirituality born of a faith in roots and continuity predict the themes and metaphors that unify the book. With a language pregnant with the images of war, armaments, and nuclear proliferation, the poet suggests that love and the greening of the mind are the only reasonable weapons in a world dangerously toying with annihilation. In the most effective vignette in the volume, "Just Don't Never Give Up on Love," the poet recounts her meeting with an eighty-four-year-old woman who inveigled her to hear her message on the power of love:

". . . C'mon over here next to me. I wants to see yo' eyes up close. You looks so uneven sittin' over there."

Did she say uneven? Did this old buddah splintering death say uneven? Couldn't she see that I had one eye shorter than the other; that my breath was painted on porcelain; that one breast crocheted keloids under this white blouse?

I moved toward her though. I scooped up the years that had stripped me to the waist and moved toward her. And she called to me to come out, come out wherever you are young woman, playing hide and go seek with scarecrow men. I gathered myself up at the gateway of her confessionals.[48]

As Mrs. Rosalie Johnson talks with her about her husbands and love, the young woman cries for herself and "for all the women who have ever stretched their bodies out anticipating civilization and finding ruins." Mrs. Johnson's message is cathartic; by allowing the old woman's healing words to slough off the bitterness and fear built up from past relationships, she is again open to love.

Moving the urgency of her message to global relationships, she concludes the volume with "A Letter to Dr. Martin Luther King" and "MIA's." Though very different in form, they are companion pieces that share Sanchez's urge to articulate the democratic evils (racism/apartheid/imperialism) that stunt the spiritual growth of black youth, corrupt hope by gradualism, and stall freedom. On the occasion of Martin Luther King's fifty-fourth year (the poet addresses the slain leader as a living spirit), she declares anew a faith in the regenerative power of blackness, which eschews fear and moves toward "freedom and justice for the universe." The letter ends with an explosion of feeling as the poet, remembering the chanting of black South African women at the death of Stephen Biko, adopts the chant "Ke wa rona" (he is ours) and calls the roll of black deliverers:

. . . On this your 54th year, listen and you will hear
the earth delivering up curfews to the missionaries and
assassins. Listen. And you will hear the tribal songs.

Ayeeee	Ayooooo	Ayeee
Ayeeee	Ayooooo	Ayeee
Malcolm . . .		Ke wa rona
Robeson . . .		Ke wa rona
Lumumba . . .		Ke wa rona
Fannie Lou . . .		Ke wa rona
Garvey . . .		Ke wa rona
Johnbrown . . .		Ke wa rona
Tubman . . .		Ke wa rona
Mandela . . .		Ke wa rona

(free Mandela
free Mandela)
Assata . . . Ke wa rona
As we go with you to the sun,
as we walk in the dawn, turn our eyes
Eastward and let the prophecy come true
and let the prophecy come true
Great God, Martin, what a morning it will be![49]

In "MIA's (missing in action and other atlantas)," the datelines—Atlanta, Johannesburg, El Salvador—serve to show the world of oppression in microcosm, and the machinations that promote death (murder / assassination / "redwhiteandblue death squads"). The centerpiece of the poem is a disturbingly accurate account of the death of Biko. Here one is aware of the substantial capacity of the poet to work with the ironic voice, which gains power by the incremental repetition of "we did all we could for the man":

sept. 13:
hear ye. hear ye. hear ye.
i regret to annouce that stephen
biko is dead. he has refused
food since sept. 5th. we did
all we could for the man.
he has hanged himself while sleeping
we did all we could for him.
he fell while answering our questions
we did all we could for the man.
he washed his face and hung him
self out to dry
we did all we could for him.
he drowned while drinking his supper
we did all we could for the man.
he fell
    hanged himself starved
drowned himself
we did all we could for him.
it's hard to keep someone alive
who won't even cooperate.
hear ye.[50]

Whether conjuring up Stephen Biko, or the "young-blood / touching and touched at random" in the killing fields of Atlanta, or the young men with "their white togas covering their / stained glass legs" in Central America, she exhorts the men and women to harvest their share of freedom.

In Sanchez's most recent volume, *Under a Soprano Sky*, she captures in the poem "for Black history month/ February 1986" the essence of her Southern sensibility as she reflects on her visit to the Great Wall of China. As she "started to climb that long winding trail of history and survival,"[51] her thoughts turned to voices and visions that propelled history, demanded survival, and forged the cultural links of which continuity is made. Moving deeply within her culture, Sanchez "had to peel away misconceptions about Blacks." As she sang the blues, hummed the spirituals, explored the myths, and walked "a piece" down the road with Nat Turner, Douglass, Harriet Tubman, Garrison, John Brown, Martin Delany, Malcolm X, Rosa Parks, David Walker . . . her racial memory nourished in Southern soil bears fruit. Her sense of reality, her sense of history rejected Old Black Joe, one of the plantation tradition's favorite sons, "Sambo-hood," and Jim Crow. Her sense of history embraced Lady Day's voice as she sang of strange fruit and blood on the magnolia, embraced Robeson's voice as he sang of deep rivers and the quest of the soul for peace on the other side of Jordan or the Mississippi or the Ohio. Her sense of the past, her roots, her ostensibly Southern imagination has allowed her to keep sight of her vision, a vision of peace and community that was first conceived in the green days of an Alabama childhood.

Notes

1. Sonia Sanchez, *Sister Son/ji*, in *New Plays from the Black Theatre*, ed. Ed Bullins (New York: Bantam, 1969), 104.
2. Sonia Sanchez, "Reflector Interview: Sonia Sanchez," *Reflector* (literary magazine of English Department, Shippensburg University, Shippensburg, Pennsylvania, 1984), 20.
3. Lateifa Hyman, "Multi-dimensional Struggle," *African Woman* 24 (November/December 1979): 18-19.
4. Haki Madhubuti, "Sonia Sanchez: The Bringer of Memories," *Black Women Writers (1950-1980): A Critical Evaluation*, ed. Mari Evans (Garden City, N.Y.: Anchor/Doubleday, 1984), 422.
5. Sonia Sanchez, *Love Poems* (New York: Third Press, 1973), 35. Also in *I've Been a Woman: New and Selected Poems* (Sausalito, Calif.: Black Scholar Press, 1978), 37.
6. *I've Been a Woman*, 39.
7. Ibid., 30.
8. Margaret Walker Alexander, review of *I've Been a Woman: New and Selected Poems* by Sonia Sanchez, *Black Scholar* 11 (January/February 1980): 92.
9. C. Hugh Holman, *The Immoderate Past: The Southern Writer and History* (Athens: University of Georgia Press, 1977), 1.
10. Sonia Sanchez, *A Blues Book for Blue Black Magical Women* (Detroit: Broadside, 1974), 21.
11. George Kent, "Notes on the 1974 Black Literary Scene," *Phylon* 6 (June 1975): 197.
12. Sanchez, *A Blues Book*, 23.
13. Ralph Ellison and James Allan McFerguson, "Indivisible Man," *Atlantic* 226 (December 1970): 59.
14. Sonia Sanchez, interview with Joanne V. Gabbin, at the poet's home in Philadelphia, 13 December 1983.
15. Sonia Sanchez, *Under a Soprano Sky* (Trenton, N.J.: Africa World Press, 1987), 54-55.
16. Ibid., 55.
17. Sanchez, *A Blues Book*, 26-27.
18. Gabbin interview.
19. Sanchez, *A Blues Book*, 28.
20. Anita Cornwell, "Attuned to the Energy: Sonia Sanchez," *Essence* 10 (July 1979): 10.
21. Richard Wright, *Black Boy: A Record of Childhood and Youth* (New York: Harper & Row, 1966), 133.
22. Ladell Payne, *Black Novelists and the Southern Literary Tradition* (Athens: University of Georgia Press, 1981), 66.
23. Gabbin interview.
24. Sonia Sanchez, *homegirls & handgrenades* (New York: Thunder's Mouth Press, 1984), 55-56.
25. Sanchez, *A Blues Book*, 31-32.
26. Ibid., 23.
27. Robert Farris Thompson, *Flash of the Spirit: African and Afro-American Art and Philosophy* (New York: Random House, 1983), 74.
28. Ibid., 79.
29. Cornwell, 10.
30. Enrico Maria Sante Pablo Neruda, *The Poetics of Prophecy* (Ithaca, N.Y.: Cornell University Press, 1982), 15-16.
31. Cornwell, 10.
32. Ruth Limmer and Louise Bogan, *Journey around My Room: The Autobiography of Louise Bogan* (New York: Viking, 1980), xix.
33. Sanchez, *A Blues Book*, 33.
34. Ibid., 37.
35. Sanchez, *I've Been a Woman*, 50.
36. Ibid., 94.
37. Ibid., 95.
38. Ibid., 95.
39. Kenneth Lincoln, *Native American Renaissance* (Berkeley: University of California Press, 1983), 45.
40. Ibid., 44.

41. Sonia Sanchez, "The Poet as a Creator of Social Values," in *Crisis in Culture: Two Speeches by Sonia Sanchez.* (New York: Black Liberation Press, 1983), 1-2.

42. Ibid., 2.

43. Sanchez, *I've Been a Woman,* 97.

44. Joyce Ann Joyce, "The Development of Sonia Sanchez: A Continuing Journey," *Indian Journal of American Studies* 13 (July 1983): 67.

45. Sanchez, *I've Been a Woman,* 99.

46. Ibid.

47. Ibid., 99-101.

48. Sanchez, *homegirls & handgrenades,* 11.

49. Ibid., 71.

50. Ibid., 73-74.

51. Sanchez, *Under a Soprano Sky,* 96.

Harriette C. Buchanan (essay date 1990)

SOURCE: Buchanan, Harriette C. "Lee Smith: The Storyteller's Voice." In *Southern Women Writers: The New Generation,* pp. 324-44. Tuscaloosa: The University of Alabama Press, 1990.

[*In the following essay, Buchanan presents an overview of Lee Smith's career, praising her talent as a natural storyteller, her flexibility in handling point of view, and her mixing of the comic and the tragic in her works.*]

"What I'm trying to do all the time is just tell a story."[1] So saying, Lee Smith modestly, or perhaps disingenuously, backs away from the complexity and richness of her narratives about life in the small-town South. Seen in context, that statement sheds light on the intentionality of her art: "I get really involved in the characters and the story, and it's hard for me to talk about whether I have any of what my [English] class calls the DHM, the Deep Hidden Meaning. What I'm trying to do all the time is just tell a story, essentially, and if the other stuff comes in, it just has to sort of creep in, I think."[2] Creep in it does. In her six novels, one volume of short stories, and uncollected stories, Lee Smith not only tells about characters and their stories, she also provides insights into the contemporary South and the realities of life in the face of change that ring true and create themes fraught with "Deep Hidden Meaning."

Often compared with such predecessors as William Faulkner, Carson McCullers, Flannery O'Connor, and Eudora Welty, Lee Smith is attaining her own stature by doing what they did so well, telling stories of her own people and places, stories told with irony and love, humor and compassion. Smith has also been compared favorably with such contemporary Southern writers as Bobbie Ann Mason. All of these writers have, in part, achieved fame because they write about their people, times, and places with warmth, humor, and ironic detachment. Lee Smith's settings are Southern, her interest in and ability for storytelling are Southern, but her characters and stories, because of their realism, even ordinariness, are universal.

Born in 1944, Lee Smith grew up in Grundy, a small mining town in the mountains of western Virginia. Smith began writing when she was a child and continued to write when she went away to school, first at St. Catherine's School, a private Episcopalian school in Richmond, Virginia, and then at Hollins College, which she selected because of its writing program. Like many novice writers, Smith first experimented with exotic characters and settings, thinking that fiction had to be about "something glamorous, something exciting."[3] Only after reading Faulkner, O'Connor, and Welty did she realize that the stuff of everyday life in the South could be the source of good fiction. With this realization, Smith began successfully to mine her personal experience for the characters and places that make her stories compelling.

Smith's first novel, *The Last Day the Dogbushes Bloomed* (1968), grew out of her senior writing project at Hollins and, like many first novels, is the coming-of-age story of a preadolescent child. The talent displayed in this first novel was recognized with a Book-of-the-Month Club Writing Fellowship. Later awards included two O. Henry awards for short fiction and the 1984 North Carolina Award for Literature. In her career, Smith juggles her writing with a teaching career (she is currently a member of the English Department at North Carolina State University) and the rearing of two sons.

The Last Day the Dogbushes Bloomed was followed in 1971 by *Something in the Wind* and in 1973 by *Fancy Strut.* During the eight-year gap between *Fancy Strut* and *Black Mountain Breakdown* (1981), Smith's publications were limited to short stories that appeared in little magazines, such as the *Carolina Quarterly,* and in popular magazines, such as *Redbook* and *Mademoiselle. Black Mountain Breakdown,* the first novel in which Smith makes full use of her Virginia mountain background, was followed in short order by *Cakewalk* (1981), a collection of short stories.

The early novels received scant critical attention, but *Black Mountain Breakdown* and *Cakewalk* were more widely and favorably received. With *Oral History* (1983), Smith's reputation as a prominent contemporary writer was firmly established. Widely and well reviewed, *Oral History* and *Family Linen* (1985) became book club selections and generated television interviews for Smith. *Oral History* and *Family Linen* deserve this attention because they demonstrate a mature novelist in full control of her material.

With this recognition, Smith has felt free to continue the vein of fiction in which she excels: the stories of a wide range of characters, told with careful detail. Attention to detail and to point of view are conscious devices that Smith deliberately manipulates in her work. She has referred to attention to detail as "art you don't normally think of as art."[4] She has also commented about "point of view and the difference it causes in the narrative. . . . different people telling and retelling the same incident."[5] Smith's use of point of view, of the voices with which she tells the story, is always true. Like a singer with perfect pitch, Smith's ear for the nuances and tones of true speech is always convincing.

The first-person narrator of *The Last Day the Dogbushes Bloomed* is Susan Tobey, a self-centered child who in the course of the story is forced to the realization that the world is not as she imagines it. During her momentous ninth summer, Susan and her friends are organized into a club by the visiting Eugene. Eugene and his mentor, the invisible, imaginary Little Arthur, destroy the innocence of the small-town children by introducing them to deliberate, heedless cruelty and to sex. On top of this change, a flood alters the valley in which they live by washing away homes and, more importantly to Susan, the "wading house," which "was not a real house. It was a soft, light green tree, a willow, that grew by the bank of the stream. . . . it was the only wading house in the world, and I was the only one that knew about it. It was a very special place" (12). Susan not only sees the tree as a house, she also sees the creatures that live at its base as "people that . . . were my good friends" (12). The flood washes the bank of the stream and her animal friends are never seen again. Another childhood illusion is gone. Susan's family also changes. Her mother, whom she calls the Queen, goes off with a man whom Susan has dubbed the Baron. The Castle is thus irrevocably changed because the Queen and the Princess, Susan's older sister, have left, and without the Queen's presence, with her shimmery dresses and flowery perfumes, the house is just a house.

The story is conventional, even predictable, but it is redeemed from the ordinary by Smith's unfailing control of Susan's voice and perspective. Susan is unaware of the conflicts within her family, including her mother's adultery, which is revealed obliquely to the reader when Susan throws reference to it in a secondary position to what she sees as the chief event, her personal situation: "I had been busy with eating a banana and listening to the radio and bending my feet, all at the same time, but then the Baron and the Queen came downstairs and when they made me turn off the radio and told me why didn't I go wash my feet, I thought about the club meeting and left" (149-50). Susan's pride at being able to eat a banana, listen to the radio, and bend her feet "all at the same time" overshadows the fact that the Queen and the Baron have been upstairs together. Their nagging about turning off the radio and washing her feet is what impinges on Susan's consciousness.

By the end of the novel, Susan has come to realize that Eugene is to be avoided, that the Queen is never coming back, and that she is no longer afraid of the dark terrors of the night, personified by Little Arthur, who now lives under the dogbushes. The thematic significance of the conventional loss-of-innocence plot is indicated in a passage in which Susan explains the meaning of the term "dogbushes": "The flowers didn't look like dogs or anything. The dogbushes I called dogbushes because one time when I was seven and one month I found a dog under the ones along the middle of the fence" (10). Susan's solipsistic view of the world is destroyed during the course of the story; therefore, her ninth summer will be the last during which the dogbushes will bloom: the next summer she will call the bushes by their more ordinary name, whatever that is.

Title is again a key to theme with *Something in the Wind* (1971), Smith's second novel. Smith quotes the line "There is something in the wind," from Shakespeare's *The Comedy of Errors* (ix). The Shakespearean line is spoken by Antipholus of Ephesus as he and his party are trying, in vain, to gain entrance to his house. Just as Antipholus feels that some outside force in the wind prevents his entering his house, Brooke Kincaid feels that some unnamed force prevents her from finding what she should do with her life.

Several thematic elements echo from Susan Tobey's story to Brooke Kincaid's. Susan's story ended with the loss of childhood fantasy and family structure. Brooke's story begins with the loss of the childhood friend with whom she had identified and to whom she had looked for guidance. At the end of her story, Susan is able to smile, unafraid, at the shadow of Little Arthur. At the end of her story, Brooke laughs, a bit hysterically, at the comedy of errors that she has lived as she tried to develop her life plan.

Brooke formulates the concept of the life plan at the first of the story: "I wrote in my notebook: 'I am the only one who knows that I am different.' I based my life plan on that. . . . The only concrete thing about the life plan was that it involved imitation. I would imitate everybody until everything became second nature . . . and I wouldn't have to bother to imitate any more, I would simply *be*" (25). In imitating her college roommate, Diana Barker, Brooke learns to be a popular, sociable coed. "At first I double-dated with Diana all the time, but then I got the hang of it. The more I acted like Diana, the more often the phone rang for me" (65). She is, however, sometimes not so sure about her qualities as an imitator. She becomes friends with Elizabeth, who "was the only threat I had. Elizabeth never knew what she was doing. She could go into a neat room, any room, and have it completely wrecked by the time she left, without any effort on her part at all. . . . Eventually, Elizabeth and I started spending a lot of time together, which was a bad thing for my life plan" (61-62).

Brooke drifts from being Diana's roommate to being Elizabeth's to moving in with Bentley, a long-haired golf jock. As she follows Brooke's progress, Smith casts an amused eye on college life of the mid-1960s. The locale is Southern, but not uniquely so. Anyone who went to college in the sixties would recognize the places, the happenings, and the people, especially the hapless Brooke. Because Brooke is eighteen rather than nine, the tone of the story she tells is more sophisticated than Susan's. While Brooke has led a sheltered existence before coming to college, she has a literary bent that enables her to describe the things that happen to her with irony, some insight, and a good vocabulary. Brooke's insight enables her to see the folly of people around her, but very little of her own. In the course of the novel, she dissociates herself from the Tri Delts, loses the notebook with the life plan and the copy of Ripley's *Believe It or Not,* to which she has resorted in times of trouble, and finally moves out of Bentley's apartment, after becoming convinced that he is not just pleasantly crazy but genuinely disturbed. By the novel's end, Brooke is in a confused state in which she is not sure whether to laugh or cry. She opts for laughter.

This laughter begins when, remaining in town after school has ended, she volunteers to walk Lady, her landlady's "medium-size, medium-age black dog of no special breed who had a lot of inertia" (234). Wearing sunglasses and half dragging Lady along the street, Brooke is approached by a stranger who insists on helping her across the street in the mistaken belief that she is blind. Brooke protests but is unable to dissuade him. She returns to the apartment disturbed and shaken by the experience: "Then all of a sudden the whole thing, everything, struck me as funny and I started laughing and once I started laughing I couldn't stop. The idea of Lady as a Seeing Eye dog was the funniest part. I rolled on the bed, laughing and laughing" (237). If Brooke survives her life, if she can truly be, rather than imitate, it will be because of the saving grace of laughter.

Something in the Wind is another novel with a conventional plot, a typical first-year-in-college story. Brooke is somewhat detached from what is happening around and to her and so is able to tell her story with a certain amount of irony and humor. The pain of her awareness that her life has no direction is buffered by her inability to feel that any of it means much. Smith's use of the first-person point of view has been flawlessly controlled but has also restricted what she could do in presenting character and plot.

With *Fancy Strut* (1973), Smith branches out by using a third-person voice. This omniscient narrator focuses not on one character whose progress is closely followed but on a whole cast of characters who act various roles in the pageantry and profiteering of the sesquicentennial celebration of Speed, Alabama. This more detached point of view enables Smith to tell the story of Speed with ironic humor. In a series of disjointed frames or segments, the narrator sees the characters as none of them would ever be able to see themselves.

Both the initial and final frames of the novel focus on Miss Iona, the self-appointed "custodian of beauty and truth in Speed, the champion of the pure and good" (4). Miss Iona's means of promoting truth and beauty, purity and goodness, is as the society and ladies' editor of the Speed *Messenger.* The narrator indicates Miss Iona's position in the community and at the same time ironically comments on social convention: "What was the good of having a party if Miss Iona didn't write it up? You might as well not have bothered. What was the good of wearing a silver lamé dress if Miss Iona wrote you up in beige lace? The truth is what you read in the paper" (4). Miss Iona, with frequency, writes not what really happens but what she would have preferred to happen, because it is her mission in life to save the younger generation from its crassness, epitomized, in her view, by the vulgarity of the majorettes who participate in the Susan Arch Findley Memorial Marching Contest.

The Majorettes, who perform the Fancy Strut figure, are not, however, important characters. Their mothers receive the narrator's focus. Mrs. Frances Pitt is the overstuffed, overzealous stage mother. The high point of her life comes when her daughter Theresa wins the Fancy Strut contest over Sharon DuBois, daughter of Frances's cousin and rival of long standing, Sandy. The Pitts and the DuBois, along with the DuBois' next-door neighbors, the Cartwrights, represent working-class Speed. All three of these families have, by dint of hard work or luck or timing, raised themselves from dirt-farm poor to respectable middle class. While they live in new tract housing, their coarse behavior and polyester pantsuits indelibly mark their origins.

The more established upper middle class is represented by the Neighbors family and the Warner family. Manly Neighbors is the owner-editor of the *Messenger.* Manly is exceedingly pleased to be editor of a small-town newspaper; his only problem is the mystery of who could be sending the paper letters threatening the celebration. His wife, Monica, inordinately proud of the new house on which she has lavished attention and money, feels her superiority to the community when she shows the house off: "'Why, it looks just like a page out of *Good Housekeeping,* honey,' Monica's bridge club had exclaimed in one breath when it was Monica's turn to be hostess. Monica winced, having had *Vogue* in mind" (27). In the novel's course, Monica has a satisfyingly sordid affair with Buck Fire, the professional manager of the pageant. While Manly and Monica are firmly of the upwardly mobile New South, the Warners represent stereotypes from the Old South. Lloyd is the dipsomaniac lawyer, an image he carefully cultivates to disguise the intelligence that would alienate him from the community. A self-consciously Faulknerian character, he sits in his dark, dusty office and observes the celebration with a mixture of amusement and despair. His mother is an Old South crazy lady who has immured herself in her home and whose view of life is expressed by the way in which she refers to her husband's suicide: "'When Mr. Warner bravely met his end' . . . exactly as if he had died in a war" (223).

Outsiders Buck Fire and Luther Fletcher have come to organize the pageant and, not incidentally, to make a large profit for the White Company. Their dreams of easy money and progressive triumph from the celebration are shattered when the pageant disintegrates as Lloyd attempts suicide during the Civil War scene and as the fire that Bevo Cartwright set consumes the scaffolding.

The novel ends with Miss Iona's indictment of the pageant: "The whole pageant had been a mockery of her heritage and the Southern way of life. It had been diametrically opposed to her own Ideal Pageant. Instead of an exalting theatrical experience, it had been nothing more than a medicine show, a carnival, pandering to the lowest possible tastes. It had deserved to be struck by fire" (328). Unable to endure further the vulgarity of the modern world, Miss Iona slips into a fantasy world in which the peacock on her dressing gown dances his own "fancy strut" (329).

Smith has orchestrated the fancy strut of her characters through the events of the sesquicentennial celebration. As each character goes through his or her own series of personal crises, Smith shows various faces of the New South, from the go-getter eagerness of Bill Higgins, Bob Pitt, and Ron-the-Mouth Skinner, to the stolid complacency of Manly Neighbors, to the bitter cynicism of Lloyd Warner. The women express a similar range, from the restless ambition of Ruthie Cartwright and Sharon DuBois, to the brassy aggression of Frances Pitt, to the bored listlessness of Anne Cartwright and Monica Neighbors, to the withdrawn unreality of Mrs. Warner and Miss Iona. Hanging the complicated maneuvering of these characters on the simple plot device of the sesquicentennial celebration, Smith gives a cross section of the small-town South during the late 1960s. She tells the stories of her characters with irony and humor, but never with scorn. The humor dominates; *Fancy Strut* is above all a funny story.

The tone of Smith's next novel, *Black Mountain Breakdown* (1981), is, despite many funny episodes, tragic. Retaining the third-person perspective, Smith returns to the narrative device of the first two novels by following the growing pains of a single female character. Crystal Spangler, like Susan Tobey and Brooke Kincaid, is roughly disabused of childhood innocence. Crystal's story, in fact, strongly echoes those of Susan and Brooke. Like Susan, the child Crystal prefers a world where phantoms are as real as family. A dreamy, artistic child, Crystal wants only to laugh, sing, and be happy. Like Susan's, her fantasy ends with family dissolution; she abruptly comes to the end of childhood when her father dies. Crystal's sense of loss of direction after her father's death echoes Brooke's. Like Brooke, Crystal vacillates between trying to follow the role of the good girl and rebelling at that role with promiscuous sexual adventures. Brooke first bases her "life plan" on imitation but eventually abandons that plan for laughter. Crystal, also trying on different, imitative roles, never learns to laugh.

Crystal's failure to find the grace of laughter or to act with stoic acceptance, as her mother does, is the source of her tragedy. In talking about this novel, Smith describes one of her motives for writing the story: "to really make a thematic point . . . that if you're entirely a passive person, you're going to get in big trouble. The way so many women, and I think particularly Southern women, are raised is to make themselves fit the image that other people set out for them, and that was Crystal's great tragedy, that she wasn't able to get her own self-definition."[6]

Black Mountain Breakdown is set in rural western Virginia during the 1960s and 1970s. In high school, Crystal participates, with her mother's permission, in beauty pageants and religious revivals and, without her mother's permission, in an affair with the disreputable Mack Stiltner, who eventually leaves her for a career in Nashville as a country singer. Crystal also eventually leaves for college.

After a five-year absence, she returns home to find her mother and the Black Rock community enjoying a new prosperity created by increasing demand and prices for coal. Crystal joins the Junior Women's Club and takes a job teaching English at the junior high school, which she "falls into . . . so easily that it's as if she had never done anything else. It's like there's a part of her which knows how to do it already. . . . She's very busy" (182) and relatively satisfied with her roles as a teacher and member of the community.

This tranquillity is shattered when, on the day of her mother's remarriage, former high school sweetheart Roger Lee Combs reappears in Crystal's life. Roger takes over, assuring her: "'I know you, sweetheart, I know everything you've been and everything you've done. I've watched you go through all these changes, one right after another. You might *think* you're happy now, Crystal, but you're not'" (199). Crystal falls under Roger's influence. They run away; he divorces his wife and marries Crystal; they begin working on his political campaigns.

Crystal settles into a new pattern as the successful candidate's wife, the darling of the society pages. There is, however, a shadow in this existence. Despite her love for Roger, Crystal shrinks from committing herself to him more fully by having a baby: "Because things are not exactly as Roger thinks, anyway. Things are more precarious. They have edges now. . . . Ever since the beginning—ever since that day when he came up to her mother's house—she has been conscious of the end" (210).

The end is precipitated by a campaign visit to a mental hospital, where the mindless face of a retarded man stirs long-repressed memories of the time she was raped by her father's half-witted brother, Devere, a trauma that Crystal has submerged in her unconscious and that represents the cloud that has apparently prevented Crystal from dealing constructively with her life. Crystal leaves Roger and returns to her mother's house, where she soon retreats into catatonia.

Crystal is cared for by her mother, Lorene, and her childhood friend Agnes McClanahan, women who have persevered and even triumphed over their experience by a devotion to duty and a determination to "deal with problems by rising above them" (21). Both women, though humorless, display a shrewd business acumen and a flair for survival in a world that offers little to independent women. Lacking their strength, Crystal simply withdraws from painful change: "And who knows what will happen in this world? Agnes reflects. . . . Why, Crystal might jump right up from that bed tomorrow and go off and get her Ph.D. . . . Or she might stay right here and atrophy to death. What Agnes really thinks, though, is that Crystal is happy, that she likes to have Agnes hold her hand and brush her hair, as outside her window the seasons come and go and the colors change on the mountain" (227-28). Crystal withdraws, but life goes on in Black Rock. Roger wins his election; Lorene and Odell go on trips; Agnes continues to expand her business interests.

Susan Tobey, Brooke Kincaid, and Crystal Spangler are all idealistic, imaginative girls who are disabused of their dreams by harsh reality. They represent artistic sensitivity crushed by the modern world. But is artistic sensitivity an unadulterated good and commercial progress an unqualified evil? No. Artistic sensitivity can lead to Crystal's paralysis or to Miss Iona's madness; commercial progress can bring the comfortable prosperity that enables Lorene and Agnes to feel satisfied with their lives. Lee Smith tells her stories with ironic humor but also with a balanced vision. She sees both sides of her characters and their stories; she does not make the kinds of opinionated judgments so frequently made by many of her characters.

The irony that shows the difference between Lee Smith's humanism and the narrow, judgmental views of her characters is especially evident in the stories collected in *Cakewalk* (1981). Mrs. Joline B. Newhouse, the narrator of the lead story, "Between the Lines," is such a judgmental character. Smith's handling of these characters is evident as Joline introduces herself by justifying the standard closing for her newspaper column. She had considered "Yours in Christ," but she rejected it because: "I am in Christ but I know for a fact that a lot of them are not. . . . 'Peace be with you,' as I see it, is sufficiently religious without laying all the cards right out on the table in plain view. I like to keep an ace or two up my sleeve. I like to write between the lines" (11). Working in a vein that Miss Iona would have recognized, Joline B. Newhouse's professed aim is to uplift her readers. If that means reporting a wife beating as: "Mrs. Alma Goodnight is enjoying a pleasant recuperation period in the lovely, modern Walker Mountain Community Hospital while she is sorely missed by her loved ones at home" (12), then so be it. The "mere facts" of human interactions are not important to Joline: "Because that is a *mystery*, and I am no detective by a long shot. I am what I am, I know what I know, and I know you've got to give folks something to hang on to, something to keep them going. That is what I have in mind when I say *uplift*" (12-13). Although Joline is pompous and self-righteous in her judgments of the needs of others, she is not an object of ridicule; rather, Smith uses her to present the major theme of the mystery of life. At the end of the story, Joline asks a question that resonates throughout Smith's fiction: "Now where will it all end? I ask you. All this pain and loving, mystery and loss. And it just goes on and on" (25). The sensitivity of this question goes far toward redeeming the self-righteousness of Joline's earlier pronouncements about her fellow citizens in Salt Lick. Mrs. Joline B. Newhouse too is human and deserves compassion.

This is true of the host of other characters who are presented in all their passivity and frailty in *Cakewalk*. "Georgia Rose," who can see the future, spends her life running from it. Helen, in "All the Days of Our Lives," prefers vicariously enjoying the houses and affairs of soap opera characters to taking a promotion at work and opportunities for solid relationships in her own life.

Debbi drifts with the drifter who strands her in "Gulfport," dreaming of life as it is lived in magazine spreads. "And it just goes on and on."

Some of the characters, including Florrie in the title story "Cakewalk," manage to break away from passivity and isolation, but whether or not this is a real victory is not clear. At the end of "Artists," Jennifer, who had identified earlier with her artistic, otherworldly grandmother and had jealously guarded the long hair her grandmother admired, finally cuts her hair. "It looked terrific. . . . So I grew up. And I never became an artist, although my career has certainly had its ups and downs, like most careers. Like most lives" (123), like the closest many Lee Smith characters come to self-realization and strong assertion.

Several of the narrative voices of *Oral History* (1983) echo the sense of assertiveness that Jennifer of "Artists" demonstrates. Granny Younger, Ludie Davenport, Ora Mae, and Sally are all assured of who they are and of their places in the community around Hoot Owl Holler. The passive heroine, yearning for some undefined and perhaps undefinable something that will deliver her into a life somehow more or better, is also present in *Oral History*. Interestingly, these passive women do not tell their own stories; rather, it is their stories that the other, stronger women tell. The beautiful and doomed Dory and her restless and talented daughter Pearl are the figures around whom the action of the story swirls. The community believes that these women have been cursed by the first Almarine Cantrell's Red Emmy; the curse is conveyed in the gold earrings owned by Almarine's wife, Pricey Jane, who mysteriously dies of the "dew pizen" (78). The earrings pass to Pricey Jane's daughter Dory, who commits suicide by lying on the railroad track. They then go to Dory's daughter Maggie, who, apparently dying of polio, gives them to her twin sister, Pearl. Maggie recovers, but Pearl, enduring an unhappy marriage, has an affair with a high school boy, after which she mysteriously dies following the premature still-birth of a baby whose paternity is uncertain. The curse is presumably expiated after Pearl's funeral, when Ora Mae, daughter of Almarine's second wife, Vashti, throws the earrings down a gorge.

More complex and broader in scope than any of Smith's previous works, *Oral History* exhibits Lee Smith's maturity and mastery of her craft. Fully in control of point of view, Smith shifts effortlessly from an omniscient third person to the first-person voices of most of the story's narrators. The novel opens and closes in a present time sequence focusing on Jennifer, Pearl's daughter from the stifling marriage, who has come to record, for her oral history course, the rumored haunted sounds from the family homestead in Hoot Owl Holler. After she has set up her tape recorder, Jennifer writes in her journal, in self-conscious student prose: "One feels that the true benefits of this trip may derive not from what is recorded or not recorded by the tape, . . . but from my new knowledge of my heritage and a new appreciation of these colorful, interesting folk. My *roots*" (19). Jennifer's condescension toward her mountain relatives and the fact that this condescension is misplaced are demonstrated when, closing her journal entry with "I shall descend now, to be with them as they go about their evening chores'" (20), she returns to the house to find no one doing "chores." Little Luther and Ora Mae are sitting on the porch, Al is puttering with his van, his children are watching *Magnum* on television. The twentieth century has come to Hoot Owl Holler; the outsider's stereotypes have little to do with reality.

Having established a late-twentieth-century reality, Smith shifts back almost one hundred years to have Granny Younger begin telling the Cantrell family saga, replete with passion, pain and loving, mystery and loss. A traditional granny-woman healer, Granny Younger tells Almarine's story by providing his family background since Civil War times and by picking up the threads of the narrative in 1902, when Almarine returned to Hoot Owl Holler after a five-year absence.

Granny Younger knows how to spin a yarn and how to keep her audience, of whom she is always conscious, on the edges of their seats. She carries the main thread of the narrative but weaves in digressionary fibers and tales, as well as throws out hints of what is to come in the story. Granny Younger's voice keens like a mountain ballad. Directly addressing her audience, she says: "I said I know moren you know and mought be I'll tell you moren you want to hear. I'll tell you a story that's truer than true, and nothing so true is so pretty. It's blood on the moon, as I said. The way I tell a story is the way I want to, and iffen you mislike it, you don't have to hear" (37). But Granny knows that by the time she issues that warning she has her audience firmly in hand; there is not one who does not want to hear.

Like the best regional writers, Smith writes not in the literal dialect than an ethnologist would record, with numerous apostrophes indicating dropped and elided syllables, but in a lyric prose that captures an authentic flavor of the speech of the people who live in the mountains around Hoot Owl Holler. Authentic rhythms, speech patterns, and expressions are recorded; peculiar vocalizations for vowel and consonant sounds are ignored. Like Granny Younger, Smith is aware of her audience and wants them to listen to and understand the human richness of the characters' voices, not to be shut out by eccentric pronunciations indicated by alien print symbols.

Granny Younger tells of Almarine Cantrell's passion for Red Emmy, of the mysterious end of their affair, of his marriage to Pricey Jane, of the birth of their daughter Dory. Along the way, she also tells a lot about folk medicine, witches, and everyday life.

The third-person narrator tells about Pricey Jane, with her beautiful black hair and golden earrings, who yearns secretly for something she cannot name but that she suspects is out there somewhere in the wider world. As Pricey Jane falls ill, the narrator shifts focus to Almarine, who returns home to find his wife and son dying and wildly brings in Granny Younger and the neighbors to try to stay the inevitable. Rose Hibbits, who is not normal, tells part of the story; then the third-person narrator closes the first part of the novel with an account of Pricey Jane's funeral.

The second section of the novel picks up the story in 1923, when Dory has grown to young womanhood. It is Dory's story now, but it is told by the outsider Richard Burlage as he writes in his journal, with a self-consciousness and arrogance that echoes Jennifer's, about what he sees as his "pilgrimage to a simpler era, back—dare I hope it—to the very roots of consciousness and belief" (97), a pilgrimage on which he hopes to find himself. Burlage fails in this quest. While he does go back in time by coming to the Hoot Owl Holler community, he does not find a simpler era. He finds the reality of a close, closed community with its own ways, suspicious of the ways of outsiders. Burlage falls hopelessly in love with Dory, an affair doomed by her family's distrust of him and by his inability to accept what she and her family really are. He finally leaves Hoot Owl Holler, Tug, and Black Rock in disgrace, his affair with Dory having been discovered, and unaware that Dory is pregnant.

When Burlage returns, some nine years later, he has fooled himself into believing that he has matured. He has become a photographer and returns hoping to record on film scenes from a past time. In the time he has been away, he has changed only externally; internally, he still has no real sense of who he is or of who the mountain people are. He can only deal with the surface reality of what can be recorded by his camera. He learns that Dory has married Luther Wade and goes past their house, hoping to see her. He catches a glimpse of her, but the lingering images are those that he has captured on film, the most haunting of these being beautiful twin girls, who he does not know are his daughters.

Richard Burlage, because of the pompous self-consciousness of his prose, is the least attractive of *Oral History*'s narrators. Yet, it is he who holds the stage the longest. In addition to the third-person omniscient narrator, there are eleven different perspectives for telling the Cantrell family's story. Eight of these perspectives are first-person narrators who tell the story as they can see and decode it. These include the important and memorably distinct voices of Granny Younger; Richard Burlage; Jink Cantrell, Dory's half-brother; and Sally, Dory's daughter by Luther Wade, as well as the lesser voices of Rose Hibbits, Little Luther Wade, Mrs. Ludie Davenport, and Ora Mae. Among these first-person voices are woven the sections told in a third-person voice, but focusing on the perspective of one of the characters, including Pricey Jane, Almarine, and Jennifer. Burlage speaks as long as Granny Younger and Sally combined. They, in turn, each speak twice as long as Jink, who speaks more than twice as long as Ora Mae. Why do these characters hold the stage for such precisely varying lengths?

The key to this mystery lies in the heart of the story, Dory. Granny Younger provides the family background and tells about the curse of Red Emmy; her story ends with Dory's birth. Sally tells about Dory's death and about the working out of the curse in the lives of Maggie and Pearl. Granny Younger and Sally are the first and last voices heard within the frame device of Jennifer's story. In the middle falls the long passage in which Burlage grapples with his love for Dory and his inability to reach out and touch and know any more than her body. He is fascinated by the enigmatic smile and golden Botticelli hair, but he never knows or understands the personality behind the smile and hair.

That personality is the central mystery of the novel. Granny Younger has set up the mystery with her tales of witches and curses. Burlage, with his air of outside rationality, tries in vain to penetrate it. Sally, with her frank openness, simply acknowledges it. She describes her mother's position in the rest of the family, using the image of a kaleidoscope they once had: "It had a bright blue spot in the middle of all the patterns, one spot that never moved no matter which way you turned it or how many pretty bright patterns came and went all around. Our family was like that, with Mama at the center, not doing anything particular but not *having* to either, and all the rest of us falling in place around" (238). The kaleidoscope image not only serves Sally as a way to describe her family, but it also serves as a way to describe and organize Lee Smith's narrative design for *Oral History*.

Jennifer, the contemporary outsider, begins and ends the story in her quest for family history. Within this frame fall Granny Younger and Sally and all the others, with Burlage at once the closest and yet the most distant from the heart, the core, the center of the design, Dory. It is Burlage's outsider, foreign status that enables him to get closest to Dory but keeps him farthest away. The other characters, by blood, by marriage, by propinquity, are physically closer, but Dory's elusive personality is absolutely beyond their ken. Burlage has clues about what Dory can be, about the nature of her vague yearnings for some kind of beauty in life that cannot be found in the mountains of western Virginia. He is, however, powerless to break the bonds that tie her to her family and place. Dory is the center, but her reality remains a mystery because her story is told by first-person narrators, not by the omniscient third-person voice that focuses only on peripheral characters.

"No matter who's telling the story, it is always the teller's tale, and you never *finally* know exactly the way it was," says Lee Smith of her work. "I guess I see some sort of central mystery at the center of the past, of any past, that you can't, no matter what a good attempt you make at understanding how it was, you never can quite get it."[7] Smith varies the narrative voices in order to produce several good attempts to get at the center of the Cantrell family past. But because each teller is telling about his or her own perception of or need from Dory, Dory herself remains elusive; the family focus keeps shifting like the pieces in Sally's kaleidoscope. Dory is the center of the family history because she most clearly, yet elusively, represents the family's yearning for something beyond themselves. Sally refers to this in her analysis of the curse that haunts the Cantrell family: "People say they're haunted and they are—every one of them all eat up with wanting something they haven't got" (235). But, of course, this is Sally's oversimplification, her need to deny the catastrophic yearning. Even though she is happily married to Roy, she too was once a lost, unhappy woman, wanting something and not even knowing it. Sally, like the other narrators, tells about Dory and about the other Cantrells' history, but the central mystery is only partially illuminated.

Jennifer's experience in Hoot Owl Holler has not given her a positive picture of her "roots"; rather, it has given her an unwelcome glimpse of the dark mystery. She does not understand Little Luther or Ora Mae or, most of all, "Uncle Al," who is no blood kin of hers. The younger Almarine shows Jennifer both a cruel brutality and a rough good ole boy humor that, along with his threatening warning that she should not return, bewilder her. She leaves in tears, but her bewilderment vanishes as physical distance from her family becomes emotional distance and comfortable stereotype. She now sees them as "primitive people, . . . some sort of early tribe. Crude jokes and animal instincts—it's the other side of the pastoral coin" (284). Unable to understand what she has experienced, Jennifer retreats into the outsider's disregard for the reality of mountain people. The passions that drive the Cantrells are conveniently labeled as attributes of a "primitive people," people whom Jennifer can pigeonhole and forget. Lee Smith has ensured, however, that the readers, hearing all the narrators' voices and following the shifting focus of the Cantrells' story, will never forget the variety of people who inhabit Hoot Owl Holler.

Attempting once again to get at the mystery of the past, Lee Smith airs the *Family Linen* (1985) of the Bird-Hess family. This time there is also a conventional mystery involved, the question of whether or not Sybill Hess really saw her mother murder her father with an ax and dump his body in the well in the backyard of the family home. As with *Oral History,* Smith uses shifting perspectives to work around the central problem. This time, however, the story is told not by an omniscient or by first-person narrators; the voice is third person, but with a focus limited to one narrator at a time. The story opens with Sybill Hess's visit to a hypnotist, who she hopes will be able to cure her recurring headaches. Under hypnosis, Sybill "sees" the murder. But the hypnotist, Bob, warns her that the vision may be a fear-generated fantasy. Determined to get to the bottom of the mystery, Sybill returns to her childhood home in Booker Creek, Virginia.

The narrative then switches to focus on Sybill's younger sister Myrtle. Where Sybill is a prim, uptight old maid, Myrtle is a yuppie housewife who, in college, had been intent primarily on "her 'MRS,' and she's got it, and that's good enough for her. . . . their three children are her 'PHD'" (46). Myrtle has returned home from a tryst with her lover, Gary Vance, the exterminator, to learn that her mother has been hospitalized with a stroke. Sybill arrives to learn of this traumatic event, which will frustrate her desire to confront her mother about the truth of her vision.

The disarray into which the family is plunged by Miss Elizabeth's stroke is next seen from a somewhat more detached viewpoint, that of Myrtle's teenage son, Sean. The family's confusion is refracted through the perspective of Sean's own adolescent confusion, indicated by his reaction to the family furor: "I looked at *Playboy* for a while, all those foxes, and then I got up and got this stupid stuffed dog, . . . don't ask me why it's still around . . . and listened to "Thriller" and thought about Mom and Aunt Sybill yelling. . . . And I could tell from their voices they were scared" (68).

The family gathers to watch at Miss Elizabeth's bedside, and Lacy, the youngest daughter, begins telling her version of the events. Lacy feels she is more Miss Elizabeth's daughter than the others, "*the poetry* took, *with me*" (69), and cannot see much further than the trauma of desertion by her husband, Jack. A Ph.D. candidate at the University of North Carolina at Chapel Hill, Lacy feels distanced from the everyday lives of her kin in Booker Creek. She scorns the blondness, blandness, and "absolute invincible belief in human perfectibility" (72) that she feels Myrtle and her husband, Don, embody. She identifies with the idealism that she sees symbolized in her mother's house, which sits on the hill that dominates Booker Creek. At the same time, she ponders the "Gothic" (76) involvements of her family, especially her Aunt Nettie's many marriages and unexplained estrangement from her mother.

By this stage in the novel, the reader recognizes that the story is not a simple murder mystery. Sybill's questions for Miss Elizabeth have taken a backseat as other mysteries of the family's past become more prominent. The reader has also begun to realize that the narrative pattern of the novel is not straightforward. It is not even so straightforward as the shifting focuses of *Oral History*. The thirdperson limited perspective is at once less personal and yet more immediate than the combination of first-person and omniscient narrator. By Lacy's section of *Family Linen*, the reader is well and truly caught up in the kaleidoscopically shifting patterns of the different family members' perspectives on the life, illness, and central mystery that is Miss Elizabeth. Just as Dory is the central, fixed spot in the kaleidoscope of *Oral History*, Miss Elizabeth is the center of *Family Linen*. The primary narrators are her children, Sybill, Arthur, Candy, Myrtle, and Lacy. In addition, her sisters, Fay, a crazy recluse whose world consists of television and such papers as the *National Enquirer*, and Nettie, whose estrangement is not explained until late in the novel, and her grandson Sean tell their versions of what is happening. Of these narrators, only Candy, a beautician and proud of it, seems satisfied with her life and herself.

When Miss Elizabeth dies without ever regaining consciousness, it is Candy who retains a sense of equilibrium. Arthur is dismayed that yet another person has died on him, and Sybill is enraged that her mother died before she could learn the truth about her father's death. Candy fixes her mother's hair for the funeral and ponders the mysteries of hair and death. Hair is "the most vital organ of the body by a long shot. . . . It will grow after death. It's one of the great mysteries. Along with death. Candy has always been good with hair. And sometimes she thinks she was born knowing all about death, too" (122).

After Miss Elizabeth's funeral, Don and Myrtle, who have inherited her house, decide to move in and remodel it. One modification they plan is the addition of a swimming pool, requiring the bulldozing of the backyard. Ever practical, Don has decided to serve his own purposes as well as to answer Sybill's mystery. Lacy, meanwhile, searches the house over for her own answer to the mystery, to the "secret here, at the heart of the house" (161). What she finds is a journal Miss Elizabeth had written more than fifty years earlier, before either of her marriages. The journal opens with an elaborate metaphor, illustrating her poetic bent and explaining her feelings about exploring her family history. "I approach the Past as a young maiden, bearing a candle, might approach a deserted mansion deep within the Enchanted woods. . . . The wind . . . is my anxiety manifest. I shield my candle with my trembling hand, and if I reach the mansion, will its paltry light be sufficient to illuminate That which lies therein?" (164). The journal recounts Miss Elizabeth's happy childhood with father, mother, and sisters Fay and Nettie. After her mother's death, the family fortunes begin to slip, sinking finally into bankruptcy with the death of her father and Elizabeth's refusal to sell the family home to try to save the family business, the beginning of her estrangement from Nettie, who had been running the business as their father's health had declined. Clinging to the home as a symbol of the beauty and good that her mother had represented, Elizabeth determines to passively await what will come. What Lacy and the reader have learned about is Elizabeth's pride and determination, but the mystery of her being and of whether or not she could have killed her husband remain.

As Lacy finishes reading Miss Elizabeth's journal, the bulldozer uncovers a body, that of Jewell Rife, Elizabeth's first husband and the father of Sybill and Arthur. Lacy confronts her Aunt Nettie with the evidence of the family rift found in the journal and demands an explanation. Nettie, who has known most of the story for a long time but has not seen any "point hanging dirty linen on the line" (213), now tells her version of the family history, including the sordid details of Elizabeth's marriage to the worthless, philandering Jewell, who had been committing adultery with Elizabeth's sister Fay as well as with other women. Nettie reveals that Fay is Candy's mother and that, in her determination to raise Candy as her own child, Elizabeth drove both Fay and Nettie away.

The kaleidoscope shifts again when Fay is discovered dead in an old car outside the One Stop where she and Nettie and Nettie's stepson, Clinus, another half-wit, live. Nettie now knows: "She must of done it, then, Fay" (271). Nettie thus solves the murder mystery; Jewell was murdered by Fay, who strongly resembled Elizabeth, because he had reneged on his promise to take her when he left for Florida. The story then settles into the essentially happy confusion, as the family continues to squabble over the division of Miss Elizabeth's things, of the arrival of Myrtle's and Don's pregnant daughter, Karen, and her boyfriend, Karl.

The last pages of the novel shift to over a month after the discovery of Jewell's body and Fay's death. Karen's wedding day is celebrated by the entire family, with Candy happily at the center fixing everyone's hair, except Karen's. The house has been remodeled, with the pool and patio completed to be the scene of the wedding and reception, and many of the family problems have been settled. Sybill is over her headaches and is in her element as the director of the wedding; Myrtle has settled into happy domesticity and a new career in real estate, wondering what she ever saw in Gary Vance; Arthur is courting the nurse Mrs. Palucci and beginning a new career as manager of the One Stop; and Lacy has begun work on her dissertation as well as seeing Jack once a week. The novel ends with a section focused on Lacy, the youngest, who is thinking about Clinus's message on the sign at the One Stop: "KAREN AND KARL, TODAY IS THE FIRST DAY OF THE REST OF YOUR LIFE. It is, too. That goes for everybody" (272). On this optimistic note, the kaleidoscope of *Family Linen* ceases to shift and leaves the reader with the image of Miss Elizabeth, her position as the idealistic matriarch of the family still firmly in place. The murder mystery has been solved, but the central mystery of the past remains somewhat murky, because the human perceptions that are our access to it are not fully resolved. Nor, according to Lee Smith, will, or should, they ever be. The exploration and representation of those mysteries, of those human lives, are the artist's endeavor, and she will continue to present them to us as her characters, in their own ways, tell us their stories.

Lee Smith's artistry has fully emerged from her early works to the mature recent works *Oral History* and *Family Linen*. The earlier work shows Smith's development in her flexibility with point of view, which becomes so practiced a device in *Oral History* and *Family Linen* that it at once dominates and disappears. Complexity of plot and character also develop through the course of the earlier works. From the simple plot and elementary character development of *The Last Day the Dogbushes Bloomed*, Smith has worked to the complex plots and intricate character interrelationships of *Oral History* and *Family Linen*. In *Something in the Wind*, character was developed in somewhat more depth and breadth; in *Fancy Strut*, plot was much more complicated; in *Black Mountain Breakdown*, character and plot were presented over a longer time span than previously. Smith's continued experimentation with point of view and plot should enable her power as a storyteller to grow even further in future fictions.

With only a few notable exceptions, the characters with whom Smith primarily deals are women hamstrung by their environments and cultures. Susan Tobey, like many Southern girls, has been, on the one hand, overprotected and sheltered from reality and, on the other hand, denied her parents' time and presence. Raised by a servant whose primary responsibility is the house, Susan understandably grows up without a strong or realistic sense of who she is or where she fits in her family or her community. She is very likely to follow in Brooke Kincaid's footsteps and be completely bewildered once she is removed from a sheltered situation. Both are likely to grow up to be like the Monica Neighbors at the first of *Fancy Strut* and the Myrtle Dotson at the first of *Family Linen*, who define themselves by the external standards presented in magazines and social conventions. Whether or not they will find the limited sense of self-assertion that Monica and Myrtle finally achieve is unclear.

Crystal Spangler is the most helpless of all of Smith's women because her life holds not even the faintest hope of self-realization. Crystal is a victim, however, not only of her environment but of her own passiveness. She allows herself to fall into the beauty queen/politician's wife pattern that is socially desirable. Her affair with Mack Stiltner is not a clear and open rebellion but is more a drifting with the currents of circumstance. While she enjoys teaching, she is unable to resist Roger's determination that she be his. Her only assertion is the retreat to her mother's home and into catatonia.

The central woman in *Oral History*, Dory, is similarly helpless and unable to break out of the bonds of family and place to try to be what she wants. Like Crystal, Dory asserts herself with self-destruction. When her daughter Pearl does attempt to shape her life positively, she fails, perhaps because she has had no role models to show her the way. Pearl's half-sister, Sally, is the only Cantrell woman who is content with a life that she has chosen for herself, but Sally had to go through drifting and an unhappy marriage before she found Roy and her job and a life to enjoy.

Miss Elizabeth, the central woman in *Family Linen*, resembles Dory in that she is limited by her environment and considerations of family, but she seizes more control, for good or for ill, by adopting Candy and marrying Verner Hess and bearing two more children, Myrtle and Lacy. The lost woman of this novel is Fay, whose right to a life, to her child, and to a mind are all denied by birth and family circumstance. The strong women of *Family Linen* are Nettie and Candy, who, from the first, are not afraid to buck social convention and be themselves; only they remain essentially unchanged from the novel's beginning to its end. Sybill, Myrtle, and Lacy all change for the better, emerging as more self-confident and self-directed as a result of the airing of the *Family Linen*.

Smith's stories are about women faced with a world for which they are unprepared. These women are not only unprepared but also have little idea of where to look for guidance, because their families and communities provide so little in the way of honest or genuinely nurturing support. The families are usually broken, with key members either physically or mentally absent. These characters are so frequently lost and spiritually impoverished that they see no solution to their problems. Women's periodicals, soap operas, and television shows offer the only consolation, and what they offer is impersonal and unrealistic. Although their hopes and dreams are unrealistic, Smith's characters sound absolutely real to the reader because their stories have been told in such strong, true voices.

While the stories of these women's lives are mostly tragic, the telling is extremely funny. Of this quality in her writing, Smith has said: "I think I tend to see life fairly tragically. If you do that, you've got two choices: you can either go in the closet and sit in the dark or you can make jokes."[8] Fortunately, Lee Smith is not in a closet sitting in the dark. She is telling her stories with as many jokes as she can muster. Like Sally, she can see the funny ironies in tragic lives. Her sad stories are told with warmth, compassion, and humor. The voices with which she tells her stories are truer than true, and the reader cannot help but want to hear them. The Deep Hidden Meaning creeps in because the stories are so true, and therefore basic patterns and meanings of human existence are there.

Lee Smith knows her characters and in her most recent work has delved more deeply into the specific times and places in which those characters live. Her storytelling is, therefore, gaining depth and breadth. Her characters, while often bizarre, are real, and their voices resound truthfully. Smith's conscious variation in narrative voice and tone not only underscores her vision of the ultimate complexity and unknowableness, the mystery, of human life, but it also forces us to read between the lines and look for answers to the ambiguities present in the shifting focuses of her narrative patterns. Smith, like Mrs. Joline B. Newhouse, asks, "Now where will it all end? I ask you. All this pain and loving, mystery and loss. And it just goes on and on." Fortunately, because the mystery of life does go on and on, Lee Smith will not run out of subject matter for her art. As readers we sit enthralled by her stories, her narrative voices, ready to hear more. Tell us another story, Lee Smith.

Notes

1. Edwin T. Arnold, "An Interview with Lee Smith," *Appalachian Journal* 11 (Spring 1984): 248.
2. Ibid.
3. Ibid., 243.
4. Michelle Lodge, "Lee Smith" *Publishers Weekly* 228 (20 September 1985): 110.
5. Ibid.
6. Arnold, 244-45.
7. Ibid., 246.
8. Ibid., 252.

Angeline Godwin Dvorak (essay date winter-spring 1992)

SOURCE: Dvorak, Angeline Godwin. "Cooking as Mission and Ministry in Southern Culture: The Nurturers of Clyde Edgerton's *Walking across Egypt,* Fannie Flagg's *Fried Green Tomatoes at the Whistlestop Cafe,* and Anne Tyler's *Dinner at the Homesick Restaurant.*" *Southern Quarterly* 30, nos. 2-3 (winter-spring 1992): 90-8.

[*In the following essay, Dvorak explores the role of cooking as it relates to a sense of community, spiritual sustenance, women's friendships, and female identity in three Southern novels.*]

The table spread with culinary delights easily triggers images of home, hearth and familial companionship. In southern culture, especially, food is nothing less than the social base of most interchanges of human experience and activity. The concept of "southern hospitality" has remained long after the demise of the antebellum era that birthed it. This graciousness surely began as much from logistics as generosity, for plantation and even tenant-farming neighbors, separated by hundreds of acres and miles of dirt roads, gathered at each other's homes for a gala "get together" that ultimately centered around food (Taylor 46). Each plantation and homestead boasted its own specialties and secret recipes, which can still be enjoyed in eating establishments across the South. Barbecue, for example, was and certainly is a southern favorite.[1] The role of cooking in southern culture, however, is even more relevant to everyday life in a common kitchen, shared by ordinary people, usually women, often mothers, frequently nurturers, but always southern cooks. It is what preparing food and feeding people mean to a southerner, especially "the cook," that makes "cookin' and eatin'" in the South an "in-culture" experience.

Southern fiction intimately captures the significance of cooking in a culture richly laced with a sense of community and Christian duty as well as a host of social facades and hypocritical masques. For the traditional, middle-class southern mother-woman, preparing food for the nourishment and enjoyment of other people plays a major role in her life. The act of cooking for and feeding someone—be it family, friend or total stranger—goes far beyond physical nurturance. Cooking is not simply a task or a chore; it is a mission that fulfills a sense of belonging as one earns a reputation for being, at least, a caretaker for her family, and at best, a very good cook. It is also a ministry that nurtures people's emotional and spiritual needs as much as their physical ones (Douglas 104, 122). Hunger of the soul and spirit drives the force behind the spoon and the skillet with the same intensity as a growling stomach. In southern culture, cooking can be an extension and sometimes a substitution for maternal nurturance, and even a token for martyrdom. Cooking serves the southern cook, likewise, as evidence of self-esteem and social status, moral soundness and spiritual faith, human compassion and community conscience.

Two contemporary southern writers, Clyde Edgerton in *Walking across Egypt* and Fannie Flagg in *Fried Green Tomatoes at the Whistle Stop Cafe* feature characters for whom cooking food and feeding people form the central core of their everyday lives and the culture. Intimate communication and personal bonding accompany the physical as well as emotional and spiritual nurturance of a meal prepared, served and consumed. Ruth and Idgie Threadgoode, proprietors of the Whistle Stop Cafe, Whistle Stop, Alabama, and Mattie Rigsbee of Listre, North Carolina, dramatize the words heard by almost any troubled, lonely, injured or estranged person who happens to stumble into a southern home—"let me fix you somethin' to eat; it will make you feel better." Whether facing abandonment, marital infidelity, a bout with arthritis, a lost loved one or a spat with the preacher, that "somethin'" becomes the solstice, the balm. That "somethin'" also becomes the impetus of doing something for someone in a situation that makes everyone involved feel helpless, insecure or inadequate.

When this hospitality is absent, when the maternal figure does not nurture those around her, even if she does cook for them literally, the ones who are "starved" may try to recreate the emotional and spiritual nurturing, possibly by feeding others and actually setting a table spread. Anne Tyler, in *Dinner at the Homesick Restaurant,* portrays the void of the nurturer and a child's attempt to become a surrogate in order to fulfill the omissions of the past. While Pearl Tull puts food on her table to feed her children, she starves them otherwise. Her son Ezra, therefore, recasts the familial milieu in his own "Homesick Restaurant" where he tries to "feed" himself, his customers and his siblings, in hopes of generating love and compassion, even tolerance, among them. Understanding the iterative impact of nurturing other people far beyond their physical needs is paramount to approaching these authors' treatment of cooking in southern culture.

In *Walking across Egypt,* the core of Mattie Rigsbee's world is cooking for people, anyone and everyone that she can entice to share her table. Preparing a meal means more to Mattie than simply completing a household chore; cooking has become a means of personal expression. However she interacts with people, she feeds them. For Mattie her cooking not only secures her reputation as "the best cook" anyone has ever known—one so good that a young man risks his freedom to steal her pound cake—it also satisfies her sense of Christian benevolence and supports her claim of independence and productivity at age seventy-eight. Joe Gray Taylor, in his "informal" history of southern hospitality, notes that when ordinary southerners open their doors, they open them wide, offering "a table loaded to the extent of [their] ability" (46-47). Mattie welcomes anyone, including the dogcatcher, the upholsterer and a fugitive juvenile delinquent, and escorts each to her table which is trimmed with the best that she has.

Even though Mattie takes pride in her cooking (and her household routines), she minimizes both its value and her own efforts. Deciding to have her kitchen-table chairs reupholstered, Mattie calls Bill Yeats to do the job and seizes the opportunity to invite him to come at lunch time, for she would "have a little bite for him to eat" (5). She assures him that having him as lunch guest has not altered her daily routine, for she cooks "three meals a day" while living on her own: "Alora brought me some corn last Friday and it was too much for one fixing, so I had some left and these potatoes are from Sunday" (7). She again reminds him that "it's not much," knowing that this young man has probably never had a better meal. Mattie deemphasizes her role in the lunch with Bill not only because she has, in fact, prepared such meals for years as part of her daily routine, but also because she doesn't want Bill to feel that he has burdened her or has been the least bit troublesome.

Not only does Mattie take great pride in her cooking, but she also treasures her independence. At seventy-eight she still cares for herself and her home with little assistance from her grown children, Robert and Elaine, even though she reminds everyone that she is "slowing down" (5). Cooking is not only part of what Mattie does but what, in fact, she is. She contributes her health and continued independence to her good diet (81). In Mattie's opinion the quality of life hinges on the kinds of food that people eat as evident in her primary concern about the dogcatcher's juvenile delinquent nephew, Wesley, because "the food he got wasn't very good" (80).

Overcoming her sense of practicality, Mattie must even feed a stray dog that wanders up at her back door, begging for food. While she repeatedly tells herself and others that she cannot keep a dog because she is "slowing down," she also continues to feed the mutt. Even after Lamar takes the dog away, Mattie asks about him and considers saving him from being put to sleep.

With her children gone and no grandchildren to occupy her time or mind, Mattie attempts to maintain a sense of purpose and normality. Structuring her life in this way and retaining her role as nurturer are Mattie's ways of dealing with the "empty nest" syndrome, "a grim reality" for most mothers (Bernard 292). She further deals with this void, however, as she dutifully "reminds" her children of their inadequacies—"It was her duty to remind them . . . a main reason mothers existed. To remind"—and as she constantly coordinates her plans to bring her family or even a surrogate one together for whom she can cook (52, 134).

Cooking for Mattie also serves her Christian ministry. She often makes reference to Matthew 25:40: "Inasmuch as ye have done it unto one of the least of these my brethren ye have done it unto me" (77). When Mattie first learns that Wesley is in the Young Men's Rehabilitation Center (YMRC), a detention facility for delinquent youth, her initial concern is his well-being there as she makes immediate plans to fix him something to eat (77). Mattie remains solid in her Christian faith, yet she realizes that she needs people, flesh and blood, preferably those that she can cook for, that faith in Jesus alone does not provide.

Mattie, in fact, addresses almost every situation and problem with her cooking. Even when a bothersome neighbor visits her, Mattie still asks her if she wants to "stay and eat a bit," while telling herself that she wishes that Alora would go home (30). This response stems not from superficiality of perception but from limitations. The seemingly obvious restrictions have been imposed by enduring seventy-eight years in the narrowness of a woman's role in a traditional southern society. As Mattie reflects, her life has been consumed with meeting other people's needs, usually the most basic ones: "I've . . . took care and took care and took care and I've done a good job of it: clothed and fed and cared for a husband and two children" (78). Robert, who seems reasonably shallow, recognizes the closely fixed parameters of his mother's life, even though he knows (and envies) her inner strength: "She had a lot of things, a lot of ways that would have served her well out in the real world if she'd ever gotten out there" (53).

Mattie's assuming the role of a surrogate mother for Wesley—even though she later tells Elaine that she is going to marry him because "*somebody* needed to get married" (222)—represents her attempt to fulfill her wishes and to stifle her fears about the genealogical death of her family as well as her own death *sans progeny*. Bringing Wesley into her home and into her care gives Mattie someone to cook for; after all, this young man did forfeit his freedom, after escaping from the YMRC, just to get some of Mattie's pound cake.

Fried Green Tomatoes at the Whistle Stop Cafe is a novel of many stories, set in places from Whistle Stop, Alabama, to Chicago, Illinois, intricately woven into years from 1917 to 1988, told through many voices, including that of an eighty-six-year-old nursing home resident who links the past and present and that of the editor of *The Weems Weekly*, the Whistle Stop weekly newsletter. Characters, connected by time and place, migrate in, and sometimes out, of each other's lives; their individual stories become part of another's and so the links are formed. Mrs. Cleo Threadgoode, "Ninny," reaching into the past which seems much more real and more immediate than the present day, resurrects her family and friends of Whistle Stop. As she pieces together the lives of her husband's family, for she has none of her own, and those around them, these figures from the past become as approachable to the reader as Ninny herself.

One of the strongest narrative streams of the novel recaptures the devotion and love between two women, Idgie (Ninnie's sister-in-law) and Ruth. Idgie, an aggressive but truly brave individual, denounces femininity but retains a powerful, nurturing maternity. After Ruth's marriage to an abusive man, it is Idgie who saves her and makes a secure life—at the Whistle Stop Cafe—where they can raise Ruth's son.

For the women of Flagg's novel, cooking is the focal point of much of their daily lives. For Ruth and Idgie, as well as the restaurant's cooks Sipsey and Onzell, cooking fundamentally serves them as a means to support themselves and thus to secure their independence. The cafe is a simple extension of the home where the "kitchen is the hub of social intercourse" (Aptheker 50). Whether selling food or giving it away to the neighboring blacks and boxcar hobos from the backdoor of the Whistle Stop, both Idgie and Ruth carry on their own isolated yet fervent efforts to combat the injustices of the South in the days before the civil rights movement and after the Depression.

For Idgie, preparing food for her "front door" customers is only the superficial function of the restaurant, not her mission or ministry. A rebellious creature, she has spent most of her life grooming a relentless determination to live out her convictions. As a child of ten or eleven, Idgie simply stood up at the dinner table "and announced, just as loud . . . 'I'm never gonna wear another dress as long as I live!' And with that . . . she marched upstairs and put on a pair of Buddy's old pants and a shirt" (13). Years later, she poses as Railroad Bill, thought to be a Negro man, who throws food off the government supply trains for the area's poor people, mostly blacks and hobos.

Ruth and Idgie share with less fortunates, even in economically strained years. With the Ku Klux Klan members paying visits, usually addressing themselves to the frank-talking, brassy Idgie, not the gentle, soft-spoken Ruth, the backdoor business of the cafe undergoes some modifications: "After that day, the only thing that changed was on the menu that hung on the back door; everything was a nickel or a dime cheaper" (55). That humble discount seems more substantial when weighed against the menu prices on the grand opening on 12 June 1929, when for breakfast a customer could get "eggs, grits, biscuits, bacon, sausage, ham and red-eye gravy, and coffee for 25¢ . . . For lunch and supper you can have: fried chicken; pork chops and gravy; catfish; chicken and dumplings; or a barbecue plate; and your choice of three vegetables, biscuits or cornbread, and your drink and dessert—for 35¢" (4).

Not only do Ruth and Idgie pursue their mission of cooking for people, but so does Sipsey, whose cooking talents brought the local consensus that "there wasn't a better cook in the state of Alabama" (48). Sipsey, in turn, "taught Idgie and Ruth everything they knew about cooking" (48). She makes a living working at the Whistle Stop Cafe, but more importantly, she spends her entire life nurturing and protecting the same people that she cooks for, including an orphan baby boy that she raises as her son. Sipsey works diligently in the cafe to feed people but also to support Ruth and Idgie. Sharing Sipsey's loyalty, Onzell nurses Ruth on her death bed, accepting no one's help or allowing no interference of "Miz" Ruth's care. These four women, over many years and many hot stoves, make a life to sustain themselves as well as nurture other people. Moreover, no color distinctions interrupt or cloud their relationships.

As the novel shifts from the primary narrator, Ninny Threadgoode, to her stories, an intense relationship between two women of different generations unfolds. During her stay at Rose Terrace Nursing Home, Ninny develops a friendship with the middle-aged Evelyn Couch. Food surfaces again and again as a bonding element in their relationship. Evelyn is starving for understanding of herself and meaning in life. Ninny is hungry for home life—"I miss the smell of coffee . . . and bacon frying in the morning" (7)—and for human companionship. Unhappy with herself as much as with anyone else, Evelyn eats and eats and eats. Ninny talks and talks and talks, comforting Evelyn with "Well, honey, a candy bar's not gonna hurt you" (67). She waits patiently for her surrogate daughter's visit to the nursing home. Evelyn, who dreaded the trips to Rose Terrace before she meets Mrs. Threadgoode and hears her stories, eagerly anticipates returning to the company and the comfort of the old woman.

On Evelyn's last visit before Ninny's death—just prior to leaving for a California "fat farm"—Evelyn prepares Ninny a special lunch:

> When Mrs. Threadgoode saw what she had on her plate, she clapped her hands, as excited as a child on Christmas. There before her was a plate of perfectly fried green tomatoes and fresh cream-white corn, six slices of bacon, with a bowl of baby lima beans on the side, and four huge light and fluffy buttermilk biscuits.
>
> (355)

So long the recipient of Ninny's patient and consistent attention, Evelyn is finally capable of nurturing Ninny, whose physical needs at the age of eighty-seven are the most immediate. Ninny leaves Evelyn Sipsey's recipes (which Flagg gives as an addendum to the novel), but in recalling the past, she gives Evelyn a recipe for salvaging her life, for nourishing herself.

When the woman in the kitchen *only* cooks the food and puts it on the table, nurturing does not exist. The literal act of frying chicken and cornbread, creaming potatoes, boiling field peas and butterbeans and baking biscuits does not constitute true southern cooking. The preparation alone is not enough; completing the task of cooking is, in fact, the least significant aspect of its role in southern culture. Rather, what is crucial is the social and emotional intercourse between the preparer and the partaker of the food.

In Tyler's *Dinner at the Homesick Restaurant*, Pearl Tull does prepare meals, though usually very bad ones, for her three children (160). She does not physically starve them, but she does not feed them emotionally or psychologically. Pearl is "a non-feeder, if ever there was one" (159). Cody, Ezra and Jenny hunger as children and throughout their adult lives for nurturance, though not simply maternal, but for a filling, satisfying source of nourishment. Ezra commits himself to complete the meal that his mother has left undone.

Discussing the sense of family and community in the novel, Paula Gallant Eckard notes that customers frequent the Homesick Restaurant to "get those foods for which they are 'homesick.' They can be nourished in body and spirit much as they would be at home" (41). Ezra is "a feeder. . . . There was something tender, almost loving, about his attitude toward people who were eating what he'd cooked them" (161), unlike his mother whose "expression, while others ate or drank, conveyed a mild distaste . . . and she implied some criticism of those who acted hungry or overinterested in what they were served" (160). She responds negatively to anyone's "neediness," including her own, stifling her needs and thus feeling more comfortable in denying anyone else's.

Ezra's efforts are materialized in his Homesick Restaurant, "a place for him to mother people, to fill them with garlicky soups 'made with love' [119], to advise them on what to eat to ease their complaints" (Elkins 128). He repeatedly bears witness to the healing powers of food that has been prepared with care and served with compassion. Mary J. Elkins, in an article which explores *Dinner at the Homesick Restaurant* and William Faulkner's *As I Lay Dying*, maintains that "Ezra's restaurant is a substitution for reality; it is in a sense a creation of a home for himself with all the elements of the women's-magazine-mothering. . . . There is no trace of Ezra's real mother here" (128). Ezra welcomes people with needs, for his ministry to feed others simultaneously achieves his own mission to restore a personal sense of home and nurture himself. Joseph C.

Voelker precisely analyzes Ezra's behavior and motivations: "In gentle but stubborn reaction to his past, Ezra opens a restaurant that is no a home but as a home might be—a consoling place, where the perfect balance of emotional closeness and distance is attained, where a meal is a source of comfort, no an occasion for bitterness, breakup, and lonely retreat. Ezra's restaurant is a extension of his own nurturing soul. His mother could not feed; she poured canned pea over the children's heads. Ezra dedicates his adult life to the sacramental aspects of dinner, a melting away of differences in a higher commonality" (129).

While Ezra does not have the strong familial bonds that he would like with his immediate family, he does secure a sense of community and even family in his restaurant. While his menu reflects the regional talents with "pot roast . . . pan-fried potatoes, black-eyed peas, beaten biscuits" (137), his restaurant ministry captures the intricate role of cooking in southern culture wherein the "feeder's" mission is to fill stomach, spirit and soul. Ezra presses on, as he "continues to cook and serve and nurture" (Eckard 43).

But why *is* cooking so intimate to southerners and so ostentatious in southern culture? Is it a patriarchally imposed, gender-designated task that southern women have embraced for a sense of purpose, willfully or subconsciously or reluctantly? Or perhaps the "nurturing values provide a counterpoint to patriarchal values" (Christ 82)? Or is it, at least for some, a readily available occasion for martyrdom?

Although the "cooks" in the three novels explored here do not set themselves up as martyrs, martyrs they could easily be. They each deal with situations and problems with a means available to them—cooking. The ability to reconcile the circumstances and the possible (and even practical) responses and reactions to them functions to confirm the ingrained determination to "do the best you can." As Bettina Aptheker notes, "[W]e see that many of our mothers [and other maternal figures] sacrificed, worked hard, nurtured, did the best they could to 'make do,' to improve the quality of our daily lives" (40). As Dilsey, in Faulkner's *The Sound and the Fury,* tries to cater to the Compson family with Caroline screaming, Benjy whining and Mrs. Compson complaining, she remains the "vital presence" (Williams 90). Dilsey alone is the "keeper of the peace, the protector and constant nourisher" (Williams 90). Faulkner captures her ultimate role as the endurer (427).

The cooks in *Walking across Egypt, Fried Green Tomatoes at the Whistle Stop Cafe* and *Dinner at the Homesick Restaurant* all endure. Mattie maintains her challenge to stay independent and to feed anyone who will let her, even if she has to adopt him as she does Wesley. The final scene of the novel finds her serving Lamar another meal as they make plans for her becoming Wesley's guardian. Although Ruth dies in *Fried Green Tomatoes at the Whistle Stop Cafe,* she remains alive to those who love her, especially Idgie, her son Stump and the hobo, Smokey Lonesome. Idgie is surely the unnamed keeper of a roadside stand on Highway 90 in Marianna, Florida, an old woman with "snow-white hair and brown weatherbeaten skin" who sustains the same sharp wit, love of fun and open generosity that she did as the owner of the Whistle Stop Cafe. Ezra, too, continues to cook and nurture, nurture and cook. Their missions and ministries prevail.

Bearing not one shred of domesticity or culinary expertise myself, I am the daughter, the granddaughter, the niece and the cousin of some extraordinary southern cooks (and extraordinary women in general, for that matter). Each is heartily praised for individual specialities; each holds a place in the hierarchy. My mother, a child nutritionist, has literally devoted her life to "feeding folks." Her traditional orientations toward meeting the physical nutritional needs of people, in concert with her feminist convictions that a woman's place is "anywhere she damned well pleases," have fostered her extending that sense of nurturance to the professional sphere. Both maternal and paternal grandmothers are known throughout our hometown community of Cool Springs, near Enterprise, Alabama, as "good cooks." While Mama's mama, "Bigmama," fancies baking "sweets"—cakes, pies, cookies and custards—my Daddy's mama, "Grandmother," is labeled by many as "the best cook that ever walked into a kitchen or greased a pan." My grandfather's reasoning for refusing to eat in a restaurant is simply, "with cooking like that, why, that woman—if she is my wife—can flat shore cook; why, it beats all I've ever seen." At seventy-eight she still cooks three meals a day.

A fear that someone may come to their house hungry drives all of these women always to "have somethin' fixed." Like Mattie, who keeps a running menu of what she can prepare in a moment's notice, they overcook and save and plan. The far-reaching scope of a problematic situation or a troublesome circumstance can be immediately addressed over "a bite to eat," which promises to soothe and heal even though it cannot cure or solve anything. Sometimes, they feel compelled to justify their value in the home and community, just as Sister, in Eudora Welty's "Why I Live at the P.O." "humbly" acknowledges her fate, standing "over the hot stove, trying to stretch two chickens over five people and a completely unexpected child into the bargain, without one moment's notice" (46). Southerners cook for themselves as they prepare food for others; the nurturance is simultaneous, just as filling, just as satisfying, just as essential.

Note

1. Linda Wagner-Martin notes how Alice Walker uses the word *barbecue* to show a "point of intersection," as she draws "parallels between the culture of the African Olinkas and the Southern blacks" in *The Color Purple* (22).

Works Cited

Apetheker, Bettina. *Tapestries of Life: Women's Work, Women's Consciousness and the Meaning of Daily Experience.* Amherst: U of Massachusetts P, 1989.

Christ, Carol P. *Diving Deep and Surfacing: Women Writers on Spiritual Quest.* Boston: Beacon, 1980.

Douglas, Mary, ed. *Food in the Social Order: Studies in Food and Festivities in Three American Communities.* New York: Sage, 1984.

Edgerton, Clyde. *Walking across Egypt.* Chapel Hill: Algonquin, 1987.

Elkins, Mary J. "*Dinner at the Homesick Restaurant*: Anne Tyler and the Faulkner Connection." *The Fiction of Anne Tyler.* Ed. C. Ralph Stephens. Jackson: UP of Mississippi, 1990. 119-35.

Flagg, Fannie. *Fried Green Tomatoes at the Whistle Stop Cafe.* New York: McGraw, 1987.

Grover, Kathryn, ed. *Dining in America: 1850-1900.* Amherst: U of Massachusetts P, 1987.

Hagood, Margaret Jarman. *Mothers of the South: Portraiture of the White Tenant Farm Woman.* New York: Norton, 1977.

Kanoza, Theresa. "Mentors and Maternal Role Models: The Healthy Mean between Extremes in Anne Tyler's Fiction." *The Fiction of Anne Tyler.* Ed. C. Ralph Stephens. Jackson: UP of Mississippi, 1990. 28-39.

Martin, Linda Wagner. "'Just the doing of it': Southern Women Writers and the Idea of Community." *Southern Literary Journal* 22.2 (1990): 19-32.

McKern, Sharon. *Redneck Mothers, Good Ol' Girls and Other Southern Belles: A Celebration of the Women of Dixie.* New York: Viking, 1979.

Prenshaw, Peggy Whitman. *Women Writers of the Contemporary South.* Jackson: UP of Mississippi, 1984.

Spruill, Julia Cherry. *Women's Life and Work in the Southern Colonies.* Chapel Hill: U of North Carolina P, 1938.

Stephens, C. Ralph. *The Fiction of Anne Tyler.* Jackson: UP of Mississippi, 1990.

Taylor, Joe Gray. *Eating, Drinking, and Visiting in the South: An Informal History.* Baton Rouge: Louisiana State UP, 1982.

Thomas, Sherry. *We Didn't Have Much, But We Sure Had Plenty.* Garden City, NY: Anchor, 1981.

Tyler, Anne. *Dinner at the Homesick Restaurant.* New York: Knopf, 1982.

Voelker, Joseph C. *Art and the Accidental in Anne Tyler.* Columbia: UP of Missouri, 1989.

Welty, Eudora. "Why I Live at the P.O." *The Collected Stories of Eudora Welty.* New York: Harcourt, 1980.

Jan Nordby Gretlund (essay date 1996)

SOURCE: Gretlund, Jan Nordby. "Josephine Humphreys's New Southerner." In *Frames of Southern Mind: Reflections on the Stoic, Bi-Racial & Existential South*, pp. 219-30. Odense, Denmark: Odense University Press, 1998.

[*In the following essay, first published in 1996, Gretlund discusses Josephine Humphreys's existentialism as seen through the choices her characters make in their daily lives and in particular Southern locales.*]

In his book on *Space and Place* Yi-Fu Tuan argues that place is different from space due to "locational qualities" associated with the contemplation of place.[1] From his mentioning of "the security and stability" of place it is clear that Yi-Fu Tuan endows place with values and complex emotions. "Place" is a more comprehensive word than "scene" or "landscape," it comprehends not only the natural physical characteristics, but also the sensory and imaginative experience of the setting. Place and sense of place both depend for their meaning on the human element, the presence of people and their feelings. We tend to measure ourselves against place and try to become a part of its more enduring identity. In this sense the psychological and existential ties that characterize a profound attachment to a place imply a universal desire to transcend the present. The critic must ask: what does consciousness of the landscape mean to the artist personally? And, how has it colored her description of the place and influenced its function in the particular story?

Like Donald Davidson's "autochthonous" Southern writer, described in his Lamar lectures, Josephine Humphreys is in a certain harmony with her social and cultural environment. But unlike Davidson's ideal writer, Humphreys *is* motivated by an urge to question, interpret, and explain the psychosocial situation in her Southern landscape. I will try to analyze the influence of the Southern landscape on Humphreys's fiction. What makes it a rewarding approach is her obvious identification with her town, her state, and its people.

It is both "natural and sensible" that our place of origin should also become the "primary proving ground" of our fiction, as Welty put it in "Place in Fiction."[2] Humphreys's fiction has come out of the particular landscape of her place of origin and is based on her long familiarity with its people, and her art is always bound to her Carolina. A sense of Charleston is "the whole foundation" on which her fiction rests, and she has devoted much time and space to it, but Humphreys never reduces her concept of her city to a simple definition.

Realism is above all what Humphreys has in common with Eudora Welty. Whatever they write, it is always wedded to place, they are "touched off by place," and place keeps them "responsible" for what they have put down for the truth. It would be difficult to find a writer who identifies with her community *more* than Humphreys does. Her favorite setting is without doubt Charleston. The city has a stubborn peculiarity of its own, and Humphreys has proved remarkably responsive to the past and present of her city. S. T. Coleridge was so taken up with German Idealism and so thoroughly convinced that the mind creates the world that he had only a limited sense of place. It is perhaps what primarily distinguishes Coleridge from his sometime friend William Wordsworth, who was totally convinced of the reality of what he saw about him, and whose sense of place is the heart of his poetry.

It was easy for Wordsworth to identify with the English landscape of his day. Today's creative artist in South Carolina has to look for the landscape behind a repetitive labyrinth of highways, motels, burger-places, gas stations, shopping malls etc. It is a modular world in which most of us are too easily at home because things are everywhere the same. What Humphreys has proved is that it is not merely pockets of virgin forests and overlooked (and therefore) unpolluted streams that awaken a feel for a place, but also cities. The city estranges us from the world *only* when it rapes and obliterates its site. Unfortunately, it has happened in Charleston and Mount Pleasant:

> Originally we had the city of Charleston, the town of Mount Pleasant, and then the country, but now they were jumbled, haphazard as a frontier settlement. . . . I was always impressed on this highway by the hordes of people stocking up on new shoes, blue jeans, groceries, hamsters, mini-vans, tomato plants, sheets of plywood, ice-cream cones. The level of shopping was an indicator, . . . , of human trust in the future. I myself sometimes woke up in the middle of the night scared to death. . . . I had studied the town of Herculaneum, buried by hot mud in the year 79 A. D. My town had been similarly engulfed, not by mud but by overflow from the city of Charleston. . . .
>
> (*Rich in Love*, 3, 5, 11)

The identification of writer and home ground is unmistakable, and it is obvious from the fidelity to every detail that a special relationship exists between the writer and her place. Her town and state are not only the geographical and sociological settings of much of her fiction, they are parts of her interior landscape.

By studying her native place and expressing its essence in fiction, Humphreys studies her own self. She may satirize the people she sees about her in Charleston and elsewhere, but the purpose is always to amuse by displaying the folly of mankind and to offer laughter as a means of questioning our concept of "sanity." It is never to expose or ridicule her own community. The Faulknerian element of pity for the individual in his misfortune is always present. If we recognize flaws and elements of the grotesque in her characters, it is probably as reflections of our own limitations. Humphreys can negate her own emotions and enter all of her characters, give them life, and bring out their humanity in all their ways wherever they live; but it is extremely important just *where* they live. The strength of her sense of place is identification in her fictional territory, *both* with her native area and its people. Without trivializing the actual landscape, Humphreys's preoccupation with Charleston goes beyond the precise, identifiably local, and mimetic descriptions of life in that city to intimations of a universal landscape of timeless joys and sorrows. The art is that the cityscape of her novels encompasses everything that happens, has happened, and will happen for as long as landscape and memory exist. And the readers know they are a part of her map of that landscape.

The contemporary Southern novel has become increasingly city-oriented with novelists such as Ann Beattie, Doris Betts, Larry Brown, Clyde Edgerton, Shelby Foote, Kaye Gibbons, Barry Hannah, Madison Jones, Bobbie Ann Mason, Walker Percy, and Peter Taylor. Even when they set their plots in rural areas, the issues are mostly those of city-people, and the problems are those of moviegoers, kidnappers, college youths in jeans, city-doctors, and city-lawyers. A preoccupation with the city is nothing new in Southern fiction, novel after novel throughout the Southern Renaissance focused on the lives of young Southerners stranded in cities. Eugene Gant in Thomas Wolfe's *Of Time and the River,* Quentin Compson in William Faulkner's *The Sound and the Fury,* and Peyton Loftis in William Styron's *Lie Down in Darkness* are classic examples. In the impersonal crowds up North the young Southerners find themselves completely cut off from everybody, and for them the city becomes a nightmare experience.

But when they try to "go home," they find it impossible. If they attempt to function as members of their native communities, they are usually unable to accept the home community as found, for to their surprise the ways of the big cities have been imported there while they were away. So on their return they often fail to find any justification for their belief in the value of a life removed from metropolitan ways. They are forced to realize that their images of an agrarian South are images of the past, and that even at home the present offers no refuge from the placelessness of the city. So the return to the rural areas around Asheville, Nashville, Clarksville, Milledgeville, Charlottesville, Louisville, or Greenville never become real homecomings. Dreams of a traditional agrarian life-pattern are easily starved in the face of what John Shelton Reed called a reality of "instant grits and plastic-wrapped crackers."[3] Their fiction profited greatly, however, from the young writers' excursions to the Northern cities, and much of the best fiction of the Southern Renaissance was constructed on the foundation of those experiences. A young Southerner in search of city-experience today need not go North. The urbanization of the South and to some extent of its culture is *the* important sociological fact of the South after the Depression. Several Southern cities have developed rapidly from rural towns to modern industrial cities. Such urbanization is nothing new for the United States in general, where three fourths of the population already long has lived on about one percent of the land, but for the South it is a fairly recent development.

Fictional portraits of city life involve an obvious selective process, and the elements selected by Humphreys to represent life in cities make it impossible to overlook an implicit judgment. In her portrait of the city she is in tune with Thomas Jefferson, who wrote in his *Notes on the State of Virginia*: "The mobs of great cities add just so much to the support of pure government, as sores do to the strength of the human body."[4] And Humphreys is in tune with ideas about the development of American history going back at least to Frederick Jackson Turner: the city leaves its mark on mind and manners, and the impact on the individual of urban life is decidedly different from that of life in the country. This is usually mentioned *not* in praise of modern cities, but to remind us of American values and ideas associated with life on the frontier in the 18th and 19th centuries. These are values that have supposedly survived into our century among Americans living on and off the country.[5]

In the "citified world" a Humphreys character may feel "twined in" and insecure:

> If there were such a thing as a safe place, she knows it would have to be here in Charleston. It was for safety these houses were built, crowded together on the peninsula behind a wall to keep out Indians, Spaniards, outlaws. And now tourists come to see the place. . . . In the suburbs as shown on television, women drink coffee together in their kitchens and men borrow tools from each other. But here [in the city] people keep to themselves.
>
> (*Dreams of Sleep*, 6-7)

It is the woman's husband who wants to live where they do, which does not mean that he is not worried:

> Maybe he shouldn't leave his children alone in the house, even for the few minutes it will take him to walk to her car and back. Maybe he ought to lock the door. "Will they be safe by themselves?" Marcella [his mother] asks. "Of course," he says. . . . He could live in a safer place. He could live downtown near the Battery instead of in this ambiguous zone between rich and poor . . . but he won't move, he has set his family here. "Courting disaster," Alice [his wife] says.
>
> (*Dreams of Sleep*, 50-51)

The loss of a sense of security in the traditional place, Leonard Lutwack talks of "the pain of placelessness," is a characteristic that makes him a typical city-dweller.[6] Will Reese is moving in the stultifying atmosphere of an acquisitive and dehumanizing civilization. The impact on him of modern urbanized life is a profound sense of loss. As Blanche H. Gelfant describes the reactions of a man in the situation, Will feels he has failed somehow and that any course of action may involve him in "serious self-contradictions, if not indeed in self-destruction."[7]

Today most Southerners are not only citified, but also city-born, and their mental states are influenced by skyscrapers and shopping-malls in the urban sprawl. Is the citizen of the Southern urban industrial setting necessarily anonymous, rootless, insecure, alienated, and cut off from human relationships? Is he also enslaved by the media, paralyzed by traffic, and victimized because of caste and class, or by crimes and violence? Humphreys does not denounce the city-tied Southerner, instead she tells us with compassion how he lives in the citified world.

The emphasis in Humphreys's fiction is always on the individual character and his emotions. But by necessity the individual is in a place and in an interrelationship with the community of that place. With her accepted sense of place comes the acceptance of a whole body of thought founded on her situatedness in place and community. A sense of a particular landscape implies a sense of continuity, and both concepts presuppose and are based on the history of the place, are bound by the emotions of the individual, and indicate a sense of community with the generations of people who lived there. It is essential to understand this element in her art to grasp Humphreys's relationship with her community.

In one of her talks Flannery O'Connor said: "The novelist is required to open his eyes on the world around him and look. If what he sees is not highly edifying, he is still required to look."[8] Throughout the 70s and 80s Southern politicians have given emphasis to the interrelationship between place and community, and they have warned against the impact of change upon the values Southerners associate with their region. In 1975 Governor Reubin Askew of Florida said: "The economic development of the South need not result in the degradation of our land or the deprivation of our people. . . . We cannot allow what has happened in the North to happen here in the South."⁹ The main reason for the concern in the midst of all the talk about growth was expressed by Gov. David Boren, who chaired the Southern Growth Policies Board in 1977. He asked: "How do we keep alive the values that make our system and our section so vital?"¹⁰ The important question for these politicians and for Southern writers is whether it is possible to urbanize and yet keep basic Agrarian values. Is it possible to avoid creating polluted and devastated cities and alienated people by simply emphasizing the old values of a sense of place, a sense of community, and an awareness of the past? When she sees the importance of traditional values and virtues for individual and community even in the *urban* South, Humphreys is in the mainstream of Southern thinking of the last two decades.

Like everybody else Humphreys's characters learn that it is tough to be anybody. Living with yourself and others means that existential choices have to be made. The decisive factors for the choice are values with their origin in the community. The existential choice takes its point of departure in the individual's sense of place and community and has consequences for the ethics of the individual and for the community. This passage is from the opening of her third novel:

> It was only by chance that the general ruin, the wreckage of the mainland city and its islands, coincided with the specific ruin of himself. The two things simply happened together: the place ravaged by hurricane, the man by something more complicated. . . . Now was the time to do it. With the whole place thrown into confusion, one man's leap into a small personal chaos would be less noticeable. . . . He saw with the eyes of a boy again. There were possibilities afoot, even in the midst of ruin.
>
> (*Fireman's Fair*, 1, 11, 14)

Humphreys describes a place in detail because she writes about human beings, and to understand and define them, it is essential in her aesthetics of place to locate them. Their meaning always bears on what they came out of, and it is defined by it. In important respects we are products of our native place, its history, its atmosphere, i. e. its essence of place. It is, of course, also true of the artist who celebrates a place.

Humphreys's idea of place involves more than memories of times past, her "—place" is also time made visible. Charleston houses a tradition-oriented and class-conscious community. Originally the physical setting still shaped the social interaction in town, but the relationship between place and social place has weakened considerably in the town. For the young generation there is now a dissociation, so that their behavior is no longer determined or defined by their physical presence in the town. Humphreys seems to be implying that the next generation may grow up without the steadying point of place to focus their minds. As Joshua Meyrowitz has shown in his *No Sense of Place*, the physical location is hardly ever the social place in the new world of electronic media.¹¹ The community is changing rapidly, it is becoming fragmented, a sense of self is no longer necessarily ingrained with a sense of community, and in as far as a social order exists, it is becoming impersonal, technological, and increasingly disneyfied. In Humphreys's fiction some of the plans for Charleston's future include:

> "A theme park." "Theme park?" "Yes, you know, like Six Flags or Carowinds." "Disney World." "No, no. . . . This will be much more low-key, more in tune with the environment and related to the historical traditions of the area." . . . "What's the theme?" "Pirates. To tie in with the riverfront. We'll have a couple of pirate ships that actually go out, take people on the river, out to Drum Island, where we'll give them maps to dig for buried treasure. Everything will have the pirate theme. Our hotel, the restaurant, the villas. It's natural because there really were pirates here. One of them was hanged on the Battery. We plan to reenact it." . . . "Oh God," Will says. "Let him have the goddamned thing. . . . We'd rather have you than those fuckers. Atlantans and Arabs! They're the same, except the Arabs are cleaner. Atlantans will mess with anything." . . . "Oh, no. This is local money. Local people. In fact the initial idea came from them.
>
> (*Dreams of Sleep*, 178, 181)

Personal relations in the community are decaying, and a chance to make a good investment could easily matter more than any residue of reverence for the historic city—even for a true son of Charleston.

Humphreys's novels come from living in South Carolina—they are *part* of living in Charleston, of her long familiarity with the thoughts and feelings of those around her in that modern landscape. She *demonstrates* that the role of place in fiction is "to attach precise local values to feeling."¹² In "Place in Fiction" Welty wrote: "Location is the ground conductor of all the currents of emotion and belief and moral conviction that charge out from the story in its course." In the most recent version of the essay the point is elaborated in an added line, which reads: "From the dawn of man's imagination, place has enshrined the spirit." Humphreys's novels are "enshrined" in her place. Her Charlestonians seem located where they stand—part of their own map.

In important respects our minds are products of our native place, its history, its atmosphere, and its essence of place. Humphreys needs the self-definition of true attachment, a sense of continuity between her past and present, and accepts her relationship with Charleston. The city, she realizes, is an inextricable part of her identity. The community provides the necessary "set of standards to struggle within or against."¹³ Like her fictional characters Humphreys has to see her life in context. She uses the identity of a place to measure herself. And she is finally measured against the enduring identity of her place, which means against all that has happened in Charleston and against all the human relationships that have been experienced there. The history of the city is an ever-present commentary on today's events. In this way the past of Charleston is integrated with its present, and contemporary Charlestonians participate in a drama of place that began before they were born and will end after they are dead. I believe that it is what C. Hugh Holman meant when in an essay on Ellen Glasgow he included "a sense of place as a dramatic dimension" among characteristics that set the best Southern writing apart from much American writing in this century.[14]

Place and writer have sustained each other, and it is obvious that "one is in a bad way without the other," as Walker Percy once put it.[15] As it reveals itself in Humphreys's changing attitude to her place, she continuously defines and redefines her own identity. In her novels she has continued her discovery and constant rediscovery of her place. For the critic it means that a study of Humphreys's idea of place, with a focus on place in fiction, becomes a way of describing her existential practices. It is the human life lived there, geographically and historically, which gives place its emotional impact in her fiction. Humphreys's characters are the place they live. Or better, their place is so much a part of them that their identity depends on the relation, whether it is the identity, present or past, of individual, family, community, city, state, or region.

What makes Humphreys's fiction art is not just the perfect evocation of a particular place, of a changing community, and a historical period, it is the analysis, discovery, and hopefully recognition of the existential landscape that is the result of the evocation of the particular place. Her hometown has changed beyond recognition. Her characters' growing disorientation and feeling of estrangement in Charleston are results of a general sense of malaise and displacement. When she writes about people as she knows them in the here and now, she is writing about everybody.[16] By seeing the particulars of her native place in time, she can successfully approach the universal.

The achievement of a national culture based on modern technology and spatial mobility, instead of a traditional culture based on a sense of place, does not necessarily appeal to Humphreys. She sees clearly what John Crowe Ransom meant when he explained that "what is called progress is often destruction."[17] Warren Odom of *Rich in Love* is Humphreys's representative of the carpeted and air-conditioned Southeast. Odom is a demolition expert, he removes the old buildings to clear the way for the new South:

> You want them to go down straight . . . , like a man shot in the knees, crumpling. . . . His last job was the old Wade Hampton Hotel in Columbia. . . . He stood in its portico, looking out past the spread of Columbia towards the sandhills, and he felt queerly lifted from his own life into a clean and quiet myth. . . . The Wade Hampton had gone down the way he had foreseen. . . . He could claim partial credit for the new look of the cities he loved: Columbia, Charlotte, Atlanta, Charleston. He had help clear the way for all their downtown Mariotts and Sheratons, office plazas and civic centers. Some of those hotels had indoor streams, and vines and trees genuinely growing in the lobby. Those buildings were proof that the Southeast had become nothing to be ashamed of.
>
> (*Rich in Love,* 80, 81, 82)

Other characters of Humphreys's novels look for a cultural continuity of traditional Agrarian ideas from their origin in the rural South to their presence in the urbanized South. Will Reese's and Rob Wyatt's mostly negative images of the city have their origin in their basically Agrarian ideas about place, identity, and a rewarding life. Lyle H. Lanier wrote in his contribution to *I'll Take My Stand*[18] that the real sense of community only exists in the agrarian community, whereas city life necessarily means a diminution of the communal experience and just serves to increase a sense of isolation. The patterns of conduct of city people are supposedly incompatible with the stability and integrity of family life. The good life is in an agrarian setting. Rob's brother Ernie is getting married to Rhonda: "Rhonda's got a little cabin and a horse pasture, horses. . . . I admit, marriage is a big step. I wasn't all for it right away. But I've thought it all out and made the decision." His brother reacts as could be expected, but he is thinking, "*a pasture, a cabin! Rhonda waiting at the cabin door in her faded jeans, the Florida greenery flashing, scrub jays in the piney woods . . .*" (*Fireman's Fair,* 196). The hope for the future based on a life in harmony with nature has been in Humphreys's novels from the start. Will Reese speculates "on the length of time required for vegetation to retake an area the size of the Old South—building, pool, parking lot. If you jackhammered the concrete and asphalt just enough to bust it up, let the seedlings through . . . With the help of kudzu the place could be green, even dense again, in two, three years" (*Dreams of Sleep,* 160). And in the same novel, Iris Moon is greatly relieved when she drives into the low marshland, down the coast of the state, and sees the still open land where Charleston does not yet touch Savannah—as she had feared. "Things are not as bad as you get to thinking they are," she said (*Dreams of Sleep,* 201). The opinion seems echoed in the most recent novel. Rob Wyatt glories in the "splendid sight" of what Hurricane Hugo had done to a golf course at the Sewee Club, he sees that nature has totally reclaimed the fairway, and he feels that "all was not lost" (*Fireman's Fair,* 79).

In his essay "Dodging Apples" Reynolds Price argues that all artists create because they believe in the "value and urgency" of what they see and attempt to understand. His point is that "all works of art came into existence to change something," "to cause some action," "in the hope of altering, literally causing movement" in the writer himself, his reader, and "the world at large."[19] Humphreys's creative principles reveal her moral principles, and her aesthetics of place is not finally distinguishable from the ethics of living in a place and finding one's identity in relation to it. She is not a sociologist trying to right social wrongs, she is not a psychologist trying to explain the origin of wrong, nor is she a preacher choosing between right and wrong. She is a novelist offering her vision of how it is with us now and how it has always been. A distinction between her moral and aesthetic values cannot be final. Like everybody else Humphreys's characters learn that living with yourself and others means that existential choices have to be made. The decisive factors for the existential choice are not abstract, but values with their origin in the community of the place, past and present. The existential choice takes its point of departure in the individual's imaginative sense of place and has consequences for the ethics of the individual and therefore for the community. Alice Reese's aesthetic impression of Charleston life on her way to the supermarket has existential implications for her, and her thoughts on "the project" become an ethical evaluation of herself, and of her time and place:

> The walk to the supermarket takes her through the black neighborhood of midtown. It is not the way she used to go; she used to detour around the project, sticking to the business streets. . . . People stared at her from windows and porches, from cars. Of course they'd stare. It is unheard of in any Southern city for a white person to walk through one of these places, the old colored town now gulped into the city and lost behind stores and hotels. . . . But this is not the worst of the city, it isn't Bayside, where old people don't leave their houses for months at a time, so frightened are they of what is on the street. No, this is just old colored town. . . . It is a pocket of slow, warm living in the middle of town, like a world coexistent with the rest but not visible from it, not from the . . . places white people go. . . . What will happen to all these black people, now the movement is dead, their heroes tucked away in public offices? Was the whole civil rights movement nothing but a minor disturbance in the succession of years? . . . Blacks and whites live farther apart than ever, like the double curve of a hyperbolic function, two human worlds of identical misery and passion but occupying opposite quadrants, nonintersecting.
>
> (*Dreams of Sleep*, 132, 133, 134)

Most of us approach the landscape focused on ourselves, looking for what agrees with our temperaments, and if we are artists, for what seems to embody our emotions, and what will suit us as setting for our creative efforts. Some people, such as Humphreys and Eudora Welty, have the good fortune to be born, and to remain, in country which is continuous with their personalities. When I see a correspondence between Josephine Humphreys's disposition and the scenery of Charleston, I am not implying an easy affinity between writer and city, or a superficial imposition of mood on a place. It is Humphreys's constant awareness of Charleston and South Carolina, and their presence in her mind as something powerfully Other to struggle with, which makes the relationship so valuable for her art.

The landscape as observed by Humphreys is a fusion of human and natural order, and the result may offer a peculiar window on the whole. The catalyst that converts the physical cityscape of Charleston into art is that Humphreys so obviously lays claim to it through her feelings for the city. The sounds and smells and sights and stories of Charleston haunt Humphreys, and it is against them that she measures the present. She responds with mind and body and claims her city and state, and out of her whole response comes her writing. When the nature of Charleston changes, Humphreys is influenced, her human values are affected, and her readers are subtly changed as well.

Josephine Humphreys is a Southern writer finding her place and defining herself in a landscape that is already crowded with talent and much-praised achievement. She is inspired by an innate historical perspective and seems to need the past to understand the present. And she is blessed by a keen sense of place and an obvious sectional pride. She is a great talent and exemplifies the continuity, change, and excellence of Southern fiction.

Notes

1. Yi-Fu Tuan, *Space and Place: The Perspective of Experience,* Minneapolis, University of Minnesota Press, (1977) 1981, p. 6.

2. Eudora Welty, *The Eye of the Story: Selected Essays and Reviews,* New York, Random House, 1978, p. 129.

3. John Shelton Reed, "Instant Grits and Plastic-Wrapped Crackers: Southern Culture and Regional Development," *The American South: Portrait of a Culture,* ed. Louis D. Rubin, Jr., Washington, Forum, 1979, p. 25.

4. Thomas Jefferson, *Notes on the State of Virginia,* ed. William Peden, Chapel Hill, 1955, p. 165.

5. Frederick Jackson Turner, "The Significance of the Frontier in American History," *The Frontier in American History,* ed. Ray Allen Billington, New York, Holt, Rinehart & Winston, 1962 (1920), pp. 1-38.

6. Leonard Lutwack, *The Role of Place in Literature,* Syracuse, New York, Syracuse University Press, 1984, p. 226.

7. Blanche Housman Gelfant, *The American City Novel,* 2nd edition, Norman, University of Oklahoma Press, 1970, p. 23.

8. Flannery O'Connor, *Mystery and Manners,* eds. Sally & Robert Fitzgerald, New York, Farrar, Straus & Giroux, 1969, p. 177.

9. Reubin Askew, "Remarks of the New Chairman," Southern Growth Policies Board, Pinehurst, North Carolina, 13 November, 1975, p. 25. Quoted in Stephen A. Smith, *Myth, Media, and the Southern Mind,* Fayetteville, The University of Arkansas Press, 1985, p. 121.

10. "Governor Boren Pays Tribute to Askew for His Leadership," *Southern Growth: Problems & Promises,* 4 (1977) 2. Quoted in Stephen A. Smith, *Myth, Media, and the Southern Mind,* 1985, p. 121.

11. Joshua Meyrowitz, *No Sense of Place: The Impact of Electronic Media on Social Behavior,* New York, Oxford University Press, 1985.

12. Frederick J. Hoffman, *The Art of Southern Fiction,* Carbondale, Ill., Southern Illinois University Press, 1967, p. 61.

13. This is also a quotation from the original version of Welty's "Place in Fiction." New York, House of Books, Ltd., 1957 [p. 23].

14. C. Hugh Holman, "Ellen Glasgow and the Southern Literary Tradition," *Southern Writers: Appraisals in Our Time,* ed. R. C. Simonni, Jr., Plainview, New York, Books for Libraries Press, (1963) reprt. 1969, p. 123.

15. Walker Percy, "Eudora Welty in Jackson," *Signposts in a Strange Land,* New York, 1991, p. 223.

16. Copy of Welty's untitled speech for the inauguration of Governor William Winter, Mississippi Department of Archives and History, Jackson, ms p. 5.

17. John Crowe Ransom, "The Aesthetic of Regionalism," *American Review* 2 (January 1934) 310.

18. *I'll Take My Stand: The South and the Agrarian Tradition,* by Twelve Southerners (1930), Gloucester, Mass., Peter Smith, 1976, pp. 122-54.

19. Reynolds Price, "Dodging Apples," *Things Themselves: Essays & Scenes,* New York, Atheneum, 1972, pp. 7-12.

John G. Cawelti (essay date 1997)

SOURCE: Cawelti, John G. "Cormac McCarthy: Restless Seekers." In *Southern Writers at Century's End,* edited by Jeffrey J. Folks and James A. Perkins, pp. 164-76. Lexington: The University Press of Kentucky, 1997.

[*In the following essay, Cawelti presents an overview of Cormac McCarthy's career, stressing that his works connect the new Western and the new Southern literature genres through a concern for a sense of the failure of white American culture.*]

Southerners have a favorite set of self-images involving associations with stability, tradition, and dedication to local communities, all the symbology of "down-home." But in fact the South was founded by a horde of restless seekers who left their home places behind them in pursuit of a plethora of dreams: wealth and grandeur, religious salvation, dreams of utopia, or all three in various combinations. Faulkner understood this well, and two of his most significant characters, Thomas Sutpen and Flem Snopes, represent different generations of poor whites seeking to rise in the world. Even Faulkner's great aristocratic families, the Sartorises, the Compsons, and the McCaslins, were founded by such pilgrims.

These men and women were driven by a restlessness and desperation of spirit that urged them on to glorious accomplishment or catastrophic destruction. Such extremities have also been a fundamental part of Southern culture and history. From the beginning, a key dynamic of Southern evangelical Protestantism featured saintly figures like Billy Graham vying for control of the Southern conscience with men athirst for wealth, lust, and power like Jim Bakker, Jimmy Swaggart, and Pat Robertson. The drive toward extremes may also account for the way in which Southern literature has been pervaded by a fascination with the gothic and the grotesque, plumbing the lower depths of society as well as fantasizing about chivalry and nobility. Flannery O'Connor, generally recognized as the most important Southern writer of the generation between the age of Faulkner and the present, was deeply imbued with this fascination as her parables of redemption and damnation in a modernizing South reveal. The most important contemporary inheritor of this stream of Southern literature and culture is a man many consider the most important living Southern writer, Cormac McCarthy.

McCarthy has developed in a very complex fashion, embarking in the last two decades on an almost completely new set of literary ventures, marked by his own restless quest from Knoxville, Tennessee, to El Paso, Texas, from the heart of the South to the edges of the West. In this way, McCarthy not only exemplifies some important aspects of the Southern identity as it is reshaping itself in the era of the Sunbelt, but in a deeper sense he can be seen as a postmodern avatar of that restless drive toward the West that has been a key motive in Southern culture since the first long hunters crossed the Appalachians in search of more game and the plantations began their long push from the Tidewater through the deep South to the plains of Texas.

McCarthy's literary journey embodies this great migration in mythical terms. In his first three novels, *The Orchard Keeper* (1965), *Outer Dark* (1968), and *Child of God* (1973), the protagonists are mountaineers driven or drawn out of their isolated home places into the modern world. *Suttree,* published in 1979, was McCarthy's most ambitious novel up to that time and it was also, as it turned out, his valediction to the middle South; for with his next novel, *Blood Meridian, or The Evening Redness in the West* (1985), McCarthy set forth on the fictional western quest that would soon lead to the first two novels of his announced "Border Trilogy," *All the Pretty Horses* (1992) and *The Crossing* (1994). The last two novels not only rise out of the Southern tradition, but are major reinventions of the Western, reminding us how the great tradition of the modern Western began when a Baltimorean went to Wyoming to recover his health and came back with a novel called *The Virginian* (1902), an epic account of a former Southerner's heroic encounter with badmen (and a New England schoolmarm) in the Wild West.

As McCarthy develops his mythos of the pilgrimage through the fictional world of his imagination, we realize that such quests are never simple. It is often difficult to tell whether McCarthy's seekers are mainly driven by something they flee or drawn by something they seek. Is their quest best defined in terms of a journey through space or into the soul? Is this journey best understood as moving into the future or into the past? Is it toward salvation or damnation? Are these mysterious quests ultimately as incomprehensible as life itself, or is there, in the end, some point to it all? One of the fascinating things about McCarthy is that the quest continues but each new book slightly shifts the grounds traversed by its predecessors. He too still seems to be engaged by the very quest he writes about with such mystery and passion.

* * *

Suttree is McCarthy's longest and most ambitious novel to date. It is also, along with *Blood Meridian,* a major work of culmination and transition in his career. It is in this novel that McCarthy says his symbolic farewell to the South and begins his move from gothic world of the Southern literary tradition to the leaner, more action-filled style of the Western. As a novel, *Suttree* is a culmination and transformation of literary modernism as well as of important aspects of its Southern inheritance. The McCarthy Home Page on the World Wide Web likens *Suttree* to Joyce's *Ulysses*—"the novel's evocation of Joyce's masterpiece, *Ulysses,* is often palpable"—with Suttree "like some latterday Bloom" and Knoxville as a Southern version of "dear, dirty Dublin." There's certainly some truth in this assertion,[1] but McCarthy's most direct predecessors are much closer. McCarthy himself offers homage to the greatest Southern modernist by making Suttree's very name allude to one of Faulkner's most important restless seekers, Thomas Sutpen. But Suttree is in some ways more like Henry than Thomas Sutpen, a latter-day revenant to the family home and the scene of the crime, though it's not at all clear what the crime is. However, the most direct prototype of *Suttree* is Flannery O'Connor's *Wise Blood*. Like an inverted Hazel Motes, Suttree is unwillingly driven toward a goal he does not want to seek. In addition, he is plagued by a sort of disciple whose penchant for the subhuman world takes Enoch Emery's gorilla suit several steps further and includes sexual intercourse with watermelons, a bizarre pursuit of pigs, and an explosion in the Knoxville sewers. Suttree even has relationships with women that are eerily reminiscent of Hazel's involvements with Leora Watts and Sabbath Lily Hawks. *Suttree*'s Knoxville is as much a variation of O'Connor's Taulkinham as it is of Joyce's Dublin.

Like O'Connor's major characters, Suttree is trapped in a world that has lost the sense of the presence of God. However, O'Connor's devout if offbeat Catholicism leads her to frame her stories of modern alienation by constantly hinting that, if we can look beyond the deceptive lights of the modern city, we can always see that "the black sky was underpinned with long silverstreaks that looked like scaffolding and depth on depth behind it were thousands and thousands of stars that all seemed to be moving very slowly as if they were about some vast construction work that involved the whole order of the universe and would take all time to complete" (*Wise Blood* 24).

In O'Connor's world it is always possible for the seeker to encounter transcendence. Sometimes even a person who is not actually seeking, like Ruby Turpin in the story "Revelation," is gifted with a moment of grace. McCarthy was raised a Catholic, but in his cosmos the audience sits in an empty and decaying theater and the minstrel show is long over. There's nothing left but death and silence. Whatever ultimate meaning there may or may not be can be summed up only in such enigmatic axioms as "ruder forms survive."

> The rest indeed is silence. It has begun to rain. . . . Faint summer lightning far downriver. A curtain is rising on the western world. A fine rain of soot, dead

beetles, anonymous small bones. The audience sits webbed in dust. Within the gutted sockets of the interlocutor's skull a spider sleeps and the jointed ruins of the hanged fool dangle from the flies, bone pendulum in motley. Fourfooted shapes go to and fro over the boards. Ruder forms survive.

[*Suttree* 5]

Suttree takes place in Knoxville in the early 1950s, a city on the verge of dramatic changes.[2] The novel ends in 1955 with the tearing down of the old slums in McAnally Flats in order to construct a new expressway, symbolizing Knoxville's hopeful participation in the Sunbelt South with its increasing commercial and industrial linkages to the rest of the country. However, the novel is not primarily concerned with the impinging of modernization on a traditional culture as it might have been had it been written by Bobbie Ann Mason, Lee Smith, Wendell Berry, or any number of other contemporary Southern writers. McCarthy chooses instead to deal with a protagonist and a group of characters whose impoverished marginality makes the new developments wholly irrelevant to them until they are suddenly dispossessed of the decaying area of the city where they live. The inhabitants of McAnally Flats form a grotesque community of exiles and escapees from the modern social order. Suttree is temporarily at home with the anarchic drunkards and grotesque thieves and madmen who live on the flats and on the waste lands along the floodplain of the Tennessee River. Deeply wounded in spirit and a restless seeker himself, Suttree is a kind of fisher king of this community of waste land outcasts. Though scion of a respectable old family, he has left the upper-middle-class world behind and become a derelict fisherman, selling carp and catfish he takes from the river to local butchers.

Yet Suttree is only hanging on in Knoxville, living marginally on its decaying fringes, held by a few residual family ties and by his loyalty to the fellow outcasts and rebels he has met along the river. Everything seems to conspire against his establishing any lasting relationships: his friends are killed by the police, hauled off to prison, or become victims of exposure and alcoholism; a perversely idyllic love affair with a beautiful girl he meets while catching mussels upriver ends tragically when his lover is killed in a rockslide; he almost settles down with a prostitute from Chicago, but just as things are going very well for them she goes violently insane and Suttree has to run for his life; finally, Suttree himself contracts typhoid fever and nearly dies. When he recovers, it is as if he has been inversely born again and everything in his former life has become dead for him. As the novel ends, Suttree passes the site of his former riverside shanty, now the construction site of a new expressway; a car stops for him, though he has not lifted a hand to signal it, and he is gone.

Whether Suttree's incessant seeking is primarily a quest for something beyond or a flight from the demons that haunt him is never fully clear. In fact, at the level of McCarthy's narrative quest and flight, seeking and running away seem to be interchangeable aspects of the same desperation of spirit. The source of this despair is McCarthy's overpowering sense of the brevity, fragility, and impermanence of human order in face of the vast but profoundly beautiful abyss of the cosmos. Above all, McCarthy's narrative gives us a sense of the macroscopic and microscopic, of the reality beyond human culture, the truth of "things known raw, unshaped by the construction of a mind obsessed with form" (427). In sudden flashes his characters reveal a primordial savagery that lurks beneath the surface of civilized society, as if "they could have been some band of stone age folk washed up out of an atavistic dream" (358). Suttree, more than most of the other characters, seems possessed with this sense of ultimate insecurity that pierces him at any moment when he lets his guard down: "he lay on his back in the gravel, the earth's core sucking his bones, a moment's giddy vertigo with this illusion of falling outward through blue and windy space, over the offside of the planet, hurtling through the high thin cirrus" (286).

Through McCarthy's vision we see that it is not the thriving New South city but the outcasts' "encampment of the damned" that is closer to reality, because it reveals the truth of man's folly and mortality: "this city constructed on no known paradigm, a mongrel architecture reading back through the works of man in a brief delineation of the aberrant disordered and mad" (3). In this world the most permanent and lyrical thing is decay, and any belief in permanence is delusion and madness. McCarthy is a veritable Tolstoy of Trash, and his pervasive and redolent poetry of rubble, garbage, and detritus are an ode to the haunting but futile beauty of the brevity and emptiness of human accomplishment against the vast geological panorama of rocks and stars.

However much he may reflect certain aspects of the Eliotic wasteland version of the grail legend, Cormac McCarthy's Suttree is no longer a Christian, nor is the possibility of Christian revelation held out to him, as is the case with Flannery O'Connor's characters. In one especially poignant scene, Suttree wanders into the unused Catholic school where he once studied, and there at this "derelict school for lechers" he finds his old desk and sits at it for a while before he notices a pathetic figure standing in the door of "this old bedroom in this old house where he'd been taught a sort of christian witchcraft." The figure is an old priest who still apparently lives in the deserted school. But there is no contact and no word. "When he came past the stairway the priest was mounted on the first landing like a piece of statuary. A catatonic shaman who spoke no word at all. Suttree went out the way that he'd come in, crossing the grass toward the lights of the street. When he looked back he could see the shape of the priest in the baywindow watching like a paper priest in a pulpit or a prophet sealed in glass" (304-5).

In *Suttree,* McCarthy's world is that of a scientific rather than a religious millenialist, though the biblical overtones of his novel are at times almost overwhelming. McCarthy views human life from the perspective of eternity, yet his version of eternity is the cosmic, geological, and biological immensity that derives from a purely naturalistic vision of the universe. In a way his characters, like O'Connor's, are "god-haunted," and his novels are secular allegories of driven souls fleeing the devil and seeking salvation in a realm across the borders of human good and evil where it is increasingly difficult to distinguish between the holy and the diabolical. This apocalyptic sense, with its implications of violence and destruction, is one aspect of the tradition of extreme individualism in religion and personal violence which John Shelton Reed identifies as a central component of the "enduring South," and which, he suggests, may be becoming an even more important characteristic of Southern culture in the postmodern era.[3]

Though he is haunted by the absence of God from the moment he first appears as a fisherman on the horribly polluted Tennessee River until he shakes the dust of Knoxville from his feet, Suttree has one significant moment of revelation during a trek up into the mountains in his second year on the river. This restless trip becomes a vision quest as Suttree gets increasingly lost and fatigue and hunger undercut his sense not only of where he is but of how long he has been there. Finally a storm that seems to have been following him for days breaks over him, and as he "crouched like an ape in the dark under the eaves of a slate bluff and watched the lightning" he has a vision of the world as a bizarre witches' sabbath with all the eras of evolutionary history mixed together:

> The storm moved off to the north. Suttree heard laughter and sounds of carnival. He saw with a madman's clarity the perishability of his flesh. Illbedowered harlots were calling from small porches in the night, in their gaudy rags like dolls panoplied out of a dirty stream. And along the little ways in the rain and lightning came a troupe of squalid merrymakers bearing a caged wivern on shoulderpoles and other alchemical game, chimeras and cacodemons skewered up on boarspears and a pharmacopeia of hellish condiments adorning a trestle and toted by trolls with an eldern gnome for guidon who shouted foul oaths from his mouthhole and a piper who piped a pipe of ploverbone and wore on his hip a glass flasket of some smoking fuel that yawed within viscid as quicksilver. A mesosaur followed above on a string like a fourlegged garfish helium filled. A tattered gonfalon embroidered with stars now extinct. Nemoral halfworld inhabitants, figures in buffoon's motley, a gross and blueback foe-
>
> tus clopping along in brogues and toga. Attendants attend. Suttree watched these puckish revelers pass with a half grin of wry doubt. Dark closed about him.
>
> [287-88]

After such knowledge, what forgiveness? This vision might serve as a symbolic prophecy of the things experienced by the protagonists of McCarthy's next three novels. For Suttree, his final year on the river brings "a season of death and epidemic violence" (416). Increasingly he feels the coming of the hunter who in some mysterious way has been dogging his steps from the beginning. Finally the destruction of McAnally Flats, the one place in Knoxville he has been able to live in, drives him off the river and onto the road, where "out across the land the lightwires and road rails were going and the telephone lines with voices shuttling on like souls" (471).

* * *

Like his own protagonist, Cormac McCarthy pulled up stakes in Knoxville, leaving there in 1976, around the same time he was completing *Suttree,* and made a major geographical and creative move to the Southwest, settling in El Paso, Texas, which stands on the border between America and Mexico. This symbolic geographical location was the point of departure for McCarthy's next three novels. The book in which McCarthy began his own literary pilgrimage from Tennessee to West Texas is the extraordinary *Blood Meridian,* which combines a nightmarish series of events redolent of Southern Gothic with an anti-heroic quest set in Mexico and the future American Southwest. In some ways a strange sequel to *Huckleberry Finn* and in others, if one can imagine such a contradiction, a pre-Western post-Western, *Blood Meridian* unites the nineteenth-century tradition of western historical fiction springing from Cooper with a postmodernist vision of madness and chaos.[4] It is about the quest-initiation of a young man from Tennessee, known only as "the kid" or "he," who runs away from home in 1841 and eventually wanders westward. He becomes a member of a gang of outlaws and thieves who work the Texas-Mexico borderlands killing Indians and anyone else they think they can plunder.

The world this unnamed young man enters is a chaotic borderland, in both geographical and historical senses. It is the literal border between the United States and Mexico just after the Mexican War, when the definition of national frontiers remained in chaos and much of the land was still occupied by Native Americans hostile to both governments. Historically, the novel covers the period when the modern world first impinged upon the vast spaces of the great Southwest. The story of *Blood Meridian* is not, however, that of the traditional Western, in which heroic pioneers bring civilization to a savage wilderness. On the contrary, what the marauding Glanton gang brings to the borderlands is, if anything, more brutal and savage than the ethos of the violent peoples it encounters and seeks to exterminate.[5] The novel is as much about the twilight of civilization as its dawning.

Like many restless and alienated young men, the kid embarks on his quest looking for adventure and fortune. What he finds everywhere is horror and violence. His wanderings might serve as a nineteenth-century paradigm for the young men whose desperate quests across the border in the aftermath of World War II were the subject of McCarthy's next two "Western" novels.

McCarthy's "Western" fiction, like the transitional *Blood Meridian,* tells a story characteristic of much contemporary Western fiction: a young man's initiation into manhood. The Western version of this archetypal theme is very often connected, as were many novels of the Southern Renascence and McCarthy's own "Southern" fiction, with a deep sense of belatedness and loss, as if the world no longer offers young men the possibilities and the satisfactions of earlier times. Larry McMurtry created an important contemporary version of this story in his two early novels of Thalia, Texas, *Horseman, Pass By* (1961) and *The Last Picture Show* (1966). In *Horseman, Pass By,* the young narrator feels a deep sense of loss: "Things used to be better around here. . . . I feel like I want something back" (123). And loss does come to characterize young Lonnie's world when his beloved grandfather's diseased cattle must be destroyed and the grandfather himself is shot after being terribly hurt in an accident. *The Last Picture Show* ends with the closing of Thalia's one movie theater and with it the mythic dream of the Old West, which inspired so many of the pictures shown there. Peter Bogdanovich effectively ended his film of the novel with the great scene from Howard Hawks's Western *Red River* (1947), in which John Wayne sets off on the first great cattle drive from Texas. In contrast to this heroic moment, the young people of Thalia are lost in the vacuous emptiness of a depressed oil boomtown.

This sense of the end of the heroic West haunts such major works of the new Western fiction as Norman Maclean's *A River Runs Through It* (1976), in which an old man, haunted by memories of his long-dead father and brother and of the fishing they shared, still broods about his inability to save his brother from the violence that destroyed him. In other stories, Maclean evokes a lost world of skill with tools and heroic physical labor and shows how powerful an experience it was to be initiated into such a world. Like the mythical Western, these works celebrate a West that is largely gone, but unlike the traditional tales of wild cow-towns and cattle drives, outlaws and marshals, gunfighters and schoolmarms that populated the nation's imagined West, these stories celebrate the heroism not of gunfighters but of loggers, miners, forest service crews, and firefighters, those ordinary people who built the West and then saw it transformed into something else.

McCarthy has rapidly made himself a central figure in this literary tradition. The two novels of his Border Trilogy are among the richest and most complex treatments of the Western themes of initiation, belatedness, and frontiers. They transmute the mythical fantasy world of wild Western gunfighters, outlaws, and savage Indians into the last remnant of an age-old world of traditional work in which men are part of the unity of life and find great fulfillment in their actions because these actions are integral with horses and the rest of nature. Horses, which have been man's primary instrument in the use of nature and the creation of culture for centuries, are, as the novel's title would suggest, the symbol of a traditional unity between man and the world that is being increasingly destroyed by modern technology and industrialism. As McCarthy portrays it, West Texas, once one of the last bastions of traditional pastoralism in America, has become a wasteland of oil derricks.

Like McMurtry's earlier work, McCarthy's 1992 National Book Award winner *All the Pretty Horses* begins in a depressed West Texas in the immediate aftermath of World War II. Its protagonist, John Grady Cole, is sixteen years old and very much alone in the world. His father is separated from his mother and is slowly dying from a condition incurred in a prison camp during the war. Cole's grandfather is a rancher and Cole himself, loving horses and ranching, would like nothing better than to continue the ranch, but the old man dies and Cole's mother plans to sell the family ranch and leave the area. To continue the work he loves, Cole crosses the border into Mexico with a young friend, and the two find work on a large hacienda where the traditional work with horses and cattle is still carried on.

This momentary recovery of paradise is disrupted, however, when Cole falls desperately in love with the daughter of the great hacienda's proprietor. When she returns his love and the two embark on a passionate affair, her powerful family has Cole wrongfully arrested. After being nearly killed in a Mexican prison, Cole is freed when his lover promises never to see him again. The last section of the novel deals with Cole's revenge on the corrupt Mexican policeman who has betrayed him and stolen his horses. Finally, hardened and matured by his ordeal and deeply saddened by the loss of his love and his encounters with death, Cole returns to Texas.

The Texas he finds is on the verge of the postwar oil boom that will utterly destroy the traditional cattle culture, the same process further portrayed by Mc-

Murtry in his series of Thalia novels and the background for television's popular Western soap opera *Dallas*. While the traditional culture still exists in the late 1940s on the great haciendas of Mexico, it too is on borrowed time. It is significant that the wealthy *hacendado* of McCarthy's novel keeps his ranch more as a hobby than a way of life and uses an airplane to fly back and forth between the hacienda and his other life in Mexico City.

John Grady Cole is not only a master of horses but something of a visionary as well and the story is punctuated by his dreams of an eternal paradise where there are always wild horses holding out hope for man's redemption. "That night as he lay in his cot he could hear music from the house and as he was drifting to sleep his thoughts were of horses and of the open country and of horses. Horses still wild on the mesa who'd never seen a man afoot and who knew nothing of him or his life yet in whose souls he would come to reside forever" (117-18).

One of the most striking moments in the novel comes in a conversation between Cole, his young friend Rawlins, and an old man who symbolizes the traditional wisdom of the world of natural work. It is this old man who expresses most clearly the full spiritual significance of horses in this traditional vision of the world:

> Finally he said that among men there was no such communion as among horses and the notion that man can be understood at all was probably an illusion. Rawlins asked him in his bad spanish if there was a heaven for horses but he shook his head and said that a horse had no need of heaven. Finally John Grady asked him if it were not true that should all horses vanish from the face of the earth the soul of the horse would not also perish for there would be nothing out of which to replenish it but the old man only said that it was pointless to speak of there being no horses in the world for God would not permit such a thing.
>
> [111]

The most important thing John Grady Cole must learn in the process of his initiation into mature life is the hardest for him to accept: that such a world no longer exists for him. The Mexican hacienda is for him a Paradise Lost. Even in Mexico, the modern world of politics and revolution, technology and cities is eroding and destroying the traditions of the countryside, while in the Texas to which he must return, the only vestiges of the traditional world of man and nature are in the few remaining Indian encampments in the midst of the oil fields:

> In four days' riding he crossed the Pecos at Iraan Texas and rode up out of the river breaks where the pumpjacks in the Yates Field ranged against the skyline rose and dipped like mechanical birds. Like great primitive birds welded up out of iron by hearsay in a land perhaps where such birds once had been. At that time there were still indians camped on the western plains and late in the day he passed in his riding a scattered group of their wickiups propped upon that scoured and trembling waste. They were perhaps a quarter mile to the north, just huts made from poles and brush with a few goathides draped across them. The indians stood watching him. He could see that none of them spoke among themselves or commented on his riding there nor did they raise a hand in greeting or call out to him. They had no curiosity about him at all. As if they knew all that they needed to know. They stood and watched him pass and watched him vanish upon that landscape solely because he was passing. Solely because he could vanish.
>
> [301]

In this profoundly elegiac conclusion McCarthy evokes that mythical Western scene of the hero riding off into the sunset, but for John Grady Cole there is no more mythical world to cross over into, there is only "the darkening land, the world to come" (302).

The Crossing, second volume of the Border Trilogy, tells a story that has many similarities to *All the Pretty Horses.* It too involves the heroic quest of a young man who seeks something he never fully understands and, in the end, discovers truths that he might prefer not to know. In fact, the hero of *The Crossing* makes three crossings into the mysterious world of Mexico, each of successively greater difficulty and risk. What he finally discovers is that life is always full of grief and evil and that perhaps the most one can hope for is to survive the night in order to struggle once again and unsuccessfully to seize the day. McCarthy's West is the world, and the true secret of the world is that it does not get any better. McCarthy's vision is as apocalyptic in its way as that of such Native American writers as Leslie Silko, though McCarthy sees only a darkening wasteland, where Silko imagines the ultimate restoration of the land through an ecological catastrophe of modern technological civilization and a return of tribal cultures.

Since the Border Trilogy is not yet complete, it is hazardous to guess where it will all come out.[6] However, there is a deep consistency throughout McCarthy's work, in spite of the dazzling changes between his "Southern" and his "Western" fiction. What haunts McCarthy as a storyteller is the way in which modern man is thrust into the world without much that he can depend on and is driven by a deep sense of frustration at being born too late for the past to be any kind of guide to action, security, and fulfillment. His desperate quest for truth and understanding is inevitably frustrated, and all the wisdom he learns cannot guarantee him anything beyond the moment in which he is alive. His heroes learn that all quests are futile, but that they have no choice but to continue their search through a world that is becoming progressively more complicated, more cruel, and more chaotic.

* * *

Cormac McCarthy links the new Western literature with that of the South through his increasing sense of the failure of white American civilization and its inescapable burden of guilt. The guilt comes from its destruction of nature and its tragic heritage of human waste represented by the extermination of great traditional cultures and by the pervasive racism of modern America. Other contemporary literary explorations of the history and culture of the South and the West, regions which were once so important as sources of romantic myths of otherness in American culture, have also produced compelling reevaluations of the basic myths of American exceptionalism and superiority and powerful critiques of the multiple failures of the American dream. It is striking, though perhaps not surprising, that these deeply critical literary movements have emerged almost simultaneously with a new surge of political conservatism and fundamentalism in America, also centered in the South and the West and seeking to manipulate the same symbolic and ideological traditions for their own very different purposes. As many commentators have noted, Ronald Reagan tried to reenact the Western myth of the shootout between the heroic marshall and the outlaw on the national and international scenes. The new breed of Southern Republicans who have recently become so important in American politics has found that a traditional Southern rhetoric of states rights, less government, family values, localism, and even a coded white supremacy skillfully disguised as opposition to affirmative action has proved highly effective on the national scene. These reactions are almost antithetical to those of serious contemporary Southern and Western writers, but they are probably different responses to the same uncertainties that have beset America in the last quarter of the twentieth century: a profound loss of confidence in America's uniqueness, moral superiority, and global omnipotence. In the context of this ongoing spiritual crisis, the South and the West, which once helped define America mythically and symbolically through their otherness, are now being pursued by both intellectual critics and conservative fundamentalists as symbols of the real truth of America.

Notes

1. Passages like the following clearly reflect the influence of Joyce's method of amassing incredibly detailed catalogues of the people and things that haunt the Dublin streets:

> Every other face goitered, twisted, tubered with some excrescence. Teeth black with rot, eyes rheumed and vacuous. Dour and diminutive people framed by paper cones of blossoms, hawkers of esoteric wares, curious electuaries ordered up in jars and elixirs decocted in the moon's dark. he went by stacks of crated pullets, plump hares with ruby eyes. Butter tubbed in ice and brown or alabaster eggs in ordered rows. Along by the meatcounters shuffling up flies out of the bloodstained sawdust. Where a calf's head rested pink and scalded on a tray and butchers honed their knives.
>
> [*Suttree* 67]

In spite of the Joycean model, McCarthy imparts his own distinctive aura to the scene.

2. Perhaps there's some hint of James Agee's nostalgically beautiful "Knoxville: Summer, 1915," that haunting evocation of a bygone way of life from *A Death in the Family,* in McCarthy's Knoxville of the 1950s.

3. Cf. John Shelton Reed, *The Enduring South: Subcultural Persistence in Mass Society* (Lexington, Mass.: Lexington Books, 1972). Also Clyde N. Wilson, ed., *Why the South Will Survive by Fifteen Southerners* (Athens: U of Georgia P, 1981).

4. The protagonist of *Blood Meridian* leaves Tennessee at the age of fourteen, about the same age Huck was when he decided to go down the river and then to run off to the "territory." The Southwest where the kid goes might well be an extension of the "territory" and the historical period is the same, the 1840s. The kid is a Huck-like innocent who encounters a world of terrible violence and corruption and grotesque characters Twain would surely have appreciated. But this is the West as well, and the theme identified by Michael Herr as "regeneration through violence" is precisely the mythos that Richard Slotkin characterizes as the dominant theme of the myth of the frontier. I'm not sure, however, that there's much regeneration in *Blood Meridian*. Rather, the book lives up to its subtitle, *The Evening Redness in the West*. (Michael Herr's comment is quoted on the cover of the paperback edition of *Blood Meridian*. Slotkin's important three-volume analysis of the myth of the frontier began with *Regeneration through Violence* [Middletown, Conn.: Wesleyan UP, 1973].)

5. It's pretty clear that *Blood Meridian* is also, like such sunnier post-Westerns as Thomas Berger's *Little Big Man,* a tacit commentary on the American invasion of Vietnam.

6. Rumor has it that the third volume tentatively titled *Cities of the Plain* will appear in the near future.

Laura Fine (essay date fall 1999)

SOURCE: Fine, Laura. "Going Nowhere Slow: The Post-South World of Bobbie-Ann Mason." *Southern Literary Journal* 32, no. 1 (fall 1999): 87-97.

[*In the following essay, Fine asserts that the Southern locale itself is tangential to Bobbie Ann Mason's fiction and that she concentrates instead on her characters' search for meaning in the wider context of pop culture.*]

In his 1930 story "A Rose for Emily," William Faulkner depicts a South in painful transition. The Old South, with its history of slavery, racism, and cruelty masked by a genteel front, battles the forces of the New South, mercantile, unconcerned with beauty. In Flannery O'Connor's stories, the South is peopled by shallow, narrow-minded whites, representatives of both the New and Old South, who assume a superiority based on their race while demonstrating a gaping ignorance of their shortcomings. O'Connor uses her bladelike humor to teach her smug characters important lessons, the ultimate being that the world is ordered by a class and colorblind God. The truth is there and knowable, but the characters are blind until O'Connor teaches them to see. Bobbie Ann Mason, in her 1980s short stories, portrays an entirely different South.

Whether factually accurate or not, a certain idea of the South has passed through the generations of southern literature. The writer Brenda Marie Osbey finds the "quilt" of southern literature threaded together by "religion, a preoccupation with death and loss, remembrance, and a love for the land" (qtd in Humphries and Lowe, 14). Virginia A. Smith sees the "issues of an economically and psychologically bruising military defeat and a defense of and guilt over an elaborately institutionalized system of chattel slavery" as well as "a tradition of story-telling, oral history and a veneration of the genteel act of writing" (4) as forming the standards of southern literature. Perhaps Jack Butler's definition of the canon of southern literature is most salient: "We think of a place; we think of the darkness and splendor of families; we think of a way of talking; we think of the Bible; and we think of black and white locked into a mutual if inharmonious fate" (35).

While Mason references her characters' southern locale and speech, and even their largely dysfunctional families, in Mason's fictional world southern history and all it represents seems irrelevant to her characters' lives. In his review of Mason's *Midnight Magic,* her new collection of stories selected from her first two volumes, Michael Gorra writes of Mason's characters as living "in a temporary world of Big Macs and *Battlestar Galactica.*" (7). Indeed, the people of Mason's stories are predominately lower-middle class white heterosexuals who could live in any subdivision or farm in the country. Robert H. Brinkmeyer, Jr. suggests that Mason's "focus is less on the Southern experience than on the American, and so for her a Southerner's quest for self—definition means coming to terms with America and not the South" (32), while Fred Hobson sees in Bobbie Ann Mason "a relative *lack* of southern self-consciousness" ("Canons" 84). Perhaps it would be more accurate to say that the characters in her stories display a lack of self-consciousness, period, and that Mason's subdivided South stands as a representation of the United States in general.

In *Civilization and its Discontents* Freud analyzes humanity's need to erect institutions and rules in order to protect people from others: "Hence . . . the use of methods . . . to incite people into . . . aim-inhibited relationships of love . . . the restriction upon sexual life . . . and the ideal's commandment to love one's neighbour as oneself—a commandment which is really justified by the fact that nothing else runs so strongly counter to the original nature of man" (66). No matter their failings, splendid and amazing in their scope, the institutions and traditions of southern culture, though justly maligned, established a framework for behavior and attitudes. In Mason's stories, the traditions of religion, the conventions of white heterosexual family life, of masculine and feminine roles, are no longer in any way sustaining. Unlike in O'Connor, no higher power orders the South Mason depicts, and no clear rules or mores remain for governing human social behavior. The only shaping force on characters' lives is popular culture. And though many of her characters are vaguely aware of their unhappiness, the cure-alls offered by popular culture are illusory and ineffective. Representative stories from her two collections, *Shiloh and Other Stories* and *Love Life,* demonstrate Mason's decidedly and, because of her mild-mannered prose and deadpan narrative voice, surprisingly bleak vision of contemporary American society.

Although O'Connor peoples her fictional world with an abundance of religious hypocrites, her vision is distinctly spiritual, and most of her characters assume that a God orders their world. Not so in Mason's fiction. In "The Retreat," the main character, Georgeann, is married to a pastor, but her husband's view of the world is a nearly obsolete one. Not only must he work as a licensed electrician to be able to afford to preach, but his faith in the value of spirituality is one not even his wife can share. As Mason critic G. O. Morphew writes, "religion is not a dominating presence in Georgeann's inner life nor does it play much of a role in the lives of any of Mason's central female characters. For them, religion is just in the landscape, like the corn fields that surround the Kentucky farm houses" (43).

Although Shelby labors at his sermons, he is not able to communicate effectively with his parishioners. When Georgeann types out a sermon he writes on sex education in the schools, she challenges a word, "pucelage." To her husband's patient explanation that it means "virginity," she retorts, "Why didn't you just say so! Nobody will know what it means" (*Shiloh* 138). And one snowy day, after he has heard that a church member has been drinking, Shelby delivers a sermon on alcohol abuse to a congregation of three, including an elderly couple and "Miss Addie Stone, the president of the WCTU chapter" (134). The vital role the church once played in southern communities is here comically diminished.

The *Love Life* stories, "Airwaves" and "Midnight Magic," portray a religion further enervated. In "Airwaves" Jane hears that her brother Joe, who has been in trouble most of his life, is now preaching and even speaking in tongues at the "Foremost Evangelical Assembly," so she goes to his church one Sunday out of curiosity. In the middle of "healing" a child, Joe starts his performance, surprising his sister: "'Shecky-beck-be-floyt-I-shecky-tibby-libby. Dab-cree-la-croo-la-crow.' He seems to be trying hard not to say 'abracadabra' or any other familiar words. Jane, disappointed, doubts that these words are messages from heaven. Joe seems afraid some repressed obscenity might rush out" (189-190). Ironically, one of the few examples of a Mason character being concertedly self-conscious involves a religious fake intent on not betraying himself. The practice of religion has become one of many revolving jobs for a con man who realizes that if he is sufficiently self-aware he is bound to fool his largely unreflective followers.

Religion is again reduced to nothing more than con artists scamming needy, gullible people in "Midnight Magic," which portrays Steve's girlfriend, Karen, attending meetings held by Sardo, "a thousand-year-old American Indian inhabiting the body of a teenage girl in Paducah" (21). The girl has enough followers and supporters that she drives a Porsche. Indeed, there is an age of difference between this teenager who is self-motivated and aware enough to heed her own preachings—"the answers are in yourself" (26)—while knowing her followers will not. Again, Mason's few characters who do sincerely subscribe to a universe ordered by God are a vanishing minority, and the vast majority of religious practitioners are money-driven fakes and their naive followers. Most of her characters are not bound by any religious traditions or moral codes.

Derived in part from the collapse of defining religious institutions, confusion abounds in Mason's stories about conventional masculine and feminine roles. As Harriet Pollack writes, "Her women have moved beyond the clear gender conceptions with which they were raised and now face the dilemma of saying what should stand in place of those conceptions" (97). In the retreat of the story's title, Georgeann participates in a workshop on Christian marriage during which one woman intones, "God made man so that he can't resist a woman's adoration. She should treat him as a priceless treasure, for man is the highest form of creation. A man is born of God—and just think, *you* get to live with him" (*Shiloh* 143). Georgeann feels wholly unable to gain sustenance from this traditional view of marital relations and yet knows no viable alternative.

Troubled by her parents' stifling view of proper masculine and feminine behavior, Jane in "Airwaves" remembers a story her late mother told her about a woman trapped in a cage with a lion who wanted to mate with her, and how, under the trainer's instructions, the woman "had to stroke the lion until he was satisfied" (*Love Life* 192). Jane recalls that that "was more or less how her mother always told her she had to be with a husband, or a rapist" (192). The rough equation of husband and rapist, and the assumption that a woman's duty is to submit to men, friendly or unfriendly, does not seem to Jane appropriate for her life. When her father lectures her, "The trouble is, too many women are working and the men can't get jobs. . . . Women should stay at home," Jane warns him to be quiet (185). The outdated gender role messages she receives from her parents make her uncertain about what rules apply to present day romances, and of what she wants with her on-again off-again boyfriend, Coy. For example, while Coy's gentleness makes him fit the *Phil Donahue* audience's criteria of the perfect man, she sometimes wishes he were more aggressive (*Love Life* 192).

In "Midnight Magic," Steve is even more confused about proper masculine behavior. When his girlfriend becomes furious with him for impersonating the neighborhood rapist and surprising her in her apartment, Steve thinks, "But it was just a game. She should have known that" (*Love Life* 27). It is as if Karen angrily refuses to play the role of the submissive woman that Jane of "Airwaves" learned from her parents, that so many women of that generation internalized and so many men expected. Steve still tries to act according to the rules of the previous generation and cannot understand why Karen does not play along. Earlier, his attempt to flirt with a woman in the laundromat goes sour when she snatches her panties away before he can grab them from her basket (26). He is thoroughly puzzled about what he is doing wrong, why women respond negatively to his best enactment of a playfully aggressive male.

Mason's world is one in which people find conventional gender roles stultifying and religious institutions irrelevant; as a result her characters have no models for their emotions and actions, no clear roles to step into. Mason critic Albert Wilhelm writes: "Painful transitions have become more frequent and more intense, but the adaptive and adjustive response previously offered by ritual is frequently lacking" (273). The only thing working to fill the void of structure and certainty is popular culture, which tries to make clean, easy sense out of our confusing, painful lives; becomes the guide for making life decisions; and takes the space of knowing oneself and others. While the characters in Mason's stories are largely inarticulate, unfulfilled, and incapable of analyzing their feelings or of communicating deeply with others, the world presented through the forms of popular culture is one in which people are happy, enjoy warm relationships with friends and family, and are able to articulate their feelings.

The simple, familiar, knowable patterns of pop culture provide its consumers a feeling of security. Whether it is half-hour situation comedies like *M*A*S*H* and *Mork and Mindy,* rock music, video games, or music videos, these forms—typically with a set beginning, a problem introduced in the middle, and neat resolution at the end—provide solace to people who can cling to no understandable patterns in their own lives. In "Love Life" Opal watches a video on her favorite channel, MTV: "Now the TV is playing a song in which all the boys are long-haired cops chasing a dangerous woman in a tweed cap and a checked shirt. The woman's picture is in all their billfolds. . . . She hops on a motorcycle, and they set up a roadblock, but she jumps it with her motorcycle. Finally, she slips onto a train and glides away from them, waving a smiling goodbye" (1). In a three minute span Opal can vicariously experience freeing herself from repressive conventions without ever having to confront the trapped feelings of her own life.

Characters throughout Mason's fictional world turn to popular culture to fill the void in their lives. In "The Retreat" Georgeann starts skipping the religious workshops to play video games in the basement of the lodge where the retreat is located. As the day passes, she improves her game: "The situation is dangerous and thrilling, but Georgeann feels in control. She isn't running away; she is chasing the aliens" (*Shiloh* 145). Georgeann, feeling less and less content with living the life of the conventional wife of a pastor and with her relationship with Shelby and increasingly confused about what to do about her unhappiness, finds a temporary solution in playing the video game, which lets her imagine taking control of her life.

On the drive home from the retreat, Shelby asks what he can do to make her happy, to which she responds, "I was happy when I was playing that game" (146). Indeed, the kind of happiness that amounts to a numbness, as Georgeann explains, making "you forget everything but who you are" (146), is the only kind she can imagine for herself. The story ends with Georgeann nonchalantly taking a sick hen and cutting its head off, the same hen whose illness she had earlier hidden from her husband because she knew if he saw a sick chicken he would kill it. Now, when she crashes the ax down on its head, "Georgeann feels nothing, only that she has done her duty" (147). Apparently, playing video games all day long has desensitized her to pain. And, since Georgeann herself was ill earlier in the story—infected by chicken mites,—and since she is in effect the "mother hen" of her family, the implication is she has become inured to her own pain through playing the video games.

In "Airwaves" Jane tries to recover from the pain of Coy's breaking up with her by blasting a rock station: "The sounds are numbing. Jane figures if she can listen to hard rock in her sleep, she won't care that Coy has gone" (*Love Life* 180). Later, as she contemplates joining the army, she imagines it as a scene on television, and likens war to rock and roll: "She pictures herself someplace remote, in a control booth, sending signals for war, like an engineer in charge of a sports special on TV. . . . The sounds of warfare would be like the sounds of rock and roll, hard-driving and satisfying" (196). Her notion of the world derives almost exclusively from what she has seen on television, so that she must filter any new experience through the lens of popular culture forms. Again, like Georgeann's experience playing video games, Jane imagines both a sense of control and of numbness. And Jane judges relationships, too, by how they fit into her slanted sense of the world. When her father suggests she move in with him after Coy leaves her, she responds that it would never work because "we don't like the same TV shows anymore" (185).

In "A New-Wave Format" Edwin drives a bus whose passengers are retarded, and, like his idol, Dr. Johnny Fever from *WKRP in Cincinnati,* he acts as disk jockey, playing tapes of carefully chosen music. The bus passengers are exaggerated representatives of the average American's anesthetized state. Freddie Johnson's ten word-vocabulary consists of "'Hot!,' "Shorts," "*Popeye* on?" "*Dukes* on!," "Cook supper," and "Go bed"' (*Shiloh* 217). Similarly, most of the concerns of Edwin and his girlfriend, Sabrina, involve television and eating: "They share a love of Fudgsicles, speed-boats, and *WKRP in Cincinnati*" (215).

When Edwin tries to adapt to the times, modernizing the music he plays for his passengers, the new-wave format creates a sensation: "Edwin believed the passengers understood what was happening. The frantic beat was a perfect expression of their aimlessness and frustration" (228). Sabrina herself likes listening to new-wave music that strikes Edwin as "violent and mindless, with a fast beat like a crazed parent abusing a child, thrashing it senseless" (227). These descriptions portray a culture of people attempting to fill the void in their lives with mindless sound, substituting numbness for self-analysis. Edwin's sense of the music's violence attests to the desperate need of these people, a need requiring extreme measures to pacify. Americans thrash themselves with the forms of popular culture in their attempt to deaden unpleasant, unacknowledged feelings; the beat of the culture's music stands in as parent, as rule-maker, but it is a crazed parent, whose only order is a frenzied thrashing. The forms of civilization that Freud saw humanity erecting in order to protect people from themselves seem here dangerously eroded.

In a world in which popular culture takes the place of formerly framing institutions and conventions, happiness comes to the few who are able to believe in popular culture's salutary power. In "Airwaves" Coy is depressed until he gets a job as a Wal-Mart floor walker. Jane visits him there and is unimpressed: "In his brown plaid pants, blue shirt, and yellow tie, he looked stylish and comfortable, as though he had finally found a place where he belonged. He seemed like a man whose ambition was to get a service award so he could have his picture in the paper, shaking hands with his boss" (*Love Life* 195). After she leaves, she thinks of "how proudly Coy had said, 'We're taking inventory,' as though he were in thick with Wal-Mart executives" (195). Floor-walking at Wal-Mart, an icon of consumer-oriented popular culture, is enough for Coy to feel like he plays an important role in society. Here Mason looks at the remarkable trend of young Americans' allying themselves with corporate culture to make themselves feel accepted. Today one may go to a mall or a college campus and be hard pressed to find anyone not wearing clothing that loudly identifies a corporation. Mason suggests one way to be happy in out popular culture is truly to believe its shallow messages.

The two other happy characters in these stories are Karen from "Midnight Magic," who enjoys feeling herself a part of the community of the religious fake Sardo, and Sabrina from "A New-Wave Format," who lands a bit part in *Oklahoma!*. Not surprisingly, Sabrina's favorite song begins, "Attention, all you K-Mart shoppers, fill your carts" (*Shiloh* 220). The high she gets from delivering her two lines in *Oklahoma!* is only the beginning: "She is full of hope, like the Christmas season. . . . she has a new job at McDonald's and a good part in *Life with Father*" (229). Working at the most powerful popular culture icon ever, and having a part, no matter how small, in a famous musical is enough to make Sabrina feel utterly fulfilled: she believes the role she plays.

But most people cannot so believe. Georgeann in "The Retreat" becomes increasingly aware of her unhappiness but manages to find only the temporary solution of playing video games to distance herself from her pain. Early in "Airwaves" Jane numbs herself by playing rock music loudly, but as the story progresses, she admits the cure has been ineffective: "Jane is not sure the hard-rock music has hardened her to pain and distraction" (*Love Life* 191). She longs to be close to people but does not know how, so she becomes obsessed with the actual physics of communication, sound waves. In this way, she is able to imagine a connection with others. She thinks that the way sound travels must be similar to the way voices from heaven travel to her brother, and when she orders food from a drive-in, she hears on the employees' radio the same station she is listening to (186) and thus feels connected to them. And indeed, this is the method popular culture offers people as a means of feeling close to others. A passing car may blast a radio station as the driver's way of proclaiming, "This is me!" and those who listen to the same station feel connected to the driver. Or a person feels close to someone sporting a Nike T-shirt, because he himself has a Nike shirt at home. Hobson notes that Mason's characters find themselves "forever riding a wave of popular culture, popular music and television programs in particular, wherever it takes them, deriving their values, their mythology, even their sense of time and family and community, their identity, from shared rock stars and television programs" (*Southern* 12). This shallow, unfulfilling means of connection is the best Jane can find, so at the end of the story she joins the Army to pursue "Communications and Electronic Operations" (195).

In "Midnight Magic," Steve realizes he is unhappy but does not know how to better his life. He feels "empty inside, doomed" (*Love Life* 21), when he thinks his relationship with his girlfriend pales in comparison to the one his friend, Doran, has with a woman he marries after six weeks. At other times Steve "has sudden feelings of desperation he can't explain" (28). Again, television and movies have taught him confusing, inadequate lessons, first among them that a good model of a relationship is one in which right from the start a couple is perfect for one another and marries after six weeks. Since his relationship with Karen does not fall into this category, he feels something is wrong. Later in the story, he finds out from Doran that all may not be well with the newlyweds, but the damage from Steve's skewed perceptions is already done. When Steve, discontent, tries but fails to spice up his relationship with Karen by pretending to be the neighborhood rapist, he finds consolation by envisioning himself expertly playing the role he has no doubt seen on television many times: "If he were the neighborhood rapist scouting out her apartment, he would hide in the dark doorway of the delivery entrance of the dry cleaner's downstairs, and when she came in at night, pointing the way with her key, he'd grab her tight around the waist" (27-28). The lessons he has learned from popular culture about relationships and self-empowerment not only fail to teach him how to be happy, but are warped.

If a character does take a step toward being more introspective, this movement is usually accompanied by a consequent increased distance in his or her relationships with others, since the other members of society remain largely unself-aware and uncommitted to change. When Jane decides she wants to become closer to the people she loves, she attempts to have a revealing conversation with her father. She asks him what he did years ago when he left his wife and children, and then proceeds to open up and tell him how she felt as a child at that time. As she recites her feelings she gets renewed courage from the way her father seems to be listening intently, patiently nodding. After she finishes he pauses so long that "Jane thinks he must be working up to a spectacular confession or apology" (*Love Life* 193). Instead, he simply remarks, "'The Constitution is damaged all to hell'" (193). His comically inadequate response both points to the way popular culture teaches people to divert attention from their psyches to less personally troubling targets and suggests that the problem really is with the constitution of America, a country whose framework is truly damaged.

In "A New Wave Format" Edwin's compassion for his passengers leads him toward introspection and to an honest attempt to look at his past and what it means. However, looking into and understanding himself means distancing himself from his girlfriend, who finds the antics of his retarded patrons alarming and disgusting. The story's end suggests their break-up is near: "The thought of her fennel toothpaste . . . fills him with something like nostalgia, as though she is already only a memory" (*Shiloh* 231).

At the end of O'Connor's "Good Country People," Manley Pointer taunts the atheist Ph.D. Hulga Hopewell with, "You ain't so smart. I been believing in nothing ever since I was born!" (291). In Mason's world, it is not only the depraved grotesques like Pointer, roaming the boundaries of southern society, who believe in nothing, but the culture as a whole. The South as Mason depicts it has degenerated into a band of more innocuous Pointers, complacent, shallow, unguided by anything besides the ideology of popular culture. But though Mason's world is free of truly evil characters like this phony Bible salesman, hers is a potentially dangerous world without the boundaries Freud saw social structures necessarily erecting. Mason examines the danger that comes from being in between, in nowhere land after the framing institutions have lost their power, replaced only by an amoral popular culture. Hers is a world in which average young American men fantasize about themselves as rapists, where young women imagine the satisfying excitement of fighting in a war, where middle-aged women chop off chickens' heads like so many video game aliens, and where a busload of pacified retarded adults waits to explode.

Works Cited

Brinkmeyer, Robert H. "Finding One's History: Bobbie Ann Mason and Contemporary Southern Literature." *Southern Literary Journal* 19.2 (1987): 20-33.

Butler, Jack. "Still Southern After All These Years." Humphries and Lowe 33-40.

Freud, Sigmund. *Civilization and its Discontents*. Trans. James Strachey. New York: Norton, 1961.

Gorra, Michael. Rev. of *Midnight Magic*, by Bobbie Ann Mason. *The New York Times Book Review*. 8 August 1998: 7.

Hobson, Fred. "Of Canons and Cultural Wars: Southern Literature and Literary Scholarship after Midcentury." Humphries and Lowe 72-86.

———. *The Southern Writer in the Postmodern World*. Athens: U of Georgia P, 1991.

Humphries, Jefferson and John Lowe, eds. *The Future of Southern Letters*. New York: Oxford UP, 1996.

Mason, Bobbie Ann. *Love Life*. New York: Harper, 1989.

———. *Midnight Magic*. Hopewell: Ecco P, 1998.

———. *Shiloh and Other Stories*. New York: Harper, 1982.

Morphew, G. O. "Downhome Feminists in *Shiloh and Other Stories*." *Southern Literary Journal*. 21 (1989): 41-49.

O'Connor, Flannery. "Good Country People." *The Complete Stories*. New York: Noonday, 1946. 271-291.

Pollack, Harriet. "From *Shiloh* to *In Country* to *Feather Crowns*: Bobbie Ann Mason, Women's History, and Southern Fiction." *Southern Literary Journal* 28 (1996): 95-116.

Smith, Virginia A. "Between the Lines: Contemporary Southern Women Writers, Gail Godwin, Bobbie Ann Mason, Lisa Alther and Lee Smith." Diss. Penn State U, 1989.

Wilhelm, Albert E. "Private Rituals: Coping with Change in the Fiction of Bobbie Ann Mason." *The Midwest Quarterly* 28 (1987): 271-282.

Martha Chew (essay date 1984)

SOURCE: Chew, Martha. "Rita Mae Brown: Feminist Theorist and Southern Novelist." In *Women Writers of the Contemporary South*, edited by Peggy Whitman Prenshaw, pp. 195-213. Jackson: University Press of Mississippi, 1984.

[*In the following essay, Chew presents an overview of Rita Mae Brown's novels and essays, focusing on her political consciousness and her treatment of social class and categories in her novels.*]

Rita Mae Brown is known both for her political writing, which consists of the essays that came out of her activism as a lesbian feminist in the late sixties and early seventies and were collected in *A Plain Brown Rapper* (1976); and for her fiction, which to date consists of five novels, *Rubyfruit Jungle* (1973), *In Her Day* (1976), *Six of One* (1978), *Southern Discomfort* (1982), and *Sudden Death* (1983). Although the two bodies of work overlap chronologically, they come out of essentially different periods in Brown's life, and the novels have been increasingly directed toward a mainstream audience.

The movement of the novels away from the political focus of the essays is reflected in the way the two types of writing diverge in their publishing histories. Brown's essays originally appeared in lesbian and feminist publications; the collected edition, *A Plain Brown Rapper,* was published by Diana Press, a west coast lesbian-feminist press (which also published her second collection of poems, *Songs to a Handsome Woman,* in 1973 and reissued in 1974 her first collection, *The Hand That Cradles the Rock*). Her first two novels, *Rubyfruit Jungle* and *In Her Day,* were published by Daughters, Inc., a Vermont feminist publishing house (co-founded by another Southern woman writer, North Carolina novelist June Arnold). When *Rubyfruit Jungle* became an underground best seller (selling 80,000 copies in hardcover), it was reissued by Bantam,[1] a subsidiary of Harper and Row, and Harper and Row simultaneously contracted for her third novel, *Six of One.* Her next two novels, *Southern Discomfort* and *Sudden Death,* were published by Harper and Row and by Bantam, respectively.

Brown had evidently anticipated and planned these two publishing tracks with a clear sense of the different audiences that her political essays and her novels would eventually have. In 1976, a year before Bantam reissued *Rubyfruit Jungle,* she responded to a questionnaire on publishing policies sent to lesbian and feminist authors, "I see my political writing going to the feminist press while in time my fiction will go to establishment presses" (Clausen, "Politics" 101).

The widening gap between Brown's essays and her fiction is marked by the disappearance from the novels of the lesbian feminist political vision that is set forth with revolutionary fervor in the early writings. This apparent shift in her ideological stance is underlined by the change in her lifestyle from that of political activist and street-level organizer to that of Hollywood scriptwriter, celebrity novelist, and member of Charlottesville's polo-playing set. This change has, predictably, been noted with favor in some camps and disfavor in others. Jan Clausen, writing in *A Movement of Poets* about the relationship of poets to the contemporary American feminist movement, notes that "it is a sobering experience . . . to read early 'underground heroine' Rita Mae Brown's musings on the joys of owning a Rolls Royce in a recent issue of *Savvy*" (14). The mainstream press, on the other hand, feels that Brown has "broken through" and that her success with standard publishers marks "the difference between being famous as a lesbian writer . . . and being a writer of greater substance and vision who is perhaps breaking new literary ground" (Holt 17, 16).

Brown, who points out that she gives ten percent of her after-tax earnings to women's political causes (Shister, 12), talks about her feminist politics as having evolved, rather than changed. In her 1976 introduction to the essays in *A Plain Brown Rapper,* she explained that, although her vision of a feminist revolution remained "unchanged," she had come to see that revolution as "the slow, steady push of people over decades" (13). And in a 1978 interview upon the publication of *Six of One,* after pointing out that fiction made her politics "more palatable," she added, "I still feel I'm part of the movement, but the form of my expression has changed" (Holt 17).

Although the distance between the political viewpoint in Brown's essays and that in her fiction clearly signals more than a change in form, the essays and fiction are linked by Brown's concern with some of the same issues. We can begin to see that link, and to define the extent to which Brown's themes in her fiction reflect her early politics, if we look first at the account her essays provide of the development of her political thinking in the early sixties and late seventies.

> There is a growing movement of Lesbians dedicated to our freedom, to your freedom, to ending all man-made oppressions. You will be part of that surge forward and you will leave your fingerprints on the shape of things to come.
>
> —Brown, "The Shape of Things to Come," 1972

Brown's political essays and speeches, which appeared from 1969 to 1975 in *The Ladder, Women: A Journal of Liberation, The Furies, Quest: A Journal of Feminist Liberation,* and other lesbian and feminist publications, chart the development of her vision of a feminist revolution. Looking back on that period in her 1976 introduction to her essays in *A Plain Brown Rapper,* Brown said, "In those days I ate, breathed and slept feminism. Nothing else mattered to me. We would bring about a revolution in this nation and we would do it now" (13).

After making the Southern writer's archetypal journey to New York, she began to move from one political group to another. She helped found the New York University Homophile League, then left it because, as she explains in her 1972 essay, "Take a Lesbian to Lunch," "the homosexual movement" was "male-dominated" (86). She joined the National Organization for Women (and was appointed national administrative coordinator), then quit, reportedly blasting the leaders as "sexist, racist, reformist clubwomen" (Alexander 112) because of their reaction to the issue of lesbianism.[2] She joined Redstockings (a New York radical feminist group that used consciousness-raising groups as a way of organizing women); found they reacted as negatively to her lebianism as had NOW; joined and then left Gay Liberation. She eventually became part of Radicalesbians, the New York collective that in 1970 issued the now-classic essay "The Woman-Identified Woman." In its definition of lesbianism as a political act, the Radicalesbians essay moves beyond "the traditional definition of women toward a concept of women defining themselves," as Brown explained in a later essay, "Living with Other Women" (76).

What Brown has called the "burning intensity" (*A Plain Brown Rapper,* Intro. 13) of her commitment to a feminist revolution led her in 1971 to help organize the Furies, a Washington, D.C., collective of lesbian feminist separatists. The impact that the collective's newsletter, *The Furies,* had on *Feminary,* a Southern feminist publication, is described by M. Segrest in her article on writing by Southern lesbians in *Southern Exposure.* "The Furies collective was a religion to us in Chapel Hill between 1971 and 1974," Segrest quotes a former *Feminary* collective member as saying (59). After Brown was purged from the Furies, she went on to become one of the founding editors of *Quest,* a journal of feminist ideology and research.

Brown's movement from one group to another was typical of the experiences of other lesbian feminist activists at the time. In *Dreamers and Dealers,* Leah Fritz's account of the second wave of the women's movement, Fritz recalls that "Lesbians began to defect from one women's group after another, to move around in search of a place where they would feel at home, a place which would serve both the totality of their needs as women and their specific needs as lesbians" (32). In documenting Brown's political odyssey during that period, the essays in *Plain Brown Rapper* are, as Brown says in the introduction, "as much a chronicle of the decade as of my own development" (22).

The essays are also important, not just as history and personal biography, but as ideology. The collection—twenty previously published essays, plus an introduction, conclusion, and a new essay—is uneven. Often the essays fire movement rhetoric at the reader in a machine-gun style that makes one piece sound very like another. And some of Brown's prescriptions for bringing about the revolution are simplistic, just as some of her predictions seem amazingly naive—"Within five years we will have our party" (117).

Yet many of the essays offer perceptive insights into class divisions and other artificial categories dividing human beings. Brown feels strongly that "Separation is what the ruling rich, white male wants: female vs. male; black vs. white; gay vs. straight; poor vs. rich" (95). Her essays attack the tendency of society to put everyone into one category or another, and she points out the ways in which these categories are restricted by what she calls "the male culture's vulgar conceptual limitations." For example, her review essay "The Last Picture Show" offers a paradigm for analyzing films that depict only "the white, middle class, heterosexual version of life" (154). A later essay, "I Am a Woman," offers an equally useful analysis, not just of the limitations of "the male concept of the female," but also of the limitations of a heterosexual view of women that ignores the fact that "even the most blatantly heterosexual woman has a relationship with her mother, her sisters, her girlfriends, aunts, grandmothers, office workers" (176).

Perhaps the best writing in the collection has to do with class, which has always been an issue of great personal significance to Brown. She identifies herself as coming from a working class background: her mother was a bakery and mill worker, and her father was a butcher. Her interviews and essays repeatedly point to lack of class consciousness in the women's movement (along with lack of consciousness about lesbianism) as the source of her problems with the different groups that she joined and then left. In a 1978 interview she recalled the New York women's groups as hostile to "lower class" issues: "the early years of the movement were bitter years, especially for me because I was from poor origins and therefore 'lower class.' Let's face it, the Women's Movement is still a white middle-class movement: I was always bringing up the basic issues that faced the poor—food, shelter and clothing. But nobody wanted to hear that. . . . With NOW and the others it was bad enough that I was a lesbian and said so, but to call into question the very process by which we were organizing ourselves—in other words the unspoken assumptions of class privilege—well, you couldn't have asked to become a more unwanted person" (Holt 16-17). Writing in the introduction to *A Plain Brown Rapper* about her experiences with the Furies, Brown says that, although the collective had tried to deal with class issues, "we ignored the psychology of class differences" and "in the end, it was this issue and the issue of identity which destroyed our collective" (16).

In "The Last Straw," perhaps her most important essay on class differences, Brown attacks two middle class assumptions: the idea that acquiring middle class income or status "removes the entire experience of our childhood and youth—working class life" (100) and also the belief in "downward mobility" embraced by some middle class revolutionaries. She points out that "for those of us who grew up without material advantages downward mobility is infuriating—here are women rejecting what we never had and can't get!" (104).

Brown's concern in her essays with class divisions is at times characterized by an ambivalence that foreshadows the movement of her novels away from her early political stance. For example, in "The Last Straw" her attack on "downward mobility" reveals an emotional defensiveness about capitalism, even though her official line in this and other essays is clearly a socialist one. Brown is not, of course, the first working class revolutionary to find her intellectual commitment to socialism in conflict with her need to protect herself by acquiring material possessions. In this defensiveness about capitalism in "The Last Straw" we can see the same conflicting feelings that turn up later in the ambivalence with which she portrays upper and middle class characters in her fiction.

On one level Brown's novels can be seen as a working and reworking of the interlocking problems of the oppressiveness of class and other artificial divisions of human beings and the isolation imposed by these divisions. As we might expect, in her essays Brown brings the expediency of the activist and the organizer to her analysis of society's readiness to put everyone in one category or another. Nonetheless, the essays reveal the intellectual basis of Brown's concern with the problems of class, race, and gender categories that her fiction explores in the lives of Southern women and in the context of the Southern environment in which Brown herself grew up.

> I'm not saying it's easy but maybe that's just what we have to do, Adele, go back where we came from and fight this out.
>
> —Brown, *In Her Day*

Although Brown's political essays were an important influence on the Southern women putting out *Feminary* in Chapel Hill, it is her novels that identify her as a Southern writer for the majority of her reading public. On promotional tours for her novels Brown has repeatedly emphasized her Southern background and indicated that she wants to be identified as a Southern writer. For example, in a Boston interview she effusively expressed her pleasure in the enthusiastic reception to her appearances in the South: "I just love the South and I'm pleased to say it loves me right back. Every time I speak there I'm just overwhelmed by love. I think Southerners are happy and proud when one of their own makes it" (White). And she clearly wanted the *New York* interviewer to see her in the tradition of Southern writers when she called *Six of One* a Southern novel and described the South as a good environment for writers. "Actually I think the book is rather southern. The South allows itself eccentrics, and, of course, if you're going to be a writer it's fabulous to grow up with that, which I did in a way" (Turner 60). In a recent interview in Philadelphia she was equally eager to identify herself as a Southern writer: "I pretty much dislike Yankees. They're no fun. They don't have a wild streak in them. They're too rational. Art is intensely emotive, and at least in the South you are allowed your emotions" (Shister 12).

Each of Brown's first four novels can be seen as a different stage in her attempt to go back to her Southern roots, either in her choice of settings or in her focus on Southern characters. Most of the first half of *Rubyfruit Jungle* is set in Fort Lauderdale; *Six of One* is set in a Pennsylvania-Maryland town on the middle of the Mason-Dixon line; and *Southern Discomfort* is set in Montgomery, Alabama. *In Her Day* takes place in New York, but a central scene, and the only flashback, focuses on Carole's trip back home to Virginia to visit her family. (Brown's fifth novel, *Sudden Death,* which is about the world of women's professional tennis and depicts a love affair that has obvious parallels to Brown's relationship with tennis star Martina Navratilova, breaks the pattern of her increasing focus on the South in her fiction. Brown wrote the novel because of a promise to a dying friend, a sports writer, and she labels it an "interruption" in her writing plans: "I was all set to go on to my next novel about the War Between the States, and this came as an interruption." The biographical note at the end of *Sudden Death* is clearly intended to alert readers to Brown's intention to return to her focus on the South: "Rita Mae Brown is currently retracing Stonewall Jackson's steps during the War Between the States in preparation for her next novel.")

Brown's first four novels go back not only to the South but to specific events and places in Brown's own life. She was born in a small Pennsylvania town and moved at an early age to Fort Lauderdale. Her adoptive parents were working class. Her biological father was French—although Brown has said that she was "without knowledge of my ethnic origins"[3]—and her biological mother at one time employed the woman who adopted her (Alexander 111). After being expelled from the University of Florida for her lesbianism and civil rights activism, Brown put herself through New York University. In the late seventies she returned to the South to live, settling in Charlottesville, Virginia, which she says is "home" now: "It's the source of my power" (Shister 12).

Different aspects of these experiences are reenacted by the various heroes of her four Southern novels. Molly in *Rubyfruit Jungle,* Carole in *In Her Day,* and Nickle in *Six of One* grow up poor in the South and leave. Brown's circuitous route from Pennsylvania to New York is specifically paralleled in Molly's move from

Pennsylvania to Fort Lauderdale, her expulsion from the state university, and her flight to New York, where she puts herself through film school. Brown's move back to the South has parallels in two of the novels: at the end of *In Her Day,* Carole and her Southern friend Adele consider going back to the South to live; and in *Six of One,* Nickel returns to Pennsylvania after publishing a successful book, buys her grandmother's house, and prepares to settle down. Although *Southern Discomfort* does not for the most part have these literal autobiographical parallels, Catherine like Brown, is adopted (as are Molly and Nickel in the two earlier novels[4]) and, like Brown, has a non-Anglo biological father. (Catherine's father is black, and there is speculation that Molly's father and Nickel's father are black, although both are identified as French.) Catherine's biological mother employs her adoptive mother, just as Brown's biological mother once employed her adoptive mother.

Brown's novels are autobiographical not only in their portrayal of these experiences but, more importantly, in their exploration of the issue that concerned her both personally and politically during her activist years. All four of the Southern novels depict people who defy society's division of human beings into artificial categories and who struggle to come to terms with the isolation imposed by those categories, and they develop this theme in more depth and with more complexity than either the scope or the purpose of her political essays permitted. In exploring this theme in autobiographical novels about Southern women, Brown is using her fiction to do what Carole in *In Her Day* tells Adele (who is also a transplanted Southerner) that they must do about the oppression they face as lesbians, "go back where we came from and fight this out."

Brown treats the problem of class and other societal categories on two levels in the novels: a realistic, or literal, level, and a symbolic level. On the literal level, she shows women running head-on into the barriers imposed by class, race, and gender categories. Locked into some categories and locked out of others, her characters have varying degrees of success in breaking through the barriers and making contact with people in other categories.

On the symbolic level, Brown suggests a bridging of these divisions through the identification of the main character with two very different types of characters, an upper or middle class character (the "aristocratic" character) and a black character. The significance of the roles of these two types of characters as the doubles of the main character is underlined by the fact that in the first, second, and fourth novels the main character is adopted. (In the third novel, *In Her Day,* Brown offers a variation on the adoption motif in that Carole's parents are dead and she has adopted a friend to replace her dead biological sister.) Although the situation of the main characters as adopted children can be emblematic of the essential loneliness of the human condition, it also functions in a more specific way to underline the extent to which societal categories cut people off from one another. As Molly puts it in *Rubyfruit Jungle,* "I had never thought I had much in common with anybody. I had no mother, no father, no roots, no biological similarities called sisters and brothers" (88).

This double-barrelled approach is evident in Brown's first novel, *Rubyfruit Jungle. Rubyfruit Jungle* became an underground best seller because of its reputation as a novel about "growing up gay in America" (as ads and reviews described it when it was reissued by Bantam in 1977),[5] but Molly Bolt is, as her name suggests, in rebellion against the restrictions imposed on her by race and class as well as gender. When her family moves from Pennsylvania to Fort Lauderdale, her father tries to explain to her that racial segregation is more obvious in Florida: "Down South things are a little different than up in York. Here the whites and the coloreds don't mix and you're not to mess with those people, although you are to be mannerly should you ever have to talk to one" (58). Her mother puts it more bluntly: "If I ever see you mixing with the wrong kind, I'm gonna wring your neck, brat" (59). Her family is poor—in her grandmother's words, "God knows with all of us working we can't make hardly enough to keep going" (23)—but it is not until they move to Florida that Molly really becomes aware of class distinctions: "Back in the Hollow we were all the same. . . . Here it was a distinct line drawn between two camps and I was certain I didn't want to be on the side with the greasy boys that leered at me and talked filthy" (61). Molly also comes up against the restrictions of gender roles. Early on her mother complains that "she don't act natural" because she "climbs trees" and "takes cars apart" instead of learning "the things she has to know to get a husband" (39), and when Molly says she wants a "candy apple red Bonneville Triumph, her cousin Leroy echoes her mother's criticism: "you ain't natural. . . . It's time you started worrying about your hair and doing those things that girls are supposed to do" (63).

Molly's reactions to the restrictions imposed on her by societal categories are in keeping with her strong sense of herself. Her reaction to racial segregation is to ignore it: "I ain't staying away from people because they look different" (59). She tackles the problem of class like the survivor she is: "It took me all of seventh grade to figure out how I would take care of myself in this new situation, but I did figure it out" (61). Her solution is to combine the traditional methods of "passing" (high grades, correct grammar, and a few good clothes) with humor: "I decided to become the funniest person in the whole school. If someone makes you laugh you have to like her" (62). Although Molly opts for "passing" in high school, later on in New York she becomes more class conscious and insists on identifying her working class background, so much so, in fact, that her friend Holly accuses her of "wearing your poverty like a badge of purity" (176). She takes an even more defiant line when faced with gender roles. When her cousin Leroy labels her interest in motorcycles unfeminine, she retorts, "I'll buy an army tank if I want to and run over anyone who tells me I can't have it" (63).

The success of Molly's defiance depends, of course, on her position in relation to the dominant culture. As white, she is a member of the dominant culture and can cross racial lines in a way that blacks cannot. As female, lesbian, and poor, she is in a more difficult position. She is able to gain the respect and liking of some people and survive the insults and attacks of others, but she can go only so far. Near the end of the novel, when she is bypassed for jobs in spite of her *summa cum laude* degree and her demonstrated talents and skills as a filmmaker, she says, "I kept hoping against hope that I'd be the bright exception, the talented token that smashed sex and class barriers" (245). The novel's closing passage records her awareness of the power of barriers erected to maintain the power of the dominant culture: "Damn, I wished the world would let me be myself. But I knew better on all counts" (246).

Molly's defiance of societal conventions concerning race, class, and sex is paralleled by the novel's symbolic identification of her with characters from different social worlds. Two of the women with whom she becomes romantically involved in New York, Holly, a beautiful black woman from a wealthy family, and Polina, an older white woman who is a medieval scholar, function as Molly's doubles, roles that are underlined by the similarity of the names of the three. Holly's role as Molly's black double is reinforced by Molly's childhood speculations about her own parents: "Since I don't know who my real folks are maybe they're colored" (59). Her other double, Polina, a medieval scholar, represents aristocratic values to Molly; she needs Polina because of "the conversations, the theater, and her stories of Europe where she grew up" (207). Although both relationships are short-lived, Holly's and Polina's roles as Molly's doubles identify her with women whose class and race are different from her own and, in doing so, foreshadow the more significant roles of the black and "aristocratic" characters in the later novels.

Brown's second novel, *In Her Day,* focuses on Carole Hanratty, a forty-four-year-old medieval art historian in New York. The break-up of her love affair with Ilse, a twenty-two-year-old lesbian feminist revolutionary from a Boston Brahmin family, is balanced against the stability of her friendship with Adele, her black friend. The novel has been described as "an embarrassing attempt to write a Lesbian-feminist novel of ideas," (Kleindeinst 3) and, with the exception of a few reviews in lesbian feminist publications, it is generally agreed to be a failure, an assessment with which Brown herself agrees.[6] Nonetheless, the novel develops the rebellion theme in *Rubyfruit Jungle* on both literal and symbolic levels. Although Carole is stately, reserved, and distrustful of Ilse's political enthusiasms, she has bucked the system in some of the same ways that Molly Bolt has. Carole's friendship with Adele in the fifties was, as Ilse reminds her, a form of "breaking the code," for "when you two became friends white and Black women weren't seen together" (93). Like Molly, Carole has fought her way up from poverty: "I worked for everything I have. I didn't come from money. Honey, I grew up in the Depression in Richmond, Virginia. . . . We lived in the Fan. It was a slum pretty much, although we didn't call it that ourselves" (76). As female and a lesbian she has rebelled against the restrictions of gender roles, first as a child ("I knew as a kid that boys got all the breaks but it made me mad—just made me fight that much harder"); then as a student at Vassar opting for a career at a time when "there wasn't a women's movement except in the direction of Yale" (26); and finally as a university professor in a department where "I would have been head . . . if I weren't a woman" (54). Carole is, as Ilse somewhat patronizingly describes her, "a proto-feminist" (26).

On the symbolic level of the novel, Adele functions as Carole's black double in a development of Holly's role in *Rubyfruit Jungle*. A beautiful black woman from a wealthy family, Adele is Carole's age and, like her, a Southerner. Her role as Carole's double is underlined by Carole's adoption of her as her sister. When Carole's biological sister is killed in an automobile accident, Adele comforts her, riding partway to Richmond with her on the train and meeting her returning train: "the hours, like a magic circle, closed around them and strengthened the bond of friendship already between them. As Carol boarded the train, finally, she turned to Adele and said, 'You're my sister now'" (62). Their identification is made even more explicit in the last scene, in which they talk about their need as Southerners to go back to their "roots" and the impossibility of their going unless they go together. "I love you more than anyone on earth" (194), Carole tells Adele.

Ilse, Carole's "aristocratic" double, attended the same college, Vassar, that Carole had attended twenty years earlier, and she looks like "white America's dream of femininity," as Carole had at her age. Ilse's role as Carole's double is underlined by Carole's internalization of upper class values. Carole acknowledges that, like Molly Bolt, she had tried to overcome class barriers by "passing": "I spent close to a decade trying to pretend I was an aristocrat" (134). Ilse remarks upon this ambivalence: "At first I thought she was some kind of aristocrat" (166). As Adele puts it in explaining Carole's attraction to Ilse, "Carole has always been fascinated and repelled by people who had it easy" (103). Although the relationship between them fails, they are, as Bernice Mennis notes in her review of the novel in *Conditions: One*, "two parts of a dialectic" and "by the end of the novel and of their relationship, each incorporates a small part of the other's vision" (119, 120). Ilse's role as Carole's "aristocratic" double builds on Polina's role in *Rubyfruit Jungle,* just as Adele's role builds on Holly's role, and the two characters prefigure the roles of the doubles in the novels that follow.

Brown's third novel, *Six of One,* portrays the women in two families in a small town in southern Pennsylvania between 1909 and 1980. The novel focuses on the lively feuding between two sisters, Juts and Louise, from their childhood (shown in flashbacks) to their old age (described by the first-person narrator, Juts's adopted daughter, Nickel). Nickel had been a "bullheaded" child, "ready to get into trouble" (284), and she had grown up to be an adult who "left the church, left the town, left [her mother] . . . writes books that disgrace the whole family" (2), and sleeps with women. She and her mother, Juts, whose "hell-raising bent" (135) she has inherited, are both reincarnations of Molly Bolt. Another hell-raiser in the novel is Celeste Chalfonte, the wealthy Southern white woman who employs Nickel's grandmother, Cora. (Cora was, Brown tells us, modeled on Brown's own grandmother and her "favorite character in the whole book").[7] Celeste defies convention by openly living with her female lover, but she cannot completely break through the class barrier. Her statement to her lover Ramelle reveals the power of the social structure in her life: "If I could choose a sister I would choose Cora. Our tragedy was to be born at opposite ends of the social spectrum. This [their employer-servant relationship] is the only way we can be part of one another's lives short of revolution" (210).

The novel symbolically bridges this class division, however, through the identification of Nickel with Celeste, her "aristocratic" double. While a black double is absent in this novel, the speculation that Nickel's biological father may have been black identifies her to some extent with blacks, much as Molly's speculation about whether her parents were black functions in *Rubyfruit Jungle.* For example, when Cora decides to adopt Nickel, her sister warns her, "For all you know, the father could be black as spades" (248), and one of the strike-breakers hired by the local munitions factory taunts Nickel, "I hear tell your father was a nigger" (291).

Celeste and Nickel are repeatedly identified with one another throughout the novel, although the two never see each other. Nickel is born on Celeste's sixty-seventh birthday, and Celeste's unexpected death the night before ushers in the birth. Celeste's thoughts on the evening of her death suggest an identification with Nickel that has undertones of reincarnation: "Celeste found herself strangely excited about the baby. She hoped it would come forth tomorrow. . . . Celebrating earthly renewal with a new person might be fun" (251). This identification of the two is continued by reminders of Nickel's resemblance to Celeste. For example, when Nickel says, "I hope I grow up to be like Celeste," her grandmother Cora replies, "I do, too" (296). When Nickel's mother tells her, "Sometimes you remind me of Celeste Chalfonte with an engine on your back," Nickel replies that one of Celeste's Vassar friends "told me . . . that I reminded her a bit of Celeste" (226). Celeste is further connected to Nickel through a bequest in her will that provides for Nickel to attend Celeste's alma mater, Vassar. The bequest links Nickel not only to Celeste but also to Celeste's social world.

The identification of Nickel with Celeste is underlined by the elaborate parallels between Celeste's two worlds. On the one hand there is her "aristocratic" world—her biological family, her lover, and her Vassar friends (who, significantly, were known as "the Furies" in college). On the other hand there is her working class family—her servant Cora, Cora's daughters Juts and Louise, and Cora's granddaughter, Nickel. When Celeste's lover becomes pregnant (by Celeste's brother), Celeste assumes the role of "a mother or mother number two" (108) to Ramelle's child. Celeste is also a second mother to Cora's daughter Juts, a relationship suggested in part through the presence of Cora's daughters in Celeste's house when their mother is working there and in part through Celeste's love for Cora. (The bond between Celeste and Cora is put in physical, although not sexual, terms when Celeste, frightened and seeking comfort in Ramelle's absence, goes to Cora's house in the middle of the night and sleeps in the same bed with her.)

The parallels between Celeste's two "daughters," her daughter by her lover Ramelle, and her daughter by her servant Cora, are continued in the implied comparison of Cora's two "granddaughters," Ramelle's granddaughter and Cora's granddaughter Nickel. Significantly, the passage in which Ramelle and Cora compare their two granddaughters ends with Cora's summing up their similarity with the phrase from which the novel takes its title, "Six of one, half dozen of the other" (284). Although attempts to break through class barriers are only partially successful on the literal level of the novel, on a symbolic level the two classes are brought together through the identification of Nickel with her "aristocratic" double, Celeste, an identification that is underlined by the complex paralleling of Celeste's two families.

Brown's recent novel, *Southern Discomfort,* takes place in Montgomery, Alabama, and is set in two periods ten years apart, 1918 and 1928. The first half of the novel focuses on the secret love affair between white society leader Hortensia Reedmuller Banastre (whose imposing demeanor recalls both Carole Hanratty in *In Her Day* and Celeste Chalfonte in *Six of One*) and Hercules Jinks, a black fifteen-year-old boxer. Their affair, which ends when Hercules is killed in a railway yard accident, leaves Hortensia pregnant with their daughter Catherine. Hortensia arranges for Catherine to be brought up by her black servant, and the second half of the novel focuses on Catherine's gradual discovery of her real heritage.

Hortensia rebels against race barriers in her love affair with Hercules, and against class barriers in her friendship with Blue Rhonda, a white prostitute. In a passage that recalls Celeste Chalfonte's envy of the "zest" and "immediacy" (124) of Cora's family in *Six of One*, Lila, Hortensia's mother, acknowledges to herself that the hope for the upper class is to break out of their rigid mold: "Half of her longed to usher her daughter into the human race and the other half of her fought to preserve the stultifying social order over which she, Lila, presided" (10).

In the end, the social order is preserved. In spite of Hortensia's love for Hercules, she is "not yet prepared to run away" (98) with him, although she does not fully realize the significance of her reluctance until ten years later.

Brown suggests a possible transcending of class barriers in a key conversation in the second half of the novel between Hortensia and Blue Rhonda. Blue Rhonda makes a fumbling speech in which she calls societal categories "God's joke" because "God put beautiful spirits into these bodies, all kinds of bodies" and "we dumb humans are confused by the outside." She ends by saying, in a tone of finality, "We are one" (131), a phrase picked up by Hortensia in their parting exchange:

"How odd that we live so close to one another . . ."

Rhonda finished her thought for her. "Same town, different worlds."

Hortensia's smile caught the moonlight. "Ah, but we are one."

(132)

But this transcending of categories is clearly only momentary. For example, when Hortensia gets Blue Rhonda and two other prostitutes invitations to a society wedding, she sees their presence there as a joke, in spite of the debt she owes them and the bond forged by that debt in their private meetings.

Rebellion against gender roles is equally short-lived. After Blue Rhonda's death, she is revealed in the epilogue to the novel to be a man who has masqueraded as a woman. The letter she leaves behind for her friends echoes her reference to "God's joke" in her conversation with Hortensia, but her statement this time, "God played a joke on me and put me in a man's body" (248-49), puts the emphasis on the power of societal categories, not their artificiality.

By virtue of her mixed heritage, Catherine defies both race and class barriers. Her feelings of isolation are movingly suggested in several scenes. When she realizes that she cannot join Hortensia's friends for drinks after a polo match, the ensuing dialogue between her and her mother reveals her sense of not fitting into any societal category:

"It's because I'm piebald, isn't it?" Catherine flatly stated. . . .

"What?" Hortensia inquired.

"Piebald, pinto—half black and half white. I don't fit anywhere, do I?"

(174)

The reaction of one of Hortensia's otherwise obtuse friends links Catherine's isolation to the "discomfort" of the novel's title: "Sugar Guerrant felt her heart sink. For one flutter of an eyelash she had a sense of the child's displacement, and worse, an insight into what Southerners used to call 'our special problem'" (174-75).

Hortensia's acknowledgment of Catherine as her daughter does not really change Catherine's sense of not belonging, as the closing of the novel's last chapter suggests:

"I don't feel like I belong to anybody but myself."

Tears filled Hortensia's eyes. "You can belong to me if you want to."

"I don't know," Catherine said thoughtfully.

"As long as you like yourself, then if you do belong only to yourself perhaps you're ahead of the game."

"I like myself." Catherine smiled, kissed Hortensia and then lay down and went right to sleep.

(246)

This last scene is inconclusive. The only time the novel suggests that these rigid divisions could be done away with permanently comes when Hortensia observes, "Still, if we wanted to, if we truly, truly wanted to, I think we could change the world" (176). Although Hortensia believes in the possibility of change, she is nonetheless resigned to accepting the "stultifying social order" in much the same way that Celeste is when she says that, although she loves Cora like a sister, there is no way "short of revolution" that she and Cora can step out of their roles as employer and servant.

Although class and race lines ultimately prevail in *Southern Discomfort*, the symbolic bridging of these divisions in the novel is more complete than it is in Brown's earlier novels. The identification of the adopted character with a black character and/or a middle or upper class character (an "aristocratic" character) in the other works is brought to the forefront of the novel here in the casting of Catherine's father as her black double and her mother as her "aristocratic" double. Her father Hercules is a variation on Molly's black double, Holly, in *Rubyfruit Jungle,* and on Carole's black double, Adele, in *In Her Day*. (Hercules also recalls the biological fathers of both Molly in *Rubyfruit Jungle* and Nickel in *Six of One* in that both men are French but are suspected of being black.) Catherine's mother Hortensia is a development of the roles of the "aristocratic" doubles in the earlier novels, Polina in *Rubyfruit Jungle,* Ilse in *In Her Day,* and Celeste in *Six of One*.

The symbolic union of Catherine with both her "aristocratic" double and her black double is climactically brought about through Hortensia's murder of the younger of her two sons, Paris. Like Celeste Chalfonte in *Six of One* with her two families, Hortensia has children in two different worlds—Paris, her beautiful and immoral son by her white husband, and Catherine, her daughter by her black lover. Paris represents the shallow side of Hortensia that she must kill in order to accept the part of her that is Catherine. This process of becoming whole began earlier when Hortensia recognized the evil in Paris and when she saw Catherine's anguish at being rejected by the white children of Montgomery: "When Paris fully revealed his twisted self, and then recently when Catherine was unmasked at the Great Witch Hunt, she was pushed into herself" (234). When Paris physically attacks Hortensia and Catherine, Hortensia kills him (in a more dramatic version of the killing or displacing of siblings than in Brown's earlier novels). The murder of Paris not only allows Hortensia to accept the part of herself that is Catherine but also brings Catherine into a fuller sense of herself. The act literally establishes Catherine in her rightful place as Hortensia's daughter and is followed by Hortensia's acknowledgment to Catherine that she is her mother. The murder also completes the union of Catherine with her black father, a process that began when Catherine had been given a picture of him and then was tutored by his mother. When the sheriff decides to report the murder as a suicide, he explains to Hortensia, "I owe Catherine's father one" (245).

Catherine and Hortensia, like Brown's heroes in her three earlier novels, rebel against a system of values that infringes on their sense of themselves. In so doing, all these characters embody the definition of "the woman-identified woman" in the essay that Brown wrote with other members of the Radicalesbians: "She is the woman who, often beginning at an extremely early age, acts in accordance with her inner compulsion to be a more complete and freer human being than her society . . . cares to allow her. These needs and actions, over a period of years, bring her into painful conflict with people, situations, the accepted ways of thinking, feeling and behaving. . . ." While the Radicalesbians essay defines the "woman-identified woman" as one who rebels against "the limitations and oppression laid on her by the most basic role of her society—the female role" ("Woman-Identified" 87), Brown's heroes rebel against all roles that reflect society's "conceptual limitations." On the literal level, this rebellion has become progressively less open in Brown's novels, moving from Molly Bolt's free-swinging defiance of everyone who gets in her way in *Rubyfruit Jungle* to Hortensia's acceptance of the social order in *Southern Discomfort*. (Anne Gottlieb, in her review of *Southern Discomfort* in the *New York Times Book Review,* sees Brown as having become aware in this novel that no one can break "*all* the rules" and that "every freedom must be understood within the bounds of a shared social structure that can, if stretched, yield painful renewal; if shattered, tragedy," 10.) At the same time, the symbolic bridging of class and race divisions has intensified, reaching its height in *Southern Discomfort* in the biological identification of the adopted character with both a black character and an "aristocratic" one.

Jill Johnston, in writing about Brown's portrayal of herself in Molly in *Rubyfruit Jungle,* says, "What I admire most is her own early, or prepolitical, refusal to compromise her identity by permitting anybody to either closet or contain her."[8] Molly Bolt is the most openly rebellious of Brown's heroes. But although the women characters in Brown's other novels do not rebel against societal categories in the same defiant way that Molly does, their rejection of the limitations that society attempts to place on them through class, race, and gender divisions is the essence of their being. It is in Brown's portrayal of the rebelliousness of her heroes that we can see how her concerns as a lesbian feminist underlie and inform her portrayal of Southern women and link her early political vision with her imaginative vision as a Southern novelist.

Notes

1. Page references are to the Bantam edition.

2. Brown also discusses the NOW experience in her 1972 essay, "Take a Lesbian to Lunch," *Plain Brown Rapper,* 87-91.

3. In "Take a Lesbian to Lunch" Brown says of NOW's attempt to co-opt her: "They got a real bargain with me. Not only was I a Lesbian, but I was poor, I was an orphan (adopted) without knowledge of my ethnic origins," *Plain Brown Rapper,* 89.

4. Judith Winn, book review editor for *Sojourner,* first pointed out to me the adoption motif in these two novels.

5. See, for example, the ad and review in *The Village Voice,* 12 Sept. 1977, 4.

6. See Kleindeinst's review in *Gay Community News,* 3, and Turner in *New York,* 60.

7. See Turner, 60.

8. Quoted by Alexander, 110.

Barbara Bennett (essay date 1998)

SOURCE: Bennett, Barbara. "Introduction: Southern Laughter and the Woman Writer." In *Comic Visions, Female Voices: Contemporary Women Novelists and Southern Humor,* pp. 1-15. Baton Rouge: Louisiana State University Press, 1998.

[*In the following essay, Bennett explores the role of humor in Southern literature, particularly as it relates to women writers, focusing on the idea that humor offers a challenge to the status quo.*]

> Laughter I declare to be blessed; you who aspire to greatness, learn how to laugh!
>
> —Friedrich Nietzsche

> Being humorous in the South is like being motorized in Los Angeles or argumentative in New York—humorous is not generally a whole calling in itself, it's just something that you're in trouble if you aren't.
>
> —Roy Blount

Dorothy Allison has described herself as "sharp, squint-eyed, determined, too caustic, stubbornly hopeful and occasionally funny as hell."[1] Allison's final phrase is perhaps the most unexpected, coming from a writer who deals with such unpleasant subjects as child abuse. Yet "funny" is an adjective that describes Allison as well as many other contemporary southern women writers, although the humor in these writers' works has long been overlooked and underappreciated, especially in the traditionally male-dominated literary world.

To be fair, literary humor in general—in male or female authors—has not received its deserved critical attention, even though, as Louis D. Rubin, Jr., points out in *The Comic Imagination in American Literature,* "There is scarcely an important American writer who does not at one time or another see the problem before him comically." This neglect is not limited to the study of literature: Freud noted that "jokes have not received nearly as much philosophical consideration as they deserve in view of the part they play in our mental life."[2] One reason humor has received such short shrift from critics is that comedy is commonly believed to be less important, and therefore less deserving of analysis, than tragedy. The ever-present Puritan within many Americans equates significance with sobriety, with the result that so-called serious writers are more highly praised than comic ones.

Southern humor has received about the same amount of attention as most other regional humor. Studies of southern humor in the nineteenth century have mainly focused on male authors—humorists of the Old Southwest and, of course, Mark Twain. As Merrill Skaggs points out, however, a "startling high percentage of the Southern writers publishing in the late nineteenth century were female."[3] In studies of twentieth-century southern humor, fair consideration has been given to Eudora Welty, Flannery O'Connor, and Carson McCullers, along with William Faulkner, but little has been published about the humor of contemporary southern writers and even less about women writers. The question could be asked if this subject is worthy of study, and the answer is "yes," for several reasons. Humor is an intricate part of many southern women writers' works, helping to define voice, communicate theme, and establish new definitions of southern literature; the tone is often more optimistic and less guilt ridden than that found in fiction written by men or by their literary predecessors. In addition, most female humor has a distinct voice and vision: iconoclastic, yet ultimately unifying; challenging traditional relationships, yet affirming the self and family.

The three issues that are most significant in this study are the "southernness" of the writing, the contemporary setting, and the female perspective. Each is intrinsic to the new voice and vision that women writers bring to the literature of today's South, and in all three, humor plays an important role. Despite its importance, though, humor is difficult to define, and in making the attempt, critics often experience frustration of the sort expressed by Dorothy Parker, who claimed that every time she tried, she "had to go and lie down with a cold wet cloth on [her] head."[4] Definitions of regional humor are even more difficult to isolate and clarify, usually tending toward generalizations. For example, the seven articles in a 1995 issue of *Southern Cultures* dedicated to southern humor deal with topics ranging from folk humor to African American humor to sexual humor and beyond; but not one writer clearly defines southern humor—or even seriously attempts to—most simply list various characteristics of it. In one article, John Shelton Reed concludes that humor "seems to be one of those 'idiomatic imponderables,'" claiming only that southern humor is "different—different enough that others don't always understand it."[5]

Perhaps the ability to define southern humor is not as important as the capacity to recognize it and distinguish it from other types of humor. Reed comes closest to describing southern humor when he quotes Jerry Clower: "I don't tell funny stories. I tell stories funny." An important characteristic, then, of southern humor is what Lee Smith calls "a love of storytelling for its own sake."[6] Twain said much the same thing in his essay "How to Tell a Story," observing that a "humorous story may be spun out to great length, and may wander around as much as it pleases, and arrive nowhere in particular." This narrative pattern can be found in his most famous short story, "The Notorious Jumping Frog of Calaveras County." Here the humor is derived mainly from the inclusion of absurd details, from the contrast between the two narrators—both of whom appear ridiculous—and from the seemingly meaningless meanderings of farfetched subplots. One doesn't look for the point of the story; the story *is* the point.

If this is true, the topic of a southern humorous story can be almost anything, and in *Roy Blount's Book of Southern Humor,* Blount lists some possibilities: "dirt, chickens, defeat, family, religion, prejudice, collard greens, politics, and diddie wa diddie."[7] By putting defeat and religion on a par with dirt and collard greens, Blount supports the claim that the humor is in the telling, not in the topic, and his inclusion of the nebulous "diddie wa diddie" implies an inability to articulate what is humorous—as well as the oral quality to southern humor. Despite Blount's encompassing list, some subjects and situations do surface more often than others in southern humor: death and violence, scatology, religion, sex, gender roles, and the place of tradition in contemporary life. Of course, these topics are not exclusively southern, but southerners—and southern women writers in particular—approach them in a distinct style.

In addition, southern humor often depends on a certain voice, tone, and use of language—which is one reason so many southern stories are told in the first person. Such stories seem meant to be read aloud, and as narrators tell their tales, readers do not just read: they hear. Again, Twain's story serves as an excellent example: when the second narrator, Simon Wheeler, begins his final tale with the words, "Well, thish-yer Smiley had a yaller one-eyed cow that didn't have no tail, only just a short stump like a bannanner," the reader laughs—not at the pathetic, afflicted cow but at the tone, the voice, the vivid language, and the fresh details.

This example highlights another important quality in southern humor: it often rises out of tragedy. If this is true, it is not surprising that writers in the South have been so prolific in creating humorous literature. Some scholars cite the Civil War as a strong factor contributing to the development of a unique humor in the South. Paradoxically enough, war does not initiate tragic creations as often as comic ones, according to Sarah Blacher Cohen, who argues that the South's defeat in the Civil War gave rise to one of the two periods of "the greatest burgeoning of American comedy"—the Depression being the other—because "travail gives rise to humor, which expresses people's rage at the senseless turn of events and dissipates their gloom." Rubin further explains this connection between tragedy and comedy: "The South has been caught up in a process of transition which has been marked by considerable turmoil and ugliness. Its literature has been one of the happier products of this process. Not merely along with, but indeed *directly out of* the turmoil and even the violence of the changing South, there have come novels and poems which have fixed the image of the South in art and have given to it the imaginative dignity of tragedy and comedy." Numerous critics and philosophers have commented on the power of humor during times of misfortune, both as respite from pain and as aid in recovery. Henri Bergson, for example, asserts that comedy produces "a momentary anesthesia of the heart." Wylie Sypher claims that "comedy is essentially a Carrying Away of Death."[8] Defeat and despair are not exclusively southern, of course, which may be one reason the literature of the South has been so popular with nonsouthern readers.

One cannot rely too heavily on tragedy and despair resulting from the Civil War as an explanation of southern humor, however, especially when analyzing southern women's humor: As women scholars have pointed out, the response to the Civil War was much different for white women than for white men. Anne Goodwyn Jones argues that southern white women, instead of being broken and depressed by the war, "gained the self-reliance and sense of competence that comes from useful work during and after the Civil War." Doris Betts muses that subsequent generations of these writers did not grow up listening to Civil War stories on front porches because they were instead probably "out in the detached kitchens baking pies at storytime."[9]

Civil War stories were quite different for freed slaves as well, since, unlike white southerners, they did not lose the war, and their contributions to southern humor are often overlooked completely. Johanna Nicol Shields believes that the roots of the humor of the Old Southwest lie in the trickster figure common in slave stories, which were often based on African tales. Trudier Harris sees African American humor as stemming not from the Civil War but from slaves who used laughter as a way to avoid tears, a technique she calls "the blues motif": "Put simply, for African Americans, humor made the South not only endurable but transcendable, for humor reduced the South to a laughably manageable level of insanity."[10] Whichever theory or combination of theories one chooses, the link between comedy and tragedy is undeniable, and although tragedy is not exclusively southern, the southerner's penchant for certain types of humor, such as gallows humor, may be directly related to feelings of defeat that, in the United States, only the South has experienced.

The southerner's tie to the past is powerful, and therefore any study of contemporary southern literature must cast at least a brief glance backward. And although there are many comprehensive studies of southern literary history, it is worthwhile here to look at the writers and movements that have influenced the ways today's women writers employ humor.

The history of southern humor begins with the history of southern literature itself. In the seventeenth and eighteenth centuries, southern writers produced a great deal of satire, but as William Ferris argues, the satire was not regionally unique; it was mainly an imitation of eighteenth-century European neoclassical comedy.[11] A uniquely southern literature did not exist until about 1840, when economic, political, and social conditions in the North and the South began to diverge and the South emerged as a distinct region.

Roughly twenty to thirty years before the Civil War, the oral tradition met print and publication in the humor of the Old Southwest. This fiction, from a region that includes what is now considered the Deep South, was written and read almost exclusively by white men. It is characterized by tall tales rife with exaggeration and the boastful recounting of humorous events, usually in the dialect of the uneducated but imaginative southwestern narrator. In a 1964 study, Hennig Cohen and William Dillingham identify the subjects, themes, and characteristics common to these humorists, many of which emerge in the writings of other nineteenth- and twentieth-century southern writers. In terms of far-reaching influences on contemporary female writers, the most salient of these include an oral quality to the tales, delight in the vivid and concrete, the frequent use of a first-person narrator, the use of black or "unhealthy" humor, and an attempt to "record realistically local customs and manners and to provide a chronicle of the times."[12]

Cohen and Dillingham describe the humor of this period as essentially "masculine" in comparison to the "genteel literature which was being enjoyed by pale young ladies in New England drawing rooms." Apparently this label was assigned because of the sometimes earthy nature of the humor, which showed a "lack of respect for delicate sensibilities";[13] however, female characters created by those male writers are far from resembling those protected and "pale" New Englanders. In the following excerpt from *The Crockett Almanacs,* entitled "Crockett's Daughters," readers discover a woman who is feisty, strong, and independent: "An' I guess I shall never forget how all horrificaciously flumexed a hull party of Indians war, the time they surprised and seized my middle darter, Thebeann. . . . The varmints knew as soon as they got hold of her that she war one of my breed, by her thunderbolt kickin', and they determined to cook half of her and eat the other half alive, out of revenge for the many lickin's I gin 'em."[14] Although such characters might not appeal to New England "ladies," it is easy to identify Thebeann's spirit in such twentieth-century literary sisters as Carson McCullers' Miss Amelia, Flannery O'Connor's Mary Grace, Fannie Flagg's Idgie Threadgoode, and Rita Mae Brown's Molly Bolt, among others, all of whom appeal to modern women readers.

Mark Twain was influenced by the humorists of the Old Southwest in several ways. Following in their patterns but refining and sharpening their techniques, Twain created literature that is far superior. In Twain's work, James Cox has identified the southwestern humorist's habit of putting "enormous imaginative pressure on both the gentleman and the bumpkin." Hugh Holman has noted the "detached, cool, amused, generally tolerant, and often sardonic" tone of the typical narrator; Pascal Covici, Jr., has remarked on another similarity: "A character is pushed by the author into a situation in which he either exposes the pretensions of others or himself emerges as ridiculous because of his pretentious behavior."[15] These aspects of Twain's writing—style, tone, and topic—have had a tremendous influence on contemporary women writers, perhaps more than the work of any other writer, male or female.

This is not to say that female authors were not prolific in the nineteenth century. Jones claims that southern women writers have "had an active and highly visible history since colonial times" and that "the South has historically accepted and praised its women writers." There are some problems with this statement, however.[16] First, despite the praise Jones mentions, until fairly recently women writers have not been adequately represented in anthologies of southern writing or mentioned in critical essays, partly because most of the writing that women produced was nonfiction—letters, diaries, journals—and much of it was published in periodicals and hence not preserved.[17] Second, fiction that included humor—by such authors as Mary Noailles Murfree, Sherwood Bonner, Sarah Barnwell Elliott, and Ruth McEnery Stuart—was often relegated to the genre of "local color," a label that connotes inferior fiction with a short lifespan for a limited audience. But the works of these women do not fit neatly into either the category of humor of the Old Southwest or that of local color. Kathryn McKee claims that these writings constitute "a previously unidentified genre" sharing characteristics with both groups. The writers whom McKee labels "Female Local Humorists" were heavily influenced by the humorists of the Old Southwest in their style, their "irreverent and ironic" tone, their regional settings, and their use of humor. But their perspective was decidedly female, allowing them to view their region in a unique way and to "redefine Southern womanhood" in the process.[18]

Despite the ironic tone they shared with the humorists of the Old Southwest, these writers have been categorized as local colorists simply because they are not male. Moreover, it has been male scholars who have generally assigned them this label, falsely assuming that men's writing has universal appeal, whereas women's writing only appeals to women. Carol S. Manning remarks on this practice of excluding women writers from collections, even though nineteenth-century men who wrote "popular, sentimental, inferior fiction" were included in such anthologies. She argues that women writers of the late nineteenth century, like Ellen Glasgow and Kate Chopin, actually began the Southern Renaissance by questioning and asserting themselves through their fiction but were overlooked because they lacked the "central circle of writers or central locale to draw the critics' spotlight" that the Fugitives had in Nashville.[19]

Thanks to the recent work of mostly female scholars, many of these women writers are being rediscovered and are finding their way back into print. Augusta Jane King, Grace King, Alice Dunbar-Nelson, and Frances Newman—as well as dozens of other authors—are finally being recognized and their works analyzed as yet another perspective from which to view the South.[20] One of these rediscovered texts is a wonderfully satiric novel by Ellen Glasgow, *The Romantic Comedians,* first published in 1926, but long out of print and unavailable until the University Press of Virginia reissued it in 1995. The novel is the first and best of what Glasgow called her "trilogy of tragicomedies," focusing on many of the same issues women writers now address: gender differences, relationships, patriarchal images of women, and the changing South.[21] Much of the novel is viewed through the eyes of Judge Honeywell, a man who claims to know everything worth knowing about life and women. Glasgow's tone, much like Twain's, is amused, detached, and ironic, and when Honeywell makes such statements as, "If there is anything wrong with the Episcopal Church or the Democratic Party, I would rather die without knowing it," one is amused at both his naïveté and his arrogance.[22] Interestingly, although other books by Glasgow have remained in print—such as *Barren Ground,* a book virtually devoid of humor—this novel has not, which may be more proof of the lack of respect accorded comedy by literary circles.

Another overlooked satirist is Frances Newman, author of *The Hard-Boiled Virgin* (1930) and *Dead Lovers Are Faithful Lovers* (1928). Although her books remained out of print until the 1980s, their relevance may simply be that they exist, evidence that women have long questioned the stereotypes of southern womanhood. In *The Hard-Boiled Virgin,* Newman exposes the superficiality of the life of the southern belle who pursues social acceptance at the expense of intellectual growth and individual achievement. Newman's prose is demanding, innovative, and sometimes impossibly convoluted, but the reader is rewarded for persevering with satiric gems such as this: "She did not suspect either the social or the biological soundness of his demonstration that southern gentlemen consider alcoholic beverages unsuited to the fragile organisms which are capable of nothing more energetic than producing twelve babies."[23] Such relatively obscure novels as *The Hard-Boiled Virgin* and *The Romantic Comedians* demonstrate that contemporary satire is merely an extension of the questioning of male and female roles that has been going on for some time; the women's movement of the 1970s only increased its strength and momentum.

A better-known author is William Faulkner, and although his presence is keenly felt in southern literary history, his work has not influenced female writers as much as it has male writers. In my own relatively informal surveys of contemporary women authors, O'Connor and Welty are mentioned more often than any others; for example, when asked about influences on her work, Dorothy Allison simply answered, "Flannery O'Connor, lord yes!" Other writers whose names appear often include Zora Neale Hurston, Harper Lee, Reynolds Price, and Walker Percy, but only Josephine Humphreys mentioned Faulkner—and then only near the end of a list of six authors. Paul Binding, a British writer who did a series of interviews with southern authors in 1979, came to a similar conclusion in his study. He claims that no writers he spoke with praised Faulkner, but virtually all mentioned Welty's work as a "creative example." Is this pattern simply a result of a fear of being compared with one of the greatest twentieth-century American writers? After all, as O'Connor noted, "Nobody wants his mule and wagon stalled on the same track the Dixie Limited is roaring down." Are contemporary writers protesting too much? Perhaps, but probably not. In terms of tone and themes that affirm life, love, and human potential, contemporary women writers are certainly, as Fred Hobson notes, "more nearly apostles of Welty than of Faulkner."[24]

In fact, exorcising Faulkner's influence from their work seems to be a preoccupation of many southern writers, who understandably feel burdened at times by his still larger-than-life presence. But women writers do not feel as threatened by the reputations of Welty and O'Connor, who are much less acknowledged and praised by critics, and writers often give a nod in their direction as a sign of appreciation. Valerie Sayers, for example, names two streets in her recurrent setting of Due East, South Carolina, O'Connor Street and Welty Street (on which can be found a restaurant called The Golden Apple), but her references to Faulkner are not so kind: few characters have read his work, and if they have, they do not understand him. In *The Track of Real Desires,* Beverly Lowry does not even mention Faulkner's name, referring ironically to his reputation and near-legendary status by disparaging people who worship him and focusing on Faulkner's role as a tourist attraction whose popularity is rivaled by good southern food: "Scholars and fans who came to the state to visit the shrine of Mississippi's dead genius writer often drove down to Eunola to eat at Moe's, and sometimes people ordered whole cheesecakes."[25] By joking about Faulkner's grip on the South, women writers clear space for themselves and their writing, showing critics that Due East, South Carolina, Hopewell, Kentucky, and Speed, Alabama, are not merely rehashed versions of Yoknapatawpha County.

Numerous writers, northern and southern, male and female, have acknowledged an inspirational indebtedness to Eudora Welty. One of those writers, Lee Smith, has said: "My teachers kept telling me, 'Write what you know' but I didn't know, for a long time, what that was. Then, in Louis Rubin's southern literature class, I came upon the stories of Eudora Welty and Flannery O'Connor. It was as though a literal light bulb snapped on in my head, exactly the way it happens in cartoons."[26] Usually, Welty's keen eye for concrete details, her near-perfect ability to characterize with a single phrase, and her expression of the profound through the simple and mundane are cited by other writers as most influential. Anne Tyler has also acknowledged many times her creative debt to Welty:

> I spent my adolescence planning to be an artist, not a writer. After all, books had to be about major events, and none had ever happened to me. All I knew were tobacco workers, stringing the leaves I handed them and talking up a storm. Then I found a book of Eudora Welty's short stories in the high school library. She was writing about Edna Earle [a character in "The Wide Net"], who was so slow-witted she could sit all day just pondering how the tail of the *C* got through the loop of the *L* on the Coca-Cola sign. Why, I knew Edna Earle. You mean you could *write* about such people?[27]

Welty describes her use of humor as "a way of entry . . . a way to get around something to make it endurable, to live with it or to shrug it off." One reviewer has noted that Welty "possesses the surest comic sense of any American writer alive." Another has said that even though her stories are very funny, the humor is there for the purpose of "providing balance, lending perspective" to the tragedy also apparent in her stories—characteristics clearly evident in the works of today's southern women novelists.[28]

Along with Welty, Flannery O'Connor's influence is acutely felt. Walter Sullivan praises O'Connor as "the only distinctly new and original [voice] to arise in the post-renascence South." Although Sullivan's opinion is undoubtedly overstated, O'Connor's influence on other writers is well documented. Her style, vision, and sense of humor are uniquely her own, however. Hugh Holman describes her conception of a human being as "a frail, weak creature, imperfect and incomplete in all his parts"; such a vision "calls for either comedy or pathos, and pathos was alien to Flannery O'Connor's nature and beliefs."[29] This statement mistakenly puts comedy and pathos at opposite extremes, when in truth, much of O'Connor's satire is aimed at characters whose lack of true religious conviction makes them targets for both pity and comedy, a focus and a technique that contemporary novelists have imitated.

O'Connor's perception that modern life is absurd is certainly apparent in contemporary southern writers, as is her belief that humor can be more than just entertainment and more than just a method for pointing out the deficiencies and inanities of life: it can become the vehicle for transcending the absurd. Many southern women writers have learned this from O'Connor, Welty, Glasgow, and Twain, among others, and although they may portray the South and the new role of women within that South differently, echoes of these earlier writers can be found throughout their work. Some aspects of their southern roots have been incorporated into southern novels by women, while other aspects have been acknowledged but subsequently rejected.

The list of literary predecessors who are female humorists is short, for the history of women and humor has been a tale of struggle for recognition and acceptance. Nancy A. Walker, author of *"A Very Serious Thing": Women's Humor and American Culture* says that "being a female humorist in America has been problematic in a number of ways that are tied closely to other issues in women's history: the tension between intellect and femininity, male and female 'separate spheres,' women's status as a minority group, and the transforming power of a feminist vision." But Walker explains that despite being told that they cannot be funny, women have continued to be "very funny indeed."[30]

Humor tests boundaries and pushes limits, doubly so for women. Although women have always known they could be funny, their humor has mainly been relegated to the kitchen, out of the range of male listeners and on the margins of patriarchal society. Giving voice to that humor in the realm of women is relatively safe, but recording that comic voice on paper is more dangerous and disruptive. Many feminist scholars have acknowledged the subversive nature of writing. In Gail Griffin's 1995 book, *Season of the Witch: Border Lines, Marginal Notes,* she claims that women instinctively have always known it, even as young girls in school: "I always saw writing, as opposed to speech, as secret, subversive, and immensely powerful, whether I was writing to a friend in class or writing poetry in my notebook instead of watching the film or taking notes. Girls write notes. It is one of the ways their little subversive voices stay alive."[31]

Since "laughter, by definition, explodes conventions," as Merrill Skaggs observes, often taking as its target—at least for women—the powerful and culturally superior, writing combined with laughter would seem to be a revolutionary act. And, in fact, for women it is. Laughter coming from the margins, from the edges, is much more powerful and threatening than laughter coming from the center, as Adrienne Rich has articulated: "Revolutionary art dwells, by its nature, on edges. That is its power: the tension between subject and means, between the is and the what can be." For Anne Jones, "The history of southern women's humor is the history of expanding the limits of what is laughable,"[32] but a more accurate phrasing may be that southern women's humor expands the limits of what is laughable *in the presence of males*. Southern women have always been funny, but until a revolution goes public, it is only the grumblings of the discontented.

Women still face many obstacles in combining writing with humor. Regina Barreca remarks in her introduction to *Last Laughs: Perspectives on Women and Comedy* that critics "do not deny that women have tried to write comedy. They argue instead that women have not been able to do it nearly so well as men." Barreca describes women's comedy as "the attempt to break free of the imposition of 'femininity,'" but the question arises of whose definition of "femininity" and whose standards of writing comedy are being used.[33] If men do not find something funny, does that mean it is *not* funny? If a man does not think a funny woman is feminine, does this mean she is *not* feminine? Researchers have found that men and women find humor in different things and do not always understand each other's jokes, in the same way that people often miss the humor in jokes from other cultures; a cultural gap exists, a lack of common experience. By reevaluating definitions and standards of humor, the study of gender-based comedy becomes an important tool in exploring the differences between the sexes: how we communicate, how we view the world and society, and how we perceive ourselves.

One difference between male and female humor concerns what Emily Toth has termed the "humane humor rule." Her claim is that women target the powerful rather than the powerless and rarely ridicule an aspect of a person or society that cannot be changed. For example, women do not usually attack the physically handicapped, choosing instead to attack those who hold narrowminded attitudes and adhere to cultural stereotypes. An example illustrating how male writers do not follow this "rule" is found in Harry Crews's 1995 novel, *The Mulching of America*; much of Crews's humor is at the expense of unfortunate characters, including the pseudo-divine hare-lipped boss of the Soaps For Life company, who utters such lines as, "My narenip was given na me by Nod!"[34] The character is an authority figure, but instead of attacking his ineffectual leadership, Crews mocks his physical deformity per se, a rare occurrence in female writing.

Southern women, especially, have had a difficult time being accepted as comic writers, since humor is often linked to intellectual aggression, which directly contradicts the stereotype of southern white females as silent, fragile, and intellectually naïve. Southern black women have had other stereotypes and barriers to overcome as humorists. Racism, cultural differences in determining what is funny, and an inadequate educational background are just a few of the factors that have limited their acceptance. Identifying these stereotypes as false and replacing them with more realistic images of southern women is an ongoing process in which humor plays a major role, a process that is redefining the southern woman.

In the course of untangling contradictions about southern women, Peggy Whitman Prenshaw has identified a "doppelgänger motif" that has created "a parade of Scarletts and Melanies." This pattern, which is not limited to but is certainly widespread in southern literature, is especially interesting in connection with humor. In *They Used to Call Me Snow White . . . But I Drifted: Women's Strategic Use of Humor*, Regina Barreca points out the same polarity found throughout popular culture as well as in literature. Instead of Melanie and Scarlett, Barreca terms the two opposites the "Good Girl" (who doesn't understand sexual jokes, doesn't laugh with her mouth open, and leaves the joke telling to the boys) and the "Bad Girl" (who laughs long and loud, rivals the boys with her own keen sense of humor, and gets all the good lines).[35]

Although Melanies and Scarletts persist in the fiction of the contemporary South, there is a tendency for female authors to bring together these two images in one woman who is both sweet and wicked. Instead of Scarlett and Melanie as rivals, we have Alice Walker's Shug Avery, Rita Mae Brown's Frazier Armstrong, and Kaye Gibbons' Charlie Kate, to name a few, relatively good women by society's standards yet possessing a sharp sense of humor and rebelling to various degrees against the still-patriarchal societies in which they live. What has been true all along for male characters (Rhett Butler, for example, is good, sexy, wicked, and desirable) is finally becoming acceptable for female characters. A sense of humor is becoming not a rarity but a standard characteristic of female protagonists.

A woman with a sense of humor is just one of the similarities of the novels under study here. In addition, all of the writers included consistently use humor to further important themes (themes especially relevant to women), all are southern either by birth or by upbringing, and all use themes, settings, and characters that are distinctly southern in nature. Finally, these writers have produced the major portion of their work since 1970. This fact is significant. Although most critics make a distinction between modern and postmodern literature, there is ample evidence showing another important break around 1970, especially in southern writing. Changes in literature at that time came about because of two powerful movements: women's liberation and civil rights. Both changed forever the face and the voice of the mainstream southern writer, which now is more often female and African American.

In *The Southern Writer in the Postmodern World,* Hobson explains that it was "in the late 1960s that perceptions and assumptions began to change radically" in the South, producing a decade that "might be seen as pivotal in southern life and letters in much the same way the 1920s was. . . . [A] watershed in southern thought resulted—and, in some ways, a new southern fiction emerged."[36] A talented and exciting group emerged from this era, some of whom are now established authors—for example, Anne Tyler, Lee Smith, and Alice Walker—and others who are just beginning to make a contribution—Dorothy Allison, Tina McElroy Ansa, Sheila Bosworth, Dori Sanders, and Michael Lee West, among others.

There have been several studies on contemporary southern women writers and an increasing number of works on gender and humor, but to my knowledge this is the first study specifically on the use of humor by contemporary southern women novelists.[37] Since humor plays such an important role in these writers' works, it is my hope that this study will be instrumental in identifying and illuminating the voice and vision of the literature of this newest of New Souths.

Notes

1. Dorothy Allison to the author, December 7, 1993.

2. Louis D. Rubin, Jr., ed., *The Comic Imagination in American Literature* (New Brunswick, N.J., 1973), viii; Sigmund Freud, *Jokes and Their Relation to the Unconscious,* trans. James Strachey (New York, 1963), 5.

3. Merrill Skaggs, "Varieties of Local Color," in *The History of Southern Literature,* ed. Louis D. Rubin, Jr. (Baton Rouge, 1985), 219.

4. Dorothy Parker, Introduction to *The Most of S. J. Perelman,* by S. J. Perelman (New York, 1958), xii.

5. John Shelton Reed, "The Front Porch," *Southern Cultures,* I (1995), 418.

6. *Ibid.,* 418-19; Lee Smith to the author, December 9, 1993.

7. Roy Blount, Jr., ed., *Roy Blount's Book of Southern Humor* (New York, 1994), 24.

8. Sarah Blacher Cohen, ed., *Comic Relief: Humor in Contemporary American Literature* (Urbana, Ill., 1978), I; Louis D. Rubin, Jr., *William Elliott Shoots a Bear: Essays on the Southern Literary Imagination* (Baton Rouge, 1975), 256; Henri Bergson, "Laughter" (1900), rpr. in *Comedy,* ed. Wylie Sypher (Garden City, N.Y., 1956), 64; Sypher, *Comedy,* 220.

9. Anne Goodwyn Jones, *Tomorrow Is Another Day: The Woman Writer in the South, 1859-1936* (Baton Rouge, 1981), 25; Doris Betts, "Daughters, Southerners, and Daisy," in *The Female Tradition in Southern Literature: Essays on Southern Women Writers,* ed. Carol S. Manning (Champaign, Ill., 1993), 266.

10. Johanna Nicol Shields, "White Honor, Black Humor, and the Making of a Southern Style," *Southern Cultures,* I (1995), 421; Trudier Harris, "Adventures in a 'Foreign Country': African American Humor and the South," *Southern Cultures,* I (1995), 458.

11. William Ferris, "Southern Literature and Folk Humor," *Southern Cultures,* I (1995), 431.

12. Hennig Cohen and William B. Dillingham, *Humor of the Old Southwest* (Boston, 1964), xiii.

13. *Ibid.,* xi, xiv.

14. Richard M. Dorson, ed., *Davy Crockett: American Comic Legend* (New York, 1977), 22.

15. James M. Cox, "Humor of the Old Southwest," in *The Comic Imagination in American Literature,* ed. Rubin, 104; C. Hugh Holman, "Detached Laughter in the South," in *Comic Relief,* ed. Cohen, 90; Pascal Covici, Jr., *Mark Twain's Humor: The Image of a World* (Dallas, 1962), 8.

16. Jones, *Tomorrow,* 41.

17. Richard H. King's *A Southern Renaissance: The Cultural Awakening of the South, 1930-1955* includes only Lillian Smith; Richard Croom Beatty identifies only one pre-twentieth-century woman writer in *The Literature of the South* (Glenview, Ill., 1968); Jay Broadus Hubbel includes only five women in his bibliography *The South in American Literature, 1607-1900* (Durham, 1954); and *The Literary South* (Baton Rouge, 1979), edited by Louis B. Rubin, Jr., gives a weak overview of women's contributions.

18. Kathryn B. McKee, "Writing in a Different Direction: Women Authors and the Tradition of South-

western Humor, 1875-1910" (Ph.D. dissertation, University of North Carolina at Chapel Hill, 1996), 25, 24, 23.

19. Manning, ed., *Female Tradition*, 3, 49.

20. For a detailed description of the work being done in the rediscovery of women's literature, I suggest reading Thadious M. Davis' essay, "Women's Art and Authorship in the Southern Region: Connections," *Ibid.*, 15-36.

21. The other two novels in the trilogy are *They Stooped to Folly* (1929) and *The Sheltered Life* (1932).

22. Ellen Glasgow, *The Romantic Comedians* (1926; rpr. Charlottesville, Va., 1995), 8.

23. Frances Newman, *The Hard-Boiled Virgin* (New York, 1930), 110-11.

24. Paul Binding, *Separate Country: A Literary Journey Through the American South* (New York, 1979), 148; Flannery O'Connor, *Mystery and Manners*, ed. Sally Fitzgerald and Robert Fitzgerald (New York, 1961), 45; Fred Hobson, *The Southern Writer in the Postmodern World* (Athens, Ga., 1991), 78.

25. Beverly Lowry, *The Track of Real Desires* (New York, 1994), 19.

26. Lee Smith, "The Voice Behind the Story," in *Friendship and Sympathy: Communities of Southern Women Writers*, ed. Rosemary M. Maggee (Jackson, Miss., 1992), 203.

27. Anne Tyler, "Still Just Writing," in *The Writer on Her Work*, ed. Janet Sternberg (New York, 1980), 13-14.

28. John Griffin Jones, "Eudora Welty," in *Conversations with Eudora Welty*, ed. Peggy Whitman Prenshaw (Jackson, Miss., 1984), 330; James Boatwright, Review of Eudora Welty's *Losing Battles*, in *New York Times Book Review*, April 12, 1970, p. I; Ruth M. Vande Kieft, "The Love Ethos of Porter, Welty, and McCullers," in *Female Tradition*, ed. Manning, 245.

29. Walter Sullivan, *Death by Melancholy: Essays on Modern Southern Fiction* (Baton Rouge, 1972), 95; Holman, "Detached," in *Comic Relief*, ed. Cohen, 103.

30. Nancy A. Walker, *"A Very Serious Thing": Women's Humor and American Culture* (Minneapolis, 1988), 7-8, ix.

31. Gail B. Griffin, *Season of the Witch: Border Lines, Marginal Notes* (Pasadena, 1995), 196.

32. Skaggs, "Varieties," in *History of Southern Literature*, ed. Rubin, 227; Adrienne Rich, *What Is Found There: Notebooks on Poetry and Politics* (New York, 1993), 242, Anne Goodwyn Jones, "The Incredible Shrinking You-Know-What: Southern Women's Humor," *Southern Cultures*, I (1995), 468.

33. Regina Barreca, ed., *Last Laughs: Perspectives on Women and Comedy* (New York, 1988), 5, 6.

34. Harry Crews, *The Mulching of America* (New York, 1995), II.

35. Peggy Whitman Prenshaw, "Southern Ladies and the Southern Literary Renaissance," in *Female Tradition*, ed. Manning, 81; Regina Barreca, *They Used to Call Me Snow White . . . But I Drifted: Women's Strategic Use of Humor* (New York, 1991), 3-7.

36. Hobson, *Southern Writer*, 7, 73.

37. Recent studies on contemporary southern women writers that are especially illuminating include Elizabeth J. Harrison's *Female Pastoral: Women Writers Revisioning the American South* (Knoxville, Tenn., 1991), and Linda Tate's *A Southern Weave of Women: Fiction of the Contemporary South* (Athens, Ga., 1994). There are also two significant collections of essays: *Women Writers of the Contemporary South* (Jackson, Miss., 1984) edited by Peggy Whitman Prenshaw, and *Southern Women Writers: The New Generation*, edited by Tonette Bond Inge (Tuscaloosa, 1990). Finally, *Friendship and Sympathy* is an interesting compilation of authors discussing the work of other writers. Among the recent works on gender and humor is Nancy A. Walker's *"A Very Serious Thing,"* which examines the history of American female humor—literary as well as cultural. Regina Barreca continues to write and edit books on women and humor, including *They Used to Call Me Snow White*, which explores the differences between male and female humor.

Patricia Yaeger (essay date 1997)

SOURCE: Yaeger, Patricia. "Beyond the Hummingbird: Southern Women Writers and the Southern Gargantua." In *Haunted Bodies: Gender and Southern Texts*, edited by Anne Goodwyn Jones and Susan V. Donaldson, pp. 287-318. Charlottesville: University Press of Virginia, 1997.

[*In the following essay, Yaeger discusses Southern women writers' frequent use of physically grotesque characters in their works and emphasizes the latter's political role in "mapping an entire region's social and psychic neuroses."*]

GIANT BODIES

This is an essay with an agenda. I want to describe the political effects of the grotesque in southern women's fiction since it is my conviction that this fiction has a politics: a politics that can be read through southern women writers' amazing inventiveness—their daunting grotesques, their mingling of dirt and desire, their tragic invention of "old" southern children.

Despite its beauty and innovation, writing by southern women has for many years taken a back seat to writing by southern men. In 1980, when Richard King published *A Southern Renaissance: The Cultural Awakening of the American South, 1930-1955,* feminists were outraged at the race and gender bias of his study. Women were excluded from *A Southern Renaissance,* as were African Americans; their fictions may have been important, but they did not measure up to King's great themes: "I will generally focus on works which take the South and its tradition as problematic. For this reason I do not deal with black writers such as Richard Wright or Ralph Ellison or with women writers such as Eudora Welty, Carson McCullers, Flannery O'Connor, and Katherine Anne Porter." To "take the South and its tradition as problematic" meant to write about the southern family romance with its mythy fathers, pithy sons, its dim wives and daughters—as these characters were conceived by white males. According to King, southern women did not, for the most part, write with the same "historical consciousness" that inspired male writers. Even when their prose imitated the grandeur of a William Faulkner or a Robert Penn Warren, southern women seemed incapable of devoting themselves to "the tortuous process of dealing with the past of the region."[1]

Of course, King was neither an artless reader nor simple chauvinist. He argued that "all of these writers would demand extensive treatment in a complete history of the Renaissance. Black writers are not taken up because for them the southern family romance was hardly problematic. It could be and was rejected out of hand. . . . The case with the women writers is more difficult, but my reading of them indicates that whatever the merits of their work—and they are considerable—they were not concerned primarily with the larger cultural, racial, and political themes that I take as my focus."[2] It will be my argument that "the larger cultural, racial, and political themes" of southern life are precisely the issues that drive southern women's writing. If critics have been blind to these themes, it is because we have not yet learned to read this writing in all of its power and intricacy, nor have we discovered the ways in which this writing exposes the deforming effects of the southern political tradition upon women, men, and children of color, upon white women and children, and even upon white men. If we fail to acknowledge this "larger" dimension in southern women's writing, we are missing a great deal, indeed.

Surprisingly, the southern woman writer's lack of thematic, stylistic, or political "largeness" is a frequent reprise in criticism of southern fiction. In *The Faraway Country: Writers of the Modern South,* Louis Rubin admits a single woman into his book's southern pantheon, and while he intends his chapter on Eudora Welty to be an eloquent defense of her writing, he flavors this defense with odd diminutions of Welty's abilities. While Faulkner's Mississippi contains combatants "larger than life," Welty's Mississippi is a "tidy, protected little world." While Faulkner flings "whole dynasties of families" into space, while he writes tribal fugues about giant men who "rage at their human limitations," Welty proffers a smaller world "in which people go about their affairs, living, marrying, getting children, diverting themselves, dying, all in tranquil, pastoral fashion." For Rubin, Welty may possess a "muscularity" that pushes her beyond those mere "local colorists," Katherine Anne Porter and Marjorie Kinnan Rawlings, but she is not quite Faulkner, not so big, nor so bold: "I am not proposing that her work is *as* important as Faulkner's, but I am maintaining that in scope and insight her two novels deserve to be compared *with* Faulkner's. She is no lightweight; she is not merely picturesque; she is a serious writer." And yet "the most startling quality of Eudora Welty's art is her style: shimmering, hovering, elusive, fanciful, fastening on little things. Entirely feminine, it moves lightly, capriciously, mirroring the bemused, diverted quality of the people whom it describes. Like the hummingbirds that appear frequently in her stories, it darts here and there, never quite coming to rest, tirelessly invoking light, color, the variety of experience."[3] In this essay I want to formulate new habits of reading that will take us beyond the hummingbird, beyond Faulkner's shadow, and into the hot southern day. My hope is to recover the political intrigue and bravura, the largeness and largesse, of fiction by southern women.

Let me start with a singular example from Eudora Welty's fiction. In her first collection of short stories, *A Curtain of Green,* we find a wonderful, puzzling story entitled "A Memory." The story seems to go nowhere—its plot line and its sense of character development are almost nil. And yet "A Memory" is Welty's own "spot of time"; the story seems entirely southern in setting and voice but resembles Wordsworthian autobiography in its side glances into the numinous terrors of the everyday. Although nothing happens, a little girl's secure southern world comes crashing down around her. In this moment the child's imaginative or writerly character is formed, and the results are the highly rebellious and political stories in Welty's first volume.

The focus of this story is a modest southern girl with a new obsession: she looks at everything through a frame made by her fingers. What she sees on the day of the story is a gargantuan woman, a ragged colossus in an old bathing suit. It is this gargantuan who will inundate any notion that southern women writers are primarily concerned with "little things": "Fat hung upon her upper arms like an arrested earthslide on a hill. With the first motion she might make, I was afraid that she would slide down upon herself into a terrifying heap. Her breasts hung heavy and widening like pears into her bathing suit. Her legs lay prone one on the other like shadowed bulwarks, uneven and deserted, upon which, from the man's hand, the sand piled higher like the teasing threat of oblivion. A slow, repetitious sound I had been hearing for a long time unconsciously, I identified as a continuous laugh which came through the motionless open pouched mouth of the woman."[4] Her crossed legs "like shadowed bulwarks" among the sands, this is woman as Ozymandias; like Ozymandias, she is vulnerable to "the teasing threat of oblivion," to visions of horror and ruin. In surveying her vast, ungainly body, Welty refuses stereotypical portraits of southern women: she refuses to replicate southern women's preoccupation with "little things." How does this human earthquake initiate a new politics of southern women's writing?

The first thing to notice about Welty's earthquake woman is her gigantism. We know that giants—as opposed to the intensely private, palm-sized world of the miniature—are associated with history writ large, with governments as they rise and fall, with the sacerdotal moments of public life. In her marvelous book *On Longing: Narratives of the Miniature, the Gigantic, the Souvenir, the Collection*, Susan Stewart argues that gigantism may also augur change: "The giant is represented through movement, through being in time. Even in the ascription of the still landscape to the giant, it is the activities of the giant, his or her legendary actions, that have resulted in the observable trace. In contrast to the still and perfect universe of the miniature, the gigantic represents the order and disorder of historical forces. The consumerism of the miniature is the consumerism of the classic; it is only fitting that consumer culture appropriates the gigantic whenever change is desired."[5] Welty's giantess is the terrible harbinger of change for a demure southern girl. Why is her body so potent? How might it be political?

When Louis Rubin describes Welty's prose as "shimmering, hovering, elusive, fanciful, fastening on little things," he is touching upon a fragility and miniaturization that haunts southern women's bodies as well. In Katherine Anne Porter's "Old Mortality" Miranda's father insists that his female relatives were all slender as sylphs:

> He sometimes glanced at the photograph and said, "It's not very good. . . . She was much slimmer than that, too. There were never any fat women in the family, thank God."
>
> When they heard their father say things like that, Maria and Miranda simply wondered, without criticism, what he meant. . . . What about great aunt Keziah, in Kentucky. Her husband, great-uncle John Jacob, had refused to allow her to ride his good horses after she had achieved two hundred and twenty pounds. . . . "Female vanity will recover," said great-uncle John Jacob, callously, "but what about my horses' backs? And if she had the proper female vanity in the first place, she would never have got into such shape." Well, great-aunt Keziah was famous for her heft, and wasn't she in the family? But something seemed to happen to their father's memory when he thought of the girls he had known in the family of his youth, and he declared steadfastly they had all been, in every generation without exception, as slim as reeds and graceful as sylphs.[6]

This willful miniaturization of the female body may seem comical, but it is also quite dangerous. "What is, in fact, lost in this idealized miniaturization of the body," as Stewart says, "is . . . the danger of power."[7] We see this loss most poignantly in the confinement of Miranda's Aunt Amy, who is reduced to "a motionless image in her dark walnut frame." Estranged by a body that is caught "forever in the pose of being photographed," her nieces wonder "why every older person who looked at the picture said, 'How lovely.' . . . The whole affair was associated, in the minds of the little girls, with dead things. . . . The woman in the picture had been Aunt Amy, but she was only a ghost in a frame, and a sad, pretty story from old times. She had been beautiful, much loved, unhappy, and she had died young" (173). These young girls recognize implicitly that miniaturization insures loss of power and provides no protection against the process of time. And yet the need to miniaturize the southern female body also works paradoxically. It not only keeps some women off horseback and out of public life, but it also embroils them in southern history in the most contorted of ways. For the miniaturized female torso does not exist in simple opposition to gigantism and history—instead, the purified, rarefied, "transcendent" female body offers a site for political labor, a place for uncoding and recording the epic disasters of the southern body politic.

How should we characterize this politicization of the intense privacy of white women's flesh? In "Identity: Skin Blood Heart," Minnie Bruce Pratt describes the ways in which public desires and private self-interest were flagrantly mapped onto her own girlish body. In the 1960s the white female body could still serve as a fulcrum for white power politics—becoming both its rallying cry and absurd rationale. At the height of the civil rights movement Pratt's father terrorized his children by lodging his own race-terrors—his flimsy beliefs in white supremacy—in his daughter's wayward, uncertain body:

> The entombment of the lady was my "protection": the physical, spiritual, sexual containment which men of my culture have used to keep "their women" pure. . . .
>
> It was this protection that I felt one evening during the height of the civil rights demonstrations in Alabama, as

the walls that had contained so many were cracking, when my father called me to his chair in the living room. He showed me a newspaper clipping . . . about Martin Luther King, Jr.; and told me that the article was about how King had sexually abused, used, young Black teen-aged girls. I believe he asked me what I thought of this; I can only guess that he wanted me to feel that my danger, my physical, sexual danger, would be the result of the release of others from containment. I felt frightened and profoundly endangered, by King, by my father: I could not answer him.[8]

It is crucial to examine the ways in which writing by modern southern women both adheres to and rebels against this ideological mask. As Anne Goodwyn Jones explains in *Tomorrow Is Another Day,* "The image wearing Dixie's Diadem" has offered, historically, a spectacular cartography for racist fears. This image

> is not a human being but a marble statue, beautiful and silent, eternally inspiring and eternally still.
>
> In that, southern womanhood is not alone. It has much in common with the ideas of the British Victorian lady and of American true womanhood. All deny to women authentic selfhood; all enjoin that women suffer and be still; all show women sexually pure, pious, deferent to external authority, and content with their place in the home. Yet southern womanhood differs in several ways from other nineteenth-century images of womanhood. Unlike them, the southern lady is at the core of a region's self-definition; the identity of the South is contingent in part upon the persistence of its tradition of the lady.[9]

We need to delve further into this tradition and what it might mean to have one's body "at the core" of the South's self-definition.

Bryan Turner suggests four different tasks that bodies create for the social systems trying to control them: "(1) the reproduction of populations in time, (2) the regulation of bodies in space, (3) the restraint of the 'interior' body through disciplines, and (4) the representation of the 'exterior' body in social space."[10] What's intriguing about this fourth category, the socially mandated miniaturization of the white southern woman's irregularly shaped frame, is that this reification of femininity—this representation of the white woman's exterior, racialized body in social space—also has stunning repercussions for the first three categories of public discipline. The racially pure and diminutive female body in need of protection becomes the motive force, the purported source for the taboo against race-mixing. As southern myth, this fragile white body helps to motivate (1) southern modes of population control reproducing black and white populations as separate, (2) the regulated segregation of these racial bodies in space, and (3) the need for deeply interiorized categories of racism that will do the work of segregation. In other words, the small compass of the ideal white woman's body is oddly at war with its epic stature in minds of white men; this fragile white body, slim as a reed and graceful as a sylph, becomes pivotal in each crucial task of bodily discipline.

What is most remarkable about southern women's fiction is the way in which it refuses such discipline. When the grotesque body marches onto the page, the ideology that controls southern bodies explodes in the most unexpected of ways. Southern women's writing is filled with bizarre somatic images that seem unnecessarily cruel or out of control, and yet this cruelty has a function: it tears at the social fabric and leaves it in shreds: "I have felt the destructive effects of personal race and class privilege first through [my mother's] life: her skin allergies that made her scratch her own white skin raw. The *her* in *me* feels the trap of that whiteness, the need to claw out. The times I have realized my own racism most, this image has come to mind: I am sitting in a white porcelain bathtub scraping my skin with Brillo pads; there is blood in rivulets in the tub."[11] This is from Mab Segrest's *My Mama's Dead Squirrel,* a text arguing that the grotesque is a neurotic, disreputable form for southern writers. And yet when Segrest wants to contemplate the terrible effects of racism—and the work of domination that the white female body performs on behalf of this racism—she resorts to a grotesque tropology. Her mother's bloody white body reveals the social agon hidden beneath the happy surfaces of feminine charisma and cleanliness. In Segrest's memoir women's open, wounded bodies become political intensifiers, spaces for mapping an entire region's social and psychic neuroses.

This is to argue that the bodies in southern women's fiction are intensely political; they are often concerned with "larger cultural, racial, and political themes" simply because southern bodies have had to endure such "themes" in daily life. As Lillian Smith recalls her childhood in *Killers of the Dream,* its lessons revolved around her body's sexual and racial markers: "Now . . . your body is a thing of shame and mystery, and curiosity about it is not good; your skin is your glory and the source of your strength and pride. It is white. And, as you have heard, whiteness is a symbol of purity and excellence. Remember this: your white skin proves that you are better than all other people on this earth. Yes, it does that. And does it simply because it is white—which, in a way, is a kind of miracle. But the Bible is full of miracles and it should not be too difficult for us to accept one more."[12] Southern women's fiction works with a similar irony; it abrades the surface of this body to bring the daily contradictions of "miraculous" whiteness to the surface. The stories we will examine work toward a massive category confusion in which the common classifications of southern life no longer make sense, in which the condensation and displacement of political contradictions onto the white female body no longer take place in secret but, instead, get held up for scrutiny.

To exemplify the female body's gargantuan labors, I want to tell the tale of another giant woman, Miss Eckhart, the foreign piano teacher in Welty's "June Recital," one of the stories in her 1949 collection *The Golden Apples*. We have already seen that Rubin's association of Welty with the miniature evokes a world of diminished associations in which Welty's style ("entirely feminine," moving "lightly, capriciously") mirrors the charming world that good southern white women were supposed to inhabit. But when we recast our image of Welty to reflect the awkward grandiosity of Miss Eckhart or the black musician Powerhouse in *A Curtain of Green*'s "Powerhouse" or the slovenly fat woman who stalks through "A Memory," these giant bodies invoke the messiness and hubris of history itself. While Miss Eckhart's body invokes a world of gender asymmetry and the gargantua in "A Memory" draws attention to southern fantasies about class, what gets magnified through Powerhouse's awkward frame is the great debacle of segregation itself. This stupendous man, "so monstrous he sends everybody into oblivion," entertains white audiences, but he is refused the right to congregate with them. During intermission Powerhouse turns his "African feet of the greatest size" and his mouth "vast and obscene," toward "Negrotown" to have a drink and then makes his way back through the pouring rain, "his mouth . . . nothing but a volcano."[13] When Welty's critics read Powerhouse as the epitome of Welty's improvisatory glee, her ability to write jazzy fiction that competes with the best boogie-woogie, they miss this story's hidden script: the fact that even the jazzman's fantasies and improvisations are restricted by segregation. Although Powerhouse mounts symbolic protests—avoiding his own sense of peril by telling thunderous tales about his wife's imagined infidelity and suicide—his powerful body still has to succumb to the illogic of Jim Crow. The merry misogyny of the stories he tells may carry the day, but they are also quite sad. His power and vastness contrast with his obsessive riffing on faithlessness and death; Powerhouse's huge frame and constricted fantasies emphasize the power and vastness of a system that still restricts this massive man's locomotion.

In Miss Eckhart we witness another kind of oppression: a great female pianist whose talent is denied because of her sex. On the thunderous summer day when she gives her concert in "June Recital," Miss Eckhart's body swells to enormous proportions; she represents new and frightening parameters for southern women's lives: "Miss Eckhart played as if it were Beethoven; she struck the music open midway and it was in soft yellow tatters like old satin. The thunder rolled and Miss Eckhart frowned and bent forward or she leaned back to play; at moments her solid body swayed from side to side like a tree trunk."[14] What is this burgeoning female body doing in the demure alcoves of southern women's fiction?

Mary Jacobus, Evelyn Fox Keller, and Sally Shuttleworth have argued that "the body, whether masculine or feminine, is imbricated in the matrices of power at all levels."[15] It is my contention that the bodies in southern women's fiction make this imbrication visible. The grotesque bodies occupying stories by Porter, Hurston, Welty, McCullers, O'Connor, Gilchrist, and Walker become premier sites for exploring the work of a southern polity in which women are barred from public power but become central players in its symbolic scripts. Miss Eckhart is a case in point. Her giant body becomes a symbol of female artistry and self-empowerment threatening beyond words; but her gigantism also becomes a battlefield for the social violence that is ordinarily scripted onto the body of the romantic white girl. When she sits down to play for her pupils, "the piece was so hard that she made mistakes and repeated to correct them, so long and stirring that it soon seemed longer than the day itself had been, and in playing it, Miss Eckhart assumed an entirely different face. Her skin flattened and drew across her cheeks, her lips changed. The face could have belonged to someone else—not even to a woman, necessarily. It was the face a mountain could have, or what might be seen behind the veil of a waterfall. There in the rainy light it was a sightless face, one for music only—though the fingers kept slipping and making mistakes they had to correct. And if the sonata had an origin in a place on earth, it was the place where Virgie, even, had never been and was not likely to go" (56). When Miss Eckhart's face blends with the huge forms of nature, she is usurping a power reserved for white males: her face changes, her music seems to come from some unearthly realm. To underline this transgressive power, Welty appropriates images from Shelley's "Mont Blanc" but with this difference.[16] While Shelley mourns—but then appropriates—Mont Blanc's grandeur and cruelty, the sublimity Shelley withholds from himself Welty gives to her heroine. Miss Eckhart *becomes* the mountain that stares back at Shelley and will not answer his call.

Ironically, it is Cassie Morrison, a child in need of giant reveries, who brings Miss Eckhart back to earth. She reimagines her piano teacher as a fallen woman, an untouchable, and reveals the policing mechanisms of the southern economy at its worst. Stunned by her piano teacher's arpeggios, Cassie protects herself by mapping communal stereotypes of race and rape onto Miss Eckhart's great body:

> She began to think of an incident that had happened to Miss Eckhart instead of about the music she was playing; that was one way.
>
> One time, at nine o'clock at night, a crazy nigger had jumped out of the school hedge and got Miss Eckhart, had pulled her down and threatened to kill her. That

was long ago. She had been walking by herself after dark; nobody had told her any better. When Dr. Loomis made her well, people were surprised that she and her mother did not move away. They wished she had moved away, everybody but poor Miss Snowdie; then they wouldn't always have to remember that a terrible thing once happened to her. But Miss Eckhart stayed, as though she considered one thing not so much more terrifying than another.

(57)

If Miss Eckhart gives us giant dreams, her listeners know how to resist them. Caught inside during an electrical storm, her pupils have listened to her music reluctantly—for like the storm itself, Miss Eckhart's playing is abusive and grand. Terrified of her newfound power and Miss Eckhart's refusal to bend her artistic talents toward the designated role of spinster-teacher, her pupils convert her harrowing body to its "proper" size.

Miss Eckhart's body is threatening because it becomes the locus for two different kinds of transgression. First, instead of a "hummingbird" style that fastens on "little things," her incredible music evokes all the elements of sublimity, transcendence, and violence that critics in search of "larger themes" could desire: "The music came with greater volume—with fewer halts—and Jinny Love tiptoed forward and began turning the music. Miss Eckhart did not even see her—her arm struck the child, making a run. Coming from Miss Eckhart, the music made all the pupils uneasy, almost alarmed; something had burst out, unwanted, exciting, from the wrong person's life. This was some brilliant thing too splendid for Miss Eckhart, piercing and striking the air around her the way a Christmas firework might almost jump out of the hand that was, each year, inexperienced anew" (56). Second, Miss Eckhart refuses the stereotypes of southern femininity. Her arm strikes a child; she wields too much creative power. But, as the editors of *Body/Politics* note, "the feminine body . . . is peculiarly the battlefield on which quite other struggles than women's own have been waged."[17] What "other" battle is raging in Miss Eckhart's body?

We have already seen the displacement of racial politics onto the white female frame in Minnie Bruce Pratt's frightened memories of Martin Luther King. What brings Pratt's and Miss Eckhart's stories together is not only an act of displacement in which white patriarchs and little white girls are so threatened by change (by the advent of black or female empowerment) that they regroup, recommit themselves to the white female's vulnerability. What's curious about this act of fetishism is that in each case the feminine body becomes prominent—turns into a battleground—when the social hierarchy is threatened, when the margins of power start to shift. As Peter Stallybrass and Allon White have suggested, "Discourses about the body have a privileged role, for transcodings between different levels and sectors of social and psychic reality are effected through the intensifying grid of the body. It is no accident . . . that transgressions and the attempt to control them obsessively return to somatic symbols, for these are the ultimate elements of social classification itself."[18] "The intensifying grid" of Miss Eckhart's body startles these children because her playing, with its brilliance and fireworks, escapes its classification and establishes a carnival moment, a temporary liberation from the established southern order. To diminish her body's grandeur, these children, well socialized by their habitus, go on the attack; they surround Miss Eckhart with a scary set of somatic symbols (their communal story about rape) to control her unwanted unruliness. When Miss Eckhart raises herself to great heights, revealing a musical brilliance reserved for great men, her pupils find a way to restore her abjection and lowliness.

Why do they impose this terrible discipline on her body? There is, of course, a regional pattern to this discipline. When Cassie converts her teacher's tempestuous playing into racial terror, she is rehearsing the perennial southern story that Jacquelyn Dowd Hall calls the "southern rape complex." Hall argues that this "complex," with its triumphant protection of white women, its calculated fear of black men, its ignorance of the abuses of black women, is an instrument of sexual and racial suppression scapegoating those players in the southern game who challenge the established order. Just as "lynching served to dramatize hierarchies among men," so stories of female victimization encourage white women to depend upon white men. Hall reminds us that the "southern rape complex" is extraindividual, a "dramatization of cultural themes, a story [white southerners] told themselves about the social arrangements and psychological strivings that lay beneath the surface of everyday life." "A woman who had just been raped, or who had been apprehended in a clandestine affair, or whose male relatives were pretending that she had been raped, stood on display before the whole community. Here was the quintessential Woman as Victim: polluted, 'ruined for life,' the object of fantasy and secret contempt. Humiliation, however, mingled with heightened worth as she played for a moment the role of Fair Maiden violated and avenged. For this privilege—if the alleged assault had in fact taken place—she might pay with suffering in the extreme. In any case, she would pay with a lifetime of subjugation to the men gathered in her behalf."[19] It is this culturally sanctioned form of "heightened worth" that Miss Eckhart tries to avoid. Even as scapegoat the pianist has maintained a public stance; she continues to teach, to take in pupils. To adapt to the trauma of rape when female honor is still a southern rallying cry means to challenge the political order at its grass roots—to acknowledge rape as an ordinary, terrible crime that should result in neither racial hysteria nor ostracism for its victims. And yet, like Powerhouse, Miss Eckhart is caught in her community's drama. Willy-nilly, her body becomes "the battleground on which quite other struggles" are waged. This means there is no need to rape this woman in fact to make her conform: she is raped repeatedly in the communal imagination. And this communal rape is not just the subject of adult brutality. In Welty's story Miss Eckhart is attacked, her rape reenacted, among the community's children, who have internalized a model of female powerlessness and continue to enforce this model upon each other and within themselves.

This is Miss Eckhart's designated story, and yet to end on this note could make us forget the scene in which she plays the piano and sways in treelike ecstasy. Miss Eckhart threatens her pupils because her body suggests a different world order in which women are allowed to be noisy and grand. The gargantuan body both maps its own limits and refuses to stay within boundaries, to serve asked-for ends. What resounds throughout this awkward female frame are the very power plays that the petite white female body tries to mask. If, as Louise Westling suggests, the southern white woman as "representative of Christian virtues was lauded in public to divert attention from the problems of slavery and racism," Westling also notes that this diversion has physical consequences: "The scope of her activities was severely limited."[20] The gargantuan body exceeds these limits and attests to the pleasures of inventing extraordinary human beings whose bodies don't follow the rules. The grotesque body is the focus for a "free play with the human body and with its organs" not permitted by southern conformity.

This giant female body offers itself as a totem, then, for our perusal of southern women's fiction: a totem that teaches two things. First, if the private bodies of white southern women are asked to become smooth public surfaces—if southern women have been compelled to inhabit pleasant, undifferentiated, fragile bodies in search of protection—Miss Eckhart's gigantism transgresses this role and renders it unstable.[21] She ushers a panoply of female giants into this study, from Carson McCullers's Amelia and Frankie to Flannery O'Connor's irate redneck matrons. We may even trace a ghostly gigantism in Kate Chopin's Edna Pontellier: "She turned her face seaward to gather in an impression of space and solitude, which the vast expanse of water, meeting and melting with the moonlit sky, conveyed to her excited fancy. As she swam she seemed to be reaching out for the unlimited in which to lose herself."[22]

At the same time, each of these giant bodies serves deliberate political ends; they give us hyperbolic visions of the systemic crises within each heroine's social milieu. By invoking the concept of systemic crisis, I want to expand upon the suggestion that female bodies are used as symbolic sites to cordon off or demarcate undesired social change. In addition, southern bodies are caught in a daily, formulaic round of hostility, tension, and emergency: a crisis that is ongoing, habitual, and monitored by white civilians and law enforcement alike. As Robin Kelley describes the pre—civil rights skirmishes that occurred on segregated southern buses in the 1940s and 1950s, "All oppositional and transgressive acts took place in a context of extreme repression. The occupants sitting in the rear who witnessed or were part of the daily guerrilla skirmishes learned that punishment was inevitable."[23] While white citizens were deputized to police the color boards, black men were denied citizenship on a daily basis. In "The Ritual of Survival" Robert Fleming testifies about this daily policing of southern race culture; he, too, describes an incessant round of racial and sexual emergency: "If a black man was to survive, he had to know his place, to step off the curb when a white person approached, and to lower his eyes whenever he spoke to a white woman. It seemed that daily lynchings of blacks were the meat-and-potatoes stories for the various Southern newspapers in those days, complete with graphic details of the grisly deed and the alleged crime for which the person of color lost his or her life."[24] Julius Lester summarizes these structural perversions, this state of perpetual emergency, in "Black and White Together." He remembers the terror of southern life during the protest movements of the 1960s when death became atmospheric: "To live in an atmosphere where the presence of death is as palpable as the smell of honeysuckle lacerated the soul in ways one dared not stop to know."[25] In the face of these repeated systematic assaults on African Americans' humanity, the fantasy of the gargantuan woman has not been limited to white women's fictions. Alice Walker's Feather Mae advances this story, as does Janie, in her reach for the horizon at the end of *Their Eyes Were Watching God*: "Then Tea Cake came prancing around her where she was and the song of the sigh flew out of the window and lit in the top of the pine trees. Tea Cake, with the sun for a shawl. Of course he wasn't dead. He could never be dead until she herself had finished feeling and thinking. The kiss of his memory made pictures of love and light against the wall. Here was peace. She pulled in her horizon like a great fishnet. Pulled it from around the waist of the world and draped it over her shoulder. So much of life in its meshes! She called in her soul to come and see."[26] The gargantuan Janie sends a promissory note. By throwing off her burdens, she refuses the boundaries of a racially constricted life, even as Tea Cake's lost, prancing body acknowledges the crises bred by racial hierarchy within a white-dominated culture all too careless of death.

In this context Miss Eckhart's refusal to be miniaturized, to fit within the confines of this system, should also remind us of the relative difficulty—for women, for people of color—of such public refusals. The stereotype of the "little woman" inheres so strictly in Miss Eckhart's habitus that it is always, already in circulation: the southern rape complex requires each woman's repeated miniaturization.[27] But southern women's fiction also contests the boundaries of these expectations, even when it gives in. When the gigantic, well-muscled Amelia, heroine of *The Ballad of the Sad Cafe,* starts winning the fight with Marvin Macy fair and square, her six-two frame is slick with body grease and the odor of victory, and we long for her success. But when Cousin Lymon comes to Macy's support, when he flies through the air and clutches "at her neck with his clawed little fingers" so that Amelia falls flat on her back, "her arms flung outward and motionless," her body also records a larger battle scene in which southern women submit to "higher" laws.[28] The exaggeration of her bodily boundaries reveals the exact location of these boundaries; the gargantuan woman becomes a political intensifier for mapping the gigantism of southern social derangements.

Miniature Bodies

In depicting the explosive body of a giant woman, Eudora Welty is exposing the southern power structure and its pervasive influence—the ways in which sexual and racial boundaries are enforced by white children as well as white men. Although King accuses southern women of writing without a sense of "historical consciousness," in "June Recital" this consciousness is all too acute. Miss Eckhart's lumbering frame exposes the quotidian social controls that keep blacks and women in their place.

It is this sense of the dailiness of history, this focus on diurnal politics, that I want to address in the second half of this essay. In reworking the image of the southern lady—in creating her grotesque or giant antitype—southern women writers do more than protest the burdens of ladyhood. Their grotesque heroines help bring the hard facts of southern racism and sexism into focus. At the same time, hard facts don't always operate through epic forms.

I've suggested that the giant body—in its outlandishness and strangeness—becomes a formal property of southern women's texts that gathers our attention and enlarges the scope of our vision so that the vagaries of southern politics (here, the southern rape complex) come to light in the sudden telescoping and shrinking of Miss Eckhart's body. We will see a similar pattern at work in "A Memory" when a fat woman's frightening body provides a moment of transformation for a staid southern child: "I saw the man lift his hand filled with crumbling sand, shaking it as the woman laughed, and pour it down inside her bathing suit between her bulbous descending breasts" (154). While the controlled body of the middle-class child promotes hierarchy, the grotesque body protests verticality. Against classicism and classism, this fat woman's sandy gigantism insists on the bodily equality of bowels, blood, and breasts. Her excess flesh will move us toward a rereading of class and gender hardship, toward an exploration of the excesses of a southern political system that inhabited little white girls as well as white men.

This suggests a turn in my argument: the giant female body relays these "larger" issues, but only insofar as she makes us pay attention to the miniature, the microcosmic, the quotidian. It is, after all, the quotidian details that express the hardest facts of southern life. Lillian Smith details this adversity in *Killers of the Dream* as she talks with one of her students about the daily struggles of the past:

> "Your parents and I lived our babyhood in those days of wrath. But always the violence was distant, the words vague and terrible for we were protected children. A lynching could happen in our county and we wouldn't know it. Yet we did know because of faces, whispers, a tightening of the whole town."
>
> I did not say more for I was caught in those old days, remembering: Sometimes it was your nurse who made you know. You loved her, and suddenly she was frightened, and you knew it. Her eyes saw things your eyes did not see. As the two of you sat in the sand playing your baby games, she'd whisper, "Lawd Jesus, when you going to help us!" And suddenly the play would leave the game and you would creep close to her begging her to shield you from her trouble. . . . Sometimes it would be your father, explaining a race incident to the older children. Even now I can feel that hush, the changed voices when they saw you listening, the talking down to the little one in false and cheerful words, saying, "Sugar, what you been playing today?"[29]

Killers of the Dream was written in 1949 and describes the vanishing world of Jasper, Florida, at the turn of the century. And yet when Julius Lester describes the South of the 1940s and 1950s from the other side of the racial divide, the details are much the same: "It is almost impossible to describe that world the civil rights movement destroyed, that world of my childhood and adolescence ruled by signs decreeing where I was and was not allowed to go, what door I had to enter at the bus station and train station, where I had to sit on the bus. How do I explain what it is to live with the absurd and pretend to its ordinariness without becoming insane? How do I explain that I cannot be sure that my sanity was not hopelessly compromised because I grew up in a world where the insane was as ordinary as margarine?"[30] To say that the "large" issues of southern history come down to bus stations and baby games is not to trivialize these issues but to acknowledge the banality of history. Racism may be epic in reach and scope, but its horror lives on in the particular. In looking at "A Memory," I want to address the intersections between the giant female body and civic life, to explore the particularity of the gargantuan body as it becomes a site of transaction for the South's "ordinary" insanities.

Welty's "A Memory" is particularly eloquent about the politics of the everyday. Like Miss Eckhart, Welty's earthquake woman does not become a public colossus or politician. Instead, we watch a middle-class girl watching a lower-class family playing at the beach. The girl, an avatar for Welty herself, is a snob; she is offended by this unsavory family's "tasteless" hijinks. In mapping her own childish aversions and offering them as an index to an entire social milieu, Welty gives us politics of a different order from the male writers of the Southern Renaissance, but she gives us politics all the same.[31]

David Held has argued that political theory has a special purpose; it "aims to offer a systematic analysis of politics and of the ways in which it is always bounded by, among other things, unacknowledged conditions of action. It can, thereby, fracture existing forms of understanding and re-form the practically generated accounts of the political in everyday life."[32] Welty's fiction may not be exhausted by the limits of "political theory," but her stories do break new ground; they help us reformulate women's relation to "the practically generated accounts of the political" in everyday southern life.

This is worth stressing because studies of southern fiction focusing on political systems have, for the most part, limited their analyses to southern politics as monument and myth.[33] When Richard King gives his definition of the Southern Renaissance, he values the ways in which male writers deal with the three *p*'s of southern studies: plantations, patriarchy, and the past. "Put briefly: the writers and intellectuals of the South after the late 1920s were engaged in an attempt to come to terms not only with the inherited values of the Southern tradition but also with a certain way of perceiving and dealing with the past, what Nietzsche called 'monumental' historical consciousness. It was vitally important for them to decide whether the past was of any use at all in the present. . . . The 'object' of their historical consciousness was a tradition whose essential figures were the father and the grandfather and whose essential structure was the literal and symbolic family. In sum, the Renaissance writers sought to come to terms with what I call the 'Southern family romance.'"[34] But there are other ways to come to terms with the legitimation crises of twentieth-century southern life. First, we need to recognize that any struggle with the use-value of the past must also be construed as a struggle within the present. It is this daily loss of legitimation, the inability of traditional or established patterns to make sense of the ebb and flow of everyday life, that southern women writers address in their obsession with the southern grotesque. We need not look to "monumental" historical consciousness—not to fathers or grandfathers or even large women—to understand the complexities that the weight of tradition brings to bear upon the diurnal round of southern life. Thus short stories, cookbooks, girlish fantasies, and personal vignettes can become sites for measuring a political crisis in the making. These private narrative forms have public dimensions implicated in the apportionment of power.[35] Welty's story also demonstrates that within a southern political schema, what a child thinks at the beach may be as telling as a trip to the statehouse; she may give us access to the ordinary dominations, the insane politics of everyday southern life.

In fact, it is just such frivolous techniques of the body that the earthquake woman engages in Welty's autobiographical story from *A Curtain of Green*. Like the little girls in "June Recital," the child who narrates "A Memory" is preoccupied with the apportionment of social space, with the division of the work of domination. All her energy goes into framing and judging her world. But as this frame breaks apart, what comes into the foreground are the "unacknowledged conditions of action" that dominate this child's caste-obsessed world, namely, her severe reliance on her position within a class that bases its Whiggish sense of superiority on warding off redneck threats to an established order.[36] The grotesque bodies in southern women's fiction give us special access to these barely acknowledged conditions of middle-class self-construction.

When "A Memory" opens, Welty's heroine is lying on the beach in the noonday sun, "looking at a rectangle brightly lit, actually glaring at me, with sun, sand, water, a little pavilion, a few solitary people in fixed attitudes, and around it all a border of dark rounded oak trees, like the engraved thunderclouds surrounding illustrations in the Bible" (147). The frame that she makes with her fingers mimics her social heritage; this child's middle-class southern Protestantism helps her frame judgments about the merits of those around her.[37] As she solemnly tells us, she sees no one at the lake but children, or "those older people whose lives are obscure, irregular, and consciously of no worth to anything" (147). What her frame offers is a system of stratification, a rectangle that designates who's in and who's out, who's valuable, and who is not.

For Welty's little girl these schemes are intricately tied up with romance. She is in love with love itself and dreams endlessly of a secret beau, meditating obsessively on the day she contrived to touch his wrist in the stairwell at school. "It was possible during that entire year for me to think endlessly on this minute and brief encounter which we endured on the stairs, until it would swell with a sudden and overwhelming beauty, like a rose forced into premature bloom for a great occasion" (149). Ironically, "A Memory" begins in the miniature world that Louis Rubin describes as typical of Welty's fiction. We see a sensitive child on her way to heterosexual stardom, preparing for the blinkered wisdom of middle-class courting where women relinquish their claim to the public world for summer cotillions and where every nerve strains toward the opposite sex.

The first hint that something is amiss in the southern romance plot is signaled with blood: "I remember with exact clarity the day in Latin class when the boy I loved (whom I watched constantly) bent suddenly over and brought his handkerchief to his face. I saw red—vermilion—blood flow over the handkerchief and his square-shaped hand; his nose had begun to bleed. I remember the very moment: several of the older girls laughed at the confusion and distraction" (150). The narrator's response is stereotypically feminine—she faints dead away. Her motive seems fairly clear; she is terrified at this splitting open of the male body, afraid of its dirtiness, its democratizing blood. Might the threat of menstruation and mortality inhere in a boy's body as well as a girl's? The older girls feel the incongruity of this reversal and laugh, but the young narrator finds her momentary superiority unbearable; when she faints, she restores her gender to its pristine passivity.

What this moment brings home is this culture's incredible anxiety about sexual difference; the heroine needs to believe that this boy is other, superior, remote from herself. But Welty also details a little girl's status anxiety in a way that is equally compelling; class hierarchy insinuates itself as another predatory worry exacerbating this child's sense of self. The narrator tells us that she knows nothing about her beau's family or background, and that "this occasioned during the year of my love a constant uneasiness in me. It was unbearable to think that his house might be slovenly and unpainted, hidden by tall trees, that his mother and father might be shabby—dishonest—crippled—dead. I speculated endlessly on the dangers of his home" (151).

The "danger" of other people's homes—the fact of class struggle—is the squalid little secret this story sets out to expose. As Pierre Bourdieu suggests, the bourgeois elite invent for themselves an "eternal sociodicy" in which "all forms of 'levelling,' 'trivialization,' or 'massification'" seem to threaten at once. The decline of modern society is associated with apocalyptic threats to the middle-class home. Welty's child, embroiled in this "sociodicy," seems particularly vulnerable to her caste's obsessive fears; she worries helplessly that her beau lives among the "undifferentiated hordes" of the underclass who threaten "to submerge the private spaces of bourgeois exclusiveness."[38]

Moreover, her obsession with squalor has the exaggerated overtone of a fairy tale or Gothic romance, and this suggests two of the gifts that Welty's story bestows.

First, the romance plot is traditionally a place where class anxiety or turmoil can be repressed. The romance usually offers (as in *Jane Eyre*) a story of assimilation, or (as in most fairy tales) a discovery that the poor little goose girl is really a queen, or (as in *Mary Barton*) a genre where love scuttles class rebellion. "A Memory" refuses these terms. Romance becomes Welty's vehicle for exploring class consciousness; for her heroine an encounter with the Other generates real terror about the flimsiness of existing social boundaries. This breaking of boundaries is an enduring characteristic of southern women's fiction. Even a novella like *Member of the Wedding* questions the race and gender confines of the white heterosexual southern myths. Frankie may become "Frances," a budding belle, but only after McCullers asks us to mourn the sacrifice of her family's African-American housekeeper, Berenice, and the death of her androgynous cousin, John Henry.

Second, like McCullers, Welty explores the odd shapes of southern class consciousness by warping our vision of the southern child. At least since Rousseau the child has functioned to circumvent rumors of "sexuality and social inequality" in the West. According to Jacqueline Rose, the storybook child "is rendered innocent of all the contradictions which flaw our interaction with the world."[39] But Welty's preadolescent offers a social fulcrum, an entrance to cultural monstrosities as the grown-up Eudora Welty takes pleasure in staging scurrilous scenes for her own childish double. As her heroine lies on the beach, "squaring" the world with her fingers and dreaming about her bleeding beau, this girlish frame is disrupted by a family that acts out her worst social fears. This family's chief distinction is its slovenliness: "Sprawled close to where I was lying . . . appeared a group of loud, squirming, ill-assorted people who seemed thrown together only by the most confused accident, and who seemed driven by a foolish intent to insult each other, all of which they enjoyed with a hilarity which astonished my heart. . . . when I was a child such people were called 'common'" (152). Their "commonness" attracts and repels the little girl: "Lying in leglike confusion together were the rest of the group, the man and the two women. The man seemed completely given over to the heat and glare of the sun; his relaxed eyes sometimes squinted with faint amusement over the brilliant water and the hot sand. His arms were flabby and at rest. He lay turned on his side, now and then scooping sand in a loose pile about the legs of the older woman" (152-53). Bourdieu reminds us that our cognitive structures, the ways we divide up the world, are not innocent schema but "internalized, 'embodied' social structures" that are chaotic and culpable; they help to enforce the most unsavory oppositions between dominant and dominated: "All the agents in a given social formation share a set of basic perceptual schemes, which receive the beginnings of objectification in the pairs of antagonistic adjectives commonly used to classify and qualify persons or objects. The network of oppositions between high . . . and low . . . fine . . . and coarse . . . unique . . . and common . . . is the matrix of all the commonplaces which find such ready acceptance because behind them lies the whole social order."[40] This is central to Welty's story. The oppositions between male and female, upper class and underclass, are the commonplaces, the building blocks of a southern class system that we may overlook because they are so ordinary. But beyond these prosaic categories of trashy white Others lies an entire social order. These distinctions are its foundations, and "A Memory" describes a child who is working hard to master these categories for herself.

This process is disrupted by an unsavory fat woman who will not take her place amidst these "antagonistic adjectives." Her body is filthy; it is covered with sand, but she refuses to accept a role of abjection: "Once when I looked up, the fat woman was standing opposite the smiling man. She bent over and in a condescending way pulled down the front of her bathing suit, turning it outward, so that the lumps of mashed and folded sand came emptying out. I felt a peak of horror, as though her breasts themselves had turned to sand, as though they were of no importance at all and she did not care" (156). This fat woman is bad taste incarnate, and her bad taste, her indecent exposure, her empty breasts have the exhilarating ability to wreck the child-narrator's delimiting frame. As sand pours out of her body, we experience an emptying out of the little girl's romance plot as well. This woman's pearlike breasts are suddenly artifactual, lightened of female allure. Her anger matters; it shakes up a little girl's sense of privilege and hierarchy, as if Welty means to give notice that those class-and-sex dramas excluded from middle-class life can return in the most ungainly forms to haunt the power structure with its guilts and desires.[41]

Have I gone too far? Can a southern female child really represent "the power structure"? The little girl in Welty's story is obsessed with evaluating her social world. While the earthquake woman is, for her, an untouchable, a social pariah, this woman's body also works to disrupt this little girl's leisured superiority, her ease with the "work of domination" that these categorical modes of otherness instill. That is, this gargantuan southern body undoes the oppressive pleasantries of middle-class "taste" by imploding this child's hoped for conformities: "I felt a necessity for absolute conformity to my ideas in any happening I witnessed. As a result, all day long in school I sat perpetually alert, fearing for the untoward to happen. The dreariness and regularity of the school day were a protection for me" (149-50). This is an amazing statement from the childish avatar of one of the foremost inventors of the southern grotesque. Within this atmosphere of anxious conformity, the gargantuan female's "untoward" explosion of the child's precarious frame seems entirely just. At the same time, the child-narrator is herself a victim of her culture's fantasies, and in perusing her role in the story, we must come full circle, returning, via the child's diminutive and minoritized body, to the interactive politics of a gargantuan woman who can disrupt the miniature framework of a haunted little girl.

Children play a double role in southern women's writing. Marginal to mainstream culture but also caught up in its process of indoctrination, the child may question her society's values and provide a narrative space for challenging its beliefs. But children also become a tragic center for exploring the effects of the political in everyday life. As the focus of adult rules and regulations, the child is a victim and seismologist who registers the costs of a classist or a sexist ethic; she becomes a vivid, painful pressure point, a site of strain and unrest within an unjust social system. What the child is busy learning, along with fractions and table manners, is a system, a framework, a set of ideological desires and constraints. And ideologies carry their own political freight; they are symbolic systems that are continually "mobilized to sustain asymmetrical power relations in the interests of dominant or hegemonic groups."[42] The effect of the earthquake woman's family upon the young Welty is to break up this hegemonic assurance:

> It seemed to me that I could hear also the thud and the fat impact of all their ugly bodies upon one another. I tried to withdraw to my most inner dream, that of touching the wrist of the boy I loved on the stair . . . but the memory itself did not come to me.
>
> . . . I sank into familiarity; but the story of my love, the long narrative of the incident on the stairs, had vanished. I did not know, any longer, the meaning of my happiness; it held me unexplained.
>
> (155-56)

At this moment Welty's story offers us the specter of a southern legitimation crisis made flesh. As we watch a young child learning her culture's norms, trying to live inside them, we also see these norms breaking apart.[43] As she moves from the superiority of a romantic framework to an altered perceptual state that admits the grotesque body in all its "untoward" irregularity, she recognizes a world outside her habitus that remains "unexplained." That is, we see the glimmer of a child who is increasingly unable to inhabit the undemocratic certainties that both discipline and support her.

Unable to withdraw into her "most inner dream," this child is experiencing a diminutive version of a southern legitimation crisis. A culture comes to a crisis in legitimation when normative structures start to change and there is a gap, a dissonance, between the demands of the framework of the social apparatus and people's expectations and needs.[44] As old norms are pushed aside, new norms are invented that lack the force of motivation and belief. Louis Rubin has argued that this dissonance is a pivotal experience in the twentieth-century South, where old sources of certitude and belief remained entrenched but failed to offer "an adequate basis for daily experience." For Rubin this becomes a world "doomed" to fall apart. "In attempting to hold onto its traditional modes of thought and behavior so far as the Negro is concerned, the South seeks to retain a social structure doomed in and by time. In so doing, it fights a losing battle, in which racial segregation is but the immediate issue."[45] The dangerous potential inherent in angry women and their redneck consorts suggests another site of conflict. Welty's story reenacts the demise of a rose-tinted, romantic southern worldview that is no longer serviceable but seems quite irreplaceable. "A Memory" reenacts that catastrophic moment when a social formation starts to break down, and the cracks or gaps in its systems of classification seem more powerful than the system itself.

Welty has inscribed the miniature catastrophes of "A Memory" in the cusp of a full-blown southern crisis. Her story comes at the center of *A Curtain of Green,* a book set in the Great Depression that dramatizes the defamiliarization of the American Dream as it is mapped onto depressed southern bodies. The regional devastation of this depression, with its displacements of entire populations, its exaggeration of the already aggravated chasm between the North's (relative) wealth and the South's greater penury, its acceleration of the breakdown of a closed agrarian world, could only drive home the object lessons (and utter inadequacy) of an impoverished worldview whose demise is half-mourned and half-celebrated in "A Memory." Unlike most of the characters in *Curtain of Green* (mainly idiots, half-wits, deaf-mutes, sideshow or plantation relics, and con men), the heroine of "A Memory" seems out of place, for she is solidly middle class and hopelessly lyrical. But by placing a formative moment from this white girl's uneventful past at the center of her story, Welty transforms the definition of an epic event; she insists that history is made by children, too. By suggesting that this story's narrator may be Welty herself, by dramatizing a moment from a southern female life when the rage for class demarcation and lyricism breaks down, Welty also suggests a mode of transformation. It is this child's youthful penchant for accurate vision, for seeing the socially unspeakable, that works to produce an adult writer who will not turn away from the grotesque but writes unflinchingly about Miss Eckhart or Powerhouse or the tenant farmers in "A Whistle." By questioning the values of a child who is at first repelled but finally feels eroticized by the grotesque world around her, "A Memory" offers the beginnings of an epistemic break, of a new era in one writer's consciousness: a suggestive description of that moment in Welty's own life when the feminine obsession with the romance ethos shatters, to be replaced with a passion for the ordinary power plays of southern life.

A similar crisis is played out in "The Power and the Glory," Robb Foreman Dew's autobiographical essay about Baton Rouge in the 1950s. As Dew describes the glory of inhabiting a white female body with the power to attract southern men—a body that also symbolizes women's supposed transcendence of class and race politics—she also describes a world where this symbolism inevitably breaks down:

> We worked so hard at being appealing! We had bedrooms that looked like beauty parlors, with stork-like hair dryers, cosmetics of every variety, fashion magazines on our bedside tables. We slept miserably with enormous, bristly rollers wound into our hair and got up at six in the morning to unwind them so that we could painstakingly backcomb and construct our page-boys. . . . We applied makeupbase, eyeliner, mascara, lipstick, and a final dusting of loose powder. . . . This was in order for us to go to school! For me each day was like a premiere, and, in fact, I went to school as little as possible, because putting in an appearance required more energy than I could muster.
>
> One morning I couldn't find my eyelash curler, and so positive was I that without curled eyelashes I would be remarkable, that I would look grotesque, that I claimed illness and did not leave the house. . . . *I* no longer felt certain of my grasp of reality. If I was elected to one thing or another I began to suspect that it was because there was something terribly wrong with me—a physical deformity or perhaps some sort of obvious mental illness . . . that elicited enormous sympathy from my schoolmates. I could no longer manage all the secrets of my own life in the face of the image I tried to sustain in public.

The fear of looking hideous, the description of southern charm as "a crippling thing that entailed turning one's whole intelligence toward an effort to be pleasing to other people," reinvokes the southern grotesque.[46] While Mab Segrest argues that southern "women who refuse to stay in their place—who refuse to be grotesque, to stay fallen—upset the whole shebang," my own thesis is exactly the opposite.[47] Following Porter's and Welty's lead, southern women writers who appropriate the grotesque are at work constructing a female tradition that refuses the genteel obsession with writing (or inhabiting) the beautiful body in exchange for something more politically active and vehement: for the angry sex- and class-conscious writing of the southern gargantua.

In Welty's story, the violence unfolding from the earthquake woman's grotesque body is threefold. First, this underclass woman possesses a vitality that shatters the complacency of the prim southern girl narrating Welty's story; her body language is so squalid and damning that it breaks the frame of the little girl's story altogether.[48] We encounter a second variety of violence in the patriarchal hand that piles sand higher and higher on this woman's body, "like the teasing threat of oblivion" (153)—smashing this girl's delusions about an idealized division of labor. Here we confront the rigid divisions of labor and the work of domination that marks southern gender relations. But this woman responds to her consort's violence with a violence of her own. ("A slow, repetitious sound I had been hearing for a long time unconsciously, I identified as a continuous laugh which came through the motionless open pouched mouth of the woman" [153].) If her slovenly body, her sandy disarray seems threatening, it is because she uncovers a world where the beautiful body fails to keep at bay the heterogeneity and injustice that southern manners are designed to hide.

Finally, Welty's story gathers new power from the fact that this earthquake woman is not the ideal southern lady, but her antitype, her mocking double. With a mirroring violence, this woman's daughter hurls her body up and down the beach. Angry and wild, she is curled in her "green bathing suit like a bottle from which she might, I felt, burst in a rage of churning smoke" (153). When this young girl explodes, she comes "running toward the bench as though she would destroy it, and with a fierceness which took my breath away, she dragged herself through the air and jumped over the bench. But no one seemed to notice" (155). Welty invents the grotesque bodies in *A Curtain of Green* to expose the small, angry dramas of southern life that everyone experiences but no one notices. And smack in the center of this volume of stories, we encounter a new female vastness: the earthquake woman's excessive body opens up the excesses of a political system that inhabits little girls as well as great men.[49]

In story after story, Welty explores a southern world that fails to support its bodies; a comical culture whose comedy evaporates when its subjects wither, die, commit suicide, choose between the insane asylum and marriage, or endure crippling pain. This pain is not just the fate of a laboring class in the midst of national depression (the world Welty depicts in "The Whistle" or "Flowers for Marjorie" or "A Worn Path") but of a southern aristocratic class as well. Southern high culture, for all its seeming power, also lacks a working thesis, a mode of synthesis, a place to sustain the body. We feel this lack most sharply in the well-born Clytie, whose story ends when she sees a repulsive reflection of her face and drowns, her legs sticking out of the rainwater barrel "like a pair of tongs" (178). This is a frightening image of the body made mechanical and robbed of its being, an immobilized body that will fit neither the feminine nor the aristocratic frame invented by high southern culture.[50]

Bourdieu suggests that "the schemes of the habitus, the primary forms of classification, owe their specific efficacy to the fact that they function below the level of consciousness and language, beyond the reach of introspective scrutiny or control by the will."[51] Welty's framing metaphor in "A Memory" brings some of these "primary forms of classification" into prominence. I have suggested that her grotesque bodies have the uncanny ability to shift our focus even farther, so that the invisible schemes of the white southern habitus move closer to consciousness, become achingly visible. Perhaps it is no accident that Welty's earthquake woman is huge and ungainly. Her body has a great weight to bear, a weight made greater because southern women writers have worked so hard and so successfully to decode their region's political unconscious via the bodies of their southern gargantuas.

Notes

1. Richard H. King, *A Southern Renaissance: The Cultural Awakening of the American South, 1930-1955* (New York: Oxford Univ. Press, 1980), 8.

2. Ibid., 8-9.

3. Louis D. Rubin Jr., *The Faraway Country: Writers of the Modern South* (Seattle: Univ. of Washington Press, 1963), 131, 133, 133-34.

4. Eudora Welty, "A Memory," in *A Curtain of Green and Other Stories* (New York: Harcourt Brace Jovanovich, 1969), 153. Subsequent references to this text are cited parenthetically within the essay.

5. Susan Stewart, *On Longing: Narratives of the Miniature, the Gigantic, the Souvenir, the Collection* (Baltimore: Johns Hopkins Univ. Press, 1984), 86.

6. Katherine Anne Porter, *The Collected Stories of Katherine Anne Porter* (New York: Harcourt Brace Jovanovich, 1969), 174. Subsequent references to this text are cited parenthetically within the essay.

7. Stewart, *On Longing,* 124.

8. Minnie Bruce Pratt, "Identity: Blood Skin Bones," in *Yours in Struggle: Three Feminist Perspectives on Anti-Semitism and Racism,* by Elly Bulkin, Minnie Bruce Pratt, and Barbara Smith (Ithaca: Firebrand Books, 1984), 37.

9. Anne Goodwyn Jones, *Tomorrow Is Another Day: The Woman Writer in the South, 1859-1936* (Baton Rouge: Louisiana State Univ. Press, 1981), 4.

10. Bryan Turner, *The Body: Social Process and Cultural Theory,* ed. Mike Featherstone, Mike Hepworth, and Bryan Turner (London: Sage Publications, 1990), 133.

11. Mab Segrest, *My Mama's Dead Squirrel: Lesbian Essays on Southern Culture* (Ithaca: Firebrand Books, 1985), 167.

12. Lillian Smith, *Killers of the Dream* (New York: Norton, 1961), 89.
13. Eudora Welty, "Powerhouse," in *A Curtain of Green*, 254-55.
14. Eudora Welty, "June Recital," in *The Golden Apples* (New York: Harcourt, Brace & World, 1949), 56. Subsequent references to this text are cited parenthetically within the essay.
15. Mary Jacobus, Evelyn Fox Keller, and Sally Shuttleworth, Introduction, *Body/Politics: Women and the Discourses of Science,* ed. Jacobus, Keller, and Shuttleworth (New York: Routledge, 1990), 2.
16. "Thine earthly rainbows stretched across the sweep / Of the aethereal waterfall, whose veil / Robes some unsculptured image. . . . Thy caverns echoing to the Arve's commotion, / A loud, lone sound no other sound can tame; / Thou art the path of that unresting sound—Dizzy Ravine!" (Percy Bysshe Shelley, "Mont Blanc").
17. Jacobus, Keller, and Shuttleworth, *Body/Politics,* 2.
18. Peter Stallybrass and Allon White, *The Politics and Poetics of Transgression* (Ithaca: Cornell Univ. Press, 1986), 26.
19. Jacquelyn Dowd Hall, "'The Mind That Burns in Each Body': Women, Rape, and Racial Violence," in *Powers of Desire: The Politics of Sexuality,* ed. Ann Snitow, Christine Stansell, and Sharon Thompson (New York: Monthly Review Press, 1983), 332, 335.
20. Louise Westling, *Sacred Groves and Ravaged Gardens: The Fiction of Eudora Welty, Carson McCullers, and Flannery O'Connor* (Athens: Univ. of Georgia Press, 1985), 8.
21. Although Miss Eckhart is foreign, an outsider, she is still expected to conform to the community's norms. Although her rebellion is non-normative, it is not especially exceptional, except in its mode of aesthetic self-expression. As Robb Foreman Dew describes her own feminine cohort in "The Power and the Glory" (in *Portraits of Southern Childhood,* ed. Alex Harris [Chapel Hill: Univ. of North Carolina Press, 1987]), "The kind of charm we aimed for was counterfeit, because it had nothing to do with any one of us; we were only learning how to make someone else believe that he or she was enchanting. And it turned some of the brightest girls into incredibly manipulative and secretly angry women. I meet these people still, all the time; they are certainly not all southern, although they are all women, and there are no other social creatures of whom I'm as wary" (121).
22. Kate Chopin, *The Awakening* (New York: Norton, 1976), 29.
23. Robin D. G. Kelley, *Race Rebels: Culture, Politics, and the Black Working Class* (New York: Free Press, 1994), 72.
24. Robert Fleming, "The Ritual of Survival," in *Up South: Stories, Studies and Letters of This Century's African-American Migrations,* ed. Malaika Adero (New York: New Press, 1993), 33. Fleming is describing his grandfather's experiences in New Orleans in 1915.
25. Julius Lester, "Black and White Together: Teaching the 'Beloved Community' in Today's Racially Divided Classrooms," *Lingua Franca* 1 (1991): 30.
26. Zora Neale Hurston, *Their Eyes Were Watching God* (Urbana: Univ. of Illinois Press, 1978), 286.
27. We see the extent to which even Miss Eckhart has internalized this miniaturization in her response to Miss Snowdie: "What were you playing, though?" Miss Snowdie asks, "holding streams of bead curtains in both hands. 'I couldn't say,' Miss Eckhart said, rising. 'I have forgotten'" (Welty, "June Recital," 58).
28. Carson McCullers, *The Ballad of the Sad Cafe and Other Stories* (New York: Bantam, 1969), 68.
29. Smith, *Killers of the Dream,* 70.
30. Lester, "Black and White Together," 30.
31. It is generally accepted that "A Memory," the only story in *A Curtain of Green* narrated by a lyrical "I," functions as a memoir or fanciful redaction of Welty's own memories.
32. David Held, *Political Theory and the Modern State* (Stanford: Stanford Univ. Press, 1989), 4.
33. There are, of course, some wonderful exceptions, including Myra Jehlen's *Class and Character in Faulkner's South* (Secaucus, N.J.: Citadel Press, 1978) and Eric J. Sundquist's *Faulkner: The House Divided* (Baltimore: Johns Hopkins Univ. Press, 1983).
34. King, *A Southern Renaissance,* 7.
35. Although Cassie's automatic aversion to Miss Eckhart's playing can be described as part and parcel of a southern rape complex that refuses women autonomy and power, her autonomic remembrance of Miss Eckhart's rape could be described, with equal devastation, as a matter of condoned or appropriate "taste." As Pierre Bourdieu suggests, "The ultimate values, as they are called, are never anything other than the primary, primitive dispositions of the body, 'visceral' tastes and distastes, in which the group's most vital interests are embedded" (*Distinction: A Social Critique of the Judgement of Taste,* trans. Richard Nice [Cambridge: Harvard Univ. Press, 1984], 474).

36. See Jehlen's *Class and Character in Faulkner's South,* 137-51.

37. Jehlen describes the narrator's use of this framing device among the southwestern humorists: "Cultural historians who thought they were reading the other side of the Southern story in the work of the humorists, who found in it a way at last to raise 'the veil of smug respectability for a refreshing view of the real thing,' were . . . largely misled by formal differences. . . . Through the wise narrator whose commentary typically framed the action of the tale, the humorists projected precisely the plantation myth's image of a cultured aristocrat who was obviously meant to rule the South" (ibid., 138). Welty is reenacting this framing—first by literalizing her child narrator's reliance on a framework to stabilize her vision, and second by thrusting a set of 'rude mechanicals' into her line of sight. But when her narrator's frame gets interrupted or broken, Welty is also disrupting the political assumptions of a long-standing literary tradition. She refuses to repeat a simplified story of southern yokels as "uncouth, unclean, [and] lawless"—as poor whites with the ominous power of deranging the South's best traditions (ibid., 139), but instead asks the white trash at the center of her story to break—or call into question—the narrator's frame.

38. Bourdieu, *Distinction,* 469. As Jehlen points out, this anxiety takes on a particularly elitist patriarchal shape in the American South: "Walker Percy has explained the 'spectacular' change in the South as resulting from the defeat of 'the old moderate tradition of the planter-lawyer-statesman class' and 'the consequent collapse of the alliance between the "good" white man and the Negro. . . . To use Faulkner's personae,' he writes succinctly, 'the Gavin Stevenses have disappeared and the Snopeses have won.' The dire prophecies of Hooper and Harris have been realized; Longstreet would have concurred, shuddering. The Whig Götterdämmerung has come and in its wake the 'uncouth, unclean, [and] lawless' poor whites have successfully taken over the ruined South" (*Class and Character,* 138-39).

39. Jacqueline Rose, *The Case of Peter Pan, or, the Impossibility of Children's Fiction* (London: Macmillan, 1984), 8-9.

40. Bourdieu, *Distinction,* 468-69.

41. This is also the subject of Peter Taylor's "The Old Forest," in which a working girl with an untold history breaks the careful framework of denial that upper-class Memphis society has constructed to maintain its wealth, security, and sense of history. The working girl's well-kept secret is that she is also working class and that her mother is the owner of a scurrilous bar (and is thoroughly frightening—a goiter-ridden, dragonlike, vestigial, but monstrous grotesque). The hero's romantic desire for this working-class heroine surfaces too late, and his new knowledge about this need to disassociate himself from his own class distorts his destined career path and underlines his alienation from the very traditions his well-bred marriage works so well to uphold (*The Old Forest and Other Stories* [New York: Ballantine, 1985], 22-82).

42. Held, *Political Theory,* 4.

43. Although the promise of heterosexual romance—of a world to be had for the marrying—offers this young girl some longed-for stability, Welty also insists upon its slenderness as a device for organizing the world.

44. Jürgen Habermas, *Legitimation Crisis,* trans. Thomas McCarthy (Boston: Beacon Press, 1975).

45. Louis D. Rubin Jr. and Robert D. Jacobs, Introduction, *South: Modern Southern Literature in Its Cultural Setting,* ed. Rubin and Jacobs (Garden City, N.Y.: Doubleday, 1961), 15.

46. Robb Foreman Dew, "The Power and the Glory," in *Portraits of Southern Childhood,* 122, 121.

47. Segrest, *My Mama's Dead Squirrel,* 29.

48. From the beginning of the story, this framework is, of course, already riven with contradictions: "I was at an age when I formed a judgment upon every person and every event which came under my eye, although I was easily frightened. When a person, or a happening, seemed to me not in keeping with my opinion, or even my hope or expectation, I was terrified by a vision of abandonment and wildness which tore my heart with a kind of sorrow" (Welty, "A Memory," 148).

49. Although this woman's body comments on the southern race-plot only indirectly (see David Roediger's *The Wages of Whiteness: Race and the Making of the American Working Class* [New York: Verso, 1992]), Welty uses its violence to begin to expose the nightmarish underside of southern fantasies about race and class inferiority, fantasies that led to historic scenes of excess resembling the mob scenes Joel Williamson describes in his biography of Faulkner—scenes where grown-ups and children alike were participants in communal acts of predation: "The details of the Patton lynching were specific to Lafayette County, but the pattern was general. The justification was rape or attempted rape, the crowd numbered hundreds and thousands, an active cadre

of several dozen men did the actual work, and the body would be mutilated, castrated, and displayed in a public, ritualistic, and dramatic way. Afterward, white people would feel a significant measure of relief. The Patton lynching was also true to the general pattern in that it was done not only by 'rednecks,' the lower orders of whites. It was done by everybody, and the white community found release in the event" (*William Faulkner and Southern History* [New York: Oxford Univ. Press, 1993], 159).

50. We have already seen that in *The Faraway Country* Rubin makes a more general suggestion about a southern world without synthesis. In the twentieth-century South "not only have towns become cities, and cities metropolises, but the moral order of the older South, the old notions of certainty and belief, have ceased to suffice as a sufficient explanation and an adequate basis for daily experience. I speak not only of religion, but of attitudes toward the values of the community, toward history, toward society. The future novelist or poet, growing up in the South in the 1900's and 1920's, did not find, as his father and grandfather had been able to find, sufficient emotional scope within the life of the community" (7). I am suggesting that Welty depicts a southern world in which this malaise has spread to the community at large. She intimates that when the upper classes forfeit the logic of their modus vivendi—their rationale for life at the top—the entire social structure is in danger of crumbling. In fact, the placement of "Clytie" in *A Curtain of Green* (it is the story following "A Memory") suggests that the traditionally gendered and elitist worldview that supports the heroine of "A Memory" has already declined past the point of use.

51. Bourdieu, *Distinction*, 466.

Peggy Whitman Prenshaw (essay date 1998)

SOURCE: Prenshaw, Peggy Whitman. "The Construction of Confluence: The Female South and Eudora Welty's Art." In *The Late Novels of Eudora Welty,* edited by Jan Nordby Gretlund and Karl-Heinz Westarp, pp. 176-94. Columbia: University of South Carolina Press, 1998.

[*In the following essay, Prenshaw examines the role of women, particularly mothers and daughters, in the fiction of Eudora Welty, noting that she depicts Southern women as a source of strength and spiritual healing in her works.*]

In the headnote that opens *One Writer's Beginnings* Eudora Welty describes her parents on a typical morning in her early childhood. Her father is shaving, preparing to leave the house for work, and her mother is frying bacon in the kitchen. Initiating what will shortly become a duet, her father begins to whistle a tune that Welty recognizes as "The Merry Widow," and her mother, who tries to whistle, responds by humming her part. Welty thus depicts her introduction to the world as an act of listening, an act of unmediated absorption of the sensual experience surrounding her. This experience is preeminently and intricately related to the domestic household, the world of her mother. Writing in her mid-seventies, Welty delineates a girl child who apprehends the worlds of father and mother. She takes delight in both worlds, acknowledging the powerful models these gave her, furnishing the imagination of the artist she would become. At the beginning of the autobiography, however, Welty explicitly links the father with what is culturally marked as "work," as well as with writing. He leaves the domestic hearth for his job as an insurance executive, and he originates tunes—a kind of paradigm for the writing career Welty will herself pursue. With her new walking shoes, she is a father's daughter, outsetting.

The inescapable association of authorship with male power in modern Western culture is a matter of continuing moment, a subject widely analyzed but hardly exhausted by numerous intellectual historians writing in recent years. Specific Southern manifestations of female authorial anxiety have also been subjected to wide-ranging study by such critics as Anne Goodwyn Jones, Lucinda MacKethan, Louise Hutchings Westling, and others, including many represented in this volume.[1] Ruth Weston, for example, discerningly analyzes the constraints acting upon Welty and other Southern contemporaries, whom Weston shows as drawing upon a Gothic tradition to mediate anxieties and offer patterns of female agency and heroism.[2]

For Eudora Welty, who was clearly aware of the identification of "male" with "author," one sustaining strategy for allaying or slaying the monster of self-doubt seems to have been the familiar habit of mind of identifying ambition and separate selfhood as the emotional and intellectual inheritance from the father, an inheritance she depicts in *One Writer's Beginnings* as wholly legitimate and natural for her. Importantly for her own development, she associates the act of writing and of "journeying" with her father, whereas she always connects reading and the passionate love of books and storytelling with her mother. To the extent that her father did read, it was for information, to equip him to act upon the world. By contrast, her mother's reading of fiction is described as an act of passion, a show of love and independence, though the independence is voluntarily surrendered to the text: "she sank as a hedonist into novels. She read Dickens in the spirit in which she would have eloped with him" (*OWB* [*One Writer's Beginnings*], 6-7).

Welty comments that it was her mother who always offered support for her ambition to be a writer; it was her father who bought her the typewriter she took with her to the University of Wisconsin. In the first section of the autobiography, Welty remembers, too, the trips she made in childhood with her brothers to her father's office, where he let them "peck at the typewriter." What they wrote on these occasions were letters to their mother, including one by the youngest, Walter, that Chestina Welty kept: "Dear Mrs. C. W. Welty. I think you know me. I think you like me." Throughout *One Writer's Beginnings* Welty explicitly associates the enterprise of journeying away from home and mother with the model of the father and with her own writing career. Time and again she would write to mother, who waited at home for her message. Welty observes, "I knew this was how she must have waited when my father had left on one of his business trips, and I thought I could guess how he, the train lover, the trip lover, must have felt too while he remained away." Welty records the "torment and guilt" she felt, "being the loved one gone," and yet, her joy, she knew, lay at a distance from home, lay in the land of publishers, editors, writers. Her "joy was connected with writing," and, despite her mother's enthusiasm for Welty's effort to become a writer, one unavoidably concludes that the actual enterprise of writing led to the most important and enduring instance in which Welty's bliss necessarily implied her "mother's deprivation or sacrifice" (*OWB*, 34, 94, 19).

In familiar patterns that many feminist critics have analyzed over the past several decades, Welty thus genders writing and art making as aligned importantly, though certainly not exclusively, with the masculine. The cost to the female writer of assuming such authority presents great risk, as Welty argues in the closing pages of *One Writer's Beginnings,* and courage is required if one is not to be undone by Medusa-like self-images that arise from a masculinist culture's perspective and transform the female artist into an unnatural monster. Danièle Pitavy-Souques's analysis of Medusa figures and Peter Schmidt's study of sibyls in Welty's fiction are helpful to an understanding of the ways such figures take shape and enact their damage in such a culture,[3] although Rebecca Mark's demurral on this point, i.e., the medusan and sibylline signification in Welty's fiction, provides a caution against such readings, which she sees as falsely demonizing the Medusa. Mark gives a persuasive interpretation of the interrelation and interdependence of the three phases of the female Gorgon figure in *The Golden Apples,* arguing that Welty not only writes a sweeping revision of "the Western myth of the literary hero in all his manifestations," but imaginatively does so by reinstating the integrity of the thrice-faced Gorgon and, indeed imaginatively reinstating thereby, the integrity and original energy of the cosmos.[4] I take Mark's point, but it seems to me that Schmidt and many other critics have in fact long been moving in the same general direction, finding and discussing various oppositions and dualities in Welty's fiction as a way of responding to her revisionary transformations of her culture's conventions.[5]

While acknowledging Welty's decentering of the culture's masculinist assumptions about authorship in her fiction, I nonetheless read in her nonfiction prose and interviews an explicit association of writing and maleness linked, as I have suggested, with her father. Furthermore, and especially interesting here, is the way in which this association also extends through the father to his native North. In Welty's cultural imagination, authorship is attached not only to gender but to region. Although Welty unhesitatingly recognizes the literary mastery of such fellow Southerners as William Faulkner, her reflections on her own psychic makeup in *One Writer's Beginnings* suggest that the singleness of mind and purposive action that she associates with her father and with the psychological makeup of the creative artist, she also associates with the North.[6] The characterization of the North as practical, progressive, and logical, and of the South as fanciful and imaginative reflects a long-running, even stereotypical, psychic drama of the American mind. When interviewer John Griffin Jones asked about her perceptions of Southern life, given "the fact that your mother and father weren't from the Deep South," she replied that her mother "considered herself a Southerner of the first water." She continued, "I think something to do with the Civil War and anti-slavery was why they moved to West Virginia. They set their slaves free—at least on one side; I don't know about the other—and went to West Virginia where there was no slavery. They were Methodist preachers, the men; one was a Baptist preacher. They went over there out of a sense of bringing up their family in West Virginia. My mother was a Southerner and a Democrat. My father was a Yankee and a Republican. They were very different in everything" (*C* [*Conversations with Eudora Welty*], 320-21).

In a 1986 BBC film documentary, Welty again makes a point of the confluent regional alliances that shaped her background. She narrates the story that brought her family to Mississippi, noting that her father offered his bride the choice of moving to upstate New York or Jackson, and that her mother made the choice of the South.[7] Significantly, in the John Griffin Jones interview, however, we see in Welty's portrait of her mother's Southern family an important revision of the plantation, slave-holding South; it is, rather, a South of preachers and teachers. For Welty, clearly, there are multiple Souths.

Although Welty repeatedly describes herself as psychically the daughter of both her mother and father, she was nonetheless a child of her time and place, and the experience that she knew most immediately growing up in Jackson, Mississippi, was the domestic life of the maternal world. Life at the roots, life known from the inside, life as emotion and feeling and intimate experience—this is experience chiefly associated with the home and hearth, with her mother, the Southerner. I suspect it was fortuitous for Welty that her family circumstance so closely matched the configuration of North-South relationships that were popularly, even stereotypically, imaged in the late nineteenth and early twentieth centuries. In the view of Northerners, at least, the public sphere of the white male had been submitted to the ultimate testing of physical might and courage in the Civil War, and the Northern male had proved the victor. Indeed, as Nina Silber has recently shown in *The Romance of Reunion,* a reiterated pattern in the popular culture of the later nineteenth century reveals a masculinized North and a feminized South frequently matched in romance plots that served a rather explicit and transparent cultural purpose: the amelioration of the bitter sectionalism of the war years. The opposition between North and South came increasingly to be figured as a family dispute, or a dispute between romantic partners, one that could be resolved by a wedding. "This gendered view of reunion and of the South," Silber writes, "offered a comfortable and familiar rubric, emphasizing as it did traditional notions of domestic harmony, through which northerners could reunite with former enemies."[8]

Although Welty's culture would confront her with a rigid gendering of male and female spheres—the South of her youth embodying an especially recalcitrant late-Victorianism in this regard—she would encounter no discordant tension between her "family romance"—to use Freud's phrase naming developmental relationships among father, mother, and child—and the regional romance. In the regional pattern the Northern patriarch operates powerfully in the public world; the Southern lady rules with verve and passion in the home and heart. What was required for Welty was to inherit male power sufficiently to energize and authorize her separation from the maternal place-bound world. As she indicates in the titles of the final two sections of *One Writer's Beginnings,* such separation was requisite to her "learning to see" and "getting her distance," that is, requisite to *writing* the truth of the multiplicitous world embodied by the maternal, writing the mother, one might say. The consequence for Welty's fiction is a fully engaged concentration upon the female and feminine, as I have discussed in an earlier essay, and as Louise Westling, Ruth D. Weston, and many other Welty critics have also noted.[9] I am not suggesting a reductionist reading of Welty's writing as limited to the feminine world her culture defined and stipulated for women; to the contrary, I think her work points the reader to a radically revised interpretation of what *that* world consisted in. In Welty's mind, it was much more expansive than that the culture typed. She pointedly notes in the BBC interview, for example, that she was the "first born" and the lone female and thereby was "awarded" the finest and largest room in the house.

Ann Romines offers a particularly suggestive reading of Welty's reminiscence about her childhood journeys to the "little store" to purchase bread for her mother, a reminiscence that shows an exposure to the world much beyond a sheltered "girl's view." Romines writes, "The necessity and delicious terror of this daughter's separation from her fruitful, housebound mother are combined with a heavy sense that her mother's myth, with the loaf of bread, is in her hands. If she fails in her mission, domestic ritual will be disrupted, and her mother will be displaced, forced to 'march' into the antidomestic world of journeys and transactions—a world that the daughter herself finds powerfully seductive." The trips enact a pattern of escapes and returns to the mother, a cyclical pattern of "daughterly birth, return, and rebirth" that becomes, Romines notes, a "powerful motif in Welty's fiction."[10]

It may be true, as one commentator has asserted, that Welty, along with other female Southern writers, has not placed the "region" at the center of her imaginative vision.[11] What is central to her work, no more or less than to a male writer's, is the direct life experience she absorbed and reflected upon. It is, of course, a capricious abstraction of thinkers to generalize the experience of one's own sex as exhaustively commensurate with and uniquely defining of the region that one inhabits, particularly in a culture that sees and inculcates vivid sex-role distinctions, but it seems that to do so is nearly inevitable (for scholars and writers). For Southern white males, the arena for discovering and enacting one's manhood has long been the public sphere of politics, a sphere undercut, however, by the Civil War defeat. Subsequently, the driving question for such men was not How could God have let us lose the war?, but rather How could the war have been lost if "real men" had been fighting it? The lessons drawn from the question-asking have been many, including an ironic, burdensome sense of man's limits, according to C. Vann Woodward.[12] But the experience of white men does not map the whole terrain of the South.

For Southern white females of Welty's era, the South was *female,* a world of matriarchs and children, a world of busy dailiness, teeming, unruly, but ruled by the mothers. It was a world of weddings and deaths and births, of gardening and feeding and preserving. It is the world of Ellen Fairchild in *Delta Wedding,* Edna Earle Ponder in *The Ponder Heart,* Becky McKelva in *The Optimist's Daughter,* and Beulah Beecham Renfro in *Losing Battles.* I have described it elsewhere as a woman's world in which males had a place, vital roles to play, but finally were peripheral to its daily enactments.[13] It is the South recorded in a long tradition of fiction and autobiography by women writers. Shirley Abbott, a generation younger than Welty, writes in *Womenfolks: Growing Up Down South* that she "grew up under the hegemony of a line of magnificent women—strong women, with an ancient pedigree, who adhered to a code of honor, who oversaw my conduct, who held (and still hold) me responsible for my actions." Like Welty, Abbott learned much of the wider world from her Yankee father, not from travel but from the books he shared with her. But her maternal ancestors in Arkansas reigned in her experience and imagination over corporeal, daily life, "representatives of a Southern feminine culture worth remembering." She continues: "They were independent almost from birth. They knew how to make do in harsh circumstances, and even in clement surroundings they maintained a stubborn equilibrium with their menfolks. To a degree that infuriated me and eventually drove me away from them, they gritted their teeth and were selfless, made sacrifices, and gave in. I am not like them. Yet I am of them, mindful of their legacy wherever I go."[14] A little later Abbott compares the extended family of women gathered around her aunt's table to members of a "corporate board," noting that "they could hardly display more intelligence and control."

It is not necessary to belabor evidence of the centrality of the domestic world in the lives of Southern girls and women of Welty's generation.[15] What I want to emphasize here is the way in which the direct impression of life that females in the South registered was affiliated with their concepts of the Southern region. No doubt it is true with Southern womanhood, as in all human societies, that idealized, unrealistic social roles and behavior have influenced the lives of the single individual, producing tensions and pain and internalized constraints for her. In the opening chapter of *Tomorrow Is Another Day*, Anne Goodwyn Jones gives a succinct and discerning discussion of the way in which Southern womanhood has been imaged in the service of a patriarchal culture and the way in which this complex image has "exerted through time tremendous power to define actual roles for Southern (perhaps all American) women of the white middle and upper classes." It is also true, of course, that Welty and many other Southern writers, the women especially, have well comprehended the diverse cultural business going on in the imaging of the Southern lady. They have also understood the complexity attending the creation of images and the inevitable duplicity enacted whenever one tries to "live" an image. Making a "marble statue live and move, and then to make it speak" is, after all, a "magician's trick," as Jones concludes.[16]

Still, I would argue that sculpting a marble statue is a considerable achievement, and to the extent that female writers have imaged women's experience to register their own direct knowledge of it and to make visible the powerful, passionate continuity of female lives, their literary efforts have seemed to me more nearly a celebration of women than a co-optation by the patriarchs.[17] Anne Jones makes the important point about the nineteenth- and early-twentieth-century women writers who are the subjects of her study (Augusta Jane Evans, Grace King, Kate Chopin, Mary Johnston, Ellen Glasgow, Frances Newman, and Margaret Mitchell) that the female authors' responses to the idea of Southern womanhood are an ambivalent meshing of idealized and realistic portrayals. One might observe that a mix of romance and realism also characterizes the fiction of the male writers of this period—Mark Twain, Stephen Crane, and William Faulkner, for example. The point may be self-evident and commonsensible, but it is one I think worth dwelling on, at least briefly. The life refracted through the lens of fiction written by Southern women originates in their felt experience as women. It is no more, or less, derived from male-dominated images than is the culture at large. And for the woman writing, for the woman "inside" this experience, as for a man, there is, alas, no way to get outside one's own skin, albeit the imagination can assuage the limitation.

Welty links "regional" and "localized raw material of life" in her essay "Place in Fiction," sensing in the opprobrium attached to regional writing a condescension to the "regional." She writes, "'Regional' is an outsider's term; it has no meaning for the insider who is doing the writing, because as far as he knows he is simply writing about life" (*ES* [*The Eye of the Story: Selected Essays and Reviews*], 132). It is far likelier that the opprobrium that Welty senses is a response to the world of female experience, a remote terrain for many male reviewers and critics and thereby thought deserving of the term "regional" to signify the exotic, the other, the inessential to one's own localized raw material of life.

"Place in Fiction" is one of Welty's early essays, initially offered as a lecture at Cambridge University and published in 1955. As she wrote it, she undoubtedly thought of Virginia Woolf's *A Room of One's Own* lectures. Welty approaches her subject in the opening paragraphs in an apologetic, defensive tone: "Place is one of the lesser angels that watch over the racing hand of fiction, perhaps the one that gazes benignly enough from off to one side, while others, like character, plot, symbolic meaning, and so on, are doing a good deal of wing-beating about her chair, and feeling, who in my eyes carries the crown, soars highest of them all and rightly relegates place into the shade" (*ES*, 116). The voice that presents "place" to us does so with teasing, ironic humor, personifying place as a heavenly female presence, though a "lesser angel," a comic one that might have been plucked from the environs of Pope's "The Rape of the Lock." With this modest disclaimer for her topic, she turns directly to the issue that interests her, namely, appropriate—and inappropriate—criteria for evaluating literary art.

Welty does not indict male traditions of socializing and intellectualizing as Woolf had. Rather, she makes an oblique and theoretical defense of her own work and circumstance as a Southern woman writer. She undertakes to deconstruct and then reconstruct "regionalism" as the term is applied to evaluations of fiction. What was and was not "regional" was a particularly lively issue in the early years of Welty's career. Both Ruth Vande Kieft and Michael Kreyling in early studies of her work address the onus of "regionalism" because they regard the term as a negative attribution.[18] In a recent study of Welty's "aesthetics of place," Jan Nordby Gretlund observes that Welty's "regionalism" is of a "subtle" nature, and he maintains that "she was never a social critic. . . ."[19]

Indeed, Welty's choice of the term "place" points up her intention from the outset to enlarge upon simplistic notions of "setting" or regional writing. What she ultimately means by "place" is the whole world of experience that a writer brings to her art—the "raw material of writing," "the achieved world of appearance," the full identity of the writer, that is, the writer's "worth." Substituting feminine for the masculine pronouns Welty employed in this 1950s essay, consider her explanation of a writer's "worth": "place is where [she] has [her] roots, place is where [she] stands; in [her] experience out of which [she] writes, it provides the base of reference; in [her] work, the point of view." Among writers who succeed in drawing upon what they directly know and realizing that experience in fiction are James, Chekhov, Emily Brontë, to begin her list. There are also stories "when the visibility is only partial or intermittent . . . as endangered as Eliza crossing the ice. Forty hounds of confusion are after it, the black waters of disbelief open up between its steps, and no matter which way it jumps it is bound to slip. Even if it has a little baby moral in its arms, it is more than likely a goner" (*ES,* 117, 120). Harriet Beecher Stowe does not fare so well with Welty, whose trope here builds upon an assumption of Stowe's inept knowledge and use of "place."

For Welty, the term "place" signifies home place, and a close reading of "Place in Fiction" reveals how closely she connects her own mother and her personality and sphere of power with both a generalized, literary conception of the term "place" and a more specific conception of "South." Welty writes that "fiction is all bound up in the local . . . *feelings* are bound up in place. The human mind is a mass of associations. . . ." One recalls that in *One Writer's Beginnings* Welty explicitly describes her mother as having a mind that was a "mass of associations" (*OWB,* 19). The art of writing, Welty continues, is "the one least likely to cut the cord that binds it to its source," whereas "music and dancing, while originating out of place—groves!—and perhaps invoking it still to minds pure or childlike, are no longer bound to dwell there" (*ES,* 118). Place furnishes an "abode" for the world of the novel, and place exerts "the most delicate control over character . . . by confining character, it defines it." "Place absorbs our earliest notice and attention, it bestows on us our original awareness. . . ." "Place heals the hurt, soothes the outrage, fills the terrible vacuum that . . . human beings make" (*ES,* 122, 128, 131). The explicit and buried metaphors in these descriptions of place (umbilical cord; sacred fertility groves; domestic habitation; nurturance that is constraining, sheltering, and directive; place as object of the child's earliest awareness, source of restorative life) all are directly associated with and invoke the image of the maternal.

The figure of artistic creation that Welty advances incorporates the great brimming world (place) and the unique imagination of the artist, which like a lamp casts interpreting light upon that world. This is, of course, the familiar paradigm of the Romantic artist, but for Welty there is a crucial difference. The artist is created by the world, linked lovingly to it, embraced, sheltered, not alienated, by it. The success of the artist is measured not by any sort of defiant struggle with the world but by her ability to create the world anew in her art and thereby to participate in the continuity of life. This conception is essentially imaged in the Psyche myth, in which the female psyche looks daringly upon the beloved so as to love more knowingly and deeply. In describing her world as "sheltered," Welty does no more than speak truly. But in directing her full imaginative vision upon this world, she is daring indeed.

How Welty manages to look upon her personal and regional experience as a Southern white woman with such candor and express her visioning with such equanimity raises interesting questions. In contrast to Carson McCullers and Flannery O'Connor, as Louise Westling observes, "she was able to be positive about the limited possibility for feminine life in the South."[20] An understanding of how and why she is so lies perhaps in Welty's identification of place just discussed. She was after bigger fish than swam in Southern waters, but fortuitously for her, her search was as suited to a specifically Southern species as to the ocean leviathan she pursued, e.g., the ancient mysteries of women, the continuity of mothers and daughters. When *Southern Review* editors Robert Penn Warren and Cleanth Brooks published her stories early in the 1940s, it is easy to imagine that they were responding not only to the literary artistry but to an invocation of the South that, with their Agrarian sympathies and affiliations, they honored. This was an elemental South, one that loomed larger and more anciently than the industrial New South. In it was manifest a mind or "temper," as Robert B. Heilman once wrote, that displayed a "sense of the concrete," "the elemental," "the ornamental," "the representative," and "the totality."[21] According to Richard Weaver in "Aspects of the Southern Philosophy," published in the 1953 *Southern Renascence,* "synthesis," the way of "religion and art," characterizes the Southern world view, whereas "analysis" and the way of "science and business" typify the North.[22] What the editors of the *Southern Review* may not have discerned, however, is how powerfully and essentially this "South" was a metaphor in Welty's imagination for "female."

One should emphasize that Welty's symbolization of the South is not one more version of the commodification of white womanhood as the South's Palladium, a flimsily romantic notion such as W. J. Cash attempted to expose in *The Mind of the South.* Here is not a feminized South that is compensatory, arising from male anxiety such as Faulkner memorably embodies in *The Sound and the Fury.* The long-standing trope of South-as-woman, employed by generations of commentators, mostly male, doubtless gave Welty a rich word and image hoard to draw upon. The significant difference here is that Welty creates and uses the trope of the female South from a nativist point of view, the native land being "herland," the world of female experience.[23]

To return to the consideration of the equanimity that Welty brings to her artistic visioning, let me suggest that Welty was able to form from her own life experience a vision of herself as daughter and Southerner and creator-artist that was, both psychologically and aesthetically, satisfying, symmetrical, and confluent. We see the elements of the self she has invented with the tools of reflection and memory; these are revealed in her written texts. In these, many emblematic images help give an understanding of this "self," but an especially compelling and inclusive moment occurs in the final pages of *One Writer's Beginnings* in which Welty relates the incident of her father's death at age fifty-two of leukemia. The year was 1931; Welty was twenty-two. The passage occurs in a section in which Welty recalls her mother, explaining how "writing a story or novel is one way of discovering *sequence* in experience, or of stumbling upon cause and effect in the happenings of a writer's own life" (*OWB,* 90). What she tells then is how, in a transfusion meant to save his life, her mother's blood killed her father. Welty's account is reportorial, noncommittal: "How much was known about compatibility of blood types then, or about the procedure itself, I'm unable to say," she writes.

> I was present when it was done, my brothers were in school. Both my parents were lying on cots, my father had been brought in on one and my mother lay on the other. Then a tube was simply run from her arm to his. My father, I believe, was unconscious. My mother was looking at him. I could see her fervent face; there was no doubt as to what she was thinking. This time, *she* would save *his* life, as he'd saved hers so long ago, when she was dying of septicemia. What he'd done for her in giving her the champagne, she would be able to do for him now in giving him her own blood. All at once his face turned dusky red all over. The doctor made a disparaging sound with his lips, the kind a woman knitting makes when she drops a stitch. What the doctor meant by it was that my father had died.
>
> My mother never recovered emotionally. Though she lived for over thirty years more, and suffered other bitter losses, she never stopped blaming herself. She saw this as her failure to save his life.
>
> (*OWB,* 94-95)

The deeply etched memory that Welty reports, the attempt to transfuse blood from her mother to her father, is not a discovery of parents fused in sexual embrace but the witnessing of a life-destroying fusion. Like her mother, who tells the child Eudora not where babies come from, but of the death of her firstborn son, Welty tells the reader of death, not sexuality. But, of course, she is talking obliquely of sexuality, and, more broadly, of the desire and pain associated with materiality, the bodiness of life.

In this scene Welty occupies the position of observer, a position of "power," as she has discussed earlier in the autobiography. She looks upon a scene that we may infer would have been "unbearable" to her restrained father, the "optimist," who in this instance lies helplessly attached by cord to Welty's mother. In the mother's power lies the realm of death—and life. By means of her art, as protective as Perseus's shield, Welty is able to gaze upon this mortal scene, despite its nearly overwhelming intensity. Her gaze matches the power of the blood; both are equally "passionate," life filled. The daughter's gaze, recorded in the written text, indeed replicates the mother's power, continuing the cycle of generation. Like a new offspring, the daughter's seeing and telling the mother's story regenerates and transforms the mother. Making the story is a daring act, requiring the direct encounter with the mother, but it is finally an act of love, an internalization of the mother's legacy.

This drama forms the core of *The Optimist's Daughter,* in which the dying father causes the daughter at last to face the mother. At the conclusion of that novel it is not Becky's, the mother's, breadboard that Laurel Hand takes away from the encounter, but her sketchbook, as she heads north to Chicago to get on with her work as a designer. Emotionally anemic when she comes home to the South, Laurel has her passion for life restored through recourse to the mother. The wandering self, the spirit, the individualized daughter comes back to the mother place to feed and be fed. Her contribution to the reunion is *sight,* the ability to see and interpret the oracular wisdom of the mother. In "Place in Fiction" Welty personifies place as just such an oracle or sibyl:

"From the dawn of man's imagination, place has enshrined the spirit; as soon as man stopped wandering and stood still and looked about him, he found a god in that place; and from then on that was where the god abided and spoke from if ever he spoke" (*ES*, 123).

Likewise, I read one of the centers of action in *Losing Battles* as Gloria's confrontation with the passionate, tragic intensity of Julia Mortimer (who reminds one of Becky McKelva) and a confronting of the fiercely communal, all-embracing family of Vaughn, Beechams, and Renfros, especially her mother-in-law, Beulah. Gloria is an orphan, probably a Sojourner, the daughter of Rachel. Like Fay and the Judge, Gloria claims she believes in the future—what is up ahead of us, she keeps insisting to Jack. But she also resembles Laurel as she listens, *hears*, internalizes Miss Julia's story—"It hurts," she says, as much in response to the account of Julia's anguished last days as to the needling she is getting from the repairing of her white organdy dress. Like Phil Hand, Jack instructs his wife in how to live and love, how to make things that work, and finally how to let go of the self.

In *Losing Battles* it is Vaughn, named for his maternal grandparents, as Laurel had been named in honor of her mother's beloved home, who holds to a vision of heroism, of separateness from the family. Vaughn sees the world as spectacle, to use Marion Montgomery's formulation, whereas it is Gloria who apprehends the limits of Julia Mortimer's pessimistic heroism and undergoes an initiation into the rites of self-sacrifice, of openness, and who begins to understand the risk and exposure of self that memory can enact.

When Welty turned from *Losing Battles* to write *The Optimist's Daughter*, I think it likely that she was working out the multiple aspects of the maternal in rather explicit ways in the figures of Becky and Fay, aspects that are figured in much greater complexity in *Losing Battles*. Peter Schmidt has elaborated the ways in which Welty suggests through her fiction the aspects of art that empower readers to "identify and change the cultural texts that confine them—to evolve from identifying with Medusa to identifying with a sibyl, from self-destructive rage and guilt to empowering acts of disguise and revision."[24] I would add that not only does Welty discern the duality of the Medusa and sibyl in the cultural raw material that furnishes the imagination; she discerns that she as well has a hand in creating them.

Certainly, one of the defining features of Eudora Welty's fiction is the iteration and reiteration of patterns of multivocality, as Rebecca Mark demonstrates in her study of *The Golden Apples*. Welty evinces an extraordinary degree of Keatsian negative capability, the capacity to resist an angry or irritable straining after resolution, the ability to understand and accept the conflicting, even contradictory nature of our own and others' being. Over the past fifty years of her writing career, many literary critics employing a variety of perspectives have addressed these patterns, which do clearly invite multiple and diverse interpretation. What I have been pursuing here is an understanding of Welty's equanimity, even delight, in the presence of an unstable signifier. And I have suggested that the synonymy, or synchronicity, of her inner experience and the outer world gave rise to a remarkable sense of self-definition for her, one might say a positionally continuous "fit" with the sexual, familial, and regional identities or subjectivities possible for her to imagine. These identities were expansive, comprising what has been culturally typed as masculinist (and modernist) attributes of separateness, "journeying," which she took to be her inheritance from her father, the Northerner who had chosen to make his life in the South. Even more multiplicitous was the identity available to her through her mother, the Southerner, an identity rendered through the symbolization of a maternal legacy that connects both mother and daughter with "place," terrestrial life, with the source of original energy.

Welty cherishes these tensions, recognizing them in her autobiographical writing as the constituents of her life. In her novels the imagined and formalized "confluence" of such tensions constitutes a central strain of her art, powerfully expressed in imagery that signifies a meeting point of separate parts of the self, that is, in images such as bridges, path crossings, and ferries, margins to be traversed, journeys from one realm of experience to another. There are also more-ominous and threatening markers of confluence, however, most notably in imagery associated with the site or sight of blood. In such imagery, she taps her deep roots of identity to imagine multiple transformations of reality.

In "A Memory," published in 1937, a work of short fiction that comes close to autobiography, the adult narrator describes a childhood memory of an appalling spectacle, a group of swimmers cavorting on the sandy beach of a public swimming lake in Jackson, Mississippi. The sight of the tanned and roughened group, some darting about, others lying in leggy confusion lumped in a pile, is as unsettling as another memory is sweetly comforting: her girlish love for one of her classmates, a boy whom she hardly knows but whom she has transformed through her dreaming into an object of love. Of direct encounters with him there have been two: a moment when her hand brushed his wrist on the stairway and a horrifying moment in the Latin class when her beloved "bent suddenly over and brought his handkerchief to his face." Then she saw "red—vermilion—blood flow over the handkerchief." It was, the narrator recalls, "a tremendous shock," "unforeseen, but at the same time dreaded" (*CS* [*The Collected Stories of Eudora Welty*], 76).

The narrator's childish notion of love was one of controlling, protecting order. She could not bear to think that her dream of love was subject to the vicissitudes of chance and messy mortality. What the child at the time does not fully comprehend, the mature narrator, however, does comprehend. The boy with the bleeding nose and the fleshy swimmers belong to the terrestrial world; they are beyond her protection, though they are subject to her discerning, interpreting eye. The memory that concludes the story is of the narrator's realization of her visioning power: "I remember continuing to lie there, squaring my vision with my hands, trying to think ahead to the time of my return to school in winter. I could imagine the boy I loved walking into a classroom, where I would watch him with this hour on the beach accompanying my recovered dream and added to my love. I could even foresee the way he would stare back, speechless and innocent, a medium-sized boy with blond hair, his unconscious eyes looking beyond me and out the window, solitary and unprotected" (*CS*, 80). In "A Memory" Welty writes of a significant threshold crossed by the narrator, a woman who recalls a childhood discovery of the irremediable but satisfying, revitalizing connectedness of love, blood, sexuality, hideous fleshy mortality and an onlooking, empathizing, participating artist—an artist whose stance and capacity for vision necessitate a separating distance.

Welty's metaphors of agency to express the process of creating a story are often derived from the domestic sphere of sewing or knitting. In "A Memory" the narrator recalls her beloved, and then, "like a needle going in and out" among her thoughts, she envisions the children running, the "upthrust oak trees," the adults lying prone and laughing on the water's edge—erotic images connecting her pubescent curiosity and desire with the rowdy, helter-skelter drama of procreation and death, a drama, one notes, that is vividly reminiscent of the feeding pigeons that are prominently associated with the maternal grandmother in *The Optimist's Daughter* and *One Writer's Beginning*. In those books, too, a revision and surer understanding of the pigeons, that is, of the vitality they represent and of the sympathetic, even grateful acceptance of the vitality, wait upon an adult narrator's sight. In stitching the fragments of memory together, the narrator creates sequence, plot, chronology. "I still would not care to say which was more real," the narrator reflects, "the dream I could make blossom at will, or the sight of the bathers. I am presenting them, you see, only as simultaneous" (*CS*, 77). The artist stitches her multiple fragments together to simulate simultaneity—domestic ritual is a central operating metaphor for artistic creativity here and elsewhere, as Ann Romines illustrates.[25] But as Danièle Pitavy-Souques argues in an earlier reading of "A Memory," the domestication of the world, the framing and ordering that is the modernist impulse designed to assuage the self's anxiety, forms only part of the girl's memory. There is also the image of death, signified by the swimmers, and there is the concluding spectacle of the devastated beach. Pitavy-Souques reads this conclusion as evidencing Welty's acknowledgment that the ordering/artist self can make only poor attempts at creating images. "It seems our lot in the end to accept the cleavage of the self, for what is the 'other' but the revelation of the non-identity of self to self."[26] Such a conclusion follows upon a reading of the artist's role as heroic, as an individual's unique confrontation with the world's resistance, but one may also find in this story an adult narrator who knows, even though the child remembered has not yet fully comprehended, that the beach will fill again and again. In "A Memory" the swimmers are equally images of life and death, as is the boy an embodiment of both beauty and horror. And all are simply and fully of the moment. One might say of "A Memory," as Rebecca Mark says of *The Golden Apples*, that the "degree of identification between artist and object collapses the duality of the subject/object split and allows for a much more fluid relationship between author and text."[27]

The tropes of stitching or of framing a scene expose the artifice of story-making and suggest the riskiness of it. Each stitch and each framed moment go forward in time, continuously susceptible to the "outside" world, the world of blood and bones, the sensible and material. The "big pattern" is forever contingent and in the process of being created by the stitcher-framer living within, part of and responsive to her world. Fusing these realities—the fields of time and blood—nearly overwhelms the child on the beach—the schoolgirl faints in response to the nosebleed, and she falls asleep in response to the disturbing, threatening swimmers. But she grows up to tell this story of an early prescience about the transformational, shape-shifting nature of her inner and outer worlds.

Like the narrator of "A Memory," Eudora Welty locates a pivotal moment of her own understanding of the complex relation between organic and word-made worlds at the site of her father's dying. In a nearly unbearable moment of seeing, she gazes upon the vitality and the limits of a powerful maternity. The sight/site marks the place of fiction for Welty, the location where she discovers a daughter's legacy and realizes the possibilities, through story-making, of continuing its generative power.

Notes

1. See Anne Goodwyn Jones, *Tomorrow Is Another Day* (Baton Rouge: Louisiana State University Press, 1981); Lucinda MacKethan, *Daughters of*

Time: Creating Woman's Voice in Southern Story (Athens: University of Georgia Press, 1990); and Louise Hutchings Westling, *Sacred Groves and Ravaged Gardens: The Fiction of Eudora Welty, Carson McCullers, and Flannery O'Connor* (Athens: University of Georgia Press, 1985).

2. Ruth D. Weston, *Gothic Traditions and Narrative Techniques in the Fiction of Eudora Welty* (Baton Rouge: Louisiana State University Press, 1994), pp. 133-72.

3. See Danièle Pitavy-Souques, *La Mort de Meduse: L'Art de la Nouvelle chez Eudora Welty* (Lyon: Presses Universitaires de Lyon, 1992); and Peter Schmidt, *The Heart of the Story: Eudora Welty's Short Fiction* (Jackson: University Press of Mississippi, 1991).

4. Rebecca Mark, *The Dragon's Blood: Feminist Intertextuality in Eudora Welty's* The Golden Apples (Jackson: University Press of Mississippi, 1994), pp. 4ff.

5. On dualities and patterns of opposition in Welty's fiction, see, for example, Merrill Maguire Skaggs, "Morgana's Apples and Pears," in *Eudora Welty: Critical Essays,* ed. Peggy Whitman Prenshaw (Jackson: University Press of Mississippi, 1979), pp. 220-41; and Susan V. Donaldson, "'Contradictors, Interferers, and Prevaricators': Opposing Modes of Discourse in Eudora Welty's *Losing Battles,*" in *Eudora Welty: Eye of the Storyteller,* ed. Dawn Trouard (Kent, Ohio: Kent State University Press, 1989), pp. 32-43.

6. Lewis P. Simpson discusses a related and parallel instance of regional identities in "Why Quentin Compson Went to Harvard," his epilogue to *Mind and the American Civil War* (Baton Rouge: Louisiana State University Press, 1989), pp. 96-105.

7. *A Writer's Beginnings,* dir. Patricia Wheatley, Omnibus Series, British Broadcasting Company, July 1987; first aired in the United States, 1988.

8. Nina Silber, *The Romance of Reunion: Northerners and the South, 1865-1900* (Chapel Hill: University of North Carolina Press, 1993), p. 10.

9. See Peggy Whitman Prenshaw, "Woman's World, Man's Place: The Fiction of Eudora Welty," in *Eudora Welty: A Form of Thanks,* ed. Louis Dollarhide and Ann J. Abadie (Jackson: University Press of Mississippi, 1979), pp. 46-77.

10. Ann Romines, *The Home Plot: Women, Writing and Domestic Ritual* (Amherst: University of Massachusetts Press, 1992), p. 193. See also Thomas McHaney's discussion of cyclical patterns in *The Golden Apples,* "Falling into Cycles: *The Golden Apples,*" in *Eudora Welty: Eye of the Storyteller,* pp. 173-89.

11. See Richard King, *A Southern Renaissance: The Cultural Awakening of the American South* (New York: Oxford University Press, 1980), pp. 8-9; see rebuttals by Carol Manning, *With Ears Opening Like Morning Glories: Eudora Welty and the Love of Storytelling* (Westport, Conn.: Greenwood Press, 1994), pp. 71-ff.; and Westling, *Sacred Groves and Ravaged Gardens,* pp. 16-ff.

12. C. Vann Woodward, *The Burden of Southern History,* rev. ed. (Baton Rouge: Louisiana State University Press, 1968).

13. See Prenshaw, "Woman's World," pp. 46-77; see also Westling, *Sacred Groves,* pp. 65-93.

14. Shirley Abbott, *Womenfolks: Growing Up Down South* (New York: Ticknor & Fields, 1983), pp. 3-4, 18.

15. See, for example, the autobiography of Virginia Foster Durr, born in 1903, who vividly describes her female-centered childhood and adolescence in Alabama, *Outside the Magic Circle: The Autobiography of Virginia Foster Durr,* ed. Hollinger F. Barnard (Tuscaloosa: University of Alabama Press, 1985; rpt. ed.: Touchstone, 1987) pp. 22-ff.

16. Jones, *Tomorrow Is Another Day,* pp. 9, 362.

17. In "Southern Ladies and the Southern Literary Renaissance," I have argued that Southern women writers have as much celebrated the strength as exposed the limitations of the "Southern lady" myth, in *The Female Tradition in Southern Literature,* ed. Carol manning (Urbana: University of Illinois Press, 1993), pp. 73-88.

18. See Ruth M. Vande Kieft, *Eudora Welty* (New York: Twayne, 1962), pp. 19ff. and *Eudora Welty, Revised Edition* (Boston: Twayne, 1987); also see Michael Kreyling, *Eudora Welty's Achievement of Order* (Jackson: University Press of Mississippi, 1980), pp. xvff.

19. Jan Nordby Gretlund, *Eudora Welty's Aesthetics of Place* (Columbia: University of South Carolina Press, 1997), pp. 32ff.

20. Westling, *Sacred Groves,* p. 55.

21. Robert B. Heilman, "The Southern Temper," in *Southern Renascence: The Literature of the Modern South,* eds. Louis D. Rubin Jr. and Robert D. Jacobs (Baltimore: Johns Hopkins University Press, 1953; rpt., 1965), pp. 3-13.

22. Richard M. Weaver, "Aspects of the Southern Philosophy," in *Southern Renascence: The Literature of the Modern South,* p. 15.

23. One might profitably investigate the relationship between the female sphere that I am discussing here as maternal and Southern and Myra Jehlen's

formulation regarding the interior life of the protagonist of the English novel, which she argues is metaphorically female. See Jehlen, "Archimedes and the Paradox of Feminist Criticism," *Signs* 6 (Summer 1981): 600.

24. Schmidt, *The Heart of the Story*, p. 263.

25. Romines, *The Home Plot*, pp. 192ff.

26. Danièle Pitavy-Souques, "A Blazing Butterfly: The Modernity of Eudora Welty," in *Welty: A Life in Literature*, ed. Albert J. Devlin (Jackson: University Press of Mississippi, 1987), p. 124.

27. Peter Schmidt in *The Heart of the Story*, pp. 3ff., Rebecca Mark in *The Dragon's Blood*, pp. 4ff., and Ruth Weston in *Gothic Traditions and Narrative Techniques*, pp. 133-72 all offer lengthy discussions of Welty's critique of the artist figured as "heroic."

FURTHER READING

Criticism

Brinkmeyer, Jr., Robert H. "Finding One's History: Bobbie Ann Mason and Contemporary Southern Literature." *Southern Literary Journal* 19, no. 2 (spring 1987): 20-33.

　　Brinkmeyer characterizes Mason's probing of history in her novels as a typically Southern concern.

Donlon, Jocelyn Hazelwood. "'Born on the Wrong Side of the Porch': Violating Traditions in *Bastard out of Carolina*." *Southern Folklore* 55, no. 2 (1998): 133-44.

　　Donlon discusses Dorothy Allison's novel and the ways in which Allison uses the symbol of the front porch to show that the main character, Bone, "operates outside of established traditions and norms."

Frega, Donnalee, and Brigette Craft. "Disabling History: Contemporary Southern Literature's Solution." *Southern Literary Journal* 29 (spring 1997): 103-21.

　　Frega and Craft assert that contemporary Southern writers depict characters who are unable to narrate, or even understand their own stories, as a way to comment on collective history.

Genovese, Eugene D. "William Styron's *The Confessions of Nat Turner*: A Meditation on Evil, Redemption, and History." In *Novel History: Historians and Novelists Confront America's Past (and Each Other)*, edited by Mark C. Carnes, pp. 209-20. New York: Simon & Schuster, 2001.

　　Genovese discusses the historical, literary, and philosophical dimensions of William Styron's *Nat Turner*.

Gray, Richard. *Southern Aberrations: Writers of the American South and the Problems of Regionalism*. Baton Rouge: Louisiana University Press, 2000, 535 p.

　　Gray explores what it means to be an author writing in and about the South, discussing a variety of literary figures from Edgar Allan Poe to contemporary Southern writers.

Jones, Anne Goodwyn, and Susan V. Donaldson, editors. *Haunted Bodies: Gender and Southern Texts*. Charlottesville: University Press of Virginia, 1998, 533 p.

　　Jones and Donaldson analyze the depiction and thematic uses of gender in Southern literature from the eighteenth century to contemporary fiction.

Krasteva, Yonka. "The South and the West in Bobbie Ann Mason's *In Country*." *Southern Literary Journal* 26, no. 2 (spring 1994): 77-90.

　　Krasteva examines Bobbie Ann Mason's *In Country* as embodying at the same time a postmodern view of the contemporary South and many of its traditional values.

Mason, Angela J., and Timothy J. Viator. "*Driving Miss Daisy*: A Sociosemiotic Analysis." *Southern Quarterly* 33, no. 1 (fall 1994): 55-63.

　　Mason and Viator explores the relationship between African Americans and Jews in the South as depicted in *Driving Miss Daisy*, noting that the theme of the play is problematized by the way language is used in it.

Metress, Christopher. "A New Father, a New Home": Styron, Faulkner, and Southern Revisionism." In *The Critical Response to William Styron*, edited by Daniel W. Ross, pp. 45-60. Westport, Conn.: Greenwood Press, 1995.

　　Metress discusses the influence of William Faulkner on William Styron and Styron's revision of the themes he "inherited" from Faulkner.

Patterson, Laura S. "Ellipsis, Ritual, and 'Real Time': Rethinking the Rape Complex in Southern Novels." *Mississippi Quarterly* 54, no. 1 (winter 2000-2001): 37-58.

　　Patterson focuses on the treatment of rape in three novels—William Faulkner's *Sanctuary*, Raymond Andrew's *Apalachee Red*, and Dorothy Allison's *Bastard out of Carolina*—and what it reveals about uses of power in the South.

Pitavy-Souques, Danielle. "'The Fictional Eye': Eudora Welty's Retranslation of the South." *South Atlantic Review* 65, no. 4 (fall 2000): 90-113.

Pitavy-Souques emphasizes Eudora Welty's unique perspective as a Southern writer that allows her to "retranslate" and reevaluate the myths that are characteristic of that region.

Polk, Noel. "Welty and Faulkner and the Southern Literary Tradition." In *Value and Vision in American Literature: Literary Essays in Honor of Ray Lewis White,* edited by Joseph Candido, pp. 132-50. Athens: Ohio University Press, 1999.

Polk explores the literary and personal relationship between Eudora Welty and William Faulkner.

Pollack, Harriet. "From *Shiloh* to *In Country* to *Feather Crowns*: Bobbie Ann Mason, Women's History, and Southern Fiction." *Southern Literary Journal* 28. no. 2 (spring 1996): 95-116.

Pollack argues that in Mason's novels "history" and "herstory" are intermixed and characters move freely in and out of their historical context.

Prenshaw, Peggy Whitman, editor. *Women Writers of the Contemporary South.* Jackson: University Press of Mississippi, 1985, 323 p.

Prenshaw presents a collection of essays on many of the most notable modern Southern women writers.

Romines, Ann. "Reading the Cakes: *Delta Wedding* and the Texts of Southern Women's Culture." *Mississippi Quarterly* 50, no. 4 (fall 1997): 601-16.

Romines examines the role of cakes in Southern culture and in *Delta Wedding* in particular, stressing the book's connection to how language is used by women.

Smith, Virginia A. "On Regionalism, Women's Writing, and Writing as a Woman: A Conversation with Lee Smith." In *Conversations with Lee Smith,* edited by Linda Tate, pp. 65-77. Jackson: University Press of Mississippi, 2001.

Smith presents a transcript of a 1989 conversation with Smith, focusing on the role of women writers in the South.

Suarez, Ernest. "Contemporary Southern Poetry and Critical Practice." *Southern Review* 30, no. 4 (autumn 1994): 674-88.

Suarez discusses several contemporary Southern poets, observing that they belong to the community of writers from and about the South.

Wimsatt, Mary Ann. "Region, Time, and Memory: *The Optimist's Daughter* as Southern Renascence Fiction." In *The Late Novels of Eudora Welty,* edited by Jan Nordby Gretlund and Karl-Heinz Westarp, pp. 134-44. Columbia: University of Southern Carolina Press, 1998.

Wimsatt examines the main themes in Eudora Welty's *The Optimist's Daughter,* especially that of the influence of the past on the present.

Winchell, Donna Haisty. "Cries of Outrage: Three Novelists' Use of History." *Mississippi Quarterly* 49, no. 4 (fall 1996): 727-42.

Winchell compares the handling of history in William Styron's *Nat Turner,* Shirley Anne Williams's *Dessa Rose,* and Toni Morrison's *The Black Book.*

York, Lamar. "From Hebe to Hippolyta: Anne Rivers Siddons's Novels." *Southern Literary Journal* 17, no. 2 (spring 1985): 91-9.

York examines the development of Siddons's treatment of women throughout her career.

Nicholas Delbanco
1942-

(Full name Nicholas Franklin Delbanco) English-born American novelist, short story writer, essayist, travel writer, critic, and nonfiction writer.

The following entry presents an overview of Delbanco's career through 2001. For further information on his life and works, see *CLC,* Volumes 6 and 13.

INTRODUCTION

Delbanco is best known for his works of fiction, most notably the Sherbrookes Trilogy, which traces five generations of a prominent New England family. His many novels include the experimental work *In the Middle Distance* (1971), a part-fictional, part-autobiographical narrative, *In the Name of Mercy* (1995), a murder mystery focused on the issue of doctor-assisted suicide, and *What Remains* (2000), the story of a German-Jewish family who fled Nazi Germany to settle in England and the United States. Delbanco's short stories, like his novels, address themes of aging, masculinity, intergenerational family dynamics, the craft of writing, and tensions between the past and the present. His style is characterized by poetic language, multiple character perspectives, and narratives that jump back and forth between distinct time periods. Delbanco's several works of nonfiction range across a variety of subjects, including travel writing, literary biography, and music history.

BIOGRAPHICAL INFORMATION

Delbanco was born on August 27, 1942, in London, England, the son of German Jews who had left Germany before World War II to escape Nazi persecution. When Delbanco was six years old, the family immigrated to the United States, where they settled in Larchmont, New York. Delbanco graduated magna cum laude from Harvard University in 1963 with a major in literature. In 1966 he completed a master's degree in English and Comparative Literature at Columbia University. Delbanco was twenty-four when his first novel, *The Martlet's Tale* (1966), was published. In 1970 he married Elena Greenhouse, with whom he has two children. Delbanco has held posts at several colleges and universities throughout the United States. He taught creative writing and English literature in the department

of language and literature at Bennington College in Bennington, Vermont, from 1966 to 1984. From 1984 to 1985 he taught as a professor of English at Skidmore College, in Saratoga Springs, New York. In 1985 Delbanco was hired as a professor of English at the University of Michigan in Ann Arbor, Michigan, where he serves as the head of the graduate program in creative writing as well as the Hopwood Awards program. Delbanco was also a staff member at the Bread Loaf Writers' Conference from 1984 to 1994. He has received numerous awards and accolades, including the National Endowment for the Arts creative writing award in 1973 and 1982, the PEN syndicated fiction award in 1983, 1985, and 1989, and the Michigan Council for the Arts award in 1986.

MAJOR WORKS

Some of Delbanco's earliest novels are modern stories based on biblical and classical texts. *The Martlet's Tale* is a reimagining of the biblical tale of the prodigal son, set in modern Greece. *Fathering* (1973) is a modern retelling of the Theban trilogy—Sophocles's series of plays about Oedipus and Antigone. *In the Middle Distance* is an experimental novel combining fiction and autobiography in a self-conscious, multi-layered narrative voice. *In the Middle Distance* alternates between first-person narration in the form of a journal kept by the protagonist—a fictional author by the name of Nicholas Delbanco—and third-person narration which describes the life of the Delbanco character. The novel intentionally blurs the distinctions between the real-life author Nicholas Delbanco and the fictional character who shares the same name. The plot concerns the writer's attempts to remodel his farmhouse in upstate New York while engaging in self-analysis and struggling with his creative process. Delbanco's Sherbrookes Trilogy—*Possession* (1977), *Sherbrookes* (1978), and *Stillness* (1980)—follows the history and genealogy of the Sherbrookes, a distinguished family from Vermont. The Sherbrookes Trilogy is written in Delbanco's characteristic poetic prose and examines the tensions between the family's past and present. *In the Name of Mercy,* set in a hospice care facility in Michigan, explores the topical issue of doctor-assisted suicide within the genre of the murder mystery. *Old Scores* (1997) describes an affair between a professor and a student on a small Vermont college campus that turns out to have a profound impact on the lives of both characters. The narrative of *Old Scores* moves back and forth between the time of the affair and the present lives of the characters. *What Remains* follows three generations of a German-Jewish family who fled Hamburg to escape the Holocaust and settled in England and the United States. The story is told from the multiple perspectives of various members of the family.

The short stories in *About My Table, and Other Stories* (1983) focus on men in their late thirties grappling with the experience of aging who are torn between marital commitments and their own escapist fantasies. The tales in *The Writer's Trade, and Other Stories* (1990) feature characters who are writers in the process of struggling with their craft and their careers. In the 1980s Delbanco began to publish various works of nonfiction, covering a wide range of topics. *Group Portrait* (1982) examines a group of famous writers—including Joseph Conrad, Stephen Crane, Ford Madox Ford, Henry James, and H. G. Wells—who all lived in the same area of England during the early twentieth century. Delbanco discusses the professional and personal relationships between the writers and the extent of their influence on each other's writing. *The Beaux Arts Trio: A Portrait* (1985) is based on Delbanco's travels with this well-known musical trio; one member of group is his wife's father. *Running in Place: Scenes from the South of France* (1989) recounts Delbanco's journey with his wife and two daughters through the region of Provence in southern France. Delbanco contrasts his current perspective of the region with his impressions from his previous journeys to the area. *The Lost Suitcase: Reflections on the Literary Life* (2000) includes a collection of fiction and essays on the craft of writing. The title piece is Delbanco's fictional reconstruction of an incident in which a suitcase full of original manuscripts by Ernest Hemingway was lost in a train station. In *The Countess of Stanlein Restored: A History of the Countess of Stanlein Ex-Paganini Stradivarius Cello of 1707* (2001) Delbanco traces the history and restoration process of his father-in-law's antique musical instrument, a rare Stradivarius cello crafted in 1707.

CRITICAL RECEPTION

Delbanco's first novel, *The Martlet's Tale,* earned him early recognition as a promising young novelist. Gregory L. Morris has extolled *In the Middle Distance* for its complex narrative structure, arguing that, "What Delbanco ultimately pursues in this novel is a triple-layered examination of self and the ability to accurately declare the truths of that examination." The novels of the Sherbrookes Trilogy have remained Delbanco's most celebrated works of fiction. Critics have complimented the poetic prose and deftly drawn characters in the trilogy and have lauded Delbanco's treatment of the family's intergenerational tensions. His novel *In the Name of Mercy* has received mixed assessments. Some critics have found the fictional narrative compelling and praised Delbanco for his ability to build suspense. Others have found the novel overly topical in addressing the issue of doctor-assisted suicide and observed that the book fails to adequately clarify the arguments on either side of the debate. Reviewers have been generally enthusiastic about *What Remains,* applauding Delbanco's skill at crafting the alternating perspectives of the novel's variety of characters. Neil Gordon has admired Delbanco's characterizations in *What Remains,* remarking that, "In a prose as evocative and clear as any being written in America today, Delbanco draws us into the very thought processes of his characters, showing us the past through their eyes and with the thick reality of their emotions." Critical response to Delbanco's short story collections has been largely positive, with commentators praising Delbanco's craftsmanship and ability to evoke strong emotion through well-chosen details. Richard Eder has observed that the stories in *About My Table* are "written with breathtaking technique and an uncanny ability to bring a penetrating emotion up out of a gesture, a pause or a random thought." Response to Delbanco's various works of nonfiction, however, has been largely mixed. Reviewers of *Group Portrait* have faulted Delbanco for failing to provide the reader with new insight or information on the authors included in the study. Despite these criticisms, the work has been commended for expressing a strong sense of affection for its subjects. Additionally, several critics have found Delbanco's accounts of his travels in *The Beaux Arts Trio* and *Running in Place* to be tedious and overwritten, offering little in the way of original observations on his subject. On the other hand, *The Countess of Stanlein Restored* has garnered an enthusiastic response by some reviewers, with Amanda Heller describing the book as "a little gem, a trove of fact, lore, and sensual description evoking two enduring and intertwined traditions—the art of the musician and the art of the luthier."

PRINCIPAL WORKS

The Martlet's Tale (novel) 1966
Grasse, 3/23/66 (novel) 1968
Consider Sappho Burning (novel) 1969
News (novel) 1970
In the Middle Distance (novel) 1971
Fathering (novel) 1973
Small Rain (novel) 1975
*Possession (novel) 1977
*Sherbrookes (novel) 1978
*Stillness (novel) 1980
Group Portrait: Joseph Conrad, Stephen Crane, Ford Madox Ford, Henry James, and H. G. Wells (criticism) 1982
About My Table, and Other Stories (short stories) 1983
The Beaux Arts Trio: A Portrait (nonfiction) 1985
Running in Place: Scenes from the South of France (travel writing) 1989
The Writer's Trade, and Other Stories (short stories) 1990
Writers and Their Craft: Short Stories and Essays on the Narrative [editor; with Laurence Goldstein] (short stories and essays) 1991
In the Name of Mercy (novel) 1995
Talking Horse: Bernard Malamud on Life and Work [editor; with Alan Cheuse] (nonfiction) 1996
Old Scores (novel) 1997
The Lost Suitcase: Reflections on the Literary Life (nonfiction) 2000
What Remains (novel) 2000
The Countess of Stanlein Restored: A History of the Countess of Stanlein Ex-Paganini Stradivarius Cello of 1707 (nonfiction) 2001

*These novels comprise Delbanco's Sherbrookes Trilogy.

CRITICISM

Allan Massie (review date 9 October 1982)

SOURCE: Massie, Allan. "Foreigners." *Spectator* 249, no. 8048 (9 October 1982): 28-9.

[*In the following review, Massie describes* Group Portrait *as interesting, perceptive, and well-crafted.*]

'Some years ago my friend H. G. Wells wrote to the papers to say that for many years he was conscious of a ring of foreign conspirators plotting against British letters at no great distance from his residence, Spade House, Sandgate'. (Ford Madox Ford: *Return to Yesterday*.) These words lie at the heart of Mr Delbanco's book, [*Group Portrait*,] though, curiously, he doesn't quote them. Three of the foreign conspirators were Henry James, Joseph Conrad and Stephen Crane. Ford tried to pretend that a fourth was W. H. Hudson, but it's more likely that Wells had Ford himself in mind—it was in his Hueffer days before his change of surname disguised his German antecedents.

And of course Wells was quite right, up to a point. James, Conrad and Ford (as it seems more convenient to call him) were indeed engaged, if not exactly on a conspiracy, at least in an attack, that gave the impression of being in some way concerted, on that 'loose baggy monster, the English novel'. The phrase was James's own, and the baggy monster was the target he had set himself to shoot down. Like almost all such consciously-selected oppositions, there was something a bit disingenuous in what James was doing. The English novel wasn't quite—had never been quite—the unstructured and rambling thing he identified. There had after all been Jane Austen; there was still Meredith, and Stevenson was only a few years dead in 1900, the year in which Mr Delbanco chooses to pitch his story. Nevertheless there was enough truth in James's strictures, and enough substance in his achievement, and in Conrad's and Ford's for us to be able to date the modern English novel from the work they did. They brought to the writing of fiction the sense of dedication and responsibility which had formerly been left to poets or to the French.

Mr Delbanco's subject is the degree of collaboration between them. Ford and Conrad worked closely together—that is well-known—and the chapter dealing with them is very properly placed at the centre of this cunningly-wrought book. Mr Delbanco is (rightly, I think) in no doubt that the collaboration was beneficial to both writers. It encouraged them to think more closely about what they were aiming at, and how it could be done. Between them, in hours of conversation, they worked out the theory of literary impressionism:

> We agreed that the general effect of a novel must be the general effect life makes on mankind. A novel must therefore not be a narration, a report . . . We saw that Life did not narrate, but made impressions on our brains. We in turn, if we wished to produce on you an effect of life, must not narrate but render impressions . . . We agreed that the whole of Art consists in selection . . .
>
> (Ford: *Joseph Conrad, a Personal Reminiscence*.)

The works they produced together were not frightfully good; it was when they resumed their separate careers that the fruits appeared. All the same they played nicely off each other. Mr Delbanco sets fascinatingly side by side passages from *Heart of Darkness* and Ford's *The Cinque Ports*; which echoes which? And of course Ford learned enough to write a good Conrad chapter. Mr Delbanco cites the example from *Nostromo*. I wish he had taken a look at the part Ford may have played in the writing of *The Secret Agent*.

The chapter or Crane is the least satisfactory, just as Crane is the most faded of the writers under review. All the same, all the others regarded him as outstandingly gifted. Conrad proposed collaboration with him before he fixed on Ford. James and Crane are said to have discussed 'style'. Crane claimed that James had sent him manuscripts. The young American struck a chord in his senior: 'during the first months of the new year', wrote Leon Edel, 'when Crane was ill most of the time, Henry James wrote *The Sacred Fount*. It may have derived some of its poignancy from the vision the novelist had of the way in which Crane was visibly dying while Cora thrived, seemingly unaware of the tragedy being lived out under her roof'. If nothing else then, Crane provided material for Jamesian art. The relation of art to life—that is an argument central to this book.

It was central to the famous quarrel between James and Wells. Here, Mr Delbanco has an advantage over most of us: he has actually read *Boon,* the novel in which Wells savaged and mocked the aged James. But, before then, there was a long record of friendship, of admiration that stopped short of understanding on either side. (Mr Delbanco also neatly points out that Wells's first sight of James was as the wretched author being catcalled on the first night of *Guy Domville*.) Mr Delbanco's sympathies lie clearly with James. He takes some satisfaction in pointing out that though '*What Maisie Knew* sold fewer copies in its first year of publication than *The Time Machine* in an average month; 80 years later, the figures are no doubt reversed.' That might not have worried Wells; he always insisted he was a journalist, that his novels were written for the here and now. What he objected to in James was in fact put more forcibly and effectively by Rebecca West: in *The Sacred Fount* 'a week-end visitor spends more intellectual force than Kant can have used on *The Critique of Pure Reason* in an unsuccessful attempt to discover whether there exists between certain of his fellow-guests a relationship not more interesting among these vacuous people than it is among sparrows.' Of course, James comes well out of the quarrel. His personal dignity is impressive, while Wells's hippety-hoppiting impertinence reminds us of a sparrow. Nevertheless, H. G.'s own claims for the novel were hardly humble: 'it is to be the social mediator, the vehicle of understanding, the instrument of self-examination, the parade of morals and exchange of manners, the factory of customs, the criticism of laws and institutions and of social dogmas and ideas'.

But, the trouble from the James-Ford-Conrad point of view was that H. G.'s loudly-trumpeted indifference to the *how* of the matter vitiated the whole enterprise. Perhaps he sensed this himself: 'the Novel proved like a blanket too small for the bed and when I tried to pull it over to cover my tossing conflict of ideas, I found I had to abandon questions of individuation. I never got "all life within the scope of the novel". What a phrase. Who could?' No one perhaps; but by 'abandoning questions of individuation', any felt life was likely to be excluded. All the same Wells's insistence on the importance of the *what* against the *how* should not be forgotten either. Mr Delbanco includes an admirable letter from Wells to Joyce, then engaged on *Finnegan's Wake,* to show how the argument was carried on to the next generation.

This is a book full of interest and intelligent perception. It occasionally irritates. Mr Delbanco frequently uses words meaninglessly. He has a ponderous way with the examination of metaphor. He is rather given to pretentious pronouncements which claim to discern significance where common sense sees none. But he has read everything on the subject, generously.

Frank Tuohy (review date 22 October 1982)

SOURCE: Tuohy, Frank. "Birds of a Feather." *Times Literary Supplement,* no. 4151 (22 October 1982): 1148.

[*In the following review,* Tuohy *comments that* Group Portrait *fails to offer the reader any new insight or information on its subject.*]

Nicholas Delbanco has planned his work [*Group Portrait*] to illustrate what he calls "colleagueship" or "collegiality": a quality that he identifies as having existed among these writers when all of them were living close to each other in West Kent or East Sussex around the turn of the century.

Today, especially when one is resident at a university, it is easy to assume that writers enjoy each other's company, and to proceed to the conclusion that in doing so they will share useful ideas about technique an so on. The idea of writers' seminars, creative writing courses and workshops, has spread from the United States to this country. If the same thing happened in the past, it must have been under the auspices of personal friendship. The popularity of books about the Bloomsbury group has strengthened this impression, though in their case friendship of the inner circle must have been helped by the fact that they were all doing different things and, to that extent at any rate, did not get in each other's light.

Delbanco quotes from Ada Galsworthy's notebook to show the large number of writers whom her husband knew between 1905 and 1910. "That constant keeping up to the mark", he notes, "could not have failed to fire ambition." But there is no reason to conclude that they spoke of anything but cricket or politics. When invited by P. H. Newby, then in charge of the Third Programme, to contribute a conversation between himself and a friend on the subject of his writing, Evelyn Waugh replied: "I am afraid this is not practical as I never mention my writing to my friends." From the English point of view it may be that collegiality is strictly for colleges.

Except for Wells, however, the group in question were a cosmopolitan lot. Conrad and James were certainly aware of a world outside, where salons and literary schools existed. But, as Delbanco points out, there was no leading lady and therefore no salon. James, in any case, had severe doubts about the gentility of the other members and their wives, and this was sufficient to keep them apart.

Because of the lack of other evidence, **Group Portrait** concentrates on three themes: the tenancy of Brede Manor by Stephen Crane and his soi-disant wife Cora, the former Madame of the Hotel de Dream; the collaboration of Conrad and Ford: and the correspondence between Henry James and H. G. Wells and their subsequent quarrel. There are other themes available—no one has yet studied the lifelong hostility between Wells and Ford, which culminated in the publication of Wells's novel *The Bulpington of Blup*. And where Henry James is concerned, there are endless complexities in all his relationships. But Delbanco's purpose is not literary research; he depends on secondary sources entirely—he even quotes Virginia Woolf as quoted by somebody else, and his citations will be familiar to anyone else with a cursory knowledge of the subject. Possibly he is aiming at students for whom the admittedly overweight biographies of James, Conrad and Hueffer which have appeared in the last twenty years are heavy-going. But his style is too allusive to provide much help. A sentence like "if Jessie Conrad never quite had veto power over Joseph's guests, her Recollections of Stephen Crane are warm" cannot mean much to anyone who is coming upon these three people for the first time.

Some of the obvious difficulties are given rather casual treatment. Ford's book on Conrad is fascinating, but how much of it is true? On points of fact, he is often right where both Conrads are wrong, but this did not matter to him very much. On the evidence of David Garnett and others (Delbanco gets the Garnetts muddled) he had no prejudice whatsoever against the manufacture of myths. His methods were demonstrated, years ago, by Simon Nowell-Smith in the preface of his *Legend of the Master*. More kindly, Rebecca West spoke of his "transforming memory which altered everything". He himself spoke of "impressionism". This word, incidentally, is a useful point of distinction between Crane, Ford and Conrad, all of whom gave it different meanings. Delbanco mentions this in passing, but the subject has been brilliantly analysed by Ian Watt.

The work that has been done on these writers recently has been the product of university departments, that world in which books are read in order to pass examinations or promote careers. Though Nicholas Delbanco is of that world himself, he is to be commended for following in the tradition of Edmund Wilson, for whom writers and their books had an importance which was on a different, fully personal level. However, **Group Portrait** does not throw enough new light on the literary characteristics of his famous five. Touches of personal autobiography in the first and last chapters come across as journalistic and perfunctory. Perhaps unjustifiably, an English reader cannot take seriously sentences such as "Sir Philip Sidney made his home in Kent and Chaucer put her on the map immortally". But in any case they seem out of place in a book where so much that is interesting and important has been passed by.

Thomas C. Moser (essay date April 1983)

SOURCE: Moser, Thomas C. "Views of Edwardian Fiction." *Sewanee Review* 91, no. 2 (April 1983): 282-91.

[*In the following review, Moser compares* Group Portrait *with two other books on Edwardian fiction. Moser comments that Delbanco's book is neatly organized and well-written, and that the strength of the book lies in the author's expression of a strong sense of affection for his subject.*]

Even though all periods, all decades, are transitional, the Edwardian age is one of the most conspicuous. Richard Ellmann's phrase is the "two faces" of Edward; Samuel Hynes's, the Edwardian "turn of mind." Between the end of Victoria's lengthy reign with its intellectual, technological revolutions and its gigantic novelists and 1914's initiation of a period of incredible, almost incessant, international violence and flashy modernist writers, the intervening years must somehow, from our point of view, account for the change. Three new books, of greatly differing approach and quality, take as their common subject the fiction of that post-Victorian period. In *Edwardian Fiction* Jefferson Hunter, of Smith College, treats the subject topically; in *The Edwardian Novelists* John Batchelor, an Oxford don, studies critically the work of six writers; in **Group**

Portrait Nicholas Delbanco, a novelist and teacher at Bennington, considers biographically five writers who were friends and neighbors at the turn of the century.

Hunter's book seems to me terrific. He determinedly resists the "dangerous illusion . . . that the Edwardian era can be comprehended by a single myth or . . . symbol." Hunter tries admirably to see the period through the eyes of those who lived in it rather than through our own eyes, which are always looking eagerly for signs of the "modern." Many Edwardians prove to have been perfectly aware both of contradictions in their ideas and of change "as the essential social fact of their time." (Still one cannot help feeling that when Hunter identifies the chief complicating facts of Edward's decade he has benefited from living in our seventies: the decline in real wages, militant suffragism, the inability to cope with either urban slums or the motor car, a deeply divisive war.) Hunter's austerity extends even to dating the period. Although he does sneak in *Heart of Darkness* (1899) and *Lord Jim* (1900), he tends to stick rigorously within Edward's reign (January 1901-May 1910). Eminently commonsensical, he nevertheless acknowledges the plausibility of going back to 1897—with its *Invisible Man, Nigger of the "Narcissus,"* and *What Maisie Knew*—or even of going forward to the guns of August 1914—when Ford finished *The Good Soldier*.

The key word in *Edwardian Fiction* is *polarities*. Hunter manages to integrate in an elegant structure his impressive historical knowledge and highly sophisticated critical responses to a welter of fictions. These include the masterpieces of James and Conrad, the works of the other major Edwardians, a host of significant minor fictions, and many best-sellers that were scorned by serious readers then and are forgotten today. The first part, "The Sense of a Period," dramatizes the polarity between the fictions' formal conservatism and their thematic adventuresomeness. Hunter is perfectly conscious of the presence of James's rich formal inventiveness, especially "his fascination with the personal and artistic difficulties of knowing." James, however, though universally admired, "still remained apart." Although Hunter laments James's lack of influence, he convincingly shows how much Forster's first Italian novels of "Continental Rescues and Autumnal Affairs" owe to *The Ambassadors*. Over a decade ago Ian Watt suggested that "James's example . . . , more than anything else, helped Conrad to evolve his mature technique." Nevertheless Hunter's main point is undeniable—that most Edwardian novelists stuck to nineteenth-century methods and ignored the examples of Conrad and James and the exhortations of Ford. He is also right that the prevailing plainness of form fitted these novelists, that *ficelles* would not have transformed Galsworthy nor the time-shift Bennett. But if these Edwardian artists were formally conservative, they nevertheless realized "that fiction might include a whole new range of personal and social observation. . . . After recovering from their fin-de-siècle weariness, Edwardians looked about them and discovered a plenitude of fictional subjects." Naturally the "prodigious" Wells is Hunter's prime instance, but he even cites a novel called *The Dream and the Business* as "representative by virtue of its title alone" of "this polarity-ridden or -blessed period."

The titles of the second and third parts of Hunter's book indicate his other major polarity—"Adventures Abroad" and "Coming Home." Each section moves from the simple to the complex; the latter deals, roughly speaking, with the latter half of the decade. "Abroad" concerns both geography (away from England) and time (away from the present to the past or the future): Conrad's settings shifted from exotic places to London, Wells's from fantasies in remote times to present realism. After observing that some Edwardian romances follow the Victorian pattern of isolating the hero against an exotic landscape, Hunter also shows how the more sensitive romancers could not overlook the implications of imperialism, could not ignore the natives. Instead of putting writers into definite pro and con camps, imperialism tended to inspire a "sense of vague disquiet." That sense gets into *Tono-Bungay* in the strange "quap" episode in which the narrator shoots a native in the back, destroying "innocent strangeness" without understanding "why he has done this." Although W. H. Hudson "never uses the word 'imperialism'" in his masterpiece, it shows "an educated white man" bringing "greed, anger, and violence into the green mansions." Hunter naturally concludes this section with Conrad; yet even in this well-trodden field he manages to look with a fresh eye: at Lord Jim, who doesn't know he is a romantic and plays his role against an unglamorous backdrop; at *Nostromo*'s childless Emilia Gould, the victim of subtle conjugal infidelity, and its titular hero, whose "passing is as ambiguous as Jim's" and whose failure makes clear "that there was no longer a place for adventurism in the world." What makes Hunter's account of how imperialism affected fiction especially persuasive is his constant, modest, self-critical awareness that "political interpretations of romance inevitably seem ponderous," that they sometimes are schematic and sometimes conflict with the authors' conscious intentions. Nevertheless "the works themselves point insistently enough in the direction of doubt about imperial ventures."

"Coming Home" explores the reaction to romance and to the human cost of empire. It concentrates upon country houses and London. Hunter lists some twenty-eight fictive country houses and deals deftly and unobtrusively with virtually all of them. But he deals with real houses as well, discussing the possible meanings of Kipling's move to Bateman's, James's to Lamb

House, Wells's to Spade House (and his even more significant leaving of it). The writers and their characters are drawn to refuges which they can humanly control and where there will be "few opportunities for bewilderment or meaningless violence." But refuges don't always work: that is true of Kate Croy's and Merton Densher's figurative refuge in their secret relationship, and of Teddy Ponderevo's frantic quest for a suitable house. Sometimes a writer's handling of a house reveals his own limitations. Soames Forsyte's building of Robin Hill dramatizes his essence, his will to control a space absolutely, to tame Irene and make of her an *objet*. Hunter says damningly that in the end Galsworthy "owns his characters in the same way . . . orders their movements with fine manipulations . . . enjoys his authorial sense of property." London is the other pole from the country in this polarity. Although some writers love London, for most, Conrad and Wells especially, it is "oppressively incomprehensible." Hunter speaks of the "bewildered return to the city" and says flatly that Edwardian novelists doubted that sense could be made of urban life. Hunter concludes by pairing *Howards End*, which retreats from social problems to celebrate human relations, with *Tono-Bungay*, which ends with the "passing of England" and "brazen irresolution." Hunter's dissatisfaction with both these "conditions of England" novels leads him—on his last page and, for me, his only disappointing one—to conclude that Edwardian fiction is a "relative failure."

For John Batchelor "the" Edwardian novelists prove unsurprisingly to be Conrad and Ford, Wells and Bennett, Galsworthy and Forster. Batchelor impressively considers them in the context not only of the voluminous critical commentary about them but also of the period's minor fiction. Thus his book is potentially as rich as Hunter's. Moreover Batchelor moves on past 1910 to consider, most appropriately, *The Good Soldier* (1915). An excellent question—"Why does Conrad look so isolated a figure?"—initiated Batchelor's inquiry, which soon came to embrace "the Edwardian period as a whole." In separate chapters on each author Batchelor, especially in the case of the "giant," Conrad, wishes "to recover the freshness of the amateur reader." This is not a bad aim, and to some extent the book profits from its author's informal, unacademic manner. Similarly Batchelor's determination not "to force these writers to resemble one another, since . . . they don't" commands at least our partial assent.

The first, longest, and, happily, the best chapter is given to Conrad. Treating him separately enables Batchelor to trace an arresting developmental theory: the novels through *Nostromo* explore the possibility that traditional heroism is still a reality; thereafter they convey a sense of the futility of human aspiration. *Lord Jim* is a great instance of "creative love," with Marlow, the rational man, celebrating a young "friend who has had a religious experience." Throughout the chapter Batchelor's lively independent mind strikes off interesting *aperçus*: Heyst is a "very successful piece of characterisation but the fiction [*Victory*] constructed round him is barely readable as a novel." But the critic's breeziness often makes for unenlightening imprecision: thus "Conrad is a *macho* novelist"; Forster had "beginner's luck" with *Where Angels Fear to Tread,* and the prose of *Howards End* is "soggy" toward the conclusion. The book occasionally gives the impression of carelessness. Batchelor yokes Stein's famous "destructive element" with life, whereas Conrad (in cloudy prose) equates it with the dream. Ford, says Batchelor, "loved the Germans, his father's people, and saw the *French* as England's natural enemy." But Ford adored France, devoted some of his loveliest prose to her, and fulfilled his wish of dying there.

Batchelor's decision to treat each writer fully has unfortunate results. For example he insists on dealing with Conrad's earliest works but has nothing significant to say about them. With good reason he dislikes all of Galsworthy except *The Man of Property,* yet he grinds out twenty-five pages on some five Galsworthy novels. What is more serious is that his method prevents his conveying much sense of the period. Instead the age has "tendencies" and "features" (the country house, urban novels). Certain potentially unifying themes do recur, but the reader must do the integrating. Probably the most interesting themes are the Edwardians' "sacramental" attitude toward "Life"; the "epistemological crisis" of the period; the inadequacy of the traditional form of the novel to portray a twentieth-century hero in a "devalued and directionless" society. Merely to list these ideas is to be reminded of Batchelor's curious and almost fatal omission—Henry James. Strether's exhortation to Little Bilham "to live" sheds light on most of the novels considered in the book, especially those of Bennett, Galsworthy, and Forster; Maisie's quest for knowledge beautifully registers the period's epistemological crisis; James's artful experimentations with form made Conrad's and Ford's possible, not to mention those of all their disciples.

Apparently a major purpose of this book is to offer fresh evaluations of the authors. These notably include confirming Galsworthy's relatively low position but elevating Wells and Bennett. Batchelor's apparent attitude toward fictive art has some strange results. In praising Wells, he insists that *Tono-Bungay* is "subtle, highly-wrought, and 'written' in as full a sense as Conrad, Ford and Henry James could wish." Nevertheless, when Ford says, in the first issue of the *English Review,* that the most important recent historical event is the publication of the New York Edition of Henry James, he also says, as Batchelor reminds us, that James's great virtues are veracity, detachment, and objectivity. For many sympathetic intelligent readers, like Walter

Allen and Bernard Bergonzi, *Tono-Bungay* is a seriously flawed novel—not because it has a form different from that of *The Ambassadors* or of *The Good Soldier* but because the narrator's love affairs are presented so sentimentally, so dishonestly. On the other hand Bennett's artistry in *The Old Wives' Tale* and *Clayhanger*, which Batchelor rightly celebrates, need not be so completely separated from Conrad's and Ford's as Batchelor asserts: "No one would ask Bennett to be Conrad. . . . To ask ultimate questions . . . one must be able to see man as free, isolated and alone, experiencing the epistemological crisis of the period. Bennett's Five Towns people are too firmly embedded in their history and their environment." Obviously Bennett, even at his best, is very different from the great impressionists. Yet it is the arch-impressionist Ford who says that the "artist must always be humble and humble and again humble, since before the greatness of his task he himself is nothing." Two of the most moving scenes in *Clayhanger* acknowledge that truth. When Miss Florence Simcox does her glorious clog-dance in the pub for those men who have all worn clogs in the winter slush, she makes charming "the clog, the very emblem of the servitude and the squalor of brutalized populations," and changes it "into the medium of grace." And when the hero, Edwin Clayhanger, observes the slow careful art of the bricklayer, he is "humbled" and "enlightened"; he realizes that such a "miracle is only the result of miraculous patience, miraculous nicety, miraculous honesty, miraculous perseverance." Conrad's Jim is, as Batchelor says, ultimately unknowable. But surely so too is Edwin to Bennett—and to himself: "The impartial and unmoved spectator that sat somewhere in Edwin . . . watching his secret life . . . thought how *strange*" it was (italics mine). Granted that, for Bennett, the puzzlement is not so psychological or moral as it is for Conrad. Rather it is a bewilderment about the mysterious effects of the inexorable passage of time. The trouble with Wells, as well as with Galsworthy—if one may make so arrogant a remark—is that, even at their best, they write without humility, write as if they think they really *know*. I, for one, am unpersuaded.

Batchelor provides interesting lore on all his writers. His account, taken from Catherine Dupré's biography of Galsworthy, of Edward Garnett's angry response to the manuscript of *The Man of Property* is especially good. Garnett insisted that Galsworthy change Bossiney's explicit suicide—by throwing himself in despair under an omnibus after hearing of Soames's rape of Irene—into an ambiguous accident. Galsworthy nevertheless kept the incident remarkably close to that of the allegedly accidental death of Sergey Stepniak in 1895 under a train engine. Stepniak was Constance Garnett's beloved and the inspiration for her Russian translations. Was Edward Garnett, reading about Bossiney's death, unconsciously reminded of a family tragedy, and could he not bear to think of a man committing suicide out of despairing love for another man's sexually estranged wife? Later Conrad was to use Stepniak's death for the climax of *Under Western Eyes*—the maiming of the distracted Razumov when he is struck by a tramcar in Geneva.

Such intimate connections remind us how small was the world of Edwardian novelists, how well they knew one another. This is the subject of Nicholas Delbanco's ***Group Portrait***. In a book explicitly "about colleagueship" among Conrad, Crane, Ford, James, and Wells the author naturally emphasizes geographical proximity and the positive aspects of the relationships. In 1900, the focal, but not exclusive, year of this portrait, these five writers were all living within an easy bicycle or dogcart ride of one another in South Kent and East Sussex. But six years before, when twenty-year-old Ford Madox Ford and his seventeen-year-old bride, Elsie Martindale, first settled in Kent, they were merely seeking cheap rent, fleeing literary London, and returning to the haunts of their childhood. (They had been schoolmates in Folkestone and lovers in Winchelsea.) And when, in 1896, James fell in love with Rye, he did so without a notion of a group forming. Yet subsequent moves south certainly suggest, as one motive, the idea of a literary circle. Delbanco celebrates this idea in a neatly organized and, for the most part, cleanly and handsomely written book. (At times the prose is perhaps a bit too cute: "The castles keep"; "The pale cast of thought has sicklied him [Crane's Henry Fleming]—yet conscience can make heroes of us all.") The terrain of literary history that Delbanco travels is familiar: chapters on the Kentish countryside, on the youthful, doomed Crane, on Ford and Conrad's collaboration, on the quarrel of James and Wells, on the group as a whole. Knowledge of the landscape will vary with the reader. Delbanco actually wrote his book in Kent, and some of his most attractive prose is devoted to evoking the setting. It made me long to drop everything and return to that benign county of Canterbury, the Romney Marsh, and the Downs, to go again to Wells's Spade House in Sandgate, Conrad's Pent Farm five miles away, then on over to Rye for Dover sole at the Mermaid and another look at James's beautiful Georgian house, then some two miles farther to Ford's clapboard cottage in Winchelsea. Though Delbanco doesn't mention it, one would want also to visit the Cearne, on the Kent-Surrey border, Edward Garnett's pseudo-medieval stone cottage where Constance entertained all these great men while translating some seventy volumes of classic Russian fiction.

Despite the familiarity of its story the book is well worth reading just for its point of view. Delbanco says he loves to read these novelists and hopes others will; he shares James's and Ford's conviction that writers flourish better in a group than as hermits; he himself writes as a novelist, as an immigrant ("born in England, of German-Jewish parents and with an Italian name"), and as one who has benefited from literary collegiality. Delbanco's affectionate attitude is particularly welcome in the case of Ford: "he has been," as Delbanco says, "unkindly discredited and is unjustly ignored." Delbanco believes, for example, that Ford's "impression" of James's pained devotion to "poor Steevie" seems truer than Edel's conviction that James felt little friendship for Crane. Quoting Eudora Welty's injunction that Ford should be approached with "the response of love," Delbanco indicates that "the trials of tracking down material . . . can vex each sleuth until he learns to hate his man." But sleuths are useful, and Delbanco should have read Mizener's biography of Ford with more care. Had he done so, he would not have yoked Violet Hunt to the last collaboration of Conrad and Ford, *The Nature of a Crime*. They wrote it in 1906; Ford and Violet met in 1907. Nor would he have said that Ford "owned" the Pent Farm; he was just renting it when he sublet it to Conrad and provided the setting for Conrad's greatest years as a writer, 1898-1907. Poor Fordie never owned much of anything. And a look at a Conrad first edition would have prevented misdating. Conrad's touching gratitude for Ford's "friendly suggestion . . . friendly pressure . . . friendly voice" that elicited Conrad's beautiful reminiscence *A Personal Record* appeared not in 1923, as Delbanco says, but in 1912. That was the brief moment of reconciliation between their 1909-11 quarrel and their 1913-15 freeze, the moment too of a fine essay on Conrad by Ford that celebrates not only *Lord Jim* but the newly published *Under Western Eyes*. These are trivial errors, unworthy of mention except because Delbanco so insists that nothing in his scholarly reliable book is "conjectural." He even cites a dissertation, J. H. Morey's useful study of the Conrad-Ford collaboration. Why then does he not cite Raymond T. Brebach's fine dissertation, "The Making of *Romance*" (1976)? Brebach identifies who wrote which sentences, who revised whose words, and documents Ford's concurrent development to the point where Ford could even improve on Conrad. These matters are germane to **Group Portrait**.

Delbanco is at his best and most engaging when he is being most personal, most speculative, when he is giving us, as he says, his "impressions of Impressionists." He yokes his authors' deepest literary themes and most innovative techniques with the idea of collegiality. Thus Conrad dreams in his fiction of "civilized solidarity," James of the "moral imperatives attendant" on being a stranger in a group, Crane and Wells of "a crowd of individuals." "It is possible to argue," Delbanco says, "that a dominant impulse in *Lord Jim* and *The Good Soldier* is precisely to find an attentive critical ear, an astute yet merciful friend," and that "books as disparate as *Kim* and *The Ambassadors* have in common some notion of a commonweal." Elsewhere Delbanco speculates that Conrad must have been a "role model" to the two young writers Crane and Ford. From the start Crane did his imaginative writing before the fact, dramatizing war in *The Red Badge* before becoming a war correspondent. He was, in short, "far more symbolist than realist." By the time of Crane's death, his "reverence was on the drift away from men of action and toward those men active in art. Conrad represented both." For all Ford's devotion to le mot juste, he was temperamentally a facile and casual writer. Conrad's "continual close scrutiny of language must have come as a surprise" to Ford. "Conrad was never casual." Conrad especially "would have influenced Ford" as to "the architectonics of the novel" (Ford's phrase). Delbanco rightly says that one of the best things about *The Good Soldier* is "the tension established between the apparently casual discourse and the tautly reined-in and organized plot." He is equally perceptive in discussing what Ford did for Conrad and persuasively proposes that in the love scene Ford wrote for *Nostromo,* when Conrad was too ill to do the next magazine installment, Ford gives Decoud's Antonia an "ease of utterance . . . elsewhere denied" her. Ford's dialogue is so convincing that it "does much to justify Decoud's ensuing action, as well as Antonia's lifelong and subsequent loss." Speaking generally, Delbanco says: "I submit that Ford released the elder man to create profound scenarios by helping him to realize the surface of his texts." Minor as the jointly written *Romance* is, its writing made greater triumphs possible; similarly an impressionistic narrator moves through "progressive revelation . . . conscious and searching but confused." Reading Delbanco's whole account of the collaboration, we have to agree that Conrad's "great creative decade comes so hard on the heels of their meeting that it is churlish to call it coincidence."

It is probably churlish too to wish from Delbanco more—more in the way of impressions, opinions, speculations, reconstructions—and to wish for fewer blocks of undigested quotations from the letters and criticism of Wells and James. Delbanco deliberately leaves out his subjects' "politics, their sexual proclivities, their neuroses, poetry, siblings, and clothes," though admitting they are "consequential." Had he considered some of these, he might have found it harder to paint so attractive a picture of colleagueship. Delbanco is right in feeling that it is a miracle that these five writers got on as well as they did—that "galaxy of talent assembled that beggars in accomplishment anything the English language has since produced." But I, the Fordian sentimentalist, keep asking why they didn't get on even better. How much did James really value the others? In conversation he spoke contemptuously of both Marlow and *Heart of Darkness*; his 1914 putdown of Conrad, Wells, and Bennett, "The Younger Generation" (those babes of fifty-seven, forty-eight, and forty-seven respectively), was "the *only time*," Conrad admitted to John Quinn, "a criticism affected me painfully." Conversely I wish that Conrad had been strong enough to have continued to bear Ford's vagaries and to have dedicated one of his many books to him. Though Conrad warmly dedicated to Wells *The Secret Agent* in 1907, Wells denigrated Conrad fictively in *Tono-Bungay* in 1909, and explicitly in *Boon* in 1915. Doubtless I am asking far too much. Writing is such a lonely, vulnerable, supremely egoistic enterprise that to expect of novelists unfailing generosity and forgiveness is even more naive than to expect it of common folk. But we, safely removed from these great men by half a century and more, can give them their due. Almost as if to answer Hunter's concluding phrase about the "relative failure of Edwardian fiction," Delbanco says flatly that at that time and in that place, south of London, the "English novel was self-consciously reinvented by a band of foreigners who chose to emulate the French." Moreover "no author writing in English today can fail to deal with Conrad and James." Hunter, of course, wants a specific kind of great novel, a quintessentially *Edwardian* work that connects the private and the public, mediates "between the poet and the statistician." How about that great novel with its Edwardian protagonist—not Edward Ponderevo, inventor of Tono-Bungay, but Edward Ashburnham, the good soldier?

Richard Eder (review date 7 August 1983)

SOURCE: Eder, Richard. "Fidelity and the Urge to Fight." *Los Angeles Times Book Review* (7 August 1983): 2, 8.

[*In the following review, Eder discusses the themes of aging and the struggle of individuals caught between marital fidelity and escapist fantasy in the stories of* About My Table.]

"We do not die from being ill; we die from being alive," Montaigne wrote. [In ***About My Table***,] Nicholas Delbanco writes of early middle life, when a certain amount of dying has already been done. Bloom has become sheen. The body's youthfulness is still there, but beginning to harden into its own memorial—it will not be renewed. It is the time when blows become cumulative, sapping resiliency and propagating their bruises.

Delbanco's nine short stories are like nine mourners at the same wake. It is a preliminary wake; there will be others. In each story the protagonist is in his late 30s and going through a climacteric of sorts. Forgotten or suppressed bits of life come back to him; but not in the final deathbed's grand retrospective of regret or rejoicing. These are data that must be lived with. It is too soon to give up and too late to hope. But life will be different.

The stories, written with breathtaking technique and an uncanny ability to bring a penetrating emotion up out of a gesture, a pause or a random thought, are independent but linked. They are linked in setting: The men are professors or professionals and live comfortably in western Massachusetts.

They are linked in theme: The protagonists are going through a crisis related to their age. They are divorced, or their marriages have stiffened. A sense of solitude has flooded in on them. They are honorably committed to their lives, they are bound to fidelity, more or less. But other lives entice them—a younger woman, the memory of a past love—to weaken the bindings and the life.

In **"The Consolidation of Philosophy,"** an architect with a wife and young daughter inhabits a no-man's-land between intimacy and estrangement. Sporadic affection alternates with sporadic fantasy. He sits in his office, spins a globe and imagines going to the Yucatan. He daydreams energetically about elaborate reunions with his first lover, who has become a well-known actress. She has, in fact, hinted once or twice that she would like to see him, but he has never pursued the hints. His real attachments stand in the way; on the other hand, his fantasies drain color from his real life.

There is a similar division in the elaborately constructed **"Some in Their Bodies' Force,"** where scenes showing the protagonist's life with his wife, and his protective, half-jealous love for his growing daughter, are intercut with memories of a Swedish girl he loved at college. Everything is told as if it were real—at the end he is a medieval adventurer sailing alone up a Norwegian fjord—and so everything has an air of hallucination.

In each of the stories, fidelity and the urge to flight are held in precarious balance, inclining sometimes one way, sometimes the other. But once youth is gone, Delbanco suggests, all choices mean pain and solitude.

In **"Traction,"** a lawyer flies to the Midwest to settle a client's case. His wife drinks heavily; his infant daughter is having a hip operation that will keep her in a cast for half a year. The trip is necessary; it is also a brief flight from the wounds that have pierced his life. A snowstorm sets in; his Ohio hosts urge him to stay over for a couple of days, and the host's seductive wife is particularly pressing.

She is Circe, he is Ulysses; and after a moment's weakness, he stops his ears and tries to get home through the storm: driving on icy roads, using feeder airlines that land in the wrong places, catching trains. "The Midwest was an obstacle course he was trying to negotiate," Delbanco writes, with a sure knowledge of how winter can make a 19th-Century ordeal out of travel in that part of the country. There is no reward in the effort; merely faithfulness.

Snow and cold, those symbols of aging, recur. In one story they frame a quarrel; in another they envelop the solitude of a museum curator whose wife has left him. She has gone because she finds he lacks ambition. What he lacks is not ambition, he says, but addition: the compulsion to add one more book, painting or exploit to the great midden of culture. As a curator he is bound to celebrate what exists, not to extend it. He has his point, but he no longer has his wife.

The stories ostensibly put their focus on the protagonist. The play of his yearning, his valor, his weakness and his endurance serves as the subject. But Delbanco is an artist, and he deals in echoes. Shadowy figures in the background manage to be the most vivid: the wives who may drink or walk out, but generally remain steadfast and plucky.

The protagonist's choice is usually to remain faithful to marriage rather than to fantasies. But it is a meager faithfulness and doesn't give much nourishment. A sunny and populated island has become, with the sun setting, a dark shape across the water. From the island's point of view, of course, life continues as before; but the setting sun sees only the shadow it has made.

Delbanco's vision is stoic, just this side of tragic. But his stories are only tangentially bleak. He writes warmly about cold things. His tormented heroes are priggish and winning at the same time, and sometimes comical. The author's gift for comedy is considerable, in fact.

In **"Ostinato"** the grave strains and reconciliations of a musician's marriage are zanily bombarded by a series of letters from a Japanese girl who had served as an *au pair* and fallen in love with him. The letters are both touching and funny; their English is sublimely broken, but what is even more broken is their thoughts. Their woozy requests for assistance suggest all manner of things ranging from love through simple cheerfulness to mild blackmail.

The struggling characters in **"About My Table"** have an enticing virtue to them; one made brittle by time. They possess a quixotic sense of life's beauty. They do not want to die and the prospect, though still distant, disrupts them. But we don't want them to die either, and that is Delbanco's success.

Ann Hulbert (review date 31 October 1983)

SOURCE: Hulbert, Ann. "Welcome the Wimps." *New Republic* 189, no. 18 (31 October 1983): 35-8.

[*In the following review, Hulbert compares* About My Table *to two other books of fiction about "men ill at ease in a post-feminist age." Hulbert asserts that Delbanco's stories are poorly plotted and lacking in variety, and that the female characters are mere caricatures, observing that the collection fails to evoke a "moral sympathy" in the reader.*]

"A man would never get the notion of writing a book on the peculiar situation of the human male," Simone de Beauvoir wrote in *The Second Sex* (1949), the book that helped inspire a flood of literature about the peculiar female predicament: manifestos and monographs, and a stream of novels—"the female sexual picaresque," one critic called the emerging genre. But to judge by the publishers' lists of the last decade or so, Beauvoir spoke too soon about men. Thanks to feminism, men have begun to feel their situation is less powerful and more peculiar, and they have gotten the notion of writing about it. Their books don't yet occupy as much space in the bookstores as women's do. But back in the how-to, pop psychology sections, a shelf has been filling up with titles like *The Male Machine, The Liberated Male, The Hazards of Being Male, On Men and Manhood*. *The New York Times* recently launched a weekly column, "About Men," to match the six-year-old "Hers" column. And now Nicholas Delbanco, Frederick Barthelme, and C. D. B. Bryan, none of them novice writers, have turned to fiction about men ill at ease in a post-feminist age.

In **About My Table,** *Moon Deluxe,* and *Beautiful Women; Ugly Scenes,* the women's movement has made its mark, and men find their lot unsettlingly altered. Where literary heroes have commonly busied themselves with physical and intellectual explorations of the world and women, the more liberated male characters in these books are preoccupied by the challenge to inhabit an unfamiliar emotional realm, once the special province of women; there's less of that old manly worry about wearing the pants, and more about wearing their hearts on their sleeves.

Twenty years ago, before such new ideals of manhood had caught on, Saul Bellow's Moses Herzog rebelled against retreating to this intimate sphere, against settling for a life that revolved around women. "What was he hanging around for?" he moaned to himself at one especially low point in *Herzog*:

> To follow this career of *personal relationships* until his strength at last gave out? Only to be a smashing success in the private realm, a king of hearts? Amorous Herzog, seeking love and embracing his Wandas, Zinkas, and Ramonas, one after another? But this is female pursuit. This hugging and heartbreak is for women. The occupation of men is in duty, in use, in civility, in politics in the Aristotelian sense.

A decade later Peter Tarnopol in Philip Roth's *My Life as a Man* also berated himself for letting amorous entanglements distract him from his higher vocation, writing. Lamenting "that sense [in women] of defenselessness and vulnerability that has come to be a mark of their sex and is often at the core of their relations with men," he too aspired to more than coping with his Maureens and Susans.

Delbanco, Barthelme, and Bryan don't give their protagonists such impatient, manly gestures, or such defenseless damsels. For their men, the career of personal relationships comes close to eclipsing all other pursuits, active or contemplative. And that career now bears the mark Tarnopol saw stamped on women's lives: the sense of vulnerability at the core of their relations with the opposite sex.

The tone of these books about newly vulnerable men is subdued—quite different from so much of what gets loosely lumped as "women's fiction," in which feminist defiance has often replaced female defenselessness. In these liberated times, Barbara Ehrenreich observes in her new book, *The Hearts of Men,* "women's issues are power issues, while male issues are human issues." The narrator of Leonard Michaels's *The Men's Club,* a parodic foray into "men's fiction" of a few years ago, reluctantly agrees that men's themes are now softer, quieter ones. "I thought again about the women," he says wistfully. "Anger, identity, politics, rights, wrongs. I envied them. It seemed attractive to be deprived in our society. Deprivation gives you something to fight for, it makes you morally superior, it makes you serious."

The male characters in these books, as well as their creators, aren't fired by such proud passions. The title of Nicholas Delbanco's collection of stories, ***About My Table,*** rather quaintly conjures up hearth and home, and his characters' dilemmas are mostly domestic. In *Beautiful Women; Ugly Scenes* C. D. B. Bryan also turns away from large-scale drama; those messy scenes mostly happen in bedrooms and backyards. And Frederick Barthelme's shy bachelors are ambivalent about venturing outside; shopping expeditions are their idea of adventure. In fact, these authors describe their post-feminist protagonists behaving surprisingly like the unassertive, dependent women of less enlightened days—an otherwise extinct species, to judge by the aggressive females who stride so conspicuously through all three of these books.

"A proper man," one of Delbanco's characters has read, "is one who has fathered a son, built a house, and completed a book." The protagonists in this collection of nine stories—all but one of them married men in their mid- to late-30s, settled in modest professional and academic careers in the Northeast—don't quite fit this image of manhood, genteel though it is. Instead, they have gentler, more womanly habits. They specialize in daughters, toward whom they are devoted and attentive—more maternally solicitous than their wives. Only one, an architect, has designed a house, but most of them are occupied with helping to keep house. And only one has completed a book, which he hardly considers a great one. It has gradually dawned on him and the other characters that fulfillment and independence have eluded them somehow, but they're docile in their discontentment. The author of ten novels, Delbanco writes stories as muted as his men's lives—lightly plotted, lacking in variety.

Most of the stories turn on the characters' realization that they have paid an unexpected price for devoting their lives to the career of personal relationships that Herzog cursed: arriving at middle age, they feel empty. As Peter Danto walks along the beach in **"Some in Their Bodies' Force,"** he reflects on his life and describes a feeling of secondary, dependent status that sounds like Beauvoir's portrait of woman as "the Other."

> He had been a "ladies' man" and now he was a "family man." He had acquaintances, of course, and men he could consult in need; he was sociable. But on the shore he felt himself abandoned, distinguished from the sea-wrack only by his sentient alertness to the distinction as such. And for an instant even this faded, even that self-consciousness was washed into transparency.

The dependency often starts even sooner. With more reverence than rancor, the narrator of **"What You Carry"** explains that he began as a mother's boy. "Through all his adolescence and young manhood, this was a constant: a continual sense . . . that his mother was someone to reckon with and serve." He can't seem to shake the courtier habit: his failure to render one duty—to deliver a grandchild to her before her death—comes to symbolize his disorientation in the world and in time.

It's the women, mothers and wives, who are autonomous and purposeful—and impatient with hapless males. "What you don't understand . . . is ambition," Edward's wife lectures him in **"The Executor."** "It's wanting to count in this world. . . . To make a difference. To be able to say, when you walk in a room, 'I matter, I'm here. This is me.'" But pushiness has no appeal for these men, who instead submit to small-scale circumstances. "Directions: he had lived his life by them," George Allison ruefully reflects in **"Marching through Georgia."** "What signs he read he followed; what turns he made he made with adequate warning and judiciously." A minor car accident—not his fault—jars him, just as a sudden surge of "rage—shock after shock of it" jolts Edward when he confronts the stark fact that "he was nothing original, never had been or would be." But they quickly compose themselves, outwardly at least. Within, they nurse "a sense of alternative possibilities," "dreams of escape," "a nostalgia for imagined opportunities that had not been, when offered, opportune." They're too demure for their own good, it's clear. Yet Delbanco only rumples their tweeds, never really roughing them up. He is ever patient with these well-meaning milquetoasts who know that without their women they would be truly, rather than only vaguely, lost.

The men in Frederick Barthelme's story collection don't have women they can rely on, and lead irresolute lives as beauties come and go. They are roughly the same age as Delbanco's characters, but the external similarities end there. Single, they live in the Southwest, in a garish landscape of bright blue pools, lobster-pink stucco bungalows, fast-food places with "oversize four-color wrapped-in-clear-vinyl menus"—worlds away from the natural hues of Delbanco's New England. Those who are employed—and most of these aimless men have no discernible occupation—work for "a company"; what kind of company, or in what kinds of jobs, we never learn. Their main activity consists in puzzling, passive encounters with women.

The interior lives of Barthelme's protagonists are more difficult to describe, even though most of the stories are narrated in the first person. These men are eerily impassive, apparently mesmerized by their gleaming surroundings—especially by sleek women (one man spends days fixated on a succession of gorgeous salesgirls at a mall). In seventeen super-realistically sharp, sometimes funny, but finally inscrutable stories (most of which previously appeared in *The New Yorker*), Barthelme probes only far enough to note that his characters are always lonely and often nervous.

Women are what make them nervous. Generally younger than the narrators, Barthelme's female characters are energetically bizarre where Delbanco's are businesslike, but they too are the assertive figures—not the men. Antonia of the title story is perhaps the most intimidating eyeful of them all:

> . . . she's huge, extraordinary, easily over six feet. Taller than you. Her skin is glass-smooth and her pale eyes are a watery turquoise. Her hair is parted on one side and brushed flat back to her scalp. She [is] . . . wearing khaki shorts and a white T-shirt with "So many men, so little time" silk-screened in two lines across the chest.

As that motto suggests, these women are hungry and in a hurry, and they seem to have Barthelme's quiet men at their mercy. They corral them into cars, jabber at them, impose on them, dump them, while the men nod and feel nervous. Like so many women of yore, the men appear to be ciphers until these manic creatures arrive and rouse them. While the men wait, Barthelme frequently describes them cleaning, like fastidious housewives—emptying the refrigerator, vacuuming the carpet. When they're out with women, they're usually eating, like children—playing with their peas, piling up one-inch squares of roast beef, arranging cream containers into football teams.

What they rarely resemble are grown-up men. They take graphic note of women's bodies, but seem strangely disembodied themselves, conveying no sign of sexual energy. In fact, they're often so aloof that women lose interest (some of them inclining instead to sinister men, or to other women). This female fickleness in turn seems to confirm the men in their cautiousness, although they never reveal their thoughts or hearts. In one story, "Lumber," the subject of relations between the sexes explicitly arises—it's the implicit theme of all of the stories—but the discussion does little to clarify the protagonist's, or Barthelme's, view of the matter. Milby, one of several peripheral brutes in the collection, has just hit his girlfriend Lois and wants to discuss his brutishness with the narrator. "So talk, already," Lois's friend Cherry tells the two men impatiently. "Go get a steak and talk. Be men all over the place. Practice spitting." The docile narrator hardly knows how to rise to this occasion, of course, and he's not sure what to tell Milby, whose anger is so alien to him. "The thing is," Milby sputters over the steak,

> "they take advantage of everything—all the differences—but you can't. You get pissed after a while."
>
> "Everybody gets pissed." I wonder why I don't tell him what I want to tell him, why he scares me. "Who's this 'they' anyway?"
>
> "The bitches—what are you, some Holy Ghost or something? I don't need catechism lessons, brother. It's jerks like you screw it up for the rest of us. I'm telling you it just happens, and you're telling me Hail Mary, full of grace. That's a big help."
>
> "Yeah, O.K.," I say, cutting through my steak. "You're probably right."

It's obvious that he doesn't really think Milby is right, but it's equally clear that this uneasy narrator, like the others in the collection, has no clue about what to expect of women—how much bitchiness, how much sympathy—or of himself.

In their confusion, Barthelme's men generally resort to some version of the gawky nerd gambit: "Hoping for quick intimacy," says the narrator of "Rain Check," "I start telling Lucille the things I'm afraid of." It's hopeless: "Lucille says she's not afraid of anything, so I shut up about loneliness." And when at the very end of the story Lucille apparently decides she's ready for intimacy and asks, "So. What about a shower?" the narrator is as insecure as ever, but cagier now:

> I give her a long look, letting the silence mount up. I stand there with her for a good two minutes, without saying a word, trying to outwait her, trying to see

what's what. . . . She smiles at me as if she really does like me. Maybe we've been there longer than two minutes, but when the smile comes, I see her lips a little bit apart and her slightly hooded eyes, and she traces her fingers down my arm from the elbow to the wrist and stops there, loosely hooking her fingernails inside my shirt cuff, pinching my skin with her nails.

However lost and lonely these men may be, they are leery about being found by the reptilian women who abound, and Barthelme doesn't seem to blame them.

With two viperous wives and countless lovers behind him, the narrator of C. D. B. Bryan's *Beautiful Women; Ugly Scenes* is as lost as any of these men, and many times more loquacious. A 40-year-old TV documentary filmmaker living in the Connecticut suburbs, he takes comfort in "the trappings of being a father, a husband, a member of a family," as Delbanco's protagonists do, yet both his marriages have failed. At the same time, he's an incorrigible adulterer and has kept up with the singles culture—slightly less plastic but hardly more personal than Barthelme's Southwest scene. Yet, for all the beautiful flesh he's fondled (there's page after page of soft porn), too many of the feelings have been ugly. "It is very hard to be a man to a woman these days. . . . To know what a man, what being a man even means," he confesses more than once:

> Difficult to know how to behave toward women. Difficult to know what they wanted. I listened to them, read their books. They said they wanted something more. They wanted equality, self-respect. They wanted to feel close, they wanted to feel passion; they wanted to feel secure; they wanted to feel *whole*.

"Sensitive" and "caring" man that the nameless narrator portrays himself to be, he's ready to confront his failure to help women enjoy any of these amorphous feelings. He's even more eager, however, to declare his own yearnings for them. He is, after all, as vulnerable, open, and unfulfilled as any woman. It's his turn to be listened to, to write a book.

And what an unheroic story of hugging and heartbreak this is from the author of *Friendly Fire,* an acclaimed chronicle of hardship on a larger scale—the trauma the Vietnam War brought to one family. With much artless talk about "mid-life crises," "psychodramas," and "the games people play," Bryan's narrator undertakes an appraisal of his busy but dismal amorous career that sounds more like the confessions that have become a convention of pop psychology literature than like full-bodied fiction. As in *Moon Deluxe* and **About My Table,** the women have a monopoly on the tough attributes now (although they certainly don't yet have a corner on the job market; most are still at home). It was the "irreverence, ballsiness, pushiness" of his second wife Alice, the narrator says, that "appealed to something I felt lacking in me. Opposites attract." He's the one who wants to "make love," as languorously as possible, while his impatient partners have a more crudely carnal view of the activity. He's emotional and uncertain, in contrast to most of the women in his life, who tend to be calculating and decisive; while he balks, bewildered, at the prospect of divorce despite a hellish marriage, Alice is coldly plotting an escape with a man who will be able to support her in style. Throughout, the narrator aspires not to the conventional heroic ideal of autonomous selfhood, but to one of dependent intimacy.

The problem is that his ideal seems to imply intimacy with a mother figure, rather than with a woman as liberated and well-rounded as he conceives himself to be. As he indirectly acknowledges, the kind of feminine strength and assertiveness that appeals to him is maternal, with no manliness about it. Thus, he finally turns to Odette, his salvation thanks to a local spouse swap: she's the French wife of a neighbor who has gone off with the narrator's wife. A woman from the old country where sexual fashions haven't changed so much, this patient angel welcomes a man whom she says "reminded me of an adolescent who had grown too fast: a little awkward, a little helpless, a little unsure of [him]self." Liberated though this man may look, he has lots of growing up left to do. His mid-life reassessment may have been purgative, but it's a protracted adolescence, not a paradise, that seems to lie ahead for him.

Most of the men in Delbanco's and Barthelme's stories are as awkward, helpless, and unsure as Bryan's narrator. They have come of age as feminism was flourishing and found that the old stern standards of masculinity and maturity don't really suit anymore. Neither, however, are new notions of manhood as comfortable as they might have hoped. Although Bryan's narrator has it on Odette's authority that "quiet and sensitive men" are what women want, the other characters in these books (and perhaps their creators as well) clearly are not sure what the ladies, often so loud and insensitive, would like. Whatever women's manly ideals might be, these men are full of ambivalence about their own aspirations for themselves. All of them may feel wiser for knowing the softer side of life. But most of them are also awash in doubts and identity problems, victims of familiar female dilemmas that threaten to leave them hollow, more wimpy than well-rounded.

If these men are not at peace with themselves, neither is the war between the sexes over. The quieter battles that continue in these books bring few victories for either life or literature. The male protagonists seem to have inherited the most debilitating of female qualities; in turn, their creators have bequeathed to the peripheral female characters the least appealing of masculine poses. Not surprisingly, the arrangement means they all lead discontented lives.

More important for the prospects of fiction, it means the men make unprepossessing literary heroes. (In the background, the women are rarely more than caricatures.) Embarked on the career of personal relationships, the protagonists have turned inward, and the uneasy narcissism that has replaced the old-style self-assertion proves to be a narrow field for fiction. The hugging and heartbreak in these stories and novel are often of more sociological than literary interest; acute observers, Delbanco, Barthelme, and Bryan get the manners just right—the décor, the relevant lusts and insecurities—but then fail to look very far beneath or beyond them. Their characters have little taste for the varied and vigorous experience of which strong plots are made. But equally rare among this lonely crowd is the moral sympathy that deepens characters and complicates their relations even in more circumscribed, domestic settings. The lives and stories of these men look thin and wan: new veins of feeling may have opened, but so has a deadly artery of anxiety.

Nicholas Delbanco and Gregory L. Morris (interview date November 1983)

SOURCE: Delbanco, Nicholas, and Gregory L. Morris. "An Interview with Nicholas Delbanco." *Contemporary Literature* 25, no. 4 (winter 1984): 386-96.

[*In the following interview, which originally took place in November 1983, Delbanco discusses connections between his fiction and his own life, developments in his writing style, and the origins of his Sherbrookes trilogy.*]

Nicholas Delbanco lives in Bennington, Vermont and teaches at Bennington College, where he directs the Bennington Writing Workshop and directs the M.F.A. in Writing program. He is the author of ten novels, including the three books of the acclaimed Sherbrookes trilogy (**Possession, Sherbrookes, Stillness**), and has most recently published a collection of short stories entitled **About My Table, and Other Stories**. He has also written two works of nonfiction—**Group Portrait: Conrad, Crane, Ford, James, and Wells,** and the forthcoming **The Beaux Arts Trio**. He is the recipient of numerous awards and fellowships, and has published and read his works widely. The interview took place in November of 1983 at Wells College in Aurora, New York.

[*Morris*]: *May we start with a little of your biography, particularly since some of your own experience seems such an integral part of your fiction?*

[Delbanco]: I was born in London of German parents who were, in my father's case, of Italian extraction. They had been living in Germany since the sixteenth century, and maybe a bit before. Hitler caused my parents, separately, to leave; they met again in England and married there. In 1948, when I was six, they came to this country to settle. How clear it was that it would be a permanent settlement, I don't know. I think it was an experiment really, but one that took. My father, who's still alive, is now living in the third country—this one—that he considers to be home. When you come from a family like that—it's a common story, God knows—but when it's built into your expectation that perhaps you don't belong somewhere, that it can be taken from you or that you might choose to leave, this idea of rootedness and inheritance becomes an open question. We are a very old and rather fancy family in that sense; I know who the Delbancos were in Venice in 1600. But on the other hand, they've always been wanderers. I traveled—I don't want to exaggerate, my passport looks pretty blank by comparison with an airline pilot or someone who's an inveterate wanderer—but I traveled a lot. From 1969 to 1972 I must have gone to Europe three or four times, around the world once, to Central America once; that kind of continual pattern of motion was established by my parents early on. Because our relatives were still in Europe we used to go back all the time; after college I went back to England and settled there—it became a habit. It's a habit that has been broken of late, in part because I've learned to love and settle in Vermont, in part because children make it much harder to move. But even this year, I was in Europe in January. I don't mean to pretend to habitual cosmopolitanism, but I feel no less at ease in London or Cannes than I do in Aurora.

It seems that the idea of transplantation is dominant in your writing.

There's no question that that's personal. When your parents live in a country that is the third country they've actually thought of as home, then you have to call that notion—home—into question.

You keep returning to specific places in your writing, seemingly turning personal traveling experience into fiction. I'm thinking of your use of such places as St. Catherine's Island and the south of France.

I went to St. Catherine's while I was still in graduate school. At Columbia I knew the people who owned that island, and the island had the fascinating history there described [in *News*], starting with Mary, Queen of the Creeks, then Button Gwinnett and Tunis G. Campbell and so forth. The husband was then an aspiring politician, and they were a very wealthy family who used to fly folk down to St. Catherine's in order to have conferences; I think the previous person to go there before me was Nixon. The husband wanted essentially a little pamphlet on the history of the island so the guests in the jet could learn where they were landing. Since I was studying International Relations and he knew I could type, he asked me to do it. In the course of what became relatively serious research about Tunis Campbell, I came out with the beginnings of a novel. I can't offhand think of any location in any of my novels in which I haven't spent time. The south of France, of course, is the locus of **Grasse 3/23/66** and of **Small Rain,** and it's a very important part of the fabric in each book.

Turning to the histories of your books, I was wondering whether they were all published in the order of their composition, or whether some were published years later or out of order?

Roughly speaking, they were published in the order of their composition. The short story collection, **About My Table,** of course, took care of itself; some of those stories were published before **Group Portrait** came out, but by and large I started to write short stories as a release from the trilogy.

It's interesting, then, that all of the stories in **About My Table** *should be so similar, considering that they were written some years apart.*

It became a desired pattern, partly. I have written and published a couple of short stories that aren't in that collection precisely because they were disparate. And the time span wasn't extraordinary, it was three or four years back.

Your first novel, **The Martlet's Tale,** *was accepted for publication while you were still at Columbia?*

Yes. It came out in July just after I left Columbia, but it was bought while I was there. Indeed, I graduated from college with a book already sold. But that was a much palmier time in American publishing; it was easier to get published then than now, and it was very easy to get attention if you were very young. So at twenty-three, when my first book appeared, I received the generic generosity given to a young author. There's still a lot of that; people routinely get more highly praised for their first book than for their second, and sometimes they can't get the second published.

And that novel was bought and turned into a movie?

Yes, but never released, fortunately. I ended up pulling out of the project.

*Your earliest novels—***The Martlet's Tale, Grasse 3/23/66, Consider Sappho Burning***—are currently out of print. Do you see any particular reason for that? Is it a result, perhaps, of their style, their experimentalism?*

It's the economics. The publisher of my first two novels, Lippincott, saw no reason to maintain or retain them, and they have long since been out of print. As far as I know **News** remains in print, and so that was probably a decision on Morrow's part; **Consider Sappho Burning** wasn't likely to burn up the salesmen's shelves. Morrow is beginning slowly—and it isn't clear to me how schematically—to bring most of them back in paper. **Group Portrait**'s going to come out in paper this summer, so they're working their way back. Faulkner, at the time of his Nobel Prize, was entirely out of print in America, and though I don't mean to compare myself to him, that's a heartening statistic; his books, which were then out of print, now sell tens of thousands yearly. And so I would like to think of that as a momentary rather than a final decision.

Do you think the success of the Sherbrookes trilogy has encouraged Morrow to bring these books out now?

I'm not sure. I think there's a certain slow but general pattern of increase in response to the work. My wife thinks, and she may be right, that books like **Grasse** and **Consider Sappho Burning** did very close to irretrievable damage to my reputation with the salesmen and the buying public. I thumbed my nose at readability and became very quickly, as far as anybody paid any attention to those other books, an obscurantist author, a recherché experimentalist writer. I think it's taken a good decade or so for me to live that down and to emerge, insofar as I have at all, into the general popular perception of an author whose books one might be able to read.

Do you see your style as having changed at all over the years, in a significant way?

No, I don't think of it as a conscious shift in emphasis or style, though it's perfectly clear to me that there has been a radical change. But it seems to me more a function of the altered emphasis of my life and experience. I was very much, in the period of **Grasse** and **Sappho,** a feisty, overeducated kid who wanted to display his book-learning. Most writers produce books that are manifestly the productions of pretentious children and gifted embryos; I don't regret or renounce those books at all, but few publish that sort of novel. I managed to, and I'm proud of them as milestones, but Lord knows it's not a road I would have liked to continue traveling.

The books seem to become more accessible, particularly the Sherbrookes Trilogy and the stories of **About My Table.**

In some degree you're no longer a very good witness either, because you're so familiar with them that if they contain a code or a private language, it's one you can speak. But I think it's objectively the case that these stories are accessible. Of the stories in **About My Table,** "Northiam Hall" is probably the most recondite and the hardest to crack, and it seemed to me at my reading last night that the fifty or so college kids who were sitting there listening to me read that story were at least able to stay without falling asleep—not something that I could have claimed a decade ago.

The book that seemed a breakthrough for you was **In the Middle Distance,** *for there you combined a more straightforward kind of style with an interesting technical experiment, in which you turn Nicholas Delbanco the writer into Nicholas Delbanco the character, and in which you interleave a journal—another common feature of your work—with your story.*

I think that is the most ambitious technical experiment I have made. It actually arose, in large part, from a course I was teaching at Bennington in autobiographies; my thesis, or the idea that emerged from teaching, was that the ratification of data can be very misleading. There's no reason, as I say in that book, to disbelieve what Proust says about his childhood just because he calls it fiction, or at least no reason to take it qualitatively differently from what Bertrand Russell says about his childhood just because he calls it an autobiography. When somebody says that something happened to him, it may have principally happened in his imagination, just as if someone says that something is principally an imagined event, it may be a true psychic revelation. So I thought I'd make the character Nicholas Delbanco like me in certain important respects; he has my house, my passport number, some of my background—but I'd shoot him forward twenty years into events that couldn't possibly have happened to me yet (although as I'm beginning to tilt toward his age, I'm feeling a little nervous). But he truly is an invented figure. He happens to have my name, and therefore it seems like an autobiographical document. On the other hand, when I was writing, I did keep an actual journal which recorded personal things that were happening, like the building of a house and so forth. That actual journal became the novel that my fictive creation tried to construct, and of course he couldn't write it very successfully. I also think it was important that that book went backwards, wound down rather than wound up, so that in the end, when he's the smallest, it really is something like my experience.

The retrogressive structure of the book is certainly one of its most puzzling, and most fascinating, features.

It forms an "X." As the journal works forward, the novel works backward, and somewhere in the middle they converge, while he's keeping notes.

And the editor's notes are notes you actually received from your editor?

I was living in the south of France during the period of composition of *In the Middle Distance.* My wife and I were about to travel around the world—we'd just gotten married and I had money from the movie deal for *The Martlet's Tale*—and so the process of editing the text, which is generally something Jim Landis and I do in person or on the phone, became one of letters. I had to send him the corrections. His letters in particular fascinated me, and somewhere around Hong Kong I sent him a telegram saying: Stop the presses. I thought we should incorporate the letters—the process of the editing ought to be part of the making of the book because it was part and parcel of the enterprise. He said, "You've got to be crazy; I'll give you till Tokyo to decide." So I sent the same telegram, and when I got back to the States he had all the letters set up in print, and we just juggled them around in the galleys and put them in. So those really do refer to the typescript text, which is what I was carrying around with me. I think it's a little precious, but it was plausible.

I'd like to move ahead a bit and talk about the origins of the Sherbrookes trilogy. You said that **Possession** *and* **Stillness** *mirror each other in a way, and that the middle book,* **Sherbrookes,** *is structurally different; it's not divided into separate books, for example.*

No, it's the pastoral interlude. It takes approximately the nine months of Jane's gestation. I think it should work that way. You have two chunks of a single day's time, with much more back and forth in memory. Then there's the more or less direct narrative drift of the period of Maggie's pregnancy. It's not accidentally a *green* book. My original working title for that work, actually, was *Spring and Fall,* which I decided was presumptuous. So then I thought of calling it *The Green Mantle.* In the play in **Stillness,** Ian does, roughly speaking, describe each of my early novels. So, yes, there is a conscious disparity.

So often the central characters in your work are erudite, artistic types—architects, poets. And in the Sherbrooke books you make Ian Sherbrooke an actor. Is this a conscious effort on your part?

I should first talk about this a little generally. My own feeling, though I don't know whether you'd share it, is that I always have had a rather surprising ability to be someone other than myself as author; I was always pretty good at old women and very old men and very young children and foreigners and folk like that. But I never, to my satisfaction, was able to create a character anything like the author, and who was nonetheless persuasive or persuasively alive. It seemed to me that the weakest figures in my fiction were always the ones closest to home. In Ian's case I knew that and was able, I hope, to make it somehow function within the novel, because as you know it's a more or less technical *Bildungsroman*; the point is that he's a beginner at the end, so that he's just working his way into something like the power and the actuality of the elder generation by the end of the trilogy. There it was functionally useful, but I still think that, of the characters in the Sherbrooke family, Ian is manifestly the least vivid. He doesn't have the kind of clarity that Judah and Hattie and Maggie and even Jane have. He's a shape-shifter, a beginner.

Even in the final book, **Stillness,** *which becomes his book?*

I mean it to be his book. As we've said, **Stillness** mirrors **Possession,** each takes place in a single day, and **Possession** is essentially Judah's book; Ian never appears, but he's always thought about. The reverse is true in the last of the trilogy. So, yes, the book's tilted downwards a generation, and the third one is Ian's, but he is not clear yet; he's becoming rather than being, and he's a more or less technical example, as I've said, of a figure in a *Bildungsroman*; he's someone who starts at the end.

Actually, I had always had trouble wrestling with figures who were somewhat, or very, similar to me, but that did not seem to be the case in the short stories in **About My Table.** I felt liberated, in that particular form, to write about a figure who in one way or another was cognate to his creator. As far as I'm concerned, in fact, all the other figures in the stories are caricatures or only partially realized; they are not stage center. It's a book about nine men and certain witnesses to their world. But I wasn't trying to make the elder generation vivid or the wives or children vivid—I just wanted to focus on the male protagonist. That was a breakthrough, because I never could do it before, and I think I can now. This is a long way around to answering your particular question: why should all those figures have that kind of culture? The answer is that I was trying to stay a little closer to home and those are worlds with which I am more or less familiar. I didn't really do any full-scale submerging into another character. Sure, I asked my brother, who's a doctor, about the influence of altitude on pulmonary statistics; and sure, I asked an architect how you build such and such a structure. But I didn't feel that I had to go very far afield at all in those stories in order to invent simulacra.

But your characters do, ultimately, claim authenticity and depth.

I hope so. I'm not sure where I acquired this distaste for books about the writing of books. It's possible that John Gardner had a lot to do with that, because as you know he went full tilt against the novelist as the center of his own fiction. Certainly, when I was writing **Grasse** and **Sappho,** the experimental mode and the shaping of the book as object were central to me. I didn't want to have my protagonist a novelist; he never was. He came perilously close a few times, as in **"Northiam Hall,"** where he writes about a dead poet and is a sort of cultural historian. Or in **"About My Table,"** of course, where he's a working journalist, and in **"Marching through Georgia,"** where he's a figure whose expertise happens to be in the subject of **"News."**

To return to Ian and the Sherbrookes trilogy, it seems, at the end of **Stillness,** *that Ian has no choice—given the forces of family and the lines of connection between generation and generation, which are always strong ideas in your work—that he almost has no choice but to return, and then not to leave, at the end of the book, when Maggie leaves with Jane and Kincannon. That he almost has to take, by force of blood, the family name.*

I wouldn't quarrel with that. I think he certainly acted as if he had an alternative, and could no doubt have remained a wanderer, but it would have been renouncing something that he finally was willing to claim.

So would you deny the validity of renunciation, which is another idea that runs throughout your work—for example, in **News***? And though Ian does renounce the family early on—*

No, I consider that Ian is making an affirmation, albeit a bleak and chilly one, at book's end. I consider that it is his first acquiescence in who he was and is. Maggie's closer to renouncing at novel's end. I think probably my reading of Henry James, which was pretty serious those years, had something to do with the way I ended **Stillness.** It's in no technical sense a closure or a foreclosure, though I don't think I left the door open to make it a quartet. It's not, however, a definitive closure; it's more James's notion of a concluded "affair."

You earlier mentioned John Gardner, who was a close friend of yours and, at one time, a colleague. Given your interest in colleagueship and collaboration, as evinced in **Group Portrait,** *I was wondering if the two of you ever actively collaborated in any way, or ever actively edited each other's work? I know, for example, that you swapped characters for your Vermont books.*

No, we never actually collaborated on anything, though we each often read the other's manuscripts. I certainly looked over his shoulder at what became *On Becoming a Novelist* and *On Moral Fiction*. And I read, for instance, the unfinished book of his, **Stillness,** the title of which John let me borrow for my own book. But I don't think he asked me for line readings, or that I offered them. When he fell very ill, he showed me stuff that he wanted my reaction to, but it was mostly critical work. Still, one doesn't have to ask, "What do you think of my paragraph?" in order to be a colleague.

Do you go along, basically, with Gardner's aesthetic, with the idea of moral fiction and art in the great tradition?

I think if the question is whether I go along basically, the answer is yes. I have quibbles and quarrels, but I don't think he's utterly wrong. I think he's more right than wrong.

You both seem to go about it differently, however, making those affirmations. I think particularly of your ideas on love, on the distinction between love and possessiveness, on "fathering," and on the confusion of family and love and lust.

These are compelling issues, problems perhaps to me, but I don't think of them as problems to be solved, as if once I get "fathering" right, then it won't be an issue any longer. I think in that way I'm far less programmatic than John was. In his best moments as a novelist I think he stepped off the soapbox and wasn't programmatic. But it's not as if I think of these as ideas to wrestle with. I can see how a critic might. Those are major themes, but I don't have actual answers. They remain interesting problems.

Do you still feel uncomfortable, to any degree, with being "an American writer"? Given the way in which your books, particularly your early books, are so "geographically frenetic," as you once put it, do you think that the Sherbrookes trilogy represents a sort of coming home for you, an acknowledgment of, or a reconciliation with, your Americanness?

There's no question that the locus of my work has shifted toward America. In the short story collection, there's only **"Northiam Hall"** that leaves the States. That is partly a geographical accident in that I spent much more time in America in the last years than I used to because my children are here and we are located. But it's also partly a sense, as the years go by and the roots go deeper, that this really is home and that there isn't any point in pretending otherwise, or even in attempting to report on any other kinds of culture. I taught a course last spring in Faulkner, Fitzgerald, and Hemingway, simply because I've never done that before, and because one pays lip-service to them as the progenitors of the American novel in the latter part of the twentieth century and takes their greatness for granted. Of course I'd read them and had my opinions, but I'd never really made a study of them; this year I did. They seem to me to be my masters and ancestors, and insofar as I hope to be an inheritor, it is of those voices and that kind of tradition. I'm actually doing an issue of *The Bennington Review* right now on Regionalism, and so I've been thinking about it to some degree, this sense of being located and fixed. I don't quarrel with it any longer, I don't resist it. I live there by choice and happily, but it's not as if I were born there.

You don't feel tied down geographically in your fiction, tying yourself to the New England region in your future fiction?

No, not in my future fiction. The novel I'm working on at the moment seems to be located in New England, and principally on the island of Martha's Vineyard, where I've gone back lately. I would like to acknowledge at some point, though it's a somewhat distant feeling, not an intellectual imperative, that, after all, the novel is principally an urban enterprise this century; I'd like to get my characters back into town a bit. No doubt their author will travel there too.

Southern Humanities Review (review date summer 1984)

SOURCE: Review of *Group Portrait*, by Nicholas Delbanco. *Southern Humanities Review* 18, no. 3 (summer 1984): 268-69.

[*In the following review, the critic asserts that* Group Portrait *offers little new factual information concerning the community of six authors in London in 1900, and that the central ideas of the book are not argued in depth.*]

In 1900 within a day's journey from each other, Joseph Conrad, Stephen Crane, Ford Madox Ford, Henry James, and H. G. Wells were neighbors in Kent and East Sussex. Comparing their situation to the expatriate Left Bank of Paris and to Bloomsbury, Nicholas Delbanco examines the community of these artists [in **Group Portrait**]. None of the writers were native to the region, and Delbanco maintains that their aggregation there was a "conscious retreat, a place of exile." Although the book jacket promises a "biographical study of writers in community," there is little biographical material in this book except what could be culled from the major previous biographies, such as Arthur Mizener's *The Saddest Story: A Biography of Ford Madox Ford* or Frederick R. Karl's *Joseph Conrad: The Three Lives*. By focusing on the single year and the communal aspects of the novelists, however, Delbanco brings a new organization and emphasis to material which is generally well known.

The romantic notion of the solitary, isolated genius at odds with his environment, joins with the notion of intellectual property as something to be possessed and created privately, so as to incline the modern reader to see writers as individuals. Delbanco does a valuable service in insisting that art creates a community, demands a reading public, serves no purpose in isolation. He argues that in their sometimes testy interchanges these five novelists provided for each other the demanding audience, the serious critic, the stimulation for new and fertile inventions. While Delbanco's position seems plausible, it is not argued in any depth. Rather than examining in detail the ideological foundations of the individuals in this community, he uses anecdotes about house parties, spats, teas, and gifts of autographed books as evidence that powerful creative impulses flowed among these men.

In treating the documents, Delbanco is incautious. Ford Madox Ford's tendency to slip from fact to richly embroidered imagination in his memoirs is notorious. Delbanco notes, "Since [Ford] is a principal witness in *Group Portrait,* it is appropriate early on to establish his veracity." Perhaps it would be even more appropriate to *test* his veracity, rather than to set out to *establish* it. Readers of Ford Madox Ford's *Joseph Conrad: A Personal Remembrance* can see at a glance that it is fictionalized. There may be a core of veracity, but the fabric of the work contains many elaborations of descriptive detail or of conversations which are extremely unlikely. Ford's memoir of Conrad is best read as an historical novel, like his Fifth Queen trilogy in which he does not hesitate to put words into the mouth of Henry VIII, for example, not because the King spoke them but because they add to his artistic characterization of the man. What he does in his novels for Henry VIII, he does in his memoir for Conrad. To recognize such novelistic or New Journalistic reportage as "perfectly pardonable tropes," is not the same as to establish "veracity."

Adding very little to factual knowledge about the five authors, accepting uncritically the fictionalized and perhaps biased anecdotes of the group, proceeding digressively from scene to unrelated scene, Delbanco's book is interesting, but puzzling. What kind of work has he written? The concluding pages give a clue: "I myself was born in England, of German-Jewish parents. . . . I make my home in Vermont. The notion of a chosen land, of momentary rootedness, and roots that are self-nurtured, has personal importance." Delbanco, himself a novelist, writes this *Group Portrait* not about Conrad, Ford, Crane, James, and Wells, so much as about himself. It is a pastoral, utopian work. Like a courtier severely restricted in his erotic life by the customs of his court, who imagines a land where shepherdesses carry crooks with lace bows and dally in the shade by clear flowing brooks, the modern writer, too, has his dream. Not an isolated, commercial, hostile world, but someplace where it is peaceful, old-fashioned and quaint, and where there are a few readers who care enough to read carefully and to comment straightforwardly. The utopia may never have existed in history, but has been created most powerfully as an imaginative fiction in Delbanco's study. It is a noble vision, attractive and compelling for any modern writer or critic who longs for some alternative to the real world, but it is probably not the same as any real world. Real shepherdesses do not carry beribboned crooks. The real relationship among Conrad, Crane, Ford, James, and Wells probably remains to be told. It is likely that there is a nexus among them which can illuminate their best work, but finding that connection will require an examination of what they thought and how their beliefs affected their art.

Ford's insistence that literary "impressionism" was a cultural wave during his collaborative years with Conrad is a promising place to begin a more serious study of their community, but it receives only perfunctory treatment in *Group Portrait.* Their attitude toward the limits of perception or the relativity of experience might also form a more enlightening area of common interest than those proposed in Delbanco's work.

Gregory L. Morris (essay date fall 1987)

SOURCE: Morris, Gregory L. "Nicholas Delbanco in the Middle Distance." *Critique* 29, no. 1 (fall 1987): 30-45.

[*In the following essay, Morris discusses* In the Middle Distance *in terms of its multilayered narrative, observing that the novel is an examination of the self and the writer's struggle to accurately represent the truth about himself.*]

Nicholas Delbanco is the author of eleven published works of fiction. The earliest of these works were experimental, dense, and highly subjective; Delbanco's emphasis here was largely upon language, and in such novels as *Grasse, 3/23/66* and *Consider Sappho Burning,* he strained the limits of allusiveness almost to the point of obsessive linguistic sport. In 1971, however, Delbanco published a book entitled *In the Middle Distance,* a sort of "fictional autobiography" that turned Nicholas Delbanco the *author* into Nicholas Delbanco the *character.* The novel's protagonist is an architect by the name of "Nicholas Delbanco," and the book's "outer narrative" details *this* "Delbanco's" self-examination of the content—and ruin—of his life. This outer narrative is told in retrogressive fashion, beginning with the present time and circumstance of "Delbanco's" life and working successively backward to his childhood. At the same time, "Delbanco," the character, keeps a journal (a typical autobiographical form), a journal he hopes to transform into a novel; the entries of this journal alternate with the chapters of the outer narrative, and basically work as counterpoint to the details of that outer narrative, moving from events in "Delbanco's" past to the events in "Delbanco's" present. Near the middle (appropriately) of *In the Middle Distance,* the two narratives intersect in a confluence of time and space.

This novel is interesting enough in its structural ingenuity, but *In the Middle Distance* boasts other elements of significance. For one, the novel tests the definitions of authorship. The Nicholas Delbanco who signs the book at the end seems to merge with the "Nicholas Delbanco" who keeps the journal and who from that journal tries unsuccessfully to build a novel. The lives of Nicholas Delbanco and "Nicholas Delbanco" are spatially and materially similar in that they share such things as name, passport number, inoculation scars, house; but they are different creatures of different times, as Delbanco vaults his character twenty years forward, into events yet unexperienced by Delbanco the author. (Delbanco is born in 1942, his character in 1922.) Thus the reader finds himself testing both the reliability of the narrative and the journal, keeping both in a sort of "middle distance" of belief. Also in that "middle distance" is the "fictional reality" of the book; time moves both forward and backward, forcing the reader to juggle two separate senses of time and space: one a creation of Nicholas Delbanco, the other a creation of Delbanco's protagonist and would-be novelist.

What Delbanco ultimately pursues in this novel is a triple-layered examination of self and the ability to accurately declare the truths of that examination. *In the Middle Distance* is a study in what Delbanco has called the "ratification of data" (Morris 391)—an imaginative look at the distinction between autobiography and fiction, at the illusory nature of presumed, apparent fact. On one level the book is an objective study of fictional character, "Nicholas Delbanco": a fictive biography of a created life. On a second level, the book is an autobiography of that created life, as "Nicholas Delbanco" the character reconstructs, in his journal, the pattern of his existence, tracing the long chain of events that has brought him to crisis and collapse. On a third level, however, *In the Middle Distance* is Nicholas the author's attempt to combine personal history with personal fiction, to turn the novel into his own apparent autobiography, to expand the bounds of concrete fact by infusing it with supposition. What is, after all, a book by Nicholas Delbanco about a man named Nicholas Delbanco? And how are we to read such a book—as fiction or as autobiography? *In the Middle Distance* seems an effort to redefine both the forms *and* the ways in which we approach those forms.

For Delbanco, the writing of *In the Middle Distance* also proved to be of personal aesthetic significance, turning Delbanco and his fiction away from the highly stylized and self-conscious work of his early career to more traditional (though still delicate and mannered) narrative modes. The book reveals a private working-out of both artistic and personal perplexities, as if the use of certain autobiographical elements aided Delbanco in advancing his own creative code. The examination of a fictional, older "Nicholas Delbanco" seemed to shed some sort of private light on mind and soul, enabling Delbanco the writer to jettison certain pieces of creative and psychological baggage, liberating his imagination from a mere servicing of technique and language to a more vital exploration of narrative and character and value.

As a fictive autobiography, *In the Middle Distance* fits rather snugly into paradigms established by traditional autobiographical theory. The novel is clearly an examination of self, Delbanco trying in earnest to get a "fix" upon the shifting image of successive past selves and to establish a firmer sense of the present (and future self). Delbanco's method here varies. He works backward in his outer narrative, moving from the present self of his protagonist, "Nicholas Delbanco," to the recollected selves of his past, on down to his earliest memories of a childhood self. All the while, though, Delbanco the novelist is suggesting a projected, proleptic self, one born some twenty years earlier than the "real" Delbanco, one who has lived in a past relatively alien to (or at least unexperienced by) his creator, and one whose future is an imaginatively educated guess. Substance, then, in the outer narrative comes of a blend of prediction, recollection, and imagination.

Delbanco's approach to the self comes in the form of the journal kept by his protagonist, a journal that the fictional "Delbanco" tries unsuccessfully to shape into a novel. The journal, we know, is the novelist Delbanco's own (Morris 391)—a sort of psychic gift from the present, realized self to an imagined and remoter self. But the journal also plays with the expectations of the reader, as it radically telescopes its perspective, at one moment a first-person revelation of heart and mind, the next a purposeful intrusion of the "real" Delbanco into the life and spirit of his created self. The journal, then, becomes a double-lensed "optical instrument" (in Proust's words), simultaneously shedding light on the life of both the fictive *and* the "real" Nicholas Delbanco.

As if to complicate the intended confusion of self already present in the novel, Delbanco includes excerpts from the letters passed between himself and his editor, James Landis, at the time of the completion of *In the Middle Distance* (Morris 392). Here the immediate contemporaneous presences of time and space directly intrude upon the fictive world of the novel. Delbanco and Landis are real identities; their words enter from a world that is more or less certain, a world abstracted from the imagined world of the novel. The letters become additional "data." Detail accretes. The selves multiply. The reader traverses boundaries of time, both real and imagined, constantly turning and returning, adjusting to the selves in each specific realm. The divided self requires, here, a divided reader. The writer becomes the subject of his own work, positing a self (or selves) that shifts with each concurrent shift in perspective; at the same time, the reader reshapes his own consciousness with each of these same shifts, shutting down certain connections with one self, re-activating other connections with another self. The reader must react to at least three Nicholas Delbancos: the author, who both removes himself from his creation *and* steps intrusively into it via the letters, the protagonist described by Delbanco the author, and the sort of double-natured Delbanco who keeps the journal.

The outer narrative begins in 1970 with "Nicholas Delbanco," architect, at age 48: "He had been married eighteen years. His wife was named Barbara, his daughter Eve . . . and he had one dead son named Michael. Michael had been named after Barbara's cousin; Barbara's cousin, too, was dead" (13). A brief flash backward to his youth, to "Delbanco's" days at Fieldston School, establishes one of the book's dominant metaphors in describing the younger "Delbanco's" record-setting broad jump: "That soaring, easeful leap, and the gathering of legs to belly in air, the final reach and curl and impact that would propel him forward—such flight had been and would remain his notion of success" (14). "Flight" here carries with it a twinned, though divergent, significance, emphasizing "Delbanco's" own "flight" from his past—the death of his son, the long affair with his lover, Jean—while at the same time figuring the sort of arc "Delbanco" seeks to draw from life and art, the necessary arc that will bridge the past and present, that will span the *distance* between memory and truth, between his several selves. ("He had a passion for bridges and wanted to build one before he retired; he dreamed of spanning the Amazon, or Ganges, or the Nile" [122].)

Truth, for "Delbanco," is something always beyond the bend in the bridge, a test of his fortitude. He is a man often "surprised by, beleaguered by faith" (25); but that faith is not enough to sustain "Delbanco" through the layers of crisis, as his psychological defenses give way, leaving him with nightmares, hauntings, suggestions of the womb:

> For seven nights running, he had slept in Michael's room. He did this for fear of strangling Barbara; he lay, arms folded, hands under his armpits, on his side. He did not sleep at all, or woke to find the pillow soaked. He ate only baby food, and little enough of that for a man of his bulk. He evolved some remedies: a glass of wine would calm him, and he chanted, regularly, "Devils, go away. Devils get lost. Devils, devils, devils."
>
> (21)

This sort of emotional regression—"Delbanco" curled in his dead son's bed, fetus-like, making that long jump from present to past—signals the same chronological regression of the outer narrative, as Delbanco takes his protagonist backward through successive selves.

What "Delbanco" will do, however, is retreat to his farm where "he would write a novel as an act of explication and an act of penance; he would expiate Michael, and Jean, and every failure embraced. He would recreate the past and resurrect it and enter into fantasy, not fact" (27). The novel will become for "Delbanco" an act of "necessity, not pleasure," a device that will *distance* him from the past, a device that he hopes will authenticate his being by explicating his private process of becoming.

The "explications" are simultaneous, for while "Delbanco" struggles with his journal-novel and with piecing together his disordered self, the other Delbanco retreats—leaps, arcing—into "Delbanco's" past, isolating specific segments of that past, working backward to the earliest bits of reliable remembrance. The first of these time-shifts is only two years removed from the novelistic present, the chapter's frame being the second honeymoon of "Nicholas" and his wife Barbara. Within this frame, Delbanco retreats further still, unraveling the various threads of their marriage, isolating the intertwined lines of pain and love and loss that have come to form the bound lives of the "Delbancos." Brought together originally by the pressures of politics (and politics is one of Delbanco's subthemes in this novel), "Nicholas" and Barbara go on to shape a marriage half-built on sacrifice and "seeming stability." Yet, a marriage that once stood as "Nicolas's" "salvation" gradually turns sour and stultifying. "Nicholas" is a man defined by growth, by distance, by the length of flight, and now he "sensed, obliquely, decline, and the chance his heights were foothills and was not reconciled. He attempted to remember, on Thursday, what he had done the ten previous Thursdays, and there was neither distinction nor growth" (57). This developing sense of decline, of failure, of loss, works to transform love into pain—"He hurt her wittingly; he believed that pain was proof of love"—love breaking down, poised, tense on the ragged edge of hatred. Marriage turns into a brew measured, unequally, of pity and love. The recollections of Michael's death, and of "Nicholas's" own protracted affair with Jean, become for "Nicolas" willed symbols of his penance; these two very different varieties of pain serve to circumscribe and authenticate his life, his self: "Pain was flagellation; pain was proof of existence and of devotion and youth. He suffered Michael's memory, and Jean's and suffered possibility; possibility, also, was pain" (48).

Where Jean becomes a symbol of the chain of women in "Nicholas's" life and of his history of infidelities ("He tabulated women and knew himself defined by them, each diminution or growth signaled by some mate"), his dead son Michael becomes the emblem—the essential, unforgettable emblem—of his failure, of his life's vastation. As Delbanco tells us in the third backward shift, "Nicholas" had "made, of his son, expectation's vehicle, and he attempted to program success." At the same time, however, "some part of him did funnel disappointment, and channel it to Michael—as if capitulation could be hedged, and the bet on failure, and age undercut" (75-76). When Michael dies, when tragedy and chance work to suddenly eliminate that hedge, the double sense of loss and failure multiplies, ramifies: "The loss would be perpetual, he thought, and the absence cumulative, and the sorrow of it, later, would be absolute. . . . Grief would come, Nicholas thought, and fury, and the sense of waste, later, when he was alone. . . . He had no love left, he decided, nor any charity" (93).

Michael's death also heightens upon "Nicholas" the twinned impresses of guilt and regret left from his affair with Jean. At the age of forty, "Nicholas thought himself a ruin of a man"; at forty, "Delbanco" senses the erosive energies of age and time. However, what wears is not only his body, his physical self, but also his emotional self, as he puzzles out his marriage and his extra-marital relationship with Jean. "Delbanco's" married self senses another sort of distance, a separateness that stretches between himself and his family, one more gap to be spanned: "He was attentive to his family and cared and provided for them and knew his love reciprocal—yet they remained discrete" (123). The failure to grow proximate seems at the heart of "Nicholas's" dilemma. Space must be filled—love's abhorrence of an emotional vacuum. Part of that space "Delbanco" occupies with the farm, bought with his wife—"and she was raveled in it past the chance of disengagement" (115). And that farm comes to occupy "Delbanco's" journal-novel.

The other portion of that vacuum—a portion lacking both physical and emotional content—"Nicholas" attempts to fill with his affair with Jean. Thirteen years earlier, he had proposed to Jean, and she had refused him, intent at the time on her career. "Delbanco" acts to resume, rekindle that relationship, not so much out of lust or want ("he had not had affairs"), but out of a wish to recapture portions of his past: "It was, he knew, his own youth he pursued in her, not someone's surrogate, and he was weary, largely, of the memory of youth" (111). Theirs is a relationship that is, indeed, wearied, exhausted, dry; their lovemaking is sterile, mechanical, a sign of love's flight and of "Nicholas's" bleak deficiency: "There was nothing, he announced, he would not foul nor could. Jean was sour and yielding and manipulated him and he was not romantic but was purposeful" (117-18). What might have been love, in the past, now over time and distance has turned bitter, lapsed into pity and self-pity and a love of weakness. Rather than forsake his marriage and his family and his present self, "Nicholas" will feign severance, will promise the consideration of divorce, align himself with fidelity, all the time admitting to a flawed nature that will periodically return him to commitments of the past (125). "Delbanco's" definition of need—or more accurately, his *inability* to define his need—renders his life, his self murky and weak and beyond reach. Resolution escapes him. Escape is resolution.

The root of this dislocated need Delbanco explores in the next retrogressive sequence, wherein "Nicholas" and Jean meet in Rome, thirteen years earlier, in July 1952. Their meeting is a reunion of sorts, a gathering together of need and lack and intense doubt: "He had proposed to her, one year previous, and she had refused. They agreed a separation would clarify choice; secretive, he had withdrawn, yet it was an act of will. She loved him, she announced, and would forever, and would marry no one else, but she had to learn of independence first" (140). Jean's *need* for independence and distance chafes at "Delbanco's" concurrent need for proximity and union (143); unable to connect emotionally, with any real hope of endurance, "Delbanco" nurtures physical desire, and its transient expression of need and dependence. In the past, at the height of their relationship, "Nicholas" and Jean had approximated that sort of marital commitment "Nicholas" now desperately seeks; but even then, the sick fruits of love—the possessiveness, the "ravening" suspicion, the quiet urge for severence—had been apparent: "He had loved, in her, unassailable distance, and attempted to obliterate it, failed. The songs he had found himself choosing to sing each heralded departure, each denied reprieve" (149).

Their relationship becomes figured in a cycle of approaches and departures, of comings and leavetakings. "Nicholas" comes to Rome, after a spring in which he had come to feel "in contact with some central part of himself, some sort of honesty long since lost" (146). He comes to collect the symbol of his supposed need, bridging distance with commitment. He proposes three times, the final offering coming during their lovemaking, his question a sort of third party in their room: "She did not answer, and he entered her and stayed on his knees in the bed, and, for the third time, this time in earnest, proposed. She came and did not answer and he deflated, sweating, determining to leave" (150). This image of radicalized need and union, appropriately enough, is shattered in the silence of Jean's refusal; "Nicholas" withdraws—physically, emotionally—chastened, intent on severance. At the airport, "Nicholas" leaves Jean "in the middle distance," his tears blurring the parting vision, his pain gearing inward:

> Pride turned to self-pity, then, he had howled for the ignominy of it, and was not contrite. He wept and traced a spiral in the window and bisected it, then traced a cone. He wept at her weeping and love and incessant exile and retrieved his boarding pass from his right vest pocket and, shivering, embarked.
>
> (156)

It is difficult to tell just how much of "Nicholas's" pain is authentic, and how much is manufactured, the product of a role—a replicated semblance of woe and want and unanticipated loss, a song long rehearsed.

It is a song that "Nicholas" first learns to sing at the age of twenty: "Nicholas first fell in love, and was reciprocated, when twenty" (168). Love's object here is Sarah—rich, willing, under analysis. The affair begins with promise, with promises. Travel, time, closeness, the imitation of commitment and union, however, bring the affair to wreckage and failure. In part, failure here is bred by the times, which are not right for a love that pretends to endure; politics, art, the tendency to analyze all conspire toward love's ruin. Failure comes, too, from a misfocused view of that world and those times, from a presumed "virginity of self": "His innocence, he decided, was intact; he had a spoiled boy's way, he said, of looking at the world. He wanted to see it unencumbered; even color-blindness served to clarify. He wanted to preserve surprise, and joy, and the sense of selfhood as receptacle; he exalted energy" (179). Young manhood, the unspoiled heart of a "spoiled boy"—ripe pickings for age and its dark, despoiling ways. "Nicholas" stands (at chapter's end) envisioning expanse, possibility, separation:

> He had, sometimes, a sense of outer limits, and that growth was not ascent. He would attend architecture school in New Haven and amass credentials and sever, haltingly, from Sarah; they aped intimacy and knew it long since gone. He was tentative about betrayal and kept a need for possession after the desire to possess.
>
> (185)

The habit of severance, for "Delbanco," is an old one. Well practiced in fraudulent, inauthentic, "aped intimacy," "Nicholas" shows early on the tendency to distance, to possession, to loneliness. Relinquishment remains unlearned—relinquishment of self and of others. "He was best, he decided, alone."

What "Nicholas" *does* learn, in a sequence some four years earlier, are the distancing capabilities of sex, of possession, of an act that is at once capitulation and gain, proximity and distance. At sixteen, "Nicholas" loses his sexual virginity in a scene that later in his life will be refigured and recolored, in Rome, with Jean. Paired, alone, "Nicholas" and his date, Jill, span time and body and consciousness in a sexual fusion (and confusion) of selves: "He pumped and gathered himself and felt a doubling distance, as though he alternated open eyes and the image leapt left, right. He touched Nicholas touching Jill and pictured her as Mary-Anne and the images were units and Nicholas exploded, making them one" (210). In a wondrous and radical union of image and act, "Nicholas" envelops himself *in* his self—balled up, cocoon-like (image of the room in Rome, of the house in which he writes his journal-novel), "gathered"—readying himself for the physical, sexual, and imaginative leap. The same sort of vision that takes him soaring in the long, record-setting arc, also takes him in and out of his self, in and out of his *partner*'s self, distancing him from the act and the actors. This "doubling of distance" also effects itself in the aesthetic, imaginative act, with the confusion or melding of images and names and characters, that novelist doubling the distance between himself and his character who, in a significant way, *is* himself. Thus, to locate the self, "Nicholas" seeks it first in the sexual act, the physical and sometimes spiritual relinquishment of self—and isolation of self. When that fails him, he turns to his journal-novel, where he seeks again to distance consciousness from self.

And in the last segment or chapter of the outer narrative, the two selves, the two skeins of time weave themselves together, as the childhood "Delbanco" shares novelistic space with the "Delbanco" the child is destined to become. (Time ramifies here: the young "Nicholas" is "twenty minutes early . . . and twenty minutes late"—these twenty minutes explode into the twenty years between the author Delbanco and his earlier-born created self—"the boy he'd been deflected in the man he was.") Delbanco removes his character to his earliest reliable memory, to his life between the ages of 7 and 10. Even at that age, "Nicholas felt he played roles. When his mother died he played the grief role; when he walked Betsy Lang home, he played the thoughtful friend" (236). The self as actor is a condition that remains consistent throughout "Delbanco's" life—that nagging sense of inauthenticity, of faked, fabricated self. Selfhood is "embellishment," love and shame are "counter-balanced." Selfhood for "Delbanco," even then, is multiplicity, indefineable variety: the self as infinite pose.

Thus, at the end of this last recollection, Delbanco has the present, still-becoming "Nicholas Delbanco" put to rest the journal-novel that he has been working on all the while Delbanco has been retelling his life. "They were in the attic. It was October sixth." Delbanco brings the narrative round to the date of the penultimate journal entry—the entry that begins *In the Middle Distance*—with "Nicholas" and wife Barbara in the attic of the farmhouse in which "Nicholas" has been laboring to reconstruct and refurbish *both* house and self: a twinned reconstruction of twinned selves. The effort, Delbanco suggests, has failed:

> He wondered if his journal might have value, if he should buy a Mosler Safe or use a safe-deposit box; he decided, no. . . . He organized the letters and the journals and the photographs. His journal was no novel, he decided, nor would be. He put the whole in boxes and aligned the boxes. He covered the boxes against leakage, with a sheet of six-inch insulation that remained.
>
> (249)

"Nicholas" gives in to—or reconciles with—failure, to the uncompleted novel and the incomplete self. He moves *on*, ascends, grows into a resumption of his life with wife and daughter, itself a measure of reconciliation and achievement.

How "Delbanco" comes to this reconciliation is, of course, the product of the inner narrative, the journal-novel that "Delbanco" constructs during his retreat to the farm in Cossayuna. Thus, while Delbanco the author writes from a "distance" of his protagonist-self and writes retrogressively, "Delbanco" the protagonist writes progressively, the journal covering a four-month summer's span. The journal itself is a composite of love letters and journals, of "college mementos and grade school looseleaf books"—most of it the actual data of Delbanco's actual life, a purposeful confusion of the fictive and the real. "People are their data's sum" (248). The question becomes, however, one of authenticity and its measure, for the nature of the data—its source, its tendency to either memory or imagination—seems to determine its acceptability as truth.

Thus, while Delbanco examines the nature of that truth—that "ratification of data"—in his novel, the fictive "Delbanco" examines the nature of individual self in his journal-novel. Incompletion and fragmentation are the ways of "Nicholas's" life. The journal is a fragment of the man's life; the passage of time occupied by the journal is but a segment of a life's passage. And still, "it's endless, it simply doesn't end." So time circles back within **In the Middle Distance**: as the two strands of "Nicholas's" life convene in the final chapter of the outer narrative, and he "buries" his would-be novel on October 6, so Delbanco begins *his* novel with an entry from that same October 6, an indication of the circularity of things.

"Delbanco's" journal is a sort of disjointed, threefold narrative that records the building (or rebuilding) of "Delbanco's" farmhouse, the construction of a novel, *and* the analysis of self—all done simultaneously, concurrently, each a function of the other. House and book are "twinned out-posts." Each comes to represent the personal disunity in "Delbanco's" life, the failure of time and force and imagination to coalesce into meaning. The house becomes an image of the self: "A house decaying over time, then fixed up with masks as to wallpaper, the fireplace stuffed, the floors covered with floors, kitchen roofed" (34). Detail and data gather over time, form strata of physical and autobiographical fact. To reconstruct, one must first deconstruct: "With each layer revealed, the house seems more its stately self, exorcising at last previous ghosts . . . let's work backwards" 67). This accumulation of material, of data, of time's residue must be stripped down, "shucked," placed and identified. The working method (like Delbanco's in the outer narrative) is retrogressive ("it's all backasswards, life"), the uncovering of layer after layer of images applied and fashioned by circumstance and wish and need. But the effort does not always match the reward. In "Delbanco's" case, deconstruction proves far simpler than reconstruction; the house turns to "shell," a lean frame of wall, a skeletal structure in need of "fleshing out."

This is exactly what "Delbanco" seeks to do with his prospective novel. As the house desires solidity, squareness, wood, so the self seeks substance, physicality as word, book, palpable creation. "Delbanco" notes of his novel: "One of the central skeins to weave is self-reflexive here, and having to do with autobiography—how this may flesh, with what sort of fabric; what's the distinction . . . between ravel and unravel; how do we wind up?" (40). How, in other words, may the subjective self be expressed and defined in the objective word? What language reliably and adequately describes the process of a life, the slow advance of being? Such is the concern of the autobiographer. But there is an opposing, yet "complementary problem": "The authentication, via data, of life that's nonexistent, word made flesh. Or, notes toward a supreme nonfiction. And perhaps, the lie can be compulsive (with farmers, women, critics), and perhaps it can be conscious. But the central and ravening paradox (how we each forge truths) should certainly apply" (64). The province proper of the novelist is adjunct to that of the autobiographer. Both deal with data, with word, with creation: distinction lies in beginning and end points. The novelist seeks to transform word into self, into believable and truth-telling flesh; the autobiographer takes flesh and consciously twists it into wishful, tendentious word. So "Delbanco's" imagined protagonist remarks: "Fiction, as I never tire telling my class in fiction is a series of strategies for truth. Autobiography, as I never tire telling my class in autobiography, is a selection of truths to adumbrate fiction" (65). Which self is genuine: that which is created, fabricated from selective and uncertain memory, or that which affirms the true, the nonfictional, through fiction? Where resides the lie—or, more appropriately, the *greater* lie? The novelist lies to attain truth. The autobiographer retells those truths that most securely underwrite a fraudulent self.

This problem of authenticity is more a concern of Delbanco's (after all, the source is, in actuality, *his* journal—confusion upon confusion—*his* script for the film adaptation of **The Martlet's Tale**). For "Delbanco," the more immediate problem is one of organization and purpose. He must first identify the nature of his effort ("Calling this a novel. That."), locate plot, protagonist, principle. Detail accumulates at random, declines toward chaos: "I'm growing weary of data, do wish for stories to tell" (131). The artist must shape his material, invest it with meaning, substance, resonance, pattern: "I need a metaphor, some sort of tale to tell. How the tomato plants found plaster at their back. Full of fits and starts, mirroring this wacky way: not the austere chronicle planned" (95). Time—*real* time—resists definition and circumscription, remains amorphous, vexatious. And so "Nicholas's" book, its pattern, abandons the linear and adopts another form, becomes a doubled medium: "What is this book but record: the motion circular, the pattern spiral, and therefore the needle transcribes a straight line" (128). The book circles inward, tracking ever-decreasing, ever-limiting circles, slowly, inexorably focusing in on self, the record's center, the end of the downward wind, of time's unraveling.

What substance and pattern the book does obtain comes from the adaptation of "Delbanco's" relationship—his failed relationship—with Jean. Jean's voice expresses itself through a series of letters inserted, italicized, into the text of the journal (perhaps one of the few *pure* fictions of this part of Delbanco's novel). In "Delbanco's" imagined reworking of this relationship, Jean (known as "K." in the working plan) and the protagonist ("Delbanco"?) are divorced; K's letters translate into pleas for reconciliation, confessions, detailed litanies of suffering. She preaches distance (72-73), but as "Nicholas" confirms, "There are certain sorts of distance one simply cannot bridge, a kind of severance apology can't heal. Trust, that difficult thing to make, is easy to break, and irrevocably" (94). The break in their relationship derives from the protagonist's (or "Nicholas's") unfaithfulness, the same sort of confused and worried lapse from grace that plagues "Nicholas" in the outer narrative: "What; sexual resentment turned to jealousy on the one hand, disdain on the other. Compounded by repeated infidelity, and the concomitant guilt" (36). "Nicholas's" distancing (or that of his protagonist's—the confusion doubles in the journal) is conscious, sought after, an insistent part of his work: "But I'm willing this separation, and writing it, and have long since decided it needful" (164). Separation becomes fact through its expression, becomes a sort of artifact generated from fragments of the imagination, a written, willed thing (188). When a by-product of love, separation is rarely unilateral. Lovers commit themselves to severance with the same fervor, the same single-mindedness that first brought them together.

Furthermore, the analysis of that severance bears little real reward, for the past leaves, at best, an ephemeral trail. The past—time—admits to no exactitude. The most one can hope for in reconstituting that past, and one's past self, is guesswork, "patchwork." Thus, "Nicholas's" attempt at reconstructing the history of his self remains scrambled, fractured, incomplete; his journal and would-be novel fail because of the inherent chaos and discontinuity of the past and of its relation to the present self. "Nicholas" feels "bloody elegiac" every time he sits at his typewriter, hunting the thread of fact and circumstance that will lead him back to a previous self—"elegiac" because that self has been necessarily buried. Too much time, too much distance intervene. Dead, outworn selves are shucked, shed, interred, almost ritualistically, to propagate the new re-imagined self.

This casting-off of the past's leavings is doubly important in **In the Middle Distance,** for it permits a double reconciliation. Just as "Nicholas" comes to terms with his present, disordered self and buries that representation of his past selves, his journal-novel—so Nicholas Delbanco, through the experience of composition and decomposition, of compilation and recovery, fixes upon a new private *and* aesthetic self at the end of **In the Middle Distance.** Delbanco's purpose here is only partly to explore the *nature* of autobiography, and its distinctness from imaginative fiction. He also *uses* the autobiographical mode as a remedy, as a sort of "talking cure." **In the Middle Distance,** in fact, conforms with some measure of consistency to the autobiographical structure described by Paul Jay in his book, *Being in the Text: Self-Representation from Wordsworth to Roland Barthes.* According to Jay, the distinction between autobiography and fictional autobiography is "finally pointless": "For if by 'fictional' we mean 'made up' 'created,' or 'imagined,'—something, that is, which is literary and not 'real'—then we have merely defined the ontological status of any text, autobiographical or not" (16). Jay goes on to argue that "each work develops out of its author's confrontation with a particular problem—the problem of literary self-representation" (21).

As for the restorative function of autobiography, Jay connects the self-reflexive literary work with the Freudian notion of a "talking cure":

> Of course, what is crucial to the transforming power of the talking cure is Freud's recognition of its doubly creative nature. The subject's cure is bound up in the ability to participate in generating a creative story in which key recollections are linked to form a therapeutic autobiographical narrative. However, the past events recollected in such a process may not in fact be "events" at all but, rather, imagined moments in a "history" being created in and by the act of analysis itself.
>
> (25)

The autobiographer effects his cure by concurrently effecting a life-story—part fact, part imagined history—that attempts to "historicize conscious memory into an eventually 'perfected' narrative" (26). The content, moreover, of that narrative derives from personal crisis. The *form,* Jay contends, "is determined in good measure by aesthetic and philosophical crises" (27). Such is the work cut out for himself by "Nicholas Delbanco," as he attempts to reconstruct and re-order his own shattered self through the narrative of his journal-novel. For "Delbanco," however, the narrative refuses to coalesce, to cohere, to form a logical, linear pattern. But the mere realization of his self's fragmentation, and of the nature of his own being, is enough to move him to a form of recovery: to a return to family and familial wholeness (even when that very family has been reduced and made unwhole by death).

For the other Delbanco, however, the novel serves as both a proof and a disproof of the self's authentication. To refute the verity of autobiographical self, Delbanco purposely shifts the viewpoint of his novel, writing in the outer narrative in the third person, moving to the first person in the inner narrative-journal. The voices grow confused, mixed, questioning. Delbanco consciously tests here the reliability of the "I," of the self-conscious, self-reflexive autobiographer, by opposing it with the distanced third-person perspective of the novelistic narrator. Delbanco multiplies this confusion with his use of "authentic" letters between himself and his editor, offering a self-conscious nod to the creative origins of *In the Middle Distance*, to its fictional roots, posing almost another sort of self in the author-editor relationship. He goes further, including a letter from editor to photographer, whose subject is the very factual photo of Nicholas Delbanco—a tangible proof of external self. Delbanco also includes a portion of his *own* script for his *own* adaptation of his *own* first novel, *The Martlet's Tale* and excerpts from the journal kept by Delbanco during the making of that film (never released).

Delbanco also disrupts the temporal flow of his novel, telling the story in the outer narrative in reverse, time shifting backwards (with further backward leaps within each specific sequence); while in the journal-inner narrative, he moves time ostensibly forward, though even then Delbanco throws time out of joint by using the original dates of *his* journal within the entries dated by "Delbanco" as he supposedly creates them: the contradiction of time by time. This sort of interrupted narrative (as Jay points out) is characteristic of twentieth-century fiction—a confusion of genres: while the novel and the autobiography share "narrative modes," and while "meaning lies in sequence," Delbanco consciously and simultaneously blurs *and* identifies the differences in genres, illuminating the several weaknesses in both.

Finally, whereas traditional autobiography conflates protagonist, narrator, and author into a single entity, Delbanco purposely multiplies these three beings into four separate forms: Nicholas Delbanco, novelist in a real world; "Nicholas Delbanco," the subject of that other Delbanco's narrative; "Nicholas Delbanco," keeper of the journal and subject of his own introspection; and Nicholas Delbanco, autobiographer of his own life, both real and fictive, author of the data of his own life and of his created character-self.

However, *In the Middle Distance* serves also as an affirmation, as an aesthetic response to an aesthetic crisis, the same sort of crisis figured, says Jay, in Proust's *A la recherche du temps perdu* and Joyce's *A Portrait of the Artist as a Young Man*. The artist, says Jay, attempts to "bridge the distance between past and present—between himself and his own textual representation of himself" (31). For Joyce and Proust, this meant finding another route to the veritable self, so that in their work, "Chronological narrative remains as the structural principle . . . but the truth becomes a function not of remembering but of fictionalizing" (36). The artist fictionalizes history because the essential self relies upon the creative process that is to "forge" it. Before that newly created self can emerge, however, old images of self must be canceled. Such, writes Jay, is the process described in *A la recherche* and *Portrait*: "For both writers, the autobiographical novel is a kind of burial place, a place in which the past is laid to rest in the very act of giving it new life in a fictional form" (146). For rebirth, there must first be a death. The artist must forget his past, must slay past selves in order to fashion one anew. The process, in fact, proves more significant than the product of that process. The artist undergoes a sort of "conversion" through his work, through the sustained effort in the *present* moments of creation, and not in the recollection of the past: "Thus, the *work* of the self-reflexive artist has an importance that transcends the importance of the *finished* work" (149). Such is the effect upon "Nicholas Delbanco," whose journal-novel remains unfinished, incomplete, but who is, in essence, redeemed by the *process* of his effort. In the end, the artist, by use of the narrative mode, "retains the vision of the self as a unified and whole metaphysical essence," even while deconstructing that self in the aesthetic process: a paradox befitting a very paradoxical self.

And such is the paradox pursued by Delbanco in *In the Middle Distance*. For his character and proleptic ego, "Nicholas Delbanco," the self remains un-unified. "Delbanco" cannot imaginatively reconstruct the self, cannot shape it into the form of a novel and a narrative, perhaps because that past is largely Nicholas Delbanco's own. "Delbanco's" imagination fails him, as does his self—all those "shucked selves" remain disparate, fractured. Yet the work *process,* as noted above, does heal him, does prove therapeutic.

For Delbanco the author, the content of *In the Middle Distance* may or may not be a response to a personal, private crisis. The novel's form, however, seems a clear aesthetic response to particular aesthetic problems afflicting Delbanco at that time in his career. *In the Middle Distance* is a pivot-point in Delbanco's career, where he shifts both the focus and the source of his art, where he subordinates memory to imagination. Delbanco, like Proust and Joyce, must "willfully forget" the past to create "an imaginatively conceived Other." Delbanco must project yet another form of *distance*—the distance between his past, autobiographical self and his present, authorial self, between memory and the aesthetic act. Before *In the Middle Distance,* Delbanco's fiction is highly autobiographical, revealing a substantial reliance upon individual experience for the stuff of his art. After *In the Middle Distance,* Delbanco tempers this mediation of memory with a greater infusion of imagination; instead of recollecting the past for his material, Delbanco collects the data of the present and of his present imaginative self. As a result, the very style of his work begins to change as well, turning from a highly allusive, recondite, referential kind of prose to a more traditional, accessible, narrative-minded style. Thus, at the end of *In the Middle Distance,* the Delbanco who signs the novel speaks out in a new, authoritative voice, issuing a declaration of aesthetic and political belief: "I hate this rhetoric. I believe it necessary now. Nor can the artist survive if only as court jester, though he might have earned the jest. Things are not amusing any more" (250). Art must serve a more serious function. The times demand it.

The times—and Delbanco's art—also demand a reaffirmed vision of self, and that redefined self is what emerges from the pages of *In the Middle Distance.* The book works as autobiography and as fiction, turning Delbanco into the "novelist of himself," figuring a proleptic Delbanco who locates the "anticipated future" in the novelistic present. Delbanco "re-authors" his past and future life, mating memory and fiction in a union that generates a whole, yet multi-faceted, imagined autobiography. The past, and the past self, lie as parts of the vastation of Delbanco's process, but the present, and the present self, emerge resurrected, strong, eager to work. Art, life, self—each awaits retrieval, resumption. Truth remains in the distance. The leap toward that truth remains, for Delbanco, to be made—and made again.

Works Cited

Delbanco, Nicholas. *In the Middle Distance.* New York: William Morrow & Company, 1971.

Jay, Paul. *Being in the Text: Self-Representation from Wordsworth to Roland Barthes.* Ithaca: Cornell Univ. Press, 1984.

Morris, Gregory L. "An Interview with Nicholas Delbanco." *Contemporary Literature* 25 (Winter 1984): 387-96.

Pascal, Roy. *Design and Truth in Autobiography.* Cambridge: Harvard Univ. Press, 1960.

Eugene Wildman (review date 23 July 1989)

SOURCE: Wildman, Eugene. "Going Away Again." *Chicago Tribune Books* (23 July 1989): 4-5.

[*In the following review, Wildman describes* Running in Place *as part autobiography, part travel literature, and observes that the book is an expression of Delbanco's "love affair" with the area of Provence, France.*]

The interplay of memory and landscape is the subject of this non-fiction offering by novelist Nicholas Delbanco. The book [*Running in Place*] is part autobiography, part travel literature and is an account of the author's several stays in Provence, that storied region of the South of France. It is a description of a love affair with the land, a deepening intimacy, an eventual, inevitable growing apart and the need to have a place to belong to.

Provence has been a favorite locale of writers and artists through the centuries. The traditions of courtly love and the troubador poetry that celebrates it were born there. In the 14th Century the papacy was there, the seat of ecclesiastical power shifting from Rome to Avignon. Cezanne and Van Gogh made its landscapes famous.

Ford Madox Ford wrote a book about Provence. Henry James and D. H. Lawrence both sang its praises. Albert Camus is buried there. James Baldwin, a longtime friend of the author, lived there, as did actor Dirk Bogarde. Of still uncertain aesthetic interest, Baby Doc Duvalier fled to Provence after his overthrow in Haiti.

Yet *Running in Place* is less a look backward than a summing up and reassessment. It opens in 1987 with Delbanco and his wife and two daughters about to embark on their latest visit. The daughters are in no way enthralled at the prospect. Then it cuts to 1961, when Delbanco, an 18-year-old student only dreaming of becoming a writer, has occasion to make his first trip. Thereafter the narrative is a kind of fugue, continually cutting to the immediate past while detailing the progress of successive trips. It is a nice strategy. Mere nostalgia never stands a chance; the present is always reasserting its claim.

Delbanco's manner is loosely anecdotal, and one of these anecdotes is a gem. He sets out for the cathedral in Aix, which houses the triptych by Nicholas Froment depicting the legendary Good King Rene. Things go wrong from the start. At the cathedral, repairs are going on. Dust is everywhere. An attendant on duty has heard of the king but knows nothing of any painting. When, after much searching, it is finally located, the triptych is closed and locked. Delbanco is crushed. Outside, a beggar accosts him, exhorting him as he is a Christian to give money. He tells the beggar he is not one and won't. Whereupon the other showers him with curses, each more spiteful and artful than the last. By the time Delbanco is out of earshot, already he feels better.

On another occasion Baldwin comes for lunch, his customary ragtag, bohemian entourage in tow. They make a spirited group. Suddenly, in the midst of their jollity, they spy through the window an elderly couple, cameras at the ready, peering curiously at them. The couple, dear friends of the landlady, are the last of the Hapsburgs and the Hohenzollerns. What their eyes registered, Delbanco notes, must have seemed the direst fulfillment of Spengler's prophecies in the "The Decline of the West."

The high point of the book may be the tale of Alex and Maija Bechstein, a 60-year-old Tristan and Isolde. He is a charming bachelor, she a proper Swiss wife. It is magic the moment they meet. She forsakes all to join him. They are ecstatically, passionately, devotedly happy. Hardly are they settled, however, than he is stricken by cancer and dies. No matter that her joy was short-lived, that her children and the townspeople at home have denounced her. She has no regrets and would do it again.

Much as Delbanco loves Provence, there is little left to hold him. A place exists to be written about. You cannot otherwise revisit it. The flirtation with expatriation is over. His daughters are the measure of what is true for him now. "What time is it back home?" one of them asks midway through. "I'm looking forward to looking back on this," the other puts in.

Perhaps the last word should be Maija's, in her own awkward, inimitable style. "Or do you finish or do you start. And both of those are simple. The hardest thing is to continue. That's what I find hard."

Merle Rubin (review date 1 September 1989)

SOURCE: Rubin, Merle. "Travel Writing that Goes No Place." *Christian Science Monitor* 81, no. 195 (1 September 1989): 13.

[*In the following review, Rubin is highly critical of* Running in Place, *describing the book as unoriginal, uninteresting, monotonous, and poorly organized.*]

Society hostess Elsa Maxwell is often credited with turning the South of France, specifically the Cote d'Azur, into a fashionable summer resort in the 1920s. (Before that, it was a place "resorted to" chiefly in the winter.) But Provence, the region of southeastern France that includes that stretch of coastline, has a long history of colorful associations: Roman Gaul, the Albigensian heresy, the medieval troubadours who virtually invented "romance." A land of sunshine, olive trees, olive oil, garlic, honey, lavender, and perfume, Provence has held a special appeal for painters, who reveled in the clear brilliant light of the region.

The South of France must hold special associations for author Nicholas Delbanco, one presumes, or he would not have written [*Running in Place*] a book on the subject. But whatever this region may mean to Mr. Delbanco, very little in the way of inspiration, information, interest, or pleasure is conveyed in the lifeless pages of this very derivative, poorly organized, and monotonously written book.

Delbanco first visited the region as a college student in 1961. He returned subsequently at various periods of his life: as an aspiring young writer carrying on a love affair with an aspiring young singer, as a newly married husband and father, and, in 1987, as a mature parent of adolescent girls.

The narrative [of *Running in Place*] shifts desultorily back and forth among time periods, a hodgepodge of banal, pretentious ruminations on predictable topics, excruciatingly tiresome snippets of Delbanco family conversations, and dull anecdotes about semi-famous people Delbanco has met, but oh-so-tastefully refuses to name for fear of invading their "privacy." (Insofar as his gifts for rendering a memorable character, telling a good story, or choosing a revealing incident are negligible, he would seem to be in little danger of delineating anyone's personality, let alone invading their privacy!)

Here is how he renders a woman he calls "Lilo Rosenthal": "She said, 'You must call me Lily,' and invited us to tea. She wore yellow trousers and a silk shirt with a floral pattern. Her jewelry was silver, and her bracelets matched her earrings and the pendant at her neck. Her hair was dark brown, meticulously coifed, with just a streak of gray; reading glasses dangled from a cord. Her eyes were brown and green." (Greenish brown or one brown eye and one green? one wonders.)

Only in the case of meeting that very famous American-in-exile, novelist James Baldwin, does Delbanco decide to drop the pseudonymity. It's just as well, because the only lively aspect of Delbanco's account is the vivid image Baldwin's name conjures up.

The descriptions of places are as weak as the descriptions of people. Driving south from Paris, Delbanco doesn't even attempt to evoke the changes in the landscape—probably because he senses he can't compete with so many other writers who have done it so well. Instead, he lists the place-names en route.

"An excellent writer is among us," proclaims the dust-jacket quote from the *New York Times* (mercifully unattributed), "and if we neglect him, we shall have to apologize to posterity." I somehow doubt apologies will be in order: This weak excuse for a book appears to have been supported by more grants than were needed to build Lincoln Center. The author of 10 less-than-memorable novels, a story collection, a disappointing book called, **Group Portrait: Conrad, Crane, Ford, James, and Wells,** recipient of Guggenheim, NEA, Yaddo, and other fellowships, Delbanco is director of the MFA in Writing at the University of Michigan and something called the Hopwood Awards Program.

Scion of a well-off banking family who fled Germany for England during the war, Delbanco grew up in America, graduated from Harvard, and began his writing career with a contract in hand for an unwritten first novel. As a young man, he toddled off to Europe, because he'd heard that's what writers (like Hemingway) did. But it would be unfair to blame Hemingway as an "influence" on Delbanco's style. This book is, indeed, underwritten: not only in the sense of being flat and colorless, but in the sense that it is the product of a career underwritten by a vast, uncoordinated, self-perpetuating system of grants, fellowships, writing programs, and awards that all too often seem to foster the overprivileged and the undertalented.

Readers in search of first-class travel writing to liven up the remaining days of summer would be well advised to skip this little side trip to Provence in favor of Ford Madox Ford's tribute to the region, or perhaps the work of the accomplished novelist, biographer, and travel writer Sybille Bedford (who spent time in the South of France herself). Bedford's splendid, *A Visit to Don Otavio: A Traveller's Tale from Mexico,* first published in 1953, has been reissued in a handsome paperback by Eland/Hippocrene Books Inc.

Here one finds the keenly observant eye, the knack for focusing on telling incidents, the elegant style, and the sense of adventure that can make travel writing as illuminating as travel itself.

Melissa Pritchard (review date 4 February 1990)

SOURCE: Pritchard, Melissa. "The Perils of Literature." *Chicago Tribune Books* (4 February 1990): 6-7.

[*In the following review, Pritchard praises* The Writer's Trade *as a brilliantly ordered and controlled book that examines the "craft and peril" of being a writer.*]

Each of us erects our hidden altars, secretly hoping for salvation from mortality. Art exists as a particularly potent religion, the artist exalted as free agent, as re-creator of the universe. In Nicholas Delbanco's 13th book and second collection of short stories, **The Writers' Trade,** the craft and peril of being a writer is scrupulously examined.

In the title story, a young man, Mark Fusco, achieves extraordinary success with the publication of his first novel. Intoxicated by language and literature, discovering joy in his solitary craft, he attends the sweet triumph of a publication party, receiving adulation as bounty and gift. Afterward, feeling "there was nothing he could not attain, no prospect unattainable," he is deep in his giddy dream of success when the train he is on hits and kills a young woman. Abruptly he is diminished by the understanding that life goes on, that "what was out there, on the track, found him irrelevant." His reaction, instinctively, is to take and absorb this stuff of life, write it down, elevate life into art.

In **"And with Advantages,"** Ben, another young, naively ambitious writer, courts elderly, eminent men of letters, hoping at once to supplant them and to earn their imprimatur. Instead he witnesses old men foolishly lapsing into adolescent humor, exchanging souvenir erotic photographs and memories. As in the title story, this young writer, led by his colossal yet innocent vanity to attempt the transformation of life into art, instead finds life implacable and largely indifferent to his powers. Like Mark Fusco, Ben learns only that he understands nothing; he is painfully humbled, his vanity and ego assaulted.

"You Can Use My Name" follows the divergent trajectories of two writers' careers. While Richard is victimized and devoured by his own overwhelming success, his friend Adam is locked into oblivion, a bohemian whose life continually misses achievement. Each seeks and fails to find easy salvation in art; Richard's potency as an artist and Adam's artistic impotence prove equally devastating.

The world leaches the artist's power, erodes the muse, mutes the voice. Acclaim is as ruinous a distraction as more moderate success, when writers, finding jobs teaching, become too tepid in their art, having failed in failing to go far enough. Repeatedly, through his characters, Delbanco warns the struggling artist to get outside life and its limitations, to not be distracted, to simply work.

In several of these stories, characters look upon the conception of a child as some vague insurance of immortality. And in many of Delbanco's tales, tensions exists between the artist's need to keep his soul and work inviolate and the need to earn a living, with its consequent encounters with worldly standards, the anguished measurement of success or failure.

"The Day's Catch" follows David, another young writer, a passionate idealist and diligent recorder of stories, through his love affair with the young woman, Alice, who becomes his wife. Delbanco poignantly observes the privacy of lovers, an isolation comparable to that of the artist. Still love, like art, is vulnerable to corruption when pulled back into life to endure its daily bruises.

A writer has two selves: the observer, the aloof outsider, and the passionate, emotional self. However much his or her published work has matched the original ambition, the writer often must face that arid loss of faith that can occur to pilgrims of any persuasion. Yet even in this struggle with darkness, impotence and despair, the artist is tempted to create once again by the fresh, sensuous detail, the pull of event and character, the voice thrown and amplified. Faced with the inadequacy of insufficient passion, the artist must push beyond quiet panic and persist. There can be subtle heroism in a writer who is serving a greater talent, reduced to the role of an acolyte, as in the story **"Palinurus."**

The young woman of **"The Day's Catch,"** Alice describes her epiphany, an experience of light in which she witnesses the world as a transparent membrane, seeing the mystical connectedness of everything. In Delbanco's final story, **"Everything,"** an old and senile writer experiences the relentless procession of time and loss—his fame and reputation of a greater density than his own failing flesh.

As Alice's experience of light gave her a sense of wholeness, senility confers upon this writer's intelligence a place where the dead and the living mingle, where memory and the present are indistinguishable, where all stories are one story, all voices one voice and life runs together like water. This involuntary disengagement from his own artistic ambitions, this collapse of the ego, suggests where true art lies, at the point of death of the self.

Contradicting the young writer's inflated sense of self, here is the stance of ultimate humility from which greatness can emerge. But in **"Everything,"** the aged author, newly wise, ironically has lost potency, the power to create.

The Writers' Trade is brilliantly ordered and controlled; its voices are many yet all perhaps are Delbanco's own—anguished, searching and stern. Both mourning and celebrating the writer's life, the bitter cost of artistic freedom, the power and gift of voice, this is an unsparing and radiant book.

Charles Simmons (review date 8 February 1990)

SOURCE: Simmons, Charles. "The Non-Telling Detail." *Washington Post* (8 February 1990): B3.

[*In the following review, Simmons comments that most of the stories in* The Writer's Trade *are flawed and bogged down by tedious details, but does reserve praise for two of the stories which he contends are well-written.*]

Most of these nine stories are full of faults, some more interesting than others. In the title story [of *The Writer's Trade*] 22-year-old Mark Fusco has just published a first novel. It gets good reviews, and he appears to be at the start of a successful writing career. Author Nicholas Delbanco describes his professional progress: "Mark was learning to provide corroborative detail for his characters: birthday parties, a distaste for lima beans, a preference in socks. 'Make a catalogue,' his writing teacher had advised. 'Make it on three-by-five cards. Know everything you can. Tell yourself the person despises lima beans. Try to decide if she likes snow peas or string beans better . . .'"

Delbanco himself follows this bad advice throughout, with wearisome results. For instance, in **"And with Advantages,"** a story about a 26-year-old writer, Ben, and his relationship with an old, ailing, famous writer, Ben goes from the old man's funeral to a girlfriend's apartment: ". . . they opened wine. The rooms were familiar, not strange. The bear rug by the bricked-up fireplace, the Indian clubs and the basket of dried flowers, the Miro prints and picture of the swimming team at Smith, the Marimekko bedspread and the rubber tree, the Exer-cycle by the dressing room and mirror on the mantel—all these remained in place." This list of cliches is presented generically and without irony. It is word-to-word specific and, all told, indefinite. These are not corroborative details, just details.

The exact detail takes some finding. Or some genius. Chekhov, who wrote fast, dropped endless exact details. When we meet the lady with the dog on vacation in Yalta she is wearing a beret. She was "always wearing the same beret," Chekhov says, "and always with the same white dog." When we learn what the story is about we understand that the dog gave the lady a certain respectability, like traveling with a child, and that the beret was sadly festive, cautiously flirtatious, a provincial's gesture. Lima beans won't do that.

Let me quote another short passage from the same story. One night Ben observes three old-timers, friends of the old novelist and now guests. Ben thinks: "They would tell me how careers are made, how their own were fashioned; they could speak of the late great. They might describe Manhattan when it was an easy town, when Harlem was an easy place to visit after dark. They had known Theodore Dreiser, Babe Ruth, Thomas Hart Benton, Josephine Baker, Chaplin, Chaliapin, Pound. They could explain the usages of the smoke-filled room, the proper measure of ambition with mete modesty, the secrets of longevity and growth." Lima beans would be more useful.

The longest story, **"The Day's Catch"** exemplifies another, more damaging fault. David, 22, fresh out of Harvard, goes to Martha's Vineyard to write. To support himself he delivers fish and takes care of a blind boy, son of a widow who is rich by having married an heir who drank himself to death. All of this is told in great detail, which leads us to believe it will come to something. Not so. David meets Alice, who moves in with him. Part 2 opens some years later. David and Alice are married and have a son. They go to Tortola to see if anything is left of their marriage. There they meet an old pal of David's who makes a pass at Alice. Alice remembers at length the last time she saw her father. He showed up with an Asian sweetheart, a nurse's aide who had taken care of him after he had been released from a prisoner-of-war camp during the Korean War. The last paragraph tells us obliquely that David and Alice's marriage is done. I suppose the point of the lengthy biographies and flashbacks is to give an impression of narrative largess; the impression I got is of a machine made of attachments but which does nothing.

Two stories work. **"His Masquerade,"** about a well-known poet's visit to a campus to give a reading, is ingenious and witty. In the concluding **"Everything,"** another aging writer ponders with what is left of his brain his long, eventful life. Delbanco's all too ready elegiac mode serves him well here. By many signs I understood that these stories intend to impart a tragic sense of life; I felt only a troubled sense of it.

Walter Cummins (review date winter 1993)

SOURCE: Cummins, Walter. Review of *Writers and Their Craft*, by Nicholas Delbanco. *Studies in Short Fiction* 30, no. 1 (winter 1993): 102-03.

[*In the following review, Cummins asserts that* Writers and Their Craft *is entertaining, but that it fails to provide new ideas or a fresh perspective on the craft of writing.*]

This collection, [*Writers and Their Craft,*] material originally contained in a two-volume issue of *Michigan Quarterly Review,* is an olio of essays, interviews, memoirs, short statements, stories, and even cartoons that the editors hoped would provide "a kind of road map through [American fiction] of the 1990s, a work whose polyphonic structure represents its subject with high fidelity." What they have produced is entertaining and frequently illuminating; but it fails to function as a road map. Anyone attempting to follow it for guidance would end up lost in a tangle of conflicting routes. The effect is a version of the logical conundrum in which a traveler at a fork in a road asks directions of a man who may belong to one of two tribes—one whose members always lie or one whose members always tell the truth. Thus, some of the 100 or so contributors consider minimalism a breakthrough, and others consider it an abomination; some despair over the vacuousness of today's writing, and others find an abundance of riches.

Equivalents of much of the material in the book—the stories and essays and interviews—could be found in many magazines, literary or otherwise. Unique is a section of almost 200 pages called "A Symposium on Contemporary American Fiction" in which 90 writers arranged alphabetically from Linsey Abrams to Jose Yglesias respond to a general question: "Granted that contemporary American fiction is a variety of things, which kind of recent writing interests you especially, and, in your opinion, is most deserving of more attention and more readers?" Some of the reactions deal specifically with those questions; others use them as an excuse to vent whatever is on the responder's mind. Some are earnest and thoughtful, others pithy or disingenuous.

However, the overall impression produced is one of déjà vu, opinions that are reruns of statements made about American fiction, say, 25 years ago. Of course, some of the vocabulary of the debate is new—postmodernism, minimalism, multiculturalism—but the basic attitudes fall into several familiar categories: e.g., nothing worthwhile is being written today, with the rare exception of work by x, y, and z; the workshops are to blame by turning out skillful writers with nothing to say; we are blessed by all the excellent work of our time; innovation is meaningless because what really matters is compelling fiction that probes the human soul; the old forms are played out; we must return to Joyce, Chekhov, Hemingway, Flannery O'Connor; publishers care only about profit; the important new writers come from Latin America or Eastern Europe or multicultural backgrounds; my own writing hasn't gotten the recognition it deserves.

Beyond the variety of opinions the symposium assemblage is useful for gathering, with photographs, the 90 current writers who responded and for offering in aggregate an extensive compilation of books and writers they recommend as the best of current fiction.

In the large majority of stories and essays they chose for the book, the editors come down on the side of tradition—familiar narrative techniques and approaches that assume fiction should illuminate the way we live now.

James Idema (review date 1 October 1995)

SOURCE: Idema, James. "Fatal Decisions." *Chicago Tribune Books* (1 October 1995): 6.

[*In the following review, Idema praises* In the Name of Mercy *as an entertaining, masterfully written novel that includes a number of compelling characters. Idema comments that, although Delbanco's views on the issue of doctor-assisted suicide seem ambiguous, the story is thoroughly engaging.*]

What seems for much of Nicholas Delbanco's riveting new novel to be an eloquent plea for legitimatizing euthanasia becomes in the long run more a cautionary tale. Man cannot be trusted with the institutionalized practice of assisted suicide, Delbanco appears to say. For all its merciful intentions, it is a deed so vulnerable to abuse as to be morally unacceptable. What is wrought "in the name of mercy" is often more wicked than good.

Meanwhile, to explore this enormously complex issue, Delbanco has [with *In the Name of Mercy*] written a terrifically entertaining book: a swift, white-knuckle thriller, with a big cast of compelling characters and a theme direct from today's news pages. That its point of view seems somewhat ambiguous detracts not at all from its engaging plot.

In the Name of Mercy is difficult to put down, even more difficult to forget once you have put it down. Never mind that it all ends in a horrific mess, with the innocent hero, an altruistic young physician, walking away from his calling, slipping into anonymous oblivion and leaving neither good nor evil ascendant in his wake.

As the story opens, Peter Julius, M.D., watching his young wife in the final agonies of her struggle with melanoma, helps her end her pain once and for all. The experience persuades him to accept an offer to direct a hospice for critically ill patients. The hospice is part of a new medical center situated in Bellehaven, a backwater town in southern Michigan. From the very beginning matters go awry.

It doesn't help that Dr. Jack Kevorkian works not far from there: an angel of mercy to one faction, the infamous "Doctor Death" to another. He "brings down this lunatic posse, these righteous right-to-lifers," as one of the center's founders complains. Nor does it help that the Bellehaven Daily is run by suspicious bigots and that it publishes unsigned letters to the editor. Like a Greek chorus, they comment periodically on the drama.

In addition to problems of public relations, desperate rivalries permeate the staff and contention over treatment is rife. The real troubles, however, begin when a long-term AIDS patient suddenly dies, and his companion charges that he was murdered. Then things really heat up, as a number of unexplained deaths occur, and it becomes apparent a killer with intimate access to hospital procedures is at work.

Several characters have both the means and the motives to do the nasty stuff, which makes the unraveling of the mystery a rewarding exercise for the reader—one that leads to a most satisfying surprise. Indeed, the finale includes a scene so balefully shocking that this reader, for one, protested aloud.

Featured players include chief resident Jim Kelly, whose troubled private life leads him to a blackmail scheme with Penny Lamson, a lusty nurse whose dream is to go to Paris, Richard Trueman and J. Harley Andrews, who founded the hospital and unexpectedly become patients there; Trip Conley, the clean-cut, ruthless president of the facility, with access to every department; and Rebecca Forsythe, a noted spokesperson on assisted suicide, whose book *Undiscovered Country* equates death and orgasm. Her love affair late in the story with Peter Julius sets up its ghastly ending.

Dr. Julius, the protagonist, is above suspicion but not always in sight, and he seems at times something of a non-participating observer—for example, his laconic response to the horror at the end, while consistent, is somehow unsatisfying.

Nevertheless, one of the chief pleasures of this book is the way the narrative moves seamlessly from one character to another—sometimes within quotation marks, more often in a kind of subconscious dialogue or soliloquy.

In one place, Trip Conley, late for a luncheon appointment with his unhappy alcoholic wife, fantasizes as he drives to their restaurant how their conversation will go after he apologizes to her: "Christine was on her second drink and staring at the menu, trying to decide if she would forgive him this once. She'd look up while he took his chair and started to apologize and, smiling that good smile of hers, the one that cost three years of orthodontia and a nose job, say, 'Don't mention it, let's not discuss it, I'm certain you had a good reason.' It would keep him guessing, and she liked to do that too.

"Or, more likely, she *would* mention it and blame him for standing her up. . . . Then she'd start in on the usual, how if it hadn't been for her there'd *be* no comfortable table, no reservation at a restaurant and nothing to buy dinner with and while he was perfecting his manners and learning the fine art of punctuality why didn't he acquire some gratitude also, you son of a bitch."

When he does actually join her, the reality is worse than what he's imagined. It is masterly writing. So is a chapter devoted to the thoughts of a dying AIDS patient, a poem of both bitter humor and pure rage.

John Leggett (review date 3 October 1995)

SOURCE: Leggett, John. "Can Death Be Humane and Cost-Effective?" *Los Angeles Times* (3 October 1995): 6.

[*In the following review, Leggett comments that the novel* In the Name of Mercy *is a provocative story, but that it fails to clarify the arguments for and against doctor-assisted suicide.*]

Nicholas Delbanco has taken on a provocative theme in his new novel, **In the Name of Mercy**.

He has seen the conflict between a doctor's Hippocratic obligation to heal, to do no harm, to leave the ending of a life to God and the contrary belief, acclaimed by Dr. Jack Kevorkian, that there is mercy in hastening the death of an incurable patient in pain.

It is certainly a timely issue, given that today's medical profession is so technically advanced that it can, at great expense, prolong life unnaturally.

Delbanco lays his tale of healing and death at the Trueman-Andrews hospital and hospice in Bellehaven, Mich.

This enterprise is part of the empire of financier J. Harley Andrews, who has acquired it from the founder, Richard Trueman. The hospital and its adjoining hospice for terminal patients are a stage for the struggle between those who believe in the right to life and those who believe in the right to a timely death.

Our expectations are raised that the two physicians in charge of the hospital will dramatize these conflicting points of view.

Dr. Peter Julius, director of the hospice, and Dr. Jim Kelly, chief resident, speak forth on the moral and practical values involved in final health care.

Dr. Julius holds that dying patients are demanding, ignorant of medical procedure and that looking after them has become too expensive. Dr. Kelly reminds himself that a doctor's mission is healing and, while he opposes health care that delivers death, cites the high cost of treatment and sees the terminal care problem as a "managerial" rather than a medical one.

Both doctors accede to the Trueman-Andrews management policy that for terminal patients a speedy demise is both the humane and cost-effective way to go.

This policy is fostered by the hospital's aggressive, businessman president, Trip Conley. He has married the founder's daughter and subsequently made her miserable with his infidelities.

One of these is with Rebecca Forsythe, an English widow who has had great success with a book about assisting her husband's suicide. Conley has brought her to the hospital from London, ostensibly to improve the hospital's poor public relations.

The local newspaper has noted the accelerating death rate among elderly patients at Trueman-Andrews, augmented by occasional suicides.

A particularly troublesome case is that of an AIDS patient, who fails his own expectations of extended life. In sudden demise. His surviving lover writes angry letters to the newspaper's editor accusing the hospital staff of murder and threatening dreadful reprisals. Whereupon the lover also dies under suspicious circumstances.

The central love story of **In the Name of Mercy** stems from the beautiful widow, Rebecca Forsythe. Trip Conley, first smitten with her in London, has found Forsythe unresponsive since her arrival in Michigan and he is further displeased to discover that she has fallen thunderously in love with Dr. Peter Julius, and he with her.

A *Grand Guignol* ending left this reader no clearer of mind over arguments for and against euthanasia, but certainly persuaded of a need for governmental oversight of the nation's health services. Some readers may vow to steer clear of all hospices whatever their need for nursing care.

As a novel, **In the Name of Mercy** has its frailties. While Delbanco is praiseworthy for taking on so grand a theme, he seems to lose heart for it along the way.

If he did reach satisfactory conclusion about the mercy-killing controversy before telling his story he did not find a character to address or portray it. We miss the figure who might show a concern for the patients of this frightening institution.

Indeed all the important characters have been bereaved, wounded in some way, so that they can respond to events only with self-concern and self-pity. The hospital management personnel who have coasted into health care on the profit motive are a particularly sleazy bunch and such punishments as Delbanco devises for them are not nearly harsh enough.

(The hospital's image is not enhanced by admitting its two sponsors as patients, J. Harley Andrews for a heart complaint and Richard Trueman for prostate cancer. Given the quality of health care at the hospital bearing their names, it is not surprising that neither man recovers.)

The narrative voice that describes the events at Trueman-Andrews has a suitably sinister tone. Its grasp of the language of medical treatment provides authenticity at occasional cost of encrypting meaning for the uninitiated. It is also a voice weighted with the irony of a man who is all too familiar with the gap between what men say and what they do.

Steven G. Kellman (review date summer 1997)

SOURCE: Kellman, Steven G. "Half in Love with Easeful Death." *Michigan Quarterly Review* 36, no. 3 (summer 1997): 520-28.

[*In the following review, Kellman discusses* In the Name of Mercy *in the context of societal debates over doctor-assisted suicide, and compares Delbanco's novel to other books addressing the same issue. Kellman asserts that* In the Name of Mercy *holds little interest as a work of fiction, beyond its topical relevance to a current social problem.*]

To be or not to be is the most compelling of all literary questions. The illustrious cases of Anna Karenina, Emma Bovary, Phaedra, Willy Loman, Ophelia, Antigone, Dido, Romeo, Hedda Gabler, Jocasta, Othello, and Quentin Compson demonstrate that the literary tradition has not exactly fixed its canon 'gainst self-slaughter. For Albert Camus, "There is but one genuinely philosophic problem, and that is suicide." It is a challenge, too, to law and medicine.

A retired pathologist named Jack Kevorkian has become the most famous Michigander since Isiah Thomas by flaunting his complicity in the deaths of more than forty human beings. Using a device he calls the Mercitron machine, he has been ending the lives of those suffering not only from terminal and racking illnesses but from merely grievous ones as well. Although Kevorkian's actions are explicitly prohibited by law, juries have consistently refused to convict him, and he reportedly receives thousands of requests for lethal assistance each week. Poised to rule on the Constitutionality of statutes prohibiting assisted suicide, the United States Supreme Court has assumed the role of laureate to an unlettered age, articulating existential insights that poets used to court. Yet poets went to court when, in Planned Parenthood v. Casey, the august justices declared: "At the heart of liberty is the right to define one's own concept of existence, of meaning, of the universe, and of the mystery of human life." Abortion was the issue that begat that judicial opinion, but contemporary debates over medicide—Kevorkian's term for death induced by a health professional—demand a similar confrontation with elemental mysteries of human life and death.

If Henrik Ibsen had lived at the end of the second millennium, he would surely have written a problem play about this dramatic problem, a topical piece in which a terminating physician is branded enemy of the people. George Eliot would have accommodated a spacious volume to a discussion of what Kevorkian calls obitriatry, the specialty of physicians who limit their practice by abetting the demise of their patients. Anthony Trollope did, in fact, publish a novel, *The Fixed Period* (1882), that depicts a society in which all citizens are put to death on their sixty-eighth birthdays. But contemporary theater and fiction have ceded turf to supermarket tabloids, movies-of-the-week, and TV talk shows. Serious novelists—those who aspire to be read long after "Dr. Death," too, dies and to be taught in the kind of university from whose faculty Kevorkian was expelled—eschew the merely topical. Anxieties over doctors dedicated to shortening rather than prolonging life are registered most directly in popular culture, and nonfiction.

Euthanasia is derived from the Greek for happy death, and the term is either oxymoronic or utopian. However, a country in which mercy-killing is legal and commonplace does exist, and it is neither Bosnia nor Rwanda but rather the Netherlands, where a government commission found that euthanasia accounts for two percent of all deaths and that more than half of the physicians admit deliberately either causing or hastening death. *Primum non nocere*, first do no harm, is the physician's solemn obligation, and for many Dutch doctors continued agony is a greater harm than loss of a hopeless life. Holland has become the Hemlock Society, and in *Seduced by Death* Herbert Hendin examines its experience. A psychiatrist active in suicide prevention, Hendin nevertheless claims to have begun his study with an open mind. But his conclusion is unequivocal, that the Dutch medical establishment is violating its ethical responsibilities: "The more I heard, the more I saw, and the more I was told by euthanasia advocates, the more shocked I was not only at the number of what could only be called wrongful deaths but at the Dutch insistence on defending what seemed indefensible."

Hendin is disturbed by the proliferation of assisted suicide in the United States, and he offers his study of the Netherlands as a polemic against legalization here. He recognizes the humanitarian and libertarian motives of its proponents, the desire to diminish suffering and to affirm the individual's autonomy and dignity. However, he argues that, in practice, assisted suicide and euthanasia enlarge the power of the doctor at the expense of the patient, particularly those most vulnerable because of age, poverty, or ethnicity. While there might be general agreement not to take extraordinary measures to sustain the functions of the terminally ill if it means unbearable, unrelenting pain, Hendin contends that moral gymnasts will soon be rationalizing murder. There is, he insists, "a 'slippery slope' that descends inexorably from assisted suicide to euthanasia, from those who are terminally ill to those who are chronically ill, from those who are physically ill to those who are mentally ill, and from those who request euthanasia to those whose lives are ended at the doctor's discretion."

Nicholas Delbanco maps that slope in his latest novel. Its very title, *In the Name of Mercy,* suggests the paradox that malign consequences proceed from benevolent intentions. The characters and events in the book so closely echo actualities, particularly in his own State of Michigan, that Delbanco begins by insisting that this is a work of fiction, set in the imaginary Michigan towns of Lakeview and Bellehaven. Yet he also thanks several doctors for their help with the manuscript. *In the Name of Mercy* is a physician-assisted *roman-à-thèse,* a literary invention designed to highlight contemporary issues in bioethics. "We live by little detail and not by large abstractions," notes one of its characters; "we believe that our personal story might stand for a general truth." Delbanco contrives details for several personal stories in order to illustrate general truths about life and death.

"I want to die," insists Julie to her husband Peter, a conscientious young physician at a clinic in Lakeview, on the east shore of Lake Michigan. She is afflicted with lentigo maligna melanoma, and, after three years of idyllic marriage, Peter reluctantly, discreetly, puts his wife permanently beyond pain. When a patient suffering from incurable Alzheimer's disease repeats the same formula, "I want to die," Peter Julius again obliges, with another fatality that is iatrogenic.

Most of *In the Name of Mercy* is set in Bellehaven, to which the widowed Peter moves in order to become director of the Harley Andrews Hospice, which specializes in the terminally ill. Crude, anonymous letters begin to alert authorities to an unusually high mortality rate among patients at the hospice and the entire Trueman-Andrews Medical Center of which it is a part. Among the principal players in Delbanco's medical whodunnit are: Penny Lampson, a cunning, randy nurse who induces Peter to take her along from Lakeview to Bellehaven; Trip Conley, a venal philanderer who got his job as head of the medical center by marrying the founder's daughter; Jim Kelly, the overwrought chief resident; Harley Andrews, a gruff old tycoon who funds the hospice and fervently believes in a mission of mercy; and Rebecca Forsythe, a British visitor whose books *Death's Kingdom* and *Undiscovered Country* have transformed her into a celebrated thanatoptician. Pressured by limited resources for urgent needs and by public concern about their profession, doctors and administrators clash over when to prolong life and when—or whether—to terminate it. While corpses accumulate, Peter and Rebecca, who share the burden of having assisted in a spouse's suicide, find renewal in each other's arms. Meanwhile, a genuine murderer is loose within the plot, and his unwitting victims appear to die in the name of mercy, rather than envy, lust, avarice, and the other base motives that truly foster slaughter.

The absent referent of much of these proceedings, Jack Kevorkian, is nevertheless explicitly invoked by Trip Conley. The rapacious hospital executive acknowledges that he invited Rebecca to Bellehaven as a winsome foil to the dour deliverer, who, by tainting the image of Michigan's medical profession, has been bad for the bottom line. Yet it is only a matter of image. The implication of the novel is that, however camouflaged, medicide is an ugly business. *In the Name of Mercy* is constructed around the paradoxical spectacle of thanatopticians hoisted on their own Mercitron machine. And Delbanco's own book is just such a mechanism, constructed to convey readers efficiently and painlessly to its end. In the merciless triage that determines literary immortality, problem novels rarely outlive the immediate social problems that they dramatize. The welfare state reduced *The Jungle* to antiquarian interest. *In the Name of Mercy* renders readers avid to turn its pages, but it diminishes life and death to merely topical matters.

If, as Wallace Stevens proclaimed, "Death is the mother of beauty," Thanatos is at least the wet nurse of the Muses. *Going to the Sun* opens with a stunning act of euthanasia, but its ambitions are loftier than a legal brief. Immobile in a hospital bed, twenty-three-year-old David St. Germaine has lost an arm, two legs, two eyes, and a penis to a feral grizzly bear. He pleads with his lover to end his misery with a covert shot of insulin. Penny Culligan met the man she nicknames "Saint" in a seminar on contemporary Irish poetry. Shortly after the two fall passionately in love, they fly off together on a camping trip. It is during their first night in Glacier National Park that David is mauled just short of death. David's distraught mother demands extraordinary measures to preserve her son, but Penny subtly ends the life of the man she has barely had the time to know.

James McManus sets most of the novel, his fourth, seven years later. Still a graduate student at the University of Illinois at Chicago, Penny has undertaken an arduous summer project; she intends to bicycle alone to Alaska, to pedal her solitary way through 3,285 miles in nine weeks. Her return to Glacier National Park will be in part an act of exorcism, enabling her to continue living without David. It is also an urgent attempt to subdue the juvenile diabetes that has dominated most of Penny's twenty-nine years and that threatens to shorten her remaining time. The bicycle trip is also a desperate strategy to overcome writer's block; she is at an impasse in her doctoral dissertation.

Her topic is the fiction of Samuel Beckett, who, along with Dante, furnishes an epigraph to *Going to the Sun*. He also functions as tutelary spirit of the entire enterprise. Throughout her long, persistent journey, through the upper Midwest and into the mountain states, Penny meditates on Molloy, the Beckett narrator whose severe assessment of human possibility resembles her own. "A solo bicycle trip is, after all, the quintessential Beckettian enterprise," she notes, mindful not only of how many Beckett characters are cyclists but also of how he uses the portrait of a man pedaling as an emblem of human identity and of the tenuous connection between body and soul. Penny's image of her frail, diabetic frame both depleted and fortified by the challenge of locomotion is Beckettian, if not Shakespearean: "a skin bag of off-kilter blood pedaling across lunar grasses." She travels across a bleak landscape that is the objective correlative of her own desolation. At a Motel 6 in Bobmars, Montana, Penny reconceives her deadlocked thesis: "I should be writing a book about what Beckett has to show about the comic and cosmic inevitability of the deterioration of the body—about accepting, even wishing for, mortality, as a return to our natural state of nonbeing. . . ."

Going to the Sun is just such a book, though it is not nearly as ponderous as that description might suggest. This picaresque novel exults in the vitality of mortality, and it rejuvenates the venerable American adventure of the open road. McManus is attentive to oddities of the natural and human landscapes through which Penny travels, and he quickens the journey by arranging encounters with Leona Marvin (aka Lee Marvin), an obsessive dissertation director who flies out to North Dakota in an awkward attempt to succor—and seduce—her student, and Ndele Rimes, a black prince in a flashy Mercedes who may be a basketball star or a fugitive carjacker. The prose is fortified by knowledgeable references to the mechanics and discipline of long-distance bicycling and to the onerous daily regimen of a careful diabetic. However, McManus's most impressive achievement is the voice of Penny Culligan, a canny young woman whom readers will gladly follow as far as she can go. Wary of self-pity, this diabetic, peripatetic ABD speaks for all, despite or because of the fact that she is dying more rapidly than most of the rest of us.

Playfully invoking both Derek Humphry, founder of the Hemlock Society and author of the suicide manual *Final Exit*, and Jack Kevorkian, Penny imagines them together in one of Dante's circles of Hell. Yet *Going to the Sun* is concerned with self-extinction less as a medical or legal issue than an existential one. "Killing myself is the last thing I'm going to do," quips Penny twice, once to her professor and once in a postcard she writes but never sends to her father. Her roommate Jane is not entirely mistaken in judging a diabetic woman's solo journey from Chicago to Alaska as "some sort of slow-motion suicide mission." Such, too, is life, though the slowness varies. Penny, whose defective metabolism is sustaining and destroying her, knows that we extinguish ourselves while distinguishing ourselves. She is intent on seizing control of a mutinous life, even if that can only be accomplished through death. Like Ibsen's Hedda Gabler, who tries to manipulate Eilert Loevborg into leaving this world "with a crown of vine-leaves in his hair," Penny envisions death as deliberate and decisive, a graphic contrast to the muddle of existence: "I'm convinced that one's death should be elegant, painless if possible, and swift—maybe even heroic and beautiful, like I hope David's was. Maybe even slightly triumphant. It should also be an adventure, and so should occur long before one becomes decrepit, since the decrepit tend to be unadventuresome." Beginning with its arresting account of ursine dismemberment and reluctant euthanasia and concluding with a thrilling dash down Logan Pass, *Going to the Sun* is just such a feat of mortal bravado.

Beckett's garrulous narrators can't go on, yet they go on, perpetuating themselves in their very wish for self-extinction. The Cumaean Sibyl's pronouncement *Apothanein thelo*, "I wish to die," is what Ira Stigman, a prolific eighty-nine-year-old author, asks to be inscribed and hung in his study in New Mexico. Stigman expresses his wish in *From Bondage* (1996), the first volume published posthumously in *Mercy of a Rude Stream*, the vast autobiographical cycle created by ailing octogenarian Henry Roth, who, like his narrator alter ego, played his wish to have done with it all against his desire to write it all down. A similar vision of the writing life as a dance with death drives *Reader's Block*, the fifth novel published by sexagenarian New Yorker David Markson. A fiction in the shape of a cento, a compendium of quotations, it at first seems merely a literary lark. But if the reader can accept its brilliant idiosyncrasy, behold, the lark ascends!

The book is composed of short, discrete assertions arranged in a series of mostly single-sentence paragraphs. Of them, 333 consist of unattributed, more or less familiar quotations, including "Exit, pursued by a bear," "*Die Welt ist alles, was der Fall ist*," and "*Delenda est Carthago*." Other brief paragraphs demonstrate the poetry of titles—e.g., "*Our Exagmination Round His Factification for Incamination of Work in Progress*," "*The Origin of Consciousness in the Breakdown of the Bicameral Mind*," and "*How Many Children Had Lady*

Macbeth?" A striking name—"Bucephalus," "Hannah Senesch," "Saxo Grammaticus"—or sequence of names—"Walter the Penniless. Peter the Hermit," "William H. McGuffey. William H. Bonney," "Brandeis. Cardozo. Frankfurter"—suffices for other paragraphs. Many others offer odd, arresting facts about literary figures—that, for example, Stephen Crane played catcher for the Syracuse University baseball team, Lautréamont, Jules Laforgue, and Jules Supervielle were all born in Montevideo, Kazantzakis's sequel to the *Odyssey* contains 33,333 lines, and Rudyard Kipling once lived in Vermont.

Two paragraphs separated by seventy-six pages each ask: "A novel of intellectual reference and allusion, so to speak minus much of the novel?" And the answer is manifestly: *Reader's Block,* a curious grab-bag of a book that also offers this self-referential snippet: "Nonlinear. Discontinuous. Collage-like. An assemblage." And what Markson's text assembles are details of the artistic life, deconstructing Western culture to reconstruct it as a theater of madness, alcoholism, poverty, and despair. Information that: "Richard Lovelace spent his last years in unimaginable poverty, sometimes scavenging for garbage to subsist" or that: "Modigliani died of tuberculosis in a pauper's ward" suggests a correlation between creativity and misery. Malice, too, is a common trait of artists, and throughout its pages *Reader's Block* takes particular pains to note that dozens of authors (Pound, Hamsun, Eliot, Aquinas, Kant, Dreiser, Tacitus, Schopenhauer, Wolfe, et al.) were anti-Semites.

But running throughout the text like a latent malignancy is the theme of self-extinction. Four pages from the end of *Reader's Block,* a two-page list catalogues sixty-one fictional characters who killed themselves. And, at least once per page throughout his book, Markson mentions another actual artist who committed suicide, often specifying the method employed—shotgun, razor blade, revolver, sleeping pills, drowning, cocaine, plastic bag, barbiturates, fire, creosote, starvation, hanging, and sword, among others. We are reminded of the famous suicides—Hemingway, Woolf, Van Gogh, Socrates, Plath, Mishima, Celan, Mayakovsky, Kleist—and no sooner learn the names of others—Kurt Tucholsky, Fanny Imlay, Thomas Heggen, Coleman Dowell, Benjamin Robert Haydon, Constance Mayer—than that they, too, ended their own lives. "There is no death and art can prove it," reads one paragraph, but the cumulative effect of all this morbid information is to establish that, though art be immortal, there are no artists and death can prove it.

"I have a narrative," asserts a statement almost halfway through the book. "But you will be put to it to find it." The narrative, such as it is, in *Reader's Block* can be found, within the context of culture as corrosion, in scattered statements about figures called "Reader" and "Protagonist." Fragmented details provide intimations about Protagonist's life—that he was born in December, 1927, that, retired from the writing life and relocated from Greenwich Village, he leads a solitary, straitened existence, eating his meals out of cans. His literary acquaintances have included Dylan Thomas, Jack Kerouac, Donald Barthelme, and Malcolm Lowry, who even drank his shaving lotion. Formerly married and involved with women of varying ages, Protagonist has been celibate for three or four years. It is not clear whether he has a telephone. Nor is it clear whether Protagonist now resides in the gatehouse to a cemetery, where he discovers his own—undisclosed—name on one of the graves, or whether he lives in a house by the beach. What does seem certain is that Protagonist, who has survived surgery for lung and prostate cancer and for cataracts, takes his own life, according to two diverging scenarios. If he lives by the beach, Protagonist is said "to saunter out among the sandpipers and the gulls one afternoon, and stand for a time abstractedly in late autumn solitude, and then walk unremarkably into the sea." In the alternative fiction, in which Protagonist lives beside a graveyard, he is thought "to pause at his accustomed window one afternoon, and gaze for a time abstractedly at the ranks of still white stone beyond, and then turn unremarkably to the gas." Thus, in the penultimate page of *Reader's Block,* does Protagonist join the ranks of all the other suicidal writers cited throughout the rest of the book.

References to Reader scattered throughout *Reader's Block* indicate that he keeps a portrait of Dante, two orange stones from Masada (site of ancient mass Jewish suicide), a ball hit foul by Ted Williams, and a human skull near his desk. Reader is presented as someone who is as responsible as the writer for imagining Protagonist into existence—and oblivion—and for synthesizing all the disparate details of this book's disconnected sentences. Reader, then, is a personification of the mechanism by which Markson's discontinuous novel is generated. But the final, stark, and devastating paragraph demonstrates that Reader also destroys the work that embodies him. With the single concluding word "Wastebasket," the novel and its connected Reader—like Chatterton or Tosca, or like Yves Tinguely's kinetic sculptures—self-destruct. Kevorkian's Mercitron machine is thus reconfigured in a litany of suicides and in the very act of reading.

Alfred Kazin (review date 9 October 1997)

SOURCE: Kazin, Alfred. "A Single Jew." *New York Review of Books* 44, no. 15 (9 October 1997): 8-9.

[*In the following review, Kazin asserts that* Talking Horse: Bernard Malamud on Life and Work *offers no new information or understanding that isn't already made clear in Malamud's fiction.*]

Bernard Malamud's *The Magic Barrel* was awarded the National Book Award for 1958 against the outraged opposition of one judge. Malamud, amazed that he had won, exclaimed, "A miracle has passed." He was delayed by a reporter in getting to the dinner in his honor. The waiter, looking him up and down, briskly informed him that the table was full and that there was no place for him. Not for the first time I was seeing a Malamud story unfold.

There was the afternoon at a Yaddo board meeting when Malcolm Cowley peremptorily addressed him as "Bernie." This was a familiarity he instantly resented (friends had to call him "Bern") and he flinched with an anger that I understood all too well. He felt he was being treated *prima facie* as just another commonplace Jew, like the Jews in immigrant Brooklyn he had raised up to a high level of American art. He identified with them, they were his blood relations and spiritual family, but he was something more—an artist, and people had better not forget it.

The readings, lectures, personal documents, and sundry analyses of his own work published in **Talking Horse: Bernard Malamud on Life and Work** all insist on one point: I am an American artist in fiction, like so many other famous American writers of fiction, and I live for my art—only death will pull us apart! As a noticeably careful, sober, but rather academic commentary on his own work, the collection says nothing to the informed reader that Malamud's wonderfully unexpected stories and his two best novels, *The Assistant* and *The Fixer*, have not made clear. His central, his essential and most remarkable subject, over and over, is a single character who is not simply "Jewish," like millions of other people, but the Jew, an individual Jew alone in an alien, ungiving environment without the company of other Jews to protect, cheer, and console him.

What could hardly be mentioned in friendly chats with students seeking lessons in "creative writing" were the long-instilled wounds in Malamud's life that did not have to bleed into his art (and they don't) although they are central to it: memories of his father's keeping a failing grocery in a hostile gentile neighborhood, his mother's death when he was fifteen, a younger brother's descent into schizophrenia, everlasting worry about poor sales.

Terror as the body palpably weakens is a principal subject. In "The Mourners," a landlord who can't get a difficult tenant to leave screams, "Don't monkey with my blood pressure. If you're not out by the fifteenth, I will personally throw you on your bony ass." The poor grocer (based on Malamud's father) whose goodness dominates his novel *The Assistant* always groans in fear of a heart attack when in the freezing dawn he has to lug in heavy cases of bottled milk.

Malamud's shopkeepers have no connection with the Jewish working class of the period, with its unions, its collective strikes, its dreams of socialism. The butcher, baker, tailor, shoemaker in these stories are on their own—their wives either dead or unstoppable complainers. No comfort comes from the faithful in the synagogue for a shopkeeper who had to keep open on the Sabbath and even, if necessary, on the holidays most sacred to a Jew. Malamud's grocer lived above the store, and could not get his rest when there was a hope of a customer coming in for a roll and a bottle of milk.

Poverty, the terror of being forced to the wall by another grocery or even a supermarket across the street, is the crucial life experience behind Malamud's recurrent figure of "the Jew." In some basic sense, he is always alone. But what Malamud could not explain in **Talking Horse** was that the Jewish experience is in some sense unbelievable to the Jew himself. What readers of Malamud's stories of the seemingly improbable often take as "fantasy" was for him just the dislocation in this supposedly common-sense world familiar to Jews *in extremis*. Primo Levi in Auschwitz asked a guard, "Why all this?" The guard: "There is no 'why' here."

Technically, Malamud made his art out of the foreign intonations he heard all through his childhood. The immigrants who still thought in Yiddish even as they spoke their self-taught English bring to Malamud's pages bitter, turbulent echoes of life in the shtetls of the Russian Pale where Jews were segregated. The voices in Malamud's slightest dialogue prepare one for *The Fixer*, Malamud's marvelous recreation of a Russia so steeped in Jew-hatred that an itinerant Jewish "fixer" and handyman could be held for three years awaiting trial on the charge of ritual murder performed according to the precepts of the Jewish religion.

In "The Loan," Mrs. Lieb, the baker's wife (his second), "alert behind the counter, . . . discerned a stranger" in the crowd waiting to buy her husband's popular white bread—"a frail, gnarled man with a hard hat who hung, disjoined, at the edge of the crowd." When he gives his name as "Kobotsky," and says he wants to see the baker she suspiciously asks, "Who Kobotsky?" adding, "What do you want to see him?" This is the language of Malamud's world, and it fits their circumstances.

> Kobotsky stared at his crippled hands. Once a cutter of furs, driven by arthritis out of the business.
>
> Lieb gazed too. The bottom of a truss bit into his belly.

The wife is right to suspect that her husband's old friend wants something—a loan. The baker is moved, and in the face of his wife's vehement disapproval, says pleadingly, "His mother—God bless her—gave me many times a plate hot soup. . . . His wife is a very fine person—Dora—you will someday meet her—" It turns out that Lieb himself has not seen "Dora" for fifteen years. In fact, she has been dead for five. Kobotsky has come to seek $200 from Lieb—he never repaid a first loan—"The money I need for a stone on her grave. She never had a stone. Next Sunday is five years that she is dead and every year I promise her, 'Dora, this year I will give you your stone,' and every year I gave her nothing."

Bessie Lieb screamed when she heard Kobotsky asking her husband for money and, "though weeping, shook her head." Her father was shot by the Bolsheviks. Her first husband died of typhus in Warsaw. An older brother sacrificed his own chances to send her to America before the war, "and himself ended, with wife and daughter, in one of Hitler's incinerators."

> So I came to America and met here a poor baker, a poor man—who was always in his life poor—without a cent and without enjoyment, and I married him, God knows why, and with my both hands, working day and night, I fixed up for him his piece of business and we make now, after twelve years, a little living. But Lieb is not a healthy man, also with eyes that he needs an operation, and this is not yet everything.

She goes on so long that she soon needs to shriek again—the all-important bread has burned to a cinder. How Malamud loved to hear his characters sound off. No one parodied Yinglish with more zest than he did and to my knowledge no one ever used it to such satiric and poignant effect. One of his funniest tales is "The Jew-bird," in which a skinny bird with frazzled black wings wearily flaps through the open kitchen window of the Cohen family's top-floor apartment on First Avenue near the East River—and turns out to be a Jew who speaks "Jewish." The bird is not welcome but won't leave or shut up. He opens up with "Gevalt, a pogrom!" and continues, "If you can't spare a lamb chop I'll settle for a piece of herring with a crust of bread. You can't live on your nerve forever." He is a Jew like any other Jew fleeing "Anti-Semeets." "What kind of anti-Semites bother a bird?" the wife asks. "'Any kind,' said the bird, 'also including eagles, vultures, and hawks. And once in a while some crows will take your eyes out.'"

The underside of Malamud's comic gift is that his frail, easily dismayed characters, seemingly driven only by fear for themselves, sometimes manage to incarnate a religious tradition they are too distracted to observe. In "The Mourners," Gruber the landlord, maddened by Kessler, the obstinate tenant he can't get out of his house, suddenly realizes that Kessler, squatting on the floor without shoes, is in mourning, doing *shiva*, in memory of him. Kessler regards him as spiritually dead. Whereupon the landlord drapes himself in a sheet that serves for a prayer shawl and joins the other in prayer.

"Take Pity" takes place in limbo, a purgatory that can be connected to Jewish experience if not to its religious tradition. The recording angel Davidov, "the census-taker," and the newly arrived Rosen, a suicide who bequeathed everything to a widow, Eva, who had refused his love on Earth, brush off all sentimentality by turning up in another world as rough, workaday Jews who talk as such Jews in Malamud usually talk. "What's the matter you don't pull the shade up?" the angel asks the suicide. "Who needs light?" "What then you need?" "Light I don't need," replied Rosen.

"Davidov, sour-faced, flipped through the closely scrawled pages of his notebook until he found a clean one. He attempted to scratch in a word with his fountain pen but it had run dry, so he fished a pencil stub out of his vest pocket and sharpened it with a cracked razor blade." Even angels have to make do in Malamud country.

No traditional afterlife ever comes to mind here, but a Jew knows what it is to be cooped up in limbo, a trying-out period between heaven and hell in which he tells his story. Rosen describes the end of Eva's husband:

> Broke in him something. . . . Broke what breaks. He was talking to me how bitter was his life, and he touched me on my sleeve to say something else, but the next minute his face got small and he fell down dead, the wife screaming, the little girls crying that it made in my heart pain. I am myself a sick man and when I saw him laying on the floor, I said to myself, "Rosen, say goodbye, this guy is finished." So I said it.

Rosen gave up his life for a woman who didn't love him. Morris Bober, the ailing, impoverished grocer in Malamud's novel *The Assistant*, so beaten up by a thug who has robbed him that he can no longer tend the store, unwittingly takes on as "assistant" the young *Italyener* Frank Alpine, the man who attacked him. Alpine doesn't know what to do with his life. Morris knows in despair all too well what to do with his. He suffers. Alpine, enviously studying Morris even as he doesn't register every sale he makes, says, "But tell me why it is that the Jews suffer so damn much, Morris. It seems to me that they like to suffer, don't they?" Morris: "If you live, you suffer. Some people suffer more, but not because they want." Frank: "What do you suffer for, Morris?" "I suffer for you," Morris said calmly.

Frank doesn't understand that last remark, and I didn't either when I first read it. Morris adds, "I mean you suffer for me," and ends up saying, "If a Jew forgets the Law, he is not a good Jew and not a good man." But Morris's saying "calmly" "I suffer for you" turns Morris into something like a Christ figure, and this is out of tune with everything else he says and does. When Morris finally dies, a rabbi he has never met, now officiating at his funeral, says, "Morris Bober was to me a true Jew because he lived in the Jewish experience, which he remembered, and with the Jewish heart.

Maybe not to our formal tradition—for this I don't excuse him—but he was true to the spirit of our life—to want for others that which he wants also for himself.... Who told me this? I know.... For such reasons he was a Jew. What more does our sweet God ask His poor people?"

Malamud wanted Morris's life—clearly drawn from his own father's life—to be more than fortitude in suffering. The Golden Rule, though versions of it are familiar in Biblical lore, is not in the Law handed down from Mount Sinai. In the "Jewish experience," which even to the most rebellious Jew has a sanctity apart from doctrine, the sense of Jewish virtue follows from all the wrong done to powerless Jews. Such virtue is what Malamud claimed for his characters. It is the most familiar theme in Yiddish fiction. But for a moment, when Morris claims to suffer for Frank, who once robbed him and assaulted him, and will rape his daughter, Malamud obviously yearns for a new moral universe based on unquestioning love for another. Malamud is perfectly aware that Christians don't dependably live up to this either. But he wants something more than fortitude and survival for his own, the long-suffering Jew—he wants him, if only once, to rise above the "Jewish experience."

Not easily done. The collected stories include an amusing fantasy, "Angel Levine," about a black Jew who is an angel "disincarnated" to live on Earth, but gets so caught up in Harlem that he gives less help than expected of a co-religionist. Typically, the story opens with the words "Manischevitz, a tailor, in his fifty-first year suffered many reverses and indignities." The tailor regards his suffering as "an affront to God," flatters and positively flirts with Him to get some help. "My dear God, sweetheart, did I deserve that this should happen to me?" But if it happens, say the pious, God wanted it to happen. Job, with his questionings, has no place here. God has swallowed the pious up: they do not complain or protest.

Yakov Bok, the victim-hero in *The Fixer*, is arrested by the Jew-hating tsarist police on a charge of ritual murder. He is enveloped in the age-old blood libel—a Jew will murder a Christian child in order to drain the blood that Jews use for baking Passover matzos. This horror, so steeped in medieval superstition that Chaucer repeated it in his tribute to the childmartyr Saint Hugh of Lincoln, was acceptable as late as 1925 to that cleverest of converts to Rome, G. K. Chesterton. In *The Everlasting Man* Chesterton charged that "the Hebrew prophets were perpetually protesting against the Hebrew race relapsing into an idolatry that involved such a war upon children; and it is probably enough that this abominable apostasy from the God of Israel has occasionally appeared in Israel since, in the form of what is called ritual murder ... by individual and irresponsible diabolists who did happen to be Jews."

Bok "the fixer" has never been a happy or agreeable man. He has no reliable trade, his wife left him because they remained childless. She turned to other men. Despite misgivings from his father-in-law, Bok leaves the shtetl to try his luck in the great city of Kiev. He is now there illegally, for Jews require special permission to live outside the Pale. Although always on the run, he manages to rescue from the freezing cold the drunken proprietor of a brick kiln, who belongs to the violently anti-Semitic "Black Hundreds," the organization most responsible for pogroms.

Not knowing that Bok is a Jew and so a fugitive from the police, the grateful proprietor hires him to oversee his employees, who are evidently cheating him. This of course makes them hate Bok, whom they already suspect to be a Jew, and when a young boy's body is discovered in a cave, Bok is promptly arrested. As a Jew illegally living in Kiev, he is on everybody's hate list. Even the kiln proprietor's crippled daughter, who coaxed Bok up to her bedroom, testifies vindictively against him. Blood is indeed at the center of the case. She hates Bok because he begged off after seeing menstrual blood on her thigh.

For three years awaiting trial, Bok is strip-searched several times a day, starved, beaten, humiliated and isolated and constantly reminded that "you Yids killed Christ." The Tsar takes a deep, vengeful interest in his case. The Russian Orthodox Church, the most anti-Semitic Christian church (it still is), vilifies him in concert with the Black Hundreds.

The Fixer is based on the historic case of Mendel Beilis in Kiev, 1913, who after suffering the many tortures Malamud unsparingly described in his novel was amazingly found innocent by a jury of Russian peasants. Leading lawyers—including Alexander Kerensky—came to his defense. Non-Jewish scholars testified that Jews have such a horror of blood that they do not tolerate a drop of it in their food. The Russian Orthodox Church built a church to commemorate Beilis's "victim." Beilis, who eventually settled in America, remained an extremely bitter man who could never forgive even the many Jews and non-Jews who backed him up against the hatred that had seeped into his prison cell.

As Dreyfus was personally not liked by many who fought for his release from Devil's Island, so Beilis was not a favorite with many who knew him best. Malamud describes Bok's gruffness, his hatred of the deserting wife, and especially his refusal to ask God for help. He is not a believer. When his father-in-law sneaks a prayer shawl into his cell, he wears it as underwear against the cold. Bok knows nothing of ritual murder. He knows that he is up against people determined to cause him pain, day after day and year after year, simply because he is a Jew. So his quarrel is with primitive, superstitious Russia, not with "God," who is not in the picture at all. Bok in jail becomes a revolutionary and imagines himself joyfully shooting the Tsar "right through the heart."

> One thing I've learned, he thought, there's no such thing as an unpolitical man, especially a Jew. You can't be one without the other, that's clear enough. You can't sit still and see yourself destroyed.
>
> Afterwards he thought, Where there's no fight for it there's no freedom. What is it Spinoza says? If the state acts in ways that are abhorrent to human nature it's the lesser evil to destroy it. Death to the anti-Semites! Long live revolution! Long live liberty!

The novel cleverly ends with Bok being taken through the streets of Kiev on his way to trial.

> The crowds lining both sides of the streets were dense again, packed tight between curb and house-front. There were faces at every window and people standing on rooftops along the way. Among those in the street were Jews of the Plossky District. Some, as the carriage clattered by and they glimpsed the fixer, were openly weeping, wringing their hands. One thinly bearded man clawed his face. One or two waved at Yakov. Some shouted his name.

Probably to Yakov's surprise, Malamud wants to say, he is not alone.

Robert Buckeye (review date spring 1998)

SOURCE: Buckeye, Robert. Review of *Old Scores*, by Nicholas Delbanco. *Review of Contemporary Fiction* 18, no. 1 (spring 1998): 250-51.

[*In the following review of* Old Scores, *Buckeye praises Delbanco's writing as intelligent, compassionate, and well-crafted.*]

We know the story: the sixties; college; the professor, Paul Ballard, and the student he becomes involved with, Elizabeth Sieverdsen; the brief flaring of their love, its near predictable failure. It was the sixties, after all, and too many mistook indulgence for love. And its sequel: to revisit, with the cold eye of experience and time, that youthful evanescence. Or, even worse, to come together again years later, marked by life, particularly divorce, and think that this time . . .

It is the story of *Old Scores* but not the one Nicholas Delbanco tells. Love is either more than we will ever understand or less than, much less than, we desire, but it is everything Paul and Elizabeth desire, all they need to understand, even if they do not know it at the time. Despite years apart, their love marks them forever, alters their lives. Delbanco gives us here an Abelard and Heloise for our time, and if his comparison, of necessity, at first diminishes, it also enlarges; Paul and Elizabeth are legitimate heirs. It is a characteristic modernist method to hold the present up against the past, and Delbanco has employed it frequently; in *Small Rain,* for example, a version of Tristan and Isolde, or *The Martlet's Tale,* an account of the prodigal son. Guy Davenport argues that modernism was determined by the discovery of the specific, and Delbanco's detail is always, Thomas Lask notes, "dense, Euclidean in its ability to focus on a particular point of time and space." Here and elsewhere, he keeps faith with the still uncompleted modernist project: his impulse utopian, standards absolute, measure the particular. We may characterize his writing at every point in this complex and difficult enterprise by its acute intelligence; by its compassion, particularly for the old; and, first and last, by its language, precise, exact. *Old Scores* is characteristic.

Jeff Gundy (essay date fall 2000)

SOURCE: Gundy, Jeff. "Handling the Truth." *Georgia Review* 106, no. 3 (fall 2000): 559-72.

[*In the following excerpt, Gundy explores notions of truth in the essay collections of several authors, including Delbanco's* The Lost Suitcase.]

Essays are often viewed as a kind of supplement, something that novelists and poets do with the leftover thoughts and stray impulses and bits of material that won't fit into their "real" work. Several aspects of the books under discussion here support this theory. One of them begins with an essay that the author breezily confesses having pieced together out of fragments from his commonplace book. And while dust-jacket notes are hardly to be trusted, if we take these at their word we learn that none of these authors is before all else an essayist. Of the whole group, only Sam Pickering is not more widely known as a poet or fiction writer, and even he, like David Brendan Hopes and Nicholas Delbanco, is described as a professor and then as an author. Turning to the others, we learn that Marjorie Sandor has won prizes for her short fiction and is also a professor, and that Hilary Masters has written eight novels. Even in their subject matter these books foreground issues related to writing fiction and poetry much more often than those related to writing nonfiction prose. Why are these authors, all of them quite capable essayists, seemingly reluctant to present themselves *as* essayists, and seemingly diffident as they offer their books for our attention?

I offer that question only for your contemplation. But as I read these books I found myself fascinated with closely related issues: just how writers present themselves, how they engage and contend with different registers of experience and inquiry, what particular elements of the world seemed to concern these novelists and poets and professors when they turn their hand to the essay. This sample is too small to be reliable, but these collections offer some tantalizing clues as to what literary artists who think of themselves as particular kinds—poets, fiction writers, or memoirists—find especially interesting and important, and to what uses they tend to put their materials.

We may view essays as mere supplements, but we also tend to have expectations about their being "true" that we don't have for fiction or even poetry. The current popularity of the unwieldy term "creative nonfiction" suggests some ambiguous balance of invention and truth, and the ways essayists handle these elements are crucial. The books under review all drew my attention to the ways their authors selected, arranged, and improvised upon the facts of their lives and interests. In what follows, then, I hope to explore how writers who define their primary identities quite differently seem to handle "the truth," even as their handling becomes itself a part of their quest for self-definition and literary creation.

Nicholas Delbanco's *The Lost Suitcase* offers an unusual combination of texts: centered among eight essays on "the literary life" we find the title novella, a re-imagining from multiple perspectives of the famous anecdote of the missing valise full of Hemingway's early manuscripts. Both the novella and the essays take up questions of literary accomplishment, judgment, and strategies in a confident, almost magisterial manner. Delbanco knows his craft and how to make even rather loose connections seem natural enough. I have already mentioned that the opening essay, **"Travel, Art, and Death,"** pieces together quite disparate entries from a commonplace book; yet by its end we believe that travels in Greece, old photographs, the deaths of Wallace Stegner and John Hersey, and the odd story of a friend—who passes his oral exam to graduate *summa cum laude* at Harvard because he happens to have memorized the first three hundred lines of *Paradise Lost*—all somehow belong together.

Lively, canny observations and anecdotes about the necessary but difficult relations among artists and their peers and mentors run through this book. Ruefully, Delbanco repeats the famous maxim that there is no arguing about taste, and he then notes the contradictory reality that those of us who teach writing or aspire to be writers must, in one way or another, spend our lives making and pressing others to make such judgments. We *have* to argue about taste; its vagaries and mysteries must be explored and examined even when they cannot be neatly summarized. One fine story tells of cellist Bernard Greenhouse studying with the master Pablo Casals until he can play a Bach suite exactly as Casals does. At this point, Casals plays through the piece once more, changing every detail and nuance of his performance. "Now you've learned how to improvise in Bach. From now on you study Bach this way."

For novelists grappling with the problem of historical accuracy, Delbanco offers the intriguing operating principle of "lazy historicity" he devised while writing a novel about the nearly forgotten Benjamin Thompson, Count Rumford. "[I]t seems to me that the domain of research in historical fiction is strangely delimited: you need to get things right but need to stop your study when imagination starts. It's a kind of starter motor: you turn that particular key until the true engine kicks in." Such a principle may trouble historians, but those concerned with the alternate avenues toward truth that fiction provides—and daunted by the nearly bottomless swamp that waits for those who pursue complete historical authenticity—will find it useful.

The essay **"Telephone"** provides some historical background in preparation for the title novella. In the standard version of the incident (Hemingway's first wife Hadley packed the suitcase to bring to him in Switzerland, and it was lost somewhere on her train journey), the loss of the early manuscripts "became an emblem for what proved irretrievable: [Hemingway's] hopeful youth, his marriage, his sense of possibility, his early close wrangling with words." Yet Delbanco resists the tragic view of the incident, pointing out that the lost work could have been "mere penny-ante prose," that surely Hemingway could have reconstructed much of what was worth saving, that Hemingway just may have, in fact, reworked some of the "lost" stories into *A Moveable Feast*.

Whatever the truth might be, **"The Lost Suitcase"** works a series of dazzling, virtuosic variations upon the story. Hadley (Delbanco calls her Anna-Lise) is naïve and earnest in the first version, a world-weary libertine in the next; in another she reads the pages and discovers, to her horror, that

> this language of his is atrocious, so very much a schoolboy's prose she cannot bring herself to think of it as Edward's work or the work of someone who could ever be a writer.
>
> There are pages about football and baseball and boxing.
>
> There are pages about fish.
>
> That which she tried to teach him he has failed entirely to learn; that which he knows is not worth knowing, but bathetic and mannered and cheap.

This is crafty stylistically as well as thematically, paying a kind of parodistic homage to Hemingway's famous prose style even as it undercuts it. Strikingly, throughout the many variations AnnaLise is a far more varied and intriguing character than Edward, who remains relatively consistent, and more or less an arrogant dope. One senses Delbanco's delight in having the master exactly where he wants him, in his own ability to retell the story with any spin he pleases, and especially in making the soon-to-be-spurned first wife the more interesting and talented character.

Yet the story's interest goes beyond the characters into the metanarrative that develops around, above, and below the kernel of incident. With the return to realism that has dominated fiction in the last twenty years or so, such postmodern maneuvers have fallen out of fashion, but Delbanco defies the currents and improvises happily, questions his own knowledge and motives, meditates on the difficulties of making fiction, and offers a droll series of lists: thirteen ways of looking at a suitcase, thirteen ways of hiding a suitcase, thirteen ways of looking *for* a suitcase, etc.

"Letter to a Young Fiction Writer" similarly pays homage to Rilke and his *Letters to a Young Poet* while drawing back a bit from the youthful admiration Delbanco once felt for the German poet. He now finds "the roses and the maidens and the lighthouses and the Orphic utterances" to be "a little humid." His own advice includes a defense of the teaching of writing: "the worst that's done is not much harm and the best is a good deal better than that." He notes the difficulty of finishing a book, of coming to terms with it as merely an "inert cultural object" rather than "fancy's flesh and bone."

The last essay of **The Lost Suitcase** deals directly with the issue of why writers write. Its highlight, and a good measure of Delbanco's method and approach, is a brief transcription of the Beaux Arts Trio in rehearsal, with commentary. The musicians speak in a kind of polyglot, shorthand babble that is both hilarious and surprisingly revealing about the process of collaborative creation:

> *Nun,* take it from D. Wubba wubba wubba wubba. *Ich habe quasi improvisatore ici.* You follow my bowing and I follow yours. Wubba wubba. You lose the whole effect of that *piano* after playing *forte* for fourteen bars through. Last night I tried going up, today I go down— the takeover shouldn't sound as if now it's *me*—but lead up, please.

Delbanco comments that his role was "to evoke the nature of the enterprise in a language faithful to the original but sufficiently distant from it to be more than mere transcription. This was a particular problem of reportage and, perhaps, extreme. But it seems to me an emblem of the novelist's ongoing task: we witness and translate." Surely he is right; yet his own practice suggests that writers must create what is effectively a *new* reality, in what is quite nearly a different language, as they move from the rich, multilayered symphony of the live situation to the comparatively flat, single instrument of the written text. Wherever that lost suitcase may be, we are fortunate to have this book about it.

Neil Gordon (review date 14 January 2001)

SOURCE: Gordon, Neil. "No Direction Home." *Washington Post Book World* (14 January 2001): 3-4.

[*In the following review, Gordon praises* What Remains *for its thoughtful, evocative, and lucid prose, as well as vivid characterization. Gordon discusses the theme of Jewish identity in the wake of the Holocaust as treated in Delbanco's novel.*]

The Holocaust is not only the brutal history of an attempted genocide nor the nightmarish story of the camps. It's also a symphony of dignity lost, of warmth and childhood forever poisoned by the knowledge that generations of Jews anchored in Europe were uprooted in a few sudden years by implacable bureaucrats and jackbooted sadists. Nowhere was this more shocking than in Germany itself, where hundreds of years of Jewish residence had created a community as inextricably interwoven into German life as Jews are today into America, Judaism being often the weaker of their cultural and political identifications. For the lucky few who were able to escape, the Holocaust was a story not of extermination but of the detailed daily cruelty of German anti-semitism: the subtle, cruel, torturous destruction of the most safe and comforting intimacies of family and home.

What Remains, Nicholas Delbanco's 15th work of fiction, is a pensive and evocative tour through three generations of an exiled German-Jewish family as they carry, first to Britain and then to America, the shameful truth of their betrayal by their country and neighbors. They were foresighted enough to flee Germany before the war, and wealthy enough to pay the 25 percent of their net worth extracted by the Nazis as the price of immigration, while immigration was still allowed. Art dealers and businessmen, they live luxuriantly and very intensely the life of the mind: Their literary references are to Schiller and Goethe, Shakespeare and Proust; they listen to Bach and Schubert, and live among Rodins and rare African masks. In England their children are educated at Cambridge, in America at Harvard. They eat Westphalian ham, they celebrate Christmas.

There is nothing affected about this: Such was the culture of bourgeois Germans of the prewar period. Sometimes it seems, looking back as if the depth of Germany's racism was a precisely opposite measure of the heights of its culture and humanity before the crash of 1929, when Nazism began to take hold.

Wherever they are, the members of the family are aware that their ancestors were expelled from Venice in the 16th century, and they themselves were expelled from Hamburg in the 20th. "And it could happen here," Delbanco writes. "On a daily basis, it is wise to be prepared. When John F. Kennedy was shot, and then Lee Harvey Oswald on TV, [Karl] had been fearful of madness, *Wahnsinn,* a national catastrophe, and they would have to leave. . . . Once you have been a refugee, you never forget it could happen again."

Delbanco begins the novel from the perspective of 1984, when Benjamin, the family's middle grandchild, visits his childhood home in London. From here the story skips in succeeding chapters back to Benjamin's father, Karl, living in a wealthy New York suburb in the '60s, then back further to Benjamin's early childhood in 1944, when the family settled in London following their early escape from Hamburg. Most of the book proceeds to explore the interior landscapes of members of Benjamin's family in London in the mid-'40s; successive chapters enter the minds of his uncle, his grandmother, his older brother. Then the narration skips forward to the '60s again, taking up Benjamin's mother's point of view in New York. In the epilogue, we return to Benjamin's point of view for a last visit to London, with his two grown daughters, in 1996.

It's a complicated structure and necessarily a bit confusing. The payoff for a little perseverance, however, is that when the book catches us, it does so very, very hard—amazingly so. In a prose as evocative and clear as any being written in America today, Delbanco draws us into the very thought processes of his characters, showing us the past through their eyes and with the thick reality of their emotions. The exactitude and plenitude of detail in this book have the authenticity of real literary imagination, a world recreated through precisely drawn objects and sensations, a deeply empathetic construction of character and place, informed by nostalgia and love. Nothing here is particularly original; this is an evocation of a very familiar world. But everything here is vivid and important.

When writing from a child's point of view, Delbanco has the gift of mixing passing images and deep observation. Ben sees his mother start to cry when she tells him, "Remember, when they take away your house and kill the people that you love they can't take what you carry in your head"; moments later he reflects on a detail of the color in a shuffleboard game, equally striking to a child. Lived memory is composed of accidental details, retained by a logic beyond our control.

The novel's multiple points of view allow unusual insight into each of the characters. So Julia, the wise and didactic mother, emerges in a complex portrait created by combining the views of Ben and his brother, Jacob, and their father, Karl. In Judaism, writes John Sanford, it is the old men who are beautiful. But the figure of this troubled, courageous, careful woman will stay with me for a great long time, and the unveiling of the trauma at the heart of her emotional life is so skillfully handled that it provides this unusually complex novel with a dimension of suspense that any mystery writer would envy.

The German philosopher Theodore Adorno's famous mistake—his assertion that there could be no art after Auschwitz—can in retrospect be paraphrased in a much surer way: There can be no home after Auschwitz. The Nazis showed the postwar world that home is an empty concept: Belonging is suspect, safety is temporary, and the roots of residence can be torn away by a racism that good governments can perhaps control but that no government, from Bonn to Washington, can ever eradicate. What remains of our identity when we know that the most unthinkable rejection can eradicate everything we hold most dear? That's the question that Delbanco's musical and wise novel asks, and his answer—a tapestry of memory, missing, art, love and a lifelong awareness of vulnerability—is as fine as will be found anywhere.

Binnie Kirshenbaum (review date January-February 2001)

SOURCE: Kirshenbaum, Binnie. "A Desire to Belong." *New Leader* 134, no. 1 (January-February 2001): 30-1.

[*In the following review, Kirshenbaum praises* What Remains *as emotionally compelling and gracefully written.*]

Nicholas Delbanco's 13th novel is a breathtakingly beautiful slim volume. But don't be misled by its size. The scope of **What Remains** is epic, spanning generations and continents. It is further testimony to Delbanco's skill as a writer that he artfully packs so much into such a compact work. There is nothing splashy here, no verbal pyrotechnics. Rather, it is the grace of language and of ideas that creates the gravitational pull which draws in the reader and swells the heart.

Told in chapters of alternating voices that skip back and forth in the time between 1944 and 1996, **What Remains** is the story of an extended family, three generations of refugees. These are not Emma Lazarus' tired, poor, huddled masses. They are rich German Jews who were among the fortunate in so far as they were able to get out of Nazi Germany largely intact, and with more than the shirts on their backs.

Although no longer fabulously wealthy—no more chauffeur-driven cars or costume balls—they are safely ensconced in bourgeois abundance (they do have a maid) in London. Yes, bombs certainly did fall and they did experience the irony of being unwanted, not for being Jewish but for being German in wartime England. Yet all in all they lived a comfortable life. In a tender detail of their safety, the father of the family's two small boys has painted a donkey, an elephant and Rafi the giraffe on the ceiling and walls of the garage that serves as their air-raid shelter.

Since this family—so warm, so loving, so morally and intellectually superior—had the prescience to see what was coming and the ability to save themselves, where is the sorrow? And make no mistake about it, this is a sorrowful novel.

The title points to the answer: It is in the ache of what is lost and of what remains behind that the author evokes in each of his wonderful characters; in the opaque patina of grief that transforms this family; in the knowledge that their lives will never be the same, innocence lost cannot be found. The sentiment is sweetly mirrored in a scene where Karl's wife Julia loses a ring. Not the whole ring, only a piece of it—the head of Minerva in gold. Her sons set about looking for it, with the promise of a pound to the one who finds it. Surely Ben will find it, because he is the one who always finds what is lost. Only this time, it is Jacob who finds the piece of gold and Ben who must face a small, but painful, truth.

This splendid family accepts what fate has dished out for them with all the courtesies, the stoicism, the strength, the dated elegance they value. Elsa, the mother of Karl and Gustave, the grandmother of Jacob and Ben, is almost eccentric. Enormous, but not so much that we don't take her seriously. She is too complicated to simply slip into an Auntie Mame type caricature, although she has her quirks: She winningly chain-smokes, leaving trails of ash in her wake. She dresses always in head-to-toe black or head-to-toe gray (the best backdrops for her silver jewelry—gold being vulgar). She teaches her grandsons the need for lovely manners. She infuses them with a love of nature, and how not to merely look but to see. She has a grand logic all her own too: If that art school had not rejected the young Adolf Hitler, nothing would have happened. It is all the fault of the art school.

But no one in this family laments or gripes or indulges in a cheap nostalgia. Even when momentarily overwhelmed with sadness while telling her grandson Ben of Germany, of the paradox of a nation that produced the music of Bach and Beethoven and Schubert yet also made Hitler (whom she often refers to as *Schicklgruber*), Granny averts her face from the boy. But, as Ben knows, it is 1946. The War is over. Hitler is gone. They could return, if only for a visit. Elsa, however, knows better:

"'And when a whole country is evil like that it's madness to think of returning. Not ever.'

"'Do you miss it?'

"'Yes,' she says. "'I miss it very much.'

"And then she gives him chocolate, and they sit and rock."

No, they can never go back. But they are German. So very, very German, and this they don't relinquish easily. There is more than a passing nod to keeping the German way of life alive in exile. They have not let go of their Goethe or their Heine or their chamber concerts or their language. Their English is liberally peppered with German, and their few friends outside the family are German refugees. In another paradox, it is their Germanness that keeps them from their Jewishness. When one of their friends, Dr. Lucas (always with the German formality of Dr.) wishes the family a good *yontiff*, he is reprimanded:

"'We don't speak Yiddish here,' says Julia. 'Not in this house.'"

No Yiddish is spoken, no synagogue attended, and they celebrate Christmas replete with a *tannenbaum* and Christmas goose. This is not, as Dr. Lucas accuses, anti-Semitism as much as perhaps an elitism and a desire to belong. Elsa may be the one who most longs for Germany, and technically she is the matriarch, but it is Julia who is the clear-eyed pragmatist. It is she who runs the show, and who is always prepared to flee if need be.

Her pragmatism results in Julia's determination to move to America, to raise her boys in a place she believes will be more congenial than England to refugees. She wants her sons to go to Harvard, and so this branch of the family—Karl, Julia, Jacob, and Benjamin—leaves England and finds further refuge in Westchester Country, where a third son is born. Again, life is more than fair to them. They live in a nice house, Karl's business is successful, Jacob and Benjamin do indeed go off to Harvard, as it seems the youngest brother will too. The American Dream come true, albeit not exactly the Horatio Alger rags-to-riches version. Rather riches to solidly upper middle class, which is a small price to pay for life and limb, for freedom from fear, for a chance to belong.

Still, the matter of what remains continues to reverberate and unfold. With her sons grown and out of the house, what remains for Julia is a loneliness that cannot be filled. It is in part a remnant of the memory of her first love—an unrequited love for a young man in Germany, Jacob Steiner, who jumped from a window to his death as the Nazis closed in. Perhaps Julia's love for Jacob was not eternal, but something of it was. After she at last married Karl and settled down, she gave her first son Jacob's name so as not to forget—to always be reminded of her initial romantic adventure, her daring intransigent wide-eyed youth that day.

Questions remain about Jacob Steiner as well, about why he rejected Julia's offer of love and what part of him feared the Nazis most. And questions remain about Karl and Julia's marriage. It was a solid marriage, a successful marriage, stable and obviously one of mutual respect, but was it a happy marriage? That is not so clear.

To be a responsible family man, Karl gave up his dream of being an artist. Instead, he is a Sunday painter, salvaging pleasure in doing self-portraits on weekends spent in his studio; a studio apart from the rest of the house because Julia cannot abide the smell of turpentine.

And what will become of Gustave's art gallery? Ben returns to England with the idea of possibly taking it over, since Gustave would like his life's work to remain in the family. But, no. It won't work out. Ben cannot stay in England, and we are left to believe that the gallery will soon be no more.

In the very end what remains is our ashes, the dust of us. Dust and memory; memory from which story is fashioned. Nicholas Delbanco opens his story with an epigram, a line from Ezra Pound:

> *What thou lovest well remains,*
> *the rest is dross*

What remains is this virtuous novel, written with love.

Amanda Heller (review date 19 August 2001)

SOURCE: Heller, Amanda. Review of *The Countess of Stanlein Restored*, by Nicholas Delbanco. *Boston Globe* (19 August 2001): D3.

[*In the following review, Heller describes* The Countess of Stanlein Restored *as an intriguing account focused on both the art of the musician and the art of the luthier.*]

It is one of those confluences of circumstance best summed up as "genius of place": For a number of variably evident reasons, about 300 years ago in the vicinity of Cremona, in northern Italy, a handful of craftsmen briefly produced the most sublime violins and cellos the world has ever known. Their names speak for themselves: Amati, Guarneri, and the most famous of all, Stradivari.

The author and scholar Nicholas Delbanco is fortunate enough to have a Stradivarius cello in the family (for such an exquisite creation is treated by its owner not as an inanimate possession but rather as a beloved, with a body and soul), belonging to his father-in-law, the master cellist Bernard Greenhouse. In this brief but intriguing essay, [*The Countess of Stanlein Restored,*] Delbanco sketches the rather murky provenance of this glorious old instrument, once owned by the violin virtuoso Paganini, and then details the painstaking surgery performed on it by a gifted artisan, Ren Morel, over a period of two years, an excruciating wait for an anxious owner approaching his mid-80s. This tiny book with its top-heavy title is a little gem, a trove of fact, lore, and sensual description evoking two enduring and intertwined traditions—the art of the musician and the art of the luthier. One suspects that Delbanco would not object to having it described, ultimately, as a love story.

Robin Elliott (review date 27 October 2001)

SOURCE: Elliott, Robin. "Lure and Lore of the Cello." *Irish Times* (27 October 2001): 69.

[*In the following excerpt, Elliott describes* The Countess of Stanlein Restored *as an engaging and affectionate portrait of a rare cello.*]

The cello is an object of such consummate perfection that it is hard to believe that it was created by the human mind. It is exquisitely beautiful to look at, and has a range of musical expression rivalled only by the violin. By turns, it can provide a sturdy yet flexible accompanying line, or take flight in full-throated song. . . .

[In *The Countess of Stanlein Restored,*] Delbanco sheds light on the mysterious art of restoration. Delbanco holds the Robert Frost Collegiate Chair of English Language and Literature at the University of Michigan, but he is also the son-in-law of Bernard Greenhouse, the semi-retired cellist of the Beaux Arts Trio. Delbanco has written an engaging and affectionate portrait of Greenhouse's Stradivarius cello, which is named after two former owners of the instrument: Stanlein, a French 19th-century aristocrat, and Paganini, the legendary Italian violin virtuoso.

This is one of about 60 surviving Strad cellos, as compared to just 12 violas but 600 or so violins.

Stradivarius made the instrument in 1707 near the start of his "Golden Period", and it is the first of his smaller-sized cellos (75 cm long, as opposed to 81 cm in his earlier period). As such it has been the model for countless imitators ever since.

Greenhouse, who played this cello every day for 40 years, decided to have the instrument completely restored when he retired from active concert giving. He entrusted the job to the New York luthier Ren Morel, who gave two years of labour and love to the job.

It was a delicate balance between keeping the original material by Stradivarius (even small strips of canvas glued to the inside for reinforcement) and respecting the history of the instrument (for instance, by not replacing the back of the peg box, which was cut out by an earlier repairer and is now a distinctive feature of the instrument). Delbanco conveys wonderfully the arcane mysteries of what went into the restoration process and what makes a Strad something very much more than the sum of its parts.

Michael Foss (review date 30 November 2001)

SOURCE: Foss, Michael. "Yours for Twenty Pence." *Times Literary Supplement,* no. 5148 (30 November 2001): 21.

[*In the following review, Foss offers a mixed assessment of* The Countess of Stanlein Restored, *faulting Delbanco for focusing too heavily on renowned persons such as cello-craftsman Antonio Stradivari and cellist Bernard Greenhouse, among others.*]

This curious little book [***The Countess of Stanlein Restored***] promises to tell the story of the life, and the restoration, of a musical instrument. The instrument is the so-called Countess of Stanlein cello, made by Antonio Stradivari in 1707 and now in the possession of the respected American cellist Bernard Greenhouse.

The history of a fine old instrument is a rich field for all kinds of investigation. In fact, a whole sociology lies implicit in such an instrument. Many tricky questions are relevant to this story: matters of craftsmanship and technology; the commercial life of Cremona in the seventeenth and eighteenth centuries; the demands of music on instruments and the relationship between compositional changes and instrument making; the requirements of performers and the pressures of audience expectation; the extreme tension, in a liberal economy, between the commodity value of an old instrument that has now become an art object and the need of none too wealthy players to release the musical potential of that object. And there is, of course, the romance of obscure histories, which, in the case of the "Stanlein", witnessed a certain Signor Merighi, in 1822, rescuing the cello from a barrow in the streets of Milan for a sum now equivalent to twenty pence.

Wisely, Nicholas Delbanco limits the interesting topics that he might have covered. Unwisely, he tells us things we don't want to know. The author is the son-in-law of Bernard Greenhouse, and (with justice) speaks of the cellist with hushed respect. But the ineffable gloss of celebrity, the spotlight of fame, washes unerringly over too many names, including the World Cello Congress, Yo-Yo Ma, Casals, Greenhouse, and in particular the restorer René Morel and the maker Antonio Stradivari. Morel and Stradivari are undoubtedly great names in their fields—Stradivari perhaps the greatest. But the point is that we would like to be given more information and more intelligent discussion, and fewer laudatory puffs for those who don't need them. For example, the author draws heavily on the judgment of the Hill brothers, those pioneers in the study of Stradivarius instruments. Well, here is their opinion of this cello: "The Stanlein bass is today only a moderate example, as it bears signs of considerable and injudicious restoration." This may be wrong, but it is worth discussing. Stradivari is a starry name, but by no means were all his instruments great. He was a craftsman, mighty but fallible, not a brand name. The sooner we learn that a mere rote of brand names is not an effective technique in the evaluation of art, the clearer our judgments will be.

FURTHER READING

Criticism

Flanagan, Thomas. "Old Masters of the Modern Novel." *Washington Post Book World* 13, no. 27 (4 July 1982): 3, 13.

> Flanagan criticizes *Group Portrait* as offering little in the way of new information, but praises Delbanco for expressing a strong sense of affection for his subject.

Ruttencutter, Helen Drees. "Working in Harmony." *Washington Post* (9 February 1985): G2.

> Ruttencutter argues that *The Beaux Arts Trio* is "disappointing" and comments that Delbanco inserts himself into the text too much.

Slung, Michele. "Aix Marks the Spot: Traveling through Provence." *Washington Post Book World* 19, no. 132 (6 August 1989): 9.

Slung asserts that the true topic of *Running in Place* is not the locations to which Delbanco travels, but the author's self-scrutiny in terms of the "powerful sensations" invoked by the experience of travel.

Additional coverage of Delbanco's life and career is contained in the following sources published by the Gale Group: *Contemporary Authors,* Vols. 17-20; *Contemporary Authors Autobiography Series,* Vols. 2, 189; *Contemporary Authors New Revision Series,* Vols. 29, 55; *Contemporary Literary Criticism,* Vols. 6, 13; *Dictionary of Literary Biography,* Vols. 6, 234; and *Literature Resource Center.*

Gao Xingjian
1940-

(Name also rendered as Xingjian Gao) Chinese-born French playwright, critic, novelist, translator, and essayist.

The following entry presents an overview of Gao's career through 2001.

INTRODUCTION

Playwright, critic, and novelist Gao was a prominent leader of the avant-garde movement in fiction and drama that emerged in the wake of the Cultural Revolution in China from 1966 to 1976. In 2000 he received the Nobel Prize in Literature from the Swedish Academy, the first time the prize had been awarded for a body of writing in the Chinese language. Gao, a self-exiled dissident writer, emigrated from China to France in 1987 in order to escape government persecution for his controversial plays, prose, and essays. His novel *La Montagne de l'âme* (1995; translated in Chinese as *Lingshan,* translated in English as *Soul Mountain*) is considered by many critics to be Gao's masterpiece, employing an experimental narrative voice to relate the story of a spiritual journey through remote China. His works typically address themes of the individual versus collective will and the search for self-identity. Despite his continual focus on topics and issues that are distinctive to Chinese culture, all of Gao's writings have been banned in China since 1989.

BIOGRAPHICAL INFORMATION

Gao Xingjian (pronounced *gow shing-jen*) was born on January 4, 1940, in Ganzhou, China. During Gao's childhood, Ganzhou—also known as Republican China—was invaded by Japanese forces. In 1949, due to the revolution led by Mao Zedong, the nation became the People's Republic of China. Gao grew up in a liberal family environment—his father was a banker and his mother was an amateur actress—and he had access to a sizable family library of Chinese literature as well as many volumes on Western Literature and art. He attended university at Beijing Foreign Languages Institute from 1957 to 1962, where he studied French language and literature. After graduating, Gao began working as a translator and editor of the French edition of *China Reconstructs,* a monthly magazine produced in all the major languages of the world to tout the successes of socialist reconstruction in China. During this period, Gao began secretly writing plays, stories, and essays, which he had to hide from the authorities due to Mao Zedong's edict that all literature and arts should solely be used to serve the masses. Gao's wife eventually denounced him to government officials. As a result, he was sent to rural China for cultural "re-education," where he worked for six years as a farm laborer and teacher. Although he continued to write during his "re-education," Gao either burned or buried all of his writings, including unpublished novels, plays, and essays, for fear of being further labelled as a subversive. Gao returned to Beijing in 1975 and began working for the Chinese Writers Association. Following the end of the Cultural Revolution, Gao's writing began to appear regularly in Chinese publications and in 1981 he was assigned to work as a writer for the Beijing People's Art Theater. His first play, *Juedui xinhao* (*Absolute Signal*), was produced in 1982 and became a popular success. That same year, Gao was diagnosed with terminal cancer, but two weeks later learned that he had been misdiagnosed and did not have cancer. His next play, *Chezhan* (1983; *Bus Stop*), was declared subversive by the Chinese government, and Gao decided to leave Beijing in order to escape a possible prison sentence. He spent the next five months on a fifteen thousand kilometer trek through rural China, an experience which later became the basis for his novel *Soul Mountain*. When the political climate in China changed in 1984, Gao returned to Beijing. His next plays received negative reactions from the Chinese government, causing Gao to emigrate to France in 1987 during a trip to Germany on an artistic fellowship. After the massacre during the student protests in Beijing's Tiananmen Square in 1989, Gao denounced the actions of the Chinese authorities to the media and applied for political asylum in France. In 1992 Gao wrote and produced a play—*Taowang* (1992; *Fleeing*)—about the Tiananmen Square massacre, resulting in the Chinese government banning all of Gao's works in China. He became a naturalized French citizen in 1998 and was awarded the Chevalier de l'Ordre des Arts et des Letters from the French government in 1992.

MAJOR WORKS

Gao's first play, *Absolute Signal,* follows an attempted train robbery that is thwarted when one of the villains decides not to go through with the crime. The play uses a variety of flashbacks and different perspectives to create an unique narrative voice. In *Bus Stop,* the thoughts and behaviors of seven characters—representing a cross-section of Chinese society—are rendered as they wait and watch buses pass without stopping. Western critics found the play reminiscent of the Theater of the Absurd movement and drew comparisons to Samuel Beckett's *Waiting for Godot*. Chinese authorities, however, condemned the play, interpreting it as an analogy for ineffective communist government. *Yeren* (1985; *Wildman*) concerns an ecologist and a newspaper reporter who travel into the wilderness of modern China in search of a mythical "wildman," who is said to be part human, part monkey. The play, defying conventional dramatic techniques, unfolds through a series of episodic scenes, interspersing traditional Chinese song, dance, and music with dialogue between the unnamed characters. In *Bi'an* (1986; *The Other Shore*)—the title refers to a term for Buddhist enlightenment—three characters, designated as The Crowd, Man, and Woman, engage in a symbolic struggle over the conflict between the individual and collective will. *The Other Shore* was the last play that Gao wrote in China before emigrating to France in 1987. His plays written in France include *Fleeing, Dialogue-interloquer* (1992; *Dialogue and Rebuttal*), *Le Somnambule* (1994; *Nocturnal Wanderer*), and *Zhoumo sichongzou* (1995; *Weekend Quartet*). *Fleeing,* set during the 1989 Tiananmen Square student protests, takes place in an abandoned warehouse where two men and a young woman have taken refuge from the military tanks sent in to stop the demonstration. *Dialogue and Rebuttal* follows two strangers who have spent the night together, examining their inability to communicate and their individual relationships with language. *Nocturnal Wanderer* is a dream play where a character named Sleepwalker battles to escape his nightmare. The structure of *Weekend Quartet* is based on the composition of a musical quartet and examines the relationships between four different characters. Gao has also received considerable critical attention for his two novels, *Soul Mountain* and *Le Livre d'un homme seul* (2000; *One Man's Bible*). *Soul Mountain*—a Buddhist term for heaven—is based on Gao's experience of being misdiagnosed with terminal cancer and his fifteen thousand kilometer, five-month long journey to the eastern coast of China. The novel employs an experimental narrative style, which includes alternating narrative points of view, as well as a bifurcation of the main character into both male and female parts. *Soul Mountain* is divided into eighty-one short, episodic chapters, with each chapter alternating between first- and second-person narration. The plot follows an individual's search for meaning by way of a spiritual journey. Through his/her encounters with the people and cultures of remote China, the main character explores the tensions between individual and collective identity. *One Man's Bible* is a historical novel, set during the Chinese Cultural Revolution. As in *Soul Mountain,* the narrative voice includes second- and third-person narration, but *One Man's Bible* purposely excludes the first-person "I" in order to symbolize the suppression of individual identity by Chinese government forces.

CRITICAL RECEPTION

There has been a direct correlation between the critical reception of Gao's writing in China and the political climate of the country. While his plays *Absolute Signal* and *Wildman* have been considered relatively politically innocuous, *Bus Stop* and *The Other Shore* have been denounced by Chinese authorities as subversive. Outside of China, Gao's plays received positive critical recognition in a number of countries during the 1980s and 1990s through theatrical productions and translated publications, although few English translations of his works existed. However, after winning the Nobel Prize in 2000, Gao gained international prominence and many of his works have become available in English. Gao's plays have been praised for their experimental theatrical techniques, episodic structures, and their focus on the recurring theme of individual versus collective identity. Critics have noted the clear influence of such Western playwrights as Samuel Beckett and Bertolt Brecht on Gao's dramatic works. Several reviewers have complimented Gao's mixture of modern Western and traditional Chinese literary and cultural influences. Critical discussion of *Soul Mountain* has focused primarily on Gao's narrative voice and structure. While many critics have found Gao's inventive storytelling techniques to be the novel's most remarkable feature, others have found the novel to be overly self-indulgent and alienating to the reader. Commentators have lauded the spiritual elements of *Soul Mountain,* with Fatima Wu observing that, "Above all, the book records one lonely individual's quest for his soul." Some reviewers, however, have questioned Gao's representations of women in his drama and fiction. Sylvia Li-chun Lin has commented that, "feminists might find his treatment of women in *Soul Mountain* bordering on male chauvinism."

PRINCIPAL WORKS

Stars on a Cold Night (novella) 1980

A Preliminary Exploration into the Techniques of Modern Fiction (criticism) 1981

*Juedui xinhao [*Absolute Signal*] (play) 1982

†*Chezhan* [*Bus Stop*] (play) 1983

Yeren [*Wildman*] (play) 1985

Bi'an [*The Other Shore*] (play) 1986

Sheng si jie [*Between Life and Death*] (play) 1991

Dialogue-interloquer [translated in Chinese as *Duihua yu fanjie*; translated in English as *Dialogue and Rebuttal*] (play) 1992

‡*Taowang* [*Fleeing*] (play) 1992

Shanhaijing zhuan [*The Story of the Classic of Seas and Mountains*] (play) 1993

Le Somnambule [translated in Chinese as *Ye you shen*; translated in English as *Nocturnal Wanderer*] (play) 1994

La Montagne de l'âme [translated in Chinese as *Lingshan*; translated in English as *Soul Mountain*] (novel) 1995

Zhoumo sichongzou [*Weekend Quartet*] (play) 1995

Au plus près du reel: Dialogues sure l'écriture, 1994-1997 (criticism) 1997

§*The Other Shore: Plays by Gao Xingjian* (plays) 1999

Le Livre d'un homme seul [translated in Chinese as *Yige ren de Shengjing*; translated in English as *One Man's Bible*] (novel) 2000

*This play has also been translated and produced under the title *Alarm Signal.*

†This play has also been translated and produced under the title *Bus Station.*

‡This play has also been translated and produced under the titles *Absconding, Escape, Exile,* and *The Fugitives.*

§This collection includes *The Other Shore, Between Life and Death, Dialogue and Rebuttal, Nocturnal Wanderer,* and *Weekend Quartet.*

CRITICISM

Xiaomei Chen (essay date fall 1992)

SOURCE: Chen, Xiaomei. "A *Wildman* Between Two Cultures: Some Paradigmatic Remarks on 'Influence Studies.'" *Comparative Literature Studies* 29, no. 4 (fall 1992): 397-416.

[*In the following essay, Chen discusses* Wildman *in terms of both Western and Chinese cultural influences.*]

In May 1985, when Gao Xingjian premiered his third play, **Wildman,** in Beijing, China, its critical reception was quite different from his first two plays, **The Alarm Signal** staged in 1982 and **The Bus Stop** in 1983.[2] Both of his earlier plays have been immediately recognized as being strongly "influenced" by the Western modern theater—by such people as "the formidable French dramatist, God-madman, Antonin Artaud," and "a host of writers and theorists of the Theater of the Absurd."[3] The Western critics were unanimous in reviewing **The Bus Stop** as "the first play to introduce elements of the Theater of the Absurd to a Chinese audience."[4] Their Chinese counterparts, likewise, expressed a similar view. One of the striking features of **The Bus Stop,** as Wang Xining argued in a review in *China Daily,* is that it successfully "dissected modern Chinese urban society in a manner reminiscent of Beckett's *Waiting for Godot.*"[5]

However, **Wildman,** the third of Gao Xingjian's plays to be performed, elicited a quite different critical response. On the one hand, some Chinese and Western critics were still enthusiastic about its Western style and technique. Others, however, pointed to a new turn in Gao's interest, one which drew on the rich resources of Chinese theatrical traditions. Those who celebrated the return of Chinese tradition in Gao's latest play insisted that it owed its success mainly to its endeavor to enrich "the range of expression open to artists in all performing arts in China."[6] What is perhaps most interesting in this critical disagreement is the way that it heightens our awareness of the complexity of cultural relations which underlie the play, and leads to what has already become a central question about it—is the play primarily founded on a Chinese or Western model? This disagreement about **Wildman** has been further complicated by Gao's own declaration of intention which stresses his allegiance to the classical Chinese traditions in theater. In the "Postscript" to the published form of the play, Gao explains that **Wildman** is an attempt to realize his ideal of establishing a "modern theater" by drawing on traditional Chinese operas characterized by its artistic techniques of *chang* (singing), *nian* (speech), *zuo* (acting), and *da* (acrobatics).[7] Interestingly enough, in characterizing this native Chinese tradition Gao uses the term "Total Theater"—a term which cannot fail to suggest to the Western consciousness the work of Antonin Artaud, and indeed the whole *Gesamtkunstwerk* tradition since Wagner—to designate his "ideal" theater in which artists would easily "recover many Chinese artistic techniques already lost in the last century."⁸

Gao explicitly claims in his "Postscript" that this play does not attempt to win over its audience by the art of dialogue, a feature which he associates with the Western drama; instead, he claims, **Wildman** seeks a full employment of the traditional Chinese operatic, and above all, non-verbal techniques of dance, music, images, costumes, and make-up to compose a "dramatic symphony" which consists of several different themes, themes which overlap harmonies and disharmonies in order to fashion a "polyphony." In **Wildman,** therefore, both language and music are used in such a way that they create a kind of "multi-voicedness." Just as a symphony seeks to create "a total musical image," Gao asserts, **Wildman** "tends to realize a total effect of action through multi-voicedness, counterpoints, contrasts and repetitions."⁹ For the visual aspect of the play, Gao symphonizes a "multi-layer-visual-image" through the use of dance, flash-back scenes, shadows, and movements. Each actor in **Wildman,** therefore, must possess the "skills required by the traditional Chinese theater": he must perform at once as a dancer, a singer, an acrobat as well as a speaking character. Costuming, our playwright demands, should not only be strikingly bright in color, as is required by the traditional theater to enhance the visual and physical effect on the senses of the audience, but it should also "truthfully reflect the local color of the mountain area along the Yellow River" which provides the play with its geographical background. A faithful portrayal of the primitive and natural lifestyle of the mountain folks, Gao Xingjian insists, is crucial for a successful production of the play. Fortunately, Lin Zhaohua, the Beijing director of **Wildman,** fundamentally preserved the "Chineseness" that Gao Xingjian so painstakingly spelled out. **Wildman** was for the most part performed in local dialect of the Sichuan Province, with episodic scenes which remind one of the traditional "opera-drama sketches," mixed up with local folk songs, national minority dances, and Han epic singing.

In addition to the traditional Chinese theatrical conventions consciously explored both by the playwright and the director, **Wildman**'s dramatic structure and theme are also indigenously Chinese. Unlike Western drama, which usually has an Aristotelian plot with a beginning, a middle, and an end, **Wildman** carries no obvious storyline. Instead, the play consists of a series of diverse episodes peopled by nameless characters who move in a more or less definite and identifiable place. The play is set in contemporary China in the rapidly-vanishing virgin forest of Sichuan province where some scientists and local people believe in the existence of wildmen, a sort of man-like monkey which is believed to offer the much sought "missing link" of traditional evolutionary theory. A nameless scientist, designated in the script only by the character name "ecologist," goes into the forest to undertake research on wildmen, hoping to learn not only something about these strange "living fossils," but also about the preservation of a living and natural environment which he believes is ultimately linked to the continuation of the human species.

In his travels the ecologist encounters lumber men, wood-cutters, and local "cadres"—bureaucrats who make their fame and living by destroying the forests. By virtue of their occupations, all of these people threaten the living environment of wildmen and thus come into conflict with the ecologist. In the course of the play he also sets himself in opposition to other city-dwellers who, like him, have ventured into the forests for the sake of tracing the whereabouts of the wildmen, though motivated by purposes quite different from his own. A newspaper man—again the character has no name and is designated only by his profession—for instance, is merely interested in hunting for "hot" or "exotic" news to please his readers in the city. Similarly, scientists representing opposing sides in a scholarly debate are at work collecting data only to prove or disprove the existence of the wildmen. Unlike the ecologist, they have no interest in investigating living creatures and their environmental conditions in order to protect them. They bribe innocent local people, especially children who cannot even understand the issues at stake, in order to prove the existence or non-existence of wildmen, thus bringing about quarrels, disputes, and disharmony in the mountain village in which peace, unity, and harmony once prevailed.

Another episodic strain of the play concerns a school teacher who devotes all his time and energy attempting to rescue an epic of the Han nationality—the only one of its kind—by writing down the performance of an old and dying epic rhapsodist. This epic, *The Song of Darkness,* recounts the history and development of the Han nationality from the time of its childhood—when it first began to separate itself from the wildman—up to the present time. Because of its nature and scope, the ecologist and teacher believe that the epic should be regarded as a "national treasure" which is "as precious as panda and wildman" for the Chinese nation. Integrated into this episode are other overlapping themes and "subplots" which deal with problematic and still unanswered questions in contemporary China about love, marriage, ethics, custom, tradition, corruption, and even ideological issues left unresolved from the Cultural Revolution.

Wildman is infinitely more complex than what I have just indicated here, but enough has been said, I think, to indicate the ways in which the play offers a view of an exceedingly problematic world that is full of contradictions and disharmonies. Yet unexpectedly at the end of the play we are offered an episode which is connected with many of the play's diverse concerns. Here a wildman appears to a little boy in a dream. The wildman imitates the boy's language and gesture, dancing with him happily, running with him into the depth of the forest. While these actions are taking place, the audience becomes increasingly aware of the epic singing and folk music which grows louder and more prominent in order to furnish an accompaniment to the scene. Central to this moment in the play's economy is a silent but nonetheless real "dialogue" between this child of modern man and his predecessor, between "mankind and Nature."[10] The image created by this last scene, one so strongly suggestive of harmony and cosmic totality, is clearly related to the spectacular ending of the traditional Chinese theater that overwhelms its audience with a *Gesamtkunstwerk*-like effect of singing, dancing and acting. Such an ending thematically embraces the Taoist vision of a harmony between nature and culture. It provides its audience with a catharsis that supposedly enabled them to come to grips with the cosmic and mythological forces in the universe. As the director of the play, Lin Zhaohua, points out: ultimately **Wildman** is about harmony, "a harmony between people and their nation, a harmony among people themselves. It urges the audience to think about its relationship to nature and to culture, especially ancient culture."[11] It seems clear, then, that both in form and content **Wildman** can be viewed as a contemporary restoration of the theatrical, cultural, and philosophical traditions of China.

Yet, it would be a serious mistake to see in Gao Xingjian's play only a recuperation of indigenous Chinese traditions. As the terminology in which Gao describes his play suggests, anyone at all acquainted with the modern Western theater will not fail to be immediately impressed by the way it seems to exploit conceptions of the theater strikingly similar to those advocated by Antonin Artaud's notion of "the total theater" and Brecht's theory of "epic theater." Artaud, of course, spent much of his life longing for a theater of "a pure action," a theater of a latent force beyond rational speech or language, beyond "a written text" and "a literary tradition." He therefore sought to create a theater wholly unlike the Western theater of his time, one which would present an "archetypal and dangerous reality, a reality of which the Principles . . . hurry to dive back into the obscurity of the deep."[12] Artaud believed that fixed text, language, reason, order, even civilization itself with its attendant traditions, were barriers to the human spirit. He therefore called for a theater of physicality that was to create "a metaphysics of speech, gesture, and expression" which would be capable of throwing its spectators back to real life, not by imitation or illusion, but by a mystical, ritual, primitive, or archetypal spectacle of signs and gestures which

spoke for the anti-rational element in human experience. Artaud therefore proposed to resort to mass spectacle, providing his audience with a "pure experience" which would create a sensation of totality, awakening in them an intuitive force which was expressed in a theater of the body. If language is used at all, Artaud observed, it must be a language beyond words and senses capable of evoking that which cannot be spoken. He therefore called his ideal theater "a sacred theater" because it was to have "the solemnity of a sacred rite."[13] Thus the Artaudian theater aims at a more universal, primordial force deeper than any psychological or social reality, a force that touches on "an idea of Chaos, an idea of the Marvelous, an idea of Equilibrium."[14]

All of these Artaudian elements of the theater can easily be identified in **Wildman**. By means of non-verbal elements, **Wildman** provides for its audiences the kind of total and physical experience that Artaud so painstakingly emphasized. The time span of 8,000 years in **Wildman**'s action and its invocation to *Pan Gu*, the Chinese God of creation in the primordial times, suggest to its spectators a cosmic view of the universe. The sharp contrast between the non-verbal, primitive wildman and the verbal but confused, problematic modern man shocks the spectators and thus attempts to throw them into a mystical and ritual experience which is "deeper than any psychological or social realities." The world of **Wildman** extends far beyond the boundaries of anything uniquely Chinese and modern; indeed, the play seems finally concerned with issues that belong to a world much larger than that which is codified in the details of its dialogue, language, and setting. Much of the effect of the play is achieved by its spectacular physicality which seeks to create the sensation that Artaud said would simultaneously "touch on Creation, Becoming, and Chaos."[15]

To a large extent, then, **Wildman** participates in the traditions of the Artaudian theater with its "passionate equation between Man, Society, Nature and Objects."[16] All of these concerns are crystallized in the last scene where, as we have already seen, amidst a mixture of pantomime, mimicry, and musical harmonies and rhythms, a wildman, the image of the primitive and the natural, dances with a little boy, a symbol of the childhood of civilization. At the end of the play, we are provided with the following stage directions:

> They [the wild man and Xi Mao, the little boy] run onto an elevation at the back of the stage. XI MAO does a forward roll. He turns expectantly to the WILD MAN, who clumsily does the same. XI MAO runs, calling to the WILD MAN, who runs after him. They play hide and seek. XI MAO looks out from behind a stone. The WILD MAN sees him and runs toward him. XI MAO runs toward the elevation, and the WILD MAN follows. Gently, music starts and their move-

ments slow down until they look as though they are in a slow-motion film. Then they perform a dance. XI MAO is nimble, the WILD MAN clumsy. When XI MAO and the WILD MAN play together, the WILD MAN tends to copy XI MAO's movements, even when in slow motion. The WILD MAN should always have his back to the audience. XI MAO draws back into an area of light at the rear of the stage, in front of a backdrop depicting the forest. All performers enter wearing makes, each mask expressing a different shade of emotion. The "happier" masks should be in the center of the stage. All move slowly toward the WILD MAN, to the rhythm of the LUMBERJACKS' dance and the melody from the song of the TEAM OF SISTERS. The sad cries of the OLD SINGER are heard, gradually fading out. XI MAO is seen and faintly heard saying, "xia, xia, a shame, xia, xia, xia. xia. A shame, a . . . shame." Curtain.[17]

All these and other theatrical conventions seek to put the audience into a state prior to language and therefore help them to break away from the intellectual subjugation of the language, thus conveying to them a sense of "a new and a deeper intellectuality which hides itself beneath the gestures and signs, raised to the dignity of particular exorcisms."[18] With this world of "the Absolutes" and "the invisible" cosmic forces, *Wildman* also meets the demands of the Artaudian theater for a "a religious ritual," and therefore moves towards what Leonard Pronko has characterized as "that meeting point where human and nonhuman, meaning and chaos, finite and infinite, come together."[19]

Yet, as soon as we have identified the similarities between *Wildman* and its Western counterparts, we are also tempted to "decenter" this claim by arguing for the opposite "truth." Artaud emphasizes the dynamics of action and the higher forces of violent physical images that "crush and hypnotize the sensibility of the spectator." He even went so far as to exclude from the theatre any "copy of life," or any concern with aspect of social and psychological realities.[20] Within his limited concern of trying to restore theater to its original direction, to "reinstate it in its religious and metaphysical aspect," Artaud makes explicit that his theater must "break with actuality," and that its object must not be to "resolve social or psychological conflicts" or "to serve as battlefield for moral passions." The function of theater, he insists, is to express objectively certain secret truths that "have been buried under forms in their encounters with Becoming."[21] For him, language, tradition, and the theatrical masterpieces of the past are responsible for the decline of the Western theater. If a contemporary public does not understand *Oedipus Rex*, he argues, it is the fault of this ancient Greek play, not of the public, since the latter has learned too well that the theater frequently deals with the themes of incest, morality, falsehood, and illusion. A concentration on social realities and their attendant problems is regarded in the Artaudian model as being outside of the legitimate concern or the proper domain of theater.

In recognizing this claim of Artaud's "total theater," we are immediately brought face-to-face with the way that *Wildman* rejects some of Artaud's demands. There can be no denying that *Wildman* is firmly foregrounded in the contemporary Chinese society; its concerns, as we have noted earlier, are occasional in the best sense of that term. Though its episodic structure forecloses the possibility of its offering a "solution" at the end of the play, *Wildman* nonetheless raises in a striking and even direct way unanswered and perhaps unanswerable questions about love, marriage, tradition, bureaucracy, science, morality, and even the current national preoccupation with ecology and environmental protection. It is true that *Wildman* can be categorized as a traditional dance and music drama, and that in this sense it seems to meet Artaud's demand for a form of theater that is closely related to ritual and religious ceremony. But it is also true that its basic thematic matter is concerned with a conflict between nature and culture that is specific to a moment in late twentieth-century Chinese history. In fact, precisely because these thematic concerns are historically so far removed from the primitive and the ritual experience in which they are theatrically mediated to us, the play is able to go beyond Artaud by combining that sense of primitive "magic culture," which Artaud's theater seeks, with much that is not Artaudian—an entirely modern world with its own social and psychological dimensions.

The same dichotomy between that which belongs to the "total theater" and that which does not becomes apparent when we attempt to locate the kinds of theatrical gestures and movements which *Wildman* employs. From one perspective the play's actions seem to look back to that moment when religious ceremony emerged from its purely ritualistic origins and was transformed into the beginnings of what we know as theater.[22] On the other hand, the play's action definitely goes beyond the first beginnings of the theater. It includes elements which we associate with a "mature" theater, with its combination of the verbal with the non-verbal, the actual with the imaginative, the social with the psychological, and above all, the sensational with the individual. *Wildman* is at once descriptive and narrative, spectacular and physical. The opposing claims for the traditional and the modern, the intellectual and the physical—seen by Artaud as irreconcilable or as hurled against each other—are here coupled together. It is perhaps in this sense that *Wildman* realizes the ideal of a theater of "totality" which goes well beyond Artaud's demands and in which the basic disparity between self and others, subject and object, reason and sensations, language and signs are finally engulfed and united.

But Artaud is not the only Western theoretician of the drama whose work is relevant to *Wildman*. Gao Xingjian observes in his "Postscript" that *Wildman*'s emphasis on the *mise en scène* and spectacle does not aim at creating verisimilitude. It is intended, on the contrary, for reminding "its audience that it is acting," not real life. Gao therefore expressly requires that masks be used in the production of *Wildman* in order to emphasize the dichotomies, contradictions or multi-voicedness within the characters. At the outset of the play, the actor who plays the part of the ecologist steps out of his character and exhorts his audience to enjoy the play fully without worrying about the whereabouts of the actors, who may sometimes appear sitting in the audience. There need not be, he implies, any barriers between the world of the audience and the world of the play. In the middle of the play, for instance, the ecologist takes off his mask more than once in order to assume his identity as an actor. In this guise he recites poems and provides background information. Earlier, at the outset of the play, he even "narrates" what would normally be regarded as stage directions and theatrical comments. In this way, the actor openly disowns his character. He calls attention to his many different roles—the ecologist, the actor who plays the ecologist, and a stage director. He is, he reminds us, at different times all of these figures, and yet he is "really" none of them. Such a discourse seems intended to prevent us from establishing an emotional identification with the ecologist or any other character. All of these devices are suggestive of the Brechtian theater, of course. In his article **"The *Wildman* and I,"** Gao Xingjian openly admits such a Brechtian influence, especially as concerns the now classic theory of the "alienation effect."[23] For him, Brechtian distancing devices help break down the conventional notion of the theater as representation of real life.[24]

But just as our observation of the Artaudian elements in *Wildman* led us also to see the presence of the opposite, so here too the Brechtian nature of the drama is undercut in our very act of recognizing its presence. Brecht's "alienation effect" aims basically and fundamentally at keeping the spectators from being emotionally involved so that they can intellectually contemplate the possible meanings of the play. In the "Postscript" to *Wildman,* however, Gao Xingjian paradoxically specifies that the director should create in the play a kind of "cordial atmosphere" in which the actors directly communicate with the audience (a Brechtian technique as well as one that recalls the works of Thornton Wilder) so that the audience can feel free and happy to participate in the total experience of the theater, as if they were enjoying an entertainment during a festival (a notion which is decidedly un-Brechtian). The production, our playwright specifies, should also leave enough time between each act so that the audience is able to think intellectually, reflect, and ponder over what they have just experienced. *Wildman,* therefore, offers its audiences a multiple, polyvalent, and even contradictory experience in which the body and mind, the primitive and the contemporary, the universal and the local, the sensational and the intellectual, the subjective and the objective, the illusionary and the actual are all joyfully united and combined. It is at once Brechtian and anti-Brechtian, Artaudian and anti-Artaudian. It is at once both and yet neither.

Gao Xingjian's *Wildman,* therefore, presents to us a strange and yet stimulating dramatic phenomenon which raises in a radical way a number of theoretical issues that are not restricted to "the dramatic" in the narrower sense of that term, but which reach into the theory of literature in general, and, as the rest of this study will suggest, into the theory and practice of Comparative Literature in particular. Gao's play raises questions of the first order about the "canonical" practice of "influence studies," and it is to this concern, both relevant for the comparative study of dramatic texts and non-dramatic texts, to which I shall now turn.

Ulrich Weisstein has said: "the notion of influence must be regarded as virtually the key concept in Comparative Literature studies, since it posits the presence of two distinct and therefore comparable entities: the work from which the influence proceeds and that [to] which it is directed."[25] That is to say, cross-cultural literary studies, as a comparative discipline, have depended largely on the "key notion of influence studies" which are characterized as one-to-one relationships between "emitter" and "receiver" texts. At first sight, the general concerns of this essay—the relationship between one national theater and that of the other—seem to be the proper subject for these kinds of "influence studies."[26] On further consideration, however, these concerns can be seen to raise, perhaps in a radical way, theoretical questions on the validity and legitimacy of such traditionally conceived "influence studies." It will be the burden of the rest of this essay to set the discussion on *Wildman,* and the Western dramatic theories on which it seems to draw, within a broader context of some critical theories of canon formation in the West and the East alike.[27]

As our discussion of *Wildman* has already suggested, it is exceedingly difficult if not impossible, to determine which cultural tradition evoked in *Wildman* is the "emitter" and which is the "receiver." Did the Chinese traditional theater influence the West by means of Brecht's theories, which, as Brecht himself admitted, were derived in some sense from Chinese sources? In that case, Chinese theories of drama made a detour through Western cultural traditions only to come back to China to exert an influence on the modern Chinese theater. Or did Artaud and Brecht influence Gao Xingjian, who, in turn, found in the West that which had been lost in the contemporary Chinese theater? Or is it, more simply, the case that Gao reached back into his own national traditions to create his play?[28] To raise these questions is to see that it is impossible simply to posit the "presence of two distinct and therefore comparable entities."

The question of whether *Wildman* is indigenously "Chinese" or characteristically "Western" can here be seen as deeply puzzling. *Wildman* appears to be both, and yet, it can never be "proven" to be one or the other. As we have seen earlier, *Wildman* has been received as the most "Chinese" play Gao has ever written, and this very "Chineseness" in the play has even been declared as part of his own attempt to rescue modern Chinese theater from being too much influenced by its Western counterparts. However, as soon as we have discovered everything that can be identified as "Chinese," these characteristics can immediately be "decentered" in order to prove just the opposite claim. We might, then, be tempted to say that the play is the product of Western influence. But clearly the matter can not be solved so facilely. Furthermore, talking about the play's "Westerness" invites yet another confusion: one perceives at the same moment the Artaudian as well as the anti-Artaudian elements, the Brechtian as well as the anti-Brechtian characteristics. It seems pertinent, therefore, to first of all attempt to "decide," if ever possible, the nature of "Chineseness" and of "Westerness" in the context of our discussion before one can even begin to discuss, and therefore to challenge, the concept of the relationship between an "emitter" and a "receiver" in the traditional mode of "influence studies."

But our difficulties are not due solely to the complications and contradictions embedded in the term "Western dramatic tradition." The words "Chineseness" and "the Chinese theater" have a similar long and seemingly "confusing" history, and this history is further complicated, in the West at least, by generations of Western critical acts of "misreading" and "misunderstanding."[29] As Leonard C. Pronko has rightly pointed out in his *Theater East* and *West,* the traditional Chinese theater "has had a history of singular mis-comprehension and mis-interpretation in the West."[30] When one considers the sheer difficulty of communicating across cultural boundaries, it is easy to agree with Pronko's claim. But Pronko's implied evaluation of misunderstanding and misreading, common as they are, constitutes at best only a partially valid view of these activities. Pronko assumes that "mis-comprehension" and "mis-interpretation" are undesirable activities, and that it is the task of cross-cultural studies to remove them. But as a good deal of recent literary theory has insisted, "misreading" and "misunderstanding" are not wholly negative actions. On the contrary, for critics like T. S. Eliot and Harold Bloom, these once-thought "negative" activities are the means by which literary history is made and—I would add—cross-cultural influence takes place.

For Eliot, Bloom, and a number of other theorists, Western literary production is motivated by an intense quest for the novel, or the apparently new. "Strong" writers and critics seek ways of escaping—or apparently escaping—the "father" tradition in which they have been formed, and the process of "misunderstanding" and "misreading" provided a convenient means for their accomplishing this goal. In an attempt to say what apparently had not been said before, some Western writers turned, and continue to turn, to the novelty of exotic literature. But the exotic literature was not studied or appropriated for its own sake. Rather it was appropriated and reworked for the apparent strangeness which it offered to audiences. Yet paradoxically, the otherness could not be allowed to remain as otherness, for in order for Western audiences to appropriate it in some way, the strange had to be made familiar; the exotic had to be domesticated, even if in the process it ceased to be exotic. To take a specific example, eighteenth-century European writers, motivated by an "anxiety of influence," turned to classical Chinese drama as a source of novelty. Yet in order to make these strange texts comprehensible, they "misread" them by making them conform to traditions of Western drama. Let us first of all consider briefly the process by which this paradoxical transformation took place.

Fan Xiheng, in his essay "From *The Orphan of Chao* to *Orphelin de la Chine*," describes for us a brief history of the transformation of a Chinese drama from the Yuan Dynasty (1279-1368) into Western dramatic repertory. This Yuan drama, known as *The Great Revenge of the Orphan of Chao* (*Zhaoshi gu'er dabaochou*), is attributed to Ji Junxiang and was first performed in China around the thirteenth century. The same play was later re-written by another anonymous author under the title of *The Story of the Orphan of Chao* (*Zhaoshi gu'er ji*). According to Fan Xiheng, Ji Junxiang's Yuan drama was first translated into French in the 1730s, which brought about other translations into English, German, Italian, and Russian.[31] This Chinese Yuan play has thus over the centuries inspired several generations of Western dramatists such as the Englishman William Hatchett, who adopted Ji's Chinese story into his *The Chinese Orphan,* and the Italian playwright Pietro Metastasio, who wrote his own version of *Eroe Cinese,* to name only a few. A better-known case, of course, is Voltaire's *Orphelin de la Chine,* which was so successful in its Paris premier that it was immediately translated into Italian and English. Yet, this process of transformation was by no means a one-way street. Not only did the original Chinese text inspire Western readers, but Chinese readers, upon reading their Western peers' re-creation of the Chinese text, did not hesitate to translate these Western texts back into Chinese language again. During the Second World War, for instance, a Chinese writer by the name of Zhang Ruogu translated Voltaire's French play, which was originally based on Ji's

Chinese orphan story, into an abridged *prose* version "in order to raise the morale of the Chinese people in their struggle against Japanese invaders."[32]

Among several Western transformations mentioned above, one of the earliest "creative misreadings" was William Hatchett's well-known adaptation of the Chinese Yuan drama, published in England in 1741. He attracted his audience and gained a certain amount of notoriety for himself by his "new" work with a borrowed "exotic" story and a foreign "parentage." Having to cope with the burden of his own Western tradition in order to find for himself a place in his own cultural tradition, Hatchett "creatively" distorted the Chinese Yuan play and actually presented it as "an English neo-classic play, observing the unity of time," though in fact his Chinese "father" story takes place over some twenty-five years.[33] It is clear that the so-called "Chinese influence" at this early stage of cultural exchange amounts to nothing more than an expression of the European taste for the exotic, the different, the dissimilar which must be garbed in Western clothing to make it attractive. The image of the "Chinese theater" that Hatchett's work suggests is only a Westerner's own arbitrary interpretation—or, better, "misinterpretation" and "misunderstanding"—of it. It is a product of a Western search for things "anew"—foreign manners, interesting events, plots or characters of curiosity. Yet in Hatchett's play these elements end up pathetically conforming to the older taste and tradition for which they were intended as an antidote, in this case, the neo-classical theater.

But this account is not complete in itself. It does not represent a naive moment in Chinese-Western cultural relationships. Attempts like Hatchett's to offer to the West such distorted and "creative" introductions of the Chinese theater decisively shape the literary and theatrical expectations of the Chinese theater. The word "Chineseness," therefore, inescapably means for the eighteenth century English audience something drastically different from what it meant in its original Chinese setting. Such audiences found in the Oriental theater what on first consideration seemed not available in their own. And these "exotic" elements "found" there and "introduced" to the West were always strikingly different from their Chinese "sources" in terms of stylization, symbolizing, movement, make-up, and music. Even in the twentieth century, despite increasing knowledge of contacts with China and Chinese scholars, the reception of the Chinese theatrical tradition by figures like Bertolt Brecht was still to some extent inspired by a "creative" misunderstanding of the ingenious works of his foreign "critical" fathers and appropriated in such a way as to enrich his own limited space of "imagination." Since Brecht appeared on the historical scene much later than his "fathers" like Hatchett and Voltaire, he explored with much more vigor than his predecessors what had been left unsaid in the Western reception of the Chinese theater. In order to outwit his Western predecessors, Brecht's "creative misreading" of the Chinese dramatic tradition was, to employ again the mechanism described in T. S. Eliot's "Tradition and the Individual Talent," a conforming and a surrendering to the two cultural traditions. At the same time, of course, it was an oedipal rebellion against both.

Brecht's concept of "*Verfremdungseffekt*" first occurred in his essay entitled "Alienation Effects in Chinese Acting," written in 1936, occasioned by Brecht's seeing Mei Lanfang's performance in Moscow. As his article reveals, Brecht was deeply impressed by the Chinese actor "who constantly keeps a distance between himself, his character, and the spectator. . . . Consequently he never loses control of himself; his performance is constantly on a conscious, artistic level with all emotion transposed."[34] As Pronko rightly points out, however, Brecht's "alienation effect" was a product of nothing more than his "misunderstanding" of the Chinese stage conventions. Chinese spectators were expected to react emotionally to the sad or happy scenes in Chinese opera. Pronko has also observed that Chinese music, originally used to appeal to deep emotions, was interpreted by Brecht as a means to break illusion and to establish a distance.[35] In terms of the present argument, Brecht rebelled against his Western "father critics," who first introduced the Chinese theater to the West, by pointing out those elements of "Chineseness" in the Chinese theater which they failed to perceive. He was therefore no longer interested in the exotic foreign manners and curious plots, as were his predecessors. Above all, he was not interested in seeing the Chinese tradition as "classical" and hence Aristotelian. His notion of "alienation effect" which he believed to be "Chinese," however, as Pronko has rightly pointed out, "inspired" only his own version of reading the Chinese performing arts. His "unfamiliarity" with the Chinese theater, however, paradoxically makes him conform to the earlier tradition of the Western "critical fathers," who revised Chinese theater in order to make it palatable to the West.

Seen from this perspective, Brecht is no "genius," nor is he a "strong" poet. For all of his attempts to do otherwise, he only repeats what his Western "father Critics" had done in the past. His "misreading" and "misunderstanding" of the Chinese theater, and as the result of it, his creative notion of "alienation effect" are no more "ingenious" than his "critical" fathers' creation of a Chinese neoclassical drama. At the same time his "misreading," or the deliberate use, of the Chinese theater also betrays Brecht as an unfaithful "critical son" to his Chinese ancestors. By an act of "creative" treason, however, he paradoxically fits himself into the foreign tradition as well as his own. He is therefore making a place for himself only by standing on the shoulders of ancient "giants" in two traditions.

Like Brecht, Gao Xingjian proved himself as no exception in following this law of the formation of a literary history. Coming quite late on the scene of the Chinese dramatic imagination, Gao Xingjian tried to create things "new" for his Chinese audience by introducing "exotic" and foreign theatrical traditions in his first two plays—*The Bus Stop* and *The Absolute Signal.* As we have already mentioned, his first two plays were heavily influenced by such Western dramatists as Artaud, Beckett, and Brecht. Later on, however, when the Chinese audience was overwhelmed by a flood of Western-style theater on the Chinese stage after the "open-door" policy was instituted, Gao Xingjian abandoned his Western critical fathers and returned to his own Chinese "parentage" in the traditional theater. In this way he was able to meet the changing literary expectations of his Chinese audience. Yet for reasons already suggested, his return to his own cultural father figures was in fact a return to the "Chineseness" of a theater which had earlier appealed to his foreign "fathers," and appropriated by them through acts of creative "misreading." Once again, then, we have an example of "belatedness" in which a son poet, in this case Gao Xingjian, felt compelled to find things "new" in a foreign culture, a culture which in fact is "originally" his own.

In this case Gao was fortunate enough to live in a time and place which enabled him to embrace simultaneously his own literary tradition—"to recover many artistic techniques already lost in the last century"—at the same time he could use something newly "created" by his Western "parental critics" out of *his* (Gao's) own tradition.[36] As a belated critical son owing his debts to numerous "parental" critics from more than one culture, Gao benefits from both cultures, the East and the West, and from both historical heritages, the ancient and the modern, but he does so in a way that depends on misreadings and misunderstanding on every hand and in every direction. Because of this he ends up belonging exclusively to neither East nor West, but inclusively to both.

These remarks help us to understand the strange reception history of *Wildman* in which the play has been claimed by more than two national "parentages" in the critical reviews. On the one hand, *Wildman* can be perceived as a Chinese play only by those whose dramatic expectations are confined to a knowledge of the traditional Chinese theater. On the other hand, however, it can be regarded as being influenced by the Western theater only by those who take the concepts of Artaud and Brecht as purely Western, thus disregarding their debts to their Oriental "critical fathers." In both cases, however, readers from different cultural backgrounds, with different dramatic and cultural expectations, inevitably receive *Wildman* differently. It could not be otherwise, even for those Chinese readers knowledgeable in Western theater or for Westerners who are acquainted with Chinese dramatic traditions. Just as producers of texts can only write from within their own historical and cultural space—and in Gao's case, that space was both Chinese and Western in paradoxical ways—so readers can only read on the basis of their own place in history. There are no ontologically grounded "truths" by which we can distinguish "Chineseness" from "Westerness." The implications of this observation seem clear: what is important for us to pursue in our critical inquiry is the dynamics of interreactions and inter-relationships between tradition and individual talents, between literary production and literary reception. Needless to say, we cannot define or even separate one "comparative entity" from the other. Neither can we fruitfully determine such things as "emitter," "receiver," "origin," "beginning," "causality," and "continuity." Each term is inextricably tied to its opposite. There is no final reference, only shared properties of *différance*. Within that *différance* all that is Chinese appears as Western, all that is Western as Chinese. For sinology, then, world literature and world culture can no longer be ignored or assigned a secondary status as mere source or influence. Rather all that is "other" and "alien" to it—which is finally to say, all that is Western—must now be recognized and inscribed within its proper interests. All future studies of "comparative" drama, therefore, and perhaps in a more general sense, all future studies of any "national literature" situated in the context of world literature, need to take their departure from this observation.

Notes

1. I wish to thank Marvin Carlson, Eugene Eoyang, Clifford C. Flanigan, Iriving Lo, and Brian Caraher for reading an earlier draft of this essay.

2. For an English translation of *Wildman,* see *Asian Theater Journal* 7.2 (Fall 1990): 195-249, trans. Bruno Boubicek.

3. For a brief survey of the Western influence in Gao Xingjian and his plays, see Geremie Barme, "A Touch of the Absurd—Introducing Gao Xingjian, and his Play *The Bus Stop*," *Renditions* 19 (1983): 373-76. For a more recent account of Gao Xingjian's indebtedness to Antonin Artaud, Jerzy Grotowski, V. E. Meyerhold, and Mei Lanfang, see William Tay, "Avant-garde Theater in Post-Mao China: *The Bus-Stop* by Gao Xingjian," *Worlds Apart: Recent Chinese Writings and its Audiences,* ed. Howard Goldblatt (Armonk, NY: M. E. Sharpe, 1990) 111-18.

4. Barme 373-76.

5. Xining Wang, "An Unconventional Blend," *China Daily* [Beijing] 21 May 1985, 5.

6. Wang 5.

7. For an informative study of the main features of traditional Chinese theater available in English, see Tao-Ching Hsu, *The Chinese Conception of the Theater* (Seattle: The U of Washington P, 1985). Hsu's work is especially helpful in the context of this essay for its comparative perspective which treats as well other theatrical conventions such as the Greek, the Elizabethan, and the Japanese.

8. Xingjian Gao, "*Guanyu yanshude jianyi yu shuoming*" ["Suggestion and Explanation for the Production of *Wildman*"], *Shiyue* [October] 2 (1985): 169.

9. Gao 169.

10. The quotations of the Chinese text in this essay are from Xingjian Gao, *Yeren* [*Wildman*], in *Shiyuan* 2 (1985): 142-68. The translations are mine unless indicated otherwise.

11. Julian Baum, "Peking's *Wildman* Jolts Theater Goers," *The Christian Science Monitor* 24 June 1985: 9.

12. Antonin Artaud, *The Theater and Its Double*, trans. Mary Caroline Richards (New York: Grove P, 1958) 48.

13. Artaud 58.

14. Artaud 36.

15. Artaud 90.

16. Artaud 90.

17. This quotation is cited from Bruno Roubicek's English translation of *Wildman* 245.

18. Artaud 91.

19. Leonard Cabell Pronko, *Theater East and West: Perspectives Toward a Total Theater* (Berkeley: U of California P, 1967) 15.

20. Artaud 83.

21. Artaud 70.

22. For a recent study in English in the primitive Chinese theater as religious ritual, see Qiuyu Yu's "Some observations on the Aesthetics of Primitive Chinese Theater," *Asian Theater Journal* 6.1 (Spring 1989): 12-30. Drawing examples from various types of exorcistic performance (nuoxi), which are still more popular than film and TV programs in the Guangxi Zhuang Autonomous Region, Yu argues that in primitive Chinese performance, the aesthetic and ritual experience are very difficult to separate and that "ancient Chinese ritual performance to a great degree reflected the principal aspects of ancient Chinese society—ritual performance actually had become a rich social ceremony" (15).

23. Gao, "*Yeren yu wo*" ["The *Wildman* and I"], *Xiju dianying bao* [*Drama and Film Newspaper*] 12 May 1985: 2.

24. For an early account of Brecht and China, see Antony Tatlow's *Brechts chinesische Gedichte* (Frankfurt am Main: Suhrkamp, 1973). For a recent study of Brecht's reception in China, see Adrian Hsia, "The Reception of Bertolt Brecht in China and Its Impact on Chinese Drama," *Brecht and East Asian Theater*, eds. Antony Tatlow and Tak-wai Wong (Hong Kong: Hong Kong UP, 1982) 47-64.

25. Ulrich Weisstein, *Comparative Literature and Literary Theory: Survey and Introduction* (Bloomington: Indiana UP, 1968) 29.

26. A number of important earlier essays on the notion of literary influence have been collected in *Influx: Essays on Literary History*, ed. Ronald Primeau (Port Washington, NY: Kennikat P, 1977). For some recent—and sharply polemical—observations that seek to defend the traditional claims of "influence study," see Anna Balakian, "Literary Theory and Comparative Literature," *Toward a Theory of Comparative Literature*, ed. and intro. Mario J. Valdes, Proc. of the XIth International Comparative Literature Congress, 20-24 August 1985 (New York; Bern; Frankfurt am Main; Paris: Lang, 1990) 3:17-24. Balakian observes that "the word 'influence' has become a bad word, been confused with 'imitation,' and has even been viewed as a threat to ethnocentrism. It has been replaced by the theoreticians with the concept of 'intertextuality,' which is random, idiosyncratic, resulting in a free play of inter-referentiality which displays the virtuosity of the critic-manipulator rather than the fruits of scholarly research in the form of deep-sea plunging into literary works. The current theoretical version of influence study has become a major feature of what could be called 'aleatory criticism'" (18).

27. For an informative survey of the recent scholarship in Chinese-Western comparative literature, see Cecile Chu-Chin Sun, "Problems of Perspective in Chinese-Western Comparative Literature Studies," *Canadian Review of Comparative Literature* 13.4 (1986): 531-48. For Sun, there are two common types of Chinese-Western comparative literature writings in the past twenty years which failed to recognize "1) what comparative literature

is about and 2) the unique role of Chinese-Western comparative literature in the field" (533). The *"myopic"* school of comparison, for example, is "characterized by an over-emphasis on surface and random aspects of the works compared. The cultural contexts and literary conventions are seldom taken into account, in order to render the similarities tenable. The main purpose of this type of comparison is to claim that, after all, Chinese literature is not all that different from Western literatures" (533). The *"hypermetropic"* school, according to Sun, primarily applies Western theories to Chinese literature, "often in a wholesale fashion" (533). Sun believes that the "danger of this kind of approach lies in its undue confidence about the universal applicability of Western theory at the expense of the distinctive (and frequently intractable) features of Chinese literature" (542). Insightful and well-documented, Sun's article focuses on the lyric, and to a much lesser degree, the narrative, without touching on the issues of Chinese-Western dramatic studies, which in many ways remain the stepchild of comparative studies of Chinese and Western culture.

28. In his essay "On Dramatic Theories," Gao Xingjian surveyed the major dramatic traditions in the West, including those of Brecht and Artaud. Exploring the reasons why in recent years Chinese audiences have increasingly lost their interest in modern Chinese drama, Gao pointed out that the predominant Ibsenique tradition of social plays on the present Chinese stage has given too much emphasis to dramatic dialogue. For him, the Ibsenique tradition should be enhanced, if not replaced, by other dramatic traditions such as those of Brecht, Artaud, Chekhov, Gorky, and especially the classical Chinese theater, which employed singing, acting, dancing, and speaking in order to provide its audiences with theatrical experiences rather than mere concepts and ideas. See Xingjian Gao, "*Lun xiju guan*" ["On Dramatic Theories"], *Xijujie* [*The Dramatic Circle*] 1 (1983): 27-34.

29. By "misunderstanding"—in quotation marks—I mean a view of a text or a cultural event by a "received" community that differs in important ways from the view of that same phenomenon in the community of its own "origins." I do not mean to suggest the preexistence of an epistemologically grounded "proper" or "correct" understanding of the text to which a "misunderstanding" can be applied.

30. Pronko 35.

31. For a recent study in Western scholarship on the receptions of this Yuan drama in the West, see, for example, A. Owen Aldridge's chapter "Voltaire and the Mirage of China," *The Reemergence of World Literature: A Study of Asia and the West* (Newark: U of Delaware P, 1986) 141-66. Aldridge's conclusions are telling in the light of the present study: "Voltaire's source was a translation of 1731 by a French Jesuit, Joseph Henri Premare, which was later included in a famous compilation by another Jesuit, Jean Baptiste Du Halde, under the title *Description geographique, historique, chronologique, politique, et physique de l'empire de la Chine et de la tartarie chinoise* (1735). Among the essential ingredients of the original Chinese work were song and music, but these were completely eliminated from Premare's translation and from Voltaire's adaptation as well. Since Voltaire's neoclassical drama departed from both the form and the substance of his Chinese source, one would be justified in asking whether his work should really be considered as an example of the penetration of Chinese culture. Should it instead be dismissed as mere Chinoiserie? The answer is that Voltaire himself understood a great deal more about Chinese civilization than his play reveals, but that he was prevented by the prevailing taste of the times from closely following his model" (145).

32. Xiheng Fan, "*Chong zhaoshi gu'er dao zhongguo gu'er—shang*" ["From *The Orphan of Chao* to *Orphelin de la Chine* (Part I)"], *Zhongguo bijiao wenxue* [*Comparative Literature in China*] 4 (1987): 159-95.

33. Pronko 37.

34. Pronko 56.

35. For more information on the paradoxical relationship between Brecht and Mei Lanfang's theories of theater, see William Huizhu Sun, "Mei Lanfang, Stanislavsky and Brecht on China's Stage and Their Aesthetic Significance," *Drama in the People's Republic of China*, eds. Constantine Tung and Colin MacKerras SUNY P, 1987) 137-50. For a more general article on the reception of Mei Lanfang's performance in the Soviet Union in 1935 on the part of European theater artists such as Stanislavsky, Meyerhold, Craig, Brecht, Eisenstein, Piscator, Tairov and Tretiakov, see George Banu's "Mei Lanfang: A Case Against and a Model for the Occidental Stage," trans. Ella L. Wiswell and June V. Gibson, *Asian Theater Journal* 3.2 (Fall 1986): 153-78. See also Zuolin Huang, "A Supplement to Brecht's 'Alienation Effects in Chinese Acting,'" *Brecht and East Asian Theater*, eds. Antony Tatlow and Tak-wai Wong (Hong Kong: Hong Kong UP, 1982) 96-110.

36. Gao, "*Guanyu yanshude jianyi yu shuoming*," 169

Harry H. Kuoshu (essay date fall 1998)

SOURCE: Kuoshu, Harry H. "Will Godot Come by Bus or through a Trace? Discussion of a Chinese Absurdist Play." *Modern Drama* 41, no. 3 (fall 1998): 461-73.

[*In the following essay, Kuoshu compares* Bus Stop *to Samuel Beckett's* Waiting for Godot, *and explores the motif of waiting in both plays in terms of their different cultural contexts.*]

The Bus-Stop, written by Gao Xingjian and performed by The People's Art Theater of Beijing, is a Chinese lyrical comedy that emerged with a group of experimental plays in Beijing in the early 1980s.[1] The play creates a bizarre situation of waiting, and its resemblance to Samuel Beckett's *Waiting for Godot* was pointed out by certain Chinese critics soon after its premiere. Since the playwright has a background in French literature, this observation came as no surprise;[2] nevertheless, it played its role in a quickly aborted political campaign of "anti-bourgeois-contamination." A Party-authorized critic used ***The Bus-Stop****'s* resemblance to Beckett's play to label it anti-socialist, assuming that the futile waiting in the play shows a loss of confidence in socialism, a loss ascribed to contamination by "bourgeois, idealistic, egoistic world views."[3] Although ***The Bus-Stop*** was degraded by Party authorities in the short-lived campaign, more experimental plays, one of them by the same playwright and performed in the same theatre, were staged with enthusiastic acceptance. Contrasted with the fact that massive non-participation actually aborted a political campaign under a regime whose functioning relied heavily and continually on new campaigns, the enthusiasm for the small experimental theatres testifies to an anxiety produced by such totalitarian control and a desire to move beyond it.

Situating these Chinese experimental plays in this political culture, one wonders about the meaning of waiting and how ***The Bus-Stop*** and *Waiting for Godot* produce a comparable situation of waiting. Clearly the same situation is almost impossible to reproduce in such different performances. This is especially true when one considers the different audiences in their historical contexts, expectations and resourcefulness in access to codes for comprehension.[4] Let's suppose that *Waiting for Godot* were staged in China. The performance would be bound to communicate through different codes and thus would produce different meanings from those of its Western performances. The performance of ***The Bus-Stop,*** on the contrary, is prescribed by known codes in a Chinese cultural context. Although sharing some surface similarities, ***The Bus-Stop*** and *Waiting for Godot* articulate different concepts of waiting. They are, to use Umberto Eco's term, two different "cultural units," that is, differed semantic units inserted into different cultural systems.[5] ***The Bus-Stop,*** nevertheless, does activate its audience's recently acquired knowledge of Godot and may serve as a cross-cultural bridge for the Chinese to enter Godot-like absurdity.[6] With these initial assumptions, I will first examine the differences between *Waiting for Godot* and ***The Bus-Stop*** and then explore the possibility of the latter as a cultural transcription, or parody, of the former. This discussion assumes that readers are familiar with *Waiting for Godot* and relatively ignorant of ***The Bus-Stop.*** It thus uses certain aspects of the former as points of departure for retrieving similar ones in the latter for comparison.

The Bus-Stop is performed, as dictated by the playwright, in a small theatre-in-the-round.[7] The bare stage contains only a bus stop sign at the center and a fence designed to keep people in line while waiting for the bus. The play begins on a Saturday afternoon but ends God knows when, since even a watch battery will run out. A group of people, eight all together, gradually gathers to catch a bus to get from their suburb into the big city. They wait and wait, mistaking some passing vehicles for their bus, which never comes. Their hopes for the bus are aroused and crushed time after time, but still they wait. Shock sets in when they realize that they have spent years waiting for the bus. At this point, they notice that a silent man among them has left long before, deciding to walk rather than to wait—a spotlight reveals him behind the audience climbing up to, and then walking on, a raised stand. They then regret that they waited; they should have walked to the city as he did. As the play ends, the theme music of "the silent man" arises with a little variation into grandeur and liveliness, and the seven performers all start talking to different parts of the audience, commenting on their waiting.

The formal similarities of ***The Bus-Stop*** and *Waiting for Godot* are obvious. They both deal with waiting for someone or something that never comes—in one case for Godot, in the other for a bus. They both treat waiting as human situation—one set in front of a tree by a country road, the other at a bus stop by the side of a suburban street. They both present the waiting group as contrasted with someone else—Gogo and Didi with Pozzo and Lucky, seven people with the silent man. These correlations—Godot and the bus, the tree and the bus stop sign, Pozzo and Lucky and the silent man—serve as convenient points of departure for revealing not the kindred codes but the striking differences between the two texts. "The codes," as Eco observes, "insofar as they are accepted by a society, set up a 'cultural' world which is neither actual nor possible in the ontological sense; its existence is linked to a cultural order, which is the way in which a society thinks, speaks and, while speaking, explains the 'purport' of its thought through other thoughts."[8] With these correlations coherently marking off two different cultural orders, it will be interesting to see if, at a certain point, a cross-cultural perspective can bring an understanding of differed expressions of kindred human dilemmas.

Markers of Codes: Godot and the Bus

In Beckett's play, Godot seems to be deprived of any practical relationship with the two tramps. Since the audience can hardly tell in any practical sense why the two tramps wait for him, it must move to a metaphysical plane to understand the tramps' relationship to Godot. This kind of move is typical in an uncoded situation, as Eco explains in *A Theory of Semiotics*:

> Faced with uncoded circumstances and complex contexts, the interpreter is obliged to recognize that the message does not rely on previous codes and yet that it must be understandable; if it is so, non-explicit conventions must exist; if not yet in existence, they have to exist (or to be posited).[9]

Since the play does not prompt the audience to see much significance in performing the details of ordinary, everyday activity, it encourages a transcended perception of them as depicting a metaphysical situation. Are there social reasons for such depiction? Yes. Herbert Blau has drawn on the words of Winston Churchill—"What is Europe now? It is a rubble-heap, a charnel house, a breeding-ground of pestilence and hate"—to establish the atmosphere out of which *Godot* was born: the despair, hunger, and disease of postwar Europe.[10] The social reasons, however, still cannot explain why the tramps should wait for Godot. The play further prompts the audience into a metaphysical contemplation: "Please note that the author doesn't say so, but he forces us to say it. In 'Godot' there is 'God.'"[11] Godot leads the audience, as one critic puts it, "toward a metaphysics of boredom."[12] The play forces the audience to face the subjective reality of the tramps.

The bus in Gao's play, by comparison, is closely related to the life of the people who wait for it. These people want to get into the city and, therefore, have to wait for the bus. In a country where there were no private cars at the time of the play's production, nothing was more familiar in one's life than the bus. People and their relationships to the bus automatically remind the audience of social problems. Often there are not enough buses for all the passengers; people have to stand in line waiting for the bus; when the bus is too full for everyone to get on it, the queue is no longer respected. Getting into the bus becomes a battle of pushing and elbowing the others away. In this chaotic situation, so-called "backdoorism" (favoritism) becomes more and more prevalent in interpersonal relationship—those who are in favor with the bus company, or the bus driver himself, will be let on the bus through the back door while the others battle to squeeze in through the front door. Being reminded of all this, the audience will worry about the deterioration of human relationships. They wonder why there cannot be more buses, realize how the huge population of the country has become a serious social problem while the planned economy cannot provide enough jobs, and so on. In Gao's play, these social problems are vividly represented in people's waiting for the bus. Each time people mistake a passing vehicle for their bus, they try to enforce the rule of the queue, an effort that always causes tension in their relationships. A rural market director, who is last to join the group on the stage, even shouts to the driver of a passing vehicle he mistakes for the bus that he has just favored the bus company with some rare commodities and demands the privilege of the back door.

While there are abundant codes for understanding the wait for the bus in practical terms, the play also pushes its social and political critique beyond everyday concerns toward the depiction of an existential boredom:

> GLASSES: Ah, life . . .
>
> GIRL: Do you call this living?
>
> GLASSES: Sure it is. Despite everything we're still alive.
>
> GIRL: We might as well be dead.
>
> GLASSES: Why don't you end it all, then?
>
> GIRL: Because it seems like such a waste to come into this world and then get nothing out of life.
>
> GLASSES: There should be some meaning to life.
>
> GIRL: To live on like this, not really alive and not dead either—it's so boring!
>
> *(All walk on the spot and then turn around in circles as if possessed.)*
>
> (***Bus*** [*The Bus-Stop*] 385)

The anxiety here, not unlike that in *Waiting for Godot*, is related to the mystery that the bus never comes and the production of meaning is blocked. In the highly politicized and Party-manipulated culture of the People's Republic of China, the ideological implication of the mystery is clear. One may argue that the play suggests a fundamental limit to the Party's conceptual system, which denies individual initiative and has blocked a diversified access to meaning in life.

Decor: A Tree and a Bus Stop Sign

While the decor of Beckett's play is accessible primarily in metaphysical codes, the decor of Gao's play communicates in social and ideological codes. Beckett's play seems set in nowhere: a tree can hardly reveal the exact location of the scene, and it can hardly contain much social meaning. This lack of social meaning endows the tree with metaphysical implications. A critic writes:

> The tree on the stage, though it is a willow, obviously stands both for the Tree of the knowledge of Good and Evil (and, when it puts on green leaves, for the Tree of Life) and for the Cross. . . . it is also the Tree of Judas, on which they (Didi and Gogo) are recurrently tempted to hang themselves.[13]

Although others may disagree with his interpretation, this critic has surely found available codes that lend Beckett's decor a richness of connotation.

A Chinese bus stop sign is a plate printed with the bus route, which is like a map showing one's location and the bus's destination. In Gao's play, this bus stop sign is connotatively rich in its communication with the audience. First of all, it sets up a rural-urban contrast, which is much sharper than the Western world can conceive of in terms of living standards. The desire of the people who wait for the bus to go into the city is really the desire for a better life—one girl says: "Whenever I see city girls all done up and wearing those high-heel shoes, it makes me feel as though they've walked all over me and are flaunting themselves in front of me just to rub it in." And a young man says: "I'm gonna have a taste of yoghurt if it's the last thing I do" (***Bus*** 384, 320). The desire may also be interpreted as a national allegory, the rural-urban contrast replaced by an international perspective. With China's opening up to the world has come an anxiety about economic underdevelopment and the desire to catch up. Reproaching his carefree companion at the bus stop, a young man releases his anger: "We've been cast aside by life, forgotten. The world is fleeting by in front of you and you don't even see it. You might be happy to muddle along like this, but I'm not" (***Bus*** 383). When asked about the value of taking the trouble to travel to the city for a chess tournament with city people, the old man retorts: "The whole point of chess is the feeling of exhilaration you get from it; it's all a matter of the spirit of the thing. The spirit of the thing, that's what life is all about" (***Bus*** 383). Exchanges like these may possibly endorse a national allegory.

Secondly, the route printed on the bus stop sign reminds the audience of the country's journey toward a utopia. With an official ideology preaching that the present-day effort is to construct a society of great human happiness and an extreme abundance of material resources; with this ideology's strong teleological beliefs that the development of the country must be set on the right route to achieve these goals; and with the country's recent history of constant "battles" between the "socialist-roaders" and the "capitalist-roaders," a Chinese audience can hardly miss the play's political allegory of the country's difficult and delayed journey from "the countryside" to "the city."

The play challenges the above-mentioned ideology with a shock technique, a technique very similar to what Brecht says about his epic theatre, "What is 'natural' must have the force of what is startling,"[14] even though Gao's earlier acknowledgment, consistent with his French background, is to Artaud's Theatre of Cruelty: to overwhelm the spectator completely and profoundly.[15] This shock technique's function of demystifying an ideology coincides with Roland Barthes' idea that what looks natural must be perceived as historical.[16] The myth being challenged by the play may not exactly be that of the utopia but rather the idea that there is a definite route for achieving this goal. In this respect, the bus stop sign posted on the stage as decor becomes crucial. It resembles Beckett's "tree of knowledge" as access to meaning. At the very beginning of the script, one finds the following description of the sign: "*Owing to years of exposure to the winds and rains, what is painted on the plate is hardly recognizable now*" (**Ch** [*Chezhan*] 119).

The passengers in the play, as a matter of habit, know this bus stop and gather here without needing to look at the sign. It is only when what appears to them as natural becomes absurd—that the bus never comes—that it occurs to them that they should have a look at the sign. They then find that the plate tells them nothing. There seem to be some stains on the plate, showing that a route change notice was probably pasted on it, but it has disappeared in "*winds and rains*," The passengers are enraged:

> OLD MAN: *(heart-brokenly)* Why is this sign still posted here? To pull our legs?
>
> GIRL: Shall we leave? Let's go!
>
> MARKET DIRECTOR: No, we have to sue them.
>
> [. . .]
>
> GLASSES: I think you have to blame yourself. Why didn't we take a good look at the sign? Why did we wait for so long? Let's go. There is nothing worth waiting for.
>
> (**Ch** 137, intervening dialogue omitted)

Failing to offer access to meaning, the bus stop sign estranges the passengers on the stage. Likewise, the political campaigns in Chinese idiom are referred to as "winds and rains." In this sense, the attention paid to the printing of a bus route faded by winds and rains gains strong ideological connotations as a challenge to the myth of the "socialist road." The cruelty of the political campaigns in defense of "the socialist road" has turned the subject into a "sacred" one, deterring careful investigation. The shock is unavoidable when one is finally forced to look at it, only to find it has faded beyond recognition, just like the printing on the sign.

Manner: Pozzo, Lucky and the Silent Man

A look at the shock technique used in ***The Bus-Stop*** leads our discussion into the manner of performance of the two plays. In Beckett's play, the waiting of Didi and Gogo is contrasted with the journey of Pozzo and Lucky. One critic writes, "Didi and Gogo stand for the contemplative life. Pozzo and Lucky stand for the life of practical action taken, mistakenly, as an end in itself. Pozzo's blindness and Lucky's dumbness in the second act rub this point in."[17] With this pessimistic contrast, walking is excluded as a solution to anxiety. The waiting in Beckett's play is a situation with no way out, similar to Sartre's *No Exit*. Waiting in this sense becomes an existential reality which, as one critic describes it, is "without past or future, irremediably present."[18]

In Gao's play, waiting produces a strong desire for its negation. The way out of it is suggested by the silent man, who not only provides a contrast to those who wait at the bus stop but also gives them hope and eventually mobilizes them to leave. The silent man communicates with those who wait at the bus stop through music, the theme of which is established when he first leaves the bus stop (the action of the play freezes briefly to draw the audience's attention to the music). Gao prescribes that the music be "*filled with painful but determined explorations.*" While waiting, people at the bus stop constantly hear "the silent man's music." When they finally decide to be on their way, the music of "the silent man" becomes a louder march (***Ch*** 138).

The different natures of the performing space and the different roles of the performers in this space also designate the different ways in which the concept of waiting is communicated between the audiences and the performers. Beckett's play is often performed in a proscenium theatre with a picture-frame stage. There is not only a physical distance between the stage and the seating area but also a purposefully created perceptual distance that keeps the audience from identifying with the performers in their immediate actions on the stage. Geneviève Serreau points out an effective moment in *Waiting for Godot* on a proscenium stage:

> . . . the spectator is involved in this process of detachment; what happens repetitively is that after a sudden destruction of theatrical illusion, the stage becomes a stage, that bounded cube which opens only into the terrifying gulf of the audience. Thus, Vladimir cries out to a frightened Gogo, who "makes a rush towards back": "Imbecile! There's no way out there." Then, gesturing towards the audience: "There! Not a soul in sight! Off you go! Quick! (*He pushes Estragon towards auditorium. Estragon recoils in horror.*) You won't? (*He contemplates auditorium.*) Well I can understand that."[19]

Although this can be perceived as a theatrical joke, it also conveys a bitter sense of human isolation that increases the perceptual distance all the more. With this distance, the clownish style of acting becomes appropriate. Serreau writes,

> . . . clowns traditionally play a parodic role, one of demystification. . . . in *Godot* the sacred monster that must be demystified is man . . . man thrown into existence and seeking to solve his own problem, or rather renouncing any solution since he cannot use his traditional tools (reality of space, time, and matter).[20]

The sense of distance and the clownish style produce an unusual parody. The parody of human existence, it seems, has to be perceived at a distance that allows for metaphysical transcendence.

Gao's play, as its actions require, has to be performed in an arena where the performance space is totally encircled by the seating area. During the performance, the members of the audience actually become each other's background for watching, decreasing the distance between the audience and the performers. The viewers are encouraged to put themselves in the position of the performers. Let's look at an example:

> OLD MAN: Maybe we should wait for the bus on the other side of the road?
>
> GLASSES: No, that's for the bus going back to the countryside.
>
> OLD MAN: (*to the audience*) You are also waiting for the bus? (*to himself*) They can't hear me. (*louder*) Are you waiting to go back to the countryside? (*to himself*) Still can't hear me. (*to the young man with spectacles*) Young man, my hearing is terrible. Could you ask them if they are going back to the countryside? If they all want to go back, we'd better not stay here to suffer as well.
>
> (***Ch*** 128)

"Going back" in this context signifies giving up hope. Faced with this option, one performer prefers waiting: "It doesn't matter too much to wait. You wait? It shows you still have hope. If you have nothing left to hope for, you're really damned . . ." (***Ch*** 137). Waiting actually builds social bonding. Through communication between the performers and the audience, the stage and the seating area gradually merge into a shared situation of waiting, a shared social space. It is with the formation of this space that the role of the silent man becomes important. While the other performers walk through the audience to get into the acting space, the silent man walks out of the acting space—his music looms from behind the audience and he appears in the spotlight overlooking this space. The silent man seems to be the only character who achieves an allegorical aloofness.

The acting style of the silent man, however, can also be seen as the accent for the whole play. It corresponds to the other performers' occasional "lyrical transcendence" of the social space mentioned above, their comic detachment from roles, and their symbolic gesturing on a basically bare stage. This style, as Gao envisions it, should be "with poetic touches," "resembling the performance of traditional operas such as Mei Lanfang while performing *The Drunken Lady*."[21] It is interesting to note that while Brecht used Chinese acting to speak for his Alienation Effects, Gao has a similar dialogue with this traditional dramaturgy so as to lend the performance of his play a small sense of absurdity. Nevertheless, he does not mention the similar Western use of this dramaturgy, which he surely knew of. One wonders if the ideological undertone of his Western predecessor deterred Gao's acknowledgment.

Godot Comes through a Trace

The silent man is a shadow of Lu Xun's Passerby, the title character from his allegorical poetic drama, written in 1925.[22] When **The Bus-Stop** was staged, *The Passerby* was performed as a prelude, with the actor who played the silent man playing the Passerby. In a discussion with the audience after the performance, Gao was asked about the possible influence of the theatre of the absurd and Beckett. He dodged the question by saying that his inspiration came mostly from Lu Xun, as indicated by using *The Passerby* as the prelude for his play. It is hard to know how much politics played a role in Gao's answer. Acknowledging Beckett's influence might have been politically problematic, while raising the battle banner of Lu Xun, a politically elevated Lu Xun, was a gesture that could not be easily attacked by official ideology.[23] The early Lu Xun as a cultural nihilist, however, had always been difficult for Party-authorized readings. In the case of **The Bus-Stop,** no one would have wondered that Lu Xun could become a vehicle for Godot, that Lu Xun's Passerby could pass on his sense of absurdity, that feeling of loss of totality and an ambivalence about walking and staying put, to Gao's silent man, making him not as naively optimistic as he might first appear.

Although written about thirty years earlier than *Waiting for Godot, The Passerby* draws **The Bus-Stop** closer to Beckett through its contemplation of meaning and the image of the road. Devoid of social connotations, the setting of *The Passerby* is clearly akin to that of *Waiting for Godot,* since the place is only a vague *"somewhere"—"to the east are a few trees and ruins, while to the west is uncultivated wasteland."* Attention, however, is drawn not to the tree, at which Beckett's characters look, but to "a trace that looks like a road yet is not a road":[24]

> PASSERBY: Do you know what kind of place lies ahead?
>
> OLD MAN: Ahead? Ahead is the grave.
>
> PASSERBY: *(Startled)* The grave?
>
> YOUNG GIRL: No, no, no! Over there are many wild lilies and wild roses.[25]

The trace, which is both there and not there, both promising and menacing, is the Godot-like entity in Lu Xun's drama. Related to this "spatial representation of a temporal dilemma," "the act of walking becomes," as Leo Ou-fan Lee shrewdly observes, "the only significant act in an existence threatened with meaninglessness."[26] Walking becomes a metaphysical allegory; even walking may not offer access to meaning, walking seems to be what life is all about. The anxiety, however, comes with the presupposition of the existence of meaning and road (or, in our Western case, meaning and tree). In Chinese intellectual history, road, or *tao,* has long been the key concept for offering a sense of totality. Lu Xun, an iconoclast in modern Chinese literature, may have denounced not only the ancient "road" but also the concept of the road as sacred—"for actually the earth had no roads to begin with, but when many men pass one way, a road is made."[27] The denunciation of a sacred road may not take place without anxiety; the life of a cultural rebel itself may turn out to be perceived as a road rarely traveled by others: "Long, long had been my road and far, far was the journey," a line Lu Xun borrowed from the ancient political exile Qu Yuan to use as the prefatory inscription to his short story collection, *Wandering.*[28] Lee remarks that the decision made by the protagonist of Lu Xun's *The Passerby* seems to be "not so much that of a nihilist as that of an existentialist"; absurdity sets in with the loss of totality, the sense that the road is not readily available and the understanding that one has to get used to a life with no definite road.[29]

The Passerby relays this sense of absurdity to **The Bus-Stop.** "Godot," designating a loss of totality of meaning, comes to the bus stop along a "Lu Xun trace" and proclaims his arrival with the performers' discovery of a blur on the bus stop sign that they believed to be the print of a definite bus route. It is a blur that can be seen as the replica of the "Lu Xun trace" along which "Godot" travels. While the printed bus route is irretrievable, and the bus does not come, one has to get used to living without them. The waiting becomes absurd when the object of waiting, which has subtly changed from the bus to the printed route, becomes unrecognizable but still commands one's attention. One character in Gao's play reflects, echoing Lu Xun's dilemma: "Should I stay or go? It's the enigma of our existence. Perhaps Fate has decreed that we must wait here forever, till we all grow old and die. But why do people accept the capricious rulings of Fate? Then again, what exactly is Fate?" (**Bus** 381).[30]

The silent man's act of walking corresponds to this contemplation. It becomes a statement of alienation, of abandoning the set road of the political totality. The silent man in Gao's play is not necessarily an allegory of achievement—that is, he is already there in the city—but he is an allegory of deviation: he is no longer yoked, as the others are, to *"turn around in circles as if possessed"* by the concept of a bus and a definite route. Although his action may not offer immediate access to meaning (his music expresses pain in exploration), the silent man draws the spotlight of admiration which differentiates him from Pozzo and Lucky and marks his action vis-à-vis the submission to totalitarian control as heroic. *The Bus-Stop,* after all, is not as nihilist as *Waiting for Godot.* It attributes existential absurdity more to the political result of totalitarian control than to an epistemological crisis. The silent man's call for deviated action and his challenge to the set route to the totality of meaning explains the artistic and ideological thrust of the Chinese experimental theatre. Its indebtedness to Western avant-gardists, in this perspective, may be not just a technical borrowing but a cultural transcription—the western codes that have produced their specific sorts of absurdity are transcribed into the codes of Chinese political culture to produce its own absurdity.

Notes

1. "Trace" is a fairly archaic word used by Leo Ou-fan Lee, in his study of the life and works of Lu Xun, to translate the term *henji* (marks on the ground) in the "stage directions" opening Lu's poetic drama *Guoke* [*The Passer-by*]: "*To the east are a few trees and ruins, while to the west is uncultivated wasteland. Between both points runs a trace that looks like a road and yet is not a road.*" Lu Xun, *Guoke,* in *Lu Xun quanji* [*Complete Works of Lu Xun*], vol. II (Beijing, 1981), 188, quoted and trans. in Leo Ou-fan Lee, *Voices from the Iron House: A Study of Lu Xun* (Bloomington, IN, 1987), 101. Yang Xianyi and Gladys Yang translate *henji* as "a faint track." See Lu Xun, *The Passer-by,* in *Selected Works,* trans. Yang Xianyi and Gladys Yang, vol. I (Beijing, 1985), 336.

2. Gao Xingjian's *The Bus-Stop* [*Chezhan*] (1983) was the second of three of his plays performed at The People's Art Theater of Beijing. The first and third were *Juedui xinhao* [*Alarm Signal*] (1982-83) and *Yeren* [*Wildman*] (1985).

    The Chinese script of *Chezhan* has been published in the bimonthly literary journal *Shi yue* [*The October*]. A partial English translation has been published in the journal *Renditions*. See Gao Xingjian, *Chezhan, Shi yue* (March 1983), 119-38; and Gao Xingjian, *The Bus-Stop,* trans. Geremie Barmé, *Renditions* 19-20 (1983), 379-86. Subsequent references to Barme's translation appear parenthetically in the text as (*Bus*), Subsequent references to the Chinese script published in *Shi yue* are my translations and appear parenthetically in the text as (*Ch*).

    Barmé's partial translation of *The Bus-Stop* was later collected into an anthology, along with an article of his on the play. See Gao Xingjian, *The Bus-Stop,* trans. Geremie Barmé, and Geremie Barmé, "A Touch of the Absurd: Introducing Gao Xingjian, and His Play *The Bus-Stop,*" both in *Trees on the Mountain: An Anthology of New Chinese Writing,* ed. Stephen C. Soong and John Minford (Hong Kong, 1984), 379-86, 373-78. For critical commentary, see also William Tay, "Avant-garde Theater in Post-Mao China: *The Bus-Stop* by Gao Xingjian," in *Worlds Apart: Recent Chinese Writing and Its Audiences,* ed. Howard Goldblatt (Armonk, NY, 1990), 111-18.

3. Gao Xingjian graduated from the French Department of Beijing Foreign Studies University.

4. See He Wen, "On Seeing the Play *The Bus-Stop,*" *Wenyi bao* [*Literary Gazette* (Beijing)] (March 1984), 21-25.

5. I am using the term "audience" in such a general sense that it may refer to almost anyone living in a certain culture. The scope of this essay does not permit sociological distinctions of varied audiences.

6. For the idea of "meaning" as "a cultural unit," see Umberto Eco, *A Theory of Semiotics* (Bloomington, IN, 1979), 66-68.

7. *Waiting for Godot* was first available to Chinese readers in an anthology of Western absurd theatre. See Samuel Beckett, "Dengdai gedno," trans. Shi Xianrong, in *Huandanpai xiju ji* [*A Collection of Absurdist Plays*] (Shanghai, 1980).

8. I attended a performance of *The Bus-Stop* and a discussion with the playwright and the director following the performance (*The Bus-Stop,* by Gao Xingjian, dir. Lin Zhaohua, prod. People's Art Theater of Beijing, summer 1983). Some of the descriptions here are based on my personal experience and observations.

9. Eco, 61. See note 6.

10. Ibid., 129.

11. Herbert Blau, "Notes from the Underground," in *Casebook on Waiting for Godot,* ed. Ruby Cohn (New York, 1967), 114.

12. Jacques Audiberti, "At the Babylone: A Fortunate Move on the Theater Checkerboard," trans. Ruby Cohn, in *Casebook on Waiting for Godot,* 14. See note 11.

13. Alfonso Sastre, "Seven Notes on *Waiting for Godot,*" trans. Leonard C. Pranko, in *Casebook on Waiting for Godot,* 106.

14. G. S. Fraser, "*Waiting for Godot,*" in *Casebook on Waiting for Godot,* 135.

15. Bertolt Brecht, "Theatre for Pleasure or Theatre for Instruction," in *Brecht on Theatre: The*

Development of an Aesthetic, trans. John Willett, 2nd ed. (New York, 1974), 71.

16. See Gao Xingjian, "Gao Xingjian, Lin Zhaohua: tan *Juedui xinhao* de yishu gousi [Gao Xingjian and Lin Zhaohua on *Alarm Signal*]," in *Juedui xinhao de yishu tansuo* [*Artistic Explorations of "Alarm Signal"*], ed. Li Baoyun and Zheng Guangsai (Beijing, 1985), 104.

17. See Roland Barthes, *Mythologies,* trans. Annette Lavers (New York, 1972), 109-111.

18. Fraser, 133. See note 14.

19. Alain Robbe-Grillet, "Samuel Beckett or Presence on the Stage," in *Casebook on Waiting for Godot,* 21.

20. Geneviève Serreau, "Beckett's Clowns," trans. Ruby Cohn, in *Casebook on Waiting for Godot,* 175.

21. Ibid., 172.

22. Gao Xingjian, "Youguan benju yanchu de jidian jianyi [Suggestions for the Performance of *The Bus-Stop*]," in *Chezhan,* 138. See note 2.

23. See Lu Xun, *Guoke,* in *Lu Xun quanji,* 188-94. See note 1.

24. The preeminence of Lu Xun (1881-1936) in the history of modern Chinese literature was posthumously enhanced by the Communist leader Mao Tse-Tung, who made Lu Xun the role model for Chinese writers. "The chief commander of China's cultural revolution," Mao writes, "he was not only a great man of letters but a great thinker and revolutionary. . . . on the cultural front he was the bravest and most correct, the firmest, the most loyal and the most ardent national hero, a hero without parallel in our history." Mao Tse-Tung, "On New Democracy," *Selected Works of Mao Tse-Tung,* vol. II (Peking, 1965), 372.

25. Lu, *Guoke,* 188, quoted and trans. in Lee, 101.

26. Lu, *Guoke,* 190, quoted and trans. in Lee, 102.

27. Lee, 102.

28. Lu Xun, "My Old Home," in *Selected Stories of Lu Hsun,* trans. Yang Hsien-yi and Gladys Yang (New York, 1977), 64.

29. Qu Yuen, *Lisao* [*Encountering Sorrow*], trans. David Hawkes, in *Anthology of Chinese Literature: From Early Times to the Fourteenth Century,* ed. Cyril Birch, vol. I (New York, 1965), 56; quoted in Lee, 43.

30. Lee, 102.

Olivier Burckhardt (essay date April 2000)

SOURCE: Burckhardt, Olivier. "The Voice of One in the Wilderness." *Quadrant* 44, no. 4 (April 2000): 54-7.

[*In the following essay, Burckhardt discusses Gao's plays in terms of the theme of self-exploration and the search for individual identity.*]

Occasionally there is an individual who has the courage not to represent, or identify with, any group whatsoever. Gao Xingjian has been described as the leading dramatist of avant-garde Chinese theatre; an author who has forged new paths in Chinese prose writing; and a painter of international repute. Although such descriptions aim to portray his activities in complimentary terms, they fail to grasp the individual. The paradox of course is with the nature of language whose primary function is to categorise—and once we have categorised we stop considering the individual as individual—but language is a supple medium, often a great deal more supple than our own thinking.

A writer-artist living in Paris since 1987, Gao Xingjian was born in China in 1940, where his earliest recollections are of fleeing the invading Japanese forces. His upbringing was exceptionally liberal. The son of an amateur actress and a bank employee, from an early age he was encouraged to paint, write and play the violin. At seventeen he went to the Beijing Foreign Languages Institute, taking a major in French language and literature, all the while developing his interest in traditional Chinese theatre alongside Western modern theatre, reading Stanislavski, Chekhov and Brecht and continuing to paint and study modern Western art. At the height of the Great Proletarian Cultural Revolution Gao Xingjian had to destroy all his early writing, a trunkful of manuscripts which included several novels, articles on aesthetics and some fifteen plays. Sent to the countryside for "rehabilitation" for six years, he continued writing in hiding, burying his texts to avoid detection—but they too are now lost.

With the easing of Sino-Western relationships he was recalled to Beijing in 1975 to work as a translator on the French edition of *China Reconstructs*. While accompanying the writer Ba Jin to France in 1978 as interpreter, Gao Xingjian was able, for the first time, to see Western oil paintings in the original. The experience had deep repercussions.

Realising that his own work in oil painting was a pale reflection of what can be achieved in the medium, he abandoned Western techniques and returned to working with Chinese ink on rice paper. His abstract paintings exploit all the gradations that Chinese ink is capable of, suffused with an eerie luminosity that permeates into the darkest shadows. Many of the works can be read as inner landscapes—landscapes that go beyond the figurative towards a vision—a state of mind. A single dab of the brush heavy with ink suggests a presence in a desolate expanse. Zen is a term often employed when describing Gao Xingjian's paintings, where the human presence is distinct but somehow detached from common reality. In a brief outline of his thoughts on painting, he concludes:

> If the self-expression of an artist becomes the direct expression of self, then one's art will be a mess. As the self (or ego) is a chaotic mass, or a black hole to begin with, unless an artist exercises self-knowledge and removes himself for dispassionate observation of the world (including the self), then what is there to see?
>
> More than self-expression I see art as a case of self-purification—observing with a pair of somewhat sober eyes the ever-changing world and one's own mainly unconnected self. And although he may not understand the riddles of life, the artist can leave behind a surprise or two.

In his writing Gao Xingjian maintains the same stance as in painting. Having been forced to destroy his literary output of some twenty years, it was only in 1980 that one of his texts was published, a novella entitled ***Stars on a Cold Night.*** This was followed in 1981 by another novella, short stories and a booklet, ***Preliminary Exploration into the Techniques of Modern Fiction,*** which caused a major debate in the Chinese literary world by challenging the social realism that was the hallmark of Chinese literature and art under Mao. The authorities condemned the work and Gao was placed under surveillance.

Rather than the Western concept of a stream of consciousness, Gao opted for a *stream of language* in which inner and outer realities criss-cross each other. Through it the *process-of-being* is brought to the fore, not only via fantasies, dreams and emotions but also via the interaction with reality as reviewed by memories. A narrative flow is kept but without adhering to fixed plots.

In June 1981 Gao Xingjian joined the Beijing People's Art Theatre and wrote ***The Bus Stop*** (*Chezhan*) (original Chinese titles to the plays are given here to avoid confusion over the various possible translations). Although the play did not take any ideological stance, shifts in the political climate made it inadvisable to produce the play and Gao wrote ***Alarm Signal*** (*Juedui xinhao*) based on a story by Liu Huiyuan. The choice of the theme was probably influenced by self-censorship. As Gilbert Fong notes in his introduction to ***The Other Shore,*** the play "is a rather didactic prodigal son story—an attempted train robbery is thwarted by one of the villains who eventually realises his mistaken ways." In form, however, its use of flashbacks, disjointed time sequences and innovative lighting and sound techniques made ***Alarm Signal*** the boldest experimental play ever staged in China at the time.

Although the authorities reacted with suspicion and threats of official sanctions, the public success of the play encouraged the staging of ***The Bus Stop*** in 1983. Run as a series of "rehearsals" for internal viewing by audiences restricted to theatrical circles, the play was preceded by *The Passer-by,* a short play by Lu Xun on whom Gao Xingjian wrote:

> It was a misfortune for literature that the writer Lu Xun was crushed to death by the politician Lu Xun. Clearly, for Lu Xun it was not necessarily a misfortune but it may have been a source of regret.

The Bus Stop, subtitled *A Lyrical Comedy Without Division of Acts,* takes place at a suburban bus stop. Transformed into the Silent Man, the Passer-by joins the queue. The story-line is simplicity itself. To quote from McDougall and Louie's *Literature of China in the Twentieth Century*:

> while a cross-section of Beijing society waits foolishly for buses that never come or never stop, the Silent Man sets off alone on his arduous journey. Skillfully employing the liveliest Beijing slang to be heard on stage since Lao She's *Teahouse,* Gao Xingjian satirises the passivity, vacillation and superficiality of key types in 1980s society, including a young hoodlum from the suburbs, a housewife preoccupied by the rising cost of food, a young woman fearful of growing too old to attract a husband, and a jovially corrupt factory boss. As the play reaches its climax, surreal effects are created by disco lights and frantic music. After endless argument (introducing the first polyphonic episode on the Chinese stage), the characters in the queue agree to walk into town, but when the stage lights darken, they are still irresolutely in place.

When news of the play reached party officials, a further series of "rehearsals" was ordered for the purpose of criticism. The attacks were virulent, with Gao being labelled a spiritual pollutant. Fearing the worst from the "Anti-Spiritual Pollution Movement" Gao took himself off to the mountains of south-western China, an area famed in ancient times for shamans and hermits.

Once assured that the political climate in Beijing had changed for the better, Gao returned there in late 1984 and wrote ***Wild Man*** (*Yeren*), a play of epic proportions that spans some eight millennia and incorporates themes from cosmology, mythology and the folk and shamanistic traditions of southern China. In his preface to the play Gao writes:

> If Western-style theatre is to succeed in China, it must blend with the traditions of Chinese theatre. In ***Wild Man*** my aim is the rejuvenation of performance

techniques associated with the distant roots of Chinese theatre, rather than adherence to established dramatic technique. Some modern thinkers, unduly concerned with the rationalisation of art, have lost the sensitivity that originally dwelt within them. In essence, the nature of drama is not to serve society but to stimulate both audience and performers alike. The loss of its utilitarian aims will bring about the self-liberation of art.

Considered politically innocuous, the play had tremendous success and, as Gilbert Fong notes, "represented the pinnacle of the development of experimental drama in China at the time."

It is a sad irony that Gao's next play, **The Other Shore** (*Bi'an*), with which the present selection by the same title opens, was to prove, in many ways, to be prophetic.

Written in early 1986, it refers to a Buddhist metaphor, wherein to reach the other shore is to become enlightened. To use Gao's words, "It is destined that the individual will never be able to acquire the ultimate truth, which is known as God or the other shore." The play's location is "from the real world to the non existent other shore." Actors play in pairs with ropes, tugging and pulling, leading and being led, resisting and co-operating, then soon the ropes are disregarded and the actors communicate and establish relations with imaginary ropes. Tired of the game with its conflicts, entanglements and fragmentation, the crowd of actors are spurred on to cross the river and reach the other shore. Once there they attempt in vain to speak. Woman teaches the Crowd language, Man emerges from the Crowd to ask Woman who she is, the Crowd explore the darker side of language and in their frenzy kill Woman. As Man reprimands them and himself, the Crowd attempt to make him their leader. Notwithstanding the fact that he refuses, they continue to follow him. A series of independent narrative segments ensues. The Crowd find a leader who makes fools of them. Throughout Man seeks to understand and explore but is constantly harangued by the Crowd, who will not admit his independence. Towards the end of the play, after Man has asked various people what they are looking for, the Crowd do not believe that he doesn't know what he is seeking or that he is not seeking anything in the first place. When he says, "I'm not going to look for anything any more. I just want to go over there," the Crowd refuse to let him go his own way.

In late 1986 yet another political shift brought about an anti-liberalism campaign and it became obvious that Gao would not be allowed to have his plays performed in China. Taking the unfinished manuscript of a novel he had been working on since the summer of 1982, Gao left Beijing in late 1987 and took up residence in Paris.

Once in Paris, Gao was able to earn his livelihood through writing and painting. In China he was not designated an "official painter," so he had not been able to exhibit or sell his paintings save through unofficial channels. He was now able to exhibit regularly and his plays were staged in Europe, Hong Kong and Taiwan. At the Guggenheim Museum, New York, in spring 1989, Chiang Ching directed Gao's **Variations on a Slow Tune** (*Sheng sheng man bianzou*), based on the poem "Grief beyond belief" by Li Qingzhao (1084-c.1151), China's greatest woman poet. The motifs of the poem were interpreted through the movements of a dancer accompanied by a monologue set to music.

Following the brutal repression in Tiananmen Square later that same year, Gao was asked to write a play based on the events. He wrote ***Taowang,*** variously translated as ***Escape, Absconding*** or ***Exile.*** The play pleased no one. In the West, the commissioning theatre asked for the play to be partially rewritten. Gao withdrew it and paid for the translation. In China the authorities reacted by publishing the play accompanied by a caricature and a vicious attack on its author. His allotted flat in Beijing was confiscated and the security police took all the papers he had left there.

Set in the basement of a disused warehouse, the play opens with a young woman and a young man taking refuge there after the tanks were ordered into Tiananmen Square. Although total strangers, they are drawn physically close. A middle-aged man, also seeking shelter, comes into the basement. Full of ideological zeal, the young man begins to discuss the situation but cannot understand the middle-aged man's refusal to belong to any faction or doctrine, that he is a bystander, free to choose whether to become involved or not become involved, that he chooses to escape from the collective will, that he has no need of any isms.

Taowang was first staged only in 1992 in Sweden and Germany and broadcast on the BBC the same year. The reaction of the Chinese authorities, of some Western academics and of pro-democracy Chinese, albeit not all to the same degree, were on a par. Like Man, the main protagonist of **The Other Shore,** Gao was told that he should not, could not, must not, criticise the collective will. To belong to no faction whatsoever is to arouse the enmity of all factions. In an essay of 1990 titled **"Bali suibi"** (**"Jottings from Paris"**) Gao gave what can be interpreted as a direct answer to many of his critics when he wrote:

> The writer is not the conscience of society nor is literature the mirror of society. The writer flees to the margin of society: he is a non-participant, an observer who looks on dispassionately. There is no need for the writer to be the conscience of society, for there has long been a surplus of social conscience. The writer simply uses his own conscience and knowledge to write his own works. He has responsibility only to himself.

In **"Without Isms"** an essay outlining his opposition to any form of indoctrination, be it political, aesthetic or philosophical, Gao Xingjian writes:

> At birth a person is without isms but after birth all sorts of isms are forced upon him and to discard these later is not a simple matter. People are permitted to convert from one ism to another but they are not permitted to be without isms.

Gao does not advocate an eradication of isms but simply the right not to adhere to any. The brand of individuality that he seeks for himself is not an egocentric claim to superiority or god-like status; his concern is foremost to plumb the inner soul, to explore what it is to be an individual human being. Art, he says, "attempts to reach a realm that is unattainable in reality. Otherwise, why go through all the trouble?"

Ultimately the bedrock of the individual *is the individual*. And it is precisely the voice of the one thrown back onto himself that pervades all Gao Xingjian's work. Unlike much of post-Mao literature, which has been called scar-literature, Gao's output is not a retrospective of the painful experiences of the past. It is a banishment of the self to find the self.

To transpose the *removal of the self to observe the self* into a stage language, Gao Xingjian developed a specific mode of acting that encourages actors to view their role from three standpoints—the self, the actor and the role—which are brought to the surface, making no attempt to disguise the fact that a play is a play. The dialogue between audience and actor is highlighted via the neutrality of the actor, who must show that he is conscious that he is acting and must make the audience aware that they are watching a play. Thus the "theatricality" of the medium is brought to the fore.

One of the means Gao employs to implement the neutrality and purification of the self is the use of pronouns. Throughout his plays actors address their role by referring to themselves as *you* or *he*. The use of a second or third person pronoun never fails to surprise or remind both audience and actor that one is watching a play. The directness and simplicity of Gao Xingjian's language prevent the device from striking an artificial chord.

In his novel **Ling Shan** (**Soul Mountain**, recently translated into English by Mabel Lee and due to be published by HarperCollins this year), Gao employs the same idea in a narrative context with artful dexterity. The novel is boldly experimental and yet never alienates the reader. In an essay on modern Chinese and literary writing Gao comments on an experimental short story which he wrote in 1991:

> The language is the simplest possible; the more the words and phrases are simple and clear, the more the reader disposes of a vast space of imagination, the more the images that are awakened in him become alive.

The simplicity of the language is also evident in Gao's plays, where the actor's role is not to embody the psychological make-up of the character but to present it to the audience, who becomes aware of the process free of artifice. The self, the "I," is embodied in the "you" of the actor who interprets the "he" or "she" of the role.

Apart from **The Other Shore**, Gao Xingjian's last play to be written in China, the collection of five plays translated from the Chinese by Gilbert Fong include his most recent works. **Between Life and Death** (**Shengsijie**, 1991) written in French and subsequently in Chinese, makes use of traditional Chinese theatre but is not set in China. Performed first in France and Australia in 1993 and in New York at the Theater for the New City in 1997 as well as broadcast on Radio Free Asia in the USA, the play explores the agonies, memories and fantasies of Woman, the main protagonist. **Between Life and Death** has no specific narrative thread or plot; as the protagonist declares, at the end of the play, it is about the self.

With **Dialogue and Rebuttal** (**Duihua yu fanjie**) of 1992, Gao focuses on the near destruction of language and the act of narration itself. Inspired by a style of question and answer prominent in Chinese Zen Buddhism, the play opens with a couple who have just met and spent the night together. Their dialogues progressively reveal an indifference to communicate and form a series of unconnected language bubbles. Of all of Gao's plays, the skill with which personal pronouns are employed to differentiate between the actor, the role and the character, best brings out the extent to which language can trap the individual.

Gao's next plays, **Nocturnal Wanderer** (**Yeyoushen**) of 1993 and **Weekend Quartet** (**Zhoumo sichongzou**) of 1995, are framed within more definite narrative contexts. The subject matter of **Nocturnal Wanderer**, performed in the Theatre des Halles in Avignon in 1999, is a nightmare that explores the traditional theme of good and evil. The Avignon performance employed a strong burlesque and circus-like mode that suited the play well. As in a real nightmare, Sleepwalker, the main character, grapples with the situations and transformations that overtake him, his attempts to extricate himself from the bad dream are to no avail, and as another character points out to him, "Good dream or bad dream, you've gotta finish it."

Gao Xingjian's most recent play, **Weekend Quartet,** is his most realistic work to date. The four protagonists have names and specific traits that characterise them. The play brings to the fore their individual viewpoints and is based on the structural elements of musical composition for a quartet. In writing the play, Gao studied some eighty quartets by Haydn, Mozart, Shostakovich, Messiaen, Gorecki and others. The role of rhythm and tonality in Chinese is of paramount importance. Gao has said that Chinese, with its loose word order and ability to forgo notions of time, can be written almost as if one were composing music. Although some of the "musicality" of the work is lost in translation, the tension, point and counterpoint that the four characters play out retain the changes of mood.

Gao's blend of traditional Chinese theatre techniques and modern Western theatre offers a radically new interpretation of drama. His tripartition of the actor forgoes Stanislavski's total immersion in the role and Brecht's alienation. In his suggestions on producing the plays he refers to Grotowski's training method which "aims at helping the actor discover his own self and to release its potential." The overwhelming impression, when watching one of Gao Xingjian's plays, is that one is watching a play—a ritual that enacts the bewilderment of modern man—and that one could walk on stage and cross the boundary to reach the surreal shore where myths are made and un-made.

Olivier Burckhardt (review date September 2000)

SOURCE: Burckhardt, Olivier. "Journey without End." *Quadrant* 44, no. 9 (September 2000): 84-5.

[*In the following review, Burckhardt examines Gao's experimental use of narrative voice in* Soul Mountain.]

Lingshan (soul-mountain) is a quasi-mythological place "where wonderful things can be seen, where suffering and pain can be forgotten, and where one can find freedom." There are many Lingshans in China but "soul-mountain" is also a Buddhist name for heaven.

Begun in 1982 when Gao returned to Beijing after a fifteen-thousand-kilometre journey through central and eastern China over a period of five months, *Soul Mountain* was finished in 1989 in Paris, where Gao currently lives. In its eighty-one short chapters, the novel alternates between an inner and outer journey. What begins as a search for the elusive mountain soon turns into an odyssey in the true sense of the word; a series of wanderings; a long adventurous journey where each episode creates a rhythmic unit of tension and counterpoise that gives the whole work a sense of unity.

Soul Mountain weaves together an intricate pattern of impressions, observations and dialogues. The critic of chapter 72 complains that the work isn't a novel and snarls, "You've slapped together travel notes, moralistic ramblings, feelings, notes, jottings, untheoretical discussions, unfable-like fables, copied out some folk songs, added some legend-like nonsense of your own invention, and are calling it fiction!"—but what the critic cannot fathom is the lack of a named protagonist and that the I, you, she and he of the book are characters.

As in many of his plays, Gao Xingjian creates a light, almost ethereal atmosphere in the novel by alternating between first- and second-person pronouns. In an essay on modern Chinese and literary writing he is careful to note that "if the narrator is truly aware of what he writes, he will realise that the changing of pronouns does not constitute a simple and skilful play of style. The three characters, I, you and he, constitute three distinctive angles of narration that procure a stable psychological base."

In her translation of Gao's Chinese, Mabel Lee has admirably succeeded in transposing the distinctive voice in which *Soul Mountain* is written. Gao's is a language where simplicity is refined to a crystalline quality. It is the total lack of artificiality or intellectual mind-games that makes *Soul Mountain* the kind of book that probes the human soul without any attempt to glorify or vilify. Reality and imagination are transposed into a flow of words which the reader can convincingly relate to and trust from the outset.

There are few modern novels that explore new forms of narration without alienating the reader to some extent or demanding various degrees of effort and skill in reading. The lyric quality of *Soul Mountain* removes such obstacles to understanding by taking a direct approach. There is no hidden meaning or an all-seeing agent to govern our perception. Rather, we are drawn into an individual's search for meaning, an individual who realises that there may be no meaning, that he means nothing, who chooses to write a book on the human self, who realises that the gods and demons summoned are summoned from within one's own self.

The "she" invoked by "he" so that the loneliness might be alleviated by telling tales which invoke more gods and demons; the patter of children's bare feet on cobbled lanes that echo his childhood; the tales of Daoist recluses, Buddhist nuns and shamans that interweave through the novel; the description of some of China's most inaccessible mountain forests and remote villages—all these elements form a kaleidoscope of images and thoughts that is constantly being shifted and realigned. *Soul Mountain* offers the reader a momentary and partial view of a transient existence seen through the eyes of a painter with a keen sense of observation who relentlessly questions himself, knowing that even while pretending to understand, he doesn't understand.

Howard Goldblatt (review date autumn 2000)

SOURCE: Goldblatt, Howard. Review of *The Other Shore*, by Gao Xingjian. *World Literature Today* 74, no. 4 (autumn 2000): 801-02.

[*In the following review of* The Other Shore, *a collection of Gao's plays in English translation, Goldblatt praises the introduction and the translation of the works by Gilbert Fong.*]

Gao Xingjian is, as the editor/translator of *The Other Shore* states in his introduction, a major figure in world drama, and the most innovative, if not the most famous, playwright China has produced in this century (one recalls Cao Yu). Yet he is not well represented in the West, if one excludes the acclaim he has garnered in France, his adopted homeland; for that and other reasons, one welcomes this collection of his plays in translation. (*Editor's Note*: This review was written and submitted three months before the announcement of Gao's receipt of the 2000 Nobel Prize in Literature.)

Gilbert Fong's introduction is, in itself, a substantial piece of scholarship/criticism and serves to open a number of windows into the structure, intent, "meaning," and idiosyncratic nature of Gao's more recent plays. Well written, well informed, thoughtful, and illuminating, this indispensable prefatory material is a boon to those who wish to appreciate the playwright's accomplishments. If there is a concern, it is that the translator appears at times to have forgotten that it is the plays for which a reader will come to the collection, not the explication. Then too, here and there, the text seems to be vying with the plays themselves for opacity. That said, given the complexity of Gao's creative work—including his long novel *Spirit Mountain* (*Lingshan*), recently published in English translation—and his finely honed views on the nature of drama, exile, marginalization, and more, Fong's comprehensive analysis is essential and rewarding. The three appendices—plays by Gao, selected criticism, and major productions—are most welcome.

The translations of the five largely experimental plays (his most famous play, *Bus Stop* [here rendered as *Bus Station*], available elsewhere, is not included) in no way do a disservice to the playwright. With Gao himself assuming the role of unofficial collaborator, the authority of the texts is unquestioned; not that Gao's English is at the level of his translator, but implications, significance of word choice, and the like are significantly aided in the finished product by his participation. Dramatic scripts and librettos are, at their best, poor substitutes for dramatic or musical creations; with Gao Xingjian, for whom stage setting and acting are so central to his work, this problem is exacerbated. Yet, since so few people will ever actually see Gao's plays performed, the volume at hand is likely the best we can hope for.

The translator, unlike many others, who seem to have a tin ear for real speech patterns, has produced smooth, idiomatic, and lively English versions of Gao's plays. Elegant when called for, colloquial when demanded, the language retains the illusion that the characters are speaking in English, and contemporary English at that. While some of the dialogue seems a bit slangy, to the detriment of that illusion, it is not a significant concern.

Readers may not always be sure where these occasionally cryptic texts are taking them, but they are sure to enjoy the journey, with the editor/translator as tour guide.

Beverly Beyette and Reed Johnson (essay date 13 October 2000)

SOURCE: Beyette, Beverly, and Reed Johnson. "Author's Seminal Work Not Yet on U.S. Shelves." *Los Angeles Times* (13 October 2000): A17.

[*In the following essay, Beyette and Johnson discuss the significance of Gao being awarded the Nobel Prize to the international recognition of Chinese literature.*]

No one was more thrilled on hearing that Gao Xingjian had won the Nobel Prize in literature than Dr. Mabel Lee, the Australian academic who translated his seminal novel, *Soul Mountain,* into English. "He is an artist, a very elegant writer," she says.

Lee, who recently retired as a professor of Chinese literature and history at the University of Sydney, worked part time for five years on the novel. "Finding a publisher," she says, "took two years."

Lee's agent, Lyn Tranter of Australian Literary Management, took the novel to HarperCollins Australia, which published it in 1999 under its Flamingo imprint. This is the only English-language edition of the book, which was first published in Taipei, Taiwan, in 1980, then in Sweden and France.

World rights have not been sold, according to Rod Morrison, Gao's editor at HarperCollins Australia. *Soul Mountain,* while on a bestseller list in Australia, is not available in the United States but is being offered to publishers here and in Britain. However, *The Other Shore: Plays by Gao Xingjian,* published by Chinese University Press in 1999, is available in English through the Internet.

Gao's plays have rarely been produced in the United States. The Yangtze Theatre Company gave 12 performances of *Between Life and Death* at an off-off-Broadway theater in 1997. "It was not living-room drama, that's for sure. It had great mythic quality," said Crystal Field, artistic director of Theater for the New City in New York. "It was a beautifully done piece."

The Nobel honor is "long overdue," said Haiping Yan, an assistant professor of theater and comparative literature at the University of Colorado who edited some of Gao's plays for an anthology of contemporary Chinese literature.

She said Gao's reputation as a dramatist was established in 1982 with a production by the state-run People's Art Theater Company in Beijing of *Bus Stop*, a play that focuses on an anxious group of commuters waiting for a bus that never arrives, a work compared by Western critics to Samuel Beckett's absurdist masterpiece *Waiting for Godot*. But, Yan said, the play's perceived Western influence, together with its implicit criticisms of Chinese society, provoked a "national controversy," and the production was closed down after only a few performances.

While Gao was influenced by European modernists such as Beckett and Eugene Ionesco, Yan added, he is "one of those authors whose artistic and humanistic social visions are deeply rooted in Chinese experience, but are also relevant to human experiences in general."

Yan's colleague, Howard Goldblatt, a professor of East Asian literature, spoke to the significance of a Chinese author winning a Nobel: "It's become a national obsession to a certain degree. I think that any sort of international recognition in whatever field is important to them, to show their standing in the world community. And a country that large, with a long literary tradition, for them to have been frozen out so long is a bit of a slap in the face, I think."

John-Thor Dahlburg (essay date 13 October 2000)

SOURCE: Dahlburg, John-Thor. "Chinese Exile Gao Xingjian of France Gets Nobel Literature Prize." *Los Angeles Times* (13 October 2000): A17.

[*In the following essay, Dahlburg provides an overview of Gao's literary career in terms of his controversial reception by the Chinese government.*]

After nearly a century of existence, the Nobel Prize in literature was awarded Thursday for the first time to a writer in the world's most-used language, dissident Chinese exile Gao Xingjian, whose works are banned in his native land.

Now a citizen of France, Gao's life and work mirror the tumult of modern China, while blending Chinese themes with narrative forms that originated in the West.

During the upheaval of Mao Tse-tung's 1966-76 Cultural Revolution, in which millions perished, the author was sent to political re-education camps and toiled for six years as an agricultural worker. During that chaotic period, he burned a suitcase filled with manuscripts to avoid their falling into the hands of government officials.

"In the writing of Gao Xingjian, literature is born anew from the struggle of the individual to survive the history of the masses," said the Swedish Academy, which selects the winner of the Nobel in literature. "He is a perspicacious skeptic who makes no claim to be able to understand the world. He asserts that he has found freedom only in writing."

"Art and propaganda are two different things," the novelist once said. Gao is also a playwright, critic and artist—he paints the covers of his own books with India ink.

The Chinese-born writer's masterpiece, the nearly 700-page novel *Soul Mountain,* was written in the 1980s. It recounts the wanderings of an ethnologist among the minorities of southern China as he searches through space and time for his origins, inner peace and freedom.

The Swedish Academy called the book "masterful," saying it recalls "the grandiose idea of German romanticism of a universal poetry."

The 60-year-old author will receive a cash prize of $915,000. He is the first literature prize winner to come from outside Europe since Japan's Kenzaburo Oe won in 1994.

Though Gao is the first Chinese to win the literature prize, that will hardly gladden the heart of Beijing authorities. His works have been outlawed in his native land for a decade, and he is officially deemed *persona non grata.*

The Swedish Academy said it had no political agenda in singling out Gao as a dissident from Chinese communism or as a writer from the world's most populous country. The Swedish judges maintained they were simply honoring great literature.

Gao was born in 1940 in Jiangxi province, the son of a banker and an actress. He attended the Peking Foreign Language Institute, specializing in French and later in translating surrealist poets.

Only in 1979 was Gao allowed to publish and to travel abroad, notably in France and Italy. In the 1980s, he became one of the most prominent avant-garde figures of post-Maoist China, publishing short stories, essays and plays. His 1982 *Alarm Signal* became the first experimental play staged in Beijing in years.

The 1983 play *Bus Stop,* which teetered on the cutting edge because of its absurdity, was denounced by Chinese officialdom as "the most pernicious text written since the creation of the People's Republic." It led to Gao being targeted in a crackdown on "spiritual pollution," a code phrase for unwelcome Western cultural influences.

When another stage production, *The Other Shore,* was banned in 1986, Gao embarked on a 10-month walking tour of Sichuan province to avoid further harassment. He left China in 1987 and was admitted to France as a political refugee.

After the 1989 massacre of protesters in Beijing's Tiananmen Square, Gao resigned his membership in the Chinese Communist Party and joined the dissident movement.

Yet another of his plays, *Fugitives,* employs that slaughter of hundreds, and perhaps thousands, of pro-democracy demonstrators in central Beijing as its backdrop. Chinese officialdom responded by outlawing Gao's entire opus and declaring him an undesirable.

In his apartment in a working-class housing complex in the Paris suburb of Bagnolet, Gao on Thursday called his Nobel Prize "a miracle." He got the news, he said, in a two-minute telephone call from Stockholm.

"It is a great happiness, a great luck," Gao, dressed in a gray sweatshirt and gray jeans, told Reuters Television in fluent French. "They announced it to me very simply and told me I had to prepare a 45-minute speech. I said that's very long."

Living in an apartment decorated with his own paintings in white, black and gray, Gao said he did not think his Chinese origins played a role in his selection. "One must first be a writer," he said.

"Gao has been one of the most important writers in creating what didn't exist before: a spoken drama in China as distinct from music drama, dance and the old traditions," Horace Engdahl, the academy's permanent secretary, told a news conference in Stockholm.

Gao renounced his Chinese citizenship and became a French national two years ago.

This year's Nobel Prizes conclude today with the announcement in Oslo of the winner of the peace prize.

Anthony Kuhn (essay date 16 October 2000)

SOURCE: Kuhn, Anthony. "To Many in China, Author's Nobel Is No Prize." *Los Angeles Times* (16 October 2000): E1, E4.

[*In the following essay, Kuhn explores the response of Chinese government officials, writers, and literary scholars to Gao's winning of the Nobel Prize in Literature.*]

For the many Chinese who have long hoped that the Nobel Prize in literature would be awarded to a Chinese cultural luminary, thereby bringing recognition to their country's rich literary traditions, last week's winner came as a rude shock.

What they got, with the selection of experimental playwright and novelist Gao Xingjian, was a writer whose works few Chinese know; whom the government considers subversive and whom the domestic media have largely been banned from discussing.

But with mainstream Chinese culture caught between unbridled commercialism and official censorship, the award may serve to draw attention to China's small but vital avant-garde arts sector, which Gao helped nurture before going into exile in France in 1987.

On Friday, China's Foreign Ministry dismissed Gao's award, saying in a statement that it "shows again the Nobel literature prize has been used for ulterior political motives, and it is not worth commenting on."

And in a move certain to make Gao even less popular with Beijing, Taiwanese President Chen Shui-bian chipped in his praise for Gao on Saturday. Taiwanese media quoted Chen as saying, "We express our highest respects for his outstanding achievement." Beijing views Taiwan as a separatist province.

The few Chinese intellectuals who had heard of Gao responded to the news of his prize with mixed emotions.

"We should congratulate him for his award," said Shu Yi, head of the recently opened National Museum of Modern Chinese Literature in Beijing. But he added: "The award is stimulating and provocative for China. It makes us feel awkward—we don't know whether to laugh or cry."

Shu said the award showed that the Nobel committee doesn't understand China, which, he said, has plenty of authors of greater stature. But he also railed at China's cultural bureaucracy for not doing a better job of translating and promoting the country's own literature.

"We can't expect foreigners to introduce China's literature to the rest of the world," Shu said. "But China no longer has any great translators."

Shu pointed out that the literary giants of early 20th century China were also translators. Novelists and playwrights such as Ba Jin, Lu Xun and Shu's father, Lao She, were typically schooled in the Chinese classics, then went overseas to study foreign languages and culture.

In much of the second half of the century, most Chinese got neither. Translators went to foreign-language schools based on the Soviet model where they were trained as technicians and taught to reject China's humanist heritage.

In Shu's opinion, the logical choice for the prize would have been the 96-year-old Ba Jin, who has previously been considered by the Nobel committee. Ba's leftist writings inspired idealistic Chinese youths to reject feudal traditions and join the Communist rebels in the caves of Yanan before they seized power in 1949.

On the fringes of China's avant-garde art world, opinions about Gao's prize were more positive.

"The Nobel Prize is not the Olympics, who's No. 1 or No. 2. It's about cultural concepts, not achievement," said Meng Jinghui, a young director at China's Central Experimental Theater. "Really, it's about a bunch of old Swedes looking for meaningful works within their limited field of vision."

"I was very happy to hear of Gao's prize. He's someone who was right next to us."

Before Gao left China, his greatest influence was in the rarefied world of avant-garde theater, and this is where his contributions are most evident today.

As a director and playwright at the People's Art Theater in the 1980s, Gao was part of a group of directors who used bold visual imagery, lighting, sound and acting techniques to introduce Chinese audiences to postmodern Western drama.

Like emerging Chinese genres from political pop and installation art to punk and rock music, the plays mocked Communist icons and the party's role as the lone arbiter of what is "true, good and beautiful" in art.

At first, the absurdity, alienation and vulgarity of these works left most Chinese audiences bewildered. Now, avant-garde art has begun to go commercial, imitated on billboards and television ads, as well as more mainstream works.

In contrast to Gao's days in China, government censors now largely ignore avant-garde theater, partly because of a political loosening, but also because the genre attracts small audiences and scarce media coverage. But this is slowly changing.

"Before, we avant-garde artists mostly just performed for each other," Meng said. Now a night of experimental theater is the in thing for college students, yuppies and foreigners.

In 1990, Meng directed Eugene Ionesco's *Bald Soprano,* which Gao had translated from French. Meng put on two shows at a 200-seat playhouse, and most of the tickets were given away as comps. His next production this year will include 40 shows at an 800-seat theater, and he even expects some box office revenues.

In 1998, Meng achieved his biggest critical success by directing *Accidental Death of an Anarchist,* by Italian playwright Dario Fo, who won the 1997 Nobel Prize in literature. In Meng's modified version of the play, police beat to death a madman who discovers evidence of official corruption, then hire a director to script a cover-up of the killing.

Comparisons to Chinese society were so obvious they didn't need to be drawn. Meng laughed, recalling, "The more we pointed out that the story was set in Italy, the happier we were."

Julia Lovell (essay date 20 October 2000)

SOURCE: Lovell, Julia. "Nobel Prize for Literature 2000." *Times Literary Supplement,* no. 5090 (20 October 2000): 15.

[*In the following essay, Lovell evaluates the significance of Gao's winning of the Nobel Prize in Literature to his status as a self-exiled dissident Chinese writer and to Western conceptions of Chinese literature.*]

"The Nobel Literature Prize has been used for ulterior political motives, and is not worth commenting on." (Chinese Foreign Ministry, October 13, 2000). The awarding, last week, of the Nobel prize for Literature to Gao Xingjian was instantly politicized, partly thanks to Beijing's hardliners, who responded to the announcement by denouncing the "political purposes" of the Prize and declaring that it had lost authority. The Western press also played its part. In the wave of panic that swept the British media last Thursday afternoon (who is he? what has he written? how is his name pronounced?), everyone reached for the first security blanket of modern Chinese studies: the playwright and novelist Gao Xingjian is an exiled dissident (he lives in France). But what significance, if any, does this political virtue have for his writing?

Born in 1940, Gao Xingjian spent the first forty-seven years of his life in China. Though he did not start writing as a professional playwright until 1981, he was active in a drama group while at university in Beijing, where he studied French literature and was introduced to Brechtian theatre. After China re-opened her doors in 1979, the literary scene was quickly deluged with Western literature and theory. Widespread debates ensued on how to reconcile China's ambition to achieve cultural and social modernity with the spiritually polluting origins of these concepts in the bourgeois West.

Gao Xingjian contributed to these debates with a much-discussed booklet on techniques in modern fiction and with *Bus Stop*, a play influenced by the Theatre of the Absurd. Seven characters spend ten years waiting for a bus that never comes, expressing their hopes, disappointments and anxieties in a public transport vacuum. Aesthetics and individual subjectivity, however, were distinctly political issues in a China emerging from an authoritarian phase of proletarian realism: ten years waiting for a bus? what kind of realism is that? what are the masses to make of it? Gao's play fell victim to the 1983 Anti-Spiritual Pollution Campaign. Rather than waiting to be sent for re-education, however, he took off on a five-month tour of China, a trip which yielded the novel *Mountain of Souls,* an exploration of the self in eighty-one chapters, a beleaguered concept both in China's past and present, but a mainstay of modern Western philosophy. All reassuringly dissident and accessible to the West.

Gao is not that easily categorized. A highly innovative playwright, in the 1980s he started developing a concept of "Total Theatre" that incorporated singing, dancing and acrobatics from Chinese sources. Chinese tradition, however, is not used for its own exotic sake, but rather as a dynamic means to create a "modern Eastern theatre" to treat wider, cross-cultural themes, such as human alienation. Set in remote rural China, his 1986 play *Wildman* aimed ambitiously to address both local questions of ecological disaster and the predicament of modern man. Nor is the West an indispensable model: Gao has written that he reads contemporary Western literature simply to avoid duplicating what others have already done.

Gao's reasons for exile emphasized the artistic over the political: on leaving China, he remarked, "an artist who wishes to express freely would not want to stay in this country unless he goes against his conscience." In exile in France, he has not been unwilling to comment on politics: his play *Fleeing* was set during the 1989 Tiananmen demonstrations, but he refused to identify with either the protesters or the Communist Party. In the 1990s, he declared that his existence as a writer hinges on expression, not on representing a nation and its people. He is one of the least political of Chinese dissidents, and it is doubtless his assertion of aesthetic neutrality that appealed to the Nobel Committee.

In an ideal world, Gao Xingjian's prize would be feted as an award to an individual writer, who happened to be born in China, for his impressive achievements in both Chinese and French. In view of the heavily politicized course of modern Chinese literature, moreover, it's easy to sympathize with Gao Xingjian's detached stance. But recent Chinese history and the marginal position occupied by modern Chinese literature in the world literary economy inevitably make his Prize a political issue. Through circumstances beyond his control, Gao, an exile practically unknown to readers in contemporary China and a French citizen since 1998, will most likely be turned into a representative of China in the West. (It remains to be seen whether Gao Xingjian's new status in World Literature will convert to cultural capital in China, whether Beijing will reclaim him as a true son of China or continue to regard him as a turncoat Frenchman.) For China, winning a Nobel Prize for Literature for the first time has been a symbol of achieving global recognition as a modern culture. Although many Chinese intellectuals have long been aware that anxiety to secure the Prize risks a capitulation to Western literary values, the money and prestige that modern Chinese literature would stand to gain are a strong draw, especially as the chances of Chinese literature breaking into the world market are influenced by the politics of international translation and publishing. (*The Economist* predicted in 1998 that the Chinese football team would qualify for the World Cup finals long before a Chinese novelist won the Nobel Prize.) The bitterness of the Chinese' government is unsurprising, in view of this abrupt end to China's century-long quest for the Prize.

Yet leaving aside the official aspect to China's search for a Nobel Literature Prize, Gao Xingjian's laureateship does not solve the problem of Western unfamiliarity with most Chinese literature. China and its literature remain a blank in average Western perceptions, filled occasionally by the writings of exiled authors. While many Chinese are doubtless privately delighted at Gao's prize, there is a feeling among contemporary Chinese writers that the country has changed enormously since 1989, and that the Western exiles are not necessarily qualified spokesmen. There is also some suspicion about the "virtuous dissident" image attached to exiled writers, an image that is ably manipulated by publishers. The Chinese government's condemnation of the Nobel Prize simply reinforces this image.

The real challenge to World Literature still remains; to build a bridge to China's contemporary literature. When copies of Gao Xingjian's work reach bookshops in a few weeks time, it is to be hoped that modern Chinese literature in general will benefit from the increased attention.

Carol J. Williams (essay date 1 November 2000)

SOURCE: Williams, Carol J. "Dubious Maneuvers Soil Nobel." *Los Angeles Times* (1 November 2000): A1, A6.

[*In the following essay, Williams contends that the Swedish Academy's Nobel Prize committee has a conflict of interest that puts into question the validity of Gao's winning of the Nobel Prize in Literature.*]

Somewhere between shameless promoter of personal interests and champion of a once little-known literary talent from China stands an unapologetic Goran Malmqvist, a member of the Swedish Academy whose behavior in this year's Nobel literature prize selection has besmirched the world of letters' sanctum sanctorum.

A retired Stockholm University professor of Chinese languages and literature, Malmqvist just happens to be the Swedish translator of this year's laureate, exiled dissident Gao Xingjian. He's also the confessed middleman in the writer's recent defection from one Swedish publisher to another just before the Nobel announcement.

The nine-month deliberations leading up to literature's most prestigious award are supposed to be held in the strictest confidence. Malmqvist insists that he neither broke the Swedish Academy's vow of silence nor did anything wrong in steering Gao into the hands of a publishing friend.

"There were no leaks from the Swedish Academy—certainly not from me. I'm not that foolish," Malmqvist said Tuesday from Stockholm in a telephone interview with *The Times*. "No member of the Swedish Academy is allowed to say anything about the prize before it is announced."

The announcement of the 60-year-old Gao's selection came Oct. 12, with a citation in which the academy said that in his writing, "literature is born anew from the struggle of the individual to survive the history of the masses." Gao, now a French citizen, has written stories, essays and plays, but the citation called his nearly 700-page novel ***Soul Mountain***, written in the 1980s, "masterful."

And while disavowing any impropriety, Malmqvist readily conceded that he advised Gao to take ***Soul Mountain*** to Kjell Petersson at Stockholm's Atlantis Publishers, where Malmqvist also tried to transfer his own translation rights from the rival house that launched Gao's works in Sweden, Forum Publishers of the Bonnier Group.

Those behind-the-scenes maneuvers stirred up unseemly squabbles in the tiny Swedish publishing realm, which takes pride in the country's outsize role in recognizing the best of the written word. But the scandal has since taken on international proportions. Cultural figures gathered at the Frankfurt Book Fair last week denounced the translator's actions as self-serving, unprofessional and damaging to both the vaunted academy and the Nobel Prize in literature.

"He has struck a severe blow against the reputation of the Swedish Academy," said German Culture Minister Michael Naumann, himself a former New York publisher.

"The eccentricity of the Swedish Academy's decisions has always vexed people," Naumann said. "But eccentricity with concomitant commercial interests puts the credibility of the entire academy in doubt."

One Swedish literary agent who was at the Frankfurt gathering explained, on condition she not be identified, that few in the interdependent business world of literature are willing to publicly criticize Malmqvist or Atlantis for fear of being "blacklisted" for future publication rights.

Jane Friedman, president and chief executive of HarperCollins, which last month bought the North American rights to ***Soul Mountain***, said: "We don't really know about this brouhaha. I was surprised to hear this."

Even Bonnier and Forum executives choose their words carefully in questioning the ethics of those they consider to be practicing the literary equivalent of insider trading.

"What should be said about the role of the academy and whether Mr. Malmqvist said things he shouldn't have, that's not for Bonnier to get involved in," said Jonas Modig, president of the publishing group. "We don't want to express open criticism of the academy. . . . We have to preserve our relations with them."

Executives at the jilted Forum, which had hoped to recoup losses from earlier Gao works that failed to sell in Sweden, said they are in principle satisfied with an out-of-court settlement reached with Atlantis in the past week that will allow them to issue a new edition of Gao short stories first published by Forum in 1988.

That compromise, for which Forum must pay Malmqvist "a small sum" for the translation it already paid for, also obliges Forum to drop its legal pursuit of the rights to other Gao works, said Forum public relations director Annelie Eldh.

Eldh and others point to a number of suspicious coincidences as evidence that ethical rules were broken. Forum was informed by letter from Petersson a couple of days before the Nobel announcement that Atlantis was taking over rights to Gao works in light of a purported letter sent to Forum by the author July 6—a letter both Bonnier and Forum say they never got.

The Swedish Academy, whose 18 members make the final selection of a Nobel laureate after a 16-person prize committee narrows the nominations to a handful, takes the public position that nothing untoward occurred in this year's decision.

"As we understand it, there was nothing inappropriate," said Carola Hermelin, the academy administrator who serves as its spokeswoman. "We only say that members should be very careful and sensitive."

Those outside the hallowed institution, however, insist that there is most certainly an academic tongue-lashing being directed at Malmqvist and other members whose private interests might compromise the academy's reputation.

The Swedish Authors Assn., of which Malmqvist is a member, brushes off any suggestion that professional standards are needed and insists that the out-of-court settlement reached by Forum and Atlantis closes the issue.

While Swedish journalists covering cultural affairs commented on the questionable actions of Malmqvist immediately after the prize announcement, they say the issue never really riled anyone in Sweden outside literary circles.

"I think he did leak information, although maybe not directly. I think he wanted something good to come of this, and I don't think he sees anything he did as wrong," said Asa Beckman, literary critic for the influential Dagens Nyheter newspaper. "I think he's just very enthusiastic about his work."

Malmqvist said he steered Gao, whose works he has translated since the 1970s, to Petersson because he thought the author's earlier works hadn't been properly promoted by Forum.

"Mr. Petersson has read 98% of Gao Xingjian's literature. He has the right to guess, as anyone else does, who would be the recipient" of the Nobel Prize, Malmqvist said of the Atlantis chief's insight into the commercial and cultural value of Gao's work. "Mr. Petersson has a nose for literature—reads books for a living—and having heard me say this is a very important talent might have had its influence. I liked it [*Soul Mountain*] and wanted him to publish it, and the fact that I'm a member of the Swedish Academy cannot hinder me from uttering my views about Chinese literature."

Malmqvist bristled at the suggestion that he was pursuing his own financial interests in promoting Gao within the academy and simultaneously attempting to shift his translation rights to Atlantis.

"I don't translate for money. It's my hobby and my pleasure," insisted the scholar, who has held an academy seat since 1985. Malmqvist said he has earned only about $8,000 from his previous translations of Gao—"less than a cleaning woman working for black-market money would accept."

Petersson, the new publisher—who expects to have *Soul Mountain* on Swedish bookstore shelves later this month—also rejected any suggestion of impropriety or profit motive. With an initial printing of 5,000 planned for a work described in the profession as "highly literary"—meaning unlikely to enrapture the masses—Atlantis has no expectations of fortune, he says.

Jennifer K. Ruark (essay date 8 December 2000)

SOURCE: Ruark, Jennifer K. "Hot Type." *Chronicle of Higher Education* 47, no. 15 (8 December 2000): A18.

[*In the following essay, Ruark assesses the publishing history of Gao's works in English translation.*]

HARD TO GET

American readers looking for books by Gao Xingjian, this year's Nobel laureate in literature, may have wondered if they were banned in the United States as well as in China. Until this week, only one volume of his works was available: a collection of plays titled *The Other Shore.*

The Swedish Academy singled out Mr. Gao's novel *Soul Mountain* for praise when it announced the prize in October, but publicists at HarperCollins in New York were bewildered when they started getting phone calls asking for copies. It turned out the book, translated by Mabel Lee, was published by the press's Australian branch. The New York office rushed an American edition into print that at press time was due out on December 5.

Until then, the University of Michigan Press has cornered the U.S. market on Gao with *The Other Shore,* which it has distributed for the Chinese University Press, of Hong Kong, since October of last year. Michigan had sold fewer than 100 copies and had only 50 more in stock when the Nobel was announced, says the press's publicist, Jessica Sysak. Editors quickly requested more, and the press has now sold 10,000 copies and ordered a third printing.

The title play—which refers to the Buddhist land of enlightenment—is a series of disjointed episodes, beginning with an improvised rope game and ending with a crowd of people who utter seemingly random sentences (including, "It's so bad, what kind of stupid play is this anyway?"). Several scenes in which a mob torments a nonconformist suggest not only the loneliness of the individual but also the dangers of collectivism. A note in the text by Mr. Gao warns that "it is best not to resort to literary analysis outside of theatrical performance or to uncover hidden meanings in the text in performing the play." Chinese authorities disagreed: They forbade the play's performance soon after it was written in 1986.

TALK OF THE TOWN

The Other Shore has since been performed under Mr. Gao's direction in Hong Kong (and Taiwan) and the book is apparently selling well there. Staff of the Chinese University Press could not be reached for comment, but a source in Hong Kong says both ***Soul Mountain*** and ***The Other Shore*** "are available in all the bookstores and there has been discussion of Gao coming to Hong Kong under Hong Kong government auspices in the near future."

That source is Colin Day, the former head of the University of Michigan Press and as of this summer the director of Hong Kong University Press, where he is also capitalizing on the Nobel laureate's sudden international acclaim. In a few months the press will publish what Mr. Day calls "the first substantial critical work on Gao's writing (and painting)," by Jessica Yeung, a lecturer in the translation department at Hong Kong's Lingnan University. It is "indicative of the degree of freedom here that Gao's ***The Other Shore*** is published by Chinese University Press, who are making a big splash about it," writes Mr. Day in an e-mail message.

"Hong Kong is still very separate from the rest of China," he writes. "Of course there is a wariness here about possible threats to basic freedoms and some things do justify such watchfulness. But the worries are about the possible implications for future freedoms, they are not about infringements of present freedoms. I, of course, asked questions about this, but was, and am, reassured that there is a very serious commitment to academic freedom in this university and in Hong Kong."

Mr. Day arrived in August, after 12 years at Michigan. "It felt time to move on and try some new kind of challenge," he writes. "Running a press in a new country seemed to meet the requirement!"

As director, he will expand the press's publications (now about 30 titles a year, most in English), focusing on studies of Hong Kong's culture and society and on building the press's lists in linguistics, Chinese history, law, and education.

Mr. Day will also increase the proportion of books the press publishes in Chinese. But he doesn't claim to be an expert. Although he has studied Mandarin Chinese off and on for years, he says now he's just trying to acquire a little "survival Cantonese."

Jonathan Levi (review date 17 December 2000)

SOURCE: Levi, Jonathan. "Internal Exile." *Los Angeles Times Book Review* (17 December 2000): 2.

[*In the following review, Levi examines the experimental narrative voice in* Soul Mountain.]

In its occasionally quixotic battle for universalism, the Swedish Academy often awards the Nobel Prize for literature to a writer whose name is greeted with surprise and ignorance by the world press. (One doesn't have to search too far back in the annals to unearth Vicente Aleixandre in 1977, or Eyvind Johnson and Harry Martinson, who shared the prize in 1974, about whom ignorance is still almost complete.)

This year's winner, Chinese expatriate Gao Xingjian, is not only relatively unknown in this country but virtually untranslated into English. A resident of Paris since the late 1980s, Gao is best known in Europe for his plays and his paintings. But it seems, according to the helpful introduction by the Australian translator Mabel Lee (who also provides a bibliography of Gao's works in English and French), that the author was also something of a political thorn in the Beijing of the early 1980s. ***Soul Mountain,*** written in 1990, is the first example of Gao's fiction to appear in English. As a true work of great literature, it ought immediately to vault Gao out of obscurity and into the ranks of the first-class laureates.

Soul Mountain is billed as a novel. But it is a novel in which the author has included "travel notes, moralistic ramblings, feelings, notes, jottings, untheoretical discussions, unfable-like fables, copied out some folk songs, added some legend-like nonsense of [his] own invention." It is a novel that threatens at first, in the style of fellow laureate Thomas Mann's *The Magic Mountain,* to join the school of bronchio-topographical fiction. The middle-aged hero, like the author himself, has recently been forced to confront his mortality thanks to a diagnosis of lung cancer. Yet, after six weeks of lying on a stone slab outside a forgotten cemetery practicing "a form of *qigong* related to the Eight Trigrams" and studying "The Book of Changes with Corrections to the Zhou Commentary," the hero has another X-ray taken and, *mirabile dictu,* the shadow on his lung is gone. In search of a new way for his new life (and because his writings have put him out of sympathy with the government), he leaves Beijing for the source of the Yangtze and the mysterious and mystical Lingshan or Soul Mountain.

Barely into the journey, however, the novel takes a turn that no tubercular dream of Hans Castorp's could ever have imagined. The identity of the hero divides. Sometimes "I," sometimes "he" and, after he creates a fictional female traveling companion with her own problems of escape and discovery, sometimes "you," the personalities of the hero mix as freely as the spirits of the folk tales and stories of the ordinary people he encounters, to whom miracles happen as easily as disasters. Split or together, the hero travels up mountains by bus and foot, down rivers by boat, across nature reserves full of mythic snakes, sleeping rough or in local inns and friendly houses where there is always the imagined company of a fellow drinker or a curious woman.

Quickly **Soul Mountain** ceases to be the story of Mann and becomes a splendid stewpot in the spirit of Bruce Chatwin's *The Songlines,* the historical mosaics of Eduardo Galeano and the hopscotch jigsaws of Julio Cortázar. Anthropology mixes with political history, stories of bear-footed Wild Men meld with tales of opium gangsters and crooked cadres, Confucian aphorisms rime chapters as barnacled as the catalogs of proverbs in *Moby-Dick.* One hallucinogenic chapter on a Tibetan plateau takes the hero past his old fear of death. "A dark blue sun circles within an even darker moon, you hold your breath enraptured, stop breathing, reach the extremity of life." To a score that could have been written by Iannis Xenakis for Stanley Kubrick's *2001: A Space Odyssey* the hero looks out from "the physical body you failed to abandon. . . . In the darkness, in the corner of the room, the line of bright red lights on your tape recorder is flashing." In another odyssey, he journeys through a nether world where the river sighs with the moans of girls who have drowned themselves in the weeds.

Occasionally the philosophy reeks more of M. Scott Peck than "Der Zauberberg." "When you think about it, life in fact doesn't have what may be called ultimate goals. It's just like this hornet's nest. It's a pity to abandon it, yet if one tries to remove it one will encounter a stinging attack. Best to leave it just hanging there so that it can be admired." Much better are the moments when Gao lets the story ripen with the tang of parable, as in one brief encounter when a beautiful young girl lets the hero take her photograph in exchange for the promise he will send her a copy in Chengdu. "Later," he writes, "when I return to Chengdu, I pass by this old street. I remember the number of her house and go past the front of it but don't go in. I don't send her the photo afterwards either. After developing my big pile of film, apart from the few I really need, I don't print most of it. I don't know," he adds, "whether or not one day I'll have all this film made into prints, nor do I know whether she will look as stunningly beautiful in the photo."

In the end, Gao's wanderer returns to Beijing, cured of the very miracle that set him on his journey. Motion has taken him not just away from himself and his past life but to the lives and—even more important—the stories of hundreds of other men and women. He has found survival not just in motion but in words. And ultimately, it is the miracle of those words that wins Nobels.

Sylvia Li-Chun Lin (essay date winter 2001)

SOURCE: Lin, Sylvia Li-Chun. "Between the Individual and the Collective: Gao Xingjian's Fiction." *World Literature Today* 75, no. 1 (winter 2001): 12-18.

[*In the following essay, Lin offers an overview of Gao's works to Western readers unfamiliar with his oeuvre, focusing on the theme of individual versus collective rights and responsibilities in Gao's plays and fiction.*]

When the winner of the Nobel Prize in Literature was announced on 12 October 2000, many people in the United States and in the People's Republic of China were wondering just who Gao Xingjian was. It was not a totally invalid question for American observers, since he was virtually unknown here outside of academic circles. What was unusual was the excitement in China over the selection of a Chinese Nobel laureate of whom most had never heard. As a self-exiled writer and naturalized French citizen, Gao Xingjian has witnessed the erasure of his name from the literary scene and the national collective memory in China for reasons that will be briefly explained in the following pages.

This is not to say that Gao's selection went unnoticed in the country of his birth; the Shanghai novelist Wang Anyi, for instance, announced that she was "very happy a Chinese writer won this award, no matter where he lives."[1] And the internationally renowned novelist Mo Yan has spoken of Gao's enormous contributions. But this essay does not concern itself with the Chinese—either the nation's youth, who were ecstatic over the choice but had no idea who the man was, or representatives of the official establishment, who were furious at what they viewed as an intentional provocation by the Swedish Academy or were utterly dismissive of his talents ("a very very average" writer, some said). Rather, I shall use this opportunity to introduce Gao's fictional works to Western readers.

Gao Xingjian was born in Jiangxi Province in 1940. As a French major in college, he obtained a broad knowledge of Western literary theories, particularly modernist writings, which prompted the publication of *A Preliminary Discussion of the Art of Modern Fiction* in 1981.[2] Published during the thaw immediately following the Cultural Revolution (1966-76), this treatise aroused heated debate among scholars and writers in China and "awakened a self-awareness in literature,"[3] but also sparked attacks of "spiritual pollution" on Gao, who was then put under surveillance.

In July 1983, his short play **Bus Stop** was banned after ten performances, for it was considered by some to be "the most pernicious work since the establishment of the People's Republic."[4] ***Bus Stop,*** in the vein of Beckett's *Waiting for Godot,* portrays a group of people waiting for a bus to take them to the city, although their bus never comes. During their ten-year wait, the individual riders reveal their dreams and desires; this was later viewed by Gao's detractors as a direct criticism of the Communist Party, which had failed to take the people into the city, the symbol of prosperity. The ten-year waiting period can also be read as a metaphor for the Cultural Revolution, during which Gao himself had burned mounds of his writings for fear of persecution, particularly since his wife at the time had reported to the authorities on the "unsavory" content of his writings.[5]

Political pressure was further compounded by a diagnosis of lung cancer, the cause of his father's death only a few years earlier. Although an X-ray later proved the diagnosis wrong, the impact on Gao was life-changing; meanwhile, the nightmare of persecution remained persistent in the form of a rumor of his imminent consignment to a prison farm in the remote province of Qinghai. Gao quickly decided to leave Beijing and set out on a roaming journey in Southern China. In 1987 he went to Germany on a fellowship and vowed not to return to Communist China until the totalitarian system was overthrown. He would go even further, by denouncing a system that allows for no dissent; in 1989 he publicly condemned the crackdown on the student movement in Tiananmen Square, an act that sealed his fate in China. His works were banned and his name was never mentioned again, except privately among small groups of intellectuals. When the October 2000 announcement came, the Chinese government dismissed the news as "a Frenchman with a Chinese name winning the Nobel." No wonder people in China did not know who he was, let alone have any familiarity with his works.

Although Gao Xingjian and his works have been politicized by supporters and detractors alike, he insists that he does not subscribe to any particular literary school of thought or align himself with any political faction, including nationalism and patriotism. "I consider literary creation to be a kind of challenge against society waged by an individual's existence," he has written; "even though this challenge may be insignificant, it is at least a gesture."[6]

In August 1989, soon after the Tiananmen massacre, a performing-arts center in Los Angeles contacted Gao with a request to write a play in support of the students' movement. When Gao gave them the play, they told him it wouldn't work for an American audience because it didn't have a hero. They needed a hero in the American fashion, but his play didn't have a single one. So they asked him to revise it; Gao responded that since the Chinese Communist Party could not make him alter his plays, he was not about to do so for the American theater.[7] It is, in part, this challenge against society and an uncompromising attitude toward his beliefs and creative principles that won such high praise from the members of the Swedish Academy.

One of the qualities that place Gao Xingjian squarely in the ranks of the most respected Nobel laureates is the universal appeal of his works, which are distinctively Chinese and yet transcend national boundaries. Unlike so many modern and contemporary Chinese writers, who seem "obsessed with China,"[8] Gao, though drawing his inspiration from Chinese culture, nevertheless ponders more fundamental issues of human existence. Among his favorite themes is the relationship between the individual and the collective entity, which can be a society or a small group of people. In addition to the famous (or "infamous") ***Bus Stop,*** which incurred official censorship, his other plays, equally well received in Europe, also tackle this issue. ***Absconding,***[9] for instance, the play rejected by the Los Angeles Center for the Performing Arts, deals with three characters who hide in a small warehouse on the night of the Tiananmen massacre. Coming from disparate backgrounds, the characters express different views on political movements. One of them, a middle-aged man, even goes so far as to claim that all mass movements are controlled by a political power from behind the scenes and thus become games of political struggle. According to Gao, when the play was performed in Germany, the setting was changed from Tiananmen Square in 1989 to Germany during the Nazi era.[10] To his European adapters, it was obvious that the choice between resistance and collaboration, as well as an individual's role in any kind of movement, is by no means uniquely Chinese, and easily finds historical resonance elsewhere; nevertheless, the Communist Party chose to read his plays as an open attack on its authority.

The conflict between individual and collective rights and responsibilities is prominently featured in Gao's plays predating the Tiananmen massacre as well. In early 1986, he completed a short play titled ***The Other Shore,*** which was immediately banned in the People's Republic and was performed only in Taiwan and Hong Kong. The notion of the other shore comes from the Buddhist concept that human life (on this shore) is full of suffering, and that one can expect salvation only after reaching the other shore. What complicates this play is the fact that the playwright does not allow the characters to obtain salvation or happiness even after they reach the other shore. Worse yet, they are further mired in manipulation and power struggles. The main character, Man, is sought out to lead the others, but then is persecuted when he refuses to be part of the collective. Representing the ultimate individualist, Man yearns for independence, but fails when the collective demands a total surrender of his individuality. Even his search for love is thwarted. Like Gao the playwright, Man becomes an outcast and leaves the stage in the form of a withered heart.

> MAN: *(Weakly)* Who are you?
>
> SHADOW: Your heart.
>
> *(As the crowd watches the drooping, blind, and deaf heart slouch past them, Shadow quietly drags Man away. The crowd slowly follows behind the heart, which is extremely old and actually invisible. All exit.)*[11]

Readers and viewers of Gao's plays in China (if the librettos were available and the plays could be staged, of course) would undoubtedly recognize them as criticisms of Chinese society, in which the individual is constantly required to participate in collective activities. It is no wonder then that the Communist Party regards Gao's work as pernicious, since such a totalitarian entity can allow no dissenting voice or quest for individuality. What readers need to bear in mind, however, is that this is by no means a uniquely Chinese problem. As shown in Gao's plays, man cannot exist alone, for he needs the Other. The Other is like a fire on a cold night; one builds a fire to keep warm, but gets burned if one gets too close to it. How to achieve a balanced, comfortable distance between Self and Other is, as Gao's works invariably demonstrate, a perennial problem for people all over the world.

This distance is essential in any society, be it Christian, Confucian, or something else, in which the dominating thought seeks to encroach upon marginal ideologies. This, however, does not mean that Gao Xingjian is a propagandist who wages a frontal attack on any dominant ideology. Rather, he approaches this issue by reflecting upon traditional Chinese culture, which, contrary to general perception, is anything but homogeneously Confucian. His long novel **Lingshan** (Eng. *Soul Mountain*) is the perfect example. Instead of questioning the impact of totalitarian Communist rule on the individual, Gao elevates the focus of examination to the level of individual versus collective in the context of dominant Confucian tenets versus marginalized cultures.

In **Soul Mountain** Gao employs two narrators, "I" and "you," clearly the two halves of one self; the absence of "we" makes this abundantly clear.[12] While the "I" explores the connection between man and nature in a wandering journey into the natural preserves of Western and Southern China, the "you" delineates the relationship between man and woman through an encounter with a "she":

> You know that I am just talking to myself to alleviate my loneliness. You know that this loneliness of mine is incurable, that no-one can save me and that I can only talk with myself as the partner of my conversation.
>
> As I listen to myself and you, I let you create a she, because you are like me and also cannot bear the loneliness and have to find a partner for your conversation. . . . Like me, you wander wherever you like. As the distance increases there is a converging of the two until unavoidably you and I merge and are inseparable. At this point there is a need to step back and to create space.[13]

Such an experiment with technique may not please every reader, but it allows Gao to reflect upon the relationship between Self and Other (be it a woman or nature itself), which is reminiscent of the existentialist question expounded in Sartre (incidentally, also a Nobel selectee, but one who refused the prize).

Through the narrator's journey in search of Soul Mountain, a physical locale and a spiritual site as well, the author incorporates local legends and supernatural tales from traditions of the Han Chinese and Chinese minorities on the borders. The critic Henry Zhao has argued that, in Gao's mind, there is an official culture represented by power and symbolized by rationalism, male power, and inculcation. This has been the dominant culture in Chinese society for centuries, one that can only be countered with an opposite culture represented by antirationalism, woman, and nature.[14] Such a view, if indeed it is held by Gao, may strike feminists and postcolonial theorists as chauvinistic and imperialistic, for the gender Other—woman—and the ethnic Other—China's minorities—can be regarded as mere foils for the Han Chinese man in quest of self-discovery. If that were the case, then this work could be considered just another male-centered intellectual exercise. But we cannot deny that in Chinese society, Confucian rationality, represented by Northern orthodoxy and the imperial government, has always been suspicious of the South and of that segment of Chinese culture that is imaginative and has an investment in the supernatural. In this sense, Gao's spiritual journey to return to nature serves the higher purpose of recognizing the legitimate status of minority cultures that are an integral part of Chinese civilization. Moreover, it is an implicit criticism of the dominant ideology—be it Communist or Confucian—and the latter's relentless demand for conformity and submission.

An inherent prerequisite for questioning the orthodox ideology and restoring the legitimacy of minority traditions is skepticism. One must reexamine ideas and beliefs that have been accepted for generations as "truth" and acknowledge that the foremost object of skepticism is history. Toward the end of the novel, the narrator "I" comes to the "historical" site where the legendary Yu, one of the earliest Chinese kings, is rumored to have eliminated the problem of flooding for the Chinese populace:

> In Yu's tomb there are now artefacts for reference but the experts still cannot decipher the tadpole-like script on the stone epitaph opposite the main hall. I look at it from various angles, ruminate for a long time, and suddenly it occurs to me that it can be read in this way: history is a riddle,

it can also be read as: history is lies
and it can also be read as: history is nonsense
and yet it can be read as: history is prediction
and then it can be read as: history is sour fruit
yet still it can be read as: history clangs like iron
and it can be read as: history is balls of wheat-flour dumplings
or it can be read as: history is shrouds for wrapping corpses
or taking it further it can be read as: history is a drug to induce sweating
or taking it further it can also be read as: history is ghosts banging on the walls
and in the same way it can be read as: history is antiques
and even: history is rational thinking
or even: history is experience
and even: history is proof
and even: history is a dish of scattered pearls
and even: history is a sequence of cause and effect
or else: history is analogy
or: history is a state of mind
and furthermore: history is history
and: history is absolutely nothing
even: history is bad sighs
Oh history oh history oh history oh history
Actually history can be read any way and this is a major discovery!

(450-51)

Such a skeptical attitude is, of course, not permitted under Communist rule, for the latter promotes a single interpretation of history that serves the Party and rejects dissent. But for Gao, it is precisely this skeptical attitude that preserves the integrity of his work; that is, his skepticism goes beyond a criticism of Communist society or even Confucian culture, as he does not subscribe to any single political belief. He questions the authoritarian view because it is only human to do so, whether one lives in China or elsewhere.

Soul Mountain is considered a highly autobiographical work, as it relates to Gao's search for a utopia after being given a second chance in life, while simultaneously dealing with the increasing pressure of political persecution. His second novel, *Yige ren de Shengjing* (*One Man's Bible*), is even more autobiographical; and yet, like **Soul Mountain,** it seeks to reach a higher level of truth and a broader humanity. As its title suggests, though it may be but one man's Bible, it is a Bible nonetheless, and deals with one man's life during a turbulent era of Chinese history while he searches for the meaning of existence in the face of human cruelty, trauma, and memory.

Read against **Soul Mountain, One Man's Bible** is strikingly different in its realistic portrayal of historical events. The major narratological difference is that the "I," "you," and "she" in **Soul Mountain** are here reduced to "you," "he," and "she." The critic Liu Zaifu argues that, as the novel deals with the Cultural Revolution, the "I" is inevitably strangled by merciless reality.[15] In other words, in the frenzy of the Great Proletarian Cultural Revolution, the individual "I" cannot survive. Unlike the "I" in **Soul Mountain,** who can embark upon self-imposed exile, the "I" in the latter novel must be eliminated. Such a narrative technique clearly sets Gao apart from the authors of the many Cultural Revolution memoirs that have flooded the market (Chinese and Western alike) in recent years. Gao's work is not an attempt to condemn the large-scale persecution so prevalent in modern Chinese history, but a sincere and sometimes brutally honest examination of the human psyche.

The story begins with an encounter between "you" and a Jewish woman in Hong Kong on the eve of the crown colony's turnover to the motherland, and cuts back and forth between the current "you" and the past "he." "You" is Gao's alter ego, one who has been living in the West and appears in Hong Kong for performances of his plays. His meeting the Jewish "she," an old acquaintance from China, calls to mind historical similarities between the Jews' fate in World War II and the fate of the Chinese during the disastrous ten-year Cultural Revolution (often referred to in China as its own "holocaust"). But the two individuals deal with the past very differently; "she" needs to remember and seems to enjoy the masochistic pleasure of shouldering the sufferings and sorrows of all Jews, while "you" wants to forget everything, which inevitably leads to the creation of "he," who travels back to the past. "He" recalls how he was once a fervent participant, until finally realizing that he was nothing but a pawn in a political struggle among higher powers. "He" tries to flee from the cruelties that one person inflicts upon another for no obvious reason other than hysteria motivated by mass madness. While "he" relives the past, "you" is also forced to reflect upon his former self and the process of writing.

> You have to liberate from memory that he, that child, that boy, that man who had yet to reach adulthood, that lucky surviving daydreamer, that insolent fellow, the one who was growing trickier by the day, the past you who had not lost your conscience, cruel and yet not without sympathy. Don't defend him and repent for him. When you observe him and listen to him, you naturally feel an uncontrollable sorrow and regret, but don't let the emotion spread and become sentimental feelings. If you stripped him of his mask to examine him, you'd have to turn him into a fictional construct, someone completely unrelated to you, awaiting your discovery. Only then would this narrative bring you the pleasure of writing, and curiosity and exploration would come naturally.[16]

You write this book for yourself. This book about exile is your One Man's Bible and you are your own God and disciple as well. You don't sacrifice yourself for others, so don't expect others to sacrifice for you. That is only fair. Everyone wants happiness; how could you have it all? You must know that there has never been much happiness in this world to begin with.

(203-4)

Critics of Gao's work have generally focused on his techniques and themes, and not much has been written about women, though they play a significant role in his novels. As mentioned earlier, feminists might find his treatment of women in *Soul Mountain* bordering on male chauvinism. While I agree that Gao gives women a prominent role in countering the male-centered Chinese culture in *Soul Mountain,* one might nonetheless find the portrayal in *One Man's Bible* less satisfying, even disturbing. Appearing in a series of encounters fraught with sexual overtones, the female characters in this long novel are somewhat flat and lack autonomy.

Gao has indicated in a private conversation with a writer friend, Ma Jian, that "of course this world could not exist without women. Men would find it impossible to survive without them, and so do I. Without women, a literary work would be boring to write, let alone to read."[17] Some might also argue that sexual desire is an integral part of the human psyche, one which should be included in an exposé of the darkest aspects of the Cultural Revolution. However, what remains debatable is the significance of juxtaposing the portrayal of relentless persecution of the individual with sexual encounters in which most of the women are passive objects for sexual gratification.

Like *Soul Mountain, One Man's Bible* does not have a clear, linear story line, but incorporates a juxtaposition of episodic recollections and meditations on life, love, and suffering. Obviously, Gao Xingjian does not intend for his two novels to be read merely as stories of the Cultural Revolution or as fantastic travelogues. Both are difficult texts because the author constantly forces readers away from the plots and into his reflections on larger issues. In this sense, they have the quality of the "alienation effect" made famous by Brecht, one of Gao's favorite Western playwrights. They also show how Gao combines dramatic techniques with novelistic themes; ultimately, he would like readers to regard him as a disciple of modernism and a practitioner of "art for art's sake," one who views his responsibility as a writer as both passionately personal and nonideological. He himself has written:

> Literature itself generally has no mission, no group, no movement, no ideology; the writer is solitary, unique. The placards of various ideologies have been attached to him by others so that he can be easily identified and put into archives or else put up for sale.[18]

For Gao, of course, those placards have also led to exile and excommunication from his homeland. The ultimate significance of Gao Xingjian's selection as winner of the 2000 Nobel Prize in Literature, one whose nationalistic and political overtones often obscure the act of writing itself, may well rest in at least one apparent victory of the individual over the collective. I suspect that "China's" first Nobel laureate takes considerable pleasure in that possibility.

Notes

1. See Jonathan Mirsky, "Chinese Writers Rejoice Over Nobel Prize to Gao," *International Herald Tribune,* 20 October 2000, p. 11.

2. This work has not been translated into English; the title is taken from Mabel Lee's introduction to *Soul Mountain,* Sydney/New York, HarperCollins, 2000, p. vii.

3. Chen Sihe, "The First Kite of Modernism," *China Times* (Taipei), 30 October 2000.

4. From *Theater & Society: An Anthology of Contemporary Chinese Drama,* ed. Haiping Yan, New York, Sharpe, 1998, p. xviii. This was uttered by a senior Party member, as quoted in Mabel Lee's introduction, p. viii.

5. From the Hong Kong newspaper *Ming Pao,* 15 October 2000.

6. Gao Xingjian, "My view on Creative Writing," *United Daily* (Taipei), 13 October 2000.

7. "I'm a Chinese After All," interview with Gao Xingjian in *Ming Pao* (Hong Kong), 15 October 2000.

8. This comment, widely quoted among scholars of Chinese literature, was made by C. T. Hsia, Emeritus Professor of Chinese at Columbia University.

9. *Absconding* is Mabel Lee's translation of the original title, *Taowang,* also rendered as *Exile* by Gilbert C. F. Fong, in the appendix to *The Other Shore: Plays by Gao Xingjian,* Hong Kong, Chinese University Press, 1999. It is also sometimes referred to as *Fugitives.*

10. "I'm a Chinese After All."

11. *The Other Shore: Plays by Gao Xingjian,* p. 40.

12. See Mabel Lee, "Pronouns as Protagonists: Gao Xingjian's *Soul Mountain* as Autobiography," in *Gao Xingjian: Critical Assessments,* ed. Kwok-kan Tam, forthcoming from the Chinese University Press in Hong Kong, 2001, n.p.

13. *Soul Mountain,* tr. Mabel Lee, pp. 312-13.

14. Henry Yiheng Zhao, introduction to *Selected Works of Gao Xingjian,* Hong Kong, Mingchuang chubanshe, 1999, p. 4.

15. Liu Zaifu, "Epilogue," in Gao Xingjian, *Yige ren de Shengjing (One Man's Bible),* Taipei, Lianjing chuban shiye youxian gongsi, 1999, pp. 451-56.

16. *Yige ren de Shengjing* (*One Man's Bible*), p. 188. The translation here is mine. A complete translation by Mabel Lee will be published in late 2001.

17. Ma Jian, "Wuxian de xiaxiang" ("Dreams with No Limits"), *Ming Pao yuekan* (Hong Kong), 11/2000, p. 48.

18. Gao Xingjian, "Bali suibi" ("Jottings from Paris"), in his *Meiyou zhuyi* (*Without Isms*), Hong Kong, Tiandi tushu youxian gongsi, 1996. Quoted and translated in Mabel Lee, "Gao Xingjian on the Issue of Literary Creation for the Modern Writer," in *Gao Xingjian: Critical Assessments,* n.p.

Yan Haiping (essay date winter 2001)

SOURCE: Haiping, Yan. "Theatrical Impulse and Posthumanism: Gao Xingjiang's 'Another Kind of Dream.'" *World Literature Today* 75, no. 1 (winter 2001): 20-9.

[*In the following essay, Haiping discusses the theme of posthumanism and the individual in Gao's dramatic works.*]

Chinese drama since the late 1970s, like other forms of art and literature of the era, began as an emotionally charged negation of the Cultural Revolution (1966-76) and developed as a multi-dimensional reflection on the turbulent history of contemporary China, fueled by the rapidly unfolding and violently changing forces of what has been called "modernization."[1] Many emerging playwrights in the early 1980s, as spiritual children of the long tradition of Chinese literary ethics,[2] viewed themselves as "speakers for the common folk" and "authors of social conscience and cultural change."[3] Connected with yet different from many of his contemporaries in this regard, Gao Xingjian appeared on the nation's cultural scene with a distinctive impulse: taking Western literary modernism in general and the theater of the absurd in particular as points of engagement, his first staged play, *Juedui xinghao* (*Absolute Signal*; 1982),[4] treats of such overt social issues as youth unemployment and juvenile delinquency to enact a mode of psychic rhythms subjectively felt by socially detached individuals.[5] Such a mode with its defining impulse enacted through a range of innovative visual images becomes crystallized in Gao's dramatic narrative, *Chezhan* (Eng. *Bus Stop*),[6] his second play, staged by the People's Art Theater Company the following year (1983).

A seemingly Beckettian play, *Bus Stop* focuses on a group of people of different social identities who have been waiting for ten years at a bus station somewhere between countryside and city for a bus that is to take them into the latter. One bus after another passes by, but none stops at their station. While waiting and agonizing over their individual dreams and desires, they hardly notice that one silent middle-aged man leaves the station after several buses have passed: "He strides away without turning his head even once. Music rises, the melody evoking a painful and persistent search" (*BS,* [*Bus Stop*] 125). By the end of the play, the people begin to realize that perhaps this bus stop has been suspended or the bus route has been changed; they finally decide to stop waiting and begin preparing to walk to the city, as the middle-aged man has just done alone.

Realistic in characterization and symbolist in structure, the play provoked immediate controversy in Beijing cultural circles, followed by heated discussion in major cultural centers throughout the nation. Some critics stressed the play's creativity, and hailed its message that people should take charge of their lives and not waste themselves in blind waiting. Others contended that the play contained a basic negation of the operations of contemporary Chinese society, a condescending attitude toward the deluded "pitiable multitude," and an "elitist" position embodied in the "silent man" walking alone to the city.[7]

Bus Stop was suspended by authorities in July 1983, after only ten performances, having been judged "seriously flawed" by decision-making officials; nevertheless, enthusiasm for Gao's "new theater experiment" intrinsically associated with Western modernist theater was spreading among an ever-growing number of dramatists across the nation. While the "Era of Cultural Pluralism" was heralded by several rising new writers in the mid-1980s,[8] it appeared clear that Western modernism and modernist theater were among the most frequently evoked categories redefining the esthetic and political bases of Chinese theater, culture, and society.

Indeed, *Bus Stop* (some sources list *Bus Station* as the title) seems to have both registered and issued a structural and ideological departure from the tradition of socialist realism of PRC theater and culture since the 1950s. Yet the implications of this departure are much more complex than what surfaced in the tense debates surrounding its public staging. It is interesting to note that those who denounced it and those who embraced it both viewed the play as "a Chinese version of Western modernism," an esthetic and political position-taking that seizes Western modernism as the transparent inspiration for the fashioning of a Chinese cultural modernity. At odds with the assertions of both its admirers and its detractors, however, *Bus Stop* with its center of dramatic gravity—the "silent middle-aged man"—is no mere imitation of European modernism. Evidently aware of the historically specific motives of modernism in post—World War II Europe—e.g., epistemological uncertainty and despair, existential agony, and ontological nothingness—and their historically specific function in deconstructing the established yet crisis-ridden Maoist culture in postrevolutionary China, Gao Xingjian articulates the features of his drama as follows in an essay titled **"Modernism and Chinese Literature"** (1987):

> The movement of contemporary Chinese literature toward modernity shares some features with Western modernism, but it cannot possibly repeat the process of development of modern Western literature. The school of modernism that has emerged in China, in general terms, is rather different from that of Western modernism. . . . Unlike Western modernism, which is underlined by a negation of the Self, Chinese modernism is founded on an affirmation of the Self; it exposes the absurdities in the realities of Chinese society but does not—as Western modernism does—take absurdity as constitutive of the existential conditions of humanity. . . . A critical skepticism about the old humanism is the point of departure for Western modernism; but for Chinese modernists, the rediscovery of humanism that was lost under the social conditions of modern and contemporary Chinese society is their core. Such rediscovered humanism is imbued, in effect, with the spirit of romanticism.[9]

Such a rediscovered humanism in the spirit of romanticism, while not overtly rejecting Chinese socialist collectivism, focuses on the individuality of the nation's citizens, which had been radically deemphasized if not erased in contemporary Chinese public discourses. One may then argue that, while Samuel Beckett's *Waiting for Godot* visibly provides a situational impulse for Gao's play, *Bus Stop* has an unmistakably Chinese quality in terms of its structural implications in the post-Mao era. Beckett's play explores the loss of humanity's ontological meaning in the postwar West; Gao's play centers on what he considers the blind multitude who have been trapped by illusory, group-bound conventions and promises throughout their lives. As an embodiment of epistemological negation of Western modernity, *Godot* offers nothing; indeed, it suspends any possibility for change. As an embodiment of disillusionment about Chinese socialist practices, **Bus Stop** offers the mode of the "silent man" who tropes humanistic enlightenment and an individual search for direction in life at a moment of social transformation and political uncertainty.

The global magnitude and the profundity of such transformation and uncertainty, which was unexpected if not unimaginable in the early 1980s to most Chinese dramatists, as the last decade of the twentieth century soon witnessed, shows just how impossibly illusory and/or heroically imperative is the life-path that Gao Xingjian's rediscovered self has to carve in its subsequent journeys within a turbulent world of posthumanist if not posthuman modernity. In another "more China-specific"[10] play written in the aftermath of the Tiananmen tragedy in 1989, *Tao wang* (Eng. ***The Fugitives***), the lyrics of the self in **Bus Stop** linger, but no longer as an unmediated emancipatory impetus. Depicting a group of three—two men and one woman—who are trapped by their social conditions as much as by the humanist configuration of their "selves," Gao writes his lyric flow of the self into an "oozy puddle" of "dirty water or blood" (***F***, [*The Fugitives,*] 67-68) in which culturally figured and disfigured desiring selves are imprisoned and of which they are physically constitutive. "The misfortune of the human not only results from external political oppression, social conformity, dominating fashions, and the will-to-power of the others," he writes in his "Afterword," tremulously close to Derrida or Foucault and their intellectual fellow travelers who demystify, displace, and suspend "the modern self" as a manufactured optic and discursive closure; "it results from the 'human self' as well. Such a self is not divine and is not issued from the gods" (***F***, 73). Yet ultimately, a non-Foucauldian but humanist spirit throbbing in a world (whether it is deemed modern, postmodern, premodern, or all of these together in a muddy mixture) that constantly decenters the human, Gao turns his dramatic writing into a personal battle of life-and-death magnitude. It is a battle against the violent practices of a humanly decentering world by persistent theatermaking, thereby opening up a liminal space between the death of the modern self and a haunting shadow that may prefigure its return as both impossible and imperative.

Sheng si jie (Eng. ***Between Life and Death***), a "woman's pouring out of the human agony," as Jean-Pierre Leonardini in Paris terms it,[11] or "a seventy-minute mad scene," as Bert Wechsler in New York prefers,[12] is a play of one extended act during which an actress shows how "she"—the protagonist, referred to only as Woman—tears through several life-and-death turns "to find out for sure if she's real or just a body without a soul."[13] As the act begins, the actress is struggling to say something, but then stops and, after an agonizing pause which suggests an abyss of bottomless agony, she suddenly erupts and "cannot control her outburst" (***BLD***, [*Between Life and Death,*] 47). The first part of this outburst, which "lasts for seventy minutes" and engages a male actor (Man) who responds to its momentum with detached and ambiguous gestures, enacts a painful rhythm of longing for "love" between intimates, a love locked in its deformation by actions of betrayal, cruelty, deception, and indifference. Displaying all the typical "feminine" features, including a body with "superfluous jewels" and a mind of "irrational jealousy," "possessiveness," and "groundless anxieties," the actress lowers her eyes and looks down, seeing "half a wooden leg, whose paint has peeled off, slowly stretch[ing] out from under her skirt," then stretching out farther "until it finally comes off her skirt" (***BLD***, 56). As the actress reacts with wide-eyed horror to what she sees, an arm appears from inside her shawl, then slowly "falls off from the shawl. From the palm up, the paint has peeled off as with the detached wooden leg" (57). In the midst of such human disembodiment, physically and figuratively, the Woman enacts how the protagonist ("she") desperately attempts to escape from this nightmare of living destruction.

> WOMAN: No! *(Runs away.)* This is too horrible, she can't continue to be cut up like this, she can't keep on butchering herself to death! She must run now, run away from this room! *(Simulates action of opening a door.)* Strange, she can't open the door, how could she be so stupid? How could she possibly lock herself in? *(Crawls all over the room in a circle around the pile of man's clothing, the jewellery box and the detached arm and leg.)* She can't find the key! How can this be possible? . . . *(Stops, staring blankly at the detached arm and leg.)* She just can't understand, can't understand what's happening here. Her home, this warm and comfortable little nest of hers, has turned into a horrifying abyss overnight, how could this be? . . . She's got to get out. *(Shouting.)* She wants to get—out—
>
> (57)

Locked in a living death accentuated by the ticking of a clock that is increasing in volume, the actress simultaneously shifts among and acts out several of "she's" real or imagined memories in a search for the always-elusive self that may or may not have ever existed. First, there was the dark, damp, locked house from which her father escaped and her mother disappeared with another man, and in which her brother broke an antique vase—"a family heirloom"—and her grandpa died of cancer which had spread to his bone marrow, forcing him to turn to opium to kill the pain. Evocative of a semidynastic and semicolonial China, with its opium-overdosed "grandpa" and its "doorless houses," the Woman's enacting of what "she" remembers intimates some temporal and spatial traces which respond to the haunting question, "How did it all begin?" (59).

Then there is the memory of her having had a modern romance with all its expected signifiers, yet all turns out to be false. Her prince wrote identical love letters to her best friend in her class: "She wants to tell a romantic story, . . . but everything has been so hypocritical . . . that it's made her utterly sick" (62). An almost unbearable memory follows: her witness to her modern mother's humiliation at the hands of various male lovers, and her own desperate seeking of her mother's love, which was met only with constant negligence and cruelty. When her mother died a strikingly modern death—in a car crash—it ended her youthful dreams and emptied them of all meaning (63). Then "she" remembers how she was once seduced by a woman and a man who jointly abused her body (the man) and mind (the woman) to sustain their moribund marriage; her escape from them sent her onto a highway "alone at night," leading to a confrontation with "a masked man who blocks her way"—death itself—in an increasingly violent and isolated postmodern "fog" that is everywhere (69-70): "She's only scared that nobody'll know when she's dead. She's even more afraid of a prolonged death, afraid of being crippled, being half dead and half living, nothing is more horrifying than that" (70).

Yet "she" seems to be coming out of her early fatal abyss and lingers on as a living entity as the play enters its final section. As she works through death scenes of what seem to be the premodern, the modern, and the postmodern moment and between the human traces of an identifiable China and an unidentifiable world in a kind of narrative fluidity, the actress's version of what "she" remembers takes on the potent force of mourning, which is also a "carrying through,"[14] a sorting-out, a leavetaking, and almost a chain-breaking liberation. As "she" resists her fear of a man in black with a mammoth policing eye on his palm and a woman without a head on her shoulders, "she" is also shown to have transferentially experienced the agony of a Buddhist nun struggling to reach "the other shore" from this world. When the nun cuts her own stomach open, pulls out her intestines, and cards them one by one to cleanse them, "she" is resonating with the nun and every physicalized emotion involved in the nun's action. Living in and out of the body of the nun and circled by an old man or his shadow whose monkhood comments on her real or illusory space, "she" reaches beyond her state of liminal being by tearing through the narrow passage between life and death, almost emerging at the other end, which may or may not mean "her true self" (57).

"She" has almost emerged at the other end, but not quite: "Everything is enshrouded in the big Chaos, only a glimmer of secret light still exists in her heart, sometimes it's bright and sometimes it's dark, and if she can't even prevent it from disappearing, then all will return to Nothingness" (77). Interweaving the Woman, "she," and the audience in overlapping rhythms of living agony, the play's performance ends with questions rather than affirmations.

> WOMAN: Is this a story? A romance? A farce? A fable? A joke? An admonishment? An essay not good enough to be a poem, or poetic prose which is not quite an essay? It's not a song, because it has meaning but no spirit, it resembles a riddle, but it has no answer. Is it an illusion, no more than the ramblings in an idiot's dream? . . . Is this about him, about you, about me, about her who is that girl, about her but not her, . . . not about me, and not about you or all of you, . . . it's merely the self, . . . that so-called self looking at her, looking at me, what more can you or I say? . . . What is the self?
>
> (78)

From a "silent man" who resolutely walks alone toward an unknown city for an individual actualization, to "a glimmer of secret light [that] still exists in her heart," but caught in a living agony under the shifting shadows of a nun and monkhood, one sees a figurative displacement that registers an immense rupture in Gao Xingjian's narrative enterprise, in his imaginative world of representation. Surely this rupture between the two figurative enactments of the self—one man and one woman—has a gendered dimension, but one would do better by taking seriously Gao's "suggestions" on how to produce the play, especially his suggestion that its staging "should not strive for naturalness" but rather "for utter theatricality" (*OS*, [*The Other Shore,*] 80). At once gender-specific and gender-exceeding, the self of romanticism or the poetics of the humanist subject initiated by Gao in his dramatic praxis of the early 1980s has profoundly transmuted with a distinct Buddhist tremor. His other major plays written since the early 1990s, including ***Duihua yu fanji*** (1992; Eng. ***Dialogue and Rebuttal***) and ***Ye you shen*** (1993; Eng. ***Nocturnal Wanderer***), also evidence such a rupturing change: the form of the former is "inspired by the *gongan* style of question and answer in Chinese Zen Buddhism" (*OS*, 136); the form of the latter is that of a dream, a nightmare that both employs and suspends the connection between reality and illusion (*OS*, 189).

Gao Xingjian himself is aware of the traces of such a Buddhist spirituality in his dramatic textures and language rhythms, and of how such spiritual fabrics intrinsic to his writing distinguish him from modern Western writers in general and Western literary modernists in particular. Informed on matters of traditional Christian metaphysics and engaged with modern psychoanalytic rewritings of foundational cultural principles, he defines his spiritual traits within the frameworks of Chinese Taoism, Zhuangzi's narratives, and a certain kind of pan-Buddhism: "What differentiates me from authors of Western traditions is perhaps an attitude of serene and reflective observation. It is the attitude that I live regarding society and the self."[15]

Still the self, however ruptured. The self as the center of Gao's experiential, observant, cognitive, imaginative, and narrative gravity persists throughout the immense rupture between the "silent man" in ***Bus Stop*** and the "outbursting woman" in ***Between Life and Death***. Gao Xingjian is, then, no Buddhist, Taoist, or practicing believer of Zhuangzi's philosophy, as he himself notes: "Zhuangzi's philosophy of 'letting things take their course' and [his adherence to] Buddhist teachings on renouncing the world seem to me a trifle excessive in their passivity; I, after all, want to *do* something. I am neither a Taoist nor a Buddhist. My writing is a method of self-rescue."[16] From his "rediscovered humanism imbued with the spirit of romanticism"[17] to his writing process as "a method" that "rescues the self," one sees a life-and-death struggle to revisit the ideal of the Enlightenment, which has become "the bone in the choking throat of Western culture" (borrowing Stephen Greenblatt's recent line on Shakespeare's *Hamlet*).[18] More ambitiously or more desperately, or both, it is also a struggle to reenact through what he calls "another kind of drama" such an ideal of the modern self, which has choked so many to death. One can hardly overemphasize the importance of Gao Xingjian's theoretical explorations in drama and his formal innovations in theater practice and stagecraft.

"Another kind of drama" as a concept was formally proposed by Gao Xingjian in 1993, in an essay bearing that very title. Recognizing the limitations of the established system of Western theater in the twentieth century, which he views as "an era of directoral dictatorship,"[19] Gao argues for a revival of the central importance of acting (or "the performance process") in theater and redefines this process in a way that both engages and extends the theory and practice of Stanislavski (who focused more on identification between the performer and his or her scripted role) and Diderot (who insisted on the separation of the two), and also revises Brecht (who refashioned Diderotian cognitive esthetics to create his own brand of political poetics using the concepts of "alienation" and "dialectics").

> I believe that the art of theater, ultimately, depends on the actor's acting for its actualization. . . . I have observed and analyzed the actor's acting in traditional Chinese music drama, and have discovered that, while Western acting theories have long been discussing the relationship between the actor and his or her scripted role, such a relationship has always been premised upon a two-dimensionally conceived dynamic, which overlooks the passage between the actor as a living human who acts and the scripted role that he or she enters. I call this passage "the medium of neutrality." It means that, before the actor enters the role, he or she needs to purify his or her body of his or her self in daily life, a leavetaking as it were. If theater acting validates this third medium of neutrality as a process, fully opens it up, reveals it, and lays it bare, then the configurations of the relationship among "the self—the actor—the role" would afford the art of acting many more new possibilities. The ways of playwriting would also be enriched.[20]

In other words, allow the human body and human action to return to, inhabit, and constitute the center stage both of the theater and of the world.

But such a return and reentry of the human self is hardly a resurrection of the ideal subject of the European Enlightenment. It is not premised upon the supremacy of the Cartesian *cogito,* the abstract individual sovereignty, and the modern apparatus with its eternalized value system as the overlord of universality. Rather, it assumes a multidimensional, constantly changing and shifting, and inherently transformative system of human relationships. It is through such a relational system that the human self (which on Gao Xingjian's stage is "a secret glimmer") might gain new possibilities to *act* in this human world, but act with an acute consciousness of its constant self-making and remaking within, against, with, and through the forces and shapes of others without the ontological certainty of its ahistorical or transhistorical "true self."

The human self, then, is a relationally conditioned process of acting, a constant remaking of itself by self-consciously inhabiting the relational system that Gao calls the "medium of neutrality." The sociocultural implications of this theatrical impulse, which is central to Gao's dramatic writing, are concisely articulated in his 1995 *Libération* interview with Gérard Meudal.

> The process of fictional narrative [and dramatic performance] involves three "persons," at least three. The self, "I," in daily life shifts almost indiscernibly into "You" when monologues engendered through meditation take place. Where does the third person, the Other, come from? When one thinks more philosophically, taking leave of one's own body, the "I" then becomes an eye of neutrality that looks back on the self's body; the Other comes from such a leavetaking from the objective, living, material world.[21]

The Other, the medium of neutrality, is therefore a system of human relations through which the possibilities of making and remaking the acting self (or the self in acting) are opened up as three-dimensional motions without the constraint of Hegelian immanence or its more secular version, humanist ontology. Enacting and enacted as a posthumanist impulse in Gao Xingjian's reenvisioning, the human self is fundamentally theatrical in its configuration, the human self in and as a theatrical agency. It is through such a reenvisioning of theater and its central dynamics—human acting—as a site of human agency in the making that the rupture between Gao's "humanist self" of the 1980s and its ghostly "secret glimmer" of the 1990s is transfigured into a source of enormous creativity.

Hence Gao Xingjian's probings into and engagements with a Chinese dramatic culture that is premised and thrives upon its theatricality are essential to an understanding of his concept of "another kind of drama," his theatrical rather than ontological process of (re)making the human self. His play **Ming jie** (1991; Eng. **Hades**, though I would prefer **City of the Dead** as more modernly evocative), drawn from many versions of the Chinese story about how the Taoist sage Zhuangzi tested his wife's love for him, is an intriguing case in point. In part 1 of the play, Zhuangzi pretends to have died and then acts as the Prince of Chu State to seduce his weeping wife, who now believes herself widowed. We then see how the wife in her "widowhood" is affected by the feigned love of this "prince," how this pretend "prince" turns out to be her "dead" husband, and how she cuts herself open with a hatchet and dies after being deranged by the unrealness of what feels real and by a perceived reality that turns out to be unreal.

In part 2, the wife's ghost, now in the City of the Dead, haunts the city's legal and political courts, making a variety of theatrically stirring sounds, facial expressions, gestures, and movements, which are witnessed and commented on by a group of human ghosts whose names and stories are all recorded in Chinese (oral) folk literature. The human effects and material consequences of Zhuangzi's play-acting are rendered physically and graphically real in the ghost-wife's highly theatrical motions, as are the rhythms and movements of this dead woman in the body of a living actress who refuses to disappear and insists on her theatrical agency with a vengeance. Indeed, the human and material realness that is embodied here through such stirringly theatrical acting is so overwhelmingly potent that it renders the play's coda—wherein Zhuangzi sings his signature song, which cancels "the real"—almost irrelevant as the point of the play.[22] Such potent realness of acting and theatrical agency, as Gao views it, is produced through the relational dynamics between the actor and the acted, the acting and the audience, an intertwined human field his poetics calls "the medium of neutrality," with temporally and spatially infinite human possibilities.[23]

Shanhaijing zhuan (1993; Eng. ***The Story of the Classic of Seas and Mountains,*** though my preference would be ***Stories of Shanhaijing: A Three-Act Tragicomedy of the Gods***), a play that is quite possibly one of the world's dramatic masterpieces of the twentieth century, is a monumental reenactment of Chinese myths originating in the Yangtze River valley and its surrounding regions, a land of human and natural abundance. The term *Shanhaijing* literally means "classics of the mountains and seas" and serves as the generic title of some eighteen volumes of written texts ranging from extended longer narratives to tales of only a few lines about enchanting rivers and hills, various tribal peoples and their customs and rituals, intriguing animals or spirits or goblins, human and nonhuman marvels, magical scenes, and legends and myths—a veritable cultural trove of ancient Chinese mythological imagining. Evidently, it was not composed by a single author at one specific time; instead, it was probably the product of many hands, most likely completed during the Period of the Warring States (475-221 B.C.), then expanded during the Qin and Han Dynasties (221 B.C.-200 A.D.). In **"Some Explanations and Suggestions on Staging Stories of Shanhaijing,"** Gao Xingjian makes certain that his readers and the producer or director of the play understand that his dramatization is based on the historical texts in close consultation with prominent scholars on the *Shanhaijing*. Even more important is his statement that he regards this trove of ancient Chinese mythology as a constantly renewable theatrical resource for the remaking of the human spirit and human drama, since, as he writes, "its richness and colorfulness matches the trove of Greek mythology."[24]

Rich and colorful indeed! And most imaginatively free and forthrightly theatrical. The play opens with a scene in which the goddess Nu Wa molds figures from the yellow earth, uses magic ropes to multiply them, then gives them life and the ability to bear children, thereby creating an ever-renewable humanity. As this process of creation is enacted against a background of furious flooding, vast rainfall, cosmic thunder, and flashes of light presaging earthquakes or auroras of unknown kinds, a folklore artist observes, narrates, comments upon and explains the action, and sings in time with the rhythms of the actress's marvelous performance, rendering Nu Wa's actions essentially those of human creativity. When, still in act 1, ten fiery suns who are also brothers are shown to be committing all kinds of outrages in the sky while burning the human lands below to cinders, along comes Yi, another mythological god, who breathes in agony with ordinary humans and kills nine of the suns with his bow and arrow, leaving only one in the sky, since he is needed by the common mortals below. Yi, portrayed by an actor whose expressions and movements are all observed and illuminated by the folklore artist and his songs, is revealed as more a farmer's son than a mythological god.

In act 2, as the gods fight for supreme dominance over the fluid and human and celestial spheres and drag every earthly and celestial being through mud and blood, there appears the Jinwei Bird. Formerly the young daughter of the Sun God who had gone to the East Sea in search of love, only to drown in the waves, she now returns in the shape of a small bird determined to fill up the sea so that it will never take another life. She picks up small stones, leaves of grass, and tree branches with her delicate beak, then flies to the sea and drops them into the water. Each and every day, she continues doing this, without cease—an impossible task, but a necessary one that gives form and meaning to her existence.

In act 3, the commingled human and celestial spheres are separated, and all the connecting passages between the two are closed off. The struggle among the gods for dominion is now over. Yet before "the century of the Emperor"[25] and its order appear on the horizon, the human world is inundated in a violent flood caused by the final battle among the gods. Taking center stage at this point is Gun, the grandson of one of the gods, whose heart weeps for the mortals caught up in the violent flood. Overhearing suggestions made by two struggling humans, Gun decides to steal from the gods the mythical soil that can multiply itself in volume and stop the floodwaters. The gods, angered by Gun's defiance of their decrees and his tenderness toward humankind, send Zhurong, the god of fire, to punish him. Gun is killed by Zhurong, yet begets a son, Dayu. Continuing his father's will and working day and night, Dayu ultimately spreads the soil across "nine ancient continents," so that the vast and consolidated land of China is finally brought into being.

Legends and mythological stories of this kind, and many others, fill the play with an epic grandeur, a stunning constellation of colorful figures, gestures, and movements that animates the acting onstage and mobilizes the sensibility of the audience, while producing an extraordinary theatricality made up of ordinary human bodies. Among the forces at work here is a poetics of the mythological creativity of ordinary humans with their distinct physical bodies and artistic abilities, showing how such larger-than-life mythological occurrences can be fully actualized in and through the extraordinary theatrical talents and actions of mere mortal human beings. Indeed, Gao Xingjian believes that poetry in drama can only be engendered in and through such human enactments of conscious theatricality, in and through the motions of acting that constitute theatrical agency.[26]

For a posthumanist if not posthuman theater and world (some call it postmodern or simply post-), the "theatrical agency" theorized and enacted by Gao Xingjian, with its promises of making "another kind of drama," another kind of world, and another kind of human subject, deserves further close, sustained examination and explication. (The limitations of and problems in Gao's dramatic theory and theatrical practice also need more study.) Suffice it to say here that, as the first Nobel laureate in literature who writes primarily in Chinese, Gao Xingjian envisions "another kind of drama" as an essentially posthumanist gesture which requires still a good deal more articulation and development. It may contain a formative impetus that prefigures certain cultural rhythms with which the human subject of the modern world can regain his or her home—in and through the varying forms and shapes of a colorful theatrical agency—in a changing world that has long exiled its human spirits.[27] If we gently probe the theatrical impulse and the posthumanism in Gao's major dramatic works, one would hope, such spirits can show us their formative momentum and indicate to us their still-unfolding, possible futures.

Notes

1. The definition of such modernization is uncertain and shifting in the Chinese context throughout the reform era. See Wang Hui, "Contemporary Chinese Thought and the Question of Modernity," *Social Text,* 16:2 (Summer 1998), pp. 8-44.

2. See Cyril Birch, "The Man—or Woman—of Letters as Hero," postscript to Yue Daiyun, *Intellectuals in Chinese Fiction,* Berkeley, University of

California Institute of East Asian Studies, 1988, pp. 134-43. For a more specific discussion of the continuity of such Chinese literary ethics in the cultural ethos of theater circles in the 1980s, please see Haiping Yan, "Theatre and Society: An Introduction to Contemporary Chinese Drama," in *Theatre and Society: An Anthology of Contemporary Chinese Drama*, ed. Haiping Yan, Armonk (N.Y.), Sharpe, 1998, pp. ix-xlvi.

3. See Yi-tsi Mei Feuerwerker, *Ideology, Power, Text*, Stanford (Ca.), Stanford University Press, 1998.

4. Gao Xingjian and Liu Huiyuan, *Juedui xinghao* [*Absolute Signal*], *Shiyue* [*October*], 1982, no. 5.

5. See Lin Zaohua, "Lin Zaohua on His Cooperation with Gao Xingjian," NetEase.www.163.com, 8 December 2000.

6. Gao Xingjian, *Chezhan* [Eng. *Bus Stop*], *Shiyue*, 1983, no. 3, pp. 119-38. (Subsequently abbreviated as *BS*.)

7. See "Bianzhe an" ["Notes from the Editor"] in "*Chezhan* sanren tan" [A Dialogue by Three Critics on *Bus Stop*], *Xijubao* [*On Theater*], March 1984, pp. 3-7.

8. See "Liu Xinwu tan xingshiqi de bianhua" ["Liu Xinwu on the Literary Changes in the New Era"], Liu Xinwu and Li Li, *Wenhui yuekan* [*Wenhui Monthly*], 1988, no. 5.

9. Gao Xingjian, "Chidao de xiandaizhuyi yu dangjin zhongguo wenxue" ["The Slow Arrival of Modernism and Contemporary Chinese Literature"], a speech given at the Hong Kong conference "Contemporary Chinese Literature and Modernism," 11 October 1987, and published in Gao Xingjian, *Meiyou zhuyi* [*No Isms*], Hong Kong, Tiandi, 1996, p. 102.

10. Gao Xingjian, *Tao wang* [Eng. *The Fugitives*], in *Gao Xingjian xi ju liu zhong* [*Six Volumes of Gao Xingjian's Plays*], Xindian, Di Jiao Chubanshe, 1995, vol. 4, p. 72. (Subsequently abbreviated as *F*.)

11. Jean Pierre Léonardini, *L'Humanité*, 21 July 1993.

12. See "One Woman's Many Problems," in "Reviews of Asian American Theatre by Bert Wechsler," taken from "NY Theatre-wire," at www.abcflash.com/arts/r_tang/wechsler.html, 22 February 1997.

13. Gao Xingjian, *Between Life and Death* [orig. *Sheng si jie*], in *The Other Shore: Plays by Gao Xingjian*, tr. Gilbert C. F. Fong, Hong Kong, Chinese University Press, 1999, p. 57. (Subsequently abbreviated as *BLD*. Subsequent references to *The Other Shore* are abbreviated as *OS*.)

14. See Sigmund Freud, "Mourning and Melancholia," in his *General Psychological Theory*, New York, Collier, 1972, pp. 164-65, 166-67.

15. Gao Xingjian, "My Views on Creative Writing," NetEase.www.163.com, 8 December 2000, p. 1.

16. Ibid., pp. 1-2.

17. Gao Xingjian, "Chidao de xiandaizhuyi . . . ," p. 102.

18. Stephen Greenblatt, "On Shakespeare's *Richard III*," public lecture, 21 February 2001, University of Michigan.

19. Gao Xingjian, "Another Kind of Drama," in *Six Volumes . . .* , vol. 5, p. 130.

20. Ibid., p. 131.

21. "How Does Gao Move the Mountains," interview with Gao Xingjian by Gérard Meudal, *Libération* (Paris), 21 December 1995.

22. Gao Xingjian, *Six Volumes . . .* , vol. 2, p. 64.

23. Gao Xingjian, "My Plays and My Key," *Six Volumes . . .* , vol. 2, p. 85.

24. Gao Xingjian, "Some Explanations and Suggestions on Staging *Stories of Shanhaijing*," *Six Volumes . . .* , vol. 3, p. 107.

25. *Six Volumes . . .* , vol. 3, p. 105.

26. "My Plays and My Key," p. 84.

27. It should be noted here that the musicality of human subjects, in both making and remaking and in their infinite variations, occurs again in *Weekend Quartet* (1996), now visualized, oralized, and explicitly theatricalized. This play is contained in *The Other Shore*, pp. 191-253. Gao's most recent drama (his eighteenth) is titled *Snow in August* and was just published in early 2001 in Taipei by Jin Lian Chubanshe; it will soon be produced by Hu Yaohen in Taipei and offers one more highly innovative instance of "another kind of drama."

Fatima Wu (review date winter 2001)

SOURCE: Wu, Fatima. Review of *Soul Mountain*, by Gao Xingjian. *World Literature Today* 75, no. 1 (winter 2001): 101.

[*In the following review, Wu explores Gao's narrative voice and the theme of the collective search for the meaning of life in* Soul Mountain.]

Gao Xingjian was diagnosed with lung cancer in 1982. Faced with imminent death, he began to gorge himself with sumptuous food and to immerse himself in reading in an old graveyard in a Beijing suburb. However, a second examination revoked the first diagnosis, and Gao was then returned to the human world. It was at this time that he left the city of Beijing to begin his 15,000-kilometer journey from central China to the east coast. This journey, which lasted over five months, gave birth to the book *Soul Mountain.*

The work is an account of Gao's odyssey, or a pagan's *Pilgrim's Progress*. In eighty-one chapters covering over five hundred pages, the author makes use of multiple narrators named "I," "you," "he," and "she" to iterate various perspectives of his ideas. One can regard the text as a traveler's journal recording Gao's feelings and routes, or even as a philosophical treatise on life, religion, culture, history, et cetera. It is also an extended monologue, bordering on stream of consciousness, by a writer who is eager to find himself and to make sense of the world around him. Above all, the book records one lonely individual's quest for his soul.

Soul Mountain distinguishes itself from contemporary Chinese literature in its form, content, and narrative technique. Maybe because Gao is also an artist, descriptions of nature in the narrative stand out in readers' eyes as paintings. The eighty-one chapters are held together not by plot or characters, but by the search for truth in a collective mind. When human beings are unhappy, whom or what can they blame? Religion? Politics? History? Culture? The opposite sex? Amid the philosophical discussions of life, Gao intersperses stories of love, tales of political persecution, and fables. These fictional narratives add to the meaning of life that Gao is searching for. They reflect the world around him, the people and the suffocating environment.

Like Wordsworth, Gao perhaps finds redemption only in nature, in its beauty and serenity. Hence the quest for Soul Mountain, of whose existence no one is certain. But unlike Wordsworth, who found meaning in nature and salvation in God, Gao renounces both the Buddhist and Taoist sects while failing to reach his destination. At the end of the narrative, he proclaims, "I comprehend nothing, I understand nothing."

Gao finished this book in 1989, and by that time he had already emigrated to Paris. The seven-year quest recounted here, presented through the eyes of a poet and a painter, enhances the work's literary and visual effect. Overall, Mabel Lee's translation can be deemed superb and outstanding, revealing not only the nihilistic and frustrated mood of the narrator but also the beauty and the all-embracing arms nature.

Gao Xingjian, Mabel Lee, and Susan Salter Reynolds (interview date 27 February 2001)

SOURCE: Xingjian, Gao, Mabel Lee, and Susan Salter Reynolds. "The World According to Gao." *Los Angeles Times* (27 February 2001): E1, E4.

[*In the following interview, Gao and Lee, the English-language translator of* Soul Mountain, *discusses the theme of love and male-female relationships in Gao's body of work.*]

There ought to be a Nobel Prize for readers. Consider the terrible isolation of the reader, for example, turning the pages of Gao Xingjian's Nobel Prize-winning novel, *Soul Mountain,* a beautiful, confusing, thought-demanding book full of questions and no answers. Whom can you talk to about the self and the soul and the constrictions of culture? Or about the perversions of social will on the pure, animal needs of the individual? On page 506, the loyal reader is told that God is a small green frog on a snowy windowsill in Sichuan province, that conclusions are bogus, the self is elusive and nothing can be understood.

And *he* gets the $900,000.

Last October, Gao Xingjian (pronounced *gow shing-jen*) became the first Chinese Nobel laureate (poet Bei Dao has been a past finalist), yet officials in Beijing were not happy about it. *Soul Mountain,* which won him the award, has been banned in China since 1985. One state newspaper, the Yangcheng Evening News, called him "an awful writer." Chinese officials refused to attend the prize ceremonies in January. In China, Gao, 61, a playwright, critic, painter and novelist, has been considered a dissident writer since his play *Bus Stop,* in which eight characters wait for a bus, was banned in 1983, described by a government official as "the most poisonous play written since 1949."

We meet here on one of the city's signature gray winter days (no wonder they read so much). Gao, who has come here from France, where he has lived since 1988, is polite and handsome in a black cashmere coat. He hardly moves when he talks. Underneath some of his answers to some questions is a well of warmth; others he has answered so much they skim the surface of his expressiveness. We talk as he heads to the University Bookstore, where the signatures he will inscribe on 80 "stock" copies of *Soul Mountain* are too beautiful for the day.

Mabel Lee, who translated *Soul Mountain,* is traveling with Gao on the book tour and translating for him; he speaks French and Mandarin but not English. Lee, who is neat, with cropped white hair and a black leather jacket, keeps saying, "I am not a translator." She does not speak French. Each time I show the slightest inclination to speak in French, she tries, albeit politely, to abandon us. An honorary associate professor of Chinese Studies at Australia's University of Sydney, Lee came to work with him almost by accident; she was visiting a friend in Paris in 1995 and decided to visit Gao. She asked if he had a translator for *Soul Mountain,* and he said no.

"The first chapter was by far the hardest," she says, "because I had never done it before. "His writing is like poetry. It can be very natural, like speech, but also classical. He is trying to depoliticize language."

"I thought *Bus Stop* was a comedy," Gao says when asked about the play that made him an enemy of the state. "But during the Cultural Revolution, it was perceived as something entirely different. Why? Because the authorities lack humor," he says, smiling mischievously.

"He's trying," Lee explains, "to force people to think."

Soul Mountain has received mixed reviews. The glowing ones compare Gao to Thomas Mann, Herman Melville and even Henry David Thoreau. The translation has been criticized as wooden. Other reviewers have grumbled about how its use of pronouns is confusing. Gao divides the author's self into "I," "you," "he" and "she," and each chapter has one of these narrators.

"I wanted," he says, "to move away from characters and to emphasize the loneliness of the narrator. There's a great deal of loneliness in Communist China. Let's say the situation in China exaggerates human loneliness, which exists everywhere. This is because at various times you were afraid to speak freely."

There is a great sense of freedom in the book and a strong feeling of what Gao calls "primitive" loneliness. "I never expected it to be published," Gao says. "I had begun to censor my own work, and I wanted to write something without self-censorship." After *Bus Stop,* government officials began to carefully scrutinize Gao's work.

In 1983 he was diagnosed with lung cancer, the disease that killed his father. After two weeks of *qui-gong* exercises (Taoist exercises not unlike tai chi), the tumor disappeared. Gao began a six-month journey, 9,300 miles into western Sichuan and the forests of Yunnan, following the Yangtze River like a pilgrim through metasequoias and linden, maple and plum trees, looking for Lingshan (which translates as "soul mountain").

"I was looking for the other China," Gao says. "The China of dragons and colors and stories." State culture, he has written, is soul-killing. Micro-cultures are soul-enhancing. Gao traveled among Daqi people and Miao, through the Ba kingdom and the Haiba in Tibet. He listened to dream sacrifice songs and watched dragon-boat ceremonies. "In the end," he wrote, "to forget one's ancestors is a crime."

Gao's current wandering in the U.S. is almost as peripatetic, a strange book tour from Washington, D.C., to Seattle to New York. Rick Simonson, manager of Elliot Bay Bookstore in Seattle, says, "Mysterious things happen," when asked how Gao ended in Seattle. ("*Par grand hazard*" is Gao's explanation.) Elliott Bay has a huge and loyal clientele. Thirteen years ago, the store had its first reading with Toni Morrison. Five years ago a secret reading with Salman Rushdie drew 1,000 people.

Soul Mountain, which was published first in Australia and only recently released by HarperCollins in the U.S., "has done well here, even before the Nobel," Simonson says. A reading Saturday night was organized by Seattle Arts and Lectures and Elliot Bay Books at A Contemporary Theatre, ACT. More than 400 tickets sold.

Gao was born in Nanjing, in eastern China, during the Japanese invasion. He had a Westernized, liberal upbringing; his father was a senior official in the Bank of China, as was his father's father. His mother, an amateur actress raised in an aristocratic household and educated by American missionaries, possessed many translations of Western writers such as Steinbeck, Balzac and Baudelaire, as well as surrealists and Russians.

In 1960, during the Great Leap Forward, Gao's mother was sent to the country to work, and she drowned in an accident. "She was very important to me," Gao says. Asked if the woman he recalls at length in *Soul Mountain* who is raped repeatedly by local boys and drowns was based on his mother, he says "yes."

Gao graduated in 1962 from the French Department of Foreign Languages Institute in Beijing. After this, he joined the Communist Party and was elected leader of a Red Guard faction. When he left the Red Guard, his wife denounced him. They divorced, and he began five years of manual labor at a cadre school in the country.

The Cultural Revolution began in 1966 and lasted until Mao's death in 1976. Gao worked as a translator of the French edition of *China Reconstructs* and also translated Beckett and Ionesco. During his "re-education" in the 1970s, Gao would wrap his manuscripts in plastic and bury them under the floor of the hut where he lived.

Gao has written 18 plays, four books of criticism and five novels (not including one he wrote when he was 10).

Conversation, slipping among French and Chinese and English, is a little awkward, but we all relax when the subject of men and women comes up, a huge and complex part of the book. "It is," Gao says in French, "the most interesting of subjects. I like, in particular, discussing it with women. There are three things that are beautiful: women, nature and art." Gao has been married two times, and will not, he says today, do it again. But he has a girlfriend.

"I couldn't live without love," he says, 'because the world is so horrible.' For a moment, we three forget which language is being spoken. "At bottom," he says, "there is no difference between men and women everywhere. At bottom, literature does not have a national identity, either. When I read translations of Western authors as a child, I wasn't reading foreign literature."

Gao renounced his party membership in 1989, after Tiananmen Square. He became a French citizen in 1998. His most appreciative audience, so far, has been in France. "My French readers think *Soul Mountain* is a book about themselves, not about China. There's a greater freedom in China now than before, but still not as much as an artist feels in France. In the past century, politics has interfered too much in peoples' lives. This is not limited to China. It's the same all over."

Gao lives in a working-class suburb of Paris called Bagnolet (he hasn't moved since winning the prize). When he first came to France, he began, after seeing Picasso's drawings, to draw in ink and to learn more about Western art. His drawings are exhibited regularly. "Painting has been my profession," he says. "It has provided the resources for me to write." His next novel to appear in English, *One Man's Bible,* about his experience with the Red Guard, is being translated by Lee and will be published by HarperCollins some time next year.

"Here are some words," I tell Gao, "that appeared frequently in *Soul Mountain.* Tell me the first thing that comes to mind when I say them." I want to see if he is still game for a little Dada exercise.

"Freedom." "Wonderful."

"Will." "Important."

"Lonely." "Necessary."

"Blood." "*J'ai peur.*" ("I am afraid.")

"Meaning." "Nonsense."

"Culture." "Ocean."

"Self." "*Quelquefois, l'enfer.*"

("Sometimes hell.")

"I may not believe in ghosts," Gao says when asked about his religion, "but I have a reverence for what can't be known. Pre-communist Chinese culture wasn't so bad. It was full of traditions that were destroyed by the communists. I have a religious feeling. Young people in China today follow fashions. Following fashion is a kind of mob mentality. I have always been antifashion, anti-trend. Even as a child, I preferred hiding in a corner and not doing what everyone else did.

"Apart from soccer," he says, "things that everyone wishes to do are suspect. And I was smart enough to know that I had no future," he says smiling, "in soccer."

David Mehegan (essay date 7 March 2001)

SOURCE: Mehegan, David. "The Man Who Can't Be 'We.'" *Boston Globe* (7 March 2001): A17.

[*In the following essay, Mehegan asserts that Gao acts as a spokesperson for individual freedoms through his works of drama and fiction.*]

Standing alone at the podium, a slender Chinese man in a black suit spoke softly. All around and high above, the concave amphitheater at Harvard University was packed to overflowing with people, primarily Chinese, of all ages, hanging on his measured words. An interpreter stood at a microphone nearby.

The room was hot and airless, but Gao Xingjian, the 2000 Nobel laureate for literature, was a kind of cool island. His short talk was on literature and freedom. The writer must break free, he said, of all constraints and external pressures: political, social, economic. "For a writer trapped by ideology," he said, "it is hard to achieve freedom. I take a stand against 'isms' of any kind; I try to jump out of all frameworks."

In the four months since he became the first Chinese winner of the Nobel Prize for literature, Gao Xingjian's selection still makes waves. His works are banned in China and his receipt of the Nobel was denounced last month by a state-controlled newspaper as "ludicrous," "disappointing," and "a kind of joke played by the Swedish Academy on the Chinese people." It's not only the government that scorns him. Some Chinese, writers and others, find his work difficult and obscure, and resent his refusal to be a spokesman for anti-Beijing elements. In a talk at a Hong Kong university in February, he angered local writers by refusing to criticize the government. His four-city American tour ended in Cambridge last week, and though most in the Harvard audience acclaimed him and lined up to take his picture and hand him books to sign, even there a few hostile voices were heard. Speaking Chinese and paraphrased by the interpreter, one young man vehemently complained that Gao was not chosen in honor of his works, but because he is a rebel—a slap to China.

Speaking of his epic novel, **Soul Mountain,** recently published in English, Gao said, "I asked that the words 'us' and 'we' not be used in the translation, since they do not appear in the original. I have an instinctive dislike of 'we.' I come from a China where 'we' has completely vanquished 'I.'"

A more radical rejection of traditional Chinese thinking, some scholars say, would be hard to imagine. Gao, 60, is a rebel of sorts, as a writer. He is an odd sort of rebel—not a political spokesman such as Vaclav Havel or Alexander Solzhenitsyn. Born in 1940, he majored in French at Beijing University. He also became a painter. Though modernist Western works were banned in China, he discovered they were available in French, so he immersed himself in Kafka, Ionesco, Beckett, Sartre, Joyce, and Thomas Mann. In the 1960s, he wrote plays, poems, and fiction, but burned most of his manuscripts during the Cultural Revolution of the 1960s. He was denounced by his wife and sent to a "reeducation camp."

A Return to Writing

In the late 1970s, Gao began to write again, and several of his plays were produced, including **Absolute Signal, Bus Stop,** and **The Wild Man.** He also published an influential short book on modernist fiction. He was gaining an audience, but in 1983 he ran afoul of Chinese leader Deng Xiaoping's "oppose spiritual pollution" campaign, and his works were blacklisted. (They still are, but Chinese writers are finding them on the Internet. That year he heard a rumor that he was about to be imprisoned, so he lit out for the territory: to the remote regions of western China, where he went on a 9,000-mile trek, following the Yangtze River from its source to its mouth. That long march through villages, to various mountaintops and river towns, provided the raw material for Gao's strange novel, **Lingshan—Soul Mountain.**

In 1987, he traveled to France and decided to stay, and began to write **Soul Mountain,** he says, "to dispel my inner loneliness." It was published in Taiwan, and later in Europe, but drew little notice. Shocked by the violence of Tiananmen Square in 1989, he resigned from the Communist Party, gained refugee status, and moved into a small apartment in a working-class neighborhood of Paris, writing and eking out a living as a painter. In 1998 he became a French citizen.

Soul Mountain is incomparable—a sort of Chinese *Canterbury Tales* with one teller, or a *Moby-Dick* on land, except that at least Captain Ahab knew who he was and what he was looking for. The unnamed traveler of **Soul Mountain** is seeking self, hometown, memories of the past, spiritual enlightenment, romantic interludes, and the truth in lore and legend. The often-lyrical, dreamlike tale has no overarching narrative or clear sequence in time. Its most remarked upon feature is its strangely shifting narrative voice. Sometimes the traveler is "I," sometimes "you." Throughout, he retells folk tales of rural indigenous peoples: mostly bitter and violent, full of rape, suicide, betrayal, and grief.

Fragmented Self

There's a sadness in **Soul Mountain** that makes one think inevitably of the man who can't be "we." The traveler can never connect. He climbs a mountain looking for a legendary Daoist monk, the last of the "Pure Unity Sect," but ends up running away in terror after the hostile monk shuns him. And whenever the traveler connects erotically with a woman, he splits so that "she" and "you" relate, while another part of himself narrates. It comes to seem that the women are only projections of his fragmented self.

But these themes apparently represent Gao's aesthetic self more than his life. In person, he's affable, and a man with friends—he hoped to reconnect with a few in Boston—and is active in theater and art circles in France. "I am not a misanthrope," he said with a smile during an interview in his Cambridge hotel. He sipped espresso and spoke of **Soul Mountain** and the writer's life through his book's translator, Mabel Lee.

"The book questions everything," he says, "all the paradigms of existence—history, society, politics. It raises doubts about consciousness, self, even the ability of language to express the self. It emphasizes how difficult it is for human beings to connect with one another."

Asked if he ever misses his cultural roots, Gao replies, "Homesickness is a drug for a writer. I have a continuous quest for new understanding and knowledge; this has made me write about China, but also about the West. If a writer cannot start something new, his life force is missing and he should give up writing. After I left China, I wrote 10 full-length plays, four of them in French."

In his Nobel address, Gao had insisted that literature is apolitical—"purely a matter of the individual." He spoke almost mystically of "cold literature," which is indifferent to fashion, criticism, or the marketplace, and which "will flee to survive." During the interview, he explained, "Cold literature confronts hot, passionate literature, which turns literature into political propaganda. It also confronts consumerist literature. It is using a dispassionate, neutral third eye to observe man and the environment."

FIRST PERSON SINGULAR

For some Chinese, Gao's individuality is hard to swallow. "In the Chinese language," explains Yaohua Shi, a professor of Chinese literature at UMass-Amherst who admires Gao's work, "one rarely uses the singular pronoun. In English we say 'my country,' but in Chinese we would say 'our country.' To call it 'my country' sounds presumptuous, as if it belongs to you."

But in a sense Gao's China, the China of *Soul Mountain,* does belong to him. In a television interview last week, he said he did not wish to return, that China is within him.

Leo Lee, professor of Chinese literature at Harvard, says China's literary establishment has been obsessed with winning the Nobel Prize as a national achievement. "They blow it out of proportion," Lee says: "two Japanese have won, one Indian has won—a Chinese must win the Nobel. When this was announced, everyone was surprised." The choice of Gao, an expatriate with French citizenship, seemed to mock the dream.

But Gao resists the idea of being a national hero. In his Harvard talk, he said, "Nations are not the boundaries of culture, nor literature, nor a text. When we read a Western author, we do not think of what country he comes from, but of what moves us."

Besides its $940,000 cash prize, the Nobel confers fame, and *Soul Mountain,* published in the United States by HarperCollins, is selling briskly. It soon will be available in a downloadable version from PerfectBound, HarperCollins's new international e-book imprint. Mabel Lee is busily translating Gao's second novel, *One Man's Bible,* which is concerned with the ravages of the Cultural Revolution.

In the interview, Gao said, "There is huge pressure on me since winning the prize. I have been totally unable to write or paint. All these interviews and invitations are a sort of task, a response to the enthusiasm that people have given me. I hope to continue writing next year, and paint as well. Saul Bellow once said that the Nobel Prize is the kiss of death. I don't want it to be so for me."

W. J. F. Jenner (review date 9 March 2001)

SOURCE: Jenner, W. J. F. "Heading for the Hills." *Times Literary Supplement,* no. 5110 (9 March 2001): 22.

[*In the following review, Jenner argues that* Soul Mountain *is a book about a male mid-life crisis and criticizes the English translation of the novel, noting the "clumsiness of expression in virtually every paragraph."*]

So you are climbing this mountain—which mountain?—almost any mountain in central or southwest China—searching for you don't quite know what. Or perhaps you are wandering around the streets of country towns, drawn by the *ambiance folklorique.* Sometimes you are catching up on a spot of archaeology and ruminating on neolithic pottery spindle whorls (or spinning wheels, as your translator so quaintly renders them). Or again, you might be talking to friends. You press-gang your reader into being a character in some parts of the book [*Soul Mountain*] by addressing him (and it evidently is him) as "you" and telling him what he is doing in the middle of the action. This allows the reviewer to "you" the author.

When you are not staggering up the misty wooded slopes or seeking the truth from sages, you occasionally like to involve your reader in a sex scene. Every few chapters you drag us poor embarrassed things into these second-person bouts with anonymous women, all desperate for your favours as you go through your prolonged mid-life crisis. Sorry about the cliché, but if ever there was a mid-life crisis, this is its book.

It was some time after 1980, and you had passed forty. As you tell it here, you had psyched yourself up to cope with a diagnosis of the lung cancer that killed your father, only to have the disease miraculously disappear. This was when the thought police were trying their hardest to take back the little spaces that some state-owned publishers had used to publish truer and more interesting things in the late 1970s. You had already made a splash with your absurdist short play *Bus Stop,* a touch of Beckett about people waiting, not for Godot but for a bus (successful state socialism, perhaps) that never comes. You were now unpublishable, and the cops may have been after you. So it was time to head for the hills. Presumably this book comes from your long journey from the mountains of the southwest to the sea. You are much too knowing to have written it straight as a novel, or a travelogue, or a diary, and too modern to have imprisoned yourself within a coherent narrative. Besides, it is fun playing transgressive and teasing the reader. You give yourself permission to pile up a jumbled heap of eighty-one chapters. You can even have a "critic" near the end tell the writer (another switch of person) that the book breaks all the rules. This gives you/him the cue to write an unpunctuated page of unconnected ramblings. You finish the book with a small green frog that you just happen to know is God looking in at you through the window, and tell your readers you don't understand anything.

If they choose to read the book, they have asked for what they get. It is amiably self-indulgent, and fun in places if one can keep going through the *longueurs* and forget about the language. At least it isn't too obviously in the dominant tradition of twentieth-century Chinese writing that tries to do the reader good and save the nation. Or is it really out to improve us? Take the eighty-one chapters, for example. That is not just nine times nine, which would be Oriental enough. It is also the same number of chapters as in the received text of the *Dao de jing*. Doesn't that suggest earnest seeking after the timeless wisdom of the East? Probably you are a little inclined that way. You enjoy sounding off about Chinese cultures, ancient and modern. You go to find people who live not in the world of politics and money, but in Buddhist monasteries, Daoist temples, isolated huts lost in the mountains. You do your Yangtze Valley version of Synge on the Aran Islands, looking for the lost authenticities of dying traditions.

Your Swedish translator must have done a good job on your book to persuade his fellow members of the Nobel Academy to give you the big prize. It is a pity about this well-intentioned English version, which clumps along in hobnailed boots. I haven't read the book you wrote, **Lingshan,** only this translated **Soul Mountain.** The problem with the English is not so much the occasional howler—we translators all make those from time to time—but the clumsiness of expression in virtually every paragraph. For that if for no other reason, this is a book best read fast.

Jeffrey Twitchell-Waas (review date summer 2001)

SOURCE: Twitchell-Waas, Jeffrey. Review of *Soul Mountain*, by Gao Xingjian. *Review of Contemporary Fiction* 21, no. 2 (summer 2001): 161.

[*In the following review, Twitchell-Waas asserts that the primary achievement of* Soul Mountain *is Gao's experimental use of narrative voice throughout the novel.*]

Although last year Gao Xingjian became China's first Nobel laureate (much to the annoyance of Beijing), until very recently little of this remarkable dramatist and fiction writer's work has appeared in English. The first of Gao's two big novels, **Soul Mountain** is an autobiographical, highly episodic epic that follows the protagonist's wanderings throughout much of southwest China, driven both by the desire to escape official persecution back in Beijing and the search for renewed spiritual grounding. This vast remote region of China—with its primeval forests, diverse minority nationalities, and remnants of authentic Buddhism and Taoism—has long represented a reservoir of oppositional cultural traditions against the dominant Han Confucianism, of which it is implied that communism is just another version. Posing as an ethnographer collecting vestiges of folk rituals and songs, the protagonist searches randomly for epiphanic moments, yet never deludes himself that these tribal or religious orders of life offer him a personal solution—if nothing else, he is too fiercely individualistic and this-worldly. Within this loose, perhaps all-too-familiar narrative structure lies the real interest and achievement of the novel. Alternating chapters switch between the protagonist's first-person account of his ramblings and a second-person narrative that apparently is his internalized dialogues and monologues addressed to himself. On both narrative levels, or trajectories, an enormous range of stories are recounted. There are many dozens of them, and all kinds—travel incidents, made-up tales, recollections, folk stories, myths, parables, dreams—as if the novel is attempting to manifest the release of repressed narratives as resources for personal and cultural renewal. However, although there are moments when the protagonist achieves a sense of nonteleological oneness, or Taoist emptying, **Lingshan** (Spirit or Soul Mountain) remains, as in the famous Buddhist parable Gao frequently alludes to, on the other shore. Both thematically and formally, **Soul Mountain** hovers between mere randomness and the prototypical meaningfulness of the unfolding search itself.

Virginia Quarterly Review (review date summer 2001)

SOURCE: Review of *Soul Mountain,* by Gao Xingjian. *Virginia Quarterly Review* 77, no. 3 (summer 2001): 98.

[*In the following review, the critic contends that Gao's narrative structure in* Soul Mountain *requires patience on the part of the reader and that the novel may not hold the attention of readers looking for a conventional storyline.*]

Soul Mountain, the 2000 Nobel Prize winner in literature, requires its readers to have patience. Patience, for example, to believe that the short, episodic chapters are leading toward a cohesive whole. Patience, to wait for a narrator split into four personal pronouns—I, you, he, and she—to deliver a comprehensible story. Though *story,* at least in the sense of most contemporary novels, is not what Xingjian is attempting in this book. Instead, he cobbles together a mix of folklore, character sketches, and snapshots of the rural Chinese countryside to create a modernist mosaic. The result is half-memoir, half-fiction, an expatriate's re-imagined journey through the Qiang, Miao, and Yi districts—places as much on the fringe of Chinese history as civilization. From biologists studying giant Pandas to Daoist masters and small-town Communist thugs, the people we meet along the way are interesting enough. Still, the interactions are minimal. After all, a traveler who gets involved is only asking for trouble. The question is whether the resulting introspective narration can hold your attention. For those readers with a steady interest in modern China and the psychological isolation of its society, the answer is yes. For those readers with a less precise motivation, who simply want to lose themselves in a story, the answer is otherwise.

FURTHER READING

Criticism

Eder, Richard. "A Dreamlike Chinese Journey Haunted by Past and Present." *New York Times* (18 December 2000): E1.

    Eder evaluates the strengths and weaknesses of *Soul Mountain*.

Goldblatt, Howard, editor. *Worlds Apart: Recent Chinese Writing and Its Audience*. Armonk, NY: M. E. Sharpe, 1990.

    Goldblatt presents a collection of essays on a variety of contemporary Chinese writers, including Gao.

Pan, Philip P. "Nobel of Little Note." *Washington Post* (14 October 2000): C3.

    Pan discusses the response of the Chinese government to Gao's winning of the Nobel Prize in Literature.

Weeks, Linton. "Chinese Exile Wins Nobel for Literature." *Washington Post* (13 October 2000): C1, C8.

    Weeks discusses the significance of Gao's status as a Chinese dissident writer to his winning of the Nobel Prize in Literature.

———. "Hard Climb to Freedom's Peak." *Washington Post* (22 February 2001): C1, C8.

    Weeks interviews Gao about how his life has been altered since winning the Nobel Prize in Literature. Weeks also discusses Gao's narrative technique in *Soul Mountain*.

Additional coverage of Gao's life and career is contained in the following sources published by the Gale Group: *Contemporary Authors,* **Vol. 193;** *Dictionary of Literary Biography Yearbook,* **2000;** *Literature Resource Center;* **and** *Reference Guide to World Literature,* **Ed. 3.**

The Color Purple

Alice Walker

(Full name Alice Malsenior Walker) American novelist, essayist, poet, short story writer, editor, memoirist, and children's writer.

The following entry presents criticism on Walker's novel *The Color Purple* (1982) through 2001. For further information on her life and complete works, see *CLC,* Volumes 5, 6, 9, 19, 27, 46, 58, and 103.

INTRODUCTION

The Color Purple is regarded as Walker's most successful and critically acclaimed work. Written in an epistolary style, the novel depicts the harsh life of a young African-American woman in the South in the early twentieth century. *The Color Purple* explores the individual identity of the African-American woman and how embracing that identity and bonding with other women affects the health of her community at large. Although some reviewers have taken issue with the novel's portrayal of Black men, the novel has largely been celebrated by critics and popular audiences alike, winning both the Pulitzer Prize and the American Book Award in 1983. In 1985 filmmaker Stephen Spielberg directed the film adaptation of *The Color Purple,* which was nominated for eleven awards—including best picture—by the Academy of Motion Picture Arts and Sciences.

BIOGRAPHICAL INFORMATION

Walker was born in Eatonton, Georgia, in 1944, the eighth and last child of sharecroppers Willie Lee and Lou Grant Walker. When she was eight years old, her brother shot her with his BB gun, leaving her scarred and blind in one eye. This disfigurement made her shy and self-conscious, and she began to use writing as a means of expressing herself. The accident also had a permanent impact on her relationship with her father: his inability to obtain proper medical treatment for her forever affected her relationship with him, and they remained estranged for the rest of his life. Despite her disadvantaged childhood, Walker won the opportunity to continue her education with a scholarship to Spelman College. After attending Spelman for two years, she became disenchanted with what she considered a puritanical atmosphere there and transferred to Sarah Lawrence College in Bronxville, New York, to complete her education. While at Sarah Lawrence, Walker wrote her first collection of poetry, entitled *Once: Poems* (1968), in reaction to a traumatic abortion. Walker shared the poems with one of her teachers, poet Muriel Rukeyser, whose agent found a publisher for Walker. After college, Walker moved to Mississippi to work as a teacher and a civil rights advocate. In 1967 she married Melvyn Leventhal, a Jewish civil rights attorney; they became the first legally married interracial couple to reside in Jackson, Mississippi. She and Leventhal had a daughter, Rebecca, but they divorced some years later. While working in Mississippi, Walker discovered the writings of Zora Neale Hurston, an author who would have great influence on her later work. Walker eventually edited a collection of Hurston's fiction called *I Love Myself when I Am Laughing . . . and Then again* when *I Am Looking Mean and Impressive: A Zora Neale Hurston Reader* (1979). In addition to poetry, Walker has written short stories, collected in *In Love and Trouble: Stories of Black Women* (1973) and *You Can't Keep a Good Woman Down* (1981), and several novels, most notably *The Color Purple*.

PLOT AND MAJOR CHARACTERS

The Color Purple begins with fourteen-year-old Celie writing a letter to God, asking for a sign. Celie is a scared, poor, African-American girl living in the South. Her mother has become ill after the most recent of her numerous pregnancies, and the man Celie believes to be her father abuses Celie sexually. He tells her, "You better not never tell nobody but God. It'd kill your mammy." Readers discover through subsequent letters that "Pa" fathers two children with Celie, but abducts them from her soon after each birth. Her mother dies during Celie's second pregnancy, and Celie is unable to confirm whether her children are living or dead. After her mother's death, Celie becomes responsible for the upkeep of the house and the rearing of her younger siblings, including her sister Nettie. Nettie is courted by a man her father's age, who asks to marry Nettie, but Pa refuses, and offers the older Celie as a wife instead. Celie marries the suitor, whom she calls Mr. ————. Nettie then becomes the object of Pa's sexual desires, causing her to move in with Celie and Mr. ————. Nettie is later forced to leave when she refuses Mr. ————'s sexual advances. Before Nettie flees, she promises Celie that she will write to her, but Celie never receives any of Nettie's letters. Celie's letters—which advance the narrative of the book—are now written to Nettie instead of God, and relate the physical, emotional, and sexual abuse that she endures in Mr. ————'s household. When Mr. ————'s son, Harpo, brings home Sophia—his prospective wife—Celie is exposed for the first time to a proud, strong female figure. Sophia is outspoken and refuses to conform to Harpo's and Mr. ————'s stereotypical model of an obedient spouse. After Harpo repeatedly beats her, Sophia leaves and is eventually arrested for assaulting a white man. A turning point in Celie's life occurs when Mr. ————'s mistress, Shug Avery, moves in to recuperate after an illness. Another strong-willed woman, Shug is a sexy, spirited blues singer, and Celie is obsessively attracted to her. After Celie nurses Shug, Shug begins to heal Celie, first as a mother figure, then as a lover. Through this relationship, Celie begins to feel loved and develops newfound feelings of self-worth. One day, when Shug gets the mail, she brings in a letter for Celie, postmarked from Africa. The letter is from Nettie, and, as Celie discovers, Nettie has been sending her letters for years. A search of the house reveals that all of Nettie's letters have been taken and hidden by Mr. ————. Celie puts the letters in chronological order and begins to read them, learning that Samuel and Corinne, a missionary couple in town, took in Nettie when she was forced to leave Mr. ————'s house. Samuel and Corrine had adopted two children and the two are Celie's lost offspring. Nettie traveled with them to Africa, where they tried to Christianize the people of the Olinka tribe. Nettie's letters also reveal that Celie's Pa is not her father, but is instead her stepfather. In a rage over the theft of these letters, Celie comes close to killing Mr. ————, but is stopped by Shug. Shug convinces Celie that it is better to create than to destroy, and Celie subsequently takes up sewing pants as a creative outlet. Celie leaves Mr. ————, whom she now calls by his given name, Albert, and travels to Memphis with Shug. After Pa dies, Celie inherits her childhood home, which also includes a dry goods store. She returns to her hometown and sets up a small business selling Folkspants—a line of pants of her own creation. Albert eventually returns to Celie as a transformed figure who now respects her, and the two work side by side, with Albert sewing matching shirts for her pants business. At the conclusion of the novel, Celie is reunited with sister Nettie and her own lost children, and she introduces Shug and Albert as her family.

MAJOR THEMES

The Color Purple dramatically underscores the oppression Black women have experienced throughout history in the rural South in America. Following the Civil War, most Black Americans remained disenfranchised and were typically viewed as less than human by many members of white society. Women were also regarded as less important than men—both Black and white—making Black women doubly disadvantaged. Black women of the era were often treated as slaves or as property, even by male members of their own families. In *The Color Purple,* Celie is passed on from Pa to Mr. ———— without any regard for her own desires. She constantly struggles to forge her own self-identity and to not accept the subservient role that society has ascribed to her. In the course of the novel, Sophia becomes Celie's first role model of a Black woman who does not allow the men surrounding her to limit her lifestyle. Additionally, the novel examines themes of sisterhood and methods of sharing among women in their quest for political, sexual, and racial equality. Celie is able to overcome her many hardships because of the love and solidarity she receives from women like Nettie, Sophia, and Shug Avery. By seeing herself as a member of a community, Celie develops a sense of identity and realizes new opportunities in her life. When Shug stops Celie from killing Mr. ————, Celie is inspired to find a new outlet for her passion and creativity. This leads to the creation of Celie's business, which offers her more personal and financial freedom. Spiritual fulfillment is also a recurring theme in *The Color*

Purple. The novel opens with Celie writing to God, an anonymous all-knowing male creator figure. Celie keeps asking for a sign from God to reveal his presence and lift her many burdens, but no signs ever appear. As the story progresses, Celie stops writing to God and begins writing to her sister Nettie. Through her relationship with Nettie and with the other Black women in her life, Celie is able to see tangible signs of hope and spirituality. Walker portrays the typical archetype of the male Christian God as aloof and absent in *The Color Purple*, while Celie's community of friends and family is portrayed as caring and emotionally nourishing.

CRITICAL RECEPTION

Walker has earned high praise for *The Color Purple*, particularly for her accurate rendering of folk idiom, her use of the oral storytelling tradition, and her characterization of Celie. Although critical response to the novel has been largely positive, there have been several widely-debated aspects of Walker's work. For example, many reviewers have criticized her portrayal of male African-American characters as archetypes of African-American men in modern society. Such commentators have condemned these portrayals as unnecessarily negative, citing the vile and unsympathetic male characters, such as Mr. ———, as evidence of enmity on Walker's part. Some critics have found fault with Walker's characterizations in general, opposing her tendency to refer to characters only with pronouns, thereby encouraging readers to consider the characters exemplary of anyone to whom that pronoun could apply. Reviewers have also noted temporal and logistic flaws in *The Color Purple*'s narrative, but most scholars have excused these faults, commenting that such lapses are a necessary sacrifice for Walker's total narrative agenda. Walker has been highly praised by feminist critics for vividly portraying the brutality that women have faced throughout the years, but some have argued that the novel's happy ending makes light of the offenses suffered by the female protagonist and runs contrary to reality. Conversely, some reviewers have defended the novel's upbeat ending, claiming that it is not disloyal to feminist concerns, but rather furthers the idea that a woman—especially one surrounded by a community of nurturing women—can overcome adversity.

PRINCIPAL WORKS

Once: Poems (poetry) 1968
The Third Life of Grange Copeland (novel) 1970
In Love and Trouble: Stories of Black Women (short stories) 1973
Revolutionary Petunias and Other Poems (poetry) 1973
*Langston Hughes: American Poet [illustrations by Don Miller] (juvenilia) 1974
Meridian (novel) 1976
Good Night, Willie Lee, I'll See You in the Morning (poetry) 1979
I Love Myself when I Am Laughing . . . and Then again when I Am Looking Mean and Impressive: A Zora Neale Hurston Reader [editor] (prose) 1979
You Can't Keep a Good Woman Down (short stories) 1981
The Color Purple (novel) 1982
In Search of Our Mothers' Gardens: Womanist Prose (essays) 1983
Horses Make a Landscape Look More Beautiful: Poems (poetry) 1984
Living by the Word: Selected Writings, 1973-1987 (essays) 1988
To Hell with Dying [illustrations by Catherine Deeter] (juvenilia) 1988
The Temple of My Familiar (novel) 1989
Finding the Green Stone [illustrations by Catherine Deeter] (juvenilia) 1991
Her Blue Body Everything We Know: Earthling Poems, 1965-1990 Complete (poetry) 1991
Possessing the Secret of Joy (novel) 1992
Warrior Marks: Female Genital Mutilation and the Sexual Blinding of Women [with Pratibha Parmar] (nonfiction) 1993
Everyday Use [edited by Barbara T. Christian] (essays and interviews) 1994
Alice Walker: Banned (nonfiction) 1996
The Same River Twice: Honoring the Difficult: A Meditation on Life, Spirit, Art, and the Making of the Film "The Color Purple" Ten Years Later (essays) 1996
Anything We Love Can Be Saved: A Writer's Activism (essays) 1997
By the Light of My Father's Smile: A Novel (novel) 1998
The Way Forward Is with a Broken Heart (memoirs and short stories) 2000
Sent by Earth: A Message from the Grandmother Spirit after the Bombing of the World Trade Center and the Pentagon (speeches) 2001

*In 2002 a revised edition was published with illustrations by Catherine Deeter.

CRITICISM

M. Teresa Tavormina (essay date fall 1986)

SOURCE: Tavormina, M. Teresa. "Dressing the Spirit: Clothworking and Language in *The Color Purple*." *Journal of Narrative Technique* 16, no. 3 (fall 1986): 220-30.

[*In the following essay, Tavormina analyzes the parallels between clothing and the perception of the charac-*

ters in *The Color Purple,* *noting how Walker's characters use sewing to create a sense of accomplishment and freedom of expression.*]

> When a message has no clothes on
> How can it be spoken?
>
> —Thomas Merton[1]

Language is the clothing of thought, the skin of the soul. The mysterious entity of self is first expressed internally, in thoughts and feelings of various degrees of clarity; yet to give that self external expression, it must be "uttered"—made outward by being dressed in language. Just as clothing protects, adorns, interprets, and helps create the first impression of the body, the outer self, so language displays the inner self, giving shape to thought and feeling, defining yet covering them, significantly influencing others' perceptions of that self. Like a membrane, like skin, language simultaneously connects and divides self to and from others. The familiar metaphors of spinning yarns and weaving words, of text as textile, suggest the purpose of language as well as the intricate manner of its making.

Thus it is not surprising to find both clothing and language playing important, related thematic roles in Alice Walker's novel *The Color Purple.*[2] Among the novel's major concerns are the discovery, definition, and expression of self, and the connections between self and other. Since both language and clothing are means of expressing—and, to our misfortune, also of repressing—the self, they are highly effective vehicles for Walker's views on the search her characters engage in. The present essay examines *The Color Purple*'s treatment of this search, as reflected in images of clothing, sewing, and quilting, and the relation of these images to her use of such personalized forms of language as dialect and letters.

I

> I had been trying to establish a respect for women and women's art; to forge a new kind of art expressing women's experience; and to find a way to make that art accessible to a large audience. I firmly believed that if art speaks clearly about something relevant to people's lives, it can change the way they perceive reality. . . . Since most of the world is illiterate in terms of women's history and contributions to culture, it seemed appropriate to relate our history through art, particularly through techniques traditionally associated with women.
>
> —Judy Chicago[3]

References to cloth, clothing, and clothworking abound in *The Color Purple.* Again and again we read about people's clothing, especially Shug's. Both Nettie and Celie have a keen eye for what people wear, and are sharply conscious of their own dress as well, at times embarrassed by it, at times pleased. Most important, sewing and designing clothes becomes Celie's refuge and then her work. The meaning of these ubiquitous references goes beyond a realistic description of a common female interest or activity, however. By the end of the novel, Walker's clothing and clothworking images have reinforced several major themes: the nature of self-definition, the creative power of the human spirit, and the growth of familial and societal bonds out of shared life and history.

As I have suggested above, clothing not only covers us but also defines us. It is usually a large part of what we see when we look at each other, and different clothes give observers quite different impressions, as the dress-for-success people are fond of reminding their readers. It is no accident that the word "habit" can refer to behavior or to dress. Clothing can express its wearer's personality, or repress it so as to conform the wearer to someone else's definition of how people should look or act. Shug tells Celie that she should make herself a pair of pants because they would suit (another bivalent term) her better, given the work she does, even if they are not traditional for a woman:

> What I need pants for? I say. I ain't no man.
>
> Don't git uppity, she say. But you don't have a dress do nothing for you. You not made like no dress pattern, neither. . . .
>
> You do all the work around here. It's a scandless, the way you look out there plowing in a dress. How you keep from falling over it or getting the plow caught in it is beyond me.
>
> (124)

Folkspants Unlimited gets its start after Celie realizes that she can make pants that truly fit the people she makes them for—not just physically, but behaviorally and emotionally too. Her pants are designed for individuals, not in terms of sexual or other stereotypes but of the wearer's own particular needs. "[Mr. ———] ast me what was so special bout my pants. Anybody can wear them, I said" (230). This is not a one-size-fits-all reductionism, but a rejection of the constraints of traditional roles and their associated outward expressions. Like native African dress as Nettie describes it, Folkspants are genuinely comfortable clothes, extensions and adornments of the people wearing them, rather than a shamefaced, constricting covering-up of the self. Only the "colorless" whites, according to *The Color Purple,* feel naked and ashamed without clothes; Walker hints that the feeling may reflect the white distance from a "natural" life in harmony with the rest of the world. For black people, it is different: "Since they are covered by color they are not naked" (232). Instead, they dress for comfort and for celebration, like the Senegalese, "these shining, blueblack people wearing brilliant blue robes with designs like fancy quilt patterns" (119). They "try to wear what feel comfortable in the heat. . . . [They] wear a little sometimes, or a lot. . . . But men and women both preshate a nice dress" (230).

When Mr. —— learns to sew from Celie, and begins designing shirts, he follows the same principles of usefulness, comfort, and attractiveness on the wearer. "Got to have pockets, he say. Got to have loose sleeves. And definitely you not spose to wear it with no tie. Folks wearing ties look like they being lynch" (239). Like Olivia's diapers, embroidered by Celie with the child's real name, the name that fits her, clothing should match the wearer's spirit, not imprison or strangle that spirit for being different; it should affirm the self, not deny it.

In proclaiming Olivia's name, the child's embroidered diapers express Celie's love for her daughter, but they also express Celie's creative spirit, a spirit that is celebratory and playful, that sews flowers and stars into a baby's diapers, that cannot be quenched even in the midst of Celie's confusion, fear, and near-despair over Fonso's brutal sexual assaults. Even before she learns to express her self by *wearing* particular products of the cloth- and needle-working arts, she expresses her self by producing such art. For the arts of needle, thread, loom, cloth are more than mere crafts, despite modern Western cultural biases. They are components of a major artistic medium, none the less valuable because its products are meant to be used, to make our lives more comfortable as well as to enrich our awareness. As the makers of medieval tapestries knew, it is a medium capable of power in all its forms, from intricate detail to huge sweeping webs of vision. It draws on potent human energies: Celie starts making pants so as to avoid killing Mr. ——; she grows as an artist by making pants for love of Shug, Squeak, Jack, Odessa, Nettie. "A needle and not a razor in my hand" (125), creation rather than destruction: this is the choice Celie makes, for Nettie's and Shug's sakes, the choice to hold fast, to remain herself. Like the quilt she has already made with Sofia, it is a "Sister's Choice," one that leads her eventually into self-possession and independence. As Shug implies in her lyric "color purple" discourse, discovering the self is a way of discovering God in the self, and God is a creative force, "always making little surprises and springing them on us when us least expect" (168).

Walker's focus on clothworking as a primary image for human creativity stresses women's creativity.[4] But she also insists that this is a human art, not limited to women unless men wish to impose artificial sex-role constraints on their own creativity. The Olinka men, who are not particularly noteworthy for respecting "women's work," nonetheless feel no threat to their masculinity from their quilt-making skills.[5] In fact, notions of "women's work" and "men's work" break down generally in *The Color Purple*: Harpo and Mr. —— find that they enjoy cooking, sewing, and cleaning house, while Sofia, Shug, and Celie all engage in various activities usually associated with men—shingling roofs, designing houses, owning a store, and so on. All human beings have the power and the calling to be both usefully and playfully creative, and we see this power at work in many characters throughout the novel. Celie of course makes quilts, curtains, and pants, and embroiders stars, flowers, and words on Olivia's diapers. The Olinka make cloth and quilts, with animals, birds, and people appliquéed on them to create little worlds in fabric. Shug and Mary Agnes make music; Harpo makes a place for people to enjoy themselves. Albert makes comfortable shirts to go with Celie's pants; Corrine and Samuel and Nettie make a school. Even the no-count Grady grows a little reefer. "You making your living, Celie," says Shug, "Girl, you on your way" (181). Making is living, destroying is death and nothingness. Even the limited destruction of meanness eats away at the soul of its perpetrator: "You know meanness kill" (191).

II

> It took me more than twenty years, nearly twenty-five, I reckon, in the evenings after supper when the children were all put to bed. My whole life is in that quilt. It scares me sometimes when I look at it. All my joys and all my sorrows are stitched into those little pieces. When I was proud of the boys and when I was downright provoked and angry with them. When the girls annoyed me or when they gave me a warm feeling around my heart. And John too. He was stitched into that quilt and all the thirty years we were married. Sometimes I loved him and sometimes I sat there hating him as I pieced the patches together. So they are all in that quilt, my hopes and fears, my joys and sorrows, my loves and hates. I tremble sometimes when I remember what that quilt knows about me.
>
> —anonymous woman in Ohio[6]

Besides providing an outlet for the creative forces within the self and offering a visual and tactile medium for presenting that self to the world, clothworking and clothing can also create the bonds between members of a community, especially a familial one. Mothers make or buy clothes for their children, or lovingly adorn those clothes as Celie does for Olivia. The only time Corrine and Celie meet is over material Corrine is buying for Olivia's new dresses, and part of Celie's pleasure at the meeting comes from helping Corrine "drape a piece of cloth close to [Olivia's] face" (14). Children are not the only recipients of lovingly made clothing: planning a pair of handsewn pants for Nettie, Celie promises that "every stitch I sew will be a kiss" (182).

Family members also share clothes at times. The reasons for such sharing are usually economic, to be sure, but the symbol of shared life is present as well. The life shared may be nurturing or constricting: if you never get to be the "first one in [your] own dress," if you are always forced to wear other people's clothes (like other people's definitions of you), this can get pretty tiresome. Celie's pleasure when Mr. ———'s sister Kate insists on her having a new dress—the first one ever made just for her—is profound. It may well be an important early step on her road to self-awareness and respect: "She say. It's all right, Celie. You deserve more than this. Maybe so. I think" (20). But sharing clothes willingly signifies genuine intimacy, as Walker illustrates *via* Corrine's suspicious refusal to let Nettie borrow her clothes and Samuel's insistence that Nettie wear them after Corrine dies.

Familial bonds can be expressed in other pieces of cloth too. Celie lends Sofia thread for sheets and makes curtains for her, curtains that are torn during one of Sofia and Harpo's fights. Sofia returns the same curtains, along with the thread and a dollar for use, when she learns that Celie had told Harpo to beat her. After Celie makes her peace with Sofia, they take the curtain scraps to start a quilt—a quilt that Sofia and Celie and Shug all work on over time, a quilt with bits of Shug's old yellow dress as well as the curtain scraps, made in the "Sister's Choice" pattern. It is a quilt made of love and trouble and dreams, of flour sacks and of "little yellow pieces, look like stars" (53). Celie thinks first of giving it to Shug, if it turns out perfect, perhaps in a kind of homage to Shug's beauty; then she thinks of keeping it for herself, if it turns out imperfect, almost as a kind of relic. But finally she gives it to Sofia to help keep her and her children warm through the winter (53, 60).

The making of this quilt underscores the fact that sewing is an act of union, of connecting pieces to make a useful whole. Furthermore, sewing with others is a comradely act, one that allows both speech and comfortable, supportive silence. The Olinka mothers sew together in the afternoons when it is too hot for anything else, and "it is in the work that the women get to know and care about each other" (141). By the end of the novel, Celie and Albert grow close enough that they can sit together sewing and making idle conversation, occupations that explain to Shug why they are "looking as fine as [they] look" (240). Sewing helps Celie get through the hate and despair she feels when she learns that Mr. ——— has been keeping Nettie's letters; its creative and unitive dimension is the only possible cure for one whose world has come apart, as the idiom goes, at the seams:

> I stutter. I mutter to myself. I stumble bout the house crazy for Mr. ——— blood. In my mind, he falling dead every which a way. . . .
>
> I really started [making pants] right here in your house to keep from killing you.
>
> (103, 214)

The depth of Celie's anguish over the telegram announcing Nettie's supposed death and the return of her unopened letters can be measured by her cry, "What good is sewing gon do? What good is anything? Being alive begin to seem like a awful strain" (216). But even in this grief, she holds things together in spite of the strain, and keeps sewing—even sharing it with Albert, multiplying creation and showing him "how to do it."[7]

Like Celie and Sofia, Corrine makes quilts too, in a mixed African and American pattern, out of "the clothes the children had outgrown, and some of her old dresses" (159); thus on both sides of the ocean, we see quilts that contain and carry on the history bound up with their pieces. Through the quilts she has made, Corrine finally remembers making the clothes they came from, remembers buying the cloth, remembers Celie, and believes. Corrine's quilts connect the moments of time that make up her own and Olivia's lives. Trying to forget such moments because they were painful, burying them in forgetfulness as the quilts are buried in Corrine's trunk, can lead to even greater pain than the original memory, as Corrine discovers. It is better to keep all of one's heritage, to keep past and present united. This concern for recognizing one's history, one's place within a community of generations, runs through many of Walker's works, from the three-generational events of her first novel, *The Third Life of Grange Copeland,* to the Johnson family quilts in **"Everyday Use,"** to the concern for keeping memory alive in **"The Abortion,"** and to many other examples.[8] Cloth, clothes, hand-ons, curtains, sheets, quilts—both individual maker, wearer, or user and the community of generations to which she belongs can be seen in these fabrics of life, created, used, re-used, shared, passed on.

III

> When I wrote **Meridian,** I realized that the chronological sequence is not one that permits me the kind of freedom I need in order to create. And I wanted to do something like a crazy quilt, or like *Cane*—if you want to be literary—something that works on the mind in different patterns. . . . A crazy quilt story is one that can jump back and forth in time, work on many different levels, and one that can include myth.
>
> —Alice Walker[9]

The quilts in *The Color Purple,* perhaps more than any of the other clothwork in the novel, may remind us of another "everyday use" art-form: language itself, especially as it finds expression in personal dialects and letters. The whole novel is crafted from these everyday materials, "pieced" from patches of memory, from patches woven of different threads and for different wear, but brought together so as to make a whole meaning from Celie's and Nettie's seemingly separated lives. The basic "threads" of the novel are the everyday voices of the two sisters, voices that are clearly distinct from each other, and clearly expressive of their distinct personal experience and sense of self, just as the personally-suited Folkspants express their wearers. Even though they are sisters, Celie and Nettie are different people, with different personal histories, and their personal dialects reflect these differences. Neither of them feels a need to "talk in a way that feel peculiar to your mind," as Celie calls the efforts made by one of her Folkspants employees to standardize Celie's speech (183-84).

But thread is only the beginning of the cloth-worker's art; the individual presence and voice embodied in one's personal dialect is only the beginning of the expressive power of language. Relatively formless in themselves, both thread and personal language can mat, ramble, pile up into inextricably incoherent tangles unless they are given a more complex and stable form by being directed to organized, purposeful ends. From individual pieces of clothing and individual letters to quilts and life-time correspondence, the creative human spirit fashions meaning from the otherwise scattered elements of life. Those elements find an initial articulation in their first use, their first wear; they "mean" a pair of pants, or an escape from self-annihilation, or a way of understanding "what is happening to me" (3). But in quilts and correspondence, they can be given a larger meaning as well by their connection to other articulations of experience, including but not limited to those experiences and articulations that lie adjacent on the thread of time. Walker makes it difficult, perhaps impossible, for her readers to determine the exact temporal relationships between letters in Celie's series and those in Nettie's. There are no dates, only a few clearly specified intervals, and even potential time-marking events—the births and ages of children or Nettie's encounter with Sofia after her release from prison—turn out to offer us little help in reconstructing precisely interlocked biographical calendars for the two sisters' lives.[10]

But no matter. The meaning is in the whole. To see linearly is to limit one's seeing. Celie does not receive Nettie's letters as soon as they are written, and Nettie does not receive Celie's at all; neither of them "answers" each other's letters in the usual sense of the word, yet their letters clearly "answers" to each other. The art—Walker's art—is not only in the creation (or the transmission) of the two lives, but also in the arrangement that juxtaposes and interlocks moments of revelation in Africa and in America (148-68), that shows both sisters coming to similar understandings of the nature of love and of God, and so on. Letters, like quilts, transcend time's boundaries. Scraps from childhood shirts border on bits of maternity smocks, patches from kitchen curtains lie alongside faded pieces of a Civil War uniform. "No matter how much the telegram said you must be drown, I still git letters from you" (233).

Yet quilts and correspondence, besides transcending time, record its parts. They create histories for us, remembering the past so as to bring it into the present. To fully understand our place in and relationship to our history, we need to see all its parts. The Olinka view of the world is limited by their refusal to understand the outside world—either that of their American brothers and sisters or that of the white planters who destroy their village. Despite her good intentions, Miss Eleanor Jane fails to understand Sofia because she only considers her own side of their relationship. Even the black missionaries' work in Africa is frequently undermined by their failure to understand African culture, despite the fact that it is ultimately a part of their own history. Celie's own understanding of the world, from clothing to black-white relations to the value of yams for controlling blood disease, is much enriched by the traditional African knowledge she rediscovers in Nettie's letters. The quilter's art has been similarly enriched by African textile techniques introduced to America by black men and women brought to this country from such areas as the Congo, Dahomey, and Angola.[11] The quilt whereby Nettie finally rekindles Corrine's memory of Celie was deliberately designed to draw on both branches of this artistic history:

> The Olinka men make beautiful quilts which are full of animals and birds and people. And as soon as Corrine saw them, she began to make a quilt that alternated one square of appliquéed figures with one nine-patch block, using the clothes the children had outgrown, and some of her old dresses.
>
> I went to her trunk and started hauling out quilts. . . .
>
> I held up first one and then another to the light, trying to find the first one I remembered her making. And trying to remember, at the same time, the dresses she and Olivia were wearing the first months I lived with them.
>
> Aha, I said, when I found what I was looking for, and laid the quilt across the bed.
>
> Do you remember buying this cloth? I asked, pointing to a flowered square. And what about this checkered bird?
>
> She traced the patterns with her finger, and slowly her eyes filled with tears.
>
> (159)

Corrine's quilt is an icon dense with history—personal, familial, artistic, national, racial, human—and with union and reunion. It brings together differences without denying them or subjugating one to another—here a flowered square, there a checkered bird. Like the full set of both Celie's and Nettie's letters, it preserves, juxtaposes, and connects; it creates a meaningful, functional beauty out of a variety that admits both pain and happiness.[12] "My whole life is [there]. . . . they are all [there], my hopes and fears, my joys and sorrows, my loves and hates."

Finally, language and sewing, cloth-working and letter-writing, quilts and correspondence share the attractive trait of being creative arts that are almost universally accessible, if at various levels of skill. Taking up a hem or writing a note to a friend are everyday, practical activities that can be practiced by people of almost any economic or social class, given access to a relatively small amount of instruction and practice. And the products of these skills, however inexpertly or occasionally practiced, have an undeniable share in the same creative forces underlying the masterful work of a great quilt-maker or novelist, the kind of work that commands our awe and profound admiration. To take needle or pen in hand, for man or woman, is to place oneself on a spectrum of creative possibility that stretches ultimately to the splendid art of experienced and inspired weavers, writers, web-workers of all kinds.

In *The Color Purple,* both clothworking and language become media for self-definition, self-expression, and self-sharing. Their distinct but similar processes and products enable Walker's characters to become more aware of themselves, of others, and of their inter-relationships with others and with the rest of the world. Both clothworking and language embody and help further the common quest of all the major characters in the novel—the quest for the Spirit, for the creative, suffering, wondering "dear God" within each individual self and shared with all other selves. We see the path toward that goal most fully in Celie's life: it begins with the need to recognize and respect the Spirit within herself, moves on to the need to communicate it clearly to those around her, and finally leads her to discover its presence in everything and to realize her share in the whole interwoven fabric of human life, history, and all creation.

With Celie and Nettie we learn that we must actively "address" the Spirit within ourselves and within others, reaching out to it with a "Dear God," "Dear Celie," or "Dear Everything." With Albert we learn that in addressing ourselves to others, we need also to listen, if we wish to hear the great ocean within the seashell. And with them and their fellow characters, we learn that we must lovingly "dress" our own and others' Spirit, helping to express it in its own terms, clothing it "preshatively" and comfortably, making it manifest in whatever creative ways we have at our disposal.

Notes

1. "A Messenger from the Horizon," in *The Collected Poems of Thomas Merton* (New York: New Dimensions, 1977), 351.
2. Alice Walker, *The Color Purple* (New York: Harcourt Brace Jovanovich, 1982). Subsequent references will be made within the text of the essay.
3. *The Dinner Party: A Symbol of Our Heritage* (Garden City, N.Y.: Anchor/Doubleday, 1979), 12.
4. The association of women with the textile arts is an old one, strikingly documented by Chicago in *The Dinner Party Needlework: Embroidering Our Heritage* (Garden City, N.Y.: Anchor/Doubleday, 1980). Its literary manifestations take such early forms as the medieval verse "When Adam dug and Eve spun" or the antifeminist proverb quoted by the cloth-making Wife of Bath, "To women by nature God has given deceit, weeping, and spinning." Still earlier are the classical tales of Penelope, Arachne, and Athena as weavers. An insightful discussion of the positive and negative implications of this connection may be found in Elaine Hedges' essay "Quilts and Women's Culture" in *In Her Own Image: Women Working in the Arts,* ed. Elaine Hedges and Ingrid Wendt (Old Westbury, N.Y.: Feminist Press, 1980), 13-19. See also the introduction to the first section of this collection, "Everyday Use: Household Work and Women's Art," 1-9.

   As Barbara Smith notes, the way Walker and other black women writers "incorporate the traditional Black female activities of rootworking, herbal medicine, conjure, and midwifery into the fabric of their stories is not mere coincidence. . . . The use of Black women's language and cultural experience in books *by* Black women *about* Black women results in a miraculously rich coalescing of form and content." ("Toward a Black Feminist Criticism," in *All the Women Are White, All the Blacks Are Men, But Some of Us Are Brave,* ed. Gloria T. Hull, Patricia Bell Scott, and Barbara Smith [Old Westbury, N.Y.: Feminist Press, 1982], 164.) A similar and perhaps more general valorizing of the commonly female activity of sewing occurs in *The Color Purple,* with its frequent associations of sewing with success, reconciliation, and self-discovery.

5. Actually, men's and women's textile work was often differentiated in Africa; but Walker chooses to stress the fact that both sexes take part in the basic activity. After all, though Celie and Albert are making different kinds of garments at the end of the novel, the important thing is that both are sewing, and sewing together.

6. Quoted by Chicago, *The Dinner Party Needlework,* 223.

7. The theme of learning and teaching "how to do like you . . . how to do it" runs throughout *The Color Purple,* from the opening Stevie Wonder epigraph to Nettie's vision of Celie writing "what life is like for [her]" (132) to Mr. ———'s tardy discovery of how to "preshate" other people as he has come to "preshate" listening to seashells. Being able to see through another's eyes, hear another's voice, and share one's own life in return

are crucial elements of communication in all the novel's relationships.

8. *The Third Life of Grange Copeland* (New York: Harcourt Brace Jovanovich, 1970); "Everyday Use," in *In Love & Trouble: Stories of Black Women* (New York: Harcourt Brace Jovanovich, 1974), 47-59; "The Abortion," in *You Can't Keep a Good Woman Down* (New York: Harcourt Brace Jovanovich, 1983), 64-76, esp. 71-76. "Everyday Use" offers an excellent gloss on the quilt-making in *The Color Purple*. For additional commentary, see Walker's "In Search of Our Mother's Gardens," *Ms.*, 2:11 (May 1974), 64-70, 105; and "Writing *The Color Purple*" (as "*The Color Purple* Didn't Come Easy"), *San Francisco Chronicle Book Review*, October 10, 1982, both reprinted in her recent collection *In Search of Our Mothers' Gardens: Womanist Prose* (New York: Harcourt Brace Jovanovich, 1983), pp. 231-43, 355-60. In the latter essay, Walker reports that while writing *The Color Purple*, she also worked on a quilt, apparently using a blue-and-red-and-purple fabric and following a pattern given her by her mother.

9. Interview in *Black Women Writers at Work*, ed. Claudia Tate (New York: Continuum, 1983), 176. I wish to thank Professor Linda Kauffman for this reference.

10. Such time references as there are in the novel seem to require Olivia to be about 13 when her family goes to Africa, and somewhere around 20 at the onset of menarche (an unusual but not impossibly late age). Nettie says that "nearly thirty years" have passed since she left Celie (217), at which time Olivia would have been six or seven years old, yet one does not have a sense of Olivia and Adam as being adults in their mid-thirties by the novel's end. It is as though time moves slower for Nettie and the children, even though the years do go by. Walker may be referring to these temporal strains in the novel when she remarks, "Fortunately, I was able to bring Celie's own children back to her (a unique power of novelists), though it took thirty years and a good bit of foreign travel. But this proved to be the largest single problem in writing the exact novel I wanted to write" ("Writing *The Color Purple*," 359-60).

11. Chicago refers in passing to the African contributions to American quilt-making in *The Dinner Party Needlework*, 220-25. See also Patsy and Myron Orlofsky, *Quilts in America* (New York: McGraw-Hill, 1974), 246, 259; and John Michael Vlach, *The Afro-American Tradition in Decorative Arts* (Cleveland: Cleveland Museum of Art, 1978), 44-75.

12. A nine-patch square also forms the center of the "Sister's Choice" pattern, perhaps coincidentally; it is intriguing to speculate as to whether there is more than a chance parallel between the nine-patch (a very common quilt element) and the three principal marital arrangements in the novel, with their three-fold structures—Celie, Mr. ———, Shug; Sofia, Harpo, Mary Agnes/Squeak; and Nettie, Samuel, Corrine.

Daniel W. Ross (essay date spring 1988)

SOURCE: Ross, Daniel W. "Celie in the Looking Glass: The Desire for Selfhood in *The Color Purple*." *Modern Fiction Studies* 34, no. 1 (spring 1988): 69-84.

[*In the following essay, Ross employs psychoanalytic methods to analyze Celie's delayed emotional growth in* The Color Purple *and examines the catalysts that shape and encourage her progress toward self-realization and self-acceptance.*]

For many readers the turning point of Alice Walker's *The Color Purple* occurs when Celie, the principal character, asserts her freedom from her husband and proclaims her right to exist: "I'm pore, I'm black, I may be ugly, and can't cook. . . . But I'm here" (187). Celie's claim is startling because throughout her life she has been subjected to a cruel form of male dominance grounded in control over speech. The novel's very first words alert us to the prohibition against speech served on Celie by her father: "You'd better not never tell nobody but God. It'd kill your mammy." Thus, Celie writes, addressing her letters to God because she has no one else to write to and because she knows she must never tell no "body." But even then Celie addresses her letters to the orthodox Christian God, another version of the father. In short, Celie's language exists through much of the book without a body or audience, just as she exists without a self or identity.

Finding the courage to speak is a major theme of *The Color Purple*. But the novel also suggests that speech cannot come from the hollow shell of selfhood that Celie presents early on. Thus, I would like to focus on the discovery that must necessarily precede Celie's discovery of speech: the discovery of desire—for selfhood, for other, for community, and for a meaningful place in the Creation. The process of discovering or developing desire begins, for Celie, with the reappropriation of her own body, which was taken from her by men—first by her brutal stepfather and then passed on to her husband, Albert. The repossession of her body encourages Celie to seek selfhood and later to assert that selfhood through spoken language. During this process Celie learns to love herself and others and to address even her written language to a body, her sister Nettie, rather than to the disembodied God she has blindly inherited from white Christian mythology. The crucial scene, I will argue, in initiating this process is the mirror scene. In this scene Celie first comes to terms with her own body, thus changing her life forever.

I

One of the primary projects of modern feminism has been to restore women's bodies, appropriated long ago by a patriarchal culture, to them. Because the female body is the most exploited target of male aggression, women have learned to fear or even to hate their bodies. According to Adrienne Rich, women must overcome these negative attitudes if they are to achieve intellectual progress:

> But fear and hatred of our bodies had often crippled our brains. Some of the most brilliant women of our time are still trying to think from somewhere outside their female bodies—hence they are still merely reproducing old forms of intellection.
>
> (284)

Coming to terms with the body can be, for women, a painful experience. Alicia Ostriker, for example, notes that although among contemporary poets females are more likely to describe the body or to use it as a source of imagery than their male counterparts are, their images often focus on strangulation, cutting, mutilation, or depictions of "psychic hurt in somatic terms" (249). Consequently, women often think of their bodies as torn or fragmented, a pattern evident in Walker's Celie. To confront the body is to confront not only an individual's abuse but also the abuse of women's bodies throughout history; as the external symbol of women's enslavement, this abuse represents for woman a reminder of her degradation and her consignment to an inferior status.

As the subject of repeated rapes and beatings, Celie tries alternately to ignore and to annihilate her body. The latter is her strategy for defense against her husband's assaults:

> He beat me like he beat the children. . . . It all I can do not to cry. I make myself wood. I say to myself, Celie, you a tree. That's how come I know trees fear man.
>
> (30)

But Celie's ignorance of her body is even more shocking than her desire to annihilate it, as her language makes clear. She describes her own hysterectomy in the words of a child: "A girl at church say you git big if you bleed every month. I don't bleed no more" (15). Even this knowledge, personal as it is, comes to Celie second hand.

Celie has no desire to get to know her body until the arrival of her husband's lover, Shug Avery. While serving Shug in the traditional female capacity of nurse, Celie feels her first erotic stirrings and associates them with a new spirituality: "I wash her body, it feel like I'm praying" (53). Celie's stirrings foreshadow her discovery, under Shug's guidance, of a new God that allows her to love sexual pleasure guiltlessly. Shug introduces Celie to the mysteries of the body and sexual experience, making possible both Celie's discovery of speech and her freedom from masculine brutality. But the introduction requires that Celie see her body and feel its components first. For this a hand-held mirror is necessary, as is Shug's encouragement that there is something worth seeing.

When Shug urges her to look at herself, Celie reacts much like a child who fears being caught by a parent: she giggles and feels "like us been doing something wrong" (80). Even Shug, for all her promiscuity, talks like a child in preparing Celie for what she will find:

> Listen, she say, right down there in your pussy is a little button that gits real hot *when you do you know what with somebody*. It gets hotter and hotter and then it melt. That the good part.
>
> (79; my emphasis)

The simplicity of Shug's language must certainly be designed in part to titillate Celie, but her uncharacteristic euphemism ("when you do you know what with somebody") suggests that even the free-spirited Shug has trouble speaking straightforwardly about sex or the body. While Celie looks in the mirror, Shug guards the door like a naughty schoolgirl, letting Celie know when the coast is clear.

Celie is astonished by what she sees in the mirror:

> Ugh. All that hair. Then my pussy lips be black. Then inside look like a wet rose.
>
> (79)

After her initial revulsion Celie sees in succession three things: the hair that shielded her vagina from view, her black lips, and, finally, her feminine beauty, symbolized as a rose. When Shug asks her what she thinks, Celie's immediate response abnegates her previous annihilation and ignorance of her body: "It mine, I say" (80). In discovering and accepting with pride her own body, Celie initiates a desire for selfhood. Next she begins to find an identity through a network of female relationships with Shug, Nettie (whose letters she soon discovers), Sofia, and Mary Agnes. With her newfound identity, Celie is able to break free from the masculine prohibition against speech and to join a community of women, thus freeing herself from dependence on and subjection to male brutality.

II

The hair, the lips, the rose. Each symbolizes an important aspect of Celie's attitude toward her body, an attitude that must change if she is ever to be free of male brutality. The hair represents Celie's old attitude of self-revulsion, evident in her spontaneous "Ugh." The pubic hair no doubt arouses Celie's memories of her stepfather's raping her; he came to her with scissors in hand, ostensibly to have her cut his hair. But inside herself Celie finds the wet rose, a symbol of her new attitude, which includes not only love but also an entirely different attitude toward God and Creation. Shug teaches Celie to find God in herself, in nature, and in her own feelings, including erotic ones: "God loves *all* them feelings," Shug tells her (178; my emphasis). In between are the lips, representing Celie's present ambivalence. Although she is gradually learning, under Shug's guidance, to discover her body, her lips are for the time being dry, indicative of her virginity (in Shug's sense of the word) and her silence. Both orifices, vagina and mouth, need moistening if Celie is to replace sexual abuse with sexual pleasure and then to assert her independence from Albert. When she and Shug make love for the first time, their pleasure is purely oral. They "kiss and kiss until [they] can't hardly kiss no more" (109). This scene culminates in an ecstasy that is both maternal and infantile for Celie:

> Then I feels something real soft and wet on my breast, feel like one of my little lost babies mouth.
>
> Way after while, I act like a lost baby too.
>
> (109)[1]

Infantilism and maternity can provoke negative memories for Celie: her stepfather raped her because her mother did not satisfy him, and her mother died screaming and cursing at Celie, who, pregnant with her first child, could not move fast enough to be an efficient nurse. But Celie does effectively nurse Shug's ills, and Shug, in turn, plays a maternal role by teaching Celie how to love. She sucks from Celie's breast as Celie's lost babies were never allowed to; we must recall here that Celie's children were taken from her before she could "nurse" them, leaving her with "breasts full of milk running down [her]self" (13). Celie's orgasm suggests a rebirth or perhaps an initial birth into a world of love, a reenactment of the primal pleasure of the child at the mother's breast. In psychoanalytic terms this scene presents the inauguration of primary narcissism that, "as a psychical reality, can only be the primal myth of a return to the maternal breast" (Laplanche 72). In essence, the story of Celie's life begins afresh here; as Terry Eagleton puts it, the desire to retrieve the mother's body drives "the narrative of our lives, impelling us to pursue substitutes for this lost paradise in the endless metonymic movement of desire" (185). I turn now to psychoanalysis to show how theories of infantile development can help explain just how far Celie comes in her development of an ego and love for another. Psychoanalysis demonstrates the crucial role Shug Avery plays in her development, especially in reconciling Celie with her own body.[2]

III

Modern psychoanalysis assigns great importance to mirror scenes. Such scenes are crucial in the development of an ego, for, as Freud noted, "the ego cannot exist in the individual from the start; the ego has to be developed" ("On Narcissism" 77). Jacques Lacan posited the beginning of that development in "the mirror stage," which normally occurs between six and eighteen months of age. The mirror stage, a metaphor for Lacan, is literally enacted by Celie and Shug in *The Color Purple*. Up until this stage a child has no perception of an external world, only of himself as, in Freud's famous phrase, "His Majesty the Baby" ("On Narcissism" 91).

Lacan believes that the mirror stage offers the child only an illusion of whole selfhood, when in fact the subject is always split. But Lacan's view of the unattainableness of whole selfhood finds a more optimistic revision in Walker's novel. *The Color Purple,* in fact, endorses another view prevalent in modern thought—that such illusions are not destructive but are positive accommodations that allow one to find meaning in life, far preferable to the desire for self-annihilation Celie voices early in the book. In Eagleton's words, if we analyze our situations in the world rationally, we are bound to conclude that we lack centering, but most of us interpret ourselves otherwise, to assure ourselves of our life's significance. Eagleton believes the relation of an individual to society, interpreted thus, resembles Lacan's view of the small child's image of itself in the mirror:

> In both cases, the human subject is supplied with a satisfying unified image of selfhood by identifying with an object which reflects this image back to it in a closed, narcissistic circle. In both cases, too, this image involves a *mis*recognition, since it idealizes the subject's real situation.
>
> (173)

But this *mis*recognition, Lacan's *meconnaissance,* says Eagleton, makes selfhood possible: "Duly enthralled by the image of myself I receive, I subject myself to it; and it is through this 'subjection' that I become a subject" (173).[3] To put it another way, the *mis*recognition fuels the desire to construct selfhood, because "the first Desire of any human is the absolute one for recognition (the Desire to be desired), itself linked to the Desire to *be* a unity" (Ragland-Sullivan 58). Spurred by this desire, the subject begins looking to others for validation. The self is an imaginary construct; what the mirror offers, says Juliet Mitchell, is a chance for a child to grasp itself "for the first time as a perfect whole, not a mess of uncoordinated movements and feelings" (40). For Celie, the mirror opens the door of her imagination, helping her envision a world of new possibilities for herself.

The dangers of pursuing an illusory wholeness of selfhood are dwarfed by those of eliding the mirror stage. The child who experiences no normal passage through a mirror stage can be arrested, trapped in a very early stage of development. Such a child may become autistic, a sign of extreme disturbance in one's sense of identity (Mahler, Pine, and Bergman 11).[4] As I will show momentarily, this is Celie's condition early in the novel, when she is arrested in the pre-mirror stage of development. Without a positive sense of him/herself as a body, and without an imago to replace the parental one, the child who does not pass through the mirror stage is left without an awareness of externality or otherness. This lack of an other is extremely critical, for Lacan links the discovery of the other to our becoming social beings: without it we become overattached to early fixations of identity, unable to adapt them as necessary to life's demands (Ragland-Sullivan 43-44).

At least one other area of development is retarded if the mirror stage is elided: speech. For Lacan speech presupposes the existence of "the Other to whom it is addressed" (Sheridan viii).[5] Thus, Celie's inability to find a listening audience for herself is another sign of her autism, another result of her arrested development.[6] Only Shug Avery is able to draw Celie out of her autism; Sofia's early attempts to get Celie to speak for herself fail because Celie has developed no concept of otherness. Celie needs not only someone who will tell her how to act and what to say but also someone who will show her. She needs a sympathetic mentor and friend, a relationship that Sharon Hymer calls a "narcissistic friendship." In the earliest stage of such a friendship, the narcissistic friend serves as "the initiator of activities as well as the provider of a value system and lifestyle which the patient embraces as a germinating ego ideal" (433).[7] Shug does initiate such activities for Celie, helping her through the mirror stage to a discovery of her own body, her capacity for speech, and her ability to love an other.

The early portions of the novel illustrate Celie's arrested development. Many girls "regress" during adolescence, returning to preoedipal or pre-mirror stage fantasies of fusion with the mother; a close friend is often the key to helping them out of such regression (Dalsimer 25-26). But Celie, fourteen and friendless at the beginning of **The Color Purple,** seems trapped in this infantile stage throughout her teenage years.[8] In Lacanian psychoanalysis, says Ragland-Sullivan, the pre-mirror stage is "a period in which an infant experiences its body as fragmented parts and images." These images include "castration, mutilation, dismemberment, dislocation, evisceration, devouring, bursting open of the body, and . . . have a formative function in composing the human subject of identity and perception" (Ragland-Sullivan 18-19). Because of male brutality, Celie defines herself in terms of such images: her symbolic castration taking the form of her premature hysterectomy; her mutilation evident in her fear of the scissors her stepfather brings to her room with him; her dislocation symbolized in her being forced to take her mother's place; her feeling of dismemberment figured in the choking her father administers while raping her; the "bursting open of the body" imagined when Celie's "stomach started moving and then that little baby come out [her] pussy chewing on it fist" (Walker 12). Celie's fragmentation is most strongly reinforced by the way her stepfather presents her as less than a whole woman to her future husband, convincing him to marry her because "God done fixed her. You can do everything just like you want to and she ain't gonna make you feed it or clothe it" (18).

To make a desire for selfhood possible, Celie must take a new perspective on her own body. Rather than defining herself in terms of fragmentation or of lack, she must learn to define herself synecdochally, seeing *part* of her body, specifically her genitalia, as a sufficient symbol of herself as a whole. According to Ellen Forst Lowery, girls need a sublimation that "depends on the additional denial of the castrated state, or as some would protest, *their intuition of an equally valuable sex organ/ identity*" (446; my emphasis). But such a radical reevaluation of the body is not likely for a woman living as Celie does. What she needs is the example of a woman who embodies sexual power; what she needs is Shug Avery.

Celie begins to fantasize about Shug before her own marriage. During the fantasy period Shug becomes Celie's ego ideal, an ideal self that "is aggrandized and exalted in the subject's mind" (Freud, "On Narcissism" 94), becoming "a model to which the subject attempts to conform" (Laplanche and Pontalis 144). Celie thinks of Shug while Albert rapes her on her wedding night, and, even though his lovemaking is as uncaring as her stepfather's, Celie begins to imagine the sexual act with some affection: "I know what he doing to me he done to Shug Avery and maybe she like it. I put my arm around him" (21). Even as an imaginary construct, Shug stirs Celie's first erotic feelings. When the real Shug steps into Celie's life, these feelings become activated.

Although Shug arrives ill and weak, she nonetheless exudes a sexual power that Celie has never before imagined in woman or man. Quickly, Celie reassesses Albert in light of Shug's sexuality:

> I look at his face. It tired and sad and I notice his chin weak. Not much chin there at all. I have more chin, I think. And his clothes dirty, dirty. When he pull them off, dust rise.
>
> (52)

Celie's three-sentence fixation on Albert's chin is revealing: by comparing her chin with his, Celie gets her first inkling of an anatomical superiority. Typical of "narcissistic friends," Celie and Shug take turns playing the supporting or, in this case, maternal role, and, interestingly enough, Celie goes first, nursing Shug through her illness. Here at last Celie is allowed the nursing role her stepfather deprived her of when he took away Celie's babies and left her with milk running from her breasts. During this nursing process Celie connects her feelings for Shug to her lost daughter and her mother: "I work on her like she a doll or like she Olivia—or like she mama" (57). The relation of the doll to the daughter and mother reflects a new development for Celie; as the psychoanalytic school of object relations would see it, the doll represents a transitional device that helps Celie come to grips with the complicated feelings of separation and ambivalence that characterize her thoughts of both Olivia and her mother. Celie, in other words, has begun to employ some typical mechanisms of psychic growth and development.

After Shug's recovery the roles shift, with Shug becoming Celie's nurse. Celie's illness, however, is not physical but psychological: Celie lacks an identity. Shug awakens Celie's desire for identity most explicitly when she sings a song she has written just for Celie. As Celie gratefully notes, "first time somebody made something and name it after me" (75). The act of naming something after Celie assures the integrity of Celie herself; she must be somebody to be a subject of a song. This act is also Celie's first clue that language need not come under the jurisdiction of male authority.

This is the background Walker gives to prepare us for the mirror scene and, after that, the first lovemaking scene between Celie and Shug. The mirror scene takes on particular meaning because the desire for ego-formation has already been sparked. From the Celie who thinks of her body as fragmented and who tries to make herself as unfeeling as a tree, Walker has taken us to a Celie whose passions allow her to begin to think about her body differently and to conceive of a relationship beyond the self, with an other. The mirror scene expedites Celie's development through the stage of primary narcissism, in which two love-objects exist—the self and the mother (Freud, "On Narcissism" 88-89)—to the onset of secondary narcissism, the stage in which self-love is "displaced onto another" (Ragland-Sullivan 37). In the scene, Shug teaches Celie first to perceive her genitals as whole and beautiful and then to masturbate.[9] That Celie and Shug act like children during this scene, giggling and running off to Celie's room "like two little prankish girls" (79), emphasizes the fact that they are engaged in an essentially juvenile drama that must be played through in order for Celie to reach a more mature stage of development.

This juvenile drama helps change Celie's perception of herself and her body. Celie's new appreciation for one part of her body allows her to revise her view of her entire body: to view her genitalia synecdochally rather than as a fragment. Celie's new synecdochally conception of her body allows her to regard her genitalia as "normal" symbols, appreciating the beauty of the part as symbol of the whole without allowing it to replace the whole completely (Laplanche 36-37). Celie's acceptance of her genitals ("It mine" [80]) clearly indicates that she no longer perceives her body as something to deny or annihilate but as a source of pleasure. Even if, as Lacan believes, the post-mirror stage forces the individual to confront again the fragmentation of the body and the self, this synecdochal process helps Celie adapt to that threat to her totality.

As part of the mirror-stage experience, the child should identify its unified image of self with the mother's body; this identification foregrounds the child's, especially the girl's, acceptance or nonacceptance of its sexual organs (Ragland-Sullivan 277-278). At the end of the mirror stage the father intervenes in the mother-child relationship, preventing total identification or fusion with the mother and thus establishing boundaries necessary to the child's individuation (Ragland-Sullivan 42, 55). This process seems clearly to have been aborted in Celie's childhood, leaving an important gap in her development that Shug Avery fills. Shug, then, not only plays the role of Celie's "narcissistic friend," but first and foremost she represents a mother-surrogate or, in Lacanian terms, a (m)Other. Under this formulation "a subject first becomes aware of itself by identification with a person (object), usually the mother," although the figure may be "any constant nurturer" (Ragland-Sullivan 16).

As (m)Other, Shug also plays a crucial role in resolving Celie's Oedipal conflict. All such conflicts are grounded in ambivalence, Celie's especially so, as Nettie's narrative of their early life reveals (160-162). Celie's father was hanged when she was two and her mother's health ruined. Celie's stepfather (whom she assumes to be her real "pa") married her mother when Celie was three to four years old, the age when the Oedipal phase begins. Every year thereafter, Celie's mother was pregnant, and her mental state gradually deteriorated. Celie's stepfather turned his lust on her when she had just passed puberty, at a time when the Oedipal drama is "internally staged for a second time," its outcome crucial in determining "adult sexuality and other vital activities and functions in later existence" (Marcus 313). Thus, Celie's early life proves to be a perverse rewriting of the Oedipal script, with Celie aware of her mother's ambivalence about yielding her wifely role to her daughter: "My mama fuss at me an look at me. She happy, cause he good to her now" (11). Celie's guilt is augmented by her mother's questioning her pregnancy and her cursing Celie on her deathbed. Given the profound guilt and confusion that Celie must have felt about replacing her mother, in addition to the disruption of her own psychic growth and the continued brutalization to follow, it is little wonder that Celie would seek to annihilate self. But the intervention of Shug as (m)Other and of Nettie's revelation that "pa is not our pa!" (162) allows Celie to reimagine the possibilities of selfhood. By taking her back to the mirror stage, Shug helps Celie identify with her more positive perceptions of selfhood, sexuality, and body.

Furthermore, as (m)Other, Shug gives Celie an unusual form of identification, at least for a woman. One of Freud's most controversial ideas is his suggestion that women tend to develop inferior object-choices to men's: where men transfer their narcissism to an other, women tend to rechannel love back into the self.[10] Such women love themselves more than anyone else, and they seek not to love but to be loved ("On Narcissism" 89). Man's "superior" object-choice is "anaclytic," in other words, based on the mother-imago; but, as we have seen, Celie also grounds her attachment in an other—Shug—who represents for her a mother-imago. As Laplanche notes, "even if one [anaclytic object-choice] is alleged to be more characteristic of men and the other [narcissistic object-choice] of women, they in fact represent two possibilities open to every human being" (77). Furthermore, if Celie's choice (both because it is based on the anaclytic model and because it is the choice of a woman) seems masculine, it is the first of several such choices she makes that help her to rise from passive submission and to develop independence and identity. Ultimately, Celie derives from her growth the power of speech that is crucial to her victory over male brutality.

IV

One sign of the mirror stage's end, for Lacan, is the coherent use of language (Ragland-Sullivan 29); another is the development of aggressivity (Lacan 19-20). Celie's progress toward gaining that coherent language in the form of speech is guided by Shug. As Elizabeth Fifer puts it, "each piece of Shug's advice changes Celie's language and becomes part of Celie's progress" (162). But aggressivity poses more sinister possibilities because Celie, once she develops her ego, cannot help but be driven to revenge against Albert. This drive peaks when she and Shug discover that Albert has been hiding Nettie's letters. Now sickened by Albert's cruelty to her, Celie believes she will feel better if she kills him. Celie gets her chance when Albert commands her to shave him, a command reminiscent of her stepfather's pretended desire for a haircut. Sharpening the razor, Celie contemplates murder, but Shug holds her back. Even after Shug takes the razor from her, Celie continues to fantasize her revenge:

> All day long I act just like Sofia. I stutter. I mutter to myself. I stumble bout the house crazy for Mr. ——— blood. In my mind, he falling dead every which a way.

> By time night come I can't even speak. Every time I open my mouth nothing come out but a little burp.
> (115)

What meager powers of speech Celie has at this time are overpowered by her desire for revenge.

Celie learns to take control over her aggressive desires by two means of sublimation: assertive speech and the substitution of one cutting instrument, the razor, for another, a needle.[11] Lowery believes that the process of acquiring language may be an early form of sublimation for children, the word standing for the desired object (443). By telling Albert that she, Nettie, and her children will "whup [his] ass" (181), Celie deflects the need to do so; speaking daggers, she need use none. Sofia has provided the lesson that only defeat can result from an attempt to quit violence with violence. Celie, in contrast, gains victory with speech. When she declares her independence from Albert, she feels almost possessed by a mysterious power: "Look like when I open my mouth the air rush in and shape words" (187). Through speech Celie establishes her freedom, breaking Albert's hold on her. She further recognizes the power of speech when her curse on Albert sinks him into a life-threatening depression. That curse is lifted and Albert's regeneration begun only when he does what Celie has demanded—return Nettie's letters to her.

Celie has previously seen the power a woman's voice has to break male domination in the example of Mary Agnes. Here too is an example of the kind of sacrifice women must make in order to bind themselves together in a community that resists the pressure of male domination. Mary Agnes, once beaten up by Sofia, her rival for Harpo, helps free Sofia from prison by submitting to rape by the warden, her illegitimate father. This act of submission gives Mary Agnes a power of guilt over the warden that expedites Sofia's release. Ironically, Mary Agnes the victim emerges from this encounter with a new power over men in general. Though she comes home with a limp, her dress torn, a heel from her shoe missing, she repudiates her derogatory nickname ("Squeak") and demands that she be called by her real name (95). Not only does Mary Agnes no longer "squeak," but she also begins to sing. Although Celie reports that "she got the kind of voice you never think of trying to sing a song" (96), Mary Agnes soon emulates Shug's success, using her voice to give her a new freedom from, and power over, men. She begins to travel, choosing when to move in and out of Harpo's life. Thus her story foreshadows the story of Celie's freedom, both stories validating the theme that strength can come from enduring oppression with as much dignity as possible and then rising to denounce it. Ultimately, the victim gains moral power over the oppressor.

Celie's aggressivity is further sublimated in the development of her own form of art: sewing. Freud of course maintained that artistic creation was a major source of sublimation. It is no small irony that Celie adopts a traditionally feminine form of art to complete her separation from the violent masculine world. By sewing, Celie narrows the gap between the sexes, making pants for both men and women. More important, sewing links Celie to woman's primordial power that predates patriarchy. As Adrienne Rich describes it, sewing or weaving emphasizes woman's "transformative power":[12]

> the conversion of raw fibers into thread was connected with the power over life and death; the spider who spins thread out of her own body, Ariadne providing the clue to the labyrinth, the figures of the Fates or Norns or old spinning-women who cut the thread of life or spin it further, are all associated with this process.
>
> (101)

Freud's interpretation of this process is more fantastical and more sexist,[13] but it also can be instructive. He regarded sewing or weaving as evidence of woman's shame, caused by her castrated genitals. Weaving, thus, is motivated by a desire to follow the pattern of Nature, who

> would seem to have given the model which this achievement imitates by causing the growth at maturity of the pubic hair that conceals the genitals. The step that remained to be taken lay in making the threads adhere to one another, while on the body they stick into the skin and are only matted together.
>
> ("Femininity" 132)

For Celie sewing represents not a means of covering up her castrated genitals but of binding together the sexes so that both male and female can "wear the pants." Furthermore, Celie's sewing associates her with a select group of female characters in American literature who use their art not to reveal their shame, as Freud suggests, but to transplant it, placing it where it really belongs—on their male oppressors. The most prominent member of this set is Hawthorne's Hester Prynne. Forced by the patriarchs of Salem to wear the scarlet letter as an emblem of shame, Hester uses her art to create a letter that represents, to the narrator who discovers it two centuries later, a "mystic symbol" (28), giving evidence "of a now forgotten art" (27). Inspired by this symbol, Hawthorne creates a story in which the bearers of shame are the Puritan patriarchs who try to dehumanize and defeminize Hester for her refusal to submit to their code. Celie's art has a similar, although more immediate, effect. Rather than revealing the source of shame to a later generation, Celie's success in sewing helps Albert face his own shame and even begin a process of self-regeneration. At the end of the book Albert is a new man, capable of loving and sharing. The change in him is symbolized by his partaking, with Celie, in the traditionally feminine activity, sewing. Having had his lifelong view that "men spose to wear the pants" (238) corrected, Albert joins Celie in a communal act that, as Celie describes it, helps eradicate the differences that make for sexual domination: "Now us sit sewing and talking and smoking our pipes" (238).

V

Very late in *The Color Purple* Celie stands before a mirror, full-length this time, again. At this time Shug has left her for a nineteen-year-old fling. This scene provides the test that proves Celie's psychic growth has continued unchecked, that she will not regress in a crisis. Standing naked before the glass, Celie asks herself, "What would she love? . . . Nothing special here for nobody to love" (229). That Celie comes through this depression signifies that she has broken free of Shug, further establishing her independence and identity. Ultimately, says Hymer, a person who relies on a narcissistic friend must "develop an identity apart from the friend" (433), just as one must split oneself from the (m)Other. Celie does develop her identity and, in the process, finds a network of friends "matrifocal" in structure but open to men who can put aside their desire to dominate.[14]

Matrifocality dissolves the hierarchies that perpetuate dominance and oppression. The loss of such hierarchies changes one's perception of the self in society and even in relation to God. Thus, it is only a short step from a belief in woman's independence from man to Shug's concept of a nonracial, genderless God: "People think pleasing God is all God care about. But any fool living in the world can see it always trying to please us back" (178). Shug carefully notes here that one must live in the world to get to know God; merely surviving and waiting for a reward in heaven, as Celie did earlier, is the patriarchal way. Shug's version of God deconstructs the fountainhead of patriarchy, the Lacanian Name-of-the-Father who is the source of law and power, replacing it with a belief that one must become engaged in the Creation as Celie does, creating one's own self, art, and community. Demonstrating a parallel commitment to matrifocality, Sofia and Mary Agnes, former rivals, learn to share Harpo and the responsibility of raising each other's children as a means of maintaining freedom while avoiding the permanent dependence on one man that perpetuates masculine power. And, in Africa, Nettie first assists Corinne in raising Adam and Olivia and, after Corrine's death, replaces her as wife and mother before yielding the children to their true mother, Celie.[15]

As I have shown, one of the climaxes in the novel is Celie's first lovemaking scene, when she and Shug reexperience the primal pleasure of the child at the mother's breast. *The Color Purple* suggests that for one who develops a sense of self and then of other, similar kinds of primal experiences can be recaptured at points throughout life and not just in sexual encounters. One kind is recaptured again at novel's end when Celie and Nettie are reunited (with Celie's children) in a fairy-tale ending:[16]

> Then us both start to moan and cry. Us totter toward one nother like us use to do when us was babies. Then us feel so weak when we touch, us knock each other down. But what us care? Us sit and lay there on the porch inside each other's arms.
>
> (250)

Such childlike joy depends on staying alive, constructing one's ego, and learning to invest love in the other. Only after that process has been completed can we, in the words of Harpo (a man), "spend the day celebrating each other" (250).

Notes

1. Lesbianism is an attempt to recapture or reexperience the mother-daughter bond. Sue Silvermarie describes the process as follows: "In loving another I discovered the deep urge to both be a mother and to find a mother in my mother. . . . When I kiss and stroke and enter my lover, I am also a child re-entering my mother" (quoted in Rich 232-233).

2. The subject of the construction of selfhood or ego has a very complicated, uneven history in psychoanalysis. Depending on the theoretical model one adopts, many views are possible. As Steven Marcus says, "the notion of the self that we can construct out of contemporary psychoanalysis contains a new enlarged admixture in it of archaic, pre-Oedipal, prephallic, and preverbal components, pieces of psychic life that remain unintegrated, and of a self that is neither stable nor coherent in its earliest vital and formative phases" (318). This being the state of things, I must draw on a wide range of theorists whose ideas are not always compatible. In seeking to describe Celie's construction of a self, I am concerned not with establishing the superiority of any school of psychoanalysis but with accurately tracing the development of her selfhood as Alice Walker dramatizes it. The terminology of psychoanalysis is extremely useful for this process, although the theorists I cite might not always agree with each other.

3. For arguments that illusions such as the type constructed here are necessary in modern life, see Ernest Becker and my own "*Lord Jim* and the Saving Illusion," forthcoming in *Conradiana*.

4. I follow Mahler, Pine, and Bergman here in distinguishing Celie's severe autism from the "normal autism" every child evinces during the early months of life. "Normal autism," a stage of primary narcissism, gives way to an awareness that "need satisfaction cannot be provided by oneself, but comes from somewhere outside the self" (42).

5. The distinction between the other (*objet petit a*) and the Other (*grand Autre*) is very complicated in Lacan. They represent algebraic signs that Lacan refused to translate. In particular, the Other does not represent, as some wrongly assume, a specific person who becomes an object of desire; Ragland-Sullivan comes closest to a definition when she says it designates "various external forces that structure a primary and secondary unconscious" (15-16). Because the lower case "other" more nearly represents a single imago or object of desire, I use it to refer to Shug's relationship with Celie. See Lacan (19).

6. Behind the principal neuroses people suffer from, Freud found unresolved conflicts traceable to one's early development. Lack of resolution leads to a point where one's development becomes arrested or fixated. See Eagleton (158).

7. Hymer finds similarities between the "narcissistic friendship" and many ancient views of friendship as described by Aristotle, Plato, Cicero, and Zeno (423). Also relevant here is Heinz Kohut's theory of "alter-ego transference" or "twinship" (115).

8. In his forthcoming book on narcissism and the novel, Jeffrey Berman notes that developmental arrest can be the result of "parental empathic failure." This sort of arrest can produce "feelings of emptiness, depression, or dehumanization." I am grateful to Professor Berman for sharing the manuscript of his book with me.

9. Freud believed that clitoral masturbation was a necessary response to penis envy. Without it the girl is likely to remain dissatisfied "with her inferior clitoris" ("Femininity" 127). Whether or not one thinks Freud is right, it seems clear that in *The Color Purple* Celie must come to accept her body as it is before she can share it with another. Masturbation is a natural means of coming to this acceptance.

10. For a harsh critique of this view, see Kate Millett (196-197).

11. The latter strategy has also been identified by Teresa M. Tavormina (222). Her article promises intriguing parallels between language and sewing, but it finally says rather little about language. Tavormina's best point is that *The Color Purple* is itself a kind of quilt, a mosaic of patches from everyday life and memory "brought together so as to make a whole meaning from Celie's and Nettie's seemingly separate lives" (225).

12. The ultimate symbol of such power, of course, is menstrual blood, "which was believed to be transformed into the infant" (Rich 101). In this light it is interesting that Walker parallels Celie's development with the story of her daughter's coming of age in Africa. In the latter story Nettie recounts how the Olinka patriarchs make menstruating women stay out of sight and how they initiate girls undergoing menarche with a ritual "so bloody and painful, I forbid Olivia to even think about it" (172).

13. *The Color Purple* strongly reinforces the feminist complaint against Freud's belief that girls resolve their Oedipal crises through a fantasy of having the father's child. Celie lives out this fantasy (until her rapist's true identity is revealed), and it proves to be a nightmare.

14. Dianne Sadoff, who calls such matrifocal structures "adaptive strategies," gives a superb account of how they grew out of slavery (10-11). Nancy Tanner explains that although matrifocal structures tend to center on the mother, they also promote sexual egalitarianism: in matrifocal societies men and women share important economic and emotional roles. Flexibility, which is assured by the "network" of kinships, is the great advantage of matrifocality, allowing its members to live together and take turns caring for each others' children (Tanner 131, 151). Although less happy with the term "matrifocality," Carol B. Stack describes the structure similarly, adding that the network may be composed of kin or non-kin, as Celie's are. Because of great social, economic, and other hardships, Stack notes, black women turn to such networks to strengthen the family, even if they threaten "any particular male-female tie" (115).

15. Corinne's suspicions of Nettie indicate her own inability to accept matrifocality. Besides reflecting her guilt for not having borne her own children, this suspiciousness seems to be a critique of Corinne's education at Spelman, which has indoctrinated her in the white, patriarchal set of mind. Walker further exploits this theme by portraying the limitations of the patriarchal perspective in Africa.

16. On the Cinderella parallels to *The Color Purple* see Margaret Walsh's article. The weakness of her reading is its reduction of Shug Avery to a "fairy godmother" or "magic helper."

Works Cited

Becker, Ernest. *The Denial of Death*. New York: Free, 1973.

Berman, Jeffrey. *Narcissism and the Novel*. New York: New York UP, forthcoming.

Dalsimer, Katharine. *Female Adolescence: Psychoanalytic Reflections on Literature*. New Haven: Yale UP, 1986.

Eagleton, Terry. *Literary Theory: An Introduction*. Minneapolis: U of Minnesota P, 1983.

Fifer, Elizabeth. "The Dialect & Letters of *The Color Purple*." *Contemporary American Women Writers: Narrative Strategies*. Eds. Catherine Rainwater and William J. Scheick. Lexington: U of Kentucky P, 1985. 155-171.

Freud, Sigmund. "Femininity." *The Standard Edition of the Complete Works of Sigmund Freud*. Vol. 22. Trans. and ed. James Strachey. London: Hogarth, 1957. 24 vols. 112-135.

———. "On Narcissism: An Introduction." *SE*. Vol. 14. 73-102.

Hawthorne, Nathaniel. *The Scarlet Letter*. Eds. Sculley Bradley, Richmond Croom Beatty, and E. Hudson Long. New York: Norton, 1961.

Hymer, Sharon. "Narcissistic Friendships." *Psychoanalytic Review* 71 (1984): 423-439.

Kohut, Heinz. *The Analysis of the Self: A Systematic Approach to the Psychoanalytic Treatment of Narcissistic Personality Disorders*. New York: International Universities P, 1971.

Lacan, Jacques. *Écrits: A Selection*. Trans. Alan Sheridan. New York: Norton, 1977.

Laplanche, Jean. *Life and Death in Psychoanalysis*. Trans. Jeffrey Mehlman. Baltimore: Johns Hopkins UP, 1976.

Laplanche, Jean, and J. B. Pontalis. *The Language of Psychoanalysis*. Trans. Donald Nicholson-Smith. New York: Norton, 1973.

Lowery, Ellen Forst. "Sublimation and Female Identity." *Psychoanalytic Review* 72 (1985): 441-455.

Marcus, Steven. "The Psychoanalytic Self." *Southern Review* 22 (1986): 308-325.

Mahler, Margaret, Fred Pine, and Anni Bergman. *The Psychological Birth of the Human Infant*. New York: Basic, 1975.

Millett, Kate. *Sexual Politics*. Garden City: Doubleday, 1970.

Mitchell, Juliet. *Psychoanalysis and Feminism: Freud, Reich, Laing, and Women*. New York: Pantheon, 1974.

Ostriker, Alicia. "Body Language: Imagery of the Body in Women's Poetry." *The State of the Language*. Eds. Leonard Michaels and Christopher Ricks. Berkeley: U of California P, 1980. 247-263.

Ragland-Sullivan, Ellie. *Jacques Lacan and the Philosophy of Psychoanalysis*. Urbana: U of Illinois P, 1986.

Rich, Adrienne. *Of Women Born: Motherhood as Experience and Institution.* New York: Norton, 1976.

Sadoff, Dianne F. "Black Matrilineage: The Case of Alice Walker and Zora Neale Hurston." *Signs* 11 (1985): 4-26.

Sheridan, Alan. "Translator's Note." Lacan. vii-xii.

Stack, Carol B. "Sex Roles and Survival Strategies in an Urban Black Community." *Women, Culture, and Society.* Eds. Michelle Zimbalist Rosaldo and Louise Lamphere. Stanford: Stanford UP, 1974. 113-128.

Tanner, Nancy. "Matrifocality in Indonesia and Africa and among Black Americans." *Women, Culture, and Society.* Eds. Michelle Zimbalist Rosaldo and Louise Lamphere. Stanford: Stanford UP, 1974. 129-156.

Tavormina, M. Teresa. "Dressing the Spirit: Clothworking and Language in *The Color Purple.*" *Journal of Narrative Technique* 16 (1986): 220-230.

Walker, Alice. *The Color Purple.* New York: Washington Square, 1982.

Walsh, Margaret. "The Enchanted World of *The Color Purple.*" *Southern Quarterly* 25 (1987): 89-101.

Wendy Wall (essay date spring 1988)

SOURCE: Wall, Wendy. "Lettered Bodies and Corporeal Texts in *The Color Purple.*" *Studies in American Fiction* 16, no. 1 (spring 1988): 83-97.

[*In the following essay, Wall examines the epistolary format of* The Color Purple, *arguing that the protagonist Celie becomes stronger by using writing as an outlet, yet hinders her emotional growth by creating private discourses instead of verbalizing her fears and needs to others.*]

In *Gyn/Ecology,* Mary Daly describes how one ideological group establishes power by imprinting its traces on the bodies of other people. Imprinting, she explains, often involves invading, cutting, impressing, and fragmenting.[1] In its depiction of rape, wife-beating, genital mutilation, and facial scarification, **The Color Purple** abounds with instances in which the human body is made to submit to and to register the forces of authority. In the text, a patriarchy maintains power by forcing the female body into a position of powerlessness, thus denying the woman's ability to shape an identity. During the course of the novel, however, Celie learns to reshape those forces of oppression and to define herself through her letters; these letters act as a "second body" that mediates her relationship to the power structure in such a way as to give her a voice. Writing becomes a means for her to define herself against the patriarchy and thus allow her to "reinscribe" those traces and wounds upon her body inflicted and imprinted by others. When Mr.——— sees Sofia giving Harpo orders, he predicts, "she going to switch the traces on you."[2] Celie's development in the novel allows her to "switch the traces" made by others, the marks of authority that limit and define her by circumscribing her within a fixed frame.

Although Celie initially writes her diary letters to heal the rift that has ensued from her sexual violation and to create an identity from fragmentation, the form of her text necessarily yokes together unity and disparity. The epistolary style divides as it unifies; it consists of a series of discrete entries that form a whole. Likewise, the "self" that emerges from Celie's development is a decentered one, precariously poised against and rift with a sense of Otherness. The novel presents a strange conflation of text and body both thematically and formally; the form and the main character's corporeal and social existence are disjunct entities with malleable, tenuous boundaries.

Celie's texts are born when she is raped and silenced; the epigraph to **The Color Purple** consists of an unattributed, pervasive threat against speech. These stark words initiate the entire text: "You better not tell nobody but God. It'd kill your mammy" (p. 11). This external silencing forces a second mode of expression to unfold, Celie's diary letters to God. She writes to understand the violation that has threatened her identity. "I am" are words literally under erasure in the first page, thus revealing the instability of her existence and the threat of "I am not" that plagues her. She crosses out the present tense of the verb, replacing it with the past: "I have always been a good girl." Her texts seek to recover that "goodness" that would allow her to state her existence without the mark of erasure; she wants to receive a reciprocal sign that will order her life and thus constitute her as whole.

Although Celie's letters provoke no reciprocal communication, her lettered plea creates a means for her to determine her identity. "Letter language" in **The Color Purple** is not merely, as Ian Watt suggests of the form, "the nearest record of . . . consciousness in ordinary life," or "instantaneous experience"[3]; it is more than a window into the mental processes of the fictionalized individual (although Nettie's claim that writing allows her to release "bottled up" emotions suggests that this function is implicit as well). Celie's naiveté and brutal honesty in self-presentation, however, negate the opposite critique of her letters as a series of concealments, erasures, or lies. Her writing is neither a pure channel of communication nor a duplicitous self-misrepresentation but a complex means of restructuring herself, an active process in which she moves toward a self-realization through the mediation of language. In her letters, she may not merely convey but reshape (by articulating in a form) her private internal experiences that remain hidden from her life of laboring acquiescence. The letters act as a second memory, a projected body that precariously holds this hidden self.

Letters are merely the culmination of a series of anti-selves that Celie creates to mediate between herself and her oppressive environment. When she describes to Harpo how she copes with Mr.———'s abuse, she reveals her strategy for relocating and thus preserving a "self." "It all I can do not to cry," she states. "I make myself wood. I say to myself, Celie, you a tree" (p. 30). She resists the impulse to rebel by becoming inanimate, a state which infects her entire world; in ministering to Harpo, she realizes that she has lost all sentience: "Patting Harpo back not even like patting a dog. It more like patting another piece of wood. Not a living tree, but a table . . ." (p. 37). Celie's attempt to negate her pain by desensitizing herself creates within her emotionally hollow spaces. In one instance, she attempts to overcome this numbness by placing a static image between herself and her world. While making love to her husband, she imagines the picture she has of Shug Avery "whirling and laughing" so that she can respond. "I know what he doing to me he done to Shug Avery and maybe she like it," Celie thinks. "I put my arm around him" (p. 21). The image of Shug is an anti-self, someone active and able to express herself; it is by clinging to this image that she is able to translate her feelings of inanimacy into passion. Emotion is mediated; it is vicarious. Art becomes a second mediation that tries to counteract this first desensitizing barrier. Celie's letters create this mediation implicitly throughout the text, as she attempts both to preserve herself from and recreate herself into sentience.

Letters become the surrogate body for Celie, an inanimate form that both fends off pain (by siphoning off her feelings of degradation) and allows her to express and feel the intensity of her emotions. It retards as well as expresses the intensity of her emotions and stimulates her ability to manipulate her position. Her self-division is imposed upon her by external circumstances; yet by displacing a part of herself onto this second body, she keeps intact that division. She compartmentalizes a suppressed "self" through her letters, dividing herself into radically different public and private beings. The letter becomes the tenuous skin of her body, framing her internal thoughts in a realm separate from her outward actions. They demarcate the border between inside and outside for Celie, persistently uncovering her inexpressible (and thus contained) thoughts. One result of this sense of a reserved self is that it conserves her social position; since her "real" feeling self is withdrawn into a separate epistolary reality, she can accept her oppression. She depends on a double-consciousness. When Mr.——— returns from hearing Shug sing, Celie has a thousand questions running through her mind; yet she merely works silently in the fields, displacing these queries onto her diary. In this way, writing perpetuates that initial fragmentation, and the letter form becomes a separate bodily frame, an alternate self.

Paradoxically, it is through this doubleness that she finds an identity. Writing allows her to keep intact a self, to unify the rift that has been inflicted upon her, to remember her violated body through language. These letters are poised against self-destruction; they are an attempt to preserve a "real" self by burying it within a diary. Celie's reason for not actively resisting the brutalities inflicted upon her is a strong sense of survival; she can survive these abuses only by recording them in a diary. She displaces her voice onto this silent (because not communicated) text. The letters become an attempt to keep her from being swallowed into anonymity; she knows that her mother's death was caused by her mother's attempt to accept the reality of an external social life, specifically by her attempt to conform to her husband's view of this world, "trying to believe his story kilt her," Celie writes (p. 15). Celie's "nonbelief," her resistance to her husband, is registered in her letters, thus preventing her from a rebellion that would cause her to be beaten, like Sofia, into submission. Nettie describes Sofia as almost inanimate: "She suddenly sort of erased herself. It was the strangest thing, Celie! One minute I was saying howdy to a living woman. The next minute nothing living was there. Only a shape" (p. 123). Celie, too, sees herself as a being riddled with negation. When she contemplates herself in the mirror, she describes not her own features but those she lacks: "Nothing special here for nobody to love. No honey-colored hair, no cuteness. Nothing young and fresh" (p. 229). Yet, it is her act of contemplating herself in the mirror that invigorates her (gives her "blooming blood") and stays those forces that would erase her, just as her contemplation of herself in her letters transforms and creates her anew.

The text of the novel functions both to contain and fragment Celie. This process is accentuated by the epistolary form which, by definition, divides the text into tiny contained "packets" of language, recorded years apart, surrounded by space and gaps. Each letter is a separate entity with a recognizable border. When collected together, these letters create a form that divides, as Janet Altman explains, one marked by "hiatuses of all sorts: time lags between event and recording, between message transmission and reception; spatial separation between writer and addressee."[4] The form is composed of a language of absence. These narrative gaps act as barriers between the writer and the outside world. Letters also, Christina Gillis notes, imprison the self in words, safely locking the person between salutation and signature, and thus shutting out dialogue.[5] The autobiographical and non-retrospective stance "cloisters" the fictional writer temporally as well as spatially; because Celie cannot reflect on her actions from a later privileged viewpoint, but instead records them *as* she lives, she becomes framed in time, sealed in what H. Porter Abbot calls the true "hermetic fiction."[6] The notion of identity is made problematic by a form that disperses and imprisons the self. "To maintain existence through epistolary communication is a risky endeavor," Gillis remarks. "Despite assertions of authenticity we are struck with the fragility of letters."[7] Celie thus is seen as a serial being, struggling to unite herself in a form that necessarily fractures identity and makes it tenuous.

Recent critical theory persistently argues that writing always fragments the self as it strives for an imposed unity; language is by definition full of displacements and slippages that deny the stability of meaning. The epistolary style, however, with its emphasis on discrete entries and its limitation to a first-person narration, emphasizes these inherent disjunctive qualities of language. It is a continually interrupted text, "a paradox of patterned disorder: spatial design against temporal,"[8] and one that continually straddles the gulf between presence and absence. Within this disorder, Gillis states, "the whole cannot be examined without regard for the individual parts."[9] This commonplace is reinvested with meaning when discussing the epistolary form, for it exists only as a collection of fragments, piece-meal sections stitched together into a whole that coheres while revealing its seams. It is difficult to talk about Alice Walker's work without invoking the metaphor of the quilt, since it is her primary means of describing her art and her characters' means of artistic expression.[10] The appropriateness of this folk craft in describing the epistolary style is obvious in that both are wholes that show the process of their construction.

The very form of **The Color Purple** produces an analogue to the female body and self within the text, as both are continually fragmented and remembered. Letters within the text, however, are similarly connected with the female body. Mr.——— conceals Nettie's letters because she refuses to be seduced by him; he rapes her language because he is denied her body. The location of these letters also links them with the body; that they are hidden in a trunk along with Shug's underwear and pornographic pictures. Mr.———'s abduction of Nettie's letters not only reveals the tenuousness of communication, evidenced by the continual interruptions in the epistolary form, but it also exposes him as a voyeur to female communication. The truncated female language, like her objectified pornographic image, becomes the object of male prurient interest. In *The Rape of Clarissa,* Terry Eagleton notes that letters are illicit intercourse: "The letter comes to signify female sexuality," he suggests, "that folded, secret place which is always open to violent intrusion."[11] Mr.———'s erotic desires are displaced onto letters as well as pornography. "The male's desire to view the female's letter is namelessly voyeuristic," Eagleton states.[12] Both the female body and their texts become subject to violation by the male, who retains the power to encroach upon these private spheres.

The text repeats this conflation of stolen letters and the fetishized female body through Nettie's description of the African rituals. African genital mutilation labeled in the text as "female initiation rites" and "a bit of bloody cutting" similarly divides and constricts the body. A clitoridectomy desensitizes the female to erotic pleasure, thus binding her as an object for male exchange, silencing the language of her body. This bodily dismemberment creates a gap within the female, making her a "cipher" or a blank, like the spaces between Celie's entries that create narrative fissures in the text.

In some African cultures, the clitoridectomy is an attempt to strip away what is masculine in the female genitalia, to deny her phallic power by removing this protrusion.[13] Likewise, circumcision is considered a defeminization of the male. Genital mutilation is, thus, an attempt to recodify gender distinctions, to use ritual to create and limit sexual identity. While the violence of these rituals polices the power structures of the society in a cruel and inhumane manner, these rites also suggest the radical notion that gender can be inscribed. Gender differentiation is not naturally defined but must be constructed through social activity.

Throughout **The Color Purple,** inherent biological gender characteristics are questioned; gender becomes a socially-imposed categorization. Harpo tries to beat Sofia into being a submissive wife but eventually learns to enjoy his domestic role as housekeeper and let her play the "masculine" role in the marriage. Shug usurps masculine power when she speaks her mind: "Shug act more manly than most men," Mr.——— comments. "She bound to live her life and be herself no matter what" (p. 236). When he realizes that "Sofia and Shug are not like men . . . but they not like women either," he implies that the social codes attached to the body that create a gendered identity can be transmuted and reconstructed (p. 236). Celie is then free to alter a socially gendered role; she may engage in a lesbian relationship with Shug, one that replaces her role as wife, and she also may undertake what is considered a masculine posture in establishing a business, albeit one that markets a female craft, sewing. Phallic power becomes a transferable quality that may be acquired and abandoned at will; like letters, these traces of power can be redirected.

The second aspect of the female initiation rite involves facial scarification, the act of inflicting wounds that emblemize submission to the traditions of the dominant power within the culture. The Olinka villagers force the young people to undergo this rite, "carving their identification as a people into their children's faces" (p. 214). This serves as the text's most obvious presentation of the authorization of the body; the human body is made to serve as the terrain upon which a culture can "mark" its heritage; the person, once marked, is circumscribed within that cultural sphere, limited to a set culture and a set gender. Adam's decision to undergo this rite of initiation, however, subverts the aim of the ritual; as an American and a man, the marks on his body misidentify. His outward signs misrepresent, and thus scramble, the means of gender and racial identification.

The novel demonstrates that the socially-circumscribed body can be dissembled and reconstructed by reimagining the self and projecting that image onto the world through language. Celie's awareness of this dynamic is evident as she learns to tear down the restrictive identity imposed upon her because of her gender. Her shift in focus from physical body to social identity follows a pattern in the text of denying the "imagized" body and instead dispersing it onto the realm of the imagination. Nettie hangs Olinka art in her cabin, "platters, mats and pieces of tribal cloth" rather than her pictures of Christ, the Apostles, Mary, the Crucifixion or other missionaries. Physical portraits make her feel "small." She feels engulfed by the representations that surround and limit her. Similarly, Nettie explains that Biblical illustrations are misleading; they depict bodies that are images of the power structure rather than drawing them to correspond to historical evidence. The skin of the Ethiopians is "whitened" in the English Bible. "It is the pictures in the bible that fool you," Nettie states. "The pictures that illustrate the words. All of the people are white and so you just think all the people from the bible were white too . . ." (p. 125). She severs the text into two parts: the word and the picture that attempts to gloss it. This division allows accepted, given pictures to be erased and redrawn.

Shug also realizes that imagining God's body reduces him to a limited entity. The only body that is powerful enough to provide a form for the divine is a white man, since he inhabits the dominant position of power within her world. This is, of course, an unfit image for the deity, since it is associated in their minds with corruption, oppression, and tyranny. Shug ridicules Celie's image of God as a man "big and old and tall and gray bearded and white" who wears "white robes and goes barefooted" and has "bluish gray" eyes (pp. 176-77). She tells Celie that her conception of God stems from a white ideological structure which is projected onto the Bible through the church. Celie's God, Shug argues, is "the one in the white folk's bible. . . . He look just like them. . . . Only bigger" (p. 177). "When I found out God was white, and a man, I lost interest," Shug concludes. Both Shug and Nettie attest to the falsity of the image of God, the depiction that "fixes" the words of scripture within a political system; from them, Celie learns to free "fixed" words for her imagination to recreate, to re-authorize God by deconstructing and reimagining his body.

Shug's conception of God both relocates and regenders him. She argues that "God ain't a her or a she, but a It" (p. 177). Gender disappears when the body is elided, and God becomes more fluid and internal; she tells Celie:

> God is inside you and inside everybody else. . . . Don't look like nothing. . . . It ain't a picture show. It ain't something you can look at apart from anything else, including yourself. I believe God is everything.
>
> (p. 177)

Celie's text of private letters to God, which have been directed toward the task of creating an internal self, are then appropriately addressed. Her letters connect her to this interior being. Once God is freed from his bodily limitations, he can pervade all of nature; Shug's pantheistic philosophy demonstrates that she can find him by dissociating herself from his image:

> My first step from the old white man was trees. Then air. Then birds. Then other people. But one day when I was sitting quiet and feeling like a motherless child, which I was, it come to me: that feeling of being part of everything, not separate at all, I knew that if I cut a tree, my arm would bleed. . . .
>
> (p. 178)

Formerly, Celie reimagined herself as a tree in order to desensitize herself to pain and abuse; she is now encouraged to recuperate that tree-state in order to feel. The mediation between herself and the world is revalued positively.

The attempt to dispel God's body, however, is a difficult task for Celie, who has bound up herself and her world in imagined, fixed states. She realizes that Shug's advice ("You have to git man off your eyeball, before you can see anything a'tall") will allow her to believe once again in a spiritual being, but her old image of the "white-haired man" stubbornly resists erasure (p. 179). "Whenever you trying to pray," Shug tells Celie, "and man plop himself on the other end of it, tell him to get lost. . . . Conjure up flowers, wind, water, a big rock" (p. 179). But Celie, who has conjured up many anti-selves as mediators, can only see these substitute bodies as weapons; "every time I conjure up a rock, I throw it," she states (p. 179). Celie's fear of rebellion reappears here; she wants to conserve the fixed image and can only dislodge it by violence. The move toward creating a porous, interchangeable body is one riddled with conflict.

Nettie writes Celie that she has undergone this same shift in perception toward internalizing God:

> God is different to us now, after all these years in Africa. More spirit than ever before, and more internal. Most people think he has to look like something or someone—a roofleaf or Christ—but we don't. And not being tied to what God look like frees us.
>
> (p. 227)

Celie can, in her last letter, write to "Dear God, dear stars, dear trees, dear sky, dear peoples. Dear everything. Dear God" (p. 249). This listing reveals that the form God inhabits has become plural and interchangeable; he is identified as a series of natural phenomena. She can give God a new form, shaped to her own contours; this allows her and God to "make love just fine" (p. 197). The sexual rift that had spawned her letters is retranslated into sexual harmony with this new understanding of a deity. Although this sexual dialogue between Celie and God replaces her letters, corporeal language still maps out the quest for identity. Once more, letter and body act as functional counterparts.

The destruction of the actual body of God is accompanied by a reinterpretation of racial traces on the body in the creation myth in Genesis. The Olinka people displace the Christian myth of origin through their belief that Adam was merely the first white man; he was an aberration, an albino, who was cast out from the African society because of his bodily disfigurement. Thus Genesis' original parents become mere societal defects within this culture, and white skin color is devalued. The Olinkas believe that snake means "parent"; within the myth, white culture attempts to crush their parents (the black people) for casting them out, rather than the devil, for causing their fall. Instead of the creation myth explaining the fall, the Olinkas read it as an explanation of white prejudice. Differences in language subvert the missionaries' myth of creation; "naked" means "white." Thus Adam and Eve cannot get rid of their nakedness, the trace of their race. The fall becomes cyclical as the bodies change in time; the outcast body recreates this societal exclusion. The Olinkas' revision of Genesis opens up the Eden story, implicating the body within a structure of interpretation; traces on the skin can be reinterpreted through myth.[14]

When Celie learns to transform her conception of the body of God and to revisualize the biblical stories, she may then shift her perceptions of her own gendered role. Both Celie's letters and her notion of the body are unravelled and reconstructed. One scene is unwittingly telling in revealing this shift. After discovering that her husband has suppressed Nettie's letters, she decides to go to Memphis with Shug. "Over my dead body, Mr.——— say," Celie replies. "It's time to leave you and enter into the Creation. And your dead body just the welcome mat I need" (p. 181). Her flippant threat to destroy her husband's body to free herself ironically notes a serious shift in her thinking, for she is liberated only through bodily experience, through refragmenting herself in her letters, and through her lesbian relationship with Shug. The function of her writing changes as her conception of her own body is changed. Celie gradually begins to assert herself, airing her covert thoughts and resisting her position as slave to her husband. She is no longer fully dependent on her alternate lettered body. After she has established her independence, however, she still is hesitant to speak these thoughts that have previously been relegated to writing. When Shug informs her of a new affair, Celie is too hurt to reply; instead she writes her response. The conversation continues with Celie writing sarcastic remarks and Shug attempting verbally to persuade Celie of her love. This scene suggests an intermediary stage in Celie's development as she dissolves this second "textual" body, her letters, and absorbs that other "self" into herself once again. Writing here is the median territory between the reserved, lettered self and the self that can "make love just fine" to God without language.

The body acts as the ground that allows her to change. She initially had been fragmented by an external force, by rape, but when she takes control of that fragmentation—solidifying the rupture by displacing part of herself into her letters—she is able to reunify herself. As she shifts her conception of her body (from ugliness to beauty, from stability to malleability), she similarly learns that she can restructure the confinements that had silenced her. Because Celie no longer writes what she cannot say, but *records* her active self-authorization, her letters cease to act as an "other" confined self. The differences between inside and outside lessen as she no longer has to compartmentalize in letters a radically different internal self; instead, she can release this self to interact with the external world. Public and private components merge into a single being. She finds that she can refuse to act as slave to her family, she can demand personal satisfaction in her relationships, she can realize her significance. In this transformation, she takes on the form of her "lettered" text, an identity that is porous and disjunct. The division between internal and external that had been erected and affirmed by her letters is transmuted as more nebulous and elastic boundaries are constructed. She no longer holds a self in reserve and contains that self completely. Celie "rewrites" the traces imprinted on her that had defined her and switches their meanings in order to establish an authority within herself.

The textual apparatus to **The Color Purple** both reinforces the notion of the malleable, fabricated self and highlights the division within the form itself. It is not unusual for epistolary works to spawn such frames. "Epistolary texts," Janet Altman states, "engender prefaces, preprefaces and postfaces . . . which are a continuation of the text's dialogical model."¹⁵ The incompleteness and energy of the form spill outside its borders. At the beginning of **The Color Purple,** Alice Walker addresses her book: "To the spirit: Without whose assistance Neither this book Nor I would have been written." These words imply a self that is "written," a body formed by an external authority. They also link her text with Celie's letters, which are later addressed to God; both invoke an ethereal, invisible audience. When Walker signs the book "A. W., author and medium" she defines herself as a vessel in which the spirit flows; this outer force reshapes the contours of her identity so as to allow her to become a medium for writing. In her essay **"Writing The Color Purple,"** she similarly defines her authority as intermediary as she describes her characters as autonomous entities she merely coordinates and situates in an environment. She explains why they could not come to life in the city. "They . . . didn't like seeing buses, cars, or other people whenever they attempted to look out," Walker says of her characters. "Us don't want to be seeing none of this," they said. "It make us can't think."¹⁶ She then proceeds to move to California to a climate that these characters can enjoy. This displacement of authorial responsibility, though not a unique literary device, nevertheless calls attention to the notion of authorship as a mediating channel between internal imaginative characters and an outside world; within this formulation, the author is linked to her main character. Like Celie, Walker is equated with the text; both are shaped by this Other form and both actively negotiate the terms of their writing. The textual apparatus reveals a clear link between the body and the linguistic text, implicating both within fields of interpretation and inscription. These words also testify to the inconclusive nature of the work; the scattered letters seek a stable frame of reference outside the narrative.

The novel also works toward creating a stable frame within the text as the conclusion celebrates a unity that totalizes and recuperates all loose stands created through the plot. The family which had been rent by incest in the opening pages is now reconstructed, the stray sister returned. Celie's biological origins are recovered through Nettie's letters. Anonymity is thwarted, as Mr.———— loses his elided name and becomes Albert; similarly, Mary Agnes has regained her voice and name, and Celie is able to give her letters a signature. Time is stayed as Celie realizes that she is growing younger in her happiness, a state founded on the communion that exists because she and her family are safely enjoined. The traditional image of the harmonious banquet is made manifest in the concluding barbeque. This form of banquet, Tashi notes, links the characters with the African community across the sea. The text thus works to coalesce into a formal supreme order. Bound up in Walker's metaphor of quilting is the notion of a final product as a pieced-together collage of assembled but disparate beings; this metaphor highlights the struggle for coherence and integrity evident in the conclusion of the text.

The unity that exists in the closure of the book, however, is a qualified one. Harpo reminds the reader that this closely-knit tie between the black family occurs only because there is a common enemy. They band together on the fourth of July, separate from the white people who celebrate a different history. Earlier in the text, the family similarly consolidated when Sofia was imprisoned. It is quite striking that Squeak, Harpo's lover, is willing to be raped by the white deputy so that Harpo's wife can be released from prison, a gesture even more unusual because the family *expects* this sacrifice. The book traces out how these internal differences are repressed so that this greater chasm can be addressed; the individual's identity and the social harmony are unities that conceal difference and disruption beneath their surface. This thematic juxtaposition of unity and disunity corresponds to the epistolary structure, where truncated pieces remain disparate even as they are drawn together into a whole. In this way, the text resists a final closure. The gaps and spaces that inhibit a continuous flow of action in the epistolary text also pervade the totality and summation of the closing moments.

The text's qualified closure foregrounds the persistent tension between fragmentation and unity that has been presented in Celie's divided female identity. In this way, the work addresses the current rift between Anglo-American feminism and French feminist theories concerning the notion of bodily fragmentation and gender construction. Mainstream American feminists, like Mary Daly, concentrate on the powerlessness of the fragmented woman, how she is silenced within the culture by forces that deny her coherence. French feminists, however, see disjunction and disunity as a desirable state. Woman's marginal position creates her as internally divisive and "partitioned." As one feminist notes, "this division-in-herself marks woman's specificity"¹⁷ and thus makes her capable of disrupting fixities within the culture. Her marginalized position is her stronghold; it gives her ground for resituating power.

In **The Color Purple,** Walker walks a thin line between these two notions, positioning herself between the two. She does not fail to point out the horrors of Celie's violent division by rape and thus resists neutralizing human pain into a mere discursive notion, yet she indicates that Celie's control of this division serves as a tool for reworking her position. Violation can be revised so as to become an empowering experience. Division remains a part of the text, even as Celie seems to emerge as an integral being. At the conclusion of the novel, Celie's merging of consciousness merely points to another existing division; the focus of the book shifts from the split within black culture along gender lines to the split between an oppressive white power structure and this unified black culture. Although Celie can resolve her double-consciousness, she still will have to suppress her desires within the culture at large, for when Eleanor Jane's baby grows up, Sofia makes it clear that he will subject her people to internal division: "I got my own troubles . . . and when Reynolds Stanley grow up, he's gon be one of them" (p. 234). When Eleanor Jane argues that her son will be different, and that she "won't let him be mean to colored," Sofia cries, "You and whose army? The first word he likely to speak won't be nothing he learn from you" (p. 234). With this dialogue, the reader is left knowing that Celie, like the others, will once again silently acquiesce externally while revolting internally. The sense of affirmation and communion invoked at the end is merely a temporary truce in an ongoing war of political division.

In describing this continuous alternation between unity and disunity, Walker furthers W. E. B. Dubois' famous remark on the Afro-American's double-consciousness, for she locates this division within the black community as well as in its relationship with a more powerful ruling class. The issue of sexism is made problematic by Nettie's letters, which root it within the patriarchal tribal system in African culture. Celie extends this criticism, directly indicting the structure of the black family as contributing to racism; she scolds Harpo: "If you hadn't tried to rule over Sofia, the white folks never would have caught her" (p. 181). For this reason, the book is quite controversial, playing off two critical camps. And it has been decried by both feminists and black literary theorists as a result. Its attempt to explore the gap between these two polemical ideologies makes the book an unsettling force.

The qualified unity at the conclusion of the book is only one aspect of the way the text foregrounds its position within a dialogue created by postmodernist inquiry. Communication in the text is thwarted at every turn. Criss-crossed letters, letters written to an absence, letters received from the dead, hidden and confiscated letters, all of these point to the instability of language and the inability of a community to consolidate itself through mutual understanding. These miscommunications also call attention to the inherent problems within the processes of reading, writing, and interpretation. Walker's use of the epistolary style introduces the reader to hermeneutical issues: "Diary fiction, by its very nature," Abbot states, "keeps the whole subject of verbal representation in focus."[18] It is a form that "explicitly articulates the problematics involved in the creation, transmission, and reception of literary texts."[19] In epistolary synecdoche, text stands for writer; there is no distanced description of the writer, but the world solely as a construction of language, with emphasis on the act of writing. Specifically, in *The Color Purple,* the fact that no letters are ever exchanged (so that a running dialogue can occur) indicates a contemporary, solipsistic view of the absence within communication or, rather, of the continuous model of sender to receiver. Exploring the fragmentation of the text and its connections to the body are also issues addressed by such contemporary theorists as Peter Brooks and Roland Barthes, who both use an erotic model to explain textual interpretation.[20]

It would be negligent to argue that *The Color Purple,* in its attempt to conserve and preserve a material grounding for artifice, is a throwback to a simpler, naive type of writing, for the work acknowledges and revises the changed relationship between a text and its reader. The epistolary form complicates the notion of audience, making the reader a voyeur (like Albert) to a private and intimate confession. This is an unsettling position; reading is portrayed as an act of intrusion, of violation. The writer is also unsettled within this form, which accentuates what Derrida terms a "crise de la destination"; it constantly questions the origin and destination of the written communication. Walter Ong notes that the form disrupts the notion of the writer:

> The audience of the diarist is . . . encased in fictions. What is easier, one might argue, than addressing oneself? As those who first begin a diary often find out, a great many things are easier. First of all, we do not normally talk to ourselves—certainly not in long, involved sentences and paragraphs. Second, the diarist pretending to be talking to himself has also, since he is writing, to pretend he is somehow not there. And to what self is he talking? To the self he imagines he is? Or would like to be?[21]

These questions destabilize the narrative voice, forcing it to recede into unfamiliarity. Celie's diary fiction is complicated further by her salutations both to God and to her sister, entities whose existence are called into question. The dislocation of the addressee and thus the audience indicates a text aware of its readers; the form's ability to engender this awareness perhaps prompts such texts as John Barth's *Letters* and Saul Bellows' *Herzog,* which, like *The Color Purple,* use the epistolary form within a postmodernist discourse.[22]

Walker's grounding of her text within a historical framework and a defined feminist polemic implicates her within a current investigation into the future of fiction. John Barth's famous essay "The Literature of Exhaustion" predicted that the novel form could only be saved by a program of self-conscious play.[23] "In the future," Raymond Federman echoes in *Surfiction,* "the primary purpose of fiction will be to unmask its own fictionality, to expose the metaphor of its own fraudulence."[24] Critics, tired of this novelistic *écriture,* have variously seen this self-exposure as evasive, unethical, or narrowly-focused. Ihab Hassan notes of recent fiction:

Whatever is truly new in it evades the social, historical and aesthetic criteria that gave an identity to the avant-garde in other periods. The force of evasion or absence in the new literature is radical indeed; it strikes at the roots and induces, metaphorically, a great silence.[25]

Walker's text re-energizes the novel by appropriating a new history and a feminist perspective that refuses social evasion and thus explodes this imminent silence.

By projecting a literary form based on a dialectical unity, one which unsettles critical communities, Walker situates her text within the postmodernist program. She echoes Borges' argument against the exhaustion of the novel: "Literature is not exhaustible for the simple and sufficient reason that no single book is. A book is not an isolated entity; it is a relationship, an axis of innumerable relationships."[26] *The Color Purple* emphasizes the plurality of these "innumerable relationships" through the epistolary form as well as through the novel's emphasis on revisionary history. Walker exploits an elusive, elliptical writing style, informed with the play between presence and absence. She resituates the novel, placing it in a liberating but precarious position, one that reveals the text's self-awareness of the subversive, fragmenting nature of language and yet absorbs that dialectical play within a new postmodern container, a new elastic form. This form attempts to work within a grounded polemic, thus responding to the challenge of social and political problems, to the frighteningly real pressures that threaten the human body. *The Color Purple* transcends a mere acknowledgment of its own fictional process of construction. It also responds by "switching the traces" that threaten to silence literary forms and by positing a qualified affirmation by "fragmented unity." It is a quilt that exposes its seams and yet still may function to accommodate the human body, simultaneously rewriting coldness into warmth, disparate interpretative axes into a mosaic and dialogic voice, oppression into self-authorization.

Notes

1. Mary Daly, *Gyn/Ecology: A Metaethics of Radical Feminism* (Boston: Beacon Press, 1978), pp. 110, 155-78.

2. Alice Walker, *The Color Purple* (New York: Washington Square Press, 1982), p. 41. Further references will be included in the text and cited by page number.

3. Ian Watt, *The Rise of the Novel* (Berkeley: Univ. of California Press, 1957), p. 192.

4. Janet Altman, *Epistolarity: Approaches to a Form* (Columbus: Ohio State Univ. 1982), p. 140.

5. Christina Gillis, *The Paradox of Privacy* (Gainesville: Univ. of Florida Press, 1984), p. 5. Gillis discusses *Clarissa*'s epistolary style in terms of a spatial metaphors; she sees the evolving consciousness of the characters in terms of breaking through barriers into private rooms, while this study locates that private space within the human body itself (pp. 1-13).

6. H. Porter Abbot, "Letters to the Self: the Cloistered Writer in Nonretrospective Fiction," *PMLA*, 95 (1980), 23.

7. Gillis, p. 9.

8. Gillis, p. 5.

9. Gillis, p. 5.

10. See, for example, Alice Walker's essay, "Writing *The Color Purple*," in which she describes her simultaneous quilting and writing, in *Black Women Writers: 1950-1980*, ed. Mari Evans (Garden City: Doubleday, 1983); and *In Search of Our Mothers' Gardens: Womanist Prose,* a collection of essays that invoke this metaphor throughout (San Diego: Harcourt, Brace and Jovanovich, 1983).

11. Terry Eagleton, *The Rape of Clarissa* (Minneapolis: Univ. of Minnesota Press, 1982), p. 54.

12. Eagleton, p. 54.

13. See Mary Daly's discussion of clitoridectomies in *Gyn/Ecology,* pp. 155-78.

14. It is also strange that Celie describes this reinterpretation of the myth; it is not included in Nettie's letters, thus indicating that either some letters are suppressed, or this mythmaking is Celie's own. In either case, Celie alone gives voice to this new interpretation within the text, her new conception of the malleable body written into history.

15. Altman, p. 163.

16. Alice Walker, "Writing *The Color Purple*," p. 454.

17. Alice Jardine, in "Gynesis," states this in discussing Eugénie Lemoine-Luccioni's ideas in particular. See *Diacritics,* 12 (1982), 62.

18. H. Porter Abbot, *Diary Fiction: Writing as Action* (Ithaca: Cornell Univ. Press, 1984), p. 39.

19. Altman, p. 212.

20. Peter Brook's *Reading for the Plot: Design and Intention in Narrative* discusses the reader's drive to work through and thus "plot" a text in terms of the "desire" for satiation (New York: Vintage Books, 1985). Roland Barthes' *The Pleasure of the Text* directly links the body and the text; he describes the reader's surrender to the jouissance of reading, the play of contradictions and immer-

sion into a world of sensation (New York: Hill and Wang, 1975). His *S/Z* also discusses the fragmentation of the female body, fracturing Balzac's *Sarrasine* into a series of codes; text and body are linked implicitly (New York: Hill and Wang, 1974).

21. Walter Ong, "The Writer's Audience Is Always a Fiction," *PMLA*, 90 (1975), 20.

22. Perhaps this argument adopts the strategy used by Jorge Borges's Pierre Menard, whose exact reconstruction of *Don Quixote* is interpreted differently in light of his historical era; Alice Walker merely appropriates the epistolary form, rather than subverting it in any significant fashion. Yet, because the form has historically been associated with women, it signals that certain issues will be at stake within the text. Walker's appropriation of this form *at this time* reveals a self-conscious attempt to address current issues of gender hermeneutics, issues that would not have existed in the same critical climate as when, for example, *Clarissa* was written.

23. John Barth, "The Literature of Exhaustion," in *Surfiction* ed. Raymond Federman (Chicago: Swallow Press, 1975), pp. 19-33.

24. Raymond Federman, in his introduction to *Surfiction* (Chicago: Swallow Press, 1975), p. 8.

25. Ihab Hassan, *The Literature of Silence* (New York: Alfred A. Knopf, 1967), p. 4.

26. Jorge L. Borges, "A Note on (Toward) B. Shaw," as quoted by Robert Altar, "Self-Conscious Moment: Reflection on the Aftermath of Postmodernism" in *Tri-Quarterly*, 33 (1975), 212.

Steven C. Weisenburger (essay date fall 1989)

SOURCE: Weisenburger, Steven C. "Errant Narrative and *The Color Purple*." *Journal of Narrative Technique* 19, no. 3 (fall 1989): 257-75.

[*In the following essay, Weisenburger examines the temporal inconsistencies in* The Color Purple, *noting the popular and critical reception of the novel's errors and themes.*]

I

What would be required in developing a poetics of narrative error? Moreover, why has none been developed? Its foundation certainly exists, in the comprehensive accounts of narrative poetics that followed the paradigm shift to structural semiotics. Indeed, colleagues in composition pedagogy have already taken up "the phenomenology of error" while narratologists have yet to frame the comparable questions: What happens when the elemental techniques of narration go astray? What interpretive potentials might analyses of error set free? In particular, what can errors disclose about the sociocultural horizon of a narrative fiction?[1]

Some examples. How did it happen that the omniscient narrator of Frank Norris's *The Octopus* relates a moment of gunplay between Annixter and Delaney, concluding with the proleptic claim that "*for years* he [Annixter] could reconstruct the scene" whenever "reminiscences began to circulate" among seated groups of men (186-7), while that narrator will also relate Annixter's death after just eight more months of story-time (367-8)? One answer might be that Norris's attention drifted away from his narrative chronometer because he was more occupied with a theme of men circulating stories, a theme handled throughout *The Octopus* as a generative dynamic standing against monopolized technology. This said, however, one would also need to ask why Norris's error has evidently gone unremarked in almost ninety years of critical commentary. Amidst the conventions of fictional realism, what blind spots have allowed such obvious glitches of verisimilitude to go unnoticed—by author, or readers, or both? Related cases certainly abound. In Harold Frederic's story "The War Widow" (1894) a first person (intradiegetic) narrator, eleven-year-old Sidney, provides crucial details of scene and event which only an omniscient (extradiegetic) narrator could glimpse through the walls of a barn. Or, in Zora Neale Hurston's novel *Their Eyes Were Watching God* (1937), a merely awkward shift into first person becomes truly erroneous when the narrator, Janey, gains omniscient access to other characters' minds; also, one cannot teach the novel without some bright-eyed cynic commenting that one of Hurston's framing devices—Janey soaking her feet at the beginning and end of an hours' long oral narrative—must have left the poor woman's feet cold and shriveled. These were obvious authorial slips, but then what shall we do with "errors" that seem parts of an authorial design? In *Gravity's Rainbow* for instance we find a variety of anachronies, false leads and cancelled-out events, all interpretable as contributing to the satire of emplotment and thus of that "paranoid style" which characterized the novel's epoch. Or, in *Goodbye, Columbus* Phillip Roth seems to have planted various errors in sports jargon that can be interpreted as clues to the fruitless yet all-American posturing of his narrator, Neil Klugman.

Alice Walker's 1982 novel, ***The Color Purple,*** is a casebook example of these problems. First of all the text is shot-through with startling errors of simple narrative chronology, or "order"; but there is still more to work with, such as errors of authority and voice. In addition, Walker's public comments about the text's composition, its reception by jurors for both the Pulitzer Prize and the American Book Award organizations, the fanfare over its cinematic translation of Stephen Spielberg and Menno Meyjes as well as the hotly politicized debate over their film, and finally a burgeoning record of the novel's scholarly interpretation as the capstone to its immense popularity—these phenomena, in addition to the fact that until now no one has noticed its errors, all make *The Color Purple* a text one has to reckon with.[2]

Walker's novel demonstrates that errors are interpretive opportunities. Errors can become windows on narrative techniques, on the "laws of genre," on political and cultural stresses thematized in the text, and finally—as I shall argue—on the ways that such stresses can be taken as influencing the production and reception of a narrative fiction. Thus *The Color Purple* demonstrates what a poetics of narrative error should entail. At a minimum, as the above examples suggest, one needs to specify that on the writer's side errors can be intended (as in a metafiction or satire) or not (errors *per se*), while on the other side readers will either perceive or not perceive the errors. Potentially, then, errors falling into the category "not intended/not perceived" should be the most engaging, for in the act of shifting them into the category "not intended/perceived" one must account for the factors of production and reception that masked the glitches themselves. In sum, beyond forcing a closer look at the elementary structures of a narrative text, errors also require explanations that inevitably turn critics toward the sociocultural horizon whose signs are there in the text's writing and reading. This is what a general "phenomenology of narrative errors" should mean. Here, more specifically, the goal is to essay how *The Color Purple* may be read as "errant" in both senses of that word: as a novel that commits errors of artifice, themselves pointing to other business—Walker's social work, or "errand."

II

First the errors themselves. Genette has taught us that between the diachronic limits of a narrative (not always its beginning and end, but the boundaries of its farthest analeptic and proleptic moments), there exist relationships of "order" by which units of narrative discourse are pegged to a presumed real time.[3] These temporal relationships may be indicated in two possible ways: through "determinants" that are "external" because referential outside the story world (i.e. "it's V-E Day"), or "internal" (i.e. "the next day"). Among the modes of narration these elements are even rather definitive: external determinants are common to the realist text but unimportant to the romance. Now, in *The Color Purple* Walker uses an epistolary and therefore essentially realist form of narrative, since Celie's letters are offered as unedited documents. Notably, however, her apparent realism depends on few external determinants. Imprecise references to automobiles, or to popular musical artists like Sophie Tucker and Duke Ellington, indicate that we are somewhere in the Thirties (*The Color Purple* 114). Or, allusions to political turmoil in Europe and to the outbreak of hostilities ("it's a big war" [282]) track us into the Forties. Otherwise, the reader's sense of order mainly depends on a strained, erroneous network of internal determinants such as births, the given ages of characters and other references.

Thus one *can* reconstruct lines of temporal order for Walker's novel, and here are the essential determinants. In the first letter Celie describes herself as 14 years old and brutally impregnated by the man she assumes is her father (1); in the second letter, she is bearing another child; and by the third that child, a boy named Adam, has been taken off like Olivia before him (4). In a trice, then, some two years have passed. By letter seven, when Pa offers Celie to Mr. ——— in marriage, Celie is "near twenty" (9). Three more months pass ("March to June" [10]) before Mr. ——— decides; at that time, with Celie now twenty, Harpo is described as twelve years old (13) and Olivia, Celie's first child, is "bout six" (14). These then are the keystone dates in a narrative so absent of external determinants and so accelerated, in its pacing, through the early letters. Indeed, when Harpo announces his intention to marry Sofia, by letter thirteen, some five more years have flown by ("I'm seventeen. She fifteen," boasts Harpo [23]). Then in the ensuing letters Sofia becomes pregnant (33), carries the baby in her arms when they marry (35), and quickly bears another child, who is old enough to "be making mud pies" by letter twenty (39). At least thirteen or fourteen years have transpired since Celie's first missive to "God": she is now in her late twenties, her children teenagers.

At this juncture the elliptical, accelerated narrative duration slows down: more letters per year. The trigger for that change of pace is Shug Avery's arrival. This occurs approximately "a month" (41) after Celie's confrontation with Sofia, attended by the two muddy children; and with it come the novel's major chronological incongruencies. At first, Shug's presence in Mr. ———'s house inspires Celie to write almost a letter per day; then while Shug heals the duration once more stretches out across the months. Sofia leaves Harpo in the fall, probably October or November ("we been having right smart cold weather long in now" [71]), and she is "gone six months" (73) by the time Harpo readies his juke-joint for Shug's coming-out celebration, set for early June (78). Yet, when Sofia arrives at Harpo's with her lover, Buster, she declares to Celie—"I got six children now" (85)—and the reader reflects that, counting the five she had when leaving in the fall ("Dilsey," "Coco," "Boo," "another one," and "the baby" [72]), Sofia has miraculously birthed four children since Celie encountered her first two sitting in the mud just nine or ten months earlier (39-40). Still more inconsistencies begin to mount up. For example, Sofia is soon arrested and given a twelve-year prison term for striking the mayor, which prompts Mr. ——— to remark that she has also been mated to Harpo "for twelve years" (91), a span of time that would allow for the six offspring but that has *not* been accounted in Celie's letters. In deference to human reproductive biology, and to subsequent references, we nonetheless have to adopt the twelve-year mark, and this would put Celie in her late thirties, her children in their middle twenties. Thus, after serving "three years" of her sentence (105) Sofia is let out of the prison wash house; and after serving a total of "five years" (108), two of them as the mayor's domestic servant, she is allowed to visit her children for the first time. Celie must be in her early forties, Celie's children in their late twenties.

Here Shug unwittingly brings Celie a letter from Nettie, the first in decades to make it through Mr. ———'s blockade of the family mailbox. Shug helps Celie find the trove of earlier missives and put them into chronological order. Then begins, as an analeptic story-within-the-story, Nettie's narrative of exile and return. Walker's chronological problems also begin to multiply. For example, in one of her earliest letters, written just before departing for Africa, Nettie describes seeing a woman serving, reluctantly, as the mayor's maid: "looking like the very last person in the world you'd expect to see waiting on anybody. . . . [who] suddenly sort of erased herself" (137). This black servant, Nettie subsequently learned, was imprisoned for having "attacked the mayor, and then the mayor and his wife took her from the prison to work in their home" (137-8). The reader's obvious inference—that this "erased" figure of wise sisterhood is none other than Sofia—will be confirmed later in the text, when Celie explains to Nettie that "It was Sofia you saw working as the mayor's maid" (205). Yet the absurdity of this coincidence should have been obvious: among Nettie's letters the description of Sofia appears in the fourth letter, "dated," as Walker even has Celie tells us, "two months later" (136) than Nettie's first three letters, themselves composed right on the heels of her expulsion from Mr. ———'s household. If so, according to events in Celie's frame narrative Celie would have had to be in her early twenties at that point and Sofia just ten or eleven years old. The error amounts to roughly twenty years.

This kind of discrepancy seems to have propagated itself throughout the subsequent pages. For instance, Nettie will soon describe having been in Africa "five years" (170), then a sixth (174); and Olivia's first menstrual period ("her friend" [195]) marks what would have to be Nettie's seventh or eighth year abroad (if Olivia is the usual twelve or thirteen at menarche). Celie should be about twenty-six or -seven. However, by this point Celie and Nettie have been *exchanging* letters for eleven pages of text; Celie therefore has to be in her middle forties; and the twenty-year chasm once more yawns between the two interwoven stories. And the most curious part of it all is, at times Walker seems cognizant of one chronology while pages later she nods towards the other. So Nettie will comment, as well she might if in her forties, that "some of my hair is gray" (232); then a few pages further she will describe "the children," Olivia and Adam, as if they were teenagers (239-46), when they should be well into their thirties. Or, Nettie will correctly remind Celie that "thirty years have passed without a word between us" (264); whereas just months earlier Celie has written Nettie about how she declared to Harpo—"I got children . . . Being brought up in Africa. Good schools, lots of fresh air" (207)—when those "children" must be mature adults long ago graduated from school. Such discrepancies fill the novel's last one hundred and fifty pages. Similar errors also crop up in subordinate plots, as when Sofia is released from prison after eleven and one-half years (having gotten "six months off for good behavior" [205]) and Henrietta, her sixth child who should be twelve or thirteen, appears to be at least half that age.

How could such remarkable errors have slipped past Walker, as well as past the novel's editors, reviewers, judges, and scholarly interpreters? (Indeed, it even slipped past movie director Stephen Spielberg and his scriptwriter Menno Meyjes, who sleepily translated every one of these errors to the screen at the same time that—incredible as it seems—they called our attention to them by using on-screen dates, fixing the opening scene in "1909," and so on.) There is some evidence that Walker herself was aware of problems. In a 1982 essay, **"Writing *The Color Purple*,"** she speaks of the novel's genesis, of how she designed it as "a historical novel" [***In Search of Our Mothers' Gardens,*** hereafter abbreviated as ***In Search***] 355), and of how she struggled to make Celie's plot jibe with Nettie's. "Fortunately I was able to bring Celie's own children back to her (a unique power of novelists), though *it took thirty years* and a good bit of foreign travel. But this proved to be *the largest single problem in writing the exact novel I wanted to write*" (***In Search*** 359-60; my emphasis). Hindsight suggests that providing each letter with a dateline, a simple convention of epistolary fictions, might have both coincided with Walker's "historical" intention *and* brought its erroneous plotting into the light. In any case the book was published without its being corrected. And perhaps, as Trudier Harris argues on thematic grounds, it was too hastily canonized. Perhaps . . . but whatever might be said along that line, the more interesting questions involve factors of genre, race and gender that shaped the writing and reading of Walker's novel.

III

More than just egregious mistakes, Walker's chronological errors spotlight the very keys to that narrative genre she chose. As a *Briefwechselroman* or "letter-exchange novel," *The Color Purple* depends for its reading on complex formal and discursive conventions that are fundamental to dialogic narrative in general, conventions that—as Bakhtin and his followers have taught us—may function in strikingly transgressive ways: to subvert the voices of authority, to disrupt hide-bound representations of Man's estate, even to undermine mimesis itself. The first two of those three functions were clearly on Alice Walker's agenda for her book.[4] And if, unlike the postmodernists around her, she never mounts a frontal assault on mimesis, her novel does seek to batter its flanks by taking on those powerful representations of gender and race that trouble American culture. What then are the functions of epistolary writing—both story and discourse—in that assault?

In its elements of story *The Color Purple* seems an almost paradigmatic epistolary novel. Its true beginning is not with a letter but with a proscription, the voice of Celie's "Pa" warning her: "You better not never tell nobody but God" (1). She does exactly that. And in writing her first letters to an omniscient deity Celie recuperates everything that was erased by her own submissions, both sexual and racial, to a brutal patriarchy. She can be audacious and free-spoken; can analyze, evaluate, and judge; give vent to spontaneous feeling; and most importantly she can be a vehicle of memory. By writing, eventually no longer to an invisible "God" but to a human correspondent (Nettie), then ultimately to the whole universe, she enters into a transactional bonding that will finally bring her out of domestic imprisonment and into the flux of ordinary talk and broader social differences—yet all in a loving, generative way. By such means *Purple* closely adheres to traditional structures, for epistolary narratives classically begin in repression (see Kauffman 20-3). Their heroines are physically cloistered or silenced, exiled and separated from the objects of generative desire: Heloise from Abelard, the nun of *Lettres Portugaises* (1669) from her beloved, Richardson's Pamela and Clarissa from their families. The epistolary heroine therefore writes, usually in secret, because it is her only available, "authentic" mode of communication. Repression, separation or violence thus serve as the very enabling conditions of story, and they provide Walker (and Spielberg) with a sensational opening. Beyond that beginning, too, the middle and end of *Purple* adhere to traditional forms. In Richardson's *Clarissa: The History of a Young Lady* (1747-8), the heroine's father first persecutes and then banishes her (from Harlowe Place); Clarissa next descends into the worldly Hell of Mrs. Sinclair's infamous house, whereupon Lovelace resumes the patriarchal persecution in more brutal and closely sequestered forms; she finally returns, albeit deceased, to her father's house. As Janet Altman observes, this pattern not only transmits the heroine's "History," it also inscribes *her story* under the aegis of biblical myth; for the novel's plot is modeled on Man's pilgrimage from Eden to Paradise (Altman 26). And this epistolary *mythos* can be closed in one of two essential ways (Altman 150-1). *Clarissa* exemplifies its tragic closure, where the letters cease because of the writer's decease; *Pamela* illustrates the comic mode, the hard won triumph of an ethically proper marriage occasioning the heroine's reunion with long-distant correspondents.

The Color Purple closely follows these conventions of form, but not without ambiguity. For when her letters begin Celie already lives in a kind of earthly inferno. Sequestered, violated and silenced by the man she mistakenly calls "Pa," Celie's only quasi-Edenic experience of family unity occurred in an age anterior to memory and is therefore absent from her autobiography until Pa (Alphonso) restores it to her, in essence also telling her how Eden ended and Hell began: "Your daddy didn't know how to git along, he say. Whitefolks lynch him" (187). There, at the farthest analeptic boundary of *The Color Purple,* Celie's story finds its true point of origin: in a violent racism that, as Darryl Pinckney observes, the novel unfortunately never examines in any significant detail. Celie is banished to the deeper inferno embodied in Mr. ———, who is (as Lovelace is to Mr. Harlowe in *Clarissa*) just another avatar of patriarchal order and its power over the (justly) subversive feelings ("sentiments") of sisters. Expressing those sentiments on paper restores Celie, like Pamela, to a world of redefined proprieties. Indeed, in the comic plotting of Walker's novel, as in *Pamela*, the "Rake's Reform" concludes a significant subplot. Similar to Richardson's "B," Walker's "Mr. ———" will declare at novel's end, "I'm satisfied this the first time I ever lived on Earth as a natural man" (267). This specifically means that Mr. ——— abandons rigid sex roles (and, not incidentally, sex) as he begins to cook, sew and "clean that house just like a woman" (229). Later he tells Celie of learning such skills by working "along with mama" (279). More broadly, however, restoring Mr. ——— to what the text so confidently assumes is a "natural" ethos will also coincide with Celie's regaining the estate of her "real daddy," an estate "passed on" to Celie and Nettie by their mother (251). The idea, quite clearly, is that the true (that is, "natural") vessels of both propriety and proprietorship are mothers. And, if *The Color Purple* is thus a novel about characters "in search of their mothers' gardens," as a type of feminist paradise, then this "argument" of its plot constitutes Walker's attempt to revise the classic epistolary *histoire*. Or is it just a contemporary variation on the form? Linda Kauffman has written extensively on the strategies of defiance and revolt in epistolary texts, in which the heroine's writing itself "is the revolution" (20). Celie's writing certainly serves to prepare her for Shug's popularized feminism.

IV

This brings one around to questions treating epistolary discourse. Story elements lay a foundation for Walker's "consciousness-raising" work, becoming a platform for the contests of her "womanist" argument,[5] but the really crucial and problematic elements of "epistolarity" can be found on its discursive side, as Altman and Kauffman argue. Epistolary discourse can stand as a model for the dialogism of the novel (in general) because the *Briefwechselroman* always involves the contrapuntal voices of letter writers, as the novelist juxtaposes them for readers. Its specific techniques for accomplishing this discursive work are what make epistolary forms unique—and problematized. On one hand the addressee of each epistle is *absent*; on the other, epistolary discourse must anchor itself in a self-consciously textualized *present*. This contrariness arises partly because writing letters means recognizing that the object of one's desire is distant, perhaps dead (as with the "God" of Celie's first letters), perhaps not yet even a differentiated part of Being (as when A. B. Cook IV addresses "his unborn child" in chapter 1:D of John Barth's *Letters*). In writing, then, the character graphs her potential for closing that gap. This is exactly why, in addition, the discursive presence of each correspondent becomes so crucial. In order for desire to close the spatio-temporal gap confronting it, everything depends on the writer's power to construct a world—literally, the illusion of presence—for her reader. As Altman phrases the problem: "To write a letter is to map one's coordinates—temporal, spatial, emotional, intellectual—in order to tell someone else where one is located at a particular time and how far one has traveled since last writing" (119). Expanding on this, we might add that the entire gambit hinges on the letter writer and her addressees sharing a world that is ultimately textual; it is events, experiences, and knowledge built (as John Barth so insistently reminds his readers) from *letters,* from alphabets on pages.

Moreover, one of the foremost qualities of that illusionary world will be its relationships of temporality. Each letter is only one frame in what appears as a continuous unfolding of cinematic scenes or episodes. The key fact, nevertheless, is that epistolary narration is *essentially* discontinuous, elliptical. It remains theoretically impossible for letters to compose an unbroken stream. Instead, each letter is composed within a unique enunciatory moment; each stands as a sovereign present around which the novel's past and future moments must be plotted.

The ramifications of this are crucial. Readers of a first- or third-person narration scarcely notice temporal ellipses or gaps because a reified narrative voice maintains the illusion of continuity. Then too, the presumed reliability of that voice would seem to foreclose on our interrogating the intervals of non-narrated time (see Genette 106-9). However, like diary fictions, epistolary novels are unique in foregrounding each hiatus; each gap between letters calls attention to the fact of non-narrated time. In addition, such gaps do not come under the authority of any primary narrator and indeed may be entirely attributable to the caprice of characters who decide whether or not to write; or the absence of a letter may be due to the impact of events beyond characters' control. For readers, this means first of all that in naturalizing an epistolary fiction the empty intervals common to narrative are suddenly more open to inquiry. And it means, secondly, that reading across the narrative lacunae depends on a certain persistence of vision, on the after-image of an "I"/"You" connection that carries over into the next letter. Indeed, those gaps might well turn disruptive if the novelist weren't using other means to sustain the illusion of ongoing presence. So in epistolary fictions some of the most striking, sometimes humorous moments come when the novelist promotes the illusion of ongoing presence by punctuating "the time of narrated action," or *erzählte Zeit,* with reminders from "the time of narrating," the *Erzählzeit* of actual letter writing. Thus Richardson has Pamela absurdly detail picking up her pen and checking her door, and continue writing even as B assails her person. Still more practically, more *realistically* (as Altman points out, 169-70), the novelist can sustain the illusion by following four basic conventions of the genre: (1) one writer/addressee relationship, (2) unfolding in a single plot, (3) which either de-emphasizes the gaps or fills them in with what readers may infer from corresponding letters, each unfolding in (4) strict chronological order. Among all of these, chronological order is certainly the most basic convention. It explains why, in **Purple,** Shug carefully arranges each of Nettie's letters *in sequence* according to its postmark—a remarkable moment when Walker's story reflects on the very discursive conventions she mishandles.

Surely this is why the erroneous chronology of **The Color Purple** is so remarkable. In brief: it was not noticed. Countless very sophisticated readers have taken Walker's letters to be just as they appear—as the spontaneous overflow of powerful feelings, a steady stream of emotions recollected in tranquility. Thus Walker's readers have wholeheartedly opted to maintain an illusion of spontaneous presence, of natural continuity, and of the heroine's evolving sentiment which seems to give the text its meaning. Put another way, they have opted to maintain the mimetic image of an unedited, continuous, documentary text.[6] Indeed, one might therefore see **Purple**'s reception as a cautionary tale about the tenacity of the metaphysics of presence among quite well-educated people.

In general, Walker's run of chronological errors seems to have begun with the necessity of coordinating her two plots—Celie's with Nettie's. However, other kinds of errors soon followed suit. A few of Walker's critics noticed that varieties of contemporary slang appear in the characters' Thirties speech. Problems of authority also crop up. For example, as *Purple* winds toward its close Celie and Albert (Mr. ———, but in his reformed mode) sit in peaceful harmony on the porch, Celie instructing him in the alternative cosmology of the Olinka (279-83). They believe, she explains, that the first white man, Adam, and all the race he spawned, were really genetic freaks of nature run out of their African village (Eden) for their naked whiteness, and destined ever afterwards to be an evil scourge on all humanity, especially people of color. One of the novel's longer didactic forays, this letter participates in Walker's "consciousness-raising" project. It seeks to relativize Judeo-Christian mythology, indeed to contain western myth inside an African cycle, and even to suggest an origin of western racist and sexist practices. The crux of it is, none of Nettie's letters has ever detailed this Olinka material (How then can Celie know it?), and even if they had it would still be illogical to have Celie write it back to Nettie (Why be so redundant?).

In epistolary narrative this common problem is usually handled by having the correspondent acknowledge her repetition of already-told detail, usually by an "I told him about what you told me." Yet there are related moments like this, as when Celie informs Nettie "I don't write to God no more" (199), when in fact Nettie can have no idea what writing Celie is speaking of. Indeed, one letter even calls attention to this very problem, when Celie writes about how Shug has laughed at her presumptiveness: "Nettie don't know these people, she say" (205). Such moments all involve the boundaries of time and space between letters, and the problem of how knowledge germane to one correspondent's unique fictional locus may be shared. In sharing knowledge between correspondents, the novelist must "choose constantly between redundancy and lack of verisimilitude" (Altman 173). Breakdowns of either sort spotlight once again the inherent discontinuity of epistolary fictions, each letter having to paradoxically function as both a self-contained unity and as a unit in that illusionary stream of narrative. Here, too, Walker's narrative fractures. The reason, no doubt, was that as *The Color Purple* neared its close the author's felt needs—to win her reader's complicity with and good opinion of her consciousness-raising work—had overridden the intradiegetic requirements for mimetic verisimilitude. Walker's "womanist" errand had taken priority over the elements of narrative art.

V

The terms of that errand need reconsideration. One ecstatic reader claims that by undertaking wholesale cultural reform Walker's novel becomes a "masterpiece that exceeds its limits as a work of fiction" (Parker-Smith 483). This was a fairly common refrain of Walker's more ardent supporters, though the novel's status as a "masterpiece" is not only arguable but even beside the point, which is that in evaluative readings of *Purple* such claims to greatness are always linked with ideas about the novel's cultural work. Clearly, it is one of those novels—like *Pamela* or *Uncle Tom's Cabin*—that not only sacrifices mimetic fidelity to the discursive demands of genre, but further sacrifices discursive precision to broader didactic goals. Withal, though, *The Color Purple* was immensely *popular*, even *effective*. The record of the book reviewers and scholarly essayists is rife with reader-witnesses who testify to the novel's didactic power in resituating, clarifying and solidifying people's lives. Such claims are worth attention no matter how many erroneous artistic strokes went unnoticed during the process of reading.

In concluding, then, I want to turn the tables. Now the idea, to paraphrase Jane Tompkins's provocative argument in *Sensational Designs,* is to put aside questions about what makes *The Color Purple* a work of "art" and ask instead what accounts for its mass-cultural popularity. This means that everything Walker's detractors have received negatively—her stock devices of melodrama, sensational turns of plot, preachy dialogue, women-in-distress and stereotyped villains—might be apprehended not only as conventions of a genre but as instruments of a cultural project. *The Color Purple* might thus be read according to the way it appears to "naturally" occupy its cultural landscape. Its archetypal story can be seen functioning as easily located, quickly decoded benchmarks. So the text becomes, as Tompkins puts it, a nexus within a network, expressing what is popularly believed, "tapping a storehouse of commonly held assumptions, reproducing what is already there in a typical and familiar form" (xvi). Here the question is: What gave the text that semblance of monumental solidity in its culture?

In *The Color Purple,* as has been suggested all along, Walker's errand involves nothing less than the recovery of an American Eden. Stephen Spielberg, his principal screenwriter Menno Meyjes and Walker herself (she collaborated on the film) all quickly intuited this theme. Their script is bracketed and punctuated by Edenic images: fields full of flowers and folks, fruitful gardens and the like—all in a landscape where machines and gridworked streets are noticeably absent. (In the novel, history's most infamous symbol of chattel slavery, the cotton gin, never actually appears; its only ghostlike appearance is managed through a brief allusion by a white girl, Miss Eleanor Jane [273]). Moreover, Spielberg and Meyjes' most significant revision of Walker's plot involved the stagey reunification of Shug with her stern preacher/father. Spielberg has the whiskey-soaked, bluesy, dionysian crowd wind its way out of Harpo's juke and bring the field into Reverend Avery's pulpit while the entire cast sings the verses of a gospel lyric ("God Is Trying to Tell You Something"). In all, it was a return to theological roots that prompted some of the most vitriolic criticisms of the film.[7] However clichéd, though, this remarkable emendation might well stand as a *mise en abyme* for Walker's whole plot, insofar as it too is concerned with reclaiming and reordering the father's house, with reclaiming Eden. (Why else send Celie's second child, Adam, back to Africa?) The point is that issues of femininity and racism, foremost in the readings of so many reviewers and critics, are just facets of a larger project. Walker's strategy was to reinscribe problems of gender and race in the context of contemporary theology.

Farfetched as this may initially seem, Walker herself has claimed that her conception of womanist concerns extends beyond gender and race to include "the spiritual survival, the survival *whole,* of my people" (***In Search*** 250). A few critics have glimpsed that commitment. Pauline Kael, for example, perceptively noted that "the glue" holding Walker's plot together "is the pop-folk religiosity that also serves to keep the book's anti-male attitudes in check" (69). Thematized (end preached) everywhere in her novel, Walker's theology is centermost in Nettie's interior narrative, when the Olinka see how "powerless" is the white peoples' God long before Samuel sees it (234), and thus himself as "A FOOL OF THE WEST" (242). In effect, Samuel and Nettie's African epiphany authorizes similar moments throughout the novel, especially Celie's own epiphany back home. Explaining why she no longer addresses letters to "God," Celie tells Shug, "The God I been praying to is a man." Like Nettie among the Olinka, Celie now finds that He "act just like all the other mens I know. Trifling, forgetful and lowdown" (199). Worse still, that God is "gray bearded and white" (201). Such a deity stands like a totem of every racist and sexist energy binding Celie's culture together in patriarchal violence.

"God" is supplanted by a god of the fields. Shug tells Celie: "My first step away from the old white man was trees. Then air. Then birds. Then other people" (203). Moreover this naturalist deity is "inside you and inside everybody else," Shug goes on to claim; and so "[y]ou can just relax, go with everything that's going, and praise God by liking what you like" (203). Shug's deity quite literally takes command of the text, authorizing its title—"I think it pisses God off if you walk by the color purple in a field somewhere and don't notice it," she says (203)—and even empowering Celie's first outbreak against nearly forty (or is it only twenty?) years of being what Zora Neale Hurston once called "the mule of the world." Reflecting on the "curse" she has put on Mr. ———, Celie writes Nettie that "it seem to come to me from the trees" (213). For Celie and those around her, this epiphany of naturalist theology quickly triggers an ethical revolution. Once they have been decentered, by cutting themselves loose from patriarchal symbols, all begin resituating family roles and reinterpreting their own racial oppression. More than any other element of the text, then, revisionist theological sentiment was designed to provide Walker's epistolary novel with its necessary appearance of mimetic continuity: in the heroine's recognition and reversal of her fate, in the interlacing of Celie's and Nettie's letters, and in the denouement which brings them all, men and women, Americans and Africans, together at last in Celie's father's field.

Here one gets right to the heart of things. **The Color Purple** has situated itself foursquare on some of the most recognizable and embattled grounds of contemporary American society: theological *and* familial. Familial because the essential locus of most epistolary fictions is domestic, as is the locus for most recent debates on sex-role stereotypes; and theological because the elemental structures of domesticity have everything to do with a culture's model of ultimate reality, its pantheon. For mere mortals, however, such things are also crucially political; an individual either fits into or rejects, or is unconsciously claimed by, the available semiotic slots. Now, if we want to define what the ideological bent of **The Color Purple** most decidedly *is not,* one can hardly do better than another "text" released just two years prior to Walker's: Senator Paul Laxalt's "Family Protection Act," a central Neoconservative manifesto that was carved up and introduced as a spate of bills before the 96th Congress in 1980. Nothing less than an attempt to roll back two decades of "consciousness-raising," these bills (if they had passed) would have struck at such things as "sex-intermingling" in school sports, family and sex education (except when taught "by a minister or church on a release-time basis"), and the relativization of Judeo-Christian morality through courses concerned with "values-clarification." In Title V, concerned with "Domestic Relations," Laxalt's manifesto would have strictly limited the powers of federal and state government in preventing spouse and child abuse, would have banned the issuance of contraceptives to minors, would have banned the use of federal legal services funds for litigation involving abortion or "homosexual rights," and would have denied any federal money to organizations presenting "homosexuality as an acceptable alternative lifestyle."[8] Right down to Walker's implied plea for acceptance of Celie and Shug's lesbian sexuality, **The Color Purple** pretty much runs the gauntlet of these Neo-conservative blows. That is precisely why the book's consumption in public school classrooms was so hotly contested.

And yet beyond these debates over domestic relations always loom the broader concerns of contemporary theology. Here again Walker's bent is clear enough; but this time if we want to define what her novel's ideology most emphatically *is,* one might well begin with a text published in 1973 and subjected to increasingly virulent attack while Walker was writing *The Color Purple.* It is the "Humanist Manifesto II," condemned by spokesmen for the fundamentalist right—such as Tim LaHaye and Senator Jesse Helms—as a "bible" for "The Most Dangerous Religion in the World."⁹ A revision of the original document published in 1933 (about the same time, by the way, as Celie's epiphany), the 1973 version begins by declaring: "humanists still believe that traditional theism, especially faith in the prayer-healing God, assumed to love and care for all persons, to hear and understand their prayers, and to be able to do something about them, is an unproved and outmoded faith." This pretty effectively restates Celie's epiphany with a sugar-coating of the standard dialect. And the ethical results of Celie's enlightenment also tally quite well with the "Manifesto"; its subsequent paragraphs affirm the "preciousness and dignity of the individual person," condemn intolerance for "the diversity of human sexual experience," call for civil liberties as a prerequisite to human spiritual growth, and accordingly deplore all forms of racial and ethnic oppression, as well as "sexism or sexual chauvinism" (quoted in Kurtz 39-47).

More precisely, Walker's spirituality neatly dovetails with definitions of what Robert N. Bellah and other sociologists of religion refer to as the "new consciousness," or "new age" faiths. Libertarian, humanist, and politically centrist or just left-of-center, new consciousness spirituality grew from countercultural movements of the Sixties and brought together many of their principal tenets: disaffection with the totalizing symbols of traditionalist faith, calls for "consciousness-raising" from civil rights groups and feminists, alternative "lifestyles," distrust of machine technologies, and "ecological awareness." To Paul Kurtz, two decisive elements in this potpourri are (1) rejecting theistic beliefs in a supernatural being, and (2) resituating that belief within the diversity of nature, including Man's embodiment of that natural diversity in his inner life. As Kurtz puts it, this new age humanist "claims that man is rooted in the soil (nature), that it is the flesh (life) that gives him satisfaction, but that it is in social harmony and creative fulfillment (the spirit) that he finds his deepest significance" (120).

Again, excepting the standard dialect (and the masculine pronouns), this almost sums up Walker's position, mediated through Shug and Celie. One might only add a further element from Bellah, who remarks that in this "post-traditional" mix "it has become possible to appropriate religious symbol systems from many times and cultures" (*Beyond Belief* 205). An example of this inter-textual, syncretic tendency: the blending of Hebraic and Olinka cosmologies, as Celie so enthusiastically describes it to Mr. ———. A further thing about this mix, apropos of Walker's novel especially, is that contemporary secularism, as well as the counter-culture which so popularly endorsed it in the Sixties, were expressions of a privileged, hegemonic white society. This is a point that Bellah has frequently driven home. And it is clearly a perception that shaped many of the more virulent attacks on *The Color Purple,* condemned as it was for pandering to white stereotypes of the black male, for being soft on the violent realities of racism in America, for blurring history, and finally for achieving sentimental popularity among a predominantly white reading public. At issue was the audience that Walker's critics saw her addressing—or mollifying, according to some.

VI

When *The Color Purple* appeared, two years into the Reagan administration's "conservative revolution," the debate over civil rights had become muted even as that over religious beliefs had become more polarized and sharply contested than at any time during this century. Still, the current strife between Fundamentalists and New Age Humanists has a lengthy pedigree in American cultural history. Essentially a split between Biblical theism and liberal utilitarianism, it has taken a variety of guises—right back to the Bay Colony/Merrymount schism. On one side stand essentially Puritan beliefs in the divine covenant, in Americans as God's elect people embarked on a millenial errand, and in the priority of communal unity. On the other side stand Cartesian doubt melded with a Lockean belief in the sovereign individual, belief therefore in self-enlightenment as the basis of creative spirit and thus of public prosperity, and acceptance also of social diversity. From 1820 to 1860, like our postwar decades also an era of profound socio-cultural change (economic turmoil, large influxes of poor immigrants, urbanization and mechanization, dissatisfaction among women, and the rise of anti-slavery movements), this rift was manifested in the growth of evangelical and revivalist sects on the one side, and on the other a more liberalist and naturalist expression of this "Second Great Awakening" in the writings of Emerson and Thoreau. During those decades, the American Temperance Society and the American Anti-Slavery Society grew, in close affiliation with organized religion, and provided many women and a few blacks their first and only outlet for socio-political involvement. Like the civil rights, antiwar, and women's liberation movements of the 1960's, these nineteenth century "societies" also provided new visions of the public covenant and the people's errand. They valorized sentiment, the individual's seemingly "natural" ability to know right feelings and just thoughts. In exactly that milieu Harriet Beecher Stowe's *Uncle Tom's Cabin* became one of the century's most popular fictions. The novel was also, as Jane Tompkins persuasively argues, "a monumental effort to reorganize culture from the woman's point of view" (124).

This historical analogy suggests that whenever critics derogatorily compare **Purple** with Stowe's novel, as Pinckney does (18), it becomes impossible to avoid questions of sexism and of whose literary canon is privileged. Terms like "sentimental" become especially problematic. Defined negatively, it means flashing all the proper badges, and at worst seems a solipsistic exercise whose only intended response would be, "We're all thinking right thoughts, now, aren't we!" To many of Walker's critics (i.e. Pinckney, Stade, Towers) this almost oxymoronic sentimentalist feminism is exactly the "error" of her fiction; it also seems to account for the "programmatic intention behind" its feminist "design" (Pinckney 17). Approached positively, however, from the perspective of an ambitiously reformist heritage of women's fictions, Walker's program is not at all surprising, much less in error. The more engaging questions involve her readers and how she intends to move them—her errand. One needs to recognize how her novel, so much in the liberal humanist tradition, composes its arguments by raiding the Biblical fundamentalist tradition for some of its most potent symbols: the new Eden, and Man's Errand. The point is, Walker may well have been attracted, as suggested earlier, to the subversive dialogism of the epistolary form, in particular its ways of disrupting patriarchal codes. Nevertheless, she wound up writing an essentially centrist, *familiar* fiction. For members of her audience—a mainly white, secular humanist group—the "argument" of Celie's letters was a known commodity.

Alice Walker's audience for **The Color Purple** is exactly the great American mass of humanist, new age believers—secular or church-going. For this great centrist majority which, we are told, is fairly literate but inherently "silent," Walker has seemingly created voices. Voices like Celie's confirm their sense that the grey-bearded old white God has passed away. With Shug, they easily assent to a contemporary naturalist theology: "just relax, go with everything that's going, and praise God by liking what you like." Inevitably, such ideas would get Walker in deep with fundamentalists who decry the apparent moral relativism of such sentiments, in just as deep with leftist readers who decry the book's lack of any "realistic" historicity capable of translating her fiction into something politically useful, and also in deep with Afro-American critics. They were quite understandably put off by the way her novel seemed to meekly recodify a long emancipatory struggle within the *mythos* of an oppressive white society. None of these groups, however, would deny that Walker intended to shift a set of benchmark cultural symbols and beliefs, all involving what Eden looks like, who gets in, and where our errand takes us in regaining it. These questions may seem (and even *be*) trivial, yet the virulence of public argument occasioned by her novel and Spielberg's film demonstrates that they may never be value-neutral. The question is: Whose values?

Indeed from one last perspective, that of French theorist Jean Baudrillard, the issue of a fiction like **The Color Purple** poses further problems. Baudrillard has detailed the way mass cultural texts advance an "implosion of meaning" which *does* neutralize the discourses of value. This eventuates from the "staging" of an audience's desire in processions of simulacra, a "hyperreality" which—because it seems "truer" to reality than reality itself—leaves the audience impassively fascinated by the apparent surmounting of their voiceless condition. By such means the "silent majority" submits itself to the tautology of myths: their common narrativity means they are easily translated for various media, and this commodification only increases their "mythic" stature. In place of a "repressive demiurgy" it is instead "a gentle *semi*urgy which control us" ("Implosion" 140). Under its aegis "the medium" is absolutely *the* event. Content, including any statement of value, dissolves in a feedback loop of media-effects, of simulacra. The cruxes of axiology become the crazes of technology, and the "message," especially the didactic social content of mass cultural texts, is according to this argument only a subterfuge on the strength of which "every hope of revolution and social change up till now has functioned" (ibid 144). Thus the only logic of such texts is their audiences' consumption of familiar metanarratives. And in the sternest moments of his jeremiad Baudrillard concludes that (excepting perhaps his own ironic, critical method) *any* symbolizing attempt to emancipate or "raise the consciousness" of individual or collective subjects is blinded by its inescapable conformity to systems whose goal is the overproduction and overvaluation of symbols, the simulacra or "fast-images" of contemporary media.

Baudrillard's optic often works with disturbing accuracy. After all, only in a fast-image culture could six-plus years slide past without anyone perceiving blatant errors of technique ("medium") like those in **The Color Purple.** Yet interpreting such errant moments should not only end with a social and ideological siting of the text's apparent message and audience. It also must involve a looping back to that narrative medium, back to its lacunae and blind spots; in short, a looping back not only to the "laws of genre" but also to the glitches of genre that can be read like the tics of its own insecurity. Put another way, if adherence to the naturalizing conventions of narrative seems to give a text "traction" (Tompkins) or solidity in its society, then the errant moments of narrative are the traces of its slippage or instability. The best sellers of contemporary mass culture should offer plentiful examples for study. Yet why stop with popular fictions? Why not also examine the errant narration (however intentional or metafictional) of self-styled "experimental" fictions, for doesn't that very term suggest a complicity with metanarratives of technical progress? Feasibly, what's under scrutiny from this perspective is the cooperation of narrative technologies with forms of socio-cultural *malaise*—these days a sort of cultural "stag-flation." In the general critique of such conditions, the example of Alice Walker's novel indicates that narrative poetics and a phenomenology of error can force a set of telling questions.

Notes

1. See for example Shaughnessy (1977), and Williams (1981).

2. Pauline Kael may have been thinking of the chronological problems when she wrote that "the cross-cutting between Nettie's experiences in Africa and Celie's life back home is staggeringly ineffective" (69), but she is never specific enough. In general, though, given the close readings of Walker's novel by everyone—from editors (at Harcourt Brace Jovanovich), early reviewers, Pulitzer and A.B.A. judges, film directors, and cultural critics, to more recent scholars and Ph.D. candidates—the common failure to notice, much less comment on such basic errors of narrative art amounts to a phenomenon in itself. For readers of *Purple* have grilled Walker and Spielberg for less obvious inconsistencies. Reviewing the book, Robert Towers saw Nettie's return with the children as "crudely contrived" and "melodramatic"; he also noted "certain improbabilities," like Celie's remarkable diction (her use of the word "amazons") and her "Folkspants" business. Still, he begged off the larger question of mimetic fidelity by noting that these might all be explainable in the context of "current male-female antagonisms within the black community," to which Walker was presumably the better witness (Towers 36). Denitia Smith pointed to an "unevenness" in the book's ideology, when the Olinka tribal patriarchy is depicted as bad, leaving one with the mistaken idea that its disruption by white colonialists is therefore "a good thing" (Smith 182). Darryl Pinckney, in a scathing review, charges that *The Color Purple* (novel and film) fails "to claim historical truth" because, with its myriad historical glitches, *The Color Purple* sacrificed accurate temporal and social context for a highly "insular" melodrama: "[it] might as well have been about a bunch of dancing eggplants for all it has to say about black history" (Pinckney 17). Thus far, M. Teresa Tavormina is the *only* critic to even begin noticing the chronological errors in Walker's novel. She hastily comments that "Walker makes it difficult, perhaps impossible, for her readers to determine the exact temporal relationships between letters in Celie's series and those in Nettie's." Then Tavormina stops short, assuming that such "time-marking events" as births and children's ages will, according to Walker's plan, only add up to a blurry picture: "The meaning is in the whole. To see linearly is to limit one's seeing" (226). Even more remarkable, in an endnote Tavormina tries to naturalize the "temporal strains in the novel"; they make sense, she argues, because it is "as though time moves slower for Nettie and the children" in their primitive, African setting (n. 10, 229-30). The sharply polarized reaction to *Purple* is also worth noting. Stade has discussed readers who have approached *The Color Purple* as "a sacred text" (264), and praiseful, near-ecstatic reviews occurred in popular periodicals such as *Ms. Magazine* (for which Alice Walker worked), and in *Newsweek*, where Peter Prescott called it "an American novel of permanent importance" (67). In *Ms.* (July 1982), Gloria Steinem seems so taken with the facts of Walker's being a woman, black, alive, and writing that she scarcely uses the fiction itself to support her praise. *The New Yorker* (September 6, 1982), relegated it to the "Briefly Noted" column of short reviews, yet still referred to *Purple* as "fiction of the highest order" (106). Denitia Smith's review was mixed, uneasy with Walker's didacticism and (what Smith saw as) ideological haziness but full of praise for the novel's qualities of voice—a common strategy for other reviewers. Smith hazarded the opinion that, with *Purple,* Alice Walker had joined "the company of Faulkner" (183). Among the downright negative reactions, Pinckney's is certainly the most outspoken and searing; he has recently been joined by Trudier Harris, who argues that the novel's too-hasty canonization resulted from "the media's ability, once again, to dictate the tastes of the reading public, and to attempt to shape what is acceptable creation by black American writers" (155). Harris also provides an excellent summary of these polarized reviews. In general, this sharply polarized reception was only exacerbated by the film's release in December, 1985. In a January 27, 1986, article the *New York Times* accurately summed up the brouhaha: feminists and liberal critics were passionately positive about the film; others, including black male writers like Nate Clay of the *Chicago Metro News* (a major black weekly), were acutely negative, usually condemning the film as "a pretext to take one more lick at society's rejects" ("Blacks in Heated" 13). Around the country, public debates aired similar opinions about issues of gender and race raised by *The Color Purple*: in New York,

over 1,000 blacks "crammed into the Progressive Community Church for a heated discussion of the film" (ibid), a scene also repeated on university campuses (later that month, for example, the University of Kentucky sponsored a heated panel discussion attended by over 200).

3. See for example Genette 116-23, and especially 140-3; also, though her terms are somewhat more general, see Rimmon-Kenan 43-6.

4. There is a striking parallel to *Purple* in a long essay Walker wrote for the July, 1982, issue of *Essence*. Almost exactly contemporaneous with the novel, "If the Present Looks Like the Past, What Does the Future Look Like" poses the two questions of blackness and femininity as they intersect in the problematic figure of that "lighter-skinned, straighter-haired" black woman who is a stock figure in many American fictions. Interestingly, the essay opens with a polemical epistle, addressed to "Dear ———." And the whole was intended to function, Walker claims, as "A Consciousness Raising Paper" (*In Search* 294). The same could well be said of *The Color Purple*.

5. In retrospect this should not be surprising. Historically, such apparently documentary fictions have often been received as if the represented characters and events were real, so powerful are the naturalizing conventions involved. As for Walker, her essay "Writing *The Color Purple*" speaks of "the people in the novel" walking in and out of her life (*In Search* 356). Then too, many of the novel's reviewers and critics have focused on the lifelike quality and naturalizing power of Celie's voice. See also Christian 470, and in particular Fifer, whose essay argues that accepting and understanding Celie's dialect, the reader comes "to understand Celie's plight within a larger cultural context" (156).

6. Here, encapsulated, is Walker's definition of a "womanist": "a black feminist or feminist of color. From the black folk expression of mothers to female children, 'You acting womanish,' i.e. like a woman. Usually referring to outrageous, audacious, courageous or *willful* behavior, [for example when a woman] loves other women, sexually and/or nonsexually. [A womanist] appreciates and prefers women's culture, women's emotional flexibility . . . and women's strength . . . [and is] committed to the survival and wholeness of entire people, male *and* female" (*In Search* xi).

7. This was the scene that prompted Pinckney's "dancing eggplants" remark (n. 3, above). Later in his essay-review he returns to it: "The preacher father is grafted onto the script not just as a way to rehabilitate the sinner, but to get the camera inside a black church because what would a black film be without a climactic scene of getting religion?" Pinckney then concludes: "it is not so much that Spielberg has revived these stock types as that he has reminded us of how present these heirlooms of folly still are, how quickly and comfortably summoned, how great is the pressure to conform to the familiar, the recognizable" (20).

8. For the full text of Laxalt's bill see the draft of it in the *Conservative Digest* 6.5/6 (May/June 1980).

9. Tim LaHaye's book, *The Battle for the Mind* (1980), was one of the most full-bore salvos of the fundamentalist right. "The Most Dangerous Religion in the World" was the subtitle of Homer Duncan's *Secular Humanism* (1981), published with a prefatory essay by Senator Jesse Helms. Both books were best sellers in the world of religious publishing.

Works Cited

Altman, Janet Gurkin. *Epistolarity: Approaches to a Form*. Columbus: Ohio State University Press, 1982.

Barth, John. *Letters: An Old Time Epistolary Novel by Seven Fictitious Drolls & Dreamers Each of Which Imagines Himself Actual*. New York: G. P. Putnams' Sons, 1979.

Baudrillard, Jean. "The Implosion of Meaning in the Media and the Implosion of the Social in the Masses." *The Myths of Information: Technology and Postindustrial Culture*. Ed. Kathleen Woodward. Madison, Wisconsin: Coda Press, 1980.

———. *In the Shadow of the Silent Majorities*. 1978. New York: Jean Baudrillard and Semiotext(e), 1983.

Bellah, Robert N. *Beyond Belief: Essays on Religion in a Post-Traditional World*. New York: Harper and Row, 1970.

———, and Charles Y. Glock, eds. *The New Religious Consciousness*. Berkeley: University of California Press, 1976.

"Blacks in Heated Debate over *The Color Purple*." *New York Times* January 27, 1986, natl. ed.: I, 13.

Christian, Barbara. "Alice Walker: The Black Woman Artist as Wayward." In Evans 457-77.

El Safar, Ruth. "Alice Walker's *The Color Purple*." *The International Fiction Review* 12.1 (1985): 11-17.

Evans, Mari, ed. *Black Women Writers: A Critical Evaluation*. Garden City: Anchor Books, 1984.

Fifer, Elizabeth. "The Dialect and Letters of *The Color Purple*." *Contemporary American Women Writers: Narrative Strategies*. Ed. Catherine Rainwater and William J. Scheick. Lexington: University Press of Kentucky, 1985.

Genette, Gerard. *Narrative Discourse: An Essay in Method.* Trans. Jane E. Lewin. Ithaca: Cornell University Press, 1980.

Harris, Trudier. "On *The Color Purple,* Stereotypes, and Silence." *Black American Literature Forum* 18.4 (1984): 155-61.

Kael, Pauline. Rev. of Spielberg's *The Color Purple. The New Yorker* December 30, 1985: 69-71.

Kauffman, Linda S. *Discourses of Desire: Gender, Genre, and Epistolary Fictions.* Ithaca: Cornell University Press, 1985.

Kurtz, Paul. *In Defense of Secular Humanism.* Buffalo: Prometheus Books, 1983.

Norris, Frank. *The Octopus.* 1900. New York: Signet, 1964.

Parker-Smith, Bettye J. "Alice Walker's Women: In Search of Peace of Mind." In Evans 478-93.

Pinckney, Darryl. "Black Victims, Black Villains." *The New York Review of Books* January 29, 1987: 17-19.

Rimmon-Kenan, Shlomith. *Narrative Fiction: Contemporary Poetics.* New York: Methuen, 1983.

Royster, Philip M. "In Search of Our Fathers' Arms: Alice Walker's Persona of the Alienated Darling." *Black American Literature Forum* 20 (1986): 347-70.

Shaughnessy, Mina P. *Errors and Expectations.* New York: Oxford University Press, 1977.

Shelton, Frank. "Alienation and Integration in Alice Walker's *The Color Purple.*" *College Language Association Journal* 28 (1985): 382-92.

Smith, Denitia. "Celie, You a Tree." *Nation* September 4, 1982: 181-3.

"Spielberg Takes His Biggest Risk With *Color Purple.*" *New York Times* December 15, 1985, natl. ed.: II, 1, 23.

Stade, George. "Womanist Fiction and Male Characters." *Partisan Review* 52 (1985): 264-70.

Tavormina, M. Teresa. "Dressing the Spirit: Clothworking and Language in *The Color Purple.*" *Journal of Narrative Technique* 16 (1986): 220-30.

Tompkins, Jane. *Sensational Designs: The Cultural Work of American Fiction, 1790-1860.* New York: Oxford University Press, 1985.

Towers, Robert. "Good Men are Hard to Find." *New York Review of Books* August 12, 1983: 35-6.

Walker, Alice. *The Color Purple.* 1982. New York: Pocket Books, 1985.

———. *In Search of Our Mothers' Gardens: Womanist Prose.* San Diego: Harcourt Brace Jovanovich, 1983.

Williams, Joseph M. "The Phenomenology of Error." *College Composition and Communication* 32 (May 1981): 152-68.

Priscilla L. Walton (essay date April 1990)

SOURCE: Walton, Priscilla L. "'What She Got to Sing About?': Comedy and *The Color Purple.*" *ARIEL* 21, no. 2 (April 1990): 59-74.

[*In the following essay, Walton defines comic theory and classifies* The Color Purple *as a comedic novel based on examples from the work.*]

> [Laughter] is a froth with a saline base. Like froth it sparkles. It is gaiety itself. But the philosopher who gathers a handful to taste may find that the substance is scanty and the aftertaste bitter.
>
> (Bergson 190)

This observation, written in 1900 by Henri Bergson, in the conclusion to his essay "Laughter," ironically anticipates the changes that occur in the comic mode of the succeeding century when laughter's "froth" virtually disappears and its "bitter aftertaste" comes to predominate. After 1900, literature—comedy in particular—becomes more acrimonious and discordant, perhaps better to represent life in our century of "disorder and irrationalism" (Sypher 201). The comic novel ceases to ring with the "silvery laughter" that George Meredith applauds; rather it reverberates to the maniacal, paranoid laughter in which Thomas Pynchon revels. In short, comedy enters the realm of the absurd and begins to reflect the individual's disorientation in a "senseless, chaotic" world.

Yet even within this context, it might seem anomalous to call Alice Walker's 1982 work, ***The Color Purple,*** a comedy. The novel is arguably bleaker than many of the others that are included in the mode, since it deals with rape, incest, and social prejudice; yet the ideal "womanist" world in which it culminates (Walker, ***In Search of Our Mothers' Gardens*** xi) is joyous and celebratory—a condition of the comic. Although its subject matter appears at times to counteract the levity expected of a comic novel and so to be at variance with the comic purpose, if we set aside our more traditional expectations of the mode and look rather at the intent of the comic, we see that ***The Color Purple*** rather closely adheres to its theoretical tenets.

While it is not my intention here to offer an absolute definition of comedy, some idea of what the comic signifies is necessary to come to an understanding of its relevance to ***The Color Purple.*** My discussion is selective: the characteristics I discuss relate more specifically to what theorists of the comic call "high comedy," or the "comedy of ideas," since Walker's novel is obviously not of the kind of comedy which elicits hearty guffaws from its readers. But this does not disqualify it from the mode, for theorists of the comic often note that laughter is a very deceptive criterion by which to assess it (Martin 74, Sypher 203). More often than not, high comedy concerns itself less with being 'funny' than with dramatizing possibilities and exploring potentials. If it does provoke laughter, it is because it mocks certain social conventions. Yet, it mocks because it devotes itself to social improvement and often provides a critique of societal limitations. James K. Feibleman suggests that comedy pursues the ideal:

> A constant reminder of the existence of the logical order as the perfect goal of actuality, comedy continually insists upon the limitations of all experience and of all actuality. The business of comedy is to dramatize and thus make more vivid and immediate the fact that contradictions in actuality must prove insupportable. It thus admonishes against the easy acceptance of interim limitations and calls for the persistent advance toward the logical order and the final elimination of limitations.
>
> (82)

Comedy seeks improvement in a "negative way," for it asserts that if it is only the limitations of actuality which prevent it from achieving perfection, then the limitations should be eliminated (96). Therefore, in a period of social change (like the twentieth-century), comedy often assumes an increasing importance because it is more subversive in nature than tragedy (96) and seeks to improve society: "Better to stress the fact that however much value any actual situation may have, it is prevented from having more only by its limitations. Why, then, be satisfied?" (96). Because comedy continually exposes the limitations of the actual to highlight the ideal, many comic theorists emphasize its potentially "dangerous" and even "revolutionary" nature. Indeed, Wylie Sypher goes so far as to suggest that the comedian

> refuses to make . . . concessions to actuality and serves, instead, as chief tactician in a permanent resistance movement, or rebellion, within the frontiers of human experience. By temperament, the comedian is often a fifth columnist in social life.
>
> (247)

All these criteria are relevant to *The Color Purple,* but of more specific interest at this point is the means by which comedy frequently displays its "revolutionary" tendency. If comedy is a subversive mode, it often succeeds in demonstrating the limitations of the social order through the incorporation of an excluded or marginalized individual. Northrop Frye perceives this as comedy's adaptation of the "*pharmakos*" or the victimized character who is "opposed to or excluded from the fictional society" and has "the sympathy of the audience" (*Anatomy* 48). The "*pharmakos*" generally appears in comedy in one of two ways and can be regarded as a "fool or worse by the fictional society, and yet impresses the real audience as having something more valuable than his [or her] society has" (48); or the "*pharmakos*" may choose to repudiate the society, and in doing so become "a kind of *pharmakos* in reverse" (48). The idea of the "*pharmakos*" also foregrounds what has been called comedy's "paradoxical nature," since in it frequently that which is "seemingly absurd [is] actually well-founded" (Martin 86) and therefore, in "the best sort of comedy," the "incongruous is finally seen to be congruent to a larger pattern than that which was originally perceived" (87).

While comedy seeks to improve society, often, particularly in its twentieth-century manifestations, it veers so close to tragedy that it is difficult to separate the comic from the tragic mode. But Frye suggests that this is because "tragedy is really implicit or uncompleted comedy [and] comedy contains a potential tragedy within itself" ("Argument" 455). If comedy completes itself, this completion is manifested in the new (or renewed) society which is evident in its conclusion. High comedy is not content to expose the limitations in a closed social order; once they have been exposed, it often offers what it perceives as the ideal, for in its aim for general improvement, it needs to provide an open society as an alternative to the closed or limited one it has dramatized. Comedy's theme, therefore, is often "the integration of society" (*Anatomy* 43) and this social integration "may emphasize the birth of an ideal society" ("Argument" 454). As a result, "that which gets born at the end of comedy" may "not impress us as true, but as desirable," since unlikely "conversions, miraculous transformations, and providential assistance are inseparable from comedy" (*Anatomy* 170).

High comedy forces its dramatized order to "open in many directions" (Sypher 249). It becomes "an achievement of man as a social being" (Sypher 252) because it compels us to recognize our potential by mocking what is less than ideal in our practice. Hence, while it exposes the limitations of our society, it either eliminates these limitations and so renews its fictional order or it posits a new, ideal order in its conclusions. Like tragedy, therefore, comedy too offers a "road to wisdom" (Sypher 254), and the comic protagonist often learns through suffering (Sypher 254); but the comic differs from the tragic in that it never "despairs of man" (Sypher 254).

And Alice Walker's novel, *The Color Purple,* does not despair of "man" either, for it incorporates these elements of comedy: it makes the incongruous congruent to a larger pattern; it refuses to accept the limitations imposed on its fictional society; and it posits a new order which is presented in the novel as ideal. Even its tragic elements are not anomalous, since they are in accord with Frye's observation of "how frequently a comic dramatist tries to bring his action as close to a catastrophic overthrow of the hero as he can get it, and then reverses the action as quickly as possible" (*Anatomy* 178).

However, if we are to apply these prescriptions to *The Color Purple,* we must first perceive it as a "high comedy," since it is only this mode which theoretically subscribes to the criteria discussed earlier. But "high comedy" invariably includes, and, in fact, culminates in the comedy of manners, and to characterize *The Color Purple* as such appears to be problematic, especially in light of M. H. Abrams's explanation that this mode

> deals with the relations and intrigues of men and women living in a polished and sophisticated society, relying for comic effect in great part on the wit and sparkle of the dialogue—often in the form of *repartee,* a witty conversational give-and-take which constitutes a kind of verbal fencing match—and to a lesser degree, on the ridiculous violations of social conventions and decorum by stupid characters such as would-be wits, jealous husbands, and foppish dandies.
>
> (26)

The male and female characters of *The Color Purple* do not live in a polished and sophisticated society, nor do they engage in what is traditionally considered sparkling and witty repartee. And the violations of social norms and decorum that occur are not perpetrated by foolish, stupid, or dandified characters but by female characters with whom we are expected to sympathize. However, the conventions of the comedy of manners are so clearly inverted in *The Color Purple* that we cannot but suspect it to be deliberate. Therefore, I would suggest that *The Color Purple* is a parodic inversion of the comedy of manners,[1] and so undercuts the form at the same time that it ironically adheres to its intentions—to improve and to open the closed social order it dramatizes.

Linda Hutcheon defines parody as "imitation with critical difference" (36). She also notes that parody too is potentially "revolutionary":

> The presupposition of both a law and its transgression bifurcates the impulses of parody: it can be normative and conservative, or it can be provocative and revolutionary. . . . [P]arody can, like the carnival, also challenge norms in order to renovate, to renew.
>
> (76)

In its parodic inversion of the comedy of manners, Walker's novel recalls the works of Jane Austen, who, as Sypher observes, "devastates our compromises and complacencies—especially male complacency" and "placidly undermines the bastions of middle-class propriety" (247). Austen too, of course, frequently parodies various literary modes, particularly "the popular romance fiction of her day" (Hutcheon 44), and through it "satirizes the traditional view of woman's role as the lover of men" (Hutcheon 44). But while she may call into question the social mores of her time, Austen presents, in the conclusions of her novels, a society in which women are integrated into the traditional order. Walker, on the other hand, recalls Austen's work with a "critical difference," since in her novel no compromises are brooked. She goes further than her predecessor and rejects the society which imposes the limitations and at the same time points out the exclusivity of literature, since traditionally few novels that have achieved significant "recognition" have dealt with anything other than a white social order or anything other than a patriarchal society. (To this end she also reworks to some extent Samuel Richardson's *Pamela* and the traditional endings of sexist fairy tales, specifically "The Frog Prince.")

By transposing the comedy of manners, Walker foregrounds the limitations she finds in it and so undercuts those social norms which it has incorporated and to which it ultimately contributes. Indeed, J. A. Cuddon suggests that the comedy of manners has "for its main subjects and themes the behaviour and deportment of men and women living under specific social codes" (139). This definition takes on new significance in relation to a novel like *The Color Purple* because it subverts the form by parodically inverting its conventional notions of expected social codes.

Walker writes from the point of view of an outsider who is rebuffed by a closed social order; yet in her novel she transcends these social restrictions and envisions a world in which they cease to exist. *The Color Purple* is an intellectual comedy in that it is a comedy of ideas: it dramatizes possibilities and completes itself in a vision of an ideal world[2]—a world which is matriarchal, a parody of the boy-gets-girl endings of most comedies and fairy tales. This world is also an ideal one which is in direct opposition to the rigidly closed society that is in evidence in the opening pages of *The Color Purple.* However, the tragic elements so apparent here are necessary to Walker's idea, since she must work through the limitations of the closed order to give credence to the utopian possibilities of her open, womanist world.

Walker dramatizes the crippling strictures of this old order through her heroine, who is a social pariah. Celie is not just a woman, she is a black woman; but she is not just a black woman, she is—as she later learns—a lesbian, and is, therefore, thrice removed from the white male heterosexual norm. By writing from the point of view of this seemingly socially aberrant individual,

Walker exposes the limitations that society imposes on anything outside the norm and the narrow, restrictive lifestyle that it upholds. The society in evidence at the beginning of the novel is a totally closed society, which would not open to include Celie even if she wished it, since she cannot change the colour of her skin or her sex. Yet this social outcast is shown to be far wiser than the white patriarchy which excludes her. She is able to manifest at the conclusion of the work a society that "opens in many directions" (Sypher 249). And in doing so, she points up the limitations of life lived under the patriarchal norm by transcending them.

But before the ideal situation is reached, virtually every bastion of society is assaulted and little is left unscathed. Walker exposes the limitations in most social values and institutions and attacks the autonomy of the white male heterosexual norm which has generated them. It is difficult to pinpoint the prescriptions of this norm, primarily because they operate as the basis of our society and so seem self-evident to us. As Feibleman writes:

> It is a notorious historical observation that customs and institutions rarely enjoy more than a comparatively brief life; and yet while they are the accepted fashion they come to be regarded as brute givens, as irreducible facts, which may be depended upon with perfect security.
>
> (81)

However, by extrapolating from the text, we can reconstruct those social mores that Walker questions.

The prescriptions are formulated in the nuclear family, which perpetuates the notion of male and female roles. The male role dictates that man perform "manly" work, such as field work and carpentry (***Purple*** 22, 27), and that he act as the head of his household and the maker of its laws (36, 37). The female role demands that woman be domestic; she must clean her house, cook, tend to the children (20), and obey her husband (37). It is not thought proper for men and women to trade these positions, and, if they do, they are subject to criticism and mockery (36). Marriage, which begins on this restrictive basis, merely perpetuates the stereotyped roles that its members are expected to play and again does not allow for deviation from them. Both the family and marriage are shown to operate on the assumption of feminine inferiority. Religion, in support of this order, preaches platitudes and casts narrow moral judgements upon those who are different or who refuse to conform to the conventions of family life (46). The laws effected by the patriarchy in the name of "equality" and "justice for all" merely function as a support to the existing order by keeping those outside that order "in their place" through the use of force (90, 91). While the theory behind the institution of the patriarchal order may have been altruistic and idealistic, Walker's novel shows how far from the ideal it has strayed in its practice. She therefore dramatizes these social values and institutions as they function in actuality and then redramatizes them in terms of the possible and the desirable.

The novel begins by portraying the family as a social unit which subjects girl children to a life of rape and terror: "First he put his thing up against my hip and sort of wiggle it around. Then he grab hold my titties. Then he push his thing inside my pussy. When that hurt, I cry. He start to choke me, saying You better shut up and git used to it" (1-2). The first three letters suggest that Celie's "father" kills her mother through abuse, at which point he ominously begins to eye her favourite sister, Nettie. Clearly, "a girl child ain't safe in a family of men" (42) and no woman in the household is inviolable. Nor is marriage a safe haven for Celie; it merely becomes an extension of her unhappy home life. Ironically, she is offered to Mr. ——— like a slave on an auction block, and Mr. ——— is more interested in her dowry than in her: "Mr. ——— say, That cow still coming? He say, Her cow" (12). In turn, Celie's wedding day is equally desolate, "I spend my wedding day running from the oldest boy. He twelve" (13). Marital sex is brutal and animalistic, and Celie later equates it with defecation, since it is hardly an act based on mutual fulfilment: "He git up on you, heist your nightgown round your waist, plunge in. Most times I pretend I ain't there. He never know the difference. Never ast me how I feel, nothing. Just do his business, get off, go to sleep" (81).

Celie's life is more a death-in-life, a life without hope, joy, or any indication of improvement. Nettie comments on this before she leaves: "I sure hate to leave you here with these rotten children, she say. Not to mention with Mr. ———. It's like seeing you buried, she say. It's worse than that, I think. If I was buried, I wouldn't have to work" (18). But Celie does not despair, and her faith sustains her: "I just say, Never mine, never mine, long as I can spell G-o-d I got somebody along" (18).

While Celie may find a vent for her anguish in writing to God, religion itself is undercut when Shug Avery comes to town. Shug, who refuses to accept the limitations that society imposes on a woman's life, becomes the target for attack:

> Even the preacher got his mouth on Shug Avery, now she down. He take her condition for his text. . . . He talk about a strumpet in short skirts, smoking cigarettes, drinking gin. Singing for money and taking other women mens. Talk bout slut, hussy, heifer and streetcleaner.
>
> (46)

Not surprisingly, however, Celie does not hold with the virtues preached from the pulpit and repudiates conventional social behaviour as prescribed by Mr.

———'s father. Independently, she rejects the "virtues" which society applauds, and takes the ill Shug in to nurse. Astutely noticing his refusal to acknowledge her as a person, Celie discounts Mr. ———'s father's words: "Celie, he say, you have my sympathy. Not many women let they husband whore lay up in they house. But he not saying to me, he saying it to Mr. ———" (57). Celie chooses instead to champion Shug and responds: "Next time he come I put a little Shug Avery pee in his glass. See how he like that" (57).

Celie identifies with the rebellious Shug from the seventh page of the novel, when she finds her picture and begins to idolize the blues singer. Shug provides an ideal for Celie, since, unlike the other women in Celie's life, she is not broken through years of abuse. Pretty and different, she offers an alternative lifestyle:

> Shug Avery was a woman. The most beautiful woman I ever saw. . . . I see her there in furs. Her face rouge. Her hair like somethin tail. She grinning with her foot up on somebody motocar. Her eyes serious tho. Sad some. . . . An now when I dream, I dream of Shug Avery. She be dress to kill, whirling and laughing.
>
> (7)

Celie is also attracted to her stepdaughter-in-law, Sofia, an Amazon who refuses to be dominated by her husband, Harpo. But an independent woman has a more difficult time than one who meekly accepts her meagre lot in life. Ironically, Harpo wants Sofia to act like the submissive Celie: "I want her to do what I say, like you do for Pa. . . . But not Sofia. She do what she want, don't pay me no mind at all. I try to beat her, she black my eyes. Oh, boo-hoo, he cry" (66). Even though he loves Sofia, Harpo's marriage is troubled because society has taught him that this is not the way a woman should behave. Celie tries to reason with him, but to no avail; social conventions are too deeply ingrained in his mind:

> Sofia *love* you. You *love* Sofia. . . . Mr. ——— marry me to take care of his children. I marry him cause my daddy made me. I don't love Mr. ——— and he don't love me. But you his wife, he say, just like Sofia mine. The wife spose to mind.
>
> (66)

Sofia becomes a victim of social injustice when she refuses to respect authority in the person of the white mayor's wife, who wants Sofia to work as her maid. When Sofia responds with a "hell no" (90), a brawl ensues and the police are called. The dangers of fighting back are clear since Sofia's punishment is hardly "just" or merited by her crime:

> When I see Sofia I don't know why she still alive. They crack her skull, they crack her ribs. They tear her nose loose on one side. They blind her in one eye. She swole from head to foot. Her tongue the size of my arm, it stick out tween her teef like a piece of rubber. She can't talk. And she just about the color of eggplant.
>
> (92)

Society's justice is again satirized when the astute women realize that the only way to get Sofia released from the prison that is killing her is to plead that "justice ought to be done" (99) and to assert that Sofia will only be sufficiently punished when she becomes "some white lady maid" (99). After raping Squeak, the sheriff promptly takes action to ensure that Sofia will be "properly punished," and she is released into the mayor's custody. We realize how correct the women's assessment of society's "compassion" is when the mayor's (white) wife wishes to be "kind" to her maid and drives her to visit the family she has not seen in five years, only to make her leave in fifteen minutes (110-11). She later berates Sofia for her ingratitude.

The novel is often criticized for its melodramatic disposition, but I would suggest that this is a result of Walker's parodic inversion of Samuel Richardson's *Pamela*. Certainly the epistolary style of **The Color Purple** reminds us of Richardson's work, which, itself, is often melodramatic.[3] **The Color Purple** deliberately recalls *Pamela,* but ironically transposes it, for Pamela becomes reconciled to the world of men, and if she is accorded any stature within it, that stature is bestowed when Mr. B. learns to appreciate her, makes her his wife, and thus allows her entry into his world. Like Pamela, Celie too suffers at the hands of men, with the "critical difference" that she is never incorporated into their society. Rather, she overturns this order and instigates a new one, into which *she* allows Mr. ——— to enter when he rehabilitates himself.

Despite the almost overwhelming oppressiveness of Celie's life, she endures and finally begins to accept herself: "I'm pore, I'm black, I may be ugly and can't cook, a voice say to everything listening. But I'm here" (214). Yet, this self-acceptance is dearly bought, and Celie suffers extreme anguish when she learns that Mr. ——— has been hiding the letters which her sister, Nettie, has written. She is so angry that she nearly kills her husband and is saved only by Shug's replacing the destructive razor in her hand with a constructive needle—a symbolic act. However, Nettie's letters provide a further source of anguish for Celie, when, through them, she learns of her true parentage. At this point, her anger turns to despair, and she rejects God:

> Yeah, I say, and he give me a lynched daddy, a crazy mama, a lowdown dog of a step pa and a sister I probably won't ever see again. Anyhow, I say, the God I been praying and writing to is a man. And act just like all the other mens I know. Trifling, forgitful and lowdown.
>
> (199)

But a woman—Shug—teaches Celie to love and to trust again, and when she offers to take Celie to Memphis, Celie's world is rejuvenated. In the pivotal dinner scene, when Celie and Squeak announce that they have decided to forge new identities by leaving their husbands, they refuse to conform to the old patriarchal order. Celie stabs Mr. ——— when he tries to slap her (271) and Squeak demands that she be called by her proper name: "Listen Squeak, say Harpo. You can't go to Memphis. That's all there is to it. Mary Agnes, say Squeak. Squeak, Mary Agnes, what difference do it make? It makes a lot, say Squeak. When I was Mary Agnes I could sing in public" (210).⁴ The final pages of the novel are spent in dramatizing the positive aspects of society, by incorporating and revitalizing the social values and institutions in light of the new order.

The family itself becomes a positive force when Sofia changes it into an entity that succours and helps its members. She extends the nuclear family when she welcomes Squeak's children into her home and heals the breach that had existed between the two women, both rivals for Harpo's affections: "Go on sing, say Sofia, I'll look after this one till you come back" (211). Family is, therefore, no longer based on blood but on mutual love and respect. Shug and Celie form a new family unit when Celie learns the truth of her parentage, and Shug's tenderness helps her to overcome her despair: "Shug say, Us each other's peoples now, and kiss me" (189). Further, Shug's relationship with Celie takes on the sanctity that Celie's marriage with Mr. ——— lacked and offers a positive view of "non-marriage" as a union which proffers acceptance and concern: "Besides, she say. You not my maid. I didn't bring you to Memphis to be that. I brought you here to love you and help you get on your feet" (218).

Even religion is revitalized when it extends to encompass the segregated, and God loses "Its" colour and gender: "God ain't a he or a she, but a It. . . . It ain't a picture show. It ain't something you can look at apart from anything else, including yourself" (202). When religion loses the limitations imposed on it by a white, male hierarchy, faith "opens in many directions" (Sypher 249), and Celie's perception of God becomes all inclusive and whole. She comes to accept Shug's belief in a God who is "everything" (202) and begins to understand "It" need not be restricted to a church:

> God love everything you love—and a mess of stuff you don't. But more than anything else, God love admiration.
>
> You say God vain? I ast.
>
> Naw, she say. Not vain, just wanting to share a good thing. I think it pisses God off if you walk by the color purple in a field somewhere and don't notice it.
>
> (203)

Society itself can become more enlightened when its members are able to repudiate the dictates of societal norms. Indeed, there is an attempt on the part of the daughters to overcome the sins of the fathers when Eleanor Jane tries to make reparation for her parents' treatment of Sofia by working for her: "Do her peoples know? I ast. They know, say Sofia. They carrying on just like you know they would. Whoever heard of a white woman working for niggers, they rave. She tell them, Whoever heard of somebody like Sofia working for trash" (288). The new society is not a closed order; it is open to all; even Mr. ——— can be included when he realizes the errors of his ways, rejects his old, narrow outlook, and learns the meaning of love:

> . . . he say something that really surprise me cause it so thoughtful and common sense. When it come to what folks do together with they bodies, he say, anybody's guess is as good as mine. But when you talk bout love I don't have to guess. I have love and I have been love. And I thank God he let me gain understanding enough to know love can't be halted just cause some peoples moan and groan. It don't surprise me you love Shug Avery, he say, I have love Shug Avery all my life.
>
> (277)

The novel's major narrative symbol is associated with the act of sewing: Celie literally sews her life back together when she begins to design pants, and Mr. ———'s salvation is symbolized when he begins to make shirts to match them. Indeed, Mr. ——— asks Celie to marry him again, "this time in the spirit as well as in the flesh" (290), but she refuses him because, as she states, "I still don't like frogs" (290). Celie's reference to frogs recalls the fairy tale, "The Frog Prince," which the novel parodically inverts. In this story, Mr. ——— may kiss the "princess," but he undergoes no miraculous transformation into a handsome prince; he remains a "frog." Celie, on the other hand, is still able to "live happily ever after" without him, which, as mentioned earlier, undercuts the traditional boy-gets-girl endings of most fairy tales and comedies. However, Celie does forgive Mr. ——— when she allows him to join in her creative process, and her forgiveness constitutes the basis for the new society, for men and even white women like Eleanor Jane, although viewed sceptically, are allowed a chance to atone.

Since the novel attacks those bastions of society—family, religion, and marriage—but also offers a rejuvenation of them in its final pages, it evidently suggests that society itself is not what Walker questions and rejects but rather the limitations that are imposed upon it and make it closed and restrictive. The womanist utopia of the conclusion signifies a renewal of the initial social order because it is more accessible and more humane. Walker's utopia is "humanist" as well as womanist in the sense that it offers a revivification of humanity as a whole. This concept is epitomized in Celie's sewing.[5] Her first pair of pants are made out of army fabric—hard, stiff to the touch—which she later rejects in favour of soft, pliable material: "Shug finger the pieces of cloth I got hanging on everything. It all soft, flowing, rich and catch the light. This a far cry from the stiff army shit us started with, she say" (219). The clothes that Celie designs out of the new fabric enhance the people who wear them; she creates pants that are comfortable and designed with their wearer in mind:

> these pants are soft, hardly wrinkle at all, and the little figures in the cloth always look perky and bright. And they full round the ankle so if she want to sing in 'em and wear 'em sort of like a long dress, she can.
>
> (219)

Mr. ———'s shirts are also devised to be extensions of their wearer; they support life rather than stifle it: "Got to have pockets, he say. Got to have loose sleeves. And definitely you not spose to wear it with no tie. Folks wearing ties look like they being lynch" (290).

The clothes that Celie and Mr. ——— design celebrate rather than restrict people; they become a symbol of the humanist/womanist utopia manifested at the end of the novel. Indeed, this utopia becomes an Edenic paradise, as Thadious M. Davis suggests, for the arrival of Celie's son, *Adam* Omatangu, and the rest of her family from Africa

> signals the continuity of generations, the return (ironically perhaps) to the 'old, unalterable roots.' Their return is cause for a larger hope for the race, and for celebration within the family and community, because they have survived 'whole,' literally since they miraculously survive a shipwreck and symbolically since they have acquired definite life-affirming attitudes.
>
> (52)

This is precisely the note on which the novel ends, since the new order, the order that opens to the once segregated, is celebratory: "White people busy celebrating they independence from England July 4th, say Harpo, so most black folks don't have to work. Us can spend the day celebrating each other" (294). To paraphrase Martin, in Walker's comedy, the female/black incongruous is seen to be more congruous than the white patriarchy, which made them incongruous in the first place by denying them entry into its closed society.

Therefore, while it may seem "incongruous" to classify *The Color Purple* as a comedy, it cannot truly be called anything else, for it seeks to improve society by eliminating the limitations prescribed by the societal norms. Meredith stresses that where "the veil is over women's faces, you cannot have society, without which the senses are barbarous and the Comic Spirit is driven to the gutters to slake its thirst" (31). In *The Color Purple*, the "veil," of which Meredith speaks, is lifted, the barriers between the sexes are razed, and a new world is erected on the ruins, in which the sexes meet on an equal footing and celebrate each other, life, and humankind.

Notes

1. I am indebted to Linda Hutcheon for showing me the significance of this aspect of the novel.

2. Romance too offers a utopia in its conclusion. However, romance offers idealized characters and incorporates other-worldly elements (Frye, *Anatomy* 186-95). To suggest that *The Color Purple* belongs to this genre, I think, would be to stretch a point. However, Frye does suggest that comedy will often overlap with romance in its conclusion (177) which seems to me to be the case here.

3. The similarity of the two male protagonists' names (Mr. ——— and Mr. B.) further supports the idea that the novel plays on Richardson's text.

4. Names are very important in this novel. Walker dramatizes the idea that when we name we possess, and as a result, the women reject the names accorded them by the patriarchy. On the other hand, Mr. ——— is also transformed into Albert when he sees the "errors of his ways" and convinces Celie of his sincere repentance. He, therefore, must be renamed to signify his renewal and his incorporation into the new order. It is also interesting to note that he loses the title—Mr.—which is used, to some extent, to subjugate Celie.

5. It is also symbolized in Celie's dialectal language which is proffered as natural and supportive of life. When she is given a chance to "improve" her speech, she says, "only a fool would want you to talk in a way that feel peculiar to your mind" (223).

Works Cited

Abrams, M. H. *A Glossary of Literary Terms*. 4th ed. New York: Holt, 1981.

Bergson, Henri. "Laughter." *Comedy*. Ed. Wylie Sypher. New York: Doubleday, 1956.

Cuddon, J. A. *A Dictionary of Literary Terms*. Harmondsworth: Penguin, 1982.

Davis, Thadious M. "Alice Walker's Celebration of Self in Southern Generations." *The Southern Quarterly: A Journal of the Arts in the South*. 21.4 (1983): 39-53.

Feibleman, James K. "The Meaning of Comedy." *Aesthetics*. Toronto: Collins, 1949.

Frye, Northrop. *Anatomy of Criticism: Four Essays.* Princeton: Princeton UP, 1973.

———. "The Argument of Comedy." *Theories of Comedy.* Ed. Paul Lauter. New York: Doubleday, 1964.

Hutcheon, Linda. *A Theory of Parody: The Teachings of Twentieth Century Art Forms.* New York: Methuen, 1985.

Martin, Robert Bernard. "Notes toward a Comic Fiction." *The Theory of the Novel.* Ed. John Halperin. New York: Oxford UP, 1974.

Meredith, George. "An Essay on Comedy." *Comedy.* Ed. Wylie Sypher. New York: Doubleday, 1956.

Sypher, Wylie. "The Meanings of Comedy." *Comedy.* Ed. Wylie Sypher. New York: Doubleday, 1956.

Walker, Alice. *In Search of Our Mothers' Gardens.* New York: Harcourt, 1983.

———. *The Color Purple.* New York: Pocket Books, 1982.

Charles L. Proudfit (essay date spring 1991)

SOURCE: Proudfit, Charles L. "Celie's Search for Identity: A Psychoanalytic Developmental Reading of Alice Walker's *The Color Purple.*" *Contemporary Literature* 32, no. 1 (spring 1991): 12-37.

[*In the following essay, Proudfit refutes the critical opinion that Celie's emotional development and actions in* The Color Purple *are unlikely literary contrivances, and uses psychoanalytic theory to argue that Celie's personal growth is realistically constructed, given her horrific childhood and adolescence.*]

> It is my belief and my faith that whenever you are trying to convey a sense of a common reality to people, they will want to read and hear about it.
>
> —Alice Walker, **"The Eighties and Me"**

Since the publication of Alice Walker's ***The Color Purple,*** both novel and author continue to elicit a wide range of praise and censure from an increasing number of black and white, female and male reviewers, literary critics, and general readers. At one extreme are those who find the work "an American novel of permanent importance" (Prescott 67); who place the author "in the company of Faulkner" (Smith 183); and who praise Walker for her creation of the unique voice of her protagonist, Celie, a "poor, ugly, uneducated [black girl] . . . [from] rural Georgia," for "the universality of the themes of redemptive love, strength in adversity, independence, and self-assertion through the values of community," and for "creating a unique set of people who speak to the *human* condition" (McFadden 139-43). At the other extreme are those who feel that the novel should be "ignored" rather than "canonized" (Harris, "On *The Color Purple*" 155); who place Walker "closer to Harriet Beecher Stowe than to [Zora Neale] Hurston" (Pinckney 18); and who censure Walker for the creation of an unrealistic plot (Towers 36), for the "depiction of violent black men who physically and psychologically abuse their wives and children . . . [and for the] depiction of lesbianism" (Royster 347), and for peopling her novel with characters who "themselves do not seem to respond to [some form of] internal logic" (Harris, "Victimization" 9). Walker herself relates that her mother finds the book's language "offensive" and humorously describes a parent's attempt to have the novel banned in a California public school system (**"Coming in from the Cold"** 55-58). Between these extreme critical positions, one finds a growing body of measured literary criticism that addresses both the novel's formal qualities and thematic concerns[1] and that validates the novel's having been awarded in 1983 both the American Book Award for Fiction and the Pulitzer Prize.

Although from the beginning critics have recognized the importance of the theme of "female bonding" in Celie's search for and development of a mature female identity,[2] no one, to my knowledge, has viewed either this theme or the protagonist's character development from the perspective of contemporary psychoanalytic developmental psychology. Such a psychoanalytic developmental reading will help illuminate Walker's literary portrayal of the importance of the mother for the female infant, child, and adult as she struggles to separate, to individuate, to develop her own identity, and to make a final choice of love object; will suggest the need to reconsider certain negative criticisms of the novel, such as unequal narrative voices, unrealistic character development, faulty plot, unbelievable events, and a lesbian relationship "that represents the height of silly romanticism" (Harris, "On *The Color Purple*" 157); and will help account for the contrasting literary portraits of Celie and Nettie.

This reading is based upon a mother-daughter bond that, according to several current psychoanalytic theorists on female development, has its origins in deep, primitive ties to the mother of infancy and is a bond that must be worked through *again and again during a woman's lifetime.*[3] Walker's descriptions of Celie's bonding, first with the biological mother of infancy and later with suitable mother surrogates, is psychologically realistic and ranges from the ministrations of Celie's younger sister Nettie, to Kate and Sofia, and to Shug's facilitating Celie's sensual awakening to adult female sexuality and a healthy emotional life. This "female bonding," which occurs over an extended period of time, enables Celie—a depressed survivor-victim of parent loss, emotional and physical neglect, rape, incest, trauma, and spousal abuse—to resume her arrested development and continue developmental processes that were thwarted in infancy and early adolescence. These processes are described with clinical accuracy; and, as they are revisited and reworked in Celie's interactions with appropriate mother surrogates, Celie is enabled to get in touch with her feelings, work through old traumas, and achieve an emotional maturity and a firm sense of identity that is psychologically convincing.

Since some readers may not be familiar with psychoanalytic developmental psychology, often referred to as object relations theory, I should first like to make several observations about this approach to the study of child development and then acquaint the reader with several concepts and theories of the English analyst and pediatrician D. W. Winnicott that inform my developmental reading of the text.[4] Stated simply, psychoanalytic developmental psychology is the study of the infant's and the child's development that focuses upon the unconscious, conscious, and maturational processes that *occur within the mother-infant/child matrix*. The infant's and child's object relations are both internal (intrapsychic) and external (the child experiences itself as separate from other objects [like mother or father] "objectively perceived" [Winnicott, *Maturational Processes* 57]). Most object relations theorists postulate that at birth the human infant is psychologically merged with its mother.[5] Winnicott asserts that "*There is no such thing as a baby*"; rather, "one sees a 'nursing couple'" (*Through Paediatrics* 99). Margaret Mahler observes that "from the beginning the child molds and unfolds in the matrix of the mother-infant dual unit" (5). Although Mahler, Winnicott, and other object relations theorists differ in their understanding of the developmental process that, if successfully "completed," allows for the emergence of a healthy, creative self, they do agree that this process occurs within the mother-infant/child matrix (Greenberg and Mitchell). Furthermore, Winnicott, Mahler, and others agree with Daniel Stern: "Development is not a succession of events left behind in history. It is a continuing process, constantly updated" (260).[6] Walker's fictional treatment of Celie's continuing development into middle age appears to be in agreement with this psychoanalytic developmental view.

Although a psychoanalytic literary critic might draw upon several schools of object relations in offering a developmental reading of Walker's ***The Color Purple***, I believe that Winnicott's concepts and theories offer the most helpful insights into the psychological dynamics that underlie Walker's literary portrayal of the significance of "female bonding" for the resumption of Celie's arrested developmental processes in the early part of the novel. Furthermore, Winnicott's view of the origin of what he calls the "True Self" and the "False Self" not only illuminates the contrasting literary portraits of Celie and her younger sister Nettie but also enables the reader to observe how Walker creatively uses diction, sentence structure, tone, and style in the sisters' letters to each other in order to create "authentic" and "inauthentic" voices. Finally, Winnicott's assertion that the developmental issues of infancy "are never fully established, and continue to be strengthened by the growth that continues in later childhood, and indeed in adult life, even in old age" (*Maturational Processes* 74) lends credence to Celie's lengthy developmental process—a process that has been severely criticized (Harris, "Victimization" 16). Since Walker's fictive description of Celie's developmental history includes a brief sketch of the first several years of her life (***Color Purple*** 160-61), I will begin with Winnicott's concept of "primary maternal preoccupation" (*Maturational Processes* 85).

Winnicott observes that many expectant mothers experience a special psychological state during the latter part of their pregnancies and for several weeks after childbirth, in which they turn their attention inward and focus on the needs of the unborn and newly born. He calls this organized state "primary maternal preoccupation" and believes that the most successful mothers experience it. He believes that the mother and her newborn should be viewed as "a unit" (*Maturational Processes* 39) and asserts that the "good-enough mother" (57, 145; *Playing* 10),[7] who is empathetically attuned to her infant's needs, provides a "holding environment" (*Maturational Processes* 44-50, 86), in which the infant moves "from being merged with the mother to being separate from her, or to relating to her as separate and 'not-me'" (45). During this time the "good-enough mother" serves both as an auxiliary ego for the immature ego of the infant (44, 56-63) and as a "mirror" in which the infant sees itself reflected: "[When] the mother is looking at the baby . . . *what she looks like is related to what she sees there*" (*Playing* 112). According to Winnicott, the "good-enough mother" provides the infant over time with enough such positive reflections of self that the infant begins to develop a "True Self" (118). If, however, a "mother [who is not good enough] reflects her own mood or, worse still, the rigidity of her own defenses" (112), then the infant perceives rather than apperceives (113), and we have the beginning of a compliant "False Self" (*Maturational Processes* 145). The origins of the "True Self" and the "False Self" begin *before* the infant has "separated off the 'not me' from the 'me'" (158), that is, roughly prior to the sixth month.

Although Winnicott eschews a strict stage theory of infant development, he does note that the infant passes through several phases on its journey toward the development of a self. In the first phase of *absolute dependence,* the mother provides a facilitating environment (womb/first few weeks of life) for the totally helpless infant (*Maturational Processes* 87-88). In the next phase of *relative dependence,* the infant comes to separate the "not me" from the "me"; and from about six months to twenty-four months the infant becomes *"aware of dependence,"* comes to *"know in his mind* that mother is necessary," and "gradually the need for the actual mother (in health) becomes fierce and truly terrible" (88). By two years of age, Winnicott believes that the infant has begun to develop inner capacities that will enable him or her to deal more effectively with loss (88). Prior to three years of age, however, loss of the mother or mothering agent can have profound adverse psychological effects upon a child. Finally, Winnicott asserts that throughout these phases of infant development "the whole procedure of infant-care has as its main characteristic a steady presentation of the world to the infant. . . . It can only be done by continuous management by a human being who is consistently herself. . . . This of course applies to father too" (87-88). These developmental concepts and theories, especially the "good-enough mother," "the holding environment," the "mirror role of the mother," and the origin of the "True Self" and the "False Self," underlie Walker's dramatic theme of "female bonding" and help illuminate the author's literary portrayal of Celie's lengthy search for and achievement of a mature female identity and healthy object relations.

Walker, like Charlotte Brontë in *Jane Eyre* (one of Walker's favorite novels in childhood [Steinem 92]) begins **The Color Purple** *in medias res*: Celie, like Jane, is poised on the edge of adolescence after a childhood of loss, deprivation, and abuse. With Celie's first anguished letter to God, Walker enables the reader to enter into the private thoughts and emotional state of her traumatized, guilt- and shame-ridden, and depressed fourteen-year-old protagonist, who has been repeatedly raped and impregnated by the man (Alphonso) whom she believes to be her biological father: "Dear God, I am fourteen years old. I have always been a good girl. Maybe you can give me a sign letting me know what is happening to me" (11). Celie draws a line through "I am" and writes "I have always been a good girl," because the child victim of rape and incest often blames herself for her trauma; or, worse still, believes that this bad thing has happened to her because *she* is bad and therefore deserves it. Celie writes to God because she is ashamed of what is happening to her (122) and because of the threat from Alphonso that immediately precedes Celie's first letter: "*You better not never tell nobody but God. It'd kill your mammy*" (11). Threats and forced secrecy are usual parts of incest (Herman 88; Russell 132-33). The style of this letter, and of those that immediately follow, is characterized by short, choppy sentences, halting rhythms, repetitive grammatical structures of subject, verb, object, concrete physical descriptions in an ongoing present, and matter-of-fact tone. It is a style that mirrors Celie's traumatized cognitive processes and depressed emotional state. We learn that Celie's depression is partly caused by her repressed rage when later in the novel Sofia asks her what she does when she gets mad: "I think. I can't even remember the last time I felt mad, I say. I used to git mad at my mammy cause she put a lot of work on me. Then I see how sick she is. Couldn't stay mad at her. Couldn't be mad at my daddy cause he my daddy. Bible say, Honor father and mother no matter what. Then after while every time I got mad, or start to feel mad, I got sick. Felt like throwing up. Terrible feeling. Then I start to feel nothing at all" (47). Even the color purple, a mixture of the primary colors red (rage) and blue (depression), suggests Celie's mood in the initial letters. The color is also symbolic of the bruises resulting from the beatings inflicted upon Celie first by Alphonso (whom she later learns is her stepfather) and then her husband Albert.

In Celie's second letter, written about a year later, Celie's mother has died, screaming and cursing her pregnant daughter. After the birth of Celie's second child, Alphonso gives her infant son away, as he had her infant daughter, though Celie believes that he has killed them. She stops menstruating after the second birth. During the next five years, Celie lives at home with Alphonso, his new young wife, and a growing number of their children; she serves as a maid, and as protector of her younger sister Nettie against Alphonso's sexual advances. At twenty, Celie is married off to Albert, a widower with children, who also abuses her. Nettie joins them but is soon told by Albert to leave.

It is not until sometime later, when Albert brings home his old flame Shug Avery, that Celie is enabled, with Shug's help, to find Nettie's letters to her. These letters, written after Nettie goes to live with the missionaries Corrine and Samuel but hidden by Albert, reveal to Celie the truth of her origin. She discovers that Alphonso is not her biological father and that she lived for the first two years of her life as the only child in a loving family. The father adored his pregnant wife and, we would expect, his daughter Celie. But one night, when she was barely two years old, her successful father's store and blacksmith shop were burned and destroyed; he and his two brothers were dragged from their homes and hanged by jealous white merchants; and, when his mutilated and burned body was brought home to his wife by neighbors, she gave birth to Nettie and suffered an emotional breakdown:

> Although the widow's body recovered, her mind was never the same. She continued to fix her husband's plate at mealtimes just as she'd always done and was always full of talk about the plans she and her husband had made. The neighbors, though not always intending to, shunned her more and more, partly because the plans she talked about were grander than anything they could even conceive of for colored people, and partly

because her attachment to the past was so pitiful. She was a good-looking woman, though, and still owned land, but there was no one to work it for her, and she didn't know how herself; besides she kept waiting for her husband to finish the meal she'd cooked for him and go to the fields himself. Soon there was nothing to eat that the neighbors did not bring, and she and her small children grubbed around in the yard as best they could.

While the second child was still a baby, a stranger appeared in the community, and lavished all his attention on the widow and her children; in a short while, they were married. Almost at once she was pregnant a third time, though her mental health was no better. Every year thereafter, she was pregnant, every year she became weaker and more mentally unstable, until, many years after she married the stranger, she died.

Two years before she died she had a baby girl that she was too sick to keep. Then a baby boy [in fact Celie's kidnapped babies (12-13)]. These children were named Olivia and Adam.

(161)

Thus, in a single evening, the two-year-old Celie experiences several catastrophic losses: (1) the death of a loving father; (2) the emotional loss of a loving mother (at first through a psychotic episode and later through sickness and depression); (3) the loss of a safe and nurturing family environment; and (4) the loss of her place as an only child. During the next several months, Celie and her newborn baby sister Nettie experience hunger, neglect, and other deprivations. When Alphonso appears on the scene within the year and "lavished all his attention on the widow and her children," Celie's and Nettie's physical needs were probably met, but their mentally unstable, ill, and often pregnant mother would not have been able to provide either of her daughters with the "good-enough mothering" that they needed. Given the description of Alphonso in Celie's early letters, he would not have been temperamentally fit to serve as a mother substitute. We can reasonably postulate that Celie became mother surrogate to Nettie, as well as to her ill and half-crazed mother's unwanted babies.[8] When Celie's mother goes "to visit her sister doctor over Macon" (11), Alphonso rapes Celie and begins to use her as a sexual replacement for his exhausted wife—a not uncommon situation in actual cases of father-daughter incest (Herman 47-49).

This dramatic literary portrait of Celie as a traumatized and depressed survivor-victim of parent loss, physical and emotional neglect, rape, incest, and spousal abuse, which one black female critic finds unbelievable (Harris, "On *The Color Purple*" 155-56), is in fact a clinically accurate description of what Leonard Shengold calls "soul murder":

> Soul, or psychic, murder involves trauma imposed from the world outside the mind that is so overwhelming that the mental apparatus is flooded with feeling. The same overstimulated state can result as a reaction to great deprivation. The terrifying too-muchness requires massive and mind-distorting defensive operations for the child to continue to think and feel and live. The child's sense of identity (that is, the emotional maintenance of the mental images of his or her self) is threatened. Our identity depends initially on good parental care and good parental caring—on the transmitted feeling that it is good that we are there. . . . What happens to the child subjected to soul murder is so terrible, so overwhelming, and usually so recurrent that the child must not feel it and cannot register it, and resorts to a massive isolation of feeling, which is maintained by brainwashing (a mixture of confusion, denial, and identifying with the aggressor). A hypnotic living deadness, a state of existing "as if" one were there, is often the result of chronic early overstimulation or deprivation. As [Sandor] Ferenczi (1933) put it, "The [abused] child changes into a mechanical obedient automaton." . . . But the automaton has murder within.
>
> (24-25)

As a survivor of deprivation in childhood and of overstimulation in adolescence and young adulthood, Celie exhibits several characteristics of those who have experienced "soul murder." When her husband Albert, whom she addresses as "Mr. ———" until the very end of the novel, orders Celie to get his belt and then beats her, she isolates her feelings: "It all I can do not to cry. I make myself wood. I say to myself, Celie, you a tree" (30). Unable to deal with her feelings of jealousy and rage (46), Celie identifies with her male aggressors: when Harpo asks her how to make his wife Sofia mind, Celie writes, "I don't mention how happy he is now. How three years pass and he still whistle and sing. I think bout how every time I jump when Mr. ——— call me, she [Sofia] look surprise. And like she pity me. Beat her, I say" (43). And Celie, like other victims of "soul murder" who have been reduced to "a mechanical obedient automaton," harbors a murderous rage that almost surfaces when Albert's father denigrates Shug (58-59) and when she learns that Albert has for many years been intercepting and hiding Nettie's letters (114-15).

How does Celie survive her early losses and subsequent "soul murder" and begin to move successfully through the developmental stages arrested in infancy and adolescence toward a mature female identity? How is she enabled to take pleasure—her own pleasure—in creative work and unselfish love as an adult? In short, how is Celie able first to verbalize and then to fulfill with her authentic living the promise inherent in those Stevie Wonder verses quoted by Walker at the beginning of her novel: "*Show me how to do like you / Show me how to do it*"?

Alice Walker writes: "Let's hope people can hear Celie's voice. There are so many people like Celie who make it who come out of nothing. People who triumph"

(Anillo and Abramson 67). According to psychoanalytic developmental psychology, however, a successful survivor does not emerge "out of nothing"; Celie, as a successful survivor, is able to learn "how to do it" because (1) her family of origin gave her "good parental care" during the first two years of her life; (2) she is able to make use of several nurturing surrogate mother figures, foremost among whom is "the Queen Honeybee" herself, Shug Avery; and (3) as a survivor of "soul murder" she uses "adaptive powers and talents" (Shengold 7).[9] In the remainder of this paper, I shall first speculate upon the psychological state of the pre-traumatized two-year-old Celie viewed from the perspective of psychoanalytic developmental psychology; then attempt to show how Celie "bonds" with developmentally appropriate mother surrogates (Winnicott's "good-enough mother") as she resumes working through several developmental processes that were traumatically halted at age two and that need to be readdressed in her skewed and delayed adolescence in order for her to achieve psychological maturity and a firm sense of identity; and, finally, compare Celie and Nettie as examples of what Winnicott calls the "True Self" and the "False Self."

Since Samuel's story of Celie's family of origin before its destruction includes a father who was a successful farmer and landowner, who prospered at whatever he turned his hand to, and who adored his wife (160), we can infer that Celie's first two years of life were spent in a supportive, caring family environment in which her basic physiological and psychological needs were met. We can assume that Celie bonded successfully with her mother and received "good-enough mothering." We find this mutually loving, triangular yet preoedipal family re-experienced by Celie in several places in the text. When Albert's father pays his son and Celie, now in her twenties, a call and denounces Shug Avery as a "whore," Albert and Celie, each of whom loves Shug, exchange a glance, and Celie writes: "This the closest us ever felt. He [Albert] say, Hand Pa his hat, Celie" (59). A little while later, Albert's brother Tobias drops by with a box of chocolate for the "Queen Honeybee." After Shug enters and sits by Celie without looking at Albert, Celie has a moment of intense self-awareness: "Then I see myself sitting there quilting tween Shug Avery and Mr. ———. Us three set together gainst Tobias and his fly speck box of chocolate. For the first time in my life, I feel just right" (61). Finally, in Celie's last letter, written in her early fifties, she describes herself and Albert and Shug "sitting out on the porch after dinner. Talking. Not talking. Rocking and fanning flies. . . . sitting on the porch with Albert and Shug feel real pleasant" (249). These adult experiences of Celie's are pleasurable because they are unconsciously experienced as that loving relationship she had had with her preoedipal father and mother during the latter part of her first two years of life. They help fulfill the need that has remained for such family object relations since the early separations.

Celie's father's adoration of his pregnant wife and mother of his daughter also strongly suggests that femaleness and femininity were highly valued by both mother and father, and that Celie's core gender identity is femaleness. According to Robert Stoller, our "core gender identity is the sense we have of our sex—of maleness in males and of femaleness in females. . . . It is a part of, but not identical with, what I have called gender identity—a broader concept, standing for the mix of masculinity and femininity found in every person. . . . Core gender identity develops first and is the central nexus around which masculinity and femininity gradually accrete" ("Primary Femininity" 61). Stoller's research leads him to believe that "core gender identity" is solidified for the most part by the end of the second year; gender identity, however, is determined by a wide variety of biological, psychological, social, and cultural influences and is usually not finalized until middle or late adolescence.[10] Thus, by two, Celie's "core gender identity," her sense of femaleness, is fairly well established, and the groundwork has been laid for the further development of her "gender identity."

Perhaps most important for Celie's ability to bond successfully with females in adolescence and young adulthood, and thus to resume her development of an identity, of a "True Self" in Winnicott's terminology, is her partial but incomplete resolution of a transitional developmental phase that occurs roughly between six and twenty-four months. Winnicott calls this phase "relative dependence" and describes the infant's need for its mother at this time as "fierce and truly terrible." Since the infant has not yet developed the permanent capacity to image mother either consciously or unconsciously when she is absent, the infant is subject to being overwhelmed with "separation anxiety." Mahler offers the term "rapprochement crisis" for this phase and describes it as a time of ambivalence, when the infant's needs for separateness and autonomy and identity formation are in conflict with its need for mother (76-120). If the mother is understanding and empathetic at this difficult time, the infant will, in the third year, go on to develop a stable sense of self and others. If, however, there are serious maternal failures, severe adult psychopathology may result, and the developmental tasks of adolescence, especially the finalizing of gender identity and a firm sense of self, will be made even more difficult. Since Celie loses her "good-enough mother" at the height of her "rapprochement crisis," when she has yet to develop stable conscious and unconscious images of mother and her identity formation is in the early stages of development, it is hardly surprising that Celie should later respond to the ministrations of women and resume the developmental tasks of separation, autonomy, and identity formation.

Although the white, patriarchal God Celie writes to in the first part of the novel never sends her a sign (175-76), life does—primarily in the form of caring and nurturing black women. These "good-enough mothers," with the notable exception of Shug Avery, take the initiative; they intuit the depressed and traumatized Celie's deeply buried needs and break through her defensive passivity. When Nettie runs away from home to escape Alphonso's unwanted sexual advances and joins Celie and Albert, she teaches Celie "spelling and everything else she think I need to know. . . . to teach me what go on in the world" (25).

Nettie not only tries to give Celie the tools that will free her, she also, even more importantly, conveys to Celie her belief that Celie is of value. Kate, one of Albert's sisters, convinces him of Celie's need for clothes and takes her to a store to select cloth so that a dress can be made. When Celie is overcome with emotion and cannot speak, Kate reassures her and says: "You deserve more than this. Maybe so. I think" (28). And when Sofia, Harpo's wife and Albert's daughter-in-law, suggests that Celie and she make quilt pieces, Celie writes: "I run git my pattern book. I sleeps like a baby now" (47).

It is the seemingly inappropriate nightclub singer Shug Avery, however, who provides Celie with an extended period of "female bonding"; who, with unconditional love, provides a "holding environment" in which Celie's nascent self is reflected back to itself; and, who, as surrogate and "good-enough mother," and lover, helps Celie to complete the development of those capacities that enable her to deal more effectively with loss, to finalize her gender identity and choice of mature love object, and to develop a stable sense of self. One might argue that the development of a nurturing and positive relationship between these two women is improbable. Celie, until she hears Shug's name spoken, appears as a passive victim. After she is married to Albert, women who become mother surrogates have to reach out to her. How then can Shug's name and her picture, provided to her by Alphonso's new wife (16), mobilize the depressed and passive Celie actively to seek a "good-enough mother" in Shug? And when the two women meet for the first time, the deathly ill Shug's first words are "You sure *is* ugly" (50).

What may appear inappropriate and improbable is seen not to be so when we acknowledge Celie's developmental history, her unconscious need to complete those developmental tasks that have been skewed and/or arrested—and most important initially, her adolescent longing for a transitional, idealized role model, figures that adolescents often draw from the entertainment and sports worlds: "Shug Avery was a woman. The most beautiful woman I ever saw. She more pretty then my mama. She bout ten thousand times more prettier then me. I see her there in furs. Her face rouge. Her hair like somethin tail. She grinning with her foot up on somebody motorcar. Her eyes serious tho. Sad some. I ast her to give me the picture. An all night long I stare at it. An now when I dream, I dream of Shug Avery" (16).

After Celie's immediate positive response to the glamorous figure in the photograph, she focuses on the singer's "serious" and "sad eyes." In so doing, she moves from her adolescent need to cathect a transitional, idealized role model to her unconscious infantile need to master the trauma of losing the emotional availability of her "good-enough mother." Her initial negative encounters with the ill Shug parallel Celie's frustrated infantile efforts to break through her mother's psychosis and later her depression and deteriorating mental and physical condition. Celie perseveres, however, for she knows from the expression of the eyes in the photograph that *this* woman has the ability to mirror Celie back to herself. "*What* [mother] *looks like is related to what she sees there,*" asserts Winnicott (*Playing* 112), and Celie's experience confirms this. When she sees Shug's "serious" and "sad" eyes, she sees into her own murdered soul. When Alphonso is trying to convince Albert that Celie would make him a good wife despite her ugliness, Celie takes out Shug's picture, looks in her eyes, and "Her eyes say Yeah, it *bees* that way sometime" (18). Celie's ability to use Shug's eyes as a mirror is predicated upon earlier, positive, and unconscious mirror reflections from a "good-enough mother" of happier days. Indeed, Celie's ability to use Shug Avery herself as a mother surrogate for female bonding is predicated upon "good-enough mothering" during the first two years of Celie's life.

Once Celie has cathected Shug's photograph, her image permeates Celie's conscious and unconscious mind. Shug serves both as a "good-enough [preoedipal] mother" and as a libidinal object. On her wedding night, Celie thinks of Shug and, knowing that Albert and Shug were lovers, puts her arm around him (21). When Kate takes her to the store to buy cloth for her dress, Celie wonders what color Shug would wear (28). After hearing that Shug and her "orkestra" are coming to town, Celie carries an announcement with Shug's picture on it in her pocket all day and wants desperately to go that night: "Not to dance. Not to drink. Not to play card. Not even to hear Shug Avery sing. I just be thankful to lay eyes on her" (33). And when Albert brings the sick Shug home to recuperate, Celie, though flooded with emotions and desiring to heal her, cannot move until she "see her eyes" (50). When Shug finally looks up at her, Celie notices those parts of Shug's face that a nursing infant would see: "her face black. . . . She got a long pointed nose and big fleshy mouth. Lips look like black plum. Eyes big, glossy" (50).

Celie not only devours Shug with her eyes but wishes to incorporate her with her mouth. As she nurses Shug back to health, Celie at first hungrily looks at her naked body: "First time I got the full sight of Shug Avery long black body with it black plum nippies, look like her mouth, I thought I had turned into a man" (53). After Celie gives Shug coffee and a cigarette, she has a compulsion to take "hold of her hand, tasting her fingers in my mouth" (55). Shug, in her capacity as a "good-enough mother," is unconsciously experienced by Celie as the maternal breast—a libidinal object. Celie's intense hunger is soon satisfied by the physical presence of this woman whose nickname, in combination with "nippies," forms a Southern expression for a pacifier. Later, Celie washes and combs Shug's hair, saving the strands that "come out in my comb. . . . I work on her like she a doll or like she Olivia—or like she mama. I comb and pat, comb and pat. First she say, hurry up and git finish. Then she melt down a little and lean back gainst my knees. That feel just right, she say. That feel like mama used to do. Or maybe not mama. Maybe grandma" (57).

Although Celie has found a "good-enough mother" in Shug, it is only when Shug can provide an extended "holding environment" that Celie can build upon the efforts of previous mother surrogates and, in bonding with Shug, complete her previously stymied psychological development. One night Shug takes the initiative and asks to sleep with Celie. When Shug asks Celie how it was making love "with your children daddy," Celie begins to tell another person for the first time about her rape and incest. Uncertain of Shug's response, Celie soon pauses: "I lay there quiet, listening to Shug breathe." After several more painful revelations, she pauses again: "Shug so quiet I think she sleep. After he through, I say, he make me finish trimming his hair. I sneak a look at Shug. Oh, Miss Celie, she say. And put her arms round me. They black and smooth and kind of glowy from the lamp-light. I start to cry too. I cry and cry and cry. Seem like it all come back to me, laying there in Shug arms. How it hurt and how much I was surprise" (108-9). This bedroom scene is the beginning of Celie's working through her rape trauma with abreaction and reconstruction of the traumatic events. Shug, as a "good-enough mother," provides a "holding environment" that enables Celie to verbalize and to get in touch with long-repressed memories and feelings and work them through. Her severe dissociative state and cognitive deficiencies improve after this abreaction, as evidenced by the increasingly grammatical, stylistic, and tonal complexity of her letters.

It is also in this bedroom scene that the two women become lovers. Once again, Shug takes the initiative. After unburdening herself with words and tears, and unable consciously to recall the love of her preoedipal parents, Celie angrily says, "Nobody ever love me." Shug immediately responds: "I love you, Miss Celie. And then she haul off and kiss me on the mouth." After Celie responds with a kiss, the two kiss repeatedly—then touch—and then Celie says: "Then I feels something real soft and wet on my breast, feel like one of my little lost babies mouth." And then: "Way after while, I act like a little lost baby too" (109).

Even though Celie's sensuous "female bonding" with Shug leads to a deeply experienced and lengthy lesbian relationship between the two women, Shug continues to serve Celie as a "good-enough mother" who ministers to the unconscious developmental needs of her child. Besides "mirroring" and providing a "holding environment," Shug also remains "consistently herself" (Winnicott, *Maturational Processes* 87) and allows for moments of quiescent transitional relatedness which, according to Winnicott, are essential for the development of a stable and personal self: "It is only when [the infant experiences himself] alone (that is to say, in the presence of someone) that the infant can discover his own personal life" (34). Celie describes the first of many such moments following their first night together: "Me and Shug sound asleep. Her back to me, my arms round her waist. What it like? Little like sleeping with mama, only I can't hardly remember ever sleeping with her. Little like sleeping with Nettie, only sleeping with Nettie never feel this good. It warm and cushiony, and I feel Shug's big tits sorta flop over my arms like suds. It feel like heaven is what it feel like, not like sleeping with Mr. ——— at all" (110).

Shug occasionally acts as an "auxiliary ego" for Celie and helps her modulate states of excitement. When Shug tells Celie that Albert has been hiding Nettie's letters to her over the years, leading her to believe that her sister was dead, Celie is flooded with murderous rage and, without Shug's intervention, would have cut Albert's throat with his razor (114-15). Later, when Celie's rage toward Albert makes her sexually impotent with Shug, Shug identifies Celie's emotional state and tells her that strong emotions, such as "being mad, grief, wanting to kill somebody" (136), make one impotent. Shug then suggests that together they make Celie a pair of pants, thus giving Celie a lesson in sublimation: "A needle and not a razor in my hand, I think" (137).[11]

Shug also helps Celie to verbalize her feelings about Albert openly and to separate from him (180-83); long before they become lovers she gives Celie a lesson in and appreciation of her female reproductive organs (79-80); and her open bisexual behavior (which offends some critics)[12] and her special blend of masculine and feminine gender identity facilitates Celie's completion of her own adult sexual orientation (choice of a love object) and gender identity. When Shug takes Celie to her house in Memphis, described by Celie as "big and pink and look sort of like a barn," in order "to love you and help you get on your feet" (188, 190), she provides Celie with a literal and psychological womblike "holding environment" in which Celie flourishes. While there, Celie discovers that she has a creative and unique talent as a designer of "perfect pants," for women and men, and, with Shug's financial backing, she establishes her own clothes business, "Folks-pants, Unlimited," and thereby achieves economic independence: "Dear Nettie, I am so happy. I got love, I got work, I got money, friends, and time" (193).

But before Celie can complete her final developmental task, the achievement of an autonomous and stable sense of self, she learns that Sofia's mother has died and returns home for the funeral. As she approaches Harpo's and Sofia's house, Celie acknowledges to herself: "I feels different. Look different. Got on some dark blue pants and a white silk shirt that look righteous. Little red flat-heel slippers, and a flower in my hair. I pass Mr. —— house and him sitting up on the porch and he didn't even know who I was" (195). When Albert walks up to Celie after the funeral, she looks "in his eyes and I see he feeling scared of me. Well, good, I think. Let him feel what I felt" (199). These internal and external changes are soon followed by an unexpected inheritance.

Sometime after returning to Memphis and Shug, Celie learns from Alphonso's wife Daisy that Alphonso is dead and that Nettie and Celie have inherited their dead parents' land and the house and dry goods store that Alphonso rebuilt. When Celie wonders what Nettie and she would sell in such a store, Shug quickly replies, "How bout pants?" (216). Celie and Shug return home to look at the property and the buildings, and Celie spends the summer getting the house ready for Nettie, her husband, Celie's grown children, Shug, and herself. When she returns home to Shug, Celie's lover and "good-enough mother" inadvertently provides her with a painful opportunity to complete her development of an autonomous and stable sense of self.

"My heart broke," Celie writes to Nettie, after hearing from Shug that she "got the hots for a boy of nineteen" (218-19). Although Shug protests that she still loves Celie and will return to her once she has had her "last fling," Celie regresses briefly, returns to *writing* about her feelings—but then is able to verbalize her love for Shug "whatever happens, whatever you do" (221). Celie finds it necessary, however, to leave Shug's house, and she returns to her own, where she undergoes a period of healthy mourning. At first Celie has little desire to live and writes Nettie that "the only thing keep me alive is watching Henrietta [Sofia's ill daughter] fight for her life" (222). She breaks into tears after telling Albert how Shug taught her how to sublimate her murderous rage for him by helping her to make her first pair of pants (223). And one of the darkest days of her life occurs when she receives both a telegram informing her that Nettie's homeward bound ship has been sunk by German mines and all of her letters written to Nettie—unopened: "I sit here in this big house by myself trying to sew, but what good is sewing gon do? What good is anything? Being alive begin to seem like a awful strain" (225). Alone and despairing, believing herself bereft of sister, adult children, and her "good-enough mother," Celie confronts her existential aloneness and struggles to complete both her mourning process and her final developmental task.

As time passes, Celie occasionally questions Shug's love: "I stand looking at my naked self in the looking glass. What would she love? I ast myself. . . . My body just any woman's body going through the changes of age. . . . My heart must be young and fresh though, it feel like it blooming blood. . . . But look at you. When Shug left, happiness desert" (229). Although she periodically receives a post card from Shug, there is no mention of her return. Celie and Albert often spend time talking about their love for Shug and sharing their happy and sad memories—an activity that furthers the mourning process. After six months have passed, Celie sums up the first part of that process:

> Well, your sister too crazy to kill herself. Most times I feels like shit but I felt like shit before in my life an what happen? I had me a fine sister name Nettie. I had me another fine woman friend name Shug. I had me some fine children growing up in Africa, singing and writing verses. The first two months was hell, though, I tell the world. But now Shug's six months is come and gone and she ain't come back. And I try to teach my heart not to want nothing it can't have.
>
> Besides, she give me so many good years. Plus, she learning new things in her new life. Now she and Germaine staying with one of her children.
>
> (235)

This extract from a letter to Nettie not only conveys the authentic voice of successful mourning but shows us that Celie is beginning to move beyond her need for a "good-enough mother" and, as a developing, autonomous, and stable self, Celie is able to express appreciation for Shug's generosity and even derive pleasure from the thought that Shug is "learning new things in her new life."

The mourning process is slow, however, and Celie is subject to a variety of contrasting thoughts and feelings about Shug: "I wish I could be traveling with her, but thank God she able to do it. Sometimes I feel mad at her. Feel like I could scratch her hair right off her head. But then I think, Shug got a right to live too. She got a right to look over the world in whatever company she choose. Just cause I love her don't take away none of her rights" (236). At times Celie regresses and unconsciously experiences Shug as the sad mother of her childhood: "What I love best bout Shug is what she been through, I say. When you look in Shug's eyes you know she been where she been, seen what she seen, did what she did. And now she know" (236). There comes a time, however, when Celie's mourning process has done its work, and she is able to consciously acknowledge and unconsciously experience Shug's separateness, uniqueness, and autonomy, as well as her own: "And then, just when I know I can live content without Shug, just when Mr. ——— done ast me to marry him again, this time in the spirit as well as in the flesh, and just after I say Naw, I still don't like frogs, but let's us be friends, Shug write me she coming home. Now. Is this life or not? *I be so calm.* If she come, I be happy. If she don't, I be content. And then I figure this the lesson I was supposed to learn" (247-48). Celie has indeed learned "*how to do like you.*" Through years of "female bonding" and "good-enough mothering," Celie has, in middle age, created a mature, stable, and autonomous identity for herself; she is what Winnicott would call a "True Self."

Nettie's literary portrait, however, contrasts sharply with Celie's; literary critics usually discuss this contrast in terms of the "narrative voices" that emerge from the letters. Whereas Celie's "voice" is praised by many,[13] including one of Walker's harshest critics (Harris, "On *The Color Purple*" 156), Nettie's "voice," and her letters, have, like the novel itself, received a wide variety of negative and positive criticism. On the negative side are those who find Nettie's voice to be nondistinctive (Towers 36) and inauthentic (Robinson 2); her letters to be "often mere monologues on African history" (Watkins 7), didactic (Smith 182), "unconvincing" (Davis 53), "preachy" (McFadden 140), and "extraneous to the central concerns of the novel" (Harris, "On *The Color Purple*" 157); and her language "dull, devitalized, too correct. . . . written in 'white' missionary language" (Tucker 92). On the positive side are those who praise Nettie's and Celie's "voices" in terms of the authentic folk voice that emanates from the novel (Watkins 7; Chambers 54) and who find that Nettie's letters provide "important thematic parallels . . . [and] essential plot information" (McFadden 140), foster change in Celie (Fifer 158; Babb 114), and "add substantially to the depth and variety of the entire novel" (Tucker 91), while Nettie's language, "conventional, educated diction," bodies forth "the new self Nettie has created with her new language" (Fifer 155, 158). Thus at one extreme Towers and Robinson assert that Nettie is "essentially uncharacterized" (Towers 36) and has "no personality" (Robinson 2), and at the other extreme Fifer argues that Nettie, through mastering a new language, standard English, has created a new self for herself (158).

Whether one views Nettie's "narrative voice" or literary portrait as superficial or complex, her intellectual and educated mind contrasts vividly with the emotional intensity of her victimized older sister. In fact, Nettie gives the appearance of having overcome the traumatic incidents of their childhood and adolescence more successfully than Celie and presents herself as a healthier character throughout her letters. But is this so? I suggest that the reverse is the case: that is, that Celie, often against overwhelming odds, works toward and achieves a stable and authentic sense of self, a "True Self," and that Nettie, who is cared for and protected by Celie until she joins the black missionaries Corrine and Samuel, the adoptive parents of Celie's two children, develops in infancy the beginning of a "False Self" that is strengthened and formed by her immediate family environment and the educational system. Approaching Nettie's literary portrait in terms of Winnicott's "False Self" helps account for the divergence of critical opinion concerning the authenticity of Nettie's "voice." Should Nettie appear to be what she is not, then those critics who find her "voice" authentic have been misled by her "False Self," and those critics who find her "voice" superficial have penetrated Nettie's "False Self." Before proceeding with this developmental reading, I should like to review Winnicott's thoughts about the origin and development of the "False Self."

Winnicott believes that the "False Self" originates during the first stage of object relationships (*Maturational Processes* 145); that is, prior to the sixth month of life, before the infant has "separated off the 'not me' from the 'me'" (58). The not "good-enough mother" mirrors her own self to the infant rather than mirroring the infant back to itself, thereby making the infant perceive rather than apperceive, and it complies with mother and her needs. The infant, according to Winnicott, begins to develop "an aspect of the personality that is false (false in that what is showing is a derivative not of the individual [True Self] but of the mothering aspect of the infant-mother coupling)" (58). The adult who has a "False Self" system uses it "to hide and protect the True Self, whatever that may be" (142); the "False Self" "does [this] by compliance with environmental demands" (147). Winnicott also posits a continuum for "False Personalities": "At one extreme: the False Self sets up as real and it is this that observers tend to think is the real person. . . . The True Self is hidden" (142-43), while "In health: the False Self is represented by the whole organization of the polite and mannered social attitude, a 'not wearing the heart on the sleeve,' as might be said" (143). Finally, Winnicott observes that "when a False Self becomes organized in an individual who has a high intellectual potential there is a very strong tendency for the mind to become the location of the False Self" (144).[14]

When Nettie's infancy is compared with Celie's, it is obvious that each is born into a "different family" and that each has a strikingly different developmental history. Whereas Celie spends the first two years of her life in an intact, loving, traditional family with "good-enough mothering," Nettie spends the first several months of her life experiencing severe physical and emotional deprivation and the first several years complying with the emotional needs of a depressed and mentally unstable mother. Although Celie was in all probability able to offer some mothering to Nettie in the early as well as the later years, she could not have been a "good-enough mother" in Winnicott's sense. Thus it is reasonable to speculate that Nettie, in order to survive, quickly learned to comply with her environment; out of necessity she developed a "False Self" at the expense of her "True Self." The text appears to corroborate this speculation.

During Nettie's adolescent years, first at home with Alphonso and later with Celie and Albert, Celie encourages Nettie "to keep at her books" (14) in order to escape her older sister's fate—and Nettie complies. When Albert decides that Nettie has to leave, Celie tells her to look up the wife of the "Reverend Mr. ———" (26)—and Nettie complies. And when Samuel and Corrine ask Nettie if she would like to join them in their African missionary enterprise, Nettie accepts, "But only if they would teach me everything they knew to make me useful as a missionary. . . . and my real education began at that time" (124).

Several critics have observed how effectively Nettie responds to and complies with her immediate environment. Valerie Babb notes that Nettie's first letter to Celie (119) "reads in a manner consistent with Celie's oral style" and that after "her missionary employers, Corrine and Samuel, have had a hand in her education . . . Nettie's letters are rendered completely in the standard" (113). Elizabeth Fifer describes Nettie as "controlled, religious, and idealistic" (163) and draws our attention to Celie's initial "bewilderment at the new self Nettie has created with her new language: 'What with being shock, crying and blowing my nose, and trying to puzzle out words us don't know, it took a long time to read just the first two or three letters'" (158). Lindsey Tucker finds Nettie's letters to be "written in 'white' missionary language. Metaphorically speaking, Nettie wears her language much like she wears Corrine's clothing—without total authenticity or comfort" (92). Tucker then asserts: "In spite of a new home, a new career, and a new self, at the end of the novel, Celie has held onto one precious possession, her language. Although urged to become 'educated,' to learn to talk as the books do, she refuses to change her speech patterns by submitting to white language" (92). Restated in psychological terms, we might say that Celie will not and, in fact, cannot compromise the integrity of her "True Self," whereas Nettie's compliance with "'white' missionary language" is in keeping with the protective nature of the "False Self." Nettie's "real education," it appears, is the final development of a "False Self" system that has found a home in Nettie's superior intellect.

In the next-to-last scene of *The Color Purple,* Celie's "True Self" and Nettie's "False Self," as well as their family and loved ones, are reunited. Although Trudier Harris calls this a "fairy-tale" ending ("On *The Color Purple*" 160), I believe that the reunification scene offers a psychological validity that transcends the contrivance of plot, and that this psychological validity consists in offering closure to the developmental processes that began with the sisters' births. Celie, feeling "real pleasant" as she sits "on the porch after dinner" between Albert and Shug (249), has developed a mature, autonomous, and "True" self, has been reunited with her lover Shug, and has also on an unconscious level been reunited with her preoedipal father (Albert) and mother (Shug). Just as it is appropriate that the altered Albert, who sent Nettie away thirty years before, should be the first to recognize her among a group of people who have gotten out of a car with their luggage at the end of the drive, so too is it psychologically appropriate that Celie's and Nettie's meeting should be described from the perspective of very little children:

> When Nettie's foot come down on the porch I almost die. . . . Then us both start to moan and cry. Us totter toward one nother like us use to do when us was babies. Then us feel so weak when us touch, us knock each other down. But what us care? Us sit and lay there on the porch inside each other's arms.
>
> After while, she say *Celie.*
>
> I say *Nettie.*
>
> Little bit more time pass. Us look round at a lot of peoples knees. Nettie never let go my waist. This my husband Samuel, she say, pointing up. These our children Olivia and Adam and this Adam's wife Tashi, she say.
>
> I point up at my peoples. This Shug and Albert, I say.
>
> (250)

Not only does this emotional meeting of two middle-aged sisters enable them to regress and re-experience unconsciously earlier infantile needs for each other, but their "True" and "False" selves are validated with this encounter. Nettie brings nothing to this reunion that is truly hers—including herself. Thirty years earlier, when she had sought refuge with Samuel and Corrine, they treated her like family, "Like family might have been, I mean" (121). In becoming a missionary and going to Africa, she assumes "'white' missionary language" and a professional role. And when she arrives at Celie's and her house, she is accompanied by a dead woman's husband and a living woman's grown children. In order to complete this developmental portrait of Nettie as a "False Self," Walker has her win a hollow "oedipal victory": "You may have guessed that I loved [Samuel] all along; but I did not know it. Oh, I loved him as a brother and respected him as a friend, but Celie, I love him bodily, *as a man!*" (211). Corrine's suspicion that Olivia and Adam are, in fact, Samuel's and Nettie's children is incorrect (158-59, 168-69); what she does sense, however, is Nettie's love for the oedipal father. Nettie, unlike Celie, was not traumatized at the height of the rapprochement period, when a child *needs* its mother. Therefore, she passes through that "triangular period" that Freud termed the "Oedipus complex" (roughly from two and a half to six years) as a "False Self." Celie, on the other hand, appears to have been largely unaffected by her passage through the oedipal years. Her traumatic losses at two and subsequent "soul murder" appear to have precluded the unfolding of this stage.

In contrast to Nettie, everything that Celie brings to this reunion is truly hers. As Nettie approaches, Celie, who "stand swaying, tween Albert and Shug" (250), is supported by her symbolic preoedipal family of origin as well as her lover Shug and now friend Albert. "Nettie stand swaying tween Samuel and . . . Adam" (250). Celie's "True Self," forged out of years of abuse and suffering and "female bonding," is face-to-face with Nettie's "False Self," created through compliance with the outside world in order to survive a chaotic infancy and childhood. Nettie, who appears to have everything, including husband, grown children, Celie, and her inheritance, lacks one essential thing—an authentic life. Celie, who has survived loss, "soul murder," incest, and physical and emotional abuse, has, in the process, acquired a home, a career, friends, and a lover and has developed an authentic self that enables her to live an authentic life. Celie, unlike Nettie, is able to participate in mature object relationships: as a "True Self," Celie can both successfully mourn the inevitable losses of life and go on to form new relationships and live authentically and deeply in the present moment (Winnicott, *Maturational Processes* 221, 148-49).

Although this psychoanalytic developmental reading of Walker's **The Color Purple** is limited in scope and makes no pretension to address the many aesthetic, moral, and sociological problems and issues raised by this complex and controversial work of fiction, I have illuminated several of the unconscious developmental processes that underlie Walker's presentation of "female bonding" and that facilitate Celie's search for and attainment of a mature, autonomous, and authentic sense of identity that enables her to live an authentic life. Drawing upon Winnicott's concepts of the "good-enough mother," the "mirror role of the mother," "the holding environment," and the origin of the "True Self" and the "False Self," I have traced the development of Celie's "True Self" and Nettie's "False Self" and, in the process, have addressed specific negative criticisms of the novel, such as unequal narrative voices, unrealistic character development, faulty plot, unbelievable events, and the "fairy-tale" quality of the lesbian relationship between Celie and Shug as well as Celie's and Nettie's reunion—arguing that a psychological reading of the text shows many of these negative criticisms to be spurious. Walker has given us in **The Color Purple** a brilliant psychological developmental novel (dedicated "*To the Spirit*: / Without whose assistance / Neither this book / Nor I / Would have been / Written"; Walker has "listened with the third ear"—her own unconscious). Celie's fictive narrative voice, that "speaks" to us though mute and that is never "heard" by those to whom she writes, transcends the limitations of her isolation and of the novel; as victim and survivor, Celie attests to the importance of "good-enough mothering" in the early years and to the healing power of human relationships.

Notes

1. See especially Fifer, Babb, Chambers, Cheung, and Tucker.

2. See Prescott 68; Smith 182; McFadden 141-42; Steinem 90; Lenhart 3; Fifer 162-63; Shelton 386-87; McKenzie 54-57; Pinckney 17; Chambers 56-57; Tucker 85-90; Cheung 168; and Lewis 79-80.

3. See Deutsch 20; Ritvo; Blos; Bergman; and Dalsimer, "Introduction" 1-12.

4. For a succinct and useful summary of D. W. Winnicott's theories of psychoanalytic developmental psychology, see Khan. For a more complete study, see Davis and Wallbridge.

   I wish to thank James E. Marquardt, psychoanalyst and colleague, for reading an earlier version of this paper and for offering clarification of several psychoanalytic developmental concepts.

5. For Winnicott, the "mother" is the infant's "primary caretaker," and the "infant" refers to that phase of life "prior to word presentation and the use of word symbols. The corollary is that [infancy] refers to a phase in which the infant depends on maternal care that is based on maternal empathy rather than on [the] understanding of what is or could be verbally expressed" (*Maturational Processes* 40).

   The terms "good-enough mother" and "primary caretaker" are, for Winnicott and other object relations theorists, not gender specific, even though in our culture the infant's primary caretaker is usually the biological mother. These terms are used to discuss the clinically observed importance of an adult person for the early psychological development of the infant. The focus of this paper is upon the importance of early object relations in the text for later change and development in adulthood, and not upon the current feminist political issues surrounding motherhood. I trust my readers will not accuse me of insensitivity to these issues.

6. See also Winnicott, *Maturational Processes* 73-74; and Mahler 3.

7. Elsewhere Winnicott writes: "If the inherited potential is to have a chance to become actual in the sense of manifesting itself in the individual's person, then the environmental provision must be adequate. It is convenient to use a phrase like 'good-enough mothering' to convey *an unidealized view* of the maternal function" (qtd. in Davis and Wallbridge 35; emphasis added).

8. Hilda S. Rollman-Branch writes: "Auxiliary mothering by older siblings supplements the mother's care and even replaces it entirely. The infant's need for attachment to a human object can be satisfied by another child" (412).

9. Shengold discusses the effects of "soul murder" upon artistic creativity in the works of three literary survivors: Dickens, Chekhov, and Kipling (181-208; 209-32; 233-83). Several critics have observed that Celie survives through the act of writing (Davis 50-52; Fifer 155-56; Chambers 59; Tucker 82-83; and Cheung 162).

10. For further psychoanalytic thinking about "core gender identity" and "gender identity," see Chodorow; Stoller, "Current Concepts" 793-96; Tyson, "Developmental Line" 61-63 and 72-84, and "Current Concepts" 796-99; and Tyson and Tyson.

11. Paul Lewis observes that Shug twice uses humor to deflect Celie's murderous rage (*Color Purple* 134-35), and that Celie likewise uses humor to make the angry and embittered Sofia laugh for the first time "in three years" (*Color Purple* 99). He identifies it as "gallows humor" and asserts that such humor both "create[s] distance from our pain, . . . liberat[ing] us at least temporarily from otherwise inescapable torment" and helps further the humanity of "Miss Celie and Sofia, [and] even Albert and his foolish son Harpo" (80). I wish to thank my colleague Professor Siegfried Mandel for bringing Lewis's book to my attention.

12. See Harris, "Victimization" 9-10; and Royster 368.

13. See Watkins 7; Smith 183; McFadden 142; Fifer 155; and Chambers 54.

14. For a brilliant contemporary psychoanalytic study of the "False Self," see Miller.

Works Cited

Anillo, Ray, and Pamela Abramson. "Characters in Search of a Book." *Newsweek* 21 June 1982: 67.

Babb, Valerie. "*The Color Purple*: Writing to Undo What Writing Has Done." *Phylon: The Atlanta University Review of Race and Culture* 47 (1986): 107-16.

Bergman, A. "On the Development of Female Identity: Issues of Mother-Daughter Interaction during the Separation-Individuation Process." Symposium on "The Many Faces of Eve." University of California at Los Angeles, Feb. 1984.

Blos, Peter. "Modifications in the Traditional Psychoanalytic Theory of Female Adolescent Development." *Adolescent Psychiatry* 8 (1980): 8-24.

Chambers, Kimberly. "Right on Time: History and Religion in Alice Walker's *The Color Purple*." *CLA Journal* 31 (1987): 44-62.

Cheung, King-Kok. "'Don't Tell': Imposed Silences in *The Color Purple* and *The Woman Warrior*." *PMLA* 103 (1988): 162-73.

Chodorow, Nancy. *The Reproduction of Mothering: Psychoanalysis and the Sociology of Gender*. Berkeley: U of California P, 1978.

Dalsimer, Katherine. *Female Adolescence: Psychoanalytic Reflections on Literature*. New Haven: Yale UP, 1986.

Davis, Madeleine, and David Wallbridge. *Boundary and Space: An Introduction to the Work of D. W. Winnicott*. New York: Brunner/Mazel, 1981.

Davis, Thadious M. "Alice Walker's Celebration of Self in Southern Generations." *Southern Quarterly Review* 21.4 (1983): 39-53.

Deutsch, H. *The Psychology of Women*. Vol. 1. New York: Grune, 1944. 2 vols.

Fifer, Elizabeth. "The Dialect and Letters of *The Color Purple*." *Contemporary American Women Writers*. Ed. Catherine Rainwater and William J. Scheick. Lexington: U of Kentucky P, 1985. 155-71.

Greenberg, Jay R., and Stephen A. Mitchell. *Object Relations in Psychoanalytic Theory*. Cambridge: Harvard UP, 1983.

Harris, Trudier. "From Victimization to Free Enterprise: Alice Walker's *The Color Purple*." *Studies in American Fiction* 14 (1986): 1-17.

———. "On *The Color Purple*, Stereotypes, and Silence." *Black American Literature Forum* 18 (1984): 155-61.

Herman, Judith Lewis. *Father-Daughter Incest*. Cambridge: Harvard UP, 1981.

M. Masud R. Khan. Introduction. Winnicott, *Through Paediatrics* xi-1.

Lenhart, Georgeann. "Inspired Purple?" *Notes on Contemporary Literature* 14.3 (1984): 2-3.

Lewis, Paul. *Comic Effects: Interdisciplinary Approaches to Humor in Literature*. New York: State U of New York P, 1989.

Mahler, Margaret, Fred Pine, and Anni Bergman. *The Psychological Birth of the Human Infant: Symbiosis and Individuation*. New York: Basic, 1975.

McFadden, Margaret. Rev. of *The Color Purple*, by Alice Walker. *Magill's Literary Annual*. Ed. Frank N. Magill. Vol. 1. Englewood Cliffs, NJ: Salem, 1983. 139-43. 2 vols.

McKenzie, Abilene Christian. "*The Color Purple*'s Celie: A Journey of Selfhood." *Conference of College Teachers of English Studies* 51 (1986): 50-58.

Miller, Alice. *Prisoners of Childhood*. Trans. Ruth Ward. New York: Basic, 1981. Rpt. as *The Drama of the Gifted Child*. Trans. Ruth Ward. New York: Basic, 1986.

Pinckney, Darryl. "Black Victims, Black Villains." Rev. of *The Color Purple*, by Alice Walker; *The Color Purple*, a film by Steven Spielberg; *Reckless Eyeballing*, by Ishmael Reed. *New York Review* 29 Jan. 1987: 17-20.

Prescott, Peter S. "A Long Road to Liberation." Rev. of *The Color Purple*, by Alice Walker. *Newsweek* 21 June 1982: 67-68.

Ritvo, S. "Adolescent to Woman." *Journal of the American Psychoanalytic Association* 24 (1976): 127-37.

Robinson, Daniel. "Problems in Form: Alice Walker's *The Color Purple*." *Notes on Contemporary Literature* 16 (1986): 2.

Rollman-Branch, Hilda S. "The First Born Child, Male Vicissitudes of Preoedipal Problems." *International Journal of Psycho-Analysis* 47 (1966): 404-15.

Royster, Philip M. "In Search of Our Fathers' Arms: Alice Walker's Persona of the Alienated Darling." *Black American Literature Forum* 20 (1986): 347-70.

Russell, Diana E. *The Secret Trauma: Incest in the Lives of Girls and Women*. New York: Basic, 1986.

Shelton, Frank W. "Alienation and Integration in Alice Walker's *The Color Purple*." *CLA Journal* 28 (1985): 382-92.

Shengold, Leonard. *Soul Murder: The Effects of Childhood Abuse and Deprivation*. New Haven: Yale UP, 1989.

Smith, Dinitia. "'Celie, You a Tree.'" Rev. of *The Color Purple*, by Alice Walker. *Nation* 4 Sept. 1982: 181-83.

Steinem, Gloria. "Do You Know This Woman? She Knows You: A Profile of Alice Walker." *Ms.* June 1982: 36-37+.

Stern, Daniel N. *The Interpersonal World of the Infant: A View from Psychoanalysis and Developmental Psychology*. New York: Basic, 1985.

Stoller, Robert J. In "Current Concepts of the Development of Sexuality." Scientific Proceedings: Panel Report by Sara A. Vogel. *Journal of the American Psychoanalytic Association* 37 (1989): 787-802.

———. "Primary Femininity." *Female Psychology: Contemporary Views*. Ed. Harold P. Blum. Spec. issue of *Journal of the American Psychoanalytic Association* 24 (1976): 59-78.

Towers, Robert. "Good Men Are Hard to Find." Rev. of *The Color Purple*, by Alice Walker. *New York Review of Books* 12 Aug. 1982: 35-36.

Tucker, Lindsey. "Alice Walker's *The Color Purple*: Emergent Woman, Emergent Text." *Black American Literature Forum* 22 (1988): 81-95.

Tyson, Phyllis. In "Current Concepts of the Development of Sexuality." Scientific Proceedings: Panel Report by Sara A. Vogel. *Journal of the American Psychoanalytic Association* 37 (1989): 787-802.

———. "A Developmental Line of Gender Identity, Gender Role, and Choice of Love Object." *Journal of the American Psychoanalytic Association* 30 (1982): 61-86.

Tyson, Phyllis, and Robert Tyson. *Psychoanalytic Theories of Development: An Integration*. New Haven: Yale UP, 1990.

Walker, Alice. *The Color Purple*. New York: Washington Square, 1983.

———. "Coming in from the Cold: Welcoming the Old, Funny-Talking Ancient Ones into the Warm Room of Present Consciousness, Or, Natty Dread Rides Again!" National Writers Union. New York, Spring 1984; Black Women's Forum. Los Angeles, 17 Nov. 1984. Rpt. in *Living by the Word*. New York: Harcourt, 1988. 54-68.

———. "The Eighties and Me." *Publishers Weekly* 5 Jan. 1990: 21.

Watkins, Mel. "Some Letters Went to God." Rev. of *The Color Purple*, by Alice Walker. *New York Times Book Review* 25 July 1982: 7.

Winnicott, D. W. *The Maturational Processes and the Facilitating Environment*. New York: International Universities, 1965.

———. *Playing and Reality*. London: Tavistock, 1971.

———. *Through Paediatrics to Psycho-Analysis*. New York: Basic, 1975.

Linda Abbandonato (essay date October 1991)

SOURCE: Abbandonato, Linda. "'A View from "Elsewhere"': Subversive Sexuality and the Rewriting of the Heroine's Story in *The Color Purple*." *PMLA* 106, no. 5 (October 1991): 1106-115.

[*In the following essay, Abbandonato explores Walker's denouncement of the caucasian, patriarchal order in* The Color Purple *by displaying Celie's claiming of an identity and sexuality outside of traditionally accepted parameters.*]

Alice Walker's novel *The Color Purple* begins with a paternal injunction of silence:

> You better not never tell nobody but God. It'd kill your mammy.
>
> (11)

Celie's story is told within the context of this threat: the narrative is about breaking silences, and, appropriately, its formal structure creates the illusion that it is filled with unmediated "voices." Trapped in a gridlock of racist, sexist, and heterosexist oppressions, Celie struggles toward linguistic self-definition. She is an "invisible woman," a character traditionally silenced and effaced in fiction; and by centering on her, Walker replots the heroine's text. I want to show how Celie's story—the story of that most marginalized of heroines the black lesbian—challenges patriarchal constructions of female subjectivity and sexuality and thus makes representation itself a compelling issue for all women, regardless of their ethnicity or sexual orientation.[1] I begin by exploring the question of representation and considering *The Color Purple* in relation to feminist theoretical discourses on femininity. I then argue that by exposing and opposing a powerful ideological constraint, institutionalized or "compulsory" heterosexuality, the novel appropriates the woman's narrative for herself, in effect reinscribing "herstory."[2]

To substantiate my claim that *The Color Purple* is a conscious rewriting of canonical male texts, I propose a literary connection that is at once obvious and unlikely: the novel's epistolary form invites us to trace its ancestry all the way to *Clarissa*. Both novels represent a woman's struggle toward linguistic self-definition in a world of disrupted signs: Celie, like Clarissa, is imprisoned, alienated, sexually abused, and driven into semiotic collapse (see Castle's excellent analysis of Clarissa's collapse). *The Color Purple,* however, stands in a parodic or at least an irreverent relation to the monolithic *Clarissa*. The comparison between two fictions so radically separate historically and culturally is appropriate, I think, because *Clarissa* fully endorses the bourgeois morality that *The Color Purple* attacks and because Samuel Richardson himself (at least as constructed in our literary histories) perfectly symbolizes white patriarchy: the founding father of the novel (by convention, if not in fact), he tells the woman's story, authorizing her on his terms, eroticizing her suffering, representing her masochism as virtue and her dying as the emblem of womanly purity. *Clarissa,* even if largely unread now, occupies a dominant place in literature: its myths and values are recirculated in many fictions, especially in the ideology of romances, with which women are most fully engaged as readers and as writers.

Buried beneath the monumental edifice of works like *Clarissa,* male-authored volumes that tell the woman's story "as an Exemplar to her sex," lie a mass of texts by women. The history of publishing is a record of female silencing; as many feminist critics have pointed out, women traditionally experienced educational and economic disadvantages and other cultural constraints that prohibited them from writing.[3] When they overcame oppressive technologies of gender and took up the forbidden pen, the technologies of print could always be deployed against them. This may seem an overrehearsed, even an outdated argument, but the problems are still acute for women of color. Feminist attempts to revise the canon and address sexism in discourse are frequently marred by their failure to recognize heterosexism and racism; the counternarratives of femininity that emerge continue to erase women who are not white or heterosexual. Sojourner Truth's lament, "Ain't I a woman?" is insistently echoed in the contemporary writings of lesbians and women of color.[4]

Alice Walker too, in her nonfictional prose, protests the exclusion of black women writers from feminist revisions of literary histories (see esp. [*In Search of Our Mothers' Gardens,* hereafter abbreviated as] *Search* 231-43, 361-83); and in *The Color Purple,* she shows her heroine trapped in the whole range of possible oppressions. Celie's struggle to create a self through language, to break free from the network of class, racial, sexual, and gender ideologies to which she is subjected, represents the woman's story in an innovative way. Can a book like *The Color Purple* make any real difference to the hegemony of patriarchal discourses? Placed beside *Clarissa* on my bookshelf, *The Color Purple* symbolically suggests in its physical size the position and power of the "womanist" text within the canon: dominated by the weight, prolixity, and authority of masculine accounts of female subjectivity, it may nonetheless challenge and displace those "masternarratives."[5]

Walker gives several definitions for the term *womanist,* which is, of course, her coinage: "A black feminist or feminist of color. . . . Usually referring to outrageous, audacious, courageous or *willful* behavior. . . . A woman who loves other women, sexually and/or nonsexually" (***Search*** xi). I choose the phrase *womanist text* in preference to *woman's text* (i.e., a book written by a woman) to stress that the problem of representation cannot be resolved simply by the inclusion of more women writers in a male-dominated canon. While it is important for women to tell their stories, to gain a voice in literary and theoretical discourses and thereby achieve a certain empowerment, the ideological constraints on representation must also be considered. Put bluntly, how can a woman define herself differently, disengage her self from the cultural scripts of sexuality and gender that produce her as feminine subject? In *Alice Doesn't*, Teresa de Lauretis distinguishes between "woman" as an ideological construct and "women" as historical subjects and argues that women experience a double consciousness in relation to their representation in film: seduced into identification with woman, they are yet aware of their exclusion, of their nonrepresentation in that construct. If women are always constituted as objects (of desire, of the gaze) or as other, if "female" is always the negative of the positive value "male," women find themselves situated in a negative space, neither participating in patriarchal discourses nor able to escape from them. When Lauren Berlant describes Celie as "falling through the cracks of a language she can barely use . . . crossing out 'I am' and situating herself squarely on the ground of negation" (838), she attributes Celie's situation to saintly self-renunciation; but I propose a different explanation. Celie's burden in building a self on a site of negation is shared by any woman who attempts to establish an identity outside patriarchal definition. If women are constituted as subjects in a man-made language, then it is only through the cracks in language, and in the places where ideology fails to cohere, that they can begin to reconstruct themselves. Luce Irigaray points out that "if [women] keep on speaking the same language together, [they're] going to reproduce the same history. Begin the same stories all over again" (205). She urges women to "come out of [men's] language." But it is no easy task for women to authorize themselves as women, to disengage their feminine identity from the ideological masternarratives that inscribe it. Feminist discourse itself is inevitably corrupt, deeply implicated in the sexism of language and in patriarchal constructions of gender. As de Lauretis argues, women's theories of reading, writing, sexuality, and ideology are based "on male narratives of gender . . . bound by the heterosexual contract; narratives which persistently tend to reproduce themselves in feminist theories." The challenge facing feminists is no less than to "rewrite cultural narratives, and to define the terms of another perspective—a view from 'elsewhere'" (*Technologies* 25).

I suggest that ***The Color Purple*** offers that "view from 'elsewhere.'" It succeeds partly because Celie's sexual orientation provides an alternative to the heterosexual paradigm of the conventional marriage plot: her choice of lesbianism is politically charged, a notion I develop later. For the moment I want only to point out that the novel is also lesbian in the much broader sense implied by Adrienne Rich's concept of the "lesbian continuum," which spans the whole spectrum of women's friendships and sisterly solidarity. Walker's own term *womanist* is clearly influenced by Rich; and in this womanist text, the eroticism of women's love for women is at once centralized and incorporated into a more diffuse model of woman-identifying women.

Another way in which ***The Color Purple*** offers a view from elsewhere is through its displacement of standard English. Aware that "*the master's tools can never dismantle the master's house*" (Lorde 99), Alice Walker has fully confronted the challenge of constructing an alternative language. The significance of her achievement here has been overlooked, partly because critics often insist on confining the novel to the genre of realism and thus evaluate the Southern black vernacular solely for its authenticity. Indeed, Walker herself disingenuously describes her role as that of a medium, communicating of behalf of the spirits who possessed her (***Search*** 355-60). She seems to intend this myth of creative inspiration literally, and it is attractive because we certainly experience the novel as filled with voices that address us directly. With Celie we undergo a metamorphosis of experience, aligning ourselves fully with her vision of the world since she insists on being taken on her own terms. Her language is indeed so compelling that we actually begin to *think* as Miss Celie—like Shug, we have her song scratched out of our heads—because by participating in her linguistic processes, we collaborate in her struggle to construct a self. For various reasons, then, we are distracted from the extreme skill with which Walker exploits her formal and linguistic resources, and thus we underestimate the degree to which the text is language as performance. There is a clue, however, in what is commonly perceived as a flaw in the novel—the sequence of letters from Nettie, which invariably disappoint readers. If signifying is "a form of meta-communication, where the surface expression and the intrinsic position diverge" (Cooke 15), we can regard ***The Color Purple*** as an elaborate act of signifying, since the apparently impoverished and inarticulate language of the illiterati turns out to be deceptively resonant and dazzlingly rich. By incorporating Nettie's letters into Celie's text, Walker illuminates the contrast between Celie's spare suggestiveness and Nettie's stilted verbosity. Thus the expressive flexibility of the black vernacular, a supposedly inferior speech, is measured against the repressed and rigid linguistic codes to which Nettie has conformed; the position of standard (white) English is challenged, and Celie's vitality is privileged over Nettie's dreary correctness. Nettie has been imaginatively stunted, her language bleached white and her ethnicity virtually erased. Always the Other Woman, one who lacks an identity of her own, she is cast in the preposterous role of a black missionary who attempts to impose the ideology of her oppressors onto a culturally self-sufficient people. Nettie's story perfectly illustrates the way society construes women as subjects (or as subject-objects, in de Lauretis's phrase): neither represented within the white mainstream nor able to construct a selfhood outside it, Nettie is internally divided, experiencing her subjectivity as otherness.

Celie, by contrast, refuses to enter the linguistic structures (and strictures) of white patriarchy, commenting that "only a fool would want you to talk in a way that feel peculiar to your mind" (194), and so retains a discourse that is potentially subversive. We might compare Walker's technique with Irigaray's linguistic playfulness, fragmented phrases, and poetic cadences, which are similar in purpose, though not in style, to the suppleness, the sharp wit, and the compression of the black vernacular: each mode of expression represents both resistance to the hegemonic discourse and the deliberate use of linguistic non-conformity to position the self outside the dominant system. In *The Color Purple* the dialect is both naturalistic and symbolic, and if we try to confine the work to realism, we may easily miss the complexity of Walker's womanist aims. Her purposeful transgression of generic boundaries has also been perceived as a lack of artistic control, although it is entirely consistent with current feminist practice; and some of the criticisms directed at Walker imply a covert form of racism—an assumption that black novelists should (or can) write only in the realistic vein established by Richard Wright.[6]

By adopting the crazy quilt, the craft of her foremothers, as the structuring principle of her fiction, Alice Walker places herself within a tradition of black female creativity. This differently crafted, quilted novel, is also differently sexual: its formal structure allows many playful variations on a sexual theme. Some designs emerge clearly, but the overall pattern is extremely complicated; themes and relationships are introduced and inverted or turned, like a piece of fabric, inside out, so that the pattern can be traced a new way. Triadic combinations proliferate: characters are constantly realigned in an intricate network of configurations, apparently in a continual state of metamorphosis until the final utopian vision, the brave new world of the ending.[7]

The novel moves freely through time and space, juxtaposing the African motifs with the African American, thus supplying a dialectical commentary on the two cultures. Comic reversals of expectation are part of the scheme: for example, the Christian missionaries, striving to impose monogamy on the Olinkas, inadvertently reinforce polygyny because the Olinkas believe (quite rightly, as it turns out) that Samuel is married to both Corinne and Nettie. The treatment of incest is particularly interesting: although in one part of her design Walker reveals the full horror of father-daughter rape, she weaves in complications, twisting her narrative thread in ways that challenge the taboo. And if the incest taboo is subverted in this novel, so too is that other taboo homosexuality. I suggest that the great twentieth-century cultural narratives of sexuality and socialization, Freud's oedipal theory and Lévi-Strauss's theory of kinship systems and the exchange of women, are played out in the drama of Celie's life. The two theories center on the incest taboo and mesh together precisely. Both also explain, and have been used to reinforce, our system of "compulsory heterosexuality." As I have suggested, Celie's lesbianism is politically significant, subverting masculine cultural narratives of femininity and desire and rewriting them from a feminist point of view.

Let us consider briefly how those narratives explain and reinforce heterosexuality, both in the construction of societies through kinship systems and in the enculturation of individuals within those societies. Lévi-Strauss describes the exchange of women as "the system of binding *men* together" (emphasis added), thus defining marriage as a social contract between men and viewing the kinship system as a means of reinforcing male power through the circulation of women. Lévi-Strauss concludes that the incest taboo is "the supreme rule of the gift," designed to ensure exogamy (481). Compulsory heterosexuality thus becomes the basis on which society operates and the exchange of women the condition whereby the patriarchy flourishes. Women are prevented from becoming subjects in an economy where they are exchanged as objects, and homosexual desire becomes taboo, like incest, because it disrupts the terms of the social contract. Naturally, this system can only operate smoothly so long as sexual nonconformity is kept invisible. An important project of feminism, then, is to make the invisible visible: to topple the dominant ideology by placing the unorthodox and the marginalized at the center of the discursive and cultural stage. Thus feminist theory constructs homosexuality as a powerfully subversive threat to the social order: Eve Sedgwick, for example, takes up René Girard's notion of "triangular desire"—which in turn develops Lévi-Strauss's theory of the exchange of women as a form of bonding between men—and argues that homophobia functions to suppress recognition of the homosociality on which patriarchal domination depends. Irigaray's coining of the word *hom(m)osexualité* plays on a pun to suggest a similar concept of society as founded on a masculine economy of sameness, so that homosexual relations must be forbidden: "*Because they openly interpret the law according to which society operates, they threaten in fact to shift the horizon of that law*" (193).

Psychoanalytic accounts of enculturation also rest on the prohibition of incest, as enforced through the castration complex; in the oedipal plot, the phallus becomes the coveted marker of sexual difference and desire. Lacan's famous diagram of the identical doors labeled "Ladies" and "Gentlemen" suggests the different ideological worlds that the subject enters according to gender; although gender, like the signs on the doors, is no more than an arbitrary and fictional construct, subjects who wish to function within the symbolic order must pass through one of those doors (147-59). The successful inscription of subjects as masculine or feminine, as "ladies" or "gentlemen," depends on acquiesence to the Law of the Father and on suppression of the polymorphously perverse drives of infancy; in the process, heterosexuality is reinforced as a cultural institution. An important objection to the oedipal scheme is that it predicates female sexuality on a masculine paradigm, thus effacing the very subject of femininity it claims to investigate. Women are effectively excluded from being desiring subjects or from having their sexuality theorized except through a distorting masculine lens. Consequently the lesbian remains outside the framework of representation, becoming, in effect, unrepresentable (for further discussion see de Lauretis, *Alice* and *Technologies*; Cixous and Clément 62-132). Feminist critiques of the oedipal theory have challenged its masculine economy of desire and exposed its inadequacy as an account of female sexuality. Adrienne Rich, for example, wonders why the female child should redirect her libidinal activity from the original object of desire, the mother, to the father and concludes that heterosexuality is a political institution into which women are conscripted ideologically, by force and through the censorship of alternative models of sexuality.[8]

But what happens when the taboo is broken and women refuse to be co-opted into a system of compulsory heterosexuality, refuse in effect to become objects of exchange between men? Or, in Irigaray's words, "*[W]hat if these 'commodities' refused to go to 'market'?*" (196).

This is, of course, the question posed by ***The Color Purple,*** which reduces the system of compulsory heterosexuality to its basic level, making it abstract. The representations of male tyranny are in one sense reductive or crude and in another sense emblematic, their implications far-reaching. The specific systems of oppression that operate in Celie's life symbolize the more or less subtle operations of patriarchal power in the lives of women everywhere.

Compulsory heterosexuality enforces Celie's subjugation and erases her subjectivity. Celie graphically represents this situation when she begins her story by placing "I am" *sous rature*. Trapped from the start into complicity in the shameful secret of incest, Celie makes a timid plea to God: "Maybe you can give me a sign letting me know what is happening to me" (11). But how can Celie be given a sign when she *is* a sign, a mere object of exchange between men? The God she conceptualizes is a cruel father whose identity merges ominously with Pa's; when asked whose baby she is carrying, Celie tells the lie that is the truth: "I say God's. I don't know no other man or what else to say" (12).

When Celie marries Mr. ———, this man with no name becomes part of the system of male oppression, joining God the Patriarch and Pa in an unholy trinity of power that displaces her identity. The marriage negotiations take place entirely between the stepfather and the husband: Celie is handed over like a beast of burden, identified with the cow that accompanies her. Physically and psychologically abused by stepfather and husband alike, Celie is denied a status as subject. Her sexuality and reproductive organs are controlled by men, her children are taken from her, and her submission is enforced through violence. In her terrified acquiescence to such blatant male brutality, Celie symbolically mirrors Everywoman. Fear of rape, for example, is so habitual that it has become naturalized and conditions women automatically; when it circumscribes their movements, we call it Common Sense, and our judicial system holds women who lack it accountable for male violence. Celie bleakly represents the plight of her more privileged sisters, who are victimized by social tyrannies like antiabortion legislation, the kidnapping of children, and state intervention in the family and in individuals' sexual orientation.

Celie's vernacular is used to poignant effect in the double negative of "I don't have nothing." Her connection with her sex is severed; doubly silenced, by father and by husband, Celie sends dead letters to an absentee God, and the only "sign" she eventually gets—the discovery that her real father was lynched—shatters an already eroded identity and precipitates her semiotic collapse. Her attempt to make sense of her new family history breaks down into the negative tautology of "Pa not Pa" (as Berlant has also argued).

This is a puzzling moment in the text. Why does Walker set up incest at the beginning and then reinscribe family relations halfway through? And what is the effect on the reader of discovering that "Pa not Pa"? At one level, I would argue, the revelation makes no difference at all: Celie was still raped, and by a man who was in every respect socially, if not biologically, her father. But suggestions of incest recur too insistently for the question to be dismissed so easily. What, for example, do we make of the marriage of "Sister Nettie" and "Brother Samuel" or of his claim that "we behave as brother and sister to each other"? Shug and Celie, sisters in spirit, become lovers in the flesh. Albert complains that Shug loves him like a brother—but Celie responds, "What so bad about that?" Shug has an affair with a boy who subsequently becomes "like a son. Maybe a grandson." Time and again, the incest taboo is symbolically dissolved as the different categories of social relations, family and sexual, are intertwined.

Perhaps this focus on incest is an honest and courageous attempt to situate sexuality where it belongs: in the heart of the family. If the family is the site of sexual repression and taboo, it is also the place where sexuality is engendered, in the fullest sense.[9] Yet, the Pa-Celie sexual relation, though initially presented as an actual violation of a primary taboo, turns out to be not literal incest but a social and symbolic equivalent. The novel seems to delve into the oedipal drama to unravel and then reweave the complexities, and the discovery that "Pa not Pa" confronts Celie with another contradiction. The Pa who is not Pa is yet—irrevocably—Pa. Her history has been shattered, and she cannot connect with the revised version sent by sister Nettie.

It is her love for Shug that enables Celie to bury her sad double narrative of paternal origins and construct a new identity within a feminine domain. In an earlier scene in the novel, Celie tells her story to Shug, breaking the father's injunction of silence and discovering a sister-lover, compassion and passion combined. Significantly, that first erotic encounter involves both women in a reciprocal mother-infant exchange: "Then I feels something real soft and wet on my breast, feel like one of my little lost babies mouth. . . . Way after while I act like a little lost baby too" (109). The anaclitic satisfaction represented here suggests a symbolic return to the preoedipal stage, an idealized state of innocent eroticism; it is, in Foucault's words, about "bodies and pleasure."[10]

Subsequently, when disconnected from her *nom-du-père* by the discovery that her paternity is indeed a legal fiction, Celie is rescued from an identity crisis by Shug, who tells her, "Us each other's people now"; the two women have mothered each other and now elect to be woman-identified women. Implicit here is an escape from patriarchal law. In breaking the taboo against homosexuality, Celie symbolically exits the masternarrative of female sexuality and abandons the position ascribed to her within the symbolic order. Instead, she chooses a mode of sexuality that Freud describes as "infantile"; but perhaps the value of that term should be reassessed. Shug, for example, is enviably infantile: as polymorphously perverse as a child, she pursues her pleasures without guilt or repression. Her sexual pluralism reminds us that sexuality is the site not only of regulation but of subversion; as Carole Vance argues, sexuality remains, in the end, "flexible, anarchic, ambiguous, layered with multiple meanings, offering doors that open to unexpected experience. The connection of both sexual behavior and fantasy to infancy, the irrational, the unconscious, is a source of both surprise and pleasure" (22). It is this highly disruptive potential—sexuality's ability to resist the ideological laws that operate through its very terrain, to survive and flourish in "aberrant" forms despite the cultural imposition of a norm—that Shug's erotic behavior suggests; she embodies and embraces the notion of jouissance as a liberating power.

Celie's initiation into eroticism is linked with her growing sense of self and her capacity to see wonder in the world. Taught by Shug, whose religious practice is to "admire," Celie metamorphoses into a Miranda, taking childlike delight in the brave new world to which her latent sensory responses have been awakened. If homosexuality involves narcissism, as Freud believes, we see its positive and empowering effect on Celie. In loving Shug, Celie becomes a desiring subject, and in being loved by Shug, she is made visible to herself as an object of desire. In contrast to the repression that Celie has experienced in accepting her social position as a "mature" woman in a phallocentric culture, her "infantile regression" is an act of radical rebellion. By choosing "deviancy," "immaturity," and the "sickness" that lesbianism signifies in a system of compulsory heterosexuality, Celie enacts a critique not of the oedipal theory itself but of the sexist socialization that it insightfully yet uncritically represents.

In a hostile review of the novel, Trudier Harris describes Celie as "a bale of cotton with a vagina" and dismisses Celie and Shug's love affair as a "schoolgirl fairytale," thereby missing the radical political implications of the shift from vagina to clitoris that the lesbian relationship involves. In Freud's theory the clitoral orgasm is notoriously immature; and within the culture, I would suggest, the notion of the mature vaginal orgasm still predominates, since it is a necessary myth within our compulsorily heterosexual society. For a long time Celie's clitoris remained "undiscovered"; and while real women in heterosexual relationships undoubtedly have lovers more skillful and sensitive than Mr. ——— (even if his being signified in this way does mischievously imply that he is the archetypal male), the ideological construct woman still seems to be experiencing orgasm without reference to her clitoris. Think of representations of sexuality in popular films, for example. In the typical love scene, the camera shows a couple commencing missionary-position sex and, eight seconds later, moves in to a close-up of the woman's face to reveal that, miraculously, she is in the throes of orgasm, her mouth wide open, perhaps to suggest that place where the camera is forbidden to go. At this climactic point, the scene dissolves from the screen in an act of self-censorship, and we are left with the dominant image of the desirable woman in our culture: passive, available, and obligingly able to reach instant vaginal orgasm. If film directors know about the clitoris, or about active female desire, film censors are surely involved in the conspiracy to keep such knowledge inadmissible.

What this practice suggests is that the ideology of popular culture subjects women to a mild form of psychological cliterodectomy, and perhaps for the same reason that real clitoridectomies are performed: as Kathleen Barry argues, they ensure that women will not form erotic attachments to one another (193). I would suggest that the erotic zone of the clitoris *has* to be censored in social constructions of sexuality, since its mapping on the female body would allow women to "just say no" to the coveted male organ.

So, for Celie, the discovery of the clitoris (and of the possibility of sexual fulfillment with a woman) is accompanied by a whole range of other discoveries that relegate man to the margins of a world he has always dominated. The most significant of these is a reconceptualization of God the Patriarch. Describing her feminist redefinition of God, Shug makes an explicit connection between spiritual and sexual jouissance.

> My first step from the old white man was trees. . . . Then birds. Then other people. But one day . . . it come to me: that feeling of being part of everything, not separate at all. . . . In fact, when it happen, you can't miss it. It sort of like you know what, she say, grinning and rubbing high up on my thigh.

In answer to Celie's shocked protest, Shug maintains, "God love all them feelings. That's some of the best stuff God did." And shortly afterward she echoes the title of the novel by observing, "I think it pisses God off if you walk by the color purple in a field somewhere and don't notice it" (178). This is a moment of epiphany for Celie, and we might notice her appropriately detumescent metaphor when, in severing the connection between "man" and "God," she observes that "[n]ext to any little scrub of a bush in my yard, Mr. ——'s evil sort of shrink." Phallocentrism has collapsed: the transformation of God from the "old white man" to a new form of otherness, the ungendered creator of the color purple, is one of the major metamorphoses of the novel.

Finally, what is meant by that richly allusive symbol, the color purple? Clearly, in part, it represents the wonder of the natural world, to which Celie's eyes have been newly awakened: "I been so busy thinking about him I never truly notice nothing God make. Not a blade of corn (how it do that?) not the color purple (where it come from?)" (179).

The color purple is encoded within the novel as a sign of indomitable female spirit. For example, Celie makes red-and-purple pants for Sofia (who has survived a brutal beating by the police that leaves her "the color of eggplant"): "I dream Sofia wearing these pants, one day she was jumping over the moon" (194). Consider also Walker's definitions of *womanist,* which are represented by the color purple. One of those definitions, quoted in part earlier, is embodied by Shug: "A woman who loves other women, sexually and/or nonsexually. . . . Sometimes loves individual men, sexually or nonsexually" (**Search** xi). Another definition refers to female joie de vivre, or exuberance; and in her fourth and final definition, Walker states suggestively, "Womanist is to feminist as purple to lavender."

But most daringly significant is the use of the color purple to encode the specifically feminine jouissance experienced by Celie. Associated with Easter and resurrection, and thus with spiritual regeneration, purple may also evoke the female genitalia; indeed, Walker makes the color connection explicit in **"One Child of One's Own"** by provocatively describing a black woman's vagina as "the color of raspberries and blackberries—or scuppernongs and muscadines" (*Search* 374). In that essay Walker complains that white women feminists "cannot imagine that black women have vaginas. Or if they can, where imagination leads them is too far to go" (373).

What I want to suggest is that in **The Color Purple,** in her representation of the unrepresentable, Walker dares us to arrive at the place where "imagination . . . is too far to go."

Notes

1. In *The Heroine's Text,* Nancy Miller defines the "euphoric text" as built on a "trajectory of ascent" and ending with the heroine's integration into society. Miller confines her study to eighteenth-century novels, but her model provides a useful contrast to *The Color Purple,* demonstrating how Walker's novel subverts the conventional plot by rewriting the story of seduction within a lesbian framework.

   In emphasizing the relevance of Celie's story for all women, I do not mean to deny the specificity of her oppression as a black lesbian. Indeed, any blanket reference to women as a category is in any case controversial; my paper does suggest briefly that in feminist discourse this usage tends to reinforce the marginalization of "minority" groups, but I should also note that some feminists would like to abandon the term altogether. Kristeva claims that "to believe that one 'is a woman' is almost as absurd and obscurantist as to believe that one 'is a man'" ("La femme, ce n'est jamais ça," *Tel quel* 59. 3 [1974]: 19-24; qtd. in Moi 163); Monique Wittig provocatively declares, "Lesbians are not women" (110).

2. The term *compulsory heterosexuality* originated with Gayle Rubin: her influential essay "The Traffic in women" synthesizes readings of Freud, Lacan, Marx, and Lévi-Strauss to account for our enculturation into the sex-gender system. See also Adrienne Rich. The term *herstory* comes from Alice Walker's feminist prose (see esp. *Search*).

3. Classic feminist texts that deal with the problem of silencing include Virginia Woolf's *Room of One's Own,* Tillie Olsen's *Silences,* Patricia Meyer Spacks's *Female Imagination,* Elaine Showalter's *Literature of Their Own,* and Sandra M. Gilbert and Susan Gubar's *Madwoman in the Attic*.

4. See, e.g., Gloria T. Hull, Patricia Bell Scott, and Barbara Smith's anthology *Some of Us Are Brave* and Cherrie Moraga and Gloria Anzaldua's *This Bridge Called My Back*. Several essays collected in Showalter's *New Feminist Criticism* also focus on writing by black women and lesbians: Barbara Smith's "Towards a Black Feminist Criticism," Deborah E. McDowell's "New Directions for Black Feminist Criticism," and Bonnie Zimmerman's "What Has Never Been: An Overview of Lesbian Feminist Literary Criticism."

   Printing presses geared toward "minority" groups have been set up recently: for example, the Kitchen Table: Women of Color Press. But in *The Sexual Mountain and Black Women Writers: Adventures in Sex, Literature, and Real Life*—a title so provocative that it invites speculation about men's place in black feminism—Calvin Hernton describes the male speaker's misogyny at a meeting set up to establish a new African American publishing company: "[The speaker] went into a tirade against black women writers . . . claiming that they had 'taken over' the publishing world in a conspiracy against black male writers" (xv). Note also Trudier Harris's allegation that Alice Walker became a media favorite by "waiting in the wings of the feminist movement and the power it had generated long enough for her curtain call to come" (155). Guilty of success, Toni Morrison and Alice Walker bear the brunt of such animosity; compare the personal and critical hostility directed at the flamboyant Zora Neale Hurston, who eventually "disappeared" under its pressure.

5. "Masternarratives" is, of course, Fredric Jameson's term, though he uses it more generally to denote the hegemonic discourse of the ruling class and intends no specific reference to gender.

6. I refer to the conventional assessment of Wright as a realistic writer, though it seems to me that this, too, is misplaced, that his works are, rather, surrealistic. Molly Hite discusses the critical blindness that has resulted from applying conventions of classic realism to *The Color Purple*.

   The feminist tradition of transgressing generic boundaries can be traced at least to Woolf's *Room of One's Own,* which inscribes its feminist social and cultural criticisms within an incisively ironic narrative framework. The strategy is most notably continued in the work of the French feminists, particularly Luce Irigaray, Hélène Cixous, and Catherine Clément; the issue here is a renegotiation of the relation between the personal and the impersonal, or the alleged objectivity of academic discourse. Disrupting generic boundaries is connected with disrupting gender boundaries: feminist writers use subversive narrative strategies to infiltrate and reshape ideological fictions of femininity.

7. For discussions of quilting in Walker's work, see Barbara Christian; Lindsey Tucker; Houston A. Baker, Jr., and Charlotte Pierce-Baker. See Showalter's "Piecing and Writing" for a critique of the revival of feminine crafts as tropes in feminist fictions and theory.

8. For an opposing view, see Cora Kaplan, who objects to Rich's concept of "intellectual" lesbianism as a political solution, arguing that it has produced among feminists a new source of sexual shame and guilt: "Any pleasure that accrues to women who take part in heterosexual acts is therefore necessarily tainted; at the extreme end of this position, women who 'go with men' are considered collaborators . . ." (52). Note also Paula Webster's argument that by privileging lesbianism, feminist discourse has constructed an alternative sexual hierarchy that creates new prohibitions and reduces women's "relationships with eroticism to issues of preference and purity . . ." (387).

9. Michel Foucault argues that "the family is the most active site of sexuality" and that incest is "constantly being solicited and refused . . . a thing that is continuously demanded in order for the family to be a hotbed of constant sexual incitement" (109).

10. One could argue that if Celie symbolically returns to a preoedipal state, her subversive language, with its poetic pulsions and absences, can be connected with Kristeva's concept of the semiotic chora.

Works Cited

Baker, Houston A., Jr., and Charlotte Pierce-Baker. "Patches, Quilts and Community in Alice Walker's 'Every Day Use.'" *Southern Review* 21 (1985): 706-21.

Barry, Kathleen. *Female Sexual Slavery.* Englewood Cliffs: Prentice, 1979.

Berlant, Lauren. "Race, Gender and Nation in *The Color Purple*." *Critical Inquiry* 14 (1988): 831-49.

Castle, Terry. *Clarissa's Ciphers*. Ithaca: Cornell UP, 1982.

Christian, Barbara, ed. *Black Feminist Criticism*. New York: Pergamon, 1985.

Cixous, Hélène, and Catherine Clément. *The Newly Born Woman*. Trans. Betsy Wing. Minneapolis: U of Minnesota P, 1986.

Cooke, Michael G. *Afro-American Literature in the Twentieth Century*. New Haven: Yale UP, 1984.

de Lauretis, Teresa. *Alice Doesn't*. Bloomington: Indiana UP, 1984.

———. *Technologies of Gender: Essays on Theory, Film, and Fiction*. Bloomington: Indiana UP, 1987.

Foucault, Michel. *The History of Sexuality*. Vol. 1. Trans. Robert Hurley. New York: Vintage-Random, 1978.

Freud, Sigmund. "On Narcissism: An Introduction." 1914. *The Standard Edition of the Complete Psychological Works of Sigmund Freud*. Ed. and trans. James Strachey. Vol. 14. London: Hogarth, 1957. 67-102.

Gilbert, Sandra M., and Susan Gubar. *The Madwoman in the Attic*. New Haven: Yale UP, 1979.

Girard, René. *Deceit, Desire, and the Novel*. Trans. Yvonne Freccero. Baltimore: Johns Hopkins UP, 1965.

Harris, Trudier. "On *The Color Purple*, Stereotypes and Silence." *Black American Literature Forum* 18 (1984): 155-61.

Hernton, Calvin C. *The Sexual Mountain and Black Women Writers: Adventures in Sex, Literature, and Real Life*. New York: Anchor-Doubleday, 1987.

Hite, Molly. "Romance, Marginality, Matrilineage: Alice Walker's *The Color Purple* and Zora Neale Hurston's *Their Eyes Were Watching God*." *Novel* 22 (1989): 257-73.

Hull, Gloria T., Patricia Bell Scott, and Barbara Smith, eds. *All the Women Are White, All the Men Are Black, but Some of Us Are Brave*. New York: Feminist, 1982.

Irigaray, Luce. *This Sex Which Is Not One*. Trans. Catherine Porter. Ithaca: Cornell UP, 1985.

Jameson, Fredric. *The Political Unconscious*. Ithaca: Cornell UP, 1981.

Kaplan, Cora. *Seachanges: Culture and Feminism*. London: Verso, 1986.

Kristeva, Julia. *Revolution in Poetic Language*. Trans. Margaret Waller. New York: Columbia UP, 1984.

Lacan, Jacques. *Ecrits*. Trans. Alan Sheridan. New York: Norton, 1977.

Lévi-Strauss, Claude. *The Elementary Structures of Kinship*. Trans. James Hurle Bell et al. 2nd ed. 1967. Oxford: Beacon, 1969.

Lorde, Audre. "The Master's Tools Will Never Dismantle the Master's House." Moraga and Anzaldua 98-101.

Miller, Nancy K. *The Heroine's Text*. New York: Columbia UP, 1980.

Moi, Toril. *Sexual/Textual Politics*. London: Methuen, 1985.

Moraga, Cherrie, and Gloria Anzaldua, eds. *This Bridge Called My Back: Writings by Radical Women of Color*. New York: Kitchen Table, 1981.

Olsen, Tillie. *Silences*. New York: Delacorte, 1979.

Rich, Adrienne. "Compulsory Heterosexuality and Lesbian Representation." *Women—Sex and Sexuality*. Ed. Catharine R. Stimpson and Ethel Spector Person. Chicago: U of Chicago P, 1980. 62-91.

Rubin, Gayle. "The Traffic in Women." *Toward an Anthropology of Women*. Ed. Rayna R. Reiter. New York: Monthly Review, 1975. 157-210.

Sedgwick, Eve. *Between Men*. New York: Columbia UP, 1985.

Showalter, Elaine. *A Literature of Their Own*. Princeton: Princeton UP, 1977.

———, ed. *The New Feminist Criticism*. New York: Pantheon, 1985.

———. "Piecing and Writing." *The Poetics of Gender*. Ed. Nancy K. Miller. New York: Columbia UP, 1986. 222-47.

Spacks, Patricia Meyer. *The Female Imagination*. New York: Knopf, 1975.

Tucker, Lindsey. "Alice Walker's *The Color Purple*: Emergent Woman, Emergent Text." *Black American Literature Forum* 21 (1988): 81-97.

Vance, Carole S., ed. *Pleasure and Danger: Exploring Female Sexuality*. Boston: Routledge, 1984.

Walker, Alice. *The Color Purple*. New York: Washington Square, 1983.

———. *In Search of Our Mothers' Gardens*. San Diego: Harcourt, 1983.

Webster, Paula. "The Forbidden: Eroticism and Taboo." Vance 385-98.

Wittig, Monique. "The Straight Mind." *Feminist Issues* 1 (1980): 103-12.

Woolf, Virginia. *A Room of One's Own.* New York: Harcourt, 1963.

James C. Hall (essay date spring 1992)

SOURCE: Hall, James C. "Towards a Map of Mis(sed) Reading: The Presence of Absence in *The Color Purple.*" *African American Review* 26, no. 1 (spring 1992): 89-97.

[*In the following essay, Hall examines Walker's portrayal of female repression in society and religion in* The Color Purple, *commenting that Celie's emotional growth depends largely on her gradual rejection of the caucasian, male God figurehead.*]

> [Some] receive the news of the death of God and the questionableness of authority with great enthusiasm. Like servants released from bondage to a harsh master or children unbound from the rule of a domineering father, such individuals feel free to become themselves.
>
> (Taylor 45)[1]

The Color Purple, Alice Walker's novel of black feminist awakening, is also a model for the reconstruction of a black feminist literary tradition. If the existence of such a tradition had previously been marked by the "white page" and historical silence, Walker subverts the space by embracing the absence. By attacking patriarchy (and patriarchal culture) at its Christian foundation, Walker celebrates the emptiness which is and has always been full. Working within and expanding the gaps, her work suggests new possibilities for the "sacred" as a tool in literary reconstruction. Her novel is at once "holy," a celebration of "wholeness," and, indeed, a hole. It is the descent necessary for the resurrection, the symbolic reversal of Christian tradition which makes lasting change possible.

If orthodox accounts of literary tradition and history treat influence and "development" with simplistic and apolitical interpretations of "genius," contemporary theories, like that of Harold Bloom, retain an attachment to a patriarchal ground. Bloom's Freudian ordering of the literary universe, in a succession of anxieties and dissatisfactions in the rupture of communication between fathers and sons, cannot provide even the briefest contextual outline for a black women's literary tradition.[2] His "daemonic" reversal, however, can be appropriated: A "misreading," the creative failure of a son's writing/righting his anxiety, can become a "mis(sed) reading," the creative success of the daughter's writing/rite-ing within the full emptiness of the page and history. Indeed, Paule Marshall has described her own literary output as writing those works that she would have liked to have read.[3] Alice Walker has also textualized this "desire" and has noted the forgotten power (and tragedy) of the silenced voice.

Walker makes clear the relationship between the emptying of the literary space and the fulfillment of female identity through her novel's epistolary structure, which subverts the predominantly male code of the Western literary tradition. This grounding celebrates an escape from history while retaining a faithfulness to the transformative power of art. It is also significant that Western and African expressive traditions combine in the epistolary mode, which is the literary/literal equivalent of call and response. Similarly, the revision of the sentimental tradition retains the importance of sororal connections and focuses attention on female bonding. Walker's women transform their own lives as Alice Walker transforms the tradition: Literary codes and conventions are seen to parallel social and sexual relations.

I would like to argue, however, that Walker's greatest accomplishment within ***The Color Purple*** is its claim for "space" through the critique of patriarchal theological structures that are, by implication, theocratic. If the adoption of the epistolary form subverts male codes of literary expression, Walker continues the daemonic subversion, further directing her attention to philosophical and political structures that are also limiting of black women. Even more complicated, perhaps, is her critique of anthropomorphic thought and its creative limitations. Walker's religious universe is "self-inventive"; it marks the clearing of debris through the embrace of absence. Insofar as it directs attention to the creative process, Walker's text tends towards the realm of metafiction. It is indeed an anti-story: anti-patriarchal, anti-sexist, anti-Western, etc. But it is not an act of nihilism or desperation, not a celebration of the end but of beginnings. It restates the power of literary creativity in a profoundly social manner.

Walker's novel begins with a threat: "*You better not never tell nobody but God. It'd kill your mammy*" (3). The irony of the triple negative goes unrecognized, and the chief significance of the voicing lies, perhaps, in its threat to the matriarchal bond. The emergence of a voice of challenge could result in the disruption of the mother-daughter covenant. The threat (based upon the sexual violation of the female) cannot be acknowledged through a cry for help or even sympathy. Celie must turn toward a personal, but distant, God. Celie's "Dear God" marks not only the emergence of a literary form (the epistolary novel) but also a ritual form (prayer). Walker immediately (if somewhat cryptically) directs our attention toward the efficacy of this ritual form: In Celie's "I am," Walker simultaneously deletes/revises the present tense of the verb *to be* and the Biblical self-designation of the Hebrew God. This radical, yet subtle, transformation is highly suggestive. Its deletion may signal a passionate turn from the Biblical religious tradition in which many black women have historically found self-definition. Equally as crucial, however, is

Walker's empowerment of her seemingly impotent protagonist. The "word" has been spoken; the refuge of the traditional ritual (and literary) form is temporary.

Celie has also asked for a sign. At this point in her narrative she perceives herself as powerless, and looks for external authorization. Although writing God, she is unable to right her situation. Somewhat immediately, however, the beneficence and the righteousness of this God is called into question. "My mama dead" (4), Celie tells us in her next letter, despite her attempts to satisfy the demands of her *father*'s curse. The victim of incest, Celie had told her mother upon the birth of her child that it was "God's" (4). Destructive patriarchal power is associated with God even though this same power is Celie's textual partner. Walker thus begins the process of clearing. Her protagonist has (in the first two pages) spoken the unspoken (the "I am") and radically revised the mythic story of Christ's birth. Celie's path to selfhood involves the evaporation of patriarchal Christianity.

Celie's marriage to Mr. ——— continues the pattern. Her husband, in a further reference to the Old Testament God, is also unnameable. This textual deletion signifies her "partner's" absolute distance, his inability to comprehend her history and future. He perceives her as livestock, and denies her not only love but humanity. She discovers her lost child in the possession of a "Reverend Mr. ———" (15). From no Mr. ——— will she receive "God help" (5). In retribution, Walker ironically denies identity to the powerful, whom she playfully makes into objects of ridicule; they possess titles of pseudo-respect, but lack "Christian" names.

It is from Nettie that Celie first learns that resistance is necessary: "You got to fight. You got to fight" (17). But as that lesson is first being learned, Nettie's safety is called into question because of Mr. ———'s advances. Nettie begins their goodbye:

> I sure hate to leave you here with these rotten children, she say. Not to mention with Mr. ———. It's like seeing you buried, she say.
>
> It's worse than that, I think. If I was buried, I wouldn't have to work. But I just say, Never mine, never mine, long as I can spell G-o-d I got somebody along.
>
> (18)

Celie's response is highly ironic, both in terms of her "never mine" comment and the silence of her respondent. It is true that that bond can never be hers. But Walker makes clear where the true bond should be. Their goodbye is completed:

> I say, Write.
>
> She say, What?

> I say, Write.
>
> She say, Nothing but death can keep me from it.
>
> She never write.
>
> (18)

The connection (a "literary" one) is based upon female ties. And what is of greatest significance is that Celie must learn to be patient with Nettie's silence; she must discover that there never was a silence, that the nexus was interrupted. The literary space is full. It is also significant that Celie herself seems to sense something. The salutation of her next letter is not "Dear God" but "G-o-d" (19). While clearly a reference to Nettie's farewell, the expression also explores the "white spaces" between the "letters." Walker's revision of the textual form (of the generic convention) exposes the ritual partner as artifice.

Although Celie must endure the indignities of her life without Nettie's support and aid, Celie's familial universe is not to be without female nurturance. Harpo's marriage to Sofia introduces Celie to an alternative mode of coping. Sofia "modifies" the requirements of marriage and child rearing. She rebels against the authority of her own father, and she is unwilling to behave deferentially to any man. Sofia's rebellion becomes a cause for Celie to reflect:

> I think bout this when Harpo ast me what he ought to do to her to make her mind. I don't mention how happy he is now. How three years pass and he still whistle and sing. I think bout how every time I jump when Mr. ——— call me, she look surprise. And like she pity me.
>
> (34)

Jealous of Sofia's autonomy, and uncomfortable with her pity, Celie suggests that Harpo beat her. Harpo's lack of success in taming Sofia and her own conscience conspire to make her realize her "sin." Not even "think[ing]" about the Bible (37) relieves her anxiety.

Sofia's confronting Celie with the fact of her betrayal leads to her considering a new possibility. Celie tells Sofia how she perseveres:

> Well, sometime Mr. ——— git on me pretty hard. I have to talk to Old Maker. But he my husband. I shrug my shoulders. This life soon be over, I say. Heaven last all ways.
>
> You ought to bash Mr. ——— head open, she say. Think bout heaven later.
>
> (39)

Sofia's suggestion participates in the clearing of the patriarchal theological ground that is part of Celie's imprisonment. Outright rejection of the future-oriented strategy is difficult, yet Sofia's combative personal style is not appropriate for Celie. Still, the suggestion introduces levity into a confrontational situation. It provides an occasion for the establishment of female bonds through the introduction of a maternal art form:

> Not much funny to me. That funny. I laugh. She laugh. Then us both laugh so hard us flop down on the step.
>
> Let's make quilt pieces out of these messed up curtains, she say. And I run git my pattern book.
>
> (39)

Whatever Sofia's contribution to Celie's enlightenment, it remains for Shug Avery to disrupt her world view radically. Shug, Mr. ———'s blues-singing lover, is clearly a threat to the patriarchal establishment, as the preacher signifies by taking Shug's "condition for his text" (40). Shug's lifestyle is a rejection of the values of the Christian-based community, and suggests both marginalization and survival. Despite her horrible condition when she enters Celie's household, she finds a way to endure:

> Ain't nothing wrong with Shug Avery. She just sick. Sicker than anybody I ever seen. She sicker than my mama was when she die. But she more evil than my mama and that keep her alive.
>
> (43)

Despite Shug's "evil," her entrance into Celie's life represents the emergence of a new religious consciousness: "I wash her body, it feel like I'm praying" (45). And surprisingly, Shug's presence seems to lessen the tension between Celie and Mr. ———; their co-commitment to her health marks a new understanding in their relationship. Shug's presence also marks Celie's ability to conceptualize things differently, to imagine another real existence: "First time I think about the world" (52), Celie considers, in clear opposition to the "other-worldly" orientation that Sofia has warned her against.

Shug's attentions to Celie are crucial to Celie's emergent self-identification. Shug helps to make Celie aware of her own sexuality, and ironically "redefines" her as "virgin" (95). Significantly, Shug as "writer" draws attention to Celie. Her "Miss Celie's song" punctuates her importance in Celie's growing self-awareness: "First time somebody made something and name it after me" (65). Still, Shug's contribution to this naming and liberating process is limited. Like Sophia, Shug cannot provide Celie with her distinctive individuality. But by encouraging Celie to provide this answer for herself and to reject the Biblical injunctions, Shug, like Sophia, participates in the theological clearing.

There is still much radical redefinition to be done. When Sofia gets into trouble for "sassing," Celie imagines a dramatic solution:

> . . . I think bout angels, God coming down by chariot, swinging down real low and carrying ole Sofia home. I see 'em all as clear as day. Angels all in white, white hair and white eyes, look like albinos. God all white too, looking like some stout white man work at the bank. Angels strike they cymbals, one of them blow his horn. God blow out a big breath of fire and suddenly Sofia free.
>
> (80)

But Celie, Shug, and Harpo's mistress Squeak do not wait for this solution. They conspire to have Squeak confront the warden in the hope of using her past to gain favor for Sofia. While their plan has limited success, it is their decision to combat patriarchal power with black female solidarity that is noteworthy. Their ability to "conspire" is significant; their "plot" is Walker's. The silence that is framed in otherworldly hope is replaced by a worldly female bonding.

Celie's discovery (with Shug's assistance) of Nettie's letters marks the radical turning point of the novel. Hidden by Mr. ——— (now named Albert), the letters are the powerful connecting metaphor for the reconstruction of a black feminist literary tradition. The text and the tradition have never been missing. They have been disguised and sequestered because of the letters' liberating power. Albert's desire to "keep" Celie, to shape her for himself, to proscribe her existence, is most powerfully expressed in his attempts to break sororal bonds through the denial of a textual connection with Nettie. The discovery of the letters, a product of ongoing self-redefinition, further promotes that process.

Nettie writes in one of her first letters:

> I remember one time you said your life made you feel so ashamed you couldn't even talk about it to God, you had to write it, bad as you thought your writing was. Well, now I know what you meant. And whether God will read letters or no, I know you will go on writing them; which is guidance enough for me.
>
> (110)

The artifice of Celie's writing structure is revealed; "God" functions as a sardonic surrogate partner in the silence created by the very patriarchal power it represents. This "revelation" produces a most dramatic change in Celie's character; Shug must try to convince her not to kill Albert, in a rage even Sofia can't conceive:

> Don't kill, she say. Nettie be coming home before long. Don't make her have to look at you like us look at Sofia.
>
> But it so hard, I say, while Shug empty her suitcase and put the letters inside.
>
> Hard to be Christ too, say Shug. But he manage. Remember that. Thou Shalt Not Kill, He said. . . .

> But Mr. —— not Christ. I'm not Christ, I say.
>
> (122)

Celie distances herself not only from the "Christ[ian]" response, but also from the tradition itself. The convincing part of Shug's argument is that Celie should not risk severing her tie to Nettie. The appeal to "Christ" is an appeal to an old rhetoric that has little hold upon Celie any more.

Walker powerfully challenges her reader (and herself) in the demythologizing of tradition by making Nettie a missionary. However, Nettie's experience in colonial Africa, rather than being a retreat, further unravels the ties between institutional Christianity and black oppression. Nettie's letters tell of the power of being faced with "the Olinka God" (131), and of physical and cultural destruction. The necessary ignorance of imperialism and the new vision of cross-cultural perspective make Corrine and Samuel appear provincial. Nettie's faithfulness in the face of such inconsistency and violence requires a radical reorientation. The "rules," it seems clear, have changed, and this shift is linked to Nettie's tie to Celie. Nettie does recognize the negative power of the vocation she represents, and distances herself accordingly. The "fact" of her one-way correspondence with Celie seems to speak to a gap in her call. "I would give anything for a picture of you, Celie," writes Nettie. ". . . the picture of Christ which generally looks good anywhere looks peculiar here" (135). Nettie has had to redefine her purpose:

> My spirits sort of drooped after being at the [Missionary] Society. On every wall there was a picture of a white man. . . . We are not white. We are not Europeans. We are black like the Africans themselves. And that we and the Africans will be working for a common goal; the uplift of black people everywhere.
>
> (115)

Celie, similarly, ceases to write to God when she learns from Nettie that "Pa is not our Pa!" (150). While literally representing the unraveling of Celie's complicated genealogy and the removal of the stigma of incest, this statement symbolically marks their joint recognition of the superfluous demands of a restrictive theocracy. The Christian "father" is not their father, not their spiritual reservoir. But, as Nettie warns (". . . unbelief is a terrible thing" [158]), a retreat into nihilism is not the answer. Celie must re-learn belief in a way that replenishes the spirit as it redefines the self.

Shug also recognizes the danger in absolute rejection:

> Just because I don't harass it like some peoples us know don't mean I ain't got religion.
>
> What God do for me? I ast. . . .
>
> She say, Miss Celie, You better hush. God might hear you.

> Let 'im hear me, I say. If he ever listened to poor colored women the world would be a different place, I can tell you.
>
> She talk and she talk, trying to budge me way from blasphemy. But I blaspheme much as I want to.
>
> (164)

Celie's claiming the power of the curse is significant. It is the most dramatic form of radical revision, but also the most dangerous.[4] Shug's and Nettie's attachment to some "form" of a god makes clear that Celie's anger endangers her bond with them; an absolute negativity could shut them out. Celie herself recognizes the risk:

> All my life I never care what people thought bout nothing I did, I say. But deep in my heart I care about God. What he going to think. And come to find out, he don't think. Just sit up there glorying in being deef, I reckon. But it ain't easy, trying to do without God. Even if you know he ain't there, trying to do without him is a strain.
>
> (164)

Celie and Shug try to renegotiate an identity and existence for "God." Shug's lesson for Celie includes recognizing that "God" isn't necessarily to be found in the institutional church, nor should "its" image be old, white, and male. Most radically, Shug rejects anthropomorphic conceptions completely:

> Here's the thing, say Shug. The thing I believe. God is inside you and inside everybody else. You come into the world with God. But only them that search for it inside find it. And sometimes it just manifest itself even if you not looking, or don't know what you looking for. . . .
>
> It? I ast.
>
> Yeah, It. God ain't a he or a she, but a It.
>
> (166-67)

Shug's rejection is the action that makes possibility; hers is a signifyin' theology that clears the way for Celie's selfhood. It reveals that Celie's writing has not been directed outward to a distant, uncaring entity, but inward, satisfying her own creativity.

But Celie must still act for herself. If Shug's lesson has provided a further opening, Celie must enter it, and claim her inheritance.

> Well, us talk and talk bout God, but I'm still adrift. Trying to chase that old white man out of my head. I been so busy thinking bout him I never truly notice nothing God make. . . .
>
> Man corrupt everything, say Shug. He on your box of grits, in your head, and all over the radio. He try to make you think he everywhere. Soon as you think he everywhere, you think he God. But he ain't. Whenever you trying to pray, and man plop himself on the other end of it, tell him to git lost, say Shug. Conjure up flowers, wind, water, a big rock.

> But this hard work, let me tell you. He been there so long, he don't want to budge. He threaten lightening, floods, and earthquakes. Us fight. I hardly pray at all. Every time I conjure up a rock, I throw it.
>
> Amen.
>
> (168)

Shug's ironic use of the orthodox account of the Genesis story becomes a tool in Celie's liberation. "Man" has corrupted the creation, and Celie must resort to conjuration to protect herself.[5] The "Amen" that ends Celie's account is a powerful one. It has been conspicuously absent from her other letters ("prayers") despite their traditional form. The "Amen" is not a note of ritual assent, but its negation. This amen indicates the power of the "specified" rather than consensus.

If conjuring provides the psychic power to prevent Celie's regression into total subservience, the "curse" is the radical negation that makes selfhood possible. "It's time to leave you and enter into the Creation," (170) she tells Mr. ———. More powerfully still:

> I curse you, I say.
>
> What that mean? he say.
>
> I say, Until you do right by me, everything you touch will crumble.
>
> He laugh. Who you think you is? he say. You can't curse nobody. Look at you. You black, you pore, you ugly, you a woman. Goddam, he say, you nothing at all. . . .
>
> I'm pore, I'm black, I may be ugly and can't cook, a voice say to everything listening. But I'm here.
>
> Amen, say Shug. Amen, amen.
>
> (176)

Mr. ———'s inability to understand "what that mean" becomes definitive of a separate tradition of voice and text. Celie's curse brings havoc upon the patriarchal household, and makes a claim for her own space within creation. Her acknowledgment of Mr. ———'s disclaimer negates its power and rejects its attempt to define appropriate roles and standards for black women. Finally, Shug's recitation of the dissenting a-men reminds the reader of the theocratic ground being cleared.

But Celie's curse is affirmative as well as negating. It instigates a new order. Not only is the restoration of Celie's family imminent, but significant changes in character are also promoted. We are told of Mr. ———'s new grooming habits and work ethic. Harpo's relationships with Sofia and his father are improved. We are even told of Harpo's going to sleep with his father in order to keep him company (191). Symbolically, the curse provides the motivation for the lamb to lie down with the lion, while it literally continues to revise gender roles.

Now Celie's troubles can be confronted in a different way. When Shug is about to leave her for a young man, Celie responds, "I write" (212). As Shug's explanation becomes more desperate, Celie's response becomes like a chant, and Walker again directs our attention to the value and function of the hidden tradition. The voice that empowers the curse also promotes and defines the tradition. Celie's "I write" (and, perhaps, I *right*) begins to provide the reader with access to that map of mis(sed) reading.

Walker's clearing of the theological ground has not been approved of universally. Indeed, the publication of her latest novel, **The Temple of My Familiar,** has heightened criticism that Walker has adopted a mushy New Age philosophy to confront a historical Christianity that has misled and misplaced black women. Gerald Early may have been Walker's harshest early critic when, in responding to **The Color Purple,** he suggested that Walker is guilty of a "fairly dim-witted pantheistic acknowledgment of the wonders of human potential that begins to sound quite suspiciously like a cross between the New Age movement and Dale Carnegie" (272). Such criticism would be appropriate if Walker claimed her novel to be "real" in the mode of either Toni Morrison or Richard Wright. But Walker may more correctly belong in a tradition of black mysticism, with Rebecca Jackson, Jean Toomer, and Howard Thurman as ancestors, and Henry Dumas as contemporary.[6] Indeed, Early goes too far when he suggests that

> . . . what Walker does in her novel is allow its social protest to become the foundation for its utopia. Not surprisingly, the book lacks any *real* intellectual or theological rigor or coherence, and the fusing of social protest and utopia is really nothing more than confounding and blundering, each seeming to subvert the reader's attention from the other. One is left thinking that Walker wishes to thwart her own ideological ends or that she simply does not know how to write novels. In essence, the book attempts to be revisionist salvation history, and fails because of its inability to use or really understand history.
>
> (273; emphasis added)

Early protests too much, and begins to be cast in the role of offended defender of the patriarchal ground. Walker has made no claim as an historian; her self-identification as "medium" suggests that **The Color Purple** is clearly meant to be outside of the historical realm. Early is correct, perhaps, when he suggests that Alice Walker does not know how to write novels—at least novels directed or shaped by a male and Western paradigm. Walker is exploring the possibilities in the text as sacrament. "Profitless play," suggests Mark

Taylor, "can overcome the unhappy consciousness of the historical agent" (4). Walker's book is not "closed"; rejecting the *telos* of the historian for the "purposeless" wandering/wondering of the blues woman, **The Color Purple** invites the play of surfaces, the interpretation of interpretation. It dismisses history to revise the present.

To have access to a *map of mis(sed) reading* is to encourage a particular kind of historic consciousness. The challenge which confronts individuals interested in the establishment of a black feminist literary history is the necessity of enacting reconstruction and imaginatively identifying new historical categories, constructing theories of influence and theories of individual creation. Walker addresses this theoretical dilemma. Despite the important contribution of *The Schomburg Library of Nineteenth-Century Black Women Writers*, Barbara Christian's *Black Women Novelists*, or even the work of the Afro-American Novel Project at Boston University to our desired historiography, we must also recognize the contribution of Walker's *fictional* transgression. What work can a new *catalog* of lost texts do towards the comprehension of black women's creative writing if we cannot also think through the problem of absent readers? If our historiographical model is to be complete, it must acknowledge a range of literary activities and desires; it must document and imaging writers and readers, perhaps even *texts,* written and dreamed. Walker recognizes the wound inflicted by canonical edict: *literary silence,* despite richness of artistic instinct, of human desire to creatively alter the world, immediate and distant. Her response is to subvert the patriarchal and racist dimensions of our *culture of the word* by questioning traditional theological and theocratic structures, while retaining through playful revision the interrelationship of speech, selfhood, and creativity. The *creative disorganization* of our very notion of tradition, while retaining commitment to humanistic values and inquiry, is no small feat. Despite a *postmodern theology*—an embrace of absent fathers—Walker has no desire to do away with meaning. She is clearly *a woman of letters.*

The reintegration offered in Celie's final letter draws attention to the *conjure*; it suggests to the reader the closing of a special period of time and space. "Dear God. Dear stars, dear trees, dear sky, dear peoples. Dear Everything. Dear God" (249)—not only is there psychic reconciliation, but also a sense of ritual completion, consistent with the notion of the text as sacrament. The reader emerges from the realm of the imaginary with a sense of new possibility. Most significantly, "Walker creates a new literary space for the black and female idiom within a traditionally Western and Eurocentric form" (Henderson 18). We begin to get some idea as to how to inscribe and describe the newness—ways of celebrating genius. And as Celie discovers the letters, and recovers her "missed reading," we are directed toward a map of tradition.

This accomplishment is best marked by Walker's quote of Stevie Wonder: "*Show me how to do like you / Show me how to do it.*" Walker's attention to the vernacular song makes clear the ways in which her text is not a passive imitation of the Western literary form. **The Color Purple** is a demand for recognition, for the acknowledgment of revision within missed reading. There is irony in the source—the black and blind (literally "vision"-less) singer asking to be *shown* as opposed to *told.* Walker's creative genius is the revision of vision, asking us to see alternatively, to see where we have not seen before.

Notes

1. Taylor's deconstruction of traditional theological conceptions is crucial to my reading of Walker.

2. Dianne F. Sadoff's "Black Matrilineage" offers an important consideration of the value of Bloom's work, particularly *The Anxiety of Influence,* for a black women's literary tradition. Sadoff also considers the value of Gilbert and Gubar's *The Madwoman in the Attic.* I wish to argue that the notion of "re-reading" or "re-voicing" can be appropriated without adopting the psychoanalytic model (and controversy). Sadoff's work demonstrates the danger inherent in confronting that tradition: Spending an inordinate amount of time delineating the complexities of one "school" over another can divert attention from the insight's constructive potential within the literary tradition. More helpful are the essays by Marjorie Pryse and Hortense Spillers in *Conjuring,* by Mae G. Henderson in *Sage,* and most especially by Walker herself (see "Saving the Life That Is Your Own," "Zora Neale Hurston: A Cautionary Tale and a Partisan View," and "Looking for Zora" in *Gardens*).

3. It must be made clear that what is being asserted here by both black women writers and myself is not the *non-existence* of a rich tradition of literature by black women, but rather a matrix of circumstances which have in the past made (conspired to make?) unlikely the placement of black women's *literary* stories in the hands of a black female readership. Benignly, one might assert that a *map of mis(sed) reading* is an analytical tool for the use of sociologists of literature; more powerfully, I think, it should be seen as a interpretive tool for the use of sympathetic critics in the *reconstruction* of the *unseen* tradition. Again, as noted above, Alice Walker's own writing on *models* is crucial.

4. Mark Taylor makes clear why it must be dangerous: "In a place of a simple reversal, it is necessary to effect a dialectical inversion that does not leave contrasting opposites unmarked but dissolves their original identities. Inversion, in other words, must simultaneously be a perversion that is subversive. Unless theological transgression becomes genuinely subversive, nothing fundamental will change. What is needed is a critical lever with which the entire inherited order can be creatively disorganized" (10).

5. Pryse and Spillers have made specific use of Walker's use of conjuration in titling their text on black women's literary tradition. I would further suggest that this is a clue to a further revision of Bloom's "ratios"; for a black women's tradition of revision we might substitute *signifyin'* for *clinamen*, *dues* for *tessara*, *steppin' out* for *kenosis*, *spirit possession* for *daemonization*, *curse* for *askesis*, and *the blues* for *apophrades*. Of course, any such revision would need to challenge more substantively Bloom's assumed historical and psychoanalytic *connections*. Walker's challenge (and my own, I hope) is more than an assault on Eurocentric paradigms—it is a needed reassertion of American pluralism against *objective* theory.

6. On Walker's knowledge of Rebecca Jackson, see "Gifts of Power: The Writings of Rebecca Jackson" (*Gardens* 71-82). One of the most disappointing aspects of the most recent assault on Walker has been the inability of critics and commentators to contextualize her more recent concerns with reference to African-American religious history.

Works Cited

Bloom, Harold. *The Anxiety of Influence: A Theory of Poetry*. New York: Oxford UP, 1973.

Christian, Barbara. *Black Women Novelists: The Development of a Tradition, 1892-1976*. Westport: Greenwood, 1980.

Early, Gerald. "Everybody's Protest Art: *The Color Purple*." *Antioch Review* 44 (1986): 261-78.

Gates, Henry Louis, Jr., gen. ed. *The Schomburg Library of Nineteenth-Century Black Women Writers*. 30 vols. New York: Oxford UP, 1988.

Gilbert, Sandra M., and Susan Gubar. *The Madwoman in the Attic: The Woman Writer and the Nineteenth-Century Imagination*. New Haven: Yale UP, 1979.

Henderson, Mae G. "*The Color Purple*: Revisions and Redefinitions." *Sage* 2.1 (1987): 14-18.

Pryse, Marjorie, "Zora Neale Hurston, Alice Walker, and the Ancient Power of Black Women." Pryse and Spillers 1-24.

Pryse, Marjorie, and Hortense J. Spillers, eds. *Conjuring: Black Women, Fiction, and Literary Tradition*. Bloomington: Indiana UP, 1985.

Sadoff, Dianne F. "Black Matrilineage: The Case of Alice Walker and Zora Neale Hurston." *Signs* 11.1 (1985): 4-26.

Spillers, Hortense J. "Cross-Currents, Discontinuities: Black Women's Fiction." Pryse and Spillers 249-61.

Taylor, Mark C. *Erring: A Postmodern A/theology*. Chicago: U of Chicago P, 1984.

Walker, Alice. *The Color Purple*. New York: Harcourt, 1982.

———. *In Search of Our Mothers' Gardens: Feminist Prose*. New York: Harcourt, 1983.

Carole Anne Taylor (essay date winter 1994)

SOURCE: Taylor, Carole Anne. "Humor, Subjectivity, Resistance: The Case of Laughter in *The Color Purple*." *Texas Studies in Literature and Language* 36, no. 4 (winter 1994): 462-82.

[*In the following essay, Taylor evaluates Walker's use of laughter in* The Color Purple, *asserting that the novel employs laughter as a shared acknowledgment of pain and camaraderie, rather than lighthearted banter.*]

> They crush and crush
> your heart;
> your humor
> escapes.
>
> —Alice Walker, **"Ndebele"**

> Postmodernism for postmodernism, politics for politics, I'd rather be an ironist than a terrorist.
>
> —Susan Suleiman, *Subversive Intent*

> Indeed, irony in the face of actual torture is arguably less worthwhile than terrorism in the face of a text. And we don't, in any event, always get to choose our contexts or our adversaries.
>
> —Lillian Robinson, "At Play in the Mind-fields"

Perhaps no text more dramatically demonstrates how differently diverse communities of readers construct literary meaning than does **The Color Purple**, the locus of ongoing debate about interlocking systems of oppression and their representation in literature. Even among generally appreciative critics, some have found a clear model for the organized struggle against oppression, and others have found a wish-fulfilling romance. Estimations of value trouble over the seemingly polarized distance between Celie's distinctive personal voice and Nettie's "essay on the history of the Olinka tribe" (Robinson, "Problems," 2), sometimes conceived as a problem of genre.¹ Is the ending too utopian to address the difficult tensions between the material oppression that writes itself on actual women's bodies and the fictional oppression that either goes away or ennobles its victims somehow too easily? Where is resistance in a world replete with incest wiped away, abuse forgiven or transformed, and a propertied Celie surrounded by extended family? What relevance has a world where black women always get up again—no matter how beaten down—to real social worlds? Such questions have strong relevance to debates about resistance in literary texts and how such resistance hooks up—or does not—to the political world. In particular, *The Color Purple* may help clarify how resistance is never purely resistance nor simply *there* in a text but always ambivalently situated in relation to what it resists.²

Significantly, different constructions of humor and the comic inform ongoing controversies about whether a postmodernism of resistance is a hopelessly conflicted idea and about whether women's writing can escape the exclusionary strategies of received Western genres.³ Theories of an extreme, parodic humor, prominent in both feminist and postmodern imagining, value the resisting laughter of a madman, a Medusa, or the *bricoleur* while absenting any "normal other" from playfulness.⁴ Concomitantly, Fredric Jameson links his critique of postmodernism to a practice "devoid of laughter," arguing that it replaces any healthy "normality" with "empty" or "neutral" parody and pastiche. And Judy Little and Clair Wills extend extant theory by fitting Bakhtin's carnival to women writers, hypothesizing an unending saturnalia, a holiday of festive inversions that never ends. Defiant, aggressive laughter exists abundantly in Walker's fictional worlds, as do festive comic inversions; and both assimilate easily into the dominant theories that identify humor as resistance with a focused attack on butts or targets.

Yet a humorous rapport among characters also celebrates a healthy normalcy and merges the subjectivities of its characters, placing *The Color Purple* somewhat outside these formulations. Its storytelling does not entirely return to an older Western realism nor entirely adapt the conventions of comic romance, just as it does not entirely abjure speech for a postmodern play among ontologies.⁵ Rather, interrogations of subjectivity itself attribute value to an intersubjectivity that has multivalent relation to readerly desire.⁶ By exploring the interrelations between humorous rapport and a merged subjectivity among characters, I want, ultimately, to consider *The Color Purple*'s genre as an expressive hybrid, one whose dialogical form of resistance has everything to do with where readings enter relations of privilege or power.⁷

And so I start with what does not console or comfort my own reading position(s) in any way: an unheard laughter, a laughter that refuses any easy desire for inclusion, a laughter that upsets any hold on the security of writerly-readerly relations. Most of the characters in *The Color Purple* ultimately share the capacity for humorous rapport, and the work's sense of an ending relies in large part on a vision of happiness incorporating a robust, vernacular humor into daily life. Yet the way humor accrues value in *The Color Purple* has little to do with funny scenes, humorous lines or narratives, or some overarching comic structure. Rather, humor develops as an interaction that in its implied normalcy provides the daily context of value. And the development of this interaction mitigates against the generic security of both Molly Hite's attempt to reconcile feminist and poststructuralist concerns in a reading of *The Color Purple* as a comic romance and, more supplementally, Henry Gates's postmodern emphasis on an epistolary transformation of "speakerly language which no character can ever speak, because it exists only in a written text" (250).⁸ In comic romance, the impulse of a sympathetic humor works through the involuted exigences of disguise and disorder until a united couple at the close represents the unthreatened norms of a society returned to its rightful order. And in an epistolary text where writing protects the reader from Gates's "tyranny of the narrative present," resisting agency resides primarily in the act of writing.⁹ Deborah McDowell's conception of character as process helps to focus on the value of humorous rapport because it usefully supplants Hite's sense of characterization and supplements Gates's emphasis, affording humor greater importance precisely because it helps to differentiate characters with fluid or merging identities from either unitary, ego-centered selves defined in contrast to some "other" or from characters subsumed by their existence in writing.¹⁰

A humor integral to the experience of interconnected relationships, dramatically presented in dialogue form, structures all of Celie's developing interactions with women, but her letters about Sofia's imprisonment and subsequent release focus on a humor contrasted to any humor "normative" to social health. Celie recounts how Sofia, at the beginning of her jail term of returning the mayor's violence, can still laugh, albeit with the quality of blues expressivity. When her extended family visits her in jail, no one present can bear the emotive force of her condition, which exists outside ordinary language:

> Mr. —— suck in his breath. Harpo groan. Miss Shug cuss. She come from Memphis special to see Sofia.
>
> I can't fix my mouth to say how I feel.
>
> (88)

Context connects this lyrical, expressive sadness with laughing alone:

> I'm a good prisoner, she [Sofia] say. Best convict they ever see. They can't believe I'm the one sass the

> mayor's wife, knock the mayor down. She laugh. It sound like something from a song. The part where everybody done gone home but you.
>
> (88)

In several subsequent letters, Celie tells of the scheming to release Sofia, a scheming that cleverly relies on white vengefulness. Then, suddenly, Sofia reappears as a participant in Celie's daily life, with a narrative ellipsis of three years marked by her presence in a relationship once again allowing mutual laughter. The absence of three years from Sofia's story, then, becomes not just some imaginary expansion of a terrible time in jail followed by a slavelike existence as resident "maid" to Miss Millie; rather, it becomes the absence of mutual, if not yet intersubjective laughter, a laughter whose disappearance and reappearance signals a gaping ellipsis in human as well as narrative time.

The capacity for this laughter marks Sofia's return to human interaction after her grotesque imprisonment, but the invocation of humor frames the opening and closing of Celie's letters rather than providing some humorous content. The first letter telling us that the scheme to release Sofia to a servitude outside the jail has worked begins with Celie's reported discourse in which she acknowledges the legitimacy of Sofia's rage but transforms it into a humorous comment on the politics of power:

> Sofia say to me today, I just can't understand it.
>
> What that? I ast.
>
> Why we ain't already kill them off.
>
> Three years after she beat she out of the wash house, got her color and her weight back, look like her old self, just all time think bout killing somebody.
>
> Too many to kill off, I say. Us outnumbered from the start. I speck we knock over one or two, though, here and there, through the years, I say.
>
> (98)

To argue that this reported dialogue represents Celie's "control" of another's speech, as do Gates's generalizations about the primacy of writing, undervalues the dramatic immediacy of the exchange and the context-specific focus on a sustaining, resisting humorous rapport. Even though Celie asserts, "Us outnumbered from the start," her attitude has nothing of impotence about it, especially since her consoling figure ("I speck we knock over one or two, though, here and there, through the years") has literal as well as figurative resonance: Sofia went to jail, after all, for knocking over "one." Internally, the letter recounts the spiteful, self-injuring kick of Miss Millie's Billy and the more needy demands of Eleanor Jane, the daughter-outsider. At the close, Sofia ponders, "I wonder why she [Eleanor Jane] was ever born," and the chapter-letter ends:

> Well, I say, us don't have to wonder that bout darkies. She giggle. Miss Celie, she say, you just as crazy as you can be. This the first giggle I heard in three years.
>
> (99)

Sofia's giggle marks the (re)created possibility for humor, taken up in the next letter. Here, Walker frames Sofia's story about Miss Millie's abusive driving experiment with explicit references to humorous rapport. Celie remarks at the outset that "Sofia would make a dog laugh, talking about those people she work for," and Sofia herself closes her narrative with "White folks is a miracle of affliction," yet the narrative itself does not represent some in-group narrative humorously targeting an out-group. The humor here, in fact, has nothing to do with the narrative per se, which has a bitter irony but nothing inviting laughter about it. Rather, the frame refers to a manner of telling, a humorous context in which even narratives of the most disturbing events—here, Miss Millie's teasing petulance with Sofia's enforced separation from her family—become occasions for laughter. Humorous rapport, here, grows out of mutual assumptions and responses within this world, and the changing humorous subject/object resides in an attitude, a tonality, a shared pleasure. Such pleasure inheres in the verbal assertions of characters resisting both others' definitions and, indeed, any easy self-other parameters. As bell hooks rightly observes, Sofia never participates in her own oppression and most radically enacts physical resistance (hooks, "Writing," 465). Thus, her return to humor does not merely introduce her once again into a world where "us giggle"; rather, it locates resistance in a laughter intimately related to suffering yet powerfully critical precisely because of the absence of any didactic, authorial assertion surrounding it.

This humor does not avoid or deny anger, but perhaps more important, its interactive rapport specifically disallows any normative view of an identity differentiated from others by greater power. Sofia's tales that "would make a dog laugh" end in her outright rejection of Eleanor Jane's desire to take part in her family's life as the still-privileged other. Subsequent invocations of humor cumulatively emphasize that relations of unequal power make humorous interaction impossible. Value accrues to the intensity and intimacy of a rapport that comes from a mutually felt pain and can only attend equitable power relations. Such humor supplements rather than displaces the more aggressive wit with which women as often as men resist domination. Walker's debt to Zora Neale Hurston may suggest some parallel between the "rebellion" of women characters here and that in *Their Eyes Were Watching God*. Janie Starks certainly devastates Joe when her verbal wit improves upon the sexual insults he has grown accustomed to heaping upon her, and when Walker's women characters stand up to men, they may do so with similarly tendentious wit. But the intimate, humorous rapport primary to my argument here, explicit in supportively embracing difference however jocular the tonality, comes much closer to Susan Willis's overall sense of the difference in black women's writing: "Black women's writing imagines the future in the present. It sees the future born out of the context of oppression" (159).[11] Such laughter as the trope for the values of improvised, spontaneous rapport, meaningful domestic activity, and a future imagined in the present—all in the context of daily activity—supplements Gates's attention to more overt rebellion and more aggressive wit. And it more closely reflects Walker's own concern for how the loss of compassion marks the end of any hopeful strategies, "whether in love or revolution," elsewhere glossed by the poetic vision of a Christ who walks with "His love in front. His love and his necessary fist behind" (Walker, [*Her Blue Body Everything We Know: Earthling Poems, 1965-1990, Complete,*] *Her Blue Body,* 289).

The daily normality of humorous rapport suggests a value at least supplemental to that of writing. Indeed, to take writing as the primary metaphor of value somewhat obscures Mae Henderson's insight that "Walker's use of the epistolary form allows her to transpose a formal tradition into a vehicle for expressing the folk voice, so her emphasis on material and popular modes of expression allows us to revise our conventional notions of 'high' art and culture" (17). To transform all emphasis on *voice* into emphasis on *writing* passes over how the power of the written word takes its place among other daily art forms distinct from elite culture, including sewing, quilting, cooking, and singing. Each of these art forms redistributes power, so that, for example, only men who have undergone transformation can participate in them. Writing as exclusive value also disregards the text's own emphasis on resistance within speech. Celie reports that Darlene aspires to correct her speech because, on grounds she reports in her own vernacular, "colored peoples think you a hick and white folks be amuse" (193). The depth of tradition inherent in that vernacular accords with Celie's frustration in trying to change it: "Every time I say something the way I say it, she correct me until I say it some other way. Pretty soon it feel like I can't think. My mind run up on a thought, git confuse, run back and sort of lay down" (193). To Darlene's assertion that Shug would love Celie more if she talked "proper," Shug gratifyingly responds, "She can talk in sign language for all I care" (194). Such explicit attention to speech and its vernacular meanings rests somewhat uncomfortably with Gates's assertion that "no one speaks in this novel," despite that assertion's reliance on a fine analytical accuracy about Celie's reportage:

> Celie only tells us what people have said to her. She never shows us their words in direct quotation. Precisely because her written dialect voice is identical in diction and idiom to the supposedly spoken words that pepper her letters, we believe that we are overhearing people speak, just as Celie did when the words were in fact uttered. We are not, however; indeed, we can never be certain whether or not Celie is showing us a telling or telling us a showing, as awkward as this sounds.
>
> (251)

Certainly, the awkwardness of explanation corresponds to the awkwardness of engaging both the primacy of Celie's speech and the voyeurism of reading another's intimate letters. Yet the intimacy of speech (just as direct, perhaps even more so, as if it were within the constraints of quotation marks) formally coincides with an intimately shared humor as an important contrast between Celie's and Nettie's (re)presentations.

That Celie's writing compels associating her with voice underscores how strongly the presentness of characters within her epistolary narration (Shug, Sofia, Mary Agnes, Harpo, Albert, e.g.) differs from that of characters within Nettie's (Samuel, Adam, Tashi, e.g.).[12] Writing does not *necessarily* transform the writer, which matters to the dramatic contrast between Celie's voiced, intimate writing and Nettie's more academic, distanced letters. As Gates notes, Celie's framing of Nettie's letters may merge voices in the manner of free indirect discourse. But the letters also give direct experience of voice that differs markedly from Celie's perceptions, especially from the character as process she will become toward the end of the work. Certainly, Nettie's letters establish the similarities between the condition of black women in the rural South and black women in Africa, giving an alternative context for female bonding; "It is in work that women get to know and care about each other," writes Nettie. But the absence of humor, or anything like the humorous rapport so important to Celie's developing relationships, suggests that Nettie's letters serve as much a judgment on missionary sensibility as upon black patriarchal culture, despite her own suspended judgment on Samuel's hopes and expectations.

In the portrayal of Samuel's missionary activity, Walker's authorial juxtapositions remove any sense of Celie-cum-character, signifying more in the manner Gates describes when showing her relation in difference to Zora Neale Hurston and Rebecca Cox Jackson. Samuel's latent bitterness about his own failure erupts just after his anecdotal tale of how Aunt Theodosia (the name says much) found herself rebuked by a young Harvard scholar named Edward DuBoyce ("or perhaps his name was Bill") for pride in a medal given her by King Leopold, a medal that symbolizes to him her "unwitting complicity" with a brutal white despot. The tonality and passionate impatience of DuBoyce invokes that of William Edward B. Dubois, also young at Harvard, whose sensibility contrasts uncomfortably with that of Samuel. Recounting DuBoyce's outrage at Aunt Theodosia's misplaced pride, Samuel uses the story to identify not with DuBoyce but with "poor Aunt Theodosia." Like Samuel, Aunt Theodosia found little gratitude among Africans who "hardly seem to care whether missionaries exist" (210). Nettie's report of Samuel's disillusioned outburst, not in quotation marks but clearly representing his voice, captures with precision the reasons why humorous rapport necessarily absents itself from the African letters:

> We love them. We try every way we can to show that love. But they reject us. They never even listen to how we've suffered. And if they listen they say stupid things. Why don't you speak our language? they ask. Why can't you remember the old ways? Why aren't you happy in America, if everyone there drives motorcars?
>
> (210)

Samuel's focus on an altruism from above, and on "our" suffering, prepares for the litany of "stupid" responses that so effectively undermine the missionary's presumption of superiority, and it explains, too, the formal justice of the text's most mystified distance: that between Nettie's story and the compellingly absent, invisible *mbeles*. (Indicatively, the *mbeles*' "place" rests "so deep in the earth" that it can be seen only "from above.") The hope for Samuel lies less in the vision of a new church "in which each person's spirit is encouraged to seek God directly," than in his entry into a world of work challenging hierarchical power relations and opportunities for dominance. Here, even Samuel might become "us" and learn to laugh.[13]

Walker takes pains to link both Celie's late-developing camaraderie with Albert and Sofia's hard-won equity with Harpo to the possibility of this already leveled humor. Celie describes her reflections on the African renaming of Adam, with Albert as participant-observer, and closes:

> [Albert] So what they name Adam?
>
> [Celie] Something sound like Omatangu, I say. It mean a unnaked man somewhere near the first one God made that knowed he was. A whole lot of the men that come before the first man was men, but none of 'em didn't know it. You know how long it take some mens to notice anything, I say.
>
> Took me long enough to notice you such good company, he say. And he laugh.
>
> He ain't Shug, but he begin to be somebody I can talk to.
>
> (241)

And when Sofia and Harpo discuss Eleanor Jane's likelihood of continuing to work for them despite the disapproval of her "menfolks," Celie reports:

> Let her quit, say Sofia. It not my salvation she working for. And if she don't learn she got to face judgment for herself, she won't even have live.
>
> Well, you got me behind you, anyway, say Harpo. And I loves every judgment you ever made. He move up and kiss her where her nose was stitch.
>
> Sofia toss her head. Everybody learn something in life, she say. And they laugh.
>
> (246)

Sofia's "Everybody learn something in life" well captures the solidarity necessary to a laughter that represents a principled resistance to white judgments and values, a laughter initially associated with women in *The Color Purple* but held out as possibility to any who sustain no felt superiority-in-difference. Celie's acceptance of Albert attends not only his abandonment of dominance but also his participation in humorous rapport, evident in the little purple frog he carves for Celie as an emblem of his acceptance of her sexuality. (She has told him earlier: "Men look like frogs to me. No matter how you kiss 'em, as far as I'm concern, frogs is what they stay" [224].) When Shug returns and senses a new intimacy between Celie and Albert, she queries about their "idle conversation." Celie puts down the impulse to provoke:

> What do you know, I think. Shug jealous. I have a good mind to make up a story just to make her feel bad. But I don't.
>
> Us talk about you, I say. How much us love you.
>
> (248)

Despite Shug's weakness for successive men and Albert's former abuse, the three achieve an intimacy without power inseparable from a prose that will merge these characters in process.

In the prose of the last pages, not only do couples disappear, but a generally shared humorous rapport effaces any individuated points of view. Thus, the ending undermines any critical argument that simply exchanges periphery for center, still trapping explanation in critical oppositions. Note, for example, how Molly Hite's sustained attempt to explicate *The Color Purple*'s dismantling of hierarchical oppositions still finds its closure in a center:

> On the basis of such redrawn lines the entire immediate society reconstitutes itself, in the manner of Shakespearean romance, around a central couple. This couple is not only black, it is aging and lesbian. Yet clearly Celie and Shug are intended to suggest the nucleus of a new and self-sustaining society: the triply marginalized become center and source.
>
> (117-18)

Such description finds a central couple in narration that blurs the couple out of existence. Yet repeatedly, in the last pages, Celie's presentation disallows either a female-centered or a couple-centered world. In the last section, often cited as the microcosm of a romantic idyll, Albert speaks first, followed by Celie's reference to "me and him and Shug." Parallel syntax foregrounds "Shug mention . . . ," "Albert say . . . ," and "I talk . . . ," followed by the reiteration of sitting on the porch "with Albert and Shug." Even the rhythms of dialogue seamlessly incorporate the vantage points:

> Could be the mailman, I say. Cept he driving a little fast.
> Could be Sofia, say Shug. You know she drive like a maniac.
> Could be Harpo, say Albert. But it not.
>
> (249)

And in the many times Celie mentions Shug and Albert in the first part of the last letter to God and "Everything," they always occur together, linked in syntactic symmetry:

> Shug reach down and give me a helping hand. Albert press me on the arm.
>
> (250)

> I stand swaying, tween Albert and Shug.
>
> (250)

> I point at my peoples. This Shug and Albert, I say.
>
> (250)

> Then Shug and Albert start to hug everybody one after the other.
>
> (250)

The last part of the letter, the book's close after Nettie and her family have arrived, begins on July Fourth as the day "us can spend celebrating each other." It invokes a panoply of characters who finally merge into an "everybody" and an "us" in a gesture that, following the global inclusiveness of the letter's address, includes everyone as subjective agency, even in contexts not normative to do so. When Tashi names her favorite African food as "barbecue," "Everybody laugh and stuff her with one more piece." Clearly, not everyone reaches for the "one more piece"; the collective gesture and the collective laugh put the closing frame on the sequence beginning with the first letter's address to an exclusionary God, followed by an opening subjectivity insecure as presence (with "I am" under the erasure of "I have") and a prose inundated in singular personal pronouns. (It also intertextually plays on Hurston's celebratory sense of "barbecue" at the end of *Dust Tracks in the Road*.)[14] After the last laugh, and before the final "Amen," comes only the felt sense of distance between how the children see them and how they feel themselves:

> I see they think me and Nettie and Shug and Albert and Samuel and Harpo and Sofia and Jack and Odessa real old and don't know much what going on. But I don't think us feel old at all. And us so happy. Matter of fact, I think this the youngest us ever felt.
>
> (251)

The prose does not differentiate among the cast of characters, and the repetition of the fluid "us" creates an expressively merged identity of characters in the process of intersubjective relation.[15]

Hite's notions about reversing hierarchical oppositions or exchanging periphery for center, especially some center "couple" consisting of Celie and Shug, ill describe such process and overlook the importance of laughter as value to resisting self-other distinctions with dominance as a defining difference. Remember that Nettie as writer does not recount episodes of laughter, nor does her standard English capture the "presentness" of humorous rapport. Only Celie's narration has used language that mitigates against a constant readerly transformation of dialogue into something written, something mediated by her own "control." In fact, the language of "control" supports a reading where characters have unambivalent agency, not a more processual characterization where dramatically presented dialogue does not threaten a "tyranny of the narrative present" precisely because "presentness" does not imply fixed identity.

And "romance" or "comic romance" suggests a teleology alien to this sense of an ending that foregrounds how "us feel." No "Edenic norm" ever existed here in a world always constrained by power relations (and with a graphic, non-Edenic enthusiasm for sexuality), and therefore no nostalgia for its return. Both Harpo and Albert must literally make themselves sick with the desire for dominance before they revive into an intimacy of work and care that allows laughter. And although the gendered tensions provide a model for "the recognition of conflict and pain, for the possibility of reconciliation,"[16] a dominance ignorant of its own presumptions still persists in the white world. Eleanor Jane helps Harpo look after the children and creates yam dishes in artful disguise for Henrietta, but must yet outlast the judgments of both her parents and "menfolks." The fact that she has learned to *sound* a little like Sofia augurs much, given the cost of Sofia's resistance:

> Do her people know? I ast.
>
> They know, say Sofia. They carrying on just like you know they would. Whoever heard of a white woman working for niggers, they rave. She tell them, whoever heard of somebody like Sofia working for trash.
>
> (246)

And "celebrating each other," with a laughter attendant upon "working together," can take place only because, as Harpo tells us, "white people busy celebrating they independence from England July 4th . . . so most black folks don't have to work" (250). This celebration has neither turned the authority of the white world upside down nor, in this instance, broken its rules. Nor has it simply inverted white norms, though "us feel" has about it the "*joyful relativity* of all structure and order" that Bakhtin locates in such inversions (184).

The model for this celebration in resistance has much to do with the spiritual reclaiming of nature in Celie's last address and the expressive work in which all engage, a communal work that in its very form disturbs T. G. A. Nelson's claim that modern comedy may not end in idyll but must in any case return us to "the awareness that life is a struggle in which nobody can always be on the winning side, and where each of us will sometimes fill the role of victim, scapegoat, or fool" (186). To be sure, Celie inherits a house and gets her extended family together, but Harpo's reference to July Fourth as providing only temporary relief from working for white people carries dissent within it.[17] **The Color Purple** rejects the terms of romantic acceptance both because it rejects the construct of "winning" and "losing" sides and because it posits as value a felt merger among different characters' multiple subject positions, whether as male/female, lover/loved, employer/employee, or manager/worker. Such bonding feels stronger than empathy because one's own health *depends* on not accepting as "natural" the process of alternating victims and victimizers.[18]

At the end of **The Color Purple,** the merger of individuated characters into a replete intersubjectivity does not necessarily refer us to an uncritical new age spiritualism; rather, celebration takes place in the midst of a gap named by Harpo as a respite from white people's work. An overtly "happy ending" invokes values inseparable from a resistance as real as Sofia's stitches and as demanding as learning to tear dominance or the comforts of privilege out of one's own life; and he who formerly most dominated, Albert, has most radically altered his position in order to participate in the merged, intersubjective identity characteristic of the closing pages.[19] The fantasy language, the trappings of generic sentiment, the closeness of characters to stereotype, all stand undermined by an intersubjective laughter that acknowledges in its very representation the pain of past and future oppressions. Analogously, the metaphysical, distancing values of romance occur within a context harshly implicating any idealized wish fulfillment, indeed, implicating all difference felt as privilege. Thus, a text with felt relation to realism, to epistolary romance, to comedy, and to comic romance closes with ambivalent recognitions and refusals, necessarily complicit in the structures its values reject.[20]

Similarly, as readers, our own positions regarding privilege in the world—as well as our diverse ways of resisting, repressing, or evading them—affect the degree to which the implications of intersubjective humor seem threatening or comfortable. Readers made aware of white, male, class, or heterosexual privilege will find themselves caught, I suspect, in unlikely combinations of desire, intimacy, and fear. Overlapping subject positions engage readers in multiple, contradictory responses to Celie's and Nettie's sections or to the judgment on righteous altruism—and by extension on the missionary venture in Africa as a whole—implied in the DuBoyce passage. **The Color Purple** blurs issues of subjective agency with cumulative expansions and mergers of identity that exclude those for whom privilege or power attend identity. An intersubjective humorous rapport moves toward an inclusive suspension of individuated subjectivity, one that bears little relation to the somewhat smarmy picture of beauty born again as fairy tale: "fanciful, heartrending, and uplifting" (Walsh, 100). Neither a nostalgic view of a prior state nor a context of wish-fulfilling changes in status diminish the cost of becoming "us" to dominant subjectivity. Oppressive power in **The Color Purple** does not recede into some abstracted, depersonalized evil. But because the text assigns yet does not essentialize blame, it proffers the possibility of transformation on the model of those specifically undergone by Harpo and Albert. The intense difficulty of such transformation inheres in the grave, embodies consequences of turning away from the abuse of power. Each has to earn a subsequent inclusion in intersubjective humorous rapport through traumatic and self-repudiating realization, through relinquishing power, and through taking up "a shared awareness of shared energy" (Snead, 245). The case does not offer anything so simple as some affirmation about humor as a kind of therapeutic transformative (a sort of Norman Cousins theory of resistance). Rather, humorous rapport becomes the textual embodiment of value, the value of an intersubjectivity most forcefully undermining the subject-object relations on which power relies.

This humor as value helps differentiate Walker's text from the several genres she uses as frames of reference and addresses, too, any felt evasions into either fantasy or didacticism. If such intersubjective humor comes closer to essentialism, to positing some chosen, constructed reality (a specifically black, women's laughter) as a first-order one, then it does so only in the partial manner of a resistance conceived as necessarily conflicted. So too, the presentness, as opposed to presence, of characters acknowledges a readerly penchant for engaging characters as analogous to embodied selves even when fluid in construction and merged in identity. Neither a comic romance with a utopian ending nor a postmodern fiction that celebrates writing as *the* figure of resistance, the very incompleteness, or partiality with which **The Color Purple** fulfills generic expectations addresses a debate about textual resistance both as conceived "inside" texts and as a negotiation made by readers "outside" texts.[21] Texts are no less resistant by virtue of double or mediated social locations than are readers interested in bringing subjectivity back to human form (not just for discourse anymore) without unifying or psychologizing it.

This humor's invitation to the reader involves not so much either the identifying empathy of realism or the intellectual/spiritual desire of romance. Here, interaction works more on the model of generative call and response, where each response acts as another call at the same time that it comments on a responding, regressive resistance to answering fully, that is, by laying down the book and changing our lives. The comic wit of Barth, Pynchon, or even Carrington relies on distancing strategies with roots in the ironic fragmentations of fantastic, apocalyptic, or abstracted modes. A humor embodying "a form of power that is exercised at the very limits of identity and authority" may well *not* take place in contexts fulfilling generic expectations;[22] humorous intersubjectivity acts as a context for storytelling that begins from an angle of passionate engagement with interlocking identities, and as such its treatment of subject-object relations refuses to engage Susan Sulieman's question about whether black women writers regard race or gender as priorities.[23] Remember that when Sofia helps Eleanor Jane, she does so because Eleanor Jane has begun to see through white altruism and has begun to understand that no less than her own "salvation" depends on finding a work not imbued with assumptions of privilege of *any kind.*

If resistance is not simply *there* in a text, but produced and reproduced through the constitutive codes necessarily embedded in genre, trope, figure, and mode (Slemon, 31), then readers who read from different subject positions will have quite different responses to this textual call. From my own reading position, the response of "I want to be like that" or "I want to have those values in my life" carries with it the cognitive dissonance attending much white, privileged admiration of black culture, the unsaid "But not at that cost, not doing that work, not relinquishing the 'I' who thinks as a separate, individuated self, and not—especially not—giving up the privilege that allows me to read from this position, the one reading, speaking, writing, thinking now."[24] (Again, Walker's poetic voice serves as gloss: "Their envy of us / has always been / our greatest crime" [**Her Blue Body,** 435].) The case of laughter here mitigates against any appropriative presumption of utopian inclusion, for its roots lie in a history specific to a felt repudiation of the mythology, indeed the metaphysics, of a unitary self.[25]

Whether thought to address an intimate sisterhood figured in the two sisters' letters, a primarily white, female audience, or a general humanity,[26] the text engages readers in reflective responses about implied analogies between how characters relate to each other, how speech relates to writing, and how writers relate to readers. The celebratory intersubjectivity that ends **The Color Purple,** however differently situated from the identity formations of readers, demands only *some* readerly relation to "what authentic solidarity with the oppressed demands" (hooks, 1990b, 188). But for reading positions of privilege, caught in the tension between desire and quite literal self-repudiation, the humorous rapport that formally links flexible, processual characterization with a valued, intersubjectivity has much to teach: it teaches that so long as theory privileges tropes "from above," it will not undermine the subjectivities it likes to declare obsolete; that resistance need not be conceived *only* in the conflictual terms of weapons, targets, and combat—or indeed any instrumentality—but also in constructions of value resisting an egocentered, individually achieving and performing self; and that only relinquishing *actual* social power—not just that in discursive formations—affords any hope of salvation.

Notes

I would like to thank Wahneema Lubiano and Beverly Guy-Sheftall for helpful comments on a first draft; though not implicated in any readerly reductions, both helped me with thinking about the relationality of resistance, its diverse relation to the subject positions of readers.

1. Both Calvin Hernton and Jacqueline Bobo provide useful overviews of the critical controversies surrounding *The Color Purple*. Specific to my purposes, Susan Willis will serve as an example of a critic treating *The Color Purple* as resistance literature and Molly Hite, Priscilla Walton, and Margaret Walsh as examples of critics who read in the direction of comic romance.

2. Perhaps those explicating colonial and postcolonial/postindependence literary resistance have argued this most strongly. Jenny Sharpe's "Figures of Colonial Resistance" finds an emphasis on the partial, complicit nature of literary resistance common to such theorists as Gayatri Spivak, Homi Bhabha, Abdul JanMohamad, and Benita Parry; and Stephen Slemon uses the "double, necessarily mediated" location of literary resistance to argue for the inclusion of "second world" texts by white Australian, New Zealander, Southern African, and Canadian writers in "post-colonial literary studies."

3. Some reject comedy as by definition representing absolute exclusivity: Umberto Eco, for example, asserts that "comic is always racist: only the others, the Barbarians, are supposed to pay" (6); and Susan Carlson argues that sexism inheres in the comic. Suleiman's sense of the avant-garde chooses as "subversive" works that ally her with McHale and others who primarily applaud parodic,

discursive play. For an overview of how theories of humor and the comic relate to critical methodologies, see my "Ideologies of the Funny."

4. Foucault widely uses mad, perverse laughter as figurative creativity, but most particularly in *Madness and Civilization,* where he elaborates "delirious discourse" at length; Hélène Cixous figures a liberating laughter in "The Laugh of the Medusa"; and Susan Suleiman, Patrick O'Neill, and others discuss the ironic, parodying laughter of postmodern pastiches. In an elegant argument for the value of playfulness and "world-travelling," values closely allied with what I call here "intersubjective humorous rapport," María Lugones describes how a sense of fun is constructed out of her by dominant constructions of play.

5. Jameson (1988a) refers to something like the possibility of an alternative realism in theory, though he has not generally explicated it in texts, when he postulates a collective subject.

6. This sense of intersubjectivity differs from that of Habermas because it dialectically negotiates among complexly plural and overlapping subject positions, not among subject individuals. Although concerned here with the meaning of a humorous rapport among characters in process, I see both laughter and play as signs of a rapport capable of becoming intersubjective.

7. I do not mean to imply that the nature of humorous rapport in *The Color Purple* is unprecedented, but rather that our theories of how to read the comic have precluded paying attention to the kind of humorous rapport so important here and have thereby tamed at least one kind of resistance out of reading.

8. Although Henry Gates's reading requires that he foreground Celie's "control" of others' language, so that we have only Celie's and "Celie-cum-characters'" speech, his explication relies on conceptualizing different characters as such, perhaps most significantly in discovering Shug as a (re)writing of Hurston herself. The distinction between speakerly and writerly texts originates with Roland Barthes, who uses it in *S/Z* to oppose an older realism (readerly texts) to a modern ideal (a writerly text) corresponding to the plural, ambiguous properties of language; when Gates refers to Hurston's *Their Eyes Were Watching God* as a speakerly text "(re)written" by Walker in *The Color Purple,* he strangely allies Hurston's passionate grounding in oral and folk traditions with the singular, imperialist language and authority Barthes identifies as readerly characteristics. Nevertheless, Gates's attention to the "simultaneous, inseparable, bonded" nature of voices suggests a resistant laughter here.

9. While brilliantly disclosing the transformative use Walker makes of both Hurston and Rebecca Cox Jackson, Gates foregrounds a resisting agency belonging to Celie's use of free indirect discourse (246-47). Humor, since it erases boundaries between individual "selves," appropriately figures some mediation between those who argue that any attention to characters as speakers suggests some unitary, regressively situated subject, and those who, like Homi Bhabha, in "Interrogating Identity," argue that some fluid, "evolving cultural agent" must connect agency with victims' capacity for resistance.

10. Deborah E. McDowell calls for a dialogical relation between this characterization as process and analogous reading strategies provocative for African American writers. Although I don't see "identification" as the only analogical link between characters with fluid identities and implied reading processes, I do attempt here to respond to her suggestion.

11. This description does not suggest any totalizing gesture toward understanding the rich number of humorous kinds used by both male and female African American writers. Carlene Young, Valerie Smith, Leslie Hill, Beverly Guy-Sheftall, and other black feminist scholars have agreed in informal discussion that qualitative difference does exist between African American men's and women's forms of humor, both in fiction and in life, but that the subject still awaits its necessarily African American, necessarily cross-gendered researchers.

12. Stanley Cavell, in his sustained refusal to ally his own skepticism with the more absolute absences of deconstruction, explicates this distinction in "The Uncanniness of the Ordinary" (174).

13. Despite my own conflictual invocations of Walker as author, whether or not Walker intended Nettie's voice as painfully devoid of humor and her situation as inimical to humorous rapport matters only if one reduces issues of resistance to issues of intentionality.

14. James Robert Saunders makes this connection between this barbecue and Hurston's "out-of-this-world" barbecue: "Maybe all of us who do not have the good fortune to meet, or meet again, in this world, will meet at a barbecue."

15. Mae Henderson aptly formulates how Celie and Mary Agnes as well as Sofia and Shug act initially as doubles, complemented by successive triadic relationships. My point here is that any "new paradigm for relationships" relies more on resisting relations of dominance than on moving from dyads to triads (but one exemplary model of symbolic dismantling and reconstructing).

16. Although hooks ("Writing," 468) has a less positive sense of Walker's success in differentiating *The Color Purple* from its sentimental frames of reference, her phrase well expresses the difficulty of an ending within the conventions of happy endings but also *not* itself simply the generic equivalent of such an ending.

17. Wall usefully relates "the persistent tension between fragmentation and unity" in the book's closure to related tensions between Anglo-American and French feminisms

18. In this emphasis, I agree with Willis that "Walker's affirmation of blackness uses racially specific traits not to define a form of Black racism but to delineate the look of a class. Black is the color of the underclass" (126). Willis's explication of *Meridian* rightly distinguishes Walker's sense of revolutionary praxis from anything resembling "the politics of counterculture."

19. Kimberly Benston's description of Celie's and Nettie's meeting as a "melting" that poses "a radical challenge to our own liminal stance as interpreters, as negotiating judges between distanced parties" (106), published after this article was written, has particular relevance to what I have called "intersubjectivity." In his context of facing traditions (here, effacing) in African American literature, the scene captures a revision "divested of the coercive powers of a specifically positioned look" (106). Taking laughter, and not the mutually reflective gaze, as trope, my reading also differs in its sense that readers' subject positions affect responses to a laughter inseparable from intersubjectivity.

20. While focusing on the autobiographical strategies that may subvert narrative expectation, Valerie Smith significantly theorizes the persistence of hybrid forms in African American literature as derived from "their alienation from the ideological content of received literary conventions" (153).

21. This seems closely related to Karla Holloway's theorizing of African American women writers' "polysignant" or "multiplied" texts, which demand something she calls "shift." As "a necessary mediation between the reader and the text," shift "encourages a dialogue among critical postures within the interpretive community" (625).

22. Bhabha uses this phrase in an eloquent, appreciative "interrogation" of Fanon, while, at the same time, himself interrogating how the black presence defeats narratives of Western personhood ("Interrogating Identity," 205).

23. I refer to a note in which Suleiman counters the possibility of considering Toni Morrison or Ntozake Shange "black women feminist postmodernists" with: "But the question of priorities (race or gender?) remains" (248). Hernton's focus on critical, largely male responses to *The Color Purple* understandably responds with a female-centered reading in the direction of romance where, "The promise in the beginning is fulfilled in the end. The ending is the beginning. The dismembered tree, the broken family, is back together again" (26). This pastoral vision overlooks the radical change in subjectivity and the fact that the "broken" family at the beginning is not the same as the "us" at the end. Even the paradigm of the "female symbol" of the porch with its "diamond of women in sisterhood" (Celie, Mary Agnes, and Shug) ignores how Albert is foregrounded in the geography of the porch.

24. This point, that reading from different subject positions implies different interpretive responses, does not suggest some imprecise or amorphous relativity (parallel, again, to Holloway's choice of the "polysignant" text). That texts may be chastening to some and discouraging to others demands rigorous examination of how and why readings separate, conflict, or overlap. Barbara Smith's reasoning and tonality captures this sense of relation in difference when she speculates on the different effects of Naylor's "The Two" for heterosexual and lesbian women readers in the context of an argument that fictional representation of black lesbian women "has crucial implications for all women's political liberation" (243).

25. The engagement of any text outside the cultural traditions that engender it perhaps necessarily risks appropriation; yet, as I try to suggest here, some forms of appropriation act as a critique of dominant presumptions and some merely reinscribe those presumptions.

26. Deborah McDowell finds affirmation in an implied intimacy between Walker and the black women readers invoked by "sisterhood," whereas hooks ("Writing") finds a voyeuristic, even pornographic presumption of a white, privileged, heterosexual female audience.

Works Cited

Appiah, Anthony. "Tolerable Falsehoods: Agency and the Interests of Theory." *Consequences of Theory.* Ed. Jonathan Arac and Barbara Johnson. Selected Papers from the English Institute, 1987-88. Baltimore: Johns Hopkins University Press, 1991.

Barthes, Roland. *S/Z* Paris: Seuil, 1970.

Benston, Kimberly W. "Facing Tradition: Revisionary Scenes in African-American Literature." *PMLA* 1 (1990): 98-109.

Bergson, Henri. *Laughter: An Essay on the Meaning of the Comic.* New York: McGraw-Hill, 1911.

Bakhtin, Mikhail. *The Dialogic Imagination.* Trans. Caryl Emerson and Michael Holquist. Austin: University of Texas Press, 1981.

Bhabha, Homi K. "Interrogating Identity: The Postcolonial Prerogative." *Anatomy of Racism.* Ed. David Greenberg. Minneapolis: University of Minnesota Press, 1990.

———. "Location, Intervention, Incommensurability: A Conversation with Homi Bhabha." *Emergences* 1 (1989): 63-88.

Carlson, Susan. "Women in Comedy: Problem, Promise, Paradox." *Themes in Drama* 7 (1985): 159-71.

Cavell, Stanley. *In Quest of the Ordinary: Line of Skepticism and Romanticism.* Chicago: University of Chicago Press, 1988.

Cixous, Hélène. "The Laugh of the Medusa." Trans. Keith Cohen and Paula Cohen. *Signs: Journal of Women in Culture and Society* 1 (1976): 875-93.

Eco, Umberto. "The Frames of Comic Freedom." *Carnival!* Ed. Thomas A. Sebeok. Berlin: Mouton, 1984.

Flax, Jane. *Thinking Fragments: Psychoanalysis, Feminism, and Postmodernism in the Contemporary West.* Berkeley: University of California Press, 1990.

Foucault, Michel. *Madness and Civilization.* Trans. Richard Howard. New York: Pantheon Books, 1965.

Freud, Sigmund. *Jokes and Their Relation to the Unconscious.* Trans. and ed. James Strachey. Harmondsworth: Penguin, 1976.

Gates, Henry Louis, Jr. *The Signifying Monkey: A Theory of African-American Literary Criticism.* New York: Oxford University Press, 1988.

Henderson, Mae. "*The Color Purple*: Revisions and Redefinitions." *Sage: A Scholarly Journal on Black Women* 2 (1985): 14-18.

Hernton, Calvin C. "Who's Afraid of Alice Walker? *The Color Purple* as Slave Narrative." *The Sexual Mountain and Black Women Writers.* New York: Doubleday, 1987.

Hite, Molly. "Romance, Marginality, Matrilineage: *The Color Purple.*" *The Other Side of the Story: Structures and Strategies of Contemporary Feminist Narratives.* Ithaca: Cornell University Press, 1989.

Holloway, Karla F. C. "Revision and (Re)membrance: A Theory of Literary Structures in Literature by African-American Women Writers." *Black American Literature Forum* 24.4 (1990): 617-31.

hooks, bell. "Postmodern Blackness." *Yearning: Race, Gender, and Cultural Politics.* Boston: South End Press, 1990a.

———. "Writing the Subject: Reading *The Color Purple.*" *Reading Black, Reading Feminist: A Critical Anthology.* Ed. Henry Louis Gates, Jr. New York: Penguin, 1990b.

———. "A Call for Militant Resistance." *Yearning: Race, Gender, and Cultural Politics.* Boston: South End Press, 1990c.

Jameson, Fredric. "Regarding Postmodernism—A Conversation with Fredric Jameson." Interview with Anders Stephanson. *Universal Abandon? The Politics of Postmodernism.* Ed. Andrew Ross. Minneapolis: University of Minnesota Press, 1988a.

———. "Postmodernism and the Consumer Society." *Postmodernism and Its Discontents: Theories, Practices.* Ed. E. Ann Kaplan. London: Verso, 1988b.

Little, Judith. *Comedy and the Woman Writer: Woolf, Spark, Feminism.* Lincoln: University of Nebraska Press, 1983.

Lugones, María. "Playfulness, 'World'-travelling, and Loving Perception." *Lesbian Philosophies and Cultures.* Ed. Jeffner Allen. Albany: State University of New York Press, 1990.

McDowell, Deborah E. "Boundaries: Or Distant Relations and Close Kin." *Afro-American Literary Study in the 1990's.* Ed. Houston A. Baker, Jr., and Patricia Redmond. Chicago: University of Chicago Press, 1989.

———. "'The Changing Same': Generational Connections and Black Women Novelists." *Reading Feminist, Reading Black: A Critical Anthology.* Ed. Henry Louis Gates, Jr. New York: Penguin, 1990.

McHale, Brian. *Postmodernist Fiction.* New York: Methuen, 1987.

McLaughlin, Andrée Nicola. "Black Women, Identity, and the Quest for Humanhood and Wholeness." *Wild Women in the Whirlwind: Afra-American Culture and the Contemporary Literary Renaissance.* Ed. Joanne M. Braxton and Andrée N. McLaughlin. New Brunswick: Rutgers University Press, 1990.

Nelson, T. G. A. *Comedy: The Theory of Comedy in Literature, Drama, and Cinema.* Oxford: Oxford University Press, 1990.

O'Neill, Patrick. *The Comedy of Entropy: Humour/Narrative/Reading.* Toronto: University of Toronto Press, 1990.

Robinson, Daniel. "Problems in Form: Alice Walker's *The Color Purple.*" *Notes on Contemporary Literature* 16.1 (1986): 2.

Robinson, Lillian. "At Play in the Mind-Fields." *Women's Review of Books* 7.10-11 (1990): 32-33.

Saunders, James Robert. "Womanism as the Key to Understanding Zora Neale Hurston's *Their Eyes Were Watching God* and Alice Walker's *The Color Purple.*" *Hollins Critic* 25.4 (1988): 2-11.

Sharpe, Jenny. "Figures of Colonial Resistance." *Modern Fiction Studies* 35.1 (1989): 137-55.

Slemon, Stephen. "Unsettling the Empire: Resistance Theory for the Second World." *World Literature Written in English* 2 (1990): 30-41.

Smith, Barbara. "Black Lesbian Fiction in the 1980's." *Wild Women in the Whirlwind: Afra-American Culture and the Contemporary Literary Renaissance*. Ed. Joanne M. Braxton and Andrée N. McLaughlin. New Brunswick: Rutgers University Press, 1990.

Smith, Valerie. *Self-Discovery and Authority in Afro-American Literature*. Cambridge: Harvard University Press, 1987.

Snead, James. "European Pedigrees/African Contagions: Nationality, Narrative, and Communality in Tutuola, Acheba, and Reed." *Nation and Narration*. Ed. Homi K. Bhabha. New York: Routledge, 1990.

Spivak, Gayatri Chakravorty. *The Post-Colonial Critic: Interviews, Strategies, Dialogues*. New York: Routledge, 1990.

———. "Theory in the Margin: Coetzee's *Foe* Reading Defoe's *Crusoe/Roxana*. Selected Papers from the English Institute, 1987-88. Ed. Jonathan Arac and Barbara Johnson. Baltimore: Johns Hopkins University Press, 1991.

Suleiman, Susan Rubin. *Subversive Intent: Gender, Politics, and the Avant-Garde*. Cambridge: Harvard University Press, 1990.

Taylor Carole Anne. "Ideologies of the Funny." *Centennial Review* 36.2 (1992): 265-98.

Walker, Alice. *The Color Purple*. New York: Washington Square Press, 1982.

———. *Her Blue Body Everything We Know: Earthling Poems, 1965-1990, Complete*. New York: Harcourt Brace Jovanovich, 1991.

Wall, Wendy. "Lettered Bodies and Corporeal Texts in *The Color Purple*." *Studies in American Fiction* 16.1 (1988): 83-97.

Walsh, Margaret. "The Enchanted World of *The Color Purple*." *Southern Quarterly* 25.2 (1987): 89-101.

Walton, Priscilla L. "'What She Got to Sing About?' Comedy and *The Color Purple*." *Ariel: A Review of International English Literature* 21.2 (1990): 59-73.

Willis, Susan. *Specifying: Black Women Writing the American Experience*. Madison: University of Wisconsin Press, 1987.

Wills, Clair. "Upsetting the Public: Carnival, Hysteria, and Women's Texts." *Bakhtin and Culture Theory*. Manchester: Manchester University Press, 1989.

Zillman, Dolf. "Disparagement Humor." *Handbook of Humor Research*. Vol. 1. Ed. Paul E. McGhee and Jeffrey H. Goldstein. New York: Springer-Verlag, 1983.

Linda Selzer (essay date spring 1995)

SOURCE: Selzer, Linda. "Race and Domesticity in *The Color Purple*." *African American Review* 29, no. 1 (spring 1995): 67-82.

[*In the following essay, Selzer discusses Walker's confrontation of race relations and class distinctions through the underlying text in* The Color Purple.]

An important juncture in Alice Walker's **The Color Purple** is reached when Celie first recovers the missing letters from her long-lost sister Nettie. This discovery not only signals the introduction of a new narrator to this epistolary novel but also begins the transformation of Celie from writer to reader. Indeed, the passage in which Celie struggles to puzzle out the markings on her first envelope from Nettie provides a concrete illustration of both Celie's particular horizon of interpretation and Walker's chosen approach to the epistolary form:

> Saturday morning Shug put Nettie letter in my lap. Little fat queen of England stamps on it, plus stamps that got peanuts, coconuts, rubber trees and say Africa. I don't know where England at. Don't know where Africa at either. So I still don't know where Nettie at.
>
> (102)

Revealing Celie's ignorance of even the most rudimentary outlines of the larger world, this passage clearly defines the "domestic" site she occupies as the novel's main narrator.[1] In particular, the difficulty Celie has interpreting this envelope underscores her tendency to understand events in terms of personal consequences rather than political categories. What matters about not knowing "where Africa at"—according to Celie—is not knowing "where Nettie at." By clarifying Celie's characteristic angle of vision, this passage highlights the intensely personal perspective that Walker brings to her tale of sexual oppression—a perspective that accounts in large part for the emotional power of the text.

But Walker's privileging of the domestic perspective of her narrators has also been judged to have other effects on the text. Indeed, critics from various aesthetic and political camps have commented on what they perceive as a tension between public and private discourse in the novel.[2] Thus, in analyzing Celie's representation of national identity, Lauren Berlant identifies a separation of "aesthetic" and "political" discourses in the novel and concludes that Celie's narrative ultimately emphasizes "individual essence in false opposition to institutional history" (868). Revealing a very different political agenda in his attacks on the novel's womanist stance, George Stade also points to a tension between personal and public elements in the text when he criticizes the novel's "narcissism" and its "championing of domesticity over the public world of masculine power plays" (266). Finally, in praising Walker's handling of sexual oppression, Elliott Butler-Evans argues that Celie's personal letters serve precisely as a "textual strategy by which the larger African-American history, focused on racial conflict and struggle, can be marginalized by its absence from the narration" (166).

By counterposing personal and public discourse in the novel, these critics could be said to have problematized the narrative's domestic perspective by suggesting that Walker's chosen treatment of the constricted viewpoint of an uneducated country woman—a woman who admits that she doesn't even know "where Africa at"—may also constrict the novel's ability to analyze issues of "race" and class.[3] Thus Butler-Evans finds that Celie's "private life preempts the exploration of the public lives of blacks" (166), while Berlant argues that Celie's family-oriented point of view and modes of expression can displace race and class analyses to the point that the "nonbiological abstraction of class relations virtually disappears" (833). And in a strongly worded rejection of the novel as "revolutionary literature," bell hooks charges that the focus upon Celie's sexual oppression ultimately deemphasizes the "collective plight of black people" and "invalidates . . . the racial agenda" of the slave narrative tradition that it draws upon ("Writing" 465).[4] In short, to many readers of *The Color Purple,* the text's ability to expose sexual oppression seems to come *at the expense of* its ability to analyze issues of race and class.[5]

But it seems to me that an examination of the representation of race in the novel leads to another conclusion: Walker's mastery of the epistolary form is revealed precisely by her ability to maintain the integrity of Celie's and Nettie's domestic perspectives even as she simultaneously undertakes an extended critique of race relations, and especially of racial integration. In particular, Walker's domestic novel engages issues of race and class through two important narrative strategies: the development of an embedded narrative line that offers a post-colonial perspective on the action, and the use of "family relations"—or kinship—as a carefully elaborated textual trope for race relations. These strategies enable Walker to foreground the personal histories of her narrators while placing those histories firmly within a wider context of race and class.

Both the novel's so-called "restriction of focus to Celie's consciousness" (Butler-Evans 166-67) and one way in which Walker's narratology complicates that perspective are illustrated by the passage quoted above. Celie's difficulty interpreting the envelope sent by Nettie at first only seems to support the claim that her domestic perspective "erases" race and class concerns from the narrative. But if this short passage delineates Celie's particular angle of vision, it also introduces textual features that invite readers to resituate her narration within a larger discourse of race and class. For where Celie sees only a "fat little queen of England," readers who recognize Queen Victoria immediately historicize the passage. And if the juxtaposition of the two stamps on the envelope—England's showcasing royalty, Africa's complete with rubber trees—suggests to Celie nothing but her own ignorance, to other readers the two images serve as a clear reminder of imperialism. Thus Africa, mentioned by name for the first time in this passage, enters the novel already situated within the context of colonialism. Importantly, Walker remains true to Celie's character even as she recontextualizes the young woman's perspective, because the features of the envelope Celie focuses upon are entirely natural ones for her to notice, even though they are politically charged in ways that other features would not be (for example, Celie might have been struck by more purely personal—and more conventional—details, such as the familiar shape of her sister's handwriting). Embedded throughout *The Color Purple,* narrative features with clear political and historical associations like these complicate the novel's point of view by inviting a post-colonial perspective on the action and by creating a layered narrative line that is used for different technical effects and thematic purposes.[6] That Celie herself is not always aware of the full political implications of her narration (although she becomes increasingly so as the novel progresses) no more erases the critique of race and class from the text than Huck's naïveté in *Huckleberry Finn* constricts that work's social criticism to the boy's opinions. This individual letter from Nettie thus provides readers with a textual analogue for the novel's larger epistolary form, illustrating one way in which the novel's domestic perspective is clearly "stamped" with signs of race and class.

But it is not only through such narrative indirection and recontextualization that the novel engages issues of race and class. Walker's domestic narrative undertakes a sustained analysis of race through the careful development of family relationships—or kinship—as an extended textual trope for race relations. Any attempt to oppose political and personal discourses in the novel collapses when one recognizes that the narrative adopts the discourse of family relations both to establish a "domestic ideal" for racial integration and to problematize that ideal through the analysis of specific integrated family groupings in Africa and America.

I. "She Says an African Daisy and an English Daisy Are Both Flowers, but Totally Different Kinds"

Important throughout the narrative, the kinship trope for race relations is articulated most explicitly late in the novel when a mature Celie and a reformed Albert enjoy some communal sewing and conversation. Celie herself raises the issue of racial conflict by drawing on the Olinka "Adam" story that has been handed down to her through Nettie's letters. Beginning with the explanation that ". . . white people is black peoples children" (231), the Olinka narrative provides an analysis of race relations expressed explicitly in terms of kinship.

According to the Olinka creation narrative, Adam was not the first man but the first white man born to an Olinka woman to be cast out for his nakedness—or for being "colorless" (231). The result of this rejection was the fallen world of racial conflict, since the outcast children were, in Celie's words, "so mad to git throwed out and told they was naked they made up they minds to crush us wherever they find us, same as they would a snake." Offered specifically as an alternative to the Judeo-Christian account of Adam, this parable also offers readers an alternative account of Original Sin— defined not in terms of appropriating knowledge or resisting authority but precisely in terms of breaking kinship bonds: "What they did, these Olinka peoples, was throw out they own children, just cause they was a little different" (232). Significantly, by retelling the Olinka narrative, Celie is able to express naturally some rather sophisticated ideas concerning the social construction of racial inferiority, since the myth defines that inferiority as a construct of power relations that will change over time. For the Olinka believe that someday the whites will "kill off so much of the earth and the colored that everybody gon hate them just like they hate us today. Then they will become the new serpent" (233).

The Olinka creation narrative also raises a question central to the novel's larger design: Is progress in race relations possible? Some Olinka, notes Celie, answer this question by predicting that the cycle of discrimination will repeat itself endlessly, that ". . . life will just go on and on like this forever," with first one race in the position of the oppressor and then the other. But others believe that progress in racial harmony is possible—that Original Sin may be ameliorated—through a new valorization of kinship bonds: ". . . the only way to stop making somebody the serpent is for everybody to accept everybody else as a child of God, or one mother's children, no matter what they look like or how they act" (233).[7] These latter Olinka, then, express a *domestic ideal* for race relations, one that counters the sin of discrimination—based on an ideology of essential difference—with an ethic of acceptance that is grounded upon a recognition of relation, or kinship.

But the universalist ethos of the domestic ideal for race relations is put to the test by the larger narrative's development of historically situated, integrated kinship groupings in both Africa and America. Of particular importance are two family groupings: the white missionary Doris Baines and her black African grandchild in Africa, and Sophia and her white charge Miss Eleanor Jane in America. In both cases the specific integrated domestic groupings serve to expose and to critique the larger pattern of racial integration found in their respective countries.

Nettie meets Doris and her adopted grandson on a trip from Africa to seek help for the recently displaced Olinka in England, a trip Nettie calls "incredible" precisely because of the presence of an integrated family on board ship: It was "impossible to ignore the presence of an aging white woman accompanied by a small black child. The ship was in a tither. Each day she and the child walked about the deck alone, groups of white people falling into silence as they passed" (193). Compared to the overtly racist actions of the other whites who ostracize Doris and her grandson, the English missionary's relationship with the boy at first seems in keeping with the ethic of treating all people as "one mother's children." Indeed, Doris describes her years as the boy's "grand*mama*" as "the happiest" years of her life (196). Furthermore, Doris's relationship with the African villagers also seems preferable to that of other white missionaries because, rather than wanting to convert "the heathen," she sees "nothing wrong with them" in the first place (195).

But the relationship between the white woman and her African grandson is actually far from ideal, and Nettie's letters subtly question the quality of their "kinship." If the boy seems "fond of his grandmother"—and, Nettie adds, "used to her"—he is also strangely reticent in her presence and reacts to Doris's conversation with "soberly observant speechlessness" (196). In contrast, the boy opens up around Adam and Olivia, suggesting that he may feel more at home with the transplanted black Americans than with his white grandmother.[8] Indeed, the boy's subdued behavior around his grandmother raises questions about the possibility of kinship across racial lines, while his ease with the black Americans suggests that feelings of kinship occur almost spontaneously within racial groups.

The nature of Doris's honorary "kinship" with the Akwee villagers is questioned more seriously still, beginning with her reasons for taking up missionary work in the first place. As a young woman Doris decided to become a missionary not out of a desire to help others but in order to escape the rarefied atmosphere of upper-class England and the probability of her eventual marriage to one of her many "milkfed" suitors, "each one more boring than the last" (194). Although Doris describes her decision to go to Africa as an attempt to escape the stultifying roles available to women in English society, it is important to note that Nettie does not take Doris's hardships very seriously and draws upon fairy-tale rhetoric to parody the woman's upper-class tribulations: "She was born to great wealth in England. Her father was Lord Somebody or Other. They were forever giving or attending boring parties that were not fun."[9] From Nettie's perspective as a black woman familiar with the trials of the displaced Olinka, Doris's aristocratic troubles seem small indeed, and Nettie further trivializes the white woman's decision to become a missionary by emphasizing that the idea struck Doris one evening when she "was getting ready for yet another tedious date" (194).

The self-interest that prompts Doris to become a missionary also characterizes the relationship she establishes with the Akwee upon her arrival in Africa. There she uses her wealth to set up an ostensibly reciprocal arrangement that in fact reflects her imperial power to buy whatever she wants: "Within a year everything as far as me and the heathen were concerned ran like clockwork. I told them right off that their souls were no concern of mine, that I wanted to write books and not be disturbed. For this pleasure I was prepared to pay. Rather handsomely." Described as a mechanism that runs "like clockwork," Doris's relationship to the Akwee clearly falls short of the maternal ideal for race relations expressed in the Olinka myths. In fact, Doris's relationship to the villagers is decidedly *pa*ternal from the outset, since her formal kinship with the Akwee begins when she is presented with "a couple of wives" (195) in recognition for her contributions to the village.[10] The fact that she continues to refer to the Olinka as "the heathen" in her discussions with Nettie implies that, in spite of her fondness for her grandson, Doris never overcomes a belief in the essential "difference" of the Africans attributed to her by the Missionary Society in England: "She thinks they are an entirely different species from what she calls Europeans. . . . She says an African daisy and an English daisy are both flowers, but totally different kinds" (115). By promoting a theory of polygenesis opposed to the Olinkan account of racial origins, Doris calls into question her own ability to treat the Akwee as kin. The true nature of her "reciprocal" relationship with the Akwee is revealed when she unselfconsciously tells Nettie that she believes she can save her villagers from the same displacement the Olinka suffered: "I am a very wealthy woman," says Doris, "and I *own* the village of Akwee" (196).

Stripped of both the religious motivation of the other missionaries and the overt racism of the other whites, Doris Baines through her relationship with the Akwee lays bare the hierarchy of self-interest and paternalism that sets the pattern for race relations in larger Africa. Indeed, from the moment that young Nettie first arrives in Africa she is surprised to find whites there "in droves," and her letters are filled with details suggestive of the hegemony of race and class. Nettie's description of Monrovia is a case in point. There she sees "bunches" of whites and a presidential palace that "looks like the American white house" (119). There Nettie also discovers that whites sit on the country's cabinet, that black cabinet members' wives dress like white women, and that the black president himself refers to his people as "natives"—as Nettie remarks, "It was the first time I'd heard a black man use that word" (120). Originally established by ex-slaves who returned to Africa but who kept "close ties to the country that bought them" (117), Monrovia clearly reveals a Western influence in more than its style of architecture, and its cocoa plantations provide the colonial model of integration that defines the white presence elsewhere in Africa—from the port town "run by a white man" who rents out "some of the stalls . . . to Africans" (127) all the way up to the governor's mansion where "the white man in charge" (144) makes the decision to build the road that ultimately destroys the Olinka village. Indeed, the later displacement of the Olinka villagers by the English roadbuilders—the main action in the African sections of ***The Color Purple***—simply recapitulates the colonial process of integration already embedded in Nettie's narrative of her travels through the less remote areas of Africa.

From her eventual vantage point within the Olinka's domestic sphere, Nettie becomes a first-hand witness to this process of colonization—a process in which she and the other black missionaries unwittingly participate. For although Nettie's reasons for going to Africa differ from Doris Baines's in that they, like those of the other black missionaries, include a concern for the "people from whom [she] sprang" (111), she is trained by a missionary society that is "run by white people" who "didn't say a thing about caring about Africa, but only about duty" (115). Indeed, missionary work is tied to national interest from the time Nettie arrives in England to prepare for the trip to Africa:

> . . . the English have been sending missionaries to Africa and India and China and God knows where all, for over a hundred years. And the things they have brought back! We spent a morning in one of their museums and it was packed with jewels, furniture, fur, carpets, swords, clothing, even *tombs* from all the countries they have been. From Africa they have *thousands* of vases, jars, masks, bowls, baskets, statues— and they are all so beautiful it is hard to imagine that the people who made them don't still exist. And yet the English assure us they do not.
>
> (116-17)

Charting the course of empire through a catalogue of the material culture appropriated by missionaries from "all the countries they have been" (and, chillingly, from peoples who no longer exist), this passage brilliantly underscores Walker's ability to maintain the integrity of the narrative's personal perspective—here that of a young girl's wonder at her first glimpse into the riches of her African heritage—even as she simultaneously invites readers to resituate that perspective in a wider context of race and class. In fact, throughout the African sections of the novel, Walker's embedded narrative enables readers to sympathize with the hopes and disappointments of the black missionaries while it simultaneously exposes the limitations of their point of view.

This narrative complexity becomes especially important in the passages concerning Samuel and Corrine's Victorian aunts, Theodosia and Althea, whom the narrative asks readers both to sympathize with and to judge harshly. On the one hand, as representatives of a group of black women missionaries who achieved much against great odds, the narrative asks readers to see these women and their accomplishments as "astonishing":

> . . . no sooner had a young woman got through Spelman Seminary than she began to put her hand to whatever work she could do for her people, anywhere in the world. It was truly astonishing. These very polite and proper young women, some of them never having set foot outside their own small country towns, except to come to the Seminary, thought nothing of packing up for India, Africa, the Orient. Or for Philadelphia or New York.
>
> (199)

On the other hand, the narrative levies its harshest criticism of missionary work not against the white missionary Doris Baines but against Aunt Theodosia—and particularly against the foolish pride she takes in a medal given to her by King Leopold for "service as an exemplary missionary in the King's colony." The criticism is levied by a young "DuBoyce," who attends one of Aunt Theodosia's "at homes" and exposes her medal as the emblem of the Victorian woman's "unwitting complicity with this despot who worked to death and brutalized and eventually exterminated thousands and thousands of African peoples" (200). Like the other political allusions embedded in Walker's narrative, the appearance of Du Bois in Aunt Theodosia's domestic sphere recontextualizes Nettie's narrative, and his comments serve as an authoritative final judgment upon the entire missionary effort in Africa.

By structuring Nettie's letters around missionary work, then, Walker achieves much. First, that work provides Nettie and the other black missionaries with a practical and credible pathway into the African domestic sphere. Second, the institutional, historical, and ideological connections between philanthropy and colonialism enable Walker to use that domestic sphere and the example of Doris Baines's integrated family to expose the missionary pattern of integration in larger Africa. Finally, the embedded narrative line enables Walker to remain true to her characters even as she anatomizes the hierarchy of race and class that is first pictured in miniature on Nettie's envelope.

II. "He Said He Wouldn't Do It to Me If He Was My Uncle"

If the integrated family of Doris Baines and her adopted African grandson exposes the missionary pattern of integration in Africa as one based on a false kinship that in fact *denies* the legitimacy of kinship bonds across racial lines, the relationship between Miss Sophia and her white charge, Miss Eleanor Jane, serves an analogous function for the American South. Sophia, of course, joins the mayor's household as a maid under conditions more overtly racist than Doris Baines's adoption of her Akwee family: Because she answers "hell no" (76) to Miss Millie's request that she come to work for her as a maid, Sophia is brutally beaten by the mayor and six policeman and is then imprisoned. Forced to do the jail's laundry and driven to the brink of madness, Sophia finally becomes Miss Millie's maid in order to escape prison. Sophia's violent confrontation with the white officers obviously foregrounds issues of race and class, as even critics who find these issues marginalized elsewhere in **The Color Purple** have noted. But it is not only through Sophia's dramatic *public* battles with white men that her story dramatizes issues of race and class. Her domestic relationship with Miss Eleanor Jane and the other members of the mayor's family offers a more finely nuanced and extended critique of racial integration, albeit one that has often been overlooked.[11]

Like Doris Baines and her black grandson, Sophia and Miss Eleanor Jane appear to have some genuine family feelings for one another. Since Sophia "practically . . . raise[s]" (222) Miss Eleanor Jane and is the one sympathetic person in her house, it is not surprising that the young girl "dote[s] on Sophia" and is "always stick[ing] up for her" (88), or that, when Sophia leaves the mayor's household (after fifteen years of service), Miss Eleanor Jane continues to seek out her approval and her help with the "mess back at the house" (174). Sophia's feelings for Miss Eleanor are of course more ambivalent. When she first joins the mayor's household, Sophia is completely indifferent to her charge, "wonder[ing] why she was ever born" (88). After rejoining her own family, Sophia resents Miss Eleanor Jane's continuing intrusions into her family life and suggests that the only reason she helps the white girl is because she's "on parole. . . . Got to act nice" (174). But later Sophia admits that she does feel "something" for Miss Eleanor Jane "because of all the people in your daddy's house, you showed me some human kindness" (225).

Whatever affection exists between the two women, however, has been shaped by the perverted "kinship" relation within which it grew—a relationship the narrative uses to expose plantation definitions of kinship in general and to explode the myth of the black mammy in particular. Separated from her own family and forced to join the mayor's household against her will, living in a room under the house and assigned the housekeeping and childraising duties, Sophia carries out a role in the mayor's household which clearly recalls that of the stereotypical mammy on the Southern plantation. However, as someone who prefers to build a roof on the house while her husband tends the children, Sophia seems particularly unsuited for that role. And that is precisely the narrative's point: Sophia *is* entirely unsuited for the role of mammy, but whites—including and perhaps especially Miss Eleanor Jane—continually *expect* her to behave according to their cultural representations of the black mother. It is, in fact, these expectations that get Sophia into trouble in the first place, for when Miss Millie happens upon Sophia's family and sees her children so "clean" (76), she assumes that Sophia would make a perfect maid and that Sophia would like to come and work in her household. Similarly, Miss Eleanor Jane assumes that Sophia must return her family feelings in kind, without considering Sophia's true position in her household. Similarly, Miss Eleanor Jane assumes that Sophia must return her family feelings in kind, without considering Sophia's true position in her household. The young white woman's stereotypical projections become clear when she can't understand why Sophia doesn't "just love" her new son, since, in her words, "all other colored women I know love children" (224-25).

An historical appropriation of domestic discourse for political ends, descriptions of the black mammy were used by apologists for slavery to argue that the plantation system benefited the people whom it enslaved by incorporating supposedly inferior blacks into productive white families.[12] And Sophia explicitly ties her employers to such plantation definitions of racial difference: "They have the nerve to try to make us think slavery fell through because of us. . . . Like us didn't have sense enough to handle it. All the time breaking hoe handles and letting the mules loose in the wheat" (89). But through Sophia's experience in the mayor's household, the narrative demonstrates that it is Miss Millie, the mayor's wife, who is actually incompetent—who must be taught to drive by Sophia, for example, and who even then can't manage a short trip by herself. Thus, when she suddenly decides to drive Sophia home for a visit, Miss Millie stalls the car and ruins the transmission, the mistress unable to master driving in reverse. Too afraid of black men to allow one of Sophia's relatives to drive her back home alone, Miss Millie reveals her childlike dependence upon Sophia, who must cut short her first visit with her children in five years to ride home with the distraught white woman. Sophia's position as domestic within the mayor's household thus enables Walker to subvert the discourse of plantation kinship by suggesting that it actually supports a group of people who are themselves incompetent or, in Sophia words, "backward, . . . clumsy, and unlucky" (89).

Predicated on this plantation model of integration, relations between whites and blacks throughout the American South reveal a false kinship not unlike that of Doris Baines and the Akwee. But in this instance the false kinship is doubly perverse because it conceals an elaborate network of actual kinship connections. Thus Miss Eleanor Jane's husband feels free to humor Sophia by referring to the importance of black mammies in the community—". . . everybody around here raise by colored. That's how come we turn out so well" (222)—while other white men refuse to recognize the children they father with black women. As Celie says of Mr. ———'s son Bub, he "look so much like the Sheriff, he and Mr. ——— almost on family terms"; that is, "just so long as Mr. ——— know he colored" (76-77). Like the apologists for slavery, then, the Southern whites in **The Color Purple** keep alive a counterfeit definition of family while denying the real ties that bind them to African Americans.

In fact, the underlying system of kinship that exists in the American South has more to do with white uncles than black mammies, as is clear from the scene in which Sophia's family and friends consider various stratagems for winning her release from prison. By asking, "Who the warden's black kinfolks?" (80), Mr. ——— reveals that kinship relations between whites and blacks are so extensive in the community that it may be assumed that *someone* will be related by blood to the warden. That someone, of course, is Squeak. Hopeful that she will be able to gain Sophia's release from the warden on the basis of their kinship, the others dress Squeak up "like she a white woman" with instructions to make the warden "see the Hodges in you" (82). In spite of the fact that the warden does recognize Squeak as kin "the minute [she] walk[s] through the door" (83)—or perhaps *because* he recognizes her—the warden rapes Squeak, denying their kinship in the very act of perverting it. As Squeak herself recounts, "He say if he was my uncle he wouldn't do it to me" (85). Both an intensely personal and highly political act, Squeak's rape exposes the denial of kinship at the heart of race relations in the South and underscores the individual and institutional power of whites to control the terms of kinship—and whatever power those definitions convey—for their own interests.[13]

It is specifically as an act of resistance to this power that Sophia comes to reject Miss Eleanor Jane's baby and thereby to challenge the Olinka kinship ideal for race relations. From the time her son is born, Miss Eleanor Jane continually tests out Sophia's maternal feelings for him, "shoving Reynolds Stanley Earl in her face" almost "every time Sofia turn[s] around" (223). When an exasperated Sophia finally admits that she doesn't love the baby, Miss Eleanor Jane accuses her of being "unnatural" and implies that Sophia should accept her son because he is "just a little baby!" (225)—an innocent who, presumably, should not be blamed for the racist sins of his fathers. From Sophia's vantage point as a persecuted black woman, however, Reynolds Stanley is not "just a sweet, smart, cute, *innocent* little baby boy." He is in fact the grandson and namesake of the man who beat her brutally in the street, a man whom he also resembles physically. A "white something without much hair" with "big stuck open eyes" (223), Reynolds Stanley also takes after his father, who is excused from the military to run the family cotton gin while Sophia's own boys are trained for service overseas. To Sophia, Reynolds Stanley is both the living embodiment of and literal heir to the system that oppresses her: "He can't even walk and already he in my house messing it up. Did I ast him to come? Do I care whether he sweet or not? Will it make any difference in the way he grow up to treat me what I think?" (224). Reminding Miss Eleanor Jane of the real social conditions that separate her from Reynolds Stanley in spite of his "innocence," Sophia articulates a strong position counter to the Olinka kinship ethic of treating everyone like one mother's children: ". . . all the colored folks talking bout loving everybody just ain't looked hard at what they thought they said" (226).

In subverting the plantation model of kinship in general and the role of mammy that it assigns to black women in particular, then, Sophia's position as an unwilling domestic in the mayor's household underscores the importance of the personal point of view to the novel's political critique of race relations. Indeed, the personal point of view of *The Color Purple* is central to its political message: It is precisely the African American woman's *subjectivity* that gives the lie to cultural attempts to reduce her—like Sophia—to the role of the contented worker in a privileged white society.[14]

III. "White People Off Celebrating Their Independence. . . . Us Can Spend the Day Celebrating Each Other"

The Color Purple closes with a celebration of kinship, its concluding action composed of a series of family reunions: Sophia patches things up with Harpo; Shug visits her estranged children (for the first time in thirty years); and the novel's two narrators, Celie and Nettie, are joyfully and tearfully reunited. Even Albert and Celie are reconciled, his change of heart signaled by his earning the right to have his first name written. Coming after Celie has achieved both economic independence and emotional security, the reunions at the end of *The Color Purple* testify to the importance of kinship to the happiness of every individual. Appropriately, then, when the two sisters fall into one another's arms at last, each identifies her kin: Nettie introduces her husband and the children, and Celie's first act is to "point up at [her] peoples . . . Shug and Albert" (243). But in addition to suggesting that the individual realizes her full potential only *within* the supporting bonds of a strong kinship group (no matter how unconventionally that group might be defined), the conclusion to *The Color Purple* also addresses the vexing question posed by the Olinka Adam narrative: Is progress in race relations possible? By bringing to closure two earlier narrative threads—one dealing with Sophia and Miss Eleanor Jane, and the other with Sophia's relationship to work—the novel suggests that progress in race relations is possible. But the narrative's ending also contains arresting images of racial segregation in both Africa and America that complicate the idea of progress and ultimately move the narrative toward a final definition of kinship based on race.

After their falling out over Reynolds Stanley, Sophia and Miss Eleanor Jane are reunited when the mayor's daughter finally learns from her family *why* Sophia came to work for them in the first place. Miss Eleanor Jane subsequently comes to work in Sophia's home, helping with the housework and taking care of Sophia's daughter Henrietta. Clearly an improvement in the domestic relationship between the two women, this new arrangement expresses Miss Eleanor Jane's new understanding of their domestic history together: To her family's question "Whoever heard of a white woman working for niggers?" Miss Eleanor Jane answers, "Whoever heard of somebody like Sophia working for trash?" For her part, Sophia's acceptance of Miss Eleanor Jane in her own home also signals progress, although when Celie asks pointedly if little Reynolds Stanley comes along with his mother, Sophia sidesteps the issue of her own feelings for the child by answering, "Henrietta say she don't mind him" (238).[15] Sophia's comment maintains the legitimacy of her own hard-earned attitudes toward the child, even as it reserves the possibility that different attitudes may be possible in future generations.

Sophia's employment in Celie's dry goods store also seems to signal an improvement in race relations, not only because it represents Sophia's final escape from her position as mammy but also because shops are used throughout *The Color Purple* to represent the status of economic and social integration between blacks and whites. Thus early in the novel Corrine, a Spelman graduate, is insulted when a white clerk calls her "Girl" (14) and intimidates her into buying some thread she doesn't want. Later the novel contrasts the histories of Celie's real Pa and Step-pa as store owners, histories that comment on the ability of African Americans to achieve economic integration into the American mainstream.[16] Celie's real father, in the tradition of the

American success story, works hard, buys his own store, and hires two of his bothers to work it for him. Ironically, his model of industry and enterprise fails, since the store's very success leads "white merchants . . . [to] complain that this store was taking all the black business away from them" (148) Refusing to tolerate free competition from a black-owned and black-operated business, whites eventually burn the store and lynch Celie's Pa and his two brothers. The tragic history of Celie's real Pa thus compels readers to reinterpret Celie's family history in terms of the historical lack of access of African Americans to the "American Dream."

Believing that Celie's real Pa "didn't know how to git along," Alphonso, her step-pa, expresses a different path to economic integration:

> Take me, he say, I know how they is. The key to all of 'em is money. The trouble with our people is as soon as they got out of slavery they didn't want to give the white man nothing else. But the fact is, you got to give 'em something. Either your money, your land, your woman or your ass. So what I did was just right off offer to give 'em money. Before I planted a seed, I made sure this one and that one knowed one seed out of three was planted for *him*. Before I ground a grain of wheat, the same thing. And when I opened up your daddy's old store in town, I bought me my own white boy to run it. And what make it so good, he say, I bought him with whitefolks' money.
>
> (155)

Alphonso's decision to pay off whites and buy a white boy to work in the dry goods store establishes him in the tradition of the trickster who plays the system for his own benefit; however, the model of integration he represents is finally seen as accommodationist. Alphonso, in fact, is identified with white power from the beginning of the novel, where he is seen going off with a group of white men armed with guns (11-12). After he has made his fortune, Alphonso recalls the compromised African president described in Nettie's letter—like him Alphonso lives in a house that now looks like a "white person's house" (153), and like him he establishes paternalistic relationships with other blacks. Thus when Shug asks Alphonso's new wife, a "child" not "more than fifteen," why her parents allowed her to marry him, the girl replies: "They work for him. . . . Live on his land" (154). Alphonso's marriage thus makes explicit the degree to which his identification with white paternalism shapes his domestic relationships with other blacks.

In the context of these earlier histories, Sophia's coming to work in Celie's dry goods store has wider significance than just her finding suitable work outside the home. Indeed, for the first time in its history the store has an integrated workforce, since Celie keeps the "white man" who works there even as she hires Sophia to "wait on" blacks and "treat 'em nice" (245). In direct contrast to the white clerk who intimidated Corrine earlier, Sophia refuses to coerce customers and turns out to be especially good at "selling stuff" because "she don't care if you buy or not." Importantly, Sophia also resists the white clerk's attempts to define their relationship in the terms of plantation kinship: When he presumes to call her "auntie," she mocks him by asking "which colored man his mama sister marry" (237-38). While race relations in Celie's integrated store are obviously not ideal, Sophia's employment there is nonetheless both a personal and a communal triumph: Sophia finds employment that suits her as an individual, and the black community is treated with new respect in the marketplace.

Significantly, these small steps toward progress in race relations come not from some realization of the Olinka ideal or any recognition of identity *between* the races but from an evolving separatism and parallel growth in racial identity *within* the African and African American communities. The possibility of treating everyone like "one mother's children" is achieved within but not between racial groups by the end of **The Color Purple**. Instead, the conclusion leaves readers with images of an emerging Pan-Africanism in Africa and a nascent black nationalism in the American South.

In Africa separatism is represented by the *mbeles,* warriors who "live deep in the jungle, refusing to work for whites or be ruled by them" (193). Composed of men and women "from dozens of African tribes," the *mbeles* are particularly significant because they comprise a remnant group defined not by traditional village bloodlines but by their common experience of racial oppression and their shared commitment to active resistance, which takes the form of "missions of sabotage against the white plantations" (234). In the *mbeles,* **The Color Purple** accurately depicts the historical origin of many African "tribes" or nations in the reorganization of older societies decimated by colonization. Their plans for the white man's "destruction—or at least for his removal from *their continent*" (217; italics added)—also reflect a nascent pan-Africanism among the disenfranchised. Including among their number "one colored man . . . from Alabama," the *mbeles* represent a form of kinship that is defined by racial rather than national identity.

In America, a parallel growth in black identity is suggested by Celie's final letter in **The Color Purple**. Indeed, the spirit of celebratory kinship with which the novel closes is achieved by Celie's group specifically in isolation from whites, as Harpo explains: "White people busy celebrating they independence from England July 4th . . . so most black folks don't have to work. Us can spend the day celebrating each other" (242). By juxtaposing "white people" and "black folks," Harpo distinguishes his kinship group from the kinship of whites, defined by privilege and national identity. Importantly, the "folks" that Harpo refers to now include Celie's African daughter-in-law, Tashi. Also significantly, that group does *not* include Miss Eleanor Jane, no matter how strained her relationship with her own family or how successful her reunion with Sophia. Tashi's easy integration into the black community effaces her earlier fears that coming to America would rob her of all kinship ties, leaving her with "no country, no people, no mother and no husband and brother" (235). Instead, Tashi's quick acceptance by the Southern women, who make a fuss over her and "stuff her" with food (244), suggests once again that feelings of black identity make it easy for people to treat others as "one mother's children."[17]

But if the conclusion to *The Color Purple* suggests that feelings of racial identity can transcend national boundaries, the novel provides no such reassurances that the boundaries between races can be successfully negotiated. That sober conclusion is confirmed by the outcome of two other attempts at integration. The first is that of Shug's son, a missionary on an Indian reservation in the American West. The American Indians refuse to accept her son, Shug explains, because "everybody not a Indian they got no use for" (237).[18] The failure of Shug's son to become integrated into the American Indian community contrasts with Mary Agnes's successful integration with the mixed peoples of Cuba, but her experience there also emphasizes the importance of racial identity to kinship definitions. Indeed, it is because she is a person of color that Mary Agnes is recognized as kin: Even though some of the Cuban people are as light as Mary Agnes while others are "real dark," Shug explains, they are "all in the same family though. Try to pass for white, somebody mention your grandma" (211). Thus in Cuba—as well as in Africa and North America—feelings of racial identity among marginalized peoples become the basis for definitions of kinship by novel's end.

Finally, it is not surprising that, in elaborating her domestic trope for race relations, Walker is able to foreground the personal experience of her narrators while simultaneously offering an extended critique of racial integration. As Walker's integrated families remind us, the black family has seldom existed as a private, middle-class space protected from the interference of the state; therefore, the African American household is particularly inscribed with social meanings available for narration. Rather than opposing public and private spheres, Walker's narrative underscores their interpenetration. If her narrative does reveal an opposition, it is not between public and private discourse but between the universalist ethos of the Olinka ideal for race relations and the historical experience of African Americans as reflected in the narrative's analysis of specific integrated family groupings. For if the Olinka ideal questions the true nature of kinship in the novel's integrated families, these families also serve to criticize the Olinka myth for tracing the origins of racial discrimination back to some imaginary sin of black people, rather than to real, historical discrimination by whites.

It may be, however, that the growing sense of racial separatism at the conclusion to the *The Color Purple* is not necessarily at odds with the Olinka ideal for race relations. Past discrimination itself may dictate that improved relations between the races must begin with the destruction of false relations—the discovery of kinship among the disenfranchised the necessary first step, perhaps, toward recognizing all others as part of the same family. Like the Olinka Adam myth, the conclusion to Walker's novel raises the question of the future of race relations, but also like that myth, the novel offers no certain predictions. One thing is certain, however. Critics who believe that *The Color Purple* sacrifices its ability to critique the public world of blacks in favor of dramatizing the personal experience of its narrators not only run the risk of reducing the narrative's technical complexity, but also of overlooking the work's sustained critique of racial integration levied from *within* the domestic sphere. Through its embedded narrative line and carefully elaborated kinship trope for race relations, *The Color Purple* offers a critique of race that explores the possibility of treating all people as "one mother's children"—while remaining unremittingly sensitive to the distance that often separates even the best of human ideals from real historical conditions.

Notes

1. By characterizing the novel's point of view as "domestic," I mean no criticism, as my paper will make clear. My approach to *The Color Purple* is in sympathy with recent revaluations of the domestic sphere in literature. See, for example, Barbara Christian, who charts in her discussion of George Simms (20) the well-known nineteenth-century denigration of sentimental fiction by male writers; and Jane Tompkins, who has argued that earlier interpretations of sentimental fiction were shaped by critics who taught "generations of students to equate popularity with debasement, emotionality with ineffectiveness, religiosity with fakery, domesticity with triviality—and all of these, implicitly, with womanly inferiority" (123). Closer at hand, Alison Light has attributed critics' "fear" of the happy ending in *The Color Purple* to similar attitudes toward sentimentality in fiction; Light points to an "'androcentricity' implicit and produced" in the "making" of public and private spheres (92) and notes that "terms like

'sentimental' and 'idealistic' are not themselves transparent descriptions of knowledge or response" but "carry with them cultural prescriptions and assumptions and have themselves to be historicized" (93). See also Susan K. Harris and Claudia Tate.

2. Called Walker's "best but most problematic" novel by Bernard Bell (263), *The Color Purple* has generated controversy since its publication in 1982 and especially since the appearance of the 1985 film of the same title. It should be noted that academic discussions of Celie's point of view in *The Color Purple* are paralleled in interesting ways by a controversy in the popular media over the representation of black men in novel and film. In "Sifting Through the Controversy: Reading *The Color Purple*," Jacqueline Bobo concludes that arguments in the public media focus on two values that sometimes seem in conflict: the need for positive images of black people in the media and the recognition of "the authority of black women writers to set the agenda for imagemaking in fiction and film" (334).

3. By placing my first reference to race in quotation marks I am following the practice of Gates and others in *"Race," Writing, and Difference*. The quotation marks indicate that "race" does not refer to some essential nature or fixed difference between people. Gates's collection illustrates a variety of critical approaches to what he calls "the complex interplay among race, writing, and difference" (15).

4. hooks also objects specifically to Walker's linking of the slave narrative form to that of the sentimental novel, an association that she believes "strips the slave narrative of its revolutionary ideological intent and content" by linking it to "Eurocentral bourgeois literary traditions" ("Writing" 465). But hooks's criticism is problematic in light of the classical slave narrative tradition itself. Female authors of slave narratives often drew heavily upon the tradition of the sentimental novel to tell their stories. Note, for example, the case of what today is probably the best known woman's narrative, Harriet Jacobs's *Incidents in the Life of a Slave Girl*. Until recently Jacobs's autobiographical narrative was thought to *be* a sentimental novel. Jean Fagan Yellin details the textual history of the narrative in her edition of *Incidents*. See also Sekora's discussion of the genre of the slave narrative as a "mixed form" that syncretizes several literary traditions. While disagreeing with hooks about the genre of slave narratives in general and with her assessment of Walker's use of that tradition in particular, I want to acknowledge my debt to her work elsewhere on plantation family structures (as discussed in n14, below).

5. Unlike George Stade and bell hooks, Lauren Berlant and Elliott Butler-Evans seek not to criticize Walker's handling of the epistolary form but to uncover one effect that they believe follows from her chosen approach. Butler-Evans believes that the "restriction of focus to Celie's consciousness enables the novel to erase the public history and permits Celie to tell her own story" (166-67). Similarly, Berlant discusses Walker's "strategy of inversion, represented in its elevation of female experience over great patriarchal events" (847). Both critics detect an opposition or separation of discourses in the text, but their analyses differ in important ways. While sympathetic to Butler-Evans's method of analyzing the "politics of narration" (17) and especially to his analysis of sexual oppression, I believe his focus on the gender issues at the center of Walker's narrative leads him to underestimate both the extent and the importance of the novel's representation of race. Berlant's sophisticated argument cannot be summarized here, but if she means to limit—as I believe she does—her analysis of "nation" to Celie's understanding of the term, then our analyses may not be so much in conflict as they first appear. My own interest is in analyzing the narrative's embedded text on racial integration rather than in defining any particular character's understanding of race or nation. In other words, I believe that the implied reader of Walker's text is provided a political vantagepoint wider than that of any particular character in the novel, including its primary narrator, Celie.

6. Gates has analyzed the extent to which *The Color Purple* signifies upon Zora Neale Hurston's *Their Eyes Were Watching God* (*Signifying* 239-58). Note that, because of its layered narrative line, Walker's text is capable of another form of "doubleness"—an ability to signify upon itself.

7. While my purpose here is to focus primarily upon the representation of racial integration rather than gender, I should also note that this domestic ideal is expressed specifically in terms of matrilineal bonds. The recognition of all people as "one mother's children" is in keeping, of course, with the construction of gender elsewhere in the novel. Woman's love, understood as growing out of the experience of identity between mother and child (rather than out of the perception of difference between the sexes) is represented throughout *The Color Purple* as love that looks beyond differences in how people "look or act." As Celie tells Shug when the singer prepares to leave her, "I'm a woman. I love you. . . . Whatever happen, whatever you do. I love you" (221). For a theoretical alternative to Oedipal theories of maturation, see Chodorow.

8. While the boy's close proximity in age to Adam and Olivia accounts for some of his demeanor, his behavior raises issues of race and class nevertheless.

9. Note that Nettie's use of fairy-tale rhetoric to parody Doris undercuts the gender issues available in the white woman's narration and emphasizes instead issues of race and class.

10. Linda Abbandonato and others have pointed to Levi-Strauss's interpretation of the exchange of women as a "system of bonding men" (1109). Similarly, historian Gerda Lemer argues in *The Creation of Patriarchy* that the control of kinship—and especially of women's sexual and reproductive powers—leads to the historical development of patriarchal political structures, as power moves from the home and into law. Ironically, Doris leaves England to avoid becoming a wife, only to become an honorary husband in Africa. Doris's money has enabled her to escape becoming an object of exchange but not to escape the patriarchal system of exchange itself, which is seen to reach across continents.

11. Thus, in an article on "alienation and integration," Frank Shelton analyzes four kinds of alienation and integration in the novel—but not racial alienation or integration, probably because he believes that one component of such an analysis is largely missing from the text: "White people," he asserts, are "called a miracle of affliction" and then are "virtually ignored" (382). Rather than being ignored, white people actually function in the latter half of the novel to underscore the presence of race and class hegemony in domestic space and to problematize the family ideal for racial integration.

12. My discussion of the black mammy builds upon the work of Hazel Carby, Barbara Christian, Trudier Harris, and bell hooks (*Ain't I a Woman*), all of whom have written on literary representations of the African American woman in the plantation household.

13. For other analyses of Squeak's rape, see Christine Froula's reading of Squeak's "self-naming" in light of the sexual violence in the novel (639), and Berlant's discussion of the rape as "the diacritical mark that organizes Squeak's insertion into the 'womanist' order" (844).

14. In doing so, Walker's novel joins the longstanding feminist critique of separate-spheres ideology as a false division used for power's self-maintenance. See Gayatri Chakravorty Spivak's comment that "the deconstruction of the opposition between the private and public" is "implicit in all feminist activity" (201).

15. Note that Celie's pointed question to Sophia about Miss Eleanor Jane's baby demonstrates her own understanding of the race issues involved in Sophia's relationship with the white baby.

16. See Berlant's reading of Celie's family history, which argues that Celie's "fairy-tale rhetoric emphasizes the personal over the institutional or political components of social relations" such that "the nonbiologized abstraction of class relations virtually disappears from the text" (841-42). According to Berlant, Celie never understands the economic or class issues implied by her family history.

17. The conclusion also suggests that feelings of kinship can transcend gender differences, even when these differences include prior wrongs as great as Albert's abuse of Celie. The novel resolves tensions between the sexes—but not those between the races—optimistically, with partners, husbands, wives, and estates well sorted out by the novel's end.

18. Shug's son may work for the same organization as Nettie, since we learn early on that the "American and African Missionary Society" has also "ministered to the Indians out west" (109). In any case, the American Indians' treatment of Shug's son underscores their own understanding of the colonial function of missionaries. By calling Shug's son the "black white man," the American Indians also complicate racial definitions of kinship by suggesting that the definition of race itself is ultimately located in social hegemony.

Works Cited

Abbandonato, Linda. "A View from Elsewhere: Subversive Sexuality and the Rewriting of the Heroine's Story in *The Color Purple*." *PMLA* 106 (1991): 1106-15.

Bell, Bernard. *The Afro-American Novel and Its Tradition*. Amherst: U of Massachusetts P, 1987.

Berlant, Lauren. "Race, Gender, and Nation in *The Color Purple*." *Critical Inquiry* 14 (1988): 831-59.

Bobo, Jacqueline. "Sifting through the Controversy: Reading *The Color Purple*." *Callaloo* 12 (1989): 332-42.

Butler-Evans, Elliott. *Race, Gender, and Desire: Narrative Strategies in the Fiction of Toni Cade Bambara, Toni Morrison, and Alice Walker*. Philadelphia: Temple UP, 1989.

Carby, Hazel. *Reconstructing Womanhood: The Emergence of the Afro-American Woman Novelist*. New York: Oxford UP, 1987.

Chodorow, Nancy. *The Reproduction of Mothering: Psychoanalysis and The Sociology of Gender*. Berkeley: U of California P, 1978.

Christian, Barbara. *Black Women Novelists: The Development of a Tradition, 1892-1976.* Westport: Greenwood, 1980.

Froula, Christine, "The Daughter's Seduction: Sexual Violence and Feminist Theory." *Signs* 2 (1986): 621-44.

Gates, Henry Louis, Jr., ed. *"Race," Writing, and Difference.* Chicago: U of Chicago P, 1986.

———. *The Signifying Monkey: A Theory of African-American Literary Criticism.* New York: Oxford UP, 1988.

Harris, Susan K. *19th-Century American Women's Novels: Interpretive Strategies.* New York: Cambridge UP, 1990.

Harris, Trudier. *From Mammies to Militants: Domestics in Black American Literature.* Philadelphia: Temple UP, 1982.

hooks, bell. *Ain't I a Woman: Black Women and Feminism.* Boston: South End, 1981.

———. "Writing the Subject: Reading *The Color Purple*." *Reading Black, Reading Feminist.* Ed. Henry Louis Gates, Jr. New York: Meridian, 1990. 454-70.

Jacobs, Harriet. *Incidents in the Life of a Slave Girl. Told by Herself.* Ed. Jean Fagan Yellin. Cambridge: Harvard UP, 1987.

Lemer, Gerda. *The Creation of Patriarchy.* New York: Oxford UP, 1986

Light, Alison. "The Fear of the Happy Ending." *Plotting Change.* Ed. Linda Anderson. London: Edward Arnold, 1993. 85-96.

Sekora, John. "Is the Slave Narrative a Species of Autobiography?" *Studies in Autobiography.* Ed. James Olney. New York: Oxford UP, 1988. 99-111.

Shelton, Frank W. "Alienation and Integration in Alice Walker's *The Color Purple*." *CLA Journal* 28 (1985): 382-92.

Spivak, Gayatri Chakravorty. "Explanation and Culture: Marginalia." *Humanities and Society* 2 (1974): 201-21.

Stade, George. "Womanist Fiction and Male Characters." *Partisan Review* 52 (1985): 264-70.

Tate, Claudia. *Domestic Allegories of Political Desire: The Black Heroine's Text at the Turn of the Century.* New York: Oxford UP, 1992.

Tompkins, Jane. *Sensational Designs: The Cultural Work of American Fiction.* New York: Oxford UP, 1985.

Walker, Alice. *The Color Purple.* New York: Harcourt, 1982.

Stacie Lynn Hankinson (essay date spring 1997)

SOURCE: Hankinson, Stacie Lynn. "From Monotheism to Pantheism: Liberation from Patriarchy in Alice Walker's *The Color Purple*." *Midwest Quarterly* 38, no. 3 (spring 1997): 320-28.

[*In the following essay, Hankinson discusses how the development of Celie's religious beliefs in* The Color Purple *are instrumental in and indicative of her spiritual growth.*]

Alice Walker's ***The Color Purple,*** in spite of its overwhelming success, has been criticized for possessing a rather superficial, fairy tale-styled ending. T. W. Lewis, for example, avows that the work appears "not as a realistic chronicle of human events but as fable" (485), and, similarly, Trudier Harris notes that "the issues are worked out at the price of realism" (6). These are valid critiques, as it is difficult to imagine any character, despite the approximately forty-year time span, arising from such utter oppression into such a state of bliss and restoration, as does Celie. Yet if we as readers can accept this ending—simply overcome our prejudice that such a conclusion is improbable—we can then ask what functions as the impetus for such change. Much critical attention has been focused on the Shug/Celie relationship as the influencing factor in the latter's growth. For instance, Margaret Walsh, who refers to Shug as Celie's "magic helper," declares that through Ms. Avery, "the love inside Celie comes forth, breaking the spell that has bound her" (90). And in like manner, Daniel Ross discusses "the crucial role" Shug plays in Celie's development (73).

However, I would like to suggest another apparently unexplored area that operates in a similar manner, and that is the pantheistic philosophy into which Celie emerges. Celie's conversion from a monotheistic view of God (or traditional Christianity) to a more pantheistic outlook represents and parallels her movement from feelings of oppression under the domination of patriarchy into a sense of connectedness with others and self-acceptance at which she ultimately arrives by the novel's end.

From early adolescence into adulthood Celie associates the biblical God with the men she knows—men who have been oppressive and cruelly insensitive to her. The male-bullying and domination begin for Celie at fourteen when the man she thinks is "Pa" rapes her on at least two occasions, rendering her unable to ever again bear children. The trauma of this event remains entrenched in Celie's mind, causing her to still cry in her adulthood: "Seem like it all come back to me, laying there in Shug's arms. How it hurt and how much I was surprise. How it stung while I finish trimming his hair. How the blood drip down my leg and mess up my stocking. How he don't never look at me straight after that" (117). This assault develops into an oppressive view of men, particularly of the father figure, for Celie. In the same way that Celie wonders whether her father killed her vanished child (4), she also begins to associate God the Father with the murderer of her children. When her mother asks where the baby is, Celie replies: "God took it." To herself she reflects: "He [God] took it. He took it while I was sleeping. Kilt it out there in the woods. Kill this one too, if he can" (3). Subtly and at an early age, Celie's notion of the monotheistic, biblical God also begins to be affiliated with fear and violence, mirroring her conception of her father, and next of Mr. ———.

Pa's relinquishment of Celie to Mr. ——— differs very little from the way one might relinquish cattle. As Harris notes, Pa essentially "barters her off" (1), when he tells Mr. ———:

> I can't let you have Nettie. . . . But I can let you have Celie. . . . She ugly. . . . But she ain't no stranger to hard work. And she clean. And God done fixed her. You can do everything just like you want to and she ain't gonna make you feed or clothe it. . . . She'd come with her own linen. . . . She ain't smart either . . . but she can work like a man.
>
> (8-9)

Pa presents Celie as "less than a whole woman" (Ross, 75), due to what Judy Elsley refers to as her "enforced hysterectomy" (73). And in the same manner in which Celie is given away, so she is treated by Mr. ———as an animal. Celie is brutalized by Mr. ———'s son, while Mr. ——— watches with indifference (13), but primarily and consistently she is beaten by Mr. ———. "He say, Celie, git the belt. The children be outside the room peeking through the cracks. It all I can do not to cry. I make myself wood. I say to myself, Celie you a tree. That's how come I know trees fear man" (23). As Ross remarks, "Celie tries alternately to ignore and to annihilate her body" (70). Celie comes to know these beatings as both arbitrary ("Sometime beat me anyhow . . . whether I do what he say or not" [66]) and simply due to her permanent identity as female ("Harpo ast his daddy why he beat me. Mr. ——— say, Cause she my wife" [23]). Additionally, Mr. ——— repeatedly performs what might be considered sanctioned rape. Celie describes to Shug her dreaded sexual experiences: "He git up on you, heist your nightgown round your waist, plunge in. Most times I pretend I ain't there. He never know the difference. Never ast me how I feel, nothing. Just do his business, get off, go to sleep" (81). This sex is both in the absence of love and against Celie's will, rendering it a vile act.

It is Celie's interpretation of the biblical God and his commands that breeds her compliance to these abusive patriarchal conditions, for her acquiescence was apparently not an all-encompassing societal norm. Sofia and Shug, who function as foil to Celie's downcast state, are both women who vehemently refuse to be dominated. It is Celie's strict adherence to traditional Christianity, to the God who looks to her "like some stout white man work at the bank" (96), which keeps her locked in the cycle of male jurisdiction. Acting as "a model of Christian behavior" (Harris, 9), Celie explains to Sofia:

> Couldn't be mad at my daddy cause he my daddy. Bible say, Honor father and mother no matter what. . . . Well, sometime Mister git on me pretty hard. I have to talk to Old Maker. But he my husband. I shrug my shoulders. This life soon be over. . . . Heaven last always.
>
> (44)

Mr. ———, who treats Celie as his slave and hides her sister's letters for several years, represents to Celie a tyrannical male figure. He explodes into an archetype—one in which Pa, Harpo, and all other men are also cast. "I don't even look at mens. That's the truth. I look at women, tho, cause I'm not scared of them. . . . Most times mens look pretty much alike to me" (6, 16). Celie's earlier experiences demonstrate "that patriarchal society puts value on women only to the degree that they serve the purpose of commodities of exchange between men" (Elsley, 73). Thus, it is not surprising that as an adult, Celie likens the monotheistic Judeo-Christian God, whom she knows to be distinctively male, to the same burdensome traits of all males, as she remarks to Shug: "the God I been praying and writing to is a man. And act just like all the other mens I know. Trifling, forgitful, and low-down" (199). This iron-fisted God keeps Celie in constant fear of being punished, bridling her into subordination; because Celie has been discarded by this "old white man" (201), she is left at the bottom of the traditional world's pecking order, as she is black, poor, female, and unattractive. Her resulting low self-esteem paralyzes her, making her a pawn, or as Charles Proudfit puts it, "a passive victim" (23), to the ubiquitous patriarchy that manifests itself both familially and spiritually.

Up to this point in the novel, Celie's life has been one of hopelessness, even longing for death as relief from life's hardships. "Celie has been fragmented into pieces which are given away to others, mostly at the insistence of the men who dominate her" (Elsley, 73). Finally, however, the story undergoes a significant turning point. When Celie discovers the long-obscured truth about her family—that her real father was lynched, her mother was crazy, and Pa was not really her father—she declares to God: "You must be sleep" (183). This is the first step Celie makes in resisting the "big and old and tall and gray bearded and white" monotheistic God (201). It is at this point that the story takes on a radically new direction even in terms of the narrative device of letter writing. Prior to this stage, Celie's letters were addressed to God, due to the threat made to her by Pa that prefaces the book: "You better not never tell nobody but God. It'd kill your mammy" (1). Thus, all these letters are cast with a fearful hue and are written to what is at best a vague entity to Celie. But after the aforementioned declaration that God is asleep in terms of her life, Celie begins addressing her letters to Nettie, underscoring the newly emerging theme of love, connectedness, and restoration, which Celie's bond with Nettie represents.

I must take issue at this point with Diane Gabrielsen Scholl who perceives the novel as having a "radically *Christian* nature" (255). Indeed, it is only as Celie rids herself of her oppressive man-God figure and emerges into a distinctly non-Christian discovery of God that she finally attains liberation from patriarchy. When Shug teaches Celie that God is in everything, including the flowers, wind, and water (204), and God is in her, and she is inherently connected to everything (203), her sense of fear and of being judged dissolves. Celie learns that she should focus on the creation, not the person of God, as Shug directs: "My first step from the old white man was trees. Then air. Then birds. Then other people. . . . I knew that if I cut a tree, my arm would bleed" (203). Celie's newfound religion links God with the power of the universe, a very pantheistic notion, and often associated with goddess religions. According to Jung, the positive aspects of the earth and nature—including fertility, growth, and abundance—are associated with "The Good Mother" (Guerin, 152). In Celie's new framework, God is posited as internal, a connecting force of all nature (202), but most significantly for Celie, God is no longer a He, but an it, erasing the male connotations she previously connected with God. Shug describes: "[It] Don't look like nothing. . . . It ain't a picture show. It ain't something you can look at apart from anything else, including yourself. I believe God is everything" (202).

This new philosophy that positions Celie as "being part of everything, not separate at all" (203), fortifies her with self-acceptance and leads her to reject male mastery. When Mr. ——— asserts Celie's low status on the white, patriarchal scale—"You black, you pore, you ugly, you a woman" (213)—it is the nature-God that literally enables her to speak and fight back. As Celie curses Mr. ———, she feels the strength "seem to come to me from the trees" (213). As Mr. ——— attempts to reassert his dominance, Celie continues to be spurred on by the air (213), and then the dirt (214), which gives utterance to her ultimate defiance against established hierarchy: "I'm pore, I'm black, I may be ugly and can't cook. . . . But I'm here" (214). Celie affirms that although she does not fulfill the standards set by the male-dominated world which surrounds her, her existence matters.

As suggested, it is only as Celie diverges from the patriarchal family structure and perspective of God that she acquires her first sense of self-acceptance. She resists the imposed negative self-image and develops a previously unprecedented confidence. Namely, she starts her own clothing business, learns to accept Shug's affair with a man, and maintains assurance that Nettie is alive, in spite of a letter's mention of her sunken boat. Most notably, Celie begins for the first time to refer to her nameless oppressor, Mr. ———, by his first name, Albert. This change in name reference is indicative of Celie's developing realization of her equality with men, in contrast to her prior feeling of subservience toward them. By finally referring to her husband (from whom she is now separated) as Albert, Celie demonstrates her rejection of the fearful reverence that the formal title Mr. ——— commands and places her husband on a level more par with herself. Celie's life rises to such heights that she writes to Nettie: "I am so happy. I got love, I got work, I got money, friends and time. And you alive and be home soon. With our children" (222). Coinciding with this newfound optimism, Celie discovers a new sense of unity and communion with the pantheistic God: "I smoke when I want to talk to God. I smoke when I want to make love. Lately I feel like me and God make love just fine anyhow" (227).

Under the masculine violence Celie is made to endure, a survival-of-the-fittest perspective had been implanted in her which pitted her against, rather than aligning her with, other women. When Harpo asks Celie "what to do to make Sophia mind" (327), Celie flatly advises him to beat her, resorting to a familiar hierarchal order system as justification: "Wives is like children. You have to let 'em know who got the upper hand. Nothing can do that better than a good sound beating" (37).

In spite of this external hostility towards other women, internally Celie is magnetized towards them, particularly towards Shug. Watching her bathe, Celie remarks: "I thought I had turned into a man" (51). Yet, in addition to the aforementioned patriarchally-instilled mentality that had set Celie in opposition to Sophia, Celie is also confronted with the moral taboo of homosexuality imposed by the white, male, Christian God. These two machinations—operating with different and yet uniform function—aim to immobilize Celie, so as to prevent her from seeking female refuge.

Celie hurdles both obstacles once again through the strength of her pantheistic god. She is liberated when Shug informs her:

> God love all them [sexual] feelings. That's some of the best stuff God did. And when you know God loves 'em you enjoys 'em a lot more. You can just relax [and] go with everything that's going.
>
> (203)

Believing in this new god that accepts alternative lifestyles and who "don't think it dirty" (203), Celie is free to venture into a lesbian relationship with Shug that for the first time merges sex and love for her. This relationship evokes so profound an erotic awakening that Celie believes she was "still a virgin" prior to it (81). Although Shug is often credited as the sole source of Celie's newfound physical and emotional nourishment, Celie may not have been receptive to Shug's advances if not for her spiritual reorientation.

Celie's final letter is addressed, "Dear God. Dear stars, dear trees, dear sky, dear peoples. Dear Everything. Dear God" (292). The novel's conclusion emphasizes Celie's discovery that God is in everything, and therefore everything is holy, a concept that defies any sense of hierarchal structure. In contrast to the unbridgeable separation Celie experienced from the remote Christian God who "sit up there glorying in being deef" (200), the ending stresses the connectedness of all existence—of God, stars, trees, the sky, and all people including herself. Celie's movement from monotheism to pantheism parallels her movement from feelings of isolation and inferiority under male authority figures, into a new sense of bonding with other women and appreciation of herself.

Among the many reasons that **The Color Purple** is considered significant, it should also be noted that the novel reveals a progression in the author's religious development and advocacy. In much of Walker's earlier work, a repudiation of traditional Christianity is evident while a viable replacement is not proposed. For instance, in *The Third Life of Grange Copeland* (1970), Grange finally rejects Christianity in the immediate moments before he is shot. While it seems to Grange "appropriate" to pray, and he even opens his mouth to do so, ultimately he "could not pray, therefore he did not" (247). Walker unshackles Grange from Christianity, but provides him with no final recourse. Similarly, Dee/Wangero in **"Everyday Use"** (1973) refuses her mother's Christian lifestyle and even her own white Christian name, only to embrace what Sylvan Barnet calls "an essentially remote heritage" (70). Walker clearly presents the Black Muslim movement in this story as a superficial solution that provides Dee with no "real connection with her heritage" (Barnet, 69). The outcome for these early characters is bleak; while they cast off what Walker exhibits as an oppressive institution, they only progress into a vast void. The pantheistic alternative propounded in **The Color Purple** represents then a newfound optimism and spiritual furtherance in the ideological framework of Walker's characters.

Bibliography

Barnet, Sylvan, Morton Berman, and William Burto. *An Introduction to Literature: Instructor's Manual*. 9th ed. New York: Harper Collins, 1989.

Elsley, Judy. "'Nothing Can Be Sole or Whole that Has Not Been Rent': Fragmentation in the Quilt and *The Color Purple*." *Weber Studies: An Interdisciplinary Humanities Journal*, 9 (1992), 71-81.

Guerin, Wilfred, et. al. *A Handbook of Critical Approaches to Literature*. 3rd ed. Oxford: Oxford University Press, 1992.

Harris, Trudier. "From Victimization to Free Enterprise: Alice Walker's *The Color Purple*." *Studies in American Fiction*, 14 (1986), 1-17.

Lewis, T. S., III. "Moral Mapping and Spiritual Guidance in *The Color Purple*." *Soundings: An Interdisciplinary Journal*, 73 (1990), 483-91.

Proudfit, Charles L. "Celie's Search for Identity: A Psychoanalytic Developmental Reading of Alice Walker's *The Color Purple*." *Contemporary Literature*, 32 (1991), 12-37.

Ross, Daniel W. "Celie in the Looking Glass: The Desire for Selfhood in *The Color Purple*." *Modern Fiction Studies*, 34 (1988), 69-84.

Scholl, Diane Gabrielson. "With Ears to Hear and Eyes to See: Alice Walker's Parable *The Color Purple*." *Christianity and Literature*, 40 (1991), 255-66.

Walker, Alice. *The Color Purple*. New York: Pocket Books, 1982.

———. *The Third Life of Grange Copeland*. New York: Harcourt Brace Jovanovich, 1970.

———. "Everyday Use." *In Love and Trouble*. New York: Harcourt Brace Javanovich, 1973.

Walsh, Margaret. "The Enchanted World of *The Color Purple*." *The Southern Quarterly: A Journal of the Arts of the South*, 25 (1987), 89-101.

Charles J. Heglar (essay date winter 2000)

SOURCE: Heglar, Charles J. "Named and Nameless: Alice Walker's Pattern of Surnames in *The Color Purple*." *ANQ* 13, no. 1 (winter 2000): 38-41.

[*In the following essay, Heglar examines Walker's withholding of surnames and use of blank lines for the names of male characters in* The Color Purple, *and studies her use of surnames for three of the novel's atypical female characters.*]

In her 1982 novel **The Color Purple,** Alice Walker skillfully erases, withholds, or supplies surnames for her characters in order to develop an alternative perspective that challenges, overturns, and regenerates the patriarchal society of the novel. Walker's erasure or withholding of surnames draws attention to her examination of male dominance; on the other hand, in the few cases when she supplies a surname for a character, Walker indicates an alternative to such domination. Namelessness and naming become a significant pattern as the novel unfolds.

Molly Hite has given an insightful reading of the most obvious instance of namelessness through erasure when she notes that "the most important agent of suffering is also a (relatively) powerful male figure, Celie's husband Mr. ———, whose unarticulated name, in the manner of epistolary fictions since Richardson's *Pamela*, suggests fearful effacement of an identity too dangerous to reveal, and whose transformation is signaled by a renaming [as Albert] that at once diminishes and humanizes" (437). However, this is only one instance of Walker's use of the ——— to erase a male surname. "Reverend Mr. ———"—the minister who brings Nettie into his home, takes her to Africa, and eventually marries her—is a representative of patriarchal religious and cultural power and becomes a person, "Samuel," much more quickly than Albert as, in Africa, his concept of God becomes less Eurocentric. The namelessness of Albert and Samuel is highlighted because the ——— draws attention to Walker's erasure of their surnames.

Closely related to erasure, withholding surnames occurs when characters are identified only by a first name or by kinship. In these cases, Walker does not even use the ———. Celie, Harpo, Corrine, Nettie, and other relatives by blood or marriage have their surnames withheld because of the erasure of Albert's and Samuel's surnames; thus, Celie and Nettie, for example, do not have married surnames because of the ——— for both Albert and Samuel. Withholding is also notable in Nettie's account of her and Celie's true origins; rather than identifying their parents by name, Nettie emphasizes their familial relationship. As Lauren Berlant points out, "Rather than naming names—her own father's, her mother's, her stepfather's—Nettie emphasized abstract kinship terms like 'the man and his two brothers,' 'the wife,' 'the widow,' 'the stranger' to describe their positions in the tale" (217). Because Nettie and Celie's stepfather is only identified as "Pa" or "Alfonso" and because their father is also presented without a surname, the sisters' maiden name is withheld. This pattern of withholding is further elaborated with Grady and Germaine, Shug Avery's two husbands, who are given no surnames, while their wife continues to be identified as "Shug Avery." Similarly, Sofia's sister's husband is only identified as "Odessa's husband" or "Jack" (191). In a minor key, Squeak—"a little nickname" given by Harpo (83)—claims a name, but not a surname, through her aid in paroling Sofia.

In *The Color Purple,* erasing and withholding men's surnames diminishes their patriarchal authority as, in contrast, supplying women's surnames establishes an alternative to male domination. This is especially important for Celie and Nettie. Critics have given deserved attention to Shug Avery and Sofia Butler as models for Celie's evolution, though not to the fact that they are surnamed; for instance, bell hooks writes of "black women . . . like Shug and Sofia [who] rebelliously place themselves outside the context of patriarchal family norms . . ." (294). The major trait of these alternatives to male domination is their ability to break through imposed stereotypes and boundaries to provide models for others, both male and female, to follow. These alternatives are clearly androgynous. Albert and Celie argue but cannot decide whether Shug and Sofia are better characterized as "manly" or "womanly" (236). In the end they agree that "Sofia and Shug not like men . . . but they not like women either" (236). However, Walker only presents this androgynous alternative in the form of female characters with surnames.

Shug Avery and Sophia Butler provide the major alternative influences that allow Celie to grow and develop. However, Miss Addie Beasley, while a minor character in the subplot of Nettie's development, is important in revealing the extent of Walker's larger pattern of surnames. Although critics have explored the roles of Avery and Butler, they have ignored Beasley. Miss Addie Beasley is the teacher who serves as Nettie's model in her effort to become an educated woman. As Celie points out, "Nettie dote on Miss Beasley. Think nobody like her in the world" (19). Significantly, with a shift of perspective, Celie's statement could as easily describe her own later relationship to Shug Avery. Like Shug Avery and Sofia Butler, Addie Beasley stands outside of and threatens the patriarchal system of the novel. Alfonso describes the school teacher with disdain for, and fear of, her androgynous power: "She run off at the mouth so much no man would have her. That how come she have to teach school" (19). Beasley even attempts to intervene when Alphonso takes Celie out of school until she realizes that Celie is pregnant.

Although Beasley cannot help Celie, her influence on Nettie is important and lasting, even after Nettie, as a missionary in Africa, has outgrown Beasley's uninformed view of Africa as a "place overrun with savages who didn't wear clothes" (123). In one of her letters to Celie, Nettie describes Beasley's influence: "one thing I do thank her for, for teaching me to learn myself by reading and studying and writing a clear hand. And for keeping alive in me somehow the desire to *know*" (123-24). *Knowing* as a process rather than a set of received facts allows Nettie to grow beyond the limits of a religious and cultural missionary and to arrive at ideas of God parallel to those Celie reaches with the aid of Shug Avery. Furthermore, both Nettie's "desire to know" and her "clear hand" are instrumental in freeing Celie: Nettie discovers their family history and writes to inform her sister of their true origins. This subtle, but important, development places Nettie's intellectual growth in direct contrast to the static development posited by Linda Abbandonato, who sees Nettie in "the preposterous role of a black missionary who attempts to impose the ideology of her oppressors onto a culturally self-sufficient people" (299).

It is tempting to see Walker's pattern of surnames as a feminization of the world of the novel. In such a reading, Sofia Butler, Shug Avery, and Addie Beasley would function as mother figures who allow not only Celie and Nettie but also Albert, Harpo, and other responsive male characters to enter a fuller, feminized life. However, given the matronly, but maidenly, status of Miss Beasley and the disruptions in Shug Avery's and Sofia Butler's mothering of their children, it is more accurate to see Walker supplying a surname to these characters as a movement away from matriarchy that complements her rejection of patriarchy. For men, Walker uses ——— as a sign of the ultimate powerlessness of patriarchal conceptions; for women, she reverses the traditional signification and gives surnames as a sign of their power as nonmatriarchal alternatives to transform the patriarchal system.

Works Cited

Abbandonato, Linda. "Rewriting the Heroine's Story in *The Color Purple*." *Alice Walker: Critical Perspectives Past and Present*. Ed. Henry Louis Gates, Jr., and K. A. Appiah. New York: Amistead, 1993. 296-308.

Berlant, Lauren. "Race, Gender, and Nation in *The Color Purple*." *Alice Walker: Critical Perspectives Past and Present*. Ed. Henry Louis Gates, Jr., and K. A. Appiah. New York: Amistead, 1993. 211-38.

Hite, Molly. "Romance, Marginality, and Matrilineage: *The Color Purple* and *Their Eyes Were Watching God*." *Reading Black, Reading Feminist: A Critical Anthology*. Ed. Henry Louis Gates, Jr. New York: Meridian, 1990. 431-53.

hooks, bell. "Reading and Resistance: *The Color Purple*." *Alice Walker: Critical Perspectives Past and Present*. Ed. Henry Louis Gates, Jr., and K. A. Appiah. New York: Amistead, 1993. 284-95.

Walker, Alice. *The Color Purple*. New York: Washington Square, 1982.

Martha J. Cutter (essay date fall-winter 2000)

SOURCE: Cutter, Martha J. "Philomela Speaks: Alice Walker's Revisioning of Rape Archetypes in *The Color Purple*." *MELUS* 25, nos. 3-4 (fall-winter 2000): 161-80.

[*In the following essay, Cutter compares and contrasts the character of Celie from* The Color Purple *with the character of Philomela from Ovid's* Metamorphoses, *noting the similarities between the women's repeated rapes and their rapists' attempts to silence them.*]

The ancient story of Philomela has resonated in the imaginations of women writers for several thousand years. The presence of this myth in contemporary texts by African American women writers marks the persistence of a powerful archetypal narrative explicitly connecting rape (a violent inscription of the female body), silencing, and the complete erasure of feminine subjectivity.[1] For in most versions of this myth Philomela is not only raped—she is also silenced. In Ovid's recounting, for example, Philomela is raped by her brother-in-law, Tereus, who then tears out her tongue. Philomela is finally transformed into a nightingale, doomed to chirp out the name of her rapist for eternity: *tereu, tereu*. The mythic narrative of Philomela therefore explicitly intertwines rape, silencing, and the destruction of feminine subjectivity.

Contemporary African American women's fiction contains allusions to this archetypal rape narrative. In Toni Morrison's *The Bluest Eye*, for example, Pecola Breedlove's rape by her father Cholly causes a fragmentation of her psyche. Pecola's attempts to tell of her rape are nullified by her disbelieving mother, and by the novel's conclusion her voice is only exercised in internal colloquies with an imaginary friend. She flutters along the edges of society, a "winged but grounded bird" (158). Similarly, in Gloria Naylor's *The Women of Brewster Place*, after Lorraine is gagged and brutally gang raped, she becomes both insane and unable to speak of her rape. Finally, she is left with only one word, a word that echoes back to Philomela's "*tereu, tereu*," the word she attempted to use to stop her attackers: "Please. Please" (173).[2] Rape is thus a central trope in these texts for the mechanisms whereby a patriarchal society writes oppressive dictates on women's bodies and minds, destroying both subjectivity and voice. Or, as Madonne Miner puts it, "Men, potential rapists, assume presence, language, and reason as their particular province. Women, potential victims, fall prey to absence, silence, and madness" (181).

For writers such as Naylor and Morrison, the myth of Philomela graphically illustrates the way a patriarchal society censors and erases women's voices. More damaging, perhaps, Philomela's story also indicates that if women find other methods of communicating, these alternatives lead only to more violence and an even deeper silence. After her rape Philomela is imprisoned in a tower of stone, but she manages to weave a tapestry (or in some accounts a robe) depicting Tereus's actions. She sends this artwork to her sister Procne, who "reads" this text and understands its import. Buried within this myth of patriarchal subjugation, then, there is a subtext that focuses on how women can "speak" across and against the limits of patriarchal discourse. However, the myth's final message seems to be that women's alternative texts fail to transform in any lasting way the social or linguistic forces of patriarchal domination. Procne's response to her sister is to first consider killing Tereus, whom she calls, as translated by Humphries, "the *author* of our evils" (149, emphasis added). Instead she kills her young son Itys, roasts and grills Itys's flesh, and serves this "feast" to her husband. When Tereus apprehends what has happened, he attempts to destroy both Philomela and Procne, but the gods intervene, transforming all three characters into birds.

The structural pattern of the myth (and its warning to women) seems clear; as Patricia Joplin explains, the myth fixes "in eternity the pattern of violation-revenge-violation. . . . The women, in yielding to violence, become just like the men. . . . The sacrifice of the innocent victim, Itys, continues, without altering it, the motion of reciprocal violence" (48-49). More importantly, the myth also instantiates an endless cycle of linguistic violence against women: violence (i.e., rape) leads to silence (the tongue is torn out); attempts to break this silence through assertions of an alternative feminine voice (the tapestry) lead only to more violence (the killing of Itys), and finally, to a more complete and final silence (the death of the characters and the loss of their human voices). The myth suggests that an assertion of alternative feminine voice merely imprisons women all the more exhaustively in pejorative master-texts that make men, as Procne says, the "author of our evils."

Like the novels of Morrison and Naylor, Alice Walker's ***The Color Purple*** invokes this archetypal rape narrative, but Walker is most interested in re-envisioning this myth through an alternative methodology of language. As Linda Abbandonato argues in her reading of the ***The Color Purple,*** it is important to consider how a woman can "define herself differently, disengage her self from the cultural scripts of sexuality and gender that produce her as feminine subject" (1107). Abbandonato argues that ***The Color Purple*** rewrites canonical male texts, but she does not discuss Walker's rewriting of the story of Philomela. Similarly, although critics such as Trudier Harris, Keith Byerman, Wendy Wall, Mae Henderson, and King-Kok Cheung have discussed Celie's acquisition of private and public languages, none of these critics has examined Walker's reconfiguration of linguistic elements of the myth of Philomela. Unlike the original mythic text, as well as the novels of Morrison and Naylor, Walker's text gives Philomela a voice that successfully resists the violent patriarchal inscription of male will onto a silent female body.

Yet Walker does more than simply allow Philomela to speak within the confines of patriarchal discourse.[3] Walker's novel revises the myth of Philomela by creating a heroine's text that reconfigures the rhetorical situation of sender-receiver-message and articulates Celie's movement away from an existence as a victim in a patriarchal plot toward a linguistic and narratological presence as the author/subject of her own story. Walker's novel also rewrites the myth through its creation of an alternative discourse that allows for the expression of both masculine and feminine subjectivity—a language of the sewn that withdraws from the violence of patriarchal domination, of patriarchal discourse.[4] Celie's skills as a seamstress both retrieve and refigure the myth of Philomela, for unlike Philomela's tapestry/text, Celie's sewing functions as an alternative methodology of language that moves her away from violence and victimization and into self-empowerment and subjectivity. The novel also deliberately conflates the pen and the needle, thereby deconstructing the binary oppositions between the masculine and the feminine, the spoken and the silenced, the lexical and the graphic. Walker's reconfiguration of the myth of Philomela thus overturns the master discourse *and* the master narrative of patriarchal society. In Walker's hands Philomela's speech becomes the instrument for a radical metamorphosis of the individual as well as a subversive deconstruction of the power structures that undergird both patriarchal language and the patriarchal world itself.

Susan Griffin argues that "more than rape itself, the fear of rape permeates our lives. . . . and the best defense against this is not to be, to deny being in the body, as a self; . . . to avert your gaze, make yourself, as a presence in this world, less felt" (83). Certainly, when Celie speaks of turning herself into wood when she is beaten or raped ("I say to myself, Celie, you a tree" [30]), the response described by Griffin is apparent; to avoid pain Celie denies her body and her presence. Walker's story begins in the familiar mythic way: Celie is told after her rape by her (presumed) father: *"You better not never tell nobody but God. It'd kill your mammy"* (11). Celie is silenced by an external source, and like Morrison's and Naylor's protagonists, she experiences the nullification of subjectivity and internal voice allied with rape by the myth of Philomela. Celie's story starts with the fact that the one identity she has always known is no longer accessible: "I am fourteen years old. I have always been a good girl" (11). No longer a "good girl," Celie has no present tense subjectivity, no present tense "I am."

Like Pecola Breedlove of Morrison's *The Bluest Eye,* who ends the novel "flail[ing] her arms like a bird in an eternal, grotesquely futile effort to fly" (158), Celie appears to have been driven into semiotic collapse by the rape. Walker's text also uses bird and blood imagery to connect Celie with her mythic prototype, Philomela as well as to revise the mythic prototext. In *Metamorphoses,* Ovid describes how Procne and Philomela are transformed, a change that silences them as humans but does not erase their bloody deeds: "One flew to the woods, the other to the roof-top, / And even so the red marks of the murder / Stayed on their breasts; the feathers were blood-colored" (151). Throughout *The Color Purple*, Celie is associated with both birds and blood. Celie tells Albert that she loves birds (223), and Albert comments, "you use to remind me of a bird. Way back when you first come to live with me. . . . And the least little thing happen, you looked about to fly away" (223). Later in the novel, when Celie returns to confront her "Pa" (Alphonso) about his actions, she comments three times on how loudly the birds are singing around his house (164, 165, 167). The singing birds of the later scene recall Celie's earlier victimization, the way she was raped, bloodied, impregnated, and deprived of voice by Alphonso's statement that "she tell lies" (18).

Paradoxically, the birds of this scene are also a positive symbol to Celie of how nature persists in displaying its beauty despite the despoiling patterns of humanity. Similarly, Walker later transforms the blood symbolism of the early rape scene ("Seem like it all come back to me. . . . How the blood drip down my leg and mess up my stocking" [108-9] into something more positive, revising the symbolism of blood in the mythic text. When Shug abandons Celie, Celie describes her heart as "blooming blood" (229). Here, although blood is painful, it is also generative: it blooms. Blood comes from Celie during her rape. It also covers her in other key scenes in the novel, such as her first meeting with Mr. ———'s (Albert's) family: "I spend my wedding day running from the oldest boy. . . . He pick up a rock and laid my head open. The blood run all down tween my breasts" (21). Like Philomela, whose breast feathers are stained "blood-colored" with the "red marks of the murder" after she is transformed into a bird (Ovid 151), Celie's breasts are stained with blood. However, Celie eventually transforms the blood of this attack into blooming blood, into a red that is creative and regenerative. A more mature Celie uses the color red as a positive element in her sewing, transforming it from a color of pain to a color of joy. She sews purple and red pants for Sofia (194), orange and red pants for Squeak (191), and blue and red pants for Shug (191). She paints her own room purple and red (248). The blood that marks Celie becomes a positive symbol of her artistic creativity, rather than (as in the myth) a negative symbol of how she is damned in perpetuity by her deed.[5]

Unlike the archetypal narrative, then, Walker's novel uses bird and blood imagery to suggest Celie's metamorphosis not from human to subhuman, but from victim to artist-heroine. The novel also differs from the mythic prototext, as well as from the novels of Morrison and Naylor, in that it begins (rather than ends) with Celie's rape, and in that the rape becomes not an instrument of silencing, but the catalyst to Celie's search for voice.

After Celie is told to be silent about the rape, she confides the details in her journal, structured at first as letters to God. In these letters Celie begins to create a resistant narratological version of events that ultimately preserves her subjectivity and voice:

> He never had a kine word to say to me. Just say You gonna do what your mammy wouldn't. First he put his thing up gainst my hip and sort of wiggle it around. Then he grab hold of my titties. Then he push his thing inside my pussy. When that hurt, I cry. He start to choke me, saying You better shut up and git used to it. But I don't never git used to it.
>
> (11)

The horror of this experience is evident, but it is also apparent that Celie narrates these events to *resist* her father. Susan Brownmiller comments that "Rape by an authority figure can befuddle a victim. . . . Authority figures emanate an aura of rightness; their actions cannot easily be challenged. What else can the victim be but 'wrong'"? (271). However, even the patent statement that "I don't never git used to it" demonstrates that Celie knows her Pa's actions are improper and that she refuses to live by his imperatives; she refuses to be the passive sheet upon which the father writes unalterable messages. By writing about her rape, Celie also externalizes her experiences so that they do not destroy her. Celie feels sorry for her mama because "Trying to believe his [the father's] story kilt her" (15). Taking one's place within a patriarchal text leads to the obliteration of feminine subjectivity. That Celie resists the father's narratives through her own writing means that she survives.

Celie's narration of these actions in her diary also enables the later moments in the novel when she speaks of her rape to Shug Avery: "While I trim his hair he look at me funny. He a little nervous too, but I don't know why, till he grab hold of me and cram me up tween his legs. . . . It hurt me, you know, I say. I was just going on fourteen. I never even thought bout men having nothing down there so big" (108). Ellen Rooney comments that scenes of sexual violence "may be privileged sites for investigating the construction of female subjectivity because they articulate questions of desire, power, and agency with a special urgency and explicitly foreground the opposition between subject and object" (92). Walker twice narrates Celie's violation in order to show how "Pa" attempts to deny Celie's subjectivity as well as how Celie creates her own spoken and written version of events which emphasizes her cognizance and functions as a counterpoint to her own earlier erasure of body and identity. Walker thus revises the archetypal paradigm depicting rape as an event that encapsulates women in patriarchal plots as the site of silence, absence, and madness. In Walker's text rape leads not to erasure, but rather to the start of a prolonged struggle toward subjectivity and voice.[6]

Celie's movement out of silence occurs despite repeated rape by her husband, who in his demeanor and behavior exactly parallels her father. Multiple or repeated rape is an important element of the violation detailed in the archetypal myth of Philomela as well as in texts by contemporary African American women. In the mythic text, after Tereus cuts out Philomela's tongue he rapes her again, perhaps more than once: "And even then—/ It seems too much to believe—even then, Tereus / Took her, and took her again, the injured body / Still giving satisfaction to his lust" (Ovid 147). In *The Women of Brewster Place,* Lorraine is repeatedly raped by six teenagers, while her "paralyzed vocal cords" cannot function because of the dirty paper bag that has been shoved in her mouth (170). In *The Bluest Eye,* Pecola's internal monologue reveals that her father, Cholly, raped her at least twice (155, 156), but her mother does not believe that either incident occurred (155).

Celie, too, is repeatedly raped by her "Pa," who impregnates her twice and then gives away her children. Celie is also raped, both actually and symbolically, by her husband, Mr. ——— (or Albert). Celie is quick to note the parallels between her husband and her father: "Mr. ——— say. . . . All women good for—he don't finish. He just tuck his chin over the paper like he do. Remind me of Pa" (30). And Celie's letters repeatedly emphasize that sex with Albert is the equivalent of rape: "He git up on you, heist your nightgown round your waist, plunge in. Most times I pretend I ain't there. He never know the difference. Never ast me how I feel, nothing. Just do his business, get off, go to sleep" (79; see also 109). In the imagery of Walker's text father and husband are conflated: both are rapists who deny that women can be anything other than objects of male abuse. This conflation echoes back to the myth of Philomela, for in Ovid's telling of the myth, when Tereus sees Philomela kissing her father, Tereus thinks that "He would like to be / Her father, at that moment; and if he were / He would be as wicked a father as he is a husband" (144-45). Furthermore, as in the myth of Philomela, in Walker's novel two women's sororal status does not stop the father/husband from wanting to have sexual intercourse with both sisters. Pa rapes Celie and then casts lascivious eyes at Nettie (13); Albert has intercourse with Celie but also attempts to rape Nettie (119). Given these parallels to the repeated rape paradigm in the myth of Philomela, Celie's resistance is all the more noteworthy.

Celie's resistant voice is enabled by her creation of an alternative conception of her audience and by a reconfiguration of the rhetorical triangle of sender-receiver-message. Rape is once again the catalyst for Celie's resistance. Albert's physical attempt to rape Nettie fails, but he finds a discursive way of "raping" both women when he refuses to deliver any of Nettie's letters to Celie. And indeed, this discursive rape is far more effective than his actual rape, as Celie's response shows. When Celie learns that Albert has suppressed all of Nettie's letters, her consciousness becomes a blank (116), and she feels "cold" and almost "dead" (115), "sickish" and "numb" (134). Moreover, as sometimes occurs in an actual rape, Celie's sexual responses to her lover Shug are deadened by Albert's symbolic rape (136). More than at any other point in the text, Celie seems on the verge of slipping into madness when she discovers Albert's suppression of her sister's letters.

However, in a text where "[c]riss-crossed letters, letters written to an absence, letters received from the dead, hidden and confiscated letters, all of these point to the instability of language" (Wall 94), perhaps it is no surprise that Albert's simplistic gesture of locking up Nettie's voice in his trunk does not actually disrupt the "conversation" between Celie and Nettie.[7] Although Nettie has never received a letter from Celie, Nettie still feels as if she is communicating with her sister: "I imagine that you really do get my letters and that you are writing back: Dear Nettie, this is what life is like for me" (144). Similarly, Celie discovers that she can converse with Nettie despite receiving no response, and even despite the possibility of Nettie's physical death: "And I don't believe you dead. How can you be dead if I still feel you? Maybe, like God, you changed into something different that I'll have to speak to in a different way, but you not dead to me Nettie. And never will be" (229-30). In a more positive version of the interchange between Philomela and Procne, Celie's letters to Nettie create an imagined linguistic persona with whom she can speak "differently." By doing so, Celie finds an alternative conception of the communicative process that allows her to bypass Albert's invalidation of her discourse and enables her survival. In most rhetorical situations, after all, the sender expects that the receiver will actually receive the message and shapes the message accordingly. But Celie subversively reconfigures her audience so that an imagined, rather than actual, person is the receiver of the message, and this allows her to shape her message in such a way that it cannot be erased or silenced, in such a way that it can exist despite Albert's attempt to deny both the communication and the communicator.

Walker also rewrites elements of the mythic paradigm of Philomela to emphasize a textual tradition in which women do more than simply defend themselves against male silencing: in Walker's new textual tradition women become active and articulate heroines of their own stories. In the myth, when Philomela is denied traditional channels of self-expression she creates an alternative text:

> . . . no power of speech
> To help her tell her wrongs. . . .
> She had a loom to work with, and with *purple*

On a white background, wove her story in,
Her story in and out. . . .

(148, my emphasis)

Walker's title may be an allusion to Philomela's text, woven in purple.[8] However, in Ovid's myth this alternative text leads only to Philomela's further victimization by Tereus and to her silence. Celie, too, finds an alternative text, a text directed at a non-patriarchal audience, for in the second half of the novel she stops writing to God—whom she perceives as "just like all the other mens I know. Trifling, forgitful and lowdown" (175)—and starts writing to Nettie.

While Philomela's alternative text leads to her destruction, Celie's alternative text, her letters to Nettie, leads to reconstruction, allowing Celie to craft an identity for herself as the heroine of her own story. Celie gets a house and a profession, and she describes both these events in heroic terms in her letters to Nettie. Both Procne and Philomela are taken away from their familial homes by Tereus. Similarly, both Nettie and Celie are driven away from their family's home by the individual they call "Pa." Unlike Procne and Philomela, both Celie and Nettie return. Celie's letter to Nettie describes her triumphant homecoming and ends with the statement that "Now you [Nettie] can come home cause you have a home to come to!" (217). Signing this letter "Your loving sister, Celie" (217), Celie asserts both her right to this home and to this text in which she is no longer a displaced wife trapped within a patriarchal plot. Although Celie seldom signs her letters, she also signs the letter in which she describes her new profession to Nettie. These two signatures, "Your loving Sister, Celie" (217), and "Your Sister, Celie, Folkspants, Unlimited" (192) indicate the contours of the heroic role Celie has shaped for herself, and contrast sharply with her earlier inability to say "I am." And only in the second half of the novel, when Celie stops writing to God and starts writing to Nettie, does she actively articulate an alternative identity for herself.

Celie's insistence on her desire for Shug also formulates an alternative to being objectified as an absence in a male plot. If, as Catharine MacKinnon argues, "A woman is a being who identifies and is identified as one whose sexuality exists for someone else, who is socially male" (533), then Celie's insistence on her desire for Shug is crucial. Celie recounts her strong sexual response to Shug Avery (53), and even goes so far as to envision voicing her passion: "All the men got they eyes glued to Shug's bosom. I got my eyes glued there too. . . . Shug, I say to her in my mind, Girl, you looks like a real good time, the Good Lord knows you do" (82). This internal voicing of desire becomes external in the letter in which Celie tells Nettie of her love for Shug (221). Celie's love for Shug and others is the fulcrum of her new brand of heroism, and her willingness to articulate it in letters to her sister indicates that she has crafted a textual tradition that allows for feminine heroism and desire.[9]

Beyond giving Celie a resistant voice that allows her to reconfigure the rhetorical situation, recreate her audience, and enunciate a heroine's text, Walker's text also creates an alternative methodology of language. In the world Walker depicts, language is often an instrument of coercion and dominance, and it is often used by men to silence women. At first Celie merely turns the tables on Albert, using language to suppress him:

> He laugh. Who you think you is? he say. You can't curse nobody. Look at you. You black, you pore, you ugly, you a woman. Goddam, he say, you nothing at all.
>
> . . . Every lick you hit me you will suffer twice, I say. Then I say, You better stop talking. . . .
>
> Shit, he say. I should have lock you up. Just let you out to work.
>
> The jail you plan for me is the one in which you will rot, I say.
>
> (187)

In the mythic pattern, Tereus doubly silences Philomela, first by pulling out her tongue and then by imprisoning her in a tower, just as Albert doubly silences Celie, denying her voice ("you can't curse nobody") and presence ("I should have lock you up"). But Celie silences and imprisons the oppressor within her own narrative: "the jail you plan for me is the one in which you will rot," "You better stop talking." Like Albert, Celie has learned how to use both physical and linguistic violence to erase others.

However, Walker is not content with showing Celie's use of "the master's tools" against the master. Celie must learn that language can be used to understand, rather than destroy, another's subjectivity. Celie's later comment about Albert that "He ain't Shug, but he begin to be somebody I can talk to" (241) is therefore revealing. Celie accepts that Albert is capable of using language in a constructive rather than destructive way, and she no longer denies his voice. In the end, Celie's and Albert's voices become agents for conversation rather than combat: "Now us [Albert and Celie] sit sewing and talking and smoking our pipes" (238).

In this passage, sewing and conversation are allied and inseparable, part of the alternative methodology of speech Walker is explicating. Indeed, in this novel sewing often functions as a language, communicating far more effectively than lexical signs. Celie sews curtains to welcome Sofia, and when Sofia is angry at Celie, she cuts down these same curtains and returns them (45). When they reconcile their differences, Celie and Sofia use the spoiled curtains as part of a quilt (47). Similarly, Celie's and Corrine's only conversation occurs in a store where Corrine buys material and thread to make a dress for her daughter. Nettie can only make Corrine remember this conversation by finding a quilt that has squares from the dress material Corrine purchased that day. Sewing is thus a key way individuals communicate with each other, signifying their friendship and interconnectedness. Commenting on Walker's ubiquitous imagery of clothworking, M. Teresa Tavormina argues that in the novel "sewing is an act of union, of connecting pieces to make a useful whole. Furthermore, sewing with others is a comradely act, one that allows both speech and comfortable, supportive silence" (224). Yet sewing does more than enable conversation: sewing *is* conversation, a language that articulates relationships and connects and reconnects networks of individuals to create a community.

Moreover, Walker's novel suggests that sewing is precisely the language that can replace the patriarchal discourse of Mr. ———, that can revise the mythic pattern of silence/violence/silence. Several critics have argued that the novel's form is quilt-like, and Walker's own comments have given strength to this interpretation.[10] The structure of the novel can also be read as an embroidered tapestry such as the one Philomela creates; in Walker's text, Celie's pen is the shuttle/needle that creates a design out of separate narrative threads. Celie's letters to God sometimes weave in quotes or threads from Nettie's and Shug's letters; for example, a short letter by Celie includes Nettie's own words, removed from the letter they came in:

> Dear God,
>
> Now I know Nettie alive I begin to strut a little bit. Think, When she come home us leave here . . . But I think bout Nettie.
>
> It's hot, here, Celie, she write. Hotter than July. Hotter than August *and* July. Hot like cooking dinner on a big stove in a little kitchen in August and July. Hot.
>
> (138; see also 235 and 238)

Furthermore, rather than allowing Nettie's letters to remain as separate blocks of narrative "fabric," Celie weaves them into her tapestry by interspersing her own voice into them: "Dear Celie, *the first letter say,*" (119), "*Next one said*" (120), "*Next one fat, dated two months later, say*" (122). Celie's narrative voice, then, is not just another square in a quilt, equal to all the other squares. Rather, in the text as a whole narrative voices are interwoven, imbricated, threaded together, and interconnected by the needle/pen of the spinner, Celie herself.

Weaving, embroidering, and sewing are thus important analogies for the novel's form, but they are also important metaphors for the kind of conversation Walker envisions replacing patriarchal discourse. Of course, there is nothing inherently peaceful about a needle, as illustrated by one character's comment that unlike Celie his wife would have taken a needle and sewn Shug's nostrils together (60). And the pen, like the needle, has a phallic shape that can rip and rend, rather than mend and stitch. What is important for Walker, however, is the use to which the instrument is put. For example, when Celie makes pants for Nettie, her sewing is envisioned as a language of love and remembering: "Nettie, I am making some pants for you to beat the heat in Africa. . . . Every stitch I sew will be a kiss" (192). Like Philomela's tapestry, Celie's sewing connects the two sisters.

But unlike Philomela's tapestry, Celie's sewn gift to her sister is an act of interconnection and rejuvenation. In Walker's telling of the myth, then, brutal retaliation is actually replaced by creativity and by sewing itself. When Celie wants to react to Albert's suppression of Nettie's letters with violence, Shug tells her to sew pants instead. Celie understands and accepts this: "everyday we going to read Nettie's letters and sew. A needle and not a razor in my hand, I think" (137). It is here that Walker's text swerves most radically from the myth of Philomela and from the mythic paradigm. Nettie's recovered letters are like Philomela's tapestry: they speak the oppression of women, they incite the sister (or all sisters) to violence. But Walker suggests that violence will only end in more silence. An alternative must be found, and this alternative is sewing and conversation, sewing *as* conversation. Sewing is a language that explicates an alternative to the violence of patriarchal discourse.

In the novel as a whole, Celie's pen stitches together the narrative fabric of the text, remaking individual relationships and roles, replacing the violence of patriarchal discourse with a language that remembers and remakes. Celie's pen becomes a needle, then. Yet Celie's needle also becomes a pen. Celie embroiders "little stars and flowers" in her daughter Olivia's diapers, but she also sews language: she sews her name for her daughter, "Olivia," into the diaper (22). The needle is, quite literally, a pen, stitching a name that fits the child, that connects mother and daughter, that is both linguistic (written in letters) and sewn (embroidered). Tavormina notes that "in ***The Color Purple***, both clothworking and language become media for self-definition, self-expression, and self-sharing," but she also claims they have "distinct but similar processes and products" (229). I would suggest, however, that Walker deliberately confuses the processes and products of cloth-working and language, of sewing and communication. Ann Bergren explains that Philomela "*huphenasa en peploi grammata*": she weaves pictures/writing since "*grammata*" can mean either (72). Like Philomela's tapestry, Celie's embroidery deconstructs the barriers between the pictorial and the lexical.

In the end, the thread and the word cannot be separated, and sewing not only helps Celie achieve self-expression, it becomes an alternative methodology of language that resists other more standard or formal discourses. When Celie's employee Darlene tries to convince Celie to speak "correctly," Celie responds "only a fool would want you to talk in a way that feel peculiar to your mind," but she also notes that she is "busy making pants for Sofia," and that she dreams of Sofia "jumping over the moon" in these pants (194). Sewing functions as an alternative methodology of speech that cannot be separated from Celie's acquisition of an alternative spoken and written language. Walker's language of the sewn denies binaries and hierarchies of the hegemonic world, such as those between oral and written language, between informal and formal diction, between art and language, and between discourse and "craft."

Nor is this alternative language of the sewn limited to women. By the end of the novel, Albert is sewing, too. Indeed, sewing facilitates a retrieval of an earlier maternal conversation in which Albert once participated: "When I was growing up, he said, I use to try to sew along with mama cause that's what she was always doing. But everybody laughed at me" (238). Through sewing, Albert becomes part of Celie's community; when Nettie returns from Africa, Celie introduces both Shug *and* Albert as "my peoples" (250). It is significant that Walker allows Albert, an image of Tereus, of the father/rapist, to participate in the conversation of sewing. His transformation and inclusion in Walker's new version of the myth of Philomela shows that indeed the violence of the cycle can be broken. In Walker's revision of the myth of Philomela, both the sisters *and* the rapist turn from the violence of patriarchal discourse and find alternative methodologies of language that speak their recapitulation of self rather than their deconstruction of self and other.

Through her depiction of Albert's metamorphosis and inclusion in the conversation of sewing, Walker also elucidates broader possibilities for social amelioration. Once rape has been renounced as an instrument of male domination, once the rapist has been transformed and included in a new social order where he can engage in "feminine" activities and be part of "feminine" language, society can move toward a more equitable relationship between the sexes. Peggy Sanday has shown that in rape-free societies, "there is no symbol system by which males define their gender identity as the antithesis of the feminine" (98), and "silencing the feminine is not necessary for becoming a proud and independent male" (94). In rape-free societies, there is "sexual equality and complementarity" (93) between the genders. It is precisely this equality between the genders and validation of the "feminine" that Walker alludes to when she includes Albert in the sewing circle (238), when she shows Harpo feeding and bathing his father (200), and when she shows Sofia making shingles (67). Critics such as Keith Byerman (66) and bell hooks (222) argue that Walker's feminization of Albert and Harpo reflects a movement away from historical and ideological conflicts. However, Sanday's research demonstrates that Walker's approach to social change is realistic. In Walker's text, the "feminine" is not silenced and it belongs entirely to neither gender. The "feminine" functions as a language that both men and women can speak, a language that offers the possibility of radical social transformation.

The novel therefore indicates that alternative methodologies of language (whether spoken by men or women) need not perpetuate the mythic cycle of feminine destruction encapsulated within patriarchal discourse and patriarchal narrative. Celie's letters allow her to reconfigure the rhetorical situation and create a resistant heroine's text in which she has a narratological existence as the author/subject of her own story. The novel as a whole also creates an alternative methodology of language that replaces the phallic and destructive patriarchal discourse of the pen, which tears and rends, with a feminine (but not female) discourse of the needle, which remends, remembers, and remakes. This discourse, the language of the sewn rather than the rent, in turn becomes the cornerstone for a reconstruction of gender roles that undermines patriarchal subjugation itself. And yet in the end, these two discourses (the discourse of the pen and of the needle) are subversively conflated, and it is finally and most incisively through this conflation and confusion that Walker's text achieves its most radical aims. After all, the pen has typically been an instrument of male empowerment, a phallic substitute instantiating men's control over women, while the needle has typically been associated with femininity, demarcating the contours and limits of women's sphere.

When Walker's text conflates needle and pen, then, it undermines the most basic binary structures of patriarchal society: male versus female, public versus private, empowered versus disempowered, spoken versus silent. For if the needle has become the pen and the pen has become the needle, if the feminine and the masculine cannot in fact be separated, if patriarchal discourse has been replaced by a discourse that admits of both masculine and feminine subject positions, what pedestal remains for the subjugation of women and other "minorities" within culture? Thus Walker's novel engages in a wholesale revision of the archetypal rape narrative of Philomela as well as the dominant master narrative of patriarchal culture itself: the silencing and objectifying of women and "others" as the basis for male subjectivity.

Notes

1. Hartman defines archetype as a narrative whose suggestiveness is not explained by its parts or its context; archetype is a text "greater than the whole of which it is a part, a text that demands a context

yet is not reducible to it" (337-38). Hartman (337), Joplin (39), and Rowe (53) view the myth of Philomela as archetypal; however, Rowe and Joplin present more positive readings of this archetype than mine. The myth of Philomela also corroborates what many recent feminist critics have argued: that rape is more than just an act of physical or sexual violence: it is an attempt to stamp out or destroy a woman's agency, and it is tied to perpetuation of gender inequality and denial of feminine subjectivity. See, for example, Brownmiller (287), Griffin (23), Sanday (85), and MacKinnon (532). For an important discussion of the treatment of rape as an archetype in contemporary women's writing, see Froula.

2. Similarly, in Angelou's autobiographical *I Know Why the Caged Bird Sings*, after the young protagonist speaks in court about her rape, she almost seems to bite off her own tongue: "I could feel the evilness flowing through my body and waiting, pent up, to rush off my tongue if I tried to open my mouth. I clamped my teeth shut, I'd hold it in" (72). However, unlike those of Morrison's and Naylor's texts, Angelou's protagonist does eventually find her voice; as Froula argues, "Angelou's powerful memoir, recovering the history that frames it, rescues the child's voice . . . by telling the prohibited story" (637). The only study of the treatment of rape in African American fiction as a whole is that of Kubitschek; she examines different texts than I do and concludes that African American literature is most likely to portray "the strength which enables the rape victim to survive and recover" (44).

3. I have found no published statements in which Walker comments on having read the myth of Philomela. However, Walker's novel *Meridian* (1976) seems to refer even more directly to this myth than *The Color Purple*. One section of *Meridian* tells of an enslaved African American woman with an extremely powerful voice. She tells stories all the children love, but one day her stories frighten the master's son to death. In punishment, the master cuts out her tongue. She buries her tongue next to a tiny tree, which eventually flourishes and grows, becoming a symbol of the master's inability to completely erase women's voice, women's tongue. I believe the resonance between this story and the myth of Philomela is too strong to be coincidental.

4. Here I am arguing that Walker does more than simply allow her heroine to speak within the confines of patriarchal discourse. I use "patriarchal discourse" to mean a language system that grants men the right to be articulate subjects, while portraying women as silent objects. Such a discursive system is embodied in the novel by various male characters who believe that they should rule over women (Albert, Harpo), that women are objects of barter and exchange (Pa, Albert), and that women's main function is to support male subjectivity (Pa. Albert, and Harpo). The idea that men have more power in language than women also is directly alluded to by comments such as Albert's to Celie that "You can't curse nobody. . . . You black, you pore, you ugly, you a woman" (187) and by Harpo's to Mary Agnes: "Shut up Squeak. . . . It bad luck for women to laugh at men" (182). Yet within the novel there are many language systems, and Celie struggles in her letters and sewing to find an alternative methodology of language in which her own subjectivity and voice are not denied. I am not arguing, then, that language is always patriarchal, or for that matter, white; rather, I am arguing that it often gets *configured* as such, and that Walker's text is in larger measure about reconfiguring it.

5. In general, Greek myths do not offer raped women many options, as Zeitlin explains: "Whatever the outcome of the particular tale, and to whatever different uses it may be put, the repertory of Greek myth leaves us in no doubt that the female body is vulnerable to sexual assault. . . . Fleeing sexual violence only entails another kind of forcible change to the body [metamorphosis], while those who succumb, especially when gods are the desirers, become pregnant and produce a hero child" (122-23).

6. Squeak/Mary Agnes's rape and movement towards voice can also be compared to Celie's. Again, Walker may be rewriting the mythic text, for after her rape Squeak becomes vocal, insisting that Harpo call her by her real name. Her creativity also seems to be unleashed; six months later she begins to sing. I am not arguing that Walker thinks rape is somehow "good" for women, nor do I agree with bell hooks's statement that Walker's treatment of the rape of a black woman by a white man shows "a benevolent portrayal of the consequences of rape" (222). Rather, Walker suggests that given the ubiquity of rape in society, women need to learn how to move beyond its victimization into agency and voice. All but one of Walker's central female characters have a rape (or an attempted rape) perpetrated against them. Celie and Squeak are actually raped, Nettie suffers an attempted rape, and even the strong-willed Sofia implies that she has learned to fight mainly to ward off unwanted sexual assaults by her male relatives (46).

7. Wall argues that in the novel, "the fact that no letters are ever exchanged (so that a running dialogue can occur) indicates a contemporary, solipsistic view of the absence within communication or, rather, of the continuous model of sender to receiver" (94).

8. Cheung also believes the title may be an allusion to the story of Philomela (172, n. 6) but does not discuss Walker's revision of this myth. For other readings of the title, see Abbandonato (1113).

9. For a corroborating view, see Abbandonato's statement that "in breaking the taboo against homosexuality, Celie symbolically exits the masternarrative of female sexuality and abandons the position ascribed to her within the symbolic order" (1111-12). But for an alternative view, see hooks's argument that "Sexual desire, initially evoked in the novel as a subversive transformative force . . . is suppressed and finally absent—a means to an end but not an end in itself (217). I would agree with hooks that desire itself is not, per se, subversive in this novel, but that Celie's willingness to *articulate* her desire both privately and publicly is subversive.

10. For critics who argue that the novel's structure is quilt-like, see Abbandonato (1109), Wall (96), and Tavormina (225). Walker herself comments that she "wanted to do something like a crazy quilt. . . . A crazy-quilt story is one that can jump back and forth in time, work on many different levels, and one that can include myth" (*Black Women Writers at Work* 176).

Works Cited

Abbandonato, Linda. "A View from 'Elsewhere': Subversive Sexuality and the Rewriting of the Heroine's Story in *The Color Purple*." *PMLA* 106 (1991): 1106-115.

Angelou, Maya. *I Know Why the Caged Bird Sings*. New York: Bantam, 1969.

Bergren, Ann L. T. "Language and the Female in Early Greek Thought." *Arethusa* 16 (1983): 69-95.

Brownmiller, Susan. *Against Our Will: Men, Women and Rape*. New York: Simon and Schuster, 1975.

Byerman, Keith. "Walker's Blues." *Alice Walker*. Ed. Harold Bloom. New York: Chelsea, 1989. 59-66.

Cheung, King-Kok. "'Don't Tell': Imposed Silences in *The Color Purple* and *The Woman Warrior*." *PMLA* 103 (1988): 162-74.

Froula, Christine. "The Daughter's Seduction: Sexual Violence and Literary History." *Signs* 11 (1986): 621-44.

Griffin, Susan. *Rape: The Politics of Consciousness*. San Francisco: Harper & Row, 1986.

Harris, Trudier. "From Victimization to Free Enterprise: Alice Walker's *The Color Purple*." *Studies in American Fiction* 14 (1986): 1-17.

Hartman, Geoffrey. "The Voice of the Shuttle: Language from the Point of View of Literature." *Beyond Formalism*. New Haven: Yale UP, 1970. 337-55.

Henderson, Mae G. "*The Color Purple*: Revisions and Redefinitions." *Alice Walker*. Ed. Harold Bloom. New York: Chelsea, 1989. 67-80.

hooks, bell. "Writing the Subject: Reading *The Color Purple*." *Alice Walker*. Ed. Harold Bloom. New York: Chelsea, 1989. 215-28.

Joplin, Patricia Klindienst. "The Voice of the Shuttle is Ours." *Rape and Representation*. Ed. Lynn Higgins and Brenda R. Silver. New York: Columbia UP, 1991. 35-64.

Kubitschek, Missy Dehn. "Subjugated Knowledge: Toward a Feminist Exploration of Rape in Afro-American Fiction." *Black Feminist Criticism and Critical Theory*. Ed. Joe Weixlmann and Houston A. Baker, Jr. Greenwood, FL: Penkeville, 1988. 43-56.

MacKinnon, Catharine A. "Feminism, Marxism, Method, and the State: An Agenda for Theory." *Signs* 7 (1982): 515-44.

Miner, Madonne. "Lady No Longer Sings the Blues: Rape, Madness, and Silence in *The Bluest Eye*." *Conjuring: Black Women, Fiction, and Literary Tradition*. Ed. Marjorie Pryse and Hortense Spillers. Bloomington: Indiana UP, 1985.

Morrison, Toni. *The Bluest Eye*. New York: Washington Square, 1970.

Naylor, Gloria. *The Women of Brewster Place*. New York: Penguin, 1980.

Ovid. *Metamorphoses*. Trans. Rolfe Humphries. Bloomington: Indiana UP, 1955.

Rooney, Ellen. "'A Little More than Persuading': Tess and the Subject of Sexual Violence." *Rape and Representation*. Ed. Lynn Higgins and Brenda R. Silver. New York: Columbia UP, 1991. 87-114.

Rowe, Karen E. "To Spin a Yarn: The Female Voice in Folklore and Fairy Tale." *Fairy Tales and Society: Illusion, Allusion, and Paradigm*. Ed. Ruth B. Bottigheimer. Philadelphia: U of Pennsylvania P, 1986. 53-74.

Sanday, Peggy Reeves. "Rape and the Silencing of the Feminine." *Rape*. Ed. Sylvana Tomaselli and Roy Porter. Oxford: Basil Blackwell, 1986. 84-101.

Tavormina, M. Teresa. "Dressing the Spirit: Clothworking and Language in *The Color Purple*." *The Journal of Narrative Technique* 16 (1986): 220-30.

Walker, Alice. *The Color Purple*. New York: Washington Square, 1982.

———. Interview in *Black Women Writers at Work*. Ed. Claudia Tate. New York: Continuum, 1983. 175-87.

———. *Meridian*. New York: Simon and Schuster, 1976.

Wall, Wendy. "Lettered Bodies and Corporeal Texts in *The Color Purple*." *Studies in American Fiction* 16 (1988): 83-97.

Zeitlin, Froma. "Configurations of Rape in Greek Myth." *Rape*. Ed. Sylvana Tomaselli and Roy Porter. Oxford: Basil Blackwell, 1986. 122-51.

Robyn R. Warhol (essay date May 2001)

SOURCE: Warhol, Robyn R. "How Narration Produces Gender: Femininity as Affect and Effect in Alice Walker's *The Color Purple*." *Narrative* 9, no. 2 (May 2001): 182-87.

[*In the following essay, Warhol explores the sentimentality of the themes and narrative in* The Color Purple, *and analyzes the reasons for a feminine gender designation to sentimental and emotional stories.*]

Having a good cry is a feminine thing to do. In British and American mainstream culture of the nineteenth and twentieth centuries, weeping openly and emotionally—whether for grief, anger, frustration, sympathy, relief, joy, triumph, or gratitude—is an activity associated with girls and women, considered appropriate to their female frames and feminine feelings. Men cry, too, of course: if they are gay men, their tears are understood as part of the penchant they are supposed to share with feminine women for "making a spectacle" of their feelings;[1] if they are straight, they must be perceived as shedding "manly tears" or run the risk of compromising their masculinity. To have a *good* cry, though, is to indulge in one of the perquisites of this culture's version of femininity, whether the person doing the crying is male or female.

In this essay I will focus on the narrative strategies that produce the good cry in narrative fiction, using as my illustrative example Alice Walker's ***The Color Purple*** (1982), an unabashedly sentimental novel, notorious for making readers cry. For me and for many of my students and fellow readers over the past fifteen years, the last letter in Walker's epistolary novel functions to invoke a "good cry" that is identical to the impact of the classics of the feminine "good-cry" genre, from the climatic moments of Louisa May Alcott's *Little Women* and Harriet Beecher Stowe's *Uncle Tom's Cabin,* to the end of *It's a Wonderful Life*.[2] I will argue that the source of the novel's affective impact is not individual readers' personal (or somehow essentially "feminine") ability to identify with the characters but, rather, the novel's narrative technique, particularly the ways it uses focalization and address to underscore the novel's affirmation of what contemporary U.S. culture understands as feminine mythologies. My larger point is that readers' femininity does not preexist our repeated and habitual encounters with gendered cultural artifacts; rather, gender gets produced and reproduced through countless cultural patterns, including narrative strategies associated with texts that are marked within a given culture as "masculine" (such as adventure stories) or "feminine" (such as good-cry novels like ***The Color Purple***). Narratology provides a useful vocabulary for describing the ways this works.

Sentimental narrative discourse requires a particular handling of "internal focalization," narratology's term for narrative discourse conveying the perceptions (vision, thoughts, feelings, etc.) not of the narrator but of a character, regardless of whether the discourse is in the narrator's or the character's voice. Scenes in sentimental novels tend to be focalized either through victims or triumphant figures who have formerly been represented as oppressed. This focalization invites the reader to participate emotionally from the subject-position of the oppressed, in the diegetic good times and the bad. Sentimental novels can use embedded first-person narratives to achieve this effect. More often, the "omniscient" (or in more properly narratological terms, "heterodiegetic") narrative focus simply shifts to the perspective of the sufferer, rendering the scene as he or she sees it. As Philip Fisher has pointed out, the focalization in sentimental narrative sometimes comes through sympathetic intermediary figures who are not, themselves, directly oppressed—such as Eva in *Uncle Tom*—but it is seldom if ever granted to those who oppress the protagonists in the fictional world. This careful limiting of the narrative point of view to those who suffer and triumph after tribulation can effect a powerful pull on the sensations of a susceptible, cooperative reader, regardless of the reader's historical orientation to the text (readers experiencing the novel twenty or a hundred years after its writing can have emotional reactions equal to those of the text's first readers).[3] In sentimental novels, moreover, the "good cry" is much more often evoked by scenes of triumph than by scenes of sadness.

Attention to the role narrative focalization plays in the affective dynamics of reading is important, as it presents a challenge to the idea that readers sympathize with suffering characters when they can "identify" with them. Michael Steig's remarkable reader-response study, *Stories of Reading* (1989), for example, attributes Steig's own crying over Charles Dickens's *Bleak House* to identification with the characters. Steig reports, "I still find my eyes filling with tears at the same old points. I have felt in the past that I must have some residue of sentimentality in my soul, and have been annoyed that Dickens manipulates me into that reaction, but that is probably unfair" (70). Steig finds the "coy" narrator, Esther Summerson, consistently irritating, "and yet at the same time I must be identifying with her strongly, on the evidence of the way my tears so easily flow"

(70). Emphasizing the intrinsically personal psychology of such identification, Steig remarks, "To get at the reasons for this will require some digging into my past" (70). Of course, a model of identification like Steig's puts the crying reader in a position of enjoying pleasures that are both individualistic and masochistic. If we think about the feminine reader's tears as, in part, a consequence of the text's technical arrangement of perspective, rather than as a reflection of the reader's consciously or subconsciously feeling that the miserable or triumphant sufferer is "just like me," however, audiences' participation in sentimentalism becomes more positively performative, less revealing of some presumed hidden truth about the readers' "real feelings."

Epistolary fiction (the form of *The Color Purple*), with its shifts in narrative voice and in temporal perspective, brings the affective mechanics of focalization into especially vivid relief. As the letter-writer relates each segment of the story, she has access only to her own consciousness (like any conventionally realist first-person narrator, she cannot read other characters' minds, but can only report their actions and expressions, both verbal and physical). Her perspective is even more strictly limited, however, than that of the intradiegetic narrators of novels that are not epistolary, in that she only knows as much about the story as she *can* know at the time of composing the letter: she has not yet "lived" beyond the moment at which she is writing, and hence cannot foreshadow, in her narration, what is to happen after that moment.[4]

Since Samuel Richardson's *Pamela,* epistolary novelists have made the most of this technique's ability to build suspense and to heighten the affective impact of fictional narratives. Like Pamela, Celie does not know, in moments when she is writing in fear and anger, that her tribulations will end happily; unlike Jane Eyre, for example, she does not tell her story with the double consciousness (and the inevitably ironic distance between the "I" who speaks and the "I" who experiences) that comes from life-long retrospection.[5] Of course, epistolary narratives are usually written retrospectively, but the retrospection is in pieces, arranged serially as it were, rather than spanning the length of the diegetic time represented within the narrative. Hence, the telos in epistolary fiction is distinct from that of nonepistolary narrative, in that the epistolary narrator can reflect no sense of his or her final outcome in the narration, even if the author has used other means to establish foreshadows. The effect, for the willing or cooperative reader of the sentimental epistolary novel, is a heightened physical experience of reading that can be readily enlisted in the service of the good cry. The actual reader is "in the moment" with the epistolary narrator; the potential for detachment that is available to the authorial audience of retrospective or otherwise distanced narration is not available in epistolary form.

Critics commenting on *The Color Purple* take it for granted that this novel inspires readerly tears with moments of intensely rendered grief (as when the adolescent Celie mourns the two babies that were born to her and then brutally taken away; or when she is separated from Nettie, seemingly forever; or when she encounters the beautifully Amazonian Sophia, physically and emotionally diminished by her time in jail). But for me, the biggest cry comes at the novel's end, with a burst of joy peculiarly foregrounded by the focalizing effect of the epistolary form. The first fifty letters in the novel are addressed by Celie to "Dear God." Up to that point, the narrative form more closely resembles a diary than an epistolary fiction; the letters to God are a chronicle of Celie's isolation, inspired by her supposed-father's injunction against her reporting his repeated, incestuous rapes: "You better not never tell nobody but God" (11). At the novel's formal turning point, the diary form gets interrupted by eight of the letters Nettie has written to Celie from Africa, hidden until this point by Celie's abusive husband, Albert. Celie's rage against Albert and against that rapist who, she learns from Nettie's letters, was *not* in fact her own father, leads her to conclude that God "must be [a]sleep" (163). At this point, with a third of the novel still to go, Celie changes her address from "Dear God" to "Dear Nettie," and though Nettie's subsequent letters are not answers to the letters Celie addresses to her, the remainder of the text takes the form of a correspondence (although it is undelivered and undeliverable) between the two sisters.

As commentators have observed, Nettie's letters serve the thematic purpose of broadening *The Color Purple*'s geographical and political horizons to include Africa and to connect that continent to Celie's little corner of the American South. The interpolation of Nettie's letters also serves a narrative function, though, as the letters provide Celie with an embodied narratee. Nettie's existence as narratee becomes the textual sign of Celie's relief from isolation, her coming into community as she comes out into her lesbian sexuality with Shug. When Celie grumbles to Shug about her religious disillusionment, Shug offers Celie an alternative view of God: "I believe God is everything, say Shug. Everything that is or ever was or ever will be. And when you can feel that, and be happy to feel that, you've found It. . . . She say, My first step from the old white man [image of God] was trees. Then air. Then birds. Then other people" (178).

As Celie renders it in a letter to Nettie, this scene's initial significance is in its romantic dimension, since it brings Celie closer to Shug. The Celie who relates this conversation cannot know how its vocabulary will return in the novel's last letter, or how the words' significance will shift, and so she cannot foreshadow its significance. The susceptible reader will be taken unawares, in the novel's final pages, by the scene's reprise.

Because the epistolary form focalizes the narrative through Celie's present state of feeling in each of her letters, the sudden happy ending does indeed carry heavy affective clout. But what makes me cry in Celie's last letter is not only—and, indeed, not primarily—the "happy-ending" events. I remain aware that these events, especially in combination, are so implausible as to be almost laughable. They include (1) the unexpected return of Nettie, who has been reunited in Africa with Celie's two lost children and has now brought them back, with their adoptive father (Nettie's own new husband) to live with Celie again; (2) the mother-and-child reunion that accompanies the sister's return; and (3) Celie's own new-found good fortune in having a place to welcome them to, having inherited the home her birth-father has left to her, thus solidifying the financial independence she has begun to establish with her pants-making business. No, it is not the situation itself that is the main source of the good cry for me. Instead, the main source is in the confluence of the narrative discourse with the novel's passionate endorsement of mythologies central to femininity (mythologies about sisters, mothers, children, and financial self-sufficiency, for instance), in the address of Celie's last letter. After having addressed fourteen consecutive letters to "Dear Nettie," Celie starts her last letter with a completely new beginning: "Dear God. Dear stars, dear trees, dear sky, dear peoples. Dear Everything. Dear God. Thank you for bringing my sister Nettie and our children home" (249). That passage gets me every time; for me, no other good-cry moment can surpass it. The way Celie's voice crosses the diegetic boundary, to include me in her address ("dear peoples. Dear Everything") and, in so doing, to assert my inclusion in Celie's newly minted concept of God; the way her address brings into being a moment of pure community embracing not just Nettie, as the previous letters had done, but all the characters and even me; the unmixed joy and triumph of the moment of ecstatic enunciation always make me cry. And that is why I'd call it a "feminine narrative," as it enforces and reinforces the physical experience of an emotion the culture marks as specifically feminine. The "femininity" of the text is not linked to the "femaleness" of the author or characters, nor to the sex of the presumed readers' bodies: it is a narrative effect.

To those who ask, "What's 'good' about 'the good cry'?" I respond (only somewhat self-consciously) that the ideals of sentimental culture—the affirmation of community, the persistence of hopefulness and of willingness, the belief that everyone matters, the sense that life has a purpose that can be traced to the links of affection between and among persons—are good ideals. Sentimentalism has a bad reputation, among general readers and critics alike; it is no coincidence that Steig, for one, reports resenting Dickens's "manipulation" of his tears. To be sure, sentimentalism is often exploited in order to promote agendas far less progressive than Walker's or even Dickens's. If manipulators of public sentiment unscrupulously deploy the narrative techniques of the sentimental tradition in the service of nationalism, capitalism, and commercialism, however, that does not drain the techniques themselves (or their potential affective impact upon actual audiences) of value. Becoming more conscious of how those techniques achieve their effects does not render readers immune to them, but it can offer us the opportunity to affirm "feelings" that constitute what is worth preserving from traditional feminine culture.

Notes

1. I am thinking of the links Joseph Litvak draws between spectacle, spectacular emotions, and homosexuality in *Caught in the Act*.

2. For an introduction to what I mean by the "good-cry genre," see my essay, "As You Stand, So You Feel and Are." That argument, and the general point I am making in the present essay, are elaborated in my book forthcoming from Ohio State University Press, *Having a Good Cry*.

3. See Sicherman for a rich account of Victorian-American feminine readers' reactions to reading sentimental fiction.

4. To be sure, the author of an epistolary narrative may foreshadow future diegetic events by including verbal details or patterns in the storyline that will recur, even though the narrator does not, at the moment of narration, realize that they will.

5. For more details on the retrospective impact of first-person narration, see my article entitled "Double Gender, Double Genre."

Works Cited

Fisher, Philip. *Hard Facts: Setting and Form in the American Novel*. New York: Oxford Univ. Press, 1987.

Litvak, Joseph. *Caught in the Act: Theatricality in the Nineteenth-Century English Novel*. Berkeley: Univ. of California Press, 1992.

Sicherman, Barbara. "Sense and Sensibility: A Case Study of Women's Reading in Late-Victorian America." In *Reading in America: Literature and Social History*, edited by Cathy N. Davidson, 201-25. Baltimore: Johns Hopkins Univ. Press, 1989.

Steig, Michael. *Stories of Reading: Subjectivity and Literary Understanding*. Baltimore: Johns Hopkins Univ. Press, 1989.

Walker, Alice. *The Color Purple*. New York: Harcourt Brace Jovanovich, 1982.

Warhol, Robyn R. "'As You Stand, So You Feel and Are': The Crying Body and the 19th-Century Text." In *Tattoo, Torture, Mutilation, and Adornment: The De-*

Naturalization of the Body in Culture and Text, edited by Fran Mascia-Lees and Patricia Sharpe, 100-25. Albany: State Univ. of New York Press, 1992.

———. "Double Gender, Double Genre in *Jane Eyre* and *Villette,*" *Studies in English Literature* 36 (Fall 1996): 857-75.

———. *Having a Good Cry.* Columbus: Ohio State Univ. Press, forthcoming.

FURTHER READING

Criticism

Berlant, Lauren. "Race, Gender, and Nation in *The Color Purple.*" *Critical Inquiry* 14, no. 4 (summer 1988): 831-59.

  Berlant presents an in-depth study of the political, racial, and gender-based agendas in *The Color Purple.*

Chambers, Kimberly R. "Right on Time: History and Religion in Alice Walker's *The Color Purple.*" *CLA Journal* 31, no. 1 (September 1987): 44-62.

  Chambers explores the effects that African-American folklore and traditions have on the temporal and religious aspects of *The Color Purple.*

Christophe, Marc A. "*The Color Purple*: An Existential Novel." *CLA Journal* 36, no. 3 (March 1993): 280-90.

  Christophe discusses the adversities Celie faces in *The Color Purple* and the various coping mechanisms she employs during her development.

Dole, Carol M. "The Return of the Father in Spielberg's *The Color Purple.*" *Literature/Film Quarterly* 24, no. 1 (1996): 12-16.

  Dole explores the differences between the novel and the film version of *The Color Purple.*

Early, Gerald. "*The Color Purple* as Everybody's Protest Art." *Antioch Review* 50, nos. 1-2 (winter 1992): 399-412.

  Early offers a negative assessment of both the novel and film *The Color Purple.*

Juneja, Om P. "The Purple Colour of Walker Women: Their Journey from Slavery to Liberation." *Literary Criterion* 25, no. 3 (1990): 66-76.

  Juneja examines the trials and tribulations of the female protagonists in Alice Walker's works.

Powers, Peter Kerry. "'Pa is not our Pa': Sacred History and Political Imagination in *The Color Purple.*" *South Atlantic Review* 60, no. 2 (May 1995): 69-92.

  Powers analyzes Celie's need to reinvent God's image in order to embrace spirituality and her own self-worth in *The Color Purple,* instead of adhering to the white, patriarchal religion which oppresses and devalues women.

Walker, Alice, and Kate Fitzsimmons. "Go Ask Alice: Alice Walker Talks about *The Color Purple* 10 Years Later." *San Francisco Review of Books* 21, no. 2 (March-April 1996): 20-3.

  Walker discusses writing *The Color Purple,* her views of the film version, and her opinions on current race and gender relations.

Additional coverage of Walker's life and career is contained in the following sources published by the Gale Group: *Authors and Artists for Young Adults,* **Vols. 3, 33;** *African American Writers,* **Eds. 1, 2;** *American Writers Supplement,* **Vol. 3;** *Beacham's Encyclopedia of Popular Fiction: Biography & Resources,* **Vol. 3;** *Bestsellers,* **Vol. 89:4;** *Black Literature Criticism,* **Ed. 3;** *Black Writers,* **Eds. 2, 3;** *Concise Dictionary of American Literary Biography, 1968-1988; Contemporary Authors,* **Vols. 37-40R;** *Contemporary Authors New Revision Series,* **Vols. 9, 27, 49, 66, 82;** *Contemporary Literary Criticism,* **Vols. 5, 6, 9, 19, 27, 46, 58, 103;** *Contemporary Novelists,* **Ed. 7;** *Contemporary Popular Writers; Contemporary Southern Writers; DISCovering Authors; DISCovering Authors: British Edition; DISCovering Authors: Canadian Edition; DISCovering Authors Modules: Most-studied Authors, Multicultural Authors, Novelists, Poets,* **and** *Popular Fiction and Genre Authors; DISCovering Authors 3.0; Dictionary of Literary Biography,* **Vols. 6, 33, 143;** *Exploring Novels; Exploring Short Stories; Feminist Writers; Literature and Its Times,* **Vol. 3;** *Literature Resource Center; Modern American Women Writers; Major 20th-Century Writers,* **Eds. 1, 2;** *Novels for Students,* **Vol. 5;** *Poetry Criticism,* **Vol. 30;** *Reference Guide to American Literature,* **Ed. 4;** *Reference Guide to Short Fiction,* **Ed. 2;** *St. James Guide to Young Adult Writers; Something about the Author,* **Vol. 31;** *Short Story Criticism,* **Vol. 5;** *Short Stories for Students,* **Vols. 2, 11; and** *World Literature Criticism Supplement.*

How to Use This Index

The main references

> Calvino, Italo
> 1923-1985 .... CLC 5, 8, 11, 22, 33, 39,
> 73; SSC 3, 48

list all author entries in the following Gale Literary Criticism series:

AAL = Asian American Literature
BLC = Black Literature Criticism
BLCS = Black Literature Criticism Supplement
CLC = Contemporary Literary Criticism
CLR = Children's Literature Review
CMLC = Classical and Medieval Literature Criticism
DC = Drama Criticism
HLC = Hispanic Literature Criticism
HLCS = Hispanic Literature Criticism Supplement
LC = Literature Criticism from 1400 to 1800
NCLC = Nineteenth-Century Literature Criticism
NNAL = Native North American Literature
PC = Poetry Criticism
SSC = Short Story Criticism
TCLC = Twentieth-Century Literary Criticism
WLC = World Literature Criticism, 1500 to the Present
WLCS = World Literature Criticism Supplement

The cross-references

> See also CA 85-88, 116; CANR 23, 61;
> DAM NOV; DLB 196; EW 13; MTCW 1, 2;
> RGSF 2; RGWL 2; SFW 4; SSFS 12

list all author entries in the following Gale biographical and literary sources:

AAYA = Authors & Artists for Young Adults
AFAW = African American Writers
AFW = African Writers
AITN = Authors in the News
AMW = American Writers
AMWR = American Writers Retrospective Supplement
AMWS = American Writers Supplement
ANW = American Nature Writers
AW = Ancient Writers
BEST = Bestsellers
BPFB = Beacham's Encyclopedia of Popular Fiction: Biography and Resources
BRW = British Writers
BRWS = British Writers Supplement
BW = Black Writers
BYA = Beacham's Guide to Literature for Young Adults
CA = Contemporary Authors
CAAS = Contemporary Authors Autobiography Series
CABS = Contemporary Authors Bibliographical Series
CAD = Contemporary American Dramatists
CANR = Contemporary Authors New Revision Series
CAP = Contemporary Authors Permanent Series
CBD = Contemporary British Dramatists
CCA = Contemporary Canadian Authors
CD = Contemporary Dramatists
CDALB = Concise Dictionary of American Literary Biography
CDALBS = Concise Dictionary of American Literary Biography Supplement
CDBLB = Concise Dictionary of British Literary Biography
CMW = St. James Guide to Crime & Mystery Writers
CN = Contemporary Novelists

CP = *Contemporary Poets*
CPW = *Contemporary Popular Writers*
CSW = *Contemporary Southern Writers*
CWD = *Contemporary Women Dramatists*
CWP = *Contemporary Women Poets*
CWRI = *St. James Guide to Children's Writers*
CWW = *Contemporary World Writers*
DA = *DISCovering Authors*
DA3 = *DISCovering Authors 3.0*
DAB = *DISCovering Authors: British Edition*
DAC = *DISCovering Authors: Canadian Edition*
DAM = *DISCovering Authors: Modules*
   DRAM: *Dramatists Module;* **MST:** *Most-studied Authors Module;*
   MULT: *Multicultural Authors Module;* **NOV:** *Novelists Module;*
   POET: *Poets Module;* **POP:** *Popular Fiction and Genre Authors Module*
DFS = *Drama for Students*
DLB = *Dictionary of Literary Biography*
DLBD = *Dictionary of Literary Biography Documentary Series*
DLBY = *Dictionary of Literary Biography Yearbook*
DNFS = *Literature of Developing Nations for Students*
EFS = *Epics for Students*
EXPN = *Exploring Novels*
EXPP = *Exploring Poetry*
EXPS = *Exploring Short Stories*
EW = *European Writers*
FANT = *St. James Guide to Fantasy Writers*
FW = *Feminist Writers*
GFL = *Guide to French Literature,* Beginnings to 1789, 1798 to the Present
GLL = *Gay and Lesbian Literature*
HGG = *St. James Guide to Horror, Ghost & Gothic Writers*
HW = *Hispanic Writers*
IDFW = *International Dictionary of Films and Filmmakers: Writers and Production Artists*
IDTP = *International Dictionary of Theatre: Playwrights*
LAIT = *Literature and Its Times*
LAW = *Latin American Writers*
JRDA = *Junior DISCovering Authors*
MAICYA = *Major Authors and Illustrators for Children and Young Adults*
MAICYAS = *Major Authors and Illustrators for Children and Young Adults Supplement*
MAWW = *Modern American Women Writers*
MJW = *Modern Japanese Writers*
MTCW = *Major 20th-Century Writers*
NCFS = *Nonfiction Classics for Students*
NFS = *Novels for Students*
PAB = *Poets: American and British*
PFS = *Poetry for Students*
RGAL = *Reference Guide to American Literature*
RGEL = *Reference Guide to English Literature*
RGSF = *Reference Guide to Short Fiction*
RGWL = *Reference Guide to World Literature*
RHW = *Twentieth-Century Romance and Historical Writers*
SAAS = *Something about the Author Autobiography Series*
SATA = *Something about the Author*
SFW = *St. James Guide to Science Fiction Writers*
SSFS = *Short Stories for Students*
TCWW = *Twentieth-Century Western Writers*
WLIT = *World Literature and Its Times*
WP = *World Poets*
YABC = *Yesterday's Authors of Books for Children*
YAW = *St. James Guide to Young Adult Writers*

Literary Criticism Series
Cumulative Author Index

20/1631
See Upward, Allen
A/C Cross
See Lawrence, T(homas) E(dward)
Abasiyanik, Sait Faik 1906-1954
See Sait Faik
Abbey, Edward 1927-1989 .... **CLC 36, 59**
See also ANW; CA 45-48; CANR 2, 41; DLB 256; MTCW 2; TCWW 2
Abbott, Lee K(ittredge) 1947- .... **CLC 48**
See also CA 124; CANR 51, 101; DLB 130
Abe, Kobo 1924-1993 .... **CLC 8, 22, 53, 81**
See also CA 65-68; CANR 24, 60; DAM NOV; DFS 14; DLB 182; MJW; MTCW 1, 2; RGWL 3; SFW 4; TCLC 121
Abe Kobo
See Abe, Kobo
Abelard, Peter c. 1079-c. 1142 ...... **CMLC 11**
See also DLB 115, 208
Abell, Kjeld 1901-1961 .... **CLC 15**
See also CA 191; DLB 214
Abish, Walter 1931- .... **CLC 22; SSC 44**
See also CA 101; CANR 37; CN 7; DLB 130, 227
Abrahams, Peter (Henry) 1919- .... **CLC 4**
See also AFW; BW 1; CA 57-60; CANR 26; CDWLB 3; CN 7; DLB 117, 225; MTCW 1, 2; RGEL 2; WLIT 2
Abrams, M(eyer) H(oward) 1912- ... **CLC 24**
See also CA 57-60; CANR 13, 33; DLB 67
Abse, Dannie 1923- .... **CLC 7, 29; PC 41**
See also CA 53-56; CAAS 1; CANR 4, 46, 74; CBD; CP 7; DAB; DAM POET; DLB 27, 245; MTCW 1
Abutsu 1222(?)-1283 .... **CMLC 46**
See also Abutsu-ni
Abutsu-ni
See Abutsu
See also DLB 203
Achebe, (Albert) Chinua(lumogu)
1930- ...... **CLC 1, 3, 5, 7, 11, 26, 51, 75, 127, 152; BLC 1; WLC**
See also AAYA 15; AFW; BPFB 1; BW 2, 3; CA 1-4R; CANR 6, 26, 47; CDWLB 3; CLR 20; CN 7; CP 7; CWRI 5; DA; DAB; DAC; DAM MST, MULT, NOV; DLB 117; DNFS 1; EXPN; EXPS; LAIT 2; MAICYA 1, 2; MTCW 1, 2; NFS 2; RGEL 2; RGSF 2; SATA 38, 40; SATA-Brief 38; SSFS 3, 13; TWA; WLIT 2
Acker, Kathy 1948-1997 .... **CLC 45, 111**
See also CA 122; CANR 55; CN 7
Ackroyd, Peter 1949- .... **CLC 34, 52, 140**
See also BRWS 6; CA 127; CANR 51, 74, 99; CN 7; DLB 155, 231; HGG; INT 127; MTCW 1; RHW; SUFW 2

Acorn, Milton 1923-1986 .... **CLC 15**
See also CA 103; CCA 1; DAC; DLB 53; INT 103
Adamov, Arthur 1908-1970 .... **CLC 4, 25**
See also CA 17-18; CAP 2; DAM DRAM; GFL 1789 to the Present; MTCW 1; RGWL 2, 3
Adams, Alice (Boyd) 1926-1999 .. **CLC 6, 13, 46; SSC 24**
See also CA 81-84; CANR 26, 53, 75, 88; CN 7; CSW; DLB 234; DLBY 1986; INT CANR-26; MTCW 1, 2; SSFS 14
Adams, Andy 1859-1935 .... **TCLC 56**
See also TCWW 2; YABC 1
Adams, Brooks 1848-1927 .... **TCLC 80**
See also DLB 47
Adams, Douglas (Noel) 1952-2001 .. **CLC 27, 60**
See also AAYA 4, 33; BEST 89:3; BYA 14; CA 106; CANR 34, 64; CPW; DAM POP; DLB 261; DLBY 1983; JRDA; MTCW 1; NFS 7; SATA 116; SATA-Obit 128; SFW 4
Adams, Francis 1862-1893 .... **NCLC 33**
Adams, Henry (Brooks)
1838-1918 .... **TCLC 4, 52**
See also AMW; CA 133; CANR 77; DA; DAB; DAC; DAM MST; DLB 12, 47, 189; MTCW 1; NCFS 1; RGAL 4; TUS
Adams, John 1735-1826 .... **NCLC 106**
See also DLB 31, 183
Adams, Richard (George) 1920- ... **CLC 4, 5, 18**
See also AAYA 16; AITN 1, 2; BPFB 1; BYA 5; CA 49-52; CANR 3, 35; CLR 20; CN 7; DAM NOV; DLB 261; FANT; JRDA; LAIT 5; MAICYA 1, 2; MTCW 1, 2; NFS 11; SATA 7, 69; YAW
Adamson, Joy(-Friederike Victoria)
1910-1980 .... **CLC 17**
See also CA 69-72; CANR 22; MTCW 1; SATA 11; SATA-Obit 22
Adcock, Fleur 1934- .... **CLC 41**
See also CA 25-28R, 182; CAAE 182; CAAS 23; CANR 11, 34, 69, 101; CP 7; CWP; DLB 40; FW
Addams, Charles (Samuel)
1912-1988 .... **CLC 30**
See also CA 61-64; CANR 12, 79
Addams, Jane 1860-1935 .... **TCLC 76**
See also AMWS 1; FW
Addams, (Laura) Jane 1860-1935 . **TCLC 76**
See also AMWS 1; CA 194; FW
Addison, Joseph 1672-1719 .... **LC 18**
See also BRW 3; CDBLB 1660-1789; DLB 101; RGEL 2; WLIT 3
Adler, Alfred (F.) 1870-1937 .... **TCLC 61**
See also CA 159

Adler, C(arole) S(chwerdtfeger)
1932- .... **CLC 35**
See also AAYA 4, 41; CA 89-92; CANR 19, 40, 101; CLR 78; JRDA; MAICYA 1, 2; SAAS 15; SATA 26, 63, 102, 126; YAW
Adler, Renata 1938- .... **CLC 8, 31**
See also CA 49-52; CANR 95; CN 7; MTCW 1
Adorno, Theodor W(iesengrund)
1903-1969 .... **TCLC 111**
See also CA 89-92; CANR 89; DLB 242
Ady, Endre 1877-1919 .... **TCLC 11**
See also CDWLB 4; DLB 215; EW 9
A.E. .... **TCLC 3, 10**
See also Russell, George William
See also DLB 19
Aelfric c. 955-c. 1010 .... **CMLC 46**
See also DLB 146
Aeschines c. 390B.C.-c. 320B.C. ..... **CMLC 47**
See also DLB 176
Aeschylus 525(?)B.C.-456(?)B.C. .. **CMLC 11, 51; DC 8; WLCS**
See also AW 1; CDWLB 1; DA; DAB; DAC; DAM DRAM, MST; DFS 5, 10; DLB 176; RGWL 2, 3; TWA
Aesop 620(?)B.C.-560(?)B.C. .... **CMLC 24**
See also CLR 14; MAICYA 1, 2; SATA 64
Affable Hawk
See MacCarthy, Sir (Charles Otto) Desmond
Africa, Ben
See Bosman, Herman Charles
Afton, Effie
See Harper, Frances Ellen Watkins
Agapida, Fray Antonio
See Irving, Washington
Agee, James (Rufus) 1909-1955 ...... **TCLC 1, 19**
See also AITN 1; AMW; CA 148; CDALB 1941-1968; DAM NOV; DLB 2, 26, 152; DLBY 1989; LAIT 3; MTCW 1; RGAL 4; TUS
Aghill, Gordon
See Silverberg, Robert
Agnon, S(hmuel) Y(osef Halevi)
1888-1970 .... **CLC 4, 8, 14; SSC 30**
See also CA 17-18; CANR 60, 102; CAP 2; MTCW 1, 2; RGSF 2; RGWL 2, 3
Agrippa von Nettesheim, Henry Cornelius
1486-1535 .... **LC 27**
Aguilera Malta, Demetrio 1909-1981
See also CA 124; CANR 87; DAM MULT, NOV; DLB 145; HLCS 1; HW 1; RGWL 3
Agustini, Delmira 1886-1914
See also CA 166; HLCS 1; HW 1, 2; LAW
Aherne, Owen
See Cassill, R(onald) V(erlin)

Ai 1947- .... **CLC 4, 14, 69**
　See also CA 85-88; CAAS 13; CANR 70; DLB 120

Aickman, Robert (Fordyce) 1914-1981 .... **CLC 57**
　See also CA 5-8R; CANR 3, 72, 100; DLB 261; HGG; SUFW 1, 2

Aiken, Conrad (Potter) 1889-1973 .... **CLC 1, 3, 5, 10, 52; PC 26; SSC 9**
　See also AMW; CA 5-8R; CANR 4, 60; CDALB 1929-1941; DAM NOV, POET; DLB 9, 45, 102; EXPS; HGG; MTCW 1, 2; RGAL 4; RGSF 2; SATA 3, 30; SSFS 8; TUS

Aiken, Joan (Delano) 1924- .... **CLC 35**
　See also AAYA 1, 25; CA 9-12R, 182; CAAE 182; CANR 4, 23, 34, 64; CLR 1, 19; DLB 161; FANT; HGG; JRDA; MAICYA 1, 2; MTCW 1; RHW; SAAS 1; SATA 2, 30, 73; SATA-Essay 109; SUFW 2; WYA; YAW

Ainsworth, William Harrison 1805-1882 .... **NCLC 13**
　See also DLB 21; HGG; RGEL 2; SATA 24; SUFW 1

Aitmatov, Chingiz (Torekulovich) 1928- .... **CLC 71**
　See also CA 103; CANR 38; MTCW 1; RGSF 2; SATA 56

Akers, Floyd
　See Baum, L(yman) Frank

Akhmadulina, Bella Akhatovna 1937- .... **CLC 53; PC 43**
　See also CA 65-68; CWP; CWW 2; DAM POET

Akhmatova, Anna 1888-1966 ..... **CLC 11, 25, 64, 126; PC 2**
　See also CA 19-20; CANR 35; CAP 1; DAM POET; EW 10; MTCW 1, 2; RGWL 2, 3

Aksakov, Sergei Timofeyvich 1791-1859 .... **NCLC 2**
　See also DLB 198

Aksenov, Vassily
　See Aksyonov, Vassily (Pavlovich)

Akst, Daniel 1956- .... **CLC 109**
　See also CA 161; CANR 110

Aksyonov, Vassily (Pavlovich) 1932- .... **CLC 22, 37, 101**
　See also CA 53-56; CANR 12, 48, 77; CWW 2

Akutagawa Ryunosuke 1892-1927 .... **TCLC 16; SSC 44**
　See also CA 154; DLB 180; MJW; RGSF 2; RGWL 2, 3

Alain 1868-1951 .... **TCLC 41**
　See also CA 163; GFL 1789 to the Present

Alain de Lille c. 1116-c. 1203 .... **CMLC 53**
　See also DLB 208

Alain-Fournier .... **TCLC 6**
　See also Fournier, Henri Alban
　See also DLB 65; GFL 1789 to the Present; RGWL 2, 3

Alanus de Insluis
　See Alain de Lille

Alarcon, Pedro Antonio de 1833-1891 .... **NCLC 1**

Alas (y Urena), Leopoldo (Enrique Garcia) 1852-1901 .... **TCLC 29**
　See also CA 131; HW 1; RGSF 2

Albee, Edward (Franklin III) 1928- . **CLC 1, 2, 3, 5, 9, 11, 13, 25, 53, 86, 113; DC 11; WLC**
　See also AITN 1; AMW; CA 5-8R; CABS 3; CAD; CANR 8, 54, 74; CD 5; CDALB 1941-1968; DA; DAB; DAC; DAM DRAM, MST; DFS 2, 3, 8, 10, 13, 14; DLB 7, 266; INT CANR-8; LAIT 4; MTCW 1, 2; RGAL 4; TUS

Alberti, Rafael 1902-1999 .... **CLC 7**
　See also CA 85-88; CANR 81; DLB 108; HW 2; RGWL 2, 3

Albert the Great 1193(?)-1280 ...... **CMLC 16**
　See also DLB 115

Alcala-Galiano, Juan Valera y
　See Valera y Alcala-Galiano, Juan

Alcayaga, Lucila Godoy
　See Godoy Alcayaga, Lucila

Alcott, Amos Bronson 1799-1888 .... **NCLC 1**
　See also DLB 1, 223

Alcott, Louisa May 1832-1888 . **NCLC 6, 58, 83; SSC 27; WLC**
　See also AAYA 20; AMWS 1; BPFB 1; BYA 2; CDALB 1865-1917; CLR 1, 38; DA; DAB; DAC; DAM MST, NOV; DLB 1, 42, 79, 223, 239, 242; DLBD 14; FW; JRDA; LAIT 2; MAICYA 1, 2; NFS 12; RGAL 4; SATA 100; TUS; WCH; WYA; YABC 1; YAW

Aldanov, M. A.
　See Aldanov, Mark (Alexandrovich)

Aldanov, Mark (Alexandrovich) 1886(?)-1957 .... **TCLC 23**
　See also CA 181

Aldington, Richard 1892-1962 .... **CLC 49**
　See also CA 85-88; CANR 45; DLB 20, 36, 100, 149; RGEL 2

Aldiss, Brian W(ilson) 1925- . **CLC 5, 14, 40; SSC 36**
　See also AAYA 42; CA 5-8R; CAAE 190; CAAS 2; CANR 5, 28, 64; CN 7; DAM NOV; DLB 14, 261, 271; MTCW 1, 2; SATA 34; SFW 4

Aldrich, Bess Streeter 1881-1954 .... **TCLC 125**
　See also CLR 70

Alegria, Claribel 1924- .... **CLC 75; HLCS 1; PC 26**
　See also CA 131; CAAS 15; CANR 66, 94; CWW 2; DAM MULT; DLB 145; HW 1; MTCW 1

Alegria, Fernando 1918- .... **CLC 57**
　See also CA 9-12R; CANR 5, 32, 72; HW 1, 2

Aleichem, Sholom .... **TCLC 1, 35; SSC 33**
　See also Rabinovitch, Sholem
　See also TWA

Aleixandre, Vicente 1898-1984 ... **TCLC 113; HLCS 1**
　See also CANR 81; DLB 108; HW 2; RGWL 2, 3

Aleman, Mateo 1547-1615(?) .... **LC 81**

Alencon, Marguerite d'
　See de Navarre, Marguerite

Alepoudelis, Odysseus
　See Elytis, Odysseus
　See also CWW 2

Aleshkovsky, Joseph 1929-
　See Aleshkovsky, Yuz
　See also CA 128

Aleshkovsky, Yuz .... **CLC 44**
　See also Aleshkovsky, Joseph

Alexander, Lloyd (Chudley) 1924- ... **CLC 35**
　See also AAYA 1, 27; BPFB 1; BYA 5, 6, 7, 9, 10, 11; CA 1-4R; CANR 1, 24, 38, 55, 113; CLR 1, 5, 48; CWRI 5; DLB 52; FANT; JRDA; MAICYA 1, 2; MAICYAS 1; MTCW 1; SAAS 19; SATA 3, 49, 81, 129, 135; SUFW; TUS; WYA; YAW

Alexander, Meena 1951- .... **CLC 121**
　See also CA 115; CANR 38, 70; CP 7; CWP; FW

Alexander, Samuel 1859-1938 .... **TCLC 77**

Alexie, Sherman (Joseph, Jr.) 1966- .... **CLC 96, 154**
　See also AAYA 28; CA 138; CANR 95; DAM MULT; DLB 175, 206; MTCW 1; NNAL

Alfau, Felipe 1902-1999 .... **CLC 66**
　See also CA 137

Alfieri, Vittorio 1749-1803 .... **NCLC 101**
　See also EW 4; RGWL 2, 3

Alfred, Jean Gaston
　See Ponge, Francis

Alger, Horatio, Jr. 1832-1899 .... **NCLC 8, 83**
　See also DLB 42; LAIT 2; RGAL 4; SATA 16; TUS

Al-Ghazali, Muhammad ibn Muhammad 1058-1111 .... **CMLC 50**
　See also DLB 115

Algren, Nelson 1909-1981 ..... **CLC 4, 10, 33; SSC 33**
　See also AMWS 9; BPFB 1; CA 13-16R; CANR 20, 61; CDALB 1941-1968; DLB 9; DLBY 1981, 1982, 2000; MTCW 1, 2; RGAL 4; RGSF 2

Ali, Ahmed 1908-1998 .... **CLC 69**
　See also CA 25-28R; CANR 15, 34

Alighieri, Dante
　See Dante

Allan, John B.
　See Westlake, Donald E(dwin)

Allan, Sidney
　See Hartmann, Sadakichi

Allan, Sydney
　See Hartmann, Sadakichi

Allard, Janet .... **CLC 59**

Allen, Edward 1948- .... **CLC 59**

Allen, Fred 1894-1956 .... **TCLC 87**

Allen, Paula Gunn 1939- .... **CLC 84**
　See also AMWS 4; CA 143; CANR 63; CWP; DAM MULT; DLB 175; FW; MTCW 1; NNAL; RGAL 4

Allen, Roland
　See Ayckbourn, Alan

Allen, Sarah A.
　See Hopkins, Pauline Elizabeth

Allen, Sidney H.
　See Hartmann, Sadakichi

Allen, Woody 1935- .... **CLC 16, 52**
　See also AAYA 10; CA 33-36R; CANR 27, 38, 63; DAM POP; DLB 44; MTCW 1

Allende, Isabel 1942- . **CLC 39, 57, 97; HLC 1; WLCS**
　See also AAYA 18; CA 130; CANR 51, 74; CDWLB 3; CWW 2; DAM MULT, NOV; DLB 145; DNFS 1; FW; HW 1, 2; INT CA-130; LAIT 5; LAWS 1; MTCW 1, 2; NCFS 1; NFS 6; RGSF 2; RGWL 3; SSFS 11; WLIT 1

Alleyn, Ellen
　See Rossetti, Christina (Georgina)

Alleyne, Carla D. .... **CLC 65**

Allingham, Margery (Louise) 1904-1966 .... **CLC 19**
　See also CA 5-8R; CANR 4, 58; CMW 4; DLB 77; MSW; MTCW 1, 2

Allingham, William 1824-1889 ...... **NCLC 25**
　See also DLB 35; RGEL 2

Allison, Dorothy E. 1949- .... **CLC 78, 153**
　See also CA 140; CANR 66, 107; CSW; FW; MTCW 1; NFS 11; RGAL 4

Alloula, Malek .... **CLC 65**

Allston, Washington 1779-1843 .... **NCLC 2**
　See also DLB 1, 235

Almedingen, E. M. .... **CLC 12**
　See also Almedingen, Martha Edith von
　See also SATA 3

Almedingen, Martha Edith von 1898-1971
　See Almedingen, E. M.
　See also CA 1-4R; CANR 1

Almodovar, Pedro 1949(?)- .... **CLC 114; HLCS 1**
　See also CA 133; CANR 72; HW 2

Almqvist, Carl Jonas Love
1793-1866 .... NCLC 42
Alonso, Damaso 1898-1990 .... CLC 14
See also CA 131; CANR 72; DLB 108; HW 1, 2
Alov
See Gogol, Nikolai (Vasilyevich)
Alta 1942- .... CLC 19
See also CA 57-60
Alter, Robert B(ernard) 1935- .... CLC 34
See also CA 49-52; CANR 1, 47, 100
Alther, Lisa 1944- .... CLC 7, 41
See also BPFB 1; CA 65-68; CAAS 30; CANR 12, 30, 51; CN 7; CSW; GLL 2; MTCW 1
Althusser, L.
See Althusser, Louis
Althusser, Louis 1918-1990 .... CLC 106
See also CA 131; CANR 102; DLB 242
Altman, Robert 1925- .... CLC 16, 116
See also CA 73-76; CANR 43
Alurista
See Urista, Alberto H.
See also DLB 82; HLCS 1
Alvarez, A(lfred) 1929- .... CLC 5, 13
See also CA 1-4R; CANR 3, 33, 63, 101; CN 7; CP 7; DLB 14, 40
Alvarez, Alejandro Rodriguez 1903-1965
See Casona, Alejandro
See also CA 131; HW 1
Alvarez, Julia 1950- .... CLC 93; HLCS 1
See also AAYA 25; AMWS 7; CA 147; CANR 69, 101; MTCW 1; NFS 5, 9; SATA 129; WLIT 1
Alvaro, Corrado 1896-1956 .... TCLC 60
See also CA 163; DLB 264
Amado, Jorge 1912-2001 ... CLC 13, 40, 106; HLC 1
See also CA 77-80; CANR 35, 74; DAM MULT, NOV; DLB 113; HW 2; LAW; LAWS 1; MTCW 1, 2; RGWL 2, 3; TWA; WLIT 1
Ambler, Eric 1909-1998 .... CLC 4, 6, 9
See also BRWS 4; CA 9-12R; CANR 7, 38, 74; CMW 4; CN 7; DLB 77; MSW; MTCW 1, 2; TEA
Ambrose, Stephen E(dward)
1936-2002 .... CLC 145
See also CA 1-4R; CANR 3, 43, 57, 83, 105; NCFS 2; SATA 40
Amichai, Yehuda 1924-2000 .. CLC 9, 22, 57, 116; PC 38
See also CA 85-88; CANR 46, 60, 99; CWW 2; MTCW 1
Amichai, Yehudah
See Amichai, Yehuda
Amiel, Henri Frederic 1821-1881 .... NCLC 4
See also DLB 217
Amis, Kingsley (William)
1922-1995 ...... CLC 1, 2, 3, 5, 8, 13, 40, 44, 129
See also AITN 2; BPFB 1; BRWS 2; CA 9-12R; CANR 8, 28, 54; CDBLB 1945-1960; CN 7; CP 7; DA; DAB; DAC; DAM MST, NOV; DLB 15, 27, 100, 139; DLBY 1996; HGG; INT CANR-8; MTCW 1, 2; RGEL 2; RGSF 2; SFW 4
Amis, Martin (Louis) 1949- .... CLC 4, 9, 38, 62, 101
See also BEST 90:3; BRWS 4; CA 65-68; CANR 8, 27, 54, 73, 95; CN 7; DLB 14, 194; INT CANR-27; MTCW 1
Ammons, A(rchie) R(andolph)
1926-2001 .... CLC 2, 3, 5, 8, 9, 25, 57, 108; PC 16
See also AITN 1; AMWS 7; CA 9-12R; CANR 6, 36, 51, 73, 107; CP 7; CSW; DAM POET; DLB 5, 165; MTCW 1, 2; RGAL 4

Amo, Tauraatua i
See Adams, Henry (Brooks)
Amory, Thomas 1691(?)-1788 .... LC 48
See also DLB 39
Anand, Mulk Raj 1905- .... CLC 23, 93
See also CA 65-68; CANR 32, 64; CN 7; DAM NOV; MTCW 1, 2; RGSF 2
Anatol
See Schnitzler, Arthur
Anaximander c. 611B.C.-c.
546B.C. .... CMLC 22
Anaya, Rudolfo A(lfonso) 1937- ...... CLC 23, 148; HLC 1
See also AAYA 20; BYA 13; CA 45-48; CAAS 4; CANR 1, 32, 51; CN 7; DAM MULT, NOV; DLB 82, 206; HW 1; LAIT 4; MTCW 1, 2; NFS 12; RGAL 4; RGSF 2; WLIT 1
Andersen, Hans Christian
1805-1875 .... NCLC 7, 79; SSC 6, 56; WLC
See also CLR 6; DA; DAB; DAC; DAM MST, POP; EW 6; MAICYA 1, 2; RGSF 2; RGWL 2, 3; SATA 100; TWA; WCH; YABC 1
Anderson, C. Farley
See Mencken, H(enry) L(ouis); Nathan, George Jean
Anderson, Jessica (Margaret) Queale
1916- .... CLC 37
See also CA 9-12R; CANR 4, 62; CN 7
Anderson, Jon (Victor) 1940- .... CLC 9
See also CA 25-28R; CANR 20; DAM POET
Anderson, Lindsay (Gordon)
1923-1994 .... CLC 20
See also CA 128; CANR 77
Anderson, Maxwell 1888-1959 .... TCLC 2
See also CA 152; DAM DRAM; DLB 7, 228; MTCW 2; RGAL 4
Anderson, Poul (William)
1926-2001 .... CLC 15
See also AAYA 5, 34; BPFB 1; BYA 6, 8, 9; CA 1-4R, 181; CAAE 181; CAAS 2; CANR 2, 15, 34, 64, 110; CLR 58; DLB 8; FANT; INT CANR-15; MTCW 1, 2; SATA 90; SATA-Brief 39; SATA-Essay 106; SCFW 2; SFW 4; SUFW 1, 2
Anderson, Robert (Woodruff)
1917- .... CLC 23
See also AITN 1; CA 21-24R; CANR 32; DAM DRAM; DLB 7; LAIT 5
Anderson, Roberta Joan
See Mitchell, Joni
Anderson, Sherwood 1876-1941 ..... TCLC 1, 10, 24, 123; SSC 1, 46; WLC
See also AAYA 30; AMW; BPFB 1; CA 121; CANR 61; CDALB 1917-1929; DA; DAB; DAC; DAM MST, NOV; DLB 4, 9, 86; DLBD 1; EXPS; GLL 2; MTCW 1, 2; NFS 4; RGAL 4; RGSF 2; SSFS 4, 10, 11; TUS
Andier, Pierre
See Desnos, Robert
Andouard
See Giraudoux, Jean(-Hippolyte)
Andrade, Carlos Drummond de ..... CLC 18
See also Drummond de Andrade, Carlos
See also RGWL 2, 3
Andrade, Mario de .... TCLC 43
See also de Andrade, Mario
See also LAW; RGWL 2, 3; WLIT 1
Andreae, Johann V(alentin)
1586-1654 .... LC 32
See also DLB 164
Andreas Capellanus fl. c. 1185- .... CMLC 45
See also DLB 208
Andreas-Salome, Lou 1861-1937 ... TCLC 56
See also CA 178; DLB 66

Andress, Lesley
See Sanders, Lawrence
Andrewes, Lancelot 1555-1626 .... LC 5
See also DLB 151, 172
Andrews, Cicily Fairfield
See West, Rebecca
Andrews, Elton V.
See Pohl, Frederik
Andreyev, Leonid (Nikolaevich)
1871-1919 .... TCLC 3
See also CA 185
Andric, Ivo 1892-1975 .... CLC 8; SSC 36
See also CA 81-84; CANR 43, 60; CDWLB 4; DLB 147; EW 11; MTCW 1; RGSF 2; RGWL 2, 3
Androvar
See Prado (Calvo), Pedro
Angelique, Pierre
See Bataille, Georges
Angell, Roger 1920- .... CLC 26
See also CA 57-60; CANR 13, 44, 70; DLB 171, 185
Angelou, Maya 1928- ..... CLC 12, 35, 64, 77, 155; BLC 1; PC 32; WLCS
See also AAYA 7, 20; AMWS 4; BPFB 1; BW 2, 3; BYA 2; CA 65-68; CANR 19, 42, 65, 111; CDALBS; CLR 53; CP 7; CPW; CSW; CWP; DA; DAB; DAC; DAM MST, MULT, POET, POP; DLB 38; EXPN; EXPP; LAIT 4; MAICYA 2; MAICYAS 1; MAWW; MTCW 1, 2; NCFS 2; NFS 2; PFS 2, 3; RGAL 4; SATA 49; WYA; YAW
Angouleme, Marguerite d'
See de Navarre, Marguerite
Anna Comnena 1083-1153 .... CMLC 25
Annensky, Innokenty (Fyodorovich)
1856-1909 .... TCLC 14
See also CA 155
Annunzio, Gabriele d'
See D'Annunzio, Gabriele
Anodos
See Coleridge, Mary E(lizabeth)
Anon, Charles Robert
See Pessoa, Fernando (Antonio Nogueira)
Anouilh, Jean (Marie Lucien Pierre)
1910-1987 . CLC 1, 3, 8, 13, 40, 50; DC 8
See also CA 17-20R; CANR 32; DAM DRAM; DFS 9, 10; EW 13; GFL 1789 to the Present; MTCW 1, 2; RGWL 2, 3; TWA
Anthony, Florence
See Ai
Anthony, John
See Ciardi, John (Anthony)
Anthony, Peter
See Shaffer, Anthony (Joshua); Shaffer, Peter (Levin)
Anthony, Piers 1934- .... CLC 35
See also AAYA 11; BYA 7; CA 21-24R; CAAE 200; CANR 28, 56, 73, 102; CPW; DAM POP; DLB 8; FANT; MAICYA 2; MAICYAS 1; MTCW 1, 2; SAAS 22; SATA 84; SATA-Essay 129; SFW 4; SUFW 1, 2; YAW
Anthony, Susan B(rownell)
1820-1906 .... TCLC 84
See also FW
Antiphon c. 480B.C.-c. 411B.C. .... CMLC 55
Antoine, Marc
See Proust, (Valentin-Louis-George-Eugene-)Marcel
Antoninus, Brother
See Everson, William (Oliver)
Antonioni, Michelangelo 1912- .... CLC 20, 144
See also CA 73-76; CANR 45, 77

Antschel, Paul 1920-1970
See Celan, Paul
See also CA 85-88; CANR 33, 61; MTCW 1

Anwar, Chairil 1922-1949 .... **TCLC 22**
See also RGWL 3

Anzaldua, Gloria (Evanjelina) 1942-
See also CA 175; CSW; CWP; DLB 122; FW; HLCS 1; RGAL 4

Apess, William 1798-1839(?) .... **NCLC 73**
See also DAM MULT; DLB 175, 243; NNAL

Apollinaire, Guillaume 1880-1918 .. **TCLC 3, 8, 51; PC 7**
See also Kostrowitzki, Wilhelm Apollinaris de
See also CA 152; DAM POET; DLB 258; EW 9; GFL 1789 to the Present; MTCW 1; RGWL 2, 3; TWA; WP

Apollonius of Rhodes
See Apollonius Rhodius
See also AW 1; RGWL 2, 3

Apollonius Rhodius c. 300B.C.-c. 220B.C. .... **CMLC 28**
See also Apollonius of Rhodes
See also DLB 176

Appelfeld, Aharon 1932- ... **CLC 23, 47; SSC 42**
See also CA 133; CANR 86; CWW 2; RGSF 2

Apple, Max (Isaac) 1941- .... **CLC 9, 33; SSC 50**
See also CA 81-84; CANR 19, 54; DLB 130

Appleman, Philip (Dean) 1926- .... **CLC 51**
See also CA 13-16R; CAAS 18; CANR 6, 29, 56

Appleton, Lawrence
See Lovecraft, H(oward) P(hillips)

Apteryx
See Eliot, T(homas) S(tearns)

Apuleius, (Lucius Madaurensis) 125(?)-175(?) .... **CMLC 1**
See also AW 2; CDWLB 1; DLB 211; RGWL 2, 3; SUFW

Aquin, Hubert 1929-1977 .... **CLC 15**
See also CA 105; DLB 53

Aquinas, Thomas 1224(?)-1274 ..... **CMLC 33**
See also DLB 115; EW 1; TWA

Aragon, Louis 1897-1982 .... **CLC 3, 22**
See also CA 69-72; CANR 28, 71; DAM NOV, POET; DLB 72, 258; EW 11; GFL 1789 to the Present; GLL 2; MTCW 1, 2; RGWL 2, 3; TCLC 123

Arany, Janos 1817-1882 .... **NCLC 34**

Aranyos, Kakay 1847-1910
See Mikszath, Kalman

Arbuthnot, John 1667-1735 .... **LC 1**
See also DLB 101

Archer, Herbert Winslow
See Mencken, H(enry) L(ouis)

Archer, Jeffrey (Howard) 1940- .... **CLC 28**
See also AAYA 16; BEST 89:3; BPFB 1; CA 77-80; CANR 22, 52, 95; CPW; DAM POP; INT CANR-22

Archer, Jules 1915- .... **CLC 12**
See also CA 9-12R; CANR 6, 69; SAAS 5; SATA 4, 85

Archer, Lee
See Ellison, Harlan (Jay)

Archilochus c. 7th cent. B.C.- .... **CMLC 44**
See also DLB 176

Arden, John 1930- .... **CLC 6, 13, 15**
See also BRWS 2; CA 13-16R; CAAS 4; CANR 31, 65, 67; CBD; CD 5; DAM DRAM; DFS 9; DLB 13, 245; MTCW 1

Arenas, Reinaldo 1943-1990 .. **CLC 41; HLC 1**
See also CA 128; CANR 73, 106; DAM MULT; DLB 145; GLL 2; HW 1; LAW; LAWS 1; MTCW 1; RGSF 2; RGWL 3; WLIT 1

Arendt, Hannah 1906-1975 .... **CLC 66, 98**
See also CA 17-20R; CANR 26, 60; DLB 242; MTCW 1, 2

Aretino, Pietro 1492-1556 .... **LC 12**
See also RGWL 2, 3

Arghezi, Tudor -1967 .... **CLC 80**
See also Theodorescu, Ion N.
See also CA 167; CDWLB 4; DLB 220

Arguedas, Jose Maria 1911-1969 .... **CLC 10, 18; HLCS 1**
See also CA 89-92; CANR 73; DLB 113; HW 1; LAW; RGWL 2, 3; WLIT 1

Argueta, Manlio 1936- .... **CLC 31**
See also CA 131; CANR 73; CWW 2; DLB 145; HW 1; RGWL 3

Arias, Ron(ald Francis) 1941-
See also CA 131; CANR 81; DAM MULT; DLB 82; HLC 1; HW 1, 2; MTCW 2

Ariosto, Ludovico 1474-1533 .... **LC 6; PC 42**
See also EW 2; RGWL 2, 3

Aristides
See Epstein, Joseph

Aristophanes 450B.C.-385B.C. .... **CMLC 4, 51; DC 2; WLCS**
See also AW 1; CDWLB 1; DA; DAB; DAC; DAM DRAM, MST; DFS 10; DLB 176; RGWL 2, 3; TWA

Aristotle 384B.C.-322B.C. .... **CMLC 31; WLCS**
See also AW 1; CDWLB 1; DA; DAB; DAC; DAM MST; DLB 176; RGEL 2, 3; TWA

Arlt, Roberto (Godofredo Christophersen) 1900-1942 .... **TCLC 29; HLC 1**
See also CA 131; CANR 67; DAM MULT; HW 1, 2; LAW

Armah, Ayi Kwei 1939- .... **CLC 5, 33, 136; BLC 1**
See also AFW; BW 1; CA 61-64; CANR 21, 64; CDWLB 3; CN 7; DAM MULT, POET; DLB 117; MTCW 1; WLIT 2

Armatrading, Joan 1950- .... **CLC 17**
See also CA 186

Armitage, Frank
See Carpenter, John (Howard)

Arnette, Robert
See Silverberg, Robert

Arnim, Achim von (Ludwig Joachim von Arnim) 1781-1831 ..... **NCLC 5; SSC 29**
See also DLB 90

Arnim, Bettina von 1785-1859 .... **NCLC 38**
See also DLB 90; RGWL 2, 3

Arnold, Matthew 1822-1888 ..... **NCLC 6, 29, 89; PC 5; WLC**
See also BRW 5; CDBLB 1832-1890; DA; DAB; DAC; DAM MST, POET; DLB 32, 57; EXPP; PAB; PFS 2; TEA; WP

Arnold, Thomas 1795-1842 .... **NCLC 18**
See also DLB 55

Arnow, Harriette (Louisa) Simpson 1908-1986 .... **CLC 2, 7, 18**
See also BPFB 1; CA 9-12R; CANR 14; DLB 6; FW; MTCW 1, 2; RHW; SATA 42; SATA-Obit 47

Arouet, Francois-Marie
See Voltaire

Arp, Hans
See Arp, Jean

Arp, Jean 1887-1966 .... **CLC 5**
See also CA 81-84; CANR 42, 77; EW 10; TCLC 115

Arrabal
See Arrabal, Fernando

Arrabal, Fernando 1932- ... **CLC 2, 9, 18, 58**
See also CA 9-12R; CANR 15

Arreola, Juan Jose 1918-2001 .... **CLC 147; HLC 1; SSC 38**
See also CA 131; CANR 81; DAM MULT; DLB 113; DNFS 2; HW 1, 2; LAW; RGSF 2

Arrian c. 89(?)-c. 155(?) .... **CMLC 43**
See also DLB 176

Arrick, Fran .... **CLC 30**
See also Gaberman, Judie Angell
See also BYA 6

Arriey, Richmond
See Delany, Samuel R(ay), Jr.

Artaud, Antonin (Marie Joseph) 1896-1948 .... **TCLC 3, 36; DC 14**
See also CA 149; DAM DRAM; DLB 258; EW 11; GFL 1789 to the Present; MTCW 1; RGWL 2, 3

Arthur, Ruth M(abel) 1905-1979 ..... **CLC 12**
See also CA 9-12R; CANR 4; CWRI 5; SATA 7, 26

Artsybashev, Mikhail (Petrovich) 1878-1927 .... **TCLC 31**
See also CA 170

Arundel, Honor (Morfydd) 1919-1973 .... **CLC 17**
See also CA 21-22; CAP 2; CLR 35; CWRI 5; SATA 4; SATA-Obit 24

Arzner, Dorothy 1900-1979 .... **CLC 98**

Asch, Sholem 1880-1957 .... **TCLC 3**
See also GLL 2

Ash, Shalom
See Asch, Sholem

Ashbery, John (Lawrence) 1927- .. **CLC 2, 3, 4, 6, 9, 13, 15, 25, 41, 77, 125; PC 26**
See also Berry, Jonas
See also AMWS 3; CA 5-8R; CANR 9, 37, 66, 102; CP 7; DAM POET; DLB 5, 165; DLBY 1981; INT CANR-9; MTCW 1, 2; PAB; PFS 11; RGAL 4; WP

Ashdown, Clifford
See Freeman, R(ichard) Austin

Ashe, Gordon
See Creasey, John

Ashton-Warner, Sylvia (Constance) 1908-1984 .... **CLC 19**
See also CA 69-72; CANR 29; MTCW 1, 2

Asimov, Isaac 1920-1992 ..... **CLC 1, 3, 9, 19, 26, 76, 92**
See also AAYA 13; BEST 90:2; BPFB 1; BYA 4, 6, 7, 9; CA 1-4R; CANR 2, 19, 36, 60; CLR 12, 79; CMW 4; CPW; DAM POP; DLB 8; DLBY 1992; INT CANR-19; JRDA; LAIT 5; MAICYA 1, 2; MTCW 1, 2; RGAL 4; SATA 1, 26, 74; SCFW 2; SFW 4; TUS; YAW

Askew, Anne 1521(?)-1546 .... **LC 81**
See also DLB 136

Assis, Joaquim Maria Machado de
See Machado de Assis, Joaquim Maria

Astell, Mary 1666-1731 .... **LC 68**
See also DLB 252; FW

Astley, Thea (Beatrice May) 1925- ... **CLC 41**
See also CA 65-68; CANR 11, 43, 78; CN 7

Astley, William 1855-1911
See Warung, Price

Aston, James
See White, T(erence) H(anbury)

Asturias, Miguel Angel 1899-1974 .... **CLC 3, 8, 13; HLC 1**
See also CA 25-28; CANR 32; CAP 2; CD-WLB 3; DAM MULT, NOV; DLB 113; HW 1; LAW; MTCW 1, 2; RGWL 2, 3; WLIT 1

Atares, Carlos Saura
See Saura (Atares), Carlos

Athanasius c. 295-c. 373 .... **CMLC 48**
Atheling, William
See Pound, Ezra (Weston Loomis)
Atheling, William, Jr.
See Blish, James (Benjamin)
Atherton, Gertrude (Franklin Horn)
1857-1948 .... **TCLC 2**
See also CA 155; DLB 9, 78, 186; HGG; RGAL 4; SUFW 1; TCWW 2
Atherton, Lucius
See Masters, Edgar Lee
Atkins, Jack
See Harris, Mark
Atkinson, Kate 1951- .... **CLC 99**
See also CA 166; CANR 101; DLB 267
Attaway, William (Alexander)
1911-1986 .... **CLC 92; BLC 1**
See also BW 2, 3; CA 143; CANR 82; DAM MULT; DLB 76
Atticus
See Fleming, Ian (Lancaster); Wilson, (Thomas) Woodrow
Atwood, Margaret (Eleanor) 1939- ... **CLC 2, 3, 4, 8, 13, 15, 25, 44, 84, 135; PC 8; SSC 2, 46; WLC**
See also AAYA 12; BEST 89:2; BPFB 1; CA 49-52; CANR 3, 24, 33, 59, 95; CN 7; CP 7; CPW; CWP; DA; DAB; DAC; DAM MST, NOV, POET; DLB 53, 251; EXPN; FW; INT CANR-24; LAIT 5; MTCW 1, 2; NFS 4, 12, 13, 14; PFS 7; RGSF 2; SATA 50; SSFS 3, 13; TWA; YAW
Aubigny, Pierre d'
See Mencken, H(enry) L(ouis)
Aubin, Penelope 1685-1731(?) .... **LC 9**
See also DLB 39
Auchincloss, Louis (Stanton) 1917- .. **CLC 4, 6, 9, 18, 45; SSC 22**
See also AMWS 4; CA 1-4R; CANR 6, 29, 55, 87; CN 7; DAM NOV; DLB 2, 244; DLBY 1980; INT CANR-29; MTCW 1; RGAL 4
Auden, W(ystan) H(ugh) 1907-1973 . **CLC 1, 2, 3, 4, 6, 9, 11, 14, 43, 123; PC 1; WLC**
See also AAYA 18; AMWS 2; BRW 7; BRWR 1; CA 9-12R; CANR 5, 61, 105; CDBLB 1914-1945; DA; DAB; DAC; DAM DRAM, MST, POET; DLB 10, 20; EXPP; MTCW 1, 2; PAB; PFS 1, 3, 4, 10; TUS; WP
Audiberti, Jacques 1900-1965 .... **CLC 38**
See also DAM DRAM
Audubon, John James 1785-1851 . **NCLC 47**
See also ANW; DLB 248
Auel, Jean M(arie) 1936- .... **CLC 31, 107**
See also AAYA 7; BEST 90:4; BPFB 1; CA 103; CANR 21, 64; CPW; DAM POP; INT CANR-21; NFS 11; RHW; SATA 91
Auerbach, Erich 1892-1957 .... **TCLC 43**
See also CA 155
Augier, Emile 1820-1889 .... **NCLC 31**
See also DLB 192; GFL 1789 to the Present
August, John
See De Voto, Bernard (Augustine)
Augustine, St. 354-430 .... **CMLC 6; WLCS**
See also DA; DAB; DAC; DAM MST; DLB 115; EW 1; RGWL 2, 3
Aunt Belinda
See Braddon, Mary Elizabeth
Aunt Weedy
See Alcott, Louisa May
Aurelius
See Bourne, Randolph S(illiman)
Aurelius, Marcus 121-180 .... **CMLC 45**
See also Marcus Aurelius
See also RGWL 2, 3

Aurobindo, Sri
See Ghose, Aurabinda
Austen, Jane 1775-1817 ...... **NCLC 1, 13, 19, 33, 51, 81, 95, 119; WLC**
See also AAYA 19; BRW 4; BRWR 2; BYA 3; CDBLB 1789-1832; DA; DAB; DAC; DAM MST, NOV; DLB 116; EXPN; LAIT 2; NFS 1, 14; TEA; WLIT 3; WYAS 1
Auster, Paul 1947- .... **CLC 47, 131**
See also CA 69-72; CANR 23, 52, 75; CMW 4; CN 7; DLB 227; MTCW 1; SUFW 2
Austin, Frank
See Faust, Frederick (Schiller)
See also TCWW 2
Austin, Mary (Hunter) 1868-1934 . **TCLC 25**
See also Stairs, Gordon
See also ANW; CA 178; DLB 9, 78, 206, 221; FW; TCWW 2
Averroes 1126-1198 .... **CMLC 7**
See also DLB 115
Avicenna 980-1037 .... **CMLC 16**
See also DLB 115
Avison, Margaret 1918- .... **CLC 2, 4, 97**
See also CA 17-20R; CP 7; DAC; DAM POET; DLB 53; MTCW 1
Axton, David
See Koontz, Dean R(ay)
Ayckbourn, Alan 1939- ...... **CLC 5, 8, 18, 33, 74; DC 13**
See also BRWS 5; CA 21-24R; CANR 31, 59; CBD; CD 5; DAB; DAM DRAM; DFS 7; DLB 13, 245; MTCW 1, 2
Aydy, Catherine
See Tennant, Emma (Christina)
Ayme, Marcel (Andre) 1902-1967 ... **CLC 11; SSC 41**
See also CA 89-92; CANR 67; CLR 25; DLB 72; EW 12; GFL 1789 to the Present; RGSF 2; RGWL 2, 3; SATA 91
Ayrton, Michael 1921-1975 .... **CLC 7**
See also CA 5-8R; CANR 9, 21
Azorin .... **CLC 11**
See also Martinez Ruiz, Jose
See also EW 9
Azuela, Mariano 1873-1952 .. **TCLC 3; HLC 1**
See also CA 131; CANR 81; DAM MULT; HW 1, 2; LAW; MTCW 1, 2
Baastad, Babbis Friis
See Friis-Baastad, Babbis Ellinor
Bab
See Gilbert, W(illiam) S(chwenck)
Babbis, Eleanor
See Friis-Baastad, Babbis Ellinor
Babel, Isaac
See Babel, Isaak (Emmanuilovich)
See also EW 11; SSFS 10
Babel, Isaak (Emmanuilovich)
1894-1941(?) .... **TCLC 2, 13; SSC 16**
See also Babel, Isaac
See also CA 104; 155; CANR 113; DLB 272; MTCW 1; RGSF 2; RGWL 2, 3; TWA
Babits, Mihaly 1883-1941 .... **TCLC 14**
See also CDWLB 4; DLB 215
Babur 1483-1530 .... **LC 18**
Babylas 1898-1962
See Ghelderode, Michel de
Baca, Jimmy Santiago 1952- .... **PC 41**
See also CA 131; CANR 81, 90; CP 7; DAM MULT; DLB 122; HLC 1; HW 1, 2
Baca, Jose Santiago
See Baca, Jimmy Santiago
Bacchelli, Riccardo 1891-1985 .... **CLC 19**
See also CA 29-32R; DLB 264

Bach, Richard (David) 1936- .... **CLC 14**
See also AITN 1; BEST 89:2; BPFB 1; BYA 5; CA 9-12R; CANR 18, 93; CPW; DAM NOV, POP; FANT; MTCW 1; SATA 13
Bache, Benjamin Franklin
1769-1798 .... **LC 74**
See also DLB 43
Bachelard, Gaston 1884-1962 ...... **TCLC 128**
See also CA 97-100; GFL 1789 to the Present
Bachman, Richard
See King, Stephen (Edwin)
Bachmann, Ingeborg 1926-1973 .... **CLC 69**
See also CA 93-96; CANR 69; DLB 85; RGWL 2, 3
Bacon, Francis 1561-1626 .... **LC 18, 32**
See also BRW 1; CDBLB Before 1660; DLB 151, 236, 252; RGEL 2; TEA
Bacon, Roger 1214(?)-1294 .... **CMLC 14**
See also DLB 115
Bacovia, George 1881-1957 .... **TCLC 24**
See also Vasiliu, Gheorghe
See also CDWLB 4; DLB 220
Badanes, Jerome 1937- .... **CLC 59**
Bagehot, Walter 1826-1877 .... **NCLC 10**
See also DLB 55
Bagnold, Enid 1889-1981 .... **CLC 25**
See also BYA 2; CA 5-8R; CANR 5, 40; CBD; CWD; CWRI 5; DAB; DAM DRAM; DLB 13, 160, 191, 245; FW; MAICYA 1, 2; RGEL 2; SATA 1, 25
Bagritsky, Eduard 1895-1934 .... **TCLC 60**
Bagrjana, Elisaveta
See Belcheva, Elisaveta Lyubomirova
Bagryana, Elisaveta -1991 .... **CLC 10**
See also Belcheva, Elisaveta Lyubomirova
See also CA 178; CDWLB 4; DLB 147
Bailey, Paul 1937- .... **CLC 45**
See also CA 21-24R; CANR 16, 62; CN 7; DLB 14, 271; GLL 2
Baillie, Joanna 1762-1851 .... **NCLC 71**
See also DLB 93; RGEL 2
Bainbridge, Beryl (Margaret) 1934- . **CLC 4, 5, 8, 10, 14, 18, 22, 62, 130**
See also BRWS 6; CA 21-24R; CANR 24, 55, 75, 88; CN 7; DAM NOV; DLB 14, 231; MTCW 1, 2
Baker, Carlos (Heard)
1909-1987 .... **TCLC 119**
See also CA 5-8R; CANR 3, 63; DLB 103
Baker, Elliott 1922- .... **CLC 8**
See also CA 45-48; CANR 2, 63; CN 7
Baker, Jean H. .... **TCLC 3, 10**
See also Russell, George William
Baker, Nicholson 1957- .... **CLC 61, 165**
See also CA 135; CANR 63; CN 7; CPW; DAM POP; DLB 227
Baker, Ray Stannard 1870-1946 .... **TCLC 47**
Baker, Russell (Wayne) 1925- .... **CLC 31**
See also BEST 89:4; CA 57-60; CANR 11, 41, 59; MTCW 1, 2
Bakhtin, M.
See Bakhtin, Mikhail Mikhailovich
Bakhtin, M. M.
See Bakhtin, Mikhail Mikhailovich
Bakhtin, Mikhail
See Bakhtin, Mikhail Mikhailovich
Bakhtin, Mikhail Mikhailovich
1895-1975 .... **CLC 83**
See also CA 128; DLB 242
Bakshi, Ralph 1938(?)- .... **CLC 26**
See also CA 138; IDFW 3
Bakunin, Mikhail (Alexandrovich)
1814-1876 .... **NCLC 25, 58**
Baldwin, James (Arthur) 1924-1987 . **CLC 1, 2, 3, 4, 5, 8, 13, 15, 17, 42, 50, 67, 90, 127; BLC 1; DC 1; SSC 10, 33; WLC**
See also AAYA 4, 34; AFAW 1, 2; AMWS 1; BPFB 1; BW 1; CA 1-4R; CABS 1; CAD; CANR 3, 24; CDALB 1941-1968;

CPW; DA; DAB; DAC; DAM MST, MULT, NOV, POP; DFS 15; DLB 2, 7, 33, 249; DLBY 1987; EXPS; LAIT 5; MTCW 1, 2; NCFS 4; NFS 4; RGAL 2; RGSF 2; SATA 9; SATA-Obit 54; SSFS 2; TUS

Bale, John 1495-1563 .... **LC 62**
See also DLB 132; RGEL 2; TEA

Ball, Hugo 1886-1927 .... **TCLC 104**

Ballard, J(ames) G(raham) 1930- . **CLC 3, 6, 14, 36, 137; SSC 1, 53**
See also AAYA 3; BRWS 5; CA 5-8R; CANR 15, 39, 65, 107; CN 7; DAM NOV, POP; DLB 14, 207, 261; HGG; MTCW 1, 2; NFS 8; RGEL 2; RGSF 2; SATA 93; SFW 4

Balmont, Konstantin (Dmitriyevich)
1867-1943 .... **TCLC 11**
See also CA 155

Baltausis, Vincas 1847-1910
See Mikszath, Kalman

Balzac, Honore de 1799-1850 ... **NCLC 5, 35, 53; SSC 5; WLC**
See also DA; DAB; DAC; DAM MST, NOV; DLB 119; EW 5; GFL 1789 to the Present; RGSF 2; RGWL 2, 3; SSFS 10; SUFW; TWA

Bambara, Toni Cade 1939-1995 ...... **CLC 19, 88; BLC 1; SSC 35; WLCS**
See also AAYA 5; AFAW 2; AMWS 11; BW 2, 3; BYA 12, 14; CA 29-32R; CANR 24, 49, 81; CDALBS; DA; DAC; DAM MST, MULT; DLB 38, 218; EXPS; MTCW 1, 2; RGAL 4; RGSF 2; SATA 112; SSFS 4, 7, 12; TCLC 116

Bamdad, A.
See Shamlu, Ahmad

Banat, D. R.
See Bradbury, Ray (Douglas)

Bancroft, Laura
See Baum, L(yman) Frank

Banim, John 1798-1842 .... **NCLC 13**
See also DLB 116, 158, 159; RGEL 2

Banim, Michael 1796-1874 .... **NCLC 13**
See also DLB 158, 159

Banjo, The
See Paterson, A(ndrew) B(arton)

Banks, Iain
See Banks, Iain M(enzies)

Banks, Iain M(enzies) 1954- .... **CLC 34**
See also CA 128; CANR 61, 106; DLB 194, 261; HGG; INT 128; SFW 4

Banks, Lynne Reid .... **CLC 23**
See also Reid Banks, Lynne
See also AAYA 6; BYA 7

Banks, Russell 1940- .... **CLC 37, 72; SSC 42**
See also AMWS 5; CA 65-68; CAAS 15; CANR 19, 52, 73; CN 7; DLB 130; NFS 13

Banville, John 1945- .... **CLC 46, 118**
See also CA 128; CANR 104; CN 7; DLB 14, 271; INT 128

Banville, Theodore (Faullain) de
1832-1891 .... **NCLC 9**
See also DLB 217; GFL 1789 to the Present

Baraka, Amiri 1934- . **CLC 1, 2, 3, 5, 10, 14, 33, 115; BLC 1; DC 6; PC 4; WLCS**
See also Jones, LeRoi
See also AFAW 1, 2; AMWS 2; BW 2, 3; CA 21-24R; CABS 3; CAD; CANR 27, 38, 61; CD 5; CDALB 1941-1968; CP 7; CPW; DA; DAC; DAM MST, MULT, POET, POP; DFS 3, 11; DLB 5, 7, 16, 38; DLBD 8; MTCW 1, 2; PFS 9; RGAL 4; TUS; WP

Baratynsky, Evgenii Abramovich
1800-1844 .... **NCLC 103**
See also DLB 205

Barbauld, Anna Laetitia
1743-1825 .... **NCLC 50**
See also DLB 107, 109, 142, 158; RGEL 2

Barbellion, W. N. P. .... **TCLC 24**
See also Cummings, Bruce F(rederick)

Barber, Benjamin R. 1939- .... **CLC 141**
See also CA 29-32R; CANR 12, 32, 64

Barbera, Jack (Vincent) 1945- .... **CLC 44**
See also CA 110; CANR 45

Barbey d'Aurevilly, Jules-Amedee
1808-1889 .... **NCLC 1; SSC 17**
See also DLB 119; GFL 1789 to the Present

Barbour, John c. 1316-1395 .... **CMLC 33**
See also DLB 146

Barbusse, Henri 1873-1935 .... **TCLC 5**
See also CA 154; DLB 65; RGWL 2, 3

Barclay, Bill
See Moorcock, Michael (John)

Barclay, William Ewert
See Moorcock, Michael (John)

Barea, Arturo 1897-1957 .... **TCLC 14**
See also CA 201

Barfoot, Joan 1946- .... **CLC 18**
See also CA 105

Barham, Richard Harris
1788-1845 .... **NCLC 77**
See also DLB 159

Baring, Maurice 1874-1945 .... **TCLC 8**
See also CA 168; DLB 34; HGG

Baring-Gould, Sabine 1834-1924 ... **TCLC 88**
See also DLB 156, 190

Barker, Clive 1952- .... **CLC 52; SSC 53**
See also AAYA 10; BEST 90:3; BPFB 1; CA 129; CANR 71, 111; CPW; DAM POP; DLB 261; HGG; INT 129; MTCW 1, 2; SUFW 2

Barker, George Granville
1913-1991 .... **CLC 8, 48**
See also CA 9-12R; CANR 7, 38; DAM POET; DLB 20; MTCW 1

Barker, Harley Granville
See Granville-Barker, Harley
See also DLB 10

Barker, Howard 1946- .... **CLC 37**
See also CA 102; CBD; CD 5; DLB 13, 233

Barker, Jane 1652-1732 .... **LC 42, 82**
See also DLB 39, 131

Barker, Pat(ricia) 1943- ...... **CLC 32, 94, 146**
See also BRWS 4; CA 122; CANR 50, 101; CN 7; DLB 271; INT 122

Barlach, Ernst (Heinrich)
1870-1938 .... **TCLC 84**
See also CA 178; DLB 56, 118

Barlow, Joel 1754-1812 .... **NCLC 23**
See also AMWS 2; DLB 37; RGAL 4

Barnard, Mary (Ethel) 1909- .... **CLC 48**
See also CA 21-22; CAP 2

Barnes, Djuna 1892-1982 .... **CLC 3, 4, 8, 11, 29, 127; SSC 3**
See also Steptoe, Lydia
See also AMWS 3; CA 9-12R; CAD; CANR 16, 55; CWD; DLB 4, 9, 45; GLL 1; MTCW 1, 2; RGAL 4; TUS

Barnes, Julian (Patrick) 1946- . **CLC 42, 141**
See also BRWS 4; CA 102; CANR 19, 54; CN 7; DAB; DLB 194; DLBY 1993; MTCW 1

Barnes, Peter 1931- .... **CLC 5, 56**
See also CA 65-68; CAAS 12; CANR 33, 34, 64, 113; CBD; CD 5; DFS 6; DLB 13, 233; MTCW 1

Barnes, William 1801-1886 .... **NCLC 75**
See also DLB 32

Baroja (y Nessi), Pio 1872-1956 ..... **TCLC 8; HLC 1**
See also EW 9

Baron, David
See Pinter, Harold

Baron Corvo
See Rolfe, Frederick (William Serafino Austin Lewis Mary)

Barondess, Sue K(aufman)
1926-1977 .... **CLC 8**
See also Kaufman, Sue
See also CA 1-4R; CANR 1

Baron de Teive
See Pessoa, Fernando (Antonio Nogueira)

Baroness Von S.
See Zangwill, Israel

Barres, (Auguste-)Maurice
1862-1923 .... **TCLC 47**
See also CA 164; DLB 123; GFL 1789 to the Present

Barreto, Afonso Henrique de Lima
See Lima Barreto, Afonso Henrique de

Barrett, Andrea 1954- .... **CLC 150**
See also CA 156; CANR 92

Barrett, Michele .... **CLC 65**

Barrett, (Roger) Syd 1946- .... **CLC 35**

Barrett, William (Christopher)
1913-1992 .... **CLC 27**
See also CA 13-16R; CANR 11, 67; INT CANR-11

Barrie, J(ames) M(atthew)
1860-1937 .... **TCLC 2**
See also BRWS 3; BYA 4, 5; CA 136; CANR 77; CDBLB 1890-1914; CLR 16; CWRI 5; DAB; DAM DRAM; DFS 7; DLB 10, 141, 156; FANT; MAICYA 1, 2; MTCW 1; SATA 100; SUFW; WCH; WLIT 4; YABC 1

Barrington, Michael
See Moorcock, Michael (John)

Barrol, Grady
See Bograd, Larry

Barry, Mike
See Malzberg, Barry N(athaniel)

Barry, Philip 1896-1949 .... **TCLC 11**
See also CA 199; DFS 9; DLB 7, 228; RGAL 4

Bart, Andre Schwarz
See Schwarz-Bart, Andre

Barth, John (Simmons) 1930- ... **CLC 1, 2, 3, 5, 7, 9, 10, 14, 27, 51, 89; SSC 10**
See also AITN 1, 2; AMW; BPFB 1; CA 1-4R; CABS 1; CANR 5, 23, 49, 64, 113; CN 7; DAM NOV; DLB 2, 227; FANT; MTCW 1; RGAL 4; RGSF 2; RHW; SSFS 6; TUS

Barthelme, Donald 1931-1989 ... **CLC 1, 2, 3, 5, 6, 8, 13, 23, 46, 59, 115; SSC 2, 55**
See also AMWS 4; BPFB 1; CA 21-24R; CANR 20, 58; DAM NOV; DLB 2, 234; DLBY 1980, 1989; FANT; MTCW 1, 2; RGAL 4; RGSF 2; SATA 7; SATA-Obit 62; SSFS 3

Barthelme, Frederick 1943- ...... **CLC 36, 117**
See also AMWS 11; CA 122; CANR 77; CN 7; CSW; DLB 244; DLBY 1985; INT CA-122

Barthes, Roland (Gerard)
1915-1980 .... **CLC 24, 83**
See also CA 130; CANR 66; EW 13; GFL 1789 to the Present; MTCW 1, 2; TWA

Barzun, Jacques (Martin) 1907- ..... **CLC 51, 145**
See also CA 61-64; CANR 22, 95

Bashevis, Isaac
See Singer, Isaac Bashevis

Bashkirtseff, Marie 1859-1884 .... **NCLC 27**

Basho, Matsuo
See Matsuo Basho
See also RGWL 2, 3; WP

Basil of Caesaria c. 330-379 .... **CMLC 35**

Bass, Kingsley B., Jr.
See Bullins, Ed

Bass, Rick 1958- .... **CLC 79, 143**
See also ANW; CA 126; CANR 53, 93; CSW; DLB 212

Bassani, Giorgio 1916-2000 .... **CLC 9**
See also CA 65-68; CANR 33; CWW 2; DLB 128, 177; MTCW 1; RGWL 2, 3

Bastian, Ann .... **CLC 70**

Bastos, Augusto (Antonio) Roa
See Roa Bastos, Augusto (Antonio)

Bataille, Georges 1897-1962 .... **CLC 29**
See also CA 101

Bates, H(erbert) E(rnest)
1905-1974 .... **CLC 46; SSC 10**
See also CA 93-96; CANR 34; DAB; DAM POP; DLB 162, 191; EXPS; MTCW 1, 2; RGSF 2; SSFS 7

Bauchart
See Camus, Albert

Baudelaire, Charles 1821-1867 . **NCLC 6, 29, 55; PC 1; SSC 18; WLC**
See also DA; DAB; DAC; DAM MST, POET; DLB 217; EW 7; GFL 1789 to the Present; RGWL 2, 3; TWA

Baudouin, Marcel
See Peguy, Charles (Pierre)

Baudouin, Pierre
See Peguy, Charles (Pierre)

Baudrillard, Jean 1929- .... **CLC 60**

Baum, L(yman) Frank 1856-1919 ... **TCLC 7**
See also CA 133; CLR 15; CWRI 5; DLB 22; FANT; JRDA; MAICYA 1, 2; MTCW 1, 2; NFS 13; RGAL 4; SATA 18, 100; WCH

Baum, Louis F.
See Baum, L(yman) Frank

Baumbach, Jonathan 1933- .... **CLC 6, 23**
See also CA 13-16R; CAAS 5; CANR 12, 66; CN 7; DLBY 1980; INT CANR-12; MTCW 1

Bausch, Richard (Carl) 1945- .... **CLC 51**
See also AMWS 7; CA 101; CAAS 14; CANR 43, 61, 87; CSW; DLB 130

Baxter, Charles (Morley) 1947- .... **CLC 45, 78**
See also CA 57-60; CANR 40, 64, 104; CPW; DAM POP; DLB 130; MTCW 2

Baxter, George Owen
See Faust, Frederick (Schiller)

Baxter, James K(eir) 1926-1972 .... **CLC 14**
See also CA 77-80

Baxter, John
See Hunt, E(verette) Howard, (Jr.)

Bayer, Sylvia
See Glassco, John

Baynton, Barbara 1857-1929 .... **TCLC 57**
See also DLB 230; RGSF 2

Beagle, Peter S(oyer) 1939- .... **CLC 7, 104**
See also AAYA 47; BPFB 1; BYA 9, 10; CA 9-12R; CANR 4, 51, 73, 110; DLBY 1980; FANT; INT CANR-4; MTCW 1; SATA 60, 130; SUFW 1, 2; YAW

Bean, Normal
See Burroughs, Edgar Rice

Beard, Charles A(ustin)
1874-1948 .... **TCLC 15**
See also CA 189; DLB 17; SATA 18

Beardsley, Aubrey 1872-1898 .... **NCLC 6**

Beattie, Ann 1947- ..... **CLC 8, 13, 18, 40, 63, 146; SSC 11**
See also AMWS 5; BEST 90:2; BPFB 1; CA 81-84; CANR 53, 73; CN 7; CPW; DAM NOV, POP; DLB 218; DLBY 1982; MTCW 1, 2; RGAL 4; RGSF 2; SSFS 9; TUS

Beattie, James 1735-1803 .... **NCLC 25**
See also DLB 109

Beauchamp, Kathleen Mansfield 1888-1923
See Mansfield, Katherine
See also CA 134; DA; DAC; DAM MST; MTCW 2; TEA

Beaumarchais, Pierre-Augustin Caron de
1732-1799 .... **LC 61; DC 4**
See also DAM DRAM; DFS 14; EW 4; GFL Beginnings to 1789; RGWL 2, 3

Beaumont, Francis 1584(?)-1616 .... **LC 33; DC 6**
See also BRW 2; CDBLB Before 1660; DLB 58; TEA

Beauvoir, Simone (Lucie Ernestine Marie Bertrand) de 1908-1986 .... **CLC 1, 2, 4, 8, 14, 31, 44, 50, 71, 124; SSC 35; WLC**
See also BPFB 1; CA 9-12R; CANR 28, 61; DA; DAB; DAC; DAM MST, NOV; DLB 72; DLBY 1986; EW 12; FW; GFL 1789 to the Present; MTCW 1, 2; RGSF 2; RGWL 2, 3; TWA

Becker, Carl (Lotus) 1873-1945 ..... **TCLC 63**
See also CA 157; DLB 17

Becker, Jurek 1937-1997 .... **CLC 7, 19**
See also CA 85-88; CANR 60; CWW 2; DLB 75

Becker, Walter 1950- .... **CLC 26**

Beckett, Samuel (Barclay)
1906-1989 .. **CLC 1, 2, 3, 4, 6, 9, 10, 11, 14, 18, 29, 57, 59, 83; SSC 16; WLC**
See also BRWR 1; BRWS 1; CA 5-8R; CANR 33, 61; CBD; CDBLB 1945-1960; DA; DAB; DAC; DAM DRAM, MST, NOV; DFS 2, 7; DLB 13, 15, 233; DLBY 1990; GFL 1789 to the Present; MTCW 1, 2; RGSF 2; RGWL 2, 3; SSFS 15; TEA; WLIT 4

Beckford, William 1760-1844 .... **NCLC 16**
See also BRW 3; DLB 39, 213; HGG; SUFW

Beckman, Gunnel 1910- .... **CLC 26**
See also CA 33-36R; CANR 15; CLR 25; MAICYA 1, 2; SAAS 9; SATA 6

Becque, Henri 1837-1899 .... **NCLC 3**
See also DLB 192; GFL 1789 to the Present

Becquer, Gustavo Adolfo
1836-1870 .... **NCLC 106; HLCS 1**
See also DAM MULT

Beddoes, Thomas Lovell
1803-1849 .... **NCLC 3; DC 15**
See also DLB 96

Bede c. 673-735 .... **CMLC 20**
See also DLB 146; TEA

Bedford, Donald F.
See Fearing, Kenneth (Flexner)

Beecher, Catharine Esther
1800-1878 .... **NCLC 30**
See also DLB 1, 243

Beecher, John 1904-1980 .... **CLC 6**
See also AITN 1; CA 5-8R; CANR 8

Beer, Johann 1655-1700 .... **LC 5**
See also DLB 168

Beer, Patricia 1924- .... **CLC 58**
See also CA 61-64; CANR 13, 46; CP 7; CWP; DLB 40; FW

Beerbohm, Max
See Beerbohm, (Henry) Max(imilian)

Beerbohm, (Henry) Max(imilian)
1872-1956 .... **TCLC 1, 24**
See also BRWS 2; CA 154; CANR 79; DLB 34, 100; FANT

Beer-Hofmann, Richard
1866-1945 .... **TCLC 60**
See also CA 160; DLB 81

Beg, Shemus
See Stephens, James

Begiebing, Robert J(ohn) 1946- .... **CLC 70**
See also CA 122; CANR 40, 88

Behan, Brendan 1923-1964 ...... **CLC 1, 8, 11, 15, 79**
See also BRWS 2; CA 73-76; CANR 33; CBD; CDBLB 1945-1960; DAM DRAM; DFS 7; DLB 13, 233; MTCW 1, 2

Behn, Aphra 1640(?)-1689 .... **LC 1, 30, 42; DC 4; PC 13; WLC**
See also BRWS 3; DA; DAB; DAC; DAM DRAM, MST, NOV, POET; DLB 39, 80, 131; FW; TEA; WLIT 3

Behrman, S(amuel) N(athaniel)
1893-1973 .... **CLC 40**
See also CA 13-16; CAD; CAP 1; DLB 7, 44; IDFW 3; RGAL 4

Belasco, David 1853-1931 .... **TCLC 3**
See also CA 168; DLB 7; RGAL 4

Belcheva, Elisaveta Lyubomirova
1893-1991 .... **CLC 10**
See also Bagryana, Elisaveta

Beldone, Phil "Cheech"
See Ellison, Harlan (Jay)

Beleno
See Azuela, Mariano

Belinski, Vissarion Grigoryevich
1811-1848 .... **NCLC 5**
See also DLB 198

Belitt, Ben 1911- .... **CLC 22**
See also CA 13-16R; CAAS 4; CANR 7, 77; CP 7; DLB 5

Bell, Gertrude (Margaret Lowthian)
1868-1926 .... **TCLC 67**
See also CA 167; CANR 110; DLB 174

Bell, J. Freeman
See Zangwill, Israel

Bell, James Madison 1826-1902 ... **TCLC 43; BLC 1**
See also BW 1; CA 124; DAM MULT; DLB 50

Bell, Madison Smartt 1957- ...... **CLC 41, 102**
See also AMWS 10; BPFB 1; CA 111, 183; CAAE 183; CANR 28, 54, 73; CN 7; CSW; DLB 218; MTCW 1

Bell, Marvin (Hartley) 1937- .... **CLC 8, 31**
See also CA 21-24R; CAAS 14; CANR 59, 102; CP 7; DAM POET; DLB 5; MTCW 1

Bell, W. L. D.
See Mencken, H(enry) L(ouis)

Bellamy, Atwood C.
See Mencken, H(enry) L(ouis)

Bellamy, Edward 1850-1898 .... **NCLC 4, 86**
See also DLB 12; NFS 15; RGAL 4; SFW 4

Belli, Gioconda 1949-
See also CA 152; CWW 2; HLCS 1; RGWL 3

Bellin, Edward J.
See Kuttner, Henry

Belloc, (Joseph) Hilaire (Pierre Sebastien Rene Swanton) 1870-1953 .... **TCLC 7, 18; PC 24**
See also CA 152; CWRI 5; DAM POET; DLB 19, 100, 141, 174; MTCW 1; SATA 112; WCH; YABC 1

Belloc, Joseph Peter Rene Hilaire
See Belloc, (Joseph) Hilaire (Pierre Sebastien Rene Swanton)

Belloc, Joseph Pierre Hilaire
See Belloc, (Joseph) Hilaire (Pierre Sebastien Rene Swanton)

Belloc, M. A.
See Lowndes, Marie Adelaide (Belloc)

Belloc-Lowndes, Mrs.
See Lowndes, Marie Adelaide (Belloc)

Bellow, Saul 1915- . **CLC 1, 2, 3, 6, 8, 10, 13, 15, 25, 33, 34, 63, 79; SSC 14; WLC**
See also AITN 2; AMW; BEST 89:3; BPFB 1; CA 5-8R; CABS 1; CANR 29, 53, 95; CDALB 1941-1968; CN 7; DA; DAB; DAC; DAM MST, NOV, POP; DLB 2, 28; DLBD 3; DLBY 1982; MTCW 1, 2; NFS 4, 14; RGAL 4; RGSF 2; SSFS 12; TUS

Belser, Reimond Karel Maria de 1929-
See Ruyslinck, Ward
See also CA 152

Bely, Andrey .... **TCLC 7; PC 11**
See also Bugayev, Boris Nikolayevich
See also EW 9; MTCW 1

Belyi, Andrei
See Bugayev, Boris Nikolayevich
See also RGWL 2, 3

Bembo, Pietro 1470-1547 .... **LC 79**
See also RGWL 2, 3

Benary, Margot
See Benary-Isbert, Margot

Benary-Isbert, Margot 1889-1979 .... **CLC 12**
See also CA 5-8R; CANR 4, 72; CLR 12; MAICYA 1, 2; SATA 2; SATA-Obit 21

Benavente (y Martinez), Jacinto
1866-1954 .... **TCLC 3; HLCS 1**
See also CA 131; CANR 81; DAM DRAM, MULT; GLL 2; HW 1, 2; MTCW 1, 2

Benchley, Peter (Bradford) 1940- .. **CLC 4, 8**
See also AAYA 14; AITN 2; BPFB 1; CA 17-20R; CANR 12, 35, 66; CPW; DAM NOV, POP; HGG; MTCW 1, 2; SATA 3, 89

Benchley, Robert (Charles)
1889-1945 .... **TCLC 1, 55**
See also CA 153; DLB 11; RGAL 4

Benda, Julien 1867-1956 .... **TCLC 60**
See also CA 154; GFL 1789 to the Present

Benedict, Ruth (Fulton)
1887-1948 .... **TCLC 60**
See also CA 158; DLB 246

Benedikt, Michael 1935- .... **CLC 4, 14**
See also CA 13-16R; CANR 7; CP 7; DLB 5

Benet, Juan 1927-1993 .... **CLC 28**
See also CA 143

Benet, Stephen Vincent 1898-1943 . **TCLC 7; SSC 10**
See also AMWS 11; CA 152; DAM POET; DLB 4, 48, 102, 249; DLBY 1997; HGG; MTCW 1; RGAL 4; RGSF 2; SUFW; WP; YABC 1

Benet, William Rose 1886-1950 ..... **TCLC 28**
See also CA 152; DAM POET; DLB 45; RGAL 4

Benford, Gregory (Albert) 1941- ..... **CLC 52**
See also BPFB 1; CA 69-72, 175; CAAE 175; CAAS 27; CANR 12, 24, 49, 95; CSW; DLBY 1982; SCFW; SFW 4

Bengtsson, Frans (Gunnar)
1894-1954 .... **TCLC 48**
See also CA 170

Benjamin, David
See Slavitt, David R(ytman)

Benjamin, Lois
See Gould, Lois

Benjamin, Walter 1892-1940 .... **TCLC 39**
See also CA 164; DLB 242; EW 11

Benn, Gottfried 1886-1956 .. **TCLC 3; PC 35**
See also CA 153; DLB 56; RGWL 2, 3

Bennett, Alan 1934- .... **CLC 45, 77**
See also BRWS 8; CA 103; CANR 35, 55, 106; CBD; CD 5; DAB; DAM MST; MTCW 1, 2

Bennett, (Enoch) Arnold
1867-1931 .... **TCLC 5, 20**
See also BRW 6; CA 155; CDBLB 1890-1914; DLB 10, 34, 98, 135; MTCW 2

Bennett, Elizabeth
See Mitchell, Margaret (Munnerlyn)

Bennett, George Harold 1930-
See Bennett, Hal
See also BW 1; CA 97-100; CANR 87

Bennett, Hal .... **CLC 5**
See also Bennett, George Harold
See also DLB 33

Bennett, Jay 1912- .... **CLC 35**
See also AAYA 10; CA 69-72; CANR 11, 42, 79; JRDA; SAAS 4; SATA 41, 87; SATA-Brief 27; WYA; YAW

Bennett, Louise (Simone) 1919- ...... **CLC 28; BLC 1**
See also BW 2, 3; CA 151; CDWLB 3; CP 7; DAM MULT; DLB 117

Benson, A. C. 1862-1925 .... **TCLC 123**
See also DLB 98

Benson, E(dward) F(rederic)
1867-1940 .... **TCLC 27**
See also CA 157; DLB 135, 153; HGG; SUFW 1

Benson, Jackson J. 1930- .... **CLC 34**
See also CA 25-28R; DLB 111

Benson, Sally 1900-1972 .... **CLC 17**
See also CA 19-20; CAP 1; SATA 1, 35; SATA-Obit 27

Benson, Stella 1892-1933 .... **TCLC 17**
See also CA 154, 155; DLB 36, 162; FANT; TEA

Bentham, Jeremy 1748-1832 .... **NCLC 38**
See also DLB 107, 158, 252

Bentley, E(dmund) C(lerihew)
1875-1956 .... **TCLC 12**
See also DLB 70; MSW

Bentley, Eric (Russell) 1916- .... **CLC 24**
See also CA 5-8R; CAD; CANR 6, 67; CBD; CD 5; INT CANR-6

Beranger, Pierre Jean de
1780-1857 .... **NCLC 34**

Berdyaev, Nicolas
See Berdyaev, Nikolai (Aleksandrovich)

Berdyaev, Nikolai (Aleksandrovich)
1874-1948 .... **TCLC 67**
See also CA 157

Berdyayev, Nikolai (Aleksandrovich)
See Berdyaev, Nikolai (Aleksandrovich)

Berendt, John (Lawrence) 1939- ...... **CLC 86**
See also CA 146; CANR 75, 93; MTCW 1

Beresford, J(ohn) D(avys)
1873-1947 .... **TCLC 81**
See also CA 155; DLB 162, 178, 197; SFW 4; SUFW 1

Bergelson, David 1884-1952 .... **TCLC 81**

Berger, Colonel
See Malraux, (Georges-)Andre

Berger, John (Peter) 1926- .... **CLC 2, 19**
See also BRWS 4; CA 81-84; CANR 51, 78; CN 7; DLB 14, 207

Berger, Melvin H. 1927- .... **CLC 12**
See also CA 5-8R; CANR 4; CLR 32; SAAS 2; SATA 5, 88; SATA-Essay 124

Berger, Thomas (Louis) 1924- .. **CLC 3, 5, 8, 11, 18, 38**
See also BPFB 1; CA 1-4R; CANR 5, 28, 51; CN 7; DAM NOV; DLB 2; DLBY 1980; FANT; INT CANR-28; MTCW 1, 2; RHW; TCWW 2

Bergman, (Ernst) Ingmar 1918- ...... **CLC 16, 72**
See also CA 81-84; CANR 33, 70; DLB 257; MTCW 2

Bergson, Henri(-Louis) 1859-1941 . **TCLC 32**
See also CA 164; EW 8; GFL 1789 to the Present

Bergstein, Eleanor 1938- .... **CLC 4**
See also CA 53-56; CANR 5

Berkeley, George 1685-1753 .... **LC 65**
See also DLB 31, 101, 252

Berkoff, Steven 1937- .... **CLC 56**
See also CA 104; CANR 72; CBD; CD 5

Berlin, Isaiah 1909-1997 .... **TCLC 105**
See also CA 85-88

Bermant, Chaim (Icyk) 1929-1998 ... **CLC 40**
See also CA 57-60; CANR 6, 31, 57, 105; CN 7

Bern, Victoria
See Fisher, M(ary) F(rances) K(ennedy)

Bernanos, (Paul Louis) Georges
1888-1948 .... **TCLC 3**
See also CA 130; CANR 94; DLB 72; GFL 1789 to the Present; RGWL 2, 3

Bernard, April 1956- .... **CLC 59**
See also CA 131

Berne, Victoria
See Fisher, M(ary) F(rances) K(ennedy)

Bernhard, Thomas 1931-1989 ..... **CLC 3, 32, 61; DC 14**
See also CA 85-88; CANR 32, 57; CDWLB 2; DLB 85, 124; MTCW 1; RGWL 2, 3

Bernhardt, Sarah (Henriette Rosine)
1844-1923 .... **TCLC 75**
See also CA 157

Bernstein, Charles 1950- .... **CLC 142**
See also CA 129; CAAS 24; CANR 90; CP 7; DLB 169

Berriault, Gina 1926-1999 .... **CLC 54, 109; SSC 30**
See also CA 129; CANR 66; DLB 130; SSFS 7,11

Berrigan, Daniel 1921- .... **CLC 4**
See also CA 33-36R; CAAE 187; CAAS 1; CANR 11, 43, 78; CP 7; DLB 5

Berrigan, Edmund Joseph Michael, Jr.
1934-1983
See Berrigan, Ted
See also CA 61-64; CANR 14, 102

Berrigan, Ted .... **CLC 37**
See also Berrigan, Edmund Joseph Michael, Jr.
See also DLB 5, 169; WP

Berry, Charles Edward Anderson 1931-
See Berry, Chuck
See also CA 115

Berry, Chuck .... **CLC 17**
See also Berry, Charles Edward Anderson

Berry, Jonas
See Ashbery, John (Lawrence)
See also GLL 1

Berry, Wendell (Erdman) 1934- ... **CLC 4, 6, 8, 27, 46; PC 28**
See also AITN 1; AMWS 10; ANW; CA 73-76; CANR 50, 73, 101; CP 7; CSW; DAM POET; DLB 5, 6, 234; MTCW 1

Berryman, John 1914-1972 ... **CLC 1, 2, 3, 4, 6, 8, 10, 13, 25, 62**
See also AMW; CA 13-16; CABS 2; CANR 35; CAP 1; CDALB 1941-1968; DAM POET; DLB 48; MTCW 1, 2; PAB; RGAL 4; WP

Bertolucci, Bernardo 1940- ...... **CLC 16, 157**
See also CA 106

Berton, Pierre (Francis Demarigny)
1920- .... **CLC 104**
See also CA 1-4R; CANR 2, 56; CPW; DLB 68; SATA 99

Bertrand, Aloysius 1807-1841 .... **NCLC 31**
See also Bertrand, Louis oAloysiusc

Bertrand, Louis oAloysiusc
See Bertrand, Aloysius
See also DLB 217

Bertran de Born c. 1140-1215 .... **CMLC 5**

Besant, Annie (Wood) 1847-1933 ..... **TCLC 9**
See also CA 185

Bessie, Alvah 1904-1985 .... **CLC 23**
See also CA 5-8R; CANR 2, 80; DLB 26

Bethlen, T. D.
See Silverberg, Robert

Beti, Mongo .... **CLC 27; BLC 1**
See also Biyidi, Alexandre
See also AFW; CANR 79; DAM MULT; WLIT 2

Betjeman, John 1906-1984 ...... **CLC 2, 6, 10, 34, 43**
See also BRW 7; CA 9-12R; CANR 33, 56; CDBLB 1945-1960; DAB; DAM MST, POET; DLB 20; DLBY 1984; MTCW 1, 2

Bettelheim, Bruno 1903-1990 .... **CLC 79**
See also CA 81-84; CANR 23, 61; MTCW 1, 2

Betti, Ugo 1892-1953 .... **TCLC 5**
See also CA 155; RGWL 2, 3

Betts, Doris (Waugh) 1932- ..... **CLC 3, 6, 28; SSC 45**
See also CA 13-16R; CANR 9, 66, 77; CN 7; CSW; DLB 218; DLBY 1982; INT CANR-9; RGAL 4

Bevan, Alistair
See Roberts, Keith (John Kingston)

Bey, Pilaff
See Douglas, (George) Norman

Bialik, Chaim Nachman
1873-1934 .... **TCLC 25**
See also CA 170

Bickerstaff, Isaac
See Swift, Jonathan

Bidart, Frank 1939- .... **CLC 33**
See also CA 140; CANR 106; CP 7

Bienek, Horst 1930- .... **CLC 7, 11**
See also CA 73-76; DLB 75

Bierce, Ambrose (Gwinett)
1842-1914(?) ..... **TCLC 1, 7, 44; SSC 9; WLC**
See also AMW; BYA 11; CA 139; CANR 78; CDALB 1865-1917; DA; DAC; DAM MST; DLB 11, 12, 23, 71, 74, 186; EXPS; HGG; LAIT 2; RGAL 4; RGSF 2; SSFS 9; SUFW 1

Biggers, Earl Derr 1884-1933 .... **TCLC 65**
See also CA 153

Billiken, Bud
See Motley, Willard (Francis)

Billings, Josh
See Shaw, Henry Wheeler

Billington, (Lady) Rachel (Mary)
1942- .... **CLC 43**
See also AITN 2; CA 33-36R; CANR 44; CN 7

Binchy, Maeve 1940- .... **CLC 153**
See also BEST 90:1; BPFB 1; CA 134; CANR 50, 96; CN 7; CPW; DAM POP; INT CA-134; MTCW 1; RHW

Binyon, T(imothy) J(ohn) 1936- .... **CLC 34**
See also CA 111; CANR 28

Bion 335B.C.-245B.C. .... **CMLC 39**

Bioy Casares, Adolfo 1914-1999 ... **CLC 4, 8, 13, 88; HLC 1; SSC 17**
See also Casares, Adolfo Bioy; Miranda, Javier; Sacastru, Martin
See also CA 29-32R; CANR 19, 43, 66; DAM MULT; DLB 113; HW 1, 2; LAW; MTCW 1, 2

Birch, Allison .... **CLC 65**

Bird, Cordwainer
See Ellison, Harlan (Jay)

Bird, Robert Montgomery
1806-1854 .... **NCLC 1**
See also DLB 202; RGAL 4

Birkerts, Sven 1951- .... **CLC 116**
See also CA 133, 176; CAAE 176; CAAS 29; INT 133

Birney, (Alfred) Earle 1904-1995 .. **CLC 1, 4, 6, 11**
See also CA 1-4R; CANR 5, 20; CP 7; DAC; DAM MST, POET; DLB 88; MTCW 1; PFS 8; RGEL 2

Biruni, al 973-1048(?) .... **CMLC 28**

Bishop, Elizabeth 1911-1979 ..... **CLC 1, 4, 9, 13, 15, 32; PC 3, 34**
See also AMWS 1; CA 5-8R; CABS 2; CANR 26, 61, 108; CDALB 1968-1988; DA; DAC; DAM MST, POET; DLB 5, 169; GLL 2; MAWW; MTCW 1, 2; PAB; PFS 6, 12; RGAL 4; SATA-Obit 24; TCLC 121; TUS; WP

Bishop, John 1935- .... **CLC 10**
See also CA 105

Bishop, John Peale 1892-1944 ..... **TCLC 103**
See also CA 155; DLB 4, 9, 45; RGAL 4

Bissett, Bill 1939- .... **CLC 18; PC 14**
See also CA 69-72; CAAS 19; CANR 15; CCA 1; CP 7; DLB 53; MTCW 1

Bissoondath, Neil (Devindra)
1955- .... **CLC 120**
See also CA 136; CN 7; DAC

Bitov, Andrei (Georgievich) 1937- ... **CLC 57**
See also CA 142

Biyidi, Alexandre 1932-
See Beti, Mongo
See also BW 1, 3; CA 124; CANR 81; MTCW 1, 2

Bjarme, Brynjolf
See Ibsen, Henrik (Johan)

Bjoernson, Bjoernstjerne (Martinius)
1832-1910 .... **TCLC 7, 37**

Black, Robert
See Holdstock, Robert P.

Blackburn, Paul 1926-1971 .... **CLC 9, 43**
See also CA 81-84; CANR 34; DLB 16; DLBY 1981

Black Elk 1863-1950 .... **TCLC 33**
See also CA 144; DAM MULT; MTCW 1; NNAL; WP

Black Hobart
See Sanders, (James) Ed(ward)

Blacklin, Malcolm
See Chambers, Aidan

Blackmore, R(ichard) D(oddridge)
1825-1900 .... **TCLC 27**
See also DLB 18; RGEL 2

Blackmur, R(ichard) P(almer)
1904-1965 .... **CLC 2, 24**
See also AMWS 2; CA 11-12; CANR 71; CAP 1; DLB 63

Black Tarantula
See Acker, Kathy

Blackwood, Algernon (Henry)
1869-1951 .... **TCLC 5**
See also CA 150; DLB 153, 156, 178; HGG; SUFW 1

Blackwood, Caroline 1931-1996 .... **CLC 6, 9, 100**
See also CA 85-88; CANR 32, 61, 65; CN 7; DLB 14, 207; HGG; MTCW 1

Blade, Alexander
See Hamilton, Edmond; Silverberg, Robert

Blaga, Lucian 1895-1961 .... **CLC 75**
See also CA 157; DLB 220

Blair, Eric (Arthur) 1903-1950 .... **TCLC 123**
See also Orwell, George
See also CA 132; DA; DAB; DAC; DAM MST, NOV; MTCW 1, 2; SATA 29

Blair, Hugh 1718-1800 .... **NCLC 75**

Blais, Marie-Claire 1939- .... **CLC 2, 4, 6, 13, 22**
See also CA 21-24R; CAAS 4; CANR 38, 75, 93; DAC; DAM MST; DLB 53; FW; MTCW 1, 2; TWA

Blaise, Clark 1940- .... **CLC 29**
See also AITN 2; CA 53-56; CAAS 3; CANR 5, 66, 106; CN 7; DLB 53; RGSF 2

Blake, Fairley
See De Voto, Bernard (Augustine)

Blake, Nicholas
See Day Lewis, C(ecil)
See also DLB 77; MSW

Blake, Sterling
See Benford, Gregory (Albert)

Blake, William 1757-1827 .... **NCLC 13, 37, 57; PC 12; WLC**
See also BRW 3; BRWR 1; CDBLB 1789-1832; CLR 52; DA; DAB; DAC; DAM MST, POET; DLB 93, 163; EXPP; MAICYA 1, 2; PAB; PFS 2, 12; SATA 30; TEA; WCH; WLIT 3; WP

Blanchot, Maurice 1907- .... **CLC 135**
See also CA 144; DLB 72

Blasco Ibanez, Vicente 1867-1928 . **TCLC 12**
See also BPFB 1; CA 131; CANR 81; DAM NOV; EW 8; HW 1, 2; MTCW 1

Blatty, William Peter 1928- .... **CLC 2**
See also CA 5-8R; CANR 9; DAM POP; HGG

Bleeck, Oliver
See Thomas, Ross (Elmore)

Blessing, Lee 1949- .... **CLC 54**
See also CAD; CD 5

Blight, Rose
See Greer, Germaine

Blish, James (Benjamin) 1921-1975 . **CLC 14**
See also BPFB 1; CA 1-4R; CANR 3; DLB 8; MTCW 1; SATA 66; SCFW 2; SFW 4

Bliss, Reginald
See Wells, H(erbert) G(eorge)

Blixen, Karen (Christentze Dinesen)
1885-1962
See Dinesen, Isak
See also CA 25-28; CANR 22, 50; CAP 2; DLB 214; MTCW 1, 2; SATA 44

Bloch, Robert (Albert) 1917-1994 .... **CLC 33**
See also AAYA 29; CA 5-8R, 179; CAAE 179; CAAS 20; CANR 5, 78; DLB 44; HGG; INT CANR-5; MTCW 1; SATA 12; SATA-Obit 82; SFW 4; SUFW 1, 2

Blok, Alexander (Alexandrovich)
1880-1921 .... **TCLC 5; PC 21**
See also CA 183; EW 9; RGWL 2, 3

Blom, Jan
See Breytenbach, Breyten

Bloom, Harold 1930- .... **CLC 24, 103**
See also CA 13-16R; CANR 39, 75, 92; DLB 67; MTCW 1; RGAL 4

Bloomfield, Aurelius
See Bourne, Randolph S(illiman)

Blount, Roy (Alton), Jr. 1941- .... **CLC 38**
See also CA 53-56; CANR 10, 28, 61; CSW; INT CANR-28; MTCW 1

Bloy, Leon 1846-1917 .... **TCLC 22**
See also CA 183; DLB 123; GFL 1789 to the Present

Bluggage, Oranthy
See Alcott, Louisa May

Blume, Judy (Sussman) 1938- ..... **CLC 12, 30**
See also AAYA 3, 26; BYA 1, 8, 12; CA 29-32R; CANR 13, 37, 66; CLR 2, 15, 69; CPW; DAM NOV, POP; DLB 52; JRDA; MAICYA 1, 2; MAICYAS 1; MTCW 1, 2; SATA 2, 31, 79; WYA; YAW

Blunden, Edmund (Charles)
1896-1974 .... **CLC 2, 56**
See also BRW 6; CA 17-18; CANR 54; CAP 2; DLB 20, 100, 155; MTCW 1; PAB

Bly, Robert (Elwood) 1926- .... **CLC 1, 2, 5, 10, 15, 38, 128; PC 39**
See also AMWS 4; CA 5-8R; CANR 41, 73; CP 7; DAM POET; DLB 5; MTCW 1, 2; RGAL 4

Boas, Franz 1858-1942 .... **TCLC 56**
See also CA 181

Bobette
See Simenon, Georges (Jacques Christian)

Boccaccio, Giovanni 1313-1375 ... **CMLC 13; SSC 10**
See also EW 2; RGSF 2; RGWL 2, 3; TWA

Bochco, Steven 1943- .... **CLC 35**
See also AAYA 11; CA 138

Bode, Sigmund
See O'Doherty, Brian

Bodel, Jean 1167(?)-1210 .... **CMLC 28**

Bodenheim, Maxwell 1892-1954 .... **TCLC 44**
See also CA 187; DLB 9, 45; RGAL 4

Bodenheimer, Maxwell
See Bodenheim, Maxwell

Bodker, Cecil 1927- .... **CLC 21**
See also CA 73-76; CANR 13, 44, 111; CLR 23; MAICYA 1, 2; SATA 14, 133

Bodker, Cecil 1927-
See Bodker, Cecil

Boell, Heinrich (Theodor) 1917-1985 ..... **CLC 2, 3, 6, 9, 11, 15, 27, 32, 72; SSC 23; WLC**
See also Boll, Heinrich
See also CA 21-24R; CANR 24; DA; DAB; DAC; DAM MST, NOV; DLB 69; DLBY 1985; MTCW 1, 2; TWA

Boerne, Alfred
See Doeblin, Alfred

Boethius c. 480-c. 524 .... **CMLC 15**
See also DLB 115; RGWL 2, 3

Boff, Leonardo (Genezio Darci) 1938- .... **CLC 70; HLC 1**
See also CA 150; DAM MULT; HW 2

Bogan, Louise 1897-1970 .... **CLC 4, 39, 46, 93; PC 12**
See also AMWS 3; CA 73-76; CANR 33, 82; DAM POET; DLB 45, 169; MAWW; MTCW 1, 2; RGAL 4

Bogarde, Dirk
See Van Den Bogarde, Derek Jules Gaspard Ulric Niven
See also DLB 14

Bogosian, Eric 1953- .... **CLC 45, 141**
See also CA 138; CAD; CANR 102; CD 5

Bograd, Larry 1953- .... **CLC 35**
See also CA 93-96; CANR 57; SAAS 21; SATA 33, 89; WYA

Boiardo, Matteo Maria 1441-1494 .... **LC 6**

Boileau-Despreaux, Nicolas 1636-1711 . **LC 3**
See also DLB 268; EW 3; GFL Beginnings to 1789; RGWL 2, 3

Boissard, Maurice
See Leautaud, Paul

Bojer, Johan 1872-1959 .... **TCLC 64**
See also CA 189

Bok, Edward W. 1863-1930 .... **TCLC 101**
See also DLB 91; DLBD 16

Boland, Eavan (Aisling) 1944- .. **CLC 40, 67, 113**
See also BRWS 5; CA 143; CANR 61; CP 7; CWP; DAM POET; DLB 40; FW; MTCW 2; PFS 12

Boll, Heinrich
See Boell, Heinrich (Theodor)
See also BPFB 1; CDWLB 2; EW 13; RGSF 2; RGWL 2, 3

Bolt, Lee
See Faust, Frederick (Schiller)

Bolt, Robert (Oxton) 1924-1995 .... **CLC 14**
See also CA 17-20R; CANR 35, 67; CBD; DAM DRAM; DFS 2; DLB 13, 233; LAIT 1; MTCW 1

Bombal, Maria Luisa 1910-1980 ...... **SSC 37; HLCS 1**
See also CA 127; CANR 72; HW 1; LAW; RGSF 2

Bombet, Louis-Alexandre-Cesar
See Stendhal

Bomkauf
See Kaufman, Bob (Garnell)

Bonaventura .... **NCLC 35**
See also DLB 90

Bond, Edward 1934- .... **CLC 4, 6, 13, 23**
See also BRWS 1; CA 25-28R; CANR 38, 67, 106; CBD; CD 5; DAM DRAM; DFS 3,8; DLB 13; MTCW 1

Bonham, Frank 1914-1989 .... **CLC 12**
See also AAYA 1; BYA 1, 3; CA 9-12R; CANR 4, 36; JRDA; MAICYA 1, 2; SAAS 3; SATA 1, 49; SATA-Obit 62; TCWW 2; YAW

Bonnefoy, Yves 1923- .... **CLC 9, 15, 58**
See also CA 85-88; CANR 33, 75, 97; CWW 2; DAM MST, POET; DLB 258; GFL 1789 to the Present; MTCW 1, 2

Bontemps, Arna(ud Wendell) 1902-1973 .... **CLC 1, 18; BLC 1**
See also BW 1; CA 1-4R; CANR 4, 35; CLR 6; CWRI 5; DAM MULT, NOV, POET; DLB 48, 51; HR 2; JRDA; MAICYA 1, 2; MTCW 1, 2; SATA 2, 44; SATA-Obit 24; WCH; WP

Booth, Martin 1944- .... **CLC 13**
See also CA 93-96; CAAE 188; CAAS 2; CANR 92

Booth, Philip 1925- .... **CLC 23**
See also CA 5-8R; CANR 5, 88; CP 7; DLBY 1982

Booth, Wayne C(layson) 1921- .... **CLC 24**
See also CA 1-4R; CAAS 5; CANR 3, 43; DLB 67

Borchert, Wolfgang 1921-1947 .... **TCLC 5**
See also CA 188; DLB 69, 124

Borel, Petrus 1809-1859 .... **NCLC 41**
See also DLB 119; GFL 1789 to the Present

Borges, Jorge Luis 1899-1986 ... **CLC 1, 2, 3, 4, 6, 8, 9, 10, 13, 19, 44, 48, 83; HLC 1; PC 22, 32; SSC 4, 41; WLC**
See also AAYA 26; BPFB 1; CA 21-24R; CANR 19, 33, 75, 105; CDWLB 3; DA; DAB; DAC; DAM MST, MULT; DLB 113; DLBY 1986; DNFS 1, 2; HW 1, 2; LAW; MSW; MTCW 1, 2; RGSF 2; RGWL 2, 3; SFW 4; SSFS 4, 9; TCLC 109; TWA; WLIT 1

Borowski, Tadeusz 1922-1951 .... **TCLC 9; SSC 48**
See also CA 154; CDWLB 4, 4; DLB 215; RGSF 2; RGWL 3; SSFS 13

Borrow, George (Henry) 1803-1881 .... **NCLC 9**
See also DLB 21, 55, 166

Bosch (Gavino), Juan 1909-2001
See also CA 151; DAM MST, MULT; DLB 145; HLCS 1; HW 1, 2

Bosman, Herman Charles 1905-1951 .... **TCLC 49**
See also Malan, Herman
See also CA 160; DLB 225; RGSF 2

Bosschere, Jean de 1878(?)-1953 ... **TCLC 19**
See also CA 186

Boswell, James 1740-1795 ... **LC 4, 50; WLC**
See also BRW 3; CDBLB 1660-1789; DA; DAB; DAC; DAM MST; DLB 104, 142; TEA; WLIT 3

Bottomley, Gordon 1874-1948 ..... **TCLC 107**
See also CA 192; DLB 10

Bottoms, David 1949- .... **CLC 53**
See also CA 105; CANR 22; CSW; DLB 120; DLBY 1983

Boucicault, Dion 1820-1890 .... **NCLC 41**

Boucolon, Maryse
See Conde, Maryse

Bourget, Paul (Charles Joseph) 1852-1935 .... **TCLC 12**
See also CA 196; DLB 123; GFL 1789 to the Present

Bourjaily, Vance (Nye) 1922- .... **CLC 8, 62**
See also CA 1-4R; CAAS 1; CANR 2, 72; CN 7; DLB 2, 143

Bourne, Randolph S(illiman) 1886-1918 .... **TCLC 16**
See also AMW; CA 155; DLB 63

Bova, Ben(jamin William) 1932- ...... **CLC 45**
See also AAYA 16; CA 5-8R; CAAS 18; CANR 11, 56, 94, 111; CLR 3; DLBY 1981; INT CANR-11; MAICYA 1, 2; MTCW 1; SATA 6, 68, 133; SFW 4

Bowen, Elizabeth (Dorothea Cole) 1899-1973 . **CLC 1, 3, 6, 11, 15, 22, 118; SSC 3, 28**
See also BRWS 2; CA 17-18; CANR 35, 105; CAP 2; CDBLB 1945-1960; DAM NOV; DLB 15, 162; EXPS; FW; HGG; MTCW 1, 2; NFS 13; RGSF 2; SSFS 5; SUFW 1; TEA; WLIT 4

Bowering, George 1935- .... **CLC 15, 47**
See also CA 21-24R; CAAS 16; CANR 10; CP 7; DLB 53

Bowering, Marilyn R(uthe) 1949- .... **CLC 32**
See also CA 101; CANR 49; CP 7; CWP

Bowers, Edgar 1924-2000 .... **CLC 9**
See also CA 5-8R; CANR 24; CP 7; CSW; DLB 5

Bowers, Mrs. J. Milton 1842-1914
See Bierce, Ambrose (Gwinett)

Bowie, David .... **CLC 17**
See also Jones, David Robert

Bowles, Jane (Sydney) 1917-1973 ..... **CLC 3, 68**
See also CA 19-20; CAP 2

Bowles, Paul (Frederick) 1910-1999 . **CLC 1, 2, 19, 53; SSC 3**
See also AMWS 4; CA 1-4R; CAAS 1; CANR 1, 19, 50, 75; CN 7; DLB 5, 6, 218; MTCW 1, 2; RGAL 4

Bowles, William Lisle 1762-1850 . **NCLC 103**
See also DLB 93

Box, Edgar
See Vidal, Gore
See also GLL 1

Boyd, James 1888-1944 .... **TCLC 115**
See also CA 186; DLB 9; DLBD 16; RGAL 4; RHW

Boyd, Nancy
See Millay, Edna St. Vincent
See also GLL 1

Boyd, Thomas (Alexander) 1898-1935 .... **TCLC 111**
See also CA 183; DLB 9; DLBD 16

Boyd, William 1952- .... **CLC 28, 53, 70**
See also CA 120; CANR 51, 71; CN 7; DLB 231

Boyle, Kay 1902-1992 .... **CLC 1, 5, 19, 58, 121; SSC 5**
See also CA 13-16R; CAAS 1; CANR 29, 61, 110; DLB 4, 9, 48, 86; DLBY 1993; MTCW 1, 2; RGAL 4; RGSF 2; SSFS 10, 13, 14

Boyle, Mark
See Kienzle, William X(avier)

Boyle, Patrick 1905-1982 .... **CLC 19**
See also CA 127

Boyle, T. C.
See Boyle, T(homas) Coraghessan
See also AMWS 8

Boyle, T(homas) Coraghessan 1948- .... **CLC 36, 55, 90; SSC 16**
See also Boyle, T. C.
See also BEST 90:4; BPFB 1; CA 120; CANR 44, 76, 89; CN 7; CPW; DAM POP; DLB 218; DLBY 1986; MTCW 2; SSFS 13

Boz
See Dickens, Charles (John Huffam)

Brackenridge, Hugh Henry
1748-1816 .... NCLC 7
See also DLB 11, 37; RGAL 4

Bradbury, Edward P.
See Moorcock, Michael (John)
See also MTCW 2

Bradbury, Malcolm (Stanley)
1932-2000 .... CLC 32, 61
See also CA 1-4R; CANR 1, 33, 91, 98; CN 7; DAM NOV; DLB 14, 207; MTCW 1, 2

Bradbury, Ray (Douglas) 1920- .... CLC 1, 3, 10, 15, 42, 98; SSC 29, 53; WLC
See also AAYA 15; AITN 1, 2; AMWS 4; BPFB 1; BYA 4, 5, 11; CA 1-4R; CANR 2, 30, 75; CDALB 1968-1988; CN 7; CPW; DA; DAB; DAC; DAM MST, NOV, POP; DLB 2, 8; EXPN; EXPS; HGG; LAIT 3, 5; MTCW 1, 2; NFS 1; RGAL 4; RGSF 2; SATA 11, 64, 123; SCFW 2; SFW 4; SSFS 1; SUFW 1, 2; TUS; YAW

Braddon, Mary Elizabeth
1837-1915 .... TCLC 111
See also BRWS 8; CA 179; CMW 4; DLB 18, 70, 156; HGG

Bradford, Gamaliel 1863-1932 .... TCLC 36
See also CA 160; DLB 17

Bradford, William 1590-1657 .... LC 64
See also DLB 24, 30; RGAL 4

Bradley, David (Henry), Jr. 1950- ... CLC 23, 118; BLC 1
See also BW 1, 3; CA 104; CANR 26, 81; CN 7; DAM MULT; DLB 33

Bradley, John Ed(mund, Jr.) 1958- . CLC 55
See also CA 139; CANR 99; CN 7; CSW

Bradley, Marion Zimmer
1930-1999 .... CLC 30
See also Chapman, Lee; Dexter, John; Gardner, Miriam; Ives, Morgan; Rivers, Elfrida
See also AAYA 40; BPFB 1; CA 57-60; CAAS 10; CANR 7, 31, 51, 75, 107; CPW; DAM POP; DLB 8; FANT; FW; MTCW 1, 2; SATA 90; SATA-Obit 116; SFW 4; SUFW 2; YAW

Bradshaw, John 1933- .... CLC 70
See also CA 138; CANR 61

Bradstreet, Anne 1612(?)-1672 ...... LC 4, 30; PC 10
See also AMWS 1; CDALB 1640-1865; DA; DAB; DAC; DAM MST, POET; DLB 24; EXPP; FW; PFS 6; RGAL 4; TUS; WP

Brady, Joan 1939- .... CLC 86
See also CA 141

Bragg, Melvyn 1939- .... CLC 10
See also BEST 89:3; CA 57-60; CANR 10, 48, 89; CN 7; DLB 14, 271; RHW

Brahe, Tycho 1546-1601 .... LC 45

Braine, John (Gerard) 1922-1986 . CLC 1, 3, 41
See also CA 1-4R; CANR 1, 33; CDBLB 1945-1960; DLB 15; DLBY 1986; MTCW 1

Bramah, Ernest 1868-1942 .... TCLC 72
See also CA 156; CMW 4; DLB 70; FANT

Brammer, William 1930(?)-1978 ...... CLC 31

Brancati, Vitaliano 1907-1954 .... TCLC 12
See also DLB 264

Brancato, Robin F(idler) 1936- .... CLC 35
See also AAYA 9; BYA 6; CA 69-72; CANR 11, 45; CLR 32; JRDA; MAICYA 2; MAICYAS 1; SAAS 9; SATA 97; WYA; YAW

Brand, Max
See Faust, Frederick (Schiller)
See also BPFB 1; TCWW 2

Brand, Millen 1906-1980 .... CLC 7
See also CA 21-24R; CANR 72

Branden, Barbara .... CLC 44
See also CA 148

Brandes, Georg (Morris Cohen)
1842-1927 .... TCLC 10
See also CA 189

Brandys, Kazimierz 1916-2000 .... CLC 62

Branley, Franklyn M(ansfield)
1915- .... CLC 21
See also CA 33-36R; CANR 14, 39; CLR 13; MAICYA 1, 2; SAAS 16; SATA 4, 68

Brathwaite, Edward Kamau 1930- . CLC 11; BLCS
See also BW 2, 3; CA 25-28R; CANR 11, 26, 47, 107; CDWLB 3; CP 7; DAM POET; DLB 125

Brathwaite, Kamau
See Brathwaite, Edward Kamau

Brautigan, Richard (Gary)
1935-1984 ..... CLC 1, 3, 5, 9, 12, 34, 42
See also BPFB 1; CA 53-56; CANR 34; DAM NOV; DLB 2, 5, 206; DLBY 1980, 1984; FANT; MTCW 1; RGAL 4; SATA 56

Brave Bird, Mary
See Crow Dog, Mary (Ellen)
See also NNAL

Braverman, Kate 1950- .... CLC 67
See also CA 89-92

Brecht, (Eugen) Bertolt (Friedrich)
1898-1956 ..... TCLC 1, 6, 13, 35; DC 3; WLC
See also CA 133; CANR 62; CDWLB 2; DA; DAB; DAC; DAM DRAM, MST; DFS 4, 5, 9; DLB 56, 124; EW 11; IDTP; MTCW 1, 2; RGWL 2, 3; TWA

Brecht, Eugen Berthold Friedrich
See Brecht, (Eugen) Bertolt (Friedrich)

Bremer, Fredrika 1801-1865 .... NCLC 11
See also DLB 254

Brennan, Christopher John
1870-1932 .... TCLC 17
See also CA 188; DLB 230

Brennan, Maeve 1917-1993 .... CLC 5
See also CA 81-84; CANR 72, 100; TCLC 124

Brent, Linda
See Jacobs, Harriet A(nn)

Brentano, Clemens (Maria)
1778-1842 .... NCLC 1
See also DLB 90; RGWL 2, 3

Brent of Bin Bin
See Franklin, (Stella Maria Sarah) Miles (Lampe)

Brenton, Howard 1942- .... CLC 31
See also CA 69-72; CANR 33, 67; CBD; CD 5; DLB 13; MTCW 1

Breslin, James 1930-
See Breslin, Jimmy
See also CA 73-76; CANR 31, 75; DAM NOV; MTCW 1, 2

Breslin, Jimmy .... CLC 4, 43
See also Breslin, James
See also AITN 1; DLB 185; MTCW 2

Bresson, Robert 1901(?)-1999 .... CLC 16
See also CA 110; CANR 49

Breton, Andre 1896-1966 .. CLC 2, 9, 15, 54; PC 15
See also CA 19-20; CANR 40, 60; CAP 2; DLB 65, 258; EW 11; GFL 1789 to the Present; MTCW 1, 2; RGWL 2, 3; TWA; WP

Breytenbach, Breyten 1939(?)- .. CLC 23, 37, 126
See also CA 129; CANR 61; CWW 2; DAM POET; DLB 225

Bridgers, Sue Ellen 1942- .... CLC 26
See also AAYA 8; BYA 7, 8; CA 65-68; CANR 11, 36; CLR 18; DLB 52; JRDA; MAICYA 1, 2; SAAS 1; SATA 22, 90; SATA-Essay 109; WYA; YAW

Bridges, Robert (Seymour)
1844-1930 .... TCLC 1; PC 28
See also BRW 6; CA 152; CDBLB 1890-1914; DAM POET; DLB 19, 98

Bridie, James .... TCLC 3
See also Mavor, Osborne Henry
See also DLB 10

Brin, David 1950- .... CLC 34
See also AAYA 21; CA 102; CANR 24, 70; INT CANR-24; SATA 65; SCFW 2; SFW 4

Brink, Andre (Philippus) 1935- . CLC 18, 36, 106
See also AFW; BRWS 6; CA 104; CANR 39, 62, 109; CN 7; DLB 225; INT CA-103; MTCW 1, 2; WLIT 2

Brinsmead, H. F(ay)
See Brinsmead, H(esba) F(ay)

Brinsmead, H. F.
See Brinsmead, H(esba) F(ay)

Brinsmead, H(esba) F(ay) 1922- ...... CLC 21
See also CA 21-24R; CANR 10; CLR 47; CWRI 5; MAICYA 1, 2; SAAS 5; SATA 18, 78

Brittain, Vera (Mary) 1893(?)-1970 . CLC 23
See also CA 13-16; CANR 58; CAP 1; DLB 191; FW; MTCW 1, 2

Broch, Hermann 1886-1951 .... TCLC 20
See also CA 133; CDWLB 2; DLB 85, 124; EW 10; RGWL 2, 3

Brock, Rose
See Hansen, Joseph
See also GLL 1

Brod, Max 1884-1968 .... TCLC 115
See also CA 5-8R; CANR 7; DLB 81

Brodkey, Harold (Roy) 1930-1996 ... CLC 56
See also CA 111; CANR 71; CN 7; DLB 130; TCLC 123

Brodskii, Iosif
See Brodsky, Joseph

Brodsky, Iosif Alexandrovich 1940-1996
See Brodsky, Joseph
See also AITN 1; CA 41-44R; CANR 37, 106; DAM POET; MTCW 1, 2; RGWL 2, 3

Brodsky, Joseph . CLC 4, 6, 13, 36, 100; PC 9
See also Brodsky, Iosif Alexandrovich
See also AMWS 8; CWW 2; MTCW 1

Brodsky, Michael (Mark) 1948- .... CLC 19
See also CA 102; CANR 18, 41, 58; DLB 244

Brodzki, Bella ed. .... CLC 65

Brome, Richard 1590(?)-1652 .... LC 61
See also DLB 58

Bromell, Henry 1947- .... CLC 5
See also CA 53-56; CANR 9

Bromfield, Louis (Brucker)
1896-1956 .... TCLC 11
See also CA 155; DLB 4, 9, 86; RGAL 4; RHW

Broner, E(sther) M(asserman)
1930- .... CLC 19
See also CA 17-20R; CANR 8, 25, 72; CN 7; DLB 28

Bronk, William (M.) 1918-1999 .... CLC 10
See also CA 89-92; CANR 23; CP 7; DLB 165

Bronstein, Lev Davidovich
See Trotsky, Leon

Bronte, Anne 1820-1849 ..... NCLC 4, 71, 102
See also BRW 5; BRWR 1; DLB 21, 199; TEA

Bronte, (Patrick) Branwell
1817-1848 .... **NCLC 109**

Bronte, Charlotte 1816-1855 ...... **NCLC 3, 8, 33, 58, 105; WLC**
See also AAYA 17; BRW 5; BRWR 1; BYA 2; CDBLB 1832-1890; DA; DAB; DAC; DAM MST, NOV; DLB 21, 159, 199; EXPN; LAIT 2; NFS 4; TEA; WLIT 4

Bronte, Emily (Jane) 1818-1848 ... **NCLC 16, 35; PC 8; WLC**
See also AAYA 17; BPFB 1; BRW 5; BRWR 1; BYA 3; CDBLB 1832-1890; DA; DAB; DAC; DAM MST, NOV, POET; DLB 21, 32, 199; EXPN; LAIT 1; TEA; WLIT 3

Brontes
See Bronte, Anne; Bronte, Charlotte; Bronte, Emily (Jane)

Brooke, Frances 1724-1789 .... **LC 6, 48**
See also DLB 39, 99

Brooke, Henry 1703(?)-1783 .... **LC 1**
See also DLB 39

Brooke, Rupert (Chawner)
1887-1915 ..... **TCLC 2, 7; PC 24; WLC**
See also BRWS 3; CA 132; CANR 61; CDBLB 1914-1945; DA; DAB; DAC; DAM MST, POET; DLB 19, 216; EXPP; GLL 2; MTCW 1, 2; PFS 7; TEA

Brooke-Haven, P.
See Wodehouse, P(elham) G(renville)

Brooke-Rose, Christine 1926(?)- ...... **CLC 40**
See also BRWS 4; CA 13-16R; CANR 58; CN 7; DLB 14, 231; SFW 4

Brookner, Anita 1928- .. **CLC 32, 34, 51, 136**
See also BRWS 4; CA 120; CANR 37, 56, 87; CN 7; CPW; DAB; DAM POP; DLB 194; DLBY 1987; MTCW 1, 2; TEA

Brooks, Cleanth 1906-1994 . **CLC 24, 86, 110**
See also CA 17-20R; CANR 33, 35; CSW; DLB 63; DLBY 1994; INT CANR-35; MTCW 1, 2

Brooks, George
See Baum, L(yman) Frank

Brooks, Gwendolyn (Elizabeth)
1917-2000 .. **CLC 1, 2, 4, 5, 15, 49, 125; BLC 1; PC 7; WLC**
See also AAYA 20; AFAW 1, 2; AITN 1; AMWS 3; BW 2, 3; CA 1-4R; CANR 1, 27, 52, 75; CDALB 1941-1968; CLR 27; CP 7; CWP; DA; DAC; DAM MST, MULT, POET; DLB 5, 76, 165; EXPP; MAWW; MTCW 1, 2; PFS 1, 2, 4, 6; RGAL 4; SATA 6; SATA-Obit 123; TUS; WP

Brooks, Mel .... **CLC 12**
See also Kaminsky, Melvin
See also AAYA 13; DLB 26

Brooks, Peter (Preston) 1938- .... **CLC 34**
See also CA 45-48; CANR 1, 107

Brooks, Van Wyck 1886-1963 .... **CLC 29**
See also AMW; CA 1-4R; CANR 6; DLB 45, 63, 103; TUS

Brophy, Brigid (Antonia)
1929-1995 .... **CLC 6, 11, 29, 105**
See also CA 5-8R; CAAS 4; CANR 25, 53; CBD; CN 7; CWD; DLB 14, 271; MTCW 1, 2

Brosman, Catharine Savage 1934- ..... **CLC 9**
See also CA 61-64; CANR 21, 46

Brossard, Nicole 1943- .... **CLC 115**
See also CA 122; CAAS 16; CCA 1; CWP; CWW 2; DLB 53; FW; GLL 2; RGWL 3

Brother Antoninus
See Everson, William (Oliver)

The Brothers Quay
See Quay, Stephen; Quay, Timothy

Broughton, T(homas) Alan 1936- ...... **CLC 19**
See also CA 45-48; CANR 2, 23, 48, 111

Broumas, Olga 1949- .... **CLC 10, 73**
See also CA 85-88; CANR 20, 69, 110; CP 7; CWP; GLL 2

Broun, Heywood 1888-1939 .... **TCLC 104**
See also DLB 29, 171

Brown, Alan 1950- .... **CLC 99**
See also CA 156

Brown, Charles Brockden
1771-1810 .... **NCLC 22, 74**
See also AMWS 1; CDALB 1640-1865; DLB 37, 59, 73; FW; HGG; RGAL 4; TUS

Brown, Christy 1932-1981 .... **CLC 63**
See also BYA 13; CA 105; CANR 72; DLB 14

Brown, Claude 1937-2002 ... **CLC 30; BLC 1**
See also AAYA 7; BW 1, 3; CA 73-76; CANR 81; DAM MULT

Brown, Dee (Alexander) 1908- ... **CLC 18, 47**
See also AAYA 30; CA 13-16R; CAAS 6; CANR 11, 45, 60; CPW; CSW; DAM POP; DLBY 1980; LAIT 2; MTCW 1, 2; SATA 5, 110; TCWW 2

Brown, George
See Wertmueller, Lina

Brown, George Douglas
1869-1902 .... **TCLC 28**
See also Douglas, George
See also CA 162

Brown, George Mackay 1921-1996 ... **CLC 5, 48, 100**
See also BRWS 6; CA 21-24R; CAAS 6; CANR 12, 37, 67; CN 7; CP 7; DLB 14, 27, 139, 271; MTCW 1; RGSF 2; SATA 35

Brown, (William) Larry 1951- .... **CLC 73**
See also CA 134; CSW; DLB 234; INT 133

Brown, Moses
See Barrett, William (Christopher)

Brown, Rita Mae 1944- .... **CLC 18, 43, 79**
See also BPFB 1; CA 45-48; CANR 2, 11, 35, 62, 95; CN 7; CPW; CSW; DAM NOV, POP; FW; INT CANR-11; MTCW 1, 2; NFS 9; RGAL 4; TUS

Brown, Roderick (Langmere) Haig-
See Haig-Brown, Roderick (Langmere)

Brown, Rosellen 1939- .... **CLC 32**
See also CA 77-80; CAAS 10; CANR 14, 44, 98; CN 7

Brown, Sterling Allen 1901-1989 .... **CLC 1, 23, 59; BLC 1**
See also AFAW 1, 2; BW 1, 3; CA 85-88; CANR 26; DAM MULT, POET; DLB 48, 51, 63; HR 2; MTCW 1, 2; RGAL 4; WP

Brown, Will
See Ainsworth, William Harrison

Brown, William Wells 1815-1884 ... **NCLC 2, 89; BLC 1; DC 1**
See also DAM MULT; DLB 3, 50, 183, 248; RGAL 4

Browne, (Clyde) Jackson 1948(?)- ... **CLC 21**
See also CA 120

Browning, Elizabeth Barrett
1806-1861 ... **NCLC 1, 16, 61, 66; PC 6; WLC**
See also BRW 4; CDBLB 1832-1890; DA; DAB; DAC; DAM MST, POET; DLB 32, 199; EXPP; PAB; PFS 2; TEA; WLIT 4; WP

Browning, Robert 1812-1889 . **NCLC 19, 79; PC 2; WLCS**
See also BRW 4; BRWR 2; CDBLB 1832-1890; DA; DAB; DAC; DAM MST, POET; DLB 32, 163; EXPP; PAB; PFS 1, 15; RGEL 2; TEA; WLIT 4; WP; YABC 1

Browning, Tod 1882-1962 .... **CLC 16**
See also CA 141

Brownmiller, Susan 1935- .... **CLC 159**
See also CA 103; CANR 35, 75; DAM NOV; FW; MTCW 1, 2

Brownson, Orestes Augustus
1803-1876 .... **NCLC 50**
See also DLB 1, 59, 73, 243

Bruccoli, Matthew J(oseph) 1931- ... **CLC 34**
See also CA 9-12R; CANR 7, 87; DLB 103

Bruce, Lenny .... **CLC 21**
See also Schneider, Leonard Alfred

Bruin, John
See Brutus, Dennis

Brulard, Henri
See Stendhal

Brulls, Christian
See Simenon, Georges (Jacques Christian)

Brunner, John (Kilian Houston)
1934-1995 .... **CLC 8, 10**
See also CA 1-4R; CAAS 8; CANR 2, 37; CPW; DAM POP; DLB 261; MTCW 1, 2; SCFW 2; SFW 4

Bruno, Giordano 1548-1600 .... **LC 27**
See also RGWL 2, 3

Brutus, Dennis 1924- ... **CLC 43; BLC 1; PC 24**
See also AFW; BW 2, 3; CA 49-52; CAAS 14; CANR 2, 27, 42, 81; CDWLB 3; CP 7; DAM MULT, POET; DLB 117, 225

Bryan, C(ourtlandt) D(ixon) B(arnes)
1936- .... **CLC 29**
See also CA 73-76; CANR 13, 68; DLB 185; INT CANR-13

Bryan, Michael
See Moore, Brian
See also CCA 1

Bryan, William Jennings
1860-1925 .... **TCLC 99**

Bryant, William Cullen 1794-1878 . **NCLC 6, 46; PC 20**
See also AMWS 1; CDALB 1640-1865; DA; DAB; DAC; DAM MST, POET; DLB 3, 43, 59, 189, 250; EXPP; PAB; RGAL 4; TUS

Bryusov, Valery Yakovlevich
1873-1924 .... **TCLC 10**
See also CA 155; SFW 4

Buchan, John 1875-1940 .... **TCLC 41**
See also CA 145; CMW 4; DAB; DAM POP; DLB 34, 70, 156; HGG; MSW; MTCW 1; RGEL 2; RHW; YABC 2

Buchanan, George 1506-1582 .... **LC 4**
See also DLB 132

Buchanan, Robert 1841-1901 .... **TCLC 107**
See also CA 179; DLB 18, 35

Buchheim, Lothar-Guenther 1918- .... **CLC 6**
See also CA 85-88

Buchner, (Karl) Georg 1813-1837 . **NCLC 26**
See also CDWLB 2; DLB 133; EW 6; RGSF 2; RGWL 2, 3; TWA

Buchwald, Art(hur) 1925- .... **CLC 33**
See also AITN 1; CA 5-8R; CANR 21, 67, 107; MTCW 1, 2; SATA 10

Buck, Pearl S(ydenstricker)
1892-1973 .... **CLC 7, 11, 18, 127**
See also AAYA 42; AITN 1; AMWS 2; BPFB 1; CA 1-4R; CANR 1, 34; CDALBS; DA; DAB; DAC; DAM MST, NOV; DLB 9, 102; LAIT 3; MTCW 1, 2; RGAL 4; RHW; SATA 1, 25; TUS

Buckler, Ernest 1908-1984 .... **CLC 13**
See also CA 11-12; CAP 1; CCA 1; DAC; DAM MST; DLB 68; SATA 47

Buckley, Christopher (Taylor)
1952- .... **CLC 165**
See also CA 139

Buckley, Vincent (Thomas)
1925-1988 .... **CLC 57**
See also CA 101

Buckley, William F(rank), Jr. 1925- . **CLC 7, 18, 37**
See also AITN 1; BPFB 1; CA 1-4R; CANR 1, 24, 53, 93; CMW 2; CPW; DAM POP; DLB 137; DLBY 1980; INT CANR-24; MTCW 1, 2; TUS

Buechner, (Carl) Frederick 1926- . **CLC 2, 4, 6, 9**
See also BPFB 1; CA 13-16R; CANR 11, 39, 64; CN 7; DAM NOV; DLBY 1980; INT CANR-11; MTCW 1, 2

Buell, John (Edward) 1927- .... **CLC 10**
See also CA 1-4R; CANR 71; DLB 53

Buero Vallejo, Antonio 1916-2000 ... **CLC 15, 46, 139; DC 18**
See also CA 106; CANR 24, 49, 75; DFS 11; HW 1; MTCW 1, 2

Bufalino, Gesualdo 1920(?)-1990 ...... **CLC 74**
See also CWW 2; DLB 196

Bugayev, Boris Nikolayevich 1880-1934 .... **TCLC 7; PC 11**
See also Bely, Andrey; Belyi, Andrei
See also CA 165; MTCW 1

Bukowski, Charles 1920-1994 ... **CLC 2, 5, 9, 41, 82, 108; PC 18; SSC 45**
See also CA 17-20R; CANR 40, 62, 105; CPW; DAM NOV, POET; DLB 5, 130, 169; MTCW 1, 2

Bulgakov, Mikhail (Afanas'evich) 1891-1940 .... **TCLC 2, 16; SSC 18**
See also BPFB 1; CA 152; DAM DRAM, NOV; DLB 272; NFS 8; RGSF 2; RGWL 2, 3; SFW 4; TWA

Bulgya, Alexander Alexandrovich 1901-1956 .... **TCLC 53**
See also Fadeev, Aleksandr Aleksandrovich; Fadeyev, Alexander
See also CA 181

Bullins, Ed 1935- ... **CLC 1, 5, 7; BLC 1; DC 6**
See also BW 2, 3; CA 49-52; CAAS 16; CAD; CANR 24, 46, 73; CD 5; DAM DRAM, MULT; DLB 7, 38, 249; MTCW 1, 2; RGAL 4

Bulwer-Lytton, Edward (George Earle Lytton) 1803-1873 .... **NCLC 1, 45**
See also DLB 21; RGEL 2; SFW 4; SUFW 1; TEA

Bunin, Ivan Alexeyevich 1870-1953 .... **TCLC 6; SSC 5**
See also RGSF 2; RGWL 2, 3; TWA

Bunting, Basil 1900-1985 ...... **CLC 10, 39, 47**
See also BRWS 7; CA 53-56; CANR 7; DAM POET; DLB 20; RGEL 2

Bunuel, Luis 1900-1983 ... **CLC 16, 80; HLC 1**
See also CA 101; CANR 32, 77; DAM MULT; HW 1

Bunyan, John 1628-1688 ..... **LC 4, 69; WLC**
See also BRW 2; BYA 5; CDBLB 1660-1789; DA; DAB; DAC; DAM MST; DLB 39; RGEL 2; TEA; WCH; WLIT 3

Buravsky, Alexandr .... **CLC 59**

Burckhardt, Jacob (Christoph) 1818-1897 .... **NCLC 49**
See also EW 6

Burford, Eleanor
See Hibbert, Eleanor Alice Burford

Burgess, Anthony . **CLC 1, 2, 4, 5, 8, 10, 13, 15, 22, 40, 62, 81, 94**
See also Wilson, John (Anthony) Burgess
See also AAYA 25; AITN 1; BRWS 1; CDBLB 1960 to Present; DAB; DLB 14, 194, 261; DLBY 1998; MTCW 1, 2; RGEL 2; RHW; SFW 4; YAW

Burke, Edmund 1729(?)-1797 .... **LC 7, 36; WLC**
See also BRW 3; DA; DAB; DAC; DAM MST; DLB 104, 252; RGEL 2; TEA

Burke, Kenneth (Duva) 1897-1993 ... **CLC 2, 24**
See also AMW; CA 5-8R; CANR 39, 74; DLB 45, 63; MTCW 1, 2; RGAL 4

Burke, Leda
See Garnett, David

Burke, Ralph
See Silverberg, Robert

Burke, Thomas 1886-1945 .... **TCLC 63**
See also CA 155; CMW 4; DLB 197

Burney, Fanny 1752-1840 .... **NCLC 12, 54, 107**
See also BRWS 3; DLB 39; RGEL 2; TEA

Burney, Frances
See Burney, Fanny

Burns, Robert 1759-1796 ... **LC 3, 29, 40; PC 6; WLC**
See also BRW 3; CDBLB 1789-1832; DA; DAB; DAC; DAM MST, POET; DLB 109; EXPP; PAB; RGEL 2; TEA; WP

Burns, Tex
See L'Amour, Louis (Dearborn)
See also TCWW 2

Burnshaw, Stanley 1906- .... **CLC 3, 13, 44**
See also CA 9-12R; CP 7; DLB 48; DLBY 1997

Burr, Anne 1937- .... **CLC 6**
See also CA 25-28R

Burroughs, Edgar Rice 1875-1950 . **TCLC 2, 32**
See also AAYA 11; BPFB 1; BYA 4, 9; CA 132; DAM NOV; DLB 8; FANT; MTCW 1, 2; RGAL 4; SATA 41; SCFW 2; SFW 4; TUS; YAW

Burroughs, William S(eward) 1914-1997 .. **CLC 1, 2, 5, 15, 22, 42, 75, 109; WLC**
See also Lee, William; Lee, Willy
See also AITN 2; AMWS 3; BPFB 1; CA 9-12R; CANR 20, 52, 104; CN 7; CPW; DA; DAB; DAC; DAM MST, NOV, POP; DLB 2, 8, 16, 152, 237; DLBY 1981, 1997; HGG; MTCW 1, 2; RGAL 4; SFW 4; TCLC 121

Burton, Sir Richard F(rancis) 1821-1890 .... **NCLC 42**
See also DLB 55, 166, 184

Burton, Robert 1577-1640 .... **LC 74**
See also DLB 151; RGEL 2

Buruma, Ian 1951- .... **CLC 163**
See also CA 128; CANR 65

Busch, Frederick 1941- ... **CLC 7, 10, 18, 47, 166**
See also CA 33-36R; CAAS 1; CANR 45, 73, 92; CN 7; DLB 6, 218

Bush, Ronald 1946- .... **CLC 34**
See also CA 136

Bustos, F(rancisco)
See Borges, Jorge Luis

Bustos Domecq, H(onorio)
See Bioy Casares, Adolfo; Borges, Jorge Luis

Butler, Octavia E(stelle) 1947- .... **CLC 38, 121; BLCS**
See also AAYA 18; AFAW 2; BPFB 1; BW 2, 3; CA 73-76; CANR 12, 24, 38, 73; CLR 65; CPW; DAM MULT, POP; DLB 33; MTCW 1, 2; NFS 8; SATA 84; SCFW 2; SFW 4; SSFS 6; YAW

Butler, Robert Olen, (Jr.) 1945- ...... **CLC 81, 162**
See also BPFB 1; CA 112; CANR 66; CSW; DAM POP; DLB 173; INT CA-112; MTCW 1; SSFS 11

Butler, Samuel 1612-1680 .... **LC 16, 43**
See also DLB 101, 126; RGEL 2

Butler, Samuel 1835-1902 .... **TCLC 1, 33; WLC**
See also BRWS 2; CA 143; CDBLB 1890-1914; DA; DAB; DAC; DAM NOV; DLB 18, 57, 174; RGEL 2; SFW 4; TEA

Butler, Walter C.
See Faust, Frederick (Schiller)

Butor, Michel (Marie Francois) 1926- .... **CLC 1, 3, 8, 11, 15, 161**
See also CA 9-12R; CANR 33, 66; DLB 83; EW 13; GFL 1789 to the Present; MTCW 1, 2

Butts, Mary 1890(?)-1937 .... **TCLC 77**
See also CA 148; DLB 240

Buxton, Ralph
See Silverstein, Alvin; Silverstein, Virginia B(arbara Opshelor)

Buzo, Alexander (John) 1944- .... **CLC 61**
See also CA 97-100; CANR 17, 39, 69; CD 5

Buzzati, Dino 1906-1972 .... **CLC 36**
See also CA 160; DLB 177; RGWL 2, 3; SFW 4

Byars, Betsy (Cromer) 1928- .... **CLC 35**
See also AAYA 19; BYA 3; CA 33-36R, 183; CAAE 183; CANR 18, 36, 57, 102; CLR 1, 16, 72; DLB 52; INT CANR-18; JRDA; MAICYA 1, 2; MAICYAS 1; MTCW 1; SAAS 1; SATA 4, 46, 80; SATA-Essay 108; WYA; YAW

Byatt, A(ntonia) S(usan Drabble) 1936- .... **CLC 19, 65, 136**
See also BPFB 1; BRWS 4; CA 13-16R; CANR 13, 33, 50, 75, 96; DAM NOV, POP; DLB 14, 194; MTCW 1, 2; RGSF 2; RHW; TEA

Byrne, David 1952- .... **CLC 26**
See also CA 127

Byrne, John Keyes 1926-
See Leonard, Hugh
See also CA 102; CANR 78; INT CA-102

Byron, George Gordon (Noel) 1788-1824 ...... **NCLC 2, 12, 109; PC 16; WLC**
See also BRW 4; CDBLB 1789-1832; DA; DAB; DAC; DAM MST, POET; DLB 96, 110; EXPP; PAB; PFS 1, 14; RGEL 2; TEA; WLIT 3; WP

Byron, Robert 1905-1941 .... **TCLC 67**
See also CA 160; DLB 195

C. 3. 3.
See Wilde, Oscar (Fingal O'Flahertie Wills)

C. 3. 3.,
See Wilde, Oscar (Fingal O'Flahertie Wills)

Caballero, Fernan 1796-1877 .... **NCLC 10**

Cabell, Branch
See Cabell, James Branch

Cabell, James Branch 1879-1958 .... **TCLC 6**
See also CA 152; DLB 9, 78; FANT; MTCW 1; RGAL 4; SUFW 1

Cabeza de Vaca, Alvar Nunez 1490-1557(?) .... **LC 61**

Cable, George Washington 1844-1925 .... **TCLC 4; SSC 4**
See also CA 155; DLB 12, 74; DLBD 13; RGAL 4; TUS

Cabral de Melo Neto, Joao 1920-1999 .... **CLC 76**
See also CA 151; DAM MULT; LAW; LAWS 1

Cabrera Infante, G(uillermo) 1929- . **CLC 5, 25, 45, 120; HLC 1; SSC 39**
See also CA 85-88; CANR 29, 65, 110; CDWLB 3; DAM MULT; DLB 113; HW 1, 2; LAW; LAWS 1; MTCW 1, 2; RGSF 2; WLIT 1

Cade, Toni
See Bambara, Toni Cade

Cadmus and Harmonia
See Buchan, John

Caedmon fl. 658-680 .... **CMLC 7**
See also DLB 146

Caeiro, Alberto
See Pessoa, Fernando (Antonio Nogueira)

Caesar, Julius .... **CMLC 47**
See also Julius Caesar
See also AW 1; RGWL 2, 3

Cage, John (Milton, Jr.) 1912-1992 . **CLC 41**
See also CA 13-16R; CANR 9, 78; DLB 193; INT CANR-9

Cahan, Abraham 1860-1951 .... **TCLC 71**
See also CA 154; DLB 9, 25, 28; RGAL 4

Cain, G.
See Cabrera Infante, G(uillermo)

Cain, Guillermo
See Cabrera Infante, G(uillermo)

Cain, James M(allahan) 1892-1977 .. **CLC 3, 11, 28**
See also AITN 1; BPFB 1; CA 17-20R; CANR 8, 34, 61; CMW 4; DLB 226; MSW; MTCW 1; RGAL 4

Caine, Hall 1853-1931 .... **TCLC 97**
See also RHW

Caine, Mark
See Raphael, Frederic (Michael)

Calasso, Roberto 1941- .... **CLC 81**
See also CA 143; CANR 89

Calderon de la Barca, Pedro
1600-1681 .... **LC 23; DC 3; HLCS 1**
See also EW 2; RGWL 2, 3; TWA

Caldwell, Erskine (Preston)
1903-1987 .... **CLC 1, 8, 14, 50, 60; SSC 19**
See also AITN 1; AMW; BPFB 1; CA 1-4R; CAAS 1; CANR 2, 33; DAM NOV; DLB 9, 86; MTCW 1, 2; RGAL 4; RGSF 2; TCLC 117; TUS

Caldwell, (Janet Miriam) Taylor (Holland)
1900-1985 .... **CLC 2, 28, 39**
See also BPFB 1; CA 5-8R; CANR 5; DAM NOV, POP; DLBD 17; RHW

Calhoun, John Caldwell
1782-1850 .... **NCLC 15**
See also DLB 3, 248

Calisher, Hortense 1911- ..... **CLC 2, 4, 8, 38, 134; SSC 15**
See also CA 1-4R; CANR 1, 22; CN 7; DAM NOV; DLB 2, 218; INT CANR-22; MTCW 1, 2; RGAL 4; RGSF 2

Callaghan, Morley Edward
1903-1990 .... **CLC 3, 14, 41, 65**
See also CA 9-12R; CANR 33, 73; DAC; DAM MST; DLB 68; MTCW 1, 2; RGEL 2; RGSF 2

Callimachus c. 305B.C.-c.
240B.C. .... **CMLC 18**
See also AW 1; DLB 176; RGWL 2, 3

Calvin, Jean
See Calvin, John
See also GFL Beginnings to 1789

Calvin, John 1509-1564 .... **LC 37**
See also Calvin, Jean

Calvino, Italo 1923-1985 ..... **CLC 5, 8, 11, 22, 33, 39, 73; SSC 3, 48**
See also CA 85-88; CANR 23, 61; DAM NOV; DLB 196; EW 13; MTCW 1, 2; RGSF 2; RGWL 2, 3; SFW 4; SSFS 12

Camden, William 1551-1623 .... **LC 77**
See also DLB 172

Cameron, Carey 1952- .... **CLC 59**
See also CA 135

Cameron, Peter 1959- .... **CLC 44**
See also CA 125; CANR 50; DLB 234; GLL 2

Camoens, Luis Vaz de 1524(?)-1580
See Camoes, Luis de
See also EW 2

Camoes, Luis de 1524(?)-1580 .... **LC 62; HLCS 1; PC 31**
See also Camoens, Luis Vaz de
See also RGWL 2, 3

Campana, Dino 1885-1932 .... **TCLC 20**
See also DLB 114

Campanella, Tommaso 1568-1639 .... **LC 32**
See also RGWL 2, 3

Campbell, John W(ood, Jr.)
1910-1971 .... **CLC 32**
See also CA 21-22; CANR 34; CAP 2; DLB 8; MTCW 1; SCFW; SFW 4

Campbell, Joseph 1904-1987 .... **CLC 69**
See also AAYA 3; BEST 89:2; CA 1-4R; CANR 3, 28, 61, 107; MTCW 1, 2

Campbell, Maria 1940- .... **CLC 85**
See also CA 102; CANR 54; CCA 1; DAC; NNAL

Campbell, Paul N. 1923-
See hooks, bell
See also CA 21-24R

Campbell, (John) Ramsey 1946- ..... **CLC 42; SSC 19**
See also CA 57-60; CANR 7, 102; DLB 261; HGG; INT CANR-7; SUFW 1, 2

Campbell, (Ignatius) Roy (Dunnachie)
1901-1957 .... **TCLC 5**
See also AFW; CA 155; DLB 20, 225; MTCW 2; RGEL 2

Campbell, Thomas 1777-1844 .... **NCLC 19**
See also DLB 93, 144; RGEL 2

Campbell, Wilfred .... **TCLC 9**
See also Campbell, William

Campbell, William 1858(?)-1918
See Campbell, Wilfred
See also DLB 92

Campion, Jane .... **CLC 95**
See also AAYA 33; CA 138; CANR 87

Campion, Thomas 1567-1620 .... **LC 78**
See also CDBLB Before 1660; DAM POET; DLB 58, 172; RGEL 2

Camus, Albert 1913-1960 ...... **CLC 1, 2, 4, 9, 11, 14, 32, 63, 69, 124; DC 2; SSC 9; WLC**
See also AAYA 36; AFW; BPFB 1; CA 89-92; DA; DAB; DAC; DAM DRAM, MST, NOV; DLB 72; EW 13; EXPN; EXPS; GFL 1789 to the Present; MTCW 1, 2; NFS 6; RGSF 2; RGWL 2, 3; SSFS 4; TWA

Canby, Vincent 1924-2000 .... **CLC 13**
See also CA 81-84

Cancale
See Desnos, Robert

Canetti, Elias 1905-1994 .. **CLC 3, 14, 25, 75, 86**
See also CA 21-24R; CANR 23, 61, 79; CDWLB 2; CWW 2; DLB 85, 124; EW 12; MTCW 1, 2; RGWL 2, 3; TWA

Canfield, Dorothea F.
See Fisher, Dorothy (Frances) Canfield

Canfield, Dorothea Frances
See Fisher, Dorothy (Frances) Canfield

Canfield, Dorothy
See Fisher, Dorothy (Frances) Canfield

Canin, Ethan 1960- .... **CLC 55**
See also CA 135

Cankar, Ivan 1876-1918 .... **TCLC 105**
See also CDWLB 4; DLB 147

Cannon, Curt
See Hunter, Evan

Cao, Lan 1961- .... **CLC 109**
See also CA 165

Cape, Judith
See Page, P(atricia) K(athleen)
See also CCA 1

Capek, Karel 1890-1938 .... **TCLC 6, 37; DC 1; SSC 36; WLC**
See also CA 140; CDWLB 4; DA; DAB; DAC; DAM DRAM, MST, NOV; DFS 7, 11 !**; DLB 215; EW 10; MTCW 1; RGSF 2; RGWL 2, 3; SCFW 2; SFW 4

Capote, Truman 1924-1984 . **CLC 1, 3, 8, 13, 19, 34, 38, 58; SSC 2, 47; WLC**
See also AMWS 3; BPFB 1; CA 5-8R; CANR 18, 62; CDALB 1941-1968; CPW; DA; DAB; DAC; DAM MST, NOV, POP; DLB 2, 185, 227; DLBY 1980, 1984; EXPS; GLL 1; LAIT 3; MTCW 1, 2; NCFS 2; RGAL 4; RGSF 2; SATA 91; SSFS 2; TUS

Capra, Frank 1897-1991 .... **CLC 16**
See also CA 61-64

Caputo, Philip 1941- .... **CLC 32**
See also CA 73-76; CANR 40; YAW

Caragiale, Ion Luca 1852-1912 ...... **TCLC 76**
See also CA 157

Card, Orson Scott 1951- .... **CLC 44, 47, 50**
See also AAYA 11, 42; BPFB 1; BYA 5, 8; CA 102; CANR 27, 47, 73, 102, 106; CPW; DAM POP; FANT; INT CANR-27; MTCW 1, 2; NFS 5; SATA 83, 127; SCFW 2; SFW 4; SUFW 2; YAW

Cardenal, Ernesto 1925- .... **CLC 31, 161; HLC 1; PC 22**
See also CA 49-52; CANR 2, 32, 66; CWW 2; DAM MULT, POET; HW 1, 2; LAWS 1; MTCW 1, 2; RGWL 2, 3

Cardozo, Benjamin N(athan)
1870-1938 .... **TCLC 65**
See also CA 164

Carducci, Giosue (Alessandro Giuseppe)
1835-1907 .... **TCLC 32**
See also CA 163; EW 7; RGWL 2, 3

Carew, Thomas 1595(?)-1640 . **LC 13; PC 29**
See also BRW 2; DLB 126; PAB; RGEL 2

Carey, Ernestine Gilbreth 1908- .... **CLC 17**
See also CA 5-8R; CANR 71; SATA 2

Carey, Peter 1943- .... **CLC 40, 55, 96**
See also CA 127; CANR 53, 76; CN 7; INT CA-127; MTCW 1, 2; RGSF 2; SATA 94

Carleton, William 1794-1869 .... **NCLC 3**
See also DLB 159; RGEL 2; RGSF 2

Carlisle, Henry (Coffin) 1926- .... **CLC 33**
See also CA 13-16R; CANR 15, 85

Carlsen, Chris
See Holdstock, Robert P.

Carlson, Ron(ald F.) 1947- .... **CLC 54**
See also CA 105; CAAE 189; CANR 27; DLB 244

Carlyle, Thomas 1795-1881 ..... **NCLC 22, 70**
See also BRW 4; CDBLB 1789-1832; DA; DAB; DAC; DAM MST; DLB 55, 144, 254; RGEL 2; TEA

Carman, (William) Bliss
1861-1929 .... **TCLC 7; PC 34**
See also CA 152; DAC; DLB 92; RGEL 2

Carnegie, Dale 1888-1955 .... **TCLC 53**

Carossa, Hans 1878-1956 .... **TCLC 48**
See also CA 170; DLB 66

Carpenter, Don(ald Richard)
1931-1995 .... **CLC 41**
See also CA 45-48; CANR 1, 71

Carpenter, Edward 1844-1929 .... **TCLC 88**
See also CA 163; GLL 1

Carpenter, John (Howard) 1948- ... **CLC 161**
See also AAYA 2; CA 134; SATA 58

Carpenter, Johnny
See Carpenter, John (Howard)

Carpentier (y Valmont), Alejo
1904-1980 . **CLC 8, 11, 38, 110; HLC 1; SSC 35**
See also CA 65-68; CANR 11, 70; CDWLB 3; DAM MULT; DLB 113; HW 1, 2; LAW; RGSF 2; RGWL 2, 3; WLIT 1

Carr, Caleb 1955(?)- .... **CLC 86**
See also CA 147; CANR 73

Carr, Emily 1871-1945 .... **TCLC 32**
See also CA 159; DLB 68; FW; GLL 2

Carr, John Dickson 1906-1977 .... **CLC 3**
See also Fairbairn, Roger
See also CA 49-52; CANR 3, 33, 60; CMW 4; MSW; MTCW 1, 2

Carr, Philippa
See Hibbert, Eleanor Alice Burford

Carr, Virginia Spencer 1929- .... **CLC 34**
See also CA 61-64; DLB 111

Carrere, Emmanuel 1957- .... **CLC 89**
See also CA 200

Carrier, Roch 1937- .... **CLC 13, 78**
See also CA 130; CANR 61; CCA 1; DAC; DAM MST; DLB 53; SATA 105

Carroll, James P. 1943(?)- .... **CLC 38**
See also CA 81-84; CANR 73; MTCW 1

Carroll, Jim 1951- .... **CLC 35, 143**
See also AAYA 17; CA 45-48; CANR 42

Carroll, Lewis ... **NCLC 2, 53; PC 18; WLC**
See also Dodgson, Charles L(utwidge)
See also AAYA 39; BRW 5; BYA 5, 13; CDBLB 1832-1890; CLR 2, 18; DLB 18, 163, 178; DLBY 1998; EXPN; EXPP; FANT; JRDA; LAIT 1; NFS 7; PFS 11; RGEL 2; SUFW 1; TEA; WCH

Carroll, Paul Vincent 1900-1968 ...... **CLC 10**
See also CA 9-12R; DLB 10; RGEL 2

Carruth, Hayden 1921- ..... **CLC 4, 7, 10, 18, 84; PC 10**
See also CA 9-12R; CANR 4, 38, 59, 110; CP 7; DLB 5, 165; INT CANR-4; MTCW 1, 2; SATA 47

Carson, Rachel Louise 1907-1964 .... **CLC 71**
See also AMWS 9; ANW; CA 77-80; CANR 35; DAM POP; FW; LAIT 4; MTCW 1, 2; NCFS 1; SATA 23

Carter, Angela (Olive) 1940-1992 ...... **CLC 5, 41, 76; SSC 13**
See also BRWS 3; CA 53-56; CANR 12, 36, 61, 106; DLB 14, 207, 261; EXPS; FANT; FW; MTCW 1, 2; RGSF 2; SATA 66; SATA-Obit 70; SFW 4; SSFS 4, 12; SUFW 2; WLIT 4

Carter, Nick
See Smith, Martin Cruz

Carver, Raymond 1938-1988 ..... **CLC 22, 36, 53, 55, 126; SSC 8, 51**
See also AMWS 3; BPFB 1; CA 33-36R; CANR 17, 34, 61, 103; CPW; DAM NOV; DLB 130; DLBY 1984, 1988; MTCW 1, 2; RGAL 4; RGSF 2; SSFS 3, 6, 12, 13; TCWW 2; TUS

Cary, Elizabeth, Lady Falkland 1585-1639 .... **LC 30**

Cary, (Arthur) Joyce (Lunel) 1888-1957 .... **TCLC 1, 29**
See also BRW 7; CA 164; CDBLB 1914-1945; DLB 15, 100; MTCW 2; RGEL 2; TEA

Casanova de Seingalt, Giovanni Jacopo 1725-1798 .... **LC 13**

Casares, Adolfo Bioy
See Bioy Casares, Adolfo
See also RGSF 2

Casas, Bartolome de las 1474-1566
See Las Casas, Bartolome de
See also WLIT 1

Casely-Hayford, J(oseph) E(phraim) 1866-1903 .... **TCLC 24; BLC 1**
See also BW 2; CA 152; DAM MULT

Casey, John (Dudley) 1939- .... **CLC 59**
See also BEST 90:2; CA 69-72; CANR 23, 100

Casey, Michael 1947- .... **CLC 2**
See also CA 65-68; CANR 109; DLB 5

Casey, Patrick
See Thurman, Wallace (Henry)

Casey, Warren (Peter) 1935-1988 .... **CLC 12**
See also CA 101; INT 101

Casona, Alejandro .... **CLC 49**
See also Alvarez, Alejandro Rodriguez

Cassavetes, John 1929-1989 .... **CLC 20**
See also CA 85-88; CANR 82

Cassian, Nina 1924- .... **PC 17**
See also CWP; CWW 2

Cassill, R(onald) V(erlin) 1919- ... **CLC 4, 23**
See also CA 9-12R; CAAS 1; CANR 7, 45; CN 7; DLB 6, 218

Cassiodorus, Flavius Magnus c. 490(?)-c. 583(?) .... **CMLC 43**

Cassirer, Ernst 1874-1945 .... **TCLC 61**
See also CA 157

Cassity, (Allen) Turner 1929- .... **CLC 6, 42**
See also CA 17-20R; CAAS 8; CANR 11; CSW; DLB 105

Castaneda, Carlos (Cesar Aranha) 1931(?)-1998 .... **CLC 12, 119**
See also CA 25-28R; CANR 32, 66, 105; DNFS 1; HW 1; MTCW 1

Castedo, Elena 1937- .... **CLC 65**
See also CA 132

Castedo-Ellerman, Elena
See Castedo, Elena

Castellanos, Rosario 1925-1974 .... **CLC 66; HLC 1; SSC 39**
See also CA 131; CANR 58; CDWLB 3; DAM MULT; DLB 113; FW; HW 1; LAW; MTCW 1; RGSF 2; RGWL 2, 3

Castelvetro, Lodovico 1505-1571 .... **LC 12**

Castiglione, Baldassare 1478-1529 ...... **LC 12**
See also Castiglione, Baldesar
See also RGWL 2, 3

Castiglione, Baldesar
See Castiglione, Baldassare
See also EW 2

Castillo, Ana (Hernandez Del) 1953- .... **CLC 151**
See also AAYA 42; CA 131; CANR 51, 86; CWP; DLB 122, 227; DNFS 2; FW; HW 1

Castle, Robert
See Hamilton, Edmond

Castro (Ruz), Fidel 1926(?)-
See also CA 129; CANR 81; DAM MULT; HLC 1; HW 2

Castro, Guillen de 1569-1631 .... **LC 19**

Castro, Rosalia de 1837-1885 ... **NCLC 3, 78; PC 41**
See also DAM MULT

Cather, Willa (Sibert) 1873-1947 .... **TCLC 1, 11, 31, 99, 125; SSC 2, 50; WLC**
See also AAYA 24; AMW; AMWR 1; BPFB 1; CA 128; CDALB 1865-1917; DA; DAB; DAC; DAM MST, NOV; DLB 9, 54, 78, 256; DLBD 1; EXPN; EXPS; LAIT 3; MAWW; MTCW 1, 2; NFS 2; RGAL 4; RGSF 2; RHW; SATA 30; SSFS 2, 7; TCWW 2; TUS

Catherine II
See Catherine the Great
See also DLB 150

Catherine the Great 1729-1796 .... **LC 69**
See also Catherine II

Cato, Marcus Porcius 234B.C.-149B.C. .... **CMLC 21**
See also Cato the Elder

Cato, Marcus Porcius, the Elder
See Cato, Marcus Porcius

Cato the Elder
See Cato, Marcus Porcius
See also DLB 211

Catton, (Charles) Bruce 1899-1978 . **CLC 35**
See also AITN 1; CA 5-8R; CANR 7, 74; DLB 17; SATA 2; SATA-Obit 24

Catullus c. 84B.C.-54B.C. .... **CMLC 18**
See also AW 2; CDWLB 1; DLB 211; RGWL 2, 3

Cauldwell, Frank
See King, Francis (Henry)

Caunitz, William J. 1933-1996 .... **CLC 34**
See also BEST 89:3; CA 130; CANR 73; INT 130

Causley, Charles (Stanley) 1917- .... **CLC 7**
See also CA 9-12R; CANR 5, 35, 94; CLR 30; CWRI 5; DLB 27; MTCW 1; SATA 3, 66

Caute, (John) David 1936- .... **CLC 29**
See also CA 1-4R; CAAS 4; CANR 1, 33, 64; CBD; CD 5; CN 7; DAM NOV; DLB 14, 231

Cavafy, C(onstantine) P(eter) ... **TCLC 2, 7; PC 36**
See also Kavafis, Konstantinos Petrou
See also CA 148; DAM POET; EW 8; MTCW 1; RGWL 2, 3; WP

Cavalcanti, Guido c. 1250-c. 1300 .... **CMLC 54**

Cavallo, Evelyn
See Spark, Muriel (Sarah)

Cavanna, Betty .... **CLC 12**
See also Harrison, Elizabeth (Allen) Cavanna
See also JRDA; MAICYA 1; SAAS 4; SATA 1, 30

Cavendish, Margaret Lucas 1623-1673 .... **LC 30**
See also DLB 131, 252; RGEL 2

Caxton, William 1421(?)-1491(?) .... **LC 17**
See also DLB 170

Cayer, D. M.
See Duffy, Maureen

Cayrol, Jean 1911- .... **CLC 11**
See also CA 89-92; DLB 83

Cela, Camilo Jose 1916-2002 .... **CLC 4, 13, 59, 122; HLC 1**
See also BEST 90:2; CA 21-24R; CAAS 10; CANR 21, 32, 76; DAM MULT; DLBY 1989; EW 13; HW 1; MTCW 1, 2; RGSF 2; RGWL 2, 3

Celan, Paul -1970 .... **CLC 10, 19, 53, 82; PC 10**
See also Antschel, Paul
See also CDWLB 2; DLB 69; RGWL 2, 3

Celine, Louis-Ferdinand .. **CLC 1, 3, 4, 7, 9, 15, 47, 124**
See also Destouches, Louis-Ferdinand
See also DLB 72; EW 11; GFL 1789 to the Present; RGWL 2, 3

Cellini, Benvenuto 1500-1571 .... **LC 7**

Cendrars, Blaise .... **CLC 18, 106**
See also Sauser-Hall, Frederic
See also DLB 258; GFL 1789 to the Present; RGWL 2, 3; WP

Centlivre, Susanna 1669(?)-1723 .... **LC 65**
See also DLB 84; RGEL 2

Cernuda (y Bidon), Luis 1902-1963 . **CLC 54**
See also CA 131; DAM POET; DLB 134; GLL 1; HW 1; RGWL 2, 3

Cervantes, Lorna Dee 1954- .... **PC 35**
See also CA 131; CANR 80; CWP; DLB 82; EXPP; HLCS 1; HW 1

Cervantes (Saavedra), Miguel de 1547-1616 .... **LC 6, 23; HLCS; SSC 12; WLC**
See also BYA 1, 14; DA; DAB; DAC; DAM MST, NOV; EW 2; LAIT 1; NFS 8; RGSF 2; RGWL 2, 3; TWA

Cesaire, Aime (Fernand) 1913- . **CLC 19, 32, 112; BLC 1; PC 25**
See also BW 2, 3; CA 65-68; CANR 24, 43, 81; DAM MULT, POET; GFL 1789 to the Present; MTCW 1, 2; WP

Chabon, Michael 1963- .... **CLC 55, 149**
See also AMWS 11; CA 139; CANR 57, 96

Chabrol, Claude 1930- .... **CLC 16**
See also CA 110

Challans, Mary 1905-1983
See Renault, Mary
See also CA 81-84; CANR 74; MTCW 2; SATA 23; SATA-Obit 36; TEA

Challis, George
See Faust, Frederick (Schiller)
See also TCWW 2

Chambers, Aidan 1934- .... **CLC 35**
See also AAYA 27; CA 25-28R; CANR 12, 31, 58; JRDA; MAICYA 1, 2; SAAS 12; SATA 1, 69, 108; WYA; YAW

Chambers, James 1948-
See Cliff, Jimmy

Chambers, Jessie
See Lawrence, D(avid) H(erbert Richards)
See also GLL 1

Chambers, Robert W(illiam)
1865-1933 .... **TCLC 41**
See also CA 165; DLB 202; HGG; SATA 107; SUFW 1

Chambers, (David) Whittaker
1901-1961 .... **TCLC 129**

Chamisso, Adelbert von
1781-1838 .... **NCLC 82**
See also DLB 90; RGWL 2, 3; SUFW 1

Chance, James T.
See Carpenter, John (Howard)

Chance, John T.
See Carpenter, John (Howard)

Chandler, Raymond (Thornton)
1888-1959 .... **TCLC 1, 7; SSC 23**
See also AAYA 25; AMWS 4; BPFB 1; CA 129; CANR 60, 107; CDALB 1929-1941; CMW 4; DLB 226, 253; DLBD 6; MSW; MTCW 1, 2; RGAL 4; TUS

Chang, Eileen 1921-1995 .... **SSC 28**
See also CA 166; CWW 2

Chang, Jung 1952- .... **CLC 71**
See also CA 142

Chang Ai-Ling
See Chang, Eileen

Channing, William Ellery
1780-1842 .... **NCLC 17**
See also DLB 1, 59, 235; RGAL 4

Chao, Patricia 1955- .... **CLC 119**
See also CA 163

Chaplin, Charles Spencer
1889-1977 .... **CLC 16**
See also Chaplin, Charlie
See also CA 81-84

Chaplin, Charlie
See Chaplin, Charles Spencer
See also DLB 44

Chapman, George 1559(?)-1634 .... **LC 22**
See also BRW 1; DAM DRAM; DLB 62, 121; RGEL 2

Chapman, Graham 1941-1989 .... **CLC 21**
See also Monty Python
See also CA 116; CANR 35, 95

Chapman, John Jay 1862-1933 .... **TCLC 7**
See also CA 191

Chapman, Lee
See Bradley, Marion Zimmer
See also GLL 1

Chapman, Walker
See Silverberg, Robert

Chappell, Fred (Davis) 1936- .... **CLC 40, 78, 162**
See also CA 5-8R; CAAE 198; CAAS 4; CANR 8, 33, 67, 110; CN 7; CP 7; CSW; DLB 6, 105; HGG

Char, Rene(-Emile) 1907-1988 .... **CLC 9, 11, 14, 55**
See also CA 13-16R; CANR 32; DAM POET; DLB 258; GFL 1789 to the Present; MTCW 1, 2; RGWL 2, 3

Charby, Jay
See Ellison, Harlan (Jay)

Chardin, Pierre Teilhard de
See Teilhard de Chardin, (Marie Joseph) Pierre

Chariton fl. 1st cent. (?)- .... **CMLC 49**

Charlemagne 742-814 .... **CMLC 37**

Charles I 1600-1649 .... **LC 13**

Charriere, Isabelle de 1740-1805 .. **NCLC 66**

Chartier, Emile-Auguste
See Alain

Charyn, Jerome 1937- .... **CLC 5, 8, 18**
See also CA 5-8R; CAAS 1; CANR 7, 61, 101; CMW 4; CN 7; DLBY 1983; MTCW 1

Chase, Adam
See Marlowe, Stephen

Chase, Mary (Coyle) 1907-1981 .... **DC 1**
See also CA 77-80; CAD; CWD; DFS 11; DLB 228; SATA 17; SATA-Obit 29

Chase, Mary Ellen 1887-1973 .... **CLC 2**
See also CA 13-16; CAP 1; SATA 10; TCLC 124

Chase, Nicholas
See Hyde, Anthony
See also CCA 1

Chateaubriand, Francois Rene de
1768-1848 .... **NCLC 3**
See also DLB 119; EW 5; GFL 1789 to the Present; RGWL 2, 3; TWA

Chatterje, Sarat Chandra 1876-1936(?)
See Chatterji, Saratchandra

Chatterji, Bankim Chandra
1838-1894 .... **NCLC 19**

Chatterji, Saratchandra .... **TCLC 13**
See also Chatterje, Sarat Chandra
See also CA 186

Chatterton, Thomas 1752-1770 .... **LC 3, 54**
See also DAM POET; DLB 109; RGEL 2

Chatwin, (Charles) Bruce
1940-1989 .... **CLC 28, 57, 59**
See also AAYA 4; BEST 90:1; BRWS 4; CA 85-88; CPW; DAM POP; DLB 194, 204

Chaucer, Daniel
See Ford, Ford Madox
See also RHW

Chaucer, Geoffrey 1340(?)-1400 .. **LC 17, 56; PC 19; WLCS**
See also BRW 1; BRWR 2; CDBLB Before 1660; DA; DAB; DAC; DAM MST, POET; DLB 146; LAIT 1; PAB; PFS 14; RGEL 2; TEA; WLIT 3; WP

Chavez, Denise (Elia) 1948-
See also CA 131; CANR 56, 81; DAM MULT; DLB 122; FW; HLC 1; HW 1, 2; MTCW 2

Chaviaras, Strates 1935-
See Haviaras, Stratis
See also CA 105

Chayefsky, Paddy .... **CLC 23**
See also Chayefsky, Sidney
See also CAD; DLB 7, 44; DLBY 1981; RGAL 4

Chayefsky, Sidney 1923-1981
See Chayefsky, Paddy
See also CA 9-12R; CANR 18; DAM DRAM

Chedid, Andree 1920- .... **CLC 47**
See also CA 145; CANR 95

Cheever, John 1912-1982 ..... **CLC 3, 7, 8, 11, 15, 25, 64; SSC 1, 38; WLC**
See also AMWS 1; BPFB 1; CA 5-8R; CABS 1; CANR 5, 27, 76; CDALB 1941-1968; CPW; DA; DAB; DAC; DAM MST, NOV, POP; DLB 2, 102, 227; DLBY 1980, 1982; EXPS; INT CANR-5; MTCW 1, 2; RGAL 4; RGSF 2; SSFS 2, 14; TUS

Cheever, Susan 1943- .... **CLC 18, 48**
See also CA 103; CANR 27, 51, 92; DLBY 1982; INT CANR-27

Chekhonte, Antosha
See Chekhov, Anton (Pavlovich)

Chekhov, Anton (Pavlovich)
1860-1904 . **TCLC 3, 10, 31, 55, 96; DC 9; SSC 2, 28, 41, 51; WLC**
See also BYA 14; CA 124; DA; DAB; DAC; DAM DRAM, MST; DFS 1, 5, 10, 12; EW 7; EXPS; LAIT 3; RGSF 2; RGWL 2, 3; SATA 90; SSFS 5, 13, 14; TWA

Cheney, Lynne V. 1941- .... **CLC 70**
See also CA 89-92; CANR 58

Chernyshevsky, Nikolai Gavrilovich
See Chernyshevsky, Nikolay Gavrilovich
See also DLB 238

Chernyshevsky, Nikolay Gavrilovich
1828-1889 .... **NCLC 1**
See also Chernyshevsky, Nikolai Gavrilovich

Cherry, Carolyn Janice 1942-
See Cherryh, C. J.
See also CA 65-68; CANR 10

Cherryh, C. J. .... **CLC 35**
See also Cherry, Carolyn Janice
See also AAYA 24; BPFB 1; DLBY 1980; FANT; SATA 93; SCFW 2; SFW 4; YAW

Chesnutt, Charles W(addell)
1858-1932 .... **TCLC 5, 39; BLC 1; SSC 7, 54**
See also AFAW 1, 2; BW 1, 3; CA 125; CANR 76; DAM MULT; DLB 12, 50, 78; MTCW 1, 2; RGAL 4; RGSF 2; SSFS 11

Chester, Alfred 1929(?)-1971 .... **CLC 49**
See also CA 196; DLB 130

Chesterton, G(ilbert) K(eith)
1874-1936 . **TCLC 1, 6, 64; PC 28; SSC 1, 46**
See also BRW 6; CA 132; CANR 73; CD-BLB 1914-1945; CMW 4; DAM NOV, POET; DLB 10, 19, 34, 70, 98, 149, 178; FANT; MSW; MTCW 1, 2; RGEL 2; RGSF 2; SATA 27; SUFW 1

Chiang, Pin-chin 1904-1986
See Ding Ling

Ch'ien, Chung-shu 1910-1998 .... **CLC 22**
See also CA 130; CANR 73; MTCW 1, 2

Chikamatsu Monzaemon 1653-1724 ... **LC 66**
See also RGWL 2, 3

Child, L. Maria
See Child, Lydia Maria

Child, Lydia Maria 1802-1880 .. **NCLC 6, 73**
See also DLB 1, 74, 243; RGAL 4; SATA 67

Child, Mrs.
See Child, Lydia Maria

Child, Philip 1898-1978 .... **CLC 19, 68**
See also CA 13-14; CAP 1; DLB 68; RHW; SATA 47

Childers, (Robert) Erskine
1870-1922 .... **TCLC 65**
See also CA 153; DLB 70

Childress, Alice 1920-1994 .. **CLC 12, 15, 86, 96; BLC 1; DC 4**
See also AAYA 8; BW 2, 3; BYA 2; CA 45-48; CAD; CANR 3, 27, 50, 74; CLR 14; CWD; DAM DRAM, MULT, NOV; DFS

2, 8, 14; DLB 7, 38, 249; JRDA; LAIT 5; MAICYA 1, 2; MAICYAS 1; MTCW 1, 2; RGAL 4; SATA 7, 48, 81; TCLC 116; TUS; WYA; YAW

Chin, Frank (Chew, Jr.) 1940-...... CLC 135; DC 7
See also CA 33-36R; CANR 71; CD 5; DAM MULT; DLB 206; LAIT 5; RGAL 4

Chin, Marilyn (Mei Ling) 1955-......... PC 40
See also CA 129; CANR 70, 113; CWP

Chislett, (Margaret) Anne 1943-...... CLC 34
See also CA 151

Chitty, Thomas Willes 1926-............. CLC 11
See also Hinde, Thomas
See also CA 5-8R; CN 7

Chivers, Thomas Holley 1809-1858..................... NCLC 49
See also DLB 3, 248; RGAL 4

Choi, Susan .... CLC 119

Chomette, Rene Lucien 1898-1981
See Clair, Rene

Chomsky, (Avram) Noam 1928-..... CLC 132
See also CA 17-20R; CANR 28, 62, 110; DLB 246; MTCW 1, 2

Chopin, Kate ..... TCLC 127; SSC 8; WLCS
See also Chopin, Katherine
See also AAYA 33; AMWS 1; CDALB 1865-1917; DA; DAB; DLB 12, 78; EXPN; EXPS; FW; LAIT 3; MAWW; NFS 3; RGAL 4; RGSF 2; SSFS 2, 13; TUS

Chopin, Katherine 1851-1904
See Chopin, Kate
See also CA 122; DAC; DAM MST, NOV

Chretien de Troyes c. 12th cent. - . CMLC 10
See also DLB 208; EW 1; RGWL 2, 3; TWA

Christie
See Ichikawa, Kon

Christie, Agatha (Mary Clarissa) 1890-1976 .. CLC 1, 6, 8, 12, 39, 48, 110
See also AAYA 9; AITN 1, 2; BPFB 1; BRWS 2; CA 17-20R; CANR 10, 37, 108; CBD; CDBLB 1914-1945; CMW 4; CPW; CWD; DAB; DAC; DAM NOV; DFS 2; DLB 13, 77, 245; MSW; MTCW 1, 2; NFS 8; RGEL 2; RHW; SATA 36; TEA; YAW

Christie, Philippa .... CLC 21
See also Pearce, Philippa
See also BYA 5; CANR 109; CLR 9; DLB 161; MAICYA 1; SATA 1, 67, 129

Christine de Pizan 1365(?)-1431(?) .... LC 9
See also DLB 208; RGWL 2, 3

Chubb, Elmer
See Masters, Edgar Lee

Chulkov, Mikhail Dmitrievich 1743-1792 .... LC 2
See also DLB 150

Churchill, Caryl 1938- .... CLC 31, 55, 157; DC 5
See also BRWS 4; CA 102; CANR 22, 46, 108; CBD; CWD; DFS 12; DLB 13; FW; MTCW 1; RGEL 2

Churchill, Charles 1731-1764 .... LC 3
See also DLB 109; RGEL 2

Churchill, Sir Winston (Leonard Spencer) 1874-1965 .... TCLC 113
See also BRW 6; CA 97-100; CDBLB 1890-1914; DLB 100; DLBD 16; LAIT 4; MTCW 1, 2

Chute, Carolyn 1947- .... CLC 39
See also CA 123

Ciardi, John (Anthony) 1916-1986 . CLC 10, 40, 44, 129
See also CA 5-8R; CAAS 2; CANR 5, 33; CLR 19; CWRI 5; DAM POET; DLB 5; DLBY 1986; INT CANR-5; MAICYA 1, 2; MTCW 1, 2; RGAL 4; SAAS 26; SATA 1, 65; SATA-Obit 46

Cibber, Colley 1671-1757 .... LC 66
See also DLB 84; RGEL 2

Cicero, Marcus Tullius 106B.C.-43B.C. .... CMLC 3
See also AW 1; CDWLB 1; DLB 211; RGWL 2, 3

Cimino, Michael 1943- .... CLC 16
See also CA 105

Cioran, E(mil) M. 1911-1995 .... CLC 64
See also CA 25-28R; CANR 91; DLB 220

Cisneros, Sandra 1954- .. CLC 69, 118; HLC 1; SSC 32
See also AAYA 9; AMWS 7; CA 131; CANR 64; CWP; DAM MULT; DLB 122, 152; EXPN; FW; HW 1, 2; LAIT 5; MAICYA 2; MTCW 2; NFS 2; RGAL 4; RGSF 2; SSFS 3, 13; WLIT 1; YAW

Cixous, Helene 1937- .... CLC 92
See also CA 126; CANR 55; CWW 2; DLB 83, 242; FW; GLL 2; MTCW 1, 2; TWA

Clair, Rene .... CLC 20
See also Chomette, Rene Lucien

Clampitt, Amy 1920-1994 .... CLC 32; PC 19
See also AMWS 9; CA 110; CANR 29, 79; DLB 105

Clancy, Thomas L., Jr. 1947-
See Clancy, Tom
See also CA 131; CANR 62, 105; INT CA-131; MTCW 1, 2

Clancy, Tom .... CLC 45, 112
See also Clancy, Thomas L., Jr.
See also AAYA 9; BEST 89:1, 90:1; BPFB 1; BYA 10, 11; CMW 4; CPW; DAM NOV, POP; DLB 227

Clare, John 1793-1864 .. NCLC 9, 86; PC 23
See also DAB; DAM POET; DLB 55, 96; RGEL 2

Clarin
See Alas (y Urena), Leopoldo (Enrique Garcia)

Clark, Al C.
See Goines, Donald

Clark, (Robert) Brian 1932- .... CLC 29
See also CA 41-44R; CANR 67; CBD; CD 5

Clark, Curt
See Westlake, Donald E(dwin)

Clark, Eleanor 1913-1996 .... CLC 5, 19
See also CA 9-12R; CANR 41; CN 7; DLB 6

Clark, J. P.
See Clark Bekederemo, J(ohnson) P(epper)
See also CDWLB 3; DLB 117

Clark, John Pepper
See Clark Bekederemo, J(ohnson) P(epper)
See also AFW; CD 5; CP 7; RGEL 2

Clark, M. R.
See Clark, Mavis Thorpe

Clark, Mavis Thorpe 1909-1999 ...... CLC 12
See also CA 57-60; CANR 8, 37, 107; CLR 30; CWRI 5; MAICYA 1, 2; SAAS 5; SATA 8, 74

Clark, Walter Van Tilburg 1909-1971 .... CLC 28
See also CA 9-12R; CANR 63, 113; DLB 9, 206; LAIT 2; RGAL 4; SATA 8

Clark Bekederemo, J(ohnson) P(epper) 1935- .... CLC 38; BLC 1; DC 5
See also Clark, J. P.; Clark, John Pepper
See also AFW; CA 65-68; CANR 16, 72; DAM DRAM, MULT; DFS 13; MTCW 1

Clarke, Arthur C(harles) 1917- .... CLC 1, 4, 13, 18, 35, 136; SSC 3
See also AAYA 4, 33; BPFB 1; BYA 13; CA 1-4R; CANR 2, 28, 55, 74; CN 7; CPW; DAM POP; DLB 261; JRDA; LAIT 5; MAICYA 1, 2; MTCW 1, 2; SATA 13, 70, 115; SCFW; SFW 4; SSFS 4; YAW

Clarke, Austin 1896-1974 .... CLC 6, 9
See also CA 29-32; CAP 2; DAM POET; DLB 10, 20; RGEL 2

Clarke, Austin C(hesterfield) 1934- .. CLC 8, 53; BLC 1; SSC 45
See also BW 1; CA 25-28R; CAAS 16; CANR 14, 32, 68; CN 7; DAC; DAM MULT; DLB 53, 125; DNFS 2; RGSF 2

Clarke, Gillian 1937- .... CLC 61
See also CA 106; CP 7; CWP; DLB 40

Clarke, Marcus (Andrew Hislop) 1846-1881 .... NCLC 19
See also DLB 230; RGEL 2; RGSF 2

Clarke, Shirley 1925-1997 .... CLC 16
See also CA 189

Clash, The
See Headon, (Nicky) Topper; Jones, Mick; Simonon, Paul; Strummer, Joe

Claudel, Paul (Louis Charles Marie) 1868-1955 .... TCLC 2, 10
See also CA 165; DLB 192, 258; EW 8; GFL 1789 to the Present; RGWL 2, 3; TWA

Claudian 370(?)-404(?) .... CMLC 46
See also RGWL 2, 3

Claudius, Matthias 1740-1815 .... NCLC 75
See also DLB 97

Clavell, James (duMaresq) 1925-1994 .... CLC 6, 25, 87
See also BPFB 1; CA 25-28R; CANR 26, 48; CPW; DAM NOV, POP; MTCW 1, 2; NFS 10; RHW

Clayman, Gregory .... CLC 65

Cleaver, (Leroy) Eldridge 1935-1998 .... CLC 30, 119; BLC 1
See also BW 1, 3; CA 21-24R; CANR 16, 75; DAM MULT; MTCW 2; YAW

Cleese, John (Marwood) 1939- .... CLC 21
See also Monty Python
See also CA 116; CANR 35; MTCW 1

Cleishbotham, Jebediah
See Scott, Sir Walter

Cleland, John 1710-1789 .... LC 2, 48
See also DLB 39; RGEL 2

Clemens, Samuel Langhorne 1835-1910
See Twain, Mark
See also CA 135; CDALB 1865-1917; DA; DAB; DAC; DAM MST, NOV; DLB 12, 23, 64, 74, 186, 189; JRDA; MAICYA 1, 2; NCFS 4; SATA 100; YABC 2

Clement of Alexandria 150(?)-215(?) .... CMLC 41

Cleophil
See Congreve, William

Clerihew, E.
See Bentley, E(dmund) C(lerihew)

Clerk, N. W.
See Lewis, C(live) S(taples)

Cliff, Jimmy .... CLC 21
See also Chambers, James
See also CA 193

Cliff, Michelle 1946- .... CLC 120; BLCS
See also BW 2; CA 116; CANR 39, 72; CDWLB 3; DLB 157; FW; GLL 2

Clifford, Lady Anne 1590-1676 .... LC 76
See also DLB 151

Clifton, (Thelma) Lucille 1936- . CLC 19, 66, 162; BLC 1; PC 17
See also AFAW 2; BW 2, 3; CA 49-52; CANR 2, 24, 42, 76, 97; CLR 5; CP 7; CSW; CWP; CWRI 5; DAM MULT, POET; DLB 5, 41; EXPP; MAICYA 1, 2; MTCW 1, 2; PFS 1, 14; SATA 20, 69, 128; WP

Clinton, Dirk
See Silverberg, Robert

Clough, Arthur Hugh 1819-1861 ... NCLC 27
See also BRW 5; DLB 32; RGEL 2

Clutha, Janet Paterson Frame 1924-
See Frame, Janet
See also CA 1-4R; CANR 2, 36, 76; MTCW 1, 2; SATA 119

Clyne, Terence
See Blatty, William Peter

Cobalt, Martin
See Mayne, William (James Carter)

Cobb, Irvin S(hrewsbury)
1876-1944 .... **TCLC 77**
See also CA 175; DLB 11, 25, 86

Cobbett, William 1763-1835 .... **NCLC 49**
See also DLB 43, 107, 158; RGEL 2

Coburn, D(onald) L(ee) 1938- .... **CLC 10**
See also CA 89-92

Cocteau, Jean (Maurice Eugene Clement)
1889-1963 ...... **CLC 1, 8, 15, 16, 43; DC 17; WLC**
See also CA 25-28; CANR 40; CAP 2; DA; DAB; DAC; DAM DRAM, MST, NOV; DLB 65, 258; EW 10; GFL 1789 to the Present; MTCW 1, 2; RGWL 2, 3; TCLC 119; TWA

Codrescu, Andrei 1946- .... **CLC 46, 121**
See also CA 33-36R; CAAS 19; CANR 13, 34, 53, 76; DAM POET; MTCW 2

Coe, Max
See Bourne, Randolph S(illiman)

Coe, Tucker
See Westlake, Donald E(dwin)

Coen, Ethan 1958- .... **CLC 108**
See also CA 126; CANR 85

Coen, Joel 1955- .... **CLC 108**
See also CA 126

The Coen Brothers
See Coen, Ethan; Coen, Joel

Coetzee, J(ohn) M(ichael) 1940- ...... **CLC 23, 33, 66, 117, 161, 162**
See also AAYA 37; AFW; BRWS 6; CA 77-80; CANR 41, 54, 74; CN 7; DAM NOV; DLB 225; MTCW 1, 2; WLIT 2

Coffey, Brian
See Koontz, Dean R(ay)

Coffin, Robert P(eter) Tristram
1892-1955 .... **TCLC 95**
See also CA 169; DLB 45

Cohan, George M(ichael)
1878-1942 .... **TCLC 60**
See also CA 157; DLB 249; RGAL 4

Cohen, Arthur A(llen) 1928-1986 ...... **CLC 7, 31**
See also CA 1-4R; CANR 1, 17, 42; DLB 28

Cohen, Leonard (Norman) 1934- ...... **CLC 3, 38**
See also CA 21-24R; CANR 14, 69; CN 7; CP 7; DAC; DAM MST; DLB 53; MTCW 1

Cohen, Matt(hew) 1942-1999 .... **CLC 19**
See also CA 61-64; CAAS 18; CANR 40; CN 7; DAC; DLB 53

Cohen-Solal, Annie 19(?)- .... **CLC 50**

Colegate, Isabel 1931- .... **CLC 36**
See also CA 17-20R; CANR 8, 22, 74; CN 7; DLB 14, 231; INT CANR-22; MTCW 1

Coleman, Emmett
See Reed, Ishmael

Coleridge, Hartley 1796-1849 .... **NCLC 90**
See also DLB 96

Coleridge, M. E.
See Coleridge, Mary E(lizabeth)

Coleridge, Mary E(lizabeth)
1861-1907 .... **TCLC 73**
See also CA 166; DLB 19, 98

Coleridge, Samuel Taylor
1772-1834 ...... **NCLC 9, 54, 99, 111; PC 11, 39; WLC**
See also BRW 4; BRWR 2; BYA 4; CDBLB 1789-1832; DA; DAB; DAC; DAM MST, POET; DLB 93, 107; EXPP; PAB; PFS 4, 5; RGEL 2; TEA; WLIT 3; WP

Coleridge, Sara 1802-1852 .... **NCLC 31**
See also DLB 199

Coles, Don 1928- .... **CLC 46**
See also CA 115; CANR 38; CP 7

Coles, Robert (Martin) 1929- .... **CLC 108**
See also CA 45-48; CANR 3, 32, 66, 70; INT CANR-32; SATA 23

Colette, (Sidonie-Gabrielle)
1873-1954 .... **TCLC 1, 5, 16; SSC 10**
See also Willy, Colette
See also CA 131; DAM NOV; DLB 65; EW 9; GFL 1789 to the Present; MTCW 1, 2; RGWL 2, 3; TWA

Collett, (Jacobine) Camilla (Wergeland)
1813-1895 .... **NCLC 22**

Collier, Christopher 1930- .... **CLC 30**
See also AAYA 13; BYA 2; CA 33-36R; CANR 13, 33, 102; JRDA; MAICYA 1, 2; SATA 16, 70; WYA; YAW 1

Collier, James Lincoln 1928- .... **CLC 30**
See also AAYA 13; BYA 2; CA 9-12R; CANR 4, 33, 60, 102; CLR 3; DAM POP; JRDA; MAICYA 1, 2; SAAS 21; SATA 8, 70; WYA; YAW 1

Collier, Jeremy 1650-1726 .... **LC 6**

Collier, John 1901-1980 . **TCLC 127; SSC 19**
See also CA 65-68; CANR 10; DLB 77, 255; FANT; SUFW 1

Collingwood, R(obin) G(eorge)
1889(?)-1943 .... **TCLC 67**
See also CA 155; DLB 262

Collins, Hunt
See Hunter, Evan

Collins, Linda 1931- .... **CLC 44**
See also CA 125

Collins, (William) Wilkie
1824-1889 .... **NCLC 1, 18, 93**
See also BRWS 6; CDBLB 1832-1890; CMW 4; DLB 18, 70, 159; MSW; RGEL 2; RGSF 2; SUFW 1; WLIT 4

Collins, William 1721-1759 .... **LC 4, 40**
See also BRW 3; DAM POET; DLB 109; RGEL 2

Collodi, Carlo .... **NCLC 54**
See also Lorenzini, Carlo
See also CLR 5; WCH

Colman, George
See Glassco, John

Colonna, Vittoria 1492-1547 .... **LC 71**
See also RGWL 2, 3

Colt, Winchester Remington
See Hubbard, L(afayette) Ron(ald)

Colter, Cyrus J. 1910-2002 .... **CLC 58**
See also BW 1; CA 65-68; CANR 10, 66; CN 7; DLB 33

Colton, James
See Hansen, Joseph
See also GLL 1

Colum, Padraic 1881-1972 .... **CLC 28**
See also BYA 4; CA 73-76; CANR 35; CLR 36; CWRI 5; DLB 19; MAICYA 1, 2; MTCW 1; RGEL 2; SATA 15; WCH

Colvin, James
See Moorcock, Michael (John)

Colwin, Laurie (E.) 1944-1992 .... **CLC 5, 13, 23, 84**
See also CA 89-92; CANR 20, 46; DLB 218; DLBY 1980; MTCW 1

Comfort, Alex(ander) 1920-2000 .... **CLC 7**
See also CA 1-4R; CANR 1, 45; CP 7; DAM POP; MTCW 1

Comfort, Montgomery
See Campbell, (John) Ramsey

Compton-Burnett, I(vy)
1892(?)-1969 .... **CLC 1, 3, 10, 15, 34**
See also BRW 7; CA 1-4R; CANR 4; DAM NOV; DLB 36; MTCW 1; RGEL 2

Comstock, Anthony 1844-1915 .... **TCLC 13**
See also CA 169

Comte, Auguste 1798-1857 .... **NCLC 54**

Conan Doyle, Arthur
See Doyle, Sir Arthur Conan
See also BPFB 1; BYA 4, 5, 11

Conde (Abellan), Carmen 1901-1996
See also CA 177; DLB 108; HLCS 1; HW 2

Conde, Maryse 1937- ..... **CLC 52, 92; BLCS**
See also BW 2, 3; CA 110; CAAE 190; CANR 30, 53, 76; CWW 2; DAM MULT; MTCW 1

Condillac, Etienne Bonnot de
1714-1780 .... **LC 26**

Condon, Richard (Thomas)
1915-1996 .... **CLC 4, 6, 8, 10, 45, 100**
See also BEST 90:3; BPFB 1; CA 1-4R; CAAS 1; CANR 2, 23; CMW 4; CN 7; DAM NOV; INT CANR-23; MTCW 1, 2

Confucius 551B.C.-479B.C. .... **CMLC 19; WLCS**
See also DA; DAB; DAC; DAM MST

Congreve, William 1670-1729 . **LC 5, 21; DC 2; WLC**
See also BRW 2; CDBLB 1660-1789; DA; DAB; DAC; DAM DRAM, MST, POET; DFS 15; DLB 39, 84; RGEL 2; WLIT 3

Connell, Evan S(helby), Jr. 1924- . **CLC 4, 6, 45**
See also AAYA 7; CA 1-4R; CAAS 2; CANR 2, 39, 76, 97; CN 7; DAM NOV; DLB 2; DLBY 1981; MTCW 1, 2

Connelly, Marc(us Cook) 1890-1980 . **CLC 7**
See also CA 85-88; CANR 30; DFS 12; DLB 7; DLBY 1980; RGAL 4; SATA-Obit 25

Connor, Ralph .... **TCLC 31**
See also Gordon, Charles William
See also DLB 92; TCWW 2

Conrad, Joseph 1857-1924 .... **TCLC 1, 6, 13, 25, 43, 57; SSC 9; WLC**
See also AAYA 26; BPFB 1; BRW 6; BRWR 2; BYA 2; CA 131; CANR 60; CDBLB 1890-1914; DA; DAB; DAC; DAM MST, NOV; DLB 10, 34, 98, 156; EXPN; EXPS; LAIT 2; MTCW 1, 2; NFS 2; RGEL 2; RGSF 2; SATA 27; SSFS 1, 12; TEA; WLIT 4

Conrad, Robert Arnold
See Hart, Moss

Conroy, (Donald) Pat(rick) 1945- ... **CLC 30, 74**
See also AAYA 8; AITN 1; BPFB 1; CA 85-88; CANR 24, 53; CPW; CSW; DAM NOV, POP; DLB 6; LAIT 5; MTCW 1, 2

Constant (de Rebecque), (Henri) Benjamin
1767-1830 .... **NCLC 6**
See also DLB 119; EW 4; GFL 1789 to the Present

Conway, Jill K(er) 1934- .... **CLC 152**
See also CA 130; CANR 94

Conybeare, Charles Augustus
See Eliot, T(homas) S(tearns)

Cook, Michael 1933-1994 .... **CLC 58**
See also CA 93-96; CANR 68; DLB 53

Cook, Robin 1940- .... **CLC 14**
See also AAYA 32; BEST 90:2; BPFB 1; CA 111; CANR 41, 90, 109; CPW; DAM POP; HGG; INT CA-111

Cook, Roy
See Silverberg, Robert

Cooke, Elizabeth 1948- .... **CLC 55**
See also CA 129

Cooke, John Esten 1830-1886 .... **NCLC 5**
See also DLB 3, 248; RGAL 4

Cooke, John Estes
See Baum, L(yman) Frank

Cooke, M. E.
See Creasey, John

Cooke, Margaret
See Creasey, John

Cooke, Rose Terry 1827-1892 ...... **NCLC 110**
See also DLB 12, 74

Cook-Lynn, Elizabeth 1930- .... **CLC 93**
See also CA 133; DAM MULT; DLB 175; NNAL

Cooney, Ray .... **CLC 62**
See also CBD

Cooper, Douglas 1960- .... **CLC 86**

Cooper, Henry St. John
See Creasey, John

Cooper, J(oan) California (?)- .... **CLC 56**
See also AAYA 12; BW 1; CA 125; CANR 55; DAM MULT; DLB 212

Cooper, James Fenimore
1789-1851 .... **NCLC 1, 27, 54**
See also AAYA 22; AMW; BPFB 1; CDALB 1640-1865; DLB 3, 183, 250, 254; LAIT 1; NFS 9; RGAL 4; SATA 19; TUS; WCH

Coover, Robert (Lowell) 1932- ...... **CLC 3, 7, 15, 32, 46, 87, 161; SSC 15**
See also AMWS 5; BPFB 1; CA 45-48; CANR 3, 37, 58; CN 7; DAM NOV; DLB 2, 227; DLBY 1981; MTCW 1, 2; RGAL 4; RGSF 2

Copeland, Stewart (Armstrong)
1952- .... **CLC 26**

Copernicus, Nicolaus 1473-1543 .... **LC 45**

Coppard, A(lfred) E(dgar)
1878-1957 .... **TCLC 5; SSC 21**
See also BRWS 8; CA 167; DLB 162; HGG; RGEL 2; RGSF 2; SUFW 1; YABC 1

Coppee, Francois 1842-1908 .... **TCLC 25**
See also CA 170; DLB 217

Coppola, Francis Ford 1939- ... **CLC 16, 126**
See also AAYA 39; CA 77-80; CANR 40, 78; DLB 44

Corbiere, Tristan 1845-1875 .... **NCLC 43**
See also DLB 217; GFL 1789 to the Present

Corcoran, Barbara (Asenath)
1911- .... **CLC 17**
See also AAYA 14; CA 21-24R; CAAE 191; CAAS 2; CANR 11, 28, 48; CLR 50; DLB 52; JRDA; MAICYA 2; MAICYAS 1; RHW; SAAS 20; SATA 3, 77, 125

Cordelier, Maurice
See Giraudoux, Jean(-Hippolyte)

Corelli, Marie .... **TCLC 51**
See also Mackay, Mary
See also DLB 34, 156; RGEL 2; SUFW 1

Corman, Cid .... **CLC 9**
See also Corman, Sidney
See also CAAS 2; DLB 5, 193

Corman, Sidney 1924-
See Corman, Cid
See also CA 85-88; CANR 44; CP 7; DAM POET

Cormier, Robert (Edmund)
1925-2000 .... **CLC 12, 30**
See also AAYA 3, 19; BYA 1, 2, 6, 8, 9; CA 1-4R; CANR 5, 23, 76, 93; CDALB 1968-1988; CLR 12, 55; DA; DAB; DAC; DAM MST, NOV; DLB 52; EXPN; INT CANR-23; JRDA; LAIT 5; MAICYA 1, 2; MTCW 1, 2; NFS 2; SATA 10, 45, 83; SATA-Obit 122; WYA; YAW

Corn, Alfred (DeWitt III) 1943- .... **CLC 33**
See also CA 179; CAAE 179; CAAS 25; CANR 44; CP 7; CSW; DLB 120; DLBY 1980

Corneille, Pierre 1606-1684 .... **LC 28**
See also DAB; DAM MST; DLB 268; EW 3; GFL Beginnings to 1789; RGWL 2, 3; TWA

Cornwell, David (John Moore)
1931- .... **CLC 9, 15**
See also le Carre, John
See also CA 5-8R; CANR 13, 33, 59, 107; DAM POP; MTCW 1, 2

Cornwell, Patricia (Daniels) 1956- . **CLC 155**
See also AAYA 16; BPFB 1; CA 134; CANR 53; CMW 4; CPW; CSW; DAM POP; MSW; MTCW 1

Corso, (Nunzio) Gregory 1930-2001 . **CLC 1, 11; PC 33**
See also CA 5-8R; CANR 41, 76; CP 7; DLB 5, 16, 237; MTCW 1, 2; WP

Cortazar, Julio 1914-1984 ... **CLC 2, 3, 5, 10, 13, 15, 33, 34, 92; HLC 1; SSC 7**
See also BPFB 1; CA 21-24R; CANR 12, 32, 81; CDWLB 3; DAM MULT, NOV; DLB 113; EXPS; HW 1, 2; LAW; MTCW 1, 2; RGSF 2; RGWL 2, 3; SSFS 3; TWA; WLIT 1

Cortes, Hernan 1485-1547 .... **LC 31**

Corvinus, Jakob
See Raabe, Wilhelm (Karl)

Corvo, Baron
See Rolfe, Frederick (William Serafino Austin Lewis Mary)
See also GLL 1; RGEL 2

Corwin, Cecil
See Kornbluth, C(yril) M.

Cosic, Dobrica 1921- .... **CLC 14**
See also CA 138; CDWLB 4; CWW 2; DLB 181

Costain, Thomas B(ertram)
1885-1965 .... **CLC 30**
See also BYA 3; CA 5-8R; DLB 9; RHW

Costantini, Humberto 1924(?)-1987 . **CLC 49**
See also CA 131; HW 1

Costello, Elvis 1954- .... **CLC 21**
See also CA 204

Costenoble, Philostene
See Ghelderode, Michel de

Cotes, Cecil V.
See Duncan, Sara Jeannette

Cotter, Joseph Seamon Sr.
1861-1949 .... **TCLC 28; BLC 1**
See also BW 1; CA 124; DAM MULT; DLB 50

Couch, Arthur Thomas Quiller
See Quiller-Couch, Sir Arthur (Thomas)

Coulton, James
See Hansen, Joseph

Couperus, Louis (Marie Anne)
1863-1923 .... **TCLC 15**
See also RGWL 2, 3

Coupland, Douglas 1961- .... **CLC 85, 133**
See also AAYA 34; CA 142; CANR 57, 90; CCA 1; CPW; DAC; DAM POP

Court, Wesli
See Turco, Lewis (Putnam)

Courtenay, Bryce 1933- .... **CLC 59**
See also CA 138; CPW

Courtney, Robert
See Ellison, Harlan (Jay)

Cousteau, Jacques-Yves 1910-1997 .. **CLC 30**
See also CA 65-68; CANR 15, 67; MTCW 1; SATA 38, 98

Coventry, Francis 1725-1754 .... **LC 46**

Coverdale, Miles c. 1487-1569 .... **LC 77**
See also DLB 167

Cowan, Peter (Walkinshaw) 1914- .... **SSC 28**
See also CA 21-24R; CANR 9, 25, 50, 83; CN 7; DLB 260; RGSF 2

Coward, Noel (Peirce) 1899-1973 . **CLC 1, 9, 29, 51**
See also AITN 1; BRWS 2; CA 17-18; CANR 35; CAP 2; CDBLB 1914-1945; DAM DRAM; DFS 3, 6; DLB 10, 245; IDFW 3, 4; MTCW 1, 2; RGEL 2; TEA

Cowley, Abraham 1618-1667 .... **LC 43**
See also BRW 2; DLB 131, 151; PAB; RGEL 2

Cowley, Malcolm 1898-1989 .... **CLC 39**
See also AMWS 2; CA 5-8R; CANR 3, 55; DLB 4, 48; DLBY 1981, 1989; MTCW 1, 2

Cowper, William 1731-1800 ..... **NCLC 8, 94; PC 40**
See also BRW 3; DAM POET; DLB 104, 109; RGEL 2

Cox, William Trevor 1928-
See Trevor, William
See also CA 9-12R; CANR 4, 37, 55, 76, 102; DAM NOV; INT CANR-37; MTCW 1, 2; TEA

Coyne, P. J.
See Masters, Hilary

Cozzens, James Gould 1903-1978 . **CLC 1, 4, 11, 92**
See also AMW; BPFB 1; CA 9-12R; CANR 19; CDALB 1941-1968; DLB 9; DLBD 2; DLBY 1984, 1997; MTCW 1, 2; RGAL 4

Crabbe, George 1754-1832 .... **NCLC 26**
See also BRW 3; DLB 93; RGEL 2

Crace, Jim 1946- .... **CLC 157**
See also CA 135; CANR 55, 70; CN 7; DLB 231; INT CA-135

Craddock, Charles Egbert
See Murfree, Mary Noailles

Craig, A. A.
See Anderson, Poul (William)

Craik, Mrs.
See Craik, Dinah Maria (Mulock)
See also RGEL 2

Craik, Dinah Maria (Mulock)
1826-1887 .... **NCLC 38**
See also Craik, Mrs.; Mulock, Dinah Maria
See also DLB 35, 163; MAICYA 1, 2; SATA 34

Cram, Ralph Adams 1863-1942 ..... **TCLC 45**
See also CA 160

Cranch, Christopher Pearse
1813-1892 .... **NCLC 115**
See also DLB 1, 42, 243

Crane, (Harold) Hart 1899-1932 .... **TCLC 2, 5, 80; PC 3; WLC**
See also AMW; CA 127; CDALB 1917-1929; DA; DAB; DAC; DAM MST, POET; DLB 4, 48; MTCW 1, 2; RGAL 4; TUS

Crane, R(onald) S(almon)
1886-1967 .... **CLC 27**
See also CA 85-88; DLB 63

Cranshaw, Stanley
See Fisher, Dorothy (Frances) Canfield

Crase, Douglas 1944- .... **CLC 58**
See also CA 106

Crashaw, Richard 1612(?)-1649 .... **LC 24**
See also BRW 2; DLB 126; PAB; RGEL 2

Cratinus c. 519B.C.-c. 422B.C. ..... **CMLC 54**

Craven, Margaret 1901-1980 .... **CLC 17**
See also BYA 2; CA 103; CCA 1; DAC; LAIT 5

Crawford, F(rancis) Marion
1854-1909 .... **TCLC 10**
See also CA 168; DLB 71; HGG; RGAL 4; SUFW 1

Crawford, Isabella Valancy
1850-1887 .... NCLC 12
See also DLB 92; RGEL 2
Crayon, Geoffrey
See Irving, Washington
Creasey, John 1908-1973 .... CLC 11
See also Marric, J. J.
See also CA 5-8R; CANR 8, 59; CMW 4; DLB 77; MTCW 1
Crebillon, Claude Prosper Jolyot de (fils)
1707-1777 .... LC 1, 28
See also GFL Beginnings to 1789
Credo
See Creasey, John
Credo, Alvaro J. de
See Prado (Calvo), Pedro
Creeley, Robert (White) 1926- .. CLC 1, 2, 4, 8, 11, 15, 36, 78
See also AMWS 4; CA 1-4R; CAAS 10; CANR 23, 43, 89; CP 7; DAM POET; DLB 5, 16, 169; DLBD 17; MTCW 1, 2; RGAL 4; WP
Crevecoeur, Hector St. John de
See Crevecoeur, Michel Guillaume Jean de
See also ANW
Crevecoeur, Michel Guillaume Jean de
1735-1813 .... NCLC 105
See also Crevecoeur, Hector St. John de
See also AMWS 1; DLB 37
Crevel, Rene 1900-1935 .... TCLC 112
See also GLL 2
Crews, Harry (Eugene) 1935- ..... CLC 6, 23, 49
See also AITN 1; AMWS 11; BPFB 1; CA 25-28R; CANR 20, 57; CN 7; CSW; DLB 6, 143, 185; MTCW 1, 2; RGAL 4
Crichton, (John) Michael 1942- .... CLC 2, 6, 54, 90
See also AAYA 10; AITN 2; BPFB 1; CA 25-28R; CANR 13, 40, 54, 76; CMW 4; CN 7; CPW; DAM NOV, POP; DLBY 1981; INT CANR-13; JRDA; MTCW 1, 2; SATA 9, 88; SFW 4; YAW
Crispin, Edmund .... CLC 22
See also Montgomery, (Robert) Bruce
See also DLB 87; MSW
Cristofer, Michael 1945(?)- .... CLC 28
See also CA 152; CAD; CD 5; DAM DRAM; DFS 15; DLB 7
Croce, Benedetto 1866-1952 .... TCLC 37
See also CA 155; EW 8
Crockett, David 1786-1836 .... NCLC 8
See also DLB 3, 11, 183, 248
Crockett, Davy
See Crockett, David
Crofts, Freeman Wills 1879-1957 .. TCLC 55
See also CA 195; CMW 4; DLB 77; MSW
Croker, John Wilson 1780-1857 .... NCLC 10
See also DLB 110
Crommelynck, Fernand 1885-1970 .. CLC 75
See also CA 189
Cromwell, Oliver 1599-1658 .... LC 43
Cronenberg, David 1943- .... CLC 143
See also CA 138; CCA 1
Cronin, A(rchibald) J(oseph)
1896-1981 .... CLC 32
See also BPFB 1; CA 1-4R; CANR 5; DLB 191; SATA 47; SATA-Obit 25
Cross, Amanda
See Heilbrun, Carolyn G(old)
See also BPFB 1; CMW; CPW; MSW
Crothers, Rachel 1878-1958 .... TCLC 19
See also CA 194; CAD; CWD; DLB 7, 266; RGAL 4
Croves, Hal
See Traven, B.
Crow Dog, Mary (Ellen) (?)- .... CLC 93
See also Brave Bird, Mary
See also CA 154

Crowfield, Christopher
See Stowe, Harriet (Elizabeth) Beecher
Crowley, Aleister .... TCLC 7
See also Crowley, Edward Alexander
See also GLL 1
Crowley, Edward Alexander 1875-1947
See Crowley, Aleister
See also HGG
Crowley, John 1942- .... CLC 57
See also BPFB 1; CA 61-64; CANR 43, 98; DLBY 1982; SATA 65; SFW 4; SUFW 2
Crud
See Crumb, R(obert)
Crumarums
See Crumb, R(obert)
Crumb, R(obert) 1943- .... CLC 17
See also CA 106; CANR 107
Crumbum
See Crumb, R(obert)
Crumski
See Crumb, R(obert)
Crum the Bum
See Crumb, R(obert)
Crunk
See Crumb, R(obert)
Crustt
See Crumb, R(obert)
Crutchfield, Les
See Trumbo, Dalton
Cruz, Victor Hernandez 1949- .... PC 37
See also BW 2; CA 65-68; CAAS 17; CANR 14, 32, 74; CP 7; DAM MULT, POET; DLB 41; DNFS 1; EXPP; HLC 1; HW 1, 2; MTCW 1; WP
Cryer, Gretchen (Kiger) 1935- .... CLC 21
See also CA 123
Csath, Geza 1887-1919 .... TCLC 13
Cudlip, David R(ockwell) 1933- .... CLC 34
See also CA 177
Cullen, Countee 1903-1946 .... TCLC 4, 37; BLC 1; PC 20; WLCS
See also AFAW 2; AMWS 4; BW 1; CA 124; CDALB 1917-1929; DA; DAC; DAM MST, MULT, POET; DLB 4, 48, 51; EXPP; HR 2; MTCW 1, 2; PFS 3; RGAL 4; SATA 18; WP
Cum, R.
See Crumb, R(obert)
Cummings, Bruce F(rederick) 1889-1919
See Barbellion, W. N. P.
Cummings, E(dward) E(stlin)
1894-1962 .. CLC 1, 3, 8, 12, 15, 68; PC 5; WLC
See also AAYA 41; AMW; CA 73-76; CANR 31; CDALB 1929-1941; DA; DAB; DAC; DAM MST, POET; DLB 4, 48; EXPP; MTCW 1, 2; PAB; PFS 1, 3, 12, 13; RGAL 4; TUS; WP
Cunha, Euclides (Rodrigues Pimenta) da
1866-1909 .... TCLC 24
See also LAW; WLIT 1
Cunningham, E. V.
See Fast, Howard (Melvin)
Cunningham, J(ames) V(incent)
1911-1985 .... CLC 3, 31
See also CA 1-4R; CANR 1, 72; DLB 5
Cunningham, Julia (Woolfolk)
1916- .... CLC 12
See also CA 9-12R; CANR 4, 19, 36; CWRI 5; JRDA; MAICYA 1, 2; SAAS 2; SATA 1, 26, 132
Cunningham, Michael 1952- .... CLC 34
See also CA 136; CANR 96; GLL 2
Cunninghame Graham, R. B.
See Cunninghame Graham, Robert (Gallnigad) Bontine

Cunninghame Graham, Robert (Gallnigad)
Bontine 1852-1936 .... TCLC 19
See also Graham, R(obert) B(ontine) Cunninghame
See also CA 184
Currie, Ellen 19(?)- .... CLC 44
Curtin, Philip
See Lowndes, Marie Adelaide (Belloc)
Curtin, Phillip
See Lowndes, Marie Adelaide (Belloc)
Curtis, Price
See Ellison, Harlan (Jay)
Cusanus, Nicolaus 1401-1464 .... LC 80
See also Nicholas of Cusa
Cutrate, Joe
See Spiegelman, Art
Cynewulf c. 770- .... CMLC 23
See also DLB 146; RGEL 2
Cyrano de Bergerac, Savinien de
1619-1655 .... LC 65
See also DLB 268; GFL Beginnings to 1789; RGWL 2, 3
Czaczkes, Shmuel Yosef Halevi
See Agnon, S(hmuel) Y(osef Halevi)
Dabrowska, Maria (Szumska)
1889-1965 .... CLC 15
See also CA 106; CDWLB 4; DLB 215
Dabydeen, David 1955- .... CLC 34
See also BW 1; CA 125; CANR 56, 92; CN 7; CP 7
Dacey, Philip 1939- .... CLC 51
See also CA 37-40R; CAAS 17; CANR 14, 32, 64; CP 7; DLB 105
Dagerman, Stig (Halvard)
1923-1954 .... TCLC 17
See also CA 155; DLB 259
D'Aguiar, Fred 1960- .... CLC 145
See also CA 148; CANR 83, 101; CP 7; DLB 157
Dahl, Roald 1916-1990 .... CLC 1, 6, 18, 79
See also AAYA 15; BPFB 1; BRWS 4; BYA 5; CA 1-4R; CANR 6, 32, 37, 62; CLR 1, 7, 41; CPW; DAB; DAC; DAM MST, NOV, POP; DLB 139, 255; HGG; JRDA; MAICYA 1, 2; MTCW 1, 2; RGSF 2; SATA 1, 26, 73; SATA-Obit 65; SSFS 4; TEA; YAW
Dahlberg, Edward 1900-1977 .. CLC 1, 7, 14
See also CA 9-12R; CANR 31, 62; DLB 48; MTCW 1; RGAL 4
Daitch, Susan 1954- .... CLC 103
See also CA 161
Dale, Colin .... TCLC 18
See also Lawrence, T(homas) E(dward)
Dale, George E.
See Asimov, Isaac
Dalton, Roque 1935-1975(?) .... PC 36
See also CA 176; HLCS 1; HW 2
Daly, Elizabeth 1878-1967 .... CLC 52
See also CA 23-24; CANR 60; CAP 2; CMW 4
Daly, Maureen 1921- .... CLC 17
See also AAYA 5; BYA 6; CANR 37, 83, 108; JRDA; MAICYA 1, 2; SAAS 1; SATA 2, 129; WYA; YAW
Damas, Leon-Gontran 1912-1978 .... CLC 84
See also BW 1; CA 125
Dana, Richard Henry Sr.
1787-1879 .... NCLC 53
Daniel, Samuel 1562(?)-1619 .... LC 24
See also DLB 62; RGEL 2
Daniels, Brett
See Adler, Renata
Dannay, Frederic 1905-1982 .... CLC 11
See also Queen, Ellery
See also CA 1-4R; CANR 1, 39; CMW 4; DAM POP; DLB 137; MTCW 1

D'Annunzio, Gabriele 1863-1938 .... **TCLC 6, 40**
   See also CA 155; EW 8; RGWL 2, 3; TWA
Danois, N. le
   See Gourmont, Remy(-Marie-Charles) de
Dante 1265-1321 .... **CMLC 3, 18, 39; PC 21; WLCS**
   See also DA; DAB; DAC; DAM MST, POET; EFS 1; EW 1; LAIT 1; RGWL 2, 3; TWA; WP
d'Antibes, Germain
   See Simenon, Georges (Jacques Christian)
Danticat, Edwidge 1969- .... **CLC 94, 139**
   See also AAYA 29; CA 152; CAAE 192; CANR 73; DNFS 1; EXPS; MTCW 1; SSFS 1; YAW
Danvers, Dennis 1947- .... **CLC 70**
Danziger, Paula 1944- .... **CLC 21**
   See also AAYA 4, 36; BYA 6, 7, 14; CA 115; CANR 37; CLR 20; JRDA; MAICYA 1, 2; SATA 36, 63, 102; SATA-Brief 30; WYA; YAW
Da Ponte, Lorenzo 1749-1838 .... **NCLC 50**
Dario, Ruben 1867-1916 ... **TCLC 4; HLC 1; PC 15**
   See also CA 131; CANR 81; DAM MULT; HW 1, 2; LAW; MTCW 1, 2; RGWL 2, 3
Darley, George 1795-1846 .... **NCLC 2**
   See also DLB 96; RGEL 2
Darrow, Clarence (Seward) 1857-1938 .... **TCLC 81**
   See also CA 164
Darwin, Charles 1809-1882 .... **NCLC 57**
   See also BRWS 7; DLB 57, 166; RGEL 2; TEA; WLIT 4
Darwin, Erasmus 1731-1802 .... **NCLC 106**
   See also DLB 93; RGEL 2
Daryush, Elizabeth 1887-1977 ...... **CLC 6, 19**
   See also CA 49-52; CANR 3, 81; DLB 20
Das, Kamala 1934- .... **PC 43**
   See also CA 101; CANR 27, 59; CP 7; CWP; FW
Dasgupta, Surendranath 1887-1952 .... **TCLC 81**
   See also CA 157
Dashwood, Edmee Elizabeth Monica de la Pasture 1890-1943
   See Delafield, E. M.
   See also CA 154
da Silva, Antonio Jose 1705-1739 .... **NCLC 114**
   See also Silva, Jose Asuncion
Daudet, (Louis Marie) Alphonse 1840-1897 .... **NCLC 1**
   See also DLB 123; GFL 1789 to the Present; RGSF 2
Daumal, Rene 1908-1944 .... **TCLC 14**
Davenant, William 1606-1668 .... **LC 13**
   See also DLB 58, 126; RGEL 2
Davenport, Guy (Mattison, Jr.) 1927- .... **CLC 6, 14, 38; SSC 16**
   See also CA 33-36R; CANR 23, 73; CN 7; CSW; DLB 130
David, Robert
   See Nezval, Vitezslav
Davidson, Avram (James) 1923-1993
   See Queen, Ellery
   See also CA 101; CANR 26; DLB 8; FANT; SFW 4; SUFW 1, 2
Davidson, Donald (Grady) 1893-1968 .... **CLC 2, 13, 19**
   See also CA 5-8R; CANR 4, 84; DLB 45
Davidson, Hugh
   See Hamilton, Edmond
Davidson, John 1857-1909 .... **TCLC 24**
   See also DLB 19; RGEL 2
Davidson, Sara 1943- .... **CLC 9**
   See also CA 81-84; CANR 44, 68; DLB 185

Davie, Donald (Alfred) 1922-1995 .... **CLC 5, 8, 10, 31; PC 29**
   See also BRWS 6; CA 1-4R; CAAS 3; CANR 1, 44; CP 7; DLB 27; MTCW 1; RGEL 2
Davie, Elspeth 1919-1995 .... **SSC 52**
   See also CA 126; DLB 139
Davies, Ray(mond Douglas) 1944- ... **CLC 21**
   See also CA 146; CANR 92
Davies, Rhys 1901-1978 .... **CLC 23**
   See also CA 9-12R; CANR 4; DLB 139, 191
Davies, (William) Robertson 1913-1995 .... **CLC 2, 7, 13, 25, 42, 75, 91; WLC**
   See also Marchbanks, Samuel
   See also BEST 89:2; BPFB 1; CA 33-36R; CANR 17, 42, 103; CN 7; CPW; DA; DAB; DAC; DAM MST, NOV, POP; DLB 68; HGG; INT CANR-17; MTCW 1, 2; RGEL 2; TWA
Davies, Walter C.
   See Kornbluth, C(yril) M.
Davies, William Henry 1871-1940 ... **TCLC 5**
   See also CA 179; DLB 19, 174; RGEL 2
Da Vinci, Leonardo 1452-1519 ..... **LC 12, 57, 60**
   See also AAYA 40
Davis, Angela (Yvonne) 1944- .... **CLC 77**
   See also BW 2, 3; CA 57-60; CANR 10, 81; CSW; DAM MULT; FW
Davis, B. Lynch
   See Bioy Casares, Adolfo; Borges, Jorge Luis
Davis, Gordon
   See Hunt, E(verette) Howard, (Jr.)
Davis, H(arold) L(enoir) 1896-1960 . **CLC 49**
   See also ANW; CA 178; DLB 9, 206; SATA 114
Davis, Rebecca (Blaine) Harding 1831-1910 .... **TCLC 6; SSC 38**
   See also CA 179; DLB 74, 239; FW; NFS 14; RGAL 4; TUS
Davis, Richard Harding 1864-1916 .... **TCLC 24**
   See also CA 179; DLB 12, 23, 78, 79, 189; DLBD 13; RGAL 4
Davison, Frank Dalby 1893-1970 ..... **CLC 15**
   See also DLB 260
Davison, Lawrence H.
   See Lawrence, D(avid) H(erbert Richards)
Davison, Peter (Hubert) 1928- .... **CLC 28**
   See also CA 9-12R; CAAS 4; CANR 3, 43, 84; CP 7; DLB 5
Davys, Mary 1674-1732 .... **LC 1, 46**
   See also DLB 39
Dawson, (Guy) Fielding (Lewis) 1930-2002 .... **CLC 6**
   See also CA 85-88; CANR 108; DLB 130
Dawson, Peter
   See Faust, Frederick (Schiller)
   See also TCWW 2, 2
Day, Clarence (Shepard, Jr.) 1874-1935 .... **TCLC 25**
   See also DLB 11
Day, John 1574(?)-1640(?) .... **LC 70**
   See also DLB 62, 170; RGEL 2
Day, Thomas 1748-1789 .... **LC 1**
   See also DLB 39; YABC 1
Day Lewis, C(ecil) 1904-1972 . **CLC 1, 6, 10; PC 11**
   See also Blake, Nicholas
   See also BRWS 3; CA 13-16; CANR 34; CAP 1; CWRI 5; DAM POET; DLB 15, 20; MTCW 1, 2; RGEL 2
Dazai Osamu .... **TCLC 11; SSC 41**
   See also Tsushima, Shuji
   See also CA 164; DLB 182; MJW; RGSF 2; RGWL 2, 3; TWA

de Andrade, Carlos Drummond
   See Drummond de Andrade, Carlos
de Andrade, Mario 1892-1945
   See Andrade, Mario de
   See also CA 178; HW 2
Deane, Norman
   See Creasey, John
Deane, Seamus (Francis) 1940- ...... **CLC 122**
   See also CA 118; CANR 42
de Beauvoir, Simone (Lucie Ernestine Marie Bertrand)
   See Beauvoir, Simone (Lucie Ernestine Marie Bertrand) de
de Beer, P.
   See Bosman, Herman Charles
de Brissac, Malcolm
   See Dickinson, Peter (Malcolm)
de Campos, Alvaro
   See Pessoa, Fernando (Antonio Nogueira)
de Chardin, Pierre Teilhard
   See Teilhard de Chardin, (Marie Joseph) Pierre
Dee, John 1527-1608 .... **LC 20**
   See also DLB 136, 213
Deer, Sandra 1940- .... **CLC 45**
   See also CA 186
De Ferrari, Gabriella 1941- .... **CLC 65**
   See also CA 146
de Filippo, Eduardo 1900-1984 ... **TCLC 127**
   See also CA 132; MTCW 1; RGWL 2, 3
Defoe, Daniel 1660(?)-1731 .. **LC 1, 42; WLC**
   See also AAYA 27; BRW 3; BRWR 1; BYA 4; CDBLB 1660-1789; CLR 61; DA; DAB; DAC; DAM MST, NOV; DLB 39, 95, 101; JRDA; LAIT 1; MAICYA 1, 2; NFS 9, 13; RGEL 2; SATA 22; TEA; WCH; WLIT 3
de Gourmont, Remy(-Marie-Charles)
   See Gourmont, Remy(-Marie-Charles) de
de Hartog, Jan 1914- .... **CLC 19**
   See also CA 1-4R; CANR 1; DFS 12
de Hostos, E. M.
   See Hostos (y Bonilla), Eugenio Maria de
de Hostos, Eugenio M.
   See Hostos (y Bonilla), Eugenio Maria de
Deighton, Len .... **CLC 4, 7, 22, 46**
   See also Deighton, Leonard Cyril
   See also AAYA 6; BEST 89:2; BPFB 1; CDBLB 1960 to Present; CMW 4; CN 7; CPW; DLB 87
Deighton, Leonard Cyril 1929-
   See Deighton, Len
   See also CA 9-12R; CANR 19, 33, 68; DAM NOV, POP; MTCW 1, 2
Dekker, Thomas 1572(?)-1632 ...... **LC 22; DC 12**
   See also CDBLB Before 1660; DAM DRAM; DLB 62, 172; RGEL 2
de Laclos, Pierre Ambroise Franois
   See Laclos, Pierre Ambroise Francois
Delafield, E. M. .... **TCLC 61**
   See also Dashwood, Edmee Elizabeth Monica de la Pasture
   See also DLB 34; RHW
de la Mare, Walter (John) 1873-1956 . **TCLC 4, 53; SSC 14; WLC**
   See also CA 163; CDBLB 1914-1945; CLR 23; CWRI 5; DAB; DAC; DAM MST, POET; DLB 19, 153, 162, 255; EXPP; HGG; MAICYA 1, 2; MTCW 1; RGEL 2; RGSF 2; SATA 16; SUFW 1; TEA; WCH
de Lamartine, Alphonse (Marie Louis Prat)
   See Lamartine, Alphonse (Marie Louis Prat) de
Delaney, Franey
   See O'Hara, John (Henry)

Delaney, Shelagh 1939- .... **CLC 29**
See also CA 17-20R; CANR 30, 67; CBD; CD 5; CDBLB 1960 to Present; CWD; DAM DRAM; DFS 7; DLB 13; MTCW 1

Delany, Martin Robison
1812-1885 .... **NCLC 93**
See also DLB 50; RGAL 4

Delany, Mary (Granville Pendarves)
1700-1788 .... **LC 12**

Delany, Samuel R(ay), Jr. 1942- . **CLC 8, 14, 38, 141; BLC 1**
See also AAYA 24; AFAW 2; BPFB 1; BW 2, 3; CA 81-84; CANR 27, 43; CN 7; DAM MULT; DLB 8, 33; FANT; MTCW 1, 2; RGAL 4; SATA 92; SCFW; SFW 4; SUFW 2

De La Ramee, (Marie) Louise 1839-1908
See Ouida
See also SATA 20

de la Roche, Mazo 1879-1961 .... **CLC 14**
See also CA 85-88; CANR 30; DLB 68; RGEL 2; RHW; SATA 64

De La Salle, Innocent
See Hartmann, Sadakichi

de Laureamont, Comte
See Lautreamont

Delbanco, Nicholas (Franklin)
1942- .... **CLC 6, 13, 167**
See also CA 17-20R; CAAE 189; CAAS 2; CANR 29, 55; DLB 6, 234

del Castillo, Michel 1933- .... **CLC 38**
See also CA 109; CANR 77

Deledda, Grazia (Cosima)
1875(?)-1936 .... **TCLC 23**
See also DLB 264; RGWL 2, 3

Deleuze, Gilles 1925-1995 .... **TCLC 116**

Delgado, Abelardo (Lalo) B(arrientos) 1930-
See also CA 131; CAAS 15; CANR 90; DAM MST, MULT; DLB 82; HLC 1; HW 1, 2

Delibes, Miguel .... **CLC 8, 18**
See also Delibes Setien, Miguel

Delibes Setien, Miguel 1920-
See Delibes, Miguel
See also CA 45-48; CANR 1, 32; HW 1; MTCW 1

DeLillo, Don 1936- ..... **CLC 8, 10, 13, 27, 39, 54, 76, 143**
See also AMWS 6; BEST 89:1; BPFB 1; CA 81-84; CANR 21, 76, 92; CN 7; CPW; DAM NOV, POP; DLB 6, 173; MTCW 1, 2; RGAL 4; TUS

de Lisser, H. G.
See De Lisser, H(erbert) G(eorge)
See also DLB 117

De Lisser, H(erbert) G(eorge)
1878-1944 .... **TCLC 12**
See also de Lisser, H. G.
See also BW 2; CA 152

Deloire, Pierre
See Peguy, Charles (Pierre)

Deloney, Thomas 1543(?)-1600 .... **LC 41**
See also DLB 167; RGEL 2

Deloria, Vine (Victor), Jr. 1933- ...... **CLC 21, 122**
See also CA 53-56; CANR 5, 20, 48, 98; DAM MULT; DLB 175; MTCW 1; NNAL; SATA 21

del Valle-Inclan, Ramon (Maria)
See Valle-Inclan, Ramon (Maria) del

Del Vecchio, John M(ichael) 1947- .. **CLC 29**
See also CA 110; DLBD 9

de Man, Paul (Adolph Michel)
1919-1983 .... **CLC 55**
See also CA 128; CANR 61; DLB 67; MTCW 1, 2

DeMarinis, Rick 1934- .... **CLC 54**
See also CA 57-60, 184; CAAE 184; CAAS 24; CANR 9, 25, 50; DLB 218

de Maupassant, (Henri Rene Albert) Guy
See Maupassant, (Henri Rene Albert) Guy de

Dembry, R. Emmet
See Murfree, Mary Noailles

Demby, William 1922- .... **CLC 53; BLC 1**
See also BW 1, 3; CA 81-84; CANR 81; DAM MULT; DLB 33

de Menton, Francisco
See Chin, Frank (Chew, Jr.)

Demetrius of Phalerum c.
307B.C.- .... **CMLC 34**

Demijohn, Thom
See Disch, Thomas M(ichael)

Deming, Richard 1915-1983
See Queen, Ellery
See also CA 9-12R; CANR 3, 94; SATA 24

Democritus c. 460B.C.-c. 370B.C. . **CMLC 47**

de Montaigne, Michel (Eyquem)
See Montaigne, Michel (Eyquem) de

de Montherlant, Henry (Milon)
See Montherlant, Henry (Milon) de

Demosthenes 384B.C.-322B.C. ...... **CMLC 13**
See also AW 1; DLB 176; RGWL 2, 3

de Musset, (Louis Charles) Alfred
See Musset, (Louis Charles) Alfred de

de Natale, Francine
See Malzberg, Barry N(athaniel)

de Navarre, Marguerite 1492-1549 ..... **LC 61**
See also Marguerite d'Angouleme; Marguerite de Navarre

Denby, Edwin (Orr) 1903-1983 .... **CLC 48**
See also CA 138

de Nerval, Gerard
See Nerval, Gerard de

Denham, John 1615-1669 .... **LC 73**
See also DLB 58, 126; RGEL 2

Denis, Julio
See Cortazar, Julio

Denmark, Harrison
See Zelazny, Roger (Joseph)

Dennis, John 1658-1734 .... **LC 11**
See also DLB 101; RGEL 2

Dennis, Nigel (Forbes) 1912-1989 ...... **CLC 8**
See also CA 25-28R; DLB 13, 15, 233; MTCW 1

Dent, Lester 1904(?)-1959 .... **TCLC 72**
See also CA 161; CMW 4; SFW 4

De Palma, Brian (Russell) 1940- ...... **CLC 20**
See also CA 109

De Quincey, Thomas 1785-1859 ..... **NCLC 4, 87**
See also BRW 4; CDBLB 1789-1832; DLB 110, 144; RGEL 2

Deren, Eleanora 1908(?)-1961
See Deren, Maya
See also CA 192

Deren, Maya .... **CLC 16, 102**
See also Deren, Eleanora

Derleth, August (William)
1909-1971 .... **CLC 31**
See also BPFB 1; BYA 9, 10; CA 1-4R; CANR 4; CMW 4; DLB 9; DLBD 17; HGG; SATA 5; SUFW 1

Der Nister 1884-1950 .... **TCLC 56**

de Routisie, Albert
See Aragon, Louis

Derrida, Jacques 1930- .... **CLC 24, 87**
See also CA 127; CANR 76, 98; DLB 242; MTCW 1; TWA

Derry Down Derry
See Lear, Edward

Dersonnes, Jacques
See Simenon, Georges (Jacques Christian)

Desai, Anita 1937- .... **CLC 19, 37, 97**
See also BRWS 5; CA 81-84; CANR 33, 53, 95; CN 7; CWRI 5; DAB; DAM NOV; DLB 271; DNFS 2; FW; MTCW 1, 2; SATA 63, 126

Desai, Kiran 1971- .... **CLC 119**
See also CA 171

de Saint-Luc, Jean
See Glassco, John

de Saint Roman, Arnaud
See Aragon, Louis

Desbordes-Valmore, Marceline
1786-1859 .... **NCLC 97**
See also DLB 217

Descartes, Rene 1596-1650 .... **LC 20, 35**
See also DLB 268; EW 3; GFL Beginnings to 1789

De Sica, Vittorio 1901(?)-1974 .... **CLC 20**

Desnos, Robert 1900-1945 .... **TCLC 22**
See also CA 151; CANR 107; DLB 258

Destouches, Louis-Ferdinand
1894-1961 .... **CLC 9, 15**
See also Celine, Louis-Ferdinand
See also CA 85-88; CANR 28; MTCW 1

de Tolignac, Gaston
See Griffith, D(avid Lewelyn) W(ark)

Deutsch, Babette 1895-1982 .... **CLC 18**
See also BYA 3; CA 1-4R; CANR 4, 79; DLB 45; SATA 1; SATA-Obit 33

Devenant, William 1606-1649 .... **LC 13**

Devkota, Laxmiprasad 1909-1959 . **TCLC 23**

De Voto, Bernard (Augustine)
1897-1955 .... **TCLC 29**
See also CA 160; DLB 9, 256

De Vries, Peter 1910-1993 ..... **CLC 1, 2, 3, 7, 10, 28, 46**
See also CA 17-20R; CANR 41; DAM NOV; DLB 6; DLBY 1982; MTCW 1, 2

Dewey, John 1859-1952 .... **TCLC 95**
See also CA 170; DLB 246, 270; RGAL 4

Dexter, John
See Bradley, Marion Zimmer
See also GLL 1

Dexter, Martin
See Faust, Frederick (Schiller)
See also TCWW 2

Dexter, Pete 1943- .... **CLC 34, 55**
See also BEST 89:2; CA 131; CPW; DAM POP; INT 131; MTCW 1

Diamano, Silmang
See Senghor, Leopold Sedar

Diamond, Neil 1941- .... **CLC 30**
See also CA 108

Diaz del Castillo, Bernal 1496-1584 .. **LC 31; HLCS 1**
See also LAW

di Bassetto, Corno
See Shaw, George Bernard

Dick, Philip K(indred) 1928-1982 ... **CLC 10, 30, 72**
See also AAYA 24; BPFB 1; BYA 11; CA 49-52; CANR 2, 16; CPW; DAM NOV, POP; DLB 8; MTCW 1, 2; NFS 5; SCFW; SFW 4

Dickens, Charles (John Huffam)
1812-1870 .... **NCLC 3, 8, 18, 26, 37, 50, 86, 105, 113; SSC 17, 49; WLC**
See also AAYA 23; BRW 5; BYA 1, 2, 3, 13, 14; CDBLB 1832-1890; CMW 4; DA; DAB; DAC; DAM MST, NOV; DLB 21, 55, 70, 159, 166; EXPN; HGG; JRDA; LAIT 1, 2; MAICYA 1, 2; NFS 4, 5, 10, 14; RGEL 2; RGSF 2; SATA 15; SUFW 1; TEA; WCH; WLIT 4; WYA

Dickey, James (Lafayette)
1923-1997 .... **CLC 1, 2, 4, 7, 10, 15, 47, 109; PC 40**
See also AITN 1, 2; AMWS 4; BPFB 1; CA 9-12R; CABS 2; CANR 10, 48, 61, 105; CDALB 1968-1988; CP 7; CPW; CSW; DAM NOV, POET, POP; DLB 5, 193; DLBD 7; DLBY 1982, 1993, 1996, 1997, 1998; INT CANR-10; MTCW 1, 2; NFS 9; PFS 6, 11; RGAL 4; TUS

Dickey, William 1928-1994 .... **CLC 3, 28**
See also CA 9-12R; CANR 24, 79; DLB 5

Dickinson, Charles 1951- .... **CLC 49**
See also CA 128

Dickinson, Emily (Elizabeth)
1830-1886 ... **NCLC 21, 77; PC 1; WLC**
See also AAYA 22; AMW; AMWR 1; CDALB 1865-1917; DA; DAB; DAC; DAM MST, POET; DLB 1, 243; EXPP; MAWW; PAB; PFS 1, 2, 3, 4, 5, 6, 8, 10, 11, 13; RGAL 4; SATA 29; TUS; WP; WYA

Dickinson, Mrs. Herbert Ward
See Phelps, Elizabeth Stuart

Dickinson, Peter (Malcolm) 1927- .. **CLC 12, 35**
See also AAYA 9; BYA 5; CA 41-44R; CANR 31, 58, 88; CLR 29; CMW 4; DLB 87, 161; JRDA; MAICYA 1, 2; SATA 5, 62, 95; SFW 4; WYA; YAW

Dickson, Carr
See Carr, John Dickson

Dickson, Carter
See Carr, John Dickson

Diderot, Denis 1713-1784 .... **LC 26**
See also EW 6; GFL Beginnings to 1789; RGWL 2, 3

Didion, Joan 1934- . **CLC 1, 3, 8, 14, 32, 129**
See also AITN 1; AMWS 4; CA 5-8R; CANR 14, 52, 76; CDALB 1968-1988; CN 7; DAM NOV; DLB 2, 173, 185; DLBY 1981, 1986; MAWW; MTCW 1, 2; NFS 3; RGAL 4; TCWW 2; TUS

Dietrich, Robert
See Hunt, E(verette) Howard, (Jr.)

Difusa, Pati
See Almodovar, Pedro

Dillard, Annie 1945- .... **CLC 9, 60, 115**
See also AAYA 6, 43; AMWS 6; ANW; CA 49-52; CANR 3, 43, 62, 90; DAM NOV; DLBY 1980; LAIT 4, 5; MTCW 1, 2; NCFS 1; RGAL 4; SATA 10; TUS

Dillard, R(ichard) H(enry) W(ilde)
1937- .... **CLC 5**
See also CA 21-24R; CAAS 7; CANR 10; CP 7; CSW; DLB 5, 244

Dillon, Eilis 1920-1994 .... **CLC 17**
See also CA 9-12R, 182; CAAE 182; CAAS 3; CANR 4, 38, 78; CLR 26; MAICYA 1, 2; MAICYAS 1; SATA 2, 74; SATA-Essay 105; SATA-Obit 83; YAW

Dimont, Penelope
See Mortimer, Penelope (Ruth)

Dinesen, Isak .... **CLC 10, 29, 95; SSC 7**
See also Blixen, Karen (Christentze Dinesen)
See also EW 10; EXPS; FW; HGG; LAIT 3; MTCW 1; NCFS 2; NFS 9; RGSF 2; RGWL 2, 3; SSFS 3, 6, 13; WLIT 2

Ding Ling .... **CLC 68**
See also Chiang, Pin-chin
See also RGWL 3

Diphusa, Patty
See Almodovar, Pedro

Disch, Thomas M(ichael) 1940- ... **CLC 7, 36**
See also AAYA 17; BPFB 1; CA 21-24R; CAAS 4; CANR 17, 36, 54, 89; CLR 18; CP 7; DLB 8; HGG; MAICYA 1, 2; MTCW 1; SAAS 15; SATA 92; SCFW; SFW 4; SUFW 2

Disch, Tom
See Disch, Thomas M(ichael)

d'Isly, Georges
See Simenon, Georges (Jacques Christian)

Disraeli, Benjamin 1804-1881 ... **NCLC 2, 39, 79**
See also BRW 4; DLB 21, 55; RGEL 2

Ditcum, Steve
See Crumb, R(obert)

Dixon, Paige
See Corcoran, Barbara (Asenath)

Dixon, Stephen 1936- .... **CLC 52; SSC 16**
See also CA 89-92; CANR 17, 40, 54, 91; CN 7; DLB 130

Doak, Annie
See Dillard, Annie

Dobell, Sydney Thompson
1824-1874 .... **NCLC 43**
See also DLB 32; RGEL 2

Doblin, Alfred .... **TCLC 13**
See also Doeblin, Alfred
See also CDWLB 2; RGWL 2, 3

Dobrolyubov, Nikolai Alexandrovich
1836-1861 .... **NCLC 5**

Dobson, Austin 1840-1921 .... **TCLC 79**
See also DLB 35, 144

Dobyns, Stephen 1941- .... **CLC 37**
See also CA 45-48; CANR 2, 18, 99; CMW 4; CP 7

Doctorow, E(dgar) L(aurence)
1931- .... **CLC 6, 11, 15, 18, 37, 44, 65, 113**
See also AAYA 22; AITN 2; AMWS 4; BEST 89:3; BPFB 1; CA 45-48; CANR 2, 33, 51, 76, 97; CDALB 1968-1988; CN 7; CPW; DAM NOV, POP; DLB 2, 28, 173; DLBY 1980; LAIT 3; MTCW 1, 2; NFS 6; RGAL 4; RHW; TUS

Dodgson, Charles L(utwidge) 1832-1898
See Carroll, Lewis
See also CLR 2; DA; DAB; DAC; DAM MST, NOV, POET; MAICYA 1, 2; SATA 100; YABC 2

Dodson, Owen (Vincent)
1914-1983 .... **CLC 79; BLC 1**
See also BW 1; CA 65-68; CANR 24; DAM MULT; DLB 76

Doeblin, Alfred 1878-1957 .... **TCLC 13**
See also Doblin, Alfred
See also CA 141; DLB 66

Doerr, Harriet 1910- .... **CLC 34**
See also CA 122; CANR 47; INT 122

Domecq, H(onorio Bustos)
See Bioy Casares, Adolfo

Domecq, H(onorio) Bustos
See Bioy Casares, Adolfo; Borges, Jorge Luis

Domini, Rey
See Lorde, Audre (Geraldine)
See also GLL 1

Dominique
See Proust, (Valentin-Louis-George-Eugene-)Marcel

Don, A
See Stephen, Sir Leslie

Donaldson, Stephen R(eeder)
1947- .... **CLC 46, 138**
See also AAYA 36; BPFB 1; CA 89-92; CANR 13, 55, 99; CPW; DAM POP; FANT; INT CANR-13; SATA 121; SFW 4; SUFW 1, 2

Donleavy, J(ames) P(atrick) 1926- .... **CLC 1, 4, 6, 10, 45**
See also AITN 2; BPFB 1; CA 9-12R; CANR 24, 49, 62, 80; CBD; CD 5; CN 7; DLB 6, 173; INT CANR-24; MTCW 1, 2; RGAL 4

Donne, John 1572-1631 ..... **LC 10, 24; PC 1, 43; WLC**
See also BRW 1; BRWR 2; CDBLB Before 1660; DA; DAB; DAC; DAM MST, POET; DLB 121, 151; EXPP; PAB; PFS 2, 11; RGEL 2; TEA; WLIT 3; WP

Donnell, David 1939(?)- .... **CLC 34**
See also CA 197

Donoghue, P. S.
See Hunt, E(verette) Howard, (Jr.)

Donoso (Yanez), Jose 1924-1996 ... **CLC 4, 8, 11, 32, 99; HLC 1; SSC 34**
See also CA 81-84; CANR 32, 73; CDWLB 3; DAM MULT; DLB 113; HW 1, 2; LAW; LAWS 1; MTCW 1, 2; RGSF 2; WLIT 1

Donovan, John 1928-1992 .... **CLC 35**
See also AAYA 20; CA 97-100; CLR 3; MAICYA 1, 2; SATA 72; SATA-Brief 29; YAW

Don Roberto
See Cunninghame Graham, Robert (Gallnigad) Bontine

Doolittle, Hilda 1886-1961 . **CLC 3, 8, 14, 31, 34, 73; PC 5; WLC**
See also H. D.
See also AMWS 1; CA 97-100; CANR 35; DA; DAC; DAM MST, POET; DLB 4, 45; FW; GLL 1; MAWW; MTCW 1, 2; PFS 6; RGAL 4

Doppo, Kunikida .... **TCLC 99**
See also Kunikida Doppo

Dorfman, Ariel 1942- .... **CLC 48, 77; HLC 1**
See also CA 130; CANR 67, 70; CWW 2; DAM MULT; DFS 4; HW 1, 2; INT CA-130; WLIT 1

Dorn, Edward (Merton)
1929-1999 .... **CLC 10, 18**
See also CA 93-96; CANR 42, 79; CP 7; DLB 5; INT 93-96; WP

Dor-Ner, Zvi .... **CLC 70**

Dorris, Michael (Anthony)
1945-1997 .... **CLC 109**
See also AAYA 20; BEST 90:1; BYA 12; CA 102; CANR 19, 46, 75; CLR 58; DAM MULT, NOV; DLB 175; LAIT 5; MTCW 2; NFS 3; NNAL; RGAL 4; SATA 75; SATA-Obit 94; TCWW 2; YAW

Dorris, Michael A.
See Dorris, Michael (Anthony)

Dorsan, Luc
See Simenon, Georges (Jacques Christian)

Dorsange, Jean
See Simenon, Georges (Jacques Christian)

Dos Passos, John (Roderigo)
1896-1970 ... **CLC 1, 4, 8, 11, 15, 25, 34, 82; WLC**
See also AMW; BPFB 1; CA 1-4R; CANR 3; CDALB 1929-1941; DA; DAB; DAC; DAM MST, NOV; DLB 4, 9; DLBD 1, 15; DLBY 1996; MTCW 1, 2; NFS 14; RGAL 4; TUS

Dossage, Jean
See Simenon, Georges (Jacques Christian)

Dostoevsky, Fedor Mikhailovich
1821-1881 .. **NCLC 2, 7, 21, 33, 43, 119; SSC 2, 33, 44; WLC**
See also Dostoevsky, Fyodor
See also AAYA 40; DA; DAB; DAC; DAM MST, NOV; EW 7; EXPN; NFS 3, 8; RGSF 2; RGWL 2, 3; SSFS 8; TWA

Dostoevsky, Fyodor
See Dostoevsky, Fedor Mikhailovich
See also DLB 238

Doughty, Charles M(ontagu)
1843-1926 .... **TCLC 27**
See also CA 178; DLB 19, 57, 174

Douglas, Ellen .... **CLC 73**
See also Haxton, Josephine Ayres; Williamson, Ellen Douglas
See also CN 7; CSW

Douglas, Gavin 1475(?)-1522 .... **LC 20**
See also DLB 132; RGEL 2

Douglas, George
See Brown, George Douglas
See also RGEL 2

Douglas, Keith (Castellain)
1920-1944 .... **TCLC 40**
See also BRW 7; CA 160; DLB 27; PAB; RGEL 2

Douglas, Leonard
See Bradbury, Ray (Douglas)

Douglas, Michael
See Crichton, (John) Michael

Douglas, (George) Norman
1868-1952 .... **TCLC 68**
See also BRW 6; CA 157; DLB 34, 195; RGEL 2

Douglas, William
See Brown, George Douglas

Douglass, Frederick 1817(?)-1895 .. **NCLC 7, 55; BLC 1; WLC**
See also AFAW 1, 2; AMWS 3; CDALB 1640-1865; DA; DAC; DAM MST, MULT; DLB 1, 43, 50, 79, 243; FW; LAIT 2; NCFS 2; RGAL 4; SATA 29

Dourado, (Waldomiro Freitas) Autran
1926- .... **CLC 23, 60**
See also CA 25-28R, 179; CANR 34, 81; DLB 145; HW 2

Dourado, Waldomiro Autran
See Dourado, (Waldomiro Freitas) Autran
See also CA 179

Dove, Rita (Frances) 1952- .... **CLC 50, 81; BLCS; PC 6**
See also AMWS 4; BW 2; CA 109; CAAS 19; CANR 27, 42, 68, 76, 97; CDALBS; CP 7; CSW; CWP; DAM MULT, POET; DLB 120; EXPP; MTCW 1; PFS 1, 15; RGAL 4

Doveglion
See Villa, Jose Garcia

Dowell, Coleman 1925-1985 .... **CLC 60**
See also CA 25-28R; CANR 10; DLB 130; GLL 2

Dowson, Ernest (Christopher)
1867-1900 .... **TCLC 4**
See also CA 150; DLB 19, 135; RGEL 2

Doyle, A. Conan
See Doyle, Sir Arthur Conan

Doyle, Sir Arthur Conan
1859-1930 .... **TCLC 7; SSC 12; WLC**
See Conan Doyle, Arthur
See also AAYA 14; BRWS 2; CA 122; CDBLB 1890-1914; CMW 4; DA; DAB; DAC; DAM MST, NOV; DLB 18, 70, 156, 178; EXPS; HGG; LAIT 2; MSW; MTCW 1, 2; RGEL 2; RGSF 2; RHW; SATA 24; SCFW 2; SFW 4; SSFS 2; TEA; WCH; WLIT 4; WYA; YAW

Doyle, Conan
See Doyle, Sir Arthur Conan

Doyle, John
See Graves, Robert (von Ranke)

Doyle, Roddy 1958(?)- .... **CLC 81**
See also AAYA 14; BRWS 5; CA 143; CANR 73; CN 7; DLB 194

Doyle, Sir A. Conan
See Doyle, Sir Arthur Conan

Dr. A
See Asimov, Isaac; Silverstein, Alvin; Silverstein, Virginia B(arbara Opshelor)

Drabble, Margaret 1939- ...... **CLC 2, 3, 5, 8, 10, 22, 53, 129**
See also BRWS 4; CA 13-16R; CANR 18, 35, 63, 112; CDBLB 1960 to Present; CN 7; CPW; DAB; DAC; DAM MST, NOV, POP; DLB 14, 155, 231; FW; MTCW 1, 2; RGEL 2; SATA 48; TEA

Drapier, M. B.
See Swift, Jonathan

Drayham, James
See Mencken, H(enry) L(ouis)

Drayton, Michael 1563-1631 .... **LC 8**
See also DAM POET; DLB 121; RGEL 2

Dreadstone, Carl
See Campbell, (John) Ramsey

Dreiser, Theodore (Herman Albert)
1871-1945 .... **TCLC 10, 18, 35, 83; SSC 30; WLC**
See also AMW; CA 132; CDALB 1865-1917; DA; DAC; DAM MST, NOV; DLB 9, 12, 102, 137; DLBD 1; LAIT 2; MTCW 1, 2; NFS 8; RGAL 4; TUS

Drexler, Rosalyn 1926- .... **CLC 2, 6**
See also CA 81-84; CAD; CANR 68; CD 5; CWD

Dreyer, Carl Theodor 1889-1968 .... **CLC 16**

Drieu la Rochelle, Pierre(-Eugene)
1893-1945 .... **TCLC 21**
See also DLB 72; GFL 1789 to the Present

Drinkwater, John 1882-1937 .... **TCLC 57**
See also CA 149; DLB 10, 19, 149; RGEL 2

Drop Shot
See Cable, George Washington

Droste-Hulshoff, Annette Freiin von
1797-1848 .... **NCLC 3**
See also CDWLB 2; DLB 133; RGSF 2; RGWL 2, 3

Drummond, Walter
See Silverberg, Robert

Drummond, William Henry
1854-1907 .... **TCLC 25**
See also CA 160; DLB 92

Drummond de Andrade, Carlos
1902-1987 .... **CLC 18**
See Andrade, Carlos Drummond de
See also CA 132; LAW

Drummond of Hawthornden, William
1585-1649 .... **LC 83**
See also DLB 121, 213; RGEL 2

Drury, Allen (Stuart) 1918-1998 .... **CLC 37**
See also CA 57-60; CANR 18, 52; CN 7; INT CANR-18

Dryden, John 1631-1700 ..... **LC 3, 21; DC 3; PC 25; WLC**
See also BRW 2; CDBLB 1660-1789; DA; DAB; DAC; DAM DRAM, MST, POET; DLB 80, 101, 131; EXPP; IDTP; RGEL 2; TEA; WLIT 3

Duberman, Martin (Bauml) 1930- ..... **CLC 8**
See also CA 1-4R; CAD; CANR 2, 63; CD 5

Dubie, Norman (Evans) 1945- .... **CLC 36**
See also CA 69-72; CANR 12; CP 7; DLB 120; PFS 12

Du Bois, W(illiam) E(dward) B(urghardt)
1868-1963 ... **CLC 1, 2, 13, 64, 96; BLC 1; WLC**
See also AAYA 40; AFAW 1, 2; AMWS 2; BW 1, 3; CA 85-88; CANR 34, 82; CDALB 1865-1917; DA; DAC; DAM MST, MULT, NOV; DLB 47, 50, 91, 246; EXPP; HR 2; LAIT 2; MTCW 1, 2; NCFS 1; PFS 13; RGAL 4; SATA 42

Dubus, Andre 1936-1999 ..... **CLC 13, 36, 97; SSC 15**
See also AMWS 7; CA 21-24R; CANR 17; CN 7; CSW; DLB 130; INT CANR-17; RGAL 4; SSFS 10

Duca Minimo
See D'Annunzio, Gabriele

Ducharme, Rejean 1941- .... **CLC 74**
See also DLB 60

Duchen, Claire .... **CLC 65**

Duclos, Charles Pinot- 1704-1772 .... **LC 1**
See also GFL Beginnings to 1789

Dudek, Louis 1918- .... **CLC 11, 19**
See also CA 45-48; CAAS 14; CANR 1; CP 7; DLB 88

Duerrenmatt, Friedrich 1921-1990 ... **CLC 1, 4, 8, 11, 15, 43, 102**
See also Durrenmatt, Friedrich
See also CA 17-20R; CANR 33; CMW 4; DAM DRAM; DLB 69, 124; MTCW 1, 2

Duffy, Bruce 1953(?)- .... **CLC 50**
See also CA 172

Duffy, Maureen 1933- .... **CLC 37**
See also CA 25-28R; CANR 33, 68; CBD; CN 7; CP 7; CWD; CWP; DFS 15; DLB 14; FW; MTCW 1

Du Fu
See Tu Fu
See also RGWL 2, 3

Dugan, Alan 1923- .... **CLC 2, 6**
See also CA 81-84; CP 7; DLB 5; PFS 10

du Gard, Roger Martin
See Martin du Gard, Roger

Duhamel, Georges 1884-1966 .... **CLC 8**
See also CA 81-84; CANR 35; DLB 65; GFL 1789 to the Present; MTCW 1

Dujardin, Edouard (Emile Louis)
1861-1949 .... **TCLC 13**
See also DLB 123

Duke, Raoul
See Thompson, Hunter S(tockton)

Dulles, John Foster 1888-1959 .... **TCLC 72**
See also CA 149

Dumas, Alexandre (pere)
1802-1870 .... **NCLC 11, 71; WLC**
See also AAYA 22; BYA 3; DA; DAB; DAC; DAM MST, NOV; DLB 119, 192; EW 6; GFL 1789 to the Present; LAIT 1, 2; NFS 14; RGWL 2, 3; SATA 18; TWA; WCH

Dumas, Alexandre (fils)
1824-1895 .... **NCLC 9; DC 1**
See also DLB 192; GFL 1789 to the Present; RGWL 2, 3

Dumas, Claudine
See Malzberg, Barry N(athaniel)

Dumas, Henry L. 1934-1968 .... **CLC 6, 62**
See also BW 1; CA 85-88; DLB 41; RGAL 4

du Maurier, Daphne 1907-1989 .. **CLC 6, 11, 59; SSC 18**
See also AAYA 37; BPFB 1; BRWS 3; CA 5-8R; CANR 6, 55; CMW 4; CPW; DAB; DAC; DAM MST, POP; DLB 191; HGG; LAIT 3; MSW; MTCW 1, 2; NFS 12; RGEL 2; RGSF 2; RHW; SATA 27; SATA-Obit 60; SSFS 14; TEA

Du Maurier, George 1834-1896 ..... **NCLC 86**
See also DLB 153, 178; RGEL 2

Dunbar, Paul Laurence 1872-1906 . **TCLC 2, 12; BLC 1; PC 5; SSC 8; WLC**
See also AFAW 1, 2; AMWS 2; BW 1, 3; CA 124; CANR 79; CDALB 1865-1917; DA; DAC; DAM MST, MULT, POET; DLB 50, 54, 78; EXPP; RGAL 4; SATA 34

Dunbar, William 1460(?)-1520(?) .... **LC 20**
See also BRWS 8; DLB 132, 146; RGEL 2

Duncan, Dora Angela
See Duncan, Isadora

Duncan, Isadora 1877(?)-1927 .... **TCLC 68**
See also CA 149

Duncan, Lois 1934- .... **CLC 26**
See also AAYA 4, 34; BYA 6, 8; CA 1-4R; CANR 2, 23, 36, 111; CLR 29; JRDA; MAICYA 1, 2; MAICYAS 1; SAAS 2; SATA 1, 36, 75, 133; WYA; YAW

Duncan, Robert (Edward)
1919-1988 .... **CLC 1, 2, 4, 7, 15, 41, 55; PC 2**
See also CA 9-12R; CANR 28, 62; DAM POET; DLB 5, 16, 193; MTCW 1, 2; PFS 13; RGAL 4; WP

Duncan, Sara Jeannette
1861-1922 .... **TCLC 60**
See also CA 157; DLB 92

Dunlap, William 1766-1839 .... **NCLC 2**
See also DLB 30, 37, 59; RGAL 4

Dunn, Douglas (Eaglesham) 1942- .... **CLC 6, 40**
See also CA 45-48; CANR 2, 33; CP 7; DLB 40; MTCW 1

Dunn, Katherine (Karen) 1945- .... **CLC 71**
See also CA 33-36R; CANR 72; HGG; MTCW 1

Dunn, Stephen (Elliott) 1939- .... **CLC 36**
See also AMWS 11; CA 33-36R; CANR 12, 48, 53, 105; CP 7; DLB 105

Dunne, Finley Peter 1867-1936 ...... **TCLC 28**
See also CA 178; DLB 11, 23; RGAL 4

Dunne, John Gregory 1932- .... **CLC 28**
See also CA 25-28R; CANR 14, 50; CN 7; DLBY 1980

Dunsany, Lord .... **TCLC 2, 59**
See also Dunsany, Edward John Moreton Drax Plunkett
See also DLB 77, 153, 156, 255; FANT; IDTP; RGEL 2; SFW 4; SUFW 1

Dunsany, Edward John Moreton Drax Plunkett 1878-1957
See Dunsany, Lord
See also CA 148; DLB 10; MTCW 1

du Perry, Jean
See Simenon, Georges (Jacques Christian)

Durang, Christopher (Ferdinand)
1949- .... **CLC 27, 38**
See also CA 105; CAD; CANR 50, 76; CD 5; MTCW 1

Duras, Marguerite 1914-1996 . **CLC 3, 6, 11, 20, 34, 40, 68, 100; SSC 40**
See also BPFB 1; CA 25-28R; CANR 50; CWW 2; DLB 83; GFL 1789 to the Present; IDFW 4; MTCW 1, 2; RGWL 2, 3; TWA

Durban, (Rosa) Pam 1947- .... **CLC 39**
See also CA 123; CANR 98; CSW

Durcan, Paul 1944- .... **CLC 43, 70**
See also CA 134; CP 7; DAM POET

Durkheim, Emile 1858-1917 .... **TCLC 55**

Durrell, Lawrence (George)
1912-1990 ..... **CLC 1, 4, 6, 8, 13, 27, 41**
See also BPFB 1; BRWS 1; CA 9-12R; CANR 40, 77; CDBLB 1945-1960; DAM NOV; DLB 15, 27, 204; DLBY 1990; MTCW 1, 2; RGEL 2; SFW 4; TEA

Durrenmatt, Friedrich
See Duerrenmatt, Friedrich
See also CDWLB 2; EW 13; RGWL 2, 3

Dutt, Michael Madhusudan
1824-1873 .... **NCLC 118**

Dutt, Toru 1856-1877 .... **NCLC 29**
See also DLB 240

Dwight, Timothy 1752-1817 .... **NCLC 13**
See also DLB 37; RGAL 4

Dworkin, Andrea 1946- .... **CLC 43, 123**
See also CA 77-80; CAAS 21; CANR 16, 39, 76, 96; FW; GLL 1; INT CANR-16; MTCW 1, 2

Dwyer, Deanna
See Koontz, Dean R(ay)

Dwyer, K. R.
See Koontz, Dean R(ay)

Dwyer, Thomas A. 1923- .... **CLC 114**
See also CA 115

Dybek, Stuart 1942- .... **CLC 114; SSC 55**
See also CA 97-100; CANR 39; DLB 130

Dye, Richard
See De Voto, Bernard (Augustine)

Dyer, Geoff 1958- .... **CLC 149**
See also CA 125; CANR 88

Dylan, Bob 1941- .... **CLC 3, 4, 6, 12, 77; PC 37**
See also CA 41-44R; CANR 108; CP 7; DLB 16

Dyson, John 1943- .... **CLC 70**
See also CA 144

E. V. L.
See Lucas, E(dward) V(errall)

Eagleton, Terence (Francis) 1943- .. **CLC 63, 132**
See also CA 57-60; CANR 7, 23, 68; DLB 242; MTCW 1, 2

Eagleton, Terry
See Eagleton, Terence (Francis)

Early, Jack
See Scoppettone, Sandra
See also GLL 1

East, Michael
See West, Morris L(anglo)

Eastaway, Edward
See Thomas, (Philip) Edward

Eastlake, William (Derry)
1917-1997 .... **CLC 8**
See also CA 5-8R; CAAS 1; CANR 5, 63; CN 7; DLB 6, 206; INT CANR-5; TCWW 2

Eastman, Charles A(lexander)
1858-1939 .... **TCLC 55**
See also CA 179; CANR 91; DAM MULT; DLB 175; NNAL; YABC 1

Eberhart, Richard (Ghormley)
1904- .... **CLC 3, 11, 19, 56**
See also AMW; CA 1-4R; CANR 2; CDALB 1941-1968; CP 7; DAM POET; DLB 48; MTCW 1; RGAL 4

Eberstadt, Fernanda 1960- .... **CLC 39**
See also CA 136; CANR 69

Echegaray (y Eizaguirre), Jose (Maria Waldo) 1832-1916 .... **TCLC 4; HLCS 1**
See also CANR 32; HW 1; MTCW 1

Echeverria, (Jose) Esteban (Antonino)
1805-1851 .... **NCLC 18**
See also LAW

Echo
See Proust, (Valentin-Louis-George-Eugene-)Marcel

Eckert, Allan W. 1931- .... **CLC 17**
See also AAYA 18; BYA 2; CA 13-16R; CANR 14, 45; INT CANR-14; MAICYA 2; MAICYAS 1; SAAS 21; SATA 29, 91; SATA-Brief 27

Eckhart, Meister 1260(?)-1327(?) ... **CMLC 9**
See also DLB 115

Eckmar, F. R.
See de Hartog, Jan

Eco, Umberto 1932- .... **CLC 28, 60, 142**
See also BEST 90:1; BPFB 1; CA 77-80; CANR 12, 33, 55, 110; CPW; CWW 2; DAM NOV, POP; DLB 196, 242; MSW; MTCW 1, 2; RGWL 3

Eddison, E(ric) R(ucker)
1882-1945 .... **TCLC 15**
See also CA 156; DLB 255; FANT; SFW 4; SUFW 1

Eddy, Mary (Ann Morse) Baker
1821-1910 .... **TCLC 71**
See also CA 174

Edel, (Joseph) Leon 1907-1997 .. **CLC 29, 34**
See also CA 1-4R; CANR 1, 22, 112; DLB 103; INT CANR-22

Eden, Emily 1797-1869 .... **NCLC 10**

Edgar, David 1948- .... **CLC 42**
See also CA 57-60; CANR 12, 61, 112; CBD; CD 5; DAM DRAM; DFS 15; DLB 13, 233; MTCW 1

Edgerton, Clyde (Carlyle) 1944- ...... **CLC 39**
See also AAYA 17; CA 134; CANR 64; CSW; INT 134; YAW

Edgeworth, Maria 1768-1849 .... **NCLC 1, 51**
See also BRWS 3; DLB 116, 159, 163; FW; RGEL 2; SATA 21; TEA; WLIT 3

Edmonds, Paul
See Kuttner, Henry

Edmonds, Walter D(umaux)
1903-1998 .... **CLC 35**
See also BYA 2; CA 5-8R; CANR 2; CWRI 5; DLB 9; LAIT 1; MAICYA 1, 2; RHW; SAAS 4; SATA 1, 27; SATA-Obit 99

Edmondson, Wallace
See Ellison, Harlan (Jay)

Edson, Russell 1935- .... **CLC 13**
See also CA 33-36R; DLB 244; WP

Edwards, Bronwen Elizabeth
See Rose, Wendy

Edwards, G(erald) B(asil)
1899-1976 .... **CLC 25**
See also CA 201

Edwards, Gus 1939- .... **CLC 43**
See also CA 108; INT 108

Edwards, Jonathan 1703-1758 .... **LC 7, 54**
See also AMW; DA; DAC; DAM MST; DLB 24, 270; RGAL 4; TUS

Efron, Marina Ivanovna Tsvetaeva
See Tsvetaeva (Efron), Marina (Ivanovna)

Egoyan, Atom 1960- .... **CLC 151**
See also CA 157

Ehle, John (Marsden, Jr.) 1925- ...... **CLC 27**
See also CA 9-12R; CSW

Ehrenbourg, Ilya (Grigoryevich)
See Ehrenburg, Ilya (Grigoryevich)

Ehrenburg, Ilya (Grigoryevich)
1891-1967 .... **CLC 18, 34, 62**
See also Erenburg, Il'ia Grigor'evich
See also CA 102

Ehrenburg, Ilyo (Grigoryevich)
See Ehrenburg, Ilya (Grigoryevich)

Ehrenreich, Barbara 1941- .... **CLC 110**
See also BEST 90:4; CA 73-76; CANR 16, 37, 62; DLB 246; FW; MTCW 1, 2

Eich, Gunter
See Eich, Gunter
See also RGWL 2, 3

Eich, Gunter 1907-1972 .... **CLC 15**
See also Eich, Gunter
See also CA 111; DLB 69, 124

Eichendorff, Joseph 1788-1857 .... **NCLC 8**
See also DLB 90; RGWL 2, 3

Eigner, Larry .... **CLC 9**
See also Eigner, Laurence (Joel)
See also CAAS 23; DLB 5; WP

Eigner, Laurence (Joel) 1927-1996
See Eigner, Larry
See also CA 9-12R; CANR 6, 84; CP 7; DLB 193

Einhard c. 770-840 .... **CMLC 50**
See also DLB 148

Einstein, Albert 1879-1955 .... **TCLC 65**
See also CA 133; MTCW 1, 2

Eiseley, Loren Corey 1907-1977 .... **CLC 7**
See also AAYA 5; ANW; CA 1-4R; CANR 6; DLBD 17

Eisenstadt, Jill 1963- .... **CLC 50**
See also CA 140

Eisenstein, Sergei (Mikhailovich)
1898-1948 .... **TCLC 57**
See also CA 149
Eisner, Simon
See Kornbluth, C(yril) M.
Ekeloef, (Bengt) Gunnar
1907-1968 .... **CLC 27; PC 23**
See also Ekelof, (Bengt) Gunnar
See also CA 123; DAM POET
Ekelof, (Bengt) Gunnar 1907-1968
See Ekeloef, (Bengt) Gunnar
See also DLB 259; EW 12
Ekelund, Vilhelm 1880-1949 .... **TCLC 75**
See also CA 189
Ekwensi, C. O. D.
See Ekwensi, Cyprian (Odiatu Duaka)
Ekwensi, Cyprian (Odiatu Duaka)
1921- .... **CLC 4; BLC 1**
See also AFW; BW 2, 3; CA 29-32R; CANR 18, 42, 74; CDWLB 3; CN 7; CWRI 5; DAM MULT; DLB 117; MTCW 1, 2; RGEL 2; SATA 66; WLIT 2
Elaine .... **TCLC 18**
See also Leverson, Ada Esther
El Crummo
See Crumb, R(obert)
Elder, Lonne III 1931-1996 .... **DC 8**
See also BLC 1; BW 1, 3; CA 81-84; CAD; CANR 25; DAM MULT; DLB 7, 38, 44
Eleanor of Aquitaine 1122-1204 ... **CMLC 39**
Elia
See Lamb, Charles
Eliade, Mircea 1907-1986 .... **CLC 19**
See also CA 65-68; CANR 30, 62; CDWLB 4; DLB 220; MTCW 1; RGWL 3; SFW 4
Eliot, A. D.
See Jewett, (Theodora) Sarah Orne
Eliot, Alice
See Jewett, (Theodora) Sarah Orne
Eliot, Dan
See Silverberg, Robert
Eliot, George 1819-1880 ...... **NCLC 4, 13, 23, 41, 49, 89, 118; PC 20; WLC**
See also BRW 5; BRWR 2; CDBLB 1832-1890; CN 7; CPW; DA; DAB; DAC; DAM MST, NOV; DLB 21, 35, 55; RGEL 2; RGSF 2; SSFS 8; TEA; WLIT 3
Eliot, John 1604-1690 .... **LC 5**
See also DLB 24
Eliot, T(homas) S(tearns)
1888-1965 ...... **CLC 1, 2, 3, 6, 9, 10, 13, 15, 24, 34, 41, 55, 57, 113; PC 5, 31; WLC**
See also AAYA 28; AMW; AMWR 1; BRW 7; BRWR 2; CA 5-8R; CANR 41; CDALB 1929-1941; DA; DAB; DAC; DAM DRAM, MST, POET; DFS 4, 13; DLB 7, 10, 45, 63, 245; DLBY 1988; EXPP; LAIT 3; MTCW 1, 2; PAB; PFS 1, 7; RGAL 4; RGEL 2; TUS; WLIT 4; WP
Elizabeth 1866-1941 .... **TCLC 41**
Elkin, Stanley L(awrence)
1930-1995 .. **CLC 4, 6, 9, 14, 27, 51, 91; SSC 12**
See also AMWS 6; BPFB 1; CA 9-12R; CANR 8, 46; CN 7; CPW; DAM NOV, POP; DLB 2, 28, 218; DLBY 1980; INT CANR-8; MTCW 1, 2; RGAL 4
Elledge, Scott .... **CLC 34**
Elliot, Don
See Silverberg, Robert
Elliott, Don
See Silverberg, Robert
Elliott, George P(aul) 1918-1980 .... **CLC 2**
See also CA 1-4R; CANR 2; DLB 244
Elliott, Janice 1931-1995 .... **CLC 47**
See also CA 13-16R; CANR 8, 29, 84; CN 7; DLB 14; SATA 119

Elliott, Sumner Locke 1917-1991 ..... **CLC 38**
See also CA 5-8R; CANR 2, 21
Elliott, William
See Bradbury, Ray (Douglas)
Ellis, A. E. .... **CLC 7**
Ellis, Alice Thomas .... **CLC 40**
See also Haycraft, Anna (Margaret)
See also DLB 194; MTCW 1
Ellis, Bret Easton 1964- ...... **CLC 39, 71, 117**
See also AAYA 2, 43; CA 123; CANR 51, 74; CN 7; CPW; DAM POP; HGG; INT CA-123; MTCW 1; NFS 11
Ellis, (Henry) Havelock
1859-1939 .... **TCLC 14**
See also CA 169; DLB 190
Ellis, Landon
See Ellison, Harlan (Jay)
Ellis, Trey 1962- .... **CLC 55**
See also CA 146; CANR 92
Ellison, Harlan (Jay) 1934- ... **CLC 1, 13, 42, 139; SSC 14**
See also AAYA 29; BPFB 1; BYA 14; CA 5-8R; CANR 5, 46; CPW; DAM POP; DLB 8; HGG; INT CANR-5; MTCW 1, 2; SCFW 2; SFW 4; SSFS 13, 14, 15; SUFW 1, 2
Ellison, Ralph (Waldo) 1914-1994 ..... **CLC 1, 3, 11, 54, 86, 114; BLC 1; SSC 26; WLC**
See also AAYA 19; AFAW 1, 2; AMWS 2; BPFB 1; BW 1, 3; BYA 2; CA 9-12R; CANR 24, 53; CDALB 1941-1968; CSW; DA; DAB; DAC; DAM MST, MULT, NOV; DLB 2, 76, 227; DLBY 1994; EXPN; EXPS; LAIT 4; MTCW 1, 2; NCFS 3; NFS 2; RGAL 4; RGSF 2; SSFS 1, 11; YAW
Ellmann, Lucy (Elizabeth) 1956- ...... **CLC 61**
See also CA 128
Ellmann, Richard (David)
1918-1987 .... **CLC 50**
See also BEST 89:2; CA 1-4R; CANR 2, 28, 61; DLB 103; DLBY 1987; MTCW 1, 2
Elman, Richard (Martin)
1934-1997 .... **CLC 19**
See also CA 17-20R; CAAS 3; CANR 47
Elron
See Hubbard, L(afayette) Ron(ald)
Eluard, Paul .... **TCLC 7, 41; PC 38**
See also Grindel, Eugene
See also GFL 1789 to the Present; RGWL 2, 3
Elyot, Thomas 1490(?)-1546 .... **LC 11**
See also DLB 136; RGEL 2
Elytis, Odysseus 1911-1996 .... **CLC 15, 49, 100; PC 21**
See also Alepoudelis, Odysseus
See also CA 102; CANR 94; CWW 2; DAM POET; EW 13; MTCW 1, 2; RGWL 2, 3
Emecheta, (Florence Onye) Buchi
1944- .... **CLC 14, 48, 128; BLC 2**
See also AFW; BW 2, 3; CA 81-84; CANR 27, 81; CDWLB 3; CN 7; CWRI 5; DAM MULT; DLB 117; FW; MTCW 1, 2; NFS 12, 14; SATA 66; WLIT 2
Emerson, Mary Moody
1774-1863 .... **NCLC 66**
Emerson, Ralph Waldo 1803-1882 . **NCLC 1, 38, 98; PC 18; WLC**
See also AMW; ANW; CDALB 1640-1865; DA; DAB; DAC; DAM MST, POET; DLB 1, 59, 73, 183, 223, 270; EXPP; LAIT 2; NCFS 3; PFS 4; RGAL 4; TUS; WP
Eminescu, Mihail 1850-1889 .... **NCLC 33**
Empedocles 5th cent. B.C.- .... **CMLC 50**
See also DLB 176

Empson, William 1906-1984 ... **CLC 3, 8, 19, 33, 34**
See also BRWS 2; CA 17-20R; CANR 31, 61; DLB 20; MTCW 1, 2; RGEL 2
Enchi, Fumiko (Ueda) 1905-1986 ..... **CLC 31**
See also Enchi Fumiko
See also CA 129; FW; MJW
Enchi Fumiko
See Enchi, Fumiko (Ueda)
See also DLB 182
Ende, Michael (Andreas Helmuth)
1929-1995 .... **CLC 31**
See also BYA 5; CA 124; CANR 36, 110; CLR 14; DLB 75; MAICYA 1, 2; MAICYAS 1; SATA 61, 130; SATA-Brief 42; SATA-Obit 86
Endo, Shusaku 1923-1996 ..... **CLC 7, 14, 19, 54, 99; SSC 48**
See also Endo Shusaku
See also CA 29-32R; CANR 21, 54; DAM NOV; MTCW 1, 2; RGSF 2; RGWL 2, 3
Endo Shusaku
See Endo, Shusaku
See also DLB 182
Engel, Marian 1933-1985 .... **CLC 36**
See also CA 25-28R; CANR 12; DLB 53; FW; INT CANR-12
Engelhardt, Frederick
See Hubbard, L(afayette) Ron(ald)
Engels, Friedrich 1820-1895 .. **NCLC 85, 114**
See also DLB 129
Enright, D(ennis) J(oseph) 1920- ... **CLC 4, 8, 31**
See also CA 1-4R; CANR 1, 42, 83; CP 7; DLB 27; SATA 25
Enzensberger, Hans Magnus
1929- .... **CLC 43; PC 28**
See also CA 119; CANR 103
Ephron, Nora 1941- .... **CLC 17, 31**
See also AAYA 35; AITN 2; CA 65-68; CANR 12, 39, 83
Epicurus 341B.C.-270B.C. .... **CMLC 21**
See also DLB 176
Epsilon
See Betjeman, John
Epstein, Daniel Mark 1948- .... **CLC 7**
See also CA 49-52; CANR 2, 53, 90
Epstein, Jacob 1956- .... **CLC 19**
See also CA 114
Epstein, Jean 1897-1953 .... **TCLC 92**
Epstein, Joseph 1937- .... **CLC 39**
See also CA 119; CANR 50, 65
Epstein, Leslie 1938- .... **CLC 27**
See also CA 73-76; CAAS 12; CANR 23, 69
Equiano, Olaudah 1745(?)-1797 .... **LC 16; BLC 2**
See also AFAW 1, 2; CDWLB 3; DAM MULT; DLB 37, 50; WLIT 2
Erasmus, Desiderius 1469(?)-1536 ...... **LC 16**
See also DLB 136; EW 2; RGWL 2, 3; TWA
Erdman, Paul E(mil) 1932- .... **CLC 25**
See also AITN 1; CA 61-64; CANR 13, 43, 84
Erdrich, Louise 1954- .... **CLC 39, 54, 120**
See also AAYA 10; AMWS 4; BEST 89:1; BPFB 1; CA 114; CANR 41, 62; CDALBS; CN 7; CP 7; CPW; CWP; DAM MULT, NOV, POP; DLB 152, 175, 206; EXPP; LAIT 5; MTCW 1; NFS 5; NNAL; PFS 14; RGAL 4; SATA 94; SSFS 14; TCWW 2
Erenburg, Ilya (Grigoryevich)
See Ehrenburg, Ilya (Grigoryevich)
Erickson, Stephen Michael 1950-
See Erickson, Steve
See also CA 129; SFW 4

Erickson, Steve .... **CLC 64**
See also Erickson, Stephen Michael
See also CANR 60, 68; SUFW 2

Ericson, Walter
See Fast, Howard (Melvin)

Eriksson, Buntel
See Bergman, (Ernst) Ingmar

Ernaux, Annie 1940- .... **CLC 88**
See also CA 147; CANR 93; NCFS 3

Erskine, John 1879-1951 .... **TCLC 84**
See also CA 159; DLB 9, 102; FANT

Eschenbach, Wolfram von
See Wolfram von Eschenbach
See also RGWL 3

Eseki, Bruno
See Mphahlele, Ezekiel

Esenin, Sergei (Alexandrovich)
1895-1925 .... **TCLC 4**
See also RGWL 2, 3

Eshleman, Clayton 1935- .... **CLC 7**
See also CA 33-36R; CAAS 6; CANR 93; CP 7; DLB 5

Espriella, Don Manuel Alvarez
See Southey, Robert

Espriu, Salvador 1913-1985 .... **CLC 9**
See also CA 154; DLB 134

Espronceda, Jose de 1808-1842 ..... **NCLC 39**

Esquivel, Laura 1951(?)- ... **CLC 141; HLCS 1**
See also AAYA 29; CA 143; CANR 68, 113; DNFS 2; LAIT 3; MTCW 1; NFS 5; WLIT 1

Esse, James
See Stephens, James

Esterbrook, Tom
See Hubbard, L(afayette) Ron(ald)

Estleman, Loren D. 1952- .... **CLC 48**
See also AAYA 27; CA 85-88; CANR 27, 74; CMW 4; CPW; DAM NOV; DLB 226; INT CANR-27; MTCW 1, 2

Etherege, Sir George 1636-1692 .... **LC 78**
See also BRW 2; DAM DRAM; DLB 80; PAB; RGEL 2

Euclid 306B.C.-283B.C. .... **CMLC 25**

Eugenides, Jeffrey 1960(?)- .... **CLC 81**
See also CA 144

Euripides c. 484B.C.-406B.C. ...... **CMLC 23, 51; DC 4; WLCS**
See also AW 1; CDWLB 1; DA; DAB; DAC; DAM DRAM, MST; DFS 1, 4, 6; DLB 176; LAIT 1; RGWL 2, 3

Evan, Evin
See Faust, Frederick (Schiller)

Evans, Caradoc 1878-1945 ... **TCLC 85; SSC 43**
See also DLB 162

Evans, Evan
See Faust, Frederick (Schiller)
See also TCWW 2

Evans, Marian
See Eliot, George

Evans, Mary Ann
See Eliot, George

Evarts, Esther
See Benson, Sally

Everett, Percival
See Everett, Percival L.
See also CSW

Everett, Percival L. 1956- .... **CLC 57**
See also Everett, Percival
See also BW 2; CA 129; CANR 94

Everson, R(onald) G(ilmour)
1903-1992 .... **CLC 27**
See also CA 17-20R; DLB 88

Everson, William (Oliver)
1912-1994 .... **CLC 1, 5, 14**
See also CA 9-12R; CANR 20; DLB 5, 16, 212; MTCW 1

Evtushenko, Evgenii Aleksandrovich
See Yevtushenko, Yevgeny (Alexandrovich)
See also RGWL 2, 3

Ewart, Gavin (Buchanan)
1916-1995 .... **CLC 13, 46**
See also BRWS 7; CA 89-92; CANR 17, 46; CP 7; DLB 40; MTCW 1

Ewers, Hanns Heinz 1871-1943 ..... **TCLC 12**
See also CA 149

Ewing, Frederick R.
See Sturgeon, Theodore (Hamilton)

Exley, Frederick (Earl) 1929-1992 .... **CLC 6, 11**
See also AITN 2; BPFB 1; CA 81-84; DLB 143; DLBY 1981

Eynhardt, Guillermo
See Quiroga, Horacio (Sylvestre)

Ezekiel, Nissim 1924- .... **CLC 61**
See also CA 61-64; CP 7

Ezekiel, Tish O'Dowd 1943- .... **CLC 34**
See also CA 129

Fadeev, Aleksandr Aleksandrovich
See Bulgya, Alexander Alexandrovich
See also DLB 272

Fadeyev, A.
See Bulgya, Alexander Alexandrovich

Fadeyev, Alexander .... **TCLC 53**
See also Bulgya, Alexander Alexandrovich

Fagen, Donald 1948- .... **CLC 26**

Fainzilberg, Ilya Arnoldovich 1897-1937
See Ilf, Ilya
See also CA 165

Fair, Ronald L. 1932- .... **CLC 18**
See also BW 1; CA 69-72; CANR 25; DLB 33

Fairbairn, Roger
See Carr, John Dickson

Fairbairns, Zoe (Ann) 1948- .... **CLC 32**
See also CA 103; CANR 21, 85; CN 7

Fairfield, Flora
See Alcott, Louisa May

Fairman, Paul W. 1916-1977
See Queen, Ellery
See also SFW 4

Falco, Gian
See Papini, Giovanni

Falconer, James
See Kirkup, James

Falconer, Kenneth
See Kornbluth, C(yril) M.

Falkland, Samuel
See Heijermans, Herman

Fallaci, Oriana 1930- .... **CLC 11, 110**
See also CA 77-80; CANR 15, 58; FW; MTCW 1

Faludi, Susan 1959- .... **CLC 140**
See also CA 138; FW; MTCW 1; NCFS 3

Faludy, George 1913- .... **CLC 42**
See also CA 21-24R

Faludy, Gyoergy
See Faludy, George

Fanon, Frantz 1925-1961 .... **CLC 74; BLC 2**
See also BW 1; CA 116; DAM MULT; WLIT 2

Fanshawe, Ann 1625-1680 .... **LC 11**

Fante, John (Thomas) 1911-1983 ..... **CLC 60**
See also AMWS 11; CA 69-72; CANR 23, 104; DLB 130; DLBY 1983

Farah, Nuruddin 1945- .. **CLC 53, 137; BLC 2**
See also AFW; BW 2, 3; CA 106; CANR 81; CDWLB 3; CN 7; DAM MULT; DLB 125; WLIT 2

Fargue, Leon-Paul 1876(?)-1947 .... **TCLC 11**
See also CANR 107; DLB 258

Farigoule, Louis
See Romains, Jules

Farina, Richard 1936(?)-1966 .... **CLC 9**
See also CA 81-84

Farley, Walter (Lorimer)
1915-1989 .... **CLC 17**
See also BYA 14; CA 17-20R; CANR 8, 29, 84; DLB 22; JRDA; MAICYA 1, 2; SATA 2, 43, 132; YAW

Farmer, Philip Jose 1918- .... **CLC 1, 19**
See also AAYA 28; BPFB 1; CA 1-4R; CANR 4, 35, 111; DLB 8; MTCW 1; SATA 93; SCFW 2; SFW 4

Farquhar, George 1677-1707 .... **LC 21**
See also BRW 2; DAM DRAM; DLB 84; RGEL 2

Farrell, J(ames) G(ordon)
1935-1979 .... **CLC 6**
See also CA 73-76; CANR 36; DLB 14, 271; MTCW 1; RGEL 2; RHW; WLIT 4

Farrell, James T(homas) 1904-1979 . **CLC 1, 4, 8, 11, 66; SSC 28**
See also AMW; BPFB 1; CA 5-8R; CANR 9, 61; DLB 4, 9, 86; DLBD 2; MTCW 1, 2; RGAL 4

Farrell, Warren (Thomas) 1943- ...... **CLC 70**
See also CA 146

Farren, Richard J.
See Betjeman, John

Farren, Richard M.
See Betjeman, John

Fassbinder, Rainer Werner
1946-1982 .... **CLC 20**
See also CA 93-96; CANR 31

Fast, Howard (Melvin) 1914- ... **CLC 23, 131**
See also AAYA 16; BPFB 1; CA 1-4R, 181; CAAE 181; CAAS 18; CANR 1, 33, 54, 75, 98; CMW 4; CN 7; CPW; DAM NOV; DLB 9; INT CANR-33; MTCW 1; RHW; SATA 7; SATA-Essay 107; TCWW 2; YAW

Faulcon, Robert
See Holdstock, Robert P.

Faulkner, William (Cuthbert)
1897-1962 .... **CLC 1, 3, 6, 8, 9, 11, 14, 18, 28, 52, 68; SSC 1, 35, 42; WLC**
See also AAYA 7; AMW; AMWR 1; BPFB 1; BYA 5; CA 81-84; CANR 33; CDALB 1929-1941; DA; DAB; DAC; DAM MST, NOV; DLB 9, 11, 44, 102; DLBD 2; DLBY 1986, 1997; EXPN; EXPS; LAIT 2; MTCW 1, 2; NFS 4, 8, 13; RGAL 4; RGSF 2; SSFS 2, 5, 6, 12; TUS

Fauset, Jessie Redmon
1882(?)-1961 .... **CLC 19, 54; BLC 2**
See also AFAW 2; BW 1; CA 109; CANR 83; DAM MULT; DLB 51; FW; HR 2; MAWW

Faust, Frederick (Schiller)
1892-1944(?) .... **TCLC 49**
See also Austin, Frank; Brand, Max; Challis, George; Dawson, Peter; Dexter, Martin; Evans, Evan; Frederick, John; Frost, Frederick; Manning, David; Silver, Nicholas
See also CA 152; DAM POP; DLB 256; TUS

Faust, Irvin 1924- .... **CLC 8**
See also CA 33-36R; CANR 28, 67; CN 7; DLB 2, 28, 218; DLBY 1980

Fawkes, Guy
See Benchley, Robert (Charles)

Fearing, Kenneth (Flexner)
1902-1961 .... **CLC 51**
See also CA 93-96; CANR 59; CMW 4; DLB 9; RGAL 4

Fecamps, Elise
See Creasey, John

Federman, Raymond 1928- .... **CLC 6, 47**
See also CA 17-20R; CAAS 8; CANR 10, 43, 83, 108; CN 7; DLBY 1980

Federspiel, J(uerg) F. 1931- .... **CLC 42**
See also CA 146
Feiffer, Jules (Ralph) 1929- ...... **CLC 2, 8, 64**
See also AAYA 3; CA 17-20R; CAD; CANR 30, 59; CD 5; DAM DRAM; DLB 7, 44; INT CANR-30; MTCW 1; SATA 8, 61, 111
Feige, Hermann Albert Otto Maximilian
See Traven, B.
Feinberg, David B. 1956-1994 .... **CLC 59**
See also CA 135
Feinstein, Elaine 1930- .... **CLC 36**
See also CA 69-72; CAAS 1; CANR 31, 68; CN 7; CP 7; CWP; DLB 14, 40; MTCW 1
Feke, Gilbert David .... **CLC 65**
Feldman, Irving (Mordecai) 1928- ..... **CLC 7**
See also CA 1-4R; CANR 1; CP 7; DLB 169
Felix-Tchicaya, Gerald
See Tchicaya, Gerald Felix
Fellini, Federico 1920-1993 .... **CLC 16, 85**
See also CA 65-68; CANR 33
Felsen, Henry Gregor 1916-1995 ..... **CLC 17**
See also CA 1-4R; CANR 1; SAAS 2; SATA 1
Felski, Rita .... **CLC 65**
Fenno, Jack
See Calisher, Hortense
Fenollosa, Ernest (Francisco) 1853-1908 .... **TCLC 91**
Fenton, James Martin 1949- .... **CLC 32**
See also CA 102; CANR 108; CP 7; DLB 40; PFS 11
Ferber, Edna 1887-1968 .... **CLC 18, 93**
See also AITN 1; CA 5-8R; CANR 68, 105; DLB 9, 28, 86, 266; MTCW 1, 2; RGAL 4; RHW; SATA 7; TCWW 2
Ferdowsi, Abu'l Qasem 940-1020 . **CMLC 43**
See also RGWL 2, 3
Ferguson, Helen
See Kavan, Anna
Ferguson, Niall 1964- .... **CLC 134**
See also CA 190
Ferguson, Samuel 1810-1886 .... **NCLC 33**
See also DLB 32; RGEL 2
Fergusson, Robert 1750-1774 .... **LC 29**
See also DLB 109; RGEL 2
Ferling, Lawrence
See Ferlinghetti, Lawrence (Monsanto)
Ferlinghetti, Lawrence (Monsanto) 1919(?)- ...... **CLC 2, 6, 10, 27, 111; PC 1**
See also CA 5-8R; CANR 3, 41, 73; CDALB 1941-1968; CP 7; DAM POET; DLB 5, 16; MTCW 1, 2; RGAL 4; WP
Fern, Fanny
See Parton, Sara Payson Willis
Fernandez, Vicente Garcia Huidobro
See Huidobro Fernandez, Vicente Garcia
Fernandez-Armesto, Felipe .... **CLC 70**
Fernandez de Lizardi, Jose Joaquin
See Lizardi, Jose Joaquin Fernandez de
Ferre, Rosario 1942- ...... **CLC 139; HLCS 1; SSC 36**
See also CA 131; CANR 55, 81; CWW 2; DLB 145; HW 1, 2; LAWS 1; MTCW 1; WLIT 1
Ferrer, Gabriel (Francisco Victor) Miro
See Miro (Ferrer), Gabriel (Francisco Victor)
Ferrier, Susan (Edmonstone) 1782-1854 .... **NCLC 8**
See also DLB 116; RGEL 2
Ferrigno, Robert 1948(?)- .... **CLC 65**
See also CA 140
Ferron, Jacques 1921-1985 .... **CLC 94**
See also CA 129; CCA 1; DAC; DLB 60

Feuchtwanger, Lion 1884-1958 .... **TCLC 3**
See also CA 187; DLB 66
Feuillet, Octave 1821-1890 .... **NCLC 45**
See also DLB 192
Feydeau, Georges (Leon Jules Marie) 1862-1921 .... **TCLC 22**
See also CA 152; CANR 84; DAM DRAM; DLB 192; GFL 1789 to the Present; RGWL 2, 3
Fichte, Johann Gottlieb 1762-1814 .... **NCLC 62**
See also DLB 90
Ficino, Marsilio 1433-1499 .... **LC 12**
Fiedeler, Hans
See Doeblin, Alfred
Fiedler, Leslie A(aron) 1917- .. **CLC 4, 13, 24**
See also CA 9-12R; CANR 7, 63; CN 7; DLB 28, 67; MTCW 1, 2; RGAL 4; TUS
Field, Andrew 1938- .... **CLC 44**
See also CA 97-100; CANR 25
Field, Eugene 1850-1895 .... **NCLC 3**
See also DLB 23, 42, 140; DLBD 13; MAI-CYA 1, 2; RGAL 4; SATA 16
Field, Gans T.
See Wellman, Manly Wade
Field, Michael 1915-1971 .... **TCLC 43**
Field, Peter
See Hobson, Laura Z(ametkin)
See also TCWW 2
Fielding, Helen 1959(?)- .... **CLC 146**
See also CA 172; DLB 231
Fielding, Henry 1707-1754 .. **LC 1, 46; WLC**
See also BRW 3; BRWR 1; CDBLB 1660-1789; DA; DAB; DAC; DAM DRAM, MST, NOV; DLB 39, 84, 101; RGEL 2; TEA; WLIT 3
Fielding, Sarah 1710-1768 .... **LC 1, 44**
See also DLB 39; RGEL 2; TEA
Fields, W. C. 1880-1946 .... **TCLC 80**
See also DLB 44
Fierstein, Harvey (Forbes) 1954- ..... **CLC 33**
See also CA 129; CAD; CD 5; CPW; DAM DRAM, POP; DFS 6; DLB 266; GLL
Figes, Eva 1932- .... **CLC 31**
See also CA 53-56; CANR 4, 44, 83; CN 7; DLB 14, 271; FW
Filippo, Eduardo de
See de Filippo, Eduardo
Finch, Anne 1661-1720 .... **LC 3; PC 21**
See also DLB 95
Finch, Robert (Duer Claydon) 1900-1995 .... **CLC 18**
See also CA 57-60; CANR 9, 24, 49; CP 7; DLB 88
Findley, Timothy 1930- .... **CLC 27, 102**
See also CA 25-28R; CANR 12, 42, 69, 109; CCA 1; CN 7; DAC; DAM MST; DLB 53; FANT; RHW
Fink, William
See Mencken, H(enry) L(ouis)
Firbank, Louis 1942-
See Reed, Lou
Firbank, (Arthur Annesley) Ronald 1886-1926 .... **TCLC 1**
See also BRWS 2; CA 177; DLB 36; RGEL 2
Fish, Stanley
See Fish, Stanley Eugene
Fish, Stanley E.
See Fish, Stanley Eugene
Fish, Stanley Eugene 1938- .... **CLC 142**
See also CA 132; CANR 90; DLB 67
Fisher, Dorothy (Frances) Canfield 1879-1958 .... **TCLC 87**
See also CA 136; CANR 80; CLR 71,; CWRI 5; DLB 9, 102; MAICYA 1, 2; YABC 1

Fisher, M(ary) F(rances) K(ennedy) 1908-1992 .... **CLC 76, 87**
See also CA 77-80; CANR 44; MTCW 1
Fisher, Roy 1930- .... **CLC 25**
See also CA 81-84; CAAS 10; CANR 16; CP 7; DLB 40
Fisher, Rudolph 1897-1934 .. **TCLC 11; BLC 2; SSC 25**
See also BW 1, 3; CA 124; CANR 80; DAM MULT; DLB 51, 102; HR 2
Fisher, Vardis (Alvero) 1895-1968 ...... **CLC 7**
See also CA 5-8R; CANR 68; DLB 9, 206; RGAL 4; TCWW 2
Fiske, Tarleton
See Bloch, Robert (Albert)
Fitch, Clarke
See Sinclair, Upton (Beall)
Fitch, John IV
See Cormier, Robert (Edmund)
Fitzgerald, Captain Hugh
See Baum, L(yman) Frank
FitzGerald, Edward 1809-1883 .... **NCLC 9**
See also BRW 4; DLB 32; RGEL 2
Fitzgerald, F(rancis) Scott (Key) 1896-1940 . **TCLC 1, 6, 14, 28, 55; SSC 6, 31; WLC**
See also AAYA 24; AITN 1; AMW; AMWR 1; BPFB 1; CA 123; CDALB 1917-1929; DA; DAB; DAC; DAM MST, NOV; DLB 4, 9, 86, 219; DLBD 1, 15, 16; DLBY 1981, 1996; EXPN; EXPS; LAIT 3; MTCW 1, 2; NFS 2; RGAL 4; RGSF 2; SSFS 4, 15; TUS
Fitzgerald, Penelope 1916-2000 . **CLC 19, 51, 61, 143**
See also BRWS 5; CA 85-88; CAAS 10; CANR 56, 86; CN 7; DLB 14, 194; MTCW 2
Fitzgerald, Robert (Stuart) 1910-1985 .... **CLC 39**
See also CA 1-4R; CANR 1; DLBY 1980
FitzGerald, Robert D(avid) 1902-1987 .... **CLC 19**
See also CA 17-20R; DLB 260; RGEL 2
Fitzgerald, Zelda (Sayre) 1900-1948 .... **TCLC 52**
See also AMWS 9; CA 126; DLBY 1984
Flanagan, Thomas (James Bonner) 1923- .... **CLC 25, 52**
See also CA 108; CANR 55; CN 7; DLBY 1980; INT 108; MTCW 1; RHW
Flaubert, Gustave 1821-1880 .... **NCLC 2, 10, 19, 62, 66; SSC 11; WLC**
See also DA; DAB; DAC; DAM MST, NOV; DLB 119; EW 7; EXPS; GFL 1789 to the Present; LAIT 2; NFS 14; RGSF 2; RGWL 2, 3; SSFS 6; TWA
Flavius Josephus
See Josephus, Flavius
Flecker, Herman Elroy
See Flecker, (Herman) James Elroy
Flecker, (Herman) James Elroy 1884-1915 .... **TCLC 43**
See also CA 150; DLB 10, 19; RGEL 2
Fleming, Ian (Lancaster) 1908-1964 . **CLC 3, 30**
See also AAYA 26; BPFB 1; CA 5-8R; CANR 59; CDBLB 1945-1960; CMW 4; CPW; DAM POP; DLB 87, 201; MSW; MTCW 1, 2; RGEL 2; SATA 9; TEA; YAW
Fleming, Thomas (James) 1927- .... **CLC 37**
See also CA 5-8R; CANR 10, 102; INT CANR-10; SATA 8
Fletcher, John 1579-1625 .... **LC 33; DC 6**
See also BRW 2; CDBLB Before 1660; DLB 58; RGEL 2; TEA
Fletcher, John Gould 1886-1950 .... **TCLC 35**
See also CA 167; DLB 4, 45; RGAL 4

Fleur, Paul
　See Pohl, Frederik
Flooglebuckle, Al
　See Spiegelman, Art
Flora, Fletcher 1914-1969
　See Queen, Ellery
　See also CA 1-4R; CANR 3, 85
Flying Officer X
　See Bates, H(erbert) E(rnest)
Fo, Dario 1926- .... **CLC 32, 109; DC 10**
　See also CA 128; CANR 68; CWW 2; DAM DRAM; DLBY 1997; MTCW 1, 2
Fogarty, Jonathan Titulescu Esq.
　See Farrell, James T(homas)
Follett, Ken(neth Martin) 1949- .... **CLC 18**
　See also AAYA 6; BEST 89:4; BPFB 1; CA 81-84; CANR 13, 33, 54, 102; CMW 4; CPW; DAM NOV, POP; DLB 87; DLBY 1981; INT CANR-33; MTCW 1
Fontane, Theodor 1819-1898 .... **NCLC 26**
　See also CDWLB 2; DLB 129; EW 6; RGWL 2, 3; TWA
Fontenot, Chester .... **CLC 65**
Fonvizin, Denis Ivanovich 1744(?)-1792 .... **LC 81**
　See also DLB 150; RGWL 2, 3
Foote, Horton 1916- .... **CLC 51, 91**
　See also CA 73-76; CAD; CANR 34, 51, 110; CD 5; CSW; DAM DRAM; DLB 26, 266; INT CANR-34
Foote, Mary Hallock 1847-1938 .. **TCLC 108**
　See also DLB 186, 188, 202, 221
Foote, Shelby 1916- .... **CLC 75**
　See also AAYA 40; CA 5-8R; CANR 3, 45, 74; CN 7; CPW; CSW; DAM NOV, POP; DLB 2, 17; MTCW 2; RHW
Forbes, Cosmo
　See Lewton, Val
Forbes, Esther 1891-1967 .... **CLC 12**
　See also AAYA 17; BYA 2; CA 13-14; CAP 1; CLR 27; DLB 22; JRDA; MAICYA 1, 2; RHW; SATA 2, 100; YAW
Forche, Carolyn (Louise) 1950- .... **CLC 25, 83, 86; PC 10**
　See also CA 117; CANR 50, 74; CP 7; CWP; DAM POET; DLB 5, 193; INT CA-117; MTCW 1; RGAL 4
Ford, Elbur
　See Hibbert, Eleanor Alice Burford
Ford, Ford Madox 1873-1939 ... **TCLC 1, 15, 39, 57**
　See also Chaucer, Daniel
　See also BRW 6; CA 132; CANR 74; CDBLB 1914-1945; DAM NOV; DLB 34, 98, 162; MTCW 1, 2; RGEL 2; TEA
Ford, Henry 1863-1947 .... **TCLC 73**
　See also CA 148
Ford, Jack
　See Ford, John
Ford, John 1586-1639 .... **LC 68; DC 8**
　See also BRW 2; CDBLB Before 1660; DAM DRAM; DFS 7; DLB 58; IDTP; RGEL 2
Ford, John 1895-1973 .... **CLC 16**
　See also CA 187
Ford, Richard 1944- ..... **CLC 46, 99; SSC 57**
　See also AMWS 5; CA 69-72; CANR 11, 47, 86; CN 7; CSW; DLB 227; MTCW 1; RGAL 4; RGSF 2
Ford, Webster
　See Masters, Edgar Lee
Foreman, Richard 1937- .... **CLC 50**
　See also CA 65-68; CAD; CANR 32, 63; CD 5
Forester, C(ecil) S(cott) 1899-1966 ... **CLC 35**
　See also CA 73-76; CANR 83; DLB 191; RGEL 2; RHW; SATA 13
Forez
　See Mauriac, Francois (Charles)

Forman, James
　See Forman, James D(ouglas)
Forman, James D(ouglas) 1932- .... **CLC 21**
　See also AAYA 17; CA 9-12R; CANR 4, 19, 42; JRDA; MAICYA 1, 2; SATA 8, 70; YAW
Forman, Milos 1932- .... **CLC 164**
　See also CA 109
Fornes, Maria Irene 1930- . **CLC 39, 61; DC 10; HLCS 1**
　See also CA 25-28R; CAD; CANR 28, 81; CD 5; CWD; DLB 7; HW 1, 2; INT CANR-28; MTCW 1; RGAL 4
Forrest, Leon (Richard) 1937-1997 .. **CLC 4; BLCS**
　See also AFAW 2; BW 2; CA 89-92; CAAS 7; CANR 25, 52, 87; CN 7; DLB 33
Forster, E(dward) M(organ) 1879-1970 ...... **CLC 1, 2, 3, 4, 9, 10, 13, 15, 22, 45, 77; SSC 27; WLC**
　See also AAYA 2, 37; BRW 6; BRWR 2; CA 13-14; CANR 45; CAP 1; CDBLB 1914-1945; DA; DAB; DAC; DAM MST, NOV; DLB 34, 98, 162, 178, 195; DLBD 10; EXPN; LAIT 3; MTCW 1, 2; NCFS 1; NFS 3, 10, 11; RGEL 2; RGSF 2; SATA 57; SUFW 1; TCLC 125; TEA; WLIT 4
Forster, John 1812-1876 .... **NCLC 11**
　See also DLB 144, 184
Forster, Margaret 1938- .... **CLC 149**
　See also CA 133; CANR 62; CN 7; DLB 155, 271
Forsyth, Frederick 1938- .... **CLC 2, 5, 36**
　See also BEST 89:4; CA 85-88; CANR 38, 62; CMW 4; CN 7; CPW; DAM NOV, POP; DLB 87; MTCW 1, 2
Forten, Charlotte L. 1837-1914 .... **TCLC 16; BLC 2**
　See also Grimke, Charlotte L(ottie) Forten
　See also DLB 50, 239
Fortinbras
　See Grieg, (Johan) Nordahl (Brun)
Foscolo, Ugo 1778-1827 .... **NCLC 8, 97**
　See also EW 5
Fosse, Bob .... **CLC 20**
　See also Fosse, Robert Louis
Fosse, Robert Louis 1927-1987
　See Fosse, Bob
Foster, Hannah Webster 1758-1840 .... **NCLC 99**
　See also DLB 37, 200; RGAL 4
Foster, Stephen Collins 1826-1864 .... **NCLC 26**
　See also RGAL 4
Foucault, Michel 1926-1984 . **CLC 31, 34, 69**
　See also CA 105; CANR 34; DLB 242; EW 13; GFL 1789 to the Present; GLL 1; MTCW 1, 2; TWA
Fouque, Friedrich (Heinrich Karl) de la Motte 1777-1843 .... **NCLC 2**
　See also DLB 90; RGWL 2, 3; SUFW 1
Fourier, Charles 1772-1837 .... **NCLC 51**
Fournier, Henri Alban 1886-1914
　See Alain-Fournier
　See also CA 179
Fournier, Pierre 1916- .... **CLC 11**
　See also Gascar, Pierre
　See also CA 89-92; CANR 16, 40
Fowles, John (Robert) 1926- . **CLC 1, 2, 3, 4, 6, 9, 10, 15, 33, 87; SSC 33**
　See also BPFB 1; BRWS 1; CA 5-8R; CANR 25, 71, 103; CDBLB 1960 to Present; CN 7; DAB; DAC; DAM MST; DLB 14, 139, 207; HGG; MTCW 1, 2; RGEL 2; RHW; SATA 22; TEA; WLIT 4

Fox, Paula 1923- .... **CLC 2, 8, 121**
　See also AAYA 3, 37; BYA 3, 8; CA 73-76; CANR 20, 36, 62, 105; CLR 1, 44; DLB 52; JRDA; MAICYA 1, 2; MTCW 1; NFS 12; SATA 17, 60, 120; WYA; YAW
Fox, William Price (Jr.) 1926- .... **CLC 22**
　See also CA 17-20R; CAAS 19; CANR 11; CSW; DLB 2; DLBY 1981
Foxe, John 1517(?)-1587 .... **LC 14**
　See also DLB 132
Frame, Janet .. **CLC 2, 3, 6, 22, 66, 96; SSC 29**
　See also Clutha, Janet Paterson Frame
　See also CN 7; CWP; RGEL 2; RGSF 2; TWA
France, Anatole .... **TCLC 9**
　See also Thibault, Jacques Anatole Francois
　See also DLB 123; GFL 1789 to the Present; MTCW 1; RGWL 2, 3; SUFW 1
Francis, Claude .... **CLC 50**
　See also CA 192
Francis, Dick 1920- .... **CLC 2, 22, 42, 102**
　See also AAYA 5, 21; BEST 89:3; BPFB 1; CA 5-8R; CANR 9, 42, 68, 100; CDBLB 1960 to Present; CMW 4; CN 7; DAM POP; DLB 87; INT CANR-9; MSW; MTCW 1, 2
Francis, Robert (Churchill) 1901-1987 .... **CLC 15; PC 34**
　See also AMWS 9; CA 1-4R; CANR 1; EXPP; PFS 12
Francis, Lord Jeffrey
　See Jeffrey, Francis
　See also DLB 107
Frank, Anne(lies Marie) 1929-1945 .... **TCLC 17; WLC**
　See also AAYA 12; BYA 1; CA 133; CANR 68; DA; DAB; DAC; DAM MST; LAIT 4; MAICYA 2; MAICYAS 1; MTCW 1, 2; NCFS 2; SATA 87; SATA-Brief 42; WYA; YAW
Frank, Bruno 1887-1945 .... **TCLC 81**
　See also CA 189; DLB 118
Frank, Elizabeth 1945- .... **CLC 39**
　See also CA 126; CANR 78; INT 126
Frankl, Viktor E(mil) 1905-1997 .... **CLC 93**
　See also CA 65-68
Franklin, Benjamin
　See Hasek, Jaroslav (Matej Frantisek)
Franklin, Benjamin 1706-1790 .... **LC 25; WLCS**
　See also AMW; CDALB 1640-1865; DA; DAB; DAC; DAM MST; DLB 24, 43, 73, 183; LAIT 1; RGAL 4; TUS
Franklin, (Stella Maria Sarah) Miles (Lampe) 1879-1954 .... **TCLC 7**
　See also CA 164; DLB 230; FW; MTCW 2; RGEL 2; TWA
Fraser, (Lady) Antonia (Pakenham) 1932- .... **CLC 32, 107**
　See also CA 85-88; CANR 44, 65; CMW; MTCW 1, 2; SATA-Brief 32
Fraser, George MacDonald 1925- ...... **CLC 7**
　See also CA 45-48; CAAE 180; CANR 2, 48, 74; MTCW 1; RHW
Fraser, Sylvia 1935- .... **CLC 64**
　See also CA 45-48; CANR 1, 16, 60; CCA 1
Frayn, Michael 1933- .... **CLC 3, 7, 31, 47**
　See also BRWS 7; CA 5-8R; CANR 30, 69; CBD; CD 5; CN 7; DAM DRAM, NOV; DLB 13, 14, 194, 245; FANT; MTCW 1, 2; SFW 4
Fraze, Candida (Merrill) 1945- .... **CLC 50**
　See also CA 126
Frazer, Andrew
　See Marlowe, Stephen

Frazer, J(ames) G(eorge)
1854-1941 .... **TCLC 32**
See also BRWS 3

Frazer, Robert Caine
See Creasey, John

Frazer, Sir James George
See Frazer, J(ames) G(eorge)

Frazier, Charles 1950- .... **CLC 109**
See also AAYA 34; CA 161; CSW

Frazier, Ian 1951- .... **CLC 46**
See also CA 130; CANR 54, 93

Frederic, Harold 1856-1898 .... **NCLC 10**
See also AMW; DLB 12, 23; DLBD 13; RGAL 4

Frederick, John
See Faust, Frederick (Schiller)
See also TCWW 2

Frederick the Great 1712-1786 .... **LC 14**

Fredro, Aleksander 1793-1876 .... **NCLC 8**

Freeling, Nicolas 1927- .... **CLC 38**
See also CA 49-52; CAAS 12; CANR 1, 17, 50, 84; CMW 4; CN 7; DLB 87

Freeman, Douglas Southall
1886-1953 .... **TCLC 11**
See also CA 195; DLB 17; DLBD 17

Freeman, Judith 1946- .... **CLC 55**
See also CA 148; DLB 256

Freeman, Mary E(leanor) Wilkins
1852-1930 .... **TCLC 9; SSC 1, 47**
See also CA 177; DLB 12, 78, 221; EXPS; FW; HGG; MAWW; RGAL 4; RGSF 2; SSFS 4, 8; SUFW 1; TUS

Freeman, R(ichard) Austin
1862-1943 .... **TCLC 21**
See also CANR 84; CMW 4; DLB 70

French, Albert 1943- .... **CLC 86**
See also BW 3; CA 167

French, Antonia
See Kureishi, Hanif

French, Marilyn 1929- .... **CLC 10, 18, 60**
See also BPFB 1; CA 69-72; CANR 3, 31; CN 7; CPW; DAM DRAM, NOV, POP; FW; INT CANR-31; MTCW 1, 2

French, Paul
See Asimov, Isaac

Freneau, Philip Morin 1752-1832 .. **NCLC 1, 111**
See also AMWS 2; DLB 37, 43; RGAL 4

Freud, Sigmund 1856-1939 .... **TCLC 52**
See also CA 133; CANR 69; EW 8; MTCW 1, 2; NCFS 3; TWA

Freytag, Gustav 1816-1895 .... **NCLC 109**
See also DLB 129

Friedan, Betty (Naomi) 1921- .... **CLC 74**
See also CA 65-68; CANR 18, 45, 74; DLB 246; FW; MTCW 1, 2

Friedlander, Saul 1932- .... **CLC 90**
See also CA 130; CANR 72

Friedman, B(ernard) H(arper)
1926- .... **CLC 7**
See also CA 1-4R; CANR 3, 48

Friedman, Bruce Jay 1930- .... **CLC 3, 5, 56**
See also CA 9-12R; CAD; CANR 25, 52, 101; CD 5; CN 7; DLB 2, 28, 244; INT CANR-25

Friel, Brian 1929- .... **CLC 5, 42, 59, 115; DC 8**
See also BRWS 5; CA 21-24R; CANR 33, 69; CBD; CD 5; DFS 11; DLB 13; MTCW 1; RGEL 2; TEA

Friis-Baastad, Babbis Ellinor
1921-1970 .... **CLC 12**
See also CA 17-20R; SATA 7

Frisch, Max (Rudolf) 1911-1991 .. **CLC 3, 9, 14, 18, 32, 44**
See also CA 85-88; CANR 32, 74; CDWLB 2; DAM DRAM, NOV; DLB 69, 124; EW 13; MTCW 1, 2; RGWL 2, 3; TCLC 121

Fromentin, Eugene (Samuel Auguste)
1820-1876 .... **NCLC 10**
See also DLB 123; GFL 1789 to the Present

Frost, Frederick
See Faust, Frederick (Schiller)
See also TCWW 2

Frost, Robert (Lee) 1874-1963 .. **CLC 1, 3, 4, 9, 10, 13, 15, 26, 34, 44; PC 1, 39; WLC**
See also AAYA 21; AMW; AMWR 1; CA 89-92; CANR 33; CDALB 1917-1929; CLR 67; DA; DAB; DAC; DAM MST, POET; DLB 54; DLBD 7; EXPP; MTCW 1, 2; PAB; PFS 1, 2, 3, 4, 5, 6, 7, 10, 13; RGAL 4; SATA 14; TUS; WP; WYA

Froude, James Anthony
1818-1894 .... **NCLC 43**
See also DLB 18, 57, 144

Froy, Herald
See Waterhouse, Keith (Spencer)

Fry, Christopher 1907- .... **CLC 2, 10, 14**
See also BRWS 3; CA 17-20R; CAAS 23; CANR 9, 30, 74; CBD; CD 5; CP 7; DAM DRAM; DLB 13; MTCW 1, 2; RGEL 2; SATA 66; TEA

Frye, (Herman) Northrop
1912-1991 .... **CLC 24, 70**
See also CA 5-8R; CANR 8, 37; DLB 67, 68, 246; MTCW 1, 2; RGAL 4; TWA

Fuchs, Daniel 1909-1993 .... **CLC 8, 22**
See also CA 81-84; CAAS 5; CANR 40; DLB 9, 26, 28; DLBY 1993

Fuchs, Daniel 1934- .... **CLC 34**
See also CA 37-40R; CANR 14, 48

Fuentes, Carlos 1928- .. **CLC 3, 8, 10, 13, 22, 41, 60, 113; HLC 1; SSC 24; WLC**
See also AAYA 4; AITN 2; BPFB 1; CA 69-72; CANR 10, 32, 68, 104; CDWLB 3; CWW 2; DA; DAB; DAC; DAM MST, MULT, NOV; DLB 113; DNFS 2; HW 1, 2; LAIT 3; LAW; LAWS 1; MTCW 1, 2; NFS 8; RGSF 2; RGWL 2, 3; TWA; WLIT 1

Fuentes, Gregorio Lopez y
See Lopez y Fuentes, Gregorio

Fuertes, Gloria 1918-1998 .... **PC 27**
See also CA 178, 180; DLB 108; HW 2; SATA 115

Fugard, (Harold) Athol 1932- . **CLC 5, 9, 14, 25, 40, 80; DC 3**
See also AAYA 17; AFW; CA 85-88; CANR 32, 54; CD 5; DAM DRAM; DFS 3, 6, 10; DLB 225; DNFS 1, 2; MTCW 1; RGEL 2; WLIT 2

Fugard, Sheila 1932- .... **CLC 48**
See also CA 125

Fukuyama, Francis 1952- .... **CLC 131**
See also CA 140; CANR 72

Fuller, Charles (H., Jr.) 1939- .... **CLC 25; BLC 2; DC 1**
See also BW 2; CA 112; CAD; CANR 87; CD 5; DAM DRAM, MULT; DFS 8; DLB 38, 266; INT CA-112; MTCW 1

Fuller, Henry Blake 1857-1929 .... **TCLC 103**
See also CA 177; DLB 12; RGAL 4

Fuller, John (Leopold) 1937- .... **CLC 62**
See also CA 21-24R; CANR 9, 44; CP 7; DLB 40

Fuller, Margaret
See Ossoli, Sarah Margaret (Fuller)
See also AMWS 2; DLB 183, 223, 239

Fuller, Roy (Broadbent) 1912-1991 ... **CLC 4, 28**
See also BRWS 7; CA 5-8R; CAAS 10; CANR 53, 83; CWRI 5; DLB 15, 20; RGEL 2; SATA 87

Fuller, Sarah Margaret
See Ossoli, Sarah Margaret (Fuller)

Fuller, Sarah Margaret
See Ossoli, Sarah Margaret (Fuller)
See also DLB 1, 59, 73

Fulton, Alice 1952- .... **CLC 52**
See also CA 116; CANR 57, 88; CP 7; CWP; DLB 193

Furphy, Joseph 1843-1912 .... **TCLC 25**
See also CA 163; DLB 230; RGEL 2

Fuson, Robert H(enderson) 1927- .... **CLC 70**
See also CA 89-92; CANR 103

Fussell, Paul 1924- .... **CLC 74**
See also BEST 90:1; CA 17-20R; CANR 8, 21, 35, 69; INT CANR-21; MTCW 1, 2

Futabatei, Shimei 1864-1909 .... **TCLC 44**
See also Futabatei Shimei
See also CA 162; MJW

Futabatei Shimei
See Futabatei, Shimei
See also DLB 180

Futrelle, Jacques 1875-1912 .... **TCLC 19**
See also CA 155; CMW 4

Gaboriau, Emile 1835-1873 .... **NCLC 14**
See also CMW 4; MSW

Gadda, Carlo Emilio 1893-1973 .... **CLC 11**
See also CA 89-92; DLB 177

Gaddis, William 1922-1998 ... **CLC 1, 3, 6, 8, 10, 19, 43, 86**
See also AMWS 4; BPFB 1; CA 17-20R; CANR 21, 48; CN 7; DLB 2; MTCW 1, 2; RGAL 4

Gaelique, Moruen le
See Jacob, (Cyprien-)Max

Gage, Walter
See Inge, William (Motter)

Gaines, Ernest J(ames) 1933- ...... **CLC 3, 11, 18, 86; BLC 2**
See also AAYA 18; AFAW 1, 2; AITN 1; BPFB 2; BW 2, 3; BYA 6; CA 9-12R; CANR 6, 24, 42, 75; CDALB 1968-1988; CLR 62; CN 7; CSW; DAM MULT; DLB 2, 33, 152; DLBY 1980; EXPN; LAIT 5; MTCW 1, 2; NFS 5, 7; RGAL 4; RGSF 2; RHW; SATA 86; SSFS 5; YAW

Gaitskill, Mary 1954- .... **CLC 69**
See also CA 128; CANR 61; DLB 244

Galdos, Benito Perez
See Perez Galdos, Benito
See also EW 7

Gale, Zona 1874-1938 .... **TCLC 7**
See also CA 153; CANR 84; DAM DRAM; DLB 9, 78, 228; RGAL 4

Galeano, Eduardo (Hughes) 1940- . **CLC 72; HLCS 1**
See also CA 29-32R; CANR 13, 32, 100; HW 1

Galiano, Juan Valera y Alcala
See Valera y Alcala-Galiano, Juan

Galilei, Galileo 1564-1642 .... **LC 45**

Gallagher, Tess 1943- .... **CLC 18, 63; PC 9**
See also CA 106; CP 7; CWP; DAM POET; DLB 120, 212, 244

Gallant, Mavis 1922- ...... **CLC 7, 18, 38, 167; SSC 5**
See also CA 69-72; CANR 29, 69; CCA 1; CN 7; DAC; DAM MST; DLB 53; MTCW 1, 2; RGEL 2; RGSF 2

Gallant, Roy A(rthur) 1924- .... **CLC 17**
See also CA 5-8R; CANR 4, 29, 54; CLR 30; MAICYA 1, 2; SATA 4, 68, 110

Gallico, Paul (William) 1897-1976 ..... **CLC 2**
See also AITN 1; CA 5-8R; CANR 23; DLB 9, 171; FANT; MAICYA 1, 2; SATA 13

Gallo, Max Louis 1932- .... **CLC 95**
See also CA 85-88

Gallois, Lucien
See Desnos, Robert

Gallup, Ralph
See Whitemore, Hugh (John)

Galsworthy, John 1867-1933 .... **TCLC 1, 45; SSC 22; WLC**
See also BRW 6; CA 141; CANR 75; CDBLB 1890-1914; DA; DAB; DAC; DAM DRAM, MST, NOV; DLB 10, 34, 98, 162; DLBD 16; MTCW 1; RGEL 2; SSFS 3; TEA

Galt, John 1779-1839 .... **NCLC 1, 110**
See also DLB 99, 116, 159; RGEL 2; RGSF 2

Galvin, James 1951- .... **CLC 38**
See also CA 108; CANR 26

Gamboa, Federico 1864-1939 .... **TCLC 36**
See also CA 167; HW 2; LAW

Gandhi, M. K.
See Gandhi, Mohandas Karamchand

Gandhi, Mahatma
See Gandhi, Mohandas Karamchand

Gandhi, Mohandas Karamchand
1869-1948 .... **TCLC 59**
See also CA 132; DAM MULT; MTCW 1, 2

Gann, Ernest Kellogg 1910-1991 ..... **CLC 23**
See also AITN 1; BPFB 2; CA 1-4R; CANR 1, 83; RHW

Gao Xingjian 1940- .... **CLC 167**
See also Xingjian, Gao
See also CA 193; RGWL 3

Garber, Eric 1943(?)-
See Holleran, Andrew
See also CANR 89

Garcia, Cristina 1958- .... **CLC 76**
See also AMWS 11; CA 141; CANR 73; DNFS 1; HW 2

Garcia Lorca, Federico 1898-1936 . **TCLC 1, 7, 49; DC 2; HLC 2; PC 3; WLC**
See also Lorca, Federico Garcia
See also CA 131; CANR 81; DA; DAB; DAC; DAM DRAM, MST, MULT, POET; DFS 10; DLB 108; HW 1, 2; MTCW 1, 2; TWA

Garcia Marquez, Gabriel (Jose)
1928- .... **CLC 2, 3, 8, 10, 15, 27, 47, 55, 68; HLC 1; SSC 8; WLC**
See also AAYA 3, 33; BEST 89:1, 90:4; BPFB 2; BYA 12; CA 33-36R; CANR 10, 28, 50, 75, 82; CDWLB 3; CPW; DA; DAB; DAC; DAM MST, MULT, NOV, POP; DLB 113; DNFS 1, 2; EXPN; EXPS; HW 1, 2; LAIT 2; LAW; LAWS 1; MTCW 1, 2; NCFS 3; NFS 1, 5, 10; RGSF 2; RGWL 2, 3; SSFS 1, 6; TWA; WLIT 1

Garcilaso de la Vega, El Inca 1503-1536
See also HLCS 1; LAW

Gard, Janice
See Latham, Jean Lee

Gard, Roger Martin du
See Martin du Gard, Roger

Gardam, Jane (Mary) 1928- .... **CLC 43**
See also CA 49-52; CANR 2, 18, 33, 54, 106; CLR 12; DLB 14, 161, 231; MAICYA 1, 2; MTCW 1; SAAS 9; SATA 39, 76, 130; SATA-Brief 28; YAW

Gardner, Herb(ert) 1934- .... **CLC 44**
See also CA 149; CAD; CD 5

Gardner, John (Champlin), Jr.
1933-1982 ...... **CLC 2, 3, 5, 7, 8, 10, 18, 28, 34; SSC 7**
See also AITN 1; AMWS 6; BPFB 2; CA 65-68; CANR 33, 73; CDALBS; CPW; DAM NOV, POP; DLB 2; DLBY 1982; FANT; MTCW 1; NFS 3; RGAL 4; RGSF 2; SATA 40; SATA-Obit 31; SSFS 8

Gardner, John (Edmund) 1926- .... **CLC 30**
See also CA 103; CANR 15, 69; CMW 4; CPW; DAM POP; MTCW 1

Gardner, Miriam
See Bradley, Marion Zimmer
See also GLL 1

Gardner, Noel
See Kuttner, Henry

Gardons, S. S.
See Snodgrass, W(illiam) D(e Witt)

Garfield, Leon 1921-1996 .... **CLC 12**
See also AAYA 8; BYA 1, 3; CA 17-20R; CANR 38, 41, 78; CLR 21; DLB 161; JRDA; MAICYA 1, 2; MAICYAS 1; SATA 1, 32, 76; SATA-Obit 90; TEA; WYA; YAW

Garland, (Hannibal) Hamlin
1860-1940 .... **TCLC 3; SSC 18**
See also DLB 12, 71, 78, 186; RGAL 4; RGSF 2; TCWW 2

Garneau, (Hector de) Saint-Denys
1912-1943 .... **TCLC 13**
See also DLB 88

Garner, Alan 1934- .... **CLC 17**
See also AAYA 18; BYA 3, 5; CA 73-76, 178; CAAE 178; CANR 15, 64; CLR 20; CPW; DAB; DAM POP; DLB 161, 261; FANT; MAICYA 1, 2; MTCW 1, 2; SATA 18, 69; SATA-Essay 108; SUFW 1, 2; YAW

Garner, Hugh 1913-1979 .... **CLC 13**
See also Warwick, Jarvis
See also CA 69-72; CANR 31; CCA 1; DLB 68

Garnett, David 1892-1981 .... **CLC 3**
See also CA 5-8R; CANR 17, 79; DLB 34; FANT; MTCW 2; RGEL 2; SFW 4; SUFW 1

Garos, Stephanie
See Katz, Steve

Garrett, George (Palmer) 1929- .. **CLC 3, 11, 51; SSC 30**
See also AMWS 7; BPFB 2; CA 1-4R; CAAE 202; CAAS 5; CANR 1, 42, 67, 109; CN 7; CP 7; CSW; DLB 2, 5, 130, 152; DLBY 1983

Garrick, David 1717-1779 .... **LC 15**
See also DAM DRAM; DLB 84, 213; RGEL 2

Garrigue, Jean 1914-1972 .... **CLC 2, 8**
See also CA 5-8R; CANR 20

Garrison, Frederick
See Sinclair, Upton (Beall)

Garro, Elena 1920(?)-1998
See also CA 131; CWW 2; DLB 145; HLCS 1; HW 1; LAWS 1; WLIT 1

Garth, Will
See Hamilton, Edmond; Kuttner, Henry

Garvey, Marcus (Moziah, Jr.)
1887-1940 .... **TCLC 41; BLC 2**
See also BW 1; CA 124; CANR 79; DAM MULT; HR 2

Gary, Romain .... **CLC 25**
See also Kacew, Romain
See also DLB 83

Gascar, Pierre .... **CLC 11**
See also Fournier, Pierre

Gascoyne, David (Emery)
1916-2001 .... **CLC 45**
See also CA 65-68; CANR 10, 28, 54; CP 7; DLB 20; MTCW 1; RGEL 2

Gaskell, Elizabeth Cleghorn
1810-1865 .... **NCLC 5, 70, 97; SSC 25**
See also BRW 5; CDBLB 1832-1890; DAB; DAM MST; DLB 21, 144, 159; RGEL 2; RGSF 2; TEA

Gass, William H(oward) 1924- . **CLC 1, 2, 8, 11, 15, 39, 132; SSC 12**
See also AMWS 6; CA 17-20R; CANR 30, 71, 100; CN 7; DLB 2, 227; MTCW 1, 2; RGAL 4

Gassendi, Pierre 1592-1655 .... **LC 54**
See also GFL Beginnings to 1789

Gasset, Jose Ortega y
See Ortega y Gasset, Jose

Gates, Henry Louis, Jr. 1950- .... **CLC 65; BLCS**
See also BW 2, 3; CA 109; CANR 25, 53, 75; CSW; DAM MULT; DLB 67; MTCW 1; RGAL 4

Gautier, Theophile 1811-1872 .. **NCLC 1, 59; PC 18; SSC 20**
See also DAM POET; DLB 119; EW 6; GFL 1789 to the Present; RGWL 2, 3; SUFW; TWA

Gawsworth, John
See Bates, H(erbert) E(rnest)

Gay, John 1685-1732 .... **LC 49**
See also BRW 3; DAM DRAM; DLB 84, 95; RGEL 2; WLIT 3

Gay, Oliver
See Gogarty, Oliver St. John

Gay, Peter (Jack) 1923- .... **CLC 158**
See also CA 13-16R; CANR 18, 41, 77; INT CANR-18

Gaye, Marvin (Pentz, Jr.)
1939-1984 .... **CLC 26**
See also CA 195

Gebler, Carlo (Ernest) 1954- .... **CLC 39**
See also CA 133; CANR 96; DLB 271

Gee, Maggie (Mary) 1948- .... **CLC 57**
See also CA 130; CN 7; DLB 207

Gee, Maurice (Gough) 1931- .... **CLC 29**
See also AAYA 42; CA 97-100; CANR 67; CLR 56; CN 7; CWRI 5; MAICYA 2; RGSF 2; SATA 46, 101

Gelbart, Larry (Simon) 1928- .... **CLC 21, 61**
See also Gelbart, Larry
See also CA 73-76; CANR 45, 94

Gelbart, Larry 1928-
See Gelbart, Larry (Simon)
See also CAD; CD 5

Gelber, Jack 1932- .... **CLC 1, 6, 14, 79**
See also CA 1-4R; CAD; CANR 2; DLB 7, 228

Gellhorn, Martha (Ellis)
1908-1998 .... **CLC 14, 60**
See also CA 77-80; CANR 44; CN 7; DLBY 1982, 1998

Genet, Jean 1910-1986 .. **CLC 1, 2, 5, 10, 14, 44, 46; TCLC 128**
See also CA 13-16R; CANR 18; DAM DRAM; DFS 10; DLB 72; DLBY 1986; EW 13; GFL 1789 to the Present; GLL 1; MTCW 1, 2; RGWL 2, 3; TWA

Gent, Peter 1942- .... **CLC 29**
See also AITN 1; CA 89-92; DLBY 1982

Gentile, Giovanni 1875-1944 .... **TCLC 96**

Gentlewoman in New England, A
See Bradstreet, Anne

Gentlewoman in Those Parts, A
See Bradstreet, Anne

Geoffrey of Monmouth c.
1100-1155 .... **CMLC 44**
See also DLB 146; TEA

George, Jean
See George, Jean Craighead

George, Jean Craighead 1919- .... **CLC 35**
See also AAYA 8; BYA 2, 4; CA 5-8R; CANR 25; CLR 1; 80; DLB 52; JRDA; MAICYA 1, 2; SATA 2, 68, 124; WYA; YAW

George, Stefan (Anton) 1868-1933 . **TCLC 2, 14**
See also CA 193; EW 8

Georges, Georges Martin
See Simenon, Georges (Jacques Christian)

Gerhardi, William Alexander
See Gerhardie, William Alexander

Gerhardie, William Alexander
1895-1977 .... **CLC 5**
See also CA 25-28R; CANR 18; DLB 36; RGEL 2

Gerson, Jean 1363-1429 .... **LC 77**
See also DLB 208
Gersonides 1288-1344 .... **CMLC 49**
See also DLB 115
Gerstler, Amy 1956- .... **CLC 70**
See also CA 146; CANR 99
Gertler, T. .... **CLC 134**
See also CA 121
Ghalib .... **NCLC 39, 78**
See also Ghalib, Asadullah Khan
Ghalib, Asadullah Khan 1797-1869
See Ghalib
See also DAM POET; RGWL 2, 3
Ghelderode, Michel de 1898-1962 ..... **CLC 6, 11; DC 15**
See also CA 85-88; CANR 40, 77; DAM DRAM; EW 11; TWA
Ghiselin, Brewster 1903-2001 .... **CLC 23**
See also CA 13-16R; CAAS 10; CANR 13; CP 7
Ghose, Aurabinda 1872-1950 .... **TCLC 63**
See also CA 163
Ghose, Zulfikar 1935- .... **CLC 42**
See also CA 65-68; CANR 67; CN 7; CP 7
Ghosh, Amitav 1956- .... **CLC 44, 153**
See also CA 147; CANR 80; CN 7
Giacosa, Giuseppe 1847-1906 .... **TCLC 7**
Gibb, Lee
See Waterhouse, Keith (Spencer)
Gibbon, Lewis Grassic .... **TCLC 4**
See Mitchell, James Leslie
See also RGEL 2
Gibbons, Kaye 1960- .... **CLC 50, 88, 145**
See also AAYA 34; AMWS 10; CA 151; CANR 75; CSW; DAM POP; MTCW 1; NFS 3; RGAL 4; SATA 117
Gibran, Kahlil 1883-1931 . **TCLC 1, 9; PC 9**
See also CA 150; DAM POET, POP; MTCW 2
Gibran, Khalil
See Gibran, Kahlil
Gibson, William 1914- .... **CLC 23**
See also CA 9-12R; CAD 2; CANR 9, 42, 75; CD 5; DA; DAB; DAC; DAM DRAM, MST; DFS 2; DLB 7; LAIT 2; MTCW 2; SATA 66; YAW
Gibson, William (Ford) 1948- ... **CLC 39, 63; SSC 52**
See also AAYA 12; BPFB 2; CA 133; CANR 52, 90, 106; CN 7; CPW; DAM POP; DLB 251; MTCW 2; SCFW 2; SFW 4
Gide, Andre (Paul Guillaume) 1869-1951 ..... **TCLC 5, 12, 36; SSC 13; WLC**
See also CA 124; DA; DAB; DAC; DAM MST, NOV; DLB 65; EW 8; GFL 1789 to the Present; MTCW 1, 2; RGSF 2; RGWL 2, 3; TWA
Gifford, Barry (Colby) 1946- .... **CLC 34**
See also CA 65-68; CANR 9, 30, 40, 90
Gilbert, Frank
See De Voto, Bernard (Augustine)
Gilbert, W(illiam) S(chwenck) 1836-1911 .... **TCLC 3**
See also CA 173; DAM DRAM, POET; RGEL 2; SATA 36
Gilbreth, Frank B(unker), Jr. 1911-2001 .... **CLC 17**
See also CA 9-12R; SATA 2
Gilchrist, Ellen (Louise) 1935- .. **CLC 34, 48, 143; SSC 14**
See also BPFB 2; CA 116; CANR 41, 61, 104; CN 7; CPW; CSW; DAM POP; DLB 130; EXPS; MTCW 1, 2; RGAL 4; RGSF 2; SSFS 9
Giles, Molly 1942- .... **CLC 39**
See also CA 126; CANR 98

Gill, Eric 1882-1940 .... **TCLC 85**
Gill, Patrick
See Creasey, John
Gillette, Douglas .... **CLC 70**
Gilliam, Terry (Vance) 1940- .... **CLC 21, 141**
See also Monty Python
See also AAYA 19; CA 113; CANR 35; INT 113
Gillian, Jerry
See Gilliam, Terry (Vance)
Gilliatt, Penelope (Ann Douglass) 1932-1993 .... **CLC 2, 10, 13, 53**
See also AITN 2; CA 13-16R; CANR 49; DLB 14
Gilman, Charlotte (Anna) Perkins (Stetson) 1860-1935 ..... **TCLC 9, 37, 117; SSC 13**
See also AMWS 11; BYA 11; CA 150; DLB 221; EXPS; FW; HGG; LAIT 2; MAWW; MTCW 1; RGAL 4; RGSF 2; SFW 4; SSFS 1
Gilmour, David 1946- .... **CLC 35**
Gilpin, William 1724-1804 .... **NCLC 30**
Gilray, J. D.
See Mencken, H(enry) L(ouis)
Gilroy, Frank D(aniel) 1925- .... **CLC 2**
See also CA 81-84; CAD; CANR 32, 64, 86; CD 5; DLB 7
Gilstrap, John 1957(?)- .... **CLC 99**
See also CA 160; CANR 101
Ginsberg, Allen 1926-1997 .... **CLC 1, 2, 3, 4, 6, 13, 36, 69, 109; PC 4; WLC**
See also AAYA 33; AITN 1; AMWS 2; CA 1-4R; CANR 2, 41, 63, 95; CDALB 1941-1968; CP 7; DA; DAB; DAC; DAM MST, POET; DLB 5, 16, 169, 237; GLL 1; MTCW 1, 2; PAB; PFS 5; RGAL 4; TCLC 120; TUS; WP
Ginzburg, Eugenia .... **CLC 59**
Ginzburg, Natalia 1916-1991 .... **CLC 5, 11, 54, 70**
See also CA 85-88; CANR 33; DFS 14; DLB 177; EW 13; MTCW 1, 2; RGWL 2, 3
Giono, Jean 1895-1970 .... **CLC 4, 11**
See also CA 45-48; CANR 2, 35; DLB 72; GFL 1789 to the Present; MTCW 1; RGWL 2, 3; TCLC 124
Giovanni, Nikki 1943- .... **CLC 2, 4, 19, 64, 117; BLC 2; PC 19; WLCS**
See also AAYA 22; AITN 1; BW 2, 3; CA 29-32R; CAAS 6; CANR 18, 41, 60, 91; CDALBS; CLR 6, 73; CP 7; CSW; CWP; CWRI 5; DA; DAB; DAC; DAM MST, MULT, POET; DLB 5, 41; EXPP; INT CANR-18; MAICYA 1, 2; MTCW 1, 2; RGAL 4; SATA 24, 107; TUS; YAW
Giovene, Andrea 1904-1998 .... **CLC 7**
See also CA 85-88
Gippius, Zinaida (Nikolayevna) 1869-1945
See Hippius, Zinaida
Giraudoux, Jean(-Hippolyte) 1882-1944 .... **TCLC 2, 7**
See also CA 196; DAM DRAM; DLB 65; EW 9; GFL 1789 to the Present; RGWL 2, 3; TWA
Gironella, Jose Maria 1917-1991 ..... **CLC 11**
See also CA 101; RGWL 2, 3
Gissing, George (Robert) 1857-1903 .... **TCLC 3, 24, 47; SSC 37**
See also BRW 5; CA 167; DLB 18, 135, 184; RGEL 2; TEA
Giurlani, Aldo
See Palazzeschi, Aldo
Gladkov, Fedor Vasil'evich
See Gladkov, Fyodor (Vasilyevich)
See also DLB 272

Gladkov, Fyodor (Vasilyevich) 1883-1958 .... **TCLC 27**
See also Gladkov, Fedor Vasil'evich
See also CA 170
Glanville, Brian (Lester) 1931- .... **CLC 6**
See also CA 5-8R; CAAS 9; CANR 3, 70; CN 7; DLB 15, 139; SATA 42
Glasgow, Ellen (Anderson Gholson) 1873-1945 .... **TCLC 2, 7; SSC 34**
See also AMW; CA 164; DLB 9, 12; MAWW; MTCW 2; RGAL 4; RHW; SSFS 9; TUS
Glaspell, Susan 1882(?)-1948 . **TCLC 55; DC 10; SSC 41**
See also AMWS 3; CA 154; DFS 8; DLB 7, 9, 78, 228; MAWW; RGAL 4; SSFS 3; TCWW 2; TUS; YABC 2
Glassco, John 1909-1981 .... **CLC 9**
See also CA 13-16R; CANR 15; DLB 68
Glasscock, Amnesia
See Steinbeck, John (Ernst)
Glasser, Ronald J. 1940(?)- .... **CLC 37**
Glassman, Joyce
See Johnson, Joyce
Gleick, James (W.) 1954- .... **CLC 147**
See also CA 137; CANR 97; INT CA-137
Glendinning, Victoria 1937- .... **CLC 50**
See also CA 127; CANR 59, 89; DLB 155
Glissant, Edouard (Mathieu) 1928- .... **CLC 10, 68**
See also CA 153; CANR 111; CWW 2; DAM MULT; RGWL 3
Gloag, Julian 1930- .... **CLC 40**
See also AITN 1; CA 65-68; CANR 10, 70; CN 7
Glowacki, Aleksander
See Prus, Boleslaw
Gluck, Louise (Elisabeth) 1943- .. **CLC 7, 22, 44, 81, 160; PC 16**
See also AMWS 5; CA 33-36R; CANR 40, 69, 108; CP 7; CWP; DAM POET; DLB 5; MTCW 2; PFS 5, 15; RGAL 4
Glyn, Elinor 1864-1943 .... **TCLC 72**
See also DLB 153; RHW
Gobineau, Joseph-Arthur 1816-1882 .... **NCLC 17**
See also DLB 123; GFL 1789 to the Present
Godard, Jean-Luc 1930- .... **CLC 20**
See also CA 93-96
Godden, (Margaret) Rumer 1907-1998 .... **CLC 53**
See also AAYA 6; BPFB 2; BYA 2, 5; CA 5-8R; CANR 4, 27, 36, 55, 80; CLR 20; CN 7; CWRI 5; DLB 161; MAICYA 1, 2; RHW; SAAS 12; SATA 3, 36; SATA-Obit 109; TEA
Godoy Alcayaga, Lucila 1899-1957 .... **TCLC 2; HLC 2; PC 32**
See also Mistral, Gabriela
See also BW 2; CA 131; CANR 81; DAM MULT; DNFS 1, 2; HW 1, 2; MTCW 1, 2
Godwin, Gail (Kathleen) 1937- ..... **CLC 5, 8, 22, 31, 69, 125**
See also BPFB 2; CA 29-32R; CANR 15, 43, 69; CN 7; CPW; CSW; DAM POP; DLB 6, 234; INT CANR-15; MTCW 1, 2
Godwin, William 1756-1836 .... **NCLC 14**
See also CDBLB 1789-1832; CMW 4; DLB 39, 104, 142, 158, 163, 262; HGG; RGEL 2
Goebbels, Josef
See Goebbels, (Paul) Joseph
Goebbels, (Paul) Joseph 1897-1945 .... **TCLC 68**
See also CA 148
Goebbels, Joseph Paul
See Goebbels, (Paul) Joseph

Goethe, Johann Wolfgang von
1749-1832 ... **NCLC 4, 22, 34, 90; PC 5; SSC 38; WLC**
See also CDWLB 2; DA; DAB; DAC; DAM DRAM, MST, POET; DLB 94; EW 5; RGWL 2, 3; TWA

Gogarty, Oliver St. John
1878-1957 .... **TCLC 15**
See also CA 150; DLB 15, 19; RGEL 2

Gogol, Nikolai (Vasilyevich)
1809-1852 .... **NCLC 5, 15, 31; DC 1; SSC 4, 29, 52; WLC**
See also DA; DAB; DAC; DAM DRAM, MST; DFS 12; DLB 198; EW 6; EXPS; RGSF 2; RGWL 2, 3; SSFS 7; TWA

Goines, Donald 1937(?)-1974 . **CLC 80; BLC 2**
See also AITN 1; BW 1, 3; CA 124; CANR 82; CMW 4; DAM MULT, POP; DLB 33

Gold, Herbert 1924- ... **CLC 4, 7, 14, 42, 152**
See also CA 9-12R; CANR 17, 45; CN 7; DLB 2; DLBY 1981

Goldbarth, Albert 1948- .... **CLC 5, 38**
See also CA 53-56; CANR 6, 40; CP 7; DLB 120

Goldberg, Anatol 1910-1982 .... **CLC 34**
See also CA 131

Goldemberg, Isaac 1945- .... **CLC 52**
See also CA 69-72; CAAS 12; CANR 11, 32; HW 1; WLIT 1

Golding, William (Gerald)
1911-1993 ..... **CLC 1, 2, 3, 8, 10, 17, 27, 58, 81; WLC**
See also AAYA 5; BPFB 2; BRWR 1; BRWS 1; BYA 2; CA 5-8R; CANR 13, 33, 54; CDBLB 1945-1960; DA; DAB; DAC; DAM MST, NOV; DLB 15, 100, 255; EXPN; HGG; LAIT 4; MTCW 1, 2; NFS 2; RGEL 2; RHW; SFW 4; TEA; WLIT 4; YAW

Goldman, Emma 1869-1940 .... **TCLC 13**
See also CA 150; DLB 221; FW; RGAL 4; TUS

Goldman, Francisco 1954- .... **CLC 76**
See also CA 162

Goldman, William (W.) 1931- ...... **CLC 1, 48**
See also BPFB 2; CA 9-12R; CANR 29, 69, 106; CN 7; DLB 44; FANT; IDFW 3, 4

Goldmann, Lucien 1913-1970 .... **CLC 24**
See also CA 25-28; CAP 2

Goldoni, Carlo 1707-1793 .... **LC 4**
See also DAM DRAM; EW 4; RGWL 2, 3

Goldsberry, Steven 1949- .... **CLC 34**
See also CA 131

Goldsmith, Oliver 1730-1774 .. **LC 2, 48; DC 8; WLC**
See also BRW 3; CDBLB 1660-1789; DA; DAB; DAC; DAM DRAM, MST, NOV, POET; DFS 1; DLB 39, 89, 104, 109, 142; IDTP; RGEL 2; SATA 26; TEA; WLIT 3

Goldsmith, Peter
See Priestley, J(ohn) B(oynton)

Gombrowicz, Witold 1904-1969 .... **CLC 4, 7, 11, 49**
See also CA 19-20; CANR 105; CAP 2; CDWLB 4; DAM DRAM; DLB 215; EW 12; RGWL 2, 3; TWA

Gomez de Avellaneda, Gertrudis
1814-1873 .... **NCLC 111**
See also LAW

Gomez de la Serna, Ramon
1888-1963 .... **CLC 9**
See also CA 153; CANR 79; HW 1, 2

Goncharov, Ivan Alexandrovich
1812-1891 .... **NCLC 1, 63**
See also DLB 238; EW 6; RGWL 2, 3

Goncourt, Edmond (Louis Antoine Huot) de
1822-1896 .... **NCLC 7**
See also DLB 123; EW 7; GFL 1789 to the Present; RGWL 2, 3

Goncourt, Jules (Alfred Huot) de
1830-1870 .... **NCLC 7**
See also DLB 123; EW 7; GFL 1789 to the Present; RGWL 2, 3

Gongora (y Argote), Luis de
1561-1627 .... **LC 72**
See also RGWL 2, 3

Gontier, Fernande 19(?)- .... **CLC 50**

Gonzalez Martinez, Enrique
1871-1952 .... **TCLC 72**
See also CA 166; CANR 81; HW 1, 2

Goodison, Lorna 1947- .... **PC 36**
See also CA 142; CANR 88; CP 7; CWP; DLB 157

Goodman, Paul 1911-1972 ..... **CLC 1, 2, 4, 7**
See also CA 19-20; CAD; CANR 34; CAP 2; DLB 130, 246; MTCW 1; RGAL 4

Gordimer, Nadine 1923- .... **CLC 3, 5, 7, 10, 18, 33, 51, 70, 123, 160, 161; SSC 17; WLCS**
See also AAYA 39; AFW; BRWS 2; CA 5-8R; CANR 3, 28, 56, 88; CN 7; DA; DAB; DAC; DAM MST, NOV; DLB 225; EXPS; INT CANR-28; MTCW 1, 2; NFS 4; RGEL 2; RGSF 2; SSFS 2, 14; TWA; WLIT 2; YAW

Gordon, Adam Lindsay
1833-1870 .... **NCLC 21**
See also DLB 230

Gordon, Caroline 1895-1981 . **CLC 6, 13, 29, 83; SSC 15**
See also AMW; CA 11-12; CANR 36; CAP 1; DLB 4, 9, 102; DLBD 17; DLBY 1981; MTCW 1, 2; RGAL 4; RGSF 2

Gordon, Charles William 1860-1937
See Connor, Ralph

Gordon, Mary (Catherine) 1949- .... **CLC 13, 22, 128**
See also AMWS 4; BPFB 2; CA 102; CANR 44, 92; CN 7; DLB 6; DLBY 1981; FW; INT CA-102; MTCW 1

Gordon, N. J.
See Bosman, Herman Charles

Gordon, Sol 1923- .... **CLC 26**
See also CA 53-56; CANR 4; SATA 11

Gordone, Charles 1925-1995 .. **CLC 1, 4; DC 8**
See also BW 1, 3; CA 93-96, 180; CAAE 180; CAD; CANR 55; DAM DRAM; DLB 7; INT 93-96; MTCW 1

Gore, Catherine 1800-1861 .... **NCLC 65**
See also DLB 116; RGEL 2

Gorenko, Anna Andreevna
See Akhmatova, Anna

Gorky, Maxim .... **TCLC 8; SSC 28; WLC**
See also Peshkov, Alexei Maximovich
See also DAB; DFS 9; EW 8; MTCW 2; TWA

Goryan, Sirak
See Saroyan, William

Gosse, Edmund (William)
1849-1928 .... **TCLC 28**
See also DLB 57, 144, 184; RGEL 2

Gotlieb, Phyllis Fay (Bloom) 1926- .. **CLC 18**
See also CA 13-16R; CANR 7; DLB 88, 251; SFW 4

Gottesman, S. D.
See Kornbluth, C(yril) M.; Pohl, Frederik

Gottfried von Strassburg fl. c.
1170-1215 .... **CMLC 10**
See also CDWLB 2; DLB 138; EW 1; RGWL 2, 3

Gotthelf, Jeremias 1797-1854 .... **NCLC 117**
See also DLB 133; RGWL 2, 3

Gottschalk, Laura Riding
See Jackson, Laura (Riding)

Gould, Lois 1932(?)-2002 .... **CLC 4, 10**
See also CA 77-80; CANR 29; MTCW 1

Gould, Stephen Jay 1941-2002 .... **CLC 163**
See also AAYA 26; BEST 90:3; CA 77-80; CANR 10, 27, 56, 75; CPW; INT CANR-27; MTCW 1, 2

Gourmont, Remy(-Marie-Charles) de
1858-1915 .... **TCLC 17**
See also CA 150; GFL 1789 to the Present; MTCW 2

Govier, Katherine 1948- .... **CLC 51**
See also CA 101; CANR 18, 40; CCA 1

Gower, John c. 1330-1408 .... **LC 76**
See also BRW 1; DLB 146; RGEL 2

Goyen, (Charles) William
1915-1983 .... **CLC 5, 8, 14, 40**
See also AITN 2; CA 5-8R; CANR 6, 71; DLB 2, 218; DLBY 1983; INT CANR-6

Goytisolo, Juan 1931- .... **CLC 5, 10, 23, 133; HLC 1**
See also CA 85-88; CANR 32, 61; CWW 2; DAM MULT; GLL 2; HW 1, 2; MTCW 1, 2

Gozzano, Guido 1883-1916 .... **PC 10**
See also CA 154; DLB 114

Gozzi, (Conte) Carlo 1720-1806 .... **NCLC 23**

Grabbe, Christian Dietrich
1801-1836 .... **NCLC 2**
See also DLB 133; RGWL 2, 3

Grace, Patricia Frances 1937- .... **CLC 56**
See also CA 176; CN 7; RGSF 2

Gracian y Morales, Baltasar
1601-1658 .... **LC 15**

Gracq, Julien .... **CLC 11, 48**
See also Poirier, Louis
See also CWW 2; DLB 83; GFL 1789 to the Present

Grade, Chaim 1910-1982 .... **CLC 10**
See also CA 93-96

Graduate of Oxford, A
See Ruskin, John

Grafton, Garth
See Duncan, Sara Jeannette

Grafton, Sue 1940- .... **CLC 163**
See also AAYA 11; BPFB 2; CA 108; CANR 31, 55, 111; CMW 4; CPW; CSW; DAM POP; DLB 226; FW; MSW

Graham, John
See Phillips, David Graham

Graham, Jorie 1951- .... **CLC 48, 118**
See also CA 111; CANR 63; CP 7; CWP; DLB 120; PFS 10

Graham, R(obert) B(ontine) Cunninghame
See Cunninghame Graham, Robert (Gallnigad) Bontine
See also DLB 98, 135, 174; RGEL 2; RGSF 2

Graham, Robert
See Haldeman, Joe (William)

Graham, Tom
See Lewis, (Harry) Sinclair

Graham, W(illiam) S(idney)
1918-1986 .... **CLC 29**
See also BRWS 7; CA 73-76; DLB 20; RGEL 2

Graham, Winston (Mawdsley)
1910- .... **CLC 23**
See also CA 49-52; CANR 2, 22, 45, 66; CMW 4; CN 7; DLB 77; RHW

Grahame, Kenneth 1859-1932 .... **TCLC 64**
See also BYA 5; CA 136; CANR 80; CLR 5; CWRI 5; DAB; DLB 34, 141, 178; FANT; MAICYA 1, 2; MTCW 2; RGEL 2; SATA 100; TEA; WCH; YABC 1

Granger, Darius John
See Marlowe, Stephen

Granin, Daniil .... **CLC 59**
Granovsky, Timofei Nikolaevich
  1813-1855 .... **NCLC 75**
  See also DLB 198
Grant, Skeeter
  See Spiegelman, Art
Granville-Barker, Harley
  1877-1946 .... **TCLC 2**
  See also Barker, Harley Granville
  See also CA 204; DAM DRAM; RGEL 2
Granzotto, Gianni
  See Granzotto, Giovanni Battista
Granzotto, Giovanni Battista
  1914-1985 .... **CLC 70**
  See also CA 166
Grass, Guenter (Wilhelm) 1927- ... **CLC 1, 2, 4, 6, 11, 15, 22, 32, 49, 88; WLC**
  See also BPFB 2; CA 13-16R; CANR 20, 75, 93; CDWLB 2; DA; DAB; DAC; DAM MST, NOV; DLB 75, 124; EW 13; MTCW 1, 2; RGWL 2, 3; TWA
Gratton, Thomas
  See Hulme, T(homas) E(rnest)
Grau, Shirley Ann 1929- .... **CLC 4, 9, 146; SSC 15**
  See also CA 89-92; CANR 22, 69; CN 7; CSW; DLB 2, 218; INT CA-89-92, CANR-22; MTCW 1
Gravel, Fern
  See Hall, James Norman
Graver, Elizabeth 1964- .... **CLC 70**
  See also CA 135; CANR 71
Graves, Richard Perceval
  1895-1985 .... **CLC 44**
  See also CA 65-68; CANR 9, 26, 51
Graves, Robert (von Ranke)
  1895-1985 .. **CLC 1, 2, 6, 11, 39, 44, 45; PC 6**
  See also BPFB 2; BRW 7; BYA 4; CA 5-8R; CANR 5, 36; CDBLB 1914-1945; DAB; DAC; DAM MST, POET; DLB 20, 100, 191; DLBD 18; DLBY 1985; MTCW 1, 2; NCFS 2; RGEL 2; RHW; SATA 45; TEA
Graves, Valerie
  See Bradley, Marion Zimmer
Gray, Alasdair (James) 1934- .... **CLC 41**
  See also CA 126; CANR 47, 69, 106; CN 7; DLB 194, 261; HGG; INT CA-126; MTCW 1, 2; RGSF 2; SUFW 2
Gray, Amlin 1946- .... **CLC 29**
  See also CA 138
Gray, Francine du Plessix 1930- ..... **CLC 22, 153**
  See also BEST 90:3; CA 61-64; CAAS 2; CANR 11, 33, 75, 81; DAM NOV; INT CANR-11; MTCW 1, 2
Gray, John (Henry) 1866-1934 ...... **TCLC 19**
  See also CA 162; RGEL 2
Gray, Simon (James Holliday)
  1936- .... **CLC 9, 14, 36**
  See also AITN 1; CA 21-24R; CAAS 3; CANR 32, 69; CD 5; DLB 13; MTCW 1; RGEL 2
Gray, Spalding 1941- ..... **CLC 49, 112; DC 7**
  See also CA 128; CAD; CANR 74; CD 5; CPW; DAM POP; MTCW 2
Gray, Thomas 1716-1771 .... **LC 4, 40; PC 2; WLC**
  See also BRW 3; CDBLB 1660-1789; DA; DAB; DAC; DAM MST; DLB 109; EXPP; PAB; PFS 9; RGEL 2; TEA; WP
Grayson, David
  See Baker, Ray Stannard
Grayson, Richard (A.) 1951- .... **CLC 38**
  See also CA 85-88; CANR 14, 31, 57; DLB 234

Greeley, Andrew M(oran) 1928- ...... **CLC 28**
  See also BPFB 2; CA 5-8R; CAAS 7; CANR 7, 43, 69, 104; CMW 4; CPW; DAM POP; MTCW 1, 2
Green, Anna Katharine
  1846-1935 .... **TCLC 63**
  See also CA 159; CMW 4; DLB 202, 221; MSW
Green, Brian
  See Card, Orson Scott
Green, Hannah
  See Greenberg, Joanne (Goldenberg)
Green, Hannah 1927(?)-1996 .... **CLC 3**
  See also CA 73-76; CANR 59, 93; NFS 10
Green, Henry .... **CLC 2, 13, 97**
  See also Yorke, Henry Vincent
  See also BRWS 2; CA 175; DLB 15; RGEL 2
Green, Julian (Hartridge) 1900-1998
  See Green, Julien
  See also CA 21-24R; CANR 33, 87; DLB 4, 72; MTCW 1
Green, Julien .... **CLC 3, 11, 77**
  See also Green, Julian (Hartridge)
  See also GFL 1789 to the Present; MTCW 2
Green, Paul (Eliot) 1894-1981 .... **CLC 25**
  See also AITN 1; CA 5-8R; CANR 3; DAM DRAM; DLB 7, 9, 249; DLBY 1981; RGAL 4
Greenaway, Peter 1942- .... **CLC 159**
  See also CA 127
Greenberg, Ivan 1908-1973
  See Rahv, Philip
  See also CA 85-88
Greenberg, Joanne (Goldenberg)
  1932- .... **CLC 7, 30**
  See also AAYA 12; CA 5-8R; CANR 14, 32, 69; CN 7; SATA 25; YAW
Greenberg, Richard 1959(?)- .... **CLC 57**
  See also CA 138; CAD; CD 5
Greenblatt, Stephen J(ay) 1943- ...... **CLC 70**
  See also CA 49-52
Greene, Bette 1934- .... **CLC 30**
  See also AAYA 7; BYA 3; CA 53-56; CANR 4; CLR 2; CWRI 5; JRDA; LAIT 4; MAICYA 1, 2; NFS 10; SAAS 16; SATA 8, 102; WYA; YAW
Greene, Gael .... **CLC 8**
  See also CA 13-16R; CANR 10
Greene, Graham (Henry)
  1904-1991 .... **CLC 1, 3, 6, 9, 14, 18, 27, 37, 70, 72, 125; SSC 29; WLC**
  See also AITN 2; BPFB 2; BRWR 2; BRWS 1; BYA 3; CA 13-16R; CANR 35, 61; CBD; CDBLB 1945-1960; CMW 4; DA; DAB; DAC; DAM MST, NOV; DLB 13, 15, 77, 100, 162, 201, 204; DLBY 1991; MSW; MTCW 1, 2; RGEL 2; SATA 20; SSFS 14; TEA; WLIT 4
Greene, Robert 1558-1592 .... **LC 41**
  See also BRWS 8; DLB 62, 167; IDTP; RGEL 2; TEA
Greer, Germaine 1939- .... **CLC 131**
  See also AITN 1; CA 81-84; CANR 33, 70; FW; MTCW 1, 2
Greer, Richard
  See Silverberg, Robert
Gregor, Arthur 1923- .... **CLC 9**
  See also CA 25-28R; CAAS 10; CANR 11; CP 7; SATA 36
Gregor, Lee
  See Pohl, Frederik
Gregory, Lady Isabella Augusta (Persse)
  1852-1932 .... **TCLC 1**
  See also BRW 6; CA 184; DLB 10; IDTP; RGEL 2
Gregory, J. Dennis
  See Williams, John A(lfred)

Grekova, I. .... **CLC 59**
Grendon, Stephen
  See Derleth, August (William)
Grenville, Kate 1950- .... **CLC 61**
  See also CA 118; CANR 53, 93
Grenville, Pelham
  See Wodehouse, P(elham) G(renville)
Greve, Felix Paul (Berthold Friedrich)
  1879-1948
  See Grove, Frederick Philip
  See also CA 141, 175; CANR 79; DAC; DAM MST
Greville, Fulke 1554-1628 .... **LC 79**
  See also DLB 62, 172; RGEL 2
Grey, Zane 1872-1939 .... **TCLC 6**
  See also BPFB 2; CA 132; DAM POP; DLB 9, 212; MTCW 1, 2; RGAL 4; TCWW 2; TUS
Grieg, (Johan) Nordahl (Brun)
  1902-1943 .... **TCLC 10**
  See also CA 189
Grieve, C(hristopher) M(urray)
  1892-1978 .... **CLC 11, 19**
  See also MacDiarmid, Hugh; Pteleon
  See also CA 5-8R; CANR 33, 107; DAM POET; MTCW 1; RGEL 2
Griffin, Gerald 1803-1840 .... **NCLC 7**
  See also DLB 159; RGEL 2
Griffin, John Howard 1920-1980 ..... **CLC 68**
  See also AITN 1; CA 1-4R; CANR 2
Griffin, Peter 1942- .... **CLC 39**
  See also CA 136
Griffith, D(avid Lewelyn) W(ark)
  1875(?)-1948 .... **TCLC 68**
  See also CA 150; CANR 80
Griffith, Lawrence
  See Griffith, D(avid Lewelyn) W(ark)
Griffiths, Trevor 1935- .... **CLC 13, 52**
  See also CA 97-100; CANR 45; CBD; CD 5; DLB 13, 245
Griggs, Sutton (Elbert)
  1872-1930 .... **TCLC 77**
  See also CA 186; DLB 50
Grigson, Geoffrey (Edward Harvey)
  1905-1985 .... **CLC 7, 39**
  See also CA 25-28R; CANR 20, 33; DLB 27; MTCW 1, 2
Grile, Dod
  See Bierce, Ambrose (Gwinett)
Grillparzer, Franz 1791-1872 . **NCLC 1, 102; DC 14; SSC 37**
  See also CDWLB 2; DLB 133; EW 5; RGWL 2, 3; TWA
Grimble, Reverend Charles James
  See Eliot, T(homas) S(tearns)
Grimke, Charlotte L(ottie) Forten
  1837(?)-1914
  See Forten, Charlotte L.
  See also BW 1; CA 124; DAM MULT, POET
Grimm, Jacob Ludwig Karl
  1785-1863 .... **NCLC 3, 77; SSC 36**
  See also DLB 90; MAICYA 1, 2; RGSF 2; RGWL 2, 3; SATA 22; WCH
Grimm, Wilhelm Karl 1786-1859 .. **NCLC 3, 77; SSC 36**
  See also CDWLB 2; DLB 90; MAICYA 1, 2; RGSF 2; RGWL 2, 3; SATA 22; WCH
Grimmelshausen, Hans Jakob Christoffel von
  See Grimmelshausen, Johann Jakob Christoffel von
  See also RGWL 2, 3
Grimmelshausen, Johann Jakob Christoffel von 1621-1676 .... **LC 6**
  See also Grimmelshausen, Hans Jakob Christoffel von
  See also CDWLB 2; DLB 168

Grindel, Eugene 1895-1952
See Eluard, Paul
See also CA 193

Grisham, John 1955- .... **CLC 84**
See also AAYA 14; BPFB 2; CA 138; CANR 47, 69; CMW 4; CN 7; CPW; CSW; DAM POP; MSW; MTCW 2

Grossman, David 1954- .... **CLC 67**
See also CA 138; CWW 2

Grossman, Vasilii Semenovich
See Grossman, Vasily (Semenovich)
See also DLB 272

Grossman, Vasily (Semenovich)
1905-1964 .... **CLC 41**
See also Grossman, Vasilii Semenovich
See also CA 130; MTCW 1

Grove, Frederick Philip .... **TCLC 4**
See also Greve, Felix Paul (Berthold Friedrich)
See also DLB 92; RGEL 2

Grubb
See Crumb, R(obert)

Grumbach, Doris (Isaac) 1918- . **CLC 13, 22, 64**
See also CA 5-8R; CAAS 2; CANR 9, 42, 70; CN 7; INT CANR-9; MTCW 2

Grundtvig, Nicolai Frederik Severin
1783-1872 .... **NCLC 1**

Grunge
See Crumb, R(obert)

Grunwald, Lisa 1959- .... **CLC 44**
See also CA 120

Guare, John 1938- .... **CLC 8, 14, 29, 67**
See also CA 73-76; CAD; CANR 21, 69; CD 5; DAM DRAM; DFS 8, 13; DLB 7, 249; MTCW 1, 2; RGAL 4

Gubar, Susan (David) 1944- .... **CLC 145**
See also CA 108; CANR 45, 70; FW; MTCW 1; RGAL 4

Gudjonsson, Halldor Kiljan 1902-1998
See Laxness, Halldor
See also CA 103; CWW 2

Guenter, Erich
See Eich, Gunter

Guest, Barbara 1920- .... **CLC 34**
See also CA 25-28R; CANR 11, 44, 84; CP 7; CWP; DLB 5, 193

Guest, Edgar A(lbert) 1881-1959 ... **TCLC 95**
See also CA 168

Guest, Judith (Ann) 1936- .... **CLC 8, 30**
See also AAYA 7; CA 77-80; CANR 15, 75; DAM NOV, POP; EXPN; INT CANR-15; LAIT 5; MTCW 1, 2; NFS 1

Guevara, Che .... **CLC 87; HLC 1**
See also Guevara (Serna), Ernesto

Guevara (Serna), Ernesto
1928-1967 .... **CLC 87; HLC 1**
See also Guevara, Che
See also CA 127; CANR 56; DAM MULT; HW 1

Guicciardini, Francesco 1483-1540 ..... **LC 49**

Guild, Nicholas M. 1944- .... **CLC 33**
See also CA 93-96

Guillemin, Jacques
See Sartre, Jean-Paul

Guillen, Jorge 1893-1984 . **CLC 11; HLCS 1; PC 35**
See also CA 89-92; DAM MULT, POET; DLB 108; HW 1; RGWL 2, 3

Guillen, Nicolas (Cristobal)
1902-1989 .... **CLC 48, 79; BLC 2; HLC 1; PC 23**
See also BW 2; CA 125; CANR 84; DAM MST, MULT, POET; HW 1; LAW; RGWL 2, 3; WP

Guillen y Alvarez, Jorge
See Guillen, Jorge

Guillevic, (Eugene) 1907-1997 .... **CLC 33**
See also CA 93-96; CWW 2

Guillois
See Desnos, Robert

Guillois, Valentin
See Desnos, Robert

Guimaraes Rosa, Joao 1908-1967
See also CA 175; HLCS 2; LAW; RGSF 2; RGWL 2, 3

Guiney, Louise Imogen
1861-1920 .... **TCLC 41**
See also CA 160; DLB 54; RGAL 4

Guinizelli, Guido c. 1230-1276 ...... **CMLC 49**

Guiraldes, Ricardo (Guillermo)
1886-1927 .... **TCLC 39**
See also CA 131; HW 1; LAW; MTCW 1

Gumilev, Nikolai (Stepanovich)
1886-1921 .... **TCLC 60**
See also CA 165

Gunesekera, Romesh 1954- .... **CLC 91**
See also CA 159; CN 7; DLB 267

Gunn, Bill .... **CLC 5**
See also Gunn, William Harrison
See also DLB 38

Gunn, Thom(son William) 1929- .. **CLC 3, 6, 18, 32, 81; PC 26**
See also BRWS 4; CA 17-20R; CANR 9, 33; CDBLB 1960 to Present; CP 7; DAM POET; DLB 27; INT CANR-33; MTCW 1; PFS 9; RGEL 2

Gunn, William Harrison 1934(?)-1989
See Gunn, Bill
See also AITN 1; BW 1, 3; CA 13-16R; CANR 12, 25, 76

Gunn Allen, Paula
See Allen, Paula Gunn

Gunnars, Kristjana 1948- .... **CLC 69**
See also CA 113; CCA 1; CP 7; CWP; DLB 60

Gunter, Erich
See Eich, Gunter

Gurdjieff, G(eorgei) I(vanovich)
1877(?)-1949 .... **TCLC 71**
See also CA 157

Gurganus, Allan 1947- .... **CLC 70**
See also BEST 90:1; CA 135; CN 7; CPW; CSW; DAM POP; GLL 1

Gurney, A. R.
See Gurney, A(lbert) R(amsdell), Jr.
See also DLB 266

Gurney, A(lbert) R(amsdell), Jr.
1930- .... **CLC 32, 50, 54**
See also Gurney, A. R.
See also AMWS 5; CA 77-80; CAD; CANR 32, 64; CD 5; DAM DRAM

Gurney, Ivor (Bertie) 1890-1937 ... **TCLC 33**
See also BRW 6; CA 167; PAB; RGEL 2

Gurney, Peter
See Gurney, A(lbert) R(amsdell), Jr.

Guro, Elena 1877-1913 .... **TCLC 56**

Gustafson, James M(oody) 1925- ... **CLC 100**
See also CA 25-28R; CANR 37

Gustafson, Ralph (Barker)
1909-1995 .... **CLC 36**
See also CA 21-24R; CANR 8, 45, 84; CP 7; DLB 88; RGEL 2

Gut, Gom
See Simenon, Georges (Jacques Christian)

Guterson, David 1956- .... **CLC 91**
See also CA 132; CANR 73; MTCW 2; NFS 13

Guthrie, A(lfred) B(ertram), Jr.
1901-1991 .... **CLC 23**
See also CA 57-60; CANR 24; DLB 6, 212; SATA 62; SATA-Obit 67

Guthrie, Isobel
See Grieve, C(hristopher) M(urray)

Guthrie, Woodrow Wilson 1912-1967
See Guthrie, Woody
See also CA 113

Guthrie, Woody .... **CLC 35**
See also Guthrie, Woodrow Wilson
See also LAIT 3

Gutierrez Najera, Manuel 1859-1895
See also HLCS 2; LAW

Guy, Rosa (Cuthbert) 1925- .... **CLC 26**
See also AAYA 4, 37; BW 2; CA 17-20R; CANR 14, 34, 83; CLR 13; DLB 33; DNFS 1; JRDA; MAICYA 1, 2; SATA 14, 62, 122; YAW

Gwendolyn
See Bennett, (Enoch) Arnold

H. D. .... **CLC 3, 8, 14, 31, 34, 73; PC 5**
See also Doolittle, Hilda

H. de V.
See Buchan, John

Haavikko, Paavo Juhani 1931- .. **CLC 18, 34**
See also CA 106

Habbema, Koos
See Heijermans, Herman

Habermas, Juergen 1929- .... **CLC 104**
See also CA 109; CANR 85; DLB 242

Habermas, Jurgen
See Habermas, Juergen

Hacker, Marilyn 1942- . **CLC 5, 9, 23, 72, 91**
See also CA 77-80; CANR 68; CP 7; CWP; DAM POET; DLB 120; FW; GLL 2

Hadrian 76-138 .... **CMLC 52**

Haeckel, Ernst Heinrich (Philipp August)
1834-1919 .... **TCLC 83**
See also CA 157

Hafiz c. 1326-1389(?) .... **CMLC 34**
See also RGWL 2, 3

Haggard, H(enry) Rider
1856-1925 .... **TCLC 11**
See also BRWS 3; BYA 4, 5; CA 148; CANR 112; DLB 70, 156, 174, 178; FANT; MTCW 2; RGEL 2; RHW; SATA 16; SCFW 1; SFW 4; SUFW 1; WLIT 4

Hagiosy, L.
See Larbaud, Valery (Nicolas)

Hagiwara, Sakutaro 1886-1942 .... **TCLC 60; PC 18**
See also CA 154; RGWL 3

Haig, Fenil
See Ford, Ford Madox

Haig-Brown, Roderick (Langmere)
1908-1976 .... **CLC 21**
See also CA 5-8R; CANR 4, 38, 83; CLR 31; CWRI 5; DLB 88; MAICYA 1, 2; SATA 12

Haight, Rip
See Carpenter, John (Howard)

Hailey, Arthur 1920- .... **CLC 5**
See also AITN 2; BEST 90:3; BPFB 2; CA 1-4R; CANR 2, 36, 75; CCA 1; CN 7; CPW; DAM NOV, POP; DLB 88; DLBY 1982; MTCW 1, 2

Hailey, Elizabeth Forsythe 1938- ..... **CLC 40**
See also CA 93-96; CAAE 188; CAAS 1; CANR 15, 48; INT CANR-15

Haines, John (Meade) 1924- .... **CLC 58**
See also CA 17-20R; CANR 13, 34; CSW; DLB 5, 212

Hakluyt, Richard 1552-1616 .... **LC 31**
See also DLB 136; RGEL 2

Haldeman, Joe (William) 1943- .... **CLC 61**
See also Graham, Robert
See also AAYA 38; CA 53-56, 179; CAAE 179; CAAS 25; CANR 6, 70, 72; DLB 8; INT CANR-6; SCFW 2; SFW 4

Hale, Sarah Josepha (Buell)
1788-1879 .... **NCLC 75**
See also DLB 1, 42, 73, 243

Halevy, Elie 1870-1937 .... **TCLC 104**
Haley, Alex(ander Murray Palmer)
  1921-1992 .... **CLC 8, 12, 76; BLC 2**
  See also AAYA 26; BPFB 2; BW 2, 3; CA 77-80; CANR 61; CDALBS; CPW; CSW; DA; DAB; DAC; DAM MST, MULT, POP; DLB 38; LAIT 5; MTCW 1, 2; NFS 9
Haliburton, Thomas Chandler
  1796-1865 .... **NCLC 15**
  See also DLB 11, 99; RGEL 2; RGSF 2
Hall, Donald (Andrew, Jr.) 1928- ...... **CLC 1, 13, 37, 59, 151**
  See also CA 5-8R; CAAS 7; CANR 2, 44, 64, 106; CP 7; DAM POET; DLB 5; MTCW 1; RGAL 4; SATA 23, 97
Hall, Frederic Sauser
  See Sauser-Hall, Frederic
Hall, James
  See Kuttner, Henry
Hall, James Norman 1887-1951 ..... **TCLC 23**
  See also CA 173; LAIT 1; RHW 1; SATA 21
Hall, (Marguerite) Radclyffe
  1880-1943 .... **TCLC 12**
  See also BRWS 6; CA 150; CANR 83; DLB 191; MTCW 1; RGEL 2; RHW
Hall, Rodney 1935- .... **CLC 51**
  See also CA 109; CANR 69; CN 7; CP 7
Hallam, Arthur Henry
  1811-1833 .... **NCLC 110**
  See also DLB 32
Halleck, Fitz-Greene 1790-1867 .... **NCLC 47**
  See also DLB 3, 250; RGAL 4
Halliday, Michael
  See Creasey, John
Halpern, Daniel 1945- .... **CLC 14**
  See also CA 33-36R; CANR 93; CP 7
Hamburger, Michael (Peter Leopold)
  1924- .... **CLC 5, 14**
  See also CA 5-8R; CAAE 196; CAAS 4; CANR 2, 47; CP 7; DLB 27
Hamill, Pete 1935- .... **CLC 10**
  See also CA 25-28R; CANR 18, 71
Hamilton, Alexander
  1755(?)-1804 .... **NCLC 49**
  See also DLB 37
Hamilton, Clive
  See Lewis, C(live) S(taples)
Hamilton, Edmond 1904-1977 .... **CLC 1**
  See also CA 1-4R; CANR 3, 84; DLB 8; SATA 118; SFW 4
Hamilton, Eugene (Jacob) Lee
  See Lee-Hamilton, Eugene (Jacob)
Hamilton, Franklin
  See Silverberg, Robert
Hamilton, Gail
  See Corcoran, Barbara (Asenath)
Hamilton, Mollie
  See Kaye, M(ary) M(argaret)
Hamilton, (Anthony Walter) Patrick
  1904-1962 .... **CLC 51**
  See also CA 176; DLB 10, 191
Hamilton, Virginia (Esther)
  1936-2002 .... **CLC 26**
  See also AAYA 2, 21; BW 2, 3; BYA 1, 2, 8; CA 25-28R; CANR 20, 37, 73; CLR 1, 11, 40; DAM MULT; DLB 33, 52; DLBY 01; INT CANR-20; JRDA; LAIT 5; MAICYA 1, 2; MAICYAS 1; MTCW 1, 2; SATA 4, 56, 79, 123; SATA-Obit 132; WYA; YAW
Hammett, (Samuel) Dashiell
  1894-1961 .... **CLC 3, 5, 10, 19, 47; SSC 17**
  See also AITN 1; AMWS 4; BPFB 2; CA 81-84; CANR 42; CDALB 1929-1941; CMW 4; DLB 226; DLBD 6; DLBY 1996; LAIT 3; MSW; MTCW 1, 2; RGAL 4; RGSF 2; TUS

Hammon, Jupiter 1720(?)-1800(?) . **NCLC 5; BLC 2; PC 16**
  See also DAM MULT, POET; DLB 31, 50
Hammond, Keith
  See Kuttner, Henry
Hamner, Earl (Henry), Jr. 1923- ...... **CLC 12**
  See also AITN 2; CA 73-76; DLB 6
Hampton, Christopher (James)
  1946- .... **CLC 4**
  See also CA 25-28R; CD 5; DLB 13; MTCW 1
Hamsun, Knut .... **TCLC 2, 14, 49**
  See also Pedersen, Knut
  See also EW 8; RGWL 2, 3
Handke, Peter 1942- .... **CLC 5, 8, 10, 15, 38, 134; DC 17**
  See also CA 77-80; CANR 33, 75, 104; CWW 2; DAM DRAM, NOV; DLB 85, 124; MTCW 1, 2; TWA
Handy, W(illiam) C(hristopher)
  1873-1958 .... **TCLC 97**
  See also BW 3; CA 167
Hanley, James 1901-1985 ..... **CLC 3, 5, 8, 13**
  See also CA 73-76; CANR 36; CBD; DLB 191; MTCW 1; RGEL 2
Hannah, Barry 1942- .... **CLC 23, 38, 90**
  See also BPFB 2; CA 110; CANR 43, 68, 113; CN 7; CSW; DLB 6, 234; INT CA-110; MTCW 1; RGSF 2
Hannon, Ezra
  See Hunter, Evan
Hansberry, Lorraine (Vivian)
  1930-1965 ... **CLC 17, 62; BLC 2; DC 2**
  See also AAYA 25; AFAW 1, 2; AMWS 4; BW 1, 3; CA 109; CABS 3; CANR 58; CDALB 1941-1968; DA; DAB; DAC; DAM DRAM, MST, MULT; DFS 2; DLB 7, 38; FW; LAIT 4; MTCW 1, 2; RGAL 4; TUS
Hansen, Joseph 1923- .... **CLC 38**
  See Brock, Rose; Colton, James
  See also BPFB 2; CA 29-32R; CAAS 17; CANR 16, 44, 66; CMW 4; DLB 226; GLL 1; INT CANR-16
Hansen, Martin A(lfred)
  1909-1955 .... **TCLC 32**
  See also CA 167; DLB 214
Hansen and Philipson eds. .... **CLC 65**
Hanson, Kenneth O(stlin) 1922- ...... **CLC 13**
  See also CA 53-56; CANR 7
Hardwick, Elizabeth (Bruce) 1916- .. **CLC 13**
  See also AMWS 3; CA 5-8R; CANR 3, 32, 70, 100; CN 7; CSW; DAM NOV; DLB 6; MAWW; MTCW 1, 2
Hardy, Thomas 1840-1928 .. **TCLC 4, 10, 18, 32, 48, 53, 72; PC 8; SSC 2; WLC**
  See also BRW 6; BRWR 1; CA 123; CD-BLB 1890-1914; DA; DAB; DAC; DAM MST, NOV, POET; DLB 18, 19, 135; EXPN; EXPP; LAIT 2; MTCW 1, 2; NFS 3, 11, 15; PFS 3, 4; RGEL 2; RGSF 2; TEA; WLIT 4
Hare, David 1947- .... **CLC 29, 58, 136**
  See also BRWS 4; CA 97-100; CANR 39, 91; CBD; CD 5; DFS 4, 7; DLB 13; MTCW 1; TEA
Harewood, John
  See Van Druten, John (William)
Harford, Henry
  See Hudson, W(illiam) H(enry)
Hargrave, Leonie
  See Disch, Thomas M(ichael)
Harjo, Joy 1951- .... **CLC 83; PC 27**
  See also CA 114; CANR 35, 67, 91; CP 7; CWP; DAM MULT; DLB 120, 175; MTCW 2; NNAL; PFS 15; RGAL 4
Harlan, Louis R(udolph) 1922- .... **CLC 34**
  See also CA 21-24R; CANR 25, 55, 80

Harling, Robert 1951(?)- .... **CLC 53**
  See also CA 147
Harmon, William (Ruth) 1938- .... **CLC 38**
  See also CA 33-36R; CANR 14, 32, 35; SATA 65
Harper, F. E. W.
  See Harper, Frances Ellen Watkins
Harper, Frances E. W.
  See Harper, Frances Ellen Watkins
Harper, Frances E. Watkins
  See Harper, Frances Ellen Watkins
Harper, Frances Ellen
  See Harper, Frances Ellen Watkins
Harper, Frances Ellen Watkins
  1825-1911 ..... **TCLC 14; BLC 2; PC 21**
  See also AFAW 1, 2; BW 1, 3; CA 125; CANR 79; DAM MULT, POET; DLB 50, 221; MAWW; RGAL 4
Harper, Michael S(teven) 1938- ... **CLC 7, 22**
  See also AFAW 2; BW 1; CA 33-36R; CANR 24, 108; CP 7; DLB 41; RGAL 4
Harper, Mrs. F. E. W.
  See Harper, Frances Ellen Watkins
Harpur, Charles 1813-1868 .... **NCLC 114**
  See also DLB 230; RGEL 2
Harris, Christie 1907-
  See Harris, Christie (Lucy) Irwin
Harris, Christie (Lucy) Irwin
  1907-2002 .... **CLC 12**
  See also CA 5-8R; CANR 6, 83; CLR 47; DLB 88; JRDA; MAICYA 1, 2; SAAS 10; SATA 6, 74; SATA-Essay 116
Harris, Frank 1856-1931 .... **TCLC 24**
  See also CA 150; CANR 80; DLB 156, 197; RGEL 2
Harris, George Washington
  1814-1869 .... **NCLC 23**
  See also DLB 3, 11, 248; RGAL 4
Harris, Joel Chandler 1848-1908 ... **TCLC 2; SSC 19**
  See also CA 137; CANR 80; CLR 49; DLB 11, 23, 42, 78, 91; LAIT 2; MAICYA 1, 2; RGSF 2; SATA 100; WCH; YABC 1
Harris, John (Wyndham Parkes Lucas) Beynon 1903-1969
  See Wyndham, John
  See also CA 102; CANR 84; SATA 118; SFW 4
Harris, MacDonald .... **CLC 9**
  See also Heiney, Donald (William)
Harris, Mark 1922- .... **CLC 19**
  See also CA 5-8R; CAAS 3; CANR 2, 55, 83; CN 7; DLB 2; DLBY 1980
Harris, Norman .... **CLC 65**
Harris, (Theodore) Wilson 1921- .... **CLC 25, 159**
  See also BRWS 5; BW 2, 3; CA 65-68; CAAS 16; CANR 11, 27, 69; CDWLB 3; CN 7; CP 7; DLB 117; MTCW 1; RGEL 2
Harrison, Barbara Grizzuti
  1934-2002 .... **CLC 144**
  See also CA 77-80; CANR 15, 48; INT CANR-15
Harrison, Elizabeth (Allen) Cavanna
  1909-2001
  See Cavanna, Betty
  See also CA 9-12R; CANR 6, 27, 85, 104; MAICYA 2; YAW
Harrison, Harry (Max) 1925- .... **CLC 42**
  See also CA 1-4R; CANR 5, 21, 84; DLB 8; SATA 4; SCFW 2; SFW 4
Harrison, James (Thomas) 1937- ...... **CLC 6, 14, 33, 66, 143; SSC 19**
  See Harrison, Jim
  See also CA 13-16R; CANR 8, 51, 79; CN 7; CP 7; DLBY 1982; INT CANR-8

Harrison, Jim
See Harrison, James (Thomas)
See also AMWS 8; RGAL 4; TCWW 2; TUS

Harrison, Kathryn 1961- .... **CLC 70, 151**
See also CA 144; CANR 68

Harrison, Tony 1937- .... **CLC 43, 129**
See also BRWS 5; CA 65-68; CANR 44, 98; CBD; CD 5; CP 7; DLB 40, 245; MTCW 1; RGEL 2

Harriss, Will(ard Irvin) 1922- .... **CLC 34**
See also CA 111

Hart, Ellis
See Ellison, Harlan (Jay)

Hart, Josephine 1942(?)- .... **CLC 70**
See also CA 138; CANR 70; CPW; DAM POP

Hart, Moss 1904-1961 .... **CLC 66**
See also CA 109; CANR 84; DAM DRAM; DFS 1; DLB 7, 266; RGAL 4

Harte, (Francis) Bret(t) 1836(?)-1902 .... **TCLC 1, 25; SSC 8; WLC**
See also AMWS 2; CA 140; CANR 80; CDALB 1865-1917; DA; DAB; DAC; DAM MST; DLB 12, 64, 74, 79, 186; EXPS; LAIT 2; RGAL 4; RGSF 2; SATA 26; SSFS 3; TUS

Hartley, L(eslie) P(oles) 1895-1972 ... **CLC 2, 22**
See also BRWS 7; CA 45-48; CANR 33; DLB 15, 139; HGG; MTCW 1, 2; RGEL 2; RGSF 2; SUFW 1

Hartman, Geoffrey H. 1929- .... **CLC 27**
See also CA 125; CANR 79; DLB 67

Hartmann, Sadakichi 1869-1944 ... **TCLC 73**
See also CA 157; DLB 54

Hartmann von Aue c. 1170-c. 1210 .... **CMLC 15**
See also CDWLB 2; DLB 138; RGWL 2, 3

Hartog, Jan de
See de Hartog, Jan

Haruf, Kent 1943- .... **CLC 34**
See also CA 149; CANR 91

Harwood, Ronald 1934- .... **CLC 32**
See also CA 1-4R; CANR 4, 55; CBD; CD 5; DAM DRAM, MST; DLB 13

Hasegawa Tatsunosuke
See Futabatei, Shimei

Hasek, Jaroslav (Matej Frantisek) 1883-1923 .... **TCLC 4**
See also CA 129; CDWLB 4; DLB 215; EW 9; MTCW 1, 2; RGSF 2; RGWL 2, 3

Hass, Robert 1941- ... **CLC 18, 39, 99; PC 16**
See also AMWS 6; CA 111; CANR 30, 50, 71; CP 7; DLB 105, 206; RGAL 4; SATA 94

Hastings, Hudson
See Kuttner, Henry

Hastings, Selina .... **CLC 44**

Hathorne, John 1641-1717 .... **LC 38**

Hatteras, Amelia
See Mencken, H(enry) L(ouis)

Hatteras, Owen .... **TCLC 18**
See also Mencken, H(enry) L(ouis); Nathan, George Jean

Hauptmann, Gerhart (Johann Robert) 1862-1946 .... **TCLC 4; SSC 37**
See also CA 153; CDWLB 2; DAM DRAM; DLB 66, 118; EW 8; RGSF 2; RGWL 2, 3; TWA

Havel, Vaclav 1936- ..... **CLC 25, 58, 65, 123; DC 6**
See also CA 104; CANR 36, 63; CDWLB 4; CWW 2; DAM DRAM; DFS 10; DLB 232; MTCW 1, 2; RGWL 3

Haviaras, Stratis .... **CLC 33**
See also Chaviaras, Strates

Hawes, Stephen 1475(?)-1529(?) .... **LC 17**
See also DLB 132; RGEL 2

Hawkes, John (Clendennin Burne, Jr.) 1925-1998 .. **CLC 1, 2, 3, 4, 7, 9, 14, 15, 27, 49**
See also BPFB 2; CA 1-4R; CANR 2, 47, 64; CN 7; DLB 2, 7, 227; DLBY 1980, 1998; MTCW 1, 2; RGAL 4

Hawking, S. W.
See Hawking, Stephen W(illiam)

Hawking, Stephen W(illiam) 1942- . **CLC 63, 105**
See also AAYA 13; BEST 89:1; CA 129; CANR 48; CPW; MTCW 2

Hawkins, Anthony Hope
See Hope, Anthony

Hawthorne, Julian 1846-1934 .... **TCLC 25**
See also CA 165; HGG

Hawthorne, Nathaniel 1804-1864 ... **NCLC 2, 10, 17, 23, 39, 79, 95; SSC 3, 29, 39; WLC**
See also AAYA 18; AMW; AMWR 1; BPFB 2; BYA 3; CDALB 1640-1865; DA; DAB; DAC; DAM MST, NOV; DLB 1, 74, 183, 223; EXPN; EXPS; HGG; LAIT 1; NFS 1; RGAL 4; RGSF 2; SSFS 1, 7, 11, 15; SUFW 1; TUS; WCH; YABC 2

Haxton, Josephine Ayres 1921-
See Douglas, Ellen
See also CA 115; CANR 41, 83

Hayaseca y Eizaguirre, Jorge
See Echegaray (y Eizaguirre), Jose (Maria Waldo)

Hayashi, Fumiko 1904-1951 .... **TCLC 27**
See also Hayashi Fumiko
See also CA 161

Hayashi Fumiko
See Hayashi, Fumiko
See also DLB 180

Haycraft, Anna (Margaret) 1932-
See Ellis, Alice Thomas
See also CA 122; CANR 85, 90; MTCW 2

Hayden, Robert E(arl) 1913-1980 . **CLC 5, 9, 14, 37; BLC 2; PC 6**
See also AFAW 1, 2; AMWS 2; BW 1, 3; CA 69-72; CABS 2; CANR 24, 75, 82; CDALB 1941-1968; DA; DAC; DAM MST, MULT, POET; DLB 5, 76; EXPP; MTCW 1, 2; PFS 1; RGAL 4; SATA 19; SATA-Obit 26; WP

Hayek, F(riedrich) A(ugust von) 1899-1992 .... **TCLC 109**
See also CA 93-96; CANR 20; MTCW 1, 2

Hayford, J(oseph) E(phraim) Casely
See Casely-Hayford, J(oseph) E(phraim)

Hayman, Ronald 1932- .... **CLC 44**
See also CA 25-28R; CANR 18, 50, 88; CD 5; DLB 155

Hayne, Paul Hamilton 1830-1886 . **NCLC 94**
See also DLB 3, 64, 79, 248; RGAL 4

Hays, Mary 1760-1843 .... **NCLC 114**
See also DLB 142, 158; RGEL 2

Haywood, Eliza (Fowler) 1693(?)-1756 .... **LC 1, 44**
See also DLB 39; RGEL 2

Hazlitt, William 1778-1830 ...... **NCLC 29, 82**
See also BRW 4; DLB 110, 158; RGEL 2; TEA

Hazzard, Shirley 1931- .... **CLC 18**
See also CA 9-12R; CANR 4, 70; CN 7; DLBY 1982; MTCW 1

Head, Bessie 1937-1986 .... **CLC 25, 67; BLC 2; SSC 52**
See also AFW; BW 2, 3; CA 29-32R; CANR 25, 82; CDWLB 3; DAM MULT; DLB 117, 225; EXPS; FW; MTCW 1, 2; RGSF 2; SSFS 5, 13; WLIT 2

Headon, (Nicky) Topper 1956(?)- ..... **CLC 30**

Heaney, Seamus (Justin) 1939- ..... **CLC 5, 7, 14, 25, 37, 74, 91; PC 18; WLCS**
See also BRWR 1; BRWS 2; CA 85-88; CANR 25, 48, 75, 91; CDBLB 1960 to Present; CP 7; DAB; DAM POET; DLB 40; DLBY 1995; EXPP; MTCW 1, 2; PAB; PFS 2, 5, 8; RGEL 2; TEA; WLIT 4

Hearn, (Patricio) Lafcadio (Tessima Carlos) 1850-1904 .... **TCLC 9**
See also CA 166; DLB 12, 78, 189; HGG; RGAL 4

Hearne, Vicki 1946-2001 .... **CLC 56**
See also CA 139

Hearon, Shelby 1931- .... **CLC 63**
See also AITN 2; AMWS 8; CA 25-28R; CANR 18, 48, 103; CSW

Heat-Moon, William Least .... **CLC 29**
See also Trogdon, William (Lewis)
See also AAYA 9

Hebbel, Friedrich 1813-1863 .... **NCLC 43**
See also CDWLB 2; DAM DRAM; DLB 129; EW 6; RGWL 2, 3

Hebert, Anne 1916-2000 .... **CLC 4, 13, 29**
See also CA 85-88; CANR 69; CCA 1; CWP; CWW 2; DAC; DAM MST, POET; DLB 68; GFL 1789 to the Present; MTCW 1, 2

Hecht, Anthony (Evan) 1923- ...... **CLC 8, 13, 19**
See also AMWS 10; CA 9-12R; CANR 6, 108; CP 7; DAM POET; DLB 5, 169; PFS 6; WP

Hecht, Ben 1894-1964 .... **CLC 8**
See also CA 85-88; DFS 9; DLB 7, 9, 25, 26, 28, 86; FANT; IDFW 3, 4; RGAL 4; TCLC 101

Hedayat, Sadeq 1903-1951 .... **TCLC 21**
See also RGSF 2

Hegel, Georg Wilhelm Friedrich 1770-1831 .... **NCLC 46**
See also DLB 90; TWA

Heidegger, Martin 1889-1976 .... **CLC 24**
See also CA 81-84; CANR 34; MTCW 1, 2

Heidenstam, (Carl Gustaf) Verner von 1859-1940 .... **TCLC 5**

Heifner, Jack 1946- .... **CLC 11**
See also CA 105; CANR 47

Heijermans, Herman 1864-1924 .... **TCLC 24**

Heilbrun, Carolyn G(old) 1926- .... **CLC 25**
See also Cross, Amanda
See also CA 45-48; CANR 1, 28, 58, 94; FW

Hein, Christoph 1944- .... **CLC 154**
See also CA 158; CANR 108; CDWLB 2; CWW 2; DLB 124

Heine, Heinrich 1797-1856 .... **NCLC 4, 54; PC 25**
See also CDWLB 2; DLB 90; EW 5; RGWL 2, 3; TWA

Heinemann, Larry (Curtiss) 1944- .. **CLC 50**
See also CA 110; CAAS 21; CANR 31, 81; DLBD 9; INT CANR-31

Heiney, Donald (William) 1921-1993
See Harris, MacDonald
See also CA 1-4R; CANR 3, 58; FANT

Heinlein, Robert A(nson) 1907-1988 . **CLC 1, 3, 8, 14, 26, 55; SSC 55**
See also AAYA 17; BPFB 2; BYA 4, 13; CA 1-4R; CANR 1, 20, 53; CLR 75; CPW; DAM POP; DLB 8; EXPS; JRDA; LAIT 5; MAICYA 1, 2; MTCW 1, 2; RGAL 4; SATA 9, 69; SATA-Obit 56; SCFW 4; SFW 4; SSFS 7; YAW

Helforth, John
See Doolittle, Hilda

Heliodorus fl. 3rd cent. - .... **CMLC 52**
Hellenhofferu, Vojtech Kapristian z
See Hasek, Jaroslav (Matej Frantisek)
Heller, Joseph 1923-1999 . **CLC 1, 3, 5, 8, 11, 36, 63; WLC**
See also AAYA 24; AITN 1; AMWS 4; BPFB 2; BYA 1; CA 5-8R; CABS 1; CANR 8, 42, 66; CN 7; CPW; DA; DAB; DAC; DAM MST, NOV, POP; DLB 2, 28, 227; DLBY 1980; EXPN; INT CANR-8; LAIT 4; MTCW 1, 2; NFS 1; RGAL 4; TUS; YAW
Hellman, Lillian (Florence) 1906-1984 .. **CLC 2, 4, 8, 14, 18, 34, 44, 52; DC 1**
See also AITN 1, 2; AMWS 1; CA 13-16R; CAD; CANR 33; CWD; DAM DRAM; DFS 1, 3, 14; DLB 7, 228; DLBY 1984; FW; LAIT 3; MAWW; MTCW 1, 2; RGAL 4; TCLC 119; TUS
Helprin, Mark 1947- .... **CLC 7, 10, 22, 32**
See also CA 81-84; CANR 47, 64; CDALBS; CPW; DAM NOV, POP; DLBY 1985; FANT; MTCW 1, 2; SUFW 2
Helvetius, Claude-Adrien 1715-1771 .. **LC 26**
Helyar, Jane Penelope Josephine 1933-
See Poole, Josephine
See also CA 21-24R; CANR 10, 26; CWRI 5; SATA 82
Hemans, Felicia 1793-1835 ...... **NCLC 29, 71**
See also DLB 96; RGEL 2
Hemingway, Ernest (Miller) 1899-1961 .... **CLC 1, 3, 6, 8, 10, 13, 19, 30, 34, 39, 41, 44, 50, 61, 80; SSC 1, 25, 36, 40; WLC**
See also AAYA 19; AMW; AMWR 1; BPFB 2; BYA 2, 3, 13; CA 77-80; CANR 34; CDALB 1917-1929; DA; DAB; DAC; DAM MST, NOV; DLB 4, 9, 102, 210; DLBD 1, 15, 16; DLBY 1981, 1987, 1996, 1998; EXPN; EXPS; LAIT 3, 4; MTCW 1, 2; NFS 1, 5, 6, 14; RGAL 4; RGSF 2; SSFS 1, 6, 8, 9, 11; TCLC 115; TUS; WYA
Hempel, Amy 1951- .... **CLC 39**
See also CA 137; CANR 70; DLB 218; EXPS; MTCW 2; SSFS 2
Henderson, F. C.
See Mencken, H(enry) L(ouis)
Henderson, Sylvia
See Ashton-Warner, Sylvia (Constance)
Henderson, Zenna (Chlarson) 1917-1983 .... **SSC 29**
See also CA 1-4R; CANR 1, 84; DLB 8; SATA 5; SFW 4
Henkin, Joshua .... **CLC 119**
See also CA 161
Henley, Beth .... **CLC 23; DC 6, 14**
See also Henley, Elizabeth Becker
See also CABS 3; CAD; CD 5; CSW; CWD; DFS 2; DLBY 1986; FW
Henley, Elizabeth Becker 1952-
See Henley, Beth
See also CA 107; CANR 32, 73; DAM DRAM, MST; MTCW 1, 2
Henley, William Ernest 1849-1903 .. **TCLC 8**
See also DLB 19; RGEL 2
Hennissart, Martha
See Lathen, Emma
See also CA 85-88; CANR 64
Henry VIII 1491-1547 .... **LC 10**
See also DLB 132
Henry, O. .... **TCLC 1, 19; SSC 5, 49; WLC**
See also Porter, William Sydney
See also AAYA 41; AMWS 2; EXPS; RGAL 4; RGSF 2; SSFS 2
Henry, Patrick 1736-1799 .... **LC 25**
See also LAIT 1

Henryson, Robert 1430(?)-1506(?) ...... **LC 20**
See also BRWS 7; DLB 146; RGEL 2
Henschke, Alfred
See Klabund
Hentoff, Nat(han Irving) 1925- .... **CLC 26**
See also AAYA 4, 42; BYA 6; CA 1-4R; CAAS 5; CANR 5, 25, 77; CLR 1, 52; INT CANR-25; JRDA; MAICYA 1, 2; SATA 42, 69, 133; SATA-Brief 27; WYA; YAW
Heppenstall, (John) Rayner 1911-1981 .... **CLC 10**
See also CA 1-4R; CANR 29
Heraclitus c. 540B.C.-c. 450B.C. ... **CMLC 22**
See also DLB 176
Herbert, Frank (Patrick) 1920-1986 .... **CLC 12, 23, 35, 44, 85**
See also AAYA 21; BPFB 2; BYA 4, 14; CA 53-56; CANR 5, 43; CDALBS; CPW; DAM POP; DLB 8; INT CANR-5; LAIT 5; MTCW 1, 2; SATA 9, 37; SATA-Obit 47; SCFW 2; SFW 4; YAW
Herbert, George 1593-1633 ...... **LC 24; PC 4**
See also BRW 2; BRWR 2; CDBLB Before 1660; DAB; DAM POET; DLB 126; EXPP; RGEL 2; TEA; WP
Herbert, Zbigniew 1924-1998 .... **CLC 9, 43**
See also CA 89-92; CANR 36, 74; CDWLB 4; CWW 2; DAM POET; DLB 232; MTCW 1
Herbst, Josephine (Frey) 1897-1969 .... **CLC 34**
See also CA 5-8R; DLB 9
Herder, Johann Gottfried von 1744-1803 .... **NCLC 8**
See also DLB 97; EW 4; TWA
Heredia, Jose Maria 1803-1839
See also HLCS 2; LAW
Hergesheimer, Joseph 1880-1954 ... **TCLC 11**
See also CA 194; DLB 102, 9; RGAL 4
Herlihy, James Leo 1927-1993 .... **CLC 6**
See also CA 1-4R; CAD; CANR 2
Herman, William
See Bierce, Ambrose (Gwinett)
Hermogenes fl. c. 175- .... **CMLC 6**
Hernandez, Jose 1834-1886 .... **NCLC 17**
See also LAW; RGWL 2, 3; WLIT 1
Herodotus c. 484B.C.-c. 420B.C. .. **CMLC 17**
See also AW 1; CDWLB 1; DLB 176; RGWL 2, 3; TWA
Herrick, Robert 1591-1674 .... **LC 13; PC 9**
See also BRW 2; DA; DAB; DAC; DAM MST, POP; DLB 126; EXPP; PFS 13; RGAL 4; RGEL 2; TEA; WP
Herring, Guilles
See Somerville, Edith Oenone
Herriot, James 1916-1995 .... **CLC 12**
See also Wight, James Alfred
See also AAYA 1; BPFB 2; CANR 40; CLR 80; CPW; DAM POP; LAIT 3; MAICYA 2; MAICYAS 1; MTCW 2; SATA 86, 135; TEA; YAW
Herris, Violet
See Hunt, Violet
Herrmann, Dorothy 1941- .... **CLC 44**
See also CA 107
Herrmann, Taffy
See Herrmann, Dorothy
Hersey, John (Richard) 1914-1993 .... **CLC 1, 2, 7, 9, 40, 81, 97**
See also AAYA 29; BPFB 2; CA 17-20R; CANR 33; CDALBS; CPW; DAM POP; DLB 6, 185; MTCW 1, 2; SATA 25; SATA-Obit 76; TUS
Herzen, Aleksandr Ivanovich 1812-1870 .... **NCLC 10, 61**
Herzl, Theodor 1860-1904 .... **TCLC 36**
See also CA 168

Herzog, Werner 1942- .... **CLC 16**
See also CA 89-92
Hesiod c. 8th cent. B.C.- .... **CMLC 5**
See also AW 1; DLB 176; RGWL 2, 3
Hesse, Hermann 1877-1962 ... **CLC 1, 2, 3, 6, 11, 17, 25, 69; SSC 9, 49; WLC**
See also AAYA 43; BPFB 2; CA 17-18; CAP 2; CDWLB 2; DA; DAB; DAC; DAM MST, NOV; DLB 66; EW 9; EXPN; LAIT 1; MTCW 1, 2; NFS 6, 15; RGWL 2, 3; SATA 50; TWA
Hewes, Cady
See De Voto, Bernard (Augustine)
Heyen, William 1940- .... **CLC 13, 18**
See also CA 33-36R; CAAS 9; CANR 98; CP 7; DLB 5
Heyerdahl, Thor 1914-2002 .... **CLC 26**
See also CA 5-8R; CANR 5, 22, 66, 73; LAIT 4; MTCW 1, 2; SATA 2, 52
Heym, Georg (Theodor Franz Arthur) 1887-1912 .... **TCLC 9**
See also CA 181
Heym, Stefan 1913-2001 .... **CLC 41**
See also CA 9-12R; CANR 4; CWW 2; DLB 69
Heyse, Paul (Johann Ludwig von) 1830-1914 .... **TCLC 8**
See also DLB 129
Heyward, (Edwin) DuBose 1885-1940 .... **TCLC 59**
See also CA 157; DLB 7, 9, 45, 249; HR 2; SATA 21
Heywood, John 1497(?)-1580(?) .... **LC 65**
See also DLB 136; RGEL 2
Hibbert, Eleanor Alice Burford 1906-1993 .... **CLC 7**
See also Holt, Victoria
See also BEST 90:4; CA 17-20R; CANR 9, 28, 59; CMW 4; CPW; DAM POP; MTCW 2; RHW; SATA 2; SATA-Obit 74
Hichens, Robert (Smythe) 1864-1950 .... **TCLC 64**
See also CA 162; DLB 153; HGG; RHW; SUFW
Higgins, George V(incent) 1939-1999 .... **CLC 4, 7, 10, 18**
See also BPFB 2; CA 77-80; CAAS 5; CANR 17, 51, 89, 96; CMW 4; CN 7; DLB 2; DLBY 1981, 1998; INT CANR-17; MSW; MTCW 1
Higginson, Thomas Wentworth 1823-1911 .... **TCLC 36**
See also CA 162; DLB 1, 64, 243
Higgonet, Margaret ed. .... **CLC 65**
Highet, Helen
See MacInnes, Helen (Clark)
Highsmith, (Mary) Patricia 1921-1995 .... **CLC 2, 4, 14, 42, 102**
See also Morgan, Claire
See also BRWS 5; CA 1-4R; CANR 1, 20, 48, 62, 108; CMW 4; CPW; DAM NOV, POP; MSW; MTCW 1, 2
Highwater, Jamake (Mamake) 1942(?)-2001 .... **CLC 12**
See also AAYA 7; BPFB 2; BYA 4; CA 65-68; CAAS 7; CANR 10, 34, 84; CLR 17; CWRI 5; DLB 52; DLBY 1985; JRDA; MAICYA 1, 2; SATA 32, 69; SATA-Brief 30
Highway, Tomson 1951- .... **CLC 92**
See also CA 151; CANR 75; CCA 1; CD 5; DAC; DAM MULT; DFS 2; MTCW 2; NNAL
Hijuelos, Oscar 1951- .... **CLC 65; HLC 1**
See also AAYA 25; AMWS 8; BEST 90:1; CA 123; CANR 50, 75; CPW; DAM MULT, POP; DLB 145; HW 1, 2; MTCW 2; RGAL 4; WLIT 1

Hikmet, Nazim 1902(?)-1963 .... **CLC 40**
See also CA 141

Hildegard von Bingen 1098-1179 . **CMLC 20**
See also DLB 148

Hildesheimer, Wolfgang 1916-1991 .. **CLC 49**
See also CA 101; DLB 69, 124

Hill, Geoffrey (William) 1932- ...... **CLC 5, 8, 18, 45**
See also BRWS 5; CA 81-84; CANR 21, 89; CDBLB 1960 to Present; CP 7; DAM POET; DLB 40; MTCW 1; RGEL 2

Hill, George Roy 1921- .... **CLC 26**
See also CA 122

Hill, John
See Koontz, Dean R(ay)

Hill, Susan (Elizabeth) 1942- ...... **CLC 4, 113**
See also CA 33-36R; CANR 29, 69; CN 7; DAB; DAM MST, NOV; DLB 14, 139; HGG; MTCW 1; RHW

Hillard, Asa G. III .... **CLC 70**

Hillerman, Tony 1925- .... **CLC 62**
See also AAYA 40; BEST 89:1; BPFB 2; CA 29-32R; CANR 21, 42, 65, 97; CMW 4; CPW; DAM POP; DLB 206; MSW; RGAL 4; SATA 6; TCWW 2; YAW

Hillesum, Etty 1914-1943 .... **TCLC 49**
See also CA 137

Hilliard, Noel (Harvey) 1929-1996 ... **CLC 15**
See also CA 9-12R; CANR 7, 69; CN 7

Hillis, Rick 1956- .... **CLC 66**
See also CA 134

Hilton, James 1900-1954 .... **TCLC 21**
See also CA 169; DLB 34, 77; FANT; SATA 34

Himes, Chester (Bomar) 1909-1984 .. **CLC 2, 4, 7, 18, 58, 108; BLC 2**
See also AFAW 2; BPFB 2; BW 2; CA 25-28R; CANR 22, 89; CMW 4; DAM MULT; DLB 2, 76, 143, 226; MSW; MTCW 1, 2; RGAL 4

Hinde, Thomas .... **CLC 6, 11**
See also Chitty, Thomas Willes

Hine, (William) Daryl 1936- .... **CLC 15**
See also CA 1-4R; CAAS 15; CANR 1, 20; CP 7; DLB 60

Hinkson, Katharine Tynan
See Tynan, Katharine

Hinojosa(-Smith), Rolando (R.) 1929-
See also CA 131; CAAS 16; CANR 62; DAM MULT; DLB 82; HLC 1; HW 1, 2; MTCW 2; RGAL 4

Hinton, S(usan) E(loise) 1950- .. **CLC 30, 111**
See also AAYA 2, 33; BPFB 2; BYA 2, 3; CA 81-84; CANR 32, 62, 92; CDALBS; CLR 3, 23; CPW; DA; DAB; DAC; DAM MST, NOV; JRDA; LAIT 5; MAICYA 1, 2; MTCW 1, 2; NFS 5, 9, 15; SATA 19, 58, 115; WYA; YAW

Hippius, Zinaida .... **TCLC 9**
See also Gippius, Zinaida (Nikolayevna)

Hiraoka, Kimitake 1925-1970
See Mishima, Yukio
See also CA 97-100; DAM DRAM; GLL 1; MTCW 1, 2

Hirsch, E(ric) D(onald), Jr. 1928- .... **CLC 79**
See also CA 25-28R; CANR 27, 51; DLB 67; INT CANR-27; MTCW 1

Hirsch, Edward 1950- .... **CLC 31, 50**
See also CA 104; CANR 20, 42, 102; CP 7; DLB 120

Hitchcock, Alfred (Joseph)
1899-1980 .... **CLC 16**
See also AAYA 22; CA 159; SATA 27; SATA-Obit 24

Hitchens, Christopher (Eric)
1949- .... **CLC 157**
See also CA 152; CANR 89

Hitler, Adolf 1889-1945 .... **TCLC 53**
See also CA 147

Hoagland, Edward 1932- .... **CLC 28**
See also ANW; CA 1-4R; CANR 2, 31, 57, 107; CN 7; DLB 6; SATA 51; TCWW 2

Hoban, Russell (Conwell) 1925- ... **CLC 7, 25**
See also BPFB 2; CA 5-8R; CANR 23, 37, 66; CLR 3, 69; CN 7; CWRI 5; DAM NOV; DLB 52; FANT; MAICYA 1, 2; MTCW 1, 2; SATA 1, 40, 78; SFW 4; SUFW 2

Hobbes, Thomas 1588-1679 .... **LC 36**
See also DLB 151, 252; RGEL 2

Hobbs, Perry
See Blackmur, R(ichard) P(almer)

Hobson, Laura Z(ametkin)
1900-1986 .... **CLC 7, 25**
See also BPFB 2; CA 17-20R; CANR 55; DLB 28; SATA 52

Hoccleve, Thomas c. 1368-c. 1437 ...... **LC 75**
See also DLB 146; RGEL 2

Hoch, Edward D(entinger) 1930-
See Queen, Ellery
See also CA 29-32R; CANR 11, 27, 51, 97; CMW 4; SFW 4

Hochhuth, Rolf 1931- .... **CLC 4, 11, 18**
See also CA 5-8R; CANR 33, 75; CWW 2; DAM DRAM; DLB 124; MTCW 1, 2

Hochman, Sandra 1936- .... **CLC 3, 8**
See also CA 5-8R; DLB 5

Hochwaelder, Fritz 1911-1986 .... **CLC 36**
See also Hochwalder, Fritz
See also CA 29-32R; CANR 42; DAM DRAM; MTCW 1; RGWL 3

Hochwalder, Fritz
See Hochwaelder, Fritz
See also RGWL 2

Hocking, Mary (Eunice) 1921- .... **CLC 13**
See also CA 101; CANR 18, 40

Hodgins, Jack 1938- .... **CLC 23**
See also CA 93-96; CN 7; DLB 60

Hodgson, William Hope
1877(?)-1918 .... **TCLC 13**
See also CA 164; CMW 4; DLB 70, 153, 156, 178; HGG; MTCW 2; SFW 4; SUFW 1

Hoeg, Peter 1957- .... **CLC 95, 156**
See also CA 151; CANR 75; CMW 4; DLB 214; MTCW 2; RGWL 3

Hoffman, Alice 1952- .... **CLC 51**
See also AAYA 37; AMWS 10; CA 77-80; CANR 34, 66, 100; CN 7; CPW; DAM NOV; MTCW 1, 2

Hoffman, Daniel (Gerard) 1923- . **CLC 6, 13, 23**
See also CA 1-4R; CANR 4; CP 7; DLB 5

Hoffman, Stanley 1944- .... **CLC 5**
See also CA 77-80

Hoffman, William 1925- .... **CLC 141**
See also CA 21-24R; CANR 9, 103; CSW; DLB 234

Hoffman, William M(oses) 1939- ..... **CLC 40**
See Hoffman, William M.
See also CA 57-60; CANR 11, 71

Hoffmann, E(rnst) T(heodor) A(madeus)
1776-1822 .... **NCLC 2; SSC 13**
See also CDWLB 2; DLB 90; EW 5; RGSF 2; RGWL 2, 3; SATA 27; SUFW 1; WCH

Hofmann, Gert 1931- .... **CLC 54**
See also CA 128

Hofmannsthal, Hugo von
1874-1929 .... **TCLC 11; DC 4**
See also CA 153; CDWLB 2; DAM DRAM; DFS 12; DLB 81, 118; EW 9; RGWL 2, 3

Hogan, Linda 1947- .... **CLC 73; PC 35**
See also AMWS 4; ANW; BYA 12; CA 120; CANR 45, 73; CWP; DAM MULT; DLB 175; NNAL; SATA 132; TCWW 2

Hogarth, Charles
See Creasey, John

Hogarth, Emmett
See Polonsky, Abraham (Lincoln)

Hogg, James 1770-1835 .... **NCLC 4, 109**
See also DLB 93, 116, 159; HGG; RGEL 2; SUFW 1

Holbach, Paul Henri Thiry Baron
1723-1789 .... **LC 14**

Holberg, Ludvig 1684-1754 .... **LC 6**
See also RGWL 2, 3

Holcroft, Thomas 1745-1809 .... **NCLC 85**
See also DLB 39, 89, 158; RGEL 2

Holden, Ursula 1921- .... **CLC 18**
See also CA 101; CAAS 8; CANR 22

Holderlin, (Johann Christian) Friedrich
1770-1843 .... **NCLC 16; PC 4**
See also CDWLB 2; DLB 90; EW 5; RGWL 2, 3

Holdstock, Robert
See Holdstock, Robert P.

Holdstock, Robert P. 1948- .... **CLC 39**
See also CA 131; CANR 81; DLB 261; FANT; HGG; SFW 4; SUFW 2

Holinshed, Raphael fl. 1580- .... **LC 69**
See also DLB 167; RGEL 2

Holland, Isabelle (Christian)
1920-2002 .... **CLC 21**
See also AAYA 11; CA 21-24R, 181; CAAE 181; CANR 10, 25, 47; CLR 57; CWRI 5; JRDA; LAIT 4; MAICYA 1, 2; SATA 8, 70; SATA-Essay 103; SATA-Obit 132; WYA

Holland, Marcus
See Caldwell, (Janet Miriam) Taylor (Holland)

Hollander, John 1929- .... **CLC 2, 5, 8, 14**
See also CA 1-4R; CANR 1, 52; CP 7; DLB 5; SATA 13

Hollander, Paul
See Silverberg, Robert

Holleran, Andrew 1943(?)- .... **CLC 38**
See also Garber, Eric
See also CA 144; GLL 1

Holley, Marietta 1836(?)-1926 .... **TCLC 99**
See also DLB 11

Hollinghurst, Alan 1954- .... **CLC 55, 91**
See also CA 114; CN 7; DLB 207; GLL 1

Hollis, Jim
See Summers, Hollis (Spurgeon, Jr.)

Holly, Buddy 1936-1959 .... **TCLC 65**

Holmes, Gordon
See Shiel, M(atthew) P(hipps)

Holmes, John
See Souster, (Holmes) Raymond

Holmes, John Clellon 1926-1988 ...... **CLC 56**
See also CA 9-12R; CANR 4; DLB 16, 237

Holmes, Oliver Wendell, Jr.
1841-1935 .... **TCLC 77**
See also CA 186

Holmes, Oliver Wendell
1809-1894 .... **NCLC 14, 81**
See also AMWS 1; CDALB 1640-1865; DLB 1, 189, 235; EXPP; RGAL 4; SATA 34

Holmes, Raymond
See Souster, (Holmes) Raymond

Holt, Victoria
See Hibbert, Eleanor Alice Burford
See also BPFB 2

Holub, Miroslav 1923-1998 .... **CLC 4**
See also CA 21-24R; CANR 10; CDWLB 4; CWW 2; DLB 232; RGWL 3

Homer c. 8th cent. B.C.- .... **CMLC 1, 16; PC 23; WLCS**
See also AW 1; CDWLB 1; DA; DAB; DAC; DAM MST, POET; DLB 176; EFS 1; LAIT 1; RGWL 2, 3; TWA; WP

Hongo, Garrett Kaoru 1951- .... **PC 23**
See also CA 133; CAAS 22; CP 7; DLB 120; EXPP; RGAL 4

Honig, Edwin 1919- .... **CLC 33**
See also CA 5-8R; CAAS 8; CANR 4, 45; CP 7; DLB 5

Hood, Hugh (John Blagdon) 1928- . **CLC 15, 28; SSC 42**
See also CA 49-52; CAAS 17; CANR 1, 33, 87; CN 7; DLB 53; RGSF 2

Hood, Thomas 1799-1845 .... **NCLC 16**
See also BRW 4; DLB 96; RGEL 2

Hooker, (Peter) Jeremy 1941- .... **CLC 43**
See also CA 77-80; CANR 22; CP 7; DLB 40

hooks, bell .... **CLC 94**
See also Watkins, Gloria Jean
See also DLB 246

Hope, A(lec) D(erwent) 1907-2000 .... **CLC 3, 51**
See also BRWS 7; CA 21-24R; CANR 33, 74; MTCW 1, 2; PFS 8; RGEL 2

Hope, Anthony 1863-1933 .... **TCLC 83**
See also CA 157; DLB 153, 156; RGEL 2; RHW

Hope, Brian
See Creasey, John

Hope, Christopher (David Tully) 1944- .... **CLC 52**
See also AFW; CA 106; CANR 47, 101; CN 7; DLB 225; SATA 62

Hopkins, Gerard Manley 1844-1889 ...... **NCLC 17; PC 15; WLC**
See also BRW 5; BRWR 2; CDBLB 1890-1914; DA; DAB; DAC; DAM MST, POET; DLB 35, 57; EXPP; PAB; RGEL 2; TEA; WP

Hopkins, John (Richard) 1931-1998 .. **CLC 4**
See also CA 85-88; CBD; CD 5

Hopkins, Pauline Elizabeth 1859-1930 .... **TCLC 28; BLC 2**
See also AFAW 2; BW 2, 3; CA 141; CANR 82; DAM MULT; DLB 50

Hopkinson, Francis 1737-1791 .... **LC 25**
See also DLB 31; RGAL 4

Hopley-Woolrich, Cornell George 1903-1968
See Woolrich, Cornell
See also CA 13-14; CANR 58; CAP 1; CMW 4; DLB 226; MTCW 2

Horace 65B.C.-8B.C. .... **CMLC 39**
See also AW 2; CDWLB 1; DLB 211; RGWL 2, 3

Horatio
See Proust, (Valentin-Louis-George-Eugene-)Marcel

Horgan, Paul (George Vincent O'Shaughnessy) 1903-1995 .. **CLC 9, 53**
See also BPFB 2; CA 13-16R; CANR 9, 35; DAM NOV; DLB 102, 212; DLBY 1985; INT CANR-9; MTCW 1, 2; SATA 13; SATA-Obit 84; TCWW 2

Horn, Peter
See Kuttner, Henry

Hornem, Horace Esq.
See Byron, George Gordon (Noel)

Horney, Karen (Clementine Theodore Danielsen) 1885-1952 .... **TCLC 71**
See also CA 165; DLB 246; FW

Hornung, E(rnest) W(illiam) 1866-1921 .... **TCLC 59**
See also CA 160; CMW 4; DLB 70

Horovitz, Israel (Arthur) 1939- .... **CLC 56**
See also CA 33-36R; CAD; CANR 46, 59; CD 5; DAM DRAM; DLB 7

Horton, George Moses 1797(?)-1883(?) .... **NCLC 87**
See also DLB 50

Horvath, odon von 1901-1938
See von Horvath, Odon

Horvath, Oedoen von -1938
See von Horvath, Odon

Horwitz, Julius 1920-1986 .... **CLC 14**
See also CA 9-12R; CANR 12

Hospital, Janette Turner 1942- .... **CLC 42, 145**
See also CA 108; CANR 48; CN 7; RGSF 2

Hostos, E. M. de
See Hostos (y Bonilla), Eugenio Maria de

Hostos, Eugenio M. de
See Hostos (y Bonilla), Eugenio Maria de

Hostos, Eugenio Maria
See Hostos (y Bonilla), Eugenio Maria de

Hostos (y Bonilla), Eugenio Maria de 1839-1903 .... **TCLC 24**
See also CA 131; HW 1

Houdini
See Lovecraft, H(oward) P(hillips)

Hougan, Carolyn 1943- .... **CLC 34**
See also CA 139

Household, Geoffrey (Edward West) 1900-1988 .... **CLC 11**
See also CA 77-80; CANR 58; CMW 4; DLB 87; SATA 14; SATA-Obit 59

Housman, A(lfred) E(dward) 1859-1936 .... **TCLC 1, 10; PC 2, 43; WLCS**
See also BRW 6; CA 125; DA; DAB; DAC; DAM MST, POET; DLB 19; EXPP; MTCW 1, 2; PAB; PFS 4, 7; RGEL 2; TEA; WP

Housman, Laurence 1865-1959 .... **TCLC 7**
See also CA 155; DLB 10; FANT; RGEL 2; SATA 25

Howard, Elizabeth Jane 1923- ..... **CLC 7, 29**
See also CA 5-8R; CANR 8, 62; CN 7

Howard, Maureen 1930- .... **CLC 5, 14, 46, 151**
See also CA 53-56; CANR 31, 75; CN 7; DLBY 1983; INT CANR-31; MTCW 1, 2

Howard, Richard 1929- .... **CLC 7, 10, 47**
See also AITN 1; CA 85-88; CANR 25, 80; CP 7; DLB 5; INT CANR-25

Howard, Robert E(rvin) 1906-1936 .... **TCLC 8**
See also BPFB 2; BYA 5; CA 157; FANT; SUFW 1

Howard, Warren F.
See Pohl, Frederik

Howe, Fanny (Quincy) 1940- .... **CLC 47**
See also CA 117; CAAE 187; CAAS 27; CANR 70; CP 7; CWP; SATA-Brief 52

Howe, Irving 1920-1993 .... **CLC 85**
See also AMWS 6; CA 9-12R; CANR 21, 50; DLB 67; MTCW 1, 2

Howe, Julia Ward 1819-1910 .... **TCLC 21**
See also CA 191; DLB 1, 189, 235; FW

Howe, Susan 1937- .... **CLC 72, 152**
See also AMWS 4; CA 160; CP 7; CWP; DLB 120; FW; RGAL 4

Howe, Tina 1937- .... **CLC 48**
See also CA 109; CAD; CD 5; CWD

Howell, James 1594(?)-1666 .... **LC 13**
See also DLB 151

Howells, W. D.
See Howells, William Dean

Howells, William D.
See Howells, William Dean

Howells, William Dean 1837-1920 .. **TCLC 7, 17, 41; SSC 36**
See also AMW; CA 134; CDALB 1865-1917; DLB 12, 64, 74, 79, 189; MTCW 2; RGAL 4; TUS

Howes, Barbara 1914-1996 .... **CLC 15**
See also CA 9-12R; CAAS 3; CANR 53; CP 7; SATA 5

Hrabal, Bohumil 1914-1997 .... **CLC 13, 67**
See also CA 106; CAAS 12; CANR 57; CWW 2; DLB 232; RGSF 2

Hrotsvit of Gandersheim c. 935-c. 1000 .... **CMLC 29**
See also DLB 148

Hsi, Chu 1130-1200 .... **CMLC 42**

Hsun, Lu
See Lu Hsun

Hubbard, L(afayette) Ron(ald) 1911-1986 .... **CLC 43**
See also CA 77-80; CANR 52; CPW; DAM POP; FANT; MTCW 2; SFW 4

Huch, Ricarda (Octavia) 1864-1947 .... **TCLC 13**
See also CA 189; DLB 66

Huddle, David 1942- .... **CLC 49**
See also CA 57-60; CAAS 20; CANR 89; DLB 130

Hudson, Jeffrey
See Crichton, (John) Michael

Hudson, W(illiam) H(enry) 1841-1922 .... **TCLC 29**
See also CA 190; DLB 98, 153, 174; RGEL 2; SATA 35

Hueffer, Ford Madox
See Ford, Ford Madox

Hughart, Barry 1934- .... **CLC 39**
See also CA 137; FANT; SFW 4; SUFW 2

Hughes, Colin
See Creasey, John

Hughes, David (John) 1930- .... **CLC 48**
See also CA 129; CN 7; DLB 14

Hughes, Edward James
See Hughes, Ted
See also DAM MST, POET

Hughes, (James Mercer) Langston 1902-1967 .... **CLC 1, 5, 10, 15, 35, 44, 108; BLC 2; DC 3; PC 1; SSC 6; WLC**
See also AAYA 12; AFAW 1, 2; AMWR 1; AMWS 1; BW 1, 3; CA 1-4R; CANR 1, 34, 82; CDALB 1929-1941; CLR 17; DA; DAB; DAC; DAM DRAM, MST, MULT, POET; DLB 4, 7, 48, 51, 86, 228; EXPP; EXPS; HR 2; JRDA; LAIT 3; MAICYA 1, 2; MTCW 1, 2; PAB; PFS 1, 3, 6, 10, 15; RGAL 4; RGSF 2; SATA 4, 33; SSFS 4, 7; TUS; WCH; WP; YAW

Hughes, Richard (Arthur Warren) 1900-1976 .... **CLC 1, 11**
See also CA 5-8R; CANR 4; DAM NOV; DLB 15, 161; MTCW 1; RGEL 2; SATA 8; SATA-Obit 25

Hughes, Ted 1930-1998 . **CLC 2, 4, 9, 14, 37, 119; PC 7**
See also Hughes, Edward James
See also BRWR 2; BRWS 1; CA 1-4R; CANR 1, 33, 66, 108; CLR 3; CP 7; DAB; DAC; DLB 40, 161; EXPP; MAICYA 1, 2; MTCW 1, 2; PAB; PFS 4; RGEL 2; SATA 49; SATA-Brief 27; SATA-Obit 107; TEA; YAW

Hugo, Richard
See Huch, Ricarda (Octavia)

Hugo, Richard F(ranklin) 1923-1982 .... **CLC 6, 18, 32**
See also AMWS 6; CA 49-52; CANR 3; DAM POET; DLB 5, 206; RGAL 4

Hugo, Victor (Marie) 1802-1885 .... **NCLC 3, 10, 21; PC 17; WLC**
See also AAYA 28; DA; DAB; DAC; DAM DRAM, MST, NOV, POET; DLB 119, 192, 217; EFS 2; EW 6; EXPN; GFL 1789 to the Present; LAIT 1, 2; NFS 5; RGWL 2, 3; SATA 47; TWA

Huidobro, Vicente
See Huidobro Fernandez, Vicente Garcia
See also LAW

Huidobro Fernandez, Vicente Garcia 1893-1948 .... TCLC 31
See also Huidobro, Vicente
See also CA 131; HW 1

Hulme, Keri 1947- .... CLC 39, 130
See also CA 125; CANR 69; CN 7; CP 7; CWP; FW; INT 125

Hulme, T(homas) E(rnest) 1883-1917 .... TCLC 21
See also BRWS 6; CA 203; DLB 19

Hume, David 1711-1776 .... LC 7, 56
See also BRWS 3; DLB 104, 252; TEA

Humphrey, William 1924-1997 .... CLC 45
See also AMWS 9; CA 77-80; CANR 68; CN 7; CSW; DLB 6, 212, 234; TCWW 2

Humphreys, Emyr Owen 1919- .... CLC 47
See also CA 5-8R; CANR 3, 24; CN 7; DLB 15

Humphreys, Josephine 1945- .... CLC 34, 57
See also CA 127; CANR 97; CSW; INT 127

Huneker, James Gibbons 1860-1921 .... TCLC 65
See also CA 193; DLB 71; RGAL 4

Hungerford, Hesba Fay
See Brinsmead, H(esba) F(ay)

Hungerford, Pixie
See Brinsmead, H(esba) F(ay)

Hunt, E(verette) Howard, (Jr.) 1918- .... CLC 3
See also AITN 1; CA 45-48; CANR 2, 47, 103; CMW 4

Hunt, Francesca
See Holland, Isabelle (Christian)

Hunt, Howard
See Hunt, E(verette) Howard, (Jr.)

Hunt, Kyle
See Creasey, John

Hunt, (James Henry) Leigh 1784-1859 .... NCLC 1, 70
See also DAM POET; DLB 96, 110, 144; RGEL 2; TEA

Hunt, Marsha 1946- .... CLC 70
See also BW 2, 3; CA 143; CANR 79

Hunt, Violet 1866(?)-1942 .... TCLC 53
See also CA 184; DLB 162, 197

Hunter, E. Waldo
See Sturgeon, Theodore (Hamilton)

Hunter, Evan 1926- .... CLC 11, 31
See also McBain, Ed
See also AAYA 39; BPFB 2; CA 5-8R; CANR 5, 38, 62, 97; CMW 4; CN 7; CPW; DAM POP; DLBY 1982; INT CANR-5; MSW; MTCW 1; SATA 25; SFW 4

Hunter, Kristin 1931-
See Lattany, Kristin (Elaine Eggleston) Hunter

Hunter, Mary
See Austin, Mary (Hunter)

Hunter, Mollie 1922- .... CLC 21
See also McIlwraith, Maureen Mollie Hunter
See also AAYA 13; BYA 6; CANR 37, 78; CLR 25; DLB 161; JRDA; MAICYA 1, 2; SAAS 7; SATA 54, 106; WYA; YAW

Hunter, Robert (?)-1734 .... LC 7

Hurston, Zora Neale 1891-1960 .... BLC 2; CLC 7, 30, 61; DC 12; SSC 4; TCLC 121; WLCS
See also AAYA 15; AFAW 1, 2; AMWS 6; BW 1; BYA 12; CA 85-88; CANR 61; CDALBS; DA; DAC; DAM MST, MULT, NOV; DFS 6; DLB 51, 86; EXPN; EXPS; FW; HR 2; LAIT 3; MAWW; MTCW 1, 2; NFS 3; RGAL 4; RGSF 2; SSFS 1, 6, 11; TUS; YAW

Husserl, E. G.
See Husserl, Edmund (Gustav Albrecht)

Husserl, Edmund (Gustav Albrecht) 1859-1938 .... TCLC 100
See also CA 133

Huston, John (Marcellus) 1906-1987 .... CLC 20
See also CA 73-76; CANR 34; DLB 26

Hustvedt, Siri 1955- .... CLC 76
See also CA 137

Hutten, Ulrich von 1488-1523 .... LC 16
See also DLB 179

Huxley, Aldous (Leonard) 1894-1963 .... CLC 1, 3, 4, 5, 8, 11, 18, 35, 79; SSC 39; WLC
See also AAYA 11; BPFB 2; BRW 7; CA 85-88; CANR 44, 99; CDBLB 1914-1945; DA; DAB; DAC; DAM MST, NOV; DLB 36, 100, 162, 195, 255; EXPN; LAIT 5; MTCW 1, 2; NFS 6; RGEL 2; SATA 63; SCFW 2; SFW 4; TEA; YAW

Huxley, T(homas) H(enry) 1825-1895 .... NCLC 67
See also DLB 57; TEA

Huysmans, Joris-Karl 1848-1907 ... TCLC 7, 69
See also CA 165; DLB 123; EW 7; GFL 1789 to the Present; RGWL 2, 3

Hwang, David Henry 1957- ... CLC 55; DC 4
See also CA 132; CAD; CANR 76; CD 5; DAM DRAM; DFS 11; DLB 212, 228; INT CA-132; MTCW 2; RGAL 4

Hyde, Anthony 1946- .... CLC 42
See Chase, Nicholas
See also CA 136; CCA 1

Hyde, Margaret O(ldroyd) 1917- .... CLC 21
See also CA 1-4R; CANR 1, 36; CLR 23; JRDA; MAICYA 1, 2; SAAS 8; SATA 1, 42, 76

Hynes, James 1956(?)- .... CLC 65
See also CA 164; CANR 105

Hypatia c. 370-415 .... CMLC 35

Ian, Janis 1951- .... CLC 21
See also CA 187

Ibanez, Vicente Blasco
See Blasco Ibanez, Vicente

Ibarbourou, Juana de 1895-1979
See also HLCS 2; HW 1; LAW

Ibarguengoitia, Jorge 1928-1983 .... CLC 37
See also CA 124; HW 1

Ibsen, Henrik (Johan) 1828-1906 ... TCLC 2, 8, 16, 37, 52; DC 2; WLC
See also CA 141; DA; DAB; DAC; DAM DRAM, MST; DFS 15; EW 7; LAIT 2; RGWL 2, 3

Ibuse, Masuji 1898-1993 .... CLC 22
See Ibuse Masuji
See also CA 127; MJW; RGWL 3

Ibuse Masuji
See Ibuse, Masuji
See also DLB 180

Ichikawa, Kon 1915- .... CLC 20
See also CA 121

Ichiyo, Higuchi 1872-1896 .... NCLC 49
See also MJW

Idle, Eric 1943-2000 .... CLC 21
See also Monty Python
See also CA 116; CANR 35, 91

Ignatow, David 1914-1997 .... CLC 4, 7, 14, 40; PC 34
See also CA 9-12R; CAAS 3; CANR 31, 57, 96; CP 7; DLB 5

Ignotus
See Strachey, (Giles) Lytton

Ihimaera, Witi 1944- .... CLC 46
See also CA 77-80; CN 7; RGSF 2

Ilf, Ilya .... TCLC 21
See also Fainzilberg, Ilya Arnoldovich

Illyes, Gyula 1902-1983 .... PC 16
See also CA 114; CDWLB 4; DLB 215; RGWL 2, 3

Immermann, Karl (Lebrecht) 1796-1840 .... NCLC 4, 49
See also DLB 133

Ince, Thomas H. 1882-1924 .... TCLC 89
See also IDFW 3, 4

Inchbald, Elizabeth 1753-1821 ...... NCLC 62
See also DLB 39, 89; RGEL 2

Inclan, Ramon (Maria) del Valle
See Valle-Inclan, Ramon (Maria) del

Infante, G(uillermo) Cabrera
See Cabrera Infante, G(uillermo)

Ingalls, Rachel (Holmes) 1940- .... CLC 42
See also CA 127

Ingamells, Reginald Charles
See Ingamells, Rex

Ingamells, Rex 1913-1955 .... TCLC 35
See also CA 167; DLB 260

Inge, William (Motter) 1913-1973 ..... CLC 1, 8, 19
See also CA 9-12R; CDALB 1941-1968; DAM DRAM; DFS 1, 5, 8; DLB 7, 249; MTCW 1, 2; RGAL 4; TUS

Ingelow, Jean 1820-1897 .... NCLC 39, 107
See also DLB 35, 163; FANT; SATA 33

Ingram, Willis J.
See Harris, Mark

Innaurato, Albert (F.) 1948(?)- ... CLC 21, 60
See also CA 122; CAD; CANR 78; CD 5; INT CA-122

Innes, Michael
See Stewart, J(ohn) I(nnes) M(ackintosh)
See also MSW

Innis, Harold Adams 1894-1952 .... TCLC 77
See also CA 181; DLB 88

Insluis, Alanus de
See Alain de Lille

Iola
See Wells-Barnett, Ida B(ell)

Ionesco, Eugene 1912-1994 ... CLC 1, 4, 6, 9, 11, 15, 41, 86; DC 12; WLC
See also CA 9-12R; CANR 55; CWW 2; DA; DAB; DAC; DAM DRAM, MST; DFS 4, 9; EW 13; GFL 1789 to the Present; MTCW 1, 2; RGWL 2, 3; SATA 7; SATA-Obit 79; TWA

Iqbal, Muhammad 1877-1938 .... TCLC 28

Ireland, Patrick
See O'Doherty, Brian

Irenaeus St. 130- .... CMLC 42

Irigaray, Luce 1930- .... CLC 164
See also CA 154; FW

Iron, Ralph
See Schreiner, Olive (Emilie Albertina)

Irving, John (Winslow) 1942- ... CLC 13, 23, 38, 112
See also AAYA 8; AMWS 6; BEST 89:3; BPFB 2; CA 25-28R; CANR 28, 73, 112; CN 7; CPW; DAM NOV, POP; DLB 6; DLBY 1982; MTCW 1, 2; NFS 12, 14; RGAL 4; TUS

Irving, Washington 1783-1859 . NCLC 2, 19, 95; SSC 2, 37; WLC
See also AMW; CDALB 1640-1865; DA; DAB; DAC; DAM MST; DLB 3, 11, 30, 59, 73, 74, 183, 186, 250, 254; EXPS; LAIT 1; RGAL 4; RGSF 2; SSFS 1, 8; SUFW 1; TUS; WCH; YABC 2

Irwin, P. K.
See Page, P(atricia) K(athleen)

Isaacs, Jorge Ricardo 1837-1895 ... NCLC 70
See also LAW

Isaacs, Susan 1943- .... CLC 32
See also BEST 89:1; BPFB 2; CA 89-92; CANR 20, 41, 65, 112; CPW; DAM POP; INT CANR-20; MTCW 1, 2

Isherwood, Christopher (William Bradshaw) 1904-1986 .... **CLC 1, 9, 11, 14, 44; SSC 56**
See also BRW 7; CA 13-16R; CANR 35, 97; DAM DRAM, NOV; DLB 15, 195; DLBY 1986; IDTP; MTCW 1, 2; RGAL 4; RGEL 2; TUS; WLIT 4

Ishiguro, Kazuo 1954- .. **CLC 27, 56, 59, 110**
See also BEST 90:2; BPFB 2; BRWS 4; CA 120; CANR 49, 95; CN 7; DAM NOV; DLB 194; MTCW 1, 2; NFS 13; WLIT 4

Ishikawa, Hakuhin
See Ishikawa, Takuboku

Ishikawa, Takuboku
1886(?)-1912 .... **TCLC 15; PC 10**
See also CA 153; DAM POET

Iskander, Fazil 1929- .... **CLC 47**
See also CA 102

Isler, Alan (David) 1934- .... **CLC 91**
See also CA 156; CANR 105

Ivan IV 1530-1584 .... **LC 17**

Ivanov, Vyacheslav Ivanovich
1866-1949 .... **TCLC 33**

Ivask, Ivar Vidrik 1927-1992 .... **CLC 14**
See also CA 37-40R; CANR 24

Ives, Morgan
See Bradley, Marion Zimmer
See also GLL 1

Izumi Shikibu c. 973-c. 1034 .... **CMLC 33**

J .... **CLC 56, 165**
See also CA 123; CCA 1; DAC; DAM MST; DLB 60; MTCW 2; RGSF 2

J .... **TCLC 11, 17, 32; SSC 7, 56; WLC**
See also AAYA 21; AMW; BPFB 1; BYA 3; CA 140; CANR 84; CDALB 1865-1917; DA; DAB; DAC; DAM MST, NOV, POET; DLB 12, 54, 78; EXPS; EXPN; LAIT 2; NFS 4; PFS 9; RGAL 4; RGSF 2; SSFS 4; TUS; WYA; YABC 2

J. R. S.
See Gogarty, Oliver St. John

Jabran, Kahlil
See Gibran, Kahlil

Jabran, Khalil
See Gibran, Kahlil

Jackson, Daniel
See Wingrove, David (John)

Jackson, Helen Hunt 1830-1885 .... **NCLC 90**
See also DLB 42, 47, 186, 189; RGAL 4

Jackson, Jesse 1908-1983 .... **CLC 12**
See also BW 1; CA 25-28R; CANR 27; CLR 28; CWRI 5; MAICYA 1, 2; SATA 2, 29; SATA-Obit 48

Jackson, Laura (Riding) 1901-1991 .... **PC 44**
See also Riding, Laura
See also CA 65-68; CANR 28, 89; DLB 48

Jackson, Sam
See Trumbo, Dalton

Jackson, Sara
See Wingrove, David (John)

Jackson, Shirley 1919-1965 . **CLC 11, 60, 87; SSC 9, 39; WLC**
See also AAYA 9; AMWS 9; BPFB 2; CA 1-4R; CANR 4, 52; CDALB 1941-1968; DA; DAC; DAM MST; DLB 6, 234; EXPS; HGG; LAIT 4; MTCW 2; RGAL 4; RGSF 2; SATA 2; SSFS 1; SUFW 1, 2

Jacob, (Cyprien-)Max 1876-1944 .... **TCLC 6**
See also CA 193; DLB 258; GFL 1789 to the Present; GLL 2; RGWL 2, 3

Jacobs, Harriet A(nn)
1813(?)-1897 .... **NCLC 67**
See also AFAW 1, 2; DLB 239; FW; LAIT 2; RGAL 4

Jacobs, Jim 1942- .... **CLC 12**
See also CA 97-100; INT 97-100

Jacobs, W(illiam) W(ymark)
1863-1943 .... **TCLC 22**
See also CA 167; DLB 135; EXPS; HGG; RGEL 2; RGSF 2; SSFS 2; SUFW 1

Jacobsen, Jens Peter 1847-1885 .... **NCLC 34**

Jacobsen, Josephine 1908- .... **CLC 48, 102**
See also CA 33-36R; CAAS 18; CANR 23, 48; CCA 1; CP 7; DLB 244

Jacobson, Dan 1929- .... **CLC 4, 14**
See also AFW; CA 1-4R; CANR 2, 25, 66; CN 7; DLB 14, 207, 225; MTCW 1; RGSF 2

Jacqueline
See Carpentier (y Valmont), Alejo

Jagger, Mick 1944- .... **CLC 17**

Jahiz, al- c. 780-c. 869 .... **CMLC 25**

Jakes, John (William) 1932- .... **CLC 29**
See also AAYA 32; BEST 89:4; BPFB 2; CA 57-60; CANR 10, 43, 66, 111; CPW; CSW; DAM NOV, POP; DLBY 1983; FANT; INT CANR-10; MTCW 1, 2; RHW; SATA 62; SFW 4; TCWW 2

James I 1394-1437 .... **LC 20**
See also RGEL 2

James, Andrew
See Kirkup, James

James, C(yril) L(ionel) R(obert)
1901-1989 .... **CLC 33; BLCS**
See also BW 2; CA 125; CANR 62; DLB 125; MTCW 1

James, Daniel (Lewis) 1911-1988
See Santiago, Danny
See also CA 174

James, Dynely
See Mayne, William (James Carter)

James, Henry Sr. 1811-1882 .... **NCLC 53**

James, Henry 1843-1916 ..... **TCLC 2, 11, 24, 40, 47, 64; SSC 8, 32, 47; WLC**
See also AMW; AMWR 1; BPFB 2; BRW 6; CA 132; CDALB 1865-1917; DA; DAB; DAC; DAM MST, NOV; DLB 12, 71, 74, 189; DLB 13; EXPS; HGG; LAIT; MTCW 1, 2; NFS 12; RGAL 4; RGEL 2; RGSF 2; SSFS 9; SUFW 1; TUS

James, M. R.
See James, Montague (Rhodes)
See also DLB 156, 201

James, Montague (Rhodes)
1862-1936 .... **TCLC 6; SSC 16**
See also James, M. R.
See also HGG; RGEL 2; RGSF 2; SUFW 1

James, P. D. .... **CLC 18, 46, 122**
See also White, Phyllis Dorothy James
See also BEST 90:2; BPFB 2; BRWS 4; CDBLB 1960 to Present; DLB 87; DLBD 17; MSW

James, Philip
See Moorcock, Michael (John)

James, Samuel
See Stephens, James

James, Seumas
See Stephens, James

James, Stephen
See Stephens, James

James, William 1842-1910 .... **TCLC 15, 32**
See also AMW; CA 193; DLB 270; RGAL 4

Jameson, Anna 1794-1860 .... **NCLC 43**
See also DLB 99, 166

Jameson, Fredric (R.) 1934- .... **CLC 142**
See also CA 196; DLB 67

Jami, Nur al-Din 'Abd al-Rahman
1414-1492 .... **LC 9**

Jammes, Francis 1868-1938 .... **TCLC 75**
See also CA 198; GFL 1789 to the Present

Jandl, Ernst 1925-2000 .... **CLC 34**
See also CA 200

Janowitz, Tama 1957- .... **CLC 43, 145**
See also CA 106; CANR 52, 89; CN 7; CPW; DAM POP

Japrisot, Sebastien 1931- .... **CLC 90**
See also Rossi, Jean Baptiste
See also CMW 4

Jarrell, Randall 1914-1965 .... **CLC 1, 2, 6, 9, 13, 49; PC 41**
See also AMW; BYA 5; CA 5-8R; CABS 2; CANR 6, 34; CDALB 1941-1968; CLR 6; CWRI 5; DAM POET; DLB 48, 52; EXPP; MAICYA 1, 2; MTCW 1, 2; PAB; PFS 2; RGAL 4; SATA 7

Jarry, Alfred 1873-1907 .... **TCLC 2, 14; SSC 20**
See also CA 153; DAM DRAM; DFS 8; DLB 192, 258; EW 9; GFL 1789 to the Present; RGWL 2, 3; TWA

Jawien, Andrzej
See John Paul II, Pope

Jaynes, Roderick
See Coen, Ethan

Jeake, Samuel, Jr.
See Aiken, Conrad (Potter)

Jean Paul 1763-1825 .... **NCLC 7**

Jefferies, (John) Richard
1848-1887 .... **NCLC 47**
See also DLB 98, 141; RGEL 2; SATA 16; SFW 4

Jeffers, (John) Robinson 1887-1962 .. **CLC 2, 3, 11, 15, 54; PC 17; WLC**
See also AMWS 2; CA 85-88; CANR 35; CDALB 1917-1929; DA; DAC; DAM MST, POET; DLB 45, 212; MTCW 1, 2; PAB; PFS 3, 4; RGAL 4

Jefferson, Janet
See Mencken, H(enry) L(ouis)

Jefferson, Thomas 1743-1826 . **NCLC 11, 103**
See also ANW; CDALB 1640-1865; DLB 31, 183; LAIT 1; RGAL 4

Jeffrey, Francis 1773-1850 .... **NCLC 33**
See also Francis, Lord Jeffrey

Jelakowitch, Ivan
See Heijermans, Herman

Jellicoe, (Patricia) Ann 1927- .... **CLC 27**
See also CA 85-88; CBD; CD 5; CWD; CWRI 5; DLB 13, 233; FW

Jemyma
See Holley, Marietta

Jen, Gish .... **CLC 70**
See also Jen, Lillian

Jen, Lillian 1956(?)-
See Jen, Gish
See also CA 135; CANR 89

Jenkins, (John) Robin 1912- .... **CLC 52**
See also CA 1-4R; CANR 1; CN 7; DLB 14, 271

Jennings, Elizabeth (Joan)
1926-2001 .... **CLC 5, 14, 131**
See also BRWS 5; CA 61-64; CAAS 5; CANR 8, 39, 66; CP 7; CWP; DLB 27; MTCW 1; SATA 66

Jennings, Waylon 1937- .... **CLC 21**

Jensen, Johannes V. 1873-1950 ...... **TCLC 41**
See also CA 170; DLB 214; RGWL 3

Jensen, Laura (Linnea) 1948- .... **CLC 37**
See also CA 103

Jerome, Saint 345-420 .... **CMLC 30**
See also RGWL 3

Jerome, Jerome K(lapka)
1859-1927 .... **TCLC 23**
See also CA 177; DLB 10, 34, 135; RGEL 2

Jerrold, Douglas William
1803-1857 .... **NCLC 2**
See also DLB 158, 159; RGEL 2

Jewett, (Theodora) Sarah Orne
1849-1909 .... **TCLC 1, 22; SSC 6, 44**
See also AMW; CA 127; CANR 71; DLB 12, 74, 221; EXPS; FW; MAWW; NFS 15; RGAL 4; RGSF 2; SATA 15; SSFS 4

Jewsbury, Geraldine (Endsor)
1812-1880 .... **NCLC 22**
See also DLB 21

Jhabvala, Ruth Prawer 1927- . **CLC 4, 8, 29, 94, 138**
See also BRWS 5; CA 1-4R; CANR 2, 29, 51, 74, 91; CN 7; DAB; DAM NOV; DLB 139, 194; IDFW 3, 4; INT CANR-29; MTCW 1, 2; RGSF 2; RGWL 2; RHW; TEA

Jibran, Kahlil
See Gibran, Kahlil

Jibran, Khalil
See Gibran, Kahlil

Jiles, Paulette 1943- .... **CLC 13, 58**
See also CA 101; CANR 70; CWP

Jimenez (Mantecon), Juan Ramon
1881-1958 .... **TCLC 4; HLC 1; PC 7**
See also CA 131; CANR 74; DAM MULT, POET; DLB 134; EW 9; HW 1; MTCW 1, 2; RGWL 2, 3

Jimenez, Ramon
See Jimenez (Mantecon), Juan Ramon

Jimenez Mantecon, Juan
See Jimenez (Mantecon), Juan Ramon

Jin, Ha .... **CLC 109**
See also Jin, Xuefei
See also CA 152; DLB 244

Jin, Xuefei 1956-
See Jin, Ha
See also CANR 91

Joel, Billy .... **CLC 26**
See also Joel, William Martin

Joel, William Martin 1949-
See Joel, Billy
See also CA 108

John, Saint 107th cent. -100 .... **CMLC 27**

John of the Cross, St. 1542-1591 .... **LC 18**
See also RGWL 2, 3

John Paul II, Pope 1920- .... **CLC 128**
See also CA 133

Johnson, B(ryan) S(tanley William)
1933-1973 .... **CLC 6, 9**
See also CA 9-12R; CANR 9; DLB 14, 40; RGEL 2

Johnson, Benjamin F., of Boone
See Riley, James Whitcomb

Johnson, Charles (Richard) 1948- .... **CLC 7, 51, 65, 163; BLC 2**
See also AFAW 2; AMWS 6; BW 2, 3; CA 116; CAAS 18; CANR 42, 66, 82; CN 7; DAM MULT; DLB 33; MTCW 2; RGAL 4

Johnson, Denis 1949- . **CLC 52, 160; SSC 56**
See also CA 121; CANR 71, 99; CN 7; DLB 120

Johnson, Diane 1934- .... **CLC 5, 13, 48**
See also BPFB 2; CA 41-44R; CANR 17, 40, 62, 95; CN 7; DLBY 1980; INT CANR-17; MTCW 1

Johnson, Eyvind (Olof Verner)
1900-1976 .... **CLC 14**
See also CA 73-76; CANR 34, 101; DLB 259; EW 12

Johnson, J. R.
See James, C(yril) L(ionel) R(obert)

Johnson, James Weldon
1871-1938 . **TCLC 3, 19; BLC 2; PC 24**
See also AFAW 1, 2; BW 1, 3; CA 125; CANR 82; CDALB 1917-1929; CLR 32; DAM MULT, POET; DLB 51; EXPP; HR 3; MTCW 1, 2; PFS 1; RGAL 4; SATA 31; TUS

Johnson, Joyce 1935- .... **CLC 58**
See also CA 129; CANR 102

Johnson, Judith (Emlyn) 1936- .... **CLC 7, 15**
See also Sherwin, Judith Johnson
See also CA 25-28R, 153; CANR 34

Johnson, Lionel (Pigot)
1867-1902 .... **TCLC 19**
See also DLB 19; RGEL 2

Johnson, Marguerite (Annie)
See Angelou, Maya

Johnson, Mel
See Malzberg, Barry N(athaniel)

Johnson, Pamela Hansford
1912-1981 .... **CLC 1, 7, 27**
See also CA 1-4R; CANR 2, 28; DLB 15; MTCW 1, 2; RGEL 2

Johnson, Paul (Bede) 1928- .... **CLC 147**
See also BEST 89:4; CA 17-20R; CANR 34, 62, 100

Johnson, Robert .... **CLC 70**

Johnson, Robert 1911(?)-1938 .... **TCLC 69**
See also BW 3; CA 174

Johnson, Samuel 1709-1784 .... **LC 15, 52; WLC**
See also BRW 3; BRWR 1; CDBLB 1660-1789; DA; DAB; DAC; DAM MST; DLB 39, 95, 104, 142, 213; RGEL 2; TEA

Johnson, Uwe 1934-1984 .. **CLC 5, 10, 15, 40**
See also CA 1-4R; CANR 1, 39; CDWLB 2; DLB 75; MTCW 1; RGWL 2, 3

Johnston, George (Benson) 1913- ..... **CLC 51**
See also CA 1-4R; CANR 5, 20; CP 7; DLB 88

Johnston, Jennifer (Prudence)
1930- .... **CLC 7, 150**
See also CA 85-88; CANR 92; CN 7; DLB 14

Joinville, Jean de 1224(?)-1317 ..... **CMLC 38**

Jolley, (Monica) Elizabeth 1923- ..... **CLC 46; SSC 19**
See also CA 127; CAAS 13; CANR 59; CN 7; RGSF 2

Jones, Arthur Llewellyn 1863-1947
See Machen, Arthur
See also CA 179; HGG

Jones, D(ouglas) G(ordon) 1929- ..... **CLC 10**
See also CA 29-32R; CANR 13, 90; CP 7; DLB 53

Jones, David (Michael) 1895-1974 .... **CLC 2, 4, 7, 13, 42**
See also BRW 6; BRWS 7; CA 9-12R; CANR 28; CDBLB 1945-1960; DLB 20, 100; MTCW 1; PAB; RGEL 2

Jones, David Robert 1947-
See Bowie, David
See also CA 103; CANR 104

Jones, Diana Wynne 1934- .... **CLC 26**
See also AAYA 12; BYA 6, 7, 9, 11, 13; CA 49-52; CANR 4, 26, 56; CLR 23; DLB 161; FANT; JRDA; MAICYA 1, 2; SAAS 7; SATA 9, 70, 108; SFW 4; SUFW 2; YAW

Jones, Edward P. 1950- .... **CLC 76**
See also BW 2, 3; CA 142; CANR 79; CSW

Jones, Gayl 1949- ...... **CLC 6, 9, 131; BLC 2**
See also AFAW 1, 2; BW 2, 3; CA 77-80; CANR 27, 66; CN 7; CSW; DAM MULT; DLB 33; MTCW 1, 2; RGAL 4

Jones, James 1921-1977 ...... **CLC 1, 3, 10, 39**
See also AITN 1, 2; AMWS 11; BPFB 2; CA 1-4R; CANR 6; DLB 2, 143; DLBD 17; DLBY 1998; MTCW 1; RGAL 4

Jones, John J.
See Lovecraft, H(oward) P(hillips)

Jones, LeRoi .... **CLC 1, 2, 3, 5, 10, 14**
See also Baraka, Amiri
See also MTCW 2

Jones, Louis B. 1953- .... **CLC 65**
See also CA 141; CANR 73

Jones, Madison (Percy, Jr.) 1925- ...... **CLC 4**
See also CA 13-16R; CAAS 11; CANR 7, 54, 83; CN 7; CSW; DLB 152

Jones, Mervyn 1922- .... **CLC 10, 52**
See also CA 45-48; CAAS 5; CANR 1, 91; CN 7; MTCW 1

Jones, Mick 1956(?)- .... **CLC 30**

Jones, Nettie (Pearl) 1941- .... **CLC 34**
See also BW 2; CA 137; CAAS 20; CANR 88

Jones, Preston 1936-1979 .... **CLC 10**
See also CA 73-76; DLB 7

Jones, Robert F(rancis) 1934- .... **CLC 7**
See also CA 49-52; CANR 2, 61

Jones, Rod 1953- .... **CLC 50**
See also CA 128

Jones, Terence Graham Parry
1942- .... **CLC 21**
See also Jones, Terry; Monty Python
See also CA 116; CANR 35, 93; INT 116; SATA 127

Jones, Terry
See Jones, Terence Graham Parry
See also SATA 67; SATA-Brief 51

Jones, Thom (Douglas) 1945(?)- ..... **CLC 81; SSC 56**
See also CA 157; CANR 88; DLB 244

Jong, Erica 1942- .... **CLC 4, 6, 8, 18, 83**
See also AITN 1; AMWS 5; BEST 90:2; BPFB 2; CA 73-76; CANR 26, 52, 75; CN 7; CP 7; CPW; DAM NOV, POP; DLB 2, 5, 28, 152; FW; INT CANR-26; MTCW 1, 2

Jonson, Ben(jamin) 1572(?)-1637 .. **LC 6, 33; DC 4; PC 17; WLC**
See also BRW 1; BRWR 1; CDBLB Before 1660; DA; DAB; DAC; DAM DRAM, MST, POET; DFS 4, 10; DLB 62, 121; RGEL 2; TEA; WLIT 3

Jordan, June 1936- .... **CLC 5, 11, 23, 114; BLCS; PC 38**
See also Meyer, June
See also AAYA 2; AFAW 1, 2; BW 2, 3; CA 33-36R; CANR 25, 70; CLR 10; CP 7; CWP; DAM MULT, POET; DLB 38; GLL 2; LAIT 5; MAICYA 1, 2; MTCW 1; SATA 4; YAW

Jordan, Neil (Patrick) 1950- .... **CLC 110**
See also CA 130; CANR 54; CN 7; GLL 2; INT 130

Jordan, Pat(rick M.) 1941- .... **CLC 37**
See also CA 33-36R

Jorgensen, Ivar
See Ellison, Harlan (Jay)

Jorgenson, Ivar
See Silverberg, Robert

Joseph, George Ghevarughese .... **CLC 70**

Josephson, Mary
See O'Doherty, Brian

Josephus, Flavius c. 37-100 .... **CMLC 13**
See also AW 2; DLB 176

Josiah Allen's Wife
See Holley, Marietta

Josipovici, Gabriel (David) 1940- ...... **CLC 6, 43, 153**
See also CA 37-40R; CAAS 8; CANR 47, 84; CN 7; DLB 14

Joubert, Joseph 1754-1824 .... **NCLC 9**

Jouve, Pierre Jean 1887-1976 .... **CLC 47**
See also DLB 258

Jovine, Francesco 1902-1950 .... **TCLC 79**
See also DLB 264

Joyce, James (Augustine Aloysius)
1882-1941 ... **TCLC 3, 8, 16, 35, 52; DC 16; PC 22; SSC 3, 26, 44; WLC**
See also AAYA 42; BRW 7; BRWR 1; BYA 11, 13; CA 126; CDBLB 1914-1945; DA; DAB; DAC; DAM MST, NOV, POET;

DLB 10, 19, 36, 162, 247; EXPN; EXPS; LAIT 3; MTCW 1, 2; NFS 7; RGSF 2; SSFS 1; TEA; WLIT 4

Jozsef, Attila 1905-1937 .... **TCLC 22**
See also CDWLB 4; DLB 215

Juana Ines de la Cruz, Sor
1651(?)-1695 ...... **LC 5; HLCS 1; PC 24**
See also FW; LAW; RGWL 2, 3; WLIT 1

Juana Inez de La Cruz, Sor
See Juana Ines de la Cruz, Sor

Judd, Cyril
See Kornbluth, C(yril) M.; Pohl, Frederik

Juenger, Ernst 1895-1998 .... **CLC 125**
See also Junger, Ernst
See also CA 101; CANR 21, 47, 106; DLB 56

Julian of Norwich 1342(?)-1416(?) . **LC 6, 52**
See also DLB 146

Julius Caesar 100B.C.-44B.C.
See Caesar, Julius
See also CDWLB 1; DLB 211

Junger, Ernst
See Juenger, Ernst
See also CDWLB 2; RGWL 2, 3

Junger, Sebastian 1962- .... **CLC 109**
See also AAYA 28; CA 165

Juniper, Alex
See Hospital, Janette Turner

Junius
See Luxemburg, Rosa

Just, Ward (Swift) 1935- .... **CLC 4, 27**
See also CA 25-28R; CANR 32, 87; CN 7; INT CANR-32

Justice, Donald (Rodney) 1925- .. **CLC 6, 19, 102**
See also AMWS 7; CA 5-8R; CANR 26, 54, 74; CP 7; CSW; DAM POET; DLBY 1983; INT CANR-26; MTCW 2; PFS 14

Juvenal c. 60-c. 130 .... **CMLC 8**
See also AW 2; CDWLB 1; DLB 211; RGWL 2, 3

Juvenis
See Bourne, Randolph S(illiman)

Kabakov, Sasha .... **CLC 59**

Kacew, Romain 1914-1980
See Gary, Romain
See also CA 108

Kadare, Ismail 1936- .... **CLC 52**
See also CA 161; RGWL 3

Kadohata, Cynthia .... **CLC 59, 122**
See also CA 140

Kafka, Franz 1883-1924 . **TCLC 2, 6, 13, 29, 47, 53, 112; SSC 5, 29, 35; WLC**
See also AAYA 31; BPFB 2; CA 126; CDWLB 2; DA; DAB; DAC; DAM MST, NOV; DLB 81; EW 9; EXPS; MTCW 1, 2; NFS 7; RGSF 2; RGWL 2, 3; SFW 4; SSFS 3, 7, 12; TWA

Kahanovitsch, Pinkhes
See Der Nister

Kahn, Roger 1927- .... **CLC 30**
See also CA 25-28R; CANR 44, 69; DLB 171; SATA 37

Kain, Saul
See Sassoon, Siegfried (Lorraine)

Kaiser, Georg 1878-1945 .... **TCLC 9**
See also CA 190; CDWLB 2; DLB 124; RGWL 2, 3

Kaledin, Sergei .... **CLC 59**

Kaletski, Alexander 1946- .... **CLC 39**
See also CA 143

Kalidasa fl. c. 400-455 .... **CMLC 9; PC 22**
See also RGWL 2, 3

Kallman, Chester (Simon)
1921-1975 .... **CLC 2**
See also CA 45-48; CANR 3

Kaminsky, Melvin 1926-
See Brooks, Mel
See also CA 65-68; CANR 16

Kaminsky, Stuart M(elvin) 1934- ..... **CLC 59**
See also CA 73-76; CANR 29, 53, 89; CMW 4

Kandinsky, Wassily 1866-1944 .... **TCLC 92**
See also CA 155

Kane, Francis
See Robbins, Harold

Kane, Henry 1918-
See Queen, Ellery
See also CA 156; CMW 4

Kane, Paul
See Simon, Paul (Frederick)

Kanin, Garson 1912-1999 .... **CLC 22**
See also AITN 1; CA 5-8R; CAD; CANR 7, 78; DLB 7; IDFW 3, 4

Kaniuk, Yoram 1930- .... **CLC 19**
See also CA 134

Kant, Immanuel 1724-1804 ..... **NCLC 27, 67**
See also DLB 94

Kantor, MacKinlay 1904-1977 .... **CLC 7**
See also CA 61-64; CANR 60, 63; DLB 9, 102; MTCW 2; RHW; TCWW 2

Kanze Motokiyo
See Zeami

Kaplan, David Michael 1946- .... **CLC 50**
See also CA 187

Kaplan, James 1951- .... **CLC 59**
See also CA 135

Karadzic, Vuk Stefanovic
1787-1864 .... **NCLC 115**
See also CDWLB 4; DLB 147

Karageorge, Michael
See Anderson, Poul (William)

Karamzin, Nikolai Mikhailovich
1766-1826 .... **NCLC 3**
See also DLB 150; RGSF 2

Karapanou, Margarita 1946- .... **CLC 13**
See also CA 101

Karinthy, Frigyes 1887-1938 .... **TCLC 47**
See also CA 170; DLB 215

Karl, Frederick R(obert) 1927- .... **CLC 34**
See also CA 5-8R; CANR 3, 44

Kastel, Warren
See Silverberg, Robert

Kataev, Evgeny Petrovich 1903-1942
See Petrov, Evgeny

Kataphusin
See Ruskin, John

Katz, Steve 1935- .... **CLC 47**
See also CA 25-28R; CAAS 14, 64; CANR 12; CN 7; DLBY 1983

Kauffman, Janet 1945- .... **CLC 42**
See also CA 117; CANR 43, 84; DLB 218; DLBY 1986

Kaufman, Bob (Garnell) 1925-1986 . **CLC 49**
See also BW 1; CA 41-44R; CANR 22; DLB 16, 41

Kaufman, George S. 1889-1961 ...... **CLC 38; DC 17**
See also CA 108; DAM DRAM; DFS 1, 10; DLB 7; INT CA-108; MTCW 2; RGAL 4; TUS

Kaufman, Sue .... **CLC 3, 8**
See also Barondess, Sue K(aufman)

Kavafis, Konstantinos Petrou 1863-1933
See Cavafy, C(onstantine) P(eter)

Kavan, Anna 1901-1968 .... **CLC 5, 13, 82**
See also BRWS 7; CA 5-8R; CANR 6, 57; DLB 255; MTCW 1; RGEL 2; SFW 4

Kavanagh, Dan
See Barnes, Julian (Patrick)

Kavanagh, Julie 1952- .... **CLC 119**
See also CA 163

Kavanagh, Patrick (Joseph)
1904-1967 .... **CLC 22; PC 33**
See also BRWS 7; CA 123; DLB 15, 20; MTCW 1; RGEL 2

Kawabata, Yasunari 1899-1972 ..... **CLC 2, 5, 9, 18, 107; SSC 17**
See also Kawabata Yasunari
See also CA 93-96; CANR 88; DAM MULT; MJW; MTCW 2; RGSF 2; RGWL 2, 3

Kawabata Yasunari
See Kawabata, Yasunari
See also DLB 180

Kaye, M(ary) M(argaret) 1909- .... **CLC 28**
See also CA 89-92; CANR 24, 60, 102; MTCW 1, 2; RHW; SATA 62

Kaye, Mollie
See Kaye, M(ary) M(argaret)

Kaye-Smith, Sheila 1887-1956 .... **TCLC 20**
See also CA 203; DLB 36

Kaymor, Patrice Maguilene
See Senghor, Leopold Sedar

Kazakov, Yuri Pavlovich 1927-1982 . **SSC 43**
See also CA 5-8R; CANR 36; MTCW 1; RGSF 2

Kazan, Elia 1909- .... **CLC 6, 16, 63**
See also CA 21-24R; CANR 32, 78

Kazantzakis, Nikos 1883(?)-1957 .... **TCLC 2, 5, 33**
See also BPFB 2; CA 132; EW 9; MTCW 1, 2; RGWL 2, 3

Kazin, Alfred 1915-1998 ..... **CLC 34, 38, 119**
See also AMWS 8; CA 1-4R; CAAS 7; CANR 1, 45, 79; DLB 67

Keane, Mary Nesta (Skrine) 1904-1996
See Keane, Molly
See also CA 114; CN 7; RHW

Keane, Molly .... **CLC 31**
See also Keane, Mary Nesta (Skrine)
See also INT 114

Keates, Jonathan 1946(?)- .... **CLC 34**
See also CA 163

Keaton, Buster 1895-1966 .... **CLC 20**
See also CA 194

Keats, John 1795-1821 ... **NCLC 8, 73; PC 1; WLC**
See also BRW 4; BRWR 1; CDBLB 1789-1832; DA; DAB; DAC; DAM MST, POET; DLB 96, 110; EXPP; PAB; PFS 1, 2, 3, 9; RGEL 2; TEA; WLIT 3; WP

Keble, John 1792-1866 .... **NCLC 87**
See also DLB 32, 55; RGEL 2

Keene, Donald 1922- .... **CLC 34**
See also CA 1-4R; CANR 5

Keillor, Garrison .... **CLC 40, 115**
See also Keillor, Gary (Edward)
See also AAYA 2; BEST 89:3; BPFB 2; DLBY 1987; SATA 58; TUS

Keillor, Gary (Edward) 1942-
See Keillor, Garrison
See also CA 117; CANR 36, 59; CPW; DAM POP; MTCW 1, 2

Keith, Carlos
See Lewton, Val

Keith, Michael
See Hubbard, L(afayette) Ron(ald)

Keller, Gottfried 1819-1890 .... **NCLC 2; SSC 26**
See also CDWLB 2; DLB 129; EW; RGSF 2; RGWL 2, 3

Keller, Nora Okja 1965- .... **CLC 109**
See also CA 187

Kellerman, Jonathan 1949- .... **CLC 44**
See also AAYA 35; BEST 90:1; CA 106; CANR 29, 51; CMW 4; CPW; DAM POP; INT CANR-29

Kelley, William Melvin 1937- .... **CLC 22**
See also BW 1; CA 77-80; CANR 27, 83; CN 7; DLB 33

Kellogg, Marjorie 1922- .... **CLC 2**
See also CA 81-84

Kellow, Kathleen
See Hibbert, Eleanor Alice Burford

Kelly, M(ilton) T(errence) 1947- ...... **CLC 55**
See also CA 97-100; CAAS 22; CANR 19, 43, 84; CN 7

Kelly, Robert 1935- .... **SSC 50**
See also CA 17-20R; CAAS 19; CANR 47; CP 7; DLB 5, 130, 165

Kelman, James 1946- .... **CLC 58, 86**
See also BRWS 5; CA 148; CANR 85; CN 7; DLB 194; RGSF 2; WLIT 4

Kemal, Yashar 1923- .... **CLC 14, 29**
See also CA 89-92; CANR 44; CWW 2

Kemble, Fanny 1809-1893 .... **NCLC 18**
See also DLB 32

Kemelman, Harry 1908-1996 .... **CLC 2**
See also AITN 1; BPFB 2; CA 9-12R; CANR 6, 71; CMW 4; DLB 28

Kempe, Margery 1373(?)-1440(?) ... **LC 6, 56**
See also DLB 146; RGEL 2

Kempis, Thomas a 1380-1471 .... **LC 11**

Kendall, Henry 1839-1882 .... **NCLC 12**
See also DLB 230

Keneally, Thomas (Michael) 1935- ... **CLC 5, 8, 10, 14, 19, 27, 43, 117**
See also BRWS 4; CA 85-88; CANR 10, 50, 74; CN 7; CPW; DAM NOV; MTCW 1, 2; RGEL 2; RHW

Kennedy, Adrienne (Lita) 1931- ..... **CLC 66; BLC 2; DC 5**
See also AFAW 2; BW 2, 3; CA 103; CAAS 20; CABS 3; CANR 26, 53, 82; CD 5; DAM MULT; DFS 9; DLB 38; FW

Kennedy, John Pendleton 1795-1870 .... **NCLC 2**
See also DLB 3, 248, 254; RGAL 4

Kennedy, Joseph Charles 1929-
See Kennedy, X. J.
See also CA 1-4R; CAAE 201; CANR 4, 30, 40; CP 7; CWRI 5; MAICYA 1; SATA 14, 86; SATA-Essay 130

Kennedy, William 1928- ... **CLC 6, 28, 34, 53**
See also AAYA 1; AMWS 7; BPFB 2; CA 85-88; CANR 14, 31, 76; DAM NOV; DLB 143; DLBY 1985; INT CANR-31; MTCW 1, 2; SATA 57

Kennedy, X. J. .... **CLC 8, 42**
See also Kennedy, Joseph Charles
See also CAAS 9; CLR 27; DLB 5; SAAS 22

Kenny, Maurice (Francis) 1929- ...... **CLC 87**
See also CA 144; CAAS 22; DAM MULT; DLB 175; NNAL

Kent, Kelvin
See Kuttner, Henry

Kenton, Maxwell
See Southern, Terry

Kenyon, Robert O.
See Kuttner, Henry

Kepler, Johannes 1571-1630 .... **LC 45**

Ker, Jill
See Conway, Jill K(er)

Kerkow, H. C.
See Lewton, Val

Kerouac, Jack 1922-1969 ...... **CLC 1, 2, 3, 5, 14, 29, 61; WLC**
See also Kerouac, Jean-Louis Lebris de
See also AAYA 25; AMWS 3; BPFB 2; CDALB 1941-1968; CPW; DLB 2, 16, 237; DLBD 3; DLBY 1995; GLL 1; MTCW 2; NFS 8; RGAL 4; TCLC 117; TUS; WP

Kerouac, Jean-Louis Lebris de 1922-1969
See Kerouac, Jack
See also AITN 1; CA 5-8R; CANR 26, 54, 95; DA; DAB; DAC; DAM MST, NOV, POET, POP; MTCW 1, 2

Kerr, Jean 1923- .... **CLC 22**
See also CA 5-8R; CANR 7; INT CANR-7

Kerr, M. E. .... **CLC 12, 35**
See also Meaker, Marijane (Agnes)
See also AAYA 2, 23; BYA 1, 7, 8; CLR 29; SAAS 1; WYA

Kerr, Robert .... **CLC 55**

Kerrigan, (Thomas) Anthony 1918- .. **CLC 4, 6**
See also CA 49-52; CAAS 11; CANR 4

Kerry, Lois
See Duncan, Lois

Kesey, Ken (Elton) 1935-2001 ... **CLC 1, 3, 6, 11, 46, 64; WLC**
See also AAYA 25; BPFB 2; CA 1-4R; CANR 22, 38, 66; CDALB 1968-1988; CN 7; CPW; DA; DAB; DAC; DAM MST, NOV, POP; DLB 2, 16, 206; EXPN; LAIT 4; MTCW 1, 2; NFS 2; RGAL 4; SATA 66; SATA-Obit 131; TUS; YAW

Kesselring, Joseph (Otto) 1902-1967 .... **CLC 45**
See also CA 150; DAM DRAM, MST

Kessler, Jascha (Frederick) 1929- .... **CLC 4**
See also CA 17-20R; CANR 8, 48, 111

Kettelkamp, Larry (Dale) 1933- .... **CLC 12**
See also CA 29-32R; CANR 16; SAAS 3; SATA 2

Key, Ellen (Karolina Sofia) 1849-1926 .... **TCLC 65**
See also DLB 259

Keyes, Daniel 1927- .... **CLC 80**
See also AAYA 23; BYA 11; CA 17-20R, 181; CAAE 181; CANR 10, 26, 54, 74; DA; DAC; DAM MST, NOV; EXPN; LAIT 4; MTCW 2; NFS 2; SATA 37; SFW 4

Keynes, John Maynard 1883-1946 .... **TCLC 64**
See also CA 162, 163; DLBD 10; MTCW 2

Khanshendel, Chiron
See Rose, Wendy

Khayyam, Omar 1048-1131 ... **CMLC 11; PC 8**
See also Omar Khayyam
See also DAM POET

Kherdian, David 1931- .... **CLC 6, 9**
See also AAYA 42; CA 21-24R; CAAE 192; CAAS 2; CANR 39, 78; CLR 24; JRDA; LAIT 3; MAICYA 1, 2; SATA 16, 74; SATA-Essay 125

Khlebnikov, Velimir .... **TCLC 20**
See also Khlebnikov, Viktor Vladimirovich
See also EW 10; RGWL 2, 3

Khlebnikov, Viktor Vladimirovich 1885-1922
See Khlebnikov, Velimir

Khodasevich, Vladislav (Felitsianovich) 1886-1939 .... **TCLC 15**

Kielland, Alexander Lange 1849-1906 .... **TCLC 5**

Kiely, Benedict 1919- .... **CLC 23, 43**
See also CA 1-4R; CANR 2, 84; CN 7; DLB 15

Kienzle, William X(avier) 1928-2001 .... **CLC 25**
See also CA 93-96; CAAS 1; CANR 9, 31, 59, 111; CMW 4; DAM POP; INT CANR-31; MSW; MTCW 1, 2

Kierkegaard, Soren 1813-1855 ..... **NCLC 34, 78**
See also EW 6; RGWL 3; TWA

Kieslowski, Krzysztof 1941-1996 .... **CLC 120**
See also CA 147

Killens, John Oliver 1916-1987 .... **CLC 10**
See also BW 2; CA 77-80; CAAS 2; CANR 26; DLB 33

Killigrew, Anne 1660-1685 .... **LC 4, 73**
See also DLB 131

Killigrew, Thomas 1612-1683 .... **LC 57**
See also DLB 58; RGEL 2

Kim
See Simenon, Georges (Jacques Christian)

Kincaid, Jamaica 1949- ..... **CLC 43, 68, 137; BLC 2**
See also AAYA 13; AFAW 2; AMWS 7; BRWS 7; BW 2, 3; CA 125; CANR 47, 59, 95; CDALBS; CDWLB 3; CLR 63; CN 7; DAM MULT, NOV; DLB 157, 227; DNFS 1; EXPS; FW; MTCW 2; NCFS 1; NFS 3; SSFS 5, 7; TUS; YAW

King, Francis (Henry) 1923- .... **CLC 8, 53, 145**
See also CA 1-4R; CANR 1, 33, 86; CN 7; DAM NOV; DLB 15, 139; MTCW 1

King, Kennedy
See Brown, George Douglas

King, Martin Luther, Jr. 1929-1968 .... **CLC 83; BLC 2; WLCS**
See also BW 2, 3; CA 25-28; CANR 27, 44; CAP 2; DA; DAB; DAC; DAM MST, MULT; LAIT 5; MTCW 1, 2; SATA 14

King, Stephen (Edwin) 1947- .... **CLC 12, 26, 37, 61, 113; SSC 17, 55**
See also AAYA 1, 17; AMWS 5; BEST 90:1; BPFB 2; CA 61-64; CANR 1, 30, 52, 76; CPW; DAM NOV, POP; DLB 143; DLBY 1980; HGG; JRDA; LAIT 5; MTCW 1, 2; RGAL 4; SATA 9, 55; SUFW 1, 2; WYAS 1; YAW

King, Steve
See King, Stephen (Edwin)

King, Thomas 1943- .... **CLC 89**
See also CA 144; CANR 95; CCA 1; CN 7; DAC; DAM MULT; DLB 175; NNAL; SATA 96

Kingman, Lee .... **CLC 17**
See also Natti, (Mary) Lee
See also CWRI 5; SAAS 3; SATA 1, 67

Kingsley, Charles 1819-1875 .... **NCLC 35**
See also CLR 77; DLB 21, 32, 163, 178, 190; FANT; MAICYA 2; MAICYAS 1; RGEL 2; WCH; YABC 2

Kingsley, Henry 1830-1876 .... **NCLC 107**
See also DLB 21, 230; RGEL 2

Kingsley, Sidney 1906-1995 .... **CLC 44**
See also CA 85-88; CAD; DFS 14; DLB 7; RGAL 4

Kingsolver, Barbara 1955- . **CLC 55, 81, 130**
See also AAYA 15; AMWS 7; CA 134; CANR 60, 96; CDALBS; CPW; CSW; DAM POP; DLB 206; INT CA-134; LAIT 5; MTCW 1; NFS 5, 10, 12; RGAL 4

Kingston, Maxine (Ting Ting) Hong 1940- .... **CLC 12, 19, 58, 121; AAL; WLCS**
See also AAYA 8; AMWS 5; BPFB 2; CA 69-72; CANR 13, 38, 74, 87; CDALBS; CN 7; DAM MULT, NOV; DLB 173, 212; DLBY 1980; FW; INT CANR-13; LAIT 5; MAWW; MTCW 1, 2; NFS 6; RGAL 4; SATA 53; SSFS 3

Kinnell, Galway 1927- ..... **CLC 1, 2, 3, 5, 13, 29, 129; PC 26**
See also AMWS 3; CA 9-12R; CANR 10, 34, 66; CP 7; DLB 5; DLBY 1987; INT CANR-34; MTCW 1, 2; PAB; PFS 9; RGAL 4; WP

Kinsella, Thomas 1928- .... **CLC 4, 19, 138**
See also BRWS 5; CA 17-20R; CANR 15; CP 7; DLB 27; MTCW 1, 2; RGEL 2; TEA

Kinsella, W(illiam) P(atrick) 1935- . **CLC 27, 43, 166**
See also AAYA 7; BPFB 2; CA 97-100; CAAS 7; CANR 21, 35, 66, 75; CN 7;

CPW; DAC; DAM NOV, POP; FANT; INT CANR-21; LAIT 5; MTCW 1, 2; NFS 15; RGSF 2

Kinsey, Alfred C(harles)
1894-1956 .... **TCLC 91**
See also CA 170; MTCW 2

Kipling, (Joseph) Rudyard
1865-1936 ... **TCLC 8, 17; PC 3; SSC 5, 54; WLC**
See also AAYA 32; BRW 6; BYA 4; CA 120; CANR 33; CDBLB 1890-1914; CLR 39, 65; CWRI 5; DA; DAB; DAC; DAM MST, POET; DLB 19, 34, 141, 156; EXPS; FANT; LAIT 3; MAICYA 1, 2; MTCW 1, 2; RGEL 2; RGSF 2; SATA 100; SFW 4; SSFS 8; SUFW 1; TEA; WCH; WLIT 4; YABC 2

Kirk, Russell (Amos) 1918-1994 .. **TCLC 119**
See also AITN 1; CA 1-4R; CAAS 9; CANR 1, 20, 60; HGG; INT CANR-20; MTCW 1, 2

Kirkland, Caroline M. 1801-1864 . **NCLC 85**
See also DLB 3, 73, 74, 250, 254; DLBD 13

Kirkup, James 1918- .... **CLC 1**
See also CA 1-4R; CAAS 4; CANR 2; CP 7; DLB 27; SATA 12

Kirkwood, James 1930(?)-1989 .... **CLC 9**
See also AITN 2; CA 1-4R; CANR 6, 40; GLL 2

Kirshner, Sidney
See Kingsley, Sidney

Kis, Danilo 1935-1989 .... **CLC 57**
See also CA 118; CANR 61; CDWLB 4; DLB 181; MTCW 1; RGSF 2; RGWL 2, 3

Kissinger, Henry A(lfred) 1923- ..... **CLC 137**
See also CA 1-4R; CANR 2, 33, 66, 109; MTCW 1

Kivi, Aleksis 1834-1872 .... **NCLC 30**

Kizer, Carolyn (Ashley) 1925- ... **CLC 15, 39, 80**
See also CA 65-68; CAAS 5; CANR 24, 70; CP 7; CWP; DAM POET; DLB 5, 169; MTCW 2

Klabund 1890-1928 .... **TCLC 44**
See also CA 162; DLB 66

Klappert, Peter 1942- .... **CLC 57**
See also CA 33-36R; CSW; DLB 5

Klein, A(braham) M(oses)
1909-1972 .... **CLC 19**
See also CA 101; DAB; DAC; DAM MST; DLB 68; RGEL 2

Klein, Joe
See Klein, Joseph

Klein, Joseph 1946- .... **CLC 154**
See also CA 85-88; CANR 55

Klein, Norma 1938-1989 .... **CLC 30**
See also AAYA 2, 35; BPFB 2; BYA 6, 7, 8; CA 41-44R; CANR 15, 37; CLR 2, 19; INT CANR-15; JRDA; MAICYA 1, 2; SAAS 1; SATA 7, 57; WYA; YAW

Klein, T(heodore) E(ibon) D(onald)
1947- .... **CLC 34**
See also CA 119; CANR 44, 75; HGG

Kleist, Heinrich von 1777-1811 ...... **NCLC 2, 37; SSC 22**
See also CDWLB 2; DAM DRAM; DLB 90; EW 5; RGSF 2; RGWL 2, 3

Klima, Ivan 1931- .... **CLC 56**
See also CA 25-28R; CANR 17, 50, 91; CDWLB 4; CWW 2; DAM NOV; DLB 232; RGWL 3

Klimentev, Andrei Platonovich
See Klimentov, Andrei Platonovich

Klimentov, Andrei Platonovich
1899-1951 .... **TCLC 14; SSC 42**
See also Platonov, Andrei Platonovich

Klinger, Friedrich Maximilian von
1752-1831 .... **NCLC 1**
See also DLB 94

Klingsor the Magician
See Hartmann, Sadakichi

Klopstock, Friedrich Gottlieb
1724-1803 .... **NCLC 11**
See also DLB 97; EW 4; RGWL 2, 3

Knapp, Caroline 1959-2002 .... **CLC 99**
See also CA 154

Knebel, Fletcher 1911-1993 .... **CLC 14**
See also AITN 1; CA 1-4R; CAAS 3; CANR 1, 36; SATA 36; SATA-Obit 75

Knickerbocker, Diedrich
See Irving, Washington

Knight, Etheridge 1931-1991 . **CLC 40; BLC 2; PC 14**
See also BW 1, 3; CA 21-24R; CANR 23, 82; DAM POET; DLB 41; MTCW 2; RGAL 4

Knight, Sarah Kemble 1666-1727 .... **LC 7**
See also DLB 24, 200

Knister, Raymond 1899-1932 .... **TCLC 56**
See also CA 186; DLB 68; RGEL 2

Knowles, John 1926-2001 ... **CLC 1, 4, 10, 26**
See also AAYA 10; BPFB 2; BYA 3; CA 17-20R; CANR 40, 74, 76; CDALB 1968-1988; CN 7; DA; DAC; DAM MST, NOV; DLB 6; EXPN; MTCW 1, 2; NFS 2; RGAL 4; SATA 8, 89; SATA-Obit 134; YAW

Knox, Calvin M.
See Silverberg, Robert

Knox, John c. 1505-1572 .... **LC 37**
See also DLB 132

Knye, Cassandra
See Disch, Thomas M(ichael)

Koch, C(hristopher) J(ohn) 1932- .... **CLC 42**
See also CA 127; CANR 84; CN 7

Koch, Christopher
See Koch, C(hristopher) J(ohn)

Koch, Kenneth 1925-2002 .... **CLC 5, 8, 44**
See also CA 1-4R; CAD; CANR 6, 36, 57, 97; CD 5; CP 7; DAM POET; DLB 5; INT CANR-36; MTCW 2; SATA 65; WP

Kochanowski, Jan 1530-1584 .... **LC 10**
See also RGWL 2, 3

Kock, Charles Paul de 1794-1871 . **NCLC 16**

Koda Rohan
See Koda Shigeyuki

Koda Rohan
See Koda Shigeyuki
See also DLB 180

Koda Shigeyuki 1867-1947 .... **TCLC 22**
See also Koda Rohan
See also CA 183

Koestler, Arthur 1905-1983 ... **CLC 1, 3, 6, 8, 15, 33**
See also BRWS 1; CA 1-4R; CANR 1, 33; CDBLB 1945-1960; DLBY 1983; MTCW 1, 2; RGEL 2

Kogawa, Joy Nozomi 1935- ...... **CLC 78, 129**
See also CA 101; CANR 19, 62; CN 7; CWP; DAC; DAM MST, MULT, FW; MTCW 2; NFS 3; SATA 99

Kohout, Pavel 1928- .... **CLC 13**
See also CA 45-48; CANR 3

Koizumi, Yakumo
See Hearn, (Patricio) Lafcadio (Tessima Carlos)

Kolmar, Gertrud 1894-1943 .... **TCLC 40**
See also CA 167

Komunyakaa, Yusef 1947- .... **CLC 86, 94; BLCS**
See also AFAW 2; CA 147; CANR 83; CP 7; CSW; DLB 120; PFS 5; RGAL 4

Konrad, George
See Konrad, Gyorgy
See also CWW 2

Konrad, Gyorgy 1933- .... **CLC 4, 10, 73**
See also Konrad, George
See also CA 85-88; CANR 97; CDWLB 4; CWW 2; DLB 232

Konwicki, Tadeusz 1926- .... **CLC 8, 28, 54, 117**
See also CA 101; CAAS 9; CANR 39, 59; CWW 2; DLB 232; IDFW 3; MTCW 1

Koontz, Dean R(ay) 1945- .... **CLC 78**
See also AAYA 9, 31; BEST 89:3, 90:2; CA 108; CANR 19, 36, 52, 95; CMW 4; CPW; DAM NOV, POP; HGG; MTCW 1; SATA 92; SFW 4; SUFW 2; YAW

Kopernik, Mikolaj
See Copernicus, Nicolaus

Kopit, Arthur (Lee) 1937- .... **CLC 1, 18, 33**
See also AITN 1; CA 81-84; CABS 3; CD 5; DAM DRAM; DFS 7, 14; DLB 7; MTCW 1; RGAL 4

Kopitar, Jernej (Bartholomaus)
1780-1844 .... **NCLC 117**

Kops, Bernard 1926- .... **CLC 4**
See also CA 5-8R; CANR 84; CBD; CN 7; CP 7; DLB 13

Kornbluth, C(yril) M. 1923-1958 .... **TCLC 8**
See also CA 160; DLB 8; SFW 4

Korolenko, V. G.
See Korolenko, Vladimir Galaktionovich

Korolenko, Vladimir
See Korolenko, Vladimir Galaktionovich

Korolenko, Vladimir G.
See Korolenko, Vladimir Galaktionovich

Korolenko, Vladimir Galaktionovich
1853-1921 .... **TCLC 22**

Korzybski, Alfred (Habdank Skarbek)
1879-1950 .... **TCLC 61**
See also CA 160

Kosinski, Jerzy (Nikodem)
1933-1991 .... **CLC 1, 2, 3, 6, 10, 15, 53, 70**
See also AMWS 7; BPFB 2; CA 17-20R; CANR 9, 46; DAM NOV; DLB 2; DLBY 1982; HGG; MTCW 1, 2; NFS 12; RGAL 4; TUS

Kostelanetz, Richard (Cory) 1940- .. **CLC 28**
See also CA 13-16R; CAAS 8; CANR 38, 77; CN 7; CP 7

Kostrowitzki, Wilhelm Apollinaris de
1880-1918
See Apollinaire, Guillaume

Kotlowitz, Robert 1924- .... **CLC 4**
See also CA 33-36R; CANR 36

Kotzebue, August (Friedrich Ferdinand) von
1761-1819 .... **NCLC 25**
See also DLB 94

Kotzwinkle, William 1938- ...... **CLC 5, 14, 35**
See also BPFB 2; CA 45-48; CANR 3, 44, 84; CLR 6; DLB 173; FANT; MAICYA 1, 2; SATA 24, 70; SFW 4; SUFW 2; YAW

Kowna, Stancy
See Szymborska, Wislawa

Kozol, Jonathan 1936- .... **CLC 17**
See also CA 61-64; CANR 16, 45, 96

Kozoll, Michael 1940(?)- .... **CLC 35**

Kramer, Kathryn 19(?)- .... **CLC 34**

Kramer, Larry 1935- .... **CLC 42; DC 8**
See also CA 126; CANR 60; DAM POP; DLB 249; GLL 1

Krasicki, Ignacy 1735-1801 .... **NCLC 8**

Krasinski, Zygmunt 1812-1859 .... **NCLC 4**
See also RGWL 2, 3

Kraus, Karl 1874-1936 .... **TCLC 5**
See also DLB 118

Kreve (Mickevicius), Vincas
1882-1954 .... **TCLC 27**
See also CA 170; DLB 220

Kristeva, Julia 1941- .... **CLC 77, 140**
See also CA 154; CANR 99; DLB 242; FW

Kristofferson, Kris 1936- .... CLC 26
See also CA 104

Krizanc, John 1956- .... CLC 57
See also CA 187

Krleza, Miroslav 1893-1981 .... CLC 8, 114
See also CA 97-100; CANR 50; CDWLB 4; DLB 147; EW 11; RGWL 2, 3

Kroetsch, Robert 1927- .. CLC 5, 23, 57, 132
See also CA 17-20R; CANR 8, 38; CCA 1; CN 7; CP 7; DAC; DAM POET; DLB 53; MTCW 1

Kroetz, Franz
See Kroetz, Franz Xaver

Kroetz, Franz Xaver 1946- .... CLC 41
See also CA 130

Kroker, Arthur (W.) 1945- .... CLC 77
See also CA 161

Kropotkin, Peter (Aleksieevich)
1842-1921 .... TCLC 36

Krotkov, Yuri 1917-1981 .... CLC 19
See also CA 102

Krumb
See Crumb, R(obert)

Krumgold, Joseph (Quincy)
1908-1980 .... CLC 12
See also BYA 1, 2; CA 9-12R; CANR 7; MAICYA 1, 2; SATA 1, 48; SATA-Obit 23; YAW

Krumwitz
See Crumb, R(obert)

Krutch, Joseph Wood 1893-1970 ..... CLC 24
See also ANW; CA 1-4R; CANR 4; DLB 63, 206

Krutzch, Gus
See Eliot, T(homas) S(tearns)

Krylov, Ivan Andreevich
1768(?)-1844 .... NCLC 1
See also DLB 150

Kubin, Alfred (Leopold Isidor)
1877-1959 .... TCLC 23
See also CA 149; CANR 104; DLB 81

Kubrick, Stanley 1928-1999 .... CLC 16
See also AAYA 30; CA 81-84; CANR 33; DLB 26; TCLC 112

Kueng, Hans 1928-
See Kung, Hans
See also CA 53-56; CANR 66; MTCW 1, 2

Kumin, Maxine (Winokur) 1925- ..... CLC 5, 13, 28, 164; PC 15
See also AITN 2; AMWS 4; ANW; CA 1-4R; CAAS 8; CANR 1, 21, 69; CP 7; CWP; DAM POET; DLB 5; EXPP; MTCW 1, 2; PAB; SATA 12

Kundera, Milan 1929- . CLC 4, 9, 19, 32, 68, 115, 135; SSC 24
See also AAYA 2; BPFB 2; CA 85-88; CANR 19, 52, 74; CDWLB 4; CWW 2; DAM NOV; DLB 232; EW 13; MTCW 1, 2; RGSF 2; RGWL 3; SSFS 10

Kunene, Mazisi (Raymond) 1930- ... CLC 85
See also BW 1, 3; CA 125; CANR 81; CP 7; DLB 117

Kung, Hans .... CLC 130
See also Kueng, Hans

Kunikida Doppo 1869(?)-1908
See Doppo, Kunikida
See also DLB 180

Kunitz, Stanley (Jasspon) 1905- .. CLC 6, 11, 14, 148; PC 19
See also AMWS 3; CA 41-44R; CANR 26, 57, 98; CP 7; DLB 48; INT CANR-26; MTCW 1, 2; PFS 11; RGAL 4

Kunze, Reiner 1933- .... CLC 10
See also CA 93-96; CWW 2; DLB 75

Kuprin, Aleksander Ivanovich
1870-1938 .... TCLC 5
See also CA 182

Kureishi, Hanif 1954(?)- .... CLC 64, 135
See also CA 139; CANR 113; CBD; CD 5; CN 7; DLB 194, 245; GLL 2; IDFW 4; WLIT 4

Kurosawa, Akira 1910-1998 ..... CLC 16, 119
See also AAYA 11; CA 101; CANR 46; DAM MULT

Kushner, Tony 1957(?)- .... CLC 81; DC 10
See also AMWS 9; CA 144; CAD; CANR 74; CD 5; DAM DRAM; DFS 5; DLB 228; GLL 1; LAIT 5; MTCW 2; RGAL 4

Kuttner, Henry 1915-1958 .... TCLC 10
See also CA 157; DLB 8; FANT; SCFW 2; SFW 4

Kutty, Madhavi
See Das, Kamala

Kuzma, Greg 1944- .... CLC 7
See also CA 33-36R; CANR 70

Kuzmin, Mikhail 1872(?)-1936 ...... TCLC 40
See also CA 170

Kyd, Thomas 1558-1594 .... LC 22; DC 3
See also BRW 1; DAM DRAM; DLB 62; IDTP; RGEL 2; TEA; WLIT 3

Kyprianos, Iossif
See Samarakis, Antonis

L. S.
See Stephen, Sir Leslie

Labrunie, Gerard
See Nerval, Gerard de

La Bruyere, Jean de 1645-1696 .... LC 17
See also DLB 268; EW 3; GFL Beginnings to 1789

Lacan, Jacques (Marie Emile)
1901-1981 .... CLC 75
See also CA 121; TWA

Laclos, Pierre Ambroise Francois
1741-1803 .... NCLC 4, 87
See also EW 4; GFL Beginnings to 1789; RGWL 2, 3

La Colere, Francois
See Aragon, Louis

Lacolere, Francois
See Aragon, Louis

La Deshabilleuse
See Simenon, Georges (Jacques Christian)

Lady Gregory
See Gregory, Lady Isabella Augusta (Persse)

Lady of Quality, A
See Bagnold, Enid

La Fayette, Marie-(Madelaine Pioche de la Vergne) 1634-1693 .... LC 2
See also Lafayette, Marie-Madeleine
See also GFL Beginnings to 1789; RGWL 2, 3

Lafayette, Marie-Madeleine
See La Fayette, Marie-(Madelaine Pioche de la Vergne)
See also DLB 268

Lafayette, Rene
See Hubbard, L(afayette) Ron(ald)

La Fontaine, Jean de 1621-1695 .... LC 50
See also DLB 268; EW 3; GFL Beginnings to 1789; MAICYA 1, 2; RGWL 2, 3; SATA 18

Laforgue, Jules 1860-1887 . NCLC 5, 53; PC 14; SSC 20
See also DLB 217; EW 7; GFL 1789 to the Present; RGWL 2, 3

Layamon
See Layamon
See also DLB 146

Lagerkvist, Paer (Fabian)
1891-1974 .... CLC 7, 10, 13, 54
See also Lagerkvist, Par
See also CA 85-88; DAM DRAM, NOV; MTCW 1, 2; TWA

Lagerkvist, Par .... SSC 12
See also Lagerkvist, Paer (Fabian)
See also DLB 259; EW 10; MTCW 2; RGSF 2; RGWL 2, 3

Lagerloef, Selma (Ottiliana Lovisa)
1858-1940 .... TCLC 4, 36
See also Lagerlof, Selma (Ottiliana Lovisa)
See also MTCW 2; SATA 15

Lagerlof, Selma (Ottiliana Lovisa)
See Lagerloef, Selma (Ottiliana Lovisa)
See also CLR 7; SATA 15

La Guma, (Justin) Alex(ander)
1925-1985 .... CLC 19; BLCS
See also AFW; BW 1, 3; CA 49-52; CANR 25, 81; CDWLB 3; DAM NOV; DLB 117, 225; MTCW 1, 2; WLIT 2

Laidlaw, A. K.
See Grieve, C(hristopher) M(urray)

Lainez, Manuel Mujica
See Mujica Lainez, Manuel
See also HW 1

Laing, R(onald) D(avid) 1927-1989 . CLC 95
See also CA 107; CANR 34; MTCW 1

Lamartine, Alphonse (Marie Louis Prat) de
1790-1869 .... NCLC 11; PC 16
See also DAM POET; DLB 217; GFL 1789 to the Present; RGWL 2, 3

Lamb, Charles 1775-1834 ..... NCLC 10, 113; WLC
See also BRW 4; CDBLB 1789-1832; DA; DAB; DAC; DAM MST; DLB 93, 107, 163; RGEL 2; SATA 17; TEA

Lamb, Lady Caroline 1785-1828 ... NCLC 38
See also DLB 116

Lamming, George (William) 1927- ... CLC 2, 4, 66, 144; BLC 2
See also BW 2, 3; CA 85-88; CANR 26, 76; CDWLB 3; CN 7; DAM MULT; DLB 125; MTCW 1, 2; NFS 15; RGEL 2

L'Amour, Louis (Dearborn)
1908-1988 .... CLC 25, 55
See also AAYA 16; AITN 2; BEST 89:2; BPFB 2; CA 1-4R; CANR 3, 25, 40; CPW; DAM NOV, POP; DLB 206; DLBY 1980; MTCW 1, 2; RGAL 4

Lampedusa, Giuseppe (Tomasi) di
.... TCLC 13
See also Tomasi di Lampedusa, Giuseppe
See also CA 164; EW 11; MTCW 2; RGWL 2, 3

Lampman, Archibald 1861-1899 ... NCLC 25
See also DLB 92; RGEL 2; TWA

Lancaster, Bruce 1896-1963 .... CLC 36
See also CA 9-10; CANR 70; CAP 1; SATA 9

Lanchester, John 1962- .... CLC 99
See also CA 194; DLB 267

Landau, Mark Alexandrovich
See Aldanov, Mark (Alexandrovich)

Landau-Aldanov, Mark Alexandrovich
See Aldanov, Mark (Alexandrovich)

Landis, Jerry
See Simon, Paul (Frederick)

Landis, John 1950- .... CLC 26
See also CA 122

Landolfi, Tommaso 1908-1979 .... CLC 11, 49
See also CA 127; DLB 177

Landon, Letitia Elizabeth
1802-1838 .... NCLC 15
See also DLB 96

Landor, Walter Savage
1775-1864 .... NCLC 14
See also BRW 4; DLB 93, 107; RGEL 2

Landwirth, Heinz 1927-
See Lind, Jakov
See also CA 9-12R; CANR 7

Lane, Patrick 1939- .... **CLC 25**
See also CA 97-100; CANR 54; CP 7; DAM POET; DLB 53; INT 97-100

Lang, Andrew 1844-1912 .... **TCLC 16**
See also CA 137; CANR 85; DLB 98, 141, 184; FANT; MAICYA 1, 2; RGEL 2; SATA 16; WCH

Lang, Fritz 1890-1976 .... **CLC 20, 103**
See also CA 77-80; CANR 30

Lange, John
See Crichton, (John) Michael

Langer, Elinor 1939- .... **CLC 34**
See also CA 121

Langland, William 1332(?)-1400(?) ..... **LC 19**
See also BRW 1; DA; DAB; DAC; DAM MST, POET; DLB 146; RGEL 2; TEA; WLIT 3

Langstaff, Launcelot
See Irving, Washington

Lanier, Sidney 1842-1881 .... **NCLC 6, 118**
See also AMWS 1; DAM POET; DLB 64; DLBD 13; EXPP; MAICYA 1; PFS 14; RGAL 4; SATA 18

Lanyer, Aemilia 1569-1645 ...... **LC 10, 30, 83**
See also DLB 121

Lao-Tzu
See Lao Tzu

Lao Tzu c. 6th cent. B.C.-3rd cent. B.C. .... **CMLC 7**

Lapine, James 1949- .... **CLC 39**
See also CA 130; CANR 54; INT 130

Larbaud, Valery (Nicolas) 1881-1957 .... **TCLC 9**
See also CA 152; GFL 1789 to the Present

Lardner, Ring
See Lardner, Ring(gold) W(ilmer)
See also BPFB 2; CDALB 1917-1929; DLB 11, 25, 86, 171; DLBD 16; RGAL 4; RGSF 2

Lardner, Ring W., Jr.
See Lardner, Ring(gold) W(ilmer)

Lardner, Ring(gold) W(ilmer) 1885-1933 .... **TCLC 2, 14; SSC 32**
See also Lardner, Ring
See also AMW; CA 131; MTCW 1, 2; TUS

Laredo, Betty
See Codrescu, Andrei

Larkin, Maia
See Wojciechowska, Maia (Teresa)

Larkin, Philip (Arthur) 1922-1985 ... **CLC 3, 5, 8, 9, 13, 18, 33, 39, 64; PC 21**
See also BRWS 1; CA 5-8R; CANR 24, 62; CDBLB 1960 to Present; DAB; DAM MST, POET; DLB 27; MTCW 1, 2; PFS 3, 4, 12; RGEL 2

Larra (y Sanchez de Castro), Mariano Jose de 1809-1837 .... **NCLC 17**

Larsen, Eric 1941- .... **CLC 55**
See also CA 132

Larsen, Nella 1893(?)-1963 . **CLC 37; BLC 2**
See also AFAW 1, 2; BW 1; CA 125; CANR 83; DAM MULT; DLB 51; FW; HR 3

Larson, Charles R(aymond) 1938- ... **CLC 31**
See also CA 53-56; CANR 4

Larson, Jonathan 1961-1996 .... **CLC 99**
See also AAYA 28; CA 156

Las Casas, Bartolome de 1474-1566 . **LC 31; HLCS**
See also Casas, Bartolome de las
See also LAW

Lasch, Christopher 1932-1994 .... **CLC 102**
See also CA 73-76; CANR 25; DLB 246; MTCW 1, 2

Lasker-Schueler, Else 1869-1945 ... **TCLC 57**
See also CA 183; DLB 66, 124

Laski, Harold J(oseph) 1893-1950 . **TCLC 79**
See also CA 188

Latham, Jean Lee 1902-1995 .... **CLC 12**
See also AITN 1; BYA 1; CA 5-8R; CANR 7, 84; CLR 50; MAICYA 1, 2; SATA 2, 68; YAW

Latham, Mavis
See Clark, Mavis Thorpe

Lathen, Emma .... **CLC 2**
See also Hennissart, Martha; Latsis, Mary J(ane)
See also BPFB 2; CMW 4

Lathrop, Francis
See Leiber, Fritz (Reuter, Jr.)

Latsis, Mary J(ane) 1927(?)-1997
See Lathen, Emma
See also CA 85-88; CMW 4

Lattany, Kristin
See Lattany, Kristin (Elaine Eggleston) Hunter

Lattany, Kristin (Elaine Eggleston) Hunter 1931- .... **CLC 35**
See also AITN 1; BW 1; BYA 3; CA 13-16R; CANR 13, 108; CLR 3; CN 7; DLB 33; INT CANR-13; MAICYA 1, 2; SAAS 10; SATA 12, 132; YAW

Lattimore, Richmond (Alexander) 1906-1984 .... **CLC 3**
See also CA 1-4R; CANR 1

Laughlin, James 1914-1997 .... **CLC 49**
See also CA 21-24R; CAAS 22; CANR 9, 47; CP 7; DLB 48; DLBY 1996, 1997

Laurence, (Jean) Margaret (Wemyss) 1926-1987 . **CLC 3, 6, 13, 50, 62; SSC 7**
See also BYA 13; CA 5-8R; CANR 33; DAC; DAM MST; DLB 53; FW; MTCW 1, 2; NFS 11; RGEL 2; RGSF 2; SATA-Obit 50; TCWW 2

Laurent, Antoine 1952- .... **CLC 50**

Lauscher, Hermann
See Hesse, Hermann

Lautreamont 1846-1870 .. **NCLC 12; SSC 14**
See also Lautreamont, Isidore Lucien Ducasse
See also GFL 1789 to the Present; RGWL 2, 3

Lautreamont, Isidore Lucien Ducasse
See Lautreamont
See also DLB 217

Laverty, Donald
See Blish, James (Benjamin)

Lavin, Mary 1912-1996 . **CLC 4, 18, 99; SSC 4**
See also CA 9-12R; CANR 33; CN 7; DLB 15; FW; MTCW 1; RGEL 2; RGSF 2

Lavond, Paul Dennis
See Kornbluth, C(yril) M.; Pohl, Frederik

Lawler, Raymond Evenor 1922- .... **CLC 58**
See also CA 103; CD 5; RGEL 2

Lawrence, D(avid) H(erbert Richards) 1885-1930 .... **TCLC 2, 9, 16, 33, 48, 61, 93; SSC 4, 19; WLC**
See also Chambers, Jessie
See also BPFB 2; BRW 7; BRWR 2; CA 121; CDBLB 1914-1945; DA; DAB; DAC; DAM MST, NOV, POET; DLB 10, 19, 36, 98, 162, 195; EXPP; EXPS; LAIT 2, 3; MTCW 1, 2; PFS 6; RGEL 2; RGSF 2; SSFS 2, 6; TEA; WLIT 4; WP

Lawrence, T(homas) E(dward) 1888-1935 .... **TCLC 18**
See also Dale, Colin
See also BRWS 2; CA 167; DLB 195

Lawrence of Arabia
See Lawrence, T(homas) E(dward)

Lawson, Henry (Archibald Hertzberg) 1867-1922 .... **TCLC 27; SSC 18**
See also CA 181; DLB 230; RGEL 2; RGSF 2

Lawton, Dennis
See Faust, Frederick (Schiller)

Laxness, Halldor .... **CLC 25**
See also Gudjonsson, Halldor Kiljan
See also EW 12; RGWL 2, 3

Layamon fl. c. 1200- .... **CMLC 10**
See also Layamon
See also RGEL 2

Laye, Camara 1928-1980 ... **CLC 4, 38; BLC 2**
See also AFW; BW 1; CA 85-88; CANR 25; DAM MULT; MTCW 1, 2; WLIT 2

Layton, Irving (Peter) 1912- .... **CLC 2, 15, 164**
See also CA 1-4R; CANR 2, 33, 43, 66; CP 7; DAC; DAM MST, POET; DLB 88; MTCW 1, 2; PFS 12; RGEL 2

Lazarus, Emma 1849-1887 ...... **NCLC 8, 109**

Lazarus, Felix
See Cable, George Washington

Lazarus, Henry
See Slavitt, David R(ytman)

Lea, Joan
See Neufeld, John (Arthur)

Leacock, Stephen (Butler) 1869-1944 .... **TCLC 2; SSC 39**
See also CA 141; CANR 80; DAC; DAM MST; DLB 92; MTCW 2; RGEL 2; RGSF 2

Lead, Jane Ward 1623-1704 .... **LC 72**
See also DLB 131

Leapor, Mary 1722-1746 .... **LC 80**
See also DLB 109

Lear, Edward 1812-1888 .... **NCLC 3**
See also BRW 5; CLR 1, 75; DLB 32, 163, 166; MAICYA 1, 2; RGEL 2; SATA 18, 100; WCH; WP

Lear, Norman (Milton) 1922- .... **CLC 12**
See also CA 73-76

Leautaud, Paul 1872-1956 .... **TCLC 83**
See also CA 203; DLB 65; GFL 1789 to the Present

Leavis, F(rank) R(aymond) 1895-1978 .... **CLC 24**
See also BRW 7; CA 21-24R; CANR 44; DLB 242; MTCW 1, 2; RGEL 2

Leavitt, David 1961- .... **CLC 34**
See also CA 122; CANR 50, 62, 101; CPW; DAM POP; DLB 130; GLL 1; INT 122; MTCW 2

Leblanc, Maurice (Marie Emile) 1864-1941 .... **TCLC 49**
See also CMW 4

Lebowitz, Fran(ces Ann) 1951(?)- ... **CLC 11, 36**
See also CA 81-84; CANR 14, 60, 70; INT CANR-14; MTCW 1

Lebrecht, Peter
See Tieck, (Johann) Ludwig

le Carre, John .... **CLC 3, 5, 9, 15, 28**
See also Cornwell, David (John Moore)
See also AAYA 42; BEST 89:4; BPFB 2; BRWS 2; CDBLB 1960 to Present; CMW 4; CN 7; CPW; DLB 87; MSW; MTCW 2; RGEL 2; TEA

Le Clezio, J(ean) M(arie) G(ustave) 1940- .... **CLC 31, 155**
See also CA 128; DLB 83; GFL 1789 to the Present; RGSF 2

Leconte de Lisle, Charles-Marie-Rene 1818-1894 .... **NCLC 29**
See also DLB 217; EW 6; GFL 1789 to the Present

Le Coq, Monsieur
See Simenon, Georges (Jacques Christian)

Leduc, Violette 1907-1972 .... **CLC 22**
See also CA 13-14; CANR 69; CAP 1; GFL 1789 to the Present; GLL 1

Ledwidge, Francis 1887(?)-1917 .... **TCLC 23**
See also CA 203; DLB 20

Lee, Andrea 1953- .... **CLC 36; BLC 2**
See also BW 1, 3; CA 125; CANR 82; DAM MULT

Lee, Andrew
See Auchincloss, Louis (Stanton)

Lee, Chang-rae 1965- .... **CLC 91**
See also CA 148; CANR 89

Lee, Don L. .... **CLC 2**
See also Madhubuti, Haki R.

Lee, George W(ashington) 1894-1976 .... **CLC 52; BLC 2**
See also BW 1; CA 125; CANR 83; DAM MULT; DLB 51

Lee, (Nelle) Harper 1926- .... **CLC 12, 60; WLC**
See also AAYA 13; AMWS 8; BPFB 2; BYA 3; CA 13-16R; CANR 51; CDALB 1941-1968; CSW; DA; DAB; DAC; DAM MST, NOV; DLB 6; EXPN; LAIT 3; MTCW 1, 2; NFS 2; SATA 11; WYA; YAW

Lee, Helen Elaine 1959(?)- .... **CLC 86**
See also CA 148

Lee, John .... **CLC 70**

Lee, Julian
See Latham, Jean Lee

Lee, Larry
See Lee, Lawrence

Lee, Laurie 1914-1997 .... **CLC 90**
See also CA 77-80; CANR 33, 73; CP 7; CPW; DAB; DAM POP; DLB 27; MTCW 1; RGEL 2

Lee, Lawrence 1941-1990 .... **CLC 34**
See also CANR 43

Lee, Li-Young 1957- .... **CLC 164; PC 24**
See also CA 153; CP 7; DLB 165; PFS 11, 15

Lee, Manfred B(ennington) 1905-1971 .... **CLC 11**
See also Queen, Ellery
See also CA 1-4R; CANR 2; CMW 4; DLB 137

Lee, Shelton Jackson 1957(?)- .... **CLC 105; BLCS**
See also Lee, Spike
See also BW 2, 3; CA 125; CANR 42; DAM MULT

Lee, Spike
See Lee, Shelton Jackson
See also AAYA 4, 29

Lee, Stan 1922- .... **CLC 17**
See also AAYA 5; CA 111; INT 111

Lee, Tanith 1947- .... **CLC 46**
See also AAYA 15; CA 37-40R; CANR 53, 102; DLB 261; FANT; SATA 8, 88, 134; SFW 4; SUFW 1, 2; YAW

Lee, Vernon .... **TCLC 5; SSC 33**
See also Paget, Violet
See also DLB 57, 153, 156, 174, 178; GLL 1; SUFW 1

Lee, William
See Burroughs, William S(eward)
See also GLL 1

Lee, Willy
See Burroughs, William S(eward)
See also GLL 1

Lee-Hamilton, Eugene (Jacob) 1845-1907 .... **TCLC 22**

Leet, Judith 1935- .... **CLC 11**
See also CA 187

Le Fanu, Joseph Sheridan 1814-1873 .... **NCLC 9, 58; SSC 14**
See also CMW 4; DAM POP; DLB 21, 70, 159, 178; HGG; RGEL 2; RGSF 2; SUFW 1

Leffland, Ella 1931- .... **CLC 19**
See also CA 29-32R; CANR 35, 78, 82; DLBY 1984; INT CANR-35; SATA 65

Leger, Alexis
See Leger, (Marie-Rene Auguste) Alexis Saint-Leger

Leger, (Marie-Rene Auguste) Alexis Saint-Leger 1887-1975 .. **CLC 4, 11, 46; PC 23**
See also Perse, Saint-John; Saint-John Perse
See also CA 13-16R; CANR 43; DAM POET; MTCW 1

Leger, Saintleger
See Leger, (Marie-Rene Auguste) Alexis Saint-Leger

Le Guin, Ursula K(roeber) 1929- ..... **CLC 8, 13, 22, 45, 71, 136; SSC 12**
See also AAYA 9, 27; AITN 1; BPFB 2; BYA 5, 8, 11, 14; CA 21-24R; CANR 9, 32, 52, 74; CDALB 1968-1988; CLR 3, 28; CN 7; CPW; DAB; DAC; DAM MST, POP; DLB 8, 52, 256; EXPS; FANT; FW; INT CANR-32; JRDA; LAIT 5; MAICYA 1, 2; MTCW 1, 2; NFS 6, 9; SATA 4, 52, 99; SCFW 4; SFW 4; SSFS 2; SUFW 1, 2; WYA; YAW

Lehmann, Rosamond (Nina) 1901-1990 .... **CLC 5**
See also CA 77-80; CANR 8, 73; DLB 15; MTCW 2; RGEL 2; RHW

Leiber, Fritz (Reuter, Jr.) 1910-1992 .... **CLC 25**
See also BPFB 2; CA 45-48; CANR 2, 40, 86; DLB 8; FANT; HGG; MTCW 1, 2; SATA 45; SATA-Obit 73; SCFW 2; SFW 4; SUFW 1, 2

Leibniz, Gottfried Wilhelm von 1646-1716 .... **LC 35**
See also DLB 168

Leimbach, Martha 1963-
See Leimbach, Marti
See also CA 130

Leimbach, Marti .... **CLC 65**
See also Leimbach, Martha

Leino, Eino .... **TCLC 24**
See also Loennbohm, Armas Eino Leopold

Leiris, Michel (Julien) 1901-1990 ..... **CLC 61**
See also CA 128; GFL 1789 to the Present

Leithauser, Brad 1953- .... **CLC 27**
See also CA 107; CANR 27, 81; CP 7; DLB 120

Lelchuk, Alan 1938- .... **CLC 5**
See also CA 45-48; CAAS 20; CANR 1, 70; CN 7

Lem, Stanislaw 1921- ...... **CLC 8, 15, 40, 149**
See also CA 105; CAAS 1; CANR 32; CWW 2; MTCW 1; SCFW 2; SFW 4

Lemann, Nancy 1956- .... **CLC 39**
See also CA 136

Lemonnier, (Antoine Louis) Camille 1844-1913 .... **TCLC 22**

Lenau, Nikolaus 1802-1850 .... **NCLC 16**

L'Engle, Madeleine (Camp Franklin) 1918- .... **CLC 12**
See also AAYA 28; AITN 2; BPFB 2; BYA 2, 4, 5, 7; CA 1-4R; CANR 3, 21, 39, 66, 107; CLR 1, 14, 57; CPW; CWRI 5; DAM POP; DLB 52; JRDA; MAICYA 1, 2; MTCW 1, 2; SAAS 15; SATA 1, 27, 75, 128; SFW 4; WYA; YAW

Lengyel, Jozsef 1896-1975 .... **CLC 7**
See also CA 85-88; CANR 71; RGSF 2

Lenin 1870-1924
See Lenin, V. I.
See also CA 168

Lenin, V. I. .... **TCLC 67**
See also Lenin

Lennon, John (Ono) 1940-1980 .. **CLC 12, 35**
See also CA 102; SATA 114

Lennox, Charlotte Ramsay 1729(?)-1804 .... **NCLC 23**
See also DLB 39; RGEL 2

Lentricchia, Frank, (Jr.) 1940- .... **CLC 34**
See also CA 25-28R; CANR 19, 106; DLB 246

Lenz, Gunter .... **CLC 65**

Lenz, Siegfried 1926- .... **CLC 27; SSC 33**
See also CA 89-92; CANR 80; CWW 2; DLB 75; RGSF 2; RGWL 2, 3

Leon, David
See Jacob, (Cyprien-)Max

Leonard, Elmore (John, Jr.) 1925- . **CLC 28, 34, 71, 120**
See also AAYA 22; AITN 1; BEST 89:1, 90:4; BPFB 2; CA 81-84; CANR 12, 28, 53, 76, 96; CMW 4; CN 7; CPW; DAM POP; DLB 173, 226; INT CANR-28; MSW; MTCW 1, 2; RGAL 4; TCWW 2

Leonard, Hugh .... **CLC 19**
See also Byrne, John Keyes
See also CBD; CD 5; DFS 13; DLB 13

Leonov, Leonid (Maximovich) 1899-1994 .... **CLC 92**
See also Leonov, Leonid Maksimovich
See also CA 129; CANR 74, 76; DAM NOV; MTCW 1, 2

Leonov, Leonid Maksimovich
See Leonov, Leonid (Maximovich)
See also DLB 272

Leopardi, (Conte) Giacomo 1798-1837 .... **NCLC 22; PC 37**
See also EW 5; RGWL 2, 3; WP

Le Reveler
See Artaud, Antonin (Marie Joseph)

Lerman, Eleanor 1952- .... **CLC 9**
See also CA 85-88; CANR 69

Lerman, Rhoda 1936- .... **CLC 56**
See also CA 49-52; CANR 70

Lermontov, Mikhail
See Lermontov, Mikhail Yuryevich

Lermontov, Mikhail Iur'evich
See Lermontov, Mikhail Yuryevich
See also DLB 205

Lermontov, Mikhail Yuryevich 1814-1841 .... **NCLC 5, 47; PC 18**
See also Lermontov, Mikhail Iur'evich
See also EW 6; RGWL 2, 3; TWA

Leroux, Gaston 1868-1927 .... **TCLC 25**
See also CA 136; CANR 69; CMW 4; SATA 65

Lesage, Alain-Rene 1668-1747 .... **LC 2, 28**
See also EW 3; GFL Beginnings to 1789; RGWL 2, 3

Leskov, N(ikolai) S(emenovich) 1831-1895
See Leskov, Nikolai (Semyonovich)

Leskov, Nikolai (Semyonovich) 1831-1895 .... **NCLC 25; SSC 34**
See also Leskov, Nikolai Semenovich

Leskov, Nikolai Semenovich
See Leskov, Nikolai (Semyonovich)
See also DLB 238

Lesser, Milton
See Marlowe, Stephen

Lessing, Doris (May) 1919- ... **CLC 1, 2, 3, 6, 10, 15, 22, 40, 94; SSC 6; WLCS**
See also AFW; BRWS 1; CA 9-12R; CAAS 14; CANR 33, 54, 76; CD 5; CDBLB 1960 to Present; CN 7; DA; DAB; DAC; DAM MST, NOV; DLB 15, 139; DLBY 1985; EXPS; FW; LAIT 4; MTCW 1, 2; RGEL 2; RGSF 2; SFW 4; SSFS 1, 12; TEA; WLIT 2, 4

Lessing, Gotthold Ephraim 1729-1781 . **LC 8**
See also CDWLB 2; DLB 97; EW 4; RGWL 2, 3

Lester, Richard 1932- .... **CLC 20**

Levenson, Jay .... **CLC 70**

Lever, Charles (James) 1806-1872 .... **NCLC 23**
See also DLB 21; RGEL 2

Leverson, Ada Esther
1862(?)-1933(?) .... **TCLC 18**
See also Elaine
See also CA 202; DLB 153; RGEL 2

Levertov, Denise 1923-1997 .. **CLC 1, 2, 3, 5, 8, 15, 28, 66; PC 11**
See also AMWS 3; CA 1-4R, 178; CAAE 178; CAAS 19; CANR 3, 29, 50, 108; CDALBS; CP 7; CWP; DAM POET; DLB 5, 165; EXPP; FW; INT CANR-29; MTCW 1, 2; PAB; PFS 7; RGAL 4; TUS; WP

Levi, Carlo 1902-1975 .... **TCLC 125**
See also CA 65-68; CANR 10; RGWL 2, 3

Levi, Jonathan .... **CLC 76**
See also CA 197

Levi, Peter (Chad Tigar)
1931-2000 .... **CLC 41**
See also CA 5-8R; CANR 34, 80; CP 7; DLB 40

Levi, Primo 1919-1987 . **CLC 37, 50; SSC 12**
See also CA 13-16R; CANR 12, 33, 61, 70; DLB 177; MTCW 1, 2; RGWL 2, 3; TCLC 109

Levin, Ira 1929- .... **CLC 3, 6**
See also CA 21-24R; CANR 17, 44, 74; CMW 4; CN 7; CPW; DAM POP; HGG; MTCW 1, 2; SATA 66; SFW 4

Levin, Meyer 1905-1981 .... **CLC 7**
See also AITN 1; CA 9-12R; CANR 15; DAM POP; DLB 9, 28; DLBY 1981; SATA 21; SATA-Obit 27

Levine, Norman 1924- .... **CLC 54**
See also CA 73-76; CAAS 23; CANR 14, 70; DLB 88

Levine, Philip 1928- .. **CLC 2, 4, 5, 9, 14, 33, 118; PC 22**
See also AMWS 5; CA 9-12R; CANR 9, 37, 52; CP 7; DAM POET; DLB 5; PFS 8

Levinson, Deirdre 1931- .... **CLC 49**
See also CA 73-76; CANR 70

Levi-Strauss, Claude 1908- .... **CLC 38**
See also CA 1-4R; CANR 6, 32, 57; DLB 242; GFL 1789 to the Present; MTCW 1, 2; TWA

Levitin, Sonia (Wolff) 1934- .... **CLC 17**
See also AAYA 13; CA 29-32R; CANR 14, 32, 79; CLR 53; JRDA; MAICYA 1, 2; SAAS 2; SATA 4, 68, 119; SATA-Essay 131; YAW

Levon, O. U.
See Kesey, Ken (Elton)

Levy, Amy 1861-1889 .... **NCLC 59**
See also DLB 156, 240

Lewes, George Henry 1817-1878 ... **NCLC 25**
See also DLB 55, 144

Lewis, Alun 1915-1944 .... **TCLC 3; SSC 40**
See also BRW 7; CA 188; DLB 20, 162; PAB; RGEL 2

Lewis, C. Day
See Day Lewis, C(ecil)

Lewis, C(live) S(taples) 1898-1963 .... **CLC 1, 3, 6, 14, 27, 124; WLC**
See also AAYA 3, 39; BPFB 2; BRWS 3; CA 81-84; CANR 33, 71; CDBLB 1945-1960; CLR 3, 27; CWRI 5; DA; DAB; DAC; DAM MST, NOV, POP; DLB 15, 100, 160, 255; FANT; JRDA; MAICYA 1, 2; MTCW 1, 2; RGEL 2; SATA 13, 100; SCFW; SFW 4; SUFW 1; TEA; WCH; WYA; YAW

Lewis, Cecil Day
See Day Lewis, C(ecil)

Lewis, Janet 1899-1998 .... **CLC 41**
See also Winters, Janet Lewis
See also CA 9-12R; CANR 29, 63; CAP 1; CN 7; DLBY 1987; RHW; TCWW 2

Lewis, Matthew Gregory
1775-1818 .... **NCLC 11, 62**
See also DLB 39, 158, 178; HGG; RGEL 2; SUFW

Lewis, (Harry) Sinclair 1885-1951 . **TCLC 4, 13, 23, 39; WLC**
See also AMW; BPFB 2; CA 133; CDALB 1917-1929; DA; DAB; DAC; DAM MST, NOV; DLB 9, 102; DLBD 1; LAIT 3; MTCW 1, 2; NFS 15; RGAL 4; TUS

Lewis, (Percy) Wyndham
1884(?)-1957 .. **TCLC 2, 9, 104; SSC 34**
See also BRW 7; CA 157; DLB 15; FANT; MTCW 2; RGEL 2

Lewisohn, Ludwig 1883-1955 .... **TCLC 19**
See also DLB 4, 9, 28, 102

Lewton, Val 1904-1951 .... **TCLC 76**
See also CA 199; IDFW 3, 4

Leyner, Mark 1956- .... **CLC 92**
See also CA 110; CANR 28, 53; MTCW 2

Lezama Lima, Jose 1910-1976 .... **CLC 4, 10, 101; HLCS 2**
See also CA 77-80; CANR 71; DAM MULT; DLB 113; HW 1, 2; LAW; RGWL 2, 3

L'Heureux, John (Clarke) 1934- ...... **CLC 52**
See also CA 13-16R; CANR 23, 45, 88; DLB 244

Liddell, C. H.
See Kuttner, Henry

Lie, Jonas (Lauritz Idemil)
1833-1908(?) .... **TCLC 5**

Lieber, Joel 1937-1971 .... **CLC 6**
See also CA 73-76

Lieber, Stanley Martin
See Lee, Stan

Lieberman, Laurence (James)
1935- .... **CLC 4, 36**
See also CA 17-20R; CANR 8, 36, 89; CP 7

Lieh Tzu fl. 7th cent. B.C.-5th cent.
B.C. .... **CMLC 27**

Lieksman, Anders
See Haavikko, Paavo Juhani

Li Fei-kan 1904-
See Pa Chin
See also CA 105; TWA

Lifton, Robert Jay 1926- .... **CLC 67**
See also CA 17-20R; CANR 27, 78; INT CANR-27; SATA 66

Lightfoot, Gordon 1938- .... **CLC 26**

Lightman, Alan P(aige) 1948- .... **CLC 81**
See also CA 141; CANR 63, 105

Ligotti, Thomas (Robert) 1953- ...... **CLC 44; SSC 16**
See also CA 123; CANR 49; HGG; SUFW 2

Li Ho 791-817 .... **PC 13**

Liliencron, (Friedrich Adolf Axel) Detlev von 1844-1909 .... **TCLC 18**

Lille, Alain de
See Alain de Lille

Lilly, William 1602-1681 .... **LC 27**

Lima, Jose Lezama
See Lezama Lima, Jose

Lima Barreto, Afonso Henrique de
1881-1922 .... **TCLC 23**
See also CA 181; LAW

Lima Barreto, Afonso Henriques de
See Lima Barreto, Afonso Henrique de

Limonov, Edward 1944- .... **CLC 67**
See also CA 137

Lin, Frank
See Atherton, Gertrude (Franklin Horn)

Lincoln, Abraham 1809-1865 .... **NCLC 18**
See also LAIT 2

Lind, Jakov .... **CLC 1, 2, 4, 27, 82**
See also Landwirth, Heinz
See also CAAS 4

Lindbergh, Anne (Spencer) Morrow
1906-2001 .... **CLC 82**
See also BPFB 2; CA 17-20R; CANR 16, 73; DAM NOV; MTCW 1, 2; SATA 33; SATA-Obit 125; TUS

Lindsay, David 1878(?)-1945 .... **TCLC 15**
See also CA 187; DLB 255; FANT; SFW 4; SUFW 1

Lindsay, (Nicholas) Vachel
1879-1931 .... **TCLC 17; PC 23; WLC**
See also AMWS 1; CA 135; CANR 79; CDALB 1865-1917; DA; DAC; DAM MST, POET; DLB 54; EXPP; RGAL 4; SATA 40; WP

Linke-Poot
See Doeblin, Alfred

Linney, Romulus 1930- .... **CLC 51**
See also CA 1-4R; CAD; CANR 40, 44, 79; CD 5; CSW; RGAL 4

Linton, Eliza Lynn 1822-1898 .... **NCLC 41**
See also DLB 18

Li Po 701-763 .... **CMLC 2; PC 29**
See also WP

Lipsius, Justus 1547-1606 .... **LC 16**

Lipsyte, Robert (Michael) 1938- .... **CLC 21**
See also AAYA 7; CA 17-20R; CANR 8, 57; CLR 23, 76; DA; DAC; DAM MST, NOV; JRDA; LAIT 5; MAICYA 1, 2; SATA 5, 68, 113; WYA; YAW

Lish, Gordon (Jay) 1934- ... **CLC 45; SSC 18**
See also CA 117; CANR 79; DLB 130; INT 117

Lispector, Clarice 1925(?)-1977 .... **CLC 43; HLCS 2; SSC 34**
See also CA 139; CANR 71; CDWLB 3; DLB 113; DNFS 1; FW; HW 2; LAW; RGSF 2; RGWL 2, 3; WLIT 1

Littell, Robert 1935(?)- .... **CLC 42**
See also CA 112; CANR 64; CMW 4

Little, Malcolm 1925-1965
See Malcolm X
See also BW 1, 3; CA 125; CANR 82; DA; DAB; DAC; DAM MST, MULT; MTCW 1, 2; NCFS 3

Littlewit, Humphrey Gent.
See Lovecraft, H(oward) P(hillips)

Litwos
See Sienkiewicz, Henryk (Adam Alexander Pius)

Liu, E. 1857-1909 .... **TCLC 15**
See also CA 190

Lively, Penelope (Margaret) 1933- .. **CLC 32, 50**
See also BPFB 2; CA 41-44R; CANR 29, 67, 79; CLR 7; CN 7; CWRI 5; DAM NOV; DLB 14, 161, 207; FANT; JRDA; MAICYA 1, 2; MTCW 1, 2; SATA 7, 60, 101; TEA

Livesay, Dorothy (Kathleen)
1909-1996 .... **CLC 4, 15, 79**
See also AITN 2; CA 25-28R; CAAS 8; CANR 36, 67; DAC; DAM MST, POET; DLB 68; FW; MTCW 1; RGEL 2; TWA

Livy c. 59B.C.-c. 12 .... **CMLC 11**
See also AW 2; CDWLB 1; DLB 211; RGWL 2, 3

Lizardi, Jose Joaquin Fernandez de
1776-1827 .... **NCLC 30**
See also LAW

Llewellyn, Richard
See Llewellyn Lloyd, Richard Dafydd Vivian
See also DLB 15

Llewellyn Lloyd, Richard Dafydd Vivian
1906-1983 .... **CLC 7, 80**
See also Llewellyn, Richard
See also CA 53-56; CANR 7, 71; SATA 11;
SATA-Obit 37

Llosa, (Jorge) Mario (Pedro) Vargas
See Vargas Llosa, (Jorge) Mario (Pedro)
See also RGWL 3

Lloyd, Manda
See Mander, (Mary) Jane

Lloyd Webber, Andrew 1948-
See Webber, Andrew Lloyd
See also AAYA 1, 38; CA 149; DAM
DRAM; SATA 56

Llull, Ramon c. 1235-c. 1316 .... **CMLC 12**

Lobb, Ebenezer
See Upward, Allen

Locke, Alain (Le Roy) 1886-1954 . **TCLC 43;
BLCS**
See also BW 1, 3; CA 124; CANR 79; HR
3; RGAL 4

Locke, John 1632-1704 .... **LC 7, 35**
See also DLB 31, 101, 213, 252; RGEL 2;
WLIT 3

Locke-Elliott, Sumner
See Elliott, Sumner Locke

Lockhart, John Gibson 1794-1854 .. **NCLC 6**
See also DLB 110, 116, 144

Lockridge, Ross (Franklin), Jr.
1914-1948 .... **TCLC 111**
See also CA 145; CANR 79; DLB 143;
DLBY 1980; RGAL 4; RHW

Lockwood, Robert
See Johnson, Robert

Lodge, David (John) 1935- .... **CLC 36, 141**
See also BEST 90:1; BRWS 4; CA 17-20R;
CANR 19, 53, 92; CN 7; CPW; DAM
POP; DLB 14, 194; INT CANR-19;
MTCW 1, 2

Lodge, Thomas 1558-1625 .... **LC 41**
See also DLB 172; RGEL 2

Loewinsohn, Ron(ald William)
1937- .... **CLC 52**
See also CA 25-28R; CANR 71

Logan, Jake
See Smith, Martin Cruz

Logan, John (Burton) 1923-1987 .... **CLC 5**
See also CA 77-80; CANR 45; DLB 5

Lo Kuan-chung 1330(?)-1400(?) .... **LC 12**

Lombard, Nap
See Johnson, Pamela Hansford

Lomotey (editor), Kofi .... **CLC 70**

London, Jack 1876-1916 ..... **TCLC 9, 15, 39;
SSC 4, 49; WLC**
See also London, John Griffith
See also AAYA 13; AITN 2; AMW; BPFB
2; BYA 4, 13; CDALB 1865-1917; DLB
8, 12, 78, 212; EXPS; LAIT 3; NFS 8;
RGAL 4; RGSF 2; SATA 18; SFW 4;
SSFS 7; TCWW 2; TUS; WYA; YAW

London, John Griffith 1876-1916
See London, Jack
See also CA 119; CANR 73; DA; DAB;
DAC; DAM MST, NOV; JRDA; MAI-
CYA 1, 2; MTCW 1, 2

Long, Emmett
See Leonard, Elmore (John, Jr.)

Longbaugh, Harry
See Goldman, William (W.)

Longfellow, Henry Wadsworth
1807-1882 .... **NCLC 2, 45, 101, 103; PC
30; WLCS**
See also AMW; CDALB 1640-1865; DA;
DAB; DAC; DAM MST, POET; DLB 1,
59, 235; EXPP; PAB; PFS 7; RGAL 4;
SATA 19; TUS; WP

Longinus c. 1st cent. - .... **CMLC 27**
See also AW 2; DLB 176

Longley, Michael 1939- .... **CLC 29**
See also BRWS 8; CA 102; CP 7; DLB 40

Longus fl. c. 2nd cent. - .... **CMLC 7**

Longway, A. Hugh
See Lang, Andrew

Lonnrot, Elias 1802-1884 .... **NCLC 53**
See also EFS 1

Lonsdale, Roger ed. .... **CLC 65**

Lopate, Phillip 1943- .... **CLC 29**
See also CA 97-100; CANR 88; DLBY
1980; INT 97-100

Lopez, Barry (Holstun) 1945- .... **CLC 70**
See also AAYA 9; ANW; CA 65-68; CANR
7, 23, 47, 68, 92; DLB 256; INT CANR-7,
-23; MTCW 1; RGAL 4; SATA 67

Lopez Portillo (y Pacheco), Jose
1920- .... **CLC 46**
See also CA 129; HW 1

Lopez y Fuentes, Gregorio
1897(?)-1966 .... **CLC 32**
See also CA 131; HW 1

Lorca, Federico Garcia
See Garcia Lorca, Federico
See also DFS 4; EW 11; RGWL 2, 3; WP

Lord, Bette Bao 1938- .... **CLC 23; AAL**
See also BEST 90:3; BPFB 2; CA 107;
CANR 41, 79; INT CA-107; SATA 58

Lord Auch
See Bataille, Georges

Lord Brooke
See Greville, Fulke

Lord Byron
See Byron, George Gordon (Noel)

Lorde, Audre (Geraldine)
1934-1992 .. **CLC 18, 71; BLC 2; PC 12**
See also Domini, Rey
See also AFAW 1, 2; BW 1, 3; CA 25-28R;
CANR 16, 26, 46, 82; DAM MULT,
POET; DLB 41; FW; MTCW 1, 2; RGAL
4

Lord Houghton
See Milnes, Richard Monckton

Lord Jeffrey
See Jeffrey, Francis

Loreaux, Nichol .... **CLC 65**

Lorenzini, Carlo 1826-1890
See Collodi, Carlo
See also MAICYA 1, 2; SATA 29, 100

Lorenzo, Heberto Padilla
See Padilla (Lorenzo), Heberto

Loris
See Hofmannsthal, Hugo von

Loti, Pierre .... **TCLC 11**
See also Viaud, (Louis Marie) Julien
See also DLB 123; GFL 1789 to the Present

Lou, Henri
See Andreas-Salome, Lou

Louie, David Wong 1954- .... **CLC 70**
See also CA 139

Louis, Father M.
See Merton, Thomas (James)

Lovecraft, H(oward) P(hillips)
1890-1937 .... **TCLC 4, 22; SSC 3, 52**
See also AAYA 14; BPFB 2; CA 133;
CANR 106; DAM POP; HGG; MTCW 1,
2; RGAL 4; SCFW; SFW 4; SUFW

Lovelace, Earl 1935- .... **CLC 51**
See also BW 2; CA 77-80; CANR 41, 72;
CD 5; CDWLB 3; CN 7; DLB 125;
MTCW 1

Lovelace, Richard 1618-1657 .... **LC 24**
See also BRW 2; DLB 131; EXPP; PAB;
RGEL 2

Lowell, Amy 1874-1925 ... **TCLC 1, 8; PC 13**
See also AMW; CA 151; DAM POET; DLB
54, 140; EXPP; MAWW; MTCW 2;
RGAL 4; TUS

Lowell, James Russell 1819-1891 ... **NCLC 2,
90**
See also AMWS 1; CDALB 1640-1865;
DLB 1, 11, 64, 79, 189, 235; RGAL 4

Lowell, Robert (Traill Spence, Jr.)
1917-1977 .... **CLC 1, 2, 3, 4, 5, 8, 9, 11,
15, 37, 124; PC 3; WLC**
See also AMW; CA 9-12R; CABS 2; CANR
26, 60; CDALBS; DA; DAB; DAC; DAM
MST, NOV; DLB 5, 169; MTCW 1, 2;
PAB; PFS 6, 7; RGAL 4; WP

Lowenthal, Michael (Francis)
1969- .... **CLC 119**
See also CA 150

Lowndes, Marie Adelaide (Belloc)
1868-1947 .... **TCLC 12**
See also CMW 4; DLB 70; RHW

Lowry, (Clarence) Malcolm
1909-1957 .... **TCLC 6, 40; SSC 31**
See also BPFB 2; BRWS 3; CA 131; CANR
62, 105; CDBLB 1945-1960; DLB 15;
MTCW 1, 2; RGAL 4

Lowry, Mina Gertrude 1882-1966
See Loy, Mina
See also CA 113

Loxsmith, John
See Brunner, John (Kilian Houston)

Loy, Mina .... **CLC 28; PC 16**
See also Lowry, Mina Gertrude
See also DAM POET; DLB 4, 54

Loyson-Bridet
See Schwob, Marcel (Mayer Andre)

Lucan 39-65 .... **CMLC 33**
See also AW 2; DLB 211; EFS 2; RGWL 2,
3

Lucas, Craig 1951- .... **CLC 64**
See also CA 137; CAD; CANR 71, 109;
CD 5; GLL 2

Lucas, E(dward) V(errall)
1868-1938 .... **TCLC 73**
See also CA 176; DLB 98, 149, 153; SATA
20

Lucas, George 1944- .... **CLC 16**
See also AAYA 1, 23; CA 77-80; CANR
30; SATA 56

Lucas, Hans
See Godard, Jean-Luc

Lucas, Victoria
See Plath, Sylvia

Lucian c. 125-c. 180 .... **CMLC 32**
See also AW 2; RGWL 2, 3

Lucretius c. 94B.C.-c. 49B.C. .... **CMLC 48**
See also AW 2; CDWLB 1; DLB 211; EFS
2; RGWL 2, 3

Ludlam, Charles 1943-1987 .... **CLC 46, 50**
See also CA 85-88; CAD; CANR 72, 86;
DLB 266

Ludlum, Robert 1927-2001 .... **CLC 22, 43**
See also AAYA 10; BEST 89:1, 90:3; BPFB
2; CA 33-36R; CANR 25, 41, 68, 105;
CMW 4; CPW; DAM NOV, POP; DLBY
1982; MSW; MTCW 1, 2

Ludwig, Ken .... **CLC 60**
See also CA 195; CAD

Ludwig, Otto 1813-1865 .... **NCLC 4**
See also DLB 129

Lugones, Leopoldo 1874-1938 ...... **TCLC 15;
HLCS 2**
See also CA 131; CANR 104; HW 1; LAW

Lu Hsun .... **TCLC 3; SSC 20**
See also Shu-Jen, Chou

Lukacs, George .... **CLC 24**
See also Lukacs, Gyorgy (Szegeny von)

Lukacs, Gyorgy (Szegeny von) 1885-1971
See Lukacs, George
See also CA 101; CANR 62; CDWLB 4;
DLB 215, 242; EW 10; MTCW 2

Luke, Peter (Ambrose Cyprian)
1919-1995 .... **CLC 38**
See also CA 81-84; CANR 72; CBD; CD 5; DLB 13

Lunar, Dennis
See Mungo, Raymond

Lurie, Alison 1926- .... **CLC 4, 5, 18, 39**
See also BPFB 2; CA 1-4R; CANR 2, 17, 50, 88; CN 7; DLB 2; MTCW 1; SATA 46, 112

Lustig, Arnost 1926- .... **CLC 56**
See also AAYA 3; CA 69-72; CANR 47, 102; CWW 2; DLB 232; SATA 56

Luther, Martin 1483-1546 .... **LC 9, 37**
See also CDWLB 2; DLB 179; EW 2; RGWL 2, 3

Luxemburg, Rosa 1870(?)-1919 ..... **TCLC 63**

Luzi, Mario 1914- .... **CLC 13**
See also CA 61-64; CANR 9, 70; CWW 2; DLB 128

L'vov, Arkady .... **CLC 59**

Lydgate, John c. 1370-1450(?) .... **LC 81**
See also BRW 1; DLB 146; RGEL 2

Lyly, John 1554(?)-1606 .... **LC 41; DC 7**
See also BRW 1; DAM DRAM; DLB 62, 167; RGEL 2

L'Ymagier
See Gourmont, Remy(-Marie-Charles) de

Lynch, B. Suarez
See Borges, Jorge Luis

Lynch, David (Keith) 1946- ...... **CLC 66, 162**
See also CA 129; CANR 111

Lynch, James
See Andreyev, Leonid (Nikolaevich)

Lyndsay, Sir David 1485-1555 .... **LC 20**
See also RGEL 2

Lynn, Kenneth S(chuyler)
1923-2001 .... **CLC 50**
See also CA 1-4R; CANR 3, 27, 65

Lynx
See West, Rebecca

Lyons, Marcus
See Blish, James (Benjamin)

Lyotard, Jean-Francois
1924-1998 .... **TCLC 103**
See also DLB 242

Lyre, Pinchbeck
See Sassoon, Siegfried (Lorraine)

Lytle, Andrew (Nelson) 1902-1995 ... **CLC 22**
See also CA 9-12R; CANR 70; CN 7; CSW; DLB 6; DLBY 1995; RGAL 4; RHW

Lyttelton, George 1709-1773 .... **LC 10**
See also RGEL 2

Lytton of Knebworth, Baron
See Bulwer-Lytton, Edward (George Earle Lytton)

Maas, Peter 1929-2001 .... **CLC 29**
See also CA 93-96; INT CA-93-96; MTCW 2

Macaulay, Catherine 1731-1791 .... **LC 64**
See also DLB 104

Macaulay, (Emilie) Rose
1881(?)-1958 .... **TCLC 7, 44**
See also DLB 36; RGEL 2; RHW

Macaulay, Thomas Babington
1800-1859 .... **NCLC 42**
See also BRW 4; CDBLB 1832-1890; DLB 32, 55; RGEL 2

MacBeth, George (Mann)
1932-1992 .... **CLC 2, 5, 9**
See also CA 25-28R; CANR 61, 66; DLB 40; MTCW 1; PFS 8; SATA 4; SATA-Obit 70

MacCaig, Norman (Alexander)
1910-1996 .... **CLC 36**
See also BRWS 6; CA 9-12R; CANR 3, 34; CP 7; DAB; DAM POET; DLB 27; RGEL 2

MacCarthy, Sir (Charles Otto) Desmond
1877-1952 .... **TCLC 36**
See also CA 167

MacDiarmid, Hugh .... **CLC 2, 4, 11, 19, 63; PC 9**
See also Grieve, C(hristopher) M(urray)
See also CDBLB 1945-1960; DLB 20; RGEL 2

MacDonald, Anson
See Heinlein, Robert A(nson)

Macdonald, Cynthia 1928- .... **CLC 13, 19**
See also CA 49-52; CANR 4, 44; DLB 105

MacDonald, George 1824-1905 .... **TCLC 9, 113**
See also BYA 5; CA 137; CANR 80; CLR 67; DLB 18, 163, 178; FANT; MAICYA 1, 2; RGEL 2; SATA 33, 100; SFW 4; SUFW; WCH

Macdonald, John
See Millar, Kenneth

MacDonald, John D(ann)
1916-1986 .... **CLC 3, 27, 44**
See also BPFB 2; CA 1-4R; CANR 1, 19, 60; CMW 4; CPW; DAM NOV, POP; DLB 8; DLBY 1986; MSW; MTCW 1, 2; SFW 4

Macdonald, John Ross
See Millar, Kenneth

Macdonald, Ross ...... **CLC 1, 2, 3, 14, 34, 41**
See also Millar, Kenneth
See also AMWS 4; BPFB 2; DLBD 6; MSW; RGAL 4

MacDougal, John
See Blish, James (Benjamin)

MacDougal, John
See Blish, James (Benjamin)

MacDowell, John
See Parks, Tim(othy Harold)

MacEwen, Gwendolyn (Margaret)
1941-1987 .... **CLC 13, 55**
See also CA 9-12R; CANR 7, 22; DLB 53, 251; SATA 50; SATA-Obit 55

Macha, Karel Hynek 1810-1846 .... **NCLC 46**

Machado (y Ruiz), Antonio
1875-1939 .... **TCLC 3**
See also CA 174; DLB 108; EW 9; HW 2; RGWL 2, 3

Machado de Assis, Joaquim Maria
1839-1908 ...... **TCLC 10; BLC 2; HLCS 2; SSC 24**
See also CA 153; CANR 91; LAW; RGSF 2; RGWL 2, 3; TWA; WLIT 1

Machen, Arthur .... **TCLC 4; SSC 20**
See also Jones, Arthur Llewellyn
See also CA 179; DLB 156, 178; RGEL 2; SUFW 1

Machiavelli, Niccolo 1469-1527 ..... **LC 8, 36; DC 16; WLCS**
See also DA; DAB; DAC; DAM MST; EW 2; LAIT 1; NFS 9; RGWL 2, 3; TWA

MacInnes, Colin 1914-1976 .... **CLC 4, 23**
See also CA 69-72; CANR 21; DLB 14; MTCW 1, 2; RGEL 2; RHW

MacInnes, Helen (Clark)
1907-1985 .... **CLC 27, 39**
See also BPFB 2; CA 1-4R; CANR 1, 28, 58; CMW 4; CPW; DAM POP; DLB 87; MSW; MTCW 1, 2; SATA 22; SATA-Obit 44

Mackay, Mary 1855-1924
See Corelli, Marie
See also CA 177; FANT; RHW

Mackenzie, Compton (Edward Montague)
1883-1972 .... **CLC 18**
See also CA 21-22; CAP 2; DLB 34, 100; RGEL 2; TCLC 116

Mackenzie, Henry 1745-1831 .... **NCLC 41**
See also DLB 39; RGEL 2

Mackintosh, Elizabeth 1896(?)-1952
See Tey, Josephine
See also CMW 4

MacLaren, James
See Grieve, C(hristopher) M(urray)

Mac Laverty, Bernard 1942- .... **CLC 31**
See also CA 118; CANR 43, 88; CN 7; DLB 267; INT CA-118; RGSF 2

MacLean, Alistair (Stuart)
1922(?)-1987 .... **CLC 3, 13, 50, 63**
See also CA 57-60; CANR 28, 61; CMW 4; CPW; DAM POP; MTCW 1; SATA 23; SATA-Obit 50; TCWW 2

Maclean, Norman (Fitzroy)
1902-1990 .... **CLC 78; SSC 13**
See also CA 102; CANR 49; CPW; DAM POP; DLB 206; TCWW 2

MacLeish, Archibald 1892-1982 ... **CLC 3, 8, 14, 68**
See also AMW; CA 9-12R; CAD; CANR 33, 63; CDALBS; DAM POET; DFS 15; DLB 4, 7, 45; DLBY 1982; EXPP; MTCW 1, 2; PAB; PFS 5; RGAL 4; TUS

MacLennan, (John) Hugh
1907-1990 .... **CLC 2, 14, 92**
See also CA 5-8R; CANR 33; DAC; DAM MST; DLB 68; MTCW 1, 2; RGEL 2; TWA

Macleod, Fiona
See Sharp, William
See also RGEL 2; SUFW

MacNeice, (Frederick) Louis
1907-1963 .... **CLC 1, 4, 10, 53**
See also BRW 7; CA 85-88; CANR 61; DAB; DAM POET; DLB 10, 20; MTCW 1, 2; RGEL 2

MacNeill, Dand
See Fraser, George MacDonald

Macpherson, James 1736-1796 .... **LC 29**
See also Ossian
See also BRWS 8; DLB 109; RGEL 2

Macpherson, (Jean) Jay 1931- .... **CLC 14**
See also CA 5-8R; CANR 90; CP 7; CWP; DLB 53

Macrobius fl. 430- .... **CMLC 48**

MacShane, Frank 1927-1999 .... **CLC 39**
See also CA 9-12R; CANR 3, 33; DLB 111

Macumber, Mari
See Sandoz, Mari(e Susette)

Madach, Imre 1823-1864 .... **NCLC 19**

Madden, (Jerry) David 1933- .... **CLC 5, 15**
See also CA 1-4R; CAAS 3; CANR 4, 45; CN 7; CSW; DLB 6; MTCW 1

Maddern, Al(an)
See Ellison, Harlan (Jay)

Madhubuti, Haki R. 1942- . **CLC 6, 73; BLC 2; PC 5**
See also Lee, Don L.
See also BW 2, 3; CA 73-76; CANR 24, 51, 73; CP 7; CSW; DAM MULT, POET; DLB 5, 41; DLBD 8; MTCW 2; RGAL 4

Maepenn, Hugh
See Kuttner, Henry

Maepenn, K. H.
See Kuttner, Henry

Maeterlinck, Maurice 1862-1949 ..... **TCLC 3**
See also CA 136; CANR 80; DAM DRAM; DLB 192; EW 8; GFL 1789 to the Present; RGWL 2, 3; SATA 66; TWA

Maginn, William 1794-1842 .... **NCLC 8**
See also DLB 110, 159

Mahapatra, Jayanta 1928- .... **CLC 33**
See also CA 73-76; CAAS 9; CANR 15, 33, 66, 87; CP 7; DAM MULT

Mahfouz, Naguib (Abdel Aziz Al-Sabilgi)
1911(?)- .... **CLC 153**
See also Mahfuz, Najib (Abdel Aziz al-Sabilgi)
See also BEST 89:2; CA 128; CANR 55, 101; CWW 2; DAM NOV; MTCW 1, 2; RGWL 2, 3; SSFS 9

Mahfuz, Najib (Abdel Aziz al-Sabilgi)
.... **CLC 52, 55**
See also Mahfouz, Naguib (Abdel Aziz Al-Sabilgi)
See also AFW; DLBY 1988; RGSF 2; WLIT 2

Mahon, Derek 1941- .... **CLC 27**
See also BRWS 6; CA 128; CANR 88; CP 7; DLB 40

Maiakovskii, Vladimir
See Mayakovski, Vladimir (Vladimirovich)
See also IDTP; RGWL 2, 3

Mailer, Norman 1923- ... **CLC 1, 2, 3, 4, 5, 8, 11, 14, 28, 39, 74, 111**
See also AAYA 31; AITN 2; AMW; BPFB 2; CA 9-12R; CABS 1; CANR 28, 74, 77; CDALB 1968-1988; CN 7; CPW; DA; DAB; DAC; DAM MST, NOV, POP; DLB 2, 16, 28, 185; DLBD 3; DLBY 1980, 1983; MTCW 1, 2; NFS 10; RGAL 4; TUS

Maillet, Antonine 1929- .... **CLC 54, 118**
See also CA 120; CANR 46, 74, 77; CCA 1; CWW 2; DAC; DLB 60; INT 120; MTCW 2

Mais, Roger 1905-1955 .... **TCLC 8**
See also BW 1, 3; CA 124; CANR 82; CDWLB 3; DLB 125; MTCW 1; RGEL 2

Maistre, Joseph 1753-1821 .... **NCLC 37**
See also GFL 1789 to the Present

Maitland, Frederic William
1850-1906 .... **TCLC 65**

Maitland, Sara (Louise) 1950- .... **CLC 49**
See also CA 69-72; CANR 13, 59; DLB 271; FW

Major, Clarence 1936- . **CLC 3, 19, 48; BLC 2**
See also AFAW 2; BW 2, 3; CA 21-24R; CAAS 6; CANR 13, 25, 53, 82; CN 7; CP 7; CSW; DAM MULT; DLB 33; MSW

Major, Kevin (Gerald) 1949- .... **CLC 26**
See also AAYA 16; CA 97-100; CANR 21, 38, 112; CLR 11; DAC; DLB 60; INT CANR-21; JRDA; MAICYA 1, 2; MAICYAS 1; SATA 32, 82, 134; WYA; YAW

Maki, James
See Ozu, Yasujiro

Malabaila, Damiano
See Levi, Primo

Malamud, Bernard 1914-1986 .. **CLC 1, 2, 3, 5, 8, 9, 11, 18, 27, 44, 78, 85; SSC 15; WLC**
See also AAYA 16; AMWS 1; BPFB 2; CA 5-8R; CABS 1; CANR 28, 62; CDALB 1941-1968; CPW; DA; DAB; DAC; DAM MST, NOV, POP; DLB 2, 28, 152; DLBY 1980, 1986; EXPS; LAIT 4; MTCW 1, 2; NFS 4, 9; RGAL 4; RGSF 2; SSFS 8, 13; TCLC 129; TUS

Malan, Herman
See Bosman, Herman Charles; Bosman, Herman Charles

Malaparte, Curzio 1898-1957 .... **TCLC 52**
See also DLB 264

Malcolm, Dan
See Silverberg, Robert

Malcolm X .... **CLC 82, 117; BLC 2; WLCS**
See also Little, Malcolm
See also LAIT 5

Malherbe, Francois de 1555-1628 .... **LC 5**
See also GFL Beginnings to 1789

Mallarme, Stephane 1842-1898 ...... **NCLC 4, 41; PC 4**
See also DAM POET; DLB 217; EW 7; GFL 1789 to the Present; RGWL 2, 3; TWA

Mallet-Joris, Francoise 1930- .... **CLC 11**
See also CA 65-68; CANR 17; DLB 83; GFL 1789 to the Present

Malley, Ern
See McAuley, James Phillip

Mallowan, Agatha Christie
See Christie, Agatha (Mary Clarissa)

Maloff, Saul 1922- .... **CLC 5**
See also CA 33-36R

Malone, Louis
See MacNeice, (Frederick) Louis

Malone, Michael (Christopher)
1942- .... **CLC 43**
See also CA 77-80; CANR 14, 32, 57

Malory, Sir Thomas 1410(?)-1471(?) . **LC 11; WLCS**
See also BRW 1; BRWR 2; CDBLB Before 1660; DA; DAB; DAC; DAM MST; DLB 146; EFS 2; RGEL 2; SATA 59; SATA-Brief 33; TEA; WLIT 3

Malouf, (George Joseph) David
1934- .... **CLC 28, 86**
See also CA 124; CANR 50, 76; CN 7; CP 7; MTCW 2

Malraux, (Georges-)Andre
1901-1976 .... **CLC 1, 4, 9, 13, 15, 57**
See also BPFB 2; CA 21-22; CANR 34, 58; CAP 2; DAM NOV; DLB 72; EW 12; GFL 1789 to the Present; MTCW 1, 2; RGWL 2, 3; TWA

Malzberg, Barry N(athaniel) 1939- ... **CLC 7**
See also CA 61-64; CAAS 4; CANR 16; CMW 4; DLB 8; SFW 4

Mamet, David (Alan) 1947- .. **CLC 9, 15, 34, 46, 91, 166; DC 4**
See also AAYA 3; CA 81-84; CABS 3; CANR 15, 41, 67, 72; CD 5; DAM DRAM; DFS 15; DLB 7; IDFW 4; MTCW 1, 2; RGAL 4

Mamoulian, Rouben (Zachary)
1897-1987 .... **CLC 16**
See also CA 25-28R; CANR 85

Mandelshtam, Osip
See Mandelstam, Osip (Emilievich)
See also EW 10; RGWL 2, 3

Mandelstam, Osip (Emilievich)
1891(?)-1943(?) .... **TCLC 2, 6; PC 14**
See also Mandelshtam, Osip
See also CA 150; MTCW 2; TWA

Mander, (Mary) Jane 1877-1949 ... **TCLC 31**
See also CA 162; RGEL 2

Mandeville, Bernard 1670-1733 .... **LC 82**
See also DLB 101

Mandeville, Sir John fl. 1350- .... **CMLC 19**
See also DLB 146

Mandiargues, Andre Pieyre de .... **CLC 41**
See also Pieyre de Mandiargues, Andre
See also DLB 83

Mandrake, Ethel Belle
See Thurman, Wallace (Henry)

Mangan, James Clarence
1803-1849 .... **NCLC 27**
See also RGEL 2

Maniere, J.-E.
See Giraudoux, Jean(-Hippolyte)

Mankiewicz, Herman (Jacob)
1897-1953 .... **TCLC 85**
See also CA 169; DLB 26; IDFW 3, 4

Manley, (Mary) Delariviere
1672(?)-1724 .... **LC 1, 42**
See also DLB 39, 80; RGEL 2

Mann, Abel
See Creasey, John

Mann, Emily 1952- .... **DC 7**
See also CA 130; CAD; CANR 55; CD 5; CWD; DLB 266

Mann, (Luiz) Heinrich 1871-1950 ... **TCLC 9**
See also CA 164, 181; DLB 66, 118; EW 8; RGWL 2, 3

Mann, (Paul) Thomas 1875-1955 ... **TCLC 2, 8, 14, 21, 35, 44, 60; SSC 5; WLC**
See also BPFB 2; CA 128; CDWLB 2; DA; DAB; DAC; DAM MST, NOV; DLB 66; EW 9; GLL 1; MTCW 1, 2; RGSF 2; RGWL 2, 3; SSFS 4, 9; TWA

Mannheim, Karl 1893-1947 .... **TCLC 65**
See also CA 204

Manning, David
See Faust, Frederick (Schiller)
See also TCWW 2

Manning, Frederic 1887(?)-1935 ... **TCLC 25**
See also DLB 260

Manning, Olivia 1915-1980 .... **CLC 5, 19**
See also CA 5-8R; CANR 29; FW; MTCW 1; RGEL 2

Mano, D. Keith 1942- .... **CLC 2, 10**
See also CA 25-28R; CAAS 6; CANR 26, 57; DLB 6

Mansfield, Katherine ... **TCLC 2, 8, 39; SSC 9, 23, 38; WLC**
See also Beauchamp, Kathleen Mansfield
See also BPFB 2; BRW 7; DAB; DLB 162; EXPS; FW; GLL 1; RGEL 2; RGSF 2; SSFS 2, 8, 10, 11

Manso, Peter 1940- .... **CLC 39**
See also CA 29-32R; CANR 44

Mantecon, Juan Jimenez
See Jimenez (Mantecon), Juan Ramon

Mantel, Hilary (Mary) 1952- .... **CLC 144**
See also CA 125; CANR 54, 101; CN 7; DLB 271; RHW

Manton, Peter
See Creasey, John

Man Without a Spleen, A
See Chekhov, Anton (Pavlovich)

Manzoni, Alessandro 1785-1873 ... **NCLC 29, 98**
See also EW 5; RGWL 2, 3; TWA

Map, Walter 1140-1209 .... **CMLC 32**

Mapu, Abraham (ben Jekutiel)
1808-1867 .... **NCLC 18**

Mara, Sally
See Queneau, Raymond

Marat, Jean Paul 1743-1793 .... **LC 10**

Marcel, Gabriel Honore 1889-1973 . **CLC 15**
See also CA 102; MTCW 1, 2

March, William 1893-1954 .... **TCLC 96**

Marchbanks, Samuel
See Davies, (William) Robertson
See also CCA 1

Marchi, Giacomo
See Bassani, Giorgio

Marcus Aurelius
See Aurelius, Marcus
See also AW 2

Marguerite
See de Navarre, Marguerite

Marguerite d'Angouleme
See de Navarre, Marguerite
See also GFL Beginnings to 1789

Marguerite de Navarre
See de Navarre, Marguerite
See also RGWL 2, 3

Margulies, Donald 1954- .... **CLC 76**
See also CA 200; DFS 13; DLB 228

Marie de France c. 12th cent. - ...... **CMLC 8; PC 22**
See also DLB 208; FW; RGWL 2, 3

Marie de l'Incarnation 1599-1672 ...... **LC 10**

Marier, Captain Victor
See Griffith, D(avid Lewelyn) W(ark)

Mariner, Scott
See Pohl, Frederik
Marinetti, Filippo Tommaso
1876-1944 .... **TCLC 10**
See also DLB 114, 264; EW 9
Marivaux, Pierre Carlet de Chamblain de
1688-1763 .... **LC 4; DC 7**
See also GFL Beginnings to 1789; RGWL 2, 3; TWA
Markandaya, Kamala .... **CLC 8, 38**
See also Taylor, Kamala (Purnaiya)
See also BYA 13; CN 7
Markfield, Wallace 1926- .... **CLC 8**
See also CA 69-72; CAAS 3; CN 7; DLB 2, 28
Markham, Edwin 1852-1940 .... **TCLC 47**
See also CA 160; DLB 54, 186; RGAL 4
Markham, Robert
See Amis, Kingsley (William)
Marks, J
See Highwater, Jamake (Mamake)
Marks, J.
See Highwater, Jamake (Mamake)
Marks-Highwater, J
See Highwater, Jamake (Mamake)
Marks-Highwater, J.
See Highwater, Jamake (Mamake)
Markson, David M(errill) 1927- .... **CLC 67**
See also CA 49-52; CANR 1, 91; CN 7
Marley, Bob .... **CLC 17**
See also Marley, Robert Nesta
Marley, Robert Nesta 1945-1981
See Marley, Bob
See also CA 107
Marlowe, Christopher 1564-1593 ...... **LC 22, 47; DC 1; WLC**
See also BRW 1; BRWR 1; CDBLB Before 1660; DA; DAB; DAC; DAM DRAM, MST; DFS 1, 5, 13; DLB 62; EXPP; RGEL 2; TEA; WLIT 3
Marlowe, Stephen 1928- .... **CLC 70**
See also Queen, Ellery
See also CA 13-16R; CANR 6, 55; CMW 4; SFW 4
Marmontel, Jean-Francois 1723-1799 .. **LC 2**
Maron, Monika 1941- .... **CLC 165**
See also CA 201
Marquand, John P(hillips)
1893-1960 .... **CLC 2, 10**
See also AMW; BPFB 2; CA 85-88; CANR 73; CMW 4; DLB 9, 102; MTCW 2; RGAL 4
Marques, Rene 1919-1979 .. **CLC 96; HLC 2**
See also CA 97-100; CANR 78; DAM MULT; DLB 113; HW 1, 2; LAW; RGSF 2
Marquez, Gabriel (Jose) Garcia
See Garcia Marquez, Gabriel (Jose)
Marquis, Don(ald Robert Perry)
1878-1937 .... **TCLC 7**
See also CA 166; DLB 11, 25; RGAL 4
Marquis de Sade
See Sade, Donatien Alphonse Francois
Marric, J. J.
See Creasey, John
See also MSW
Marryat, Frederick 1792-1848 .... **NCLC 3**
See also DLB 21, 163; RGEL 2; WCH
Marsden, James
See Creasey, John
Marsh, Edward 1872-1953 .... **TCLC 99**
Marsh, (Edith) Ngaio 1899-1982 .. **CLC 7, 53**
See also CA 9-12R; CANR 6, 58; CMW 4; CPW; DAM POP; DLB 77; MSW; MTCW 1, 2; RGEL 2; TEA
Marshall, Garry 1934- .... **CLC 17**
See also AAYA 3; CA 111; SATA 60

Marshall, Paule 1929- .. **CLC 27, 72; BLC 3; SSC 3**
See also AFAW 1, 2; AMWS 11; BPFB 2; BW 2, 3; CA 77-80; CANR 25, 73; CN 7; DAM MULT; DLB 33, 157, 227; MTCW 1, 2; RGAL 4; SSFS 15
Marshallik
See Zangwill, Israel
Marsten, Richard
See Hunter, Evan
Marston, John 1576-1634 .... **LC 33**
See also BRW 2; DAM DRAM; DLB 58, 172; RGEL 2
Martha, Henry
See Harris, Mark
Marti (y Perez), Jose (Julian)
1853-1895 .... **NCLC 63; HLC 2**
See also DAM MULT; HW 2; LAW; RGWL 2, 3; WLIT 1
Martial c. 40-c. 104 .... **CMLC 35; PC 10**
See also AW 2; CDWLB 1; DLB 211; RGWL 2, 3
Martin, Ken
See Hubbard, L(afayette) Ron(ald)
Martin, Richard
See Creasey, John
Martin, Steve 1945- .... **CLC 30**
See also CA 97-100; CANR 30, 100; MTCW 1
Martin, Valerie 1948- .... **CLC 89**
See also BEST 90:2; CA 85-88; CANR 49, 89
Martin, Violet Florence
1862-1915 .... **TCLC 51; SSC 56**
Martin, Webber
See Silverberg, Robert
Martindale, Patrick Victor
See White, Patrick (Victor Martindale)
Martin du Gard, Roger
1881-1958 .... **TCLC 24**
See also CANR 94; DLB 65; GFL 1789 to the Present; RGWL 2, 3
Martineau, Harriet 1802-1876 .... **NCLC 26**
See also DLB 21, 55, 159, 163, 166, 190; FW; RGEL 2; YABC 2
Martines, Julia
See O'Faolain, Julia
Martinez, Enrique Gonzalez
See Gonzalez Martinez, Enrique
Martinez, Jacinto Benavente y
See Benavente (y Martinez), Jacinto
Martinez de la Rosa, Francisco de Paula
1787-1862 .... **NCLC 102**
See also TWA
Martinez Ruiz, Jose 1873-1967
See Azorin; Ruiz, Jose Martinez
See also CA 93-96; HW 1
Martinez Sierra, Gregorio
1881-1947 .... **TCLC 6**
Martinez Sierra, Maria (de la O'LeJarraga)
1874-1974 .... **TCLC 6**
Martinsen, Martin
See Follett, Ken(neth Martin)
Martinson, Harry (Edmund)
1904-1978 .... **CLC 14**
See also CA 77-80; CANR 34; DLB 259
Martyn, Edward 1859-1923 .... **TCLC 121**
See also CA 179; DLB 10; RGEL 2
Marut, Ret
See Traven, B.
Marut, Robert
See Traven, B.
Marvell, Andrew 1621-1678 .... **LC 4, 43; PC 10; WLC**
See also BRW 2; BRWR 2; CDBLB 1660-1789; DA; DAB; DAC; DAM MST, POET; DLB 131; EXPP; PFS 5; RGEL 2; TEA; WP

Marx, Karl (Heinrich)
1818-1883 .... **NCLC 17, 114**
See also DLB 129; TWA
Masaoka, Shiki -1902 .... **TCLC 18**
See also Masaoka, Tsunenori
See also RGWL 3
Masaoka, Tsunenori 1867-1902
See Masaoka, Shiki
See also CA 191; TWA
Masefield, John (Edward)
1878-1967 .... **CLC 11, 47**
See also CA 19-20; CANR 33; CAP 2; CD-BLB 1890-1914; DAM POET; DLB 10, 19, 153, 160; EXPP; FANT; MTCW 1, 2; PFS 5; RGEL 2; SATA 19
Maso, Carole 19(?)- .... **CLC 44**
See also CA 170; GLL 2; RGAL 4
Mason, Bobbie Ann 1940- ... **CLC 28, 43, 82, 154; SSC 4**
See also AAYA 5, 42; AMWS 8; BPFB 2; CA 53-56; CANR 11, 31, 58, 83; CDALBS; CN 7; CSW; DLB 173; DLBY 1987; EXPS; INT CANR-31; MTCW 1, 2; NFS 4; RGAL 4; RGSF 2; SSFS 3,8; YAW
Mason, Ernst
See Pohl, Frederik
Mason, Hunni B.
See Sternheim, (William Adolf) Carl
Mason, Lee W.
See Malzberg, Barry N(athaniel)
Mason, Nick 1945- .... **CLC 35**
Mason, Tally
See Derleth, August (William)
Mass, Anna .... **CLC 59**
Mass, William
See Gibson, William
Massinger, Philip 1583-1640 .... **LC 70**
See also DLB 58; RGEL 2
Master Lao
See Lao Tzu
Masters, Edgar Lee 1868-1950 .... **TCLC 2, 25; PC 1, 36; WLCS**
See also AMWS 1; CA 133; CDALB 1865-1917; DA; DAC; DAM MST, POET; DLB 54; EXPP; MTCW 1, 2; RGAL 4; TUS; WP
Masters, Hilary 1928- .... **CLC 48**
See also CA 25-28R; CANR 13, 47, 97; CN 7; DLB 244
Mastrosimone, William 19(?)- .... **CLC 36**
See also CA 186; CAD; CD 5
Mathe, Albert
See Camus, Albert
Mather, Cotton 1663-1728 .... **LC 38**
See also AMWS 2; CDALB 1640-1865; DLB 24, 30, 140; RGAL 4; TUS
Mather, Increase 1639-1723 .... **LC 38**
See also DLB 24
Matheson, Richard (Burton) 1926- .. **CLC 37**
See also AAYA 31; CA 97-100; CANR 88, 99; DLB 8, 44; HGG; INT 97-100; SCFW 2; SFW 4; SUFW 2
Mathews, Harry 1930- .... **CLC 6, 52**
See also CA 21-24R; CAAS 6; CANR 18, 40, 98; CN 7
Mathews, John Joseph 1894-1979 .... **CLC 84**
See also CA 19-20; CANR 45; CAP 2; DAM MULT; DLB 175; NNAL
Mathias, Roland (Glyn) 1915- .... **CLC 45**
See also CA 97-100; CANR 19, 41; CP 7; DLB 27
Matsuo Basho 1644-1694 .... **LC 62; PC 3**
See also Basho, Matsuo
See also DAM POET; PFS 2, 7
Mattheson, Rodney
See Creasey, John

Matthews, (James) Brander
1852-1929 .... **TCLC 95**
See also DLB 71, 78; DLBD 13

Matthews, Greg 1949- .... **CLC 45**
See also CA 135

Matthews, William (Procter III)
1942-1997 .... **CLC 40**
See also AMWS 9; CA 29-32R; CAAS 18; CANR 12, 57; CP 7; DLB 5

Matthias, John (Edward) 1941- .... **CLC 9**
See also CA 33-36R; CANR 56; CP 7

Matthiessen, F(rancis) O(tto)
1902-1950 .... **TCLC 100**
See also CA 185; DLB 63

Matthiessen, Peter 1927- ... **CLC 5, 7, 11, 32, 64**
See also AAYA 6, 40; AMWS 5; ANW; BEST 90:4; BPFB 2; CA 9-12R; CANR 21, 50, 73, 100; CN 7; DAM NOV; DLB 6, 173; MTCW 1, 2; SATA 27

Maturin, Charles Robert
1780(?)-1824 .... **NCLC 6**
See also BRWS 8; DLB 178; HGG; RGEL 2; SUFW

Matute (Ausejo), Ana Maria 1925- ... **CLC 11**
See also CA 89-92; MTCW 1; RGSF 2

Maugham, W. S.
See Maugham, W(illiam) Somerset

Maugham, W(illiam) Somerset
1874-1965 .. **CLC 1, 11, 15, 67, 93; SSC 8; WLC**
See also BPFB 2; BRW 6; CA 5-8R; CANR 40; CDBLB 1914-1945; CMW 4; DA; DAB; DAC; DAM DRAM, MST, NOV; DLB 10, 36, 77, 100, 162, 195; LAIT 3; MTCW 1, 2; RGEL 2; RGSF 2; SATA 54

Maugham, William Somerset
See Maugham, W(illiam) Somerset

Maupassant, (Henri Rene Albert) Guy de
1850-1893 .... **NCLC 1, 42, 83; SSC 1; WLC**
See also BYA 14; DA; DAB; DAC; DAM MST; DLB 123; EW 7; EXPS; GFL 1789 to the Present; LAIT 2; RGSF 2; RGWL 2, 3; SSFS 4; SUFW; TWA

Maupin, Armistead (Jones, Jr.)
1944- .... **CLC 95**
See also CA 130; CANR 58, 101; CPW; DAM POP; GLL 1; INT 130; MTCW 2

Maurhut, Richard
See Traven, B.

Mauriac, Claude 1914-1996 .... **CLC 9**
See also CA 89-92; CWW 2; DLB 83; GFL 1789 to the Present

Mauriac, Francois (Charles)
1885-1970 .... **CLC 4, 9, 56; SSC 24**
See also CA 25-28; CAP 2; DLB 65; EW 10; GFL 1789 to the Present; MTCW 1, 2; RGWL 2, 3; TWA

Mavor, Osborne Henry 1888-1951
See Bridie, James

Maxwell, William (Keepers, Jr.)
1908-2000 .... **CLC 19**
See also AMWS 8; CA 93-96; CANR 54, 95; CN 7; DLB 218; DLBY 1980; INT CA-93-96; SATA-Obit 128

May, Elaine 1932- .... **CLC 16**
See also CA 142; CAD; CWD; DLB 44

Mayakovski, Vladimir (Vladimirovich)
1893-1930 .... **TCLC 4, 18**
See also Maiakovskii, Vladimir; Mayakovsky, Vladimir
See also CA 158; MTCW 2; SFW 4; TWA

Mayakovsky, Vladimir
See Mayakovski, Vladimir (Vladimirovich)
See also EW 11; WP

Mayhew, Henry 1812-1887 .... **NCLC 31**
See also DLB 18, 55, 190

Mayle, Peter 1939(?)- .... **CLC 89**
See also CA 139; CANR 64, 109

Maynard, Joyce 1953- .... **CLC 23**
See also CA 129; CANR 64

Mayne, William (James Carter)
1928- .... **CLC 12**
See also AAYA 20; CA 9-12R; CANR 37, 80, 100; CLR 25; FANT; JRDA; MAI-CYA 1, 2; MAICYAS 1; SAAS 11; SATA 6, 68, 122; SUFW 2; YAW

Mayo, Jim
See L'Amour, Louis (Dearborn)
See also TCWW 2

Maysles, Albert 1926- .... **CLC 16**
See also CA 29-32R

Maysles, David 1932-1987 .... **CLC 16**
See also CA 191

Mazer, Norma Fox 1931- .... **CLC 26**
See also AAYA 5, 36; BYA 1, 8; CA 69-72; CANR 12, 32, 66; CLR 23; JRDA; MAI-CYA 1, 2; SAAS 1; SATA 24, 67, 105; WYA; YAW

Mazzini, Guiseppe 1805-1872 .... **NCLC 34**

McAlmon, Robert (Menzies)
1895-1956 .... **TCLC 97**
See also CA 168; DLB 4, 45; DLBD 15; GLL 1

McAuley, James Phillip 1917-1976 .. **CLC 45**
See also CA 97-100; DLB 260; RGEL 2

McBain, Ed
See Hunter, Evan
See also MSW

McBrien, William (Augustine)
1930- .... **CLC 44**
See also CA 107; CANR 90

McCabe, Patrick 1955- .... **CLC 133**
See also CA 130; CANR 50, 90; CN 7; DLB 194

McCaffrey, Anne (Inez) 1926- .... **CLC 17**
See also AAYA 6, 34; AITN 2; BEST 89:2; BPFB 2; BYA 5; CA 25-28R; CANR 15, 35, 55, 96; CLR 49; CPW; DAM NOV, POP; DLB 8; JRDA; MAICYA 1, 2; MTCW 1, 2; SAAS 11; SATA 8, 70, 116; SFW 4; SUFW 2; WYA; YAW

McCall, Nathan 1955(?)- .... **CLC 86**
See also BW 3; CA 146; CANR 88

McCann, Arthur
See Campbell, John W(ood, Jr.)

McCann, Edson
See Pohl, Frederik

McCarthy, Charles, Jr. 1933-
See McCarthy, Cormac
See also CANR 42, 69, 101; CN 7; CPW; CSW; DAM POP; MTCW 2

McCarthy, Cormac .... **CLC 4, 57, 59, 101**
See also McCarthy, Charles, Jr.
See also AAYA 41; AMWS 8; BPFB 2; CA 13-16R; CANR 10; DLB 6, 143, 256; TCWW 2

McCarthy, Mary (Therese)
1912-1989 .. **CLC 1, 3, 5, 14, 24, 39, 59; SSC 24**
See also AMW; BPFB 2; CA 5-8R; CANR 16, 50, 64; DLB 2; DLBY 1981; FW; INT CANR-16; MAWW; MTCW 1, 2; RGAL 4; TUS

McCartney, (James) Paul 1942- . **CLC 12, 35**
See also CA 146; CANR 111

McCauley, Stephen (D.) 1955- .... **CLC 50**
See also CA 141

McClaren, Peter .... **CLC 70**

McClure, Michael (Thomas) 1932- ... **CLC 6, 10**
See also CA 21-24R; CAD; CANR 17, 46, 77; CD 5; CP 7; DLB 16; WP

McCorkle, Jill (Collins) 1958- .... **CLC 51**
See also CA 121; CANR 113; CSW; DLB 234; DLBY 1987

McCourt, Frank 1930- .... **CLC 109**
See also CA 157; CANR 97; NCFS 1

McCourt, James 1941- .... **CLC 5**
See also CA 57-60; CANR 98

McCourt, Malachy 1932- .... **CLC 119**
See also SATA 126

McCoy, Horace (Stanley)
1897-1955 .... **TCLC 28**
See also CA 155; CMW 4; DLB 9

McCrae, John 1872-1918 .... **TCLC 12**
See also DLB 92; PFS 5

McCreigh, James
See Pohl, Frederik

McCullers, (Lula) Carson (Smith)
1917-1967 .... **CLC 1, 4, 10, 12, 48, 100; SSC 9, 24; WLC**
See also AAYA 21; AMW; BPFB 2; CA 5-8R; CABS 1, 3; CANR 18; CDALB 1941-1968; DA; DAB; DAC; DAM MST, NOV; DFS 5; DLB 2, 7, 173, 228; EXPS; FW; GLL 1; LAIT 3, 4; MAWW; MTCW 1, 2; NFS 6, 13; RGAL 4; RGSF 2; SATA 27; SSFS 5; TUS; YAW

McCulloch, John Tyler
See Burroughs, Edgar Rice

McCullough, Colleen 1938(?)- .. **CLC 27, 107**
See also AAYA 36; BPFB 2; CA 81-84; CANR 17, 46, 67, 98; CPW; DAM NOV, POP; MTCW 1, 2; RHW

McDermott, Alice 1953- .... **CLC 90**
See also CA 109; CANR 40, 90

McElroy, Joseph 1930- .... **CLC 5, 47**
See also CA 17-20R; CN 7

McEwan, Ian (Russell) 1948- ..... **CLC 13, 66**
See also BEST 90:4; BRWS 4; CA 61-64; CANR 14, 41, 69, 87; CN 7; DAM NOV; DLB 14, 194; HGG; MTCW 1, 2; RGSF 2; SUFW 2; TEA

McFadden, David 1940- .... **CLC 48**
See also CA 104; CP 7; DLB 60; INT 104

McFarland, Dennis 1950- .... **CLC 65**
See also CA 165; CANR 110

McGahern, John 1934- ... **CLC 5, 9, 48, 156; SSC 17**
See also CA 17-20R; CANR 29, 68, 113; CN 7; DLB 14, 231; MTCW 1

McGinley, Patrick (Anthony) 1937- . **CLC 41**
See also CA 127; CANR 56; INT 127

McGinley, Phyllis 1905-1978 .... **CLC 14**
See also CA 9-12R; CANR 19; CWRI 5; DLB 11, 48; PFS 9, 13; SATA 2, 44; SATA-Obit 24

McGinniss, Joe 1942- .... **CLC 32**
See also AITN 2; BEST 89:2; CA 25-28R; CANR 26, 70; CPW; DLB 185; INT CANR-26

McGivern, Maureen Daly
See Daly, Maureen

McGrath, Patrick 1950- .... **CLC 55**
See also CA 136; CANR 65; CN 7; DLB 231; HGG; SUFW 2

McGrath, Thomas (Matthew)
1916-1990 .... **CLC 28, 59**
See also AMWS 10; CA 9-12R; CANR 6, 33, 95; DAM POET; MTCW 1; SATA 41; SATA-Obit 66

McGuane, Thomas (Francis III)
1939- .... **CLC 3, 7, 18, 45, 127**
See also AITN 2; BPFB 2; CA 49-52; CANR 5, 24, 49, 94; CN 7; DLB 2, 212; DLBY 1980; INT CANR-24; MTCW 1; TCWW 2

McGuckian, Medbh 1950- ... **CLC 48; PC 27**
See also BRWS 5; CA 143; CP 7; CWP; DAM POET; DLB 40

McHale, Tom 1942(?)-1982 .... **CLC 3, 5**
See also AITN 1; CA 77-80

McIlvanney, William 1936- .... **CLC 42**
See also CA 25-28R; CANR 61; CMW 4; DLB 14, 207

McIlwraith, Maureen Mollie Hunter
See Hunter, Mollie
See also SATA 2

McInerney, Jay 1955- .... **CLC 34, 112**
See also AAYA 18; BPFB 2; CA 123; CANR 45, 68; CN 7; CPW; DAM POP; INT 123; MTCW 2

McIntyre, Vonda N(eel) 1948- .... **CLC 18**
See also CA 81-84; CANR 17, 34, 69; MTCW 1; SFW 4; YAW

McKay, Claude .... **TCLC 7, 41; BLC 3; PC 2; WLC**
See also McKay, Festus Claudius
See also AFAW 1, 2; AMWS 10; DAB; DLB 4, 45, 51, 117; EXPP; GLL 2; HR 3; LAIT 3; PAB; PFS 4; RGAL 4; WP

McKay, Festus Claudius 1889-1948
See McKay, Claude
See also BW 1, 3; CA 124; CANR 73; DA; DAC; DAM MST, MULT, NOV, POET; MTCW 1, 2; TUS

McKuen, Rod 1933- .... **CLC 1, 3**
See also AITN 1; CA 41-44R; CANR 40

McLoughlin, R. B.
See Mencken, H(enry) L(ouis)

McLuhan, (Herbert) Marshall 1911-1980 .... **CLC 37, 83**
See also CA 9-12R; CANR 12, 34, 61; DLB 88; INT CANR-12; MTCW 1, 2

McManus, Declan Patrick Aloysius
See Costello, Elvis

McMillan, Terry (L.) 1951- .... **CLC 50, 61, 112; BLCS**
See also AAYA 21; BPFB 2; BW 2, 3; CA 140; CANR 60, 104; CPW; DAM MULT, NOV, POP; MTCW 2; RGAL 4; YAW

McMurtry, Larry (Jeff) 1936- .. **CLC 2, 3, 7, 11, 27, 44, 127**
See also AAYA 15; AITN 2; AMWS 5; BEST 89:2; BPFB 2; CA 5-8R; CANR 19, 43, 64, 103; CDALB 1968-1988; CN 7; CPW; CSW; DAM NOV, POP; DLB 2, 143, 256; DLBY 1980, 1987; MTCW 1, 2; RGAL 4; TCWW 2

McNally, T. M. 1961- .... **CLC 82**

McNally, Terrence 1939- .... **CLC 4, 7, 41, 91**
See also CA 45-48; CANR 2, 56; CD 5; DAM DRAM; DLB 7, 249; GLL 1; MTCW 2

McNamer, Deirdre 1950- .... **CLC 70**

McNeal, Tom .... **CLC 119**

McNeile, Herman Cyril 1888-1937
See Sapper
See also CA 184; CMW 4; DLB 77

McNickle, (William) D'Arcy 1904-1977 .... **CLC 89**
See also CA 9-12R; CANR 5, 45; DAM MULT; DLB 175, 212; NNAL; RGAL 4; SATA-Obit 22

McPhee, John (Angus) 1931- .... **CLC 36**
See also AMWS 3; ANW; BEST 90:1; CA 65-68; CANR 20, 46, 64, 69; CPW; DLB 185; MTCW 1, 2; TUS

McPherson, James Alan 1943- .. **CLC 19, 77; BLCS**
See also BW 1, 3; CA 25-28R; CAAS 17; CANR 24, 74; CN 7; CSW; DLB 38, 244; MTCW 1, 2; RGAL 4; RGSF 2

McPherson, William (Alexander) 1933- .... **CLC 34**
See also CA 69-72; CANR 28; INT CANR-28

McTaggart, J. McT. Ellis
See McTaggart, John McTaggart Ellis

McTaggart, John McTaggart Ellis 1866-1925 .... **TCLC 105**
See also DLB 262

Mead, George Herbert 1863-1931 . **TCLC 89**
See also DLB 270

Mead, Margaret 1901-1978 .... **CLC 37**
See also AITN 1; CA 1-4R; CANR 4; FW; MTCW 1, 2; SATA-Obit 20

Meaker, Marijane (Agnes) 1927-
See Kerr, M. E.
See also CA 107; CANR 37, 63; INT 107; JRDA; MAICYA 1, 2; MAICYAS 1; MTCW 1; SATA 20, 61, 99; SATA-Essay 111; YAW

Medoff, Mark (Howard) 1940- .... **CLC 6, 23**
See also AITN 1; CA 53-56; CAD; CANR 5; CD 5; DAM DRAM; DFS 4; DLB 7; INT CANR-5

Medvedev, P. N.
See Bakhtin, Mikhail Mikhailovich

Meged, Aharon
See Megged, Aharon

Meged, Aron
See Megged, Aharon

Megged, Aharon 1920- .... **CLC 9**
See also CA 49-52; CAAS 13; CANR 1

Mehta, Ved (Parkash) 1934- .... **CLC 37**
See also CA 1-4R; CANR 2, 23, 69; MTCW 1

Melanter
See Blackmore, R(ichard) D(oddridge)

Meleager c. 140B.C.-c. 70B.C. ...... **CMLC 53**

Melies, Georges 1861-1938 .... **TCLC 81**

Melikow, Loris
See Hofmannsthal, Hugo von

Melmoth, Sebastian
See Wilde, Oscar (Fingal O'Flahertie Wills)

Meltzer, Milton 1915- .... **CLC 26**
See also AAYA 8; BYA 2, 6; CA 13-16R; CANR 38, 92, 107; CLR 13; DLB 61; JRDA; MAICYA 1, 2; SAAS 1; SATA 1, 50, 80, 128; SATA-Essay 124; WYA; YAW

Melville, Herman 1819-1891 ..... **NCLC 3, 12, 29, 45, 49, 91, 93; SSC 1, 17, 46; WLC**
See also AAYA 25; AMW; AMWR 1; CDALB 1640-1865; DA; DAB; DAC; DAM MST, NOV; DLB 3, 74, 250, 254; EXPN; EXPS; LAIT 1, 2; NFS 7, 9; RGAL 4; RGSF 2; SATA 59; SSFS 3; TUS

Members, Mark
See Powell, Anthony (Dymoke)

Membreno, Alejandro .... **CLC 59**

Menander c. 342B.C.-c. 293B.C. .... **CMLC 9, 51; DC 3**
See also AW 1; CDWLB 1; DAM DRAM; DLB 176; RGWL 2, 3

Menchu, Rigoberta 1959- .. **CLC 160; HLCS 2**
See also CA 175; DNFS 1; WLIT 1

Mencken, H(enry) L(ouis) 1880-1956 .... **TCLC 13**
See also AMW; CA 125; CDALB 1917-1929; DLB 11, 29, 63, 137, 222; MTCW 1, 2; NCFS 4; RGAL 4; TUS

Mendelsohn, Jane 1965- .... **CLC 99**
See also CA 154; CANR 94

Menton, Francisco de
See Chin, Frank (Chew, Jr.)

Mercer, David 1928-1980 .... **CLC 5**
See also CA 9-12R; CANR 23; CBD; DAM DRAM; DLB 13; MTCW 1; RGEL 2

Merchant, Paul
See Ellison, Harlan (Jay)

Meredith, George 1828-1909 ... **TCLC 17, 43**
See also CA 153; CANR 80; CDBLB 1832-1890; DAM POET; DLB 18, 35, 57, 159; RGEL 2; TEA

Meredith, William (Morris) 1919- .... **CLC 4, 13, 22, 55; PC 28**
See also CA 9-12R; CAAS 14; CANR 6, 40; CP 7; DAM POET; DLB 5

Merezhkovsky, Dmitry Sergeyevich 1865-1941 .... **TCLC 29**
See also CA 169

Merimee, Prosper 1803-1870 ... **NCLC 6, 65; SSC 7**
See also DLB 119, 192; EW 6; EXPS; GFL 1789 to the Present; RGSF 2; RGWL 2, 3; SSFS 8; SUFW

Merkin, Daphne 1954- .... **CLC 44**
See also CA 123

Merlin, Arthur
See Blish, James (Benjamin)

Merrill, James (Ingram) 1926-1995 .. **CLC 2, 3, 6, 8, 13, 18, 34, 91; PC 28**
See also AMWS 3; CA 13-16R; CANR 10, 49, 63, 108; DAM POET; DLB 5, 165; DLBY 1985; INT CANR-10; MTCW 1, 2; PAB; RGAL 4

Merriman, Alex
See Silverberg, Robert

Merriman, Brian 1747-1805 .... **NCLC 70**

Merritt, E. B.
See Waddington, Miriam

Merton, Thomas (James) 1915-1968 . **CLC 1, 3, 11, 34, 83; PC 10**
See also AMWS 8; CA 5-8R; CANR 22, 53, 111; DLB 48; DLBY 1981; MTCW 1, 2

Merwin, W(illiam) S(tanley) 1927- ... **CLC 1, 2, 3, 5, 8, 13, 18, 45, 88**
See also AMWS 3; CA 13-16R; CANR 15, 51, 112; CP 7; DAM POET; DLB 5, 169; INT CANR-15; MTCW 1, 2; PAB; PFS 5, 15; RGAL 4

Metcalf, John 1938- .... **CLC 37; SSC 43**
See also CA 113; CN 7; DLB 60; RGSF 2; TWA

Metcalf, Suzanne
See Baum, L(yman) Frank

Mew, Charlotte (Mary) 1870-1928 .. **TCLC 8**
See also CA 189; DLB 19, 135; RGEL 2

Mewshaw, Michael 1943- .... **CLC 9**
See also CA 53-56; CANR 7, 47; DLBY 1980

Meyer, Conrad Ferdinand 1825-1905 .... **NCLC 81**
See also DLB 129; EW; RGWL 2, 3

Meyer, Gustav 1868-1932
See Meyrink, Gustav
See also CA 190

Meyer, June
See Jordan, June
See also GLL 2

Meyer, Lynn
See Slavitt, David R(ytman)

Meyers, Jeffrey 1939- .... **CLC 39**
See also CA 73-76; CAAE 186; CANR 54, 102; DLB 111

Meynell, Alice (Christina Gertrude Thompson) 1847-1922 .... **TCLC 6**
See also CA 177; DLB 19, 98; RGEL 2

Meyrink, Gustav .... **TCLC 21**
See also Meyer, Gustav
See also DLB 81

Michaels, Leonard 1933- .... **CLC 6, 25; SSC 16**
See also CA 61-64; CANR 21, 62; CN 7; DLB 130; MTCW 1

Michaux, Henri 1899-1984 .... **CLC 8, 19**
See also CA 85-88; DLB 258; GFL 1789 to the Present; RGWL 2, 3

Micheaux, Oscar (Devereaux) 1884-1951 .... **TCLC 76**
See also BW 3; CA 174; DLB 50; TCWW 2

Michelangelo 1475-1564 .... **LC 12**
See also AAYA 43
Michelet, Jules 1798-1874 .... **NCLC 31**
See also EW 5; GFL 1789 to the Present
Michels, Robert 1876-1936 .... **TCLC 88**
Michener, James A(lbert)
1907(?)-1997 .. **CLC 1, 5, 11, 29, 60, 109**
See also AAYA 27; AITN 1; BEST 90:1; BPFB 2; CA 5-8R; CANR 21, 45, 68; CN 7; CPW; DAM NOV, POP; DLB 6; MTCW 1, 2; RHW
Mickiewicz, Adam 1798-1855 . **NCLC 3, 101; PC 38**
See also EW 5; RGWL 2, 3
Middleton, Christopher 1926- .... **CLC 13**
See also CA 13-16R; CANR 29, 54; CP 7; DLB 40
Middleton, Richard (Barham)
1882-1911 .... **TCLC 56**
See also CA 187; DLB 156; HGG
Middleton, Stanley 1919- .... **CLC 7, 38**
See also CA 25-28R; CAAS 23; CANR 21, 46, 81; CN 7; DLB 14
Middleton, Thomas 1580-1627 .... **LC 33; DC 5**
See also BRW 2; DAM DRAM, MST; DLB 58; RGEL 2
Migueis, Jose Rodrigues 1901- .... **CLC 10**
Mikszath, Kalman 1847-1910 .... **TCLC 31**
See also CA 170
Miles, Jack .... **CLC 100**
See also CA 200
Miles, John Russiano
See Miles, Jack
Miles, Josephine (Louise)
1911-1985 .... **CLC 1, 2, 14, 34, 39**
See also CA 1-4R; CANR 2, 55; DAM POET; DLB 48
Militant
See Sandburg, Carl (August)
Mill, Harriet (Hardy) Taylor
1807-1858 .... **NCLC 102**
See also FW
Mill, John Stuart 1806-1873 .... **NCLC 11, 58**
See also CDBLB 1832-1890; DLB 55, 190, 262; FW 1; RGEL 2; TEA
Millar, Kenneth 1915-1983 .... **CLC 14**
See also Macdonald, Ross
See also CA 9-12R; CANR 16, 63, 107; CMW 4; CPW; DAM POP; DLB 2, 226; DLBD 6; DLBY 1983; MTCW 1, 2
Millay, E. Vincent
See Millay, Edna St. Vincent
Millay, Edna St. Vincent
1892-1950 ... **TCLC 4, 49; PC 6; WLCS**
See also Boyd, Nancy
See also AMW; CA 130; CDALB 1917-1929; DA; DAB; DAC; DAM MST, POET; DLB 45, 249; EXPP; MAWW; MTCW 1, 2; PAB; PFS 3; RGAL 4; TUS; WP
Miller, Arthur 1915- ...... **CLC 1, 2, 6, 10, 15, 26, 47, 78; DC 1; WLC**
See also AAYA 15; AITN 1; AMW; CA 1-4R; CABS 3; CAD; CANR 2, 30, 54, 76; CD 5; CDALB 1941-1968; DA; DAB; DAC; DAM DRAM, MST; DFS 1, 3; DLB 7, 266; LAIT 1, 4; MTCW 1, 2; RGAL 4; TUS; WYAS 1
Miller, Henry (Valentine)
1891-1980 .... **CLC 1, 2, 4, 9, 14, 43, 84; WLC**
See also AMW; BPFB 2; CA 9-12R; CANR 33, 64; CDALB 1929-1941; DA; DAB; DAC; DAM MST, NOV; DLB 4, 9; DLBY 1980; MTCW 1, 2; RGAL 4; TUS
Miller, Jason 1939(?)-2001 .... **CLC 2**
See also AITN 1; CA 73-76; CAD; DFS 12; DLB 7

Miller, Sue 1943- .... **CLC 44**
See also BEST 90:3; CA 139; CANR 59, 91; DAM POP; DLB 143
Miller, Walter M(ichael, Jr.)
1923-1996 .... **CLC 4, 30**
See also BPFB 2; CA 85-88; CANR 108; DLB 8; SCFW; SFW 4
Millett, Kate 1934- .... **CLC 67**
See also AITN 1; CA 73-76; CANR 32, 53, 76, 110; DLB 246; FW; GLL 1; MTCW 1, 2
Millhauser, Steven (Lewis) 1943- .... **CLC 21, 54, 109**
See also CA 111; CANR 63; CN 7; DLB 2; FANT; INT CA-111; MTCW 2
Millin, Sarah Gertrude 1889-1968 ... **CLC 49**
See also CA 102; DLB 225
Milne, A(lan) A(lexander)
1882-1956 .... **TCLC 6, 88**
See also BRWS 5; CA 133; CLR 1, 26; CMW 4; CWRI 5; DAB; DAC; DAM MST; DLB 10, 77, 100, 160; FANT; MAICYA 1, 2; MTCW 1, 2; RGEL 2; SATA 100; WCH; YABC 1
Milner, Ron(ald) 1938- .... **CLC 56; BLC 3**
See also AITN 1; BW 1; CA 73-76; CAD; CANR 24, 81; CD 5; DAM MULT; DLB 38; MTCW 1
Milnes, Richard Monckton
1809-1885 .... **NCLC 61**
See also DLB 32, 184
Milosz, Czeslaw 1911- ...... **CLC 5, 11, 22, 31, 56, 82; PC 8; WLCS**
See also CA 81-84; CANR 23, 51, 91; CDWLB 4; CWW 2; DAM MST, POET; DLB 215; EW 13; MTCW 1, 2; RGWL 2, 3
Milton, John 1608-1674 ..... **LC 9, 43; PC 19, 29; WLC**
See also BRW 2; BRWR 2; CDBLB 1660-1789; DA; DAB; DAC; DAM MST, POET; DLB 131, 151; EFS 1; EXPP; LAIT 1; PAB; PFS 3; RGEL 2; TEA; WLIT 3; WP
Min, Anchee 1957- .... **CLC 86**
See also CA 146; CANR 94
Minehaha, Cornelius
See Wedekind, (Benjamin) Frank(lin)
Miner, Valerie 1947- .... **CLC 40**
See also CA 97-100; CANR 59; FW; GLL 2
Minimo, Duca
See D'Annunzio, Gabriele
Minot, Susan 1956- .... **CLC 44, 159**
See also AMWS 6; CA 134; CN 7
Minus, Ed 1938- .... **CLC 39**
See also CA 185
Miranda, Javier
See Bioy Casares, Adolfo
See also CWW 2
Mirbeau, Octave 1848-1917 .... **TCLC 55**
See also DLB 123, 192; GFL 1789 to the Present
Miro (Ferrer), Gabriel (Francisco Victor)
1879-1930 .... **TCLC 5**
See also CA 185
Misharin, Alexandr .... **CLC 59**
Mishima, Yukio ... **CLC 2, 4, 6, 9, 27; DC 1; SSC 4**
See also Hiraoka, Kimitake
See also BPFB 2; GLL 1; MJW; MTCW 2; RGSF 2; RGWL 2, 3; SSFS 5, 12
Mistral, Frederic 1830-1914 .... **TCLC 51**
See also GFL 1789 to the Present
Mistral, Gabriela
See Godoy Alcayaga, Lucila
See also DNFS 1; LAW; RGWL 2, 3; WP

Mistry, Rohinton 1952- .... **CLC 71**
See also CA 141; CANR 86; CCA 1; CN 7; DAC; SSFS 6
Mitchell, James Leslie 1901-1935
See Gibbon, Lewis Grassic
See also CA 188; DLB 15
Mitchell, Joni 1943- .... **CLC 12**
See also CA 112; CCA 1
Mitchell, Joseph (Quincy)
1908-1996 .... **CLC 98**
See also CA 77-80; CANR 69; CN 7; CSW; DLB 185; DLBY 1996
Mitchell, Margaret (Munnerlyn)
1900-1949 .... **TCLC 11**
See also AAYA 23; BPFB 2; BYA 1; CA 125; CANR 55, 94; CDALBS; DAM NOV, POP; DLB 9; LAIT 2; MTCW 1, 2; NFS 9; RGAL 4; RHW; TUS; WYAS 1; YAW
Mitchell, Peggy
See Mitchell, Margaret (Munnerlyn)
Mitchell, S(ilas) Weir 1829-1914 .... **TCLC 36**
See also CA 165; DLB 202; RGAL 4
Mitchell, W(illiam) O(rmond)
1914-1998 .... **CLC 25**
See also CA 77-80; CANR 15, 43; CN 7; DAC; DAM MST; DLB 88
Mitchell, William 1879-1936 .... **TCLC 81**
Mitford, Mary Russell 1787-1855 ... **NCLC 4**
See also DLB 110, 116; RGEL 2
Mitford, Nancy 1904-1973 .... **CLC 44**
See also CA 9-12R; DLB 191; RGEL 2
Miyamoto, (Chujo) Yuriko
1899-1951 .... **TCLC 37**
See also CA 170, 174
Miyamoto Yuriko
See Miyamoto, (Chujo) Yuriko
See also DLB 180
Miyazawa, Kenji 1896-1933 .... **TCLC 76**
See also CA 157; RGWL 3
Mizoguchi, Kenji 1898-1956 .... **TCLC 72**
See also CA 167
Mo, Timothy (Peter) 1950(?)- ... **CLC 46, 134**
See also CA 117; CN 7; DLB 194; MTCW 1; WLIT 4
Modarressi, Taghi (M.) 1931-1997 ... **CLC 44**
See also CA 134; INT 134
Modiano, Patrick (Jean) 1945- .... **CLC 18**
See also CA 85-88; CANR 17, 40; CWW 2; DLB 83
Mofolo, Thomas (Mokopu)
1875(?)-1948 .... **TCLC 22; BLC 3**
See also AFW; CA 153; CANR 83; DAM MULT; DLB 225; MTCW 2; WLIT 2
Mohr, Nicholasa 1938- .... **CLC 12; HLC 2**
See also AAYA 8; CA 49-52; CANR 1, 32, 64; CLR 22; DAM MULT; DLB 145; HW 1, 2; JRDA; LAIT 5; MAICYA 1, 2; MAICYAS 1; RGAL 4; SAAS 8; SATA 8, 97; SATA-Essay 113; WYA; YAW
Mojtabai, A(nn) G(race) 1938- ..... **CLC 5, 9, 15, 29**
See also CA 85-88; CANR 88
Moliere 1622-1673 ..... **LC 10, 28, 64; DC 13; WLC**
See also DA; DAB; DAC; DAM DRAM, MST; DFS 13; DLB 268; EW 3; GFL Beginnings to 1789; RGWL 2, 3; TWA
Molin, Charles
See Mayne, William (James Carter)
Molnar, Ferenc 1878-1952 .... **TCLC 20**
See also CA 153; CANR 83; CDWLB 4; DAM DRAM; DLB 215; RGWL 2, 3
Momaday, N(avarre) Scott 1934- ...... **CLC 2, 19, 85, 95, 160; PC 25; WLCS**
See also AAYA 11; AMWS 4; ANW; BPFB 2; CA 25-28R; CANR 14, 34, 68; CDALBS; CN 7; CPW; DA; DAB; DAC;

DAM MST, MULT, NOV, POP; DLB 143, 175, 256; EXPP; INT CANR-14; LAIT 4; MTCW 1, 2; NFS 10; NNAL; PFS 2, 11; RGAL 4; SATA 48; SATA-Brief 30; WP; YAW

Monette, Paul 1945-1995 .... **CLC 82**
See also AMWS 10; CA 139; CN 7; GLL 1

Monroe, Harriet 1860-1936 .... **TCLC 12**
See also CA 204; DLB 54, 91

Monroe, Lyle
See Heinlein, Robert A(nson)

Montagu, Elizabeth 1720-1800 .... **NCLC 7, 117**
See also FW

Montagu, Mary (Pierrepont) Wortley 1689-1762 .... **LC 9, 57; PC 16**
See also DLB 95, 101; RGEL 2

Montagu, W. H.
See Coleridge, Samuel Taylor

Montague, John (Patrick) 1929- ..... **CLC 13, 46**
See also CA 9-12R; CANR 9, 69; CP 7; DLB 40; MTCW 1; PFS 12; RGEL 2

Montaigne, Michel (Eyquem) de 1533-1592 .... **LC 8; WLC**
See also DA; DAB; DAC; DAM MST; EW 2; GFL Beginnings to 1789; RGWL 2, 3; TWA

Montale, Eugenio 1896-1981 ... **CLC 7, 9, 18; PC 13**
See also CA 17-20R; CANR 30; DLB 114; EW 11; MTCW 1; RGWL 2, 3; TWA

Montesquieu, Charles-Louis de Secondat 1689-1755 .... **LC 7, 69**
See also EW 3; GFL Beginnings to 1789; TWA

Montessori, Maria 1870-1952 .... **TCLC 103**
See also CA 147

Montgomery, (Robert) Bruce 1921(?)-1978
See Crispin, Edmund
See also CA 179; CMW 4

Montgomery, L(ucy) M(aud) 1874-1942 .... **TCLC 51**
See also AAYA 12; BYA 1; CA 137; CLR 8; DAC; DAM MST; DLB 92; DLBD 14; JRDA; MAICYA 1, 2; MTCW 2; RGEL 2; SATA 100; TWA; WCH; WYA; YABC 1

Montgomery, Marion H., Jr. 1925- .... **CLC 7**
See also AITN 1; CA 1-4R; CANR 3, 48; CSW; DLB 6

Montgomery, Max
See Davenport, Guy (Mattison, Jr.)

Montherlant, Henry (Milon) de 1896-1972 .... **CLC 8, 19**
See also CA 85-88; DAM DRAM; DLB 72; EW 11; GFL 1789 to the Present; MTCW 1

Monty Python
See Chapman, Graham; Cleese, John (Marwood); Gilliam, Terry (Vance); Idle, Eric; Jones, Terence Graham Parry; Palin, Michael (Edward)
See also AAYA 7

Moodie, Susanna (Strickland) 1803-1885 .... **NCLC 14, 113**
See also DLB 99

Moody, Hiram (F. III) 1961-
See Moody, Rick
See also CA 138; CANR 64, 112

Moody, Minerva
See Alcott, Louisa May

Moody, Rick .... **CLC 147**
See also Moody, Hiram (F. III)

Moody, William Vaughan 1869-1910 .... **TCLC 105**
See also CA 178; DLB 7, 54; RGAL 4

Mooney, Edward 1951-
See Mooney, Ted
See also CA 130

Mooney, Ted .... **CLC 25**
See also Mooney, Edward

Moorcock, Michael (John) 1939- ...... **CLC 5, 27, 58**
See also Bradbury, Edward P.
See also AAYA 26; CA 45-48; CAAS 5; CANR 2, 17, 38, 64; CN 7; DLB 14, 231, 261; FANT; MTCW 1, 2; SATA 93; SCFW 2; SFW 4; SUFW 1, 2

Moore, Brian 1921-1999 ... **CLC 1, 3, 5, 7, 8, 19, 32, 90**
See also Bryan, Michael
See also CA 1-4R; CANR 1, 25, 42, 63; CCA 1; CN 7; DAB; DAC; DAM MST; DLB 251; FANT; MTCW 1, 2; RGEL 2

Moore, Edward
See Muir, Edwin
See also RGEL 2

Moore, G. E. 1873-1958 .... **TCLC 89**
See also DLB 262

Moore, George Augustus 1852-1933 .... **TCLC 7; SSC 19**
See also BRW 6; CA 177; DLB 10, 18, 57, 135; RGEL 2; RGSF 2

Moore, Lorrie .... **CLC 39, 45, 68**
See also Moore, Marie Lorena
See also AMWS 10; DLB 234

Moore, Marianne (Craig) 1887-1972 .... **CLC 1, 2, 4, 8, 10, 13, 19, 47; PC 4; WLCS**
See also AMW; CA 1-4R; CANR 3, 61; CDALB 1929-1941; DA; DAB; DAC; DAM MST, POET; DLB 45; DLBD 7; EXPP; MAWW; MTCW 1, 2; PAB; PFS 14; RGAL 4; SATA 20; TUS; WP

Moore, Marie Lorena 1957- .... **CLC 165**
See also Moore, Lorrie
See also CA 116; CANR 39, 83; CN 7; DLB 234

Moore, Thomas 1779-1852 .... **NCLC 6, 110**
See also DLB 96, 144; RGEL 2

Moorhouse, Frank 1938- .... **SSC 40**
See also CA 118; CANR 92; CN 7; RGSF 2

Mora, Pat(ricia) 1942-
See also CA 129; CANR 57, 81, 112; CLR 58; DAM MULT; DLB 209; HLC 1; HW 1, 2; MAICYA 2; SATA 92, 134

Moraga, Cherrie 1952- .... **CLC 126**
See also CA 131; CANR 66; DAM MULT; DLB 82, 249; FW; GLL 1; HW 1, 2

Morand, Paul 1888-1976 .... **CLC 41; SSC 22**
See also CA 184; DLB 65

Morante, Elsa 1918-1985 .... **CLC 8, 47**
See also CA 85-88; CANR 35; DLB 177; MTCW 1, 2; RGWL 2, 3

Moravia, Alberto .... **CLC 2, 7, 11, 27, 46; SSC 26**
See also Pincherle, Alberto
See also DLB 177; EW 12; MTCW 2; RGSF 2; RGWL 2, 3

More, Hannah 1745-1833 .... **NCLC 27**
See also DLB 107, 109, 116, 158; RGEL 2

More, Henry 1614-1687 .... **LC 9**
See also DLB 126, 252

More, Sir Thomas 1478(?)-1535 .... **LC 10, 32**
See also BRWS 7; DLB 136; RGEL 2; TEA

Moreas, Jean .... **TCLC 18**
See also Papadiamantopoulos, Johannes
See also GFL 1789 to the Present

Moreton, Andrew Esq.
See Defoe, Daniel

Morgan, Berry 1919- .... **CLC 6**
See also CA 49-52; DLB 6

Morgan, Claire
See Highsmith, (Mary) Patricia
See also GLL 1

Morgan, Edwin (George) 1920- .... **CLC 31**
See also CA 5-8R; CANR 3, 43, 90; CP 7; DLB 27

Morgan, (George) Frederick 1922- .. **CLC 23**
See also CA 17-20R; CANR 21; CP 7

Morgan, Harriet
See Mencken, H(enry) L(ouis)

Morgan, Jane
See Cooper, James Fenimore

Morgan, Janet 1945- .... **CLC 39**
See also CA 65-68

Morgan, Lady 1776(?)-1859 .... **NCLC 29**
See also DLB 116, 158; RGEL 2

Morgan, Robin (Evonne) 1941- .... **CLC 2**
See also CA 69-72; CANR 29, 68; FW; GLL 2; MTCW 1; SATA 80

Morgan, Scott
See Kuttner, Henry

Morgan, Seth 1949(?)-1990 .... **CLC 65**
See also CA 185

Morgenstern, Christian (Otto Josef Wolfgang) 1871-1914 .... **TCLC 8**
See also CA 191

Morgenstern, S.
See Goldman, William (W.)

Mori, Rintaro
See Mori Ogai

Moricz, Zsigmond 1879-1942 .... **TCLC 33**
See also CA 165; DLB 215

Morike, Eduard (Friedrich) 1804-1875 .... **NCLC 10**
See also DLB 133; RGWL 2, 3

Mori Ogai 1862-1922 .... **TCLC 14**
See also Ogai
See also CA 164; DLB 180; RGWL 3; TWA

Moritz, Karl Philipp 1756-1793 .... **LC 2**
See also DLB 94

Morland, Peter Henry
See Faust, Frederick (Schiller)

Morley, Christopher (Darlington) 1890-1957 .... **TCLC 87**
See also DLB 9; RGAL 4

Morren, Theophil
See Hofmannsthal, Hugo von

Morris, Bill 1952- .... **CLC 76**

Morris, Julian
See West, Morris L(anglo)

Morris, Steveland Judkins 1950(?)-
See Wonder, Stevie

Morris, William 1834-1896 .... **NCLC 4**
See also BRW 5; CDBLB 1832-1890; DLB 18, 35, 57, 156, 178, 184; FANT; RGEL 2; SFW 4; SUFW

Morris, Wright 1910-1998 .. **CLC 1, 3, 7, 18, 37**
See also AMW; CA 9-12R; CANR 21, 81; CN 7; DLB 2, 206, 218; DLBY 1981; MTCW 1, 2; RGAL 4; TCLC 107; TCWW 2

Morrison, Arthur 1863-1945 .... **TCLC 72; SSC 40**
See also CA 157; CMW 4; DLB 70, 135, 197; RGEL 2

Morrison, James Douglas 1943-1971
See Morrison, Jim
See also CA 73-76; CANR 40

Morrison, Jim .... **CLC 17**
See also Morrison, James Douglas

Morrison, Toni 1931- . **CLC 4, 10, 22, 55, 81, 87; BLC 3**
See also AAYA 1, 22; AFAW 1, 2; AMWS 3; BPFB 2; BW 2, 3; CA 29-32R; CANR 27, 42, 67, 113; CDALB 1968-1988; CN 7; CPW; DA; DAB; DAC; DAM MST, MULT, NOV, POP; DLB 6, 33, 143;

DLBY 1981; EXPN; FW; LAIT 2, 4; MAWW; MTCW 1, 2; NFS 1, 6, 8, 14; RGAL 4; RHW; SATA 57; SSFS 5; TUS; YAW

Morrison, Van 1945- .... **CLC 21**
See also CA 168

Morrissy, Mary 1957- .... **CLC 99**
See also CA 205; DLB 267

Mortimer, John (Clifford) 1923- ..... **CLC 28, 43**
See also CA 13-16R; CANR 21, 69, 109; CD 5; CDBLB 1960 to Present; CMW 4; CN 7; CPW; DAM DRAM, POP; DLB 13, 245, 271; INT CANR-21; MSW; MTCW 1, 2; RGEL 2

Mortimer, Penelope (Ruth) 1918-1999 .... **CLC 5**
See also CA 57-60; CANR 45, 88; CN 7

Mortimer, Sir John
See Mortimer, John (Clifford)

Morton, Anthony
See Creasey, John

Morton, Thomas 1579(?)-1647(?) .... **LC 72**
See also DLB 24; RGEL 2

Mosca, Gaetano 1858-1941 .... **TCLC 75**

Mosher, Howard Frank 1943- .... **CLC 62**
See also CA 139; CANR 65

Mosley, Nicholas 1923- .... **CLC 43, 70**
See also CA 69-72; CANR 41, 60, 108; CN 7; DLB 14, 207

Mosley, Walter 1952- .... **CLC 97; BLCS**
See also AAYA 17; BPFB 2; BW 2; CA 142; CANR 57, 92; CMW 4; CPW; DAM MULT, POP; MSW; MTCW 2

Moss, Howard 1922-1987 . **CLC 7, 14, 45, 50**
See also CA 1-4R; CANR 1, 44; DAM POET; DLB 5

Mossgiel, Rab
See Burns, Robert

Motion, Andrew (Peter) 1952- .... **CLC 47**
See also BRWS 7; CA 146; CANR 90; CP 7; DLB 40

Motley, Willard (Francis) 1909-1965 .... **CLC 18**
See also BW 1; CA 117; CANR 88; DLB 76, 143

Motoori, Norinaga 1730-1801 .... **NCLC 45**

Mott, Michael (Charles Alston) 1930- .... **CLC 15, 34**
See also CA 5-8R; CAAS 7; CANR 7, 29

Mountain Wolf Woman 1884-1960 .. **CLC 92**
See also CA 144; CANR 90; NNAL

Moure, Erin 1955- .... **CLC 88**
See also CA 113; CP 7; CWP; DLB 60

Mowat, Farley (McGill) 1921- .... **CLC 26**
See also AAYA 1; BYA 2; CA 1-4R; CANR 4, 24, 42, 68, 108; CLR 20; CPW; DAC; DAM MST; DLB 68; INT CANR-24; JRDA; MAICYA 1; MTCW 1, 2; SATA 3, 55; YAW

Mowatt, Anna Cora 1819-1870 ..... **NCLC 74**
See also RGAL 4

Moyers, Bill 1934- .... **CLC 74**
See also AITN 2; CA 61-64; CANR 31, 52

Mphahlele, Es'kia
See Mphahlele, Ezekiel
See also AFW; CDWLB 3; DLB 125, 225; RGSF 2; SSFS 11

Mphahlele, Ezekiel 1919- .... **CLC 25, 133; BLC 3**
See also Mphahlele, Es'kia
See also BW 2, 3; CA 81-84; CANR 26, 76; CN 7; DAM MULT; MTCW 2; SATA 119

Mqhayi, S(amuel) E(dward) K(rune Loliwe) 1875-1945 .... **TCLC 25; BLC 3**
See also CA 153; CANR 87; DAM MULT

Mrozek, Slawomir 1930- .... **CLC 3, 13**
See also CA 13-16R; CAAS 10; CANR 29; CDWLB 4; CWW 2; DLB 232; MTCW 1

Mrs. Belloc-Lowndes
See Lowndes, Marie Adelaide (Belloc)

M'Taggart, John M'Taggart Ellis
See McTaggart, John McTaggart Ellis

Mtwa, Percy (?)- .... **CLC 47**

Mueller, Lisel 1924- .... **CLC 13, 51; PC 33**
See also CA 93-96; CP 7; DLB 105; PFS 9, 13

Muggeridge, Malcolm (Thomas) 1903-1990 .... **TCLC 120**
See also AITN 1; CA 101; CANR 33, 63; MTCW 1, 2

Muir, Edwin 1887-1959 .... **TCLC 2, 87**
See also Moore, Edward
See also BRWS 6; CA 193; DLB 20, 100, 191; RGEL 2

Muir, John 1838-1914 .... **TCLC 28**
See also AMWS 9; ANW; CA 165; DLB 186

Mujica Lainez, Manuel 1910-1984 ... **CLC 31**
See also Lainez, Manuel Mujica
See also CA 81-84; CANR 32; HW 1

Mukherjee, Bharati 1940- .... **CLC 53, 115; AAL; SSC 38**
See also BEST 89:2; CA 107; CANR 45, 72; CN 7; DAM NOV; DLB 60, 218; DNFS 1, 2; FW; MTCW 1, 2; RGAL 4; RGSF 2; SSFS 7; TUS

Muldoon, Paul 1951- .... **CLC 32, 72, 166**
See also BRWS 4; CA 129; CANR 52, 91; CP 7; DAM POET; DLB 40; INT 129; PFS 7

Mulisch, Harry 1927- .... **CLC 42**
See also CA 9-12R; CANR 6, 26, 56, 110

Mull, Martin 1943- .... **CLC 17**
See also CA 105

Muller, Wilhelm .... **NCLC 73**

Mulock, Dinah Maria
See Craik, Dinah Maria (Mulock)
See also RGEL 2

Munford, Robert 1737(?)-1783 .... **LC 5**
See also DLB 31

Mungo, Raymond 1946- .... **CLC 72**
See also CA 49-52; CANR 2

Munro, Alice 1931- .... **CLC 6, 10, 19, 50, 95; SSC 3; WLCS**
See also AITN 2; BPFB 2; CA 33-36R; CANR 33, 53, 75; CCA 1; CN 7; DAC; DAM MST, NOV; DLB 53; MTCW 1, 2; RGEL 2; RGSF 2; SATA 29; SSFS 5, 13

Munro, H(ector) H(ugh) 1870-1916
See Saki
See also CA 130; CANR 104; CDBLB 1890-1914; DA; DAB; DAC; DAM MST, NOV; DLB 34, 162; EXPS; MTCW 1, 2; RGEL 2; SSFS 15; WLC

Murakami, Haruki 1949- .... **CLC 150**
See also Murakami Haruki
See also CA 165; CANR 102; MJW; RGWL 3; SFW 4

Murakami Haruki
See Murakami, Haruki
See also DLB 182

Murasaki, Lady
See Murasaki Shikibu

Murasaki Shikibu 978(?)-1026(?) ... **CMLC 1**
See also EFS 2; RGWL 2, 3

Murdoch, (Jean) Iris 1919-1999 ... **CLC 1, 2, 3, 4, 6, 8, 11, 15, 22, 31, 51**
See also BRWS 1; CA 13-16R; CANR 8, 43, 68, 103; CDBLB 1960 to Present; CN 7; DAB; DAC; DAM MST, NOV; DLB 14, 194, 233; INT CANR-8; MTCW 1, 2; RGEL 2; TEA; WLIT 4

Murfree, Mary Noailles 1850-1922 ... **SSC 22**
See also CA 176; DLB 12, 74; RGAL 4

Murnau, Friedrich Wilhelm
See Plumpe, Friedrich Wilhelm

Murphy, Richard 1927- .... **CLC 41**
See also BRWS 5; CA 29-32R; CP 7; DLB 40

Murphy, Sylvia 1937- .... **CLC 34**
See also CA 121

Murphy, Thomas (Bernard) 1935- ... **CLC 51**
See also CA 101

Murray, Albert L. 1916- .... **CLC 73**
See also BW 2; CA 49-52; CANR 26, 52, 78; CSW; DLB 38

Murray, James Augustus Henry 1837-1915 .... **TCLC 117**

Murray, Judith Sargent 1751-1820 .... **NCLC 63**
See also DLB 37, 200

Murray, Les(lie Allan) 1938- .... **CLC 40**
See also BRWS 7; CA 21-24R; CANR 11, 27, 56, 103; CP 7; DAM POET; DLBY 01; RGEL 2

Murry, J. Middleton
See Murry, John Middleton

Murry, John Middleton 1889-1957 .... **TCLC 16**
See also DLB 149

Musgrave, Susan 1951- .... **CLC 13, 54**
See also CA 69-72; CANR 45, 84; CCA 1; CP 7; CWP

Musil, Robert (Edler von) 1880-1942 .... **TCLC 12, 68; SSC 18**
See also CANR 55, 84; CDWLB 2; DLB 81, 124; EW 9; MTCW 2; RGSF 2; RGWL 2, 3

Muske, Carol .... **CLC 90**
See also Muske-Dukes, Carol (Anne)

Muske-Dukes, Carol (Anne) 1945-
See Muske, Carol
See also CA 65-68; CAAE 203; CANR 32, 70; CWP

Musset, (Louis Charles) Alfred de 1810-1857 .... **NCLC 7**
See also DLB 192, 217; EW 6; GFL 1789 to the Present; RGWL 2, 3; TWA

Mussolini, Benito (Amilcare Andrea) 1883-1945 .... **TCLC 96**

My Brother's Brother
See Chekhov, Anton (Pavlovich)

Myers, L(eopold) H(amilton) 1881-1944 .... **TCLC 59**
See also CA 157; DLB 15; RGEL 2

Myers, Walter Dean 1937- .. **CLC 35; BLC 3**
See also AAYA 4, 23; BW 2; BYA 6, 8, 11; CA 33-36R; CANR 20, 42, 67, 108; CLR 4, 16, 35; DAM MULT, NOV; DLB 33; INT CANR-20; JRDA; LAIT 5; MAICYA 1, 2; MAICYAS 1; MTCW 2; SAAS 2; SATA 41, 71, 109; SATA-Brief 27; WYA; YAW

Myers, Walter M.
See Myers, Walter Dean

Myles, Symon
See Follett, Ken(neth Martin)

Nabokov, Vladimir (Vladimirovich) 1899-1977 .... **CLC 1, 2, 3, 6, 8, 11, 15, 23, 44, 46, 64; SSC 11; WLC**
See also AMW; AMWR 1; BPFB 2; CA 5-8R; CANR 20, 102; CDALB 1941-1968; DA; DAB; DAC; DAM MST, NOV; DLB 2, 244; DLBD 3; DLBY 1980, 1991; EXPS; MTCW 1, 2; NCFS 4; NFS 9; RGAL 4; RGSF 2; SSFS 6, 15; TCLC 108; TUS

Naevius c. 265B.C.-201B.C. .... **CMLC 37**
See also DLB 211

Nagai, Kafu .... **TCLC 51**
See also Nagai, Sokichi
See also DLB 180

Nagai, Sokichi 1879-1959
 See Nagai, Kafu
Nagy, Laszlo 1925-1978 .... **CLC 7**
 See also CA 129
Naidu, Sarojini 1879-1949 .... **TCLC 80**
 See also RGEL 2
Naipaul, Shiva(dhar Srinivasa)
 1945-1985 .... **CLC 32, 39**
 See also CA 112; CANR 33; DAM NOV; DLB 157; DLBY 1985; MTCW 1, 2
Naipaul, V(idiadhar) S(urajprasad)
 1932- .... **CLC 4, 7, 9, 13, 18, 37, 105; SSC 38**
 See also BPFB 2; BRWS 1; CA 1-4R; CANR 1, 33, 51, 91; CDBLB 1960 to Present; CDWLB 3; CN 7; DAB; DAC; DAM MST, NOV; DLB 125, 204, 207; DLBY 1985, 2001; MTCW 1, 2; RGEL 2; RGSF 2; TWA; WLIT 4
Nakos, Lilika 1899(?)- .... **CLC 29**
Narayan, R(asipuram) K(rishnaswami)
 1906-2001 . **CLC 7, 28, 47, 121; SSC 25**
 See also BPFB 2; CA 81-84; CANR 33, 61, 112; CN 7; DAM NOV; DNFS 1; MTCW 1, 2; RGEL 2; RGSF 2; SATA 62; SSFS 5
Nash, (Frediric) Ogden 1902-1971 . **CLC 23; PC 21**
 See also CA 13-14; CANR 34, 61; CAP 1; DAM POET; DLB 11; MAICYA 1, 2; MTCW 1, 2; RGAL 4; SATA 2, 46; TCLC 109; WP
Nashe, Thomas 1567-1601(?) .... **LC 41**
 See also DLB 167; RGEL 2
Nathan, Daniel
 See Dannay, Frederic
Nathan, George Jean 1882-1958 .... **TCLC 18**
 See also Hatteras, Owen
 See also CA 169; DLB 137
Natsume, Kinnosuke
 See Natsume, Soseki
Natsume, Soseki 1867-1916 .... **TCLC 2, 10**
 See also Natsume Soseki; Soseki
 See also CA 195; RGWL 2, 3; TWA
Natsume Soseki
 See Natsume, Soseki
 See also DLB 180
Natti, (Mary) Lee 1919-
 See Kingman, Lee
 See also CA 5-8R; CANR 2
Navarre, Marguerite de
 See de Navarre, Marguerite
Naylor, Gloria 1950- . **CLC 28, 52, 156; BLC 3; WLCS**
 See also AAYA 6, 39; AFAW 1, 2; AMWS 8; BW 2, 3; CA 107; CANR 27, 51, 74; CN 7; CPW; DA; DAC; DAM MST, MULT, NOV, POP; DLB 173; FW; MTCW 1, 2; NFS 4, 7; RGAL 4; TUS
Neff, Debra .... **CLC 59**
Neihardt, John Gneisenau
 1881-1973 .... **CLC 32**
 See also CA 13-14; CANR 65; CAP 1; DLB 9, 54, 256; LAIT 2
Nekrasov, Nikolai Alekseevich
 1821-1878 .... **NCLC 11**
Nelligan, Emile 1879-1941 .... **TCLC 14**
 See also DLB 92
Nelson, Willie 1933- .... **CLC 17**
 See also CA 107
Nemerov, Howard (Stanley)
 1920-1991 .... **CLC 2, 6, 9, 36; PC 24**
 See also AMW; CA 1-4R; CABS 2; CANR 1, 27, 53; DAM POET; DLB 5, 6; DLBY 1983; INT CANR-27; MTCW 1, 2; PFS 10, 14; RGAL 4; TCLC 124

Neruda, Pablo 1904-1973 .. **CLC 1, 2, 5, 7, 9, 28, 62; HLC 2; PC 4; WLC**
 See also CA 19-20; CAP 2; DA; DAB; DAC; DAM MST, MULT, POET; DNFS 2; HW 1; LAW; MTCW 1, 2; PFS 11; RGWL 2, 3; TWA; WLIT 1; WP
Nerval, Gerard de 1808-1855 ... **NCLC 1, 67; PC 13; SSC 18**
 See also DLB 217; EW 6; GFL 1789 to the Present; RGSF 2; RGWL 2, 3
Nervo, (Jose) Amado (Ruiz de)
 1870-1919 .... **TCLC 11; HLCS 2**
 See also CA 131; HW 1; LAW
Nesbit, Malcolm
 See Chester, Alfred
Nessi, Pio Baroja y
 See Baroja (y Nessi), Pio
Nestroy, Johann 1801-1862 .... **NCLC 42**
 See also DLB 133; RGWL 2, 3
Netterville, Luke
 See O'Grady, Standish (James)
Neufeld, John (Arthur) 1938- .... **CLC 17**
 See also AAYA 11; CA 25-28R; CANR 11, 37, 56; CLR 52; MAICYA 1, 2; SAAS 3; SATA 6, 81; SATA-Essay 131; YAW
Neumann, Alfred 1895-1952 .... **TCLC 100**
 See also CA 183; DLB 56
Neumann, Ferenc
 See Molnar, Ferenc
Neville, Emily Cheney 1919- .... **CLC 12**
 See also BYA 2; CA 5-8R; CANR 3, 37, 85; JRDA; MAICYA 1, 2; SAAS 2; SATA 1; YAW
Newbound, Bernard Slade 1930-
 See Slade, Bernard
 See also CA 81-84; CANR 49; CD 5; DAM DRAM
Newby, P(ercy) H(oward)
 1918-1997 .... **CLC 2, 13**
 See also CA 5-8R; CANR 32, 67; CN 7; DAM NOV; DLB 15; MTCW 1; RGEL 2
Newcastle
 See Cavendish, Margaret Lucas
Newlove, Donald 1928- .... **CLC 6**
 See also CA 29-32R; CANR 25
Newlove, John (Herbert) 1938- .... **CLC 14**
 See also CA 21-24R; CANR 9, 25; CP 7
Newman, Charles 1938- .... **CLC 2, 8**
 See also CA 21-24R; CANR 84; CN 7
Newman, Edwin (Harold) 1919- .... **CLC 14**
 See also AITN 1; CA 69-72; CANR 5
Newman, John Henry 1801-1890 . **NCLC 38, 99**
 See also BRWS 7; DLB 18, 32, 55; RGEL 2
Newton, (Sir) Isaac 1642-1727 ...... **LC 35, 53**
 See also DLB 252
Newton, Suzanne 1936- .... **CLC 35**
 See also BYA 7; CA 41-44R; CANR 14; JRDA; SATA 5, 77
New York Dept. of Ed. .... **CLC 70**
Nexo, Martin Andersen
 1869-1954 .... **TCLC 43**
 See also CA 202; DLB 214
Nezval, Vitezslav 1900-1958 .... **TCLC 44**
 See also CDWLB 4; DLB 215
Ng, Fae Myenne 1957(?)- .... **CLC 81**
 See also CA 146
Ngema, Mbongeni 1955- .... **CLC 57**
 See also BW 2; CA 143; CANR 84; CD 5
Ngugi, James T(hiong'o) .... **CLC 3, 7, 13**
 See also Ngugi wa Thiong'o
Ngugi wa Thiong'o
 See Ngugi wa Thiong'o
 See also DLB 125

Ngugi wa Thiong'o 1938- .... **CLC 36; BLC 3**
 See also Ngugi, James T(hiong'o); Ngugi wa Thiong'o
 See also AFW; BRWS 8; BW 2; CA 81-84; CANR 27, 58; CDWLB 3; DAM MULT, NOV; DNFS 2; MTCW 1, 2; RGEL 2
Nichol, B(arrie) P(hillip) 1944-1988 . **CLC 18**
 See also CA 53-56; DLB 53; SATA 66
Nicholas of Cusa 1401-1464 .... **LC 80**
 See also DLB 115
Nichols, John (Treadwell) 1940- .... **CLC 38**
 See also CA 9-12R; CAAE 190; CAAS 2; CANR 6, 70; DLBY 1982; TCWW 2
Nichols, Leigh
 See Koontz, Dean R(ay)
Nichols, Peter (Richard) 1927- .... **CLC 5, 36, 65**
 See also CA 104; CANR 33, 86; CBD; CD 5; DLB 13, 245; MTCW 1
Nicholson, Linda ed. .... **CLC 65**
Ni Chuilleanain, Eilean 1942- .... **PC 34**
 See also CA 126; CANR 53, 83; CP 7; CWP; DLB 40
Nicolas, F. R. E.
 See Freeling, Nicolas
Niedecker, Lorine 1903-1970 ..... **CLC 10, 42; PC 42**
 See also CA 25-28; CAP 2; DAM POET; DLB 48
Nietzsche, Friedrich (Wilhelm)
 1844-1900 .... **TCLC 10, 18, 55**
 See also CA 121; CDWLB 2; DLB 129; EW 7; RGWL 2, 3; TWA
Nievo, Ippolito 1831-1861 .... **NCLC 22**
Nightingale, Anne Redmon 1943-
 See Redmon, Anne
 See also CA 103
Nightingale, Florence 1820-1910 ... **TCLC 85**
 See also CA 188; DLB 166
Nijo Yoshimoto 1320-1388 .... **CMLC 49**
 See also DLB 203
Nik. T. O.
 See Annensky, Innokenty (Fyodorovich)
Nin, Anais 1903-1977 ..... **CLC 1, 4, 8, 11, 14, 60, 127; SSC 10**
 See also AITN 2; AMWS 10; BPFB 2; CA 13-16R; CANR 22, 53; DAM NOV, POP; DLB 2, 4, 152; GLL 2; MAWW; MTCW 1, 2; RGAL 4; RGSF 2
Nisbet, Robert A(lexander)
 1913-1996 .... **TCLC 117**
 See also CA 25-28R; CANR 17; INT CANR-17
Nishida, Kitaro 1870-1945 .... **TCLC 83**
Nishiwaki, Junzaburo
 See Nishiwaki, Junzaburo
 See also CA 194
Nishiwaki, Junzaburo 1894-1982 .... **PC 15**
 See also Nishiwaki, Junzaburo
 See also CA 194; MJW; RGWL 3
Nissenson, Hugh 1933- .... **CLC 4, 9**
 See also CA 17-20R; CANR 27, 108; CN 7; DLB 28
Niven, Larry .... **CLC 8**
 See also Niven, Laurence Van Cott
 See also AAYA 27; BPFB 2; BYA 10; DLB 8; SCFW 2
Niven, Laurence Van Cott 1938-
 See Niven, Larry
 See also CA 21-24R; CAAS 12; CANR 14, 44, 66, 113; CPW; DAM POP; MTCW 1, 2; SATA 95; SFW 4
Nixon, Agnes Eckhardt 1927- .... **CLC 21**
 See also CA 110
Nizan, Paul 1905-1940 .... **TCLC 40**
 See also CA 161; DLB 72; GFL 1789 to the Present

Nkosi, Lewis 1936- .... **CLC 45; BLC 3**
See also BW 1, 3; CA 65-68; CANR 27, 81; CBD; CD 5; DAM MULT; DLB 157, 225

Nodier, (Jean) Charles (Emmanuel) 1780-1844 .... **NCLC 19**
See also DLB 119; GFL 1789 to the Present

Noguchi, Yone 1875-1947 .... **TCLC 80**

Nolan, Christopher 1965- .... **CLC 58**
See also CA 111; CANR 88

Noon, Jeff 1957- .... **CLC 91**
See also CA 148; CANR 83; DLB 267; SFW 4

Norden, Charles
See Durrell, Lawrence (George)

Nordhoff, Charles (Bernard) 1887-1947 .... **TCLC 23**
See also DLB 9; LAIT 1; RHW 1; SATA 23

Norfolk, Lawrence 1963- .... **CLC 76**
See also CA 144; CANR 85; CN 7; DLB 267

Norman, Marsha 1947- .... **CLC 28; DC 8**
See also CA 105; CABS 3; CAD; CANR 41; CD 5; CSW; CWD; DAM DRAM; DFS 2; DLB 266; DLBY 1984; FW

Normyx
See Douglas, (George) Norman

Norris, (Benjamin) Frank(lin, Jr.) 1870-1902 .... **TCLC 24; SSC 28**
See also AMW; BPFB 2; CA 160; CDALB 1865-1917; DLB 12, 71, 186; NFS 12; RGAL 4; TCWW 2; TUS

Norris, Leslie 1921- .... **CLC 14**
See also CA 11-12; CANR 14; CAP 1; CP 7; DLB 27, 256

North, Andrew
See Norton, Andre

North, Anthony
See Koontz, Dean R(ay)

North, Captain George
See Stevenson, Robert Louis (Balfour)

North, Captain George
See Stevenson, Robert Louis (Balfour)

North, Milou
See Erdrich, Louise

Northrup, B. A.
See Hubbard, L(afayette) Ron(ald)

North Staffs
See Hulme, T(homas) E(rnest)

Northup, Solomon 1808-1863 ...... **NCLC 105**

Norton, Alice Mary
See Norton, Andre
See also MAICYA 1; SATA 1, 43

Norton, Andre 1912- .... **CLC 12**
See also Norton, Alice Mary
See also AAYA 14; BPFB 2; BYA 4, 10, 12; CA 1-4R; CANR 68; CLR 50; DLB 8, 52; JRDA; MAICYA 1; MTCW 1; SATA 91; SUFW 1, 2; YAW

Norton, Caroline 1808-1877 .... **NCLC 47**
See also DLB 21, 159, 199

Norway, Nevil Shute 1899-1960
See Shute, Nevil
See also CA 102; CANR 85; MTCW 2

Norwid, Cyprian Kamil 1821-1883 .... **NCLC 17**
See also RGWL 3

Nosille, Nabrah
See Ellison, Harlan (Jay)

Nossack, Hans Erich 1901-1978 .... **CLC 6**
See also CA 93-96; DLB 69

Nostradamus 1503-1566 .... **LC 27**

Nosu, Chuji
See Ozu, Yasujiro

Notenburg, Eleanora (Genrikhovna) von
See Guro, Elena

Nova, Craig 1945- .... **CLC 7, 31**
See also CA 45-48; CANR 2, 53

Novak, Joseph
See Kosinski, Jerzy (Nikodem)

Novalis 1772-1801 .... **NCLC 13**
See also CDWLB 2; DLB 90; EW 5; RGWL 2, 3

Novick, Peter 1934- .... **CLC 164**
See also CA 188

Novis, Emile
See Weil, Simone (Adolphine)

Nowlan, Alden (Albert) 1933-1983 ... **CLC 15**
See also CA 9-12R; CANR 5; DAC; DAM MST; DLB 53; PFS 12

Noyes, Alfred 1880-1958 ...... **TCLC 7; PC 27**
See also CA 188; DLB 20; EXPP; FANT; PFS 4; RGEL 2

Nunn, Kem .... **CLC 34**
See also CA 159

Nwapa, Flora 1931-1993 .... **CLC 133; BLCS**
See also BW 2; CA 143; CANR 83; CDWLB 3; CWRI 5; DLB 125; WLIT 2

Nye, Robert 1939- .... **CLC 13, 42**
See also CA 33-36R; CANR 29, 67, 107; CN 7; CP 7; CWRI 5; DAM NOV; DLB 14, 271; FANT; HGG; MTCW 1; RHW; SATA 6

Nyro, Laura 1947-1997 .... **CLC 17**
See also CA 194

Oates, Joyce Carol 1938- .. **CLC 1, 2, 3, 6, 9, 11, 15, 19, 33, 52, 108, 134; SSC 6; WLC**
See also AAYA 15; AITN 1; AMWS 2; BEST 89:2; BPFB 2; BYA 11; CA 5-8R; CANR 25, 45, 74, 113, 113; CDALB 1968-1988; CN 7; CP 7; CPW; CWP; DA; DAB; DAC; DAM MST, NOV, POP; DLB 2, 5, 130; DLBY 1981; EXPS; FW; HGG; INT CANR-25; LAIT 4; MAWW; MTCW 1, 2; NFS 8; RGAL 4; RGSF 2; SSFS 1, 8; SUFW 2; TUS

O'Brian, E. G.
See Clarke, Arthur C(harles)

O'Brian, Patrick 1914-2000 .... **CLC 152**
See also CA 144; CANR 74; CPW; MTCW 2; RHW

O'Brien, Darcy 1939-1998 .... **CLC 11**
See also CA 21-24R; CANR 8, 59

O'Brien, Edna 1936- ...... **CLC 3, 5, 8, 13, 36, 65, 116; SSC 10**
See also BRWS 5; CA 1-4R; CANR 6, 41, 65, 102; CDBLB 1960 to Present; CN 7; DAM NOV; DLB 14, 231; FW; MTCW 1, 2; RGSF 2; WLIT 4

O'Brien, Fitz-James 1828-1862 ...... **NCLC 21**
See also DLB 74; RGAL 4; SUFW

O'Brien, Flann .... **CLC 1, 4, 5, 7, 10, 47**
See also O Nuallain, Brian
See also BRWS 2; DLB 231; RGEL 2

O'Brien, Richard 1942- .... **CLC 17**
See also CA 124

O'Brien, (William) Tim(othy) 1946- . **CLC 7, 19, 40, 103**
See also AAYA 16; AMWS 5; CA 85-88; CANR 40, 58; CDALBS; CN 7; CPW; DAM POP; DLB 152; DLBD 9; DLBY 1980; MTCW 2; RGAL 4; SSFS 5, 15

Obstfelder, Sigbjoern 1866-1900 .... **TCLC 23**

O'Casey, Sean 1880-1964 .... **CLC 1, 5, 9, 11, 15, 88; DC 12; WLCS**
See also BRW 7; CA 89-92; CANR 62; CBD; CDBLB 1914-1945; DAB; DAC; DAM DRAM, MST; DLB 10; MTCW 1, 2; RGEL 2; TEA; WLIT 4

O'Cathasaigh, Sean
See O'Casey, Sean

Occom, Samson 1723-1792 .... **LC 60**
See also DLB 175; NNAL

Ochs, Phil(ip David) 1940-1976 .... **CLC 17**
See also CA 185

O'Connor, Edwin (Greene) 1918-1968 .... **CLC 14**
See also CA 93-96

O'Connor, (Mary) Flannery 1925-1964 .... **CLC 1, 2, 3, 6, 10, 13, 15, 21, 66, 104; SSC 1, 23; WLC**
See also AAYA 7; AMW; BPFB 3; CA 1-4R; CANR 3, 41; CDALB 1941-1968; DA; DAB; DAC; DAM MST, NOV; DLB 2, 152; DLBD 12; DLBY 1980; EXPS; LAIT 5; MAWW; MTCW 1, 2; NFS 3; RGAL 4; RGSF 2; SSFS 2, 7, 10; TUS

O'Connor, Frank .... **CLC 23; SSC 5**
See also O'Donovan, Michael John
See also DLB 162; RGSF 2; SSFS 5

O'Dell, Scott 1898-1989 .... **CLC 30**
See also AAYA 3; BPFB 3; BYA 1, 2, 3, 5; CA 61-64; CANR 12, 30, 112; CLR 1, 16; DLB 52; JRDA; MAICYA 1, 2; SATA 12, 60, 134; WYA; YAW

Odets, Clifford 1906-1963 ...... **CLC 2, 28, 98; DC 6**
See also AMWS 2; CA 85-88; CAD; CANR 62; DAM DRAM; DFS 3; DLB 7, 26; MTCW 1, 2; RGAL 4; TUS

O'Doherty, Brian 1928- .... **CLC 76**
See also CA 105; CANR 108

O'Donnell, K. M.
See Malzberg, Barry N(athaniel)

O'Donnell, Lawrence
See Kuttner, Henry

O'Donovan, Michael John 1903-1966 .... **CLC 14**
See also O'Connor, Frank
See also CA 93-96; CANR 84

Oe, Kenzaburo 1935- .. **CLC 10, 36, 86; SSC 20**
See also Oe Kenzaburo
See also CA 97-100; CANR 36, 50, 74; DAM NOV; DLBY 1994; MTCW 1, 2; RGWL 3

Oe Kenzaburo
See Oe, Kenzaburo
See also CWW 2; DLB 182; EWL 3; MJW; RGSF 2; RGWL 2

O'Faolain, Julia 1932- .... **CLC 6, 19, 47, 108**
See also CA 81-84; CAAS 2; CANR 12, 61; CN 7; DLB 14, 231; FW; MTCW 1; RHW

O'Faolain, Sean 1900-1991 .... **CLC 1, 7, 14, 32, 70; SSC 13**
See also CA 61-64; CANR 12, 66; DLB 15, 162; MTCW 1, 2; RGEL 2; RGSF 2

O'Flaherty, Liam 1896-1984 .... **CLC 5, 34; SSC 6**
See also CA 101; CANR 35; DLB 36, 162; DLBY 1984; MTCW 1, 2; RGEL 2; RGSF 2; SSFS 5

Ogai
See Mori Ogai
See also MJW

Ogilvy, Gavin
See Barrie, J(ames) M(atthew)

O'Grady, Standish (James) 1846-1928 .... **TCLC 5**
See also CA 157

O'Grady, Timothy 1951- .... **CLC 59**
See also CA 138

O'Hara, Frank 1926-1966 .. **CLC 2, 5, 13, 78**
See also CA 9-12R; CANR 33; DAM POET; DLB 5, 16, 193; MTCW 1, 2; PFS 8; 12; RGAL 4; WP

O'Hara, John (Henry) 1905-1970 . **CLC 1, 2, 3, 6, 11, 42; SSC 15**
See also AMW; BPFB 3; CA 5-8R; CANR 31, 60; CDALB 1929-1941; DAM NOV; DLB 9, 86; DLBD 2; MTCW 1, 2; NFS 11; RGAL 4; RGSF 2

O Hehir, Diana 1922- .... **CLC 41**
See also CA 93-96

Ohiyesa
See Eastman, Charles A(lexander)

Okigbo, Christopher (Ifenayichukwu)
1932-1967 .... **CLC 25, 84; BLC 3; PC 7**
See also AFW; BW 1, 3; CA 77-80; CANR 74; CDWLB 3; DAM MULT, POET; DLB 125; MTCW 1, 2; RGEL 2

Okri, Ben 1959- .... **CLC 87**
See also AFW; BRWS 5; BW 2, 3; CA 138; CANR 65; CN 7; DLB 157, 231; INT CA-138; MTCW 2; RGSF 2; WLIT 2

Olds, Sharon 1942- .. **CLC 32, 39, 85; PC 22**
See also AMWS 10; CA 101; CANR 18, 41, 66, 98; CP 7; CPW; CWP; DAM POET; DLB 120; MTCW 2

Oldstyle, Jonathan
See Irving, Washington

Olesha, Iurii
See Olesha, Yuri (Karlovich)
See also RGWL 2

Olesha, Iurii Karlovich
See Olesha, Yuri (Karlovich)
See also DLB 272

Olesha, Yuri (Karlovich) 1899-1960 .. **CLC 8**
See also Olesha, Iurii; Olesha, Iurii Karlovich
See also CA 85-88; EW 11; RGWL 3

Oliphant, Mrs.
See Oliphant, Margaret (Oliphant Wilson)
See also SUFW

Oliphant, Laurence 1829(?)-1888 .. **NCLC 47**
See also DLB 18, 166

Oliphant, Margaret (Oliphant Wilson)
1828-1897 .... **NCLC 11, 61; SSC 25**
See also Oliphant, Mrs.
See also DLB 18, 159, 190; HGG; RGEL 2; RGSF 2

Oliver, Mary 1935- .... **CLC 19, 34, 98**
See also AMWS 7; CA 21-24R; CANR 9, 43, 84, 92; CP 7; CWP; DLB 5, 193; PFS 15

Olivier, Laurence (Kerr) 1907-1989 . **CLC 20**
See also CA 150

Olsen, Tillie 1912- ... **CLC 4, 13, 114; SSC 11**
See also BYA 11; CA 1-4R; CANR 1, 43, 74; CDALBS; CN 7; DA; DAB; DAC; DAM MST; DLB 28, 206; DLBY 1980; EXPS; FW; MTCW 1, 2; RGAL 4; RGSF 2; SSFS 1; TUS

Olson, Charles (John) 1910-1970 .. **CLC 1, 2, 5, 6, 9, 11, 29; PC 19**
See also AMWS 2; CA 13-16; CABS 2; CANR 35, 61; CAP 1; DAM POET; DLB 5, 16, 193; MTCW 1, 2; RGAL 4; WP

Olson, Toby 1937- .... **CLC 28**
See also CA 65-68; CANR 9, 31, 84; CP 7

Olyesha, Yuri
See Olesha, Yuri (Karlovich)

Omar Khayyam
See Khayyam, Omar
See also RGWL 2, 3

Ondaatje, (Philip) Michael 1943- .... **CLC 14, 29, 51, 76; PC 28**
See also CA 77-80; CANR 42, 74, 109; CN 7; CP 7; DAB; DAC; DAM MST; DLB 60; MTCW 2; PFS 8; TWA

Oneal, Elizabeth 1934-
See Oneal, Zibby
See also CA 106; CANR 28, 84; MAICYA 1, 2; SATA 30, 82; YAW

Oneal, Zibby .... **CLC 30**
See also Oneal, Elizabeth
See also AAYA 5, 41; BYA 13; CLR 13; JRDA; WYA

O'Neill, Eugene (Gladstone)
1888-1953 ...... **TCLC 1, 6, 27, 49; WLC**
See also AITN 1; AMW; CA 132; CAD; CDALB 1929-1941; DA; DAB; DAC; DAM DRAM, MST; DFS 9, 11, 12; DLB 7; LAIT 3; MTCW 1, 2; RGAL 4; TUS

Onetti, Juan Carlos 1909-1994 ... **CLC 7, 10; HLCS 2; SSC 23**
See also CA 85-88; CANR 32, 63; CDWLB 3; DAM MULT, NOV; DLB 113; HW 1, 2; LAW; MTCW 1, 2; RGSF 2

O Nuallain, Brian 1911-1966
See O'Brien, Flann
See also CA 21-22; CAP 2; DLB 231; FANT; TEA

Ophuls, Max 1902-1957 .... **TCLC 79**

Opie, Amelia 1769-1853 .... **NCLC 65**
See also DLB 116, 159; RGEL 2

Oppen, George 1908-1984 ..... **CLC 7, 13, 34; PC 35**
See also CA 13-16R; CANR 8, 82; DLB 5, 165; TCLC 107

Oppenheim, E(dward) Phillips
1866-1946 .... **TCLC 45**
See also CA 202; CMW 4; DLB 70

Opuls, Max
See Ophuls, Max

Origen c. 185-c. 254 .... **CMLC 19**

Orlovitz, Gil 1918-1973 .... **CLC 22**
See also CA 77-80; DLB 2, 5

Orris
See Ingelow, Jean

Ortega y Gasset, Jose 1883-1955 ... **TCLC 9; HLC 2**
See also CA 130; DAM MULT; EW 9; HW 1, 2; MTCW 1, 2

Ortese, Anna Maria 1914-1998 .... **CLC 89**
See also DLB 177

Ortiz, Simon J(oseph) 1941- ..... **CLC 45; PC 17**
See also AMWS 4; CA 134; CANR 69; CP 7; DAM MULT, POET; DLB 120, 175, 256; EXPP; NNAL; PFS 4; RGAL 4

Orton, Joe .... **CLC 4, 13, 43; DC 3**
See also Orton, John Kingsley
See also BRWS 5; CBD; CDBLB 1960 to Present; DFS 3, 6; DLB 13; GLL 1; MTCW 2; RGEL 2; TEA; WLIT 4

Orton, John Kingsley 1933-1967
See Orton, Joe
See also CA 85-88; CANR 35, 66; DAM DRAM; MTCW 1, 2

Orwell, George . **TCLC 2, 6, 15, 31, 51, 123, 128, 129; WLC**
See also Blair, Eric (Arthur)
See also BPFB 3; BRW 7; BYA 5; CDBLB 1945-1960; CLR 68; DAB; DLB 15, 98, 195, 255; EXPN; LAIT 4, 5; NFS 3, 7; RGEL 2; SCFW 2; SFW 4; SSFS 4; TEA; WLIT 4; YAW

Osborne, David
See Silverberg, Robert

Osborne, George
See Silverberg, Robert

Osborne, John (James) 1929-1994 .... **CLC 1, 2, 5, 11, 45; WLC**
See also BRWS 1; CA 13-16R; CANR 21, 56; CDBLB 1945-1960; DA; DAB; DAC; DAM DRAM, MST; DFS 4; DLB 13; MTCW 1, 2; RGEL 2

Osborne, Lawrence 1958- .... **CLC 50**
See also CA 189

Osbourne, Lloyd 1868-1947 .... **TCLC 93**

Oshima, Nagisa 1932- .... **CLC 20**
See also CA 121; CANR 78

Oskison, John Milton 1874-1947 ... **TCLC 35**
See also CA 144; CANR 84; DAM MULT; DLB 175; NNAL

Ossian c. 3rd cent. - .... **CMLC 28**
See also Macpherson, James

Ossoli, Sarah Margaret (Fuller)
1810-1850 .... **NCLC 5, 50**
See also Fuller, Margaret; Fuller, Sarah Margaret
See also CDALB 1640-1865; FW; SATA 25

Ostriker, Alicia (Suskin) 1937- .... **CLC 132**
See also CA 25-28R; CANR 10, 30, 62, 99; CWP; DLB 120; EXPP

Ostrovsky, Alexander 1823-1886 .. **NCLC 30, 57**

Otero, Blas de 1916-1979 .... **CLC 11**
See also CA 89-92; DLB 134

Otto, Rudolf 1869-1937 .... **TCLC 85**

Otto, Whitney 1955- .... **CLC 70**
See also CA 140

Ouida .... **TCLC 43**
See also De La Ramee, (Marie) Louise
See also DLB 18, 156; RGEL 2

Ouologuem, Yambo 1940- .... **CLC 146**
See also CA 176

Ousmane, Sembene 1923- ... **CLC 66; BLC 3**
See also Sembene, Ousmane
See also BW 1, 3; CA 125; CANR 81; CWW 2; MTCW 1

Ovid 43B.C.-17 .... **CMLC 7; PC 2**
See also AW 2; CDWLB 1; DAM POET; DLB 211; RGWL 2, 3; WP

Owen, Hugh
See Faust, Frederick (Schiller)

Owen, Wilfred (Edward Salter)
1893-1918 ... **TCLC 5, 27; PC 19; WLC**
See also BRW 6; CA 141; CDBLB 1914-1945; DA; DAB; DAC; DAM MST, POET; DLB 20; EXPP; MTCW 2; PFS 10; RGEL 2; WLIT 4

Owens, Rochelle 1936- .... **CLC 8**
See also CA 17-20R; CAAS 2; CAD; CANR 39; CD 5; CP 7; CWD; CWP

Oz, Amos 1939- .... **CLC 5, 8, 11, 27, 33, 54**
See also CA 53-56; CANR 27, 47, 65, 113; CWW 2; DAM NOV; MTCW 1, 2; RGSF 2; RGWL 3

Ozick, Cynthia 1928- .... **CLC 3, 7, 28, 62, 155; SSC 15**
See also AMWS 5; BEST 90:1; CA 17-20R; CANR 23, 58; CN 7; CPW; DAM NOV, POP; DLB 28, 152; DLBY 1982; EXPS; INT CANR-23; MTCW 1, 2; RGAL 4; RGSF 2; SSFS 3, 12

Ozu, Yasujiro 1903-1963 .... **CLC 16**
See also CA 112

Pabst, G. W. 1885-1967 .... **TCLC 127**

Pacheco, C.
See Pessoa, Fernando (Antonio Nogueira)

Pacheco, Jose Emilio 1939-
See also CA 131; CANR 65; DAM MULT; HLC 2; HW 1, 2; RGSF 2

Pa Chin .... **CLC 18**
See also Li Fei-kan

Pack, Robert 1929- .... **CLC 13**
See also CA 1-4R; CANR 3, 44, 82; CP 7; DLB 5; SATA 118

Padgett, Lewis
See Kuttner, Henry

Padilla (Lorenzo), Heberto
1932-2000 .... **CLC 38**
See also AITN 1; CA 131; HW 1

Page, James Patrick 1944-
See Page, Jimmy
See also CA 204

Page, Jimmy 1944- .... **CLC 12**
See also Page, James Patrick

Page, Louise 1955- .... **CLC 40**
See also CA 140; CANR 76; CBD; CD 5; CWD; DLB 233

Page, P(atricia) K(athleen) 1916- ...... **CLC 7, 18; PC 12**
See also Cape, Judith
See also CA 53-56; CANR 4, 22, 65; CP 7; DAC; DAM MST; DLB 68; MTCW 1; RGEL 2

Page, Stanton
See Fuller, Henry Blake

Page, Stanton
See Fuller, Henry Blake

Page, Thomas Nelson 1853-1922 .... **SSC 23**
See also CA 177; DLB 12, 78; DLBD 13; RGAL 4

Pagels, Elaine Hiesey 1943- .... **CLC 104**
See also CA 45-48; CANR 2, 24, 51; FW; NCFS 4

Paget, Violet 1856-1935
See Lee, Vernon
See also CA 166; GLL 1; HGG

Paget-Lowe, Henry
See Lovecraft, H(oward) P(hillips)

Paglia, Camille (Anna) 1947- .... **CLC 68**
See also CA 140; CANR 72; CPW; FW; GLL 2; MTCW 2

Paige, Richard
See Koontz, Dean R(ay)

Paine, Thomas 1737-1809 .... **NCLC 62**
See also AMWS 1; CDALB 1640-1865; DLB 31, 43, 73, 158; LAIT 1; RGAL 4; RGEL 2; TUS

Pakenham, Antonia
See Fraser, (Lady) Antonia (Pakenham)

Palamas, Costis
See Palamas, Kostes

Palamas, Kostes 1859-1943 .... **TCLC 5**
See also CA 190; RGWL 2, 3

Palamas, Kostis
See Palamas, Kostes

Palazzeschi, Aldo 1885-1974 .... **CLC 11**
See also CA 89-92; DLB 114, 264

Pales Matos, Luis 1898-1959
See Pales Matos, Luis
See also HLCS 2; HW 1; LAW

Paley, Grace 1922- .. **CLC 4, 6, 37, 140; SSC 8**
See also AMWS 6; CA 25-28R; CANR 13, 46, 74; CN 7; CPW; DAM POP; DLB 28, 218; EXPS; FW; INT CANR-13; MAWW; MTCW 1, 2; RGAL 4; RGSF 2; SSFS 3

Palin, Michael (Edward) 1943- .... **CLC 21**
See also Monty Python
See also CA 107; CANR 35, 109; SATA 67

Palliser, Charles 1947- .... **CLC 65**
See also CA 136; CANR 76; CN 7

Palma, Ricardo 1833-1919 .... **TCLC 29**
See also CA 168; LAW

Pancake, Breece Dexter 1952-1979
See Pancake, Breece D'J
See also CA 123

Pancake, Breece D'J .... **CLC 29**
See also Pancake, Breece Dexter
See also DLB 130

Panchenko, Nikolai .... **CLC 59**

Pankhurst, Emmeline (Goulden) 1858-1928 .... **TCLC 100**
See also FW

Panko, Rudy
See Gogol, Nikolai (Vasilyevich)

Papadiamantis, Alexandros 1851-1911 .... **TCLC 29**
See also CA 168

Papadiamantopoulos, Johannes 1856-1910
See Moreas, Jean

Papini, Giovanni 1881-1956 .... **TCLC 22**
See also CA 180; DLB 264

Paracelsus 1493-1541 .... **LC 14**
See also DLB 179

Parasol, Peter
See Stevens, Wallace

Pardo Bazan, Emilia 1851-1921 .... **SSC 30**
See also FW; RGSF 2; RGWL 2, 3

Pareto, Vilfredo 1848-1923 .... **TCLC 69**
See also CA 175

Paretsky, Sara 1947- .... **CLC 135**
See also AAYA 30; BEST 90:3; CA 129; CANR 59, 95; CMW 4; CPW; DAM POP; INT CA-129; MSW; RGAL 4

Parfenie, Maria
See Codrescu, Andrei

Parini, Jay (Lee) 1948- .... **CLC 54, 133**
See also CA 97-100; CAAS 16; CANR 32, 87

Park, Jordan
See Kornbluth, C(yril) M.; Pohl, Frederik

Park, Robert E(zra) 1864-1944 ..... **TCLC 73**
See also CA 165

Parker, Bert
See Ellison, Harlan (Jay)

Parker, Dorothy (Rothschild) 1893-1967 .. **CLC 15, 68; PC 28; SSC 2**
See also AMWS 9; CA 19-20; CAP 2; DAM POET; DLB 11, 45, 86; EXPP; FW; MAWW; MTCW 1, 2; RGAL 4; RGSF 2; TUS

Parker, Robert B(rown) 1932- .... **CLC 27**
See also AAYA 28; BEST 89:4; BPFB 3; CA 49-52; CANR 1, 26, 52, 89; CMW 4; CPW; DAM NOV, POP; INT CANR-26; MSW; MTCW 1

Parkin, Frank 1940- .... **CLC 43**
See also CA 147

Parkman, Francis, Jr. 1823-1893 .. **NCLC 12**
See also AMWS 2; DLB 1, 30, 183, 186, 235; RGAL 4

Parks, Gordon (Alexander Buchanan) 1912- .... **CLC 1, 16; BLC 3**
See also AAYA 36; AITN 2; BW 2, 3; CA 41-44R; CANR 26, 66; DAM MULT; DLB 33; MTCW 2; SATA 8, 108

Parks, Tim(othy Harold) 1954- ...... **CLC 147**
See also CA 131; CANR 77; DLB 231; INT CA-131

Parmenides c. 515B.C.-c. 450B.C. .... **CMLC 22**
See also DLB 176

Parnell, Thomas 1679-1718 .... **LC 3**
See also DLB 95; RGEL 2

Parra, Nicanor 1914- ... **CLC 2, 102; HLC 2; PC 39**
See also CA 85-88; CANR 32; CWW 2; DAM MULT; HW 1; LAW; MTCW 1

Parra Sanojo, Ana Teresa de la 1890-1936
See de la Parra, (Ana) Teresa (Sonojo)
See also HLCS 2; LAW

Parrish, Mary Frances
See Fisher, M(ary) F(rances) K(ennedy)

Parshchikov, Aleksei .... **CLC 59**

Parson, Professor
See Coleridge, Samuel Taylor

Parson Lot
See Kingsley, Charles

Parton, Sara Payson Willis 1811-1872 .... **NCLC 86**
See also DLB 43, 74, 239

Partridge, Anthony
See Oppenheim, E(dward) Phillips

Pascal, Blaise 1623-1662 .... **LC 35**
See also DLB 268; EW 3; GFL Beginnings to 1789; RGWL 2, 3; TWA

Pascoli, Giovanni 1855-1912 .... **TCLC 45**
See also CA 170; EW 7

Pasolini, Pier Paolo 1922-1975 .. **CLC 20, 37, 106; PC 17**
See also CA 93-96; CANR 63; DLB 128, 177; MTCW 1; RGWL 2, 3

Pasquini
See Silone, Ignazio

Pastan, Linda (Olenik) 1932- .... **CLC 27**
See also CA 61-64; CANR 18, 40, 61, 113; CP 7; CSW; CWP; DAM POET; DLB 5; PFS 8

Pasternak, Boris (Leonidovich) 1890-1960 ...... **CLC 7, 10, 18, 63; PC 6; SSC 31; WLC**
See also BPFB 3; CA 127; DA; DAB; DAC; DAM MST, NOV, POET; EW 10; MTCW 1, 2; RGSF 2; RGWL 2, 3; TWA; WP

Patchen, Kenneth 1911-1972 .... **CLC 1, 2, 18**
See also CA 1-4R; CANR 3, 35; DAM POET; DLB 16, 48; MTCW 1; RGAL 4

Pater, Walter (Horatio) 1839-1894 . **NCLC 7, 90**
See also BRW 5; CDBLB 1832-1890; DLB 57, 156; RGEL 2; TEA

Paterson, A(ndrew) B(arton) 1864-1941 .... **TCLC 32**
See also CA 155; DLB 230; RGEL 2; SATA 97

Paterson, Katherine (Womeldorf) 1932- .... **CLC 12, 30**
See also AAYA 1, 31; BYA 1, 2, 7; CA 21-24R; CANR 28, 59, 111; CLR 7, 50; CWRI 5; DLB 52; JRDA; MAI-CYA 1, 2; MAICYAS 1; MTCW 1; SATA 13, 53, 92, 133; WYA; YAW

Patmore, Coventry Kersey Dighton 1823-1896 .... **NCLC 9**
See also DLB 35, 98; RGEL 2; TEA

Paton, Alan (Stewart) 1903-1988 ...... **CLC 4, 10, 25, 55, 106; WLC**
See also AAYA 26; AFW; BPFB 3; BRWS 2; BYA 1; CA 13-16; CANR 22; CAP 1; DA; DAB; DAC; DAM MST, NOV; DLB 225; DLBD 17; EXPN; LAIT 4; MTCW 1, 2; NFS 3; RGEL 2; SATA 11; SATA-Obit 56; TWA; WLIT 2

Paton Walsh, Gillian 1937- .... **CLC 35**
See also Paton Walsh, Jill; Walsh, Jill Paton
See also AAYA 11; CANR 38, 83; CLR 2, 65; DLB 161; JRDA; MAICYA 1, 2; SAAS 3; SATA 4, 72, 109; YAW

Paton Walsh, Jill
See Paton Walsh, Gillian
See also BYA 1, 8

Patton, George S(mith), Jr. 1885-1945 .... **TCLC 79**
See also CA 189

Paulding, James Kirke 1778-1860 ... **NCLC 2**
See also DLB 3, 59, 74, 250; RGAL 4

Paulin, Thomas Neilson 1949-
See Paulin, Tom
See also CA 128; CANR 98; CP 7

Paulin, Tom .... **CLC 37**
See also Paulin, Thomas Neilson
See also DLB 40

Pausanias c. 1st cent. - .... **CMLC 36**

Paustovsky, Konstantin (Georgievich) 1892-1968 .... **CLC 40**
See also CA 93-96; DLB 272

Pavese, Cesare 1908-1950 .. **TCLC 3; PC 13; SSC 19**
See also CA 169; DLB 128, 177; EW 12; RGSF 2; RGWL 2, 3; TWA

Pavic, Milorad 1929- .... **CLC 60**
See also CA 136; CDWLB 4; CWW 2; DLB 181; RGWL 2

Pavlov, Ivan Petrovich 1849-1936 . **TCLC 91**
See also CA 180

Payne, Alan
See Jakes, John (William)

Paz, Gil
See Lugones, Leopoldo

Paz, Octavio 1914-1998 . **CLC 3, 4, 6, 10, 19, 51, 65, 119; HLC 2; PC 1; WLC**
See also CA 73-76; CANR 32, 65, 104; CWW 2; DA; DAB; DAC; DAM MST, MULT, POET; DLBY 1990, 1998; DNFS 1; HW 1, 2; LAW; LAWS 1; MTCW 1, 2; RGWL 2, 3; SSFS 13; TWA; WLIT 1

p'Bitek, Okot 1931-1982 ..... **CLC 96; BLC 3**
See also AFW; BW 2, 3; CA 124; CANR 82; DAM MULT; DLB 125; MTCW 1, 2; RGEL 2; WLIT 2

Peacock, Molly 1947- .... **CLC 60**
See also CA 103; CAAS 21; CANR 52, 84; CP 7; CWP; DLB 120

Peacock, Thomas Love 1785-1866 .... **NCLC 22**
See also BRW 4; DLB 96, 116; RGEL 2; RGSF 2

Peake, Mervyn 1911-1968 .... **CLC 7, 54**
See also CA 5-8R; CANR 3; DLB 15, 160, 255; FANT; MTCW 1; RGEL 2; SATA 23; SFW 4

Pearce, Philippa
See Christie, Philippa
See also CA 5-8R; CANR 4, 109; CWRI 5; FANT; MAICYA 2

Pearl, Eric
See Elman, Richard (Martin)

Pearson, T(homas) R(eid) 1956- .... **CLC 39**
See also CA 130; CANR 97; CSW; INT 130

Peck, Dale 1967- .... **CLC 81**
See also CA 146; CANR 72; GLL 2

Peck, John (Frederick) 1941- .... **CLC 3**
See also CA 49-52; CANR 3, 100; CP 7

Peck, Richard (Wayne) 1934- .... **CLC 21**
See also AAYA 1, 24; BYA 1, 6, 8, 11; CA 85-88; CANR 19, 38; CLR 15; INT CANR-19; JRDA; MAICYA 1, 2; SAAS 2; SATA 18, 55, 97; SATA-Essay 110; WYA; YAW

Peck, Robert Newton 1928- .... **CLC 17**
See also AAYA 3, 43; BYA 1, 6; CA 81-84, 182; CAAE 182; CANR 31, 63; CLR 45; DA; DAC; DAM MST; JRDA; LAIT 3; MAICYA 1, 2; SAAS 1; SATA 21, 62, 111; SATA-Essay 108; WYA; YAW

Peckinpah, (David) Sam(uel) 1925-1984 .... **CLC 20**
See also CA 109; CANR 82

Pedersen, Knut 1859-1952
See Hamsun, Knut
See also CA 119; CANR 63; MTCW 1, 2

Peeslake, Gaffer
See Durrell, Lawrence (George)

Peguy, Charles (Pierre) 1873-1914 .... **TCLC 10**
See also CA 193; DLB 258; GFL 1789 to the Present

Peirce, Charles Sanders 1839-1914 .... **TCLC 81**
See also CA 194; DLB 270

Pellicer, Carlos 1900(?)-1977
See also CA 153; HLCS 2; HW 1

Pena, Ramon del Valle y
See Valle-Inclan, Ramon (Maria) del

Pendennis, Arthur Esquir
See Thackeray, William Makepeace

Penn, William 1644-1718 .... **LC 25**
See also DLB 24

PEPECE
See Prado (Calvo), Pedro

Pepys, Samuel 1633-1703 ... **LC 11, 58; WLC**
See also BRW 2; CDBLB 1660-1789; DA; DAB; DAC; DAM MST; DLB 101, 213; NCFS 4; RGEL 2; TEA; WLIT 3

Percy, Thomas 1729-1811 .... **NCLC 95**
See also DLB 104

Percy, Walker 1916-1990 .... **CLC 2, 3, 6, 8, 14, 18, 47, 65**
See also AMWS 3; BPFB 3; CA 1-4R; CANR 1, 23, 64; CPW; CSW; DAM NOV, POP; DLB 2; DLBY 1980, 1990; MTCW 1, 2; RGAL 4; TUS

Percy, William Alexander 1885-1942 .... **TCLC 84**
See also CA 163; MTCW 2

Perec, Georges 1936-1982 .... **CLC 56, 116**
See also CA 141; DLB 83; GFL 1789 to the Present; RGWL 3

Pereda (y Sanchez de Porrua), Jose Maria de 1833-1906 .... **TCLC 16**

Pereda y Porrua, Jose Maria de
See Pereda (y Sanchez de Porrua), Jose Maria de

Peregoy, George Weems
See Mencken, H(enry) L(ouis)

Perelman, S(idney) J(oseph) 1904-1979 .. **CLC 3, 5, 9, 15, 23, 44, 49; SSC 32**
See also AITN 1, 2; BPFB 3; CA 73-76; CANR 18; DAM DRAM; DLB 11, 44; MTCW 1, 2; RGAL 4

Peret, Benjamin 1899-1959 .... **TCLC 20; PC 33**
See also CA 186; GFL 1789 to the Present

Peretz, Isaac Loeb 1851(?)-1915 ... **TCLC 16; SSC 26**

Peretz, Yitzkhok Leibush
See Peretz, Isaac Loeb

Perez Galdos, Benito 1843-1920 ... **TCLC 27; HLCS 2**
See also Galdos, Benito Perez
See also CA 153; HW 1; RGWL 2, 3

Peri Rossi, Cristina 1941- .. **CLC 156; HLCS 2**
See also CA 131; CANR 59, 81; DLB 145; HW 1, 2

Perlata
See Peret, Benjamin

Perloff, Marjorie G(abrielle) 1931- .... **CLC 137**
See also CA 57-60; CANR 7, 22, 49, 104

Perrault, Charles 1628-1703 ... **LC 2, 56; DC 12**
See also BYA 4; CLR 79; DLB 268; GFL Beginnings to 1789; MAICYA 1, 2; RGWL 2, 3; SATA 25; WCH

Perry, Anne 1938- .... **CLC 126**
See also CA 101; CANR 22, 50, 84; CMW 4; CN 7; CPW

Perry, Brighton
See Sherwood, Robert E(mmet)

Perse, St.-John
See Leger, (Marie-Rene Auguste) Alexis Saint-Leger

Perse, Saint-John
See Leger, (Marie-Rene Auguste) Alexis Saint-Leger
See also DLB 258; RGWL 3

Perutz, Leo(pold) 1882-1957 .... **TCLC 60**
See also CA 147; DLB 81

Peseenz, Tulio F.
See Lopez y Fuentes, Gregorio

Pesetsky, Bette 1932- .... **CLC 28**
See also CA 133; DLB 130

Peshkov, Alexei Maximovich 1868-1936
See Gorky, Maxim
See also CA 141; CANR 83; DA; DAC; DAM DRAM, MST, NOV; MTCW 2

Pessoa, Fernando (Antonio Nogueira) 1898-1935 ..... **TCLC 27; HLC 2; PC 20**
See also CA 183; DAM MULT; EW 10; RGWL 2, 3; WP

Peterkin, Julia Mood 1880-1961 ...... **CLC 31**
See also CA 102; DLB 9

Peters, Joan K(aren) 1945- .... **CLC 39**
See also CA 158; CANR 109

Peters, Robert L(ouis) 1924- .... **CLC 7**
See also CA 13-16R; CAAS 8; CP 7; DLB 105

Petofi, Sandor 1823-1849 .... **NCLC 21**
See also RGWL 2, 3

Petrakis, Harry Mark 1923- .... **CLC 3**
See also CA 9-12R; CANR 4, 30, 85; CN 7

Petrarch 1304-1374 .... **CMLC 20; PC 8**
See also DAM POET; EW 2; RGWL 2, 3

Petronius c. 20-66 .... **CMLC 34**
See also AW 2; CDWLB 1; DLB 211; RGWL 2, 3

Petrov, Evgeny .... **TCLC 21**
See also Kataev, Evgeny Petrovich

Petry, Ann (Lane) 1908-1997 ... **CLC 1, 7, 18**
See also AFAW 1, 2; BPFB 3; BW 1, 3; BYA 2; CA 5-8R; CAAS 6; CANR 4, 46; CLR 12; CN 7; DLB 76; JRDA; LAIT 1; MAICYA 1, 2; MAICYAS 1; MTCW 1; RGAL 4; SATA 5; SATA-Obit 94; TCLC 112; TUS

Petursson, Halligrimur 1614-1674 .... **LC 8**

Peychinovich
See Vazov, Ivan (Minchov)

Phaedrus c. 15B.C.-c. 50 .... **CMLC 25**
See also DLB 211

Phelps (Ward), Elizabeth Stuart
See Phelps, Elizabeth Stuart
See also FW

Phelps, Elizabeth Stuart 1844-1911 .... **TCLC 113**
See also Phelps (Ward), Elizabeth Stuart
See also DLB 74

Philips, Katherine 1632-1664 . **LC 30; PC 40**
See also DLB 131; RGEL 2

Philipson, Morris H. 1926- .... **CLC 53**
See also CA 1-4R; CANR 4

Phillips, Caryl 1958- .... **CLC 96; BLCS**
See also BRWS 5; BW 2; CA 141; CANR 63, 104; CBD; CD 5; CN 7; DAM MULT; DLB 157; MTCW 2; WLIT 4

Phillips, David Graham 1867-1911 .... **TCLC 44**
See also CA 176; DLB 9, 12; RGAL 4

Phillips, Jack
See Sandburg, Carl (August)

Phillips, Jayne Anne 1952- .... **CLC 15, 33, 139; SSC 16**
See also BPFB 3; CA 101; CANR 24, 50, 96; CN 7; CSW; DLBY 1980; INT CANR-24; MTCW 1, 2; RGAL 4; RGSF 2; SSFS 4

Phillips, Richard
See Dick, Philip K(indred)

Phillips, Robert (Schaeffer) 1938- ..... **CLC 28**
See also CA 17-20R; CAAS 13; CANR 8; DLB 105

Phillips, Ward
See Lovecraft, H(oward) P(hillips)

Piccolo, Lucio 1901-1969 .... **CLC 13**
See also CA 97-100; DLB 114

Pickthall, Marjorie L(owry) C(hristie) 1883-1922 .... **TCLC 21**
See also DLB 92

Pico della Mirandola, Giovanni 1463-1494 .... **LC 15**

Piercy, Marge 1936- .... **CLC 3, 6, 14, 18, 27, 62, 128; PC 29**
See also BPFB 3; CA 21-24R; CAAE 187; CAAS 1; CANR 13, 43, 66, 111; CN 7; CP 7; CWP; DLB 120, 227; EXPP; FW; MTCW 1, 2; PFS 9; SFW 4

Piers, Robert
See Anthony, Piers

Pieyre de Mandiargues, Andre 1909-1991
See Mandiargues, Andre Pieyre de
See also CA 103; CANR 22, 82; GFL 1789 to the Present

Pilnyak, Boris 1894-1938 . **TCLC 23; SSC 48**
See also Vogau, Boris Andreyevich

Pinchback, Eugene
See Toomer, Jean

Pincherle, Alberto 1907-1990 ...... **CLC 11, 18**
See also Moravia, Alberto
See also CA 25-28R; CANR 33, 63; DAM NOV; DLB ; MTCW 1

Pinckney, Darryl 1953- .... **CLC 76**
See also BW 2, 3; CA 143; CANR 79

Pindar 518(?)B.C.-438(?)B.C. .... **CMLC 12; PC 19**
See also AW 1; CDWLB 1; DLB 176; RGWL 2

Pineda, Cecile 1942- .... **CLC 39**
See also CA 118; DLB 209

Pinero, Arthur Wing 1855-1934 .... **TCLC 32**
See also CA 153; DAM DRAM; DLB 10; RGEL 2

Pinero, Miguel (Antonio Gomez) 1946-1988 .... **CLC 4, 55**
See also CA 61-64; CAD; CANR 29, 90; DLB 266; HW 1

Pinget, Robert 1919-1997 .... **CLC 7, 13, 37**
See also CA 85-88; CWW 2; DLB 83; GFL 1789 to the Present

Pink Floyd
See Barrett, (Roger) Syd; Gilmour, David; Mason, Nick; Waters, Roger; Wright, Rick

Pinkney, Edward 1802-1828 .... **NCLC 31**
See also DLB 248

Pinkwater, Daniel
See Pinkwater, Daniel Manus

Pinkwater, Daniel Manus 1941- .... **CLC 35**
See also AAYA 1; BYA 9; CA 29-32R; CANR 12, 38, 89; CLR 4; CSW; FANT; JRDA; MAICYA 1, 2; SAAS 3; SATA 8, 46, 76, 114; SFW 4; YAW

Pinkwater, Manus
See Pinkwater, Daniel Manus

Pinsky, Robert 1940- .... **CLC 9, 19, 38, 94, 121; PC 27**
See also AMWS 6; CA 29-32R; CAAS 4; CANR 58, 97; CP 7; DAM POET; DLBY 1982, 1998; MTCW 2; RGAL 4

Pinta, Harold
See Pinter, Harold

Pinter, Harold 1930- .. **CLC 1, 3, 6, 9, 11, 15, 27, 58, 73; DC 15; WLC**
See also BRWR 1; BRWS 1; CA 5-8R; CANR 33, 65, 112; CBD; CD 5; CDBLB 1960 to Present; DA; DAB; DAC; DAM DRAM, MST; DFS 3, 5, 7, 14; DLB 13; IDFW 3, 4; MTCW 1, 2; RGEL 2; TEA

Piozzi, Hester Lynch (Thrale) 1741-1821 .... **NCLC 57**
See also DLB 104, 142

Pirandello, Luigi 1867-1936 ...... **TCLC 4, 29; DC 5; SSC 22; WLC**
See also CA 153; CANR 103; DA; DAB; DAC; DAM DRAM, MST; DFS 4, 9; DLB 264; EW 8; MTCW 2; RGSF 2; RGWL 2, 3

Pirsig, Robert M(aynard) 1928- ... **CLC 4, 6, 73**
See also CA 53-56; CANR 42, 74; CPW 1; DAM POP; MTCW 1, 2; SATA 39

Pisarev, Dmitry Ivanovich 1840-1868 .... **NCLC 25**

Pix, Mary (Griffith) 1666-1709 .... **LC 8**
See also DLB 80

Pixerecourt, (Rene Charles) Guilbert de 1773-1844 .... **NCLC 39**
See also DLB 192; GFL 1789 to the Present

Plaatje, Sol(omon) T(shekisho) 1878-1932 .... **TCLC 73; BLCS**
See also BW 2, 3; CA 141; CANR 79; DLB 125, 225

Plaidy, Jean
See Hibbert, Eleanor Alice Burford

Planche, James Robinson 1796-1880 .... **NCLC 42**
See also RGEL 2

Plant, Robert 1948- .... **CLC 12**

Plante, David (Robert) 1940- . **CLC 7, 23, 38**
See also CA 37-40R; CANR 12, 36, 58, 82; CN 7; DAM NOV; DLBY 1983; INT CANR-12; MTCW 1

Plath, Sylvia 1932-1963 ..... **CLC 1, 2, 3, 5, 9, 11, 14, 17, 50, 51, 62, 111; PC 1, 37; WLC**
See also AAYA 13; AMWS 1; BPFB 3; CA 19-20; CANR 34, 101; CAP 2; CDALB 1941-1968; DA; DAB; DAC; DAM MST, POET; DLB 5, 6, 152; EXPN; EXPP; FW; LAIT 4; MAWW; MTCW 1, 2; NFS 1; PAB; PFS 1, 15; RGAL 4; SATA 96; TUS; WP; YAW

Plato c. 428B.C.-347B.C. ... **CMLC 8; WLCS**
See also AW 1; CDWLB 1; DA; DAB; DAC; DAM MST; DLB 176; LAIT 1; RGWL 2, 3

Platonov, Andrei
See Klimentov, Andrei Platonovich

Platonov, Andrei Platonovich
See Klimentov, Andrei Platonovich
See also DLB 272

Platt, Kin 1911- .... **CLC 26**
See also AAYA 11; CA 17-20R; CANR 11; JRDA; SAAS 17; SATA 21, 86; WYA

Plautus c. 254B.C.-c. 184B.C. ...... **CMLC 24; DC 6**
See also AW 1; CDWLB 1; DLB 211; RGWL 2, 3

Plick et Plock
See Simenon, Georges (Jacques Christian)

Plieksans, Janis
See Rainis, Janis

Plimpton, George (Ames) 1927- .... **CLC 36**
See also AITN 1; CA 21-24R; CANR 32, 70, 103; DLB 185, 241; MTCW 1, 2; SATA 10

Pliny the Elder c. 23-79 .... **CMLC 23**
See also DLB 211

Plomer, William Charles Franklin 1903-1973 .... **CLC 4, 8**
See also AFW; CA 21-22; CANR 34; CAP 2; DLB 20, 162, 191, 225; MTCW 1; RGEL 2; RGSF 2; SATA 24

Plotinus 204-270 .... **CMLC 46**
See also CDWLB 1; DLB 176

Plowman, Piers
See Kavanagh, Patrick (Joseph)

Plum, J.
See Wodehouse, P(elham) G(renville)

Plumly, Stanley (Ross) 1939- .... **CLC 33**
See also CA 110; CANR 97; CP 7; DLB 5, 193; INT 110

Plumpe, Friedrich Wilhelm 1888-1931 .... **TCLC 53**

Po Chu-i 772-846 .... **CMLC 24**

Poe, Edgar Allan 1809-1849 ..... **NCLC 1, 16, 55, 78, 94, 97, 117; PC 1; SSC 1, 22, 34, 35, 54; WLC**
See also AAYA 14; AMW; BPFB 3; BYA 5, 11; CDALB 1640-1865; CMW 4; DA; DAB; DAC; DAM MST, POET; DLB 3, 59, 73, 74, 248, 254; EXPP; EXPS; HGG; LAIT 2; MSW; PAB; PFS 1, 3, 9; RGAL 4; RGSF 2; SATA 23; SCFW 2; SFW 4; SSFS 2, 4, 7, 8; SUFW; TUS; WP; WYA

Poet of Titchfield Street, The
See Pound, Ezra (Weston Loomis)

Pohl, Frederik 1919- .... **CLC 18; SSC 25**
See also AAYA 24; CA 61-64; CAAE 188; CAAS 1; CANR 11, 37, 81; CN 7; DLB 8; INT CANR-11; MTCW 1, 2; SATA 24; SCFW 2; SFW 4

Poirier, Louis 1910-
See Gracq, Julien
See also CA 126; CWW 2

Poitier, Sidney 1927- .... **CLC 26**
See also BW 1; CA 117; CANR 94

Polanski, Roman 1933- .... **CLC 16**
See also CA 77-80

Poliakoff, Stephen 1952- .... **CLC 38**
See also CA 106; CBD; CD 5; DLB 13

Police, The
See Copeland, Stewart (Armstrong); Summers, Andrew James; Sumner, Gordon Matthew

Polidori, John William 1795-1821 . **NCLC 51**
See also DLB 116; HGG

Pollitt, Katha 1949- .... **CLC 28, 122**
See also CA 122; CANR 66, 108; MTCW 1, 2

Pollock, (Mary) Sharon 1936- .... **CLC 50**
See also CA 141; CD 5; CWD; DAC; DAM DRAM, MST; DFS 3; DLB 60; FW

Polo, Marco 1254-1324 .... **CMLC 15**

Polonsky, Abraham (Lincoln) 1910-1999 .... **CLC 92**
See also CA 104; DLB 26; INT 104

Polybius c. 200B.C.-c. 118B.C. .... **CMLC 17**
See also AW 1; DLB 176; RGWL 2, 3

Pomerance, Bernard 1940- .... **CLC 13**
See also CA 101; CAD; CANR 49; CD 5; DAM DRAM; DFS 9; LAIT 2

Ponge, Francis 1899-1988 .... **CLC 6, 18**
See also CA 85-88; CANR 40, 86; DAM POET; GFL 1789 to the Present; RGWL 2, 3

Poniatowska, Elena 1933- . **CLC 140; HLC 2**
See also CA 101; CANR 32, 66, 107; CDWLB 3; DAM MULT; DLB 113; HW 1, 2; LAWS 1; WLIT 1

Pontoppidan, Henrik 1857-1943 .... **TCLC 29**
See also CA 170

Poole, Josephine .... **CLC 17**
See also Helyar, Jane Penelope Josephine
See also SAAS 2; SATA 5

Popa, Vasko 1922-1991 .... **CLC 19**
See also CA 148; CDWLB 4; DLB 181; RGWL 2, 3

Pope, Alexander 1688-1744 ...... **LC 3, 58, 60, 64; PC 26; WLC**
See also BRW 3; BRWR 1; CDBLB 1660-1789; DA; DAB; DAC; DAM MST, POET; DLB 95, 101, 213; EXPP; PAB; PFS 12; RGEL 2; WLIT 3; WP

Popov, Yevgeny .... **CLC 59**

Poquelin, Jean-Baptiste
See Moliere

Porter, Connie (Rose) 1959(?)- .... **CLC 70**
See also AAYA 65; BW 2, 3; CA 142; CANR 90, 109; SATA 81, 129

Porter, Gene(va Grace) Stratton .. **TCLC 21**
See also Stratton-Porter, Gene(va Grace)
See also BPFB 3; CWRI 5; RHW

Porter, Katherine Anne 1890-1980 ... **CLC 1, 3, 7, 10, 13, 15, 27, 101; SSC 4, 31, 43**
See also AAYA 42; AITN 2; AMW; BPFB 3; CA 1-4R; CANR 1, 65; CDALBS; DA; DAB; DAC; DAM MST, NOV; DLB 4, 9, 102; DLBD 12; DLBY 1980; EXPS; LAIT 3; MAWW; MTCW 1, 2; NFS 14; RGAL 4; RGSF 2; SATA 39; SATA-Obit 23; SSFS 1, 8, 11; TUS

Porter, Peter (Neville Frederick) 1929- .... **CLC 5, 13, 33**
See also CA 85-88; CP 7; DLB 40

Porter, William Sydney 1862-1910
See Henry, O.
See also CA 131; CDALB 1865-1917; DA; DAB; DAC; DAM MST; DLB 12, 78, 79; MTCW 1, 2; TUS; YABC 2

Portillo (y Pacheco), Jose Lopez
See Lopez Portillo (y Pacheco), Jose

Portillo Trambley, Estela 1927-1998
See Trambley, Estela Portillo
See also CANR 32; DAM MULT; DLB 209; HLC 2; HW 1

Posse, Abel .... CLC 70

Post, Melville Davisson
1869-1930 .... TCLC 39
See also CA 202; CMW 4

Potok, Chaim 1929-2002 ... CLC 2, 7, 14, 26, 112
See also AAYA 15; AITN 1, 2; BPFB 3; BYA 1; CA 17-20R; CANR 19, 35, 64, 98; CN 7; DAM NOV; DLB 28, 152; EXPN; INT CANR-19; LAIT 4; MTCW 1, 2; NFS 4; SATA 33, 106; SATA-Obit 134; TUS; YAW

Potter, Dennis (Christopher George)
1935-1994 .... CLC 58, 86, 123
See also CA 107; CANR 33, 61; CBD; DLB 233; MTCW 1

Pound, Ezra (Weston Loomis)
1885-1972 .. CLC 1, 2, 3, 4, 5, 7, 10, 13, 18, 34, 48, 50, 112; PC 4; WLC
See also AMW; AMWR 1; CA 5-8R; CANR 40; CDALB 1917-1929; DA; DAB; DAC; DAM MST, POET; DLB 4, 45, 63; DLBD 15; EFS 2; EXPP; MTCW 1, 2; PAB; PFS 2, 8; RGAL 4; TUS; WP

Povod, Reinaldo 1959-1994 .... CLC 44
See also CA 136; CANR 83

Powell, Adam Clayton, Jr.
1908-1972 .... CLC 89; BLC 3
See also BW 1, 3; CA 102; CANR 86; DAM MULT

Powell, Anthony (Dymoke)
1905-2000 .... CLC 1, 3, 7, 9, 10, 31
See also BRW 7; CA 1-4R; CANR 1, 32, 62, 107; CDBLB 1945-1960; CN 7; DLB 15; MTCW 1, 2; RGEL 2; TEA

Powell, Dawn 1896(?)-1965 .... CLC 66
See also CA 5-8R; DLBY 1997

Powell, Padgett 1952- .... CLC 34
See also CA 126; CANR 63, 101; CSW; DLB 234; DLBY 01

Powell, (Oval) Talmage 1920-2000
See Queen, Ellery
See also CA 5-8R; CANR 2, 80

Power, Susan 1961- .... CLC 91
See also BYA 14; CA 160; NFS 11

Powers, J(ames) F(arl) 1917-1999 ..... CLC 1, 4, 8, 57; SSC 4
See also CA 1-4R; CANR 2, 61; CN 7; DLB 130; MTCW 1; RGAL 4; RGSF 2

Powers, John J(ames) 1945-
See Powers, John R.
See also CA 69-72

Powers, John R. .... CLC 66
See also Powers, John J(ames)

Powers, Richard (S.) 1957- .... CLC 93
See also AMWS 9; BPFB 3; CA 148; CANR 80; CN 7

Pownall, David 1938- .... CLC 10
See also CA 89-92, 180; CAAS 18; CANR 49, 101; CBD; CD 5; CN 7; DLB 14

Powys, John Cowper 1872-1963 ... CLC 7, 9, 15, 46, 125
See also CA 85-88; CANR 106; DLB 15, 255; FANT; MTCW 1, 2; RGEL 2; SUFW

Powys, T(heodore) F(rancis)
1875-1953 .... TCLC 9
See also BRWS 8; CA 189; DLB 36, 162; FANT; RGEL 2; SUFW

Prado (Calvo), Pedro 1886-1952 ... TCLC 75
See also CA 131; HW 1; LAW

Prager, Emily 1952- .... CLC 56
See also CA 204

Pratolini, Vasco 1913-1991 .... TCLC 124
See also DLB 177; RGWL 2, 3

Pratt, E(dwin) J(ohn) 1883(?)-1964 . CLC 19
See also CA 141; CANR 77; DAC; DAM POET; DLB 92; RGEL 2; TWA

Premchand .... TCLC 21
See also Srivastava, Dhanpat Rai

Preussler, Otfried 1923- .... CLC 17
See also CA 77-80; SATA 24

Prevert, Jacques (Henri Marie)
1900-1977 .... CLC 15
See also CA 77-80; CANR 29, 61; DLB 258; GFL 1789 to the Present; IDFW 3, 4; MTCW 1; RGWL 2, 3; SATA-Obit 30

Prevost, (Antoine Francois)
1697-1763 .... LC 1
See also EW 4; GFL Beginnings to 1789; RGWL 2, 3

Price, (Edward) Reynolds 1933- ... CLC 3, 6, 13, 43, 50, 63; SSC 22
See also AMWS 6; CA 1-4R; CANR 1, 37, 57, 87; CN 7; CSW; DAM NOV; DLB 2, 218; INT CANR-37

Price, Richard 1949- .... CLC 6, 12
See also CA 49-52; CANR 3; DLBY 1981

Prichard, Katharine Susannah
1883-1969 .... CLC 46
See also CA 11-12; CANR 33; CAP 1; DLB 260; MTCW 1; RGEL 2; RGSF 2; SATA 66

Priestley, J(ohn) B(oynton)
1894-1984 .... CLC 2, 5, 9, 34
See also BRW 7; CA 9-12R; CANR 33; CDBLB 1914-1945; DAM DRAM, NOV; DLB 10, 34, 77, 100, 139; DLBY 1984; MTCW 1, 2; RGEL 2; SFW 4

Prince 1958(?)- .... CLC 35

Prince, F(rank) T(empleton) 1912- .. CLC 22
See also CA 101; CANR 43, 79; CP 7; DLB 20

Prince Kropotkin
See Kropotkin, Peter (Aleksieevich)

Prior, Matthew 1664-1721 .... LC 4
See also DLB 95; RGEL 2

Prishvin, Mikhail 1873-1954 .... TCLC 75
See also Prishvin, Mikhail Mikhailovich

Prishvin, Mikhail Mikhailovich
See Prishvin, Mikhail
See also DLB 272

Pritchard, William H(arrison)
1932- .... CLC 34
See also CA 65-68; CANR 23, 95; DLB 111

Pritchett, V(ictor) S(awdon)
1900-1997 ... CLC 5, 13, 15, 41; SSC 14
See also BPFB 3; BRWS 3; CA 61-64; CANR 31, 63; CN 7; DAM NOV; DLB 15, 139; MTCW 1, 2; RGEL 2; RGSF 2; TEA

Private 19022
See Manning, Frederic

Probst, Mark 1925- .... CLC 59
See also CA 130

Prokosch, Frederic 1908-1989 ...... CLC 4, 48
See also CA 73-76; CANR 82; DLB 48; MTCW 2

Propertius, Sextus c. 50B.C.-c. 16B.C. .... CMLC 32
See also AW 2; CDWLB 1; DLB 211; RGWL 2, 3

Prophet, The
See Dreiser, Theodore (Herman Albert)

Prose, Francine 1947- .... CLC 45
See also CA 112; CANR 46, 95; DLB 234; SATA 101

Proudhon
See Cunha, Euclides (Rodrigues Pimenta) da

Proulx, Annie
See Proulx, E(dna) Annie

Proulx, E(dna) Annie 1935- ...... CLC 81, 158
See also AMWS 7; BPFB 3; CA 145; CANR 65, 110; CN 7; CPW 1; DAM POP; MTCW 2

Proust,
(Valentin-Louis-George-Eugene-)Marcel 1871-1922 .... TCLC 7, 13, 33; WLC
See also BPFB 3; CA 120; CANR 110; DA; DAB; DAC; DAM MST, NOV; DLB 65; EW 8; GFL 1789 to the Present; MTCW 1, 2; RGWL 2, 3; TWA

Prowler, Harley
See Masters, Edgar Lee

Prus, Boleslaw 1845-1912 .... TCLC 48
See also RGWL 2, 3

Pryor, Richard (Franklin Lenox Thomas)
1940- .... CLC 26
See also CA 152

Przybyszewski, Stanislaw
1868-1927 .... TCLC 36
See also CA 160; DLB 66

Pteleon
See Grieve, C(hristopher) M(urray)
See also DAM POET

Puckett, Lute
See Masters, Edgar Lee

Puig, Manuel 1932-1990 .... CLC 3, 5, 10, 28, 65, 133; HLC 2
See also BPFB 3; CA 45-48; CANR 2, 32, 63; CDWLB 3; DAM MULT; DLB 113; DNFS 1; GLL 1; HW 1, 2; LAW; MTCW 1, 2; RGWL 2, 3; TWA; WLIT 1

Pulitzer, Joseph 1847-1911 .... TCLC 76
See also DLB 23

Purchas, Samuel 1577(?)-1626 .... LC 70
See also DLB 151

Purdy, A(lfred) W(ellington)
1918-2000 .... CLC 3, 6, 14, 50
See also CA 81-84; CAAS 17; CANR 42, 66; CP 7; DAC; DAM MST, POET; DLB 88; PFS 5; RGEL 2

Purdy, James (Amos) 1923- .... CLC 2, 4, 10, 28, 52
See also AMWS 7; CA 33-36R; CAAS 1; CANR 19, 51; CN 7; DLB 2, 218; INT CANR-19; MTCW 1; RGAL 4

Pure, Simon
See Swinnerton, Frank Arthur

Pushkin, Aleksandr Sergeevich
See Pushkin, Alexander (Sergeyevich)
See also DLB 205

Pushkin, Alexander (Sergeyevich)
1799-1837 .... NCLC 3, 27, 83; PC 10; SSC 27, 55; WLC
See also Pushkin, Aleksandr Sergeevich
See also DA; DAB; DAC; DAM DRAM, MST, POET; EW 5; EXPS; RGSF 2; RGWL 2, 3; SATA 61; SSFS 9; TWA

P'u Sung-ling 1640-1715 .... LC 49; SSC 31

Putnam, Arthur Lee
See Alger, Horatio, Jr.

Puzo, Mario 1920-1999 .... CLC 1, 2, 6, 36, 107
See also BPFB 3; CA 65-68; CANR 4, 42, 65, 99; CN 7; CPW; DAM NOV, POP; DLB 6; MTCW 1, 2; RGAL 4

Pygge, Edward
See Barnes, Julian (Patrick)

Pyle, Ernest Taylor 1900-1945
See Pyle, Ernie
See also CA 160

Pyle, Ernie .... TCLC 75
See also Pyle, Ernest Taylor
See also DLB 29; MTCW 2

Pyle, Howard 1853-1911 .... **TCLC 81**
See also BYA 2, 4; CA 137; CLR 22; DLB 42, 188; DLBD 13; LAIT 1; MAICYA 1, 2; SATA 16, 100; WCH; YAW

Pym, Barbara (Mary Crampton)
1913-1980 .... **CLC 13, 19, 37, 111**
See also BPFB 3; BRWS 2; CA 13-14; CANR 13, 34; CAP 1; DLB 14, 207; DLBY 1987; MTCW 1, 2; RGEL 2; TEA

Pynchon, Thomas (Ruggles, Jr.)
1937- ...... **CLC 2, 3, 6, 9, 11, 18, 33, 62, 72, 123; SSC 14; WLC**
See also AMWS 2; BEST 90:2; BPFB 3; CA 17-20R; CANR 22, 46, 73; CN 7; CPW 1; DA; DAB; DAC; DAM MST, NOV, POP; DLB 2, 173; MTCW 1, 2; RGAL 4; SFW 4; TUS

Pythagoras c. 582B.C.-c. 507B.C. . **CMLC 22**
See also DLB 176

Q
See Quiller-Couch, Sir Arthur (Thomas)

Qian, Chongzhu
See Ch'ien, Chung-shu

Qian Zhongshu
See Ch'ien, Chung-shu

Qroll
See Dagerman, Stig (Halvard)

Quarrington, Paul (Lewis) 1953- ..... **CLC 65**
See also CA 129; CANR 62, 95

Quasimodo, Salvatore 1901-1968 ..... **CLC 10**
See also CA 13-16; CAP 1; DLB 114; EW 12; MTCW 1; RGWL 2, 3

Quatermass, Martin
See Carpenter, John (Howard)

Quay, Stephen 1947- .... **CLC 95**
See also CA 189

Quay, Timothy 1947- .... **CLC 95**
See also CA 189

Queen, Ellery .... **CLC 3, 11**
See also Dannay, Frederic; Davidson, Avram (James); Deming, Richard; Fairman, Paul W.; Flora, Fletcher; Hoch, Edward D(entinger); Kane, Henry; Lee, Manfred B(ennington); Marlowe, Stephen; Powell, (Oval) Talmage; Sheldon, Walter J(ames); Sturgeon, Theodore (Hamilton); Tracy, Don(ald Fiske); Vance, John Holbrook
See also BPFB 3; CMW 4; MSW; RGAL 4

Queen, Ellery, Jr.
See Dannay, Frederic; Lee, Manfred B(ennington)

Queneau, Raymond 1903-1976 ..... **CLC 2, 5, 10, 42**
See also CA 77-80; CANR 32; DLB 72, 258; EW 12; GFL 1789 to the Present; MTCW 1, 2; RGWL 2, 3

Quevedo, Francisco de 1580-1645 .... **LC 23**

Quiller-Couch, Sir Arthur (Thomas)
1863-1944 .... **TCLC 53**
See also CA 166; DLB 135, 153, 190; HGG; RGEL 2; SUFW 1

Quin, Ann (Marie) 1936-1973 .... **CLC 6**
See also CA 9-12R; DLB 14, 231

Quincey, Thomas de
See De Quincey, Thomas

Quinn, Martin
See Smith, Martin Cruz

Quinn, Peter 1947- .... **CLC 91**
See also CA 197

Quinn, Simon
See Smith, Martin Cruz

Quintana, Leroy V. 1944- .... **PC 36**
See also CA 131; CANR 65; DAM MULT; DLB 82; HLC 2; HW 1, 2

Quiroga, Horacio (Sylvestre)
1878-1937 .... **TCLC 20; HLC 2**
See also CA 131; DAM MULT; HW 1; LAW; MTCW 1; RGSF 2; WLIT 1

Quoirez, Francoise 1935- .... **CLC 9**
See also Sagan, Francoise
See also CA 49-52; CANR 6, 39, 73; CWW 2; MTCW 1, 2; TWA

Raabe, Wilhelm (Karl) 1831-1910 . **TCLC 45**
See also CA 167; DLB 129

Rabe, David (William) 1940- .. **CLC 4, 8, 33; DC 16**
See also CA 85-88; CABS 3; CAD; CANR 59; CD 5; DAM DRAM; DFS 3, 8, 13; DLB 7, 228

Rabelais, Francois 1494-1553 .... **LC 5, 60; WLC**
See also DA; DAB; DAC; DAM MST; EW 2; GFL Beginnings to 1789; RGWL 2, 3; TWA

Rabinovitch, Sholem 1859-1916
See Aleichem, Sholom

Rabinyan, Dorit 1972- .... **CLC 119**
See also CA 170

Rachilde
See Vallette, Marguerite Eymery

Racine, Jean 1639-1699 .... **LC 28**
See also DAB; DAM MST; DLB 268; EW 3; GFL Beginnings to 1789; RGWL 2, 3; TWA

Radcliffe, Ann (Ward) 1764-1823 ... **NCLC 6, 55, 106**
See also DLB 39, 178; HGG; RGEL 2; SUFW; WLIT 3

Radclyffe-Hall, Marguerite
See Hall, (Marguerite) Radclyffe

Radiguet, Raymond 1903-1923 ...... **TCLC 29**
See also CA 162; DLB 65; GFL 1789 to the Present; RGWL 2, 3

Radnoti, Miklos 1909-1944 .... **TCLC 16**
See also CDWLB 4; DLB 215; RGWL 2, 3

Rado, James 1939- .... **CLC 17**
See also CA 105

Radvanyi, Netty 1900-1983
See Seghers, Anna
See also CA 85-88; CANR 82

Rae, Ben
See Griffiths, Trevor

Raeburn, John (Hay) 1941- .... **CLC 34**
See also CA 57-60

Ragni, Gerome 1942-1991 .... **CLC 17**
See also CA 105

Rahv, Philip .... **CLC 24**
See also Greenberg, Ivan
See also DLB 137

Raimund, Ferdinand Jakob
1790-1836 .... **NCLC 69**
See also DLB 90

Raine, Craig (Anthony) 1944- .. **CLC 32, 103**
See also CA 108; CANR 29, 51, 103; CP 7; DLB 40; PFS 7

Raine, Kathleen (Jessie) 1908- ..... **CLC 7, 45**
See also CA 85-88; CANR 46, 109; CP 7; DLB 20; MTCW 1; RGEL 2

Rainis, Janis 1865-1929 .... **TCLC 29**
See also CA 170; CDWLB 4; DLB 220

Rakosi, Carl .... **CLC 47**
See also Rawley, Callman
See also CAAS 5; CP 7; DLB 193

Ralegh, Sir Walter
See Raleigh, Sir Walter
See also BRW 1; RGEL 2; WP

Raleigh, Richard
See Lovecraft, H(oward) P(hillips)

Raleigh, Sir Walter 1554(?)-1618 .... **LC 31, 39; PC 31**
See also Ralegh, Sir Walter
See also CDBLB Before 1660; DLB 172; EXPP; PFS 14; TEA

Rallentando, H. P.
See Sayers, Dorothy L(eigh)

Ramal, Walter
See de la Mare, Walter (John)

Ramana Maharshi 1879-1950 .... **TCLC 84**

Ramoacn y Cajal, Santiago
1852-1934 .... **TCLC 93**

Ramon, Juan
See Jimenez (Mantecon), Juan Ramon

Ramos, Graciliano 1892-1953 .... **TCLC 32**
See also CA 167; HW 2; LAW; WLIT 1

Rampersad, Arnold 1941- .... **CLC 44**
See also BW 2, 3; CA 133; CANR 81; DLB 111; INT 133

Rampling, Anne
See Rice, Anne
See also GLL 2

Ramsay, Allan 1686(?)-1758 .... **LC 29**
See also DLB 95; RGEL 2

Ramsay, Jay
See Campbell, (John) Ramsey

Ramuz, Charles-Ferdinand
1878-1947 .... **TCLC 33**
See also CA 165

Rand, Ayn 1905-1982 ...... **CLC 3, 30, 44, 79; WLC**
See also AAYA 10; AMWS 4; BPFB 3; BYA 12; CA 13-16R; CANR 27, 73; CDALBS; CPW; DA; DAC; DAM MST, NOV, POP; DLB 227; MTCW 1, 2; NFS 10; RGAL 4; SFW 4; TUS; YAW

Randall, Dudley (Felker) 1914-2000 . **CLC 1, 135; BLC 3**
See also BW 1, 3; CA 25-28R; CANR 23, 82; DAM MULT; DLB 41; PFS 5

Randall, Robert
See Silverberg, Robert

Ranger, Ken
See Creasey, John

Rank, Otto 1884-1939 .... **TCLC 115**

Ransom, John Crowe 1888-1974 .. **CLC 2, 4, 5, 11, 24**
See also AMW; CA 5-8R; CANR 6, 34; CDALBS; DAM POET; DLB 45, 63; EXPP; MTCW 1, 2; RGAL 4; TUS

Rao, Raja 1909- .... **CLC 25, 56**
See also CA 73-76; CANR 51; CN 7; DAM NOV; MTCW 1, 2; RGEL 2; RGSF 2

Raphael, Frederic (Michael) 1931- ... **CLC 2, 14**
See also CA 1-4R; CANR 1, 86; CN 7; DLB 14

Ratcliffe, James P.
See Mencken, H(enry) L(ouis)

Rathbone, Julian 1935- .... **CLC 41**
See also CA 101; CANR 34, 73

Rattigan, Terence (Mervyn)
1911-1977 .... **CLC 7; DC 18**
See also BRWS 7; CA 85-88; CBD; CDBLB 1945-1960; DAM DRAM; DFS 8; DLB 13; IDFW 3, 4; MTCW 1, 2; RGEL 2

Ratushinskaya, Irina 1954- .... **CLC 54**
See also CA 129; CANR 68; CWW 2

Raven, Simon (Arthur Noel)
1927-2001 .... **CLC 14**
See also CA 81-84; CANR 86; CN 7; DLB 271

Ravenna, Michael
See Welty, Eudora (Alice)

Rawley, Callman 1903-
See Rakosi, Carl
See also CA 21-24R; CANR 12, 32, 91

Rawlings, Marjorie Kinnan
1896-1953 .... **TCLC 4**
See also AAYA 20; AMWS 10; ANW; BPFB 3; BYA 3; CA 137; CANR 74; CLR 63; DLB 9, 22, 102; DLBD 17; JRDA; MAICYA 1, 2; MTCW 2; RGAL 4; SATA 100; WCH; YABC 1; YAW

Ray, Satyajit 1921-1992 .... **CLC 16, 76**
See also CA 114; DAM MULT

Read, Herbert Edward 1893-1968 ..... **CLC 4**
See also BRW 6; CA 85-88; DLB 20, 149; PAB; RGEL 2

Read, Piers Paul 1941- .... **CLC 4, 10, 25**
See also CA 21-24R; CANR 38, 86; CN 7; DLB 14; SATA 21

Reade, Charles 1814-1884 .... **NCLC 2, 74**
See also DLB 21; RGEL 2

Reade, Hamish
See Gray, Simon (James Holliday)

Reading, Peter 1946- .... **CLC 47**
See also BRWS 8; CA 103; CANR 46, 96; CP 7; DLB 40

Reaney, James 1926- .... **CLC 13**
See also CA 41-44R; CAAS 15; CANR 42; CD 5; CP 7; DAC; DAM MST; DLB 68; RGEL 2; SATA 43

Rebreanu, Liviu 1885-1944 .... **TCLC 28**
See also CA 165; DLB 220

Rechy, John (Francisco) 1934- ...... **CLC 1, 7, 14, 18, 107; HLC 2**
See also CA 5-8R; CAAE 195; CAAS 4; CANR 6, 32, 64; CN 7; DAM MULT; DLB 122; DLBY 1982; HW 1, 2; INT CANR-6; RGAL 4

Redcam, Tom 1870-1933 .... **TCLC 25**

Reddin, Keith .... **CLC 67**
See also CAD

Redgrove, Peter (William) 1932- . **CLC 6, 41**
See also BRWS 6; CA 1-4R; CANR 3, 39, 77; CP 7; DLB 40

Redmon, Anne .... **CLC 22**
See Nightingale, Anne Redmon
See also DLBY 1986

Reed, Eliot
See Ambler, Eric

Reed, Ishmael 1938- .. **CLC 2, 3, 5, 6, 13, 32, 60; BLC 3**
See also AFAW 1, 2; AMWS 10; BPFB 3; BW 2, 3; CA 21-24R; CANR 25, 48, 74; CN 7; CP 7; CSW; DAM MULT; DLB 2, 5, 33, 169, 227; DLBD 8; MSW; MTCW 1, 2; PFS 6; RGAL 4; TCWW 2

Reed, John (Silas) 1887-1920 .... **TCLC 9**
See also CA 195; TUS

Reed, Lou .... **CLC 21**
See also Firbank, Louis

Reese, Lizette Woodworth 1856-1935 . **PC 29**
See also CA 180; DLB 54

Reeve, Clara 1729-1807 .... **NCLC 19**
See also DLB 39; RGEL 2

Reich, Wilhelm 1897-1957 .... **TCLC 57**
See also CA 199

Reid, Christopher (John) 1949- .... **CLC 33**
See also CA 140; CANR 89; CP 7; DLB 40

Reid, Desmond
See Moorcock, Michael (John)

Reid Banks, Lynne 1929-
See Banks, Lynne Reid
See also CA 1-4R; CANR 6, 22, 38, 87; CLR 24; CN 7; JRDA; MAICYA 1, 2; SATA 22, 75, 111; YAW

Reilly, William K.
See Creasey, John

Reiner, Max
See Caldwell, (Janet Miriam) Taylor (Holland)

Reis, Ricardo
See Pessoa, Fernando (Antonio Nogueira)

Remarque, Erich Maria 1898-1970 . **CLC 21**
See also AAYA 27; BPFB 3; CA 77-80; CDWLB 2; DA; DAB; DAC; DAM MST, NOV; DLB 56; EXPN; LAIT 3; MTCW 1, 2; NFS 4; RGWL 2, 3

Remington, Frederic 1861-1909 ..... **TCLC 89**
See also CA 169; DLB 12, 186, 188; SATA 41

Remizov, A.
See Remizov, Aleksei (Mikhailovich)

Remizov, A. M.
See Remizov, Aleksei (Mikhailovich)

Remizov, Aleksei (Mikhailovich) 1877-1957 .... **TCLC 27**
See also CA 133

Renan, Joseph Ernest 1823-1892 .. **NCLC 26**
See also GFL 1789 to the Present

Renard, Jules(-Pierre) 1864-1910 .. **TCLC 17**
See also CA 202; GFL 1789 to the Present

Renault, Mary .... **CLC 3, 11, 17**
See also Challans, Mary
See also BPFB 3; BYA 2; DLBY 1983; GLL 1; LAIT 1; MTCW 2; RGEL 2; RHW

Rendell, Ruth (Barbara) 1930- .. **CLC 28, 48**
See also Vine, Barbara
See also BPFB 3; CA 109; CANR 32, 52, 74; CN 7; CPW; DAM POP; DLB 87; INT CANR-32; MSW; MTCW 1, 2

Renoir, Jean 1894-1979 .... **CLC 20**
See also CA 129

Resnais, Alain 1922- .... **CLC 16**

Reverdy, Pierre 1889-1960 .... **CLC 53**
See also CA 97-100; DLB 258; GFL 1789 to the Present

Rexroth, Kenneth 1905-1982 .... **CLC 1, 2, 6, 11, 22, 49, 112; PC 20**
See also CA 5-8R; CANR 14, 34, 63; CDALB 1941-1968; DAM POET; DLB 16, 48, 165, 212; DLBY 1982; INT CANR-14; MTCW 1, 2; RGAL 4

Reyes, Alfonso 1889-1959 .. **TCLC 33; HLCS 2**
See also CA 131; HW 1; LAW

Reyes y Basoalto, Ricardo Eliecer Neftali
See Neruda, Pablo

Reymont, Wladyslaw (Stanislaw) 1868(?)-1925 .... **TCLC 5**

Reynolds, Jonathan 1942- .... **CLC 6, 38**
See also CA 65-68; CANR 28

Reynolds, Joshua 1723-1792 .... **LC 15**
See also DLB 104

Reynolds, Michael S(hane) 1937-2000 .... **CLC 44**
See also CA 65-68; CANR 9, 89, 97

Reznikoff, Charles 1894-1976 .... **CLC 9**
See also CA 33-36; CAP 2; DLB 28, 45; WP

Rezzori (d'Arezzo), Gregor von 1914-1998 .... **CLC 25**
See also CA 136

Rhine, Richard
See Silverstein, Alvin; Silverstein, Virginia B(arbara Opshelor)

Rhodes, Eugene Manlove 1869-1934 .... **TCLC 53**
See also CA 198; DLB 256

R'hoone, Lord
See Balzac, Honore de

Rhys, Jean 1894(?)-1979 ...... **CLC 2, 4, 6, 14, 19, 51, 124; SSC 21**
See also BRWS 2; CA 25-28R; CANR 35, 62; CDBLB 1945-1960; CDWLB 3; DAM NOV; DLB 36, 117, 162; DNFS 1; MTCW 1, 2; RGEL 2; RGSF 2; RHW; TEA

Ribeiro, Darcy 1922-1997 .... **CLC 34**
See also CA 33-36R

Ribeiro, Joao Ubaldo (Osorio Pimentel) 1941- .... **CLC 10, 67**
See also CA 81-84

Ribman, Ronald (Burt) 1932- .... **CLC 7**
See also CA 21-24R; CAD; CANR 46, 80; CD 5

Ricci, Nino 1959- .... **CLC 70**
See also CA 137; CCA 1

Rice, Anne 1941- .... **CLC 41, 128**
See also Rampling, Anne
See also AAYA 9; AMWS 7; BEST 89:2; BPFB 3; CA 65-68; CANR 12, 36, 53, 74, 100; CN 7; CPW; CSW; DAM POP; GLL 2; HGG; MTCW 2; SUFW 2; YAW

Rice, Elmer (Leopold) 1892-1967 ...... **CLC 7, 49**
See also CA 21-22; CAP 2; DAM DRAM; DFS 12; DLB 4, 7; MTCW 1, 2; RGAL 4

Rice, Tim(othy Miles Bindon) 1944- .... **CLC 21**
See also CA 103; CANR 46; DFS 7

Rich, Adrienne (Cecile) 1929- ... **CLC 3, 6, 7, 11, 18, 36, 73, 76, 125; PC 5**
See also AMWS 1; CA 9-12R; CANR 20, 53, 74; CDALBS; CP 7; CSW; CWP; DAM POET; DLB 5, 67; EXPP; FW; MAWW; MTCW 1, 2; PAB; PFS 15; RGAL 4; WP

Rich, Barbara
See Graves, Robert (von Ranke)

Rich, Robert
See Trumbo, Dalton

Richard, Keith .... **CLC 17**
See also Richards, Keith

Richards, David Adams 1950- .... **CLC 59**
See also CA 93-96; CANR 60, 110; DAC; DLB 53

Richards, I(vor) A(rmstrong) 1893-1979 .... **CLC 14, 24**
See also BRWS 2; CA 41-44R; CANR 34, 74; DLB 27; MTCW 1, 2; RGEL 2

Richards, Keith 1943-
See Richard, Keith
See also CA 107; CANR 77

Richardson, Anne
See Roiphe, Anne (Richardson)

Richardson, Dorothy Miller 1873-1957 .... **TCLC 3**
See also CA 192; DLB 36; FW; RGEL 2

Richardson (Robertson), Ethel Florence Lindesay 1870-1946
See Richardson, Henry Handel
See also CA 190; DLB 230; RHW

Richardson, Henry Handel .... **TCLC 4**
See also Richardson (Robertson), Ethel Florence Lindesay
See also DLB 197; RGEL 2; RGSF 2

Richardson, John 1796-1852 .... **NCLC 55**
See also CCA 1; DAC; DLB 99

Richardson, Samuel 1689-1761 ...... **LC 1, 44; WLC**
See also BRW 3; CDBLB 1660-1789; DA; DAB; DAC; DAM MST, NOV; DLB 39; RGEL 2; TEA; WLIT 3

Richler, Mordecai 1931-2001 .... **CLC 3, 5, 9, 13, 18, 46, 70**
See also AITN 1; CA 65-68; CANR 31, 62, 111; CCA 1; CLR 17; CWRI 5; DAC; DAM MST, NOV; DLB 53; MAICYA 1, 2; MTCW 1, 2; RGEL 2; SATA 44, 98; SATA-Brief 27; TWA

Richter, Conrad (Michael) 1890-1968 .... **CLC 30**
See also AAYA 21; BYA 2; CA 5-8R; CANR 23; DLB 9, 212; LAIT 1; MTCW 1, 2; RGAL 4; SATA 3; TCWW 2; TUS; YAW

Ricostranza, Tom
See Ellis, Trey

Riddell, Charlotte 1832-1906 .... **TCLC 40**
See also Riddell, Mrs. J. H.
See also CA 165; DLB 156

Riddell, Mrs. J. H.
See Riddell, Charlotte
See also HGG; SUFW

Ridge, John Rollin 1827-1867 .... **NCLC 82**
See also CA 144; DAM MULT; DLB 175; NNAL

Ridgeway, Jason
See Marlowe, Stephen

Ridgway, Keith 1965- .... **CLC 119**
See also CA 172

Riding, Laura .... **CLC 3, 7**
See also Jackson, Laura (Riding)
See also RGAL 4

Riefenstahl, Berta Helene Amalia 1902-
See Riefenstahl, Leni
See also CA 108

Riefenstahl, Leni .... **CLC 16**
See also Riefenstahl, Berta Helene Amalia

Riffe, Ernest
See Bergman, (Ernst) Ingmar

Riggs, (Rolla) Lynn 1899-1954 .... **TCLC 56**
See also CA 144; DAM MULT; DLB 175; NNAL

Riis, Jacob A(ugust) 1849-1914 ..... **TCLC 80**
See also CA 168; DLB 23

Riley, James Whitcomb
1849-1916 .... **TCLC 51**
See also CA 137; DAM POET; MAICYA 1, 2; RGAL 4; SATA 17

Riley, Tex
See Creasey, John

Rilke, Rainer Maria 1875-1926 .. **TCLC 1, 6, 19; PC 2**
See also CA 132; CANR 62, 99; CDWLB 2; DAM POET; DLB 81; EW 9; MTCW 1, 2; RGWL 2, 3; TWA; WP

Rimbaud, (Jean Nicolas) Arthur
1854-1891 .... **NCLC 4, 35, 82; PC 3; WLC**
See also DA; DAB; DAC; DAM MST, POET; DLB 217; EW 7; GFL 1789 to the Present; RGWL 2, 3; TWA; WP

Rinehart, Mary Roberts
1876-1958 .... **TCLC 52**
See also BPFB 3; CA 166; RGAL 4; RHW

Ringmaster, The
See Mencken, H(enry) L(ouis)

Ringwood, Gwen(dolyn Margaret) Pharis
1910-1984 .... **CLC 48**
See also CA 148; DLB 88

Rio, Michel 1945(?)- .... **CLC 43**
See also CA 201

Ritsos, Giannes
See Ritsos, Yannis

Ritsos, Yannis 1909-1990 .... **CLC 6, 13, 31**
See also CA 77-80; CANR 39, 61; EW 12; MTCW 1; RGWL 2, 3

Ritter, Erika 1948(?)- .... **CLC 52**
See also CD 5; CWD

Rivera, Jose Eustasio 1889-1928 ... **TCLC 35**
See also CA 162; HW 1, 2; LAW

Rivera, Tomas 1935-1984
See also CA 49-52; CANR 32; DLB 82; HLCS 2; HW 1; RGAL 4; SSFS 15; TCWW 2; WLIT 1

Rivers, Conrad Kent 1933-1968 .... **CLC 1**
See also BW 1; CA 85-88; DLB 41

Rivers, Elfrida
See Bradley, Marion Zimmer
See also GLL 1

Riverside, John
See Heinlein, Robert A(nson)

Rizal, Jose 1861-1896 .... **NCLC 27**

Roa Bastos, Augusto (Antonio)
1917- .... **CLC 45; HLC 2**
See also CA 131; DAM MULT; DLB 113; HW 1; LAW; RGSF 2; WLIT 1

Robbe-Grillet, Alain 1922- .... **CLC 1, 2, 4, 6, 8, 10, 14, 43, 128**
See also BPFB 3; CA 9-12R; CANR 33, 65; DLB 83; EW 13; GFL 1789 to the Present; IDFW 3, 4; MTCW 1, 2; RGWL 2, 3; SSFS 15

Robbins, Harold 1916-1997 .... **CLC 5**
See also BPFB 3; CA 73-76; CANR 26, 54, 112; DAM NOV; MTCW 1, 2

Robbins, Thomas Eugene 1936-
See Robbins, Tom
See also CA 81-84; CANR 29, 59, 95; CN 7; CPW; CSW; DAM NOV, POP; MTCW 1, 2

Robbins, Tom .... **CLC 9, 32, 64**
See also Robbins, Thomas Eugene
See also AAYA 32; AMWS 10; BEST 90:3; BPFB 3; DLBY 1980; MTCW 2

Robbins, Trina 1938- .... **CLC 21**
See also CA 128

Roberts, Charles G(eorge) D(ouglas)
1860-1943 .... **TCLC 8**
See also CA 188; CLR 33; CWRI 5; DLB 92; RGEL 2; RGSF 2; SATA 88; SATA-Brief 29

Roberts, Elizabeth Madox
1886-1941 .... **TCLC 68**
See also CA 166; CWRI 5; DLB 9, 54, 102; RGAL 4; RHW; SATA 33; SATA-Brief 27; WCH

Roberts, Kate 1891-1985 .... **CLC 15**
See also CA 107

Roberts, Keith (John Kingston)
1935-2000 .... **CLC 14**
See also CA 25-28R; CANR 46; DLB 261; SFW 4

Roberts, Kenneth (Lewis)
1885-1957 .... **TCLC 23**
See also CA 199; DLB 9; RGAL 4; RHW

Roberts, Michele (Brigitte) 1949- ..... **CLC 48**
See also CA 115; CANR 58; CN 7; DLB 231; FW

Robertson, Ellis
See Ellison, Harlan (Jay); Silverberg, Robert

Robertson, Thomas William
1829-1871 .... **NCLC 35**
See also Robertson, Tom
See also DAM DRAM

Robertson, Tom
See Robertson, Thomas William
See also RGEL 2

Robeson, Kenneth
See Dent, Lester

Robinson, Edwin Arlington
1869-1935 .... **TCLC 5, 101; PC 1, 35**
See also AMW; CA 133; CDALB 1865-1917; DA; DAC; DAM MST, POET; DLB 54; EXPP; MTCW 1, 2; PAB; PFS 4; RGAL 4; WP

Robinson, Henry Crabb
1775-1867 .... **NCLC 15**
See also DLB 107

Robinson, Jill 1936- .... **CLC 10**
See also CA 102; INT 102

Robinson, Kim Stanley 1952- .... **CLC 34**
See also AAYA 26; CA 126; CANR 113; CN 7; SATA 109; SCFW 2; SFW 4

Robinson, Lloyd
See Silverberg, Robert

Robinson, Marilynne 1944- .... **CLC 25**
See also CA 116; CANR 80; CN 7; DLB 206

Robinson, Smokey .... **CLC 21**
See also Robinson, William, Jr.

Robinson, William, Jr. 1940-
See Robinson, Smokey

Robison, Mary 1949- .... **CLC 42, 98**
See also CA 116; CANR 87; CN 7; DLB 130; INT 116; RGSF 2

Rochester
See Wilmot, John
See also RGEL 2

Rod, Edouard 1857-1910 .... **TCLC 52**

Roddenberry, Eugene Wesley 1921-1991
See Roddenberry, Gene
See also CA 110; CANR 37; SATA 45; SATA-Obit 69

Roddenberry, Gene .... **CLC 17**
See also Roddenberry, Eugene Wesley
See also AAYA 5; SATA-Obit 69

Rodgers, Mary 1931- .... **CLC 12**
See also BYA 5; CA 49-52; CANR 8, 55, 90; CLR 20; CWRI 5; INT CANR-8; JRDA; MAICYA 1, 2; SATA 8, 130

Rodgers, W(illiam) R(obert)
1909-1969 .... **CLC 7**
See also CA 85-88; DLB 20; RGEL 2

Rodman, Eric
See Silverberg, Robert

Rodman, Howard 1920(?)-1985 .... **CLC 65**
See also CA 118

Rodman, Maia
See Wojciechowska, Maia (Teresa)

Rodo, Jose Enrique 1871(?)-1917
See also CA 178; HLCS 2; HW 2; LAW

Rodolph, Utto
See Ouologuem, Yambo

Rodriguez, Claudio 1934-1999 .... **CLC 10**
See also CA 188; DLB 134

Rodriguez, Richard 1944- .... **CLC 155; HLC 2**
See also CA 110; CANR 66; DAM MULT; DLB 82, 256; HW 1, 2; LAIT 5; NCFS 3; WLIT 1

Roelvaag, O(le) E(dvart) 1876-1931
See Rolvaag, O(le) E(dvart)
See also CA 171

Roethke, Theodore (Huebner)
1908-1963 .... **CLC 1, 3, 8, 11, 19, 46, 101; PC 15**
See also AMW; CA 81-84; CABS 2; CDALB 1941-1968; DAM POET; DLB 5, 206; EXPP; MTCW 1, 2; PAB; PFS 3; RGAL 4; WP

Rogers, Carl R(ansom)
1902-1987 .... **TCLC 125**
See also CA 1-4R; CANR 1, 18; MTCW 1

Rogers, Samuel 1763-1855 .... **NCLC 69**
See also DLB 93; RGEL 2

Rogers, Thomas Hunton 1927- .... **CLC 57**
See also CA 89-92; INT 89-92

Rogers, Will(iam Penn Adair)
1879-1935 .... **TCLC 8, 71**
See also CA 144; DAM MULT; DLB 11; MTCW 2; NNAL

Rogin, Gilbert 1929- .... **CLC 18**
See also CA 65-68; CANR 15

Rohan, Koda
See Koda Shigeyuki

Rohlfs, Anna Katharine Green
See Green, Anna Katharine

Rohmer, Eric .... **CLC 16**
See also Scherer, Jean-Marie Maurice

Rohmer, Sax .... **TCLC 28**
See also Ward, Arthur Henry Sarsfield
See also DLB 70; MSW; SUFW

Roiphe, Anne (Richardson) 1935- .. **CLC 3, 9**
See also CA 89-92; CANR 45, 73; DLBY 1980; INT 89-92

Rojas, Fernando de 1475-1541 .... **LC 23; HLCS 1**
See also RGWL 2, 3

Rojas, Gonzalo 1917-
See also CA 178; HLCS 2; HW 2; LAWS 1

Rolfe, Frederick (William Serafino Austin Lewis Mary) 1860-1913 .... **TCLC 12**
See also Corvo, Baron
See also DLB 34, 156; RGEL 2

Rolland, Romain 1866-1944 .... **TCLC 23**
See also CA 197; DLB 65; GFL 1789 to the Present; RGWL 2, 3

Rolle, Richard c. 1300-c. 1349 ...... **CMLC 21**
See also DLB 146; RGEL 2

Rolvaag, O(le) E(dvart) .... **TCLC 17**
See also Roelvaag, O(le) E(dvart)
See also DLB 9, 212; NFS 5; RGAL 4

Romain Arnaud, Saint
See Aragon, Louis

Romains, Jules 1885-1972 .... **CLC 7**
See also CA 85-88; CANR 34; DLB 65; GFL 1789 to the Present; MTCW 1

Romero, Jose Ruben 1890-1952 .... **TCLC 14**
See also CA 131; HW 1; LAW

Ronsard, Pierre de 1524-1585 . **LC 6, 54; PC 11**
See also EW 2; GFL Beginnings to 1789; RGWL 2, 3; TWA

Rooke, Leon 1934- .... **CLC 25, 34**
See also CA 25-28R; CANR 23, 53; CCA 1; CPW; DAM POP

Roosevelt, Franklin Delano 1882-1945 .... **TCLC 93**
See also CA 173; LAIT 3

Roosevelt, Theodore 1858-1919 ..... **TCLC 69**
See also CA 170; DLB 47, 186

Roper, William 1498-1578 .... **LC 10**

Roquelaure, A. N.
See Rice, Anne

Rosa, Joao Guimaraes 1908-1967 ... **CLC 23; HLCS 1**
See also DLB 113; WLIT 1

Rose, Wendy 1948- .... **CLC 85; PC 13**
See also CA 53-56; CANR 5, 51; CWP; DAM MULT; DLB 175; NNAL; PFS 13; RGAL 4; SATA 12

Rosen, R. D.
See Rosen, Richard (Dean)

Rosen, Richard (Dean) 1949- .... **CLC 39**
See also CA 77-80; CANR 62; CMW 4; INT CANR-30

Rosenberg, Isaac 1890-1918 .... **TCLC 12**
See also BRW 6; CA 188; DLB 20, 216; PAB; RGEL 2

Rosenblatt, Joe .... **CLC 15**
See also Rosenblatt, Joseph

Rosenblatt, Joseph 1933-
See Rosenblatt, Joe
See also CA 89-92; CP 7; INT 89-92

Rosenfeld, Samuel
See Tzara, Tristan

Rosenstock, Sami
See Tzara, Tristan

Rosenstock, Samuel
See Tzara, Tristan

Rosenthal, M(acha) L(ouis) 1917-1996 .... **CLC 28**
See also CA 1-4R; CAAS 6; CANR 4, 51; CP 7; DLB 5; SATA 59

Ross, Barnaby
See Dannay, Frederic

Ross, Bernard L.
See Follett, Ken(neth Martin)

Ross, J. H.
See Lawrence, T(homas) E(dward)

Ross, John Hume
See Lawrence, T(homas) E(dward)

Ross, Martin 1862-1915
See Martin, Violet Florence
See also DLB 135; GLL 2; RGEL 2; RGSF 2

Ross, (James) Sinclair 1908-1996 ... **CLC 13; SSC 24**
See also CA 73-76; CANR 81; CN 7; DAC; DAM MST; DLB 88; RGEL 2; RGSF 2; TCWW 2

Rossetti, Christina (Georgina) 1830-1894 .... **NCLC 2, 50, 66; PC 7; WLC**
See also BRW 5; BYA 4; DA; DAB; DAC; DAM MST, POET; DLB 35, 163, 240; EXPP; MAICYA 1, 2; PFS 10, 14; RGEL 2; SATA 20; TEA; WCH

Rossetti, Dante Gabriel 1828-1882 . **NCLC 4, 77; PC 44; WLC**
See also BRW 5; CDBLB 1832-1890; DA; DAB; DAC; DAM MST, POET; DLB 35; EXPP; RGEL 2; TEA

Rossi, Cristina Peri
See Peri Rossi, Cristina

Rossi, Jean Baptiste 1931-
See Japrisot, Sebastien
See also CA 201

Rossner, Judith (Perelman) 1935- . **CLC 6, 9, 29**
See also AITN 2; BEST 90:3; BPFB 3; CA 17-20R; CANR 18, 51, 73; CN 7; DLB 6; INT CANR-18; MTCW 1, 2

Rostand, Edmond (Eugene Alexis) 1868-1918 .... **TCLC 6, 37; DC 10**
See also CA 126; DA; DAB; DAC; DAM DRAM, MST; DFS 1; DLB 192; LAIT 1; MTCW 1; RGWL 2, 3; TWA

Roth, Henry 1906-1995 ...... **CLC 2, 6, 11, 104**
See also AMWS 9; CA 11-12; CANR 38, 63; CAP 1; CN 7; DLB 28; MTCW 1, 2; RGAL 4

Roth, (Moses) Joseph 1894-1939 ... **TCLC 33**
See also CA 160; DLB 85; RGWL 2, 3

Roth, Philip (Milton) 1933- ... **CLC 1, 2, 3, 4, 6, 9, 15, 22, 31, 47, 66, 86, 119; SSC 26; WLC**
See also AMWS 3; BEST 90:3; BPFB 3; CA 1-4R; CANR 1, 22, 36, 55, 89; CDALB 1968-1988; CN 7; CPW 1; DA; DAB; DAC; DAM MST, NOV, POP; DLB 2, 28, 173; DLBY 1982; MTCW 1, 2; RGAL 4; RGSF 2; SSFS 12; TUS

Rothenberg, Jerome 1931- .... **CLC 6, 57**
See also CA 45-48; CANR 1, 106; CP 7; DLB 5, 193

Rotter, Pat ed. .... **CLC 65**

Roumain, Jacques (Jean Baptiste) 1907-1944 .... **TCLC 19; BLC 3**
See also BW 1; CA 125; DAM MULT

Rourke, Constance Mayfield 1885-1941 .... **TCLC 12**
See also CA 200; YABC 1

Rousseau, Jean-Baptiste 1671-1741 ...... **LC 9**

Rousseau, Jean-Jacques 1712-1778 .... **LC 14, 36; WLC**
See also DA; DAB; DAC; DAM MST; EW 4; GFL Beginnings to 1789; RGWL 2, 3; TWA

Roussel, Raymond 1877-1933 .... **TCLC 20**
See also CA 201; GFL 1789 to the Present

Rovit, Earl (Herbert) 1927- .... **CLC 7**
See also CA 5-8R; CANR 12

Rowe, Elizabeth Singer 1674-1737 ..... **LC 44**
See also DLB 39, 95

Rowe, Nicholas 1674-1718 .... **LC 8**
See also DLB 84; RGEL 2

Rowlandson, Mary 1637(?)-1678 .... **LC 66**
See also DLB 24, 200; RGAL 4

Rowley, Ames Dorrance
See Lovecraft, H(oward) P(hillips)

Rowling, J(oanne) K(athleen) 1965- .... **CLC 137**
See also AAYA 34; BYA 13, 14; CA 173; CLR 66, 80; MAICYA 2; SATA 109; SUFW 2

Rowson, Susanna Haswell 1762(?)-1824 .... **NCLC 5, 69**
See also DLB 37, 200; RGAL 4

Roy, Arundhati 1960(?)- .... **CLC 109**
See also CA 163; CANR 90; DLBY 1997

Roy, Gabrielle 1909-1983 .... **CLC 10, 14**
See also CA 53-56; CANR 5, 61; CCA 1; DAB; DAC; DAM MST; DLB 68; MTCW 1; RGWL 2, 3; SATA 104

Royko, Mike 1932-1997 .... **CLC 109**
See also CA 89-92; CANR 26, 111; CPW

Rozanov, Vassili 1856-1919 .... **TCLC 104**

Rozewicz, Tadeusz 1921- ...... **CLC 9, 23, 139**
See also CA 108; CANR 36, 66; CWW 2; DAM POET; DLB 232; MTCW 1, 2; RGWL 3

Ruark, Gibbons 1941- .... **CLC 3**
See also CA 33-36R; CAAS 23; CANR 14, 31, 57; DLB 120

Rubens, Bernice (Ruth) 1923- .... **CLC 19, 31**
See also CA 25-28R; CANR 33, 65; CN 7; DLB 14, 207; MTCW 1

Rubin, Harold
See Robbins, Harold

Rudkin, (James) David 1936- .... **CLC 14**
See also CA 89-92; CBD; CD 5; DLB 13

Rudnik, Raphael 1933- .... **CLC 7**
See also CA 29-32R

Ruffian, M.
See Hasek, Jaroslav (Matej Frantisek)

Ruiz, Jose Martinez .... **CLC 11**
See also Martinez Ruiz, Jose

Rukeyser, Muriel 1913-1980 . **CLC 6, 10, 15, 27; PC 12**
See also AMWS 6; CA 5-8R; CANR 26, 60; DAM POET; DLB 48; FW; GLL 2; MTCW 1, 2; PFS 10; RGAL 4; SATA-Obit 22

Rule, Jane (Vance) 1931- .... **CLC 27**
See also CA 25-28R; CAAS 18; CANR 12, 87; CN 7; DLB 60; FW

Rulfo, Juan 1918-1986 .. **CLC 8, 80; HLC 2; SSC 25**
See also CA 85-88; CANR 26; CDWLB 3; DAM MULT; DLB 113; HW 1, 2; LAW; MTCW 1, 2; RGSF 2; RGWL 2, 3; WLIT 1

Rumi, Jalal al-Din 1207-1273 .... **CMLC 20**
See also RGWL 2, 3; WP

Runeberg, Johan 1804-1877 .... **NCLC 41**

Runyon, (Alfred) Damon 1884(?)-1946 .... **TCLC 10**
See also CA 165; DLB 11, 86, 171; MTCW 2; RGAL 4

Rush, Norman 1933- .... **CLC 44**
See also CA 126; INT 126

Rushdie, (Ahmed) Salman 1947- .... **CLC 23, 31, 55, 100; WLCS**
See also BEST 89:3; BPFB 3; BRWS 4; CA 111; CANR 33, 56, 108; CN 7; CPW 1; DAB; DAC; DAM MST, NOV, POP; DLB 194; FANT; INT CA-111; MTCW 1, 2; RGEL 2; RGSF 2; TEA; WLIT 4

Rushforth, Peter (Scott) 1945- .... **CLC 19**
See also CA 101

Ruskin, John 1819-1900 .... **TCLC 63**
See also BRW 5; BYA 5; CA 129; CDBLB 1832-1890; DLB 55, 163, 190; RGEL 2; SATA 24; TEA; WCH

Russ, Joanna 1937- .... **CLC 15**
See also BPFB 3; CA 5-28R; CANR 11, 31, 65; CN 7; DLB 8; FW; GLL 1; MTCW 1; SCFW 2; SFW 4

Russ, Richard Patrick
See O'Brian, Patrick

Russell, George William 1867-1935
See A.E.; Baker, Jean H.
See also BRWS 8; CA 153; CDBLB 1890-1914; DAM POET; RGEL 2

Russell, Jeffrey Burton 1934- .... **CLC 70**
See also CA 25-28R; CANR 11, 28, 52

Russell, (Henry) Ken(neth Alfred)
1927- .... CLC 16
See also CA 105
Russell, William Martin 1947-
See Russell, Willy
See also CA 164; CANR 107
Russell, Willy .... CLC 60
See also Russell, William Martin
See also CBD; CD 5; DLB 233
Rutherford, Mark .... TCLC 25
See also White, William Hale
See also DLB 18; RGEL 2
Ruyslinck, Ward .... CLC 14
See also Belser, Reimond Karel Maria de
Ryan, Cornelius (John) 1920-1974 ..... CLC 7
See also CA 69-72; CANR 38
Ryan, Michael 1946- .... CLC 65
See also CA 49-52; CANR 109; DLBY 1982
Ryan, Tim
See Dent, Lester
Rybakov, Anatoli (Naumovich)
1911-1998 .... CLC 23, 53
See also CA 135; SATA 79; SATA-Obit 108
Ryder, Jonathan
See Ludlum, Robert
Ryga, George 1932-1987 .... CLC 14
See also CA 101; CANR 43, 90; CCA 1; DAC; DAM MST; DLB 60
S. H.
See Hartmann, Sadakichi
S. S.
See Sassoon, Siegfried (Lorraine)
Saba, Umberto 1883-1957 .... TCLC 33
See also CA 144; CANR 79; DLB 114; RGWL 2, 3
Sabatini, Rafael 1875-1950 .... TCLC 47
See also BPFB 3; CA 162; RHW
Sabato, Ernesto (R.) 1911- .... CLC 10, 23; HLC 2
See also CA 97-100; CANR 32, 65; CD-WLB 3; DAM MULT; DLB 145; HW 1, 2; LAW; MTCW 1, 2
Sa-Carniero, Mario de 1890-1916 . TCLC 83
Sacastru, Martin
See Bioy Casares, Adolfo
See also CWW 2
Sacher-Masoch, Leopold von
1836(?)-1895 .... NCLC 31
Sachs, Marilyn (Stickle) 1927- .... CLC 35
See also AAYA 2; BYA 6; CA 17-20R; CANR 13, 47; CLR 2; JRDA; MAICYA 1, 2; SAAS 2; SATA 3, 68; SATA-Essay 110; WYA; YAW
Sachs, Nelly 1891-1970 .... CLC 14, 98
See also CA 17-18; CANR 87; CAP 2; MTCW 2; RGWL 2, 3
Sackler, Howard (Oliver)
1929-1982 .... CLC 14
See also CA 61-64; CAD; CANR 30; DFS 15; DLB 7
Sacks, Oliver (Wolf) 1933- .... CLC 67
See also CA 53-56; CANR 28, 50, 76; CPW; INT CANR-28; MTCW 1, 2
Sadakichi
See Hartmann, Sadakichi
Sade, Donatien Alphonse Francois
1740-1814 .... NCLC 3, 47
See also EW 4; GFL Beginnings to 1789; RGWL 2, 3
Sade, Marquis de
See Sade, Donatien Alphonse Francois
Sadoff, Ira 1945- .... CLC 9
See also CA 53-56; CANR 5, 21, 109; DLB 120
Saetone
See Camus, Albert
Safire, William 1929- .... CLC 10
See also CA 17-20R; CANR 31, 54, 91

Sagan, Carl (Edward) 1934-1996 .... CLC 30, 112
See also AAYA 2; CA 25-28R; CANR 11, 36, 74; CPW; MTCW 1, 2; SATA 58; SATA-Obit 94
Sagan, Francoise .... CLC 3, 6, 9, 17, 36
See also Quoirez, Francoise
See also CWW 2; DLB 83; GFL 1789 to the Present; MTCW 2
Sahgal, Nayantara (Pandit) 1927- .... CLC 41
See also CA 9-12R; CANR 11, 88; CN 7
Said, Edward W. 1935- .... CLC 123
See also CA 21-24R; CANR 45, 74, 107; DLB 67; MTCW 2
Saint, H(arry) F. 1941- .... CLC 50
See also CA 127
St. Aubin de Teran, Lisa 1953-
See Teran, Lisa St. Aubin de
See also CA 126; CN 7; INT 126
Saint Birgitta of Sweden c.
1303-1373 .... CMLC 24
Sainte-Beuve, Charles Augustin
1804-1869 .... NCLC 5
See also DLB 217; EW 6; GFL 1789 to the Present
Saint-Exupery, Antoine (Jean Baptiste
Marie Roger) de 1900-1944 .... TCLC 2, 56; WLC
See also BPFB 3; BYA 3; CA 132; CLR 10; DAM NOV; DLB 72; EW 12; GFL 1789 to the Present; LAIT 3; MAICYA 1, 2; MTCW 1, 2; RGWL 2, 3; SATA 20; TWA
St. John, David
See Hunt, E(verette) Howard, (Jr.)
St. John, J. Hector
See Crevecoeur, Michel Guillaume Jean de
Saint-John Perse
See Leger, (Marie-Rene Auguste) Alexis Saint-Leger
See also EW 10; GFL 1789 to the Present; RGWL 2
Saintsbury, George (Edward Bateman)
1845-1933 .... TCLC 31
See also CA 160; DLB 57, 149
Sait Faik .... TCLC 23
See also Abasiyanik, Sait Faik
Saki .... TCLC 3; SSC 12
See also Munro, H(ector) H(ugh)
See also BRWS 6; LAIT 2; MTCW 2; RGEL 2; SSFS 1; SUFW
Sakutaro, Hagiwara
See Hagiwara, Sakutaro
Sala, George Augustus 1828-1895 . NCLC 46
Saladin 1138-1193 .... CMLC 38
Salama, Hannu 1936- .... CLC 18
Salamanca, J(ack) R(ichard) 1922- .. CLC 4, 15
See also CA 25-28R; CAAE 193
Salas, Floyd Francis 1931-
See also CA 119; CAAS 27; CANR 44, 75, 93; DAM MULT; DLB 82; HLC 2; HW 1, 2; MTCW 2
Sale, J. Kirkpatrick
See Sale, Kirkpatrick
Sale, Kirkpatrick 1937- .... CLC 68
See also CA 13-16R; CANR 10
Salinas, Luis Omar 1937- ... CLC 90; HLC 2
See also CA 131; CANR 81; DAM MULT; DLB 82; HW 1, 2
Salinas (y Serrano), Pedro
1891(?)-1951 .... TCLC 17
See also DLB 134
Salinger, J(erome) D(avid) 1919- .. CLC 1, 3, 8, 12, 55, 56, 138; SSC 2, 28; WLC
See also AAYA 2, 36; AMW; BPFB 3; CA 5-8R; CANR 39; CDALB 1941-1968; CLR 18; CN 7; CPW 1; DA; DAB; DAC;
DAM MST, NOV, POP; DLB 2, 102, 173; EXPN; LAIT 4; MAICYA 1, 2; MTCW 1, 2; NFS 1; RGAL 4; RGSF 2; SATA 67; TUS; WYA; YAW
Salisbury, John
See Caute, (John) David
Salter, James 1925- .... CLC 7, 52, 59
See also AMWS 9; CA 73-76; CANR 107; DLB 130
Saltus, Edgar (Everton) 1855-1921 . TCLC 8
See also DLB 202; RGAL 4
Saltykov, Mikhail Evgrafovich
1826-1889 .... NCLC 16
See also DLB 238:
Saltykov-Shchedrin, N.
See Saltykov, Mikhail Evgrafovich
Samarakis, Antonis 1919- .... CLC 5
See also CA 25-28R; CAAS 16; CANR 36
Sanchez, Florencio 1875-1910 .... TCLC 37
See also CA 153; HW 1; LAW
Sanchez, Luis Rafael 1936- .... CLC 23
See also CA 128; DLB 145; HW 1; WLIT 1
Sanchez, Sonia 1934- .... CLC 5, 116; BLC 3; PC 9
See also BW 2, 3; CA 33-36R; CANR 24, 49, 74; CLR 18; CP 7; CSW; CWP; DAM MULT; DLB 41; DLBD 8; MAICYA 1, 2; MTCW 1, 2; SATA 22; WP
Sancho, Ignatius 1729-1780 .... LC 84
Sand, George 1804-1876 ..... NCLC 2, 42, 57; WLC
See also DA; DAB; DAC; DAM MST, NOV; DLB 119, 192; EW 6; FW; GFL 1789 to the Present; RGWL 2, 3; TWA
Sandburg, Carl (August) 1878-1967 . CLC 1, 4, 10, 15, 35; PC 2, 41; WLC
See also AAYA 24; AMW; BYA 1, 3; CA 5-8R; CANR 35; CDALB 1865-1917; CLR 67; DA; DAB; DAC; DAM MST, POET; DLB 17, 54; EXPP; LAIT 2; MAICYA 1, 2; MTCW 1, 2; PAB; PFS 3, 6, 12; RGAL 4; SATA 8; TUS; WCH; WP; WYA
Sandburg, Charles
See Sandburg, Carl (August)
Sandburg, Charles A.
See Sandburg, Carl (August)
Sanders, (James) Ed(ward) 1939- .... CLC 53
See also Sanders, Edward
See also CA 13-16R; CAAS 21; CANR 13, 44, 78; CP 7; DAM POET; DLB 16, 244
Sanders, Edward
See Sanders, (James) Ed(ward)
See also DLB 244
Sanders, Lawrence 1920-1998 .... CLC 41
See also BEST 89:4; BPFB 3; CA 81-84; CANR 33, 62; CMW 4; CPW; DAM POP; MTCW 1
Sanders, Noah
See Blount, Roy (Alton), Jr.
Sanders, Winston P.
See Anderson, Poul (William)
Sandoz, Mari(e Susette) 1900-1966 .. CLC 28
See also CA 1-4R; CANR 17, 64; DLB 9, 212; LAIT 2; MTCW 1, 2; SATA 5; TCWW 2
Sandys, George 1578-1644 .... LC 80
See also DLB 24, 121
Saner, Reg(inald Anthony) 1931- .... CLC 9
See also CA 65-68; CP 7
Sankara 788-820 .... CMLC 32
Sannazaro, Jacopo 1456(?)-1530 .... LC 8
See also RGWL 2, 3
Sansom, William 1912-1976 . CLC 2, 6; SSC 21
See also CA 5-8R; CANR 42; DAM NOV; DLB 139; MTCW 1; RGEL 2; RGSF 2

Santayana, George 1863-1952 .... **TCLC 40**
See also AMW; CA 194; DLB 54, 71, 246, 270; DLBD 13; RGAL 4; TUS

Santiago, Danny .... **CLC 33**
See also James, Daniel (Lewis)
See also DLB 122

Santmyer, Helen Hooven
1895-1986 .... **CLC 33**
See also CA 1-4R; CANR 15, 33; DLBY 1984; MTCW 1; RHW

Santoka, Taneda 1882-1940 .... **TCLC 72**

Santos, Bienvenido N(uqui)
1911-1996 .... **CLC 22**
See also CA 101; CANR 19, 46; DAM MULT; RGAL 4

Sapir, Edward 1884-1939 .... **TCLC 108**
See also DLB 92

Sapper .... **TCLC 44**
See also McNeile, Herman Cyril

Sapphire
See Sapphire, Brenda

Sapphire, Brenda 1950- .... **CLC 99**

Sappho fl. 6th cent. B.C.- ...... **CMLC 3; PC 5**
See also CDWLB 1; DAM POET; DLB 176; RGWL 2, 3; WP

Saramago, Jose 1922- ..... **CLC 119; HLCS 1**
See also CA 153; CANR 96

Sarduy, Severo 1937-1993 .... **CLC 6, 97; HLCS 2**
See also CA 89-92; CANR 58, 81; CWW 2; DLB 113; HW 1, 2; LAW

Sargeson, Frank 1903-1982 .... **CLC 31**
See also CA 25-28R; CANR 38, 79; GLL 2; RGEL 2; RGSF 2

Sarmiento, Domingo Faustino 1811-1888
See also HLCS 2; LAW; WLIT 1

Sarmiento, Felix Ruben Garcia
See Dario, Ruben

Saro-Wiwa, Ken(ule Beeson)
1941-1995 .... **CLC 114**
See also BW 2; CA 142; CANR 60; DLB 157

Saroyan, William 1908-1981 ... **CLC 1, 8, 10, 29, 34, 56; SSC 21; WLC**
See also CA 5-8R; CAD; CANR 30; CDALBS; DA; DAB; DAC; DAM DRAM, MST, NOV; DLB 7, 9, 86; DLBY 1981; LAIT 4; MTCW 1, 2; RGAL 4; RGSF 2; SATA 23; SATA-Obit 24; SSFS 14; TUS

Sarraute, Nathalie 1900-1999 .... **CLC 1, 2, 4, 8, 10, 31, 80**
See also BPFB 3; CA 9-12R; CANR 23, 66; CWW 2; DLB 83; EW 12; GFL 1789 to the Present; MTCW 1, 2; RGWL 2, 3

Sarton, (Eleanor) May 1912-1995 ..... **CLC 4, 14, 49, 91; PC 39**
See also AMWS 8; CA 1-4R; CANR 1, 34, 55; CN 7; CP 7; DAM POET; DLB 48; DLBY 1981; FW; INT CANR-34; MTCW 1, 2; RGAL 4; SATA 36; SATA-Obit 86; TCLC 120; TUS

Sartre, Jean-Paul 1905-1980 . **CLC 1, 4, 7, 9, 13, 18, 24, 44, 50, 52; DC 3; SSC 32; WLC**
See also CA 9-12R; CANR 21; DA; DAB; DAC; DAM DRAM, MST, NOV; DFS 5; DLB 72; EW 12; GFL 1789 to the Present; MTCW 1, 2; RGSF 2; RGWL 2, 3; SSFS 9; TWA

Sassoon, Siegfried (Lorraine)
1886-1967 .... **CLC 36, 130; PC 12**
See also BRW 6; CA 104; CANR 36; DAB; DAM MST, NOV, POET; DLB 20, 191; DLBD 18; MTCW 1, 2; PAB; RGEL 2; TEA

Satterfield, Charles
See Pohl, Frederik

Satyremont
See Peret, Benjamin

Saul, John (W. III) 1942- .... **CLC 46**
See also AAYA 10; BEST 90:4; CA 81-84; CANR 16, 40, 81; CPW; DAM NOV, POP; HGG; SATA 98

Saunders, Caleb
See Heinlein, Robert A(nson)

Saura (Atares), Carlos 1932-1998 .... **CLC 20**
See also CA 131; CANR 79; HW 1

Sauser-Hall, Frederic 1887-1961 ...... **CLC 18**
See also Cendrars, Blaise
See also CA 102; CANR 36, 62; MTCW 1

Saussure, Ferdinand de
1857-1913 .... **TCLC 49**
See also DLB 242

Savage, Catharine
See Brosman, Catharine Savage

Savage, Thomas 1915- .... **CLC 40**
See also CA 132; CAAS 15; CN 7; INT 132; TCWW 2

Savan, Glenn (?)- .... **CLC 50**

Sax, Robert
See Johnson, Robert

Saxton, Robert
See Johnson, Robert

Sayers, Dorothy L(eigh)
1893-1957 .... **TCLC 2, 15**
See also BPFB 3; BRWS 3; CA 119; CANR 60; CDBLB 1914-1945; CMW 4; DAM POP; DLB 10, 36, 77, 100; MSW; MTCW 1, 2; RGEL 2; SSFS 12; TEA

Sayers, Valerie 1952- .... **CLC 50, 122**
See also CA 134; CANR 61; CSW

Sayles, John (Thomas) 1950- . **CLC 7, 10, 14**
See also CA 57-60; CANR 41, 84; DLB 44

Scammell, Michael 1935- .... **CLC 34**
See also CA 156

Scannell, Vernon 1922- .... **CLC 49**
See also CA 5-8R; CANR 8, 24, 57; CP 7; CWRI 5; DLB 27; SATA 59

Scarlett, Susan
See Streatfeild, (Mary) Noel

Scarron 1847-1910
See Mikszath, Kalman

Schaeffer, Susan Fromberg 1941- ..... **CLC 6, 11, 22**
See also CA 49-52; CANR 18, 65; CN 7; DLB 28; MTCW 1, 2; SATA 22

Schama, Simon (Michael) 1945- ..... **CLC 150**
See also BEST 89:4; CA 105; CANR 39, 91

Schary, Jill
See Robinson, Jill

Schell, Jonathan 1943- .... **CLC 35**
See also CA 73-76; CANR 12

Schelling, Friedrich Wilhelm Joseph von
1775-1854 .... **NCLC 30**
See also DLB 90

Scherer, Jean-Marie Maurice 1920-
See Rohmer, Eric
See also CA 110

Schevill, James (Erwin) 1920- .... **CLC 7**
See also CA 5-8R; CAAS 12; CAD; CD 5

Schiller, Friedrich von
1759-1805 .... **NCLC 39, 69; DC 12**
See also CDWLB 2; DAM DRAM; DLB 94; EW 5; RGWL 2, 3; TWA

Schisgal, Murray (Joseph) 1926- .... **CLC 6**
See also CA 21-24R; CAD; CANR 48, 86; CD 5

Schlee, Ann 1934- .... **CLC 35**
See also CA 101; CANR 29, 88; SATA 44; SATA-Brief 36

Schlegel, August Wilhelm von
1767-1845 .... **NCLC 15**
See also DLB 94; RGWL 2, 3

Schlegel, Friedrich 1772-1829 .... **NCLC 45**
See also DLB 90; EW 5; RGWL 2, 3; TWA

Schlegel, Johann Elias (von)
1719(?)-1749 .... **LC 5**

Schleiermacher, Friedrich
1768-1834 .... **NCLC 107**
See also DLB 90

Schlesinger, Arthur M(eier), Jr.
1917- .... **CLC 84**
See also AITN 1; CA 1-4R; CANR 1, 28, 58, 105; DLB 17; INT CANR-28; MTCW 1, 2; SATA 61

Schmidt, Arno (Otto) 1914-1979 ...... **CLC 56**
See also CA 128; DLB 69

Schmitz, Aron Hector 1861-1928
See Svevo, Italo
See also CA 122; MTCW 1

Schnackenberg, Gjertrud (Cecelia)
1953- .... **CLC 40**
See also CANR 100; CP 7; CWP; DLB 120; PFS 13

Schneider, Leonard Alfred 1925-1966
See Bruce, Lenny
See also CA 89-92

Schnitzler, Arthur 1862-1931 ... **TCLC 4; DC 17; SSC 15**
See also CDWLB 2; DLB 81, 118; EW 8; RGSF 2; RGWL 2, 3

Schoenberg, Arnold Franz Walter
1874-1951 .... **TCLC 75**
See also CA 188

Schonberg, Arnold
See Schoenberg, Arnold Franz Walter

Schopenhauer, Arthur 1788-1860 .. **NCLC 51**
See also DLB 90; EW 5

Schor, Sandra (M.) 1932(?)-1990 ..... **CLC 65**

Schorer, Mark 1908-1977 .... **CLC 9**
See also CA 5-8R; CANR 7; DLB 103

Schrader, Paul (Joseph) 1946- .... **CLC 26**
See also CA 37-40R; CANR 41; DLB 44

Schreber, Daniel 1842-1911 .... **TCLC 123**

Schreiner, Olive (Emilie Albertina)
1855-1920 .... **TCLC 9**
See also AFW; BRWS 2; CA 154; DLB 18, 156, 190, 225; FW; RGEL 2; TWA; WLIT 2

Schulberg, Budd (Wilson) 1914- .. **CLC 7, 48**
See also BPFB 3; CA 25-28R; CANR 19, 87; CN 7; DLB 6, 26, 28; DLBY 1981, 2001

Schulman, Arnold
See Trumbo, Dalton

Schulz, Bruno 1892-1942 .. **TCLC 5, 51; SSC 13**
See also CA 123; CANR 86; CDWLB 4; DLB 215; MTCW 2; RGSF 2; RGWL 2, 3

Schulz, Charles M(onroe)
1922-2000 .... **CLC 12**
See also AAYA 39; CA 9-12R; CANR 6; INT CANR-6; SATA 10; SATA-Obit 118

Schumacher, E(rnst) F(riedrich)
1911-1977 .... **CLC 80**
See also CA 81-84; CANR 34, 85

Schuyler, James Marcus 1923-1991 .. **CLC 5, 23**
See also CA 101; DAM POET; DLB 5, 169; INT 101; WP

Schwartz, Delmore (David)
1913-1966 ... **CLC 2, 4, 10, 45, 87; PC 8**
See also AMWS 2; CA 17-18; CANR 35; CAP 2; DLB 28, 48; MTCW 1, 2; PAB; RGAL 4; TUS

Schwartz, Ernst
See Ozu, Yasujiro

Schwartz, John Burnham 1965- .... **CLC 59**
See also CA 132

Schwartz, Lynne Sharon 1939- .... **CLC 31**
See also CA 103; CANR 44, 89; DLB 218; MTCW 2

Schwartz, Muriel A.
See Eliot, T(homas) S(tearns)

Schwarz-Bart, Andre 1928- .... **CLC 2, 4**
See also CA 89-92; CANR 109

Schwarz-Bart, Simone 1938- . **CLC 7; BLCS**
See also BW 2; CA 97-100

Schwerner, Armand 1927-1999 .... **PC 42**
See also CA 9-12R; CANR 50, 85; CP 7; DLB 165

Schwitters, Kurt (Hermann Edward Karl Julius) 1887-1948 .... **TCLC 95**
See also CA 158

Schwob, Marcel (Mayer Andre) 1867-1905 .... **TCLC 20**
See also CA 168; DLB 123; GFL 1789 to the Present

Sciascia, Leonardo 1921-1989 .. **CLC 8, 9, 41**
See also CA 85-88; CANR 35; DLB 177; MTCW 1; RGWL 2, 3

Scoppettone, Sandra 1936- .... **CLC 26**
See also Early, Jack
See also AAYA 11; BYA 8; CA 5-8R; CANR 41, 73; GLL 1; MAICYA 2; MAICYAS 1; SATA 9, 92; WYA; YAW

Scorsese, Martin 1942- .... **CLC 20, 89**
See also AAYA 38; CA 114; CANR 46, 85

Scotland, Jay
See Jakes, John (William)

Scott, Duncan Campbell 1862-1947 .... **TCLC 6**
See also CA 153; DAC; DLB 92; RGEL 2

Scott, Evelyn 1893-1963 .... **CLC 43**
See also CA 104; CANR 64; DLB 9, 48; RHW

Scott, F(rancis) R(eginald) 1899-1985 .... **CLC 22**
See also CA 101; CANR 87; DLB 88; INT CA-101; RGEL 2

Scott, Frank
See Scott, F(rancis) R(eginald)

Scott, Joan .... **CLC 65**

Scott, Joanna 1960- .... **CLC 50**
See also CA 126; CANR 53, 92

Scott, Paul (Mark) 1920-1978 ...... **CLC 9, 60**
See also BRWS 1; CA 81-84; CANR 33; DLB 14, 207; MTCW 1; RGEL 2; RHW

Scott, Sarah 1723-1795 .... **LC 44**
See also DLB 39

Scott, Sir Walter 1771-1832 .... **NCLC 15, 69, 110; PC 13; SSC 32; WLC**
See also AAYA 22; BRW 4; BYA 2; CDBLB 1789-1832; DA; DAB; DAC; DAM MST, NOV, POET; DLB 93, 107, 116, 144, 159; HGG; LAIT 1; RGEL 2; RGSF 2; SSFS 10; SUFW 1; TEA; WLIT 3; YABC 2

Scribe, (Augustin) Eugene 1791-1861 .... **NCLC 16; DC 5**
See also DAM DRAM; DLB 192; GFL 1789 to the Present; RGWL 2, 3

Scrum, R.
See Crumb, R(obert)

Scudery, Georges de 1601-1667 .... **LC 75**
See also GFL Beginnings to 1789

Scudery, Madeleine de 1607-1701 .. **LC 2, 58**
See also DLB 268; GFL Beginnings to 1789

Scum
See Crumb, R(obert)

Scumbag, Little Bobby
See Crumb, R(obert)

Seabrook, John
See Hubbard, L(afayette) Ron(ald)

Sealy, I(rwin) Allan 1951- .... **CLC 55**
See also CA 136; CN 7

Search, Alexander
See Pessoa, Fernando (Antonio Nogueira)

Sebastian, Lee
See Silverberg, Robert

Sebastian Owl
See Thompson, Hunter S(tockton)

Sebestyen, Igen
See Sebestyen, Ouida

Sebestyen, Ouida 1924- .... **CLC 30**
See also AAYA 8; BYA 7; CA 107; CANR 40; CLR 17; JRDA; MAICYA 1, 2; SAAS 10; SATA 39; WYA; YAW

Secundus, H. Scriblerus
See Fielding, Henry

Sedges, John
See Buck, Pearl S(ydenstricker)

Sedgwick, Catharine Maria 1789-1867 .... **NCLC 19, 98**
See also DLB 1, 74, 183, 239, 243, 254; RGAL 4

Seelye, John (Douglas) 1931- .... **CLC 7**
See also CA 97-100; CANR 70; INT 97-100; TCWW 2

Seferiades, Giorgos Stylianou 1900-1971
See Seferis, George
See also CA 5-8R; CANR 5, 36; MTCW 1

Seferis, George .... **CLC 5, 11**
See also Seferiades, Giorgos Stylianou
See also EW 12; RGWL 2, 3

Segal, Erich (Wolf) 1937- .... **CLC 3, 10**
See also BEST 89:1; BPFB 3; CA 25-28R; CANR 20, 36, 65, 113; CPW; DAM POP; DLBY 1986; INT CANR-20; MTCW 1

Seger, Bob 1945- .... **CLC 35**

Seghers, Anna -1983 .... **CLC 7**
See also Radvanyi, Netty
See also CDWLB 2; DLB 69

Seidel, Frederick (Lewis) 1936- .... **CLC 18**
See also CA 13-16R; CANR 8, 99; CP 7; DLBY 1984

Seifert, Jaroslav 1901-1986 .. **CLC 34, 44, 93**
See also CA 127; CDWLB 4; DLB 215; MTCW 1, 2

Sei Shonagon c. 966-1017(?) .... **CMLC 6**

Sejour, Victor 1817-1874 .... **DC 10**
See also DLB 50

Sejour Marcou et Ferrand, Juan Victor
See Sejour, Victor

Selby, Hubert, Jr. 1928- .... **CLC 1, 2, 4, 8; SSC 20**
See also CA 13-16R; CANR 33, 85; CN 7; DLB 2, 227

Selzer, Richard 1928- .... **CLC 74**
See also CA 65-68; CANR 14, 106

Sembene, Ousmane
See Ousmane, Sembene
See also AFW; CWW 2; WLIT 2

Senancour, Etienne Pivert de 1770-1846 .... **NCLC 16**
See also DLB 119; GFL 1789 to the Present

Sender, Ramon (Jose) 1902-1982 .... **CLC 8; HLC 2**
See also CA 5-8R; CANR 8; DAM MULT; HW 1; MTCW 1; RGWL 2, 3

Seneca, Lucius Annaeus c. 4B.C.-c. 65 .... **CMLC 6; DC 5**
See also AW 2; CDWLB 1; DAM DRAM; DLB 211; RGWL 2, 3; TWA

Senghor, Leopold Sedar 1906-2001 . **CLC 54, 130; BLC 3; PC 25**
See also AFW; BW 2; CA 125; CANR 47, 74; DAM MULT, POET; DNFS 2; GFL 1789 to the Present; MTCW 1, 2; TWA

Senna, Danzy 1970- .... **CLC 119**
See also CA 169

Serling, (Edward) Rod(man) 1924-1975 .... **CLC 30**
See also AAYA 14; AITN 1; CA 162; DLB 26; SFW 4

Serna, Ramon Gomez de la
See Gomez de la Serna, Ramon

Serpieres
See Guillevic, (Eugene)

Service, Robert
See Service, Robert W(illiam)
See also BYA 4; DAB; DLB 92

Service, Robert W(illiam) 1874(?)-1958 .... **TCLC 15; WLC**
See also Service, Robert
See also CA 140; CANR 84; DA; DAC; DAM MST, POET; PFS 10; RGEL 2; SATA 20

Seth, Vikram 1952- .... **CLC 43, 90**
See also CA 127; CANR 50, 74; CN 7; CP 7; DAM MULT; DLB 120, 271; INT 127; MTCW 2

Seton, Cynthia Propper 1926-1982 .. **CLC 27**
See also CA 5-8R; CANR 7

Seton, Ernest (Evan) Thompson 1860-1946 .... **TCLC 31**
See also ANW; BYA 3; CA 204; CLR 59; DLB 92; DLBD 13; JRDA; SATA 18

Seton-Thompson, Ernest
See Seton, Ernest (Evan) Thompson

Settle, Mary Lee 1918- .... **CLC 19, 61**
See also BPFB 3; CA 89-92; CAAS 1; CANR 44, 87; CN 7; CSW; DLB 6; INT 89-92

Seuphor, Michel
See Arp, Jean

Sevigne, Marie (de Rabutin-Chantal) 1626-1696 .... **LC 11**
See also Sevigne, Marie de Rabutin Chantal
See also GFL Beginnings to 1789; TWA

Sevigne, Marie de Rabutin Chantal
See Sevigne, Marie (de Rabutin-Chantal)
See also DLB 268

Sewall, Samuel 1652-1730 .... **LC 38**
See also DLB 24; RGAL 4

Sexton, Anne (Harvey) 1928-1974 ..... **CLC 2, 4, 6, 8, 10, 15, 53, 123; PC 2; WLC**
See also AMWS 2; CA 1-4R; CABS 2; CANR 3, 36; CDALB 1941-1968; DA; DAB; DAC; DAM MST, POET; DLB 5, 169; EXPP; FW; MAWW; MTCW 1, 2; PAB; PFS 4, 14; RGAL 4; SATA 10; TUS

Shaara, Jeff 1952- .... **CLC 119**
See also CA 163; CANR 109

Shaara, Michael (Joseph, Jr.) 1929-1988 .... **CLC 15**
See also AITN 1; BPFB 3; CA 102; CANR 52, 85; DAM POP; DLBY 1983

Shackleton, C. C.
See Aldiss, Brian W(ilson)

Shacochis, Bob .... **CLC 39**
See also Shacochis, Robert G.

Shacochis, Robert G. 1951-
See Shacochis, Bob
See also CA 124; CANR 100; INT 124

Shaffer, Anthony (Joshua) 1926-2001 .... **CLC 19**
See also CA 116; CBD; CD 5; DAM DRAM; DFS 13; DLB 13

Shaffer, Peter (Levin) 1926- .. **CLC 5, 14, 18, 37, 60; DC 7**
See also BRWS 1; CA 25-28R; CANR 25, 47, 74; CBD; CD 5; CDBLB 1960 to Present; DAB; DAM DRAM, MST; DFS 5, 13; DLB 13, 233; MTCW 1, 2; RGEL 2; TEA

Shakey, Bernard
See Young, Neil

Shalamov, Varlam (Tikhonovich) 1907(?)-1982 .... **CLC 18**
See also CA 129; RGSF 2

Shamlu, Ahmad 1925-2000 .... **CLC 10**
See also CWW 2

Shammas, Anton 1951- .... **CLC 55**
See also CA 199

Shandling, Arline
See Berriault, Gina

Shange, Ntozake 1948- .... **CLC 8, 25, 38, 74, 126; BLC 3; DC 3**
See also AAYA 9; AFAW 1, 2; BW 2; CA 85-88; CABS 3; CAD; CANR 27, 48, 74; CD 5; CP 7; CWD; CWP; DAM DRAM, MULT; DFS 2, 11; DLB 38, 249; FW; LAIT 5; MTCW 1, 2; NFS 11; RGAL 4; YAW

Shanley, John Patrick 1950- .... **CLC 75**
See also CA 133; CAD; CANR 83; CD 5

Shapcott, Thomas W(illiam) 1935- .. **CLC 38**
See also CA 69-72; CANR 49, 83, 103; CP 7

Shapiro, Jane 1942- .... **CLC 76**
See also CA 196

Shapiro, Karl (Jay) 1913-2000 ...... **CLC 4, 8, 15, 53; PC 25**
See also AMWS 2; CA 1-4R; CAAS 6; CANR 1, 36, 66; CP 7; DLB 48; EXPP; MTCW 1, 2; PFS 3; RGAL 4

Sharp, William 1855-1905 .... **TCLC 39**
See also Macleod, Fiona
See also CA 160; DLB 156; RGEL 2

Sharpe, Thomas Ridley 1928-
See Sharpe, Tom
See also CA 122; CANR 85; INT CA-122

Sharpe, Tom .... **CLC 36**
See also Sharpe, Thomas Ridley
See also CN 7; DLB 14, 231

Shatrov, Mikhail .... **CLC 59**

Shaw, Bernard
See Shaw, George Bernard
See also DLB 190

Shaw, G. Bernard
See Shaw, George Bernard

Shaw, George Bernard 1856-1950 .. **TCLC 3, 9, 21, 45; WLC**
See also Shaw, Bernard
See also BRW 6; BRWR 2; CA 128; CD-BLB 1914-1945; DA; DAB; DAC; DAM DRAM, MST; DFS 1, 3, 6, 11; DLB 10, 57; LAIT 3; MTCW 1, 2; RGEL 2; TEA; WLIT 4

Shaw, Henry Wheeler 1818-1885 .. **NCLC 15**
See also DLB 11; RGAL 4

Shaw, Irwin 1913-1984 .... **CLC 7, 23, 34**
See also AITN 1; BPFB 3; CA 13-16R; CANR 21; CDALB 1941-1968; CPW; DAM DRAM, POP; DLB 6, 102; DLBY 1984; MTCW 1, 21

Shaw, Robert 1927-1978 .... **CLC 5**
See also AITN 1; CA 1-4R; CANR 4; DLB 13, 14

Shaw, T. E.
See Lawrence, T(homas) E(dward)

Shawn, Wallace 1943- .... **CLC 41**
See also CA 112; CAD; CD 5; DLB 266

Shchedrin, N.
See Saltykov, Mikhail Evgrafovich

Shea, Lisa 1953- .... **CLC 86**
See also CA 147

Sheed, Wilfrid (John Joseph) 1930- . **CLC 2, 4, 10, 53**
See also CA 65-68; CANR 30, 66; CN 7; DLB 6; MTCW 1, 2

Sheldon, Alice Hastings Bradley 1915(?)-1987
See Tiptree, James, Jr.
See also CA 108; CANR 34; INT 108; MTCW 1

Sheldon, John
See Bloch, Robert (Albert)

Sheldon, Walter J(ames) 1917-1996
See Queen, Ellery
See also AITN 1; CA 25-28R; CANR 10

Shelley, Mary Wollstonecraft (Godwin) 1797-1851 ...... **NCLC 14, 59, 103; WLC**
See also AAYA 20; BPFB 3; BRW 3; BRWS 3; BYA 5; CDBLB 1789-1832; DA; DAB; DAC; DAM MST, NOV; DLB 110, 116, 159, 178; EXPN; HGG; LAIT 1; NFS 1; RGEL 2; SATA 29; SCFW; SFW 4; TEA; WLIT 3

Shelley, Percy Bysshe 1792-1822 .. **NCLC 18, 93; PC 14; WLC**
See also BRW 4; BRWR 1; CDBLB 1789-1832; DA; DAB; DAC; DAM MST, POET; DLB 96, 110, 158; EXPP; PAB; PFS 2; RGEL 2; TEA; WLIT 3; WP

Shepard, Jim 1956- .... **CLC 36**
See also CA 137; CANR 59, 104; SATA 90

Shepard, Lucius 1947- .... **CLC 34**
See also CA 141; CANR 81; HGG; SCFW 2; SFW 4; SUFW 2

Shepard, Sam 1943- .... **CLC 4, 6, 17, 34, 41, 44; DC 5**
See also AAYA 1; AMWS 3; CA 69-72; CABS 3; CAD; CANR 22; CD 5; DAM DRAM; DFS 3, 6, 7, 14; DLB 7, 212; IDFW 3, 4; MTCW 1, 2; RGAL 4

Shepherd, Michael
See Ludlum, Robert

Sherburne, Zoa (Lillian Morin) 1912-1995 .... **CLC 30**
See also AAYA 13; CA 1-4R; CANR 3, 37; MAICYA 1, 2; SAAS 18; SATA 3; YAW

Sheridan, Frances 1724-1766 .... **LC 7**
See also DLB 39, 84

Sheridan, Richard Brinsley 1751-1816 .... **NCLC 5, 91; DC 1; WLC**
See also BRW 3; CDBLB 1660-1789; DA; DAB; DAC; DAM DRAM, MST; DFS 15; DLB 89; WLIT 3

Sherman, Jonathan Marc .... **CLC 55**
Sherman, Martin 1941(?)- .... **CLC 19**
See also CA 123; CAD; CANR 86; CD 5; DLB 228; GLL 1; IDTP

Sherwin, Judith Johnson
See Johnson, Judith (Emlyn)
See also CANR 85; CP 7; CWP

Sherwood, Frances 1940- .... **CLC 81**
See also CA 146

Sherwood, Robert E(mmet) 1896-1955 .... **TCLC 3**
See also CA 153; CANR 86; DAM DRAM; DFS 15; DLB 7, 26, 249; IDFW 3, 4; RGAL 4

Shestov, Lev 1866-1938 .... **TCLC 56**
Shevchenko, Taras 1814-1861 .... **NCLC 54**
Shiel, M(atthew) P(hipps) 1865-1947 .... **TCLC 8**
See also Holmes, Gordon
See also CA 160; DLB 153; HGG; MTCW 2; SFW 4; SUFW

Shields, Carol 1935- .... **CLC 91, 113**
See also AMWS 7; CA 81-84; CANR 51, 74, 98; CCA 1; CN 7; CPW; DAC; MTCW 2

Shields, David 1956- .... **CLC 97**
See also CA 124; CANR 48, 99, 112

Shiga, Naoya 1883-1971 ..... **CLC 33; SSC 23**
See also Shiga Naoya
See also CA 101; MJW; RGWL 3

Shiga Naoya
See Shiga, Naoya
See also DLB 180; RGWL 3

Shilts, Randy 1951-1994 .... **CLC 85**
See also AAYA 19; CA 127; CANR 45; GLL 1; INT 127; MTCW 2

Shimazaki, Haruki 1872-1943
See Shimazaki Toson
See also CA 134; CANR 84; RGWL 3

Shimazaki Toson .... **TCLC 5**
See also Shimazaki, Haruki
See also DLB 180

Sholokhov, Mikhail (Aleksandrovich) 1905-1984 .... **CLC 7, 15**
See also CA 101; DLB 272; MTCW 1, 2; RGWL 2, 3; SATA-Obit 36

Shone, Patric
See Hanley, James

Shreve, Susan Richards 1939- .... **CLC 23**
See also CA 49-52; CAAS 5; CANR 5, 38, 69, 100; MAICYA 1, 2; SATA 46, 95; SATA-Brief 41

Shue, Larry 1946-1985 .... **CLC 52**
See also CA 145; DAM DRAM; DFS 7

Shu-Jen, Chou 1881-1936
See Lu Hsun

Shulman, Alix Kates 1932- .... **CLC 2, 10**
See also CA 29-32R; CANR 43; FW; SATA 7

Shusaku, Endo
See Endo, Shusaku

Shuster, Joe 1914-1992 .... **CLC 21**

Shute, Nevil .... **CLC 30**
See also Norway, Nevil Shute
See also BPFB 3; DLB 255; NFS 9; RHW; SFW 4

Shuttle, Penelope (Diane) 1947- .... **CLC 7**
See also CA 93-96; CANR 39, 84, 92, 108; CP 7; CWP; DLB 14, 40

Sidney, Mary 1561-1621 .... **LC 19, 39**
See also Sidney Herbert, Mary

Sidney, Sir Philip 1554-1586 . **LC 19, 39; PC 32**
See also BRW 1; BRWR 2; CDBLB Before 1660; DA; DAB; DAC; DAM MST, POET; DLB 167; EXPP; PAB; RGEL 2; TEA; WP

Sidney Herbert, Mary
See Sidney, Mary
See also DLB 167

Siegel, Jerome 1914-1996 .... **CLC 21**
See also CA 169

Siegel, Jerry
See Siegel, Jerome

Sienkiewicz, Henryk (Adam Alexander Pius) 1846-1916 .... **TCLC 3**
See also CA 134; CANR 84; RGSF 2; RGWL 2, 3

Sierra, Gregorio Martinez
See Martinez Sierra, Gregorio

Sierra, Maria (de la O'LeJarraga) Martinez
See Martinez Sierra, Maria (de la O'LeJarraga)

Sigal, Clancy 1926- .... **CLC 7**
See also CA 1-4R; CANR 85; CN 7

Sigourney, Lydia H.
See Sigourney, Lydia Howard (Huntley)
See also DLB 73, 183

Sigourney, Lydia Howard (Huntley) 1791-1865 .... **NCLC 21, 87**
See also Sigourney, Lydia H.; Sigourney, Lydia Huntley
See also DLB 1

Sigourney, Lydia Huntley
See Sigourney, Lydia Howard (Huntley)
See also DLB 42, 239, 243

Siguenza y Gongora, Carlos de 1645-1700 .... **LC 8; HLCS 2**
See also LAW

Sigurjonsson, Johann 1880-1919 ... **TCLC 27**
See also CA 170

Sikelianos, Angelos 1884-1951 ...... **TCLC 39; PC 29**
See also RGWL 2, 3

Silkin, Jon 1930-1997 .... **CLC 2, 6, 43**
See also CA 5-8R; CAAS 5; CANR 89; CP 7; DLB 27

Silko, Leslie (Marmon) 1948- .... **CLC 23, 74, 114; SSC 37; WLCS**
See also AAYA 14; AMWS 4; ANW; BYA 12; CA 122; CANR 45, 65; CN 7; CP 7; CPW 1; CWP; DA; DAC; DAM MST, MULT, POP; DLB 143, 175, 256; EXPP; EXPS; LAIT 4; MTCW 2; NFS 4; NNAL; PFS 9; RGAL 4; RGSF 2; SSFS 4, 8, 10, 11

Sillanpaa, Frans Eemil 1888-1964 ... **CLC 19**
See also CA 129; MTCW 1

Sillitoe, Alan 1928- .. **CLC 1, 3, 6, 10, 19, 57, 148**
See also AITN 1; BRWS 5; CA 9-12R; CAAE 191; CAAS 2; CANR 8, 26, 55; CDBLB 1960 to Present; CN 7; DLB 14, 139; MTCW 1, 2; RGEL 2; RGSF 2; SATA 61

Silone, Ignazio 1900-1978 .... **CLC 4**
See also CA 25-28; CANR 34; CAP 2; DLB 264; EW 12; MTCW 1; RGSF 2; RGWL 2, 3

Silone, Ignazione
See Silone, Ignazio

Silva, Jose Asuncion
See da Silva, Antonio Jose
See also LAW

Silver, Joan Micklin 1935- .... **CLC 20**
See also CA 121; INT 121

Silver, Nicholas
See Faust, Frederick (Schiller)
See also TCWW 2

Silverberg, Robert 1935- .... **CLC 7, 140**
See also AAYA 24; BPFB 3; BYA 7, 9; CA 1-4R, 186; CAAE 186; CANR 1, 20, 36, 85; CLR 59; CN 7; CPW; DAM POP; DLB 8; INT CANR-20; MAICYA 1, 2; MTCW 1, 2; SATA 13, 91; SATA-Essay 104; SCFW 2; SFW 4; SUFW 2

Silverstein, Alvin 1933- .... **CLC 17**
See also CA 49-52; CANR 2; CLR 25; JRDA; MAICYA 1, 2; SATA 8, 69, 124

Silverstein, Virginia B(arbara Opshelor) 1937- .... **CLC 17**
See also CA 49-52; CANR 2; CLR 25; JRDA; MAICYA 1, 2; SATA 8, 69, 124

Sim, Georges
See Simenon, Georges (Jacques Christian)

Simak, Clifford D(onald) 1904-1988 . **CLC 1, 55**
See also CA 1-4R; CANR 1, 35; DLB 8; MTCW 1; SATA-Obit 56; SFW 4

Simenon, Georges (Jacques Christian) 1903-1989 .... **CLC 1, 2, 3, 8, 18, 47**
See also BPFB 3; CA 85-88; CANR 35; CMW 4; DAM POP; DLB 72; DLBY 1989; EW 12; GFL 1789 to the Present; MSW; MTCW 1, 2; RGWL 2, 3

Simic, Charles 1938- .... **CLC 6, 9, 22, 49, 68, 130**
See also AMWS 8; CA 29-32R; CAAS 4; CANR 12, 33, 52, 61, 96; CP 7; DAM POET; DLB 105; MTCW 2; PFS 7; RGAL 4; WP

Simmel, Georg 1858-1918 .... **TCLC 64**
See also CA 157

Simmons, Charles (Paul) 1924- .... **CLC 57**
See also CA 89-92; INT 89-92

Simmons, Dan 1948- .... **CLC 44**
See also AAYA 16; CA 138; CANR 53, 81; CPW; DAM POP; HGG; SUFW 2

Simmons, James (Stewart Alexander) 1933- .... **CLC 43**
See also CA 105; CAAS 21; CP 7; DLB 40

Simms, William Gilmore 1806-1870 .... **NCLC 3**
See also DLB 3, 30, 59, 73, 248, 254; RGAL 4

Simon, Carly 1945- .... **CLC 26**
See also CA 105

Simon, Claude 1913-1984 ... **CLC 4, 9, 15, 39**
See also CA 89-92; CANR 33; DAM NOV; DLB 83; EW 13; GFL 1789 to the Present; MTCW 1

Simon, Myles
See Follett, Ken(neth Martin)

Simon, (Marvin) Neil 1927- ... **CLC 6, 11, 31, 39, 70; DC 14**
See also AAYA 32; AITN 1; AMWS 4; CA 21-24R; CANR 26, 54, 87; CD 5; DAM DRAM; DFS 2, 6, 12; DLB 7, 266; LAIT 4; MTCW 1, 2; RGAL 4; TUS

Simon, Paul (Frederick) 1941(?)- ..... **CLC 17**
See also CA 153

Simonon, Paul 1956(?)- .... **CLC 30**

Simonson, Rick ed. .... **CLC 70**

Simpson, Harriette
See Arnow, Harriette (Louisa) Simpson

Simpson, Louis (Aston Marantz) 1923- .... **CLC 4, 7, 9, 32, 149**
See also AMWS 9; CA 1-4R; CAAS 4; CANR 1, 61; CP 7; DAM POET; DLB 5; MTCW 1, 2; PFS 7, 11, 14; RGAL 4

Simpson, Mona (Elizabeth) 1957- ... **CLC 44, 146**
See also CA 135; CANR 68, 103; CN 7

Simpson, N(orman) F(rederick) 1919- .... **CLC 29**
See also CA 13-16R; CBD; DLB 13; RGEL 2

Sinclair, Andrew (Annandale) 1935- . **CLC 2, 14**
See also CA 9-12R; CAAS 5; CANR 14, 38, 91; CN 7; DLB 14; FANT; MTCW 1

Sinclair, Emil
See Hesse, Hermann

Sinclair, Iain 1943- .... **CLC 76**
See also CA 132; CANR 81; CP 7; HGG

Sinclair, Iain MacGregor
See Sinclair, Iain

Sinclair, Irene
See Griffith, D(avid Lewelyn) W(ark)

Sinclair, Mary Amelia St. Clair 1865(?)-1946
See Sinclair, May
See also HGG; RHW

Sinclair, May .... **TCLC 3, 11**
See also Sinclair, Mary Amelia St. Clair
See also CA 166; DLB 36, 135; RGEL 2; SUFW

Sinclair, Roy
See Griffith, D(avid Lewelyn) W(ark)

Sinclair, Upton (Beall) 1878-1968 ..... **CLC 1, 11, 15, 63; WLC**
See also AMWS 5; BPFB 3; BYA 2; CA 5-8R; CANR 7; CDALB 1929-1941; DA; DAB; DAC; DAM MST, NOV; DLB 9; INT CANR-7; LAIT 3; MTCW 1, 2; NFS 6; RGAL 4; SATA 9; TUS; YAW

Singer, Isaac
See Singer, Isaac Bashevis

Singer, Isaac Bashevis 1904-1991 .. **CLC 1, 3, 6, 9, 11, 15, 23, 38, 69, 111; SSC 3, 53; WLC**
See also AAYA 32; AITN 1, 2; AMW; BPFB 3; BYA 1, 4; CA 1-4R; CANR 1, 39, 106; CDALB 1941-1968; CLR 1; CWRI 5; DA; DAB; DAC; DAM MST, NOV; DLB 6, 28, 52; DLBY 1991; EXPS; HGG; JRDA; LAIT 3; MAICYA 1, 2; MTCW 1, 2; RGAL 4; RGSF 2; SATA 3, 27; SATA-Obit 68; SSFS 2, 12; TUS; TWA

Singer, Israel Joshua 1893-1944 .... **TCLC 33**
See also CA 169

Singh, Khushwant 1915- .... **CLC 11**
See also CA 9-12R; CAAS 9; CANR 6, 84; CN 7; RGEL 2

Singleton, Ann
See Benedict, Ruth (Fulton)

Singleton, John 1968(?)- .... **CLC 156**
See also BW 2, 3; CA 138; CANR 67, 82; DAM MULT

Sinjohn, John
See Galsworthy, John

Sinyavsky, Andrei (Donatevich) 1925-1997 .... **CLC 8**
See also Tertz, Abram
See also CA 85-88

Sirin, V.
See Nabokov, Vladimir (Vladimirovich)

Sissman, L(ouis) E(dward) 1928-1976 .... **CLC 9, 18**
See also CA 21-24R; CANR 13; DLB 5

Sisson, C(harles) H(ubert) 1914- .... **CLC 8**
See also CA 1-4R; CAAS 3; CANR 3, 48, 84; CP 7; DLB 27

Sitwell, Dame Edith 1887-1964 ..... **CLC 2, 9, 67; PC 3**
See also BRW 7; CA 9-12R; CANR 35; CDBLB 1945-1960; DAM POET; DLB 20; MTCW 1, 2; RGEL 2; TEA

Siwaarmill, H. P.
See Sharp, William

Sjoewall, Maj 1935- .... **CLC 7**
See also Sjowall, Maj
See also CA 65-68; CANR 73

Sjowall, Maj
See Sjoewall, Maj
See also BPFB 3; CMW 4; MSW

Skelton, John 1460(?)-1529 ..... **LC 71; PC 25**
See also BRW 1; DLB 136; RGEL 2

Skelton, Robin 1925-1997 .... **CLC 13**
See also Zuk, Georges
See also AITN 2; CA 5-8R; CAAS 5; CANR 28, 89; CCA 1; CP 7; DLB 27, 53

Skolimowski, Jerzy 1938- .... **CLC 20**
See also CA 128

Skram, Amalie (Bertha) 1847-1905 .... **TCLC 25**
See also CA 165

Skvorecky, Josef (Vaclav) 1924- ...... **CLC 15, 39, 69, 152**
See also CA 61-64; CAAS 1; CANR 10, 34, 63, 108; CDWLB 4; DAC; DAM NOV; DLB 232; MTCW 1, 2

Slade, Bernard .... **CLC 11, 46**
See also Newbound, Bernard Slade
See also CAAS 9; CCA 1; DLB 53

Slaughter, Carolyn 1946- .... **CLC 56**
See also CA 85-88; CANR 85; CN 7

Slaughter, Frank G(ill) 1908-2001 .... **CLC 29**
See also AITN 2; CA 5-8R; CANR 5, 85; INT CANR-5; RHW

Slavitt, David R(ytman) 1935- ...... **CLC 5, 14**
See also CA 21-24R; CAAS 3; CANR 41, 83; CP 7; DLB 5, 6

Slesinger, Tess 1905-1945 .... **TCLC 10**
See also CA 199; DLB 102

Slessor, Kenneth 1901-1971 .... **CLC 14**
See also CA 102; DLB 260; RGEL 2

Slowacki, Juliusz 1809-1849 .... **NCLC 15**
See also RGWL 3

Smart, Christopher 1722-1771 . **LC 3; PC 13**
See also DAM POET; DLB 109; RGEL 2

Smart, Elizabeth 1913-1986 .... **CLC 54**
See also CA 81-84; DLB 88

Smiley, Jane (Graves) 1949- ...... **CLC 53, 76, 144**
See also AMWS 6; BPFB 3; CA 104; CANR 30, 50, 74, 96; CN 7; CPW 1; DAM POP; DLB 227, 234; INT CANR-30

Smith, A(rthur) J(ames) M(arshall) 1902-1980 .... **CLC 15**
See also CA 1-4R; CANR 4; DAC; DLB 88; RGEL 2

Smith, Adam 1723(?)-1790 .... **LC 36**
See also DLB 104, 252; RGEL 2

Smith, Alexander 1829-1867 .... **NCLC 59**
See also DLB 32, 55

Smith, Anna Deavere 1950- .... **CLC 86**
See also CA 133; CANR 103; CD 5; DFS 2

Smith, Betty (Wehner) 1904-1972 .... **CLC 19**
See also BPFB 3; BYA 1; CA 5-8R; DLBY 1982; LAIT 3; RGAL 4; SATA 6

Smith, Charlotte (Turner)
1749-1806 .... **NCLC 23, 115**
See also DLB 39, 109; RGEL 2; TEA

Smith, Clark Ashton 1893-1961 .... **CLC 43**
See also CA 143; CANR 81; FANT; HGG; MTCW 2; SCFW 2; SFW 4; SUFW

Smith, Dave .... **CLC 22, 42**
See also Smith, David (Jeddie)
See also CAAS 7; DLB 5

Smith, David (Jeddie) 1942-
See Smith, Dave
See also CA 49-52; CANR 1, 59; CP 7; CSW; DAM POET

Smith, Florence Margaret 1902-1971
See Smith, Stevie
See also CA 17-18; CANR 35; CAP 2; DAM POET; MTCW 1, 2; TEA

Smith, Iain Crichton 1928-1998 .... **CLC 64**
See also CA 21-24R; CN 7; CP 7; DLB 40, 139; RGSF 2

Smith, John 1580(?)-1631 .... **LC 9**
See also DLB 24, 30; TUS

Smith, Johnston
See J

Smith, Joseph, Jr. 1805-1844 .... **NCLC 53**

Smith, Lee 1944- .... **CLC 25, 73**
See also CA 119; CANR 46; CSW; DLB 143; DLBY 1983; INT CA-119; RGAL 4

Smith, Martin
See Smith, Martin Cruz

Smith, Martin Cruz 1942- .... **CLC 25**
See also BEST 89:4; BPFB 3; CA 85-88; CANR 6, 23, 43, 65; CMW 4; CPW; DAM MULT, POP; HGG; INT CANR-23; MTCW 2; NNAL; RGAL 4

Smith, Patti 1946- .... **CLC 12**
See also CA 93-96; CANR 63

Smith, Pauline (Urmson)
1882-1959 .... **TCLC 25**
See also DLB 225

Smith, Rosamond
See Oates, Joyce Carol

Smith, Sheila Kaye
See Kaye-Smith, Sheila

Smith, Stevie .... **CLC 3, 8, 25, 44; PC 12**
See also Smith, Florence Margaret
See also BRWS 2; DLB 20; MTCW 2; PAB; PFS 3; RGEL 2

Smith, Wilbur (Addison) 1933- .... **CLC 33**
See also CA 13-16R; CANR 7, 46, 66; CPW; MTCW 1, 2

Smith, William Jay 1918- .... **CLC 6**
See also CA 5-8R; CANR 44, 106; CP 7; CSW; CWRI 5; DLB 5; MAICYA 1, 2; SAAS 22; SATA 2, 68

Smith, Woodrow Wilson
See Kuttner, Henry

Smith, Zadie 1976- .... **CLC 158**
See also CA 193

Smolenskin, Peretz 1842-1885 .... **NCLC 30**

Smollett, Tobias (George) 1721-1771 ... **LC 2, 46**
See also BRW 3; CDBLB 1660-1789; DLB 39, 104; RGEL 2; TEA

Snodgrass, W(illiam) D(e Witt)
1926- .... **CLC 2, 6, 10, 18, 68**
See also AMWS 6; CA 1-4R; CANR 6, 36, 65, 85; CP 7; DAM POET; DLB 5; MTCW 1, 2; RGAL 4

Snow, C(harles) P(ercy) 1905-1980 ... **CLC 1, 4, 6, 9, 13, 19**
See also BRW 7; CA 5-8R; CANR 28; CDBLB 1945-1960; DAM NOV; DLB 15, 77; DLBD 17; MTCW 1, 2; RGEL 2; TEA

Snow, Frances Compton
See Adams, Henry (Brooks)

Snyder, Gary (Sherman) 1930- . **CLC 1, 2, 5, 9, 32, 120; PC 21**
See also AMWS 8; ANW; CA 17-20R; CANR 30, 60; CP 7; DAM POET; DLB 5, 16, 165, 212, 237; MTCW 2; PFS 9; RGAL 4; WP

Snyder, Zilpha Keatley 1927- .... **CLC 17**
See also AAYA 15; BYA 1; CA 9-12R; CANR 38; CLR 31; JRDA; MAICYA 1, 2; SAAS 2; SATA 1, 28, 75, 110; SATA-Essay 112; YAW

Soares, Bernardo
See Pessoa, Fernando (Antonio Nogueira)

Sobh, A.
See Shamlu, Ahmad

Sobol, Joshua 1939- .... **CLC 60**
See also Sobol, Yehoshua
See also CA 200; CWW 2

Sobol, Yehoshua 1939-
See Sobol, Joshua
See also CWW 2

Socrates 470B.C.-399B.C. .... **CMLC 27**

Soderberg, Hjalmar 1869-1941 ...... **TCLC 39**
See also DLB 259; RGSF 2

Soderbergh, Steven 1963- .... **CLC 154**
See also AAYA 43

Sodergran, Edith (Irene) 1892-1923
See Soedergran, Edith (Irene)
See also CA 202; DLB 259; EW 11; RGWL 2, 3

Soedergran, Edith (Irene)
1892-1923 .... **TCLC 31**
See also Sodergran, Edith (Irene)

Softly, Edgar
See Lovecraft, H(oward) P(hillips)

Softly, Edward
See Lovecraft, H(oward) P(hillips)

Sokolov, Raymond 1941- .... **CLC 7**
See also CA 85-88

Sokolov, Sasha .... **CLC 59**

Solo, Jay
See Ellison, Harlan (Jay)

Sologub, Fyodor .... **TCLC 9**
See also Teternikov, Fyodor Kuzmich

Solomons, Ikey Esquir
See Thackeray, William Makepeace

Solomos, Dionysios 1798-1857 .... **NCLC 15**

Solwoska, Mara
See French, Marilyn

Solzhenitsyn, Aleksandr I(sayevich)
1918- .. **CLC 1, 2, 4, 7, 9, 10, 18, 26, 34, 78, 134; SSC 32; WLC**
See also AITN 1; BPFB 3; CA 69-72; CANR 40, 65; DA; DAB; DAC; DAM MST, NOV; EW 13; EXPS; LAIT 4; MTCW 1, 2; NFS 6; RGSF 2; RGWL 2, 3; SSFS 9; TWA

Somers, Jane
See Lessing, Doris (May)

Somerville, Edith Oenone
1858-1949 .... **TCLC 51; SSC 56**
See also CA 196; DLB 135; RGEL 2; RGSF 2

Somerville & Ross
See Martin, Violet Florence; Somerville, Edith Oenone

Sommer, Scott 1951- .... **CLC 25**
See also CA 106

Sondheim, Stephen (Joshua) 1930- . **CLC 30, 39, 147**
See also AAYA 11; CA 103; CANR 47; DAM DRAM; LAIT 4

Song, Cathy 1955- .... **PC 21**
See also AAL; CA 154; CWP; DLB 169; EXPP; FW; PFS 5

Sontag, Susan 1933- .... **CLC 1, 2, 10, 13, 31, 105**
See also AMWS 3; CA 17-20R; CANR 25, 51, 74, 97; CN 7; CPW; DAM POP; DLB 2, 67; MAWW; MTCW 1, 2; RGAL 4; RHW; SSFS 10

Sophocles 496(?)B.C.-406(?)B.C. .... **CMLC 2, 47, 51; DC 1; WLCS**
See also AW 1; CDWLB 1; DA; DAB; DAC; DAM DRAM, MST; DFS 1, 4, 8; DLB 176; LAIT 1; RGWL 2, 3; TWA

Sordello 1189-1269 .... **CMLC 15**

Sorel, Georges 1847-1922 .... **TCLC 91**
See also CA 188

Sorel, Julia
See Drexler, Rosalyn

Sorokin, Vladimir .... **CLC 59**

Sorrentino, Gilbert 1929- .. **CLC 3, 7, 14, 22, 40**
See also CA 77-80; CANR 14, 33; CN 7; CP 7; DLB 5, 173; DLBY 1980; INT CANR-14

Soseki
See Natsume, Soseki
See also MJW

Soto, Gary 1952- ... **CLC 32, 80; HLC 2; PC 28**
See also AAYA 10, 37; BYA 11; CA 125; CANR 50, 74, 107; CLR 38; CP 7; DAM MULT; DLB 82; EXPP; HW 1, 2; INT CA-125; JRDA; MAICYA 2; MAICYAS 1; MTCW 2; PFS 7; RGAL 4; SATA 80, 120; WYA; YAW

Soupault, Philippe 1897-1990 .... **CLC 68**
See also CA 147; GFL 1789 to the Present

Souster, (Holmes) Raymond 1921- .... **CLC 5, 14**
See also CA 13-16R; CAAS 14; CANR 13, 29, 53; CP 7; DAC; DAM POET; DLB 88; RGEL 2; SATA 63

Southern, Terry 1924(?)-1995 .... **CLC 7**
See also AMWS 11; BPFB 3; CA 1-4R; CANR 1, 55, 107; CN 7; DLB 2; IDFW 3, 4

Southey, Robert 1774-1843 .... **NCLC 8, 97**
See also BRW 4; DLB 93, 107, 142; RGEL 2; SATA 54

Southworth, Emma Dorothy Eliza Nevitte
1819-1899 .... **NCLC 26**
See also DLB 239

Souza, Ernest
See Scott, Evelyn

Soyinka, Wole 1934- .... **CLC 3, 5, 14, 36, 44; BLC 3; DC 2; WLC**
See also AFW; BW 2, 3; CA 13-16R; CANR 27, 39, 82; CD 5; CDWLB 3; CN 7; CP 7; DA; DAB; DAC; DAM DRAM, MST, MULT; DFS 10; DLB 125; MTCW 1, 2; RGEL 2; TWA; WLIT 2

Spackman, W(illiam) M(ode)
1905-1990 .... **CLC 46**
See also CA 81-84

Spacks, Barry (Bernard) 1931- .... **CLC 14**
See also CA 154; CANR 33, 109; CP 7; DLB 105

Spanidou, Irini 1946- .... **CLC 44**
See also CA 185

Spark, Muriel (Sarah) 1918- ...... **CLC 2, 3, 5, 8, 13, 18, 40, 94; SSC 10**
See also BRWS 1; CA 5-8R; CANR 12, 36, 76, 89; CDBLB 1945-1960; CN 7; CP 7; DAB; DAC; DAM MST, NOV; DLB 15, 139; FW; INT CANR-12; LAIT 4; MTCW 1, 2; RGEL 2; TEA; WLIT 4; YAW

Spaulding, Douglas
See Bradbury, Ray (Douglas)

Spaulding, Leonard
See Bradbury, Ray (Douglas)

Spelman, Elizabeth .... **CLC 65**

Spence, J. A. D.
See Eliot, T(homas) S(tearns)

Spencer, Elizabeth 1921- .... **CLC 22**
See also CA 13-16R; CANR 32, 65, 87; CN 7; CSW; DLB 6, 218; MTCW 1; RGAL 4; SATA 14

Spencer, Leonard G.
See Silverberg, Robert

Spencer, Scott 1945- .... **CLC 30**
See also CA 113; CANR 51; DLBY 1986

Spender, Stephen (Harold)
1909-1995 .... **CLC 1, 2, 5, 10, 41, 91**
See also BRWS 2; CA 9-12R; CANR 31, 54; CDBLB 1945-1960; CP 7; DAM POET; DLB 20; MTCW 1, 2; PAB; RGEL 2; TEA

Spengler, Oswald (Arnold Gottfried)
1880-1936 .... **TCLC 25**
See also CA 189

Spenser, Edmund 1552(?)-1599 ..... **LC 5, 39; PC 8, 42; WLC**
See also BRW 1; CDBLB Before 1660; DA; DAB; DAC; DAM MST, POET; DLB 167; EFS 2; EXPP; PAB; RGEL 2; TEA; WLIT 3; WP

Spicer, Jack 1925-1965 .... **CLC 8, 18, 72**
See also CA 85-88; DAM POET; DLB 5, 16, 193; GLL 1; WP

Spiegelman, Art 1948- .... **CLC 76**
See also AAYA 10; CA 125; CANR 41, 55, 74; MTCW 2; SATA 109; YAW

Spielberg, Peter 1929- .... **CLC 6**
See also CA 5-8R; CANR 4, 48; DLBY 1981

Spielberg, Steven 1947- .... **CLC 20**
See also AAYA 8, 24; CA 77-80; CANR 32; SATA 32

Spillane, Frank Morrison 1918-
See Spillane, Mickey
See also CA 25-28R; CANR 28, 63; MTCW 1, 2; SATA 66

Spillane, Mickey .... **CLC 3, 13**
See also Spillane, Frank Morrison
See also BPFB 3; CMW 4; DLB 226; MSW; MTCW 2

Spinoza, Benedictus de 1632-1677 .. **LC 9, 58**

Spinrad, Norman (Richard) 1940- ... **CLC 46**
See also BPFB 3; CA 37-40R; CAAS 19; CANR 20, 91; DLB 8; INT CANR-20; SFW 4

Spitteler, Carl (Friedrich Georg)
1845-1924 .... **TCLC 12**
See also DLB 129

Spivack, Kathleen (Romola Drucker)
1938- .... **CLC 6**
See also CA 49-52

Spoto, Donald 1941- .... **CLC 39**
See also CA 65-68; CANR 11, 57, 93

Springsteen, Bruce (F.) 1949- .... **CLC 17**
See also CA 111

Spurling, Hilary 1940- .... **CLC 34**
See also CA 104; CANR 25, 52, 94

Spyker, John Howland
See Elman, Richard (Martin)

Squires, (James) Radcliffe
1917-1993 .... **CLC 51**
See also CA 1-4R; CANR 6, 21

Srivastava, Dhanpat Rai 1880(?)-1936
See Premchand
See also CA 197

Stacy, Donald
See Pohl, Frederik

Stael
See Stael-Holstein, Anne Louise Germaine Necker
See also EW 5; RGWL 2, 3

Stael, Germaine de
See Stael-Holstein, Anne Louise Germaine Necker
See also DLB 119, 192; FW; GFL 1789 to the Present; TWA

Stael-Holstein, Anne Louise Germaine Necker 1766-1817 .... **NCLC 3, 91**
See also Stael; Stael, Germaine de

Stafford, Jean 1915-1979 .. **CLC 4, 7, 19, 68; SSC 26**
See also CA 1-4R; CANR 3, 65; DLB 2, 173; MTCW 1, 2; RGAL 4; RGSF 2; SATA-Obit 22; TCWW 2; TUS

Stafford, William (Edgar)
1914-1993 .... **CLC 4, 7, 29**
See also AMWS 11; CA 5-8R; CAAS 3; CANR 5, 22; DAM POET; DLB 5, 206; EXPP; INT CANR-22; PFS 2, 8; RGAL 4; WP

Stagnelius, Eric Johan 1793-1823 . **NCLC 61**

Staines, Trevor
See Brunner, John (Kilian Houston)

Stairs, Gordon
See Austin, Mary (Hunter)
See also TCWW 2

Stalin, Joseph 1879-1953 .... **TCLC 92**

Stampa, Gaspara c. 1524-1554 .... **PC 43**
See also RGWL 2, 3

Stancykowna
See Szymborska, Wislawa

Stannard, Martin 1947- .... **CLC 44**
See also CA 142; DLB 155

Stanton, Elizabeth Cady
1815-1902 .... **TCLC 73**
See also CA 171; DLB 79; FW

Stanton, Maura 1946- .... **CLC 9**
See also CA 89-92; CANR 15; DLB 120

Stanton, Schuyler
See Baum, L(yman) Frank

Stapledon, (William) Olaf
1886-1950 .... **TCLC 22**
See also CA 162; DLB 15, 255; SFW 4

Starbuck, George (Edwin)
1931-1996 .... **CLC 53**
See also CA 21-24R; CANR 23; DAM POET

Stark, Richard
See Westlake, Donald E(dwin)

Staunton, Schuyler
See Baum, L(yman) Frank

Stead, Christina (Ellen) 1902-1983 ... **CLC 2, 5, 8, 32, 80**
See also BRWS 4; CA 13-16R; CANR 33, 40; DLB 260; FW; MTCW 1, 2; RGEL 2; RGSF 2

Stead, William Thomas
1849-1912 .... **TCLC 48**
See also CA 167

Stebnitsky, M.
See Leskov, Nikolai (Semyonovich)

Steele, Sir Richard 1672-1729 .... **LC 18**
See also BRW 3; CDBLB 1660-1789; DLB 84, 101; RGEL 2; WLIT 3

Steele, Timothy (Reid) 1948- .... **CLC 45**
See also CA 93-96; CANR 16, 50, 92; CP 7; DLB 120

Steffens, (Joseph) Lincoln
1866-1936 .... **TCLC 20**

Stegner, Wallace (Earle) 1909-1993 .. **CLC 9, 49, 81; SSC 27**
See also AITN 1; AMWS 4; ANW; BEST 90:3; BPFB 3; CA 1-4R; CAAS 9; CANR 1, 21, 46; DAM NOV; DLB 9, 206; DLBY 1993; MTCW 1, 2; RGAL 4; TCWW 2; TUS

Stein, Gertrude 1874-1946 .... **TCLC 1, 6, 28, 48; PC 18; SSC 42; WLC**
See also AMW; CA 132; CANR 108; CDALB 1917-1929; DA; DAB; DAC; DAM MST, NOV, POET; DLB 4, 54, 86, 228; DLBD 15; EXPS; GLL 1; MAWW; MTCW 1, 2; NCFS 4; RGAL 4; RGSF 2; SSFS 5; TUS; WP

Steinbeck, John (Ernst) 1902-1968 ... **CLC 1, 5, 9, 13, 21, 34, 45, 75, 124; SSC 11, 37; WLC**
See also AAYA 12; AMW; BPFB 3; BYA 2, 3, 13; CA 1-4R; CANR 1, 35; CDALB 1929-1941; DA; DAB; DAC; DAM DRAM, MST, NOV; DLB 7, 9, 212; DLBD 2; EXPS; LAIT 3; MTCW 1, 2; NFS 1, 5, 7; RGAL 4; RGSF 2; RHW; SATA 9; SSFS 3, 6; TCWW 2; TUS; WYA; YAW

Steinem, Gloria 1934- .... **CLC 63**
See also CA 53-56; CANR 28, 51; DLB 246; FW; MTCW 1, 2

Steiner, George 1929- .... **CLC 24**
See also CA 73-76; CANR 31, 67, 108; DAM NOV; DLB 67; MTCW 1, 2; SATA 62

Steiner, K. Leslie
See Delany, Samuel R(ay), Jr.

Steiner, Rudolf 1861-1925 .... **TCLC 13**

Stendhal 1783-1842 .. **NCLC 23, 46; SSC 27; WLC**
See also DA; DAB; DAC; DAM MST, NOV; DLB 119; EW 5; GFL 1789 to the Present; RGWL 2, 3; TWA

Stephen, Adeline Virginia
See Woolf, (Adeline) Virginia

Stephen, Sir Leslie 1832-1904 .... **TCLC 23**
See also BRW 5; DLB 57, 144, 190

Stephen, Sir Leslie
See Stephen, Sir Leslie

Stephen, Virginia
See Woolf, (Adeline) Virginia

Stephens, James 1882(?)-1950 .... **TCLC 4; SSC 50**
See also CA 192; DLB 19, 153, 162; FANT; RGEL 2; SUFW

Stephens, Reed
See Donaldson, Stephen R(eeder)

Steptoe, Lydia
See Barnes, Djuna
See also GLL 1

Sterchi, Beat 1949- .... **CLC 65**
See also CA 203

Sterling, Brett
See Bradbury, Ray (Douglas); Hamilton, Edmond

Sterling, Bruce 1954- .... **CLC 72**
See also CA 119; CANR 44; SCFW 2; SFW 4

Sterling, George 1869-1926 .... **TCLC 20**
See also CA 165; DLB 54

Stern, Gerald 1925- .... **CLC 40, 100**
See also AMWS 9; CA 81-84; CANR 28, 94; CP 7; DLB 105; RGAL 4

Stern, Richard (Gustave) 1928- .... **CLC 4, 39**
See also CA 1-4R; CANR 1, 25, 52; CN 7; DLB 218; DLBY 1987; INT CANR-25

Sternberg, Josef von 1894-1969 .... **CLC 20**
See also CA 81-84

Sterne, Laurence 1713-1768 .... **LC 2, 48; WLC**
See also BRW 3; CDBLB 1660-1789; DA; DAB; DAC; DAM MST, NOV; DLB 39; RGEL 2; TEA

Sternheim, (William Adolf) Carl
1878-1942 .... **TCLC 8**
See also CA 193; DLB 56, 118; RGWL 2, 3

Stevens, Mark 1951- .... **CLC 34**
See also CA 122

Stevens, Wallace 1879-1955 ...... **TCLC 3, 12, 45; PC 6; WLC**
See also AMW; AMWR 1; CA 124; CDALB 1929-1941; DA; DAB; DAC; DAM MST, POET; DLB 54; EXPP; MTCW 1, 2; PAB; PFS 13; RGAL 4; TUS; WP

Stevenson, Anne (Katharine) 1933- .. **CLC 7, 33**
See also BRWS 6; CA 17-20R; CAAS 9; CANR 9, 33; CP 7; CWP; DLB 40; MTCW 1; RHW

Stevenson, Robert Louis (Balfour) 1850-1894 ...... **NCLC 5, 14, 63; SSC 11, 51; WLC**
See also AAYA 24; BPFB 3; BRW 5; BRWR 1; BYA 1, 2, 4, 13; CDBLB 1890-1914; CLR 10, 11; DA; DAB; DAC; DAM MST, NOV; DLB 18, 57, 141, 156, 174; DLBD 13; HGG; JRDA; LAIT 1, 3; MAICYA 1, 2; NFS 11; RGEL 2; RGSF 2; SATA 100; SUFW; TEA; WCH; WLIT 4; WYA; YABC 2; YAW

Stewart, J(ohn) I(nnes) M(ackintosh) 1906-1994 .... **CLC 7, 14, 32**
See also Innes, Michael
See also CA 85-88; CAAS 3; CANR 47; CMW 4; MTCW 1, 2

Stewart, Mary (Florence Elinor) 1916- .... **CLC 7, 35, 117**
See also AAYA 29; BPFB 3; CA 1-4R; CANR 1, 59; CMW 4; CPW; DAB; FANT; RHW; SATA 12; YAW

Stewart, Mary Rainbow
See Stewart, Mary (Florence Elinor)

Stifle, June
See Campbell, Maria

Stifter, Adalbert 1805-1868 .. **NCLC 41; SSC 28**
See also CDWLB 2; DLB 133; RGSF 2; RGWL 2, 3

Still, James 1906-2001 .... **CLC 49**
See also CA 65-68; CAAS 17; CANR 10, 26; CSW; DLB 9; DLBY 01; SATA 29; SATA-Obit 127

Sting 1951-
See Sumner, Gordon Matthew
See also CA 167

Stirling, Arthur
See Sinclair, Upton (Beall)

Stitt, Milan 1941- .... **CLC 29**
See also CA 69-72

Stockton, Francis Richard 1834-1902
See Stockton, Frank R.
See also CA 137; MAICYA 1, 2; SATA 44; SFW 4

Stockton, Frank R. .... **TCLC 47**
See also Stockton, Francis Richard
See also BYA 4, 13; DLB 42, 74; DLBD 13; EXPS; SATA-Brief 32; SSFS 3; SUFW; WCH

Stoddard, Charles
See Kuttner, Henry

Stoker, Abraham 1847-1912 .... **SSC 55, 56**
See also Stoker, Bram
See also CA 150; DA; DAC; DAM MST, NOV; HGG; SATA 29

Stoker, Bram .... **TCLC 8; WLC**
See also Stoker, Abraham
See also AAYA 23; BPFB 3; BRWS 3; BYA 5; CDBLB 1890-1914; DAB; DLB 36, 70, 178; RGEL 2; SUFW; TEA; WLIT 4

Stolz, Mary (Slattery) 1920- .... **CLC 12**
See also AAYA 8; AITN 1; CA 5-8R; CANR 13, 41, 112; JRDA; MAICYA 1, 2; SAAS 3; SATA 10, 71, 133; YAW

Stone, Irving 1903-1989 .... **CLC 7**
See also AITN 1; BPFB 3; CA 1-4R; CAAS 3; CANR 1, 23; CPW; DAM POP; INT CANR-23; MTCW 1, 2; RHW; SATA 3; SATA-Obit 64

Stone, Oliver (William) 1946- .... **CLC 73**
See also AAYA 15; CA 110; CANR 55

Stone, Robert (Anthony) 1937- ... **CLC 5, 23, 42**
See also AMWS 5; BPFB 3; CA 85-88; CANR 23, 66, 95; CN 7; DLB 152; INT CANR-23; MTCW 1

Stone, Zachary
See Follett, Ken(neth Martin)

Stoppard, Tom 1937- ... **CLC 1, 3, 4, 5, 8, 15, 29, 34, 63, 91; DC 6; WLC**
See also BRWR 2; BRWS 1; CA 81-84; CANR 39, 67; CBD; CD 5; CDBLB 1960 to Present; DA; DAB; DAC; DAM DRAM, MST; DFS 2, 5, 8, 11, 13; DLB 13, 233; DLBY 1985; MTCW 1, 2; RGEL 2; TEA; WLIT 4

Storey, David (Malcolm) 1933- . **CLC 2, 4, 5, 8**
See also BRWS 1; CA 81-84; CANR 36; CBD; CD 5; CN 7; DAM DRAM; DLB 13, 14, 207, 245; MTCW 1; RGEL 2

Storm, Hyemeyohsts 1935- .... **CLC 3**
See also CA 81-84; CANR 45; DAM MULT; NNAL

Storm, Theodor 1817-1888 .... **SSC 27**
See also CDWLB 2; RGSF 2; RGWL 2

Storm, (Hans) Theodor (Woldsen) 1817-1888 .... **NCLC 1; SSC 27**
See also DLB 129; EW; RGWL 3

Storni, Alfonsina 1892-1938 .. **TCLC 5; HLC 2; PC 33**
See also CA 131; DAM MULT; HW 1; LAW

Stoughton, William 1631-1701 .... **LC 38**
See also DLB 24

Stout, Rex (Todhunter) 1886-1975 ..... **CLC 3**
See also AITN 2; BPFB 3; CA 61-64; CANR 71; CMW 4; MSW; RGAL 4

Stow, (Julian) Randolph 1935- ... **CLC 23, 48**
See also CA 13-16R; CANR 33; CN 7; DLB 260; MTCW 1; RGEL 2

Stowe, Harriet (Elizabeth) Beecher 1811-1896 .... **NCLC 3, 50; WLC**
See also AMWS 1; CDALB 1865-1917; DA; DAB; DAC; DAM MST, NOV; DLB 1, 12, 42, 74, 189, 239, 243; EXPN; JRDA; LAIT 2; MAICYA 1, 2; NFS 6; RGAL 4; TUS; YABC 1

Strabo c. 64B.C.-c. 25 .... **CMLC 37**
See also DLB 176

Strachey, (Giles) Lytton 1880-1932 .... **TCLC 12**
See also BRWS 2; CA 178; DLB 149; DLBD 10; MTCW 2; NCFS 4

Strand, Mark 1934- .... **CLC 6, 18, 41, 71**
See also AMWS 4; CA 21-24R; CANR 40, 65, 100; CP 7; DAM POET; DLB 5; PAB; PFS 9; RGAL 4; SATA 41

Stratton-Porter, Gene(va Grace) 1863-1924
See Porter, Gene(va Grace) Stratton
See also ANW; CA 137; DLB 221; DLBD 14; MAICYA 1, 2; SATA 15

Straub, Peter (Francis) 1943- ... **CLC 28, 107**
See also BEST 89:1; BPFB 3; CA 85-88; CANR 28, 65, 109; CPW; DAM POP; DLBY 1984; HGG; MTCW 1, 2; SUFW

Strauss, Botho 1944- .... **CLC 22**
See also CA 157; CWW 2; DLB 124

Streatfeild, (Mary) Noel 1897(?)-1986 .... **CLC 21**
See also CA 81-84; CANR 31; CLR 17, 83; CWRI 5; DLB 160; MAICYA 1, 2; SATA 20; SATA-Obit 48

Stribling, T(homas) S(igismund) 1881-1965 .... **CLC 23**
See also CA 189; CMW 4; DLB 9; RGAL 4

Strindberg, (Johan) August 1849-1912 ... **TCLC 1, 8, 21, 47; DC 18; WLC**
See also CA 135; DA; DAB; DAC; DAM DRAM, MST; DFS 4, 9; DLB 259; EW 7; IDTP; MTCW 2; RGWL 2, 3; TWA

Stringer, Arthur 1874-1950 .... **TCLC 37**
See also CA 161; DLB 92

Stringer, David
See Roberts, Keith (John Kingston)

Stroheim, Erich von 1885-1957 ..... **TCLC 71**

Strugatskii, Arkadii (Natanovich) 1925-1991 .... **CLC 27**
See also CA 106; SFW 4

Strugatskii, Boris (Natanovich) 1933- .... **CLC 27**
See also CA 106; SFW 4

Strummer, Joe 1953(?)- .... **CLC 30**

Strunk, William, Jr. 1869-1946 ...... **TCLC 92**
See also CA 164

Stryk, Lucien 1924- .... **PC 27**
See also CA 13-16R; CANR 10, 28, 55, 110; CP 7

Stuart, Don A.
See Campbell, John W(ood, Jr.)

Stuart, Ian
See MacLean, Alistair (Stuart)

Stuart, Jesse (Hilton) 1906-1984 ... **CLC 1, 8, 11, 14, 34; SSC 31**
See also CA 5-8R; CANR 31; DLB 9, 48, 102; DLBY 1984; SATA 2; SATA-Obit 36

Stubblefield, Sally
See Trumbo, Dalton

Sturgeon, Theodore (Hamilton) 1918-1985 .... **CLC 22, 39**
See also Queen, Ellery
See also BPFB 3; BYA 9, 10; CA 81-84; CANR 32, 103; DLB 8; DLBY 1985; HGG; MTCW 1, 2; SCFW; SFW 4; SUFW

Sturges, Preston 1898-1959 .... **TCLC 48**
See also CA 149; DLB 26

Sturluson, Snorri 1179-1241 .... **CMLC 56**
See also RGWL 2, 3

Styron, William 1925- .... **CLC 1, 3, 5, 11, 15, 60; SSC 25**
See also AMW; BEST 90:4; BPFB 3; CA 5-8R; CANR 6, 33, 74; CDALB 1968-1988; CN 7; CPW; CSW; DAM NOV, POP; DLB 2, 143; DLBY 1980; INT CANR-6; LAIT 2; MTCW 1, 2; NCFS 1; RGAL 4; RHW; TUS

Su, Chien 1884-1918
See Su Man-shu

Suarez Lynch, B.
See Bioy Casares, Adolfo; Borges, Jorge Luis

Suassuna, Ariano Vilar 1927-
See also CA 178; HLCS 1; HW 2; LAW

Suckert, Kurt Erich
See Malaparte, Curzio

Suckling, Sir John 1609-1642 . **LC 75; PC 30**
See also BRW 2; DAM POET; DLB 58, 126; EXPP; PAB; RGEL 2

Suckow, Ruth 1892-1960 .... **SSC 18**
See also CA 193; DLB 9, 102; RGAL 4; TCWW 2

Sudermann, Hermann 1857-1928 .. **TCLC 15**
See also CA 201; DLB 118

Sue, Eugene 1804-1857 .... **NCLC 1**
See also DLB 119

Sueskind, Patrick 1949- .... **CLC 44**
See also Suskind, Patrick

Sukenick, Ronald 1932- .... **CLC 3, 4, 6, 48**
See also CA 25-28R; CAAS 8; CANR 32, 89; CN 7; DLB 173; DLBY 1981

Suknaski, Andrew 1942- .... **CLC 19**
See also CA 101; CP 7; DLB 53

Sullivan, Vernon
See Vian, Boris

Sully Prudhomme, Rene-Francois-Armand 1839-1907 .... **TCLC 31**
See also GFL 1789 to the Present

Su Man-shu .... **TCLC 24**
See also Su, Chien

Summerforest, Ivy B.
See Kirkup, James

Summers, Andrew James 1942- ...... **CLC 26**

Summers, Andy
See Summers, Andrew James

Summers, Hollis (Spurgeon, Jr.) 1916- .... **CLC 10**
See also CA 5-8R; CANR 3; DLB 6

Summers, (Alphonsus Joseph-Mary Augustus) Montague 1880-1948 .... **TCLC 16**
See also CA 163

Sumner, Gordon Matthew .... **CLC 26**
See also Police, The; Sting

Surtees, Robert Smith 1805-1864 .. **NCLC 14**
See also DLB 21; RGEL 2

Susann, Jacqueline 1921-1974 .... **CLC 3**
See also AITN 1; BPFB 3; CA 65-68; MTCW 1, 2

Su Shi
See Su Shih
See also RGWL 2, 3

Su Shih 1036-1101 .... **CMLC 15**
See also Su Shi

Suskind, Patrick
See Sueskind, Patrick
See also BPFB 3; CA 145; CWW 2

Sutcliff, Rosemary 1920-1992 .... **CLC 26**
See also AAYA 10; BYA 1, 4; CA 5-8R; CANR 37; CLR 1, 37; CPW; DAB; DAC; DAM MST, POP; JRDA; MAICYA 1, 2; MAICYAS 1; RHW; SATA 6, 44, 78; SATA-Obit 73; WYA; YAW

Sutro, Alfred 1863-1933 .... **TCLC 6**
See also CA 185; DLB 10; RGEL 2

Sutton, Henry
See Slavitt, David R(ytman)

Suzuki, D. T.
See Suzuki, Daisetz Teitaro

Suzuki, Daisetz T.
See Suzuki, Daisetz Teitaro

Suzuki, Daisetz Teitaro 1870-1966 .... **TCLC 109**
See also CA 121; MTCW 1, 2

Suzuki, Teitaro
See Suzuki, Daisetz Teitaro

Svevo, Italo .... **TCLC 2, 35; SSC 25**
See also Schmitz, Aron Hector
See also DLB 264; EW 8; RGWL 2, 3

Swados, Elizabeth (A.) 1951- .... **CLC 12**
See also CA 97-100; CANR 49; INT 97-100

Swados, Harvey 1920-1972 .... **CLC 5**
See also CA 5-8R; CANR 6; DLB 2

Swan, Gladys 1934- .... **CLC 69**
See also CA 101; CANR 17, 39

Swanson, Logan
See Matheson, Richard (Burton)

Swarthout, Glendon (Fred) 1918-1992 .... **CLC 35**
See also CA 1-4R; CANR 1, 47; LAIT 5; SATA 26; TCWW 2; YAW

Sweet, Sarah C.
See Jewett, (Theodora) Sarah Orne

Swenson, May 1919-1989 ...... **CLC 4, 14, 61, 106; PC 14**
See also AMWS 4; CA 5-8R; CANR 36, 61; DA; DAB; DAC; DAM MST, POET; DLB 5; EXPP; GLL 1; MTCW 1, 2; SATA 15; WP

Swift, Augustus
See Lovecraft, H(oward) P(hillips)

Swift, Graham (Colin) 1949- ...... **CLC 41, 88**
See also BRWS 5; CA 122; CANR 46, 71; CN 7; DLB 194; MTCW 2; RGSF 2

Swift, Jonathan 1667-1745 .. **LC 1, 42; PC 9; WLC**
See also AAYA 41; BRW 3; BRWR 1; BYA 5, 14; CDBLB 1660-1789; CLR 53; DA; DAB; DAC; DAM MST, NOV, POET; DLB 39, 95, 101; EXPN; LAIT 1; NFS 6; RGEL 2; SATA 19; TEA; WCH; WLIT 3

Swinburne, Algernon Charles 1837-1909 ... **TCLC 8, 36; PC 24; WLC**
See also BRW 5; CA 140; CDBLB 1832-1890; DA; DAB; DAC; DAM MST, POET; DLB 35, 57; PAB; RGEL 2; TEA

Swinfen, Ann .... **CLC 34**
See also CA 202

Swinnerton, Frank Arthur 1884-1982 .... **CLC 31**
See also DLB 34

Swithen, John
See King, Stephen (Edwin)

Sylvia
See Ashton-Warner, Sylvia (Constance)

Symmes, Robert Edward
See Duncan, Robert (Edward)

Symonds, John Addington 1840-1893 .... **NCLC 34**
See also DLB 57, 144

Symons, Arthur 1865-1945 .... **TCLC 11**
See also CA 189; DLB 19, 57, 149; RGEL 2

Symons, Julian (Gustave) 1912-1994 .... **CLC 2, 14, 32**
See also CA 49-52; CAAS 3; CANR 3, 33, 59; CMW 4; DLB 87, 155; DLBY 1992; MSW; MTCW 1

Synge, (Edmund) J(ohn) M(illington) 1871-1909 .... **TCLC 6, 37; DC 2**
See also BRW 6; BRWR 1; CA 141; CDBLB 1890-1914; DAM DRAM; DLB 10, 19; RGEL 2; TEA; WLIT 4

Syruc, J.
See Milosz, Czeslaw

Szirtes, George 1948- .... **CLC 46**
See also CA 109; CANR 27, 61; CP 7

Szymborska, Wislawa 1923- ...... **CLC 99; PC 44**
See also CA 154; CANR 91; CDWLB 4; CWP; CWW 2; DLB 232; DLBY 1996; MTCW 2; PFS 15; RGWL 3

T. O., Nik
See Annensky, Innokenty (Fyodorovich)

Tabori, George 1914- .... **CLC 19**
See also CA 49-52; CANR 4, 69; CBD; CD 5; DLB 245

Tacitus c. 55-c. 117 .... **CMLC 56**
See also AW 2; CDWLB 1; DLB 211; RGWL 2, 3

Tagore, Rabindranath 1861-1941 ... **TCLC 3, 53; PC 8; SSC 48**
See also CA 120; DAM DRAM, POET; MTCW 1, 2; RGEL 2; RGSF 2; RGWL 2, 3; TWA

Taine, Hippolyte Adolphe 1828-1893 .... **NCLC 15**
See also EW 7; GFL 1789 to the Present

Talese, Gay 1932- .... **CLC 37**
See also AITN 1; CA 1-4R; CANR 9, 58; DLB 185; INT CANR-9; MTCW 1, 2

Tallent, Elizabeth (Ann) 1954- .... **CLC 45**
See also CA 117; CANR 72; DLB 130

Tally, Ted 1952- .... **CLC 42**
See also CA 124; CAD; CD 5; INT 124

Talvik, Heiti 1904-1947 .... **TCLC 87**

Tamayo y Baus, Manuel 1829-1898 .... **NCLC 1**

Tammsaare, A(nton) H(ansen) 1878-1940 .... **TCLC 27**
See also CA 164; CDWLB 4; DLB 220

Tam'si, Tchicaya U
See Tchicaya, Gerald Felix

Tan, Amy (Ruth) 1952- .... **CLC 59, 120, 151; AAL**
See also AAYA 9; AMWS 10; BEST 89:3; BPFB 3; CA 136; CANR 54, 105; CDALBS; CN 7; CPW 1; DAM MULT, NOV, POP; DLB 173; EXPN; FW; LAIT 3, 5; MTCW 2; NFS 1, 13; RGAL 4; SATA 75; SSFS 9; YAW

Tandem, Felix
See Spitteler, Carl (Friedrich Georg)

Tanizaki, Jun'ichiro 1886-1965 ... **CLC 8, 14, 28; SSC 21**
See also Tanizaki Jun'ichiro
See also CA 93-96; MJW; MTCW 2; RGSF 2; RGWL 2

Tanizaki Jun'ichiro
See Tanizaki, Jun'ichiro
See also DLB 180

Tanner, William
See Amis, Kingsley (William)

Tao Lao
See Storni, Alfonsina

Tarantino, Quentin (Jerome) 1963- .... **CLC 125**
See also CA 171

Tarassoff, Lev
See Troyat, Henri

Tarbell, Ida M(inerva) 1857-1944 . **TCLC 40**
See also CA 181; DLB 47

Tarkington, (Newton) Booth 1869-1946 .... **TCLC 9**
See also BPFB 3; BYA 3; CA 143; CWRI 5; DLB 9, 102; MTCW 2; RGAL 4; SATA 17

Tarkovskii, Andrei Arsen'evich
See Tarkovsky, Andrei (Arsenyevich)

Tarkovsky, Andrei (Arsenyevich) 1932-1986 .... **CLC 75**
See also CA 127

Tartt, Donna 1964(?)- .... **CLC 76**
See also CA 142

Tasso, Torquato 1544-1595 .... **LC 5**
See also EFS 2; EW 2; RGWL 2, 3

Tate, (John Orley) Allen 1899-1979 .. **CLC 2, 4, 6, 9, 11, 14, 24**
See also AMW; CA 5-8R; CANR 32, 108; DLB 4, 45, 63; DLBD 17; MTCW 1, 2; RGAL 4; RHW

Tate, Ellalice
See Hibbert, Eleanor Alice Burford

Tate, James (Vincent) 1943- ...... **CLC 2, 6, 25**
See also CA 21-24R; CANR 29, 57; CP 7; DLB 5, 169; PFS 10, 15; RGAL 4; WP

Tauler, Johannes c. 1300-1361 .... **CMLC 37**
See also DLB 179

Tavel, Ronald 1940- .... **CLC 6**
See also CA 21-24R; CAD; CANR 33; CD 5

Taviani, Paolo 1931- .... **CLC 70**
See also CA 153

Taylor, Bayard 1825-1878 .... **NCLC 89**
See also DLB 3, 189, 250, 254; RGAL 4

Taylor, C(ecil) P(hilip) 1929-1981 .... **CLC 27**
See also CA 25-28R; CANR 47; CBD

Taylor, Edward 1642(?)-1729 .... **LC 11**
See also AMW; DA; DAB; DAC; DAM MST, POET; DLB 24; EXPP; RGAL 4; TUS

Taylor, Eleanor Ross 1920- .... **CLC 5**
See also CA 81-84; CANR 70

Taylor, Elizabeth 1932-1975 ..... **CLC 2, 4, 29**
See also CA 13-16R; CANR 9, 70; DLB 139; MTCW 1; RGEL 2; SATA 13

Taylor, Frederick Winslow
1856-1915 .... **TCLC 76**
See also CA 188

Taylor, Henry (Splawn) 1942- .... **CLC 44**
See also CA 33-36R; CAAS 7; CANR 31; CP 7; DLB 5; PFS 10

Taylor, Kamala (Purnaiya) 1924-
See Markandaya, Kamala
See also CA 77-80; NFS 13

Taylor, Mildred D(elois) 1943- .... **CLC 21**
See also AAYA 10; BW 1; BYA 3, 8; CA 85-88; CANR 25; CLR 9, 59; CSW; DLB 52; JRDA; LAIT 3; MAICYA 1, 2; SAAS 5; SATA 135; WYA; YAW

Taylor, Peter (Hillsman) 1917-1994 .. **CLC 1, 4, 18, 37, 44, 50, 71; SSC 10**
See also AMWS 5; BPFB 3; CA 13-16R; CANR 9, 50; CSW; DLB 218; DLBY 1981, 1994; EXPS; INT CANR-9; MTCW 1, 2; RGSF 2; SSFS 9; TUS

Taylor, Robert Lewis 1912-1998 .... **CLC 14**
See also CA 1-4R; CANR 3, 64; SATA 10

Tchekhov, Anton
See Chekhov, Anton (Pavlovich)

Tchicaya, Gerald Felix 1931-1988 .. **CLC 101**
See also CA 129; CANR 81

Tchicaya U Tam'si
See Tchicaya, Gerald Felix

Teasdale, Sara 1884-1933 .... **TCLC 4; PC 31**
See also CA 163; DLB 45; GLL 1; PFS 14; RGAL 4; SATA 32; TUS

Tegner, Esaias 1782-1846 .... **NCLC 2**

Teilhard de Chardin, (Marie Joseph) Pierre
1881-1955 .... **TCLC 9**
See also GFL 1789 to the Present

Temple, Ann
See Mortimer, Penelope (Ruth)

Tennant, Emma (Christina) 1937- .. **CLC 13, 52**
See also CA 65-68; CAAS 9; CANR 10, 38, 59, 88; CN 7; DLB 14; SFW 4

Tenneshaw, S. M.
See Silverberg, Robert

Tennyson, Alfred 1809-1892 ... **NCLC 30, 65, 115; PC 6; WLC**
See also BRW 4; CDBLB 1832-1890; DA; DAB; DAC; DAM MST, POET; DLB 32; EXPP; PAB; PFS 1, 2, 4, 11, 15; RGEL 2; TEA; WLIT 4; WP

Teran, Lisa St. Aubin de .... **CLC 36**
See also St. Aubin de Teran, Lisa

Terence c. 184B.C.-c. 159B.C. ...... **CMLC 14; DC 7**
See also AW 1; CDWLB 1; DLB 211; RGWL 2, 3; TWA

Teresa de Jesus, St. 1515-1582 .... **LC 18**

Terkel, Louis 1912-
See Terkel, Studs
See also CA 57-60; CANR 18, 45, 67; MTCW 1, 2

Terkel, Studs .... **CLC 38**
See also Terkel, Louis
See also AAYA 32; AITN 1; MTCW 2; TUS

Terry, C. V.
See Slaughter, Frank G(ill)

Terry, Megan 1932- .... **CLC 19; DC 13**
See also CA 77-80; CABS 3; CAD; CANR 43; CD 5; CWD; DLB 7, 249; GLL 2

Tertullian c. 155-c. 245 .... **CMLC 29**

Tertz, Abram
See Sinyavsky, Andrei (Donatevich)
See also CWW 2; RGSF 2

Tesich, Steve 1943(?)-1996 .... **CLC 40, 69**
See also CA 105; CAD; DLBY 1983

Tesla, Nikola 1856-1943 .... **TCLC 88**

Teternikov, Fyodor Kuzmich 1863-1927
See Sologub, Fyodor

Tevis, Walter 1928-1984 .... **CLC 42**
See also CA 113; SFW 4

Tey, Josephine .... **TCLC 14**
See also Mackintosh, Elizabeth
See also DLB 77; MSW

Thackeray, William Makepeace
1811-1863 .... **NCLC 5, 14, 22, 43; WLC**
See also BRW 5; CDBLB 1832-1890; DA; DAB; DAC; DAM MST, NOV; DLB 21, 55, 159, 163; NFS 13; RGEL 2; SATA 23; TEA; WLIT 3

Thakura, Ravindranatha
See Tagore, Rabindranath

Thames, C. H.
See Marlowe, Stephen

Tharoor, Shashi 1956- .... **CLC 70**
See also CA 141; CANR 91; CN 7

Thelwell, Michael Miles 1939- .... **CLC 22**
See also BW 2; CA 101

Theobald, Lewis, Jr.
See Lovecraft, H(oward) P(hillips)

Theocritus c. 310B.C.- .... **CMLC 45**
See also AW 1; DLB 176; RGWL 2, 3

Theodorescu, Ion N. 1880-1967
See Arghezi, Tudor

Theriault, Yves 1915-1983 .... **CLC 79**
See also CA 102; CCA 1; DAC; DAM MST; DLB 88

Theroux, Alexander (Louis) 1939- .... **CLC 2, 25**
See also CA 85-88; CANR 20, 63; CN 7

Theroux, Paul (Edward) 1941- ..... **CLC 5, 8, 11, 15, 28, 46**
See also AAYA 28; AMWS 8; BEST 89:4; BPFB 3; CA 33-36R; CANR 20, 45, 74; CDALBS; CN 7; CPW 1; DAM POP; DLB 2, 218; HGG; MTCW 1, 2; RGAL 4; SATA 44, 109; TUS

Thesen, Sharon 1946- .... **CLC 56**
See also CA 163; CP 7; CWP

Thespis fl. 6th cent. B.C.- .... **CMLC 51**

Thevenin, Denis
See Duhamel, Georges

Thibault, Jacques Anatole Francois
1844-1924
See France, Anatole
See also CA 127; DAM NOV; MTCW 1, 2; TWA

Thiele, Colin (Milton) 1920- .... **CLC 17**
See also CA 29-32R; CANR 12, 28, 53, 105; CLR 27; MAICYA 1, 2; SAAS 2; SATA 14, 72, 125; YAW

Thistlethwaite, Bel
See Wetherald, Agnes Ethelwyn

Thomas, Audrey (Callahan) 1935- .... **CLC 7, 13, 37, 107; SSC 20**
See also AITN 2; CA 21-24R; CAAS 19; CANR 36, 58; CN 7; DLB 60; MTCW 1; RGSF 2

Thomas, Augustus 1857-1934 .... **TCLC 97**

Thomas, D(onald) M(ichael) 1935- . **CLC 13, 22, 31, 132**
See also BPFB 3; BRWS 4; CA 61-64; CAAS 11; CANR 17, 45, 75; CDBLB 1960 to Present; CN 7; CP 7; DLB 40, 207; HGG; INT CANR-17; MTCW 1, 2; SFW 4

Thomas, Dylan (Marlais)
1914-1953 ... **TCLC 1, 8, 45, 105; PC 2; SSC 3, 44; WLC**
See also BRWS 1; CA 120; CANR 65; CDBLB 1945-1960; DA; DAB; DAC; DAM DRAM, MST, POET; DLB 13, 20, 139; EXPP; LAIT 3; MTCW 1, 2; PAB; PFS 1, 3, 8; RGEL 2; RGSF 2; SATA 60; TEA; WLIT 4; WP

Thomas, (Philip) Edward
1878-1917 .... **TCLC 10**
See also BRW 6; BRWS 3; CA 153; DAM POET; DLB 19, 98, 156, 216; PAB; RGEL 2

Thomas, Joyce Carol 1938- .... **CLC 35**
See also AAYA 12; BW 2, 3; CA 116; CANR 48; CLR 19; DLB 33; INT CA-116; JRDA; MAICYA 1, 2; MTCW 1, 2; SAAS 7; SATA 40, 78, 123; WYA; YAW

Thomas, Lewis 1913-1993 .... **CLC 35**
See also ANW; CA 85-88; CANR 38, 60; MTCW 1, 2

Thomas, M. Carey 1857-1935 .... **TCLC 89**
See also FW

Thomas, Paul
See Mann, (Paul) Thomas

Thomas, Piri 1928- .... **CLC 17; HLCS 2**
See also CA 73-76; HW 1

Thomas, R(onald) S(tuart)
1913-2000 .... **CLC 6, 13, 48**
See also CA 89-92; CAAS 4; CANR 30; CDBLB 1960 to Present; CP 7; DAB; DAM POET; DLB 27; MTCW 1; RGEL 2

Thomas, Ross (Elmore) 1926-1995 .. **CLC 39**
See also CA 33-36R; CANR 22, 63; CMW 4

Thompson, Francis (Joseph)
1859-1907 .... **TCLC 4**
See also BRW 5; CA 189; CDBLB 1890-1914; DLB 19; RGEL 2; TEA

Thompson, Francis Clegg
See Mencken, H(enry) L(ouis)

Thompson, Hunter S(tockton)
1937(?)- .... **CLC 9, 17, 40, 104**
See also BEST 89:1; BPFB 3; CA 17-20R; CANR 23, 46, 74, 77, 111; CPW; CSW; DAM POP; DLB 185; MTCW 1, 2; TUS

Thompson, James Myers
See Thompson, Jim (Myers)

Thompson, Jim (Myers)
1906-1977(?) .... **CLC 69**
See also BPFB 3; CA 140; CMW 4; CPW; DLB 226; MSW

Thompson, Judith .... **CLC 39**
See also CWD

Thomson, James 1700-1748 .... **LC 16, 29, 40**
See also BRWS 3; DAM POET; DLB 95; RGEL 2

Thomson, James 1834-1882 .... **NCLC 18**
See also DAM POET; DLB 35; RGEL 2

Thoreau, Henry David 1817-1862 .. **NCLC 7, 21, 61; PC 30; WLC**
See also AAYA 42; AMW; ANW; BYA 3; CDALB 1640-1865; DA; DAB; DAC; DAM MST; DLB 1, 183, 223, 270; LAIT 2; NCFS 3; RGAL 4; TUS

Thorndike, E. L.
See Thorndike, Edward L(ee)

Thorndike, Edward L(ee)
1874-1949 .... **TCLC 107**

Thornton, Hall
See Silverberg, Robert

Thubron, Colin (Gerald Dryden)
1939- .... **CLC 163**
See also CA 25-28R; CANR 12, 29, 59, 95; CN 7; DLB 204, 231

Thucydides c. 455B.C.-c. 395B.C. . **CMLC 17**
See also AW 1; DLB 176; RGWL 2, 3

Thumboo, Edwin Nadason 1933- .... **PC 30**
See also CA 194

Thurber, James (Grover)
1894-1961 .. **CLC 5, 11, 25, 125; SSC 1, 47**
See also AMWS 1; BPFB 3; BYA 5; CA 73-76; CANR 17, 39; CDALB 1929-1941; CWRI 5; DA; DAB; DAC; DAM DRAM, MST, NOV; DLB 4, 11, 22, 102; EXPS; FANT; LAIT 3; MAICYA 1, 2; MTCW 1, 2; RGAL 4; RGSF 2; SATA 13; SSFS 1, 10; SUFW; TUS

Thurman, Wallace (Henry)
1902-1934 .... **TCLC 6; BLC 3**
See also BW 1, 3; CA 124; CANR 81; DAM MULT; DLB 51; HR 3

Tibullus c. 54B.C.-c. 18B.C. .... **CMLC 36**
See also AW 2; DLB 211; RGWL 2, 3

Ticheburn, Cheviot
See Ainsworth, William Harrison

Tieck, (Johann) Ludwig
1773-1853 .... **NCLC 5, 46; SSC 31**
See also CDWLB 2; DLB 90; EW 5; IDTP; RGSF 2; RGWL 2, 3; SUFW

Tiger, Derry
See Ellison, Harlan (Jay)

Tilghman, Christopher 1948(?)- .... **CLC 65**
See also CA 159; CSW; DLB 244

Tillich, Paul (Johannes)
1886-1965 .... **CLC 131**
See also CA 5-8R; CANR 33; MTCW 1, 2

Tillinghast, Richard (Williford)
1940- .... **CLC 29**
See also CA 29-32R; CAAS 23; CANR 26, 51, 96; CP 7; CSW

Timrod, Henry 1828-1867 .... **NCLC 25**
See also DLB 3, 248; RGAL 4

Tindall, Gillian (Elizabeth) 1938- ...... **CLC 7**
See also CA 21-24R; CANR 11, 65, 107; CN 7

Tiptree, James, Jr. .... **CLC 48, 50**
See also Sheldon, Alice Hastings Bradley
See also DLB 8; SCFW 2; SFW 4

Tirone Smith, Mary-Ann 1944- .... **CLC 39**
See also CA 136; CANR 113

Tirso de Molina 1580(?)-1648 ..... **LC 73; DC 13; HLCS 2**
See also RGWL 2, 3

Titmarsh, Michael Angelo
See Thackeray, William Makepeace

Tocqueville, Alexis (Charles Henri Maurice Clerel Comte) de 1805-1859 .. **NCLC 7, 63**
See also EW 6; GFL 1789 to the Present; TWA

Toibin, Colm
See Toibin, Colm
See also DLB 271

Toibin, Colm 1955- .... **CLC 162**
See also Toibin, Colm
See also CA 142; CANR 81

Tolkien, J(ohn) R(onald) R(euel)
1892-1973 .... **CLC 1, 2, 3, 8, 12, 38; WLC**
See also AAYA 10; AITN 1; BPFB 3; BRWS 2; CA 17-18; CANR 36; CAP 2; CDBLB 1914-1945; CLR 56; CPW 1; CWRI 5; DA; DAB; DAC; DAM MST, NOV, POP; DLB 15, 160, 255; EFS 2; FANT; JRDA; LAIT 1; MAICYA 1, 2; MTCW 1, 2; NFS 8; RGEL 2; SATA 2, 32, 100; SATA-Obit 24; SFW 4; SUFW; TEA; WCH; WYA; YAW

Toller, Ernst 1893-1939 .... **TCLC 10**
See also CA 186; DLB 124; RGWL 2, 3

Tolson, M. B.
See Tolson, Melvin B(eaunorus)

Tolson, Melvin B(eaunorus)
1898(?)-1966 .... **CLC 36, 105; BLC 3**
See also AFAW 1, 2; BW 1, 3; CA 124; CANR 80; DAM MULT, POET; DLB 48, 76; RGAL 4

Tolstoi, Aleksei Nikolaevich
See Tolstoy, Alexey Nikolaevich

Tolstoi, Lev
See Tolstoy, Leo (Nikolaevich)
See also RGSF 2; RGWL 2, 3

Tolstoy, Aleksei Nikolaevich
See Tolstoy, Alexey Nikolaevich
See also DLB 272

Tolstoy, Alexey Nikolaevich
1882-1945 .... **TCLC 18**
See also Tolstoi, Aleksei Nikolaevich
See also CA 158; SFW 4

Tolstoy, Leo (Nikolaevich)
1828-1910 .. **TCLC 4, 11, 17, 28, 44, 79; SSC 9, 30, 45, 54; WLC**
See also Tolstoi, Lev
See also CA 123; DA; DAB; DAC; DAM MST, NOV; DLB 238; EFS 2; EW 7; EXPS; IDTP; LAIT 2; NFS 10; SATA 26; SSFS 5; TWA

Tolstoy, Count Leo
See Tolstoy, Leo (Nikolaevich)

Tomalin, Claire 1933- .... **CLC 166**
See also CA 89-92; CANR 52, 88; DLB 155

Tomasi di Lampedusa, Giuseppe 1896-1957
See Lampedusa, Giuseppe (Tomasi) di
See also DLB 177

Tomlin, Lily .... **CLC 17**
See also Tomlin, Mary Jean

Tomlin, Mary Jean 1939(?)-
See Tomlin, Lily

Tomline, F. Latour
See Gilbert, W(illiam) S(chwenck)

Tomlinson, (Alfred) Charles 1927- .... **CLC 2, 4, 6, 13, 45; PC 17**
See also CA 5-8R; CANR 33; CP 7; DAM POET; DLB 40

Tomlinson, H(enry) M(ajor)
1873-1958 .... **TCLC 71**
See also CA 161; DLB 36, 100, 195

Tonson, Jacob
See Bennett, (Enoch) Arnold

Toole, John Kennedy 1937-1969 ..... **CLC 19, 64**
See also BPFB 3; CA 104; DLBY 1981; MTCW 2

Toomer, Eugene
See Toomer, Jean

Toomer, Eugene Pinchback
See Toomer, Jean

Toomer, Jean 1892-1967 .... **CLC 1, 4, 13, 22; BLC 3; PC 7; SSC 1, 45; WLCS**
See also AFAW 1, 2; AMWS 3, 9; BW 1; CA 85-88; CDALB 1917-1929; DAM MULT; DLB 45, 51; EXPP; EXPS; HR 3; MTCW 1, 2; NFS 11; RGAL 4; RGSF 2; SSFS 5

Toomer, Nathan Jean
See Toomer, Jean

Toomer, Nathan Pinchback
See Toomer, Jean

Torley, Luke
See Blish, James (Benjamin)

Tornimparte, Alessandra
See Ginzburg, Natalia

Torre, Raoul della
See Mencken, H(enry) L(ouis)

Torrence, Ridgely 1874-1950 .... **TCLC 97**
See also DLB 54, 249

Torrey, E(dwin) Fuller 1937- .... **CLC 34**
See also CA 119; CANR 71

Torsvan, Ben Traven
See Traven, B.

Torsvan, Benno Traven
See Traven, B.

Torsvan, Berick Traven
See Traven, B.

Torsvan, Berwick Traven
See Traven, B.

Torsvan, Bruno Traven
See Traven, B.

Torsvan, Traven
See Traven, B.

Tourneur, Cyril 1575(?)-1626 .... **LC 66**
See also BRW 2; DAM DRAM; DLB 58; RGEL 2

Tournier, Michel (Edouard) 1924- .... **CLC 6, 23, 36, 95**
See also CA 49-52; CANR 3, 36, 74; DLB 83; GFL 1789 to the Present; MTCW 1, 2; SATA 23

Tournimparte, Alessandra
See Ginzburg, Natalia

Towers, Ivar
See Kornbluth, C(yril) M.

Towne, Robert (Burton) 1936(?)- ..... **CLC 87**
See also CA 108; DLB 44; IDFW 3, 4

Townsend, Sue .... **CLC 61**
See also Townsend, Susan Lilian
See also AAYA 28; CA 127; CANR 65, 107; CBD; CD 5; CPW; CWD; DAB; DAC; DAM MST; DLB 271; INT 127; SATA 55, 93; SATA-Brief 48; YAW

Townsend, Susan Lilian 1946-
See Townsend, Sue

Townshend, Pete
See Townshend, Peter (Dennis Blandford)

Townshend, Peter (Dennis Blandford)
1945- .... **CLC 17, 42**
See also CA 107

Tozzi, Federigo 1883-1920 .... **TCLC 31**
See also CA 160; CANR 110; DLB 264

Tracy, Don(ald Fiske) 1905-1970(?)
See Queen, Ellery
See also CA 1-4R; CANR 2

Trafford, F. G.
See Riddell, Charlotte

Traill, Catharine Parr 1802-1899 .. **NCLC 31**
See also DLB 99

Trakl, Georg 1887-1914 .... **TCLC 5; PC 20**
See also CA 165; EW 10; MTCW 2; RGWL 2, 3

Tranquilli, Secondino
See Silone, Ignazio

Transtroemer, Tomas (Goesta)
1931- .... **CLC 52, 65**
See also Transtromer, Tomas
See also CA 129; CAAS 17; DAM POET

Transtromer, Tomas
See Transtroemer, Tomas (Goesta)
See also DLB 257

Transtromer, Tomas Gosta
See Transtroemer, Tomas (Goesta)

Traven, B. 1882(?)-1969 .... **CLC 8, 11**
See also CA 19-20; CAP 2; DLB 9, 56; MTCW 1; RGAL 4

Trediakovsky, Vasilii Kirillovich
1703-1769 .... **LC 68**
See also DLB 150

Treitel, Jonathan 1959- .... **CLC 70**
See also DLB 267

Trelawny, Edward John
1792-1881 .... **NCLC 85**
See also DLB 110, 116, 144

Tremain, Rose 1943- .... **CLC 42**
See also CA 97-100; CANR 44, 95; CN 7; DLB 14, 271; RGSF 2; RHW

Tremblay, Michel 1942- .... **CLC 29, 102**
See also CA 128; CCA 1; CWW 2; DAC; DAM MST; DLB 60; GLL 1; MTCW 1, 2

Trevanian .... **CLC 29**
See also Whitaker, Rod(ney)

Trevor, Glen
See Hilton, James

Trevor, William .. **CLC 7, 9, 14, 25, 71, 116; SSC 21**
See also Cox, William Trevor
See also BRWS 4; CBD; CD 5; CN 7; DLB 14, 139; MTCW 2; RGEL 2; RGSF 2; SSFS 10

Trifonov, Iurii (Valentinovich)
See Trifonov, Yuri (Valentinovich)
See also RGWL 2, 3

Trifonov, Yuri (Valentinovich)
1925-1981 .... **CLC 45**
See also Trifonov, Iurii (Valentinovich)
See also CA 126; MTCW 1

Trilling, Diana (Rubin) 1905-1996 . **CLC 129**
See also CA 5-8R; CANR 10, 46; INT CANR-10; MTCW 1, 2

Trilling, Lionel 1905-1975 .... **CLC 9, 11, 24**
See also AMWS 3; CA 9-12R; CANR 10, 105; DLB 28, 63; INT CANR-10; MTCW 1, 2; RGAL 4; TUS

Trimball, W. H.
See Mencken, H(enry) L(ouis)

Tristan
See Gomez de la Serna, Ramon

Tristram
See Housman, A(lfred) E(dward)

Trogdon, William (Lewis) 1939-
See Heat-Moon, William Least
See also CA 119; CANR 47, 89; CPW; INT CA-119

Trollope, Anthony 1815-1882 .... **NCLC 6, 33, 101; SSC 28; WLC**
See also BRW 5; CDBLB 1832-1890; DA; DAB; DAC; DAM MST, NOV; DLB 21, 57, 159; RGEL 2; RGSF 2; SATA 22

Trollope, Frances 1779-1863 .... **NCLC 30**
See also DLB 21, 166

Trotsky, Leon 1879-1940 .... **TCLC 22**
See also CA 167

Trotter (Cockburn), Catharine
1679-1749 .... **LC 8**
See also DLB 84, 252

Trotter, Wilfred 1872-1939 .... **TCLC 97**

Trout, Kilgore
See Farmer, Philip Jose

Trow, George W. S. 1943- .... **CLC 52**
See also CA 126; CANR 91

Troyat, Henri 1911- .... **CLC 23**
See also CA 45-48; CANR 2, 33, 67; GFL 1789 to the Present; MTCW 1

Trudeau, G(arretson) B(eekman) 1948-
See Trudeau, Garry B.
See also CA 81-84; CANR 31; SATA 35

Trudeau, Garry B. .... **CLC 12**
See also Trudeau, G(arretson) B(eekman)
See also AAYA 10; AITN 2

Truffaut, Francois 1932-1984 ... **CLC 20, 101**
See also CA 81-84; CANR 34

Trumbo, Dalton 1905-1976 .... **CLC 19**
See also CA 21-24R; CANR 10; DLB 26; IDFW 3, 4; YAW

Trumbull, John 1750-1831 .... **NCLC 30**
See also DLB 31; RGAL 4

Trundlett, Helen B.
See Eliot, T(homas) S(tearns)

Truth, Sojourner 1797(?)-1883 .... **NCLC 94**
See also DLB 239; FW; LAIT 2

Tryon, Thomas 1926-1991 .... **CLC 3, 11**
See also AITN 1; BPFB 3; CA 29-32R; CANR 32, 77; CPW; DAM POP; HGG; MTCW 1

Tryon, Tom
See Tryon, Thomas

Ts'ao Hsueh-ch'in 1715(?)-1763 .... **LC 1**

Tsushima, Shuji 1909-1948
See Dazai Osamu

Tsvetaeva (Efron), Marina (Ivanovna)
1892-1941 .... **TCLC 7, 35; PC 14**
See also CA 128; CANR 73; EW 11; MTCW 1, 2; RGWL 2, 3

Tuck, Lily 1938- .... **CLC 70**
See also CA 139; CANR 90

Tu Fu 712-770 .... **PC 9**
See also Du Fu
See also DAM MULT; TWA; WP

Tunis, John R(oberts) 1889-1975 ..... **CLC 12**
See also BYA 1; CA 61-64; CANR 62; DLB 22, 171; JRDA; MAICYA 1, 2; SATA 37; SATA-Brief 30; YAW

Tuohy, Frank .... **CLC 37**
See also Tuohy, John Francis
See also DLB 14, 139

Tuohy, John Francis 1925-
See Tuohy, Frank
See also CA 5-8R; CANR 3, 47; CN 7

Turco, Lewis (Putnam) 1934- ..... **CLC 11, 63**
See also CA 13-16R; CAAS 22; CANR 24, 51; CP 7; DLBY 1984

Turgenev, Ivan (Sergeevich)
1818-1883 .... **NCLC 21, 37; DC 7; SSC 7; WLC**
See also DA; DAB; DAC; DAM MST, NOV; DFS 6; DLB 238; EW 6; RGSF 2; RGWL 2, 3; TWA

Turgot, Anne-Robert-Jacques
1727-1781 .... **LC 26**

Turner, Frederick 1943- .... **CLC 48**
See also CA 73-76; CAAS 10; CANR 12, 30, 56; DLB 40

Turton, James
See Crace, Jim

Tutu, Desmond M(pilo) 1931- .... **CLC 80; BLC 3**
See also BW 1, 3; CA 125; CANR 67, 81; DAM MULT

Tutuola, Amos 1920-1997 ...... **CLC 5, 14, 29; BLC 3**
See also AFW; BW 2, 3; CA 9-12R; CANR 27, 66; CDWLB 3; CN 7; DAM MULT; DLB 125; DNFS 2; MTCW 1, 2; RGEL 2; WLIT 2

Twain, Mark .... **TCLC 6, 12, 19, 36, 48, 59; SSC 34; WLC**
See also Clemens, Samuel Langhorne
See also AAYA 20; AMW; BPFB 3; BYA 2, 3, 11, 14; CLR 58, 60, 66; DLB 11; EXPN; EXPS; FANT; LAIT 2; NFS 1, 6; RGAL 4; RGSF 2; SFW 4; SSFS 1, 7; SUFW; TUS; WCH; WYA; YAW

Tyler, Anne 1941- . **CLC 7, 11, 18, 28, 44, 59, 103**
See also AAYA 18; AMWS 4; BEST 89:1; BPFB 3; BYA 12; CA 9-12R; CANR 11, 33, 53, 109; CDALBS; CN 7; CPW; CSW; DAM NOV, POP; DLB 6, 143; DLBY 1982; EXPN; MAWW; MTCW 1, 2; NFS 2, 7, 10; RGAL 4; SATA 7, 90; TUS; YAW

Tyler, Royall 1757-1826 .... **NCLC 3**
See also DLB 37; RGAL 4

Tynan, Katharine 1861-1931 .... **TCLC 3**
See also CA 167; DLB 153, 240; FW

Tyutchev, Fyodor 1803-1873 .... **NCLC 34**

Tzara, Tristan 1896-1963 ..... **CLC 47; PC 27**
See also CA 153; DAM POET; MTCW 2

Udall, Nicholas 1504-1556 .... **LC 84**
See also DLB 62; RGEL 2

Uhry, Alfred 1936- .... **CLC 55**
See also CA 133; CAD; CANR 112; CD 5; CSW; DAM DRAM, POP; DFS 15; INT CA-133

Ulf, Haerved
See Strindberg, (Johan) August

Ulf, Harved
See Strindberg, (Johan) August

Ulibarri, Sabine R(eyes) 1919- .... **CLC 83; HLCS 2**
See also CA 131; CANR 81; DAM MULT; DLB 82; HW 1, 2; RGSF 2

Unamuno (y Jugo), Miguel de
1864-1936 . **TCLC 2, 9; HLC 2; SSC 11**
See also CA 131; CANR 81; DAM MULT, NOV; DLB 108; EW 8; HW 1, 2; MTCW 1, 2; RGSF 2; RGWL 2, 3; TWA

Undercliffe, Errol
See Campbell, (John) Ramsey

Underwood, Miles
See Glassco, John

Undset, Sigrid 1882-1949 ..... **TCLC 3; WLC**
See also CA 129; DA; DAB; DAC; DAM MST, NOV; EW 9; FW; MTCW 1, 2; RGWL 2, 3

Ungaretti, Giuseppe 1888-1970 ... **CLC 7, 11, 15**
See also CA 19-20; CAP 2; DLB 114; EW 10; RGWL 2, 3

Unger, Douglas 1952- .... **CLC 34**
See also CA 130; CANR 94

Unsworth, Barry (Forster) 1930- .... **CLC 76, 127**
See also BRWS 7; CA 25-28R; CANR 30, 54; CN 7; DLB 194

Updike, John (Hoyer) 1932- . **CLC 1, 2, 3, 5, 7, 9, 13, 15, 23, 34, 43, 70, 139; SSC 13, 27; WLC**
See also AAYA 36; AMW; AMWR 1; BPFB 3; BYA 12; CA 1-4R; CABS 1; CANR 4, 33, 51, 94; CDALB 1968-1988; CN 7; CP 7; CPW 1; DA; DAB; DAC; DAM MST, NOV, POET, POP; DLB 2, 5, 143, 218, 227; DLBD 3; DLBY 1980, 1982, 1997; EXPP; HGG; MTCW 1, 2; NFS 12; RGAL 4; RGSF 2; SSFS 3; TUS

Upshaw, Margaret Mitchell
See Mitchell, Margaret (Munnerlyn)

Upton, Mark
See Sanders, Lawrence

Upward, Allen 1863-1926 .... **TCLC 85**
See also CA 187; DLB 36

Urdang, Constance (Henriette)
1922-1996 .... **CLC 47**
See also CA 21-24R; CANR 9, 24; CP 7; CWP

Uriel, Henry
See Faust, Frederick (Schiller)

Uris, Leon (Marcus) 1924- .... **CLC 7, 32**
See also AITN 1, 2; BEST 89:2; BPFB 3; CA 1-4R; CANR 1, 40, 65; CN 7; CPW 1; DAM NOV, POP; MTCW 1, 2; SATA 49

Urista, Alberto H. 1947- .... **PC 34**
See also Alurista
See also CA 45-48, 182; CANR 2, 32; HLCS 1; HW 1

Urmuz
See Codrescu, Andrei

Urquhart, Guy
See McAlmon, Robert (Menzies)

Urquhart, Jane 1949- .... **CLC 90**
See also CA 113; CANR 32, 68; CCA 1; DAC

Usigli, Rodolfo 1905-1979
See also CA 131; HLCS 1; HW 1; LAW

Ustinov, Peter (Alexander) 1921- .... **CLC 1**
See also AITN 1; CA 13-16R; CANR 25, 51; CBD; CD 5; DLB 13; MTCW 2

U Tam'si, Gerald Felix Tchicaya
See Tchicaya, Gerald Felix

U Tam'si, Tchicaya
See Tchicaya, Gerald Felix

Vachss, Andrew (Henry) 1942- .... **CLC 106**
See also CA 118; CANR 44, 95; CMW 4
Vachss, Andrew H.
See Vachss, Andrew (Henry)
Vaculik, Ludvik 1926- .... **CLC 7**
See also CA 53-56; CANR 72; CWW 2; DLB 232
Vaihinger, Hans 1852-1933 .... **TCLC 71**
See also CA 166
Valdez, Luis (Miguel) 1940- ..... **CLC 84; DC 10; HLC 2**
See also CA 101; CAD; CANR 32, 81; CD 5; DAM MULT; DFS 5; DLB 122; HW 1; LAIT 4
Valenzuela, Luisa 1938- .... **CLC 31, 104; HLCS 2; SSC 14**
See also CA 101; CANR 32, 65; CDWLB 3; CWW 2; DAM MULT; DLB 113; FW; HW 1, 2; LAW; RGSF 2; RGWL 3
Valera y Alcala-Galiano, Juan 1824-1905 .... **TCLC 10**
Valery, (Ambroise) Paul (Toussaint Jules) 1871-1945 .... **TCLC 4, 15; PC 9**
See also CA 122; DAM POET; DLB 258; EW 8; GFL 1789 to the Present; MTCW 1, 2; RGWL 2, 3; TWA
Valle-Inclan, Ramon (Maria) del 1866-1936 .... **TCLC 5; HLC 2**
See also CA 153; CANR 80; DAM MULT; DLB 134; EW 8; HW 2; RGSF 2; RGWL 2, 3
Vallejo, Antonio Buero
See Buero Vallejo, Antonio
Vallejo, Cesar (Abraham) 1892-1938 .... **TCLC 3, 56; HLC 2**
See also CA 153; DAM MULT; HW 1; LAW; RGWL 2, 3
Valles, Jules 1832-1885 .... **NCLC 71**
See also DLB 123; GFL 1789 to the Present
Vallette, Marguerite Eymery 1860-1953 .... **TCLC 67**
See also CA 182; DLB 123, 192
Valle Y Pena, Ramon del
See Valle-Inclan, Ramon (Maria) del
Van Ash, Cay 1918- .... **CLC 34**
Vanbrugh, Sir John 1664-1726 .... **LC 21**
See also BRW 2; DAM DRAM; DLB 80; IDTP; RGEL 2
Van Campen, Karl
See Campbell, John W(ood, Jr.)
Vance, Gerald
See Silverberg, Robert
Vance, Jack .... **CLC 35**
See also Vance, John Holbrook
See also DLB 8; FANT; SCFW 2; SFW 4; SUFW 1, 2
Vance, John Holbrook 1916-
See Queen, Ellery; Vance, Jack
See also CA 29-32R; CANR 17, 65; CMW 4; MTCW 1
Van Den Bogarde, Derek Jules Gaspard Ulric Niven 1921-1999 .... **CLC 14**
See also Bogarde, Dirk
See also CA 77-80
Vandenburgh, Jane .... **CLC 59**
See also CA 168
Vanderhaeghe, Guy 1951- .... **CLC 41**
See also BPFB 3; CA 113; CANR 72
van der Post, Laurens (Jan) 1906-1996 .... **CLC 5**
See also AFW; CA 5-8R; CANR 35; CN 7; DLB 204; RGEL 2
van de Wetering, Janwillem 1931- ... **CLC 47**
See also CA 49-52; CANR 4, 62, 90; CMW 4
Van Dine, S. S. .... **TCLC 23**
See also Wright, Willard Huntington
See also MSW

Van Doren, Carl (Clinton) 1885-1950 .... **TCLC 18**
See also CA 168
Van Doren, Mark 1894-1972 .... **CLC 6, 10**
See also CA 1-4R; CANR 3; DLB 45; MTCW 1, 2; RGAL 4
Van Druten, John (William) 1901-1957 .... **TCLC 2**
See also CA 161; DLB 10; RGAL 4
Van Duyn, Mona (Jane) 1921- ...... **CLC 3, 7, 63, 116**
See also CA 9-12R; CANR 7, 38, 60; CP 7; CWP; DAM POET; DLB 5
Van Dyne, Edith
See Baum, L(yman) Frank
van Itallie, Jean-Claude 1936- .... **CLC 3**
See also CA 45-48; CAAS 2; CAD; CANR 1, 48; CD 5; DLB 7
Van Loot, Cornelius Obenchain
See Roberts, Kenneth (Lewis)
van Ostaijen, Paul 1896-1928 .... **TCLC 33**
See also CA 163
Van Peebles, Melvin 1932- .... **CLC 2, 20**
See also BW 2, 3; CA 85-88; CANR 27, 67, 82; DAM MULT
van Schendel, Arthur(-Francois-Emile) 1874-1946 .... **TCLC 56**
Vansittart, Peter 1920- .... **CLC 42**
See also CA 1-4R; CANR 3, 49, 90; CN 7; RHW
Van Vechten, Carl 1880-1964 .... **CLC 33**
See also AMWS 2; CA 183; DLB 4, 9; HR 3; RGAL 4
van Vogt, A(lfred) E(lton) 1912-2000 . **CLC 1**
See also BPFB 3; BYA 13, 14; CA 21-24R; CANR 28; DLB 8, 251; SATA 14; SATA-Obit 124; SCFW; SFW 4
Vara, Madeleine
See Jackson, Laura (Riding)
Varda, Agnes 1928- .... **CLC 16**
See also CA 122
Vargas Llosa, (Jorge) Mario (Pedro) 1936- .... **CLC 3, 6, 9, 10, 15, 31, 42, 85; HLC 2**
See also Llosa, (Jorge) Mario (Pedro) Vargas
See also BPFB 3; CA 73-76; CANR 18, 32, 42, 67; CDWLB 3; DA; DAB; DAC; DAM MST, MULT, NOV; DLB 145; DNFS 2; HW 1, 2; LAIT 5; LAW; LAWS 1; MTCW 1, 2; RGWL 2; SSFS 14; TWA; WLIT 1
Vasiliu, George
See Bacovia, George
Vasiliu, Gheorghe
See Bacovia, George
See also CA 189
Vassa, Gustavus
See Equiano, Olaudah
Vassilikos, Vassilis 1933- .... **CLC 4, 8**
See also CA 81-84; CANR 75
Vaughan, Henry 1621-1695 .... **LC 27**
See also BRW 2; DLB 131; PAB; RGEL 2
Vaughn, Stephanie .... **CLC 62**
Vazov, Ivan (Minchov) 1850-1921 .. **TCLC 25**
See also CA 167; CDWLB 4; DLB 147
Veblen, Thorstein B(unde) 1857-1929 .... **TCLC 31**
See also AMWS 1; CA 165; DLB 246
Vega, Lope de 1562-1635 .... **LC 23; HLCS 2**
See also EW 2; RGWL 2, 3
Vendler, Helen (Hennessy) 1933- ... **CLC 138**
See also CA 41-44R; CANR 25, 72; MTCW 1, 2
Venison, Alfred
See Pound, Ezra (Weston Loomis)
Verdi, Marie de
See Mencken, H(enry) L(ouis)

Verdu, Matilde
See Cela, Camilo Jose
Verga, Giovanni (Carmelo) 1840-1922 .... **TCLC 3; SSC 21**
See also CA 123; CANR 101; EW 7; RGSF 2; RGWL 2, 3
Vergil 70B.C.-19B.C. ... **CMLC 9, 40; PC 12; WLCS**
See also Virgil
See also AW 2; DA; DAB; DAC; DAM MST, POET; EFS 1
Verhaeren, Emile (Adolphe Gustave) 1855-1916 .... **TCLC 12**
See also GFL 1789 to the Present
Verlaine, Paul (Marie) 1844-1896 .. **NCLC 2, 51; PC 2, 32**
See also DAM POET; DLB 217; EW 7; GFL 1789 to the Present; RGWL 2, 3; TWA
Verne, Jules (Gabriel) 1828-1905 ... **TCLC 6, 52**
See also AAYA 16; BYA 4; CA 131; DLB 123; GFL 1789 to the Present; JRDA; LAIT 2; MAICYA 1, 2; RGWL 2, 3; SATA 21; SCFW; SFW 4; TWA; WCH
Verus, Marcus Annius
See Aurelius, Marcus
Very, Jones 1813-1880 .... **NCLC 9**
See also DLB 1, 243; RGAL 4
Vesaas, Tarjei 1897-1970 .... **CLC 48**
See also CA 190; EW 11; RGWL 3
Vialis, Gaston
See Simenon, Georges (Jacques Christian)
Vian, Boris 1920-1959 .... **TCLC 9**
See also CA 164; CANR 111; DLB 72; GFL 1789 to the Present; MTCW 2; RGWL 2, 3
Viaud, (Louis Marie) Julien 1850-1923
See Loti, Pierre
Vicar, Henry
See Felsen, Henry Gregor
Vicker, Angus
See Felsen, Henry Gregor
Vidal, Gore 1925- ...... **CLC 2, 4, 6, 8, 10, 22, 33, 72, 142**
See also Box, Edgar
See also AITN 1; AMWS 4; BEST 90:2; BPFB 3; CA 5-8R; CAD; CANR 13, 45, 65, 100; CD 5; CDALBS; CN 7; CPW; DAM NOV, POP; DFS 2; DLB 6, 152; INT CANR-13; MTCW 1, 2; RGAL 4; RHW; TUS
Viereck, Peter (Robert Edwin) 1916- .... **CLC 4; PC 27**
See also CA 1-4R; CANR 1, 47; CP 7; DLB 5; PFS 9, 14
Vigny, Alfred (Victor) de 1797-1863 .... **NCLC 7, 102; PC 26**
See also DAM POET; DLB 119, 192, 217; EW 5; GFL 1789 to the Present; RGWL 2, 3
Vilakazi, Benedict Wallet 1906-1947 .... **TCLC 37**
See also CA 168
Villa, Jose Garcia 1914-1997 .... **PC 22**
See also AAL; CA 25-28R; CANR 12; EXPP
Villarreal, Jose Antonio 1924-
See also CA 133; CANR 93; DAM MULT; DLB 82; HLC 2; HW 1; LAIT 4; RGAL 4
Villaurrutia, Xavier 1903-1950 .... **TCLC 80**
See also CA 192; HW 1; LAW
Villehardouin, Geoffroi de 1150(?)-1218(?) .... **CMLC 38**
Villiers de l'Isle Adam, Jean Marie Mathias Philippe Auguste 1838-1889 ... **NCLC 3; SSC 14**
See also DLB 123, 192; GFL 1789 to the Present; RGSF 2

Villon, Francois 1431-1463(?) . **LC 62; PC 13**
See also DLB 208; EW 2; RGWL 2, 3; TWA

Vine, Barbara .... **CLC 50**
See also Rendell, Ruth (Barbara)
See also BEST 90:4

Vinge, Joan (Carol) D(ennison)
1948- .... **CLC 30; SSC 24**
See also AAYA 32; BPFB 3; CA 93-96; CANR 72; SATA 36, 113; SFW 4; YAW

Viola, Herman J(oseph) 1938- .... **CLC 70**
See also CA 61-64; CANR 8, 23, 48, 91; SATA 126

Violis, G.
See Simenon, Georges (Jacques Christian)

Viramontes, Helena Maria 1954-
See also CA 159; DLB 122; HLCS 2; HW 2

Virgil
See Vergil
See also CDWLB 1; DLB 211; LAIT 1; RGWL 2, 3; WP

Visconti, Luchino 1906-1976 .... **CLC 16**
See also CA 81-84; CANR 39

Vittorini, Elio 1908-1966 .... **CLC 6, 9, 14**
See also CA 133; DLB 264; EW 12; RGWL 2, 3

Vivekananda, Swami 1863-1902 .... **TCLC 88**

Vizenor, Gerald Robert 1934- .... **CLC 103**
See also CA 13-16R; CAAE 205; CAAS 22; CANR 5, 21, 44, 67; DAM MULT; DLB 175, 227; MTCW 2; NNAL; TCWW 2

Vizinczey, Stephen 1933- .... **CLC 40**
See also CA 128; CCA 1; INT 128

Vliet, R(ussell) G(ordon)
1929-1984 .... **CLC 22**
See also CA 37-40R; CANR 18

Vogau, Boris Andreyevich 1894-1937(?)
See Pilnyak, Boris

Vogel, Paula A(nne) 1951- ... **CLC 76; DC 18**
See also CA 108; CAD; CD 5; CWD; DFS 14; RGAL 4

Voigt, Cynthia 1942- .... **CLC 30**
See also AAYA 3, 30; BYA 1, 3, 6, 7, 8; CA 106; CANR 18, 37, 40, 94; CLR 13, 48; INT CANR-18; JRDA; LAIT 5; MAICYA 1, 2; MAICYAS 1; SATA 48, 79, 116; SATA-Brief 33; WYA; YAW

Voigt, Ellen Bryant 1943- .... **CLC 54**
See also CA 69-72; CANR 11, 29, 55; CP 7; CSW; CWP; DLB 120

Voinovich, Vladimir (Nikolaevich)
1932- .... **CLC 10, 49, 147**
See also CA 81-84; CAAS 12; CANR 33, 67; MTCW 1

Vollmann, William T. 1959- .... **CLC 89**
See also CA 134; CANR 67; CPW; DAM NOV, POP; MTCW 2

Voloshinov, V. N.
See Bakhtin, Mikhail Mikhailovich

Voltaire 1694-1778 .... **LC 14, 79; SSC 12; WLC**
See also BYA 13; DA; DAB; DAC; DAM DRAM, MST; EW 4; GFL Beginnings to 1789; NFS 7; RGWL 2, 3; TWA

von Aschendrof, Baron Ignatz
See Ford, Ford Madox

von Chamisso, Adelbert
See Chamisso, Adelbert von

von Daeniken, Erich 1935- .... **CLC 30**
See also AITN 1; CA 37-40R; CANR 17, 44

von Daniken, Erich
See von Daeniken, Erich

von der Vogelweide, Walther c. 1170-1228 .... **CMLC 56**

von Hartmann, Eduard
1842-1906 .... **TCLC 96**

von Hayek, Friedrich August
See Hayek, F(riedrich) A(ugust von)

von Heidenstam, (Carl Gustaf) Verner
See Heidenstam, (Carl Gustaf) Verner von

von Heyse, Paul (Johann Ludwig)
See Heyse, Paul (Johann Ludwig von)

von Hofmannsthal, Hugo
See Hofmannsthal, Hugo von

von Horvath, Odon
See von Horvath, Odon

von Horvath, Odon
See von Horvath, Odon

von Horvath, Odon 1901-1938 .... **TCLC 45**
See also von Horvath, Oedoen
See also CA 194; DLB 85, 124; RGWL 2, 3

von Horvath, Oedoen
See von Horvath, Odon
See also CA 184

von Kleist, Heinrich
See Kleist, Heinrich von

von Liliencron, (Friedrich Adolf Axel) Detlev
See Liliencron, (Friedrich Adolf Axel) Detlev von

Vonnegut, Kurt, Jr. 1922- . **CLC 1, 2, 3, 4, 5, 8, 12, 22, 40, 60, 111; SSC 8; WLC**
See also AAYA 6; AITN 1; AMWS 2; BEST 90:4; BPFB 3; BYA 3, 14; CA 1-4R; CANR 1, 25, 49, 75, 92; CDALB 1968-1988; CN 7; CPW 1; DA; DAB; DAC; DAM MST, NOV, POP; DLB 2, 8, 152; DLBD 3; DLBY 1980; EXPN; EXPS; LAIT 4; MTCW 1, 2; NFS 3; RGAL 4; SCFW; SFW 4; SSFS 5; TUS; YAW

Von Rachen, Kurt
See Hubbard, L(afayette) Ron(ald)

von Rezzori (d'Arezzo), Gregor
See Rezzori (d'Arezzo), Gregor von

von Sternberg, Josef
See Sternberg, Josef von

Vorster, Gordon 1924- .... **CLC 34**
See also CA 133

Vosce, Trudie
See Ozick, Cynthia

Voznesensky, Andrei (Andreievich)
1933- .... **CLC 1, 15, 57**
See also CA 89-92; CANR 37; CWW 2; DAM POET; MTCW 1

Wace, Robert c. 1100-c. 1175 .... **CMLC 55**
See also DLB 146

Waddington, Miriam 1917- .... **CLC 28**
See also CA 21-24R; CANR 12, 30; CCA 1; CP 7; DLB 68

Wagman, Fredrica 1937- .... **CLC 7**
See also CA 97-100; INT 97-100

Wagner, Linda W.
See Wagner-Martin, Linda (C.)

Wagner, Linda Welshimer
See Wagner-Martin, Linda (C.)

Wagner, Richard 1813-1883 ..... **NCLC 9, 119**
See also DLB 129; EW 6

Wagner-Martin, Linda (C.) 1936- .... **CLC 50**
See also CA 159

Wagoner, David (Russell) 1926- .... **CLC 3, 5, 15; PC 33**
See also AMWS 9; CA 1-4R; CAAS 3; CANR 2, 71; CN 7; CP 7; DLB 5, 256; SATA 14; TCWW 2

Wah, Fred(erick James) 1939- .... **CLC 44**
See also CA 141; CP 7; DLB 60

Wahloo, Per 1926-1975 .... **CLC 7**
See also BPFB 3; CA 61-64; CANR 73; CMW 4; MSW

Wahloo, Peter
See Wahloo, Per

Wain, John (Barrington) 1925-1994 . **CLC 2, 11, 15, 46**
See also CA 5-8R; CAAS 4; CANR 23, 54; CDBLB 1960 to Present; DLB 15, 27, 139, 155; MTCW 1, 2

Wajda, Andrzej 1926- .... **CLC 16**
See also CA 102

Wakefield, Dan 1932- .... **CLC 7**
See also CA 21-24R; CAAS 7; CN 7

Wakefield, Herbert Russell
1888-1965 .... **TCLC 120**
See also CA 5-8R; CANR 77; HGG; SUFW

Wakoski, Diane 1937- ...... **CLC 2, 4, 7, 9, 11, 40; PC 15**
See also CA 13-16R; CAAS 1; CANR 9, 60, 106; CP 7; CWP; DAM POET; DLB 5; INT CANR-9; MTCW 2

Wakoski-Sherbell, Diane
See Wakoski, Diane

Walcott, Derek (Alton) 1930- .... **CLC 2, 4, 9, 14, 25, 42, 67, 76, 160; BLC 3; DC 7**
See also BW 2; CA 89-92; CANR 26, 47, 75, 80; CBD; CD 5; CDWLB 3; CP 7; DAB; DAC; DAM MST, MULT, POET; DLB 117; DLBY 1981; DNFS 1; EFS 1; MTCW 1, 2; PFS 6; RGEL 2; TWA

Waldman, Anne (Lesley) 1945- .... **CLC 7**
See also CA 37-40R; CAAS 17; CANR 34, 69; CP 7; CWP; DLB 16

Waldo, E. Hunter
See Sturgeon, Theodore (Hamilton)

Waldo, Edward Hamilton
See Sturgeon, Theodore (Hamilton)

Walker, Alice (Malsenior) 1944- ... **CLC 5, 6, 9, 19, 27, 46, 58, 103, 167; BLC 3; PC 30; SSC 5; WLCS**
See also AAYA 3, 33; AFAW 1, 2; AMWS 3; BEST 89:4; BPFB 3; BW 2, 3; CA 37-40R; CANR 9, 27, 49, 66, 82; CDALB 1968-1988; CN 7; CPW; CSW; DA; DAB; DAC; DAM MST, MULT, NOV, POET, POP; DLB 6, 33, 143; EXPN; EXPS; FW; INT CANR-27; LAIT 3; MAWW; MTCW 1, 2; NFS 5; RGAL 4; RGSF 2; SATA 31; SSFS 2, 11; TUS; YAW

Walker, David Harry 1911-1992 ...... **CLC 14**
See also CA 1-4R; CANR 1; CWRI 5; SATA 8; SATA-Obit 71

Walker, Edward Joseph 1934-
See Walker, Ted
See also CA 21-24R; CANR 12, 28, 53; CP 7

Walker, George F. 1947- .... **CLC 44, 61**
See also CA 103; CANR 21, 43, 59; CD 5; DAB; DAC; DAM MST; DLB 60

Walker, Joseph A. 1935- .... **CLC 19**
See also BW 1, 3; CA 89-92; CAD; CANR 26; CD 5; DAM DRAM, MST; DFS 12; DLB 38

Walker, Margaret (Abigail)
1915-1998 .... **CLC 1, 6; BLC; PC 20**
See also AFAW 1, 2; BW 2, 3; CA 73-76; CANR 26, 54, 76; CN 7; CP 7; CSW; DAM MULT; DLB 76, 152; EXPP; FW; MTCW 1, 2; RGAL 4; RHW; TCLC 129

Walker, Ted .... **CLC 13**
See also Walker, Edward Joseph
See also DLB 40

Wallace, David Foster 1962- ..... **CLC 50, 114**
See also AMWS 10; CA 132; CANR 59; MTCW 2

Wallace, Dexter
See Masters, Edgar Lee

Wallace, (Richard Horatio) Edgar
1875-1932 .... **TCLC 57**
See also CMW 4; DLB 70; MSW; RGEL 2

Wallace, Irving 1916-1990 .... **CLC 7, 13**
See also AITN 1; BPFB 3; CA 1-4R; CAAS 1; CANR 1, 27; CPW; DAM NOV, POP; INT CANR-27; MTCW 1, 2

Wallant, Edward Lewis 1926-1962 ... **CLC 5, 10**
See also CA 1-4R; CANR 22; DLB 2, 28, 143; MTCW 1, 2; RGAL 4

Wallas, Graham 1858-1932 .... **TCLC 91**

Walley, Byron
See Card, Orson Scott

Walpole, Horace 1717-1797 .... **LC 2, 49**
See also BRW 3; DLB 39, 104, 213; HGG; RGEL 2; SUFW 1; TEA

Walpole, Hugh (Seymour)
1884-1941 .... **TCLC 5**
See also CA 165; DLB 34; HGG; MTCW 2; RGEL 2; RHW

Walser, Martin 1927- .... **CLC 27**
See also CA 57-60; CANR 8, 46; CWW 2; DLB 75, 124

Walser, Robert 1878-1956 .... **TCLC 18; SSC 20**
See also CA 165; CANR 100; DLB 66

Walsh, Gillian Paton
See Paton Walsh, Gillian

Walsh, Jill Paton .... **CLC 35**
See also Paton Walsh, Gillian
See also CLR 2, 65; WYA

Walter, Villiam Christian
See Andersen, Hans Christian

Walton, Izaak 1593-1683 .... **LC 72**
See also BRW 2; CDBLB Before 1660; DLB 151, 213; RGEL 2

Wambaugh, Joseph (Aloysius, Jr.)
1937- .... **CLC 3, 18**
See also AITN 1; BEST 89:3; BPFB 3; CA 33-36R; CANR 42, 65; CMW 4; CPW 1; DAM NOV, POP; DLB 6; DLBY 1983; MSW; MTCW 1, 2

Wang Wei 699(?)-761(?) .... **PC 18**
See also TWA

Ward, Arthur Henry Sarsfield 1883-1959
See Rohmer, Sax
See also CA 173; CMW 4; HGG

Ward, Douglas Turner 1930- .... **CLC 19**
See also BW 1; CA 81-84; CAD; CANR 27; CD 5; DLB 7, 38

Ward, E. D.
See Lucas, E(dward) V(errall)

Ward, Mrs. Humphry 1851-1920
See Ward, Mary Augusta
See also RGEL 2

Ward, Mary Augusta 1851-1920 ... **TCLC 55**
See also Ward, Mrs. Humphry
See also DLB 18

Ward, Peter
See Faust, Frederick (Schiller)

Warhol, Andy 1928(?)-1987 .... **CLC 20**
See also AAYA 12; BEST 89:4; CA 89-92; CANR 34

Warner, Francis (Robert le Plastrier)
1937- .... **CLC 14**
See also CA 53-56; CANR 11

Warner, Marina 1946- .... **CLC 59**
See also CA 65-68; CANR 21, 55; CN 7; DLB 194

Warner, Rex (Ernest) 1905-1986 .... **CLC 45**
See also CA 89-92; DLB 15; RGEL 2; RHW

Warner, Susan (Bogert)
1819-1885 .... **NCLC 31**
See also DLB 3, 42, 239, 250, 254

Warner, Sylvia (Constance) Ashton
See Ashton-Warner, Sylvia (Constance)

Warner, Sylvia Townsend
1893-1978 .... **CLC 7, 19; SSC 23**
See also BRWS 7; CA 61-64; CANR 16, 60, 104; DLB 34, 139; FANT; FW; MTCW 1, 2; RGEL 2; RGSF 2; RHW

Warren, Mercy Otis 1728-1814 ..... **NCLC 13**
See also DLB 31, 200; RGAL 4; TUS

Warren, Robert Penn 1905-1989 .. **CLC 1, 4, 6, 8, 10, 13, 18, 39, 53, 59; PC 37; SSC 4; WLC**
See also AITN 1; AMW; BPFB 3; BYA 1; CA 13-16R; CANR 10, 47; CDALB 1968-1988; DA; DAB; DAC; DAM MST, NOV, POET; DLB 2, 48, 152; DLBY 1980, 1989; INT CANR-10; MTCW 1, 2; NFS 13; RGAL 4; RGSF 2; RHW; SATA 46; SATA-Obit 63; SSFS 8; TUS

Warshofsky, Isaac
See Singer, Isaac Bashevis

Warton, Joseph 1722-1800 .... **NCLC 118**
See also DLB 104, 109; RGEL 2

Warton, Thomas 1728-1790 .... **LC 15, 82**
See also DAM POET; DLB 104, 109; RGEL 2

Waruk, Kona
See Harris, (Theodore) Wilson

Warung, Price .... **TCLC 45**
See also Astley, William
See also DLB 230; RGEL 2

Warwick, Jarvis
See Garner, Hugh
See also CCA 1

Washington, Alex
See Harris, Mark

Washington, Booker T(aliaferro)
1856-1915 .... **TCLC 10; BLC 3**
See also BW 1; CA 125; DAM MULT; LAIT 2; RGAL 4; SATA 28

Washington, George 1732-1799 .... **LC 25**
See also DLB 31

Wassermann, (Karl) Jakob
1873-1934 .... **TCLC 6**
See also CA 163; DLB 66

Wasserstein, Wendy 1950- .. **CLC 32, 59, 90; DC 4**
See also CA 129; CABS 3; CAD; CANR 53, 75; CD 5; CWD; DAM DRAM; DFS 5; DLB 228; FW; INT CA-129; MTCW 2; SATA 94

Waterhouse, Keith (Spencer) 1929- . **CLC 47**
See also CA 5-8R; CANR 38, 67, 109; CBD; CN 7; DLB 13, 15; MTCW 1, 2

Waters, Frank (Joseph) 1902-1995 .. **CLC 88**
See also CA 5-8R; CAAS 13; CANR 3, 18, 63; DLB 212; DLBY 1986; RGAL 4; TCWW 2

Waters, Mary C. .... **CLC 70**

Waters, Roger 1944- .... **CLC 35**

Watkins, Frances Ellen
See Harper, Frances Ellen Watkins

Watkins, Gerrold
See Malzberg, Barry N(athaniel)

Watkins, Gloria Jean 1952(?)-
See hooks, bell
See also BW 2; CA 143; CANR 87; MTCW 2; SATA 115

Watkins, Paul 1964- .... **CLC 55**
See also CA 132; CANR 62, 98

Watkins, Vernon Phillips
1906-1967 .... **CLC 43**
See also CA 9-10; CAP 1; DLB 20; RGEL 2

Watson, Irving S.
See Mencken, H(enry) L(ouis)

Watson, John H.
See Farmer, Philip Jose

Watson, Richard F.
See Silverberg, Robert

Waugh, Auberon (Alexander)
1939-2001 .... **CLC 7**
See also CA 45-48; CANR 6, 22, 92; DLB 14, 194

Waugh, Evelyn (Arthur St. John)
1903-1966 .. **CLC 1, 3, 8, 13, 19, 27, 44, 107; SSC 41; WLC**
See also BPFB 3; BRW 7; CA 85-88; CANR 22; CDBLB 1914-1945; DA; DAB; DAC; DAM MST, NOV, POP; DLB 15, 162, 195; MTCW 1, 2; NFS 13; RGEL 2; RGSF 2; TEA; WLIT 4

Waugh, Harriet 1944- .... **CLC 6**
See also CA 85-88; CANR 22

Ways, C. R.
See Blount, Roy (Alton), Jr.

Waystaff, Simon
See Swift, Jonathan

Webb, Beatrice (Martha Potter)
1858-1943 .... **TCLC 22**
See also CA 162; DLB 190; FW

Webb, Charles (Richard) 1939- .... **CLC 7**
See also CA 25-28R

Webb, James H(enry), Jr. 1946- ...... **CLC 22**
See also CA 81-84

Webb, Mary Gladys (Meredith)
1881-1927 .... **TCLC 24**
See also CA 182; DLB 34; FW

Webb, Mrs. Sidney
See Webb, Beatrice (Martha Potter)

Webb, Phyllis 1927- .... **CLC 18**
See also CA 104; CANR 23; CCA 1; CP 7; CWP; DLB 53

Webb, Sidney (James) 1859-1947 .. **TCLC 22**
See also CA 163; DLB 190

Webber, Andrew Lloyd .... **CLC 21**
See also Lloyd Webber, Andrew
See also DFS 7

Weber, Lenora Mattingly
1895-1971 .... **CLC 12**
See also CA 19-20; CAP 1; SATA 2; SATA-Obit 26

Weber, Max 1864-1920 .... **TCLC 69**
See also CA 189

Webster, John 1580(?)-1634(?) ..... **LC 33, 84; DC 2; WLC**
See also BRW 2; CDBLB Before 1660; DA; DAB; DAC; DAM DRAM, MST; DLB 58; IDTP; RGEL 2; WLIT 3

Webster, Noah 1758-1843 .... **NCLC 30**
See also DLB 1, 37, 42, 43, 73, 243

Wedekind, (Benjamin) Frank(lin)
1864-1918 .... **TCLC 7**
See also CA 153; CDWLB 2; DAM DRAM; DLB 118; EW 8; RGWL 2, 3

Wehr, Demaris .... **CLC 65**

Weidman, Jerome 1913-1998 .... **CLC 7**
See also AITN 2; CA 1-4R; CAD; CANR 1; DLB 28

Weil, Simone (Adolphine)
1909-1943 .... **TCLC 23**
See also CA 159; EW 12; FW; GFL 1789 to the Present; MTCW 2

Weininger, Otto 1880-1903 .... **TCLC 84**

Weinstein, Nathan
See West, Nathanael

Weinstein, Nathan von Wallenstein
See West, Nathanael

Weir, Peter (Lindsay) 1944- .... **CLC 20**
See also CA 123

Weiss, Peter (Ulrich) 1916-1982 .. **CLC 3, 15, 51**
See also CA 45-48; CANR 3; DAM DRAM; DFS 3; DLB 69, 124; RGWL 2, 3

Weiss, Theodore (Russell) 1916- ... **CLC 3, 8, 14**
See also CA 9-12R; CAAE 189; CAAS 2; CANR 46, 94; CP 7; DLB 5

Welch, (Maurice) Denton
1915-1948 .... **TCLC 22**
See also BRWS 8; CA 148; RGEL 2
Welch, James 1940- .... **CLC 6, 14, 52**
See also CA 85-88; CANR 42, 66, 107; CN 7; CP 7; CPW; DAM MULT, POP; DLB 175, 256; NNAL; RGAL 4; TCWW 2
Weldon, Fay 1931- . **CLC 6, 9, 11, 19, 36, 59, 122**
See also BRWS 4; CA 21-24R; CANR 16, 46, 63, 97; CDBLB 1960 to Present; CN 7; CPW; DAM POP; DLB 14, 194; FW; HGG; INT CANR-16; MTCW 1, 2; RGEL 2; RGSF 2
Wellek, Rene 1903-1995 .... **CLC 28**
See also CA 5-8R; CAAS 7; CANR 8; DLB 63; INT CANR-8
Weller, Michael 1942- .... **CLC 10, 53**
See also CA 85-88; CAD; CD 5
Weller, Paul 1958- .... **CLC 26**
Wellershoff, Dieter 1925- .... **CLC 46**
See also CA 89-92; CANR 16, 37
Welles, (George) Orson 1915-1985 .. **CLC 20, 80**
See also AAYA 40; CA 93-96
Wellman, John McDowell 1945-
See Wellman, Mac
See also CA 166; CD 5
Wellman, Mac .... **CLC 65**
See also Wellman, John McDowell; Wellman, John McDowell
See also CAD; RGAL 4
Wellman, Manly Wade 1903-1986 ... **CLC 49**
See also CA 1-4R; CANR 6, 16, 44; FANT; SATA 6; SATA-Obit 47; SFW 4; SUFW
Wells, Carolyn 1869(?)-1942 .... **TCLC 35**
See also CA 185; CMW 4; DLB 11
Wells, H(erbert) G(eorge)
1866-1946 .... **TCLC 6, 12, 19; SSC 6; WLC**
See also AAYA 18; BPFB 3; BRW 6; CA 121; CDBLB 1914-1945; CLR 64; DA; DAB; DAC; DAM MST, NOV; DLB 34, 70, 156, 178; EXPS; HGG; LAIT 3; MTCW 1, 2; RGEL 2; RGSF 2; SATA 20; SCFW; SFW 4; SSFS 3; SUFW; TEA; WCH; WLIT 4; YAW
Wells, Rosemary 1943- .... **CLC 12**
See also AAYA 13; BYA 7, 8; CA 85-88; CANR 48; CLR 16, 69; CWRI 5; MAICYA 1, 2; SAAS 1; SATA 18, 69, 114; YAW
Wells-Barnett, Ida B(ell)
1862-1931 .... **TCLC 125**
See also CA 182; DLB 23, 221
Welsh, Irvine 1958- .... **CLC 144**
See also CA 173; DLB 271
Welty, Eudora (Alice) 1909-2001 .. **CLC 1, 2, 5, 14, 22, 33, 105; SSC 1, 27, 51; WLC**
See also AMW; AMWR 1; BPFB 3; CA 9-12R; CABS 1; CANR 32, 65; CDALB 1941-1968; CN 7; CSW; DA; DAB; DAC; DAM MST, NOV; DLB 2, 102, 143; DLBD 12; DLBY 1987, 2001; EXPS; HGG; LAIT 3; MAWW; MTCW 1, 2; NFS 13, 15; RGAL 4; RGSF 2; RHW; SSFS 2, 10; TUS
Wen I-to 1899-1946 .... **TCLC 28**
Wentworth, Robert
See Hamilton, Edmond
Werfel, Franz (Viktor) 1890-1945 ... **TCLC 8**
See also CA 161; DLB 81, 124; RGWL 2, 3
Wergeland, Henrik Arnold
1808-1845 .... **NCLC 5**
Wersba, Barbara 1932- .... **CLC 30**
See also AAYA 2, 30; BYA 6, 12, 13; CA 29-32R, 182; CAAE 182; CANR 16, 38; CLR 3, 78; DLB 52; JRDA; MAICYA 1, 2; SAAS 2; SATA 1, 58; SATA-Essay 103; WYA; YAW

Wertmueller, Lina 1928- .... **CLC 16**
See also CA 97-100; CANR 39, 78
Wescott, Glenway 1901-1987 .. **CLC 13; SSC 35**
See also CA 13-16R; CANR 23, 70; DLB 4, 9, 102; RGAL 4
Wesker, Arnold 1932- .... **CLC 3, 5, 42**
See also CA 1-4R; CAAS 7; CANR 1, 33; CBD; CD 5; CDBLB 1960 to Present; DAB; DAM DRAM; DLB 13; MTCW 1; RGEL 2; TEA
Wesley, Richard (Errol) 1945- .... **CLC 7**
See also BW 1; CA 57-60; CAD; CANR 27; CD 5; DLB 38
Wessel, Johan Herman 1742-1785 .... **LC 7**
West, Anthony (Panther)
1914-1987 .... **CLC 50**
See also CA 45-48; CANR 3, 19; DLB 15
West, C. P.
See Wodehouse, P(elham) G(renville)
West, Cornel (Ronald) 1953- .... **CLC 134; BLCS**
See also CA 144; CANR 91; DLB 246
West, Delno C(loyde), Jr. 1936- .... **CLC 70**
See also CA 57-60
West, Dorothy 1907-1998 .... **TCLC 108**
See also BW 2; CA 143; DLB 76; HR 3
West, (Mary) Jessamyn 1902-1984 ... **CLC 7, 17**
See also CA 9-12R; CANR 27; DLB 6; DLBY 1984; MTCW 1, 2; RGAL 4; RHW; SATA-Obit 37; TCWW 2; TUS; YAW
West, Morris L(anglo) 1916-1999 ..... **CLC 6, 33**
See also BPFB 3; CA 5-8R; CANR 24, 49, 64; CN 7; CPW; MTCW 1, 2
West, Nathanael 1903-1940 .... **TCLC 1, 14, 44; SSC 16**
See also AMW; BPFB 3; CA 125; CDALB 1929-1941; DLB 4, 9, 28; MTCW 1, 2; RGAL 4; TUS
West, Owen
See Koontz, Dean R(ay)
West, Paul 1930- .... **CLC 7, 14, 96**
See also CA 13-16R; CAAS 7; CANR 22, 53, 76, 89; CN 7; DLB 14; INT CANR-22; MTCW 2
West, Rebecca 1892-1983 ... **CLC 7, 9, 31, 50**
See also BPFB 3; BRWS 3; CA 5-8R; CANR 19; DLB 36; DLBY 1983; FW; MTCW 1, 2; NCFS 4; RGEL 2; TEA
Westall, Robert (Atkinson)
1929-1993 .... **CLC 17**
See also AAYA 12; BYA 2, 6, 7, 8, 9; CA 69-72; CANR 18, 68; CLR 13; FANT; JRDA; MAICYA 1, 2; MAICYAS 1; SAAS 2; SATA 23, 69; SATA-Obit 75; WYA; YAW
Westermarck, Edward 1862-1939 . **TCLC 87**
Westlake, Donald E(dwin) 1933- . **CLC 7, 33**
See also BPFB 3; CA 17-20R; CAAS 13; CANR 16, 44, 65, 94; CMW 4; CPW; DAM POP; INT CANR-16; MSW; MTCW 2
Westmacott, Mary
See Christie, Agatha (Mary Clarissa)
Weston, Allen
See Norton, Andre
Wetcheek, J. L.
See Feuchtwanger, Lion
Wetering, Janwillem van de
See van de Wetering, Janwillem
Wetherald, Agnes Ethelwyn
1857-1940 .... **TCLC 81**
See also CA 202; DLB 99
Wetherell, Elizabeth
See Warner, Susan (Bogert)

Whale, James 1889-1957 .... **TCLC 63**
Whalen, Philip 1923- .... **CLC 6, 29**
See also CA 9-12R; CANR 5, 39; CP 7; DLB 16; WP
Wharton, Edith (Newbold Jones)
1862-1937 .... **TCLC 3, 9, 27, 53, 129; SSC 6; WLC**
See also AAYA 25; AMW; AMWR 1; BPFB 3; CA 132; CDALB 1865-1917; DA; DAB; DAC; DAM MST, NOV; DLB 4, 9, 12, 78, 189; DLBD 13; EXPS; HGG; LAIT 2, 3; MAWW; MTCW 1, 2; NFS 5, 11, 15; RGAL 4; RGSF 2; RHW; SSFS 6, 7; SUFW; TUS
Wharton, James
See Mencken, H(enry) L(ouis)
Wharton, William (a pseudonym) . **CLC 18, 37**
See also CA 93-96; DLBY 1980; INT 93-96
Wheatley (Peters), Phillis
1753(?)-1784 ... **LC 3, 50; BLC 3; PC 3; WLC**
See also AFAW 1, 2; CDALB 1640-1865; DA; DAC; DAM MST, MULT, POET; DLB 31, 50; EXPP; PFS 13; RGAL 4
Wheelock, John Hall 1886-1978 ..... **CLC 14**
See also CA 13-16R; CANR 14; DLB 45
White, Babington
See Braddon, Mary Elizabeth
White, E(lwyn) B(rooks)
1899-1985 .... **CLC 10, 34, 39**
See also AITN 2; AMWS 1; CA 13-16R; CANR 16, 37; CDALBS; CLR 1, 21; CPW; DAM POP; DLB 11, 22; FANT; MAICYA 1, 2; MTCW 1, 2; RGAL 4; SATA 2, 29, 100; SATA-Obit 44; TUS
White, Edmund (Valentine III)
1940- .... **CLC 27, 110**
See also AAYA 7; CA 45-48; CANR 3, 19, 36, 62, 107; CN 7; DAM POP; DLB 227; MTCW 1, 2
White, Hayden V. 1928- .... **CLC 148**
See also CA 128; DLB 246
White, Patrick (Victor Martindale)
1912-1990 ...... **CLC 3, 4, 5, 7, 9, 18, 65, 69; SSC 39**
See also BRWS 1; CA 81-84; CANR 43; DLB 260; MTCW 1; RGEL 2; RGSF 2; RHW; TWA
White, Phyllis Dorothy James 1920-
See James, P. D.
See also CA 21-24R; CANR 17, 43, 65, 112; CMW 4; CN 7; CPW; DAM POP; MTCW 1, 2; TEA
White, T(erence) H(anbury)
1906-1964 .... **CLC 30**
See also AAYA 22; BPFB 3; BYA 4, 5; CA 73-76; CANR 37; DLB 160; FANT; JRDA; LAIT 1; MAICYA 1, 2; RGEL 2; SATA 12; SUFW 1; YAW
White, Terence de Vere 1912-1994 ... **CLC 49**
See also CA 49-52; CANR 3
White, Walter
See White, Walter F(rancis)
White, Walter F(rancis)
1893-1955 .... **TCLC 15; BLC 3**
See also BW 1; CA 124; DAM MULT; DLB 51; HR 3
White, William Hale 1831-1913
See Rutherford, Mark
See also CA 189
Whitehead, Alfred North
1861-1947 .... **TCLC 97**
See also CA 165; DLB 100, 262
Whitehead, E(dward) A(nthony)
1933- .... **CLC 5**
See also CA 65-68; CANR 58; CBD; CD 5
Whitehead, Ted
See Whitehead, E(dward) A(nthony)

Whitemore, Hugh (John) 1936- .... **CLC 37**
See also CA 132; CANR 77; CBD; CD 5; INT CA-132

Whitman, Sarah Helen (Power) 1803-1878 .... **NCLC 19**
See also DLB 1, 243

Whitman, Walt(er) 1819-1892 .. **NCLC 4, 31, 81; PC 3; WLC**
See also AAYA 42; AMW; AMWR 1; CDALB 1640-1865; DA; DAB; DAC; DAM MST, POET; DLB 3, 64, 224, 250; EXPP; LAIT 2; PAB; PFS 2, 3, 13; RGAL 4; SATA 20; TUS; WP; WYAS 1

Whitney, Phyllis A(yame) 1903- .... **CLC 42**
See also AAYA 36; AITN 2; BEST 90:3; CA 1-4R; CANR 3, 25, 38, 60; CLR 59; CMW 4; CPW; DAM POP; JRDA; MAICYA 1, 2; MTCW 2; RHW; SATA 1, 30; YAW

Whittemore, (Edward) Reed (Jr.) 1919- .... **CLC 4**
See also CA 9-12R; CAAS 8; CANR 4; CP 7; DLB 5

Whittier, John Greenleaf 1807-1892 .... **NCLC 8, 59**
See also AMWS 1; DLB 1, 243; RGAL 4

Whittlebot, Hernia
See Coward, Noel (Peirce)

Wicker, Thomas Grey 1926-
See Wicker, Tom
See also CA 65-68; CANR 21, 46

Wicker, Tom .... **CLC 7**
See also Wicker, Thomas Grey

Wideman, John Edgar 1941- ...... **CLC 5, 34, 36, 67, 122; BLC 3**
See also AFAW 1, 2; AMWS 10; BPFB 1; BW 2, 3; CA 85-88; CANR 14, 42, 67, 109; CN 7; DAM MULT; DLB 33, 143; MTCW 2; RGAL 4; RGSF 2; SSFS 6, 12

Wiebe, Rudy (Henry) 1934- .. **CLC 6, 11, 14, 138**
See also CA 37-40R; CANR 42, 67; CN 7; DAC; DAM MST; DLB 60; RHW

Wieland, Christoph Martin 1733-1813 .... **NCLC 17**
See also DLB 97; EW 4; RGWL 2, 3

Wiene, Robert 1881-1938 .... **TCLC 56**

Wieners, John 1934- .... **CLC 7**
See also CA 13-16R; CP 7; DLB 16; WP

Wiesel, Elie(zer) 1928- .... **CLC 3, 5, 11, 37, 165; WLCS**
See also AAYA 7; AITN 1; CA 5-8R; CAAS 4; CANR 8, 40, 65; CDALBS; DA; DAB; DAC; DAM MST, NOV; DLB 83; DLBY 1987; INT CANR-8; LAIT 4; MTCW 1, 2; NCFS 4; NFS 4; RGWL 3; SATA 56; YAW

Wiggins, Marianne 1947- .... **CLC 57**
See also BEST 89:3; CA 130; CANR 60

Wiggs, Susan .... **CLC 70**
See also CA 201

Wight, James Alfred 1916-1995
See Herriot, James
See also CA 77-80; SATA 55; SATA-Brief 44

Wilbur, Richard (Purdy) 1921- ..... **CLC 3, 6, 9, 14, 53, 110**
See also AMWS 3; CA 1-4R; CABS 2; CANR 2, 29, 76, 93; CDALBS; CP 7; DA; DAB; DAC; DAM MST, POET; DLB 5, 169; EXPP; INT CANR-29; MTCW 1, 2; PAB; PFS 11, 12; RGAL 4; SATA 9, 108; WP

Wild, Peter 1940- .... **CLC 14**
See also CA 37-40R; CP 7; DLB 5

Wilde, Oscar (Fingal O'Flahertie Wills) 1854(?)-1900 ..... **TCLC 1, 8, 23, 41; DC 17; SSC 11; WLC**
See also BRW 5; BRWR 2; CA 119; CANR 112; CDBLB 1890-1914; DA; DAB; DAC; DAM DRAM, MST, NOV; DFS 4, 8, 9; DLB 10, 19, 34, 57, 141, 156, 190; EXPS; FANT; RGEL 2; RGSF 2; SATA 24; SSFS 7; SUFW; TEA; WCH; WLIT 4

Wilder, Billy .... **CLC 20**
See also Wilder, Samuel
See also DLB 26

Wilder, Samuel 1906-2002
See Wilder, Billy
See also CA 89-92

Wilder, Stephen
See Marlowe, Stephen

Wilder, Thornton (Niven) 1897-1975 .. **CLC 1, 5, 6, 10, 15, 35, 82; DC 1; WLC**
See also AAYA 29; AITN 2; AMW; CA 13-16R; CAD; CANR 40; CDALBS; DA; DAB; DAC; DAM DRAM, MST, NOV; DFS 1, 4; DLB 4, 7, 9, 228; DLBY 1997; LAIT 3; MTCW 1, 2; RGAL 4; RHW; WYAS 1

Wilding, Michael 1942- ...... **CLC 73; SSC 50**
See also CA 104; CANR 24, 49, 106; CN 7; RGSF 2

Wiley, Richard 1944- .... **CLC 44**
See also CA 129; CANR 71

Wilhelm, Kate .... **CLC 7**
See also Wilhelm, Katie (Gertrude)
See also AAYA 20; CAAS 5; DLB 8; INT CANR-17; SCFW 2

Wilhelm, Katie (Gertrude) 1928-
See Wilhelm, Kate
See also CA 37-40R; CANR 17, 36, 60, 94; MTCW 1; SFW 4

Wilkins, Mary
See Freeman, Mary E(leanor) Wilkins

Willard, Nancy 1936- .... **CLC 7, 37**
See also BYA 5; CA 89-92; CANR 10, 39, 68, 107; CLR 5; CWP; CWRI 5; DLB 5, 52; FANT; MAICYA 1, 2; MTCW 1; SATA 37, 71, 127; SATA-Brief 30; SUFW 2

William of Ockham 1290-1349 ..... **CMLC 32**

Williams, Ben Ames 1889-1953 ..... **TCLC 89**
See also CA 183; DLB 102

Williams, C(harles) K(enneth) 1936- .... **CLC 33, 56, 148**
See also CA 37-40R; CAAS 26; CANR 57, 106; CP 7; DAM POET; DLB 5

Williams, Charles
See Collier, James Lincoln

Williams, Charles (Walter Stansby) 1886-1945 .... **TCLC 1, 11**
See also CA 163; DLB 100, 153, 255; FANT; RGEL 2; SUFW 1

Williams, (George) Emlyn 1905-1987 .... **CLC 15**
See also CA 104; CANR 36; DAM DRAM; DLB 10, 77; MTCW 1

Williams, Hank 1923-1953 .... **TCLC 81**
See also Williams, Hiram King

Williams, Hiram Hank
See Williams, Hank

Williams, Hiram King
See Williams, Hank
See also CA 188

Williams, Hugo 1942- .... **CLC 42**
See also CA 17-20R; CANR 45; CP 7; DLB 40

Williams, J. Walker
See Wodehouse, P(elham) G(renville)

Williams, John A(lfred) 1925- ..... **CLC 5, 13; BLC 3**
See also AFAW 2; BW 2, 3; CA 53-56; CAAE 195; CAAS 3; CANR 6, 26, 51; CN 7; CSW; DAM MULT; DLB 2, 33; INT CANR-6; RGAL 4; SFW 4

Williams, Jonathan (Chamberlain) 1929- .... **CLC 13**
See also CA 9-12R; CAAS 12; CANR 8, 108; CP 7; DLB 5

Williams, Joy 1944- .... **CLC 31**
See also CA 41-44R; CANR 22, 48, 97

Williams, Norman 1952- .... **CLC 39**
See also CA 118

Williams, Sherley Anne 1944-1999 . **CLC 89; BLC 3**
See also AFAW 2; BW 2, 3; CA 73-76; CANR 25, 82; DAM MULT, POET; DLB 41; INT CANR-25; SATA 78; SATA-Obit 116

Williams, Shirley
See Williams, Sherley Anne

Williams, Tennessee 1911-1983 . **CLC 1, 2, 5, 7, 8, 11, 15, 19, 30, 39, 45, 71, 111; DC 4; WLC**
See also AAYA 31; AITN 1, 2; AMW; CA 5-8R; CABS 3; CAD; CANR 31; CDALB 1941-1968; DA; DAB; DAC; DAM DRAM, MST, NOV; DFS 1, 3, 7, 12; DLB 7; DLBD 4; DLBY 1983; GLL 1; LAIT 4; MTCW 1, 2; RGAL 4; TUS

Williams, Thomas (Alonzo) 1926-1990 .... **CLC 14**
See also CA 1-4R; CANR 2

Williams, William C.
See Williams, William Carlos

Williams, William Carlos 1883-1963 .... **CLC 1, 2, 5, 9, 13, 22, 42, 67; PC 7; SSC 31**
See also AMW; AMWR 1; CA 89-92; CANR 34; CDALB 1917-1929; DA; DAB; DAC; DAM MST, POET; DLB 4, 16, 54, 86; EXPP; MTCW 1, 2; NCFS 4; PAB; PFS 1, 6, 11; RGAL 4; RGSF 2; TUS; WP

Williamson, David (Keith) 1942- ...... **CLC 56**
See also CA 103; CANR 41; CD 5

Williamson, Ellen Douglas 1905-1984
See Douglas, Ellen
See also CA 17-20R; CANR 39

Williamson, Jack .... **CLC 29**
See also Williamson, John Stewart
See also CAAS 8; DLB 8; SCFW 2

Williamson, John Stewart 1908-
See Williamson, Jack
See also CA 17-20R; CANR 23, 70; SFW 4

Willie, Frederick
See Lovecraft, H(oward) P(hillips)

Willingham, Calder (Baynard, Jr.) 1922-1995 .... **CLC 5, 51**
See also CA 5-8R; CANR 3; CSW; DLB 2, 44; IDFW 3, 4; MTCW 1

Willis, Charles
See Clarke, Arthur C(harles)

Willy
See Colette, (Sidonie-Gabrielle)

Willy, Colette
See Colette, (Sidonie-Gabrielle)
See also GLL 1

Wilmot, John 1647-1680 .... **LC 75**
See also Rochester
See also BRW 2; DLB 131; PAB

Wilson, A(ndrew) N(orman) 1950- .. **CLC 33**
See also BRWS 6; CA 122; CN 7; DLB 14, 155, 194; MTCW 2

Wilson, Angus (Frank Johnstone) 1913-1991 . **CLC 2, 3, 5, 25, 34; SSC 21**
See also BRWS 1; CA 5-8R; CANR 21; DLB 15, 139, 155; MTCW 1, 2; RGEL 2; RGSF 2

Wilson, August 1945- ... **CLC 39, 50, 63, 118; BLC 3; DC 2; WLCS**
See also AAYA 16; AFAW 2; AMWS 8; BW 2, 3; CA 122; CAD; CANR 42, 54, 76; CD 5; DA; DAB; DAC; DAM DRAM, MST, MULT; DFS 15; DLB 228; LAIT 4; MTCW 1, 2; RGAL 4

Wilson, Brian 1942- .... **CLC 12**

Wilson, Colin 1931- .... **CLC 3, 14**
See also CA 1-4R; CAAS 5; CANR 1, 22, 33, 77; CMW 4; CN 7; DLB 14, 194; HGG; MTCW 1; SFW 4

Wilson, Dirk
See Pohl, Frederik

Wilson, Edmund 1895-1972 .. **CLC 1, 2, 3, 8, 24**
See also AMW; CA 1-4R; CANR 1, 46, 110; DLB 63; MTCW 1, 2; RGAL 4; TUS

Wilson, Ethel Davis (Bryant)
1888(?)-1980 .... **CLC 13**
See also CA 102; DAC; DAM POET; DLB 68; MTCW 1; RGEL 2

Wilson, Harriet
See Wilson, Harriet E. Adams
See also DLB 239

Wilson, Harriet E.
See Wilson, Harriet E. Adams
See also DLB 243

Wilson, Harriet E. Adams
1827(?)-1863(?) .... **NCLC 78; BLC 3**
See also Wilson, Harriet; Wilson, Harriet E.
See also DAM MULT; DLB 50

Wilson, John 1785-1854 .... **NCLC 5**

Wilson, John (Anthony) Burgess 1917-1993
See Burgess, Anthony
See also CA 1-4R; CANR 2, 46; DAC; DAM NOV; MTCW 1, 2; NFS 15; TEA

Wilson, Lanford 1937- .... **CLC 7, 14, 36**
See also CA 17-20R; CABS 3; CAD; CANR 45, 96; CD 5; DAM DRAM; DFS 4, 9, 12; DLB 7; TUS

Wilson, Robert M. 1944- .... **CLC 7, 9**
See also CA 49-52; CAD; CANR 2, 41; CD 5; MTCW 1

Wilson, Robert McLiam 1964- .... **CLC 59**
See also CA 132; DLB 267

Wilson, Sloan 1920- .... **CLC 32**
See also CA 1-4R; CANR 1, 44; CN 7

Wilson, Snoo 1948- .... **CLC 33**
See also CA 69-72; CBD; CD 5

Wilson, William S(mith) 1932- .... **CLC 49**
See also CA 81-84

Wilson, (Thomas) Woodrow
1856-1924 .... **TCLC 79**
See also CA 166; DLB 47

Wilson and Warnke eds. .... **CLC 65**

Winchilsea, Anne (Kingsmill) Finch
1661-1720
See Finch, Anne
See also RGEL 2

Windham, Basil
See Wodehouse, P(elham) G(renville)

Wingrove, David (John) 1954- .... **CLC 68**
See also CA 133; SFW 4

Winnemucca, Sarah 1844-1891 ..... **NCLC 79**
See also DAM MULT; DLB 175; NNAL; RGAL 4

Winstanley, Gerrard 1609-1676 .... **LC 52**

Wintergreen, Jane
See Duncan, Sara Jeannette

Winters, Janet Lewis .... **CLC 41**
See also Lewis, Janet
See also DLBY 1987

Winters, (Arthur) Yvor 1900-1968 .... **CLC 4, 8, 32**
See also AMWS 2; CA 11-12; CAP 1; DLB 48; MTCW 1; RGAL 4

Winterson, Jeanette 1959- .... **CLC 64, 158**
See also BRWS 4; CA 136; CANR 58; CN 7; CPW; DAM POP; DLB 207, 261; FANT; FW; GLL 1; MTCW 1; RHW

Winthrop, John 1588-1649 .... **LC 31**
See also DLB 24, 30

Wirth, Louis 1897-1952 .... **TCLC 92**

Wiseman, Frederick 1930- .... **CLC 20**
See also CA 159

Wister, Owen 1860-1938 .... **TCLC 21**
See also BPFB 3; CA 162; DLB 9, 78, 186; RGAL 4; SATA 62; TCWW 2

Witkacy
See Witkiewicz, Stanislaw Ignacy

Witkiewicz, Stanislaw Ignacy
1885-1939 .... **TCLC 8**
See also CA 162; CDWLB 4; DLB 215; EW 10; RGWL 2, 3; SFW 4

Wittgenstein, Ludwig (Josef Johann)
1889-1951 .... **TCLC 59**
See also CA 164; DLB 262; MTCW 2

Wittig, Monique 1935(?)- .... **CLC 22**
See also CA 135; CWW 2; DLB 83; FW; GLL 1

Wittlin, Jozef 1896-1976 .... **CLC 25**
See also CA 49-52; CANR 3

Wodehouse, P(elham) G(renville)
1881-1975 ... **CLC 1, 2, 5, 10, 22; SSC 2**
See also AITN 2; BRWS 3; CA 45-48; CANR 3, 33; CDBLB 1914-1945; CPW 1; DAB; DAC; DAM NOV; DLB 34, 162; MTCW 1, 2; RGEL 2; RGSF 2; SATA 22; SSFS 10; TCLC 108

Woiwode, L.
See Woiwode, Larry (Alfred)

Woiwode, Larry (Alfred) 1941- ... **CLC 6, 10**
See also CA 73-76; CANR 16, 94; CN 7; DLB 6; INT CANR-16

Wojciechowska, Maia (Teresa)
1927-2002 .... **CLC 26**
See also AAYA 8; BYA 3; CA 9-12R, 183; CAAE 183; CANR 4, 41; CLR 1; JRDA; MAICYA 1, 2; SAAS 1; SATA 1, 28, 83; SATA-Essay 104; SATA-Obit 134; YAW

Wojtyla, Karol
See John Paul II, Pope

Wolf, Christa 1929- .... **CLC 14, 29, 58, 150**
See also CA 85-88; CANR 45; CDWLB 2; CWW 2; DLB 75; FW; MTCW 1; RGWL 2, 3; SSFS 14

Wolf, Naomi 1962- .... **CLC 157**
See also CA 141; CANR 110; FW

Wolfe, Gene (Rodman) 1931- .... **CLC 25**
See also AAYA 35; CA 57-60; CAAS 9; CANR 6, 32, 60; CPW; DAM POP; DLB 8; FANT; MTCW 2; SATA 118; SCFW 2; SFW 4; SUFW 2

Wolfe, George C. 1954- .... **CLC 49; BLCS**
See also CA 149; CAD; CD 5

Wolfe, Thomas (Clayton)
1900-1938 .... **TCLC 4, 13, 29, 61; SSC 33; WLC**
See also AMW; BPFB 3; CA 132; CANR 102; CDALB 1929-1941; DA; DAB; DAC; DAM MST, NOV; DLB 9, 102, 229; DLBD 2, 16; DLBY 1985, 1997; MTCW 1, 2; RGAL 4; TUS

Wolfe, Thomas Kennerly, Jr.
1930- .... **CLC 147**
See also Wolfe, Tom
See also CA 13-16R; CANR 9, 33, 70, 104; DAM POP; DLB 185; INT CANR-9; MTCW 1, 2; TUS

Wolfe, Tom .... **CLC 1, 2, 9, 15, 35, 51**
See also Wolfe, Thomas Kennerly, Jr.
See also AAYA 8; AITN 2; AMWS 3; BEST 89:1; BPFB 3; CN 7; CPW; CSW; DLB 152; LAIT 5; RGAL 4

Wolff, Geoffrey (Ansell) 1937- .... **CLC 41**
See also CA 29-32R; CANR 29, 43, 78

Wolff, Sonia
See Levitin, Sonia (Wolff)

Wolff, Tobias (Jonathan Ansell)
1945- .... **CLC 39, 64**
See also AAYA 16; AMWS 7; BEST 90:2; BYA 12; CA 117; CAAS 22; CANR 54, 76, 96; CN 7; CSW; DLB 130; INT CA-117; MTCW 2; RGAL 4; RGSF 2; SSFS 4, 11

Wolfram von Eschenbach c. 1170-c. 1220 .... **CMLC 5**
See also Eschenbach, Wolfram von
See also CDWLB 2; DLB 138; EW 1; RGWL 2

Wolitzer, Hilma 1930- .... **CLC 17**
See also CA 65-68; CANR 18, 40; INT CANR-18; SATA 31; YAW

Wollstonecraft, Mary 1759-1797 ..... **LC 5, 50**
See also BRWS 3; CDBLB 1789-1832; DLB 39, 104, 158, 252; FW; LAIT 1; RGEL 2; TEA; WLIT 3

Wonder, Stevie .... **CLC 12**
See also Morris, Steveland Judkins

Wong, Jade Snow 1922- .... **CLC 17**
See also CA 109; CANR 91; SATA 112

Woodberry, George Edward
1855-1930 .... **TCLC 73**
See also CA 165; DLB 71, 103

Woodcott, Keith
See Brunner, John (Kilian Houston)

Woodruff, Robert W.
See Mencken, H(enry) L(ouis)

Woolf, (Adeline) Virginia
1882-1941 .. **TCLC 1, 5, 20, 43, 56, 101, 123, 128; SSC 7; WLC**
See also BPFB 3; BRW 7; BRWR 1; CA 130; CANR 64; CDBLB 1914-1945; DA; DAB; DAC; DAM MST, NOV; DLB 36, 100, 162; DLBD 10; EXPS; FW; LAIT 3; MTCW 1, 2; NCFS 2; NFS 8, 12; RGEL 2; RGSF 2; SSFS 4, 12; TEA; WLIT 4

Woollcott, Alexander (Humphreys)
1887-1943 .... **TCLC 5**
See also CA 161; DLB 29

Woolrich, Cornell .... **CLC 77**
See also Hopley-Woolrich, Cornell George
See also MSW

Woolson, Constance Fenimore
1840-1894 .... **NCLC 82**
See also DLB 12, 74, 189, 221; RGAL 4

Wordsworth, Dorothy 1771-1855 .. **NCLC 25**
See also DLB 107

Wordsworth, William 1770-1850 .. **NCLC 12, 38, 111; PC 4; WLC**
See also BRW 4; CDBLB 1789-1832; DA; DAB; DAC; DAM MST, POET; DLB 93, 107; EXPP; PAB; PFS 2; RGEL 2; TEA; WLIT 3; WP

Wotton, Sir Henry 1568-1639 .... **LC 68**
See also DLB 121; RGEL 2

Wouk, Herman 1915- .... **CLC 1, 9, 38**
See also BPFB 2, 3; CA 5-8R; CANR 6, 33, 67; CDALBS; CN 7; CPW; DAM NOV, POP; DLBY 1982; INT CANR-6; LAIT 4; MTCW 1, 2; NFS 7; TUS

Wright, Charles (Penzel, Jr.) 1935- .. **CLC 6, 13, 28, 119, 146**
See also AMWS 5; CA 29-32R; CAAS 7; CANR 23, 36, 62, 88; CP 7; DLB 165; DLBY 1982; MTCW 1, 2; PFS 10

Wright, Charles Stevenson 1932- ... **CLC 49; BLC 3**
See also BW 1; CA 9-12R; CANR 26; CN 7; DAM MULT, POET; DLB 33

Wright, Frances 1795-1852 .... **NCLC 74**
See also DLB 73

Wright, Frank Lloyd 1867-1959 ...... **TCLC 95**
See also AAYA 33; CA 174

Wright, Jack R.
See Harris, Mark

Wright, James (Arlington)
1927-1980 .... **CLC 3, 5, 10, 28; PC 36**
See also AITN 2; AMWS 3; CA 49-52; CANR 4, 34, 64; CDALBS; DAM POET; DLB 5, 169; EXPP; MTCW 1, 2; PFS 7, 8; RGAL 4; TUS; WP

Wright, Judith (Arundell)
1915-2000 .... **CLC 11, 53; PC 14**
See also CA 13-16R; CANR 31, 76, 93; CP 7; CWP; DLB 260; MTCW 1, 2; PFS 8; RGEL 2; SATA 14; SATA-Obit 121

Wright, L(aurali) R. 1939- .... **CLC 44**
See also CA 138; CMW 4

Wright, Richard (Nathaniel)
1908-1960 .... **CLC 1, 3, 4, 9, 14, 21, 48, 74; BLC 3; SSC 2; WLC**
See also AAYA 5, 42; AFAW 1, 2; AMW; BPFB 3; BW 1; BYA 2; CA 108; CANR 64; CDALB 1929-1941; DA; DAB; DAC; DAM MST, MULT, NOV; DLB 76, 102; DLBD 2; EXPN; LAIT 3, 4; MTCW 1, 2; NCFS 1; NFS 1, 7; RGAL 4; RGSF 2; SSFS 3, 9, 15; TUS; YAW

Wright, Richard B(ruce) 1937- .... **CLC 6**
See also CA 85-88; DLB 53

Wright, Rick 1945- .... **CLC 35**

Wright, Rowland
See Wells, Carolyn

Wright, Stephen 1946- .... **CLC 33**

Wright, Willard Huntington 1888-1939
See Van Dine, S. S.
See also CA 189; CMW 4; DLBD 16

Wright, William 1930- .... **CLC 44**
See also CA 53-56; CANR 7, 23

Wroth, Lady Mary 1587-1653(?) .... **LC 30; PC 38**
See also DLB 121

Wu Ch'eng-en 1500(?)-1582(?) .... **LC 7**

Wu Ching-tzu 1701-1754 .... **LC 2**

Wurlitzer, Rudolph 1938(?)- .... **CLC 2, 4, 15**
See also CA 85-88; CN 7; DLB 173

Wyatt, Sir Thomas c. 1503-1542 . **LC 70; PC 27**
See also BRW 1; DLB 132; EXPP; RGEL 2; TEA

Wycherley, William 1640-1716 .... **LC 8, 21**
See also BRW 2; CDBLB 1660-1789; DAM DRAM; DLB 80; RGEL 2

Wylie, Elinor (Morton Hoyt)
1885-1928 .... **TCLC 8; PC 23**
See also AMWS 1; CA 162; DLB 9, 45; EXPP; RGAL 4

Wylie, Philip (Gordon) 1902-1971 ... **CLC 43**
See also CA 21-22; CAP 2; DLB 9; SFW 4

Wyndham, John .... **CLC 19**
See also Harris, John (Wyndham Parkes Lucas) Beynon
See also DLB 255; SCFW 2

Wyss, Johann David Von
1743-1818 .... **NCLC 10**
See also JRDA; MAICYA 1, 2; SATA 29; SATA-Brief 27

Xenophon c. 430B.C.-c. 354B.C. ... **CMLC 17**
See also AW 1; DLB 176; RGWL 2, 3

Xingjian, Gao 1940- .... **CLC 167**
See also Gao Xingjian
See also CA 193; RGWL 3

Yakumo Koizumi
See Hearn, (Patricio) Lafcadio (Tessima Carlos)

Yamada, Mitsuye (May) 1923- .... **PC 44**
See also CA 77-80

Yamamoto, Hisaye 1921- .... **SSC 34; AAL**
See also DAM MULT; LAIT 4; SSFS 14

Yanez, Jose Donoso
See Donoso (Yanez), Jose

Yanovsky, Basile S.
See Yanovsky, V(assily) S(emenovich)

Yanovsky, V(assily) S(emenovich)
1906-1989 .... **CLC 2, 18**
See also CA 97-100

Yates, Richard 1926-1992 .... **CLC 7, 8, 23**
See also AMWS 11; CA 5-8R; CANR 10, 43; DLB 2, 234; DLBY 1981, 1992; INT CANR-10

Yeats, W. B.
See Yeats, William Butler

Yeats, William Butler 1865-1939 .... **TCLC 1, 11, 18, 31, 93, 116; PC 20; WLC**
See also BRW 6; BRWR 1; CA 127; CANR 45; CDBLB 1890-1914; DA; DAB; DAC; DAM DRAM, MST, POET; DLB 10, 19, 98, 156; EXPP; MTCW 1, 2; NCFS 3; PAB; PFS 1, 2, 5, 7, 13, 15; RGEL 2; TEA; WLIT 4; WP

Yehoshua, A(braham) B. 1936- .. **CLC 13, 31**
See also CA 33-36R; CANR 43, 90; RGSF 2; RGWL 3

Yellow Bird
See Ridge, John Rollin

Yep, Laurence Michael 1948- .... **CLC 35**
See also AAYA 5, 31; BYA 7; CA 49-52; CANR 1, 46, 92; CLR 3, 17, 54; DLB 52; FANT; JRDA; MAICYA 1, 2; MAICYAS 1; SATA 7, 69, 123; WYA; YAW

Yerby, Frank G(arvin) 1916-1991 . **CLC 1, 7, 22; BLC 3**
See also BPFB 3; BW 1, 3; CA 9-12R; CANR 16, 52; DAM MULT; DLB 76; INT CANR-16; MTCW 1; RGAL 4; RHW

Yesenin, Sergei Alexandrovich
See Esenin, Sergei (Alexandrovich)

Yevtushenko, Yevgeny (Alexandrovich)
1933- .... **CLC 1, 3, 13, 26, 51, 126; PC 40**
See also Evtushenko, Evgenii Aleksandrovich
See also CA 81-84; CANR 33, 54; CWW 2; DAM POET; MTCW 1

Yezierska, Anzia 1885(?)-1970 .... **CLC 46**
See also CA 126; DLB 28, 221; FW; MTCW 1; RGAL 4; SSFS 15

Yglesias, Helen 1915- .... **CLC 7, 22**
See also CA 37-40R; CAAS 20; CANR 15, 65, 95; CN 7; INT CANR-15; MTCW 1

Yokomitsu, Riichi 1898-1947 .... **TCLC 47**
See also CA 170

Yonge, Charlotte (Mary)
1823-1901 .... **TCLC 48**
See also CA 163; DLB 18, 163; RGEL 2; SATA 17; WCH

York, Jeremy
See Creasey, John

York, Simon
See Heinlein, Robert A(nson)

Yorke, Henry Vincent 1905-1974 ..... **CLC 13**
See also Green, Henry
See also CA 85-88

Yosano Akiko 1878-1942 .... **TCLC 59; PC 11**
See also CA 161; RGWL 3

Yoshimoto, Banana .... **CLC 84**
See also Yoshimoto, Mahoko
See also NFS 7

Yoshimoto, Mahoko 1964-
See Yoshimoto, Banana
See also CA 144; CANR 98

Young, Al(bert James) 1939- . **CLC 19; BLC 3**
See also BW 2, 3; CA 29-32R; CANR 26, 65, 109; CN 7; CP 7; DAM MULT; DLB 33

Young, Andrew (John) 1885-1971 ...... **CLC 5**
See also CA 5-8R; CANR 7, 29; RGEL 2

Young, Collier
See Bloch, Robert (Albert)

Young, Edward 1683-1765 .... **LC 3, 40**
See also DLB 95; RGEL 2

Young, Marguerite (Vivian)
1909-1995 .... **CLC 82**
See also CA 13-16; CAP 1; CN 7

Young, Neil 1945- .... **CLC 17**
See also CA 110; CCA 1

Young Bear, Ray A. 1950- .... **CLC 94**
See also CA 146; DAM MULT; DLB 175; NNAL

Yourcenar, Marguerite 1903-1987 ... **CLC 19, 38, 50, 87**
See also BPFB 3; CA 69-72; CANR 23, 60, 93; DAM NOV; DLB 72; DLBY 1988; EW 12; GFL 1789 to the Present; GLL 1; MTCW 1, 2; RGWL 2, 3

Yuan, Chu 340(?)B.C.-278(?)B.C. . **CMLC 36**

Yurick, Sol 1925- .... **CLC 6**
See also CA 13-16R; CANR 25; CN 7

Zabolotsky, Nikolai Alekseevich
1903-1958 .... **TCLC 52**
See also CA 164

Zagajewski, Adam 1945- .... **PC 27**
See also CA 186; DLB 232

Zalygin, Sergei -2000 .... **CLC 59**

Zamiatin, Evgenii
See Zamyatin, Evgeny Ivanovich
See also RGSF 2; RGWL 2, 3

Zamiatin, Evgenii Ivanovich
See Zamyatin, Evgeny Ivanovich

Zamiatin, Yevgenii
See Zamyatin, Evgeny Ivanovich

Zamora, Bernice (B. Ortiz) 1938- .. **CLC 89; HLC 2**
See also CA 151; CANR 80; DAM MULT; DLB 82; HW 1, 2

Zamyatin, Evgeny Ivanovich
1884-1937 .... **TCLC 8, 37**
See also Zamiatin, Evgenii; Zamiatin, Evgenii Ivanovich
See also CA 166; EW 10; SFW 4

Zangwill, Israel 1864-1926 ... **TCLC 16; SSC 44**
See also CA 167; CMW 4; DLB 10, 135, 197; RGEL 2

Zappa, Francis Vincent, Jr. 1940-1993
See Zappa, Frank
See also CA 108; CANR 57

Zappa, Frank .... **CLC 17**
See also Zappa, Francis Vincent, Jr.

Zaturenska, Marya 1902-1982 ..... **CLC 6, 11**
See also CA 13-16R; CANR 22

Zeami 1363-1443 .... **DC 7**
See also DLB 203; RGWL 2, 3

Zelazny, Roger (Joseph) 1937-1995 . **CLC 21**
See also AAYA 7; BPFB 3; CA 21-24R; CANR 26, 60; CN 7; DLB 8; FANT; MTCW 1, 2; SATA 57; SATA-Brief 39; SCFW; SFW 4; SUFW 1, 2

Zhdanov, Andrei Alexandrovich
1896-1948 .... **TCLC 18**
See also CA 167

Zhukovsky, Vasilii Andreevich
See Zhukovsky, Vasily (Andreevich)
See also DLB 205

Zhukovsky, Vasily (Andreevich)
1783-1852 .... **NCLC 35**
See also Zhukovsky, Vasilii Andreevich

Ziegenhagen, Eric .... **CLC 55**

Zimmer, Jill Schary
See Robinson, Jill

Zimmerman, Robert
See Dylan, Bob

Zindel, Paul 1936- .... **CLC 6, 26; DC 5**
See also AAYA 2, 37; BYA 2, 3, 8, 11, 14; CA 73-76; CAD; CANR 31, 65, 108; CD 5; CDALBS; CLR 3, 45; DA; DAB;

Zinov'Ev, A. A.
See Zinoviev, Alexander (Aleksandrovich)

Zinoviev, Alexander (Aleksandrovich)
1922- .... **CLC 19**
See also CA 133; CAAS 10

Zoilus
See Lovecraft, H(oward) P(hillips)

Zola, Emile (Edouard Charles Antoine)
1840-1902 ...... **TCLC 1, 6, 21, 41; WLC**
See also CA 138; DA; DAB; DAC; DAM MST, NOV; DLB 123; EW 7; GFL 1789 to the Present; IDTP; RGWL 2; TWA

Zoline, Pamela 1941- .... **CLC 62**
See also CA 161; SFW 4

Zoroaster 628(?)B.C.-551(?)B.C. ... **CMLC 40**

Zorrilla y Moral, Jose 1817-1893 .... **NCLC 6**

Zoshchenko, Mikhail (Mikhailovich)
1895-1958 .... **TCLC 15; SSC 15**
See also CA 160; RGSF 2; RGWL 3

Zuckmayer, Carl 1896-1977 .... **CLC 18**
See also CA 69-72; DLB 56, 124; RGWL 2, 3

Zuk, Georges
See Skelton, Robin
See also CCA 1

Zukofsky, Louis 1904-1978 ... **CLC 1, 2, 4, 7, 11, 18; PC 11**
See also AMWS 3; CA 9-12R; CANR 39; DAM POET; DLB 5, 165; MTCW 1; RGAL 4

Zweig, Paul 1935-1984 .... **CLC 34, 42**
See also CA 85-88

Zweig, Stefan 1881-1942 .... **TCLC 17**
See also CA 170; DLB 81, 118

Zwingli, Huldreich 1484-1531 .... **LC 37**
See also DLB 179

[Entry continued from previous page:]
DAC; DAM DRAM, MST, NOV; DFS 12; DLB 7, 52; JRDA; LAIT 5; MAICYA 1, 2; MTCW 1, 2; NFS 14; SATA 16, 58, 102; WYA; YAW

Literary Criticism Series
Cumulative Topic Index

This index lists all topic entries in Gale's *Classical and Medieval Literature Criticism* (CMLC), *Contemporary Literary Criticism* (CLC), *Drama Criticism* (DC), *Literature Criticism from 1400 to 1800* (LC), *Nineteenth-Century Literature Criticism* (NCLC), and *Twentieth-Century Literary Criticism* (TCLC). The index also lists topic entries in the Gale Critical Companion Collection, which includes the following publication: *Harlem Renaissance* (HR).

The Aesopic Fable LC 51: 1-100
    the British Aesopic Fable, 1-54
    the Aesopic tradition in non-English-speaking cultures, 55-66
    political uses of the Aesopic fable, 67-88
    the evolution of the Aesopic fable, 89-99

African-American Folklore and Literature TCLC 126: 1-67
    African-American folk tradition, 1-16
    representative writers, 16-34
    hallmark works, 35-48
    the study of African-American literature and folklore, 48-64

Age of Johnson LC 15: 1-87
    Johnson's London, 3-15
    aesthetics of neoclassicism, 15-36
    "age of prose and reason," 36-45
    clubmen and bluestockings, 45-56
    printing technology, 56-62
    periodicals: "a map of busy life," 62-74
    transition, 74-86

Age of Spenser LC 39: 1-70
    overviews and general studies, 2-21
    literary style, 22-34
    poets and the crown, 34-70

AIDS in Literature CLC 81: 365-416

Alcohol and Literature TCLC 70: 1-58
    overview, 2-8
    fiction, 8-48
    poetry and drama, 48-58

American Abolitionism NCLC 44: 1-73
    overviews and general studies, 2-26
    abolitionist ideals, 26-46
    the literature of abolitionism, 46-72

American Autobiography TCLC 86: 1-115
    overviews and general studies, 3-36
    American authors and autobiography, 36-82
    African-American autobiography, 82-114

American Black Humor Fiction TCLC 54: 1-85
    characteristics of black humor, 2-13
    origins and development, 13-38
    black humor distinguished from related literary trends, 38-60
    black humor and society, 60-75
    black humor reconsidered, 75-83

American Civil War in Literature NCLC 32: 1-109
    overviews and general studies, 2-20
    regional perspectives, 20-54
    fiction popular during the war, 54-79
    the historical novel, 79-108

American Frontier in Literature NCLC 28: 1-103
    definitions, 2-12
    development, 12-17
    nonfiction writing about the frontier, 17-30
    frontier fiction, 30-45
    frontier protagonists, 45-66
    portrayals of Native Americans, 66-86
    feminist readings, 86-98
    twentieth-century reaction against frontier literature, 98-100

American Humor Writing NCLC 52: 1-59
    overviews and general studies, 2-12
    the Old Southwest, 12-42
    broader impacts, 42-5
    women humorists, 45-58

American Mercury, **The** TCLC 74: 1-80

American Popular Song, Golden Age of TCLC 42: 1-49
    background and major figures, 2-34
    the lyrics of popular songs, 34-47

American Proletarian Literature TCLC 54: 86-175
    overviews and general studies, 87-95
    American proletarian literature and the American Communist Party, 95-111
    ideology and literary merit, 111-7
    novels, 117-36
    Gastonia, 136-48
    drama, 148-54
    journalism, 154-9
    proletarian literature in the United States, 159-74

American Romanticism NCLC 44: 74-138
    overviews and general studies, 74-84
    sociopolitical influences, 84-104
    Romanticism and the American frontier, 104-15
    thematic concerns, 115-37

American Western Literature TCLC 46: 1-100
    definition and development of American Western literature, 2-7
    characteristics of the Western novel, 8-23
    Westerns as history and fiction, 23-34
    critical reception of American Western literature, 34-41
    the Western hero, 41-73
    women in Western fiction, 73-91
    later Western fiction, 91-9

American Writers in Paris TCLC 98: 1-156
    overviews and general studies, 2-155

Anarchism NCLC 84: 1-97
    overviews and general studies, 2-23
    the French anarchist tradition, 23-56
    Anglo-American anarchism, 56-68
    anarchism: incidents and issues, 68-97

Animals in Literature TCLC 106: 1-120
    overviews and general studies, 2-8
    animals in American literature, 8-45
    animals in Canadian literature, 45-57
    animals in European literature, 57-100
    animals in Latin American literature, 100-06
    animals in women's literature, 106-20

Antebellum South, Literature of the NCLC 112:1-188
    overviews, 4-55
    culture of the Old South, 55-68
    antebellum fiction: pastoral and heroic romance, 68-120
    role of women: a subdued rebellion, 120-59
    slavery and the slave narrative, 159-85

The Apocalyptic Movement TCLC 106: 121-69

Aristotle CMLC 31:1-397
    philosophy, 3-100
    poetics, 101-219
    rhetoric, 220-301
    science, 302-397

Art and Literature TCLC 54: 176-248
    overviews and general studies, 176-93
    definitions, 193-219
    influence of visual arts on literature, 219-31
    spatial form in literature, 231-47

Arthurian Literature CMLC 10: 1-127
    historical context and literary beginnings, 2-27
    development of the legend through Malory, 27-64
    development of the legend from Malory to the Victorian Age, 65-81
    themes and motifs, 81-95
    principal characters, 95-125

Arthurian Revival NCLC 36: 1-77
overviews and general studies, 2-12
Tennyson and his influence, 12-43
other leading figures, 43-73
the Arthurian legend in the visual arts, 73-6

Australian Literature TCLC 50: 1-94
origins and development, 2-21
characteristics of Australian literature, 21-33
historical and critical perspectives, 33-41
poetry, 41-58
fiction, 58-76
drama, 76-82
Aboriginal literature, 82-91

Beat Generation, Literature of the TCLC 42: 50-102
overviews and general studies, 51-9
the Beat generation as a social phenomenon, 59-62
development, 62-5
Beat literature, 66-96
influence, 97-100

The Bell Curve Controversy CLC 91: 281-330

***Bildungsroman* in Nineteenth-Century Literature** NCLC 20: 92-168
surveys, 93-113
in Germany, 113-40
in England, 140-56
female *Bildungsroman,* 156-67

Bloomsbury Group TCLC 34: 1-73
history and major figures, 2-13
definitions, 13-7
influences, 17-27
thought, 27-40
prose, 40-52
and literary criticism, 52-4
political ideals, 54-61
response to, 61-71

The Blues in Literature TCLC 82: 1-71

Bly, Robert, *Iron John: A Book about Men and Men's Work* CLC 70: 414-62

The Book of J CLC 65: 289-311

British Ephemeral Literature LC 59: 1-70
overviews and general studies, 1-9
broadside ballads, 10-40
chapbooks, jestbooks, pamphlets, and newspapers, 40-69

Buddhism and Literature TCLC 70: 59-164
eastern literature, 60-113
western literature, 113-63

The *Bulletin* and the Rise of Australian Literary Nationalism NCLC 116: 1-121
overviews, 3-32
legend of the nineties, 32-55
Bulletin style, 55-71
Australian literary nationalism, 71-98
myth of the bush, 98-120

Businessman in American Literature TCLC 26: 1-48
portrayal of the businessman, 1-32
themes and techniques in business fiction, 32-47

The Calendar LC 55: 1-92
overviews and general studies, 2-19
measuring time, 19-28
calendars and culture, 28-60
calendar reform, 60-92

Captivity Narratives LC 82: 71-172
overviews, 72-107
captivity narratives and Puritanism, 108-34
captivity narratives and Native Americans, 134-49
influence on American literature, 149-72

Catholicism in Nineteenth-Century American Literature NCLC 64: 1-58
overviews, 3-14
polemical literature, 14-46
Catholicism in literature, 47-57

Celtic Mythology CMLC 26: 1-111
overviews and general studies, 2-22
Celtic myth as literature and history, 22-48
Celtic religion: Druids and divinities, 48-80
Fionn MacCuhaill and the Fenian cycle, 80-111

Celtic Twilight See Irish Literary Renaissance

Chartist Movement and Literature, The NCLC 60: 1-84
overview: nineteenth-century working-class fiction, 2-19
Chartist fiction and poetry, 19-73
the Chartist press, 73-84

Child Labor in Nineteenth-Century Literature NCLC 108: 1-133
overviews, 3-10
climbing boys and chimney sweeps, 10-16
the international traffic in children, 16-45
critics and reformers, 45-82
fictional representations of child laborers, 83-132

Children's Literature, Nineteenth-Century NCLC 52: 60-135
overviews and general studies, 61-72
moral tales, 72-89
fairy tales and fantasy, 90-119
making men/making women, 119-34

Christianity in Twentieth-Century Literature TCLC 110: 1-79
overviews and general studies, 2-31
Christianity in twentieth-century fiction, 31-78

The City and Literature TCLC 90: 1-124
overviews and general studies, 2-9
the city in American literature, 9-86
the city in European literature, 86-124

Civic Critics, Russian NCLC 20: 402-46
principal figures and background, 402-9
and Russian Nihilism, 410-6
aesthetic and critical views, 416-45

The Cockney School NCLC 68: 1-64
overview, 2-7
Blackwood's Magazine and the contemporary critical response, 7-24
the political and social import of the Cockneys and their critics, 24-63

Colonial America: The Intellectual Background LC 25: 1-98
overviews and general studies, 2-17
philosophy and politics, 17-31
early religious influences in Colonial America, 31-60
consequences of the Revolution, 60-78
religious influences in post-revolutionary America, 78-87
colonial literary genres, 87-97

Colonialism in Victorian English Literature NCLC 56: 1-77
overviews and general studies, 2-34
colonialism and gender, 34-51
monsters and the occult, 51-76

Columbus, Christopher, Books on the Quincentennial of His Arrival in the New World CLC 70: 329-60

Comic Books TCLC 66: 1-139
historical and critical perspectives, 2-48
superheroes, 48-67
underground comix, 67-88
comic books and society, 88-122
adult comics and graphic novels, 122-36

Commedia dell'Arte LC 83: 1-147
overviews, 2-7
origins and development, 7-23
characters and actors, 23-45
performance, 45-62
texts and authors, 62-100
influence in Europe, 100-46

Connecticut Wits NCLC 48: 1-95
overviews and general studies, 2-40
major works, 40-76
intellectual context, 76-95

Contemporary Southern Literature CLC 167: 1-132
criticism, 2-131

Crime in Literature TCLC 54: 249-307
evolution of the criminal figure in literature, 250-61
crime and society, 261-77
literary perspectives on crime and punishment, 277-88
writings by criminals, 288-306

The Crusades CMLC 38: 1-144
history of the Crusades, 3-60
literature of the Crusades, 60-116
the Crusades and the people: attitudes and influences, 116-44

Cyberpunk TCLC 106: 170-366
overviews and general studies, 171-88
feminism and cyberpunk, 188-230
history and cyberpunk, 230-70
sexuality and cyberpunk, 270-98
social issues and cyberpunk, 299-366

Czechoslovakian Literature of the Twentieth Century TCLC 42:103-96
through World War II, 104-35
de-Stalinization, the Prague Spring, and contemporary literature, 135-72
Slovak literature, 172-85
Czech science fiction, 185-93

Dadaism TCLC 46: 101-71
background and major figures, 102-16
definitions, 116-26
manifestos and commentary by Dadaists, 126-40
theater and film, 140-58
nature and characteristics of Dadaist writing, 158-70

Darwinism and Literature NCLC 32: 110-206
background, 110-31
direct responses to Darwin, 131-71
collateral effects of Darwinism, 171-205

Death in American Literature NCLC 92: 1-170
overviews and general studies, 2-32
death in the works of Emily Dickinson, 32-72
death in the works of Herman Melville, 72-101
death in the works of Edgar Allan Poe, 101-43
death in the works of Walt Whitman, 143-70

Death in Nineteenth-Century British Literature NCLC 68: 65-142
overviews and general studies, 66-92
responses to death, 92-102
feminist perspectives, 103-17
striving for immortality, 117-41

Death in Literature TCLC 78:1-183
fiction, 2-115
poetry, 115-46
drama, 146-81

de Man, Paul, Wartime Journalism of CLC 55: 382-424

Detective Fiction, Nineteenth-Century NCLC 36: 78-148
origins of the genre, 79-100

history of nineteenth-century detective fiction, 101-33
significance of nineteenth-century detective fiction, 133-46

Detective Fiction, Twentieth-Century TCLC 38: 1-96
genesis and history of the detective story, 3-22
defining detective fiction, 22-32
evolution and varieties, 32-77
the appeal of detective fiction, 77-90

Dime Novels NCLC 84: 98-168
overviews and general studies, 99-123
popular characters, 123-39
major figures and influences, 139-52
socio-political concerns, 152-167

Disease and Literature TCLC 66: 140-283
overviews and general studies, 141-65
disease in nineteenth-century literature, 165-81
tuberculosis and literature, 181-94
women and disease in literature, 194-221
plague literature, 221-53
AIDS in literature, 253-82

El Dorado, The Legend of See Legend of El Dorado, The

The Double in Nineteenth-Century Literature NCLC 40: 1-95
genesis and development of the theme, 2-15
the double and Romanticism, 16-27
sociological views, 27-52
psychological interpretations, 52-87
philosophical considerations, 87-95

Dramatic Realism NCLC 44: 139-202
overviews and general studies, 140-50
origins and definitions, 150-66
impact and influence, 166-93
realist drama and tragedy, 193-201

Drugs and Literature TCLC 78: 184-282
overviews and general studies, 185-201
pre-twentieth-century literature, 201-42
twentieth-century literature, 242-82

Eastern Mythology CMLC 26: 112-92
heroes and kings, 113-51
cross-cultural perspective, 151-69
relations to history and society, 169-92

Eighteenth-Century British Periodicals LC 63: 1-123
rise of periodicals, 2-31
impact and influence of periodicals, 31-64
periodicals and society, 64-122

Eighteenth-Century Travel Narratives LC 77: 252-355
overviews and general studies, 254-79
eighteenth-century European travel narratives, 279-334
non-European eighteenth-century travel narratives, 334-55

Electronic "Books": Hypertext and Hyperfiction CLC 86: 367-404
books vs. CD-ROMS, 367-76
hypertext and hyperfiction, 376-95
implications for publishing, libraries, and the public, 395-403

Eliot, T. S., Centenary of Birth CLC 55: 345-75

Elizabethan Drama LC 22: 140-240
origins and influences, 142-67
characteristics and conventions, 167-83
theatrical production, 184-200
histories, 200-12
comedy, 213-20
tragedy, 220-30

Elizabethan Prose Fiction LC 41: 1-70
overviews and general studies, 1-15
origins and influences, 15-43
style and structure, 43-69

Enclosure of the English Common NCLC 88: 1-57
overviews and general studies, 1-12
early reaction to enclosure, 12-23
nineteenth-century reaction to enclosure, 23-56

The Encyclopedists LC 26: 172-253
overviews and general studies, 173-210
intellectual background, 210-32
views on esthetics, 232-41
views on women, 241-52

English Caroline Literature LC 13: 221-307
background, 222-41
evolution and varieties, 241-62
the Cavalier mode, 262-75
court and society, 275-91
politics and religion, 291-306

English Decadent Literature of the 1890s NCLC 28: 104-200
fin de siècle: the Decadent period, 105-19
definitions, 120-37
major figures: "the tragic generation," 137-50
French literature and English literary Decadence, 150-7
themes, 157-61
poetry, 161-82
periodicals, 182-96

English Essay, Rise of the LC 18: 238-308
definitions and origins, 236-54
influence on the essay, 254-69
historical background, 269-78
the essay in the seventeenth century, 279-93
the essay in the eighteenth century, 293-307

English Mystery Cycle Dramas LC 34: 1-88
overviews and general studies, 1-27
the nature of dramatic performances, 27-42
the medieval worldview and the mystery cycles, 43-67
the doctrine of repentance and the mystery cycles, 67-76
the fall from grace in the mystery cycles, 76-88

The English Realist Novel, 1740-1771 LC 51: 102-98
overviews and general studies, 103-22
from Romanticism to Realism, 123-58
women and the novel, 159-175
the novel and other literary forms, 176-197

English Revolution, Literature of the LC 43: 1-58
overviews and general studies, 2-24
pamphlets of the English Revolution, 24-38
political sermons of the English Revolution, 38-48
poetry of the English Revolution, 48-57

English Romantic Hellenism NCLC 68: 143-250
overviews and general studies, 144-69
historical development of English Romantic Hellenism, 169-91
influence of Greek mythology on the Romantics, 191-229
influence of Greek literature, art, and culture on the Romantics, 229-50

English Romantic Poetry NCLC 28: 201-327
overviews and reputation, 202-37
major subjects and themes, 237-67
forms of Romantic poetry, 267-78
politics, society, and Romantic poetry, 278-99
philosophy, religion, and Romantic poetry, 299-324

The Epistolary Novel LC 59: 71-170
overviews and general studies, 72-96
women and the Epistolary novel, 96-138
principal figures: Britain, 138-53
principal figures: France, 153-69

Espionage Literature TCLC 50: 95-159
overviews and general studies, 96-113
espionage fiction/formula fiction, 113-26
spies in fact and fiction, 126-38
the female spy, 138-44
social and psychological perspectives, 144-58

European Debates on the Conquest of the Americas LC 67: 1-129
overviews and general studies, 3-56
major Spanish figures, 56-98
English perceptions of Native Americans, 98-129

European Romanticism NCLC 36: 149-284
definitions, 149-77
origins of the movement, 177-82
Romantic theory, 182-200
themes and techniques, 200-23
Romanticism in Germany, 223-39
Romanticism in France, 240-61
Romanticism in Italy, 261-4
Romanticism in Spain, 264-8
impact and legacy, 268-82

Exile in Literature TCLC 122: 1-129
overviews and general studies, 2-33
exile in fiction, 33-92
German literature in exile, 92-129

Existentialism and Literature TCLC 42: 197-268
overviews and definitions, 198-209
history and influences, 209-19
Existentialism critiqued and defended, 220-35
philosophical and religious perspectives, 235-41
Existentialist fiction and drama, 241-67

Familiar Essay NCLC 48: 96-211
definitions and origins, 97-130
overview of the genre, 130-43
elements of form and style, 143-59
elements of content, 159-73
the Cockneys: Hazlitt, Lamb, and Hunt, 173-91
status of the genre, 191-210

The Faust Legend LC 47: 1-117

Fear in Literature TCLC 74: 81-258
overviews and general studies, 81
pre-twentieth-century literature, 123
twentieth-century literature, 182

Feminism in the 1990s: Commentary on Works by Naomi Wolf, Susan Faludi, and Camille Paglia CLC 76: 377-415

Feminist Criticism in 1990 CLC 65: 312-60

Fifteenth-Century English Literature LC 17: 248-334
background, 249-72
poetry, 272-315
drama, 315-23
prose, 323-33

Film and Literature TCLC 38: 97-226
overviews and general studies, 97-119
film and theater, 119-34
film and the novel, 134-45
the art of the screenplay, 145-66
genre literature/genre film, 167-79
the writer and the film industry, 179-90
authors on film adaptations of their works, 190-200
fiction into film: comparative essays, 200-23

Finance and Money as Represented in Nineteenth-Century Literature NCLC 76: 1-69

historical perspectives, 2-20
the image of money, 20-37
the dangers of money, 37-50
women and money, 50-69

Folklore and Literature TCLC 86: 116-293
overviews and general studies, 118-144
Native American literature, 144-67
African-American literature, 167-238
folklore and the American West, 238-57
modern and postmodern literature, 257-91

Food in Literature TCLC 114: 1-133
food and children's literature, 2-14
food as a literary device, 14-32
rituals involving food, 33-45
food and social and ethnic identity, 45-90
women's relationship with food, 91-132

Food in Nineteenth-Century Literature NCLC 108: 134-288
overviews, 136-74
food and social class, 174-85
food and gender, 185-219
food and love, 219-31
food and sex, 231-48
eating disorders, 248-70
vegetarians, carnivores, and cannibals, 270-87

French Drama in the Age of Louis XIV LC 28: 94-185
overview, 95-127
tragedy, 127-46
comedy, 146-66
tragicomedy, 166-84

French Enlightenment LC 14: 81-145
the question of definition, 82-9
le siècle des lumières, 89-94
women and the salons, 94-105
censorship, 105-15
the philosophy of reason, 115-31
influence and legacy, 131-44

French New Novel TCLC 98: 158-234
overviews and general studies, 158-92
influences, 192-213
themes, 213-33

French Realism NCLC 52: 136-216
origins and definitions, 137-70
issues and influence, 170-98
realism and representation, 198-215

French Revolution and English Literature NCLC 40: 96-195
history and theory, 96-123
romantic poetry, 123-50
the novel, 150-81
drama, 181-92
children's literature, 192-5

Futurism, Italian TCLC 42: 269-354
principles and formative influences, 271-9
manifestos, 279-88
literature, 288-303
theater, 303-19
art, 320-30
music, 330-6
architecture, 336-9
and politics, 339-46
reputation and significance, 346-51

Gaelic Revival See Irish Literary Renaissance

Gates, Henry Louis, Jr., and African-American Literary Criticism CLC 65: 361-405

Gay and Lesbian Literature CLC 76: 416-39

German Exile Literature TCLC 30: 1-58
the writer and the Nazi state, 1-10
definition of, 10-4
life in exile, 14-32
surveys, 32-50
Austrian literature in exile, 50-2

German publishing in the United States, 52-7

German Expressionism TCLC 34: 74-160
history and major figures, 76-85
aesthetic theories, 85-109
drama, 109-26
poetry, 126-38
film, 138-42
painting, 142-7
music, 147-53
and politics, 153-8

The Gilded Age NCLC 84: 169-271
popular themes, 170-90
Realism, 190-208
Aestheticism, 208-26
socio-political concerns, 226-70

Glasnost **and Contemporary Soviet Literature** CLC 59: 355-97

Gothic Novel NCLC 28: 328-402
development and major works, 328-34
definitions, 334-50
themes and techniques, 350-78
in America, 378-85
in Scotland, 385-91
influence and legacy, 391-400

The Governess in Nineteenth-Century Literature NCLC 104: 1-131
overviews and general studies, 3-28
social roles and economic conditions, 28-86
fictional governesses, 86-131

Graphic Narratives CLC 86: 405-32
history and overviews, 406-21
the "Classics Illustrated" series, 421-2
reviews of recent works, 422-32

Graveyard Poets LC 67: 131-212
origins and development, 131-52
major figures, 152-75
major works, 175-212

Greek Historiography CMLC 17: 1-49

Greek Mythology CMLC 26: 193-320
overviews and general studies, 194-209
origins and development of Greek mythology, 209-29
cosmogonies and divinities in Greek mythology, 229-54
heroes and heroines in Greek mythology, 254-80
women in Greek mythology, 280-320

Greek Theater CMLC 51: 1-58
criticism, 2-58

Hard-Boiled Fiction TCLC 118: 1-109
overviews and general studies, 2-39
major authors, 39-76
women and hard-boiled fiction, 76-109

The Harlem Renaissance HR 1: 1-563
overviews and general studies of the Harlem Renaissance, 1-137
primary sources, 3-12
overviews, 12-38
background and sources of the Harlem Renaissance, 38-56
the New Negro aesthetic, 56-91
patrons, promoters, and the New York Public Library, 91-121
women of the Harlem Renaissance, 121-37
social, economic, and political factors that influenced the Harlem Renaissance, 139-240
primary sources, 141-53
overviews, 153-87
social and economic factors, 187-213
Black intellectual and political thought, 213-40
publishing and periodicals during the Harlem Renaissance, 243-339
primary sources, 246-52

overviews, 252-68
African American writers and mainstream publishers, 268-91
anthologies: *The New Negro* and others, 291-309
African American periodicals and the Harlem Renaissance, 309-39
performing arts during the Harlem Renaissance, 341-465
primary sources, 343-48
overviews, 348-64
drama of the Harlem Renaissance, 364-92
influence of music on Harlem Renaissance writing, 437-65
visual arts during the Harlem Renaissance, 467-563
primary sources, 470-71
overviews, 471-517
painters, 517-36
sculptors, 536-58
photographers, 558-63

Harlem Renaissance TCLC 26: 49-125
principal issues and figures, 50-67
the literature and its audience, 67-74
theme and technique in poetry, fiction, and drama, 74-115
and American society, 115-21
achievement and influence, 121-2

Havel, Václav, Playwright and President CLC 65: 406-63

Historical Fiction, Nineteenth-Century NCLC 48: 212-307
definitions and characteristics, 213-36
Victorian historical fiction, 236-65
American historical fiction, 265-88
realism in historical fiction, 288-306

Hollywood and Literature TCLC 118: 110-251
overviews and general studies, 111-20
adaptations, 120-65
socio-historical and cultural impact, 165-206
theater and hollywood, 206-51

Holocaust and the Atomic Bomb: Fifty Years Later CLC 91: 331-82
the Holocaust remembered, 333-52
Anne Frank revisited, 352-62
the atomic bomb and American memory, 362-81

Holocaust Denial Literature TCLC 58: 1-110
overviews and general studies, 1-30
Robert Faurisson and Noam Chomsky, 30-52
Holocaust denial literature in America, 52-71
library access to Holocaust denial literature, 72-5
the authenticity of Anne Frank's diary, 76-90
David Irving and the "normalization" of Hitler, 90-109

Holocaust, Literature of the TCLC 42: 355-450
historical overview, 357-61
critical overview, 361-70
diaries and memoirs, 370-95
novels and short stories, 395-425
poetry, 425-41
drama, 441-8

Homosexuality in Nineteenth-Century Literature NCLC 56: 78-182
defining homosexuality, 80-111
Greek love, 111-44
trial and danger, 144-81

Hungarian Literature of the Twentieth Century TCLC 26: 126-88
surveys of, 126-47

Nyugat and early twentieth-century literature, 147-56
mid-century literature, 156-68
and politics, 168-78
since the 1956 revolt, 178-87

Hysteria in Nineteenth-Century Literature NCLC 64: 59-184
the history of hysteria, 60-75
the gender of hysteria, 75-103
hysteria and women's narratives, 103-57
hysteria in nineteenth-century poetry, 157-83

Image of the Noble Savage in Literature LC 79: 136-252
overviews and development, 136-76
the Noble Savage in the New World, 176-221
Rousseau and the French Enlightenment's view of the noble savage, 221-51

Imagism TCLC 74: 259-454
history and development, 260
major figures, 288
sources and influences, 352
Imagism and other movements, 397
influence and legacy, 431

Immigrants in Nineteenth-Century Literature, Representation of NCLC 112: 188-298
overview, 189-99
immigrants in America, 199-223
immigrants and labor, 223-60
immigrants in England, 260-97

Incest in Nineteenth-Century American Literature NCLC 76: 70-141
overview, 71-88
the concern for social order, 88-117
authority and authorship, 117-40

Incest in Victorian Literature NCLC 92: 172-318
overviews and general studies, 173-85
novels, 185-276
plays, 276-84
poetry, 284-318

Indian Literature in English TCLC 54: 308-406
overview, 309-13
origins and major figures, 313-25
the Indo-English novel, 325-55
Indo-English poetry, 355-67
Indo-English drama, 367-72
critical perspectives on Indo-English literature, 372-80
modern Indo-English literature, 380-9
Indo-English authors on their work, 389-404

The Industrial Revolution in Literature NCLC 56: 183-273
historical and cultural perspectives, 184-201
contemporary reactions to the machine, 201-21
themes and symbols in literature, 221-73

The Irish Famine as Represented in Nineteenth-Century Literature NCLC 64: 185-261
overviews and general studies, 187-98
historical background, 198-212
famine novels, 212-34
famine poetry, 234-44
famine letters and eye-witness accounts, 245-61

Irish Literary Renaissance TCLC 46: 172-287
overview, 173-83
development and major figures, 184-202
influence of Irish folklore and mythology, 202-22
Irish poetry, 222-34
Irish drama and the Abbey Theatre, 234-56
Irish fiction, 256-86

Irish Nationalism and Literature NCLC 44: 203-73
the Celtic element in literature, 203-19
anti-Irish sentiment and the Celtic response, 219-34
literary ideals in Ireland, 234-45
literary expressions, 245-73

Irish Novel, The NCLC 80: 1-130
overviews and general studies, 3-9
principal figures, 9-22
peasant and middle class Irish novelists, 22-76
aristocratic Irish and Anglo-Irish novelists, 76-129

Israeli Literature TCLC 94: 1-137
overviews and general studies, 2-18
Israeli fiction, 18-33
Israeli poetry, 33-62
Israeli drama, 62-91
women and Israeli literature, 91-112
Arab characters in Israeli literature, 112-36

Italian Futurism See **Futurism, Italian**

Italian Humanism LC 12: 205-77
origins and early development, 206-18
revival of classical letters, 218-23
humanism and other philosophies, 224-39
humanism and humanists, 239-46
the plastic arts, 246-57
achievement and significance, 258-76

Italian Romanticism NCLC 60: 85-145
origins and overviews, 86-101
Italian Romantic theory, 101-25
the language of Romanticism, 125-45

Jacobean Drama LC 33: 1-37
the Jacobean worldview: an era of transition, 2-14
the moral vision of Jacobean drama, 14-22
Jacobean tragedy, 22-3
the Jacobean masque, 23-36

Jazz and Literature TCLC 102: 3-124

Jewish-American Fiction TCLC 62: 1-181
overviews and general studies, 2-24
major figures, 24-48
Jewish writers and American life, 48-78
Jewish characters in American fiction, 78-108
themes in Jewish-American fiction, 108-43
Jewish-American women writers, 143-59
the Holocaust and Jewish-American fiction, 159-81

Jews in Literature TCLC 118: 252-417
overviews and general studies, 253-97
representing the Jew in literature, 297-351
the Holocaust in literature, 351-416

Journals of Lewis and Clark, The NCLC 100: 1-88
overviews and general studies, 4-30
journal-keeping methods, 30-46
Fort Mandan, 46-51
the Clark journal, 51-65
the journals as literary texts, 65-87

Kabuki LC 73: 118-232
overviews and general studies, 120-40
the development of Kabuki, 140-65
major works, 165-95
Kabuki and society, 195-231

Kit-Kat Club, The LC 71: 66-112
overviews and general studies, 67-88
major figures, 88-107
attacks on the Kit-Kat Club, 107-12

Knickerbocker Group, The NCLC 56: 274-341
overviews and general studies, 276-314
Knickerbocker periodicals, 314-26
writers and artists, 326-40

Lake Poets, The NCLC 52: 217-304
characteristics of the Lake Poets and their works, 218-27
literary influences and collaborations, 227-66
defining and developing Romantic ideals, 266-84
embracing Conservatism, 284-303

Language Poets TCLC 126: 66-172
overviews and general studies, 67-122
selected major figures in language poetry, 122-72

Larkin, Philip, Controversy CLC 81: 417-64

Latin American Literature, Twentieth-Century TCLC 58: 111-98
historical and critical perspectives, 112-36
the novel, 136-45
the short story, 145-9
drama, 149-60
poetry, 160-7
the writer and society, 167-86
Native Americans in Latin American literature, 186-97

Law and Literature TCLC 126: 173-347
overviews and general studies, 174-253
fiction critiquing the law, 253-88
literary responses to the law, 289-346

Legend of El Dorado, The LC 74: 248-350
overviews, 249-308
major explorations for El Dorado, 308-50

The Levellers LC 51: 200-312
overviews and general studies, 201-29
principal figures, 230-86
religion, political philosophy, and pamphleteering, 287-311

Literary Prizes TCLC 122: 130-203
overviews and general studies, 131-34
the Nobel Prize in Literature, 135-83
the Pulitzer Prize, 183-203

Literature and Millenial Lists CLC 119: 431-67
The Modern Library list, 433
The Waterstone list, 438-439

Literature of the American Cowboy NCLC 96: 1-60
overview, 3-20
cowboy fiction, 20-36
cowboy poetry and songs, 36-59

Literature of the California Gold Rush NCLC 92: 320-85
overviews and general studies, 322-24
early California Gold Rush fiction, 324-44
Gold Rush folklore and legend, 344-51
the rise of Western local color, 351-60
social relations and social change, 360-385

Living Theatre, The DC 16: 154-214

Madness in Nineteenth-Century Literature NCLC 76: 142-284
overview, 143-54
autobiography, 154-68
poetry, 168-215
fiction, 215-83

Madness in Twentieth-Century Literature TCLC 50: 160-225
overviews and general studies, 161-71
madness and the creative process, 171-86
suicide, 186-91
madness in American literature, 191-207
madness in German literature, 207-13
madness and feminist artists, 213-24

Magic Realism TCLC 110: 80-327
overviews and general studies, 81-94
magic realism in African literature, 95-110
magic realism in American literature, 110-32

magic realism in Canadian literature, 132-46
magic realism in European literature, 146-66
magic realism in Asian literature, 166-79
magic realism in Latin-American literature, 179-223
magic realism in Israeli literature and the novels of Salman Rushdie, 223-38
magic realism in literature written by women, 239-326

The Masque LC 63: 124-265
development of the masque, 125-62
sources and structure, 162-220
race and gender in the masque, 221-64

Medical Writing LC 55: 93-195
colonial America, 94-110
enlightenment, 110-24
medieval writing, 124-40
sexuality, 140-83
vernacular, 185-95

Memoirs of Trauma CLC 109: 419-466
overview, 420
criticism, 429

Metaphysical Poets LC 24: 356-439
early definitions, 358-67
surveys and overviews, 367-92
cultural and social influences, 392-406
stylistic and thematic variations, 407-38

Missionaries in the Nineteenth-Century, Literature of NCLC 112: 299-392
history and development, 300-16
uses of ethnography, 316-31
sociopolitical concerns, 331-82
David Livingstone, 382-91

Modern Essay, The TCLC 58: 199-273
overview, 200-7
the essay in the early twentieth century, 207-19
characteristics of the modern essay, 219-32
modern essayists, 232-45
the essay as a literary genre, 245-73

Modern French Literature TCLC 122: 205-359
overviews and general studies, 207-43
French theater, 243-77
gender issues and French women writers, 277-315
ideology and politics, 315-24
modern French poetry, 324-41
resistance literature, 341-58

Modern Irish Literature TCLC 102: 125-321
overview, 129-44
dramas, 144-70
fiction, 170-247
poetry, 247-321

Modern Japanese Literature TCLC 66: 284-389
poetry, 285-305
drama, 305-29
fiction, 329-61
western influences, 361-87

Modernism TCLC 70: 165-275
definitions, 166-184
Modernism and earlier influences, 184-200
stylistic and thematic traits, 200-229
poetry and drama, 229-242
redefining Modernism, 242-275

Muckraking Movement in American Journalism TCLC 34: 161-242
development, principles, and major figures, 162-70
publications, 170-9
social and political ideas, 179-86
targets, 186-208
fiction, 208-19
decline, 219-29

impact and accomplishments, 229-40

Multiculturalism in Literature and Education CLC 70: 361-413

Music and Modern Literature TCLC 62: 182-329
overviews and general studies, 182-211
musical form/literary form, 211-32
music in literature, 232-50
the influence of music on literature, 250-73
literature and popular music, 273-303
jazz and poetry, 303-28

Native American Literature CLC 76: 440-76

Natural School, Russian NCLC 24: 205-40
history and characteristics, 205-25
contemporary criticism, 225-40

Naturalism NCLC 36: 285-382
definitions and theories, 286-305
critical debates on Naturalism, 305-16
Naturalism in theater, 316-32
European Naturalism, 332-61
American Naturalism, 361-72
the legacy of Naturalism, 372-81

Negritude TCLC 50: 226-361
origins and evolution, 227-56
definitions, 256-91
Negritude in literature, 291-343
Negritude reconsidered, 343-58

New Criticism TCLC 34: 243-318
development and ideas, 244-70
debate and defense, 270-99
influence and legacy, 299-315

New South, Literature of the NCLC 116: 122-240
overviews, 124-66
the novel in the New South, 166-209
myth of the Old South in the New, 209-39

The New World in Renaissance Literature LC 31: 1-51
overview, 1-18
utopia vs. terror, 18-31
explorers and Native Americans, 31-51

New York Intellectuals and *Partisan Review* TCLC 30: 117-98
development and major figures, 118-28
influence of Judaism, 128-39
Partisan Review, 139-57
literary philosophy and practice, 157-75
political philosophy, 175-87
achievement and significance, 187-97

The New Yorker TCLC 58: 274-357
overviews and general studies, 274-95
major figures, 295-304
New Yorker style, 304-33
fiction, journalism, and humor at *The New Yorker,* 333-48
the new *New Yorker,* 348-56

Newgate Novel NCLC 24: 166-204
development of Newgate literature, 166-73
Newgate Calendar, 173-7
Newgate fiction, 177-95
Newgate drama, 195-204

Nigerian Literature of the Twentieth Century TCLC 30: 199-265
surveys of, 199-227
English language and African life, 227-45
politics and the Nigerian writer, 245-54
Nigerian writers and society, 255-62

Nihilism and Literature TCLC 110: 328-93
overviews and general studies, 328-44
European and Russian nihilism, 344-73
nihilism in the works of Albert Camus, Franz Kafka, and John Barth, 373-92

Nineteenth-Century Captivity Narratives NCLC 80:131-218
overview, 132-37

the political significance of captivity narratives, 137-67
images of gender, 167-96
moral instruction, 197-217

Nineteenth-Century Euro-American Literary Representations of Native Americans NCLC 104: 132-264
overviews and general studies, 134-53
Native American history, 153-72
the Indians of the Northeast, 172-93
the Indians of the Southeast, 193-212
the Indians of the West, 212-27
Indian-hater fiction, 227-43
the Indian as exhibit, 243-63

Nineteenth-Century Native American Autobiography NCLC 64: 262-389
overview, 263-8
problems of authorship, 268-81
the evolution of Native American autobiography, 281-304
political issues, 304-15
gender and autobiography, 316-62
autobiographical works during the turn of the century, 362-88

Norse Mythology CMLC 26: 321-85
history and mythological tradition, 322-44
Eddic poetry, 344-74
Norse mythology and other traditions, 374-85

Northern Humanism LC 16: 281-356
background, 282-305
precursor of the Reformation, 305-14
the Brethren of the Common Life, the Devotio Moderna, and education, 314-40
the impact of printing, 340-56

Novel of Manners, The NCLC 56: 342-96
social and political order, 343-53
domestic order, 353-73
depictions of gender, 373-83
the American novel of manners, 383-95

Novels of the Ming and Early Ch'ing Dynasties LC 76: 213-356
overviews and historical development, 214-45
major works—overview, 245-85
genre studies, 285-325
cultural and social themes, 325-55

Nuclear Literature: Writings and Criticism in the Nuclear Age TCLC 46: 288-390
overviews and general studies, 290-301
fiction, 301-35
poetry, 335-8
nuclear war in Russo-Japanese literature, 338-55
nuclear war and women writers, 355-67
the nuclear referent and literary criticism, 367-88

Occultism in Modern Literature TCLC 50: 362-406
influence of occultism on literature, 363-72
occultism, literature, and society, 372-87
fiction, 387-96
drama, 396-405

Opium and the Nineteenth-Century Literary Imagination NCLC 20:250-301
original sources, 250-62
historical background, 262-71
and literary society, 271-9
and literary creativity, 279-300

Orientalism NCLC 96: 149-364
overviews and general studies, 150-98
Orientalism and imperialism, 198-229
Orientalism and gender, 229-59
Orientalism and the nineteenth-century novel, 259-321
Orientalism in nineteenth-century poetry, 321-63

The Oxford Movement NCLC 72: 1-197
   overviews and general studies, 2-24
   background, 24-59
   and education, 59-69
   religious responses, 69-128
   literary aspects, 128-178
   political implications, 178-196

The Parnassian Movement NCLC 72: 198-241
   overviews and general studies, 199-231
   and epic form, 231-38
   and positivism, 238-41

Pastoral Literature of the English Renaissance LC 59: 171-282
   overviews and general studies, 172-214
   principal figures of the Elizabethan period, 214-33
   principal figures of the later Renaissance, 233-50
   pastoral drama, 250-81

Periodicals, Nineteenth-Century British NCLC 24: 100-65
   overviews and general studies, 100-30
   in the Romantic Age, 130-41
   in the Victorian era, 142-54
   and the reviewer, 154-64

Picaresque Literature of the Sixteenth and Seventeenth Centuries LC 78: 223-355
   context and development, 224-71
   genre, 271-98
   the picaro, 299-326
   the picara, 326-53

Plath, Sylvia, and the Nature of Biography CLC 86: 433-62
   the nature of biography, 433-52
   reviews of *The Silent Woman*, 452-61

Political Theory from the 15th to the 18th Century LC 36: 1-55
   overview, 1-26
   natural law, 26-42
   empiricism, 42-55

Polish Romanticism NCLC 52: 305-71
   overviews and general studies, 306-26
   major figures, 326-40
   Polish Romantic drama, 340-62
   influences, 362-71

Politics and Literature TCLC 94: 138-61
   overviews and general studies, 139-96
   Europe, 196-226
   Latin America, 226-48
   Africa and the Caribbean, 248-60

Popular Literature TCLC 70: 279-382
   overviews and general studies, 280-324
   "formula" fiction, 324-336
   readers of popular literature, 336-351
   evolution of popular literature, 351-382

The Portrayal of Jews in Nineteenth-Century English Literature NCLC 72: 242-368
   overviews and general studies, 244-77
   Anglo-Jewish novels, 277-303
   depictions by non-Jewish writers, 303-44
   Hebraism versus Hellenism, 344-67

The Portrayal of Mormonism NCLC 96: 61-148
   overview, 63-72
   early Mormon literature, 72-100
   Mormon periodicals and journals, 100-10
   women writers, 110-22
   Mormonism and nineteenth-century literature, 122-42
   Mormon poetry, 142-47

Postcolonialism TCLC 114: 134-239
   overviews and general studies, 135-153
   African postcolonial writing, 153-72
   Asian/Pacific literature, 172-78
   postcolonial literary theory, 178-213
   postcolonial women's writing, 213-38

Postmodernism TCLC 90:125-307
   overview, 126-166
   criticism, 166-224
   fiction, 224-282
   poetry, 282-300
   drama, 300-307

Pre-Raphaelite Movement NCLC 20: 302-401
   overview, 302-4
   genesis, 304-12
   Germ and *Oxford and Cambridge Magazine*, 312-20
   Robert Buchanan and the "Fleshly School of Poetry," 320-31
   satires and parodies, 331-4
   surveys, 334-51
   aesthetics, 351-75
   sister arts of poetry and painting, 375-94
   influence, 394-9

Pre-romanticism LC 40: 1-56
   overviews and general studies, 2-14
   defining the period, 14-23
   new directions in poetry and prose, 23-45
   the focus on the self, 45-56

Pre-Socratic Philosophy CMLC 22: 1-56
   overviews and general studies, 3-24
   the Ionians and the Pythagoreans, 25-35
   Heraclitus, the Eleatics, and the Atomists, 36-47
   the Sophists, 47-55

Prison in Nineteenth-Century Literature, The NCLC 116: 241-357
   overview, 242-60
   romantic prison, 260-78
   domestic prison, 278-316
   America as prison, 316-24
   physical prisons and prison authors, 324-56

Protestant Hagiography and Martyrology LC 84: 106-217
   overview, 106-37
   John Foxe's *Book of Martyrs*, 137-97
   martyrology and the feminine perspective, 198-216

Protestant Reformation, Literature of the LC 37: 1-83
   overviews and general studies, 1-49
   humanism and scholasticism, 49-69
   the reformation and literature, 69-82

Psychoanalysis and Literature TCLC 38: 227-338
   overviews and general studies, 227-46
   Freud on literature, 246-51
   psychoanalytic views of the literary process, 251-61
   psychoanalytic theories of response to literature, 261-88
   psychoanalysis and literary criticism, 288-312
   psychoanalysis as literature/literature as psychoanalysis, 313-34

The Quarrel between the Ancients and the Moderns LC 63: 266-381
   overviews and general studies, 267-301
   Renaissance origins, 301-32
   Quarrel between the Ancients and the Moderns in France, 332-58
   Battle of the Books in England, 358-80

Rap Music CLC 76: 477-50

Renaissance Natural Philosophy LC 27: 201-87
   cosmology, 201-28
   astrology, 228-54
   magic, 254-86

Representations of the Devil in Nineteenth-Century Literature NCLC 100: 89-223
   overviews and general studies, 90-115
   the Devil in American fiction, 116-43
   English Romanticism: the satanic school, 143-89
   Luciferian discourse in European literature, 189-222

Restoration Drama LC 21: 184-275
   general overviews and general studies, 185-230
   Jeremy Collier stage controversy, 230-9
   other critical interpretations, 240-75

Revenge Tragedy LC 71: 113-242
   overviews and general studies, 113-51
   Elizabethan attitudes toward revenge, 151-88
   the morality of revenge, 188-216
   reminders and remembrance, 217-41

Revising the Literary Canon CLC 81: 465-509

Revising the Literary Canon TCLC 114: 240-84
   overviews and general studies, 241-85
   canon change in American literature, 285-339
   gender and the literary canon, 339-59
   minority and third-world literature and the canon, 359-84

Revolutionary Astronomers LC 51: 314-65
   overviews and general studies, 316-25
   principal figures, 325-51
   Revolutionary astronomical models, 352-64

Robin Hood, Legend of LC 19: 205-58
   origins and development of the Robin Hood legend, 206-20
   representations of Robin Hood, 220-44
   Robin Hood as hero, 244-56

Rushdie, Salman, *Satanic Verses* Controversy CLC 55: 214-63; 59:404-56

Russian Nihilism NCLC 28: 403-47
   definitions and overviews, 404-17
   women and Nihilism, 417-27
   literature as reform: the Civic Critics, 427-33
   Nihilism and the Russian novel: Turgenev and Dostoevsky, 433-47

Russian Thaw TCLC 26: 189-247
   literary history of the period, 190-206
   theoretical debate of socialist realism, 206-11
   Novy Mir, 211-7
   Literary Moscow, 217-24
   Pasternak, *Zhivago*, and the Nobel prize, 224-7
   poetry of liberation, 228-31
   Brodsky trial and the end of the Thaw, 231-6
   achievement and influence, 236-46

Salem Witch Trials LC 38: 1-145
   overviews and general studies, 2-30
   historical background, 30-65
   judicial background, 65-78
   the search for causes, 78-115
   the role of women in the trials, 115-44

Salinger, J. D., Controversy Surrounding *In Search of J. D. Salinger* CLC 55: 325-44

Science and Modern Literature TCLC 90: 308-419
   overviews and general studies, 295-333
   fiction, 333-95
   poetry, 395-405
   drama, 405-19

Science in Nineteenth-Century Literature NCLC 100: 224-366
   overviews and general studies, 225-65
   major figures, 265-336
   sociopolitical concerns, 336-65

Science Fiction, Nineteenth-Century NCLC 24: 241-306

background, 242-50
definitions of the genre, 251-56
representative works and writers, 256-75
themes and conventions, 276-305

Scottish Chaucerians LC 20: 363-412

Scottish Poetry, Eighteenth-Century LC 29: 95-167
overviews and general studies, 96-114
the Scottish Augustans, 114-28
the Scots Vernacular Revival, 132-63
Scottish poetry after Burns, 163-66

Sea in Literature, The TCLC 82: 72-191
drama, 73-9
poetry, 79-119
fiction, 119-91

Sea in Nineteenth-Century English and American Literature, The NCLC 104: 265-362
overviews and general studies, 267-306
major figures in American sea fiction—Cooper and Melville, 306-29
American sea poetry and short stories, 329-45
English sea literature, 345-61

Sensation Novel, The NCLC 80: 219-330
overviews and general studies, 221-46
principal figures, 246-62
nineteenth-century reaction, 262-91
feminist criticism, 291-329

Sentimental Novel, The NCLC 60: 146-245
overviews and general studies, 147-58
the politics of domestic fiction, 158-79
a literature of resistance and repression, 179-212
the reception of sentimental fiction, 213-44

Sex and Literature TCLC 82: 192-434
overviews and general studies, 193-216
drama, 216-63
poetry, 263-87
fiction, 287-431

Sherlock Holmes Centenary TCLC 26: 248-310
Doyle's life and the composition of the Holmes stories, 248-59
life and character of Holmes, 259-78
method, 278-79
Holmes and the Victorian world, 279-92
Sherlockian scholarship, 292-301
Doyle and the development of the detective story, 301-07
Holmes's continuing popularity, 307-09

The Silver Fork Novel NCLC 88: 58-140
criticism, 59-139

Slave Narratives, American NCLC 20: 1-91
background, 2-9
overviews and general studies, 9-24
contemporary responses, 24-7
language, theme, and technique, 27-70
historical authenticity, 70-5
antecedents, 75-83
role in development of Black American literature, 83-8

The Slave Trade in British and American Literature LC 59: 283-369
overviews and general studies, 284-91
depictions by white writers, 291-331
depictions by former slaves, 331-67

Social Conduct Literature LC 55: 196-298
overviews and general studies, 196-223
prescriptive ideology in other literary forms, 223-38
role of the press, 238-63
impact of conduct literature, 263-87
conduct literature and the perception of women, 287-96
women writing for women, 296-98

Socialism NCLC 88: 141-237
origins, 142-54
French socialism, 154-83
Anglo-American socialism, 183-205
Socialist-Feminism, 205-36

Southern Literature See **Contemporary Southern Literature**

Southern Literature of the Reconstruction NCLC 108: 289-369
overview, 290-91
reconstruction literature: the consequences of war, 291-321
old south to new: continuities in southern culture, 321-68

Spanish Civil War Literature TCLC 26: 311-85
topics in, 312-33
British and American literature, 333-59
French literature, 359-62
Spanish literature, 362-73
German literature, 373-75
political idealism and war literature, 375-83

Spanish Golden Age Literature LC 23: 262-332
overviews and general studies, 263-81
verse drama, 281-304
prose fiction, 304-19
lyric poetry, 319-31

Spasmodic School of Poetry NCLC 24: 307-52
history and major figures, 307-21
the Spasmodics on poetry, 321-7
Firmilian and critical disfavor, 327-39
theme and technique, 339-47
influence, 347-51

Sports in Literature TCLC 86: 294-445
overviews and general studies, 295-324
major writers and works, 324-402
sports, literature, and social issues, 402-45

Steinbeck, John, Fiftieth Anniversary of *The Grapes of Wrath* CLC 59: 311-54

Sturm und Drang NCLC 40: 196-276
definitions, 197-238
poetry and poetics, 238-58
drama, 258-75

Supernatural Fiction in the Nineteenth Century NCLC 32: 207-87
major figures and influences, 208-35
the Victorian ghost story, 236-54
the influence of science and occultism, 254-66
supernatural fiction and society, 266-86

Supernatural Fiction, Modern TCLC 30: 59-116
evolution and varieties, 60-74
"decline" of the ghost story, 74-86
as a literary genre, 86-92
technique, 92-101
nature and appeal, 101-15

Surrealism TCLC 30: 334-406
history and formative influences, 335-43
manifestos, 343-54
philosophic, aesthetic, and political principles, 354-75
poetry, 375-81
novel, 381-6
drama, 386-92
film, 392-8
painting and sculpture, 398-403
achievement, 403-5

Symbolism, Russian TCLC 30: 266-333
doctrines and major figures, 267-92
theories, 293-8
and French Symbolism, 298-310
themes in poetry, 310-4
theater, 314-20
and the fine arts, 320-32

Symbolist Movement, French NCLC 20: 169-249
background and characteristics, 170-86
principles, 186-91
attacked and defended, 191-7
influences and predecessors, 197-211
and Decadence, 211-6
theater, 216-26
prose, 226-33
decline and influence, 233-47

Television and Literature TCLC 78: 283-426
television and literacy, 283-98
reading vs. watching, 298-341
adaptations, 341-62
literary genres and television, 362-90
television genres and literature, 390-410
children's literature/children's television, 410-25

Theater of the Absurd TCLC 38: 339-415
"The Theater of the Absurd," 340-7
major plays and playwrights, 347-58
and the concept of the absurd, 358-86
theatrical techniques, 386-94
predecessors of, 394-402
influence of, 402-13

Tin Pan Alley See **American Popular Song, Golden Age of**

Tobacco Culture LC 55: 299-366
social and economic attitudes toward tobacco, 299-344
tobacco trade between the old world and the new world, 344-55
tobacco smuggling in Great Britain, 355-66

Transcendentalism, American NCLC 24: 1-99
overviews and general studies, 3-23
contemporary documents, 23-41
theological aspects of, 42-52
and social issues, 52-74
literature of, 74-96

Travel Writing in the Nineteenth Century NCLC 44: 274-392
the European grand tour, 275-303
the Orient, 303-47
North America, 347-91

Travel Writing in the Twentieth Century TCLC 30: 407-56
conventions and traditions, 407-27
and fiction writing, 427-43
comparative essays on travel writers, 443-54

Tristan and Isolde Legend CMLC 42: 311-404

True-Crime Literature CLC 99: 333-433
history and analysis, 334-407
reviews of true-crime publications, 407-23
writing instruction, 424-29
author profiles, 429-33

***Ulysses* and the Process of Textual Reconstruction** TCLC 26:386-416
evaluations of the new *Ulysses,* 386-94
editorial principles and procedures, 394-401
theoretical issues, 401-16

Utilitarianism NCLC 84: 272-340
J. S. Mill's Utilitarianism: liberty, equality, justice, 273-313
Jeremy Bentham's Utilitarianism: the science of happiness, 313-39

Utopianism NCLC 88: 238-346
overviews: Utopian literature, 239-59
Utopianism in American literature, 259-99
Utopianism in British literature, 299-311
Utopianism and Feminism, 311-45

Utopian Literature, Nineteenth-Century NCLC 24: 353-473
definitions, 354-74

overviews and general studies, 374-88
theory, 388-408
communities, 409-26
fiction, 426-53
women and fiction, 454-71

Utopian Literature, Renaissance LC 32: 1-63
overviews and general studies, 2-25
classical background, 25-33
utopia and the social contract, 33-9
origins in mythology, 39-48
utopia and the Renaissance country house, 48-52
influence of millenarianism, 52-62

Vampire in Literature TCLC 46: 391-454
origins and evolution, 392-412
social and psychological perspectives, 413-44
vampire fiction and science fiction, 445-53

Vernacular Bibles LC 67: 214-388
overviews and general studies, 215-59
the English Bible, 259-355
the German Bible, 355-88

Victorian Autobiography NCLC 40: 277-363
development and major characteristics, 278-88
themes and techniques, 289-313
the autobiographical tendency in Victorian prose and poetry, 313-47
Victorian women's autobiographies, 347-62

Victorian Fantasy Literature NCLC 60: 246-384
overviews and general studies, 247-91
major figures, 292-366
women in Victorian fantasy literature, 366-83

Victorian Hellenism NCLC 68: 251-376
overviews and general studies, 252-78
the meanings of Hellenism, 278-335
the literary influence, 335-75

Victorian Novel NCLC 32: 288-454
development and major characteristics, 290-310
themes and techniques, 310-58
social criticism in the Victorian novel, 359-97
urban and rural life in the Victorian novel, 397-406
women in the Victorian novel, 406-25
Mudie's Circulating Library, 425-34
the late-Victorian novel, 434-51

Vietnamese Literature TCLC 102: 322-386

Vietnam War in Literature and Film CLC 91: 383-437
overview, 384-8
prose, 388-412
film and drama, 412-24
poetry, 424-35

Violence in Literature TCLC 98: 235-358
overviews and general studies, 236-74
violence in the works of modern authors, 274-358

Vorticism TCLC 62: 330-426
Wyndham Lewis and Vorticism, 330-8
characteristics and principles of Vorticism, 338-65
Lewis and Pound, 365-82
Vorticist writing, 382-416
Vorticist painting, 416-26

Well-Made Play, The NCLC 80: 331-370
overviews and general studies, 332-45
Scribe's style, 345-56
the influence of the well-made play, 356-69

Women's Autobiography, Nineteenth Century NCLC 76: 285-368
overviews and general studies, 287-300
autobiographies concerned with religious and political issues, 300-15
autobiographies by women of color, 315-38
autobiographies by women pioneers, 338-51
autobiographies by women of letters, 351-68

Women's Diaries, Nineteenth-Century NCLC 48: 308-54
overview, 308-13
diary as history, 314-25
sociology of diaries, 325-34
diaries as psychological scholarship, 334-43
diary as autobiography, 343-8
diary as literature, 348-53

Women in Modern Literature TCLC 94: 262-425
overviews and general studies, 263-86
American literature, 286-304
other national literatures, 304-33
fiction, 333-94
poetry, 394-407
drama, 407-24

Women Writers, Seventeenth-Century LC 30: 2-58
overview, 2-15
women and education, 15-9
women and autobiography, 19-31
women's diaries, 31-9
early feminists, 39-58

World War I Literature TCLC 34: 392-486
overview, 393-403
English, 403-27
German, 427-50
American, 450-66
French, 466-74
and modern history, 474-82

Yellow Journalism NCLC 36: 383-456
overviews and general studies, 384-96
major figures, 396-413

Young Playwrights Festival
1988 CLC 55: 376-81
1989 CLC 59: 398-403
1990 CLC 65: 444-8

CLC Cumulative Nationality Index

ALBANIAN

Kadare, Ismail **52**

ALGERIAN

Althusser, Louis **106**
Camus, Albert **1, 2, 4, 9, 11, 14, 32, 63, 69, 124**
Cixous, Hélène **92**
Cohen-Solal, Annie **50**

AMERICAN

Abbey, Edward **36, 59**
Abbott, Lee K(ittredge) **48**
Abish, Walter **22**
Abrams, M(eyer) H(oward) **24**
Acker, Kathy **45, 111**
Adams, Alice (Boyd) **6, 13, 46**
Addams, Charles (Samuel) **30**
Adler, C(arole) S(chwerdtfeger) **35**
Adler, Renata **8, 31**
Ai **4, 14, 69**
Aiken, Conrad (Potter) **1, 3, 5, 10, 52**
Albee, Edward (Franklin III) **1, 2, 3, 5, 9, 11, 13, 25, 53, 86, 113**
Alexander, Lloyd (Chudley) **35**
Alexie, Sherman (Joseph Jr.) **96, 154**
Algren, Nelson **4, 10, 33**
Allen, Edward **59**
Allen, Paula Gunn **84**
Allen, Woody **16, 52**
Allison, Dorothy E. **78, 153**
Alta **19**
Alter, Robert B(ernard) **34**
Alther, Lisa **7, 41**
Altman, Robert **16, 116**
Alvarez, Julia **93**
Ambrose, Stephen E(dward) **145**
Ammons, A(rchie) R(andolph) **2, 3, 5, 8, 9, 25, 57, 108**
L'Amour, Louis (Dearborn) **25, 55**
Anaya, Rudolfo A(lfonso) **23, 148**
Anderson, Jon (Victor) **9**
Anderson, Poul (William) **15**
Anderson, Robert (Woodruff) **23**
Angell, Roger **26**
Angelou, Maya **12, 35, 64, 77, 155**
Anthony, Piers **35**
Apple, Max (Isaac) **9, 33**
Appleman, Philip (Dean) **51**
Archer, Jules **12**
Arendt, Hannah **66, 98**
Arnow, Harriette (Louisa) Simpson **2, 7, 18**
Arrick, Fran **30**
Arzner, Dorothy **98**
Ashbery, John (Lawrence) **2, 3, 4, 6, 9, 13, 15, 25, 41, 77, 125**
Asimov, Isaac **1, 3, 9, 19, 26, 76, 92**
Attaway, William (Alexander) **92**
Auchincloss, Louis (Stanton) **4, 6, 9, 18, 45**
Auden, W(ystan) H(ugh) **1, 2, 3, 4, 6, 9, 11, 14, 43, 123**
Auel, Jean M(arie) **31, 107**

Auster, Paul **47, 131**
Bach, Richard (David) **14**
Badanes, Jerome **59**
Baker, Elliott **8**
Baker, Nicholson **61, 165**
Baker, Russell (Wayne) **31**
Bakshi, Ralph **26**
Baldwin, James (Arthur) **1, 2, 3, 4, 5, 8, 13, 15, 17, 42, 50, 67, 90, 127**
Bambara, Toni Cade **19, 88**
Banks, Russell **37, 72**
Baraka, Amiri **1, 2, 3, 5, 10, 14, 33, 115**
Barber, Benjamin R. **141**
Barbera, Jack (Vincent) **44**
Barnard, Mary (Ethel) **48**
Barnes, Djuna **3, 4, 8, 11, 29, 127**
Barondess, Sue K(aufman) **8**
Barrett, Andrea **150**
Barrett, William (Christopher) **27**
Barth, John (Simmons) **1, 2, 3, 5, 7, 9, 10, 14, 27, 51, 89**
Barthelme, Donald **1, 2, 3, 5, 6, 8, 13, 23, 46, 59, 115**
Barthelme, Frederick **36, 117**
Barzun, Jacques (Martin) **51, 145**
Bass, Rick **79, 143**
Baumbach, Jonathan **6, 23**
Bausch, Richard (Carl) **51**
Baxter, Charles (Morley) **45, 78**
Beagle, Peter S(oyer) **7, 104**
Beattie, Ann **8, 13, 18, 40, 63, 146**
Becker, Walter **26**
Beecher, John **6**
Begiebing, Robert J(ohn) **70**
Behrman, S(amuel) N(athaniel) **40**
Belitt, Ben **22**
Bell, Madison Smartt **41, 102**
Bell, Marvin (Hartley) **8, 31**
Bellow, Saul **1, 2, 3, 6, 8, 10, 13, 15, 25, 33, 34, 63, 79**
Benary-Isbert, Margot **12**
Benchley, Peter (Bradford) **4, 8**
Benedikt, Michael **4, 14**
Benford, Gregory (Albert) **52**
Bennett, Jay **35**
Benson, Jackson J. **34**
Benson, Sally **17**
Bentley, Eric (Russell) **24**
Berendt, John (Lawrence) **86**
Berger, Melvin H. **12**
Berger, Thomas (Louis) **3, 5, 8, 11, 18, 38**
Bergstein, Eleanor **4**
Bernard, April **59**
Bernstein, Charles **142,**
Berriault, Gina **54, 109**
Berrigan, Daniel **4**
Berry, Chuck **17**
Berry, Wendell (Erdman) **4, 6, 8, 27, 46**
Berryman, John **1, 2, 3, 4, 6, 8, 10, 13, 25, 62**
Bessie, Alvah **23**
Bettelheim, Bruno **79**
Betts, Doris (Waugh) **3, 6, 28**

Bidart, Frank **33**
Birkerts, Sven **116**
Bishop, Elizabeth **1, 4, 9, 13, 15, 32**
Bishop, John **10**
Blackburn, Paul **9, 43**
Blackmur, R(ichard) P(almer) **2, 24**
Blaise, Clark **29**
Blatty, William Peter **2**
Blessing, Lee **54**
Blish, James (Benjamin) **14**
Bloch, Robert (Albert) **33**
Bloom, Harold **24, 103**
Blount, Roy (Alton) Jr. **38**
Blume, Judy (Sussman) **12, 30**
Bly, Robert (Elwood) **1, 2, 5, 10, 15, 38, 128**
Bochco, Steven **35**
Bogan, Louise **4, 39, 46, 93**
Bogosian, Eric **45, 141**
Bograd, Larry **35**
Bonham, Frank **12**
Bontemps, Arna(ud Wendell) **1, 18**
Booth, Philip **23**
Booth, Wayne C(layson) **24**
Bottoms, David **53**
Bourjaily, Vance (Nye) **8, 62**
Bova, Ben(jamin William) **45**
Bowers, Edgar **9**
Bowles, Jane (Sydney) **3, 68**
Bowles, Paul (Frederick) **1, 2, 19, 53**
Boyle, Kay **1, 5, 19, 58, 121**
Boyle, T(homas) Coraghessan **36, 55, 90**
Bradbury, Ray (Douglas) **1, 3, 10, 15, 42, 98**
Bradley, David (Henry) Jr. **23, 118**
Bradley, John Ed(mund Jr.) **55**
Bradley, Marion Zimmer **30**
Bradshaw, John **70**
Brady, Joan **86**
Brammer, William **31**
Brancato, Robin F(idler) **35**
Brand, Millen **7**
Branden, Barbara **44**
Branley, Franklyn M(ansfield) **21**
Brautigan, Richard (Gary) **1, 3, 5, 9, 12, 34, 42**
Braverman, Kate **67**
Brennan, Maeve **5**
Bridgers, Sue Ellen **26**
Brin, David **34**
Brodkey, Harold (Roy) **56**
Brodsky, Joseph **4, 6, 13, 36, 100**
Brodsky, Michael (Mark) **19**
Bromell, Henry **5**
Broner, E(sther) M(asserman) **19**
Bronk, William (M.) **10**
Brooks, Cleanth **24, 86, 110**
Brooks, Gwendolyn (Elizabeth) **1, 2, 4, 5, 15, 49, 125**
Brooks, Mel **12**
Brooks, Peter **34**
Brooks, Van Wyck **29**
Brosman, Catharine Savage **9**
Broughton, T(homas) Alan **19**
Broumas, Olga **10, 73**

Brown, Claude **30**
Brown, Dee (Alexander) **18, 47**
Brown, Rita Mae **18, 43, 79**
Brown, Rosellen **32**
Brown, Sterling Allen **1, 23, 59**
Brown, (William) Larry **73**
Brownmiller, Susan **159**
Browne, (Clyde) Jackson **21**
Browning, Tod **16**
Bruccoli, Matthew J(oseph) **34**
Bruce, Lenny **21**
Bryan, C(ourtlandt) D(ixon) B(arnes) **29**
Buchwald, Art(hur) **33**
Buck, Pearl S(ydenstricker) **7, 11, 18, 127**
Buckley, Christopher **165**
Buckley, William F(rank) Jr. **7, 18, 37**
Buechner, (Carl) Frederick **2, 4, 6, 9**
Bukowski, Charles **2, 5, 9, 41, 82, 108**
Bullins, Ed **1, 5, 7**
Burke, Kenneth (Duva) **2, 24**
Burnshaw, Stanley **3, 13, 44**
Burr, Anne **6**
Burroughs, William S(eward) **1, 2, 5, 15, 22, 42, 75, 109**
Busch, Frederick **7, 10, 18, 47, 166**
Bush, Ronald **34**
Butler, Octavia E(stelle) **38, 121**
Butler, Robert Olen (Jr.) **81, 162**
Byars, Betsy (Cromer) **35**
Byrne, David **26**
Cage, John (Milton Jr.) **41**
Cain, James M(allahan) **3, 11, 28**
Caldwell, Erskine (Preston) **1, 8, 14, 50, 60**
Caldwell, (Janet Miriam) Taylor (Holland) **2, 28, 39**
Calisher, Hortense **2, 4, 8, 38, 134**
Cameron, Carey **59**
Cameron, Peter **44**
Campbell, John W(ood Jr.) **32**
Campbell, Joseph **69**
Campion, Jane **95**
Canby, Vincent **13**
Canin, Ethan **55**
Capote, Truman **1, 3, 8, 13, 19, 34, 38, 58**
Capra, Frank **16**
Caputo, Philip **32**
Card, Orson Scott **44, 47, 50**
Carey, Ernestine Gilbreth **17**
Carlisle, Henry (Coffin) **33**
Carlson, Ron(ald F.) **54**
Carpenter, Don(ald Richard) **41**
Carpenter, John **161**
Carr, Caleb **86**
Carr, John Dickson **3**
Carr, Virginia Spencer **34**
Carroll, James P. **38**
Carroll, Jim **35, 143**
Carruth, Hayden **4, 7, 10, 18, 84**
Carson, Rachel Louise **71**
Carver, Raymond **22, 36, 53, 55, 126**
Casey, John (Dudley) **59**
Casey, Michael **2**
Casey, Warren (Peter) **12**
Cassavetes, John **20**
Cassill, R(onald) V(erlin) **4, 23**
Cassity, (Allen) Turner **6, 42**
Castaneda, Carlos (Cesar Aranha) **12, 119**
Castedo, Elena **65**
Castillo, Ana (Hernandez Del) **151**
Catton, (Charles) Bruce **35**
Caunitz, William J. **34**
Chabon, Michael **55, 149**
Chappell, Fred (Davis) **40, 78, 162**
Charyn, Jerome **5, 8, 18**
Chase, Mary Ellen **2**
Chayefsky, Paddy **23**
Cheever, John **3, 7, 8, 11, 15, 25, 64**
Cheever, Susan **18, 48**
Cheney, Lynne V. **70**
Chester, Alfred **49**
Childress, Alice **12, 15, 86, 96**
Chin, Frank (Chew Jr.) **135**

Choi, Susan **119**
Chomsky, (Avram) Noam **132**
Chute, Carolyn **39**
Ciardi, John (Anthony) **10, 40, 44, 129**
Cimino, Michael **16**
Cisneros, Sandra **69, 118**
Clampitt, Amy **32**
Clancy, Tom **45, 112**
Clark, Eleanor **5, 19**
Clark, Walter Van Tilburg **28**
Clarke, Shirley **16**
Clavell, James (duMaresq) **6, 25, 87**
Cleaver, (Leroy) Eldridge **30, 119**
Clifton, (Thelma) Lucille **19, 66, 162**
Coburn, D(onald) L(ee) **10**
Codrescu, Andrei **46, 121**
Coen, Ethan **108**
Coen, Joel **108**
Cohen, Arthur A(llen) **7, 31**
Coles, Robert (Martin) **108**
Collier, Christopher **30**
Collier, James Lincoln **30**
Collins, Linda **44**
Colter, Cyrus **58**
Colum, Padraic **28**
Colwin, Laurie (E.) **5, 13, 23, 84**
Condon, Richard (Thomas) **4, 6, 8, 10, 45, 100**
Connell, Evan S(helby) Jr. **4, 6, 45**
Connelly, Marc(us Cook) **7**
Conroy, (Donald) Pat(rick) **30, 74**
Cook, Robin **14**
Cooke, Elizabeth **55**
Cook-Lynn, Elizabeth **93**
Cooper, J(oan) California **56**
Coover, Robert (Lowell) **3, 7, 15, 32, 46, 87, 161**
Coppola, Francis Ford **16, 126**
Corcoran, Barbara (Asenath) **17**
Corman, Cid **9**
Cormier, Robert (Edmund) **12, 30**
Corn, Alfred (DeWitt III) **33**
Cornwell, Patricia (Daniels) **155**
Corso, (Nunzio) Gregory **1, 11**
Costain, Thomas B(ertram) **30**
Cowley, Malcolm **39**
Cozzens, James Gould **1, 4, 11, 92**
Crane, R(onald) S(almon) **27**
Crase, Douglas **58**
Creeley, Robert (White) **1, 2, 4, 8, 11, 15, 36, 78**
Crews, Harry (Eugene) **6, 23, 49**
Crichton, (John) Michael **2, 6, 54, 90**
Cristofer, Michael **28**
Cronenberg, David **143**
Crow Dog, Mary (Ellen) **93**
Crowley, John **57**
Crumb, R(obert) **17**
Cryer, Gretchen (Kiger) **21**
Cudlip, David R(ockwell) **34**
Cummings, E(dward) E(stlin) **1, 3, 8, 12, 15, 68**
Cunningham, J(ames) V(incent) **3, 31**
Cunningham, Julia (Woolfolk) **12**
Cunningham, Michael **34**
Currie, Ellen **44**
Dacey, Philip **51**
Dahlberg, Edward **1, 7, 14**
Daitch, Susan **103**
Daly, Elizabeth **52**
Daly, Maureen **17**
Dannay, Frederic **11**
Danvers, Dennis **70**
Danziger, Paula **21**
Davenport, Guy (Mattison Jr.) **6, 14, 38**
Davidson, Donald (Grady) **2, 13, 19**
Davidson, Sara **9**
Davis, Angela (Yvonne) **77**
Davis, H(arold) L(enoir) **49**
Davison, Peter (Hubert) **28**
Dawson, Fielding **6**
Deer, Sandra **45**

Delany, Samuel R(ay) Jr. **8, 14, 38, 141**
Delbanco, Nicholas (Franklin) **6, 13, 167**
DeLillo, Don **8, 10, 13, 27, 39, 54, 76, 143**
Deloria, Vine (Victor) Jr. **21, 122**
Del Vecchio, John M(ichael) **29**
de Man, Paul (Adolph Michel) **55**
DeMarinis, Rick **54**
Demby, William **53**
Denby, Edwin (Orr) **48**
De Palma, Brian (Russell) **20**
Deren, Maya **16, 102**
Derleth, August (William) **31**
Deutsch, Babette **18**
De Vries, Peter **1, 2, 3, 7, 10, 28, 46**
Dexter, Pete **34, 55**
Diamond, Neil **30**
Dick, Philip K(indred) **10, 30, 72**
Dickey, James (Lafayette) **1, 2, 4, 7, 10, 15, 47, 109**
Dickey, William **3, 28**
Dickinson, Charles **49**
Didion, Joan **1, 3, 8, 14, 32, 129**
Dillard, Annie **9, 60, 115**
Dillard, R(ichard) H(enry) W(ilde) **5**
Disch, Thomas M(ichael) **7, 36**
Dixon, Stephen **52**
Dobyns, Stephen **37**
Doctorow, E(dgar) L(aurence) **6, 11, 15, 18, 37, 44, 65, 113**
Dodson, Owen (Vincent) **79**
Doerr, Harriet **34**
Donaldson, Stephen R(eeder) **46, 138**
Donleavy, J(ames) P(atrick) **1, 4, 6, 10, 45**
Donovan, John **35**
Doolittle, Hilda **3, 8, 14, 31, 34, 73**
Dorn, Edward (Merton) **10, 18**
Dorris, Michael (Anthony) **109**
Dos Passos, John (Roderigo) **1, 4, 8, 11, 15, 25, 34, 82**
Douglas, Ellen **73**
Dove, Rita (Frances) **50, 81**
Dowell, Coleman **60**
Drexler, Rosalyn **2, 6**
Drury, Allen (Stuart) **37**
Duberman, Martin (Bauml) **8**
Dubie, Norman (Evans) **36**
Du Bois, W(illiam) E(dward) B(urghardt) **1, 2, 13, 64, 96**
Dubus, André **13, 36, 97**
Duffy, Bruce **50**
Dugan, Alan **2, 6**
Dumas, Henry L. **6, 62**
Duncan, Lois **26**
Duncan, Robert (Edward) **1, 2, 4, 7, 15, 41, 55**
Dunn, Katherine (Karen) **71**
Dunn, Stephen (Elliott) **36**
Dunne, John Gregory **28**
Durang, Christopher (Ferdinand) **27, 38**
Durban, (Rosa) Pam **39**
Dworkin, Andrea **43, 123**
Dwyer, Thomas A. **114**
Dybek, Stuart **114**
Dylan, Bob **3, 4, 6, 12, 77**
Eastlake, William (Derry) **8**
Eberhart, Richard (Ghormley) **3, 11, 19, 56**
Eberstadt, Fernanda **39**
Eckert, Allan W. **17**
Edel, (Joseph) Leon **29, 34**
Edgerton, Clyde (Carlyle) **39**
Edmonds, Walter D(umaux) **35**
Edson, Russell **13**
Edwards, Gus **43**
Ehle, John (Marsden Jr.) **27**
Ehrenreich, Barbara **110**
Eigner, Larry **9**
Eiseley, Loren Corey **7**
Eisenstadt, Jill **50**
Eliade, Mircea **19**
Eliot, T(homas) S(tearns) **1, 2, 3, 6, 9, 10, 13, 15, 24, 34, 41, 55, 57, 113**

Elkin, Stanley L(awrence) **4, 6, 9, 14, 27, 51, 91**
Elledge, Scott **34**
Elliott, George P(aul) **2**
Ellis, Bret Easton **39, 71, 117**
Ellison, Harlan (Jay) **1, 13, 42, 139**
Ellison, Ralph (Waldo) **1, 3, 11, 54, 86, 114**
Ellmann, Lucy (Elizabeth) **61**
Ellmann, Richard (David) **50**
Elman, Richard (Martin) **19**
L'Engle, Madeleine (Camp Franklin) **12**
Ephron, Nora **17, 31**
Epstein, Daniel Mark **7**
Epstein, Jacob **19**
Epstein, Joseph **39**
Epstein, Leslie **27**
Erdman, Paul E(mil) **25**
Erdrich, Louise **39, 54, 120**
Erickson, Steve **64**
Eshleman, Clayton **7**
Estleman, Loren D. **48**
Eugenides, Jeffrey **81**
Everett, Percival L. **57**
Everson, William (Oliver) **1, 5, 14**
Exley, Frederick (Earl) **6, 11**
Ezekiel, Tish O'Dowd **34**
Fagen, Donald **26**
Fair, Ronald L. **18**
Faludi, Susan **140**
Fante, John (Thomas) **60**
Farina, Richard **9**
Farley, Walter (Lorimer) **17**
Farmer, Philip José **1, 19**
Farrell, James T(homas) **1, 4, 8, 11, 66**
Fast, Howard (Melvin) **23, 131**
Faulkner, William (Cuthbert) **1, 3, 6, 8, 9, 11, 14, 18, 28, 52, 68**
Fauset, Jessie Redmon **19, 54**
Faust, Irvin **8**
Fearing, Kenneth (Flexner) **51**
Federman, Raymond **6, 47**
Feiffer, Jules (Ralph) **2, 8, 64**
Feinberg, David B. **59**
Feldman, Irving (Mordecai) **7**
Felsen, Henry Gregor **17**
Ferber, Edna **18, 93**
Ferlinghetti, Lawrence (Monsanto) **2, 6, 10, 27, 111**
Ferrigno, Robert **65**
Fiedler, Leslie A(aron) **4, 13, 24**
Field, Andrew **44**
Fierstein, Harvey (Forbes) **33**
Fish, Stanley Eugene **142**
Fisher, M(ary) F(rances) K(ennedy) **76, 87**
Fisher, Vardis (Alvero) **7**
Fitzgerald, Robert (Stuart) **39**
Flanagan, Thomas (James Bonner) **25, 52**
Fleming, Thomas (James) **37**
Foote, Horton **51, 91**
Foote, Shelby **75**
Forbes, Esther **12**
Forché, Carolyn (Louise) **25, 83, 86**
Ford, John **16**
Ford, Richard **46, 99**
Foreman, Richard **50**
Forman, James Douglas **21**
Fornés, María Irene **39, 61**
Forrest, Leon (Richard) **4**
Fosse, Bob **20**
Fox, Paula **2, 8, 121**
Fox, William Price (Jr.) **22**
Francis, Robert (Churchill) **15**
Frank, Elizabeth **39**
Fraze, Candida (Merrill) **50**
Frazier, Ian **46**
Freeman, Judith **55**
French, Albert **86**
French, Marilyn **10, 18, 60**
Friedan, Betty (Naomi) **74**
Friedman, B(ernard) H(arper) **7**
Friedman, Bruce Jay **3, 5, 56**
Frost, Robert (Lee) **1, 3, 4, 9, 10, 13, 15, 26, 34, 44**
Frye, (Herman) Northrop **24, 70**
Fuchs, Daniel **34**
Fuchs, Daniel **8, 22**
Fukuyama, Francis **131**
Fuller, Charles (H. Jr.) **25**
Fulton, Alice **52**
Fuson, Robert H(enderson) **70**
Fussell, Paul **74**
Gaddis, William **1, 3, 6, 8, 10, 19, 43, 86**
Gaines, Ernest J(ames) **3, 11, 18, 86**
Gaitskill, Mary **69**
Gallagher, Tess **18, 63**
Gallant, Roy A(rthur) **17**
Gallico, Paul (William) **2**
Galvin, James **38**
Gann, Ernest Kellogg **23**
Garcia, Cristina **76**
Gardner, Herb(ert) **44**
Gardner, John (Champlin) Jr. **2, 3, 5, 7, 8, 10, 18, 28, 34**
Garrett, George (Palmer) **3, 11, 51**
Garrigue, Jean **2, 8**
Gass, William H(oward) **1, 2, 8, 11, 15, 39, 132**
Gates, Henry Louis Jr. **65**
Gay, Peter (Jack) **158**
Gaye, Marvin (Pentz Jr.) **26**
Gelbart, Larry (Simon) **21, 61**
Gelber, Jack **1, 6, 14, 79**
Gellhorn, Martha (Ellis) **14, 60**
Gent, Peter **29**
George, Jean Craighead **35**
Gertler, T. **134**
Ghiselin, Brewster **23**
Gibbons, Kaye **50, 88, 145**
Gibson, William **23**
Gibson, William (Ford) **39, 63**
Gifford, Barry (Colby) **34**
Gilbreth, Frank B(unker) Jr. **17**
Gilchrist, Ellen (Louise) **34, 48, 143**
Giles, Molly **39**
Gilliam, Terry (Vance) **21, 141**
Gilroy, Frank D(aniel) **2**
Gilstrap, John **99**
Ginsberg, Allen **1, 2, 3, 4, 6, 13, 36, 69, 109**
Giovanni, Nikki **2, 4, 19, 64, 117**
Glasser, Ronald J. **37**
Gleick, James (W.) **147**
Glück, Louise (Elisabeth) **7, 22, 44, 81, 160**
Godwin, Gail (Kathleen) **5, 8, 22, 31, 69, 125**
Goines, Donald **80**
Gold, Herbert **4, 7, 14, 42, 152**
Goldbarth, Albert **5, 38**
Goldman, Francisco **76**
Goldman, William (W.) **1, 48**
Goldsberry, Steven **34**
Goodman, Paul **1, 2, 4, 7**
Gordon, Caroline **6, 13, 29, 83**
Gordon, Mary (Catherine) **13, 22, 128**
Gordon, Sol **26**
Gordone, Charles **1, 4**
Gould, Lois **4, 10**
Gould, Stephen Jay **163**
Goyen, (Charles) William **5, 8, 14, 40**
Grafton, Sue **163**
Graham, Jorie **48, 118**
Grau, Shirley Ann **4, 9, 146**
Graver, Elizabeth **70**
Gray, Amlin **29**
Gray, Francine du Plessix **22, 153**
Gray, Spalding **49, 112**
Grayson, Richard (A.) **38**
Greeley, Andrew M(oran) **28**
Green, Hannah **3**
Green, Julien **3, 11, 77**
Green, Paul (Eliot) **25**
Greenberg, Joanne (Goldenberg) **7, 30**
Greenberg, Richard **57**
Greenblatt, Stephen J(ay) **70**
Greene, Bette **30**
Greene, Gael **8**
Gregor, Arthur **9**
Griffin, John Howard **68**
Griffin, Peter **39**
Grisham, John **84**
Grumbach, Doris (Isaac) **13, 22, 64**
Grunwald, Lisa **44**
Guare, John **8, 14, 29, 67**
Gubar, Susan (David) **145**
Guest, Barbara **34**
Guest, Judith (Ann) **8, 30**
Guild, Nicholas M. **33**
Gunn, Bill **5**
Gurganus, Allan **70**
Gurney, A(lbert) R(amsdell) Jr. **32, 50, 54**
Gustafson, James M(oody) **100**
Guterson, David **91**
Guthrie, A(lfred) B(ertram) Jr. **23**
Guy, Rosa (Cuthbert) **26**
Hacker, Marilyn **5, 9, 23, 72, 91**
Hailey, Elizabeth Forsythe **40**
Haines, John (Meade) **58**
Haldeman, Joe (William) **61**
Haley, Alex(ander Murray Palmer) **8, 12, 76**
Hall, Donald (Andrew Jr.) **1, 13, 37, 59, 151**
Halpern, Daniel **14**
Hamill, Pete **10**
Hamilton, Edmond **1**
Hamilton, Virginia (Esther) **26**
Hammett, (Samuel) Dashiell **3, 5, 10, 19, 47**
Hamner, Earl (Henry) Jr. **12**
Hannah, Barry **23, 38, 90**
Hansberry, Lorraine (Vivian) **17, 62**
Hansen, Joseph **38**
Hanson, Kenneth O(stlin) **13**
Hardwick, Elizabeth (Bruce) **13**
Harjo, Joy **83**
Harlan, Louis R(udolph) **34**
Harling, Robert **53**
Harmon, William (Ruth) **38**
Harper, Michael S(teven) **7, 22**
Harris, MacDonald **9**
Harris, Mark **19**
Harrison, Barbara Grizzuti **144**
Harrison, Harry (Max) **42**
Harrison, James (Thomas) **6, 14, 33, 66, 143**
Harrison, Kathryn **70, 151**
Harriss, Will(ard Irvin) **34**
Hart, Moss **66**
Hartman, Geoffrey H. **27**
Haruf, Kent **34**
Hass, Robert **18, 39, 99**
Haviaras, Stratis **33**
Hawkes, John (Clendennin Burne Jr.) **1, 2, 3, 4, 7, 9, 14, 15, 27, 49**
Hayden, Robert E(arl) **5, 9, 14, 37**
Hayman, Ronald **44**
H. D. **3, 8, 14, 31, 34, 73**
Hearne, Vicki **56**
Hearon, Shelby **63**
Hecht, Anthony (Evan) **8, 13, 19**
Hecht, Ben **8**
Heifner, Jack **11**
Heilbrun, Carolyn G(old) **25**
Heinemann, Larry (Curtiss) **50**
Heinlein, Robert A(nson) **1, 3, 8, 14, 26, 55**
Heller, Joseph **1, 3, 5, 8, 11, 36, 63**
Hellman, Lillian (Florence) **2, 4, 8, 14, 18, 34, 44, 52**
Helprin, Mark **7, 10, 22, 32**
Hemingway, Ernest (Miller) **1, 3, 6, 8, 10, 13, 19, 30, 34, 39, 41, 44, 50, 61, 80**
Hempel, Amy **39**
Henley, Beth **23**
Hentoff, Nat(han Irving) **26**
Herbert, Frank (Patrick) **12, 23, 35, 44, 85**
Herbst, Josephine (Frey) **34**
Herlihy, James Leo **6**
Herrmann, Dorothy **44**
Hersey, John (Richard) **1, 2, 7, 9, 40, 81, 97**
L'Heureux, John (Clarke) **52**

Heyen, William **13, 18**
Higgins, George V(incent) **4, 7, 10, 18**
Highsmith, (Mary) Patricia **2, 4, 14, 42, 102**
Highwater, Jamake (Mamake) **12**
Hijuelos, Oscar **65**
Hill, George Roy **26**
Hillerman, Tony **62**
Himes, Chester (Bomar) **2, 4, 7, 18, 58, 108**
Hinton, S(usan) E(loise) **30, 111**
Hirsch, Edward **31, 50**
Hirsch, E(ric) D(onald) Jr. **79**
Hoagland, Edward **28**
Hoban, Russell (Conwell) **7, 25**
Hobson, Laura Z(ametkin) **7, 25**
Hochman, Sandra **3, 8**
Hoffman, Alice **51**
Hoffman, Daniel (Gerard) **6, 13, 23**
Hoffman, Stanley **5**
Hoffman, William **141**
Hoffman, William M(oses) **40**
Hogan, Linda **73**
Holland, Isabelle **21**
Hollander, John **2, 5, 8, 14**
Holleran, Andrew **38**
Holmes, John Clellon **56**
Honig, Edwin **33**
Horgan, Paul (George Vincent O'Shaughnessy) **9, 53**
Horovitz, Israel (Arthur) **56**
Horwitz, Julius **14**
Hougan, Carolyn **34**
Howard, Maureen **5, 14, 46, 151**
Howard, Richard **7, 10, 47**
Howe, Fanny (Quincy) **47**
Howe, Irving **85**
Howe, Susan **72, 152**
Howe, Tina **48**
Howes, Barbara **15**
Hubbard, L(afayette) Ron(ald) **43**
Huddle, David **49**
Hughart, Barry **39**
Hughes, (James) Langston **1, 5, 10, 15, 35, 44, 108**
Hugo, Richard F(ranklin) **6, 18, 32**
Humphrey, William **45**
Humphreys, Josephine **34, 57**
Hunt, E(verette) Howard (Jr.) **3**
Hunt, Marsha **70**
Hunter, Evan **11, 31**
Hunter, Kristin (Eggleston) **35**
Hurston, Zora Neale **7, 30, 61**
Huston, John (Marcellus) **20**
Hustvedt, Siri **76**
Huxley, Aldous (Leonard) **1, 3, 4, 5, 8, 11, 18, 35, 79**
Hwang, David Henry **55**
Hyde, Margaret O(ldroyd) **21**
Hynes, James **65**
Ian, Janis **21**
Ignatow, David **4, 7, 14, 40**
Ingalls, Rachel (Holmes) **42**
Inge, William (Motter) **1, 8, 19**
Innaurato, Albert (F.) **21, 60**
Irving, John (Winslow) **13, 23, 38, 112**
Isaacs, Susan **32**
Isler, Alan (David) **91**
Ivask, Ivar Vidrik **14**
Jackson, Jesse **12**
Jackson, Shirley **11, 60, 87**
Jacobs, Jim **12**
Jacobsen, Josephine **48, 102**
Jakes, John (William) **29**
Jameson, Fredric (R.) **142**
Janowitz, Tama **43, 145**
Jarrell, Randall **1, 2, 6, 9, 13, 49**
Jeffers, (John) Robinson **2, 3, 11, 15, 54**
Jen, Gish **70**
Jennings, Waylon **21**
Jensen, Laura (Linnea) **37**
Jin, Xuefei **109**
Joel, Billy **26**
Johnson, Charles (Richard) **7, 51, 65, 163**

Johnson, Denis **52, 160**
Johnson, Diane **5, 13, 48**
Johnson, Joyce **58**
Johnson, Judith (Emlyn) **7, 15**
Jones, Edward P. **76**
Jones, Gayl **6, 9, 131**
Jones, James **1, 3, 10, 39**
Jones, LeRoi **1, 2, 3, 5, 10, 14**
Jones, Louis B. **65**
Jones, Madison (Percy Jr.) **4**
Jones, Nettie (Pearl) **34**
Jones, Preston **10**
Jones, Robert F(rancis) **7**
Jones, Thom (Douglas) **81**
Jong, Erica **4, 6, 8, 18, 83**
Jordan, June **5, 11, 23, 114**
Jordan, Pat(rick M.) **37**
Just, Ward (Swift) **4, 27**
Justice, Donald (Rodney) **6, 19, 102**
Kadohata, Cynthia **59, 122**
Kahn, Roger **30**
Kaletski, Alexander **39**
Kallman, Chester (Simon) **2**
Kaminsky, Stuart M(elvin) **59**
Kanin, Garson **22**
Kantor, MacKinlay **7**
Kaplan, David Michael **50**
Kaplan, James **59**
Karl, Frederick R(obert) **34**
Katz, Steve **47**
Kauffman, Janet **42**
Kaufman, Bob (Garnell) **49**
Kaufman, George S. **38**
Kaufman, Sue **3, 8**
Kazan, Elia **6, 16, 63**
Kazin, Alfred **34, 38, 119**
Keaton, Buster **20**
Keene, Donald **34**
Keillor, Garrison **40, 115**
Kellerman, Jonathan **44**
Kelley, William Melvin **22**
Kellogg, Marjorie **2**
Kemelman, Harry **2**
Kennedy, Adrienne (Lita) **66**
Kennedy, William **6, 28, 34, 53**
Kennedy, X. J. **8, 42**
Kenny, Maurice (Francis) **87**
Kerouac, Jack **1, 2, 3, 5, 14, 29, 61**
Kerr, Jean **22**
Kerr, M. E. **12, 35**
Kerr, Robert **55**
Kerrigan, (Thomas) Anthony **4, 6**
Kesey, Ken (Elton) **1, 3, 6, 11, 46, 64**
Kesselring, Joseph (Otto) **45**
Kessler, Jascha (Frederick) **4**
Kettelkamp, Larry (Dale) **12**
Keyes, Daniel **80**
Kherdian, David **6, 9**
Kienzle, William X(avier) **25**
Killens, John Oliver **10**
Kincaid, Jamaica **43, 68, 137**
King, Martin Luther Jr. **83**
King, Stephen (Edwin) **12, 26, 37, 61, 113**
King, Thomas **89**
Kingman, Lee **17**
Kingsley, Sidney **44**
Kingsolver, Barbara **55, 81, 130**
Kingston, Maxine (Ting Ting) Hong **12, 19, 58, 121**
Kinnell, Galway **1, 2, 3, 5, 13, 29, 129**
Kirkwood, James **9**
Kissinger, Henry A(lfred) **137**
Kizer, Carolyn (Ashley) **15, 39, 80**
Klappert, Peter **57**
Klein, Joe **154**
Klein, Norma **30**
Klein, T(heodore) E(ibon) D(onald) **34**
Knapp, Caroline **99**
Knebel, Fletcher **14**
Knight, Etheridge **40**
Knowles, John **1, 4, 10, 26**
Koch, Kenneth **5, 8, 44**

Komunyakaa, Yusef **86, 94**
Koontz, Dean R(ay) **78**
Kopit, Arthur (Lee) **1, 18, 33**
Kosinski, Jerzy (Nikodem) **1, 2, 3, 6, 10, 15, 53, 70**
Kostelanetz, Richard (Cory) **28**
Kotlowitz, Robert **4**
Kotzwinkle, William **5, 14, 35**
Kozol, Jonathan **17**
Kozoll, Michael **35**
Kramer, Kathryn **34**
Kramer, Larry **42**
Kristofferson, Kris **26**
Krumgold, Joseph (Quincy) **12**
Krutch, Joseph Wood **24**
Kubrick, Stanley **16**
Kumin, Maxine (Winokur) **5, 13, 28, 164**
Kunitz, Stanley (Jasspon) **6, 11, 14, 148**
Kushner, Tony **81**
Kuzma, Greg **7**
Lancaster, Bruce **36**
Landis, John **26**
Langer, Elinor **34**
Lapine, James (Elliot) **39**
Larsen, Eric **55**
Larsen, Nella **37**
Larson, Charles R(aymond) **31**
Lasch, Christopher **102**
Latham, Jean Lee **12**
Lattimore, Richmond (Alexander) **3**
Laughlin, James **49**
Lear, Norman (Milton) **12**
Leavitt, David **34**
Lebowitz, Fran(ces Ann) **11, 36**
Lee, Andrea **36**
Lee, Chang-rae **91**
Lee, Don L. **2**
Lee, George W(ashington) **52**
Lee, Helen Elaine **86**
Lee, Lawrence **34**
Lee, Manfred B(ennington) **11**
Lee, (Nelle) Harper **12, 60**
Lee, Shelton Jackson **105**
Lee, Stan **17**
Leet, Judith **11**
Leffland, Ella **19**
Le Guin, Ursula K(roeber) **8, 13, 22, 45, 71, 136**
Leiber, Fritz (Reuter Jr.) **25**
Leimbach, Marti **65**
Leithauser, Brad **27**
Lelchuk, Alan **5**
Lemann, Nancy **39**
Lentricchia, Frank (Jr.) **34**
Leonard, Elmore (John Jr.) **28, 34, 71, 120**
Lerman, Eleanor **9**
Lerman, Rhoda **56**
Lester, Richard **20**
Levertov, Denise **1, 2, 3, 5, 8, 15, 28, 66**
Levi, Jonathan **76**
Levin, Ira **3, 6**
Levin, Meyer **7**
Levine, Philip **2, 4, 5, 9, 14, 33, 118**
Levinson, Deirdre **49**
Levitin, Sonia (Wolff) **17**
Lewis, Janet **41**
Leyner, Mark **92**
Lieber, Joel **6**
Lieberman, Laurence (James) **4, 36**
Lifton, Robert Jay **67**
Lightman, Alan P(aige) **81**
Ligotti, Thomas (Robert) **44**
Lindbergh, Anne (Spencer) Morrow **82**
Linney, Romulus **51**
Lipsyte, Robert (Michael) **21**
Lish, Gordon (Jay) **45**
Littell, Robert **42**
Loewinsohn, Ron(ald William) **52**
Logan, John (Burton) **5**
Lopate, Phillip **29**
Lopez, Barry (Holstun) **70**
Lord, Bette Bao **23**

Lorde, Audre (Geraldine) **18, 71**
Louie, David Wong **70**
Lowell, Robert (Traill Spence Jr.) **1, 2, 3, 4, 5, 8, 9, 11, 15, 37, 124**
Loy, Mina **28**
Lucas, Craig **64**
Lucas, George **16**
Ludlam, Charles **46, 50**
Ludlum, Robert **22, 43**
Ludwig, Ken **60**
Lurie, Alison **4, 5, 18, 39**
Lynch, David (K.) **66, 162**
Lynn, Kenneth S(chuyler) **50**
Lytle, Andrew (Nelson) **22**
Maas, Peter **29**
Macdonald, Cynthia **13, 19**
MacDonald, John D(ann) **3, 27, 44**
MacInnes, Helen (Clark) **27, 39**
Maclean, Norman (Fitzroy) **78**
MacLeish, Archibald **3, 8, 14, 68**
MacShane, Frank **39**
Madden, (Jerry) David **5, 15**
Madhubuti, Haki R. **6, 73**
Mailer, Norman **1, 2, 3, 4, 5, 8, 11, 14, 28, 39, 74, 111**
Major, Clarence **3, 19, 48**
Malamud, Bernard **1, 2, 3, 5, 8, 9, 11, 18, 27, 44, 78, 85**
Malcolm X **82, 117**
Maloff, Saul **5**
Malone, Michael (Christopher) **43**
Malzberg, Barry N(athaniel) **7**
Mamet, David (Alan) **9, 15, 34, 46, 91, 166**
Mamoulian, Rouben (Zachary) **16**
Mano, D. Keith **2, 10**
Manso, Peter **39**
Margulies, Donald **76**
Markfield, Wallace **8**
Markson, David M(errill) **67**
Marlowe, Stephen **70**
Marquand, John P(hillips) **2, 10**
Marqués, René **96**
Marshall, Garry **17**
Marshall, Paule **27, 72**
Martin, Steve **30**
Martin, Valerie **89**
Maso, Carole **44**
Mason, Bobbie Ann **28, 43, 82, 154**
Masters, Hilary **48**
Mastrosimone, William **36**
Matheson, Richard (Burton) **37**
Mathews, Harry **6, 52**
Mathews, John Joseph **84**
Matthews, William (Procter III) **40**
Matthias, John (Edward) **9**
Matthiessen, Peter **5, 7, 11, 32, 64**
Maupin, Armistead (Jones Jr.) **95**
Maxwell, William (Keepers Jr.) **19**
May, Elaine **16**
Maynard, Joyce **23**
Maysles, Albert **16**
Maysles, David **16**
Mazer, Norma Fox **26**
McBrien, William (Augustine) **44**
McCaffrey, Anne (Inez) **17**
McCall, Nathan **86**
McCarthy, Mary (Therese) **1, 3, 5, 14, 24, 39, 59**
McCauley, Stephen (D.) **50**
McClure, Michael (Thomas) **6, 10**
McCorkle, Jill (Collins) **51**
McCourt, James **5**
McCourt, Malachy **119**
McCullers, (Lula) Carson (Smith) **1, 4, 10, 12, 48, 100**
McDermott, Alice **90**
McElroy, Joseph **5, 47**
McFarland, Dennis **65**
McGinley, Phyllis **14**
McGinniss, Joe **32**
McGrath, Thomas (Matthew) **28, 59**

McGuane, Thomas (Francis III) **3, 7, 18, 45, 127**
McHale, Tom **3, 5**
McInerney, Jay **34, 112**
McIntyre, Vonda N(eel) **18**
McKuen, Rod **1, 3**
McMillan, Terry (L.) **50, 61, 112**
McMurtry, Larry (Jeff) **2, 3, 7, 11, 27, 44, 127**
McNally, Terrence **4, 7, 41, 91**
McNally, T. M. **82**
McNamer, Deirdre **70**
McNeal, Tom **119**
McNickle, (William) D'Arcy **89**
McPhee, John (Angus) **36**
McPherson, James Alan **19, 77**
McPherson, William (Alexander) **34**
Mead, Margaret **37**
Medoff, Mark (Howard) **6, 23**
Mehta, Ved (Parkash) **37**
Meltzer, Milton **26**
Mendelsohn, Jane **99**
Meredith, William (Morris) **4, 13, 22, 55**
Merkin, Daphne **44**
Merrill, James (Ingram) **2, 3, 6, 8, 13, 18, 34, 91**
Merton, Thomas **1, 3, 11, 34, 83**
Merwin, W(illiam) S(tanley) **1, 2, 3, 5, 8, 13, 18, 45, 88**
Mewshaw, Michael **9**
Meyers, Jeffrey **39**
Michaels, Leonard **6, 25**
Michener, James A(lbert) **1, 5, 11, 29, 60, 109**
Miles, Jack **100**
Miles, Josephine (Louise) **1, 2, 14, 34, 39**
Millar, Kenneth **14**
Miller, Arthur **1, 2, 6, 10, 15, 26, 47, 78**
Miller, Henry (Valentine) **1, 2, 4, 9, 14, 43, 84**
Miller, Jason **2**
Miller, Sue **44**
Miller, Walter M(ichael Jr.) **4, 30**
Millett, Kate **67**
Millhauser, Steven (Lewis) **21, 54, 109**
Milner, Ron(ald) **56**
Miner, Valerie **40**
Minot, Susan **44, 159**
Minus, Ed **39**
Mitchell, Joseph (Quincy) **98**
Modarressi, Taghi (M.) **44**
Mohr, Nicholasa **12**
Mojtabai, A(nn) G(race) **5, 9, 15, 29**
Momaday, N(avarre) Scott **2, 19, 85, 95, 160**
Monette, Paul **82**
Montague, John (Patrick) **13, 46**
Montgomery, Marion H. Jr. **7**
Moody, Rick **147**
Mooney, Ted **25**
Moore, Lorrie **39, 45, 68, 165**
Moore, Marianne (Craig) **1, 2, 4, 8, 10, 13, 19, 47**
Moraga, Cherrie **126**
Morgan, Berry **6**
Morgan, (George) Frederick **23**
Morgan, Robin (Evonne) **2**
Morgan, Seth **65**
Morris, Bill **76**
Morris, Wright **1, 3, 7, 18, 37**
Morrison, Jim **17**
Morrison, Toni **4, 10, 22, 55, 81, 87**
Mosher, Howard Frank **62**
Mosley, Walter **97**
Moss, Howard **7, 14, 45, 50**
Motley, Willard (Francis) **18**
Mountain Wolf Woman **92**
Moyers, Bill **74**
Mueller, Lisel **13, 51**
Mull, Martin **17**
Mungo, Raymond **72**
Murphy, Sylvia **34**
Murray, Albert L. **73**

Muske, Carol **90**
Myers, Walter Dean **35**
Nabokov, Vladimir (Vladimirovich) **1, 2, 3, 6, 8, 11, 15, 23, 44, 46, 64**
Nash, (Frediric) Ogden **23**
Naylor, Gloria **28, 52, 156**
Neihardt, John Gneisenau **32**
Nelson, Willie **17**
Nemerov, Howard (Stanley) **2, 6, 9, 36**
Neufeld, John (Arthur) **17**
Neville, Emily Cheney **12**
Newlove, Donald **6**
Newman, Charles **2, 8**
Newman, Edwin (Harold) **14**
Newton, Suzanne **35**
Nichols, John (Treadwell) **38**
Niedecker, Lorine **10, 42**
Nin, Anaïs **1, 4, 8, 11, 14, 60, 127**
Nissenson, Hugh **4, 9**
Nixon, Agnes Eckhardt **21**
Norman, Marsha **28**
Norton, Andre **12**
Nova, Craig **7, 31**
Nunn, Kem **34**
Nyro, Laura **17**
Oates, Joyce Carol **1, 2, 3, 6, 9, 11, 15, 19, 33, 52, 108, 134**
O'Brien, Darcy **11**
O'Brien, (William) Tim(othy) **7, 19, 40, 103**
Ochs, Phil(ip David) **17**
O'Connor, Edwin (Greene) **14**
O'Connor, (Mary) Flannery **1, 2, 3, 6, 10, 13, 15, 21, 66, 104**
O'Dell, Scott **30**
Odets, Clifford **2, 28, 98**
O'Donovan, Michael John **14**
O'Grady, Timothy **59**
O'Hara, Frank **2, 5, 13, 78**
O'Hara, John (Henry) **1, 2, 3, 6, 11, 42**
O Hehir, Diana **41**
Olds, Sharon **32, 39, 85**
Oliver, Mary **19, 34, 98**
Olsen, Tillie **4, 13, 114**
Olson, Charles (John) **1, 2, 5, 6, 9, 11, 29**
Olson, Toby **28**
Oppen, George **7, 13, 34**
Orlovitz, Gil **22**
Ortiz, Simon J(oseph) **45**
Ostriker, Alicia (Suskin) **132**
Otto, Whitney **70**
Owens, Rochelle **8**
Ozick, Cynthia **3, 7, 28, 62, 155**
Pack, Robert **13**
Pagels, Elaine Hiesey **104**
Paglia, Camille (Anna) **68**
Paley, Grace **4, 6, 37, 140**
Palliser, Charles **65**
Pancake, Breece D'J **29**
Paretsky, Sara **135**
Parini, Jay (Lee) **54, 133**
Parker, Dorothy (Rothschild) **15, 68**
Parker, Robert B(rown) **27**
Parks, Gordon (Alexander Buchanan) **1, 16**
Pastan, Linda (Olenik) **27**
Patchen, Kenneth **1, 2, 18**
Paterson, Katherine (Womeldorf) **12, 30**
Peacock, Molly **60**
Pearson, T(homas) R(eid) **39**
Peck, John (Frederick) **3**
Peck, Richard (Wayne) **21**
Peck, Robert Newton **17**
Peckinpah, (David) Sam(uel) **20**
Percy, Walker **2, 3, 6, 8, 14, 18, 47, 65**
Perelman, S(idney) J(oseph) **3, 5, 9, 15, 23, 44, 49**
Perloff, Marjorie G(abrielle) **137**
Pesetsky, Bette **28**
Peterkin, Julia Mood **31**
Peters, Joan K(aren) **39**
Peters, Robert L(ouis) **7**
Petrakis, Harry Mark **3**
Petry, Ann (Lane) **1, 7, 18**

Philipson, Morris H. **53**
Phillips, Jayne Anne **15, 33, 139**
Phillips, Robert (Schaeffer) **28**
Piercy, Marge **3, 6, 14, 18, 27, 62, 128**
Pinckney, Darryl **76**
Pineda, Cecile **39**
Pinkwater, Daniel Manus **35**
Pinsky, Robert **9, 19, 38, 94, 121**
Pirsig, Robert M(aynard) **4, 6, 73**
Plante, David (Robert) **7, 23, 38**
Plath, Sylvia **1, 2, 3, 5, 9, 11, 14, 17, 50, 51, 62, 111**
Platt, Kin **26**
Plimpton, George (Ames) **36**
Plumly, Stanley (Ross) **33**
Pohl, Frederik **18**
Poitier, Sidney **26**
Pollitt, Katha **28, 122**
Polonsky, Abraham (Lincoln) **92**
Pomerance, Bernard **13**
Porter, Connie (Rose) **70**
Porter, Katherine Anne **1, 3, 7, 10, 13, 15, 27, 101**
Potok, Chaim **2, 7, 14, 26, 112**
Pound, Ezra (Weston Loomis) **1, 2, 3, 4, 5, 7, 10, 13, 18, 34, 48, 50, 112**
Povod, Reinaldo **44**
Powell, Adam Clayton Jr. **89**
Powell, Dawn **66**
Powell, Padgett **34**
Power, Susan **91**
Powers, J(ames) F(arl) **1, 4, 8, 57**
Powers, John R. **66**
Powers, Richard (S.) **93**
Prager, Emily **56**
Price, (Edward) Reynolds **3, 6, 13, 43, 50, 63**
Price, Richard **6, 12**
Prince **35**
Pritchard, William H(arrison) **34**
Probst, Mark **59**
Prokosch, Frederic **4, 48**
Prose, Francine **45**
Proulx, E(dna) Annie **81, 158**
Pryor, Richard (Franklin Lenox Thomas) **26**
Purdy, James (Amos) **2, 4, 10, 28, 52**
Puzo, Mario **1, 2, 6, 36, 107**
Pynchon, Thomas (Ruggles Jr.) **2, 3, 6, 9, 11, 18, 33, 62, 72, 123**
Quay, Stephen **95**
Quay, Timothy **95**
Queen, Ellery **3, 11**
Quinn, Peter **91**
Rabe, David (William) **4, 8, 33**
Rado, James **17**
Raeburn, John (Hay) **34**
Ragni, Gerome **17**
Rahv, Philip **24**
Rakosi, Carl **47**
Rampersad, Arnold **44**
Rand, Ayn **3, 30, 44, 79**
Randall, Dudley (Felker) **1, 135**
Ransom, John Crowe **2, 4, 5, 11, 24**
Raphael, Frederic (Michael) **2, 14**
Rechy, John (Francisco) **1, 7, 14, 18, 107**
Reddin, Keith **67**
Redmon, Anne **22**
Reed, Ishmael **2, 3, 5, 6, 13, 32, 60**
Reed, Lou **21**
Remarque, Erich Maria **21**
Rexroth, Kenneth **1, 2, 6, 11, 22, 49, 112**
Reynolds, Jonathan **6, 38**
Reynolds, Michael S(hane) **44**
Reznikoff, Charles **9**
Ribman, Ronald (Burt) **7**
Rice, Anne **41, 128**
Rice, Elmer (Leopold) **7, 49**
Rich, Adrienne (Cecile) **3, 6, 7, 11, 18, 36, 73, 76, 125**
Richter, Conrad (Michael) **30**
Riding, Laura **3, 7**
Ringwood, Gwen(dolyn Margaret) Pharis **48**

Rivers, Conrad Kent **1**
Robbins, Harold **5**
Robbins, Trina **21**
Robinson, Jill **10**
Robinson, Kim Stanley **34**
Robinson, Marilynne **25**
Robinson, Smokey **21**
Robison, Mary **42, 98**
Roddenberry, Gene **17**
Rodgers, Mary **12**
Rodman, Howard **65**
Rodriguez, Richard **155**
Roethke, Theodore (Huebner) **1, 3, 8, 11, 19, 46, 101**
Rogers, Thomas Hunton **57**
Rogin, Gilbert **18**
Roiphe, Anne (Richardson) **3, 9**
Rooke, Leon **25, 34**
Rose, Wendy **85**
Rosen, Richard (Dean) **39**
Rosenthal, M(acha) L(ouis) **28**
Rossner, Judith (Perelman) **6, 9, 29**
Roth, Henry **2, 6, 11, 104**
Roth, Philip (Milton) **1, 2, 3, 4, 6, 9, 15, 22, 31, 47, 66, 86, 119**
Rothenberg, Jerome **6, 57**
Rovit, Earl (Herbert) **7**
Royko, Mike **109**
Ruark, Gibbons **3**
Rudnik, Raphael **7**
Rukeyser, Muriel **6, 10, 15, 27**
Rule, Jane (Vance) **27**
Rush, Norman **44**
Russ, Joanna **15**
Russell, Jeffrey Burton **70**
Ryan, Cornelius (John) **7**
Ryan, Michael **65**
Sachs, Marilyn (Stickle) **35**
Sackler, Howard (Oliver) **14**
Sadoff, Ira **9**
Safire, William **10**
Sagan, Carl (Edward) **30, 112**
Said, Edward W. **123**
Saint, H(arry) F. **50**
Salamanca, J(ack) R(ichard) **4, 15**
Sale, Kirkpatrick **68**
Salinas, Luis Omar **90**
Salinger, J(erome) D(avid) **1, 3, 8, 12, 55, 56, 138**
Salter, James **7, 52, 59**
Sanchez, Sonia **5, 116**
Sandburg, Carl (August) **1, 4, 10, 15, 35**
Sanders, (James) Ed(ward) **53**
Sanders, Lawrence **41**
Sandoz, Mari(e Susette) **28**
Saner, Reg(inald Anthony) **9**
Santiago, Danny **33**
Santmyer, Helen Hooven **33**
Santos, Bienvenido N(uqui) **22**
Sapphire, Brenda **99**
Saroyan, William **1, 8, 10, 29, 34, 56**
Sarton, (Eleanor) May **4, 14, 49, 91**
Saul, John (W. III) **46**
Savage, Thomas **40**
Savan, Glenn **50**
Sayers, Valerie **50, 122**
Sayles, John (Thomas) **7, 10, 14**
Schaeffer, Susan Fromberg **6, 11, 22**
Schell, Jonathan **35**
Schevill, James (Erwin) **7**
Schisgal, Murray (Joseph) **6**
Schlesinger, Arthur M(eier) Jr. **84**
Schnackenberg, Gjertrud (Cecelia) **40**
Schor, Sandra (M.) **65**
Schorer, Mark **9**
Schrader, Paul (Joseph) **26**
Schulberg, Budd (Wilson) **7, 48**
Schulz, Charles M(onroe) **12**
Schuyler, James Marcus **5, 23**
Schwartz, Delmore (David) **2, 4, 10, 45, 87**
Schwartz, John Burnham **59**
Schwartz, Lynne Sharon **31**

Scoppettone, Sandra **26**
Scorsese, Martin **20, 89**
Scott, Evelyn **43**
Scott, Joanna **50**
Sebestyen, Ouida **30**
Seelye, John (Douglas) **7**
Segal, Erich (Wolf) **3, 10**
Seger, Bob **35**
Seidel, Frederick (Lewis) **18**
Selby, Hubert Jr. **1, 2, 4, 8**
Selzer, Richard **74**
Serling, (Edward) Rod(man) **30**
Seton, Cynthia Propper **27**
Settle, Mary Lee **19, 61**
Sexton, Anne (Harvey) **2, 4, 6, 8, 10, 15, 53, 123**
Shaara, Michael (Joseph Jr.) **15**
Shacochis, Bob **39**
Shange, Ntozake **8, 25, 38, 74, 126**
Shanley, John Patrick **75**
Shapiro, Jane **76**
Shapiro, Karl (Jay) **4, 8, 15, 53**
Shaw, Irwin **7, 23, 34**
Shawn, Wallace **41**
Shea, Lisa **86**
Sheed, Wilfrid (John Joseph) **2, 4, 10, 53**
Shepard, Jim **36**
Shepard, Lucius **34**
Shepard, Sam **4, 6, 17, 34, 41, 44**
Sherburne, Zoa (Lillian Morin) **30**
Sherman, Jonathan Marc **55**
Sherman, Martin **19**
Shields, Carol **91, 113**
Shields, David **97**
Shilts, Randy **85**
Shreve, Susan Richards **23**
Shue, Larry **52**
Shulman, Alix Kates **2, 10**
Shuster, Joe **21**
Siegel, Jerome **21**
Sigal, Clancy **7**
Silko, Leslie (Marmon) **23, 74, 114**
Silver, Joan Micklin **20**
Silverberg, Robert **7, 140**
Silverstein, Alvin **17**
Silverstein, Virginia B(arbara Opshelor) **17**
Simak, Clifford D(onald) **1, 55**
Simic, Charles **6, 9, 22, 49, 68, 130**
Simmons, Charles (Paul) **57**
Simmons, Dan **44**
Simon, Carly **26**
Simon, (Marvin) Neil **6, 11, 31, 39, 70**
Simon, Paul (Frederick) **17**
Simpson, Louis (Aston Marantz) **4, 7, 9, 32, 149**
Simpson, Mona (Elizabeth) **44, 146**
Sinclair, Upton (Beall) **1, 11, 15, 63**
Singer, Isaac Bashevis **1, 3, 6, 9, 11, 15, 23, 38, 69, 111**
Singleton, John **156**
Sissman, L(ouis) E(dward) **9, 18**
Slaughter, Frank G(ill) **29**
Slavitt, David R(ytman) **5, 14**
Smiley, Jane (Graves) **53, 76, 144**
Smith, Anna Deavere **86**
Smith, Betty (Wehner) **19**
Smith, Clark Ashton **43**
Smith, Dave **22, 42**
Smith, Lee **25, 73**
Smith, Martin Cruz **25**
Smith, Mary-Ann Tirone **39**
Smith, Patti **12**
Smith, William Jay **6**
Snodgrass, W(illiam) D(e Witt) **2, 6, 10, 18, 68**
Snyder, Gary (Sherman) **1, 2, 5, 9, 32, 120**
Snyder, Zilpha Keatley **17**
Soderbergh, Steven **154**
Sokolov, Raymond **7**
Sommer, Scott **25**
Sondheim, Stephen (Joshua) **30, 39, 147**
Sontag, Susan **1, 2, 10, 13, 31, 105**

Sorrentino, Gilbert **3, 7, 14, 22, 40**
Soto, Gary **32, 80**
Southern, Terry **7**
Spackman, W(illiam) M(ode) **46**
Spacks, Barry (Bernard) **14**
Spanidou, Irini **44**
Spencer, Elizabeth **22**
Spencer, Scott **30**
Spicer, Jack **8, 18, 72**
Spiegelman, Art **76**
Spielberg, Peter **6**
Spielberg, Steven **20**
Spinrad, Norman (Richard) **46**
Spivack, Kathleen (Romola Drucker) **6**
Spoto, Donald **39**
Springsteen, Bruce (F.) **17**
Squires, (James) Radcliffe **51**
Stafford, Jean **4, 7, 19, 68**
Stafford, William (Edgar) **4, 7, 29**
Stanton, Maura **9**
Starbuck, George (Edwin) **53**
Steele, Timothy (Reid) **45**
Stegner, Wallace (Earle) **9, 49, 81**
Steinbeck, John (Ernst) **1, 5, 9, 13, 21, 34, 45, 75, 124**
Steinem, Gloria **63**
Steiner, George **24**
Sterling, Bruce **72**
Stern, Gerald **40, 100**
Stern, Richard (Gustave) **4, 39**
Sternberg, Josef von **20**
Stevens, Mark **34**
Stevenson, Anne (Katharine) **7, 33**
Still, James **49**
Stitt, Milan **29**
Stolz, Mary (Slattery) **12**
Stone, Irving **7**
Stone, Oliver (William) **73**
Stone, Robert (Anthony) **5, 23, 42**
Storm, Hyemeyohsts **3**
Stout, Rex (Todhunter) **3**
Strand, Mark **6, 18, 41, 71**
Straub, Peter (Francis) **28, 107**
Stribling, T(homas) S(igismund) **23**
Stuart, Jesse (Hilton) **1, 8, 11, 14, 34**
Sturgeon, Theodore (Hamilton) **22, 39**
Styron, William **1, 3, 5, 11, 15, 60**
Sukenick, Ronald **3, 4, 6, 48**
Summers, Hollis (Spurgeon Jr.) **10**
Susann, Jacqueline **3**
Swados, Elizabeth (A.) **12**
Swados, Harvey **5**
Swan, Gladys **69**
Swarthout, Glendon (Fred) **35**
Swenson, May **4, 14, 61, 106**
Talese, Gay **37**
Tallent, Elizabeth (Ann) **45**
Tally, Ted **42**
Tan, Amy (Ruth) **59, 120, 151**
Tartt, Donna **76**
Tate, James (Vincent) **2, 6, 25**
Tate, (John Orley) Allen **2, 4, 6, 9, 11, 14, 24**
Tavel, Ronald **6**
Taylor, Eleanor Ross **5**
Taylor, Henry (Splawn) **44**
Taylor, Mildred D(elois) **21**
Taylor, Peter (Hillsman) **1, 4, 18, 37, 44, 50, 71**
Taylor, Robert Lewis **14**
Terkel, Studs **38**
Terry, Megan **19**
Tesich, Steve **40, 69**
Tevis, Walter **42**
Theroux, Alexander (Louis) **2, 25**
Theroux, Paul (Edward) **5, 8, 11, 15, 28, 46, 159**
Thomas, Audrey (Callahan) **7, 13, 37, 107**
Thomas, Joyce Carol **35**
Thomas, Lewis **35**
Thomas, Piri **17**
Thomas, Ross (Elmore) **39**
Thompson, Hunter S(tockton) **9, 17, 40, 104**

Thompson, Jim (Myers) **69**
Thurber, James (Grover) **5, 11, 25, 125**
Tilghman, Christopher **65**
Tillich, Paul (Johannes) **131**
Tillinghast, Richard (Williford) **29**
Tolson, Melvin B(eaunorus) **36, 105**
Tomlin, Lily **17**
Toole, John Kennedy **19, 64**
Toomer, Jean **1, 4, 13, 22**
Torrey, E(dwin) Fuller **34**
Towne, Robert (Burton) **87**
Traven, B. **8, 11**
Trevanian **29**
Trilling, Diana (Rubin) **129**
Trilling, Lionel **9, 11, 24**
Trow, George W. S. **52**
Trudeau, Garry B. **12**
Trumbo, Dalton **19**
Tryon, Thomas **3, 11**
Tuck, Lily **70**
Tunis, John R(oberts) **12**
Turco, Lewis (Putnam) **11, 63**
Turner, Frederick **48**
Tyler, Anne **7, 11, 18, 28, 44, 59, 103**
Uhry, Alfred **55**
Ulibarrí, Sabine R(eyes) **83**
Unger, Douglas **34**
Updike, John (Hoyer) **1, 2, 3, 5, 7, 9, 13, 15, 23, 34, 43, 70, 139**
Urdang, Constance (Henriette) **47**
Uris, Leon (Marcus) **7, 32**
Vachss, Andrew (Henry) **106**
Valdez, Luis (Miguel) **84**
Van Ash, Cay **34**
Vandenburgh, Jane **59**
Van Doren, Mark **6, 10**
Van Duyn, Mona (Jane) **3, 7, 63, 116**
Van Peebles, Melvin **2, 20**
Van Vechten, Carl **33**
Vaughn, Stephanie **62**
Vendler, Helen (Hennessy) **138**
Vidal, Gore **2, 4, 6, 8, 10, 22, 33, 72, 142**
Viereck, Peter (Robert Edwin) **4**
Vinge, Joan (Carol) D(ennison) **30**
Viola, Herman J(oseph) **70**
Vizenor, Gerald Robert **103**
Vliet, R(ussell) G(ordon) **22**
Vogel, Paula A(nne) **76**
Voigt, Cynthia **30**
Voigt, Ellen Bryant **54**
Vollmann, William T. **89**
Vonnegut, Kurt Jr. **1, 2, 3, 4, 5, 8, 12, 22, 40, 60, 111**
Wagman, Fredrica **7**
Wagner-Martin, Linda (C.) **50**
Wagoner, David (Russell) **3, 5, 15**
Wakefield, Dan **7**
Wakoski, Diane **2, 4, 7, 9, 11, 40**
Waldman, Anne (Lesley) **7**
Walker, Alice (Malsenior) **5, 6, 9, 19, 27, 46, 58, 103, 167**
Walker, Joseph A. **19**
Walker, Margaret (Abigail) **1, 6**
Wallace, David Foster **50, 114**
Wallace, Irving **7, 13**
Wallant, Edward Lewis **5, 10**
Wambaugh, Joseph (Aloysius Jr.) **3, 18**
Ward, Douglas Turner **19**
Warhol, Andy **20**
Warren, Robert Penn **1, 4, 6, 8, 10, 13, 18, 39, 53, 59**
Wasserstein, Wendy **32, 59, 90**
Waters, Frank (Joseph) **88**
Watkins, Paul **55**
Webb, Charles (Richard) **7**
Webb, James H(enry) Jr. **22**
Weber, Lenora Mattingly **12**
Weidman, Jerome **7**
Weiss, Theodore (Russell) **3, 8, 14**
Welch, James **6, 14, 52**
Wellek, Rene **28**
Weller, Michael **10, 53**

Welles, (George) Orson **20, 80**
Wellman, Mac **65**
Wellman, Manly Wade **49**
Wells, Rosemary **12**
Welty, Eudora **1, 2, 5, 14, 22, 33, 105**
Wersba, Barbara **30**
Wescott, Glenway **13**
Wesley, Richard (Errol) **7**
West, Cornel (Ronald) **134**
West, Delno C(loyde) Jr. **70**
West, (Mary) Jessamyn **7, 17**
West, Paul **7, 14, 96**
Westlake, Donald E(dwin) **7, 33**
Whalen, Philip **6, 29**
Wharton, William (a pseudonym) **18, 37**
Wheelock, John Hall **14**
White, Edmund (Valentine III) **27, 110**
White, E(lwyn) B(rooks) **10, 34, 39**
White, Hayden V. **148**
Whitney, Phyllis A(yame) **42**
Whittemore, (Edward) Reed (Jr.) **4**
Wicker, Tom **7**
Wideman, John Edgar **5, 34, 36, 67, 122**
Wieners, John **7**
Wiesel, Elie(zer) **3, 5, 11, 37, 165**
Wiggins, Marianne **57**
Wilbur, Richard (Purdy) **3, 6, 9, 14, 53, 110**
Wild, Peter **14**
Wilder, Billy **20**
Wilder, Thornton (Niven) **1, 5, 6, 10, 15, 35, 82**
Wiley, Richard **44**
Willard, Nancy **7, 37**
Williams, C(harles) K(enneth) **33, 56, 148**
Williams, John A(lfred) **5, 13**
Williams, Jonathan (Chamberlain) **13**
Williams, Joy **31**
Williams, Norman **39**
Williams, Sherley Anne **89**
Williams, Tennessee **1, 2, 5, 7, 8, 11, 15, 19, 30, 39, 45, 71, 111**
Williams, Thomas (Alonzo) **14**
Williams, William Carlos **1, 2, 5, 9, 13, 22, 42, 67**
Willingham, Calder (Baynard Jr.) **5, 51**
Wilson, August **39, 50, 63, 118**
Wilson, Brian **12**
Wilson, Edmund **1, 2, 3, 8, 24**
Wilson, Lanford **7, 14, 36**
Wilson, Robert M. **7, 9**
Wilson, Sloan **32**
Wilson, William S(mith) **49**
Winters, (Arthur) Yvor **4, 8, 32**
Winters, Janet Lewis **41**
Wiseman, Frederick **20**
Wodehouse, P(elham) G(renville) **1, 2, 5, 10, 22**
Woiwode, Larry (Alfred) **6, 10**
Wojciechowska, Maia (Teresa) **26**
Wolf, Naomi **157**
Wolfe, Gene (Rodman) **25**
Wolfe, George C. **49**
Wolfe, Thomas Kennerly Jr. **147**
Wolff, Geoffrey (Ansell) **41**
Wolff, Tobias (Jonathan Ansell) **39, 64**
Wolitzer, Hilma **17**
Wonder, Stevie **12**
Wong, Jade Snow **17**
Woolrich, Cornell **77**
Wouk, Herman **1, 9, 38**
Wright, Charles (Penzel Jr.) **6, 13, 28, 119, 146**
Wright, Charles Stevenson **49**
Wright, James (Arlington) **3, 5, 10, 28**
Wright, Richard (Nathaniel) **1, 3, 4, 9, 14, 21, 48, 74**
Wright, Stephen **33**
Wright, William **44**
Wurlitzer, Rudolph **2, 4, 15**
Wylie, Philip (Gordon) **43**
Yates, Richard **7, 8, 23**
Yep, Laurence Michael **35**

Yerby, Frank G(arvin) **1, 7, 22**
Yglesias, Helen **7, 22**
Young, Al(bert James) **19**
Young, Marguerite (Vivian) **82**
Young Bear, Ray A. **94**
Yurick, Sol **6**
Zamora, Bernice (B. Ortiz) **89**
Zappa, Frank **17**
Zaturenska, Marya **6, 11**
Zelazny, Roger (Joseph) **21**
Ziegenhagen, Eric **55**
Zindel, Paul **6, 26**
Zoline, Pamela **62**
Zukofsky, Louis **1, 2, 4, 7, 11, 18**
Zweig, Paul **34, 42**

ANGOLAN

Wellman, Manly Wade **49**

ANTIGUAN

Edwards, Gus **43**
Kincaid, Jamaica **43, 68, 137**

ARGENTINIAN

Bioy Casares, Adolfo **4, 8, 13, 88**
Borges, Jorge Luis **1, 2, 3, 4, 6, 8, 9, 10, 13, 19, 44, 48, 83**
Cortázar, Julio **2, 3, 5, 10, 13, 15, 33, 34, 92**
Costantini, Humberto **49**
Dorfman, Ariel **48, 77**
Guevara, Che **87**
Guevara (Serna), Ernesto **87**
Mujica Lainez, Manuel **31**
Puig, Manuel **3, 5, 10, 28, 65, 133**
Sabato, Ernesto (R.) **10, 23**
Valenzuela, Luisa **31, 104**

ARMENIAN

Mamoulian, Rouben (Zachary) **16**

AUSTRALIAN

Anderson, Jessica (Margaret) Queale **37**
Astley, Thea (Beatrice May) **41**
Brinsmead, H(esba) F(ay) **21**
Buckley, Vincent (Thomas) **57**
Buzo, Alexander (John) **61**
Carey, Peter **40, 55, 96**
Clark, Mavis Thorpe **12**
Clavell, James (duMaresq) **6, 25, 87**
Conway, Jill K(er) **152**
Courtenay, Bryce **59**
Davison, Frank Dalby **15**
Elliott, Sumner Locke **38**
FitzGerald, Robert D(avid) **19**
Greer, Germaine **131**
Grenville, Kate **61**
Hall, Rodney **51**
Hazzard, Shirley **18**
Hope, A(lec) D(erwent) **3, 51**
Hospital, Janette Turner **42, 145**
Jolley, (Monica) Elizabeth **46**
Jones, Rod **50**
Keneally, Thomas (Michael) **5, 8, 10, 14, 19, 27, 43, 117**
Koch, C(hristopher) J(ohn) **42**
Lawler, Raymond Evenor **58**
Malouf, (George Joseph) David **28, 86**
Matthews, Greg **45**
McAuley, James Phillip **45**
McCullough, Colleen **27, 107**
Murray, Les(lie Allan) **40**
Porter, Peter (Neville Frederick) **5, 13, 33**
Prichard, Katharine Susannah **46**
Shapcott, Thomas W(illiam) **38**
Slessor, Kenneth **14**
Stead, Christina (Ellen) **2, 5, 8, 32, 80**
Stow, (Julian) Randolph **23, 48**
Thiele, Colin (Milton) **17**
Weir, Peter (Lindsay) **20**
West, Morris L(anglo) **6, 33**

White, Patrick (Victor Martindale) **3, 4, 5, 7, 9, 18, 65, 69**
Wilding, Michael **73**
Williamson, David (Keith) **56**
Wright, Judith (Arundell) **11, 53**

AUSTRIAN

Adamson, Joy(-Friederike Victoria) **17**
Bachmann, Ingeborg **69**
Bernhard, Thomas **3, 32, 61**
Bettelheim, Bruno **79**
Frankl, Viktor E(mil) **93**
Gregor, Arthur **9**
Handke, Peter **5, 8, 10, 15, 38, 134**
Hochwaelder, Fritz **36**
Jandl, Ernst **34**
Lang, Fritz **20, 103**
Lind, Jakov **1, 2, 4, 27, 82**
Perloff, Marjorie G(abrielle) **137**
Sternberg, Josef von **20**
Wellek, Rene **28**
Wilder, Billy **20**

BARBADIAN

Brathwaite, Edward (Kamau) **11**
Clarke, Austin C(hesterfield) **8, 53**
Kennedy, Adrienne (Lita) **66**
Lamming, George (William) **2, 4, 66, 144**

BELGIAN

Crommelynck, Fernand **75**
Ghelderode, Michel de **6, 11**
Lévi-Strauss, Claude **38**
Mallet-Joris, Françoise **11**
Michaux, Henri **8, 19**
Sarton, (Eleanor) May **4, 14, 49, 91**
Simenon, Georges (Jacques Christian) **1, 2, 3, 8, 18, 47**
van Itallie, Jean-Claude **3**
Yourcenar, Marguerite **19, 38, 50, 87**

BOTSWANAN

Head, Bessie **25, 67**

BRAZILIAN

Amado, Jorge **13, 40, 106**
Boff, Leonardo (Genezio Darci) **70**
Cabral de Melo Neto, João **76**
Castaneda, Carlos (Cesar Aranha) **12, 119**
Dourado, (Waldomiro Freitas) Autran **23, 60**
Drummond de Andrade, Carlos **18**
Lispector, Clarice **43**
Ribeiro, Darcy **34**
Ribeiro, Joao Ubaldo (Osorio Pimentel) **10, 67**
Rosa, João Guimarães **23**

BULGARIAN

Belcheva, Elisaveta Lyubomirova **10**
Canetti, Elias **3, 14, 25, 75, 86**
Kristeva, Julia **77, 140**

CAMEROONIAN

Beti, Mongo **27**

CANADIAN

Acorn, Milton **15**
Aquin, Hubert **15**
Atwood, Margaret (Eleanor) **2, 3, 4, 8, 13, 15, 25, 44, 84, 135**
Avison, Margaret **2, 4, 97**
Barfoot, Joan **18**
Bellow, Saul **1, 2, 3, 6, 8, 10, 13, 15, 25, 33, 34, 63, 79**
Berton, Pierre (Francis Demarigny) **104**
Birney, (Alfred) Earle **1, 4, 6, 11**
Bissett, Bill **18**
Blais, Marie-Claire **2, 4, 6, 13, 22**
Blaise, Clark **29**

Bowering, George **15, 47**
Bowering, Marilyn R(uthe) **32**
Brossard, Nicole **115**
Buckler, Ernest **13**
Buell, John (Edward) **10**
Callaghan, Morley Edward **3, 14, 41, 65**
Campbell, Maria **85**
Carrier, Roch **13, 78**
Child, Philip **19, 68**
Chislett, (Margaret) Anne **34**
Clarke, Austin C(hesterfield) **8, 53**
Cohen, Leonard (Norman) **3, 38**
Cohen, Matt(hew) **19**
Coles, Don **46**
Cook, Michael **58**
Cooper, Douglas **86**
Coupland, Douglas **85, 133**
Craven, Margaret **17**
Cronenberg, David **143**
Davies, (William) Robertson **2, 7, 13, 25, 42, 75, 91**
de la Roche, Mazo **14**
Donnell, David **34**
Ducharme, Rejean **74**
Dudek, Louis **11, 19**
Egoyan, Atom **151**
Engel, Marian **36**
Everson, R(onald) G(ilmour) **27**
Faludy, George **42**
Ferron, Jacques **94**
Finch, Robert (Duer Claydon) **18**
Findley, Timothy **27, 102**
Fraser, Sylvia **64**
Frye, (Herman) Northrop **24, 70**
Gallant, Mavis **7, 18, 38**
Garner, Hugh **13**
Gibson, William (Ford) **39, 63**
Gilmour, David **35**
Glassco, John **9**
Gotlieb, Phyllis Fay (Bloom) **18**
Govier, Katherine **51**
Gunnars, Kristjana **69**
Gustafson, Ralph (Barker) **36**
Haig-Brown, Roderick (Langmere) **21**
Hailey, Arthur **5**
Harris, Christie (Lucy) Irwin **12**
Hébert, Anne **4, 13, 29**
Highway, Tomson **92**
Hillis, Rick **66**
Hine, (William) Daryl **15**
Hodgins, Jack **23**
Hood, Hugh (John Blagdon) **15, 28**
Hyde, Anthony **42**
Jacobsen, Josephine **48, 102**
Jiles, Paulette **13, 58**
Johnston, George (Benson) **51**
Jones, D(ouglas) G(ordon) **10**
Kelly, M(ilton) T(errence) **55**
King, Thomas **89**
Kinsella, W(illiam) P(atrick) **27, 43, 166**
Klein, A(braham) M(oses) **19**
Kogawa, Joy Nozomi **78, 129**
Krizanc, John **57**
Kroetsch, Robert **5, 23, 57, 132**
Kroker, Arthur (W.) **77**
Lane, Patrick **25**
Laurence, (Jean) Margaret (Wemyss) **3, 6, 13, 50, 62**
Layton, Irving (Peter) **2, 15, 164**
Levine, Norman **54**
Lightfoot, Gordon **26**
Livesay, Dorothy (Kathleen) **4, 15, 79**
MacEwen, Gwendolyn (Margaret) **13, 55**
MacLennan, (John) Hugh **2, 14, 92**
MacLeod, Alistair **56, 165**
Macpherson, (Jean) Jay **14**
Maillet, Antonine **54, 118**
Major, Kevin (Gerald) **26**
McFadden, David **48**
McLuhan, (Herbert) Marshall **37, 83**
Metcalf, John **37**
Mistry, Rohinton **71**

Mitchell, Joni **12**
Mitchell, W(illiam) O(rmond) **25**
Moore, Brian **1, 3, 5, 7, 8, 19, 32, 90**
Morgan, Janet **39**
Moure, Erin **88**
Mowat, Farley (McGill) **26**
Mukherjee, Bharati **53, 115**
Munro, Alice **6, 10, 19, 50, 95**
Musgrave, Susan **13, 54**
Newlove, John (Herbert) **14**
Nichol, B(arrie) P(hillip) **18**
Nowlan, Alden (Albert) **15**
Ondaatje, (Philip) Michael **14, 29, 51, 76**
Page, P(atricia) K(athleen) **7, 18**
Pollock, (Mary) Sharon **50**
Pratt, E(dwin) J(ohn) **19**
Purdy, A(lfred) W(ellington) **3, 6, 14, 50**
Quarrington, Paul (Lewis) **65**
Reaney, James **13**
Ricci, Nino **70**
Richards, David Adams **59**
Richler, Mordecai **3, 5, 9, 13, 18, 46, 70**
Ringwood, Gwen(dolyn Margaret) Pharis **48**
Ritter, Erika **52**
Rooke, Leon **25, 34**
Rosenblatt, Joe **15**
Ross, (James) Sinclair **13**
Roy, Gabrielle **10, 14**
Rule, Jane (Vance) **27**
Ryga, George **14**
Scott, F(rancis) R(eginald) **22**
Shields, Carol **91, 113**
Skelton, Robin **13**
Škvorecký, Josef (Vaclav) **15, 39, 69, 152**
Slade, Bernard **11, 46**
Smart, Elizabeth **54**
Smith, A(rthur) J(ames) M(arshall) **15**
Souster, (Holmes) Raymond **5, 14**
Suknaski, Andrew **19**
Theriault, Yves **79**
Thesen, Sharon **56**
Thomas, Audrey (Callahan) **7, 13, 37, 107**
Thompson, Judith **39**
Tremblay, Michel **29, 102**
Urquhart, Jane **90**
Vanderhaeghe, Guy **41**
van Vogt, A(lfred) E(lton) **1**
Vizinczey, Stephen **40**
Waddington, Miriam **28**
Wah, Fred(erick James) **44**
Walker, David Harry **14**
Walker, George F. **44, 61**
Webb, Phyllis **18**
Wiebe, Rudy (Henry) **6, 11, 14, 138**
Wilson, Ethel Davis (Bryant) **13**
Wright, L(aurali) R. **44**
Wright, Richard B(ruce) **6**
Young, Neil **17**

CHILEAN

Alegria, Fernando **57**
Allende, Isabel **39, 57, 97**
Donoso (Yañez), José **4, 8, 11, 32, 99**
Dorfman, Ariel **48, 77**
Neruda, Pablo **1, 2, 5, 7, 9, 28, 62**
Parra, Nicanor **2, 102**

CHINESE

Chang, Jung **71**
Ch'ien, Chung-shu **22**
Ding Ling **68**
Lord, Bette Bao **23**
Mo, Timothy (Peter) **46, 134**
Pa Chin **18**
Peake, Mervyn **7, 54**
Wong, Jade Snow **17**

COLOMBIAN

García Márquez, Gabriel (Jose) **2, 3, 8, 10, 15, 27, 47, 55, 68**

CONGOLESE

Tchicaya, Gerald Felix **101**

CUBAN

Arenas, Reinaldo **41**
Cabrera Infante, G(uillermo) **5, 25, 45, 120**
Calvino, Italo **5, 8, 11, 22, 33, 39, 73**
Carpentier (y Valmont), Alejo **8, 11, 38, 110**
Fornés, María Irene **39, 61**
Garcia, Cristina **76**
Guevara, Che **87**
Guillén, Nicolás (Cristobal) **48, 79**
Lezama Lima, José **4, 10, 101**
Padilla (Lorenzo), Heberto **38**
Sarduy, Severo **6, 97**

CZECH

Forman, Milos **164**
Friedlander, Saul **90**
Havel, Václav **25, 58, 65, 123**
Holub, Miroslav **4**
Hrabal, Bohumil **13, 67**
Klima, Ivan **56**
Kohout, Pavel **13**
Kundera, Milan **4, 9, 19, 32, 68, 115, 135**
Lustig, Arnost **56**
Seifert, Jaroslav **34, 44, 93**
Škvorecký, Josef (Vaclav) **15, 39, 69, 152**
Vaculik, Ludvik **7**

DANISH

Abell, Kjeld **15**
Bodker, Cecil **21**
Dreyer, Carl Theodor **16**
Hoeg, Peter **95, 156**

DOMINICAN REPUBLICAN

Alvarez, Julia **93**

DUTCH

Bernhard, Thomas **3, 32, 61**
Buruma, Ian **163**
de Hartog, Jan **19**
Mulisch, Harry **42**
Ruyslinck, Ward **14**
van de Wetering, Janwillem **47**

EGYPTIAN

Chedid, Andree **47**
Mahfouz, Naguīb (Abdel Azīz Al-Sabilgi) **153**

ENGLISH

Ackroyd, Peter **34, 52, 140**
Adams, Douglas (Noel) **27, 60**
Adams, Richard (George) **4, 5, 18**
Adcock, Fleur **41**
Aickman, Robert (Fordyce) **57**
Aiken, Joan (Delano) **35**
Aldington, Richard **49**
Aldiss, Brian W(ilson) **5, 14, 40**
Allingham, Margery (Louise) **19**
Almedingen, E. M. **12**
Alvarez, A(lfred) **5, 13**
Ambler, Eric **4, 6, 9**
Amis, Kingsley (William) **1, 2, 3, 5, 8, 13, 40, 44, 129**
Amis, Martin (Louis) **4, 9, 38, 62, 101**
Anderson, Lindsay (Gordon) **20**
Anthony, Piers **35**
Archer, Jeffrey (Howard) **28**
Arden, John **6, 13, 15**
Armatrading, Joan **17**
Arthur, Ruth M(abel) **12**
Arundel, Honor (Morfydd) **17**
Atkinson, Kate **99**
Auden, W(ystan) H(ugh) **1, 2, 3, 4, 6, 9, 11, 14, 43, 123**
Ayckbourn, Alan **5, 8, 18, 33, 74**
Ayrton, Michael **7**
Bagnold, Enid **25**
Bailey, Paul **45**
Bainbridge, Beryl (Margaret) **4, 5, 8, 10, 14, 18, 22, 62, 130**
Ballard, J(ames) G(raham) **3, 6, 14, 36, 137**
Banks, Lynne Reid **23**
Barker, Clive **52**
Barker, George Granville **8, 48**
Barker, Howard **37**
Barker, Pat(ricia) **32, 94, 146**
Barnes, Julian (Patrick) **42, 141**
Barnes, Peter **5, 56**
Barrett, (Roger) Syd **35**
Bates, H(erbert) E(rnest) **46**
Beer, Patricia **58**
Bennett, Alan **45, 77**
Berger, John (Peter) **2, 19**
Berkoff, Steven **56**
Bermant, Chaim (Icyk) **40**
Betjeman, John **2, 6, 10, 34, 43**
Billington, (Lady) Rachel (Mary) **43**
Binyon, T(imothy) J(ohn) **34**
Blunden, Edmund (Charles) **2, 56**
Bolt, Robert (Oxton) **14**
Bond, Edward **4, 6, 13, 23**
Booth, Martin **13**
Bowen, Elizabeth (Dorothea Cole) **1, 3, 6, 11, 15, 22, 118**
Bowie, David **17**
Boyd, William **28, 53, 70**
Bradbury, Malcolm (Stanley) **32, 61**
Bragg, Melvyn **10**
Braine, John (Gerard) **1, 3, 41**
Brenton, Howard **31**
Brittain, Vera (Mary) **23**
Brooke-Rose, Christine **40**
Brookner, Anita **32, 34, 51, 136**
Brophy, Brigid (Antonia) **6, 11, 29, 105**
Brunner, John (Kilian Houston) **8, 10**
Bunting, Basil **10, 39, 47**
Burgess, Anthony **1, 2, 4, 5, 8, 10, 13, 15, 22, 40, 62, 81, 94**
Byatt, A(ntonia) S(usan Drabble) **19, 65, 136**
Caldwell, (Janet Miriam) Taylor (Holland) **2, 28, 39**
Campbell, (John) Ramsey **42**
Carter, Angela (Olive) **5, 41, 76**
Causley, Charles (Stanley) **7**
Caute, (John) David **29**
Chambers, Aidan **35**
Chaplin, Charles Spencer **16**
Chapman, Graham **21**
Chatwin, (Charles) Bruce **28, 57, 59**
Chitty, Thomas Willes **11**
Christie, Agatha (Mary Clarissa) **1, 6, 8, 12, 39, 48, 110**
Churchill, Caryl **31, 55, 157**
Clark, (Robert) Brian **29**
Clarke, Arthur C(harles) **1, 4, 13, 18, 35, 136**
Cleese, John (Marwood) **21**
Colegate, Isabel **36**
Comfort, Alex(ander) **7**
Compton-Burnett, I(vy) **1, 3, 10, 15, 34**
Cooney, Ray **62**
Copeland, Stewart (Armstrong) **26**
Cornwell, David (John Moore) **9, 15**
Costello, Elvis **21**
Coward, Noël (Peirce) **1, 9, 29, 51**
Crace, Jim **157**
Creasey, John **11**
Crispin, Edmund **22**
Dabydeen, David **34**
D'Aguiar, Fred **145**
Dahl, Roald **1, 6, 18, 79**
Daryush, Elizabeth **6, 19**
Davie, Donald (Alfred) **5, 8, 10, 31**
Davies, Rhys **23**
Day Lewis, C(ecil) **1, 6, 10**
Deighton, Len **4, 7, 22, 46**
Delaney, Shelagh **29**
Dennis, Nigel (Forbes) **8**

CUMULATIVE NATIONALITY INDEX

Dickinson, Peter (Malcolm) **12, 35**
Drabble, Margaret **2, 3, 5, 8, 10, 22, 53, 129**
Duffy, Maureen **37**
du Maurier, Daphne **6, 11, 59**
Durrell, Lawrence (George) **1, 4, 6, 8, 13, 27, 41**
Dyer, Geoff **149**
Eagleton, Terence (Francis) **63, 132**
Edgar, David **42**
Edwards, G(erald) B(asil) **25**
Eliot, T(homas) S(tearns) **1, 2, 3, 6, 9, 10, 13, 15, 24, 34, 41, 55, 57, 113**
Elliott, Janice **47**
Ellis, A. E. **7**
Ellis, Alice Thomas **40**
Empson, William **3, 8, 19, 33, 34**
Enright, D(ennis) J(oseph) **4, 8, 31**
Ewart, Gavin (Buchanan) **13, 46**
Fairbairns, Zoe (Ann) **32**
Farrell, J(ames) G(ordon) **6**
Feinstein, Elaine **36**
Fenton, James Martin **32**
Ferguson, Niall **134**
Fielding, Helen **146**
Figes, Eva **31**
Fisher, Roy **25**
Fitzgerald, Penelope **19, 51, 61, 143**
Fleming, Ian (Lancaster) **3, 30**
Follett, Ken(neth Martin) **18**
Forester, C(ecil) S(cott) **35**
Forster, E(dward) M(organ) **1, 2, 3, 4, 9, 10, 13, 15, 22, 45, 77**
Forster, Margaret **149**
Forsyth, Frederick **2, 5, 36**
Fowles, John (Robert) **1, 2, 3, 4, 6, 9, 10, 15, 33, 87**
Francis, Dick **2, 22, 42, 102**
Fraser, George MacDonald **7**
Frayn, Michael **3, 7, 31, 47**
Freeling, Nicolas **38**
Fry, Christopher **2, 10, 14**
Fugard, Sheila **48**
Fuller, John (Leopold) **62**
Fuller, Roy (Broadbent) **4, 28**
Gardam, Jane (Mary) **43**
Gardner, John (Edmund) **30**
Garfield, Leon **12**
Garner, Alan **17**
Garnett, David **3**
Gascoyne, David (Emery) **45**
Gee, Maggie (Mary) **57**
Gerhardie, William Alexander **5**
Gilliatt, Penelope (Ann Douglass) **2, 10, 13, 53**
Glanville, Brian (Lester) **6**
Glendinning, Victoria **50**
Gloag, Julian **40**
Godden, (Margaret) Rumer **53**
Golding, William (Gerald) **1, 2, 3, 8, 10, 17, 27, 58, 81**
Graham, Winston (Mawdsley) **23**
Graves, Richard Perceval **44**
Graves, Robert (von Ranke) **1, 2, 6, 11, 39, 44, 45**
Gray, Simon (James Holliday) **9, 14, 36**
Green, Henry **2, 13, 97**
Greenaway, Peter **159**
Greene, Graham (Henry) **1, 3, 6, 9, 14, 18, 27, 37, 70, 72, 125**
Griffiths, Trevor **13, 52**
Grigson, Geoffrey (Edward Harvey) **7, 39**
Gunn, Thom(son William) **3, 6, 18, 32, 81**
Haig-Brown, Roderick (Langmere) **21**
Hailey, Arthur **5**
Hall, Rodney **51**
Hamburger, Michael (Peter Leopold) **5, 14**
Hamilton, (Anthony Walter) Patrick **51**
Hampton, Christopher (James) **4**
Hare, David **29, 58, 136**
Harris, (Theodore) Wilson **25, 159**
Harrison, Tony **43, 129**
Hartley, L(eslie) P(oles) **2, 22**

Harwood, Ronald **32**
Hastings, Selina **44**
Hawking, Stephen W(illiam) **63, 105**
Headon, (Nicky) Topper **30**
Heppenstall, (John) Rayner **10**
Hibbert, Eleanor Alice Burford **7**
Hill, Geoffrey (William) **5, 8, 18, 45**
Hill, Susan (Elizabeth) **4, 113**
Hinde, Thomas **6, 11**
Hitchcock, Alfred (Joseph) **16**
Hitchens, Christopher **157**
Hocking, Mary (Eunice) **13**
Holden, Ursula **18**
Holdstock, Robert P. **39**
Hollinghurst, Alan **55, 91**
Hooker, (Peter) Jeremy **43**
Hopkins, John (Richard) **4**
Household, Geoffrey (Edward West) **11**
Howard, Elizabeth Jane **7, 29**
Hughes, David (John) **48**
Hughes, Richard (Arthur Warren) **1, 11**
Hughes, Ted **2, 4, 9, 14, 37, 119**
Huxley, Aldous (Leonard) **1, 3, 4, 5, 8, 11, 18, 35, 79**
Idle, Eric **21**
Ingalls, Rachel (Holmes) **42**
Isherwood, Christopher (William Bradshaw) **1, 9, 11, 14, 44**
Ishiguro, Kazuo **27, 56, 59, 110**
Jacobson, Dan **4, 14**
Jagger, Mick **17**
James, C(yril) L(ionel) R(obert) **33**
James, P. D. **18, 46, 122**
Jellicoe, (Patricia) Ann **27**
Jennings, Elizabeth (Joan) **5, 14, 131**
Jhabvala, Ruth Prawer **4, 8, 29, 94, 138**
Johnson, B(ryan) S(tanley William) **6, 9**
Johnson, Pamela Hansford **1, 7, 27**
Johnson, Paul (Bede) **147**
Jolley, (Monica) Elizabeth **46**
Jones, David (Michael) **2, 4, 7, 13, 42**
Jones, Diana Wynne **26**
Jones, Mervyn **10, 52**
Jones, Mick **30**
Josipovici, Gabriel (David) **6, 43, 153**
Kavan, Anna **5, 13, 82**
Kaye, M(ary) M(argaret) **28**
Keates, Jonathan **34**
King, Francis (Henry) **8, 53, 145**
Kirkup, James **1**
Koestler, Arthur **1, 3, 6, 8, 15, 33**
Kops, Bernard **4**
Kureishi, Hanif **64, 135**
Lanchester, John **99**
Larkin, Philip (Arthur) **3, 5, 8, 9, 13, 18, 33, 39, 64**
Leavis, F(rank) R(aymond) **24**
Lee, Laurie **90**
Lee, Tanith **46**
Lehmann, Rosamond (Nina) **5**
Lennon, John (Ono) **12, 35**
Lessing, Doris (May) **1, 2, 3, 6, 10, 15, 22, 40, 94**
Levertov, Denise **1, 2, 3, 5, 8, 15, 28, 66**
Levi, Peter (Chad Tigar) **1**
Lewis, C(live) S(taples) **1, 3, 6, 14, 27, 124**
Lively, Penelope (Margaret) **32, 50**
Lodge, David (John) **36, 141**
Loy, Mina **28**
Luke, Peter (Ambrose Cyprian) **38**
MacInnes, Colin **4, 23**
Mackenzie, Compton (Edward Montague) **18**
Macpherson, (Jean) Jay **14**
Maitland, Sara (Louise) **49**
Manning, Olivia **5, 19**
Mantel, Hilary (Mary) **144**
Masefield, John (Edward) **11, 47**
Mason, Nick **35**
Maugham, W(illiam) Somerset **1, 11, 15, 67, 93**
Mayle, Peter **89**
Mayne, William (James Carter) **12**

McEwan, Ian (Russell) **13, 66**
McGrath, Patrick **55**
Mercer, David **5**
Middleton, Christopher **13**
Middleton, Stanley **7, 38**
Mitford, Nancy **44**
Mo, Timothy (Peter) **46, 134**
Moorcock, Michael (John) **5, 27, 58**
Mortimer, John (Clifford) **28, 43**
Mortimer, Penelope (Ruth) **5**
Mosley, Nicholas **43, 70**
Motion, Andrew (Peter) **47**
Mott, Michael (Charles Alston) **15, 34**
Murdoch, (Jean) Iris **1, 2, 3, 4, 6, 8, 11, 15, 22, 31, 51**
Naipaul, V(idiadhar) S(urajprasad) **4, 7, 9, 13, 18, 37, 105**
Newby, P(ercy) H(oward) **2, 13**
Nichols, Peter (Richard) **5, 36, 65**
Noon, Jeff **91**
Norfolk, Lawrence **76**
Nye, Robert **13, 42**
O'Brien, Richard **17**
O'Faolain, Julia **6, 19, 47, 108**
Olivier, Laurence (Kerr) **20**
Orton, Joe **4, 13, 43**
Osborne, John (James) **1, 2, 5, 11, 45**
Osborne, Lawrence **50**
Page, Jimmy **12**
Page, Louise **40**
Page, P(atricia) K(athleen) **7, 18**
Palin, Michael (Edward) **21**
Parkin, Frank **43**
Parks, Tim(othy Harold) **147**
Paton Walsh, Gillian **35**
Paulin, Tom **37**
Peake, Mervyn **7, 54**
Perry, Anne **126**
Phillips, Caryl **96**
Pinter, Harold **1, 3, 6, 9, 11, 15, 27, 58, 73**
Plant, Robert **12**
Poliakoff, Stephen **38**
Potter, Dennis (Christopher George) **58, 86, 123**
Powell, Anthony (Dymoke) **1, 3, 7, 9, 10, 31**
Pownall, David **10**
Powys, John Cowper **7, 9, 15, 46, 125**
Priestley, J(ohn) B(oynton) **2, 5, 9, 34**
Prince, F(rank) T(empleton) **22**
Pritchett, V(ictor) S(awdon) **5, 13, 15, 41**
Pym, Barbara (Mary Crampton) **13, 19, 37, 111**
Quin, Ann (Marie) **6**
Raine, Craig (Anthony) **32, 103**
Raine, Kathleen (Jessie) **7, 45**
Rathbone, Julian **41**
Rattigan, Terence (Mervyn) **7**
Raven, Simon (Arthur Noel) **14**
Read, Herbert Edward **4**
Read, Piers Paul **4, 10, 25**
Reading, Peter **47**
Redgrove, Peter (William) **6, 41**
Reid, Christopher (John) **33**
Rendell, Ruth (Barbara) **28, 48**
Rhys, Jean **2, 4, 6, 14, 19, 51, 124**
Rice, Tim(othy Miles Bindon) **21**
Richard, Keith **17**
Richards, I(vor) A(rmstrong) **14, 24**
Roberts, Keith (John Kingston) **14**
Roberts, Michele (Brigitte) **48**
Rowling, J(oanne) K(athleen) **137**
Rudkin, (James) David **14**
Rushdie, (Ahmed) Salman **23, 31, 55, 100**
Rushforth, Peter (Scott) **19**
Russell, (Henry) Ken(neth Alfred) **16**
Russell, William Martin **60**
Sacks, Oliver (Wolf) **67**
Sansom, William **2, 6**
Sassoon, Siegfried (Lorraine) **36, 130**
Scammell, Michael **34**
Scannell, Vernon **49**
Schama, Simon (Michael) **150**

Schlee, Ann **35**
Schumacher, E(rnst) F(riedrich) **80**
Scott, Paul (Mark) **9, 60**
Shaffer, Anthony (Joshua) **19**
Shaffer, Peter (Levin) **5, 14, 18, 37, 60**
Sharpe, Tom **36**
Shaw, Robert **5**
Sheed, Wilfrid (John Joseph) **2, 4, 10, 53**
Shute, Nevil **30**
Shuttle, Penelope (Diane) **7**
Silkin, Jon **2, 6, 43**
Sillitoe, Alan **1, 3, 6, 10, 19, 57, 148**
Simonon, Paul **30**
Simpson, N(orman) F(rederick) **29**
Sinclair, Andrew (Annandale) **2, 14**
Sinclair, Iain **76**
Sisson, C(harles) H(ubert) **8**
Sitwell, Edith **2, 9, 67**
Slaughter, Carolyn **56**
Smith, Stevie **3, 8, 25, 44**
Smith, Zadie **158**
Snow, C(harles) P(ercy) **1, 4, 6, 9, 13, 19**
Spender, Stephen (Harold) **1, 2, 5, 10, 41, 91**
Spurling, Hilary **34**
Stannard, Martin **44**
Stewart, J(ohn) I(nnes) M(ackintosh) **7, 14, 32**
Stewart, Mary (Florence Elinor) **7, 35, 117**
Stoppard, Tom **1, 3, 4, 5, 8, 15, 29, 34, 63, 91**
Storey, David (Malcolm) **2, 4, 5, 8**
Streatfeild, (Mary) Noel **21**
Strummer, Joe **30**
Summers, Andrew James **26**
Sumner, Gordon Matthew **26**
Sutcliff, Rosemary **26**
Swift, Graham (Colin) **41, 88**
Swinfen, Ann **34**
Swinnerton, Frank Arthur **31**
Symons, Julian (Gustave) **2, 14, 32**
Szirtes, George **46**
Taylor, Elizabeth **2, 4, 29**
Tennant, Emma (Christina) **13, 52**
Teran, Lisa St. Aubin de **36**
Thomas, D(onald) M(ichael) **13, 22, 31, 132**
Thubron, Colin (Gerald Dryden) **163**
Tindall, Gillian (Elizabeth) **7**
Tolkien, J(ohn) R(onald) R(euel) **1, 2, 3, 8, 12, 38**
Tomalin, Claire **166**
Tomlinson, (Alfred) Charles **2, 4, 6, 13, 45**
Townshend, Peter (Dennis Blandford) **17, 42**
Treitel, Jonathan **70**
Tremain, Rose **42**
Tuohy, Frank **37**
Turner, Frederick **48**
Unsworth, Barry (Forster) **76, 127**
Ustinov, Peter (Alexander) **1**
Van Den Bogarde, Derek Jules Gaspard Ulric Niven
Vansittart, Peter **42**
Wain, John (Barrington) **2, 11, 15, 46**
Walker, Ted **13**
Walsh, Jill Paton **35**
Warner, Francis (Robert le Plastrier) **14**
Warner, Marina **59**
Warner, Rex (Ernest) **45**
Warner, Sylvia Townsend **7, 19**
Waterhouse, Keith (Spencer) **47**
Waters, Roger **35**
Waugh, Auberon (Alexander) **7**
Waugh, Evelyn (Arthur St. John) **1, 3, 8, 13, 19, 27, 44, 107**
Waugh, Harriet **6**
Webber, Andrew Lloyd **21**
Weldon, Fay **6, 9, 11, 19, 36, 59, 122**
Weller, Paul **26**
Wesker, Arnold **3, 5, 42**
West, Anthony (Panther) **50**
West, Paul **7, 14, 96**
West, Rebecca **7, 9, 31, 50**
Westall, Robert (Atkinson) **17**
White, Patrick (Victor Martindale) **3, 4, 5, 7, 9, 18, 65, 69**
White, T(erence) H(anbury) **30**
Whitehead, E(dward) A(nthony) **5**
Whitemore, Hugh (John) **37**
Wilding, Michael **73**
Williams, Hugo **42**
Wilson, A(ndrew) N(orman) **33**
Wilson, Angus (Frank Johnstone) **2, 3, 5, 25, 34**
Wilson, Colin **3, 14**
Wilson, Snoo **33**
Wingrove, David (John) **68**
Winterson, Jeanette **64, 158**
Wodehouse, P(elham) G(renville) **1, 2, 5, 10, 22**
Wright, Rick **35**
Yorke, Henry Vincent **13**
Young, Andrew (John) **5**

ESTONIAN

Ivask, Ivar Vidrik **14**

FIJI ISLANDER

Prichard, Katharine Susannah **46**

FILIPINO

Santos, Bienvenido N(uqui) **22**

FINNISH

Haavikko, Paavo Juhani **18, 34**
Salama, Hannu **18**
Sillanpaa, Frans Eemil **19**

FRENCH

Adamov, Arthur **4, 25**
Anouilh, Jean (Marie Lucien Pierre) **1, 3, 8, 13, 40, 50**
Aragon, Louis **3, 22**
Arp, Jean **5**
Audiberti, Jacques **38**
Aymé, Marcel (Andre) **11**
Barthes, Roland (Gérard) **24, 83**
Barzun, Jacques (Martin) **51, 145**
Bataille, Georges **29**
Baudrillard, Jean **60**
Beauvoir, Simone (Lucie Ernestine Marie Bertrand) de **1, 2, 4, 8, 14, 31, 44, 50, 71, 124**
Beckett, Samuel (Barclay) **1, 2, 3, 4, 6, 9, 10, 11, 14, 18, 29, 57, 59, 83**
Blanchot, Maurice **135**
Bonnefoy, Yves **9, 15, 58**
Bresson, Robert **16**
Breton, André **2, 9, 15, 54**
Butor, Michel (Marie François) **1, 3, 8, 11, 15, 161**
Camus, Albert **1, 2, 4, 9, 11, 14, 32, 63, 69, 124**
Carrere, Emmanuel **89**
Cayrol, Jean **11**
Chabrol, Claude **16**
Char, René(-émile) **9, 11, 14, 55**
Chedid, Andree **47**
Cixous, Hélène **92**
Clair, Rene **20**
Cocteau, Jean (Maurice Eugène Clément) **1, 8, 15, 16, 43**
Cousteau, Jacques-Yves **30**
del Castillo, Michel **38**
Derrida, Jacques **24, 87**
Destouches, Louis-Ferdinand **9, 15**
Duhamel, Georges **8**
Duras, Marguerite **3, 6, 11, 20, 34, 40, 68, 100**
Ernaux, Annie **88**
Federman, Raymond **6, 47**
Foucault, Michel **31, 34, 69**
Fournier, Pierre **11**
Francis, Claude **50**
Gallo, Max Louis **95**
Gao Xingjian **167**
Gary, Romain **25**
Gascar, Pierre **11**
Genet, Jean **1, 2, 5, 10, 14, 44, 46**
Giono, Jean **4, 11**
Godard, Jean-Luc **20**
Goldmann, Lucien **24**
Gontier, Fernande **50**
Gray, Francine du Plessix **22, 153**
Green, Julien **3, 11, 77**
Guillevic, (Eugene) **33**
Ionesco, Eugène **1, 4, 6, 9, 11, 15, 41, 86**
Irigarary, Luce **164**
Japrisot, Sebastien **90**
Josipovici, Gabriel (David) **6, 43, 153**
Jouve, Pierre Jean **47**
Kristeva, Julia **77, 140**
Lacan, Jacques (Marie Emile) **75**
Laurent, Antoine **50**
Le Clézio, J(ean) M(arie) G(ustave) **31, 155**
Leduc, Violette **22**
Leger, (Marie-Rene Auguste) Alexis Saint-Leger **4, 11, 46**
Leiris, Michel (Julien) **61**
Lévi-Strauss, Claude **38**
Mallet-Joris, Françoise **11**
Malraux, (Georges-)André **1, 4, 9, 13, 15, 57**
Mandiargues, Andre Pieyre de **41**
Marcel, Gabriel Honore **15**
Mauriac, Claude **9**
Mauriac, François (Charles) **4, 9, 56**
Merton, Thomas **1, 3, 11, 34, 83**
Modiano, Patrick (Jean) **18**
Montherlant, Henry (Milon) de **8, 19**
Morand, Paul **41**
Nin, Anaïs **1, 4, 8, 11, 14, 60, 127**
Perec, Georges **56, 116**
Pinget, Robert **7, 13, 37**
Ponge, Francis **6, 18**
Poniatowska, Elena **140**
Prévert, Jacques (Henri Marie) **15**
Queneau, Raymond **2, 5, 10, 42**
Quoirez, Francoise **9**
Renoir, Jean **20**
Resnais, Alain **16**
Reverdy, Pierre **53**
Rio, Michel **43**
Robbe-Grillet, Alain **1, 2, 4, 6, 8, 10, 14, 43, 128**
Rohmer, Eric **16**
Romains, Jules **7**
Sachs, Nelly **14, 98**
Sarraute, Nathalie **1, 2, 4, 8, 10, 31, 80**
Sartre, Jean-Paul **1, 4, 7, 9, 13, 18, 24, 44, 50, 52**
Sauser-Hall, Frederic **18**
Schwarz-Bart, André **2, 4**
Schwarz-Bart, Simone **7**
Simenon, Georges (Jacques Christian) **1, 2, 3, 8, 18, 47**
Simon, Claude **4, 9, 15, 39**
Soupault, Philippe **68**
Steiner, George **24**
Tournier, Michel (édouard) **6, 23, 36, 95**
Troyat, Henri **23**
Truffaut, Francois **20, 101**
Tuck, Lily **70**
Tzara, Tristan **47**
Varda, Agnes **16**
Wittig, Monique **22**
Yourcenar, Marguerite **19, 38, 50, 87**

FRENCH GUINEAN

Damas, Leon-Gontran **84**

GERMAN

Amichai, Yehuda **9, 22, 57, 116**
Arendt, Hannah **66, 98**
Arp, Jean **5**
Becker, Jurek **7, 19**

Benary-Isbert, Margot 12
Bienek, Horst 7, 11
Boell, Heinrich (Theodor) 2, 3, 6, 9, 11, 15, 27, 32, 72
Buchheim, Lothar-Guenther 6
Bukowski, Charles 2, 5, 9, 41, 82, 108
Eich, Guenter 15
Ende, Michael (Andreas Helmuth) 31
Enzensberger, Hans Magnus 43
Fassbinder, Rainer Werner 20
Figes, Eva 31
Grass, Guenter (Wilhelm) 1, 2, 4, 6, 11, 15, 22, 32, 49, 88
Habermas, Juergen 104
Hamburger, Michael (Peter Leopold) 5, 14
Handke, Peter 5, 8, 10, 15, 38, 134
Heidegger, Martin 24
Hein, Christoph 154
Herzog, Werner 16
Hesse, Hermann 1, 2, 3, 6, 11, 17, 25, 69
Heym, Stefan 41
Hildesheimer, Wolfgang 49
Hochhuth, Rolf 4, 11, 18
Hofmann, Gert 54
Jhabvala, Ruth Prawer 4, 8, 29, 94, 138
Johnson, Uwe 5, 10, 15, 40
Juenger, Ernst 125
Kissinger, Henry A(lfred) 137
Kroetz, Franz Xaver 41
Kunze, Reiner 10
Lenz, Siegfried 27
Levitin, Sonia (Wolff) 17
Maron, Monika 165
Mueller, Lisel 13, 51
Nossack, Hans Erich 6
Preussler, Otfried 17
Remarque, Erich Maria 21
Riefenstahl, Leni 16
Sachs, Nelly 14, 98
Schmidt, Arno (Otto) 56
Schumacher, E(rnst) F(riedrich) 80
Seghers, Anna 7
Strauss, Botho 22
Sueskind, Patrick 44
Tillich, Paul (Johannes) 131
Walser, Martin 27
Weiss, Peter (Ulrich) 3, 15, 51
Wellershoff, Dieter 46
Wolf, Christa 14, 29, 58, 150
Zuckmayer, Carl 18

GHANIAN

Armah, Ayi Kwei 5, 33, 136

GREEK

Broumas, Olga 10, 73
Elytis, Odysseus 15, 49, 100
Haviaras, Stratis 33
Karapanou, Margarita 13
Nakos, Lilika 29
Ritsos, Yannis 6, 13, 31
Samarakis, Antonis 5
Seferis, George 5, 11
Spanidou, Irini 44
Vassilikos, Vassilis 4, 8

GUADELOUPEAN

Condé, Maryse 52, 92
Schwarz-Bart, Simone 7

GUATEMALAN

Asturias, Miguel Ángel 3, 8, 13

GUINEAN

Laye, Camara 4, 38

GUYANESE

Dabydeen, David 34
Harris, (Theodore) Wilson 25

HAITIAN

Danticat, Edwidge 94, 139

HUNGARIAN

Faludy, George 42
Koestler, Arthur 1, 3, 6, 8, 15, 33
Konrád, György 4, 10, 73
Lengyel, József 7
Lukacs, George 24
Nagy, Laszlo 7
Szirtes, George 46
Tabori, George 19
Vizinczey, Stephen 40

ICELANDIC

Gunnars, Kristjana 69

INDIAN

Alexander, Meena 121
Ali, Ahmed 69
Anand, Mulk Raj 23, 93
Desai, Anita 19, 37, 97
Ezekiel, Nissim 61
Ghosh, Amitav 44, 153
Mahapatra, Jayanta 33
Mehta, Ved (Parkash) 37
Mistry, Rohinton 71
Mukherjee, Bharati 53, 115
Narayan, R(asipuram) K(rishnaswami) 7, 28, 47, 121
Rao, Raja 25, 56
Ray, Satyajit 16, 76
Rushdie, (Ahmed) Salman 23, 31, 55, 100
Sahgal, Nayantara (Pandit) 41
Sealy, I(rwin) Allan 55
Seth, Vikram 43, 90
Singh, Khushwant 11
Tharoor, Shashi 70
White, T(erence) H(anbury) 30

INDONESIAN

Lee, Li-Young 164

IRANIAN

Modarressi, Taghi (M.) 44
Shamlu, Ahmad 10

IRISH

Banville, John 46, 118
Beckett, Samuel (Barclay) 1, 2, 3, 4, 6, 9, 10, 11, 14, 18, 29, 57, 59, 83
Behan, Brendan 1, 8, 11, 15, 79
Binchy, Maeve 153
Blackwood, Caroline 6, 9, 100
Boland, Eavan (Aisling) 40, 67, 113
Bowen, Elizabeth (Dorothea Cole) 1, 3, 6, 11, 15, 22, 118
Boyle, Patrick 19
Brennan, Maeve 5
Brown, Christy 63
Carroll, Paul Vincent 10
Clarke, Austin 6, 9
Colum, Padraic 28
Day Lewis, C(ecil) 1, 6, 10
Dillon, Eilis 17
Donleavy, J(ames) P(atrick) 1, 4, 6, 10, 45
Doyle, Roddy 81
Durcan, Paul 43, 70
Friel, Brian 5, 42, 59, 115
Gébler, Carlo (Ernest) 39
Hanley, James 3, 5, 8, 13
Hart, Josephine 70
Heaney, Seamus (Justin) 5, 7, 14, 25, 37, 74, 91
Johnston, Jennifer (Prudence) 7, 150
Jordan, Neil (Patrick) 110
Kavanagh, Patrick (Joseph) 22
Keane, Molly 31
Kiely, Benedict 23, 43
Kinsella, Thomas 4, 19, 138
Lavin, Mary 4, 18, 99
Leonard, Hugh 19
Longley, Michael 29
Mac Laverty, Bernard 31
MacNeice, (Frederick) Louis 1, 4, 10, 53
Mahon, Derek 27
McCabe, Patrick 133
McGahern, John 5, 9, 48, 156
McGinley, Patrick (Anthony) 41
McGuckian, Medbh 48
Montague, John (Patrick) 13, 46
Moore, Brian 1, 3, 5, 7, 8, 19, 32, 90
Morrison, Van 21
Morrissy, Mary 99
Muldoon, Paul 32, 72, 166
Murphy, Richard 41
Murphy, Thomas (Bernard) 51
Nolan, Christopher 58
O'Brian, Patrick 152
O'Brien, Edna 3, 5, 8, 13, 36, 65, 116
O'Casey, Sean 1, 5, 9, 11, 15, 88
O'Doherty, Brian 76
O'Faolain, Julia 6, 19, 47, 108
O'Faolain, Sean 1, 7, 14, 32, 70
O'Flaherty, Liam 5, 34
Paulin, Tom 37
Rodgers, W(illiam) R(obert) 7
Simmons, James (Stewart Alexander) 43
Toibin, Colm 162
Trevor, William 7, 9, 14, 25, 71, 116
White, Terence de Vere 49
Wilson, Robert McLiam 59

ISRAELI

Agnon, S(hmuel) Y(osef Halevi) 4, 8, 14
Amichai, Yehuda 9, 22, 57, 116
Appelfeld, Aharon 23, 47
Bakshi, Ralph 26
Friedlander, Saul 90
Grossman, David 67
Kaniuk, Yoram 19
Levin, Meyer 7
Megged, Aharon 9
Oz, Amos 5, 8, 11, 27, 33, 54
Shammas, Anton 55
Sobol, Joshua 60
Yehoshua, A(braham) B. 13, 31

ITALIAN

Antonioni, Michelangelo 20, 144
Bacchelli, Riccardo 19
Bassani, Giorgio 9
Bertolucci, Bernardo 16, 157
Bufalino, Gesualdo 74
Buzzati, Dino 36
Calasso, Roberto 81
Calvino, Italo 5, 8, 11, 22, 33, 39, 73
De Sica, Vittorio 20
Eco, Umberto 28, 60, 142
Fallaci, Oriana 11, 110
Fellini, Federico 16, 85
Fo, Dario 32, 109
Gadda, Carlo Emilio 11
Ginzburg, Natalia 5, 11, 54, 70
Giovene, Andrea 7
Landolfi, Tommaso 11, 49
Levi, Primo 37, 50
Luzi, Mario 13
Montale, Eugenio 7, 9, 18
Morante, Elsa 8, 47
Moravia, Alberto 2, 7, 11, 27, 46
Ortese, Anna Maria 89
Palazzeschi, Aldo 11
Pasolini, Pier Paolo 20, 37, 106
Piccolo, Lucio 13
Pincherle, Alberto 11, 18
Quasimodo, Salvatore 10
Ricci, Nino 70
Sciascia, Leonardo 8, 9, 41
Silone, Ignazio 4

Ungaretti, Giuseppe **7, 11, 15**
Visconti, Luchino **16**
Vittorini, Elio **6, 9, 14**
Wertmueller, Lina **16**

JAMAICAN

Bennett, Louise (Simone) **28**
Cliff, Jimmy **21**
Cliff, Michelle **120**
Marley, Bob **17**
Thelwell, Michael Miles **22**

JAPANESE

Abe, Kōbō **8, 22, 53, 81**
Enchi, Fumiko (Ueda) **31**
Endō, Shūsaku **7, 14, 19, 54, 99**
Ibuse, Masuji **22**
Ichikawa, Kon **20**
Ishiguro, Kazuo **27, 56, 59, 110**
Kawabata, Yasunari **2, 5, 9, 18, 107**
Kurosawa, Akira **16, 119**
Murakami, Haruki
Oe, Kenzaburo **10, 36, 86**
Oshima, Nagisa **20**
Ozu, Yasujiro **16**
Shiga, Naoya **33**
Tanizaki, Jun'ichirō **8, 14, 28**
Whitney, Phyllis A(yame) **42**
Yoshimoto, Banana **84**

KENYAN

Ngugi, James T(hiong'o) **3, 7, 13**
Ngũgĩ wa Thiong'o **36**

MALIAN

Ouologuem, Yambo **146**

MARTINICAN

Césaire, Aimé (Fernand) **19, 32, 112**
Fanon, Frantz **74**
Glissant, Edouard **10, 68**

MEXICAN

Arreola, Juan José **147**
Castellanos, Rosario **66**
Esquivel, Laura **141**
Fuentes, Carlos **3, 8, 10, 13, 22, 41, 60, 113**
Ibarguengoitia, Jorge **37**
Lopez Portillo (y Pacheco), Jose **46**
Lopez y Fuentes, Gregorio **32**
Paz, Octavio **3, 4, 6, 10, 19, 51, 65, 119**
Poniatowska, Elena **140**
Rulfo, Juan **8, 80**

MOROCCAN

Arrabal, Fernando **2, 9, 18, 58**

NEW ZEALANDER

Adcock, Fleur **41**
Ashton-Warner, Sylvia (Constance) **19**
Baxter, James K(eir) **14**
Campion, Jane **95**
Gee, Maurice (Gough) **29**
Grace, Patricia Frances **56**
Hilliard, Noel (Harvey) **15**
Hulme, Keri **39, 130**
Ihimaera, Witi **46**
Marsh, (Edith) Ngaio **7, 53**
Sargeson, Frank **31**

NICARAGUAN

Alegria, Claribel **75**
Cardenal, Ernesto **31, 161**

NIGERIAN

Achebe, (Albert) Chinua(lumogu) **1, 3, 5, 7, 11, 26, 51, 75, 127, 152**
Clark Bekedermo, J(ohnson) P(epper) **38**

Ekwensi, Cyprian (Odiatu Duaka) **4**
Emecheta, (Florence Onye) Buchi **14, 48, 128**
Nwapa, Flora **133**
Okigbo, Christopher (Ifenayichukwu) **25, 84**
Okri, Ben **87**
Saro-Wiwa, Ken(ule Beeson) **114**
Soyinka, Wole **3, 5, 14, 36, 44**
Tutuola, Amos **5, 14, 29**

NORTHERN IRISH

Deane, Seamus (Francis) **122**
Simmons, James (Stewart Alexander) **43**
Wilson, Robert McLiam **59**

NORWEGIAN

Friis-Baastad, Babbis Ellinor **12**
Heyerdahl, Thor **26**
Vesaas, Tarjei **48**

PAKISTANI

Ali, Ahmed **69**
Ghose, Zulfikar **42**

PARAGUAYAN

Roa Bastos, Augusto (Antonio) **45**

PERUVIAN

Allende, Isabel **39, 57, 97**
Arguedas, José María **10, 18**
Goldemberg, Isaac **52**
Vargas Llosa, (Jorge) Mario (Pedro) **3, 6, 9, 10, 15, 31, 42, 85**

POLISH

Agnon, S(hmuel) Y(osef Halevi) **4, 8, 14**
Becker, Jurek **7, 19**
Bermant, Chaim (Icyk) **40**
Bienek, Horst **7, 11**
Brandys, Kazimierz **62**
Dabrowska, Maria (Szumska) **15**
Gombrowicz, Witold **4, 7, 11, 49**
Herbert, Zbigniew **9, 43**
John Paul II, Pope **128**
Kieslowski, Krzysztof **120**
Konwicki, Tadeusz **8, 28, 54, 117**
Kosinski, Jerzy (Nikodem) **1, 2, 3, 6, 10, 15, 53, 70**
Lem, Stanislaw **8, 15, 40, 149**
Milosz, Czeslaw **5, 11, 22, 31, 56, 82**
Mrozek, Slawomir **3, 13**
Polanski, Roman **16**
Rozewicz, Tadeusz **9, 23, 139**
Singer, Isaac Bashevis **1, 3, 6, 9, 11, 15, 23, 38, 69, 111**
Skolimowski, Jerzy **20**
Szymborska, Wislawa **99**
Wajda, Andrzej **16**
Wittlin, Jozef **25**
Wojciechowska, Maia (Teresa) **26**

PORTUGUESE

Migueis, Jose Rodrigues **10**
Saramago, José **119**

PUERTO RICAN

Ferré, Rosario **139**
Marqués, René **96**
Piñero, Miguel (Antonio Gomez) **4, 55**
Sánchez, Luis Rafael **23**

ROMANIAN

Celan, Paul **10, 19, 53, 82**
Cioran, E(mil) M. **64**
Codrescu, Andrei **46, 121**
Ionesco, Eugène **1, 4, 6, 9, 11, 15, 41, 86**
Rezzori (d'Arezzo), Gregor von **25**
Tzara, Tristan **47**
Wiesel, Elie(zer) **3, 5, 11, 37**

RUSSIAN

Aitmatov, Chingiz (Torekulovich) **71**
Akhmadulina, Bella Akhatovna **53**
Akhmatova, Anna **11, 25, 64, 126**
Aksyonov, Vassily (Pavlovich) **22, 37, 101**
Aleshkovsky, Yuz **44**
Almedingen, E. M. **12**
Asimov, Isaac **1, 3, 9, 19, 26, 76, 92**
Bakhtin, Mikhail Mikhailovich **83**
Bitov, Andrei (Georgievich) **57**
Brodsky, Joseph **4, 6, 13, 36, 100**
Deren, Maya **16, 102**
Ehrenburg, Ilya (Grigoryevich) **18, 34, 62**
Eliade, Mircea **19**
Gary, Romain **25**
Goldberg, Anatol **34**
Grade, Chaim **10**
Grossman, Vasily (Semenovich) **41**
Iskander, Fazil **47**
Kabakov, Sasha **59**
Kaletski, Alexander **39**
Krotkov, Yuri **19**
Leonov, Leonid (Maximovich) **92**
Limonov, Edward **67**
Nabokov, Vladimir (Vladimirovich) **1, 2, 3, 6, 8, 11, 15, 23, 44, 46, 64**
Olesha, Yuri (Karlovich) **8**
Pasternak, Boris (Leonidovich) **7, 10, 18, 63**
Paustovsky, Konstantin (Georgievich) **40**
Rahv, Philip **24**
Rand, Ayn **3, 30, 44, 79**
Ratushinskaya, Irina **54**
Rybakov, Anatoli (Naumovich) **23, 53**
Sarraute, Nathalie **1, 2, 4, 8, 10, 31, 80**
Shalamov, Varlam (Tikhonovich) **18**
Shatrov, Mikhail **59**
Sholokhov, Mikhail (Aleksandrovich) **7, 15**
Sinyavsky, Andrei (Donatevich) **8**
Solzhenitsyn, Aleksandr I(sayevich) **1, 2, 4, 7, 9, 10, 18, 26, 34, 78, 134**
Strugatskii, Arkadii (Natanovich) **27**
Strugatskii, Boris (Natanovich) **27**
Tarkovsky, Andrei (Arsenyevich) **75**
Trifonov, Yuri (Valentinovich) **45**
Troyat, Henri **23**
Voinovich, Vladimir (Nikolaevich) **10, 49, 147**
Voznesensky, Andrei (Andreievich) **1, 15, 57**
Yanovsky, V(assily) S(emenovich) **2, 18**
Yevtushenko, Yevgeny (Alexandrovich) **1, 3, 13, 26, 51, 126**
Yezierska, Anzia **46**
Zaturenska, Marya **6, 11**
Zinoviev, Alexander (Aleksandrovich) **19**

SALVADORAN

Alegria, Claribel **75**
Argueta, Manlio **31**

SCOTTISH

Banks, Iain M(enzies) **34**
Brown, George Mackay **5, 48, 100**
Cronin, A(rchibald) J(oseph) **32**
Dunn, Douglas (Eaglesham) **6, 40**
Graham, W(illiam) S(idney) **29**
Gray, Alasdair (James) **41**
Grieve, C(hristopher) M(urray) **11, 19**
Hunter, Mollie **21**
Jenkins, (John) Robin **52**
Kelman, James **58, 86**
Laing, R(onald) D(avid) **95**
MacBeth, George (Mann) **2, 5, 9**
MacCaig, Norman (Alexander) **36**
MacInnes, Helen (Clark) **27, 39**
MacLean, Alistair (Stuart) **3, 13, 50, 63**
McIlvanney, William **42**
Morgan, Edwin (George) **31**
Smith, Iain Crichton **64**
Spark, Muriel (Sarah) **2, 3, 5, 8, 13, 18, 40, 94**
Taylor, C(ecil) P(hilip) **27**

Walker, David Harry **14**
Welsh, Irvine **144**
Young, Andrew (John) **5**

SENEGALESE

Ousmane, Sembene **66**
Senghor, Léopold Sédar **54, 130**

SOMALIAN

Farah, Nuruddin **53, 137**

SOUTH AFRICAN

Abrahams, Peter (Henry) **4**
Breytenbach, Breyten **23, 37, 126**
Brink, André (Philippus) **18, 36, 106**
Brutus, Dennis **43**
Coetzee, J(ohn) M(ichael) **23, 33, 66, 117, 161, 162**
Courtenay, Bryce **59**
Fugard, (Harold) Athol **5, 9, 14, 25, 40, 80**
Fugard, Sheila **48**
Gordimer, Nadine **3, 5, 7, 10, 18, 33, 51, 70, 123, 160, 161**
Harwood, Ronald **32**
Head, Bessie **25, 67**
Hope, Christopher (David Tully) **52**
Kunene, Mazisi (Raymond) **85**
La Guma, (Justin) Alex(ander) **19**
Millin, Sarah Gertrude **49**
Mphahlele, Ezekiel **25, 133**
Mtwa, Percy **47**
Ngema, Mbongeni **57**
Nkosi, Lewis **45**
Paton, Alan (Stewart) **4, 10, 25, 55, 106**
Plomer, William Charles Franklin **4, 8**
Prince, F(rank) T(empleton) **22**
Smith, Wilbur (Addison) **33**
Tolkien, J(ohn) R(onald) R(euel) **1, 2, 3, 8, 12, 38**
Tutu, Desmond M(pilo) **80**
van der Post, Laurens (Jan) **5**
Vorster, Gordon **34**

SPANISH

Alberti, Rafael **7**
Alfau, Felipe **66**
Almodovar, Pedro **114**
Alonso, Damaso **14**
Arrabal, Fernando **2, 9, 18, 58**
Benet, Juan **28**
Buero Vallejo, Antonio **15, 46, 139**
Bunuel, Luis **16, 80**
Casona, Alejandro **49**
Castedo, Elena **65**
Cela, Camilo José **4, 13, 59, 122**
Cernuda (y Bidón), Luis **54**
del Castillo, Michel **38**
Delibes, Miguel **8, 18**
Espriu, Salvador **9**
Gironella, José María **11**
Gomez de la Serna, Ramon **9**
Goytisolo, Juan **5, 10, 23, 133**
Guillén, Jorge **11**
Matute (Ausejo), Ana María **11**
Otero, Blas de **11**
Rodriguez, Claudio **10**
Ruiz, Jose Martinez **11**
Saura (Atares), Carlos **20**
Sender, Ramón (José) **8**

SRI LANKAN

Gunesekera, Romesh **91**

ST. LUCIAN

Walcott, Derek (Alton) **2, 4, 9, 14, 25, 42, 67, 76, 160**

SWEDISH

Beckman, Gunnel **26**
Bergman, (Ernst) Ingmar **16, 72**
Ekeloef, (Bengt) Gunnar **27**
Johnson, Eyvind (Olof Verner) **14**
Lagerkvist, Paer (Fabian) **7, 10, 13, 54**
Martinson, Harry (Edmund) **14**
Sjoewall, Maj **7**
Spiegelman, Art **76**
Transtroemer, Tomas (Goesta) **52, 65**
Wahlöö, Per **7**
Weiss, Peter (Ulrich) **3, 15, 51**

SWISS

Canetti, Elias **3, 14, 25, 75, 86**
Duerrenmatt, Friedrich **1, 4, 8, 11, 15, 43, 102**
Frisch, Max (Rudolf) **3, 9, 14, 18, 32, 44**
Hesse, Hermann **1, 2, 3, 6, 11, 17, 25, 69**
King, Francis (Henry) **8, 53, 145**
Kung, Hans **130**
Pinget, Robert **7, 13, 37**
Sauser-Hall, Frederic **18**
Sterchi, Beat **65**
von Daeniken, Erich **30**

TRINIDADIAN

Guy, Rosa (Cuthbert) **26**
James, C(yril) L(ionel) R(obert) **33**
Lovelace, Earl **51**
Naipaul, Shiva(dhar Srinivasa) **32, 39**
Naipaul, V(idiadhar) S(urajprasad) **4, 7, 9, 13, 18, 37, 105**
Rampersad, Arnold **44**

TURKISH

Hikmet, Nazim **40**
Kemal, Yashar **14, 29**
Seferis, George **5, 11**

UGANDAN

p'Bitek, Okot **96**

URUGUAYAN

Galeano, Eduardo (Hughes) **72**
Onetti, Juan Carlos **7, 10**
Peri Rossi, Cristina **156**

WELSH

Abse, Dannie **7, 29**
Arundel, Honor (Morfydd) **17**
Clarke, Gillian **61**
Dahl, Roald **1, 6, 18, 79**
Davies, Rhys **23**
Francis, Dick **2, 22, 42, 102**
Hughes, Richard (Arthur Warren) **1, 11**
Humphreys, Emyr Owen **47**
Jones, David (Michael) **2, 4, 7, 13, 42**
Jones, Terence Graham Parry **21**
Levinson, Deirdre **49**
Llewellyn Lloyd, Richard Dafydd Vivian **7, 80**
Mathias, Roland (Glyn) **45**
Norris, Leslie **14**
Roberts, Kate **15**
Rubens, Bernice (Ruth) **19, 31**
Thomas, R(onald) S(tuart) **6, 13, 48**
Watkins, Vernon Phillips **43**
Williams, (George) Emlyn **15**

YUGOSLAVIAN

Andrić, Ivo **8**
Cosic, Dobrica **14**
Kǐ, Danilo **57**
Krlěa, Miroslav **8, 114**
Pavic, Milorad **60**
Popa, Vasko **19**
Simic, Charles **6, 9, 22, 49, 68, 130**
Tesich, Steve **40, 69**

CLC-167 Title Index

"The Abortion" (Walker) **167**:237
"About My Table" (Delbanco) **167**:143, 150
About My Table, and Other Stories (Delbanco) **167**:142-44, 146-50
Absconding (Gao Xingjian)
 See *Taowang*
Absolute Signal (Gao Xingjian)
 See *Juedui xinhao*
The Alarm Signal (Gao Xingjian)
 See *Juedui xinhao*
"And With Advantages" (Delbanco) **167**:162-63
"Bali suibi" (Gao Xingjian) **167**:202
The Beaux Arts Trio (Delbanco) **167**:147
Between Life and Death (Gao Xingjian)
 See *Sheng si jie*
Bi'an (Gao Xingjian) **167**:202-3, 207, 212, 214, 221
Bus Station (Gao Xingjian)
 See *Chezhan*
Bus Stop (Gao Xingjian)
 See *Chezhan*
Chezhan (Gao Xingjian) **167**:184, 191, 194-99, 201, 205-6, 209, 213-14, 218-19, 221, 225-26, 228-29
City of the Dead (Gao Xingjian)
 See *Ming Jie*
The Color Purple (Walker) **167**:232-341
"Coming in from the Cold" (Walker) **167**:275
Consider Sappho Burning (Delbanco) **167**:148, 150, 152
"The Consolidation of Philosophy" (Delbanco) **167**:142
The Countess of Stanlein Restored (Delbanco) **167**:179-80
"The Day's Catch" (Delbanco) **167**:163-64
Dialogue and Rebuttal (Gao Xingjian)
 See *Dialogue-interloquer*
Dialogue-interloquer (Gao Xingjian) **167**:203, 221
Duihua yu fanjie (Gao Xingjian)
 See *Dialogue-interloquer*
"The Eighties and Me" (Walker) **167**:275
Escape (Gao Xingjian)
 See *Taowang*
"Everyday Use" (Walker) **167**:237, 327
"Everything" (Delbanco) **167**:163-64
"The Executor" (Delbanco) **167**:144
Exile (Gao Xingjian)
 See *Taowang*
Fleeing (Gao Xingjian)
 See *Taowang*
The Fugitives (Gao Xingjian)
 See *Taowang*
Grasse, 3/23/66 (Delbanco) **167**:148, 150, 152
Group Portrait: Joseph Conrad, Stephen Crane, Ford Madox Ford, Henry James, and H.G. Wells (Delbanco) **167**:135-38, 140-42, 147-48, 150-52, 162

Hades (Gao Xingjian)
 See *Ming Jie*
Her Blue Body Everything We Know: Earthling Poems, 1965-1990, Complete (Walker) **167**:305, 309
"His Masquerade" (Delbanco) **167**:164
In Search of Our Mothers' Gardens (Walker) **167**:259, 263, 268, 288-89, 293
In the Middle Distance (Delbanco) **167**:149, 152-53, 156-60
In the Name of Mercy (Delbanco) **167**:165-66, 168
"Jottings from Paris" (Gao Xingjian)
 See "Bali suibi"
Juedui xinhao (Gao Xingjian) **167**:184, 191, 201, 206, 218, 228
"Letter to a Young Fiction Writer" (Delbanco) **167**:176
Lingshan (Gao Xingjian)
 See *La Montagne de l'âme*
Le Livre d'un homme seul (Gao Xingjian) **167**:216-17, 227, 229
The Lost Suitcase: Reflections on the Literary Life (Delbanco) **167**:175-76
"The Lost Suitcase" (Delbanco) **167**:175
"Marching through Georgia" (Delbanco) **167**:144, 150
The Martlet's Tale (Delbanco) **167**:148-49, 157, 159, 174
Meridian (Walker) **167**:237
Ming Jie (Gao Xingjian) **167**:222
"Modernism and Chinese Literature" (Gao Xingjian) **167**:219
La Montagne de l'âme (Gao Xingjian) **167**:203-6, 209-13, 215-17, 225-30
Mountain of Souls (Gao Xingjian)
 See *La Montagne de l'âme*
News (Delbanco) **167**:147-48, 150
Nocturnal Wanderer (Gao Xingjian)
 See *Le Somnambule*
"Northiam Hall" (Delbanco) **167**:150-51
Old Scores (Delbanco) **167**:174
"One Child of One's Own" (Walker) **167**:293
One Man's Bible (Gao Xingjian)
 See *Le Livre d'un homme seul*
"Ostinato" (Delbanco) **167**:143
The Other Shore: Plays by Gao Xingjian (Gao Xingjian) **167**:201, 205, 211
The Other Shore (Gao Xingjian)
 See *Bi'an*
"Palinurus" (Delbanco) **167**:163
Possession (Delbanco) **167**:147, 149-50
A Preliminary Exploration into the Techniques of Modern Fiction (Gao Xingjian) **167**:201, 213
Running in Place (Delbanco) **167**:160-61
Shanhaijing zhuan (Gao Xingjian) **167**:222
Sheng sheng man bianzou (Gao Xingjian) **167**:202

Sheng si jie (Gao Xingjian) **167**:203, 205, 219, 221
Sherbrookes (Delbanco) **167**:147, 149
Small Rain (Delbanco) **167**:148, 174
"Some Explanations and Suggestions on Staging *Stories of Shanhaijing*" (Gao Xingjian) **167**:222
"Some in Their Bodies' Force" (Delbanco) **167**:142, 144
Le Somnambule (Gao Xingjian) **167**:203, 221
Soul Mountain (Gao Xingjian)
 See *La Montagne de l'âme*
Spirit Mountain (Gao Xingjian)
 See *La Montagne de l'âme*
Stars on a Cold Night (Gao Xingjian) **167**:201
Stillness (Delbanco) **167**:147, 149-50
Stories of Shanhaijing: A Three-Act Tragicomedy of the Gods (Gao Xingjian)
 See *Shanhaijing zhuan*
The Story of the Classic of Seas and Mountains (Gao Xingjian)
 See *Shanhaijing zhuan*
Talking Horse: Bernard Malamud on Life and Work (Delbanco) **167**:171
Taowang (Gao Xingjian) **167**:202, 207, 209, 214, 219
"Telephone" (Delbanco) **167**:175
The Temple of My Familiar (Walker) **167**:300
The Third Life of Grange Copeland (Walker) **167**:237, 327
"Traction" (Delbanco) **167**:142
"Travel, Art, and Death" (Delbanco) **167**:175
Variations on a Slow Tune (Gao Xingjian)
 See *Sheng sheng man bianzou*
Weekend Quartet (Gao Xingjian)
 See *Zhoumo sichongzou*
What Remains (Delbanco) **167**:176-77
"What You Carry" (Delbanco) **167**:144
"The *Wildman* and I" (Gao Xingjian) **167**:188
Wildman (Gao Xingjian)
 See *Yeren*
"Without Isms" (Gao Xingjian) **167**:202
Writers and Their Craft: Short Stories and Essays on the Narrative (Delbanco) **167**:164
"The Writer's Trade" (Delbanco) **167**:163
The Writer's Trade, and Other Stories (Delbanco) **167**:162-63
"Writing *The Color Purple*" (Walker) **167**:254, 259
Ye you shen (Gao Xingjian)
 See *Le Somnambule*
Yeren (Gao Xingjian) **167**:184-89, 191, 201, 209, 228
Yige ren de Shengjing (Gao Xingjian)
 See *Le Livre d'un homme seul*
"You Can Use My Name" (Delbanco) **167**:162
Zhoumo sichongzou (Gao Xingjian) **167**:203

ISBN 0-7876-5963-0